Sam Peckinpah's *The W*

Sam Peckinpah's *The Wild Bunch* is one of the most influential films in American cinema. The intensity of its violence was unprecedented, while the director's use of multiple cameras, montage editing, and slow motion quickly became the normative style for rendering screen violence. Demonstrating to filmmakers the power of irony as a narrative voice and its effectiveness as a tool for exploring and portraying brutality, *The Wild Bunch* fundamentally changed the Western, moving it into a more brutal and psychopathic territory than it had ever inhabited before. This volume includes freshly commissioned essays by several leading scholars of Peckinpah's work. Examining the film's production history from script to screen, its rich and ambivalent vision of American society, and its relationship to the western genre, among other topics, it provides a definitive reinterpretation of an enduring film classic.

Stephen Prince is Associate Professor of Communication Studies at Virginia Polytechnic Institute and State University. He is the author of *Savage Cinema: Sam Peckinpah and the Rise of Ultra-Violent Movies; Movies and Meaning: An Introduction to Film;* and *Visions of Empire: Political Imagery in Contemporary American Film.*

CAMBRIDGE FILM HANDBOOKS SERIES

General Editor

Andrew Horton, *University of Oklahoma*

Each CAMBRIDGE FILM HANDBOOK is intended to focus on a single film from a variety of theoretical, critical, and contextual perspectives. This "prism" approach is designed to give students and general readers valuable background and insight into the cinematic, artistic, cultural, and sociopolitical importance of individual films by including essays by leading film scholars and critics. Furthermore, these handbooks, by their very nature, are meant to help the reader better grasp the nature of the critical and theoretical discourse on cinema as an art form, as a visual medium, and as a cultural product. Filmographies and selected bibliographies are added to help the reader go further on his or her own exploration of the film under consideration.

Sam Peckinpah's
The Wild Bunch

Edited by

Stephen Prince

PUBLISHED BY THE PRESS SYNDICATE OF THE UNIVERSITY OF CAMBRIDGE
The Pitt Building, Trumpington Street, Cambridge, United Kingdom

CAMBRIDGE UNIVERSITY PRESS
The Edinburgh Building, Cambridge CB2 2RU, UK   http://www.cup.cam.ac.uk
40 West 20th Street, New York, NY 10011-4211, USA   http://www.cup.org
10 Stamford Road, Oakleigh, Melbourne 3166, Australia

First published 1999

Printed in the United States of America

Typeset in 10/14 Stone Serif, in QuarkXPress, AG
All illustrations courtesy Jerry Ohlinger s.

*A catalog record for this book is available from
the British Library*

Library of Congress Cataloging-in-Publication Data
Sam Peckinpah s The wild bunch / edited by Stephen Prince.
     p.   cm   (Cambridge film handbook series)
   Filmography: p.
   Includes bibliographical references and index.
   ISBN 0-521-58433-7 (hardcover).   ISBN 0-521-58606-2 (pbk.)
   1. Wild bunch (Motion picture)   I. Prince, Stephen, 1955   .
II. Series.
PN1997.W53613S26   1998
791.43'72 dc21   98-25117
                                                              CIP

hardback 0-521-58433-7
paperback 0-521-58606-2

For My Parents
and Tami
and Kim

Contents

Contributors

Michael Bliss, a teacher of English and film at Virginia Polytechnic Institute and State University, is the author of *Justified Lives: Morality and Narrative in the Films of Sam Peckinpah,* coauthor (with Christina Banks) of *What Goes Around Comes Around: The Films of Jonathan Demme,* and editor of *Doing It Right: The Best Criticism of Sam Peckinpah's "The Wild Bunch."* Having just completed *Dreams Within a Dream: The Films of Peter Weir,* Bliss is now cowriting *A Sense of Loss: John Woo, Hong Kong Cinema, and 1997.*

David A. Cook directs the Film Studies Program at Emory University. He is the author of *A History of Narrative Film,* a major text in its field that is now in its third edition.

Wheeler Winston Dixon is Chair of the Film Studies Program and Professor of English at the University of Nebraska, Lincoln. His books include *The Films of Jean-Luc Godard, It Looks at You: The Returned Gaze of Cinema,* and *The Early Film Criticism of François Truffaut.*

Devin McKinney is a freelance writer living in New York City. He is a frequent contributor to *Film Quarterly* and is currently writing a novel.

Stephen Prince is Associate Professor of Communication Studies at Virginia Polytechnic Institute and State University. He is the author of *Savage Cinema: Sam Peckinpah and the Rise of Ultra-Violent Movies, Movies and Meaning: An Introduction to Film,* and *Visions of Empire: Political Imagery in Contemporary American Film.*

Paul Seydor is a film editor who lives in Los Angeles. His recent work includes *Tin Cup, Cobb, White Men Can't Jump,* and *Turner and Hooch.* He is the author of *Peckinpah: The Western Films: Reconsideration.*

Christopher Sharrett is Associate Professor of Communication at Seton Hall University. He is the editor of *Crisis Cinema: The Apocalyptic Idea in Postmodern Narrative Film.* His work has appeared in *Cineaste, Film Quarterly, Persistence of Vision, Journal of Popular Film and Television, Millennium, CineAction,* and elsewhere. His essays have been anthologized in *The Dread of Difference: Gender and the Horror Film, Perspectives on German Cinema, The New American Cinema,* and other books. His book *Mythologies of Violence in Postmodern Media* is forthcoming from Wayne State University Press.

Introduction:
Sam Peckinpah, Savage
Poet of American Cinema

Running out of space and time in a modernizing West,
a band of outlaws led by Pike Bishop (William Holden) rides into
the Texas border town of San Rafael to stick up the railroad office.
The railroad, however, has hired a passel of bounty hunters to an-
nihilate the Bunch. Led by Pike's old friend Deke Thornton, the
vulturelike bounty hunters ambush the Bunch from the rooftops
of the town, killing outlaws and townspeople with indiscriminate
glee. Pike escapes, along with Dutch (Ernest Borgnine), Lyle and
Tector Gorch (Warren Oates, Ben Johnson), and Angel (Jamie Sanchez). They are joined outside town by old Freddie Sykes (Edmond
O'Brien), whereupon they discover that the bags of cash they took
from the depot are dummies stuffed with worthless washer rings.
Broke, they cross into Mexico, pursued by Thornton and his gang.
The Bunch go to work for General Mapache (Emilio Fernandez),
a cruel despot fighting on behalf of a corrupt government and
against a popular revolution. After the Bunch steals guns for the
general, Mapache seizes and tortures Angel. To avenge Angel, the
Bunch confronts and kills Mapache, precipitating a sustained
slaughter during which the members of the Bunch wipe out
most of Mapache's army and are themselves killed. The survivors,

1

Freddie Sykes and Deke Thornton, join forces with the peasant revolutionaries.

Sam Peckinpah modestly said that with *The Wild Bunch* he wasn't trying to make an epic but only to tell a simple story about bad men in changing times. But *The Wild Bunch* is an epic work, and it has had an epic impact on the American cinema. The scale and scope of its bloodletting were unprecedented, and Peckinpah's use of multiple cameras, montage editing, and slow motion quickly became the normative style for rendering screen violence. The film helped move the Western into a mud-spattered, more brutal, and psychopathic territory, and it showed subsequent filmmakers the power of irony as a narrative voice and its effectiveness as a tool for exploring, and portraying, a brutal screen world. Director Martin Scorsese called the film "savage poetry."[1]

Part of this savagery lies in Peckinpah's unflinching depiction of the characters. The outlaws led by Pike Bishop are stone killers, and the film presents them without apology. Pike coldly executes a wounded comrade after the botched holdup in San Rafael that opens the film, and astride his horse, he remorselessly tramples a woman during the confusion ensuing from the rooftop ambush. In the prelude to this ambush, as the Bunch ride into town, a group of smiling, laughing children look up from their play. But these are not the typical children, icons of sentimentality and innocence, that were so prominent in earlier generations of film. These children are patiently, joyously torturing a scorpion to death. By intercutting this torture with the following action, the shootout in town, Peckinpah encapsulated in striking imagery a vision of brutality and violence unfolding within an implacably cruel world, and he ensured that the depicted violence assumed a metaphysical dimension, as a force observable throughout human life, evident in the behavior of children as in that of adults.

Peckinpah, though, went beyond the immediate savagery of the material to search out the humanity that coexists in the Bunch with their remorseless use of violence. Typically, and in keeping with his other work as a filmmaker, Peckinpah located this redemptive humanity in the experience of psychological an-

FIGURE I

Peckinpah confers with actor William Holden, who plays Pike Bishop. Pike's anguish provides the psychological foundation of the film.

guish and torture. *The Wild Bunch* is Pike Bishop's film, and it is Bishop's anguished awareness of his terrible failings that gives the film its psychological depth and the violence its emotional resonance. The Gorch brothers are not well individuated as characters, and Dutch, though a forceful character, lacks the inner darkness of self-betrayal and the lacerated consciousness that Peckinpah would locate here, and in his other films, as indexes of the spiritual suffering that transforms and ennobles his fallen heroes. Through this psychological suffering, the inner humanity of these characters, otherwise debased through violence, asserts itself. Pike's call to his gang to confront Mapache and reclaim Angel follows from his horrified, haunted glimpse of his inner corruption, and this defiant assertion of loyalty to a comrade is Pike's means of refuting and overcoming everything that he has become and that he hates. But this transcendent assertion of humanity precipitates and accompanies a scene of apocalyptic violence as the outlaws massacre Mapache's men and are themselves annihilated. Peckinpah audaciously mixes ferocious, orgiastic violence with humanistic assertions about the importance of honor and loyalty and about the internal, psychological suffering that is the spiritual accompaniment, and consequence, of physical violence. Through this volatile mix, he achieves what Scorsese perceptively recognized as savage poetry, going inside the hurricane of violence to reveal its internal features and the residual, if deformed, humanity that exists, frighteningly, inside acts of brutality.

Peckinpah showed this brutality more candidly than any American filmmaker had before, but he went beyond its mechanical stylization to explore its effects upon heart and mind. He aimed to prod audiences into an ambivalent response, excited by the aesthetic stylization of slow-motion violence while being appalled by its physical effects and emotional and moral consequences. Peckinpah's explicit screen violence was not exploitive, nor was it a cold calculation for box-office effect. Peckinpah was a serious artist and moralist, and his use of violence in *The Wild Bunch* was sober and didactic. It was also so spectacular that he would forever after be identified with the turn in modern cinema toward graphic bloodshed. We will turn to these issues and explore the significance of the film's violence in a moment. First, it will be helpful to place *The Wild Bunch* within Peckinpah's career and to consider his decisive impact upon the Western genre.

PECKINPAH'S EARLY CAREER

Peckinpah started work in the film industry in the 1950s as a dialogue director working with Don Siegel, a filmmaker under contract with Allied Artists. Siegel had apprenticed as an editor in the montage unit at Warner Bros., and his pictures as a director (which would include the cult hit *Dirty Harry* [1972]) were distinguished by their crisp and efficient editing. Thus, it is fitting that Peckinpah trained under Siegel because Peckinpah's mature work as a director features a remarkable style of editing. As a dialogue director, Peckinpah worked on five Siegel pictures: *Riot in Cell Block 11* (1954), *Private Hell 36* (1954), *Annapolis Story* (1955), *Invasion of the Body Snatchers* (1956), and *Crime in the Streets* (1956). Peckinpah also appeared in *Body Snatchers* in a cameo role. In later years, he affectionately recalled Siegel's formative influence:

> I must say he was kind enough not to laugh openly while watching me run about with both of my feet in my mouth and my thumb up my ass. (This is not easy.) . . . He was my "patron" and he made me work and made me mad and made me think. Finally, he asked me what his next set-up was and for once I was ready, and he used it. I guess that was the beginning.[2]

Following the training with Siegel, Peckinpah worked for the next several years primarily in television, where he quickly established the Western as his special metier. From 1955 to 1960, Peckinpah wrote scripts for *Gunsmoke* and other popular television series including *Tales of Wells Fargo, Broken Arrow, Zane Grey Theater,* and *The Rifleman.* Peckinpah helped create this last series, and wrote and directed several episodes, but he left the show because of a difference of interpretation over the material. Peckinpah wanted the show to have an adult and serious focus in showing the passage of young Lucas McCain (Johnny Crawford) into manhood. The other producers, however, envisioned the series as a kids' show and preferred that Lucas remain a child and not be depicted as growing up. Following this spat, which prefigured the later stormy relationships with film producers that would eventually help derail Peckinpah's career, Sam got the chance to direct and produce his own series, *The Westerner,* about a wandering drifter, Dave Blassingame (Brian Keith). Though the series was canceled in 1960 by the network before completing its first season, Peckinpah had brought to television a markedly more adult tone, a harder-edged violence, and an unsentimental depiction of Western riffraff and lowlifes that clearly foreshadowed the direction in which he would take the genre in his feature films. In a letter to Chuck Connors, who starred in *The Rifleman,* Peckinpah described Blassingame as "a drifter and a bum; illiterate, usually inarticulate. He is as realistic a cowboy as I could create."[3]

Peckinpah continued to write Western film scripts, some of which were eventually made by other filmmakers (*One-Eyed Jacks*, 1961; *The Glory Guys*, 1965; *Villa Rides*, 1968), and when the opportunity to do features arose, he quickly achieved a mature artistic success with the magisterial and now-classic *Ride the High Country* (1962), his second feature. Peckinpah infused this simple story of two aging gunfighters (Randolph Scott and Joel McCrea) in the twilight of their career with remarkable feeling and the sneaky affection for slopbucket, redneck, peckerwood trash (in the randy Hammond clan, the film's villains) that would surface again so memorably in *The Wild Bunch*'s bounty hunters. *Ride the High Country* was tossed away by its studio, MGM, as a drive-in movie, but its evident artistry suggested that Peckinpah might indeed be the most important director of Westerns since John Ford (*Stagecoach* [1939], *The Searchers* [1956], *The Man Who Shot Liberty Valance* [1962]).

Certification of that potential had to await *The Wild Bunch*, however, because Peckinpah's next film, *Major Dundee* (1964), was a troubled production – over budget, over schedule, cut by the studio against the director's wishes – and it earned Peckinpah the reputation of a troublemaker. The studio cut up to twenty-seven minutes from the film, rendering its story about a unit of Union and Confederate soldiers pursuing a band of Apaches into Mexico nearly incomprehensible. The resulting mess that the studio released badly damaged Peckinpah's reputation, but the director fought back. He wrote to the film's producer, Jerry Bresler, "The 18 minutes that you have cut, disregarding my strongest objections, have in my opinion effectively destroyed my concept of story, character development, mood and meaning. . . . You are a well-poisoner, Jerry, and I damn you for it."[4]

To a reviewer who complained that the film was bewildering and confusing, Peckinpah wrote, "You are absolutely correct. After seeing it at the Press Screening, February 4th, 1965, I didn't know what in hell it was about and I was the director. . . . The film I made is on the cutting room floor."[5] While this experience was undeniably a bitter one for Peckinpah, and while *Major Dundee* was not the great film Peckinpah would claim it to be, he retained the ability to joke about it. He maintained a warm correspondence with star Charlton Heston (who played Major Dundee), and while in Mexico working on *The Wild Bunch,* Peckinpah wrote to Heston, who had just scored a big success with *Planet of the Apes* (1968).

> I am sitting here with Gordon Dawson, in Torreon, in the middle of a dust-rain-hail storm, thinking of new projects and we have decided to make a new picture. It will be called "Major Dundee Goes Ape" – grabs you, doesn't it? Sex, sentiment, and security – security, that is, if we can get Jerry Bresler to come back.

Peckinpah closed by saying, modestly, that *The Wild Bunch* "might turn out to be a reasonably good film."[6]

PRODUCTION OF *THE WILD BUNCH*

He was absolutely correct, and the picture was so great, defiant, and trend-setting that it relaunched Peckinpah's career after the *Dundee* disaster and his firing that same year as director of *The Cincinnati Kid,* a Steve McQueen picture. In 1967, Peckinpah had submitted a script called *The Wild Bunch* to Kenneth Hyman, a young vice-president at Warner Bros.–Seven Arts, who was committed to the policy and philosophy of a film director exercising artistic control over a film's design and production. The script, rewritten by Peckinpah, originally had been penned by Walon Green from a story by Roy Sickner. The narrative itself is fairly simple, but Peckinpah transformed it into an epic portrait of loyalty and honor and filmed it with ferocity and passion. The picture was cast in early 1968, and, with the decision to film entirely on location in Mexico, principal photography began on March 25, 1968. Seventy days were allotted for filming the 541 scenes in the script. As a measure of the intensity and responsibility with which Peckinpah worked (he told Ken Hyman, "Of all the projects I have ever worked on, this is closest to me."[7]),

FIGURE 2
Peckinpah (far right) watches as his crew films the Bunch as the outlaws ride into San Rafael before the ambush.

principal photography was concluded on June 27, 1968, only nine and one-half days behind schedule.

The first two weeks of shooting were devoted to one of the film's most complicated sequences, the payroll robbery in San Rafael and the consequent shoot-out, filmed on location in Parras, Coahuila, Mexico. On day one, the company was called at 6:30 A.M., had gotten their first shot by 9:30 A.M., and wrapped at 6:30 P.M.[8] Shooting the San Rafael material required the presence of up to 244 extras and 80 animals. Despite the complexity of this material, Peckinpah successfully captured his footage within the allotted two-week time frame.

The Aqua Verde material, the film's other most structurally complex sequence, was filmed over a period of thirty-two days, from the twenty-seventh day of shooting through the fifty-sixth day. Despite the intensity of the physical action depicted on screen during the gun battle between the Bunch and Mapache, physical accidents were relatively infrequent. On day fifty-one, a misfiring squib burned actor William Holden's arm, and two days after that,

FIGURE 3
Peckinpah plans the filming of the Aqua Verde sequences.

actor Ben Johnson (as Tector Gorch) broke his middle finger while firing the machine gun. The Aqua Verde filming required that Peckinpah coordinate over 300 extras and more than 500 animals. This scale of production makes his achievement of a 79-day shoot all the more impressive, especially given the necessity of solving each day's routine but aggravating problems. Peckinpah outlined some of these in his memos to producer Phil Feldman. They included badly functioning special effects, hazards posed by weather and locale, and the logistical difficulties of moving a large production company from place to place:

> During the first weeks of the show props, namely guns, were inoperative. Special effects were worse than inoperative, a situation which still exists. Sets are not ready and dressed when needed.[9]

> Whether to save money, water or just lack of planning, the water trucks have been watering less than one half of the road and

stopping after one trip. At least half of us are eating dust all the way.[10]

Grenade explosion timed correctly, however had not been pretested and dust obscured two-thirds of the action. . . . Impossible to make next shot before lunch as shoulder squib placed in Lyle's shirt did not match master shot . . . all squibs in Lyle's shirt have to be replaced because they are visible to the camera.[11]

Wind storm and rain; 1 hour, lost the light but finished sequence with brutes. Moved to the bridge; people, horses and props, 30 minutes to two hours late. Returned, rehearsed, broke for lunch, overcast could not shoot.[12]

Working with a sustained level of commitment and passion that he never again achieved in his career, Peckinpah surmounted these and other problems. With the completion of shooting, Peckinpah and editor Lou Lombardo had the difficult task of turning miles of raw footage into a disciplined, organized narrative. To appreciate what Peckinpah and his crew accomplished, it is instructive to consider how some of the film's scenes and story structure were shaped during the critical phase of postproduction. (Postproduction is the work of filmmaking that follows cinematography, including, chiefly, picture and sound editing.) The shaping in postproduction of narrative and theme is a routine occurrence on every film. Filmmakers never get things exactly right at the point of shooting, and very often, considerable reshaping of the material occurs on a postproduction basis. Perhaps the film's most memorable imagery is the opening scene's tableau of the children with the scorpion and ants. Initial plans also called for the incorporation of a train in the opening since the Bunch rides into San Rafael through the railroad yards. This did not work out, however, as Peckinpah explained to Feldman. "We have decided that the value of the train in the opening sequence is negligible because there is no way to get any speed in that area. We are therefore concentrating on scorpions and ants."[13]

The design and cutting of this sequence were the subjects of several memos from producer Phil Feldman to Peckinpah. Feldman was concerned that an initial cut spent too much time – two and one-half minutes – on the ants and scorpions, seemingly used every take of the children's faces, and, by starting on the scorpion and ants rather than the children, might prove confusing for the audience. (Feldman also wished to discuss with Peckinpah the symbolism of this imagery to determine whether it should be used elsewhere in the film – specifically, before the Aqua Verde shootout.)[14]

In general, in this initial cut, the picture was getting off to a slow start, with nearly seventeen minutes elapsing before the shootout in San Rafael. Feldman specifically urged Peckinpah to connect and integrate the ants with the children by using a shot that panned along a stick that one child was holding in the nest of ants. The pan would connect the children and their prey in an explicit fashion that would be necessary, Feldman believed, if the picture opened, as Peckinpah wanted, on a contextless close-up of the ants. In its revised design, after the children are established, Peckinpah goes to the first close-up of the insects when the boy shoves his stick forward, establishing a matching element for the close-up in which the stick is prominent. In response to Feldman's recommendations, the sequence was reshaped so that the scorpion–ant imagery is integrated more efficiently with the surrounding material and the children are established first, before the close-ups of the insects and scorpion. The result was a memorably poetic and symbolic sequence commenting on the human appetite for cruelty and savagery that Peckinpah believed underlay so much of recorded history.

The narrative of the film is cast as an extended pursuit, with the Bunch chased by the bounty hunters until each group is destroyed. The story alternates between scenes depicting each group with the emotional dynamics and conflicts among their members, and one of the creative challenges in editing the picture involved finding the right balance between the scenes depicting the outlaws and those depicting the bounty hunters. During post-production, Peckinpah explained to Feldman that the bounty hunters ought to be treated as a subsidiary element of the narrative. "I feel very strongly that our story is tied in primarily with the Wild Bunch and that the Bounty Hunters should be used as counterpoint."[15] Treating them as a counterpoint element influenced the cutting of the film's concluding Aqua Verde battle. In an initial cut of the picture, the bounty hunters had seemingly vanished from the screen for a protracted period of time, leading to some awkwardness upon their reintroduction and some concern from Feldman that the viewer might lose touch with these characters. Peckinpah, accordingly, inserted footage of the bounty hunters, hovering nearby, during the Aqua Verde battle. He reassured Feldman, "We will intercut the last fight to keep the Bounty Hunters alive."[16] Treating the bounty hunters as a counterpoint element also helped influence the decision about how to handle their deaths. Footage had been shot showing them killed by the Mexican revolutionaries, but at Feldman's suggestion, Peckinpah wisely decided to let their deaths occur as an off-screen event. Peckinpah thanked Feldman for this idea. "Your idea of taking out the killing of the bounty hunters was *absolutely correct.*"[17]

Postproduction work on the film helped eliminate an excruciatingly terrible line of dialogue. During the final fight, Peckinpah had filmed Dutch looking at Pike and saying, "We're doing it right this time," a remark that plays off of an earlier comment by Pike, made just before the train robbery. Feldman pointed out to Peckinpah that viewers would find the line silly, and he recommended that the idea be communicated nonverbally between Dutch and Pike. Feldman wrote to Peckinpah, "I agree that it could be considered camp and laughable. It is the one line in the picture that I think should be deleted because of audience reaction. . . . I know you think it's necessary, but I think it should be cut and we should do it all with just looks between Borgnine and Holden."[18] Here, and elsewhere, Feldman offered exceptionally keen advice to Peckinpah on the artistic shaping of the film, demonstrating how important it can be for a good director to have a supportive and intelligent producer.

Postproduction fine-tuning on the film helped sharpen its focus and make the presentation of its themes more sophisticated. Peck-

FIGURE 4
Peckinpah filmed the death of the bounty hunters, but producer
Phil Feldman persuaded him to treat it as an off-screen event.

inpah had shot a ton of footage, and the requisite trimming of this
material, unfortunately, made some of the subsidiary characters
less defined and coherent. For example, the woman who shoots
Pike in the back does so because of her close relationship with Mapache, a relationship Peckinpah tried to convey at various points
in the film. The fine-tuning of the picture, however, minimized
this connection. Peckinpah warned Feldman that the editing of
the scene where Mapache's forces are attacked by Villa was in danger of muddying the relationship between Mapache and Yolonda.

(Ultimately, this entire scene was cut from the film by the studio, but it has since then been restored.) Peckinpah wrote to Feldman,

> I have now seen the La Goma battle with Mapache's reaction cut out as per your request, two times. I think it is obvious to us both, as previously cut, that Yolonda looks at the General and his reaction to her was overdone but not having *any* reaction is now even worse. I find it is possible . . . to cut short her looking at him and to add a brief reaction to her which, as I'm sure you'll know, will tie the two together. I have tried to do this throughout the picture, as the position she has is inevitably close to the General. She is "his woman." . . . It is because of this that she shoots Holden in the back.[19]

As the film is now cut, Yolonda's shooting of Pike in the back seems somewhat gratuitous and minimally motivated. But this is

FIGURE 5
Pike, moments before he is shot in the back by Yolonda. Her character was a casualty of postproduction.

a function of the reduction (probably necessary to preserve narrative economy and efficiency) of her character to what is now essentially an extra, someone who appears as part of a group but lacks a defined identity. Yolonda's fate, victim of postproduction, exemplifies the trade-offs that are a routine part of film production, especially when the film in question is as complex as this one.

Much of the postproduction work on the film involved Peckinpah and Feldman's efforts to meet the objections to content of the Motion Picture Association of America's (MPAA) Code and Rating Administration. The MPAA was (and is) the film industry's administrative agency charged with helping to regulate movie content. Accordingly, it is very sensitive to depictions of profanity, sexuality, and violence. During production of *The Wild Bunch,* the MPAA retired its old (but recently revised) Production Code, which had shaped movie content for decades, and instituted a new G–M–R–X ratings system administered by the Code and Rating Administration (CARA). The MPAA's initial reaction to and evaluation of the script reflected the realities of the revised Production Code during the pre-CARA period when production of the film commenced. Given the existing parameters governing movie content, the MPAA deemed the proposed film, as scripted, to be largely unacceptable. "In its present form this story is so viol and bloody and filled with so many crudities of language would hesitate to say that a picture based on this ma be approved under the Production Code."[20] The MPA ed, however, that if the material was toned down, an SMA (Suggested for Mature Audiences) label might be possible.

MPAA concerns centered on the script's abundant profanity and on several sequences where the bloodletting was considered excessive or unacceptably graphic. These included the action during the opening shoot-out in which a farm boy on a wagon fires a shotgun into Buck's face, blinding him, after which Lyle Gorch shoots and kills the boy. According to the MPAA, this action "will have to be handled with great care not to be visually sickening."[21] Other objectionable material cited by the MPAA included Pike's killing of Buck in the arroyo (deemed "excessively brutal"[22]), Mapache cutting Angel's throat (deemed "unacceptable"[23]), and the extensive crowd killings during the Aqua Verde massacre (deemed "a blood bath").[24] Despite the MPAA's concerns, production on the picture commenced under the revised Production Code. However, by the time the picture was being edited, the Code was gone and the new ratings system was in place. This new system gave filmmakers in the late 1960s greatly expanded creative freedom because the ratings designated certain films, for the first time, as being unsuitable for children. Without the relaxation of censorship policies that the new CARA system represented, Peckinpah could not have released *The Wild Bunch* with its explicit images of bloodshed.

In the negotiations with the MPAA that followed principal photography, none of the episodes to which the MPAA had originally objected, or others (Angel being dragged by the automobile, Lyle at the machine gun, and Crazy Lee riddled with bullets), were deleted from the film, but they were rendered less graphic through careful editing. The SMA category was now history, and the CARA system gave Peckinpah and his producer enhanced freedom and flexibility in retaining and shaping their graphic screen violence. Of key importance for this film's remarkable production history, Peckinpah and his editors could cut the film to achieve an R rating rather than to satisfy a (revised) Production Code.

With respect to the boy in the wagon who is shot by Lyle, the MPAA objected to the bullet hit and the blood, so editor Lou Lombardo omitted these and caught the boy in mid-fall, well after he has been struck by Lyle's shot. (Producer Phil Feldman outlined the necessity for this manner of editing the footage in a letter to Warners executive Ken Hyman, which discussed specific editing solutions to the MPAA's objections.)[25] The editing feels a little jagged here, and the action may even seem a bit confusing. Critics have sometimes contrasted the optical confusions in the film's opening massacre with the clarity of perspective in the Aqua Verde shootout and have interpreted this as a stylistic statement about the unity of purpose with which the Bunch is fighting at the end. By contrast, at the beginning of the film, they are a more fractious group. The most confusing imagery in the opening shoot-out is the action in which the boy in the wagon shoots Buck, but this raggedness arose for very pragmatic reasons rather than for ones of thematic symbolism. The raggedness of the cutting was a function of having to pare back this very fast-moving material to satisfy the MPAA.

With respect to Buck's killing in the arroyo, this scene was edited to play mainly on his back, with very few quick, flash glimpses of his bloody face. Angel's drag by the automobile was shortened, with fewer close-ups of his ragged body. The editing of Mapache slitting Angel's throat deleted a side view of this action and the gush of blood that followed. This alteration enabled producer Feldman to reassure the MPAA that "all that happens is that Mapache completes his stroke over Angel's throat. There is no spurt of blood, but merely a show."[26] This is the one revision that has clearly dated the film's violence. By today's standards, the throat cutting seems somewhat anticlimactic because it is so abbreviated and without evident bloodshed. But the film could not have been released (as an R-rated picture) without this change.

In discussing with his director the need to alter the film to minimize its bloodshed, producer Phil Feldman was keenly supportive of Peckinpah's desire to push the limits of what was acceptable, and he interpreted the MPAA's objections as proof that their intentions for the film would be successful. Prior to the onset of principal photography, Feldman sent Peckinpah a copy of the MPAA's script report and included this assessment: "I am sending you a copy of the MPAA report from Shurlock. I think you can disregard this on the whole. As a matter of fact, I am rather pleased, as I am sure you are, that he finds it objectionable."[27] At the same time, Feldman urged Peckinpah to assess carefully the extent of the picture's bloodshed in relation to other prominent and trend-setting films of the period. This would help Peckinpah gauge tolerance levels for violence in potential viewers of the film. Feldman specifically urged Peckinpah to look at Sergio Leone's films (*A Fistful of Dollars, For a Few Dollars More*). "I think it might be good for you to have a comparative basis before you finally decide just how

FIGURE 6
Villa's attack on Mapache's army was among the sequences deleted
following the film's premiere.

far other people have gone in the field of blood and gore and what
the public is comparing us to."[28] The importance of Feldman's
support for Peckinpah's audacity in designing the film's extreme
violence has been overshadowed by subsequent events, chiefly the
film's Feldman-sanctioned recutting for distribution (and not for
censorship). Feldman, however, was a fine producer, and, as his
memos to Peckinpah demonstrate, he was exceptionally dedicated
to helping to make this an outstanding production and was closely
involved with Peckinpah in shaping the film's artistic design.

The most unfortunate editing of the picture was prompted not
by artistic or narrative considerations but solely by commercial
calculation. Shortly after its national premiere, the picture was recalled by the studio, and several key sequences were deleted: the

1) "Being sure is my business" flashback Pike and Deke share showing Deke's capture by police in the bordello; 2)dialogue between
Pike and Freddie Sykes about Freddie's grandson Crazy Lee, coupled with a flashback showing Pike's abandonment of Crazy Lee
during the San Rafael holdup; 3)incidental business in Angel's village when the Bunch visit; 4)and the attack of Villa's forces upon
Mapache. Much of this footage, particularly the crucial flashback
material, deepens the characters, particularly Pike, and adds complexity to their behavior. Peckinpah felt betrayed by Feldman,
who made the cuts without telling him, and this helped darken
and sour his outlook on producers. From this point on, he generally had his hackles up when dealing with studios. To the end of
his life, Peckinpah was haunted by the loss of this film in an edited assembly of which he approved. In 1980, he wrote to Lucien
Ballard, the film's cinematographer:

> Lucien, it has just come to my attention that there are rumors
> that the first married print of *The Wild Bunch* still exists. If so,
> and someone is lucky enough to get their hands on it, would
> you know of a lab to do a good CRI and re-time it so that cer-
> tain people might have a chance to see what it was really about.
> (Undercover, of course).[29]

Though Peckinpah did not live to see his greatest film restored to
its theatrical glory, it was so restored in 1995. New 35mm and
70mm prints were struck, 5)including the deleted footage and an
additional flashback showing how Pike received his leg wound,
which had never been in the American release prints. Thus restored, the film can now rightfully take its place among the classics of the American cinema and among the essential works of the
Western genre.

PECKINPAH AND THE WESTERN

With *The Wild Bunch*, Peckinpah summarized, revised,
and transcended much previous work in this genre. Peckinpah's
West is a much nastier, dirtier place than the polite, sanitized

frontier of previous Westerns. Peckinpah's reshaping of the genre is apparent in the film's extraordinary violence and in its jaundiced presentation of character. The bounty hunters T.C. (L.Q. Jones) and Coffer (Strother Martin), for example, are gleeful partners in filth and depravity ("Help me get his boots, T.C.!"), and their lusty celebration of theft, corpse mutilation, and backshooting went well beyond established genre conventions of taste and decorum. (Sergio Leone's cynical, brutal spaghetti Westerns had helped prepare the way.) They go happily off to their doom, loaded down with fresh corpses, singing "Polly Wolly Doodle," in one of the most memorable exits in the history of American film.

Peckinpah was one of the last great directors of Westerns for clear and good reasons. The classic Western filmmakers, such as John Ford, took the West seriously. They knew its geography firsthand and had a sincere commitment to, and belief in, its mythic symbolism. When Wyatt Earp escorts Clementine to the church services in John Ford's *My Darling Clementine* (1943), the surpassing beauty of this simply filmed scene is due to Ford's conviction about the resonance and meaning of the mythic imagery he has fashioned. The half-built church dwarfed by the barrenness of the surrounding desert and mountains eloquently visualizes the fragility of civilization in a harsh land and the hope for progress that the church embodies. Ford took the Western seriously because he believed in its materials and rituals and in the idea of the West as the crucible of the nation, an outlook on which the genre rests.

For Peckinpah, too, the West was a living reality, though one that he regarded and interpreted very differently than Ford. Peckinpah was born in 1925 into a family of prominent California lawyers, and he spent his boyhood summering at his grandfather's sprawling ranch in the Sierra Nevadas, where he learned to hunt, ride, and herd his grandfather's cattle. The area was still rough in those days, with old-time cowboys and prospectors hanging around, spinning yarns and tall tales, and with nearby towns with colorful names like Coarsegold and Finegold, a naming tradition that Peckinpah incorporated into his films (*Ride the High County*'s Coarsegold and *The Ballad of Cable Hogue*'s Gila and Dead Dog).

Meeting the old-timers, imbibing their stories, learning to shoot and hunt from his grandfather, and learning that the high country was a place of pristine beauty that embodied and engendered a rigorously virtuous moral philosophy ("Pick that up. These mountains don't need your trash," the hero tells a young whipper-snapper and litterbug in *Ride the High Country*) – these youthful experiences were extremely influential on Peckinpah's imagination, his veneration for the West, and particularly the melancholy tone that his Westerns assume. After his grandfather died, Peckinpah's mother sold the ranch. The loss of this property was a paradigmatic experience for young Sam and for his saddened perception that the West he knew and loved had vanished. In his interviews and recorded remarks, Peckinpah continually returned to the theme of the ranch's significance and the disturbing impact of its loss. "I grew up on a ranch. But that world is gone. . . . I feel rootless, completely. It's disturbing, very much so. But there's nothing you can do about it, nothing."[30] Peckinpah grasped the connection between the nostalgia he felt for the good times on his grandfather's ranch and his sensitivity for the Western genre and his skill for working within it. "I am a child of the old West," he said. "I knew at first hand the life of cowboys, I participated in some of their adventures and I actually witnessed the disintegration of a world. It was then inevitable that I should speak of it one day through a genre which is itself slowly dying: the Western."[31]

The Western genre permitted Peckinpah to show nostalgically the eclipse of what he considered to be a more primitive but vital world and to show caustically and critically the kind of modernity and progress that replaced it. *The Wild Bunch* is located at just such a transitional time, in 1913, on the eve of World War I, a holocaust of mechanized slaughter that was a clear harbinger of the modern brutalities of the twentieth century. The machine gun that wreaks such havoc in the film's climax embodies the modern technologies of violence that, Peckinpah believed, had so deformed contemporary life and were partly responsible for systematic savageries like the Vietnam War, a conflict he bitterly opposed. The Bunch, led by Pike Bishop, are outlaws of an old West who refuse to change with the times. Pike says, "We gotta start thinking beyond our guns," but they cannot do so. They must die with their world as a measure of the scorn that Peckinpah feels for a modern, corporate America and as a gesture of the integrity with which they embody his nostalgia for a vanquished era. "We represent the law," snarls the capitalist Harrigan just after he instigates the massacre in San Rafael, signaling his own corruption and that of the business empire he represents and the legal institutions he controls. Like the machine gun, Harrigan's boast emblematizes the looming historical forces – the concentration of ruthless political and economic power sustained by violence – that Peckinpah believed posed a significant antidemocratic threat in the twentieth century.

But counterposed to the incipient bleakness of the modern era in the film is a band of killers. As an ironist, Peckinpah provides no explicit moral condemnation of these characters. He expects that viewers will recognize their morally problematic nature. Except for Angel, Pike and his gang are aging outlaws, no longer as fast or smart as they used to be. That they will be losers in this historical contest is inevitable. It is the manner of their losing that commands such extraordinary interest in the film. This is partly due to the intense bond Peckinpah felt for these characters. "The outlaws of the West have always fascinated me," he remarked. "They were strong individuals, in a land for all intents and purposes without law, they made their own. I suppose I'm something of an outlaw myself. I identify with them. . . . I've always wondered what happened to the outlaw leaders of the Old West when it changed."[32] Yet despite this attachment he also recognized that these men are "limited and adolescent, they're not too bright."[33]

Furthermore, and most strikingly, he realized that despite their being violent bandits and despite the shattering effects of the film's graphic bloodshed, many viewers would grow attached to the Bunch and lament their passing. "The strange thing is you feel a great sense of loss when these killers reach the end of the line," Peckinpah said. This is because the film forecloses on the future of America, already in the clutches of Harrigan and his ilk, and

FIGURE 7
Flawed heroes caught in a period of historical transition, Pike and his gang die and are reborn into legend.

because the Bunch, in their violence and vitality and renegade individualism, represent the mythological center of the American spirit. Like most of Peckinpah's other Westerns (*Ride the High Country, The Ballad of Cable Hogue* [1970], *Pat Garrett and Billy the Kid* [1973]), *The Wild Bunch* deals with flawed heroes caught in a period of historical transition. They cannot change with the times, and their violent resistance to the forces of historical change (embodied in Harrigan and Mohr, the German military advisor working for Mapache, who represents the approach of World War I and, beyond it, the modern era) works, in the film's mythography, to validate the idea of a vanished West and a frontier that no longer exists, save, symbolically for these wild gringos, in Mexico.

The Western emerged as a genre in theater and literature (and subsequently in cinema) in the late 1880s at a time when the frontier was declared closed. Thus, the genre is inherently a melancholy one, dealing at its most profound level with a world that no longer exists and had ceased to do so when the genre took off.

FIGURE 8
Peckinpah showed the agony of violence with greater intensity than any previous American filmmaker.

Few films, though, have shown the death throes of an era with the passion and intensity of *The Wild Bunch*. When the Bunch go down in Aqua Verde, the film laments the passing of that robust vitality in the American heart and soul that Harrigan and all of his dollars and machinery will choke and stamp out. As these outlaws die and are reborn into legend in the film's closing moments, the loss viewers feel is connected to the renegade self in the national heritage that has been repressed and displaced by the bureaucracy and technology of today. Peckinpah was right, then, when he said that the Western was about now. "The Western is a universal frame within which it is possible to comment on today."[34] This helps ensure the continuing relevance of *The Wild Bunch*. It is not an old, dated movie. It remains fresh and vibrant today because viewers can see in it a vexing reflection upon, and a striking visualization of, the connection between an eclipsed national past and a disturbing present.

PECKINPAH AND SCREEN VIOLENCE

No feature of *The Wild Bunch* was more notorious in its day, and continues to be so, than its unprecedentedly graphic and sustained violence. Audience reactions to the film split on this issue. Some viewers at initial sneak previews of the picture were outraged, writing on their response cards "Nauseating, unending, offensive bloody violence" and "It's plain sadism. Only a sadist or one who is mentally deranged would enjoy this film."[35] Others believed the picture was making an antiviolence point. "The really shocking horror of this mass killing definitely makes one think." "I hope the viciousness of the fights stays in the film so people can really know how bad killing is."[36] Peckinpah noted these divergent responses and replied in a letter to a friend who had criticized the film's brutality that "better than 50% of the people who saw the picture felt as you did. However, better than 30% of the people thought it was an outstanding and much needed statement against violence."[37]

Peckinpah's intention, which he stated on many occasions,

was to use film to show audiences how awful violence is. However, he also realized that by stylizing violence, using slow motion and montage editing, he could render it poetically fascinating and aesthetically attractive. He noted that "in *The Wild Bunch* I wanted to show that violence could be at the same time repulsive and fascinating."[38] He thus placed viewers in an uncomfortable position, stimulating them to respond excitedly to, while recoiling morally from, the film's graphic bloodletting. In contrast to the cartoon violence of today's Arnold Schwarzenegger action films in which violence carries no pain, Peckinpah's screen violence hurts, and it is situated within a context of loss and sadness that works against the exciting stylistics of the montage editing. The Aqua Verde massacre is framed by the scene of Pike's alcoholic despair, as he silently reflects upon his wasted, failed life, and by the magnificent vulture kingdom imagery that follows the massacre as the maimed, dispossessed survivors hobble past the camera while the vultures feast on their inheritance.

Peckinpah aimed to bring suffering back to movie violence, and in doing this, he responded to the artificiality of previous decades of screen violence in which killing was quick, polite, and carried no sting. "*The Wild Bunch* was my way of reacting against all the films in which violence seemed facile, factitious and unreal. I was always fascinated to see how one died easily in the movies. . . . People die without suffering and violence provokes no pain."[39] As I discuss more fully in *Savage Cinema: Sam Peckinpah and the Rise of Ultra-Violent Movies,*[40] Peckinpah aimed to bring the nastiness and painfulness of violence onto the American screen in a way that would align film with the social realities of the traumatic violence sweeping America in the form of the Vietnam War, urban riots, and political assassinations. Peckinpah shared his nation's grieving, shocked response to these events, and he thus insisted that the violence in *The Wild Bunch* carry the disturbing force of human pain and anguish.

At the same time, he and editor Lou Lombardo stylized the gun battles in a highly artificial way by intercutting the multiple, ongoing lines of action and by employing slow motion to impose a different time scheme on the action and to render it balletic. Peck-inpah's insertion of brief slow-motion shots into the body of a normal tempo scene derives from the work of Akira Kurosawa (*Seven Samurai* [1954]) and Arthur Penn (*Bonnie and Clyde* [1967]), and the slow-motion inserts create a dynamic contrast with, and are energized by, the surrounding normal-tempo imagery. While Peckinpah continued to use slow motion in scenes of violence throughout his subsequent career (indeed, his work is closely identified with this device), the slow motion in *The Wild Bunch* is integrated into montages of great structural complexity (many critics erroneously claim that the cutting here is similar to Eisen-stein's work in *Battleship Potemkin*). Much of this complexity, and the exhilaration it produces in the viewer, are due to the way Peckinpah and Lombardo "mesh" together the separate lines of action[41] into a collage of colliding events. In this design, they slow down, interrupt, parallel, and return to ongoing lines of action. In the film's opening massacre, the Bunch have just robbed the depot and are being fired upon by the rooftop snipers. The out-laws return the fire, hitting two victims on the rooftop. The edit-ing parallels the falls of both rooftop victims by cross-cutting be-tween them, but it also interrupts these actions by cutting away to other ongoing events. As victim one topples forward, off the roof, the first cutaway appears, a shot of Pike running out of the depot office. The next shot returns to a continuation of the pre-vious action as victim one falls below the bottom of the frame. The next three shots are cutaways to other lines of action – Angel running out of the depot office, the rooftop snipers, and several of the Bunch shooting at the snipers from inside the depot. After these three cutaways, the editing returns to victim one, now falling in slow motion.

The next three shots are more cutaways, but they now also in-troduce the fate of the second rooftop victim. In the first cutaway, a medium shot shows the Bunch firing from inside the depot. Then, in the next shot, the second rooftop victim is struck and falls forward. Next, a medium shot shows Angel running from the depot, firing, continuing an action introduced six shots previously.

The next shot, in slow motion, returns to the first victim, continuing his protracted descent to earth. Next, the montage cuts to the second victim still toppling forward but not off the roof. His fall will be broken by the rooftop ledge. A medium close-up shows Deke Thornton shooting from the roof. Then, in the next two shots, both victims land simultaneously, in a matched cut, victim one in the street and victim two on the rooftop ledge.

The complexity of this editing takes us a long way from simple realism. The editing parallels the fates of both victims but introduces a highly artificial stylistic transformation of the action. The action cuts away from the fall of victim one four times, initially for one shot, then for three shots, again for three shots, and finally for two shots. Two cutaways interrupt the fall of the second victim for two shots each time. These cutaways and the slow motion markedly distort the time and space of the represented action. The editing creates a false parallel between the fates of the two victims because the relationships of time that prevail between these events are impossible. Victim one falls off the roof in slow motion and victim two falls at normal speed, yet they strike ledge and street at precisely the same moment, as the matched cut that closes off these events indicates. The simultaneous impact of the two victims represents an impossible time–space relationship within the sequence, yet Peckinpah and Lombardo convincingly intercut normal speed and slow motion to extend this discontinuity of time and space. This is certainly an example of what Peckinpah meant when he rejected allegations that his work represented a greater realism, stressing instead that it stylized violence, heightening it through an elaborate artistic transformation.

The film's montage editing adds tremendous excitement to its action sequences, yet, as several of this volume's authors point out, Peckinpah's use of montage to turn screen violence into an exciting spectacle tended to counteract his expressed intent to show viewers how powerful and nasty real violence could be. In *The Wild Bunch*, Peckinpah tends to get caught in the spectacle of violence as he evokes it through editing and slow motion. Thus evoked, it becomes a redemptive and heroic rite of passage for his

FIGURE 9
Peckinpah continued to explore the ugliness and pain of violence
in his subsequent works, especially the horrific *Straw Dogs*.

band of outlaws, enabling them to achieve a warror's apotheosis.
This is a long way from Peckinpah's alternate desire to show the
horror of violence. That does not come through consistently in
this film because, in the Aqua Verde climax, the Bunch's suicidal
gambit to reclaim Angel is both heroic and redemptive.

Peckinpah's subsequent films are more successful than *The Wild
Bunch* at showing the psychological waste and pain that violence
begets. *Straw Dogs* (1971), widely misunderstood by the critics, offers a horrific vision of how emotional rage and physical violence
corrupt and destroy the possibilities of human love and inter-
connection. The narrative of a meek college professor slaughter-
ing a gang of thugs that tries to break into his house conspicuously lacks the transcendent heroics of the violence in *The Wild
Bunch*. At the end of this bleak and icy film, the professor's house
is a shambles, he is estranged from his wife, and he is alienated

and adrift in strange and dark psychological territory. Violence has unhinged his world, and horror, not transcendence, is the result.

With *Pat Garrett and Billy the Kid* (1973), Peckinpah returned to the Western (*The Ballad of Cable Hogue,* also a Western, was comic and largely nonviolent) and the place of violence on the frontier. Unlike in *The Wild Bunch,* though, Peckinpah avoids extended and exciting montage spectacles of choreographed slaughter. In its style and narrative, the film is a fatigued, weary contemplation of Garrett's psychological and physical self-destruction, ensuing from his decision to hunt and kill his friend in return for money and what he thinks will be a secure future. The film's climactic image of Garrett, after he has killed the Kid, shooting his mirrored reflection and then gazing at himself through the shattered glass, is Peckinpah's most poetic image of the mutilation of human potential by violence. In his next film, *Bring Me the Head of Alfredo Garcia* (1974), Peckinpah showed, more bleakly than ever before, the perversion of human identity that accompanies the use of violence. A down-on-his-luck musician agrees to cut off the head of a corpse in order to collect a bounty placed on the head, but his bloody quest destroys everything in his life and leads him, in turn, to the grave. Again, the visual pyrotechnics of *The Wild Bunch* are conspicuously absent because Peckinpah realized after that film that extended scenes of uncontrolled spectacle were inconsistent with the sober and tragic portraits of human violence that he wished to evoke in *Straw Dogs, Pat Garrett* and *Alfredo Garcia.*

His work after *Alfredo Garcia* is marred by a consistently bad choice of scripts. The narrative problems in these scripts were so severe that they corrupted the resulting productions. *The Killer Elite* (1975), *Cross of Iron* (1977), *Convoy* (1978), and *The Osterman Weekend* (1983) achieve only fitful moments of narrative coherence and stylistic grace, and they collectively demonstrate Peckinpah's rapid artistic decline and failure to sustain a career as a major American director.

The Wild Bunch, therefore, finds Peckinpah at the summit of his powers and on the threshold of an incredible, if short-lived, burst of productivity that saw the release of seven remarkable films (*The Wild Bunch, The Ballad of Cable Hogue, Straw Dogs, Junior Bonner* [1972], *The Getaway* [1972], *Pat Garrett and Billy the Kid,* and *Bring Me the Head of Alfredo Garcia*) in six years. These were the peak years of Peckinpah's career, and he audaciously announced their onset with his definitive revision of the Western. As we have seen, Peckinpah's attitudes toward the screen violence he orchestrates in *The Wild Bunch* are not clearly worked out and have not yet achieved the coherence they would have in his later work. But, despite this, Peckinpah went places in this film that directors before him had not dared to go or had been permitted to go by the industry.

In *The Wild Bunch,* Peckinpah pushed violence as far as it could go within the confines of the Western, a genre in which control, discipline, and restraint, embodied in the ritual of the gunfight, had always conditioned the display of violence. Substituting for them the orgiastic frenzy of the film's opening and closing gun battles, with their mass killing, Peckinpah took violence in *The Wild Bunch* to the outer edge of what was permissible and possible in the Western. With more of the mechanized mass slaughter that caps the film at Aqua Verde, the filmmaker and viewer would find themselves in a different genre, one, like the war film or gangster film, that can accommodate more sophisticated technologies of violence and a higher body count than can the Western. By amplifying the level of violence, and by detailing the impact of bullets on flesh and the eruptions of blood, intercutting slow-motion with normal-speed imagery, Peckinpah established (but did not invent) the essential cinematic stylistics that virtually all filmmakers today employ when they present graphic violence. He also showed how powerful it could be to place bad characters at the center of a narrative, and long before *Pulp Fiction* (1995) and *Natural Born Killers* (1995) (which take special delight in their bad boy and bad girl characters), he showed the searing potential of an authorial voice fixed in irony and cynicism. There is American cinema before *The Wild Bunch,* and there is American cinema after *The Wild Bunch.* This before and after are two very different places, and Peckinpah, more than any other filmmaker of the period, took industry and audience from the one to the other.

THE ESSAYS AND REVIEWS

The richness of *The Wild Bunch* is evident in the range of discussion contained in the following essays. The authors bring a variety of critical and historical perspectives to bear on the film, but while each recognizes the film's centrality for postwar American cinema, they offer differing explanations for its importance.

Every film begins with a script during the vital pre-production phase of filmmaking. Paul Seydor traces the evolution of the film's script and discusses Peckinpah's collaboration with his screenwriters. In filming this picture, Peckinpah went well beyond the scripted material, and Seydor shows the extent to which the film originated on paper and how Peckinpah enlarged and embellished it during production. Seydor offers a valuable dissection of the film's evolution from page to screen.

Though it is a Western, *The Wild Bunch* transcends its genre. Peckinpah noted that he was using the Western to speak about the world of today. The next two essays show how he did this. Christopher Sharrett and Michael Bliss offer provocative accounts of *The Wild Bunch* as a portrait of America. Sharrett examines the vision of society contained in *The Wild Bunch,* arguing that Peckinpah was a politically radical director and his film a scathing critique of the ideals and the failures of American society. Sharrett argues that the film remains vital and contemporary because it is "more than homage for a dead past; it is a recognition of how that past was probably always a deceit."

Michael Bliss offers a differing interpretation of this film's vision of American society, and he locates a concrete basis for the film's portrait in the way that Peckinpah's visual design structures physical space in the film's shots and scenes. Proceeding from a discussion of how Peckinpah's screen space encloses and traps the characters, Bliss explores the ethical, social, and historical implications of this design, particularly in the predatory behaviors enacted by each of the film's main groups of characters – the Bunch, Harrigan and his bounty hunters, and Mapache and his army.

The next two essays place the film in historical context according to issues of style and genre. David Cook examines the history of movie gunplay in relation to *The Wild Bunch* and how the film helped inaugurate a new style of "ballistic balletics" that has now become the normative method of presenting screen violence. Cook places the film in relation to the cultural factors and film industry regulations that helped sanitize screen violence in earlier decades, and he then explains why the limits on what was permissible to show on screen changed so decisively in the late sixties. Throughout his historical discussion, Cook emphasizes the "uneasy relationship between spectators and on-screen gunplay that has been tempered by the cultural/political status of real armed violence in American society."

Wheeler Winston Dixon places the film in relation to the traditions and conventions of the Western genre, as Peckinpah inherited that genre when he began work on the film and as he transformed and recast it in ways that could not be undone by subsequent filmmakers.

In the final essay, Devin McKinney takes a provocatively different view of *The Wild Bunch*. McKinney accepts that the film deserves the extraordinary critical fascination it has received, but he argues that it is not the masterpiece it is generally considered to be. He finds that the film's style of violence – the slow motion and montage editing – "still communicates death in a way that is both insanely urgent and reflectively distanced." But, he argues, Peckinpah retreated from the radical implications of this style by telling a story that retains the conventional melodrama and sentimentality of ordinary Hollywood pictures and he was unable, in this film, to get beyond the treatment of death as a purely visual phenomenon.

These authors have the advantage of writing about *The Wild Bunch* as a film they have known and lived with for years. By contrast, newspaper and magazine movie reviewers must write about their immediate response to a new film that they have just seen.

In the concluding section of this volume, the reviewers for *Time* magazine and *The New York Times* provide an assessment of the film upon its initial release in 1969. Consequently, their reactions are more hurried, and they cannot (yet) assess the film's place in cinema history. The reviews, though, tell us much about the immediate responses of first-time viewers. Each of the reviewers spends considerable time talking about the impact of the film's extraordinary violence. While both reviewers recognize the audacious visual style of the picture, the reader will note that neither reviewer yet saw that this film would become a modern classic. Vincent Canby's closing remark, in the first *Times* piece reprinted here, that the film did not induce him to commit real violence once outside the theater was meant as a rejoinder to the controversies about the effects of movie violence that this film, and *Bonnie and Clyde* two years earlier, had helped trigger.

Canby and the reviewer for *Time* both complain about the awkwardness with which the film's flashback material was introduced. Both critics had seen the initial, complete American assembly of the film, but Warners–Seven Arts quickly withdrew this version from distribution, replacing it with a shorter version that lacked the flashbacks, one additional entire scene (Villa's attack on Mapache), and some of the material from the scene where the Bunch visit Angel's village. This abbreviated version of the film became the only one that viewers could see for many years. In the second article, Vincent Canby laments the loss of this footage, discusses the studio's reasons for making the cuts, and compares his reactions to both versions.

The outrage of many critics and viewers, who were appalled at the ferocity of the film's bloodshed, is vividly recorded in the press conference held by Peckinpah, the producer, and the cast of the film in June 1969 following a preview screening for newspaper and magazine movie reviewers. The reader will note the hostility of the questioning that Peckinpah and his associates endured and the way that the Vietnam War, then ongoing, formed a background and context for the discussion, occasioning Peckinpah's memorable proclamation, "The Western is a universal frame within which it is possible to talk about today." No better explanation for the film's enduring importance can be offered.

NOTES

The Sam Peckinpah Collection is housed at the Margaret Herrick Library, Academy of Motion Picture Arts and Sciences, Los Angeles.

1 Marshall Fine, *Bloody Sam: The Life and Films of Sam Peckinpah* (New York: Donald I. Fine, Inc., 1991), p. 153.
2 Sam Peckinpah Collection, Correspondence – Don Siegel, folder no. 89.
3 Sam Peckinpah Collection, Correspondence – misc., letter of 9/30/60, folder no. 18.
4 Sam Peckinpah Collection, *Major Dundee* – Jerry Bresler correspondence, folder no. 8.
5 Sam Peckinpah Collection, *Major Dundee,* letter of 3/23/65, folder no. 18.
6 Sam Peckinpah Collection, Correspondence – Charlton Heston, letter of 8/6/68, folder no. 46.
7 Sam Peckinpah Collection, *The Wild Bunch* – Peckinpah memos, memo of 10/12/67, folder no. 62.
8 All of the information about the film's shooting schedule is derived from the daily production log, Sam Peckinpah Collection, *Wild Bunch* production reports, folder no. 84.
9 Sam Peckinpah Collection, *The Wild Bunch* – Peckinpah memos, memo of 5/6/68, folder no. 62.
10 Ibid., memo of 5/18/68.
11 Ibid., memo of 5/20/68.
12 Ibid., memo of 6/13/68.
13 Ibid., memo of 5/9/68.
14 Sam Peckinpah Collection, Feldman memos, memo of 8/5/68, folder no. 45.
15 Sam Peckinpah Collection, *The Wild Bunch* – Peckinpah memos, memo of 10/25/68, folder no. 62.
16 Ibid., memo of 5/3/69.
17 Ibid.
18 Sam Peckinpah Collection, *Wild Bunch* – Feldman memos, memo of 2/1/69, folder no. 46.
19 Sam Peckinpah Collection, *Wild Bunch* – Peckinpah memos, memo of 5/3/69, folder no. 62.

20 Sam Peckinpah Collection, Feldman memos, letter of 1/30/68 from MPAA's Geoffrey Shurlock, folder no. 45.
21 Ibid.
22 Ibid.
23 Ibid.
24 Ibid.
25 Sam Peckinpah Collection, Feldman memos, letter of 3/17/69, folder no. 46.
26 Ibid., letter of 4/8/69, folder no. 46.
27 Ibid., memo of 2/9/68, folder no. 45.
28 Ibid., memo of 5/13/69, folder no. 46.
29 Sam Peckinpah Collection, Correspondence – Lucien Ballard, letter of 10/21/80, folder no. 5.
30 Dan Yergin, "Peckinpah's Progress," *The New York Times Magazine,* Oct. 31, 1971, p. 92.
31 Sam Peckinpah Collection, *Le Devoir* interview, Oct. 10, 1974, folder no. 96.
32 Stephen Farber, "Peckinpah's Return," *Film Quarterly* 23, no. 1 (Fall, 1969), p. 9.
33 Ibid.
34 "Press Violent About Film's Violence, Prod Sam Peckinpah Following 'Bunch'," *Variety,* July 2, 1969, p. 15.
35 Sam Peckinpah Collection, folder no. 74, 75.
36 Ibid.
37 Sam Peckinpah Collection, *Wild Bunch* – response letters, letter of May 13, 1969, folder no. 92.
38 Sam Peckinpah Collection, *Le Devoir* interview, folder no. 96.
39 Ibid.
40 Stephen Prince, *Savage Cinema: Sam Peckinpah and the Rise of Ultraviolent Movies* (Austin: University of Texas Press, 1998).
41 Lombardo described his work as the meshing or intercutting of the separate lines of action. See David Weddle, *If They Move . . . Kill 'Em* (New York: Grove Press, 1994), p. 355.

▐ *The Wild Bunch:* The Screenplay

> Any script that's written changes at least thirty percent from the time you begin preproduction: ten percent while you fit your script to what you discover about your locations, ten percent while your ideas are growing as you rehearse your actors who must grow into their parts because the words mean nothing alone, and ten percent while the film is finally being edited. It may change more than this but rarely less.
>
> Sam Peckinpah

I

If ever there was a film that absolutely demonstrates the validity of the auteur theory as it is commonly understood – that the director is the "author" of a film – it is surely *The Wild Bunch*. Of the hundreds of pieces written about this film, I can't think of a single one that doesn't rest upon – indeed, that even thinks of questioning – the assumption that it is, first, last, and always, Peckinpah's and only Peckinpah's creation. Yet he did not come up with the original story, nor did he write the first screenplay.

And though he did a substantial rewrite that transformed the material, amazingly little is known for certain about how the project began or, for that matter, about the precise contours of the way he developed the story and made it his own. What did he keep, what did he drop, what did he change, invent, or reinvent for himself?

For a long time these questions were unanswerable in any detail because the requisite materials, namely, the various versions and drafts of the screenplay, were scattered around and unavailable. However, in 1986, two years after his death, Peckinpah's family donated his papers to the Margaret Herrick Library of the Academy of Motion Picture Arts and Sciences in Beverly Hills, California. There was a daunting amount of material that took the research archivist Valentin Almendarez four years to sort, organize, and file. But since 1990 the Peckinpah Collection has been available to members of the Academy and anyone else who cares to make an appointment with the library's Special Collections department. The papers are filed in folders kept in numbered boxes measuring about 15 × 12 × 10 inches. The Peckinpah Collection fills ninety-five boxes and has an annotated inventory that requires 164 pages just to list, briefly describe, and cross reference each document to its box number.[1] Five and a half pages are devoted to the *The Wild Bunch* alone, and two boxes, numbers 30 and 31, contain treatments and several drafts of the screenplay.

They make for fascinating reading, exciting discoveries, but they do not yield their treasures easily. Peckinpah's hand – he rarely used pens, only pencils – is a nearly indecipherable hodgepodge of writing and printing. Judging from the drafts in the Collection, his typical practice was to scribble changes over or in the margin next to passages he wanted to revise, continuing on the back of the page at the same relative spot, down to the bottom, up to the unused space at the top, then onto the backs of other pages if necessary.[2] Tracking the revisions is both thrilling – the heat of inspiration is sometimes palpable – and challenging, as the effort required to decipher the scrawl is considerable. (Peckinpah did not do his own typing, and your heart goes out to his typists.)

But the rewards are worth it. They lead us, for example, to the exact moment when Peckinpah began to conceive of the Bunch in mythic terms, in two key places in the draft dated 16 June 1967. When Pike climbs back onto his horse after the stirrup strap has broken, Peckinpah added a sentence: "He turns and rides toward the mountains, the men following." The description is deceptively simple, the moment almost thrown away, yet it led to the lovely epiphany of the beleaguered outlaw riding over the dune. The other is the celebrated walk to retrieve Angel, missing from the original but scribbled onto these pages, three pregnant sentences that became perhaps the greatest filming of a Western convention in the history of motion pictures:

> THEY CROSS TO THEIR HORSES, THEIR DRUNKENNESS LESSENING with every step.

> Pike and Dutch pull rifles or shotguns from their saddle scabbards as do Lyle and Tector, then they move up the village street.

> FOUR MEN IN LINE AND THE AIR OF IMPENDING VIOLENCE IS SO STRONG around them that as they pass through the celebrating soldiers, the song and the laughter begin to die.[3]

At the time *The Wild Bunch* came out, Peckinpah played down both the epic aspirations and the romantic feelings of his greatest film. He hated pretentiousness, he didn't want to come out pompous or high-sounding, and he had not forgotten the drubbing he had taken four years earlier for what several critics perceived as o'er reaching ambition in the ill-fated *Major Dundee* (1965). But the way he developed the screenplay and eventually shot the film demonstrates pretty clearly that the largeness of vision in *The Wild Bunch,* its epic romanticism, did not happen by accident. However gradually it may have developed, it was something he saw in the material from the moment he first read the script, something he started building in from the moment he began rewriting it.

But this gets us ahead of our story, which begins with Peckinpah's previous film, *Major Dundee.*[4]

II

Roy Sickner was a stuntman at the top of his profession by the time he accepted a job as Richard Harris's double for the action sequences in *Major Dundee*. Sickner had regularly ridden stunts for Marlon Brando, Yul Brynner, Rod Taylor, and others. Classically handsome in the rugged Western mode, he was the first "Marlboro man" in the cigarette commercials. But he had ambitions of producing, his dream to do a big violent Western movie, heavy on stunts and elaborate action set pieces, starring his close friend Lee Marvin. Sickner and a friend of his, Chuck Hayward, also a stuntman, came up with a story about a gang of outlaws involved in escapades on both sides of the U.S.–Mexico border. Sickner pitched the idea to Peckinpah on the *Dundee* location in Mexico in 1964. Sometime in 1965 Marvin expressed a keen interest in a property attached to Sickner that was called *The Wild Bunch*.

This is just about all that is known with any certainty about the early history of *The Wild Bunch*. What shape it had at the very beginning is anybody's guess because nothing was written down and the evidence is largely anecdotal, most of it recollections by parties once or more removed. Of the three early principals, Peckinpah and Marvin are dead, and Sickner is too incapacitated to be of help.[5] As best the story can be pieced together, Sickner returned from Mexico soon after pitching the idea to Peckinpah, excited to get his ideas on paper but inundated with offers for more work, which he accepted.[6] He was so restless and energetic that his attention span was, to put it mildly, limited under the best of circumstances. His friends loved him, but he was the original "man's man," a wild and, when drunk, quite literally crazy and sometimes mean guy who did everything to excess – drinking, smoking, womanizing, gambling, spending, brawling, and just plain hell-raising. Like most movie-industry dreams, his would have remained unfulfilled and probably been forgotten entirely except for a change in the fortunes of Marvin's career. To the surprise of virtually everyone, including himself, he won the 1965 Academy Award as best actor for his dual performance as the drunken gunfighter and the villain in the comedy Western *Cat Ballou*. Before this a character actor known for playing villains and other tough lowlifes (he was Liberty Valance in John Ford's *The Man Who Shot Liberty Valance* [1962]), all of a sudden he found himself a star. His next picture was Richard Brooks's *The Professionals* (1966), a big-budget, star-driven Western that, like *Cat Ballou,* became a huge hit. Now Marvin wasn't just a star; he was a star whose mere interest could get a project off the ground. And he was still interested in *The Wild Bunch.*

Suddenly Sickner needed a screenwriter, as nobody, even a pal like Marvin, was going to commit to anything without a screenplay. Whatever his abilities, Sickner was no writer; he couldn't even manage a treatment (in industry parlance, a detailed synopsis of the story in narrative form, usually between twenty and fifty pages). Enter Walon Green, a documentary filmmaker in his early thirties, eager to break into writing features.[7] Green and Sickner had met in 1964 when Green was a dialogue director on *Saboteur: Code Name Morituri,* where Sickner was doubling stunts for the picture's star, Marlon Brando. A year later Sickner was directing the second unit on *Winter à Go-Go,* a low-budget comedy in need of a script polish. Sickner recommended Green to the producer, Reno Carell, who hired the writer. It was around this time that Sickner pitched his idea for *The Wild Bunch* to Carell, with Sickner himself as director. With the producer's interest and presumably his backing, Sickner offered Green $1,500 to write a treatment. "Roy came over to my house," Green recalls,

> and I remember, I had this little reel-to-reel tape recorder, and Roy dictated an outline of the plot. As best I can remember, it went something like this: these guys rob a train depot in Texas, then run across the border to Mexico with a posse chasing them. They meet some Mexican bandits who hire them to steal guns from the US army. The outlaws steal the guns, sell them to the Mexicans, and then take off. The Mexicans, who planned a double-cross all along, pursue the outlaws, eventually catching up with them just as the railroad posse closes in from the other direction. The outlaws are caught in a big gun fight that ends the movie.

From this sketch Green wrote a treatment, then the screenplay. When Carell had a budget breakdown done of the script and was informed that the picture would cost about $4 million, ten times the highest budget his company could manage, he passed. Sickner then shopped it around elsewhere, meeting with varying degrees of interest but no firm offers. Meanwhile, Green went back to directing documentaries and soon lost track of it altogether. He was not even aware that it was about to go into production at Warner Brothers until a friend read an item in the trade papers and phoned him.

The story Sickner dictated to Green was bare almost beyond skeletal, and to say that Green fleshed it out is hugely to understate the magnitude of his efforts. Even the plot, which Green, a remarkably generous, rather self-effacing man, has always credited to Sickner, needed extensive development (the whole last part following the exchange of rifles, for example, is unrecognizable even as a blueprint for the completed film). None of the characters had names, few of them were individuated enough to be called characters as such, and Thornton, Angel, and Old Sykes (among others) Green doesn't remember existing at all. It goes almost without saying that there was no suggestion of the complex relationships among the several characters and groups that distinguish the film.

Sickner had set the story in the early 1880s, but Green told him there wasn't much happening in Mexico at that time and changed it to 1911–13 (which made possible the twin themes of the end of an era and the West in transition that Peckinpah inflected so powerfully). Next Green turned to the plot. His first alteration was to have the sacks the Bunch steal at the beginning turn out to be filled with washers instead of the gold Sickner had dictated. Though apparently small, this change had large implications. Having just pulled a robbery that nets them nothing and puts a posse on their trail, the Bunch can't return to the States and are thus forced deeper into Mexico, where, out of money, they hire themselves out on a job that eventually embroils them in a civil war. Overall Green made the plot both more elaborate and more tightly knit.

He also tied the story much more closely to its milieu by creating Angel, his village, and by extension all the scenes involving Angel and the revolution (except those later contributed by Peckinpah). Finally, he worked out a much more satisfactory second half that included such scenes as the one where the *federales* try to take the guns without paying for them and that dispensed with such ludicrous coincidences as the Mexicans and the posse catching up with the robbers at the same time.

"The main genesis of the screenplay comes from several things," Green recalls. "I lived in Mexico and worked there for about a year and a half. *The Wild Bunch* was partly written as my love letter to Mexico" (interestingly, one of the same reasons Peckinpah later gave for wanting to make it). He continues:

> I had just read Barbara Tuchman's book *The Zimmerman Telegram,* which is about the Germans' efforts to get the Americans into a war with Mexico to keep them out of Europe. I wanted to allude to some of that, so I gave Mapache German advisors whose commander says that line about how useful it would be if they knew of some Americans who didn't share their government's naive sentiments. I had also seen this amazing documentary, *Memorias de Un Mexicano,* that was shot while the revolution was actually happening – it's three hours of film taken during the revolution itself. That film had a big influence on the look of *The Wild Bunch.* I didn't know Sam at this time, but I had Roy see it, and he told me that he made Sam watch it.
>
> To give you some idea of how important this film was for *The Wild Bunch,* you remember in my screenplay that Agua Verde was originally called Parras, which I used because it was the birthplace of Francisco Madero. But I had never been there. When the location scouts came back they told me it was just like I had described it. I can only assume that my descriptions were accurate because I probably saw some of Parras in *Memorias.*

The most obvious historical antecedent for the outlaws themselves is Butch Cassidy's Hole-in-the-Wall Gang, whom the newspapers nicknamed "the Wild Bunch" and who were chased out of the country by a posse of Pinkerton detectives. Though Green claimed to have known almost nothing then about the history of Cassidy (see Segaloff, p. 140), his screenplay has Lyle Gorch telling Pike, "I've heard it's like the old times in Argentina . . . Butch Cassidy went there three years ago and he's making a killing . . ." (14) and mentions the Pinkertons by name (10). And while Harrigan's occupation is not absolutely clear in Green's screenplay – he doesn't seem to be an officer of the railroad – in the treatment he is positively identified as "a private agent" employed by the railroad. There are other parallels as well. When I asked Green about these, he remembered that he learned about the Cassidy history from his story conferences with Sickner (who also came up with the title). (Much later the historical parallels were strengthened by Peckinpah, e.g., Final, p. 21.)[8]

Though Green and Peckinpah had never met or talked with one another until the director was already shooting the picture, it is amazing how close their ideas for developing the story were. One explanation is that independently they had covered a lot of the same ground: Peckinpah was researching the Mexican Revolution for *Villa Rides* (1968), an original script he was writing at Paramount immediately prior to tackling *The Wild Bunch*.[9] Another is that they shared a love for some of the same films and directors, in particular Huston and Kurosawa. Green specifically created the character of Freddie Sykes "as my homage to Howard, the old man played by Walter Huston in *The Treasure of the Sierra Madre*. You know, everybody tried to get me to drop Sykes – *everybody* – no one liked him until Sam came along, and Sam loved him." Though he couldn't possibly have known Green's intentions, Peckinpah too saw in Howard a progenitor of Sykes and an opportunity to acknowledge a film he loved. The same coincidence operated in respect to Kurosawa. Having just seen *The Seven Samurai* (1954) and been bowled over by it, Green asked Sickner if some of the violence and action in *The Wild Bunch* might be filmed in slow motion. Unbeknownst to the writer, Peckinpah also revered Kurosawa (though much preferring *Rashomon* [1954] to *The Seven Samurai*) and had already experimented with slow motion, exposing thousands of feet of high-speed footage in *Major Dundee* (see Weddle, pp. 243, 249–50). Although none of it made the final cut, by the time he got back to Mexico in 1968, Peckinpah clearly had this particular bit in his teeth and was champing at it with a vengeance.[10]

Green expended his greatest efforts on bringing the characters to life. He took unusual care assigning them names:

> Thornton was named for a kid I went to grammar school with. Pike was a name I always wanted to use, it's a kind of carnivorous fish and it suggested someone who is tough and predatory. Dutch for me is a warm and comfortable-sounding name, and I wanted to indicate something of those qualities in the man. Gorch was after a real mill-trash family I knew; I don't know where I got Lyle, but Tector was a guy I cleaned swimming pools with from West Virginia. Angel is pretty obvious, he was the good guy. Mapache means raccoon in Spanish, and it seemed to me something a peasant risen to a general might call himself, after a smart but wily and devious animal. Coffer was named for a stuntman I knew named Jack Coffer who was killed. Jack was a real inspiration to me for the kind of guys who are *really* wild and crazy. Railroad men were often Irish. Harrigan was a hard-sounding Irish name that felt right for this kind of man.[11]

In view of both the substance and the sheer number of Green's contributions, Sickner must have been aware how thoroughly his threadbare plot had been transformed into a real story, for when the treatment was registered with the Screen Writers Guild, the title page put the writer first: "*The Wild Bunch* by Walon Green from an Original Story by Roy Sickner." The on-screen credit for original story is even more decisive, attributing it to Green and Sickner in that order, suggesting that as far as the Writers Guild, which arbitrates such matters, was concerned, whatever form Sickner's story was in when it first came to Green, it required so much work as to get Green the first position.

Green's treatment, a twenty-eight-page narrative that is undated, is in the Peckinpah Collection, as is a shorter treatment, fifteen pages long and dated 28 March 1967, that is essentially a condensed version of the same narrative. Together these are the two earliest written forms of *The Wild Bunch* known to exist. The Collection also contains a copy of Green's first screenplay, though it too is undated. The first *Wild Bunch* script to carry a date – 16 June 1967 – is nearly identical to Green's original but with some notes that appear to be in Peckinpah's hand. This copy is incomplete, as is another that has many handwritten changes on it, definitely by Peckinpah and still dated 16 June. After this there is a complete script that incorporates the handwritten changes from the previous one, also dated 16 June. Then there is a complete screenplay with a title page that reads: "*The Wild Bunch,* Written by Walon Green and Sam Peckinpah, Story by Roy Sickner. FIRST DRAFT," dated 28 June 1967.

Without some explanation, none of these dates makes sense, and the date on the shorter treatment has to be wrong. To begin with, if the date is accurate, it means that Green wrote the first screenplay and that Peckinpah read it and did his first revision all in the three months between 28 March and 28 June 1967. Practically speaking, this would have been impossible; and in any case, it can't be true because Green wrote the screenplay the previous year (perhaps ever earlier) and because Sickner shopped it a while before it was purchased by Warner Brothers.[12] The history of the project clouds up again here, particularly on the matter of Peckinpah's involvement or reinvolvement, as the case may be. Sickner said that Peckinpah not only listened carefully when he and Hayward told him their ideas on the *Major Dundee* set, but even made some suggestions. For his part, Peckinpah always said that he first heard about *The Wild Bunch* from Lee Marvin. In 1977 Peckinpah wrote me:

> Roy Sickner brought me an outline of some 32 pages by Walon Green and himself, and a rough screenplay including some of the dialogue that was used in the picture. I did three drafts and submitted it to Warner Brothers. Ken Hyman bought it. I did it because Roy Sickner got some money for me from a Chicago banker. I first read it on a recommendation from Lee Marvin.[13]

Much of this is consistent with the materials in the Collection, most of which came from Peckinpah's files. The Green–Sickner treatment is there. (Though it is twenty-eight rather than thirty-two pages, David Weddle and I both believe that it is the outline Peckinpah referred to in his letter to me and that he simply mis-remembered the number of pages. No thirty-two-page treatment is known to exist.) The three drafts of the screenplay, culminating in the first complete draft of 28 June 1967, are also there. The Chicago banker is one Anthony M. Ryerson, from whom Sickner got some development money that enabled him to attract Peckinpah's attention. Peckinpah's statement that he first read "it" – meaning the outline – on a recommendation from Lee Marvin jibes with remarks he made to others. As Peckinpah was usually pretty generous when it came to giving credit, it is entirely possible that his conversations with Sickner on the location of *Major Dundee* slipped his mind. Directors are always being told about "great ideas" for movies, and Peckinpah was no exception.

It is also possible that Sickner exaggerated Peckinpah's initial interest. There is almost no question that they talked about *The Wild Bunch* at least once, probably more than once, on the location of *Major Dundee*. But between Peckinpah's being fired from *The Cincinnati Kid* in December 1964 and December 1966 – a two-year period when he was effectively blacklisted by the major studios and was frantically writing to get himself a directing job (five full-length screenplays and several teleplays) – there is little to suggest that he paid more than passing attention to Sickner's pipe dream. Though Sickner's friends believe he always intended *The Wild Bunch* for Peckinpah, Sickner's attempt to sell it to Carell with himself as director demonstrates otherwise, as does Carell's brief ownership, plainly stated on the title page of Green's treatment. Indeed, for all his talk about Peckinpah's attachment, Sickner raised the money for a treatment only *after* he had managed to maneuver himself into the director's chair. And who can blame him? This was a time when nobody was hiring Peckinpah for features.[14]

No one can say for certain, therefore, how committed Peckinpah was to *The Wild Bunch* before he read the Green screenplay or when exactly he first acquired it.[15] But it next turns up in a pile of scripts he brought with him when Ken Hyman (the Seven Arts half of Warner Brothers–Seven Arts) and Phil Feldman set him up in a studio office to begin work on *The Diamond Story,* a modern-day action-adventure property set in Africa that was supposed to star Charlton Heston. Whenever Peckinpah acquired *The Wild Bunch,* the most likely time that he would have thought seriously about revising it is late April or May 1967. There are two reasons for this supposition. Much before that he was too busy at Paramount writing *Villa Rides,* which he didn't turn in until almost the last week in April. The other is that it wasn't until late winter or early spring that Sickner seemed to have had any real money. On 21 December 1966 a letter of agreement was drafted between Sickner and Ryerson giving Peckinpah a 25 percent share of *The Wild Bunch,* in lieu of money, for rewriting the screenplay and eventually directing it. Throughout the winter of the following year, Sickner continued negotiating with Peckinpah, whose interest by then had certainly been aroused. But he still doesn't appear to have done any actual work on the script until Sickner got him some hard money, as opposed to a promised "ownership" of a property that might never get into production.[16] Still pretty strapped for cash from his two-years-plus run of bad luck, he could not afford to work on speculation.[17] Once he turned to *The Wild Bunch,* however, he finished his first revision in two months – entirely possible, even likely, given how furiously he pursued anything in those months that looked as though it might land him a directing stint.

How, then, to explain the two versions of the same treatment and a date on one of them that can't be correct? It is a matter of fact that the undated longer treatment was written by Green much earlier. But Green can't remember writing the shorter one, which makes sense: if we recall that by then he had gone off to other projects and lost track of *The Wild Bunch* altogether, he probably didn't. If not Green, then who, and why? My guess – with which Green concurs – is that Peckinpah, Sickner, or someone else close to the project had Green's treatment condensed, in the process removing Carell's name, as he no longer owned it, and assigning it a date that would keep the studio from thinking it was a reject that had been lying around. (This is often done when projects considered dead are resurrected; more often than not, the title is also changed.) As for identical dates on the director's three different copies of the Green screenplay, these were for him private working drafts only, nothing he was ready to submit to a producer or studio. He obviously felt no need to redate them each time he did some work on them. The various drafts dated 16 June are simply stages of a work-in-progress that became the 28 June screenplay. That Peckinpah considered this his first *complete* revision is evidenced by his unambiguously calling it *his* "first draft" right on the title page and taking a credit as cowriter (in the second position).[18]

Despite the work he was supposed to be doing on *The Diamond Story,* once he started rewriting *The Wild Bunch,* it consumed him for the remainder of spring and the whole summer. Some time in August, when *The Diamond Story* looked as if it would fall through for good and Feldman wondered what they might turn to next, Peckinpah handed him the revised *The Wild Bunch* and reminded him of Marvin's continued interest. Feldman liked what he read, liked also the director's ideas for further changes, and liked most of all the prospect of Marvin, whose brutal but exciting World War II action picture, *The Dirty Dozen,* had just recently hit the theaters to spectacular box office. Ken Hyman was likewise enthusiastic, as *The Dirty Dozen* was his last work as an independent producer before becoming head of production at Warners. Suddenly, *The Wild Bunch* was born, studio chief and producer both confident they had a "Western" *Dirty Dozen* in the making. Little did they know that their director was nurturing a quite different creature, though soon enough he would send Hyman a note that in retrospect contains some portent of how passionate and personal would be his investment: "Of all the projects I have worked on," Peckinpah declared, "this is the closest to me."[19]

III

The Peckinpah Collection contains several drafts of *Wild Bunch* screenplays, some complete, some not, all dated between

June 1967 and May 1968. The last changes of any sort consist of some loose pages of revisions dated 20 May 1968, by which time Peckinpah was almost two months into principal photography (which had begun on 25 March). It would be tedious, misleading, and far beyond the scope of this essay to note each and every change, revision, and addition by Peckinpah. He did so substantial a dialogue rewrite, for example, that few scenes were left untouched; but to detail every last line or word change is to indulge in minutiae that would obscure the overall pattern of his changes.[20] My task here is to set forth this pattern and chart the major changes by which it is defined. To this end, I have tried to keep critical commentary as such to a minimum. Readers interested in a full-length analysis that addresses many of the implications of these changes are directed to the chapter on *The Wild Bunch* in my critical study of Peckinpah's Western films (137–212).

"There was nothing elegant, witty, or slick about" the original screenplay, David Weddle has pointed out, and it lacked any "trace of romanticism" (309). This was Walon Green's intention. "I always liked Westerns," he has said, but

> I always felt they were too heroic and too glamorous. I'd read enough to know that Billy the Kid shot people in the back of the head while they were drinking coffee; it had to be lot meaner than that. Plus I knew a lot of ranchers and cowboys, and they were *mean*. I wrote it, thinking that I would like to see a Western that was as mean and ugly and brutal as the times, and the only nobility in men was their dedication to each other. (Segaloff, p. 143)

This was Peckinpah's point of departure too. Ever since his television series *The Westerner* (1960), he had been obsessed with portraying cowboys, outlaws, and gunfighters as realistically as he knew how. But he seems to have realized fairly early on that men who are merely bad don't make for very interesting characters, themes, or dramas. So while he retained most of Green's grit and realism, Peckinpah developed *The Wild Bunch* in two apparently antithetical directions. In the one, he went down and in, making it intimate and subjective, the characters and their relationships far more emotionally and psychologically compelling. In the other, he moved up and out, enlarging the scale, increasing and intensifying the conflicts, and investing what he liked to call "a simple adventure story" with an almost unprecedented richness, density, and complexity of theme and texture.

It was for a while rather fashionable to denigrate Green's *Wild Bunch,* but Peckinpah himself always spoke highly of it, saying that it set up and dramatized the story "very well" (Farber, p. 42). Green's is an exceptionally accomplished piece of work (astonishingly so for a first screenplay) that is in fact far closer to the completed film than is the norm for most original screenplays. By any standards it was an excellent start and a protean effort that gave Peckinpah the structure, the plot, the characters, and the canvas he needed to release his imagination to its fullest. Though the director added many scenes, he rarely altered the basic shape of those by Green that he kept, which was most of them.

A typical example is the famous scene when Pike's stirrup breaks. In Green, Sykes's horse stumbles on some loose stones, sending the group tumbling down a slope; an angry Tector throws a rock at the old man; the Bunch start to mount back up; Pike's stirrup breaks, sending him crashing to the ground; he lies there in pain, no one moving to help him ("he doesn't expect them to"), the Gorch brothers making "little effort to cover the fact that they enjoy Pike's misery"; Pike mounts up and tells them where they're headed; and they all ride off (27). As Peckinpah rewrote and eventually staged it, Tector doesn't just throw a rock at Sykes, he reaches for his gun, aiming to kill him; Pike stops him and delivers the famous speech about sticking together; the Gorch brothers' enjoyment of his misery is no longer silent but openly contemptuous ("How are you going to side with a man when you can't even get on your horse?"). When Pike climbs back onto his horse, he turns, not saying a word, and rides on ahead alone, the others watching without moving. Peckinpah added virtually all of the dialogue, brought out the barely latent animosities among the group, found a dramatically and psychologically plausible place

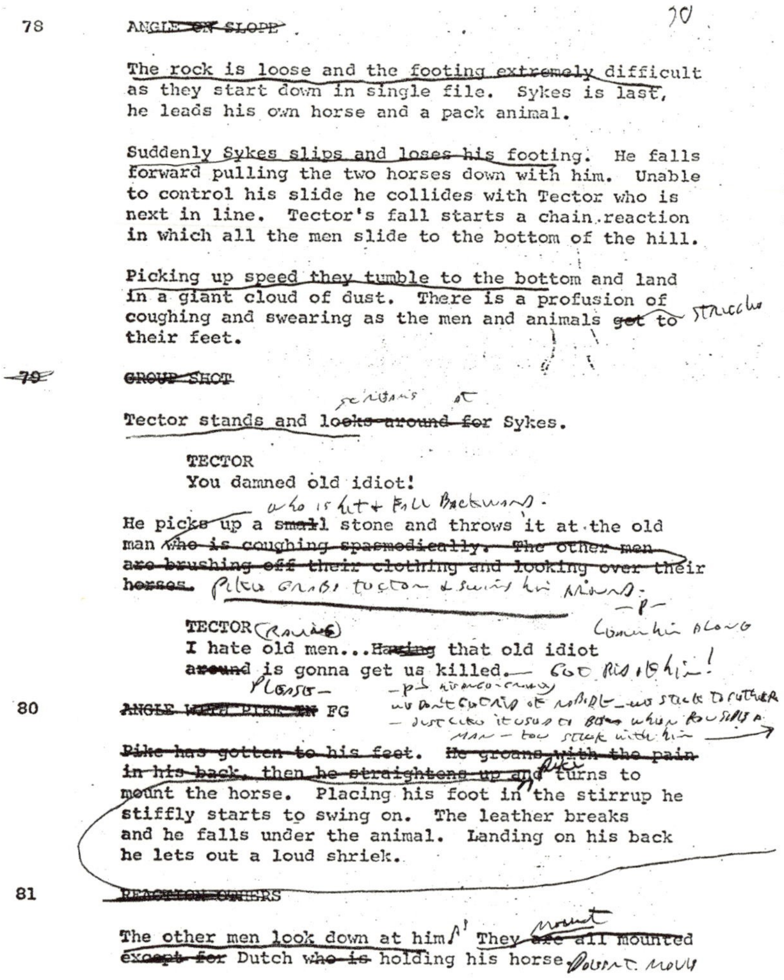

78   ~~ANGLE ON SLOPE~~ .   *10*

The rock is loose and the ~~footing extremely~~ difficult
as they start down in single file. Sykes is last,
he leads his own horse and a pack animal.

Suddenly ~~Sykes slips and loses his~~ footing. He falls
forward pulling the two horses down with him. Unable
to control his slide he collides with Tector who is
next in line. Tector's fall starts a chain reaction
in which all the men slide to the bottom of the hill.

Picking up ~~speed they tumble~~ to the bottom and land
in a giant cloud of dust. There is a profusion of
coughing and swearing as the men and animals ~~get to~~ *struggle*
their feet.

~~79~~   ~~GROUP SHOT~~

                    screams *at*
Tector stands and ~~looks around for~~ Sykes.

          TECTOR
          You damned old idiot!
                      who is hit + fall backward.
He picks up a ~~small~~ stone and throws it at the old
man ~~who is coughing spasmodically. The other men~~
~~are brushing off their clothing and looking over their~~
~~horses.~~ *Pike grabs Tector & swings him around.*
                                              —P—
          TECTOR ~~(Raving)~~   *Come him along*
          I hate old men...~~Having~~ that old idiot
          ~~around~~ is gonna get us killed.— *Got rid of him!*
            P loses—   —*p! never conserning*
80   ~~ANGLE WITH PIKE IN~~ FG   *no but concerd of nobile—no stick to ruther*
                           — just cause it used of been when pushing a
~~Pike has gotten to his feet. He groans with the pain~~   *man — too stuck with him*
~~in his back, then he straightens up and~~ *he* turns to
mount the horse. Placing his foot in the stirrup he
stiffly starts to swing on. The leather breaks
and he falls under the animal. Landing on his back
he lets out a loud shriek.

81   ~~REACTION OTHERS~~
                                      mount
The other men look down at him. They ~~are all mounted~~
~~except for~~ Dutch ~~who is~~ holding his horse *doesn't move*

FIGURE 10

Figures 10–15 are typical of the way Peckinpah reworked screenplays.

Figures 10 through 13, from one of the 16 June 1967 drafts, show how Peckinpah revised and added to the scene where Pike's stirrup breaks. Note that about two-thirds of the way down page 30 (Fig. 10) is the first appearance of Pike's "when you side with a man" speech, starting on the front and continuing on the back (Fig. 11). Notice also that midway down page 31 (Fig. 12) Peckinpah has indicated an interpolation, continued on the back (Fig. 13), of new

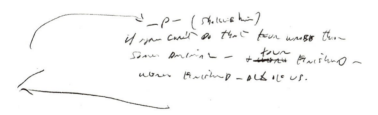

FIGURE 11

dialogue by the Gorch brothers ("Riding with him and old man Sykes makes a man wonder if it ain't time to pick up his chips and find another gam," etc.).

Figures 14 and 15 are from the 26 October 1967 draft, where Peckinpah added a new scene in Thornton's camp. Coffer asks Thornton, "You rode with Pike. What kind of man we up against?" Thornton answers, "The best. He never got caught" (Fig. 15).

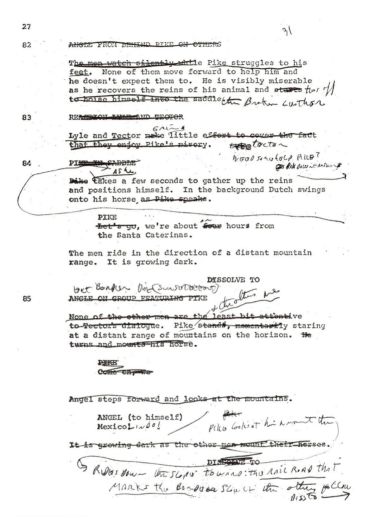

FIGURE 12

to have Pike declare his code, and in the lyrical finish suggested Pike's essential loneliness, the pain he constantly endures, and a nascent heroism. It's fair enough to say that Peckinpah transformed the scene; but he did so by building upon, not obliterating, what Green wrote.

The disposition of the groups of characters and the overall sequence of events in Green are very close to what they are in the

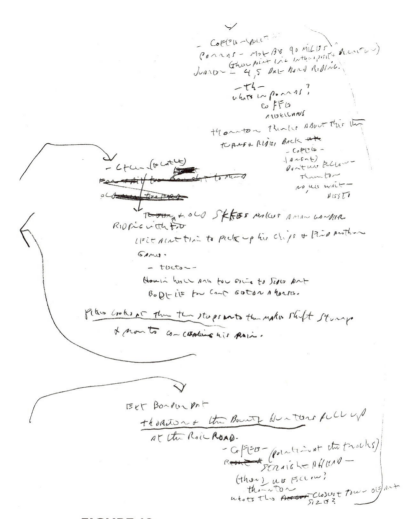

FIGURE 13

film. The most obvious differences in the first half are the character of Crazy Lee, whom Peckinpah created; the flashbacks, also Peckinpah's, which I'll treat later; and the scene in Angel's village.[21] Green did not have the Bunch go to the village: Angel goes there alone and hears his father recount Mapache's raid in a long, nightmarish flashback that actually shows what happened; when Angel asks about his fiancée, Teresa, he is told that she left, willingly,

27.

114   THE MEN ARE SILENT FOR A LONG MOMENT, then they break into
soft laughter which builds slowly.

                        LYLE
                    (after a moment)
         He -- He was making plans while
         me and Tector was --

He breaks up and can't continue.

                        DUTCH
                  (his laughter
                  growing)
         While you was getting your bell
         rope pulled by -- *(standing ~~...~~ almost staggering with laughter)*

He ~~staggers up, laughing, goes down to one knee.~~

                     ~~DUTCH~~
         By two -- mind you, two -- Hondo
         whores -- while Pike's dreaming
         of washers -- you're matching two
         of them -- in tandem --'

And the wild bunch falls apart in laughter -- even Pike is
caught, but as he laughs, he knows that they are together
again.

                                        DISSOLVE TO:

Pikus

115   EXT. CAMP - NIGHT

    PIKE AND DUTCH ARE SIDE BY SIDE in their blankets listening
to Angel play the guitar. For several moments they are
silent, then:

                        PIKE
         Didn't you run some kind of mine --
         in Sonora?

                       DUTCH
         Yeah, I helped run a little copper --
         nothing for us there except day wages.

116   PIKE FINDS IT IMPOSSIBLE to get comfortable. Groaning and
wincing with pain he shifts on the bedroll.

                       PIKE
         Why in the hell did you ever
         quit?

                                   CONTINUED

FIGURE 14

happily, with Mapache. Realizing that all this would have made
for a scene of at least ten minutes' length that was missing all but
one of the main characters and reduced that one to a passive au-
ditor, Peckinpah dropped the flashback completely and had the
Bunch accompany Angel to his village. He retained the betrayal
by Teresa but made Mapache the murderer of Angel's father. The

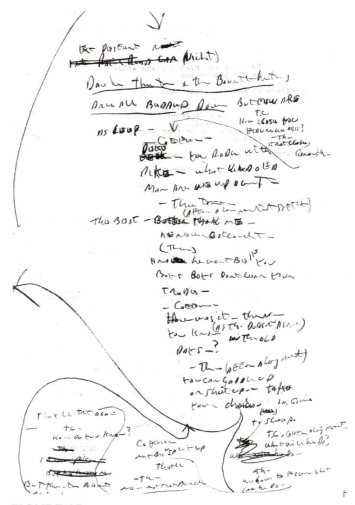

FIGURE 15

survivor who tells about the raid became a new character, Don José, Angel's grandfather and the village elder.[22]

Peckinpah had clear ideas about both the dramatic and thematic function of Angel's village. "The natural beauty of this location should contrast with other landscapes in the picture," he wrote. "This village and its inhabitants represent a complete and green contrast to the arid world of the Wild Bunch" (Final, p. 45). He also wanted to establish a rapport between the Bunch and the villagers. He invented the bit about the Gorch brothers playing cat's cradle with Angel's sister and the dialogue among Pike, Old Sykes, and Don José, three aging bandits talking about love, life, and lost innocence ("We all dream of being a child again, even the worst of us. Perhaps the worst most of all"). Peckinpah also added the nighttime festivities that conclude with Pike's admonition to a drunken Angel thirsting for revenge, "Either you learn to live with it or we'll leave you here." The last and most important addition, the Bunch's exit from the village, Peckinpah improvised on the set; it was never in any version of the screenplay.

In the second half, the beginning of the train robbery through to the locomotive crashing into the boxcar is pretty much as in the original script. However, in Green the wagon carrying the stolen rifles has barrels lashed to its sides as flotation devices and is pulled across the river by cables. Peckinpah continually fussed with this sequence, making it more and more elaborate and complicated, all the way to the eve of principal photography, where he had *both* a cable crossing and a bridge explosion. Once down in Mexico, however, he simplified the action to much greater effect, dropping the business with the cables entirely and substituting the bridge crossing. He used the whole train sequence to heighten the contrast between the efficiency and teamwork of the Bunch vis-à-vis the inept bounty hunters and the inexperienced cavalry. These twin themes of competence and incompetence are present in Green's original, but the director heightened them and added new material and new scenes until they became a running counterpoint throughout the story. The additions, which also served to keep Thornton and his posse more alive throughout the film, include such scenes as the early exchange at the river where Thornton glares at his posse for laughing at a stupid joke; Coffer pretending to draw his pistol on a pensive, unsuspecting Thornton, who goes for his gun, only to be greeted by a burst of derisive laughter; Thornton's exasperated outburst to the posse following the train robbery ("What have I got? Nothing but you egg-sucking, chicken-stealing gutter trash"); right to the very end when the bounty hunters, stupidly singing as they ride into hostile territory, are killed by Sykes and the Indians.[23] Peckinpah also added the quiet moment following the bridge explosion when Pike painfully hoists himself into his saddle on his bad leg and Tector offers him a drink, which contrasts with and resolves the Gorches' earlier ridicule when Pike fell to the ground.

Major Dundee revealed Peckinpah's interest in the clash between peasant cultures and European imperialism. In *The Wild Bunch* he highlighted the presence of the Germans wherever he could, adding the important reference to the First World War and involving them in the final battle, most significantly when their leader becomes Pike's first target after Mapache is killed. (He also brought back Mapache's automobile; in the original, Angel is dragged around by a mangy old burro.) Green wrote in the boy soldier who delivers the telegram to Mapache, which inspired Peckinpah to one of his proudest achievements in the film: the silent interplay that shows how the boy views Mapache as a hero, thus adumbrating the moment in the final battle when another boy soldier fires the first fatal bullet into Pike Bishop (which was Peckinpah's invention). The director then added the attack by Villa's forces as Mapache awaits the telegram. Those months he spent at Paramount researching *Villa Rides* really got his blood up on the whole subject of the Mexican Revolution, and he was not about to make a film set in that period without an appearance by Villa, which is necessary to clarify the urgency behind stealing the guns. An actual appearance by Villa's men also heightens our sense of how much danger the Bunch are in as they navigate the stolen weapons through bandit territory before the exchange with Mapache.

Green came up with the scene where Mapache's men try to take the guns without paying for them. But in Green's confrontation Pike merely threatens to light the fuse, which is how it remained throughout the revisions, save getting larger in scale (the original twenty soldiers became seventy or eighty). Not until the filming did Peckinpah push the situation to its logical, revelatory extreme by having Pike actually *light* the fuse. The later scene of Mapache trying to operate the machine gun without a tripod is Green's invention. But the machine gun itself is absent from his climax, which takes place at night in a cantina and, though bloody, is small in scale. Nor does the machine gun figure much into Peckinpah's written revisions until the loose pages dated 20 May 1968, but even they do not suggest anything of the apocalyptic scale, the sheer bacchanalian intensity of the final battle as we know it from the film. By contrast, the opening ambush was written out in considerable detail, some bits dating back to Sickner's suggestions that Green put into his treatment and his script. Interestingly, none of the revisions contains the business that still shocks most audiences right from the outset: the children playing with the ants and the scorpions, the epic simile by which Peckinpah unified the entire film.[24]

Not all of what Peckinpah put or left in the screenplay was necessarily meant to be used. Some things he shot just to cover himself. Three examples: Dutch's line that Angel "will have to show up with us when we deliver" (Final, p. 69); Sykes saying, "We've got to get him [Angel] out," Dutch asking, "How?" (109);[25] and an exchange between Pike and Mapache when the Bunch return to Agua Verde in which Pike tells Mapache about Thornton's posse and Mapache orders Herrera to take twenty men, find, and kill them (118). Dutch's line and his exchange with Sykes were both obviously cut because they telegraphed important turns in the plot, yet did not supply any vital information that wasn't adequately covered elsewhere (e.g., Dutch's "He played his string right out to the end" is all the explanation we need for why Angel goes along to deliver the last of the guns). Peckinpah's reasons for dropping the Pike–Mapache exchange are a little more complicated. He and Feldman argued about it just before the picture was locked, the producer wanting to keep it in. The main reason Peckinpah removed it, I would guess, is that it drops just one shoe in a place where there is no room to drop the other one. The quiet moment with the young prostitute when Pike makes the decision to reclaim Angel is the pivotal scene of the entire film. The last thing Peckinpah would have wanted here is a distraction of any sort, especially an irrelevant plot point as to whether Herrera and his men will find Thornton and his posse. Moreover, if Peckinpah shot this scene the way he wrote it, then Herrera would have to leave with the cavalry, yet Herrera is also around a short while later for all the partying and is present in the final battle. Since Mapache ordered him to kill the posse, would he return without doing so? And if so, when? Plainly, the whole business was more trouble than it was worth. Narratively speaking, Peckinpah's solution – dropping the line and putting in a brief scene of Thornton warning his men that an army patrol is nearby – was the cleanest option. I also suspect that when Peckinpah saw the film whole, he didn't care for the way the exchange reflects upon Pike, whom he had already brought pretty low by this juncture. It is enough that after abandoning the wounded Sykes, Pike says he'll let Mapache take care of Thornton's posse; I don't think he wanted to show Pike actually *asking* the General to do so.

Peckinpah used to tell his editors, "Introduce, develop, finish."[26] *The Wild Bunch* illustrates this principle more than any other film he had ever made. For all its violence, he saw in it a story of reunion, renewal, and redemption. In Green, the bounty hunters kill Sykes in the ambush on the trail; when they arrive in Agua Verde at the end, they find the bodies of the Bunch piled up and the village already sacked. Thornton remarks to himself, "with admiration," "They were a wild bunch," the last line of the script. There is not the slightest hint of Peckinpah's magnificent extended coda, with its gradually shifting moods that modulate from devastation through grief to melancholy and laughter and finally to a kind of communal celebration: Thornton reclaiming Pike's pistol, the vultures circling overhead while the human vultures strip the bodies, the revolutionaries clearing the village of supplies, the off-screen deaths of the bounty hunters at the hands of Sykes and the Indians, the reunion of Thornton and Sykes in what some viewers have affectionately called a "neo–wild bunch," and the reprise of the exit from Angel's village.

A story about redemption is by definition a story about failure, betrayal, and guilt. Accordingly, the two characters Peckinpah did the most work on are Pike Bishop and Deke Thornton. When *The Wild Bunch* was first released, it was a not uncommon observation that the members of the Bunch didn't have much individual characterization and were best thought of as a group. This was always a specious criticism, even in the studio-truncated version. The first major changes that Peckinpah made were to further deepen, humanize, and individuate not just the members of the Bunch, but Thornton, two of the bounty hunters (T.C. and Coffer), Harrigan, and Mapache and his men. The Gorch brothers remain perhaps closest to the original screenplay, but even with them Peckinpah added a great many things (the whole sequence in the wine cellar with the prostitutes, for example), including new dialogue, that made them more rounded as characters and, what was vital, that made them really *feel* like brothers.[27] They even bicker like men with a long family history:

> LYLE: They made damn fools out of us, Mr. Bishop. It's getting so's a fellow can't sleep with both eyes closed for fear of getting his throat cut. Where in the hell were you [indicates Tector]?

> TECTOR: Now you listen here, Lyle, you get up off your ass and help once in awhile and I wouldn't got caught near so easy.

Jim Silke, the director's close friend and sometime collaborator, says that from the beginning Peckinpah felt that all that was necessary to lift the decision to reclaim Angel from cliché was for the picture to answer the question "What kind of guys would really do that, sacrifice themselves like that?" (Weddle, 1994, p. 313). The key, he told Silke, lay in the characters' pasts, in particular the kind of man Pike was before the film proper begins, the things (especially the losses) that shaped him, and his relationship to his closest friend, Deke Thornton. Green's Pike is distinguished from the rest of the Bunch mostly insofar as he is their leader and is older than any of them except Sykes. On the first page of his revision, Peckinpah immediately described him as more "thoughtful," "a self-educated top gun with a penchant for violence who is afraid of nothing – except the changes in himself and those around him": "Make no mistake, Pike Bishop is not a hero – his values are not ours. . . . He lives outside and against society because he believes in that way of life." If Peckinpah wanted to emphasize that Pike's values are not ours, he nevertheless gave him a principle that any of us might readily identify with: When you side with a man, you stay with him. Pike is also much more haunted by an ethos of honor almost as a principle than, say, Dutch, for whom the word given and kept is entirely personal and conditional (the Gorch brothers are united by their family ties).

Peckinpah did a lot more with Pike's physical infirmities, emphasizing that he is always in pain. It is a portrait of a tired, lonely man with a desire to make enough money to "back off" but who carries a lot of very unquiet ghosts inside that remind him of how often he has failed to live up to his own best image of himself. These reveal themselves in the three flashbacks that Peckinpah wrote in – Pike's desertion of Thornton, his abandonment of Crazy Lee, and his failure to keep the woman he loved from being killed. Only the last is present in any form in Green:

> PIKE: I met a woman once I wanted to marry. . . . She had a husband and I should have had sense enough to kill him. . . . One night I woke up and saw him watching me over a shotgun. He fired one barrel into her face. I was running for my gun on the other side of the room when he caught me down here. I wriggled around on that floor for more than an hour and he just sat on the bed and watched me. He never took his eyes off me and I've never stopped remembering him. He made his big mistake not reloading and giving me a second blast. (53)

Pike then tells how he was reduced to begging for a year in Waco before he recovered strength enough to move around, how he took five years to catch up with the man's son, killing him after finding out that the man had gone to Cuba, and how there "hasn't been a day or an hour that I haven't thought about getting even with him."

Peckinpah retained the business of the unfinished vengeance, but how different the rest of it is from what he finally put on the screen! To start with, he mitigated, then eliminated entirely the gruesome physical details (the husband's shotgun becomes a handgun, the wife is no longer blasted in the face) and all the stuff about Pike's being a crippled beggar in Waco (the wound eventually transferred from his back to his leg). Next, he made it a true flashback that, unlike the other two flashbacks, depicts a clear disparity between the images and the commentary. In the original, Pike hardly seems to care about at all about Aurora (she isn't even given a name);[28] he talks mostly about getting even with the husband, the emphasis being on vengeance and violence. But in Peckinpah's revision, though the words Pike speaks to Dutch are about getting even, the images are about love and loss and suggest Pike's anguish, guilt, and shame. Peckinpah also added an introductory bit that shows Pike arriving two days late for a rendezvous without explanation or apology; and in one draft, he experimented with having the husband burst in on the couple after they've made love and had Aurora throw herself in front of Pike, taking the fatal shot for him. His reasons for deciding against this were apparently that he wanted it absolutely clear that Aurora's husband *means* to kill her and that the lovers' last moments together be of passion anticipated, not passion fulfilled.

About midway into preproduction, Lee Marvin, who was to play Pike, accepted a million-dollar offer to do *Paint Your Wagon* (1969) and bowed out of *The Wild Bunch*. Few clouds in Peckinpah's career ever had a silver lining, but this one did. He and Feldman immediately turned to other stars on their A list, which included Burt Lancaster, Charlton Heston, Gregory Peck, James Stewart, and William Holden. Peckinpah was a great admirer of *The Bridge on the River Kwai* (1957), and he had just recently watched *Stalag 17* (1953). Convinced that Holden was "tough enough" to play the part (Simmons, p. 84), Peckinpah seemed to realize that he had here an actor of considerably greater range and depth of feeling than Marvin, one who could take the character much further in the tormented, guilt-ridden direction he was already developing anyhow. The most immediate effects of the new casting were two. Without losing any of the exterior toughness Peckinpah considered essential, Pike became both more sensitive and stronger. His toughness was now, artistically speaking, more valid because it no longer functioned as a mere given (in other words, a convention), but rather as part of the humanity of the character, the necessary shield he has developed against both the physical and emotional pain he must constantly endure.[29]

As with Pike, so with Thornton: Peckinpah wanted the character to be contrasted with the group he is leading. In Green's opening ambush Thornton loses his head like the other bounty hunters and in the excitement kills some innocent townspeople. Unlike them, he admits to his mistake. Peckinpah kept this for a good while but eventually dropped it. The casting was probably an influence here too – Robert Ryan, with his brooding, troubled dignity, is not a man to lose control quite that way. But by then Peckinpah had already substantially reconceived both Thornton and his thematic function in the story. With his sense of form and structure – almost unerring in those days – and his obsession with paired characters who find themselves reluctant antagonists, he knew that a deepened characterization of Pike required its equivalent in the man who pursues him. Otherwise, both characters are cheapened, as are the conflict itself and the issues it focuses. In Ryan he found an actor whose screen presence would balance Holden's.

Peckinpah began by making Thornton far more integral to the plot. Thornton's relationship to Harrigan was made considerably more acrimonious, to the point of outright hatred, to which end Peckinpah made Harrigan an actual railroad executive.[30] In a curious missed opportunity, Green had Harrigan discover by accident, and only after the opening ambush, that Thornton and Pike used to ride together. Peckinpah made it the *reason* Harrigan gets him out of prison. There was a lot of talk in Peckinpah's early drafts about Thornton selling out, getting old, and changing, about his having been "broken." Along the way from revision to final cut the director eliminated all of this because it was too neat and easy, too formulaic. In a scene written just a few days before the beginning of principal photography, Peckinpah came up with the flashback of Thornton's capture, showing how it was due essentially to Pike's carelessness. In the Collection it first appears in additional pages – marked "change," dated 21 March 1968 – that were interpolated into the 7 February 1968 (Final) shooting script. It was part of a larger scene of the Bunch on the trail that Peckinpah placed between the "decent burial" scene and the bunkhouse where Harrigan chews out the bounty hunters for letting the Bunch escape. The dialogue leading up to the flashback concludes with Pike remarking of Thornton, "He got old and tired, and when that happens, things change." Dutch replies, "He changed – you didn't." Then we see Thornton's capture and Pike's escape. When we return to the present, Lyle is talking about Butch Cassidy down in Argentina "making a killing." The scene ends with Pike hoping that Thornton "ain't on our tail – but don't bet on it" (20–21).

Peckinpah constantly layered his characters' relationships with motivations and emotions that are tangled, complex, and conflicted. Not only did he want us to understand that Pike feels guilty about Thornton's capture because his carelessness was largely responsible for it, but he also wrote in two flashbacks of Thornton in prison – one of him lashed to a post and being whipped, the other of him on a rock pile, both intended to be used as quick, almost subliminal dissolves – suggesting that Harrigan used his influence to have Thornton punished as a way of forcing him to join the posse.[31] If Thornton was to be seen as "broken" – and it is by no means clear that Peckinpah felt this way by the time he finished the fine cut – then he would at least be revealed as a man who had faced hard choices and suffered cruel consequences that Pike, through guile, deceit, and desertion, had managed to escape. As always in Peckinpah, our judgments about his characters and what they do are made complicated and difficult because the basis of judgment itself is shown to be slippery and unsure, constantly shifting, often eroded entirely. "Things are always mixed" was his constant refrain.

Jim Silke told me that Peckinpah thought of Pike as the character who didn't change (because he couldn't) and Thornton as the character who did change. But Silke was here recalling some very early conversations about the script when the director was just beginning to map out the background story of the Bishop–Thornton friendship. Peckinpah made many changes quickly and decisively, but this relationship, which he regarded as the key to the whole story, he took a long time working and reworking. He wrote the crucial flashback virtually on the eve of production; the two prison flashbacks were added less than a month earlier; and even by his extraordinary standards, he was unusually sensitive to the personalities his two stars would bring to bear on their roles. It is my view – comparing the material that was written and shot with what was retained and how it was shaped in the editing – that Peckinpah went so far beyond his initial formulation as virtually to have reversed it. Whether Pike was any longer incapable of changing or afraid of it is a matter of debate; but it is beyond question that by the time Peckinpah finished rewriting, the story picked up his outlaw leader when he *wants* a change. And by making Thornton Pike's nemesis and thus his moral touchstone, the director surely encouraged us to see Thornton as more than a broken or, at least, a merely broken, man.[32]

In the process, Thornton was transformed into something of an equivalent to what Philip Young described as the "code hero" in Hemingway: the man, usually a professional of some sort, who makes a basic compromise, but once he has done so, he abides by the rules and terms of his decision absolutely.[33] He represents, in short, the principle of honor – in Thornton's case, the honor of keeping one's word once it is given, which Peckinpah developed with great care throughout his revisions. In the original script, when Harrigan threatens Thornton with a return to prison if the Bunch are not caught, Thornton replies, "You make it pretty clear." Peckinpah changed this to "I gave you my word," thus sounding a theme that he will extend ("Damn that Deke Thornton to hell!!" "What would you do? He gave his word"), ramify (Angel "played his string right out to the end"), and eventually resolve ("I sent them back, that's all I said I'd do"). Introduce, develop, finish.

I have remarked how extensive Peckinpah's dialogue rewrite was and incidentally adduced examples of it. But it should be noted that most of the lines that everyone quotes are by the director: "It's not what you meant to do," "I'll hold 'em here until hell freezes over or you say different," "How'd you like to kiss my sister's black cat's ass?," "How does it feel to be so goddamned right?," "I wouldn't have it any other way," "When you side with a man," "We all dream of being a child again," "We don't *hang* nobody," "He played his string," "It ain't like it used to be, but it'll do." This last is a striking example of how Peckinpah never stopped working on something until it was as right as he could possibly make it. Throughout the script revisions this line read, "It ain't like it used to be, but it's better than nothing," which is how it was often quoted by critics who read the publicity synopsis but didn't bother to take another look at the film itself. The final change was not made until the scene was shot, and though seemingly small, it opens onto a world of difference between the lines: The one is nihilistic, the other affirmative with a purpose behind it.

IV

In a way, that difference reflects the pattern of Peckinpah's changes. By the time he finished his fine cut, Walon Green's hard, gritty screenplay about a band of ruthless, cynical outlaws would be transformed into a violent epic of great romantic sweep and deep personal feeling, built upon themes of betrayal, guilt, vengeance, and redemption. When Thornton joins up with Sykes's band of Indian revolutionaries and Peckinpah reprises the exit from Angel's village as the Bunch are serenaded by the peasants, death really does lead to transfiguration, realism gives way to romance, and our last image of these outlaws, in what is perhaps the single most self-reflexive moment of the film, is as heroes of an adventure that has already become the stuff of mythmaking and storytelling.

It is instructive that both the exit from Angel's village and its reprise at the very end of the film were never in any version of the screenplay. The exit itself we know Peckinpah invented during shooting, while the idea of reprising it, which lifts the entire story to a whole new level of meaning, came to him only during the last weeks of the editing.[34] From this perspective it is obvious that the writing and rewriting represent only one stage in the creation of this film, and perhaps not the most important stage. The rest lies outside the scope of this essay because it consists in how Peckinpah worked with his actors; how he used his locations; how he set up, shot, and composed the scenes; how he improvised dialogue, scenes, even whole sequences on the spot; and finally, how he and his editors, Lou Lombardo and Robert Wolfe, put all the footage together in the cutting room. (At the time, the massiveness of his coverage was all but unprecedented.)

By way of conclusion, I'd like to describe three examples that illustrate how much "rewriting," as it were, Peckinpah left to the actual making of the film. "No matter how good a script is," he once said, "you have to adapt it to the needs of the actors."[35] It is almost impossible to overestimate his collaborations with his actors, how much exploration and discovery he encouraged in rehearsals and filming. We have seen how his reconception of Pike Bishop was influenced by William Holden. The casting of Ernest Borgnine likewise influenced Dutch, though in a very different way. Green's Dutch is a young man. Once Borgnine was signed, making him older and eliminating a few anomalous lines of dialogue are about all that Peckinpah did in the writing (apart, of course, from new dialogue when he added new scenes). Otherwise, on the page Dutch appears to change less from the original than any of the rest of the Bunch, even the Gorch brothers. But go to the film and observe how Peckinpah used Borgnine. Consider in particular how thoroughly *grounded* the film became through Borgnine's performance, and how ironic this was in many respects. Peckinpah agreed to Borgnine only reluctantly, as a concession to Hyman (who had used him in *The Dirty Dozen*), and one can understand his reservations: before *The Wild Bunch* (and even after) it is hard to recall really quiet, subtle work by this actor. But he and the director became fast colleagues. Playing a blunt, forthright man, Borgnine was coaxed to give the most nuanced and inward-looking performance of his career. For Peckinpah, Dutch was the conscience of *The Wild Bunch*.[36] His simple strength, his direct, unadorned line readings, and the values of loyalty, solidarity, and comradeship that he embodies provide our first access to the Bunch as a group and keep us from losing contact with them throughout. Yet little of this is apparent from a mere reading of the script, except by hindsight.

Nor from the screenplay alone, even Peckinpah's considerably worked-over revisions, would we have any idea of how genuinely *funny* much of it would be in the playing. Critics were quick enough to recognize Peckinpah's black humor and his extraordinary gift for comic relief. But as Robert Becker has pointed out, "If you think beyond the violence and the tragic ending for a moment, you discover there's a lot of *party* energy in this movie."[37] This is not just in the way laughter rounds off so many scenes or in the bawdy carousing in Agua Verde; it goes right to the heart of the polarities that constitute the basic structural unit of the film itself: how violence, dissension, death, and both failure *and* success are repeatedly resolved in toasting, celebration, music, song, dance, and laughter, sometimes hale and hearty, as in the toast after the bridge is exploded, sometimes sinister and mocking, as in the grotesque hilarity of the *federales* after Angel is caught. The scene in Angel's village Peckinpah conceived as an actual party, with drinking, feasting, and music making, followed the next morning by one of his favorite formal devices, a procession: the peasants line up and sing to the departing Bunch.[38] This sequence, a kind of celebration, contains in embryo both the structure of the extended coda of the film and by implication the basic structure of the entire film. The differences between Thornton and Sykes are dissolved in laughter that, in turn, is cinematically dissolved into images of the Bunch at their most appealing, which are next dissolved into the exit from the village of the Bunch, who are then fixed in a final apotheosis as figures of legend. In these years Peckinpah's structural sense was supreme: the whole always crystallized in the details, the details always mirroring the large design.

We know that the opening robbery was described in detail in the screenplay, but the closing battle was not. Why the difference? For one thing, though films are rarely shot in sequence, here the beginning of the story coincided with the beginning of the schedule, and Peckinpah knew that preparation was everything. But this only begs the question. The climax was scheduled later because he wasn't *ready* to shoot it. (Even if he had been ready, it is doubtful that he would have allowed it to be scheduled much earlier: it's never a good idea to film the end of the story at the beginning of production.) It wasn't until he was well into shooting that he fully discovered what the final battle was about and how he wanted to do it. My guess is that the impact of seeing the opening as Lombardo had first cut it together on location cannot be overemphasized here: once Peckinpah saw on film how horrifyingly violent yet spectacular a beginning he had, everything he knew about drama intellectually and intuitively told him that the closing battle would have to be not just longer or more intense and exciting, but something truly tremendous. And not in size and scope only, but in the very depiction of the violence itself: he would have to take it into waters literally uncharted by previous films with violent subjects, even the very good and great ones, like *Bonnie and Clyde* (1967) and *The Seven Samurai*. What form it would take he did not know, not quite yet, but he knew the immensity of the task that lay before him.

In the early eighties, he told a group of students at the University of Southern California that it wasn't until he saw the location – an old hacienda with a still-functioning aqueduct and bullet holes in the crumbling walls that were made in the revolution itself – that he realized his ideas for the final battle had been "all wrong." Yet he still had no clear idea of how he would stage it right up to the day he directed the famous moment-of-silence standoff between the Bunch and the slain Mapache's army, another on-the-spot inspiration. Then he became absolutely stymied, one of the few times his legendary improvisational ability deserted him. But once he figured it out and started back in shooting – the hiatus less than a day – everyone had to scramble to keep up. "Sam went way beyond what anybody expected he would do with that sequence," his assistant Chalo Gonzalez recalls (Weddle, p. 343). Yet again we find none of it in the screenplays, not just because it wasn't written but because it is something that *could not be written:* it could come into full being only in front of the cameras and in the editing room.

One of the continuing debates in film criticism ever since the auteur theory first burst into international prominence over three decades ago is the relative importance of writing vis-à-vis directing. I'm hardly about to resolve the matter here, except to suggest that if a director is not the first author of a film, then he or she is at the very least the *last* author of a film, and for that reason arguably the most decisive. This is because *everything* prior to the actual filming of the story, even the most polished screenplay ever written, is only so much material, not necessarily raw but certainly unborn, waiting to be brought to life in front of the camera. A film exists only in what is captured *on* film and how it is later cut together during the long months in the editing room.

"Persistence of vision," science tells us, is the phenomenon that makes motion in motion pictures possible. But persistence of vision differently defined is also what makes the *art* of motion pictures possible. Though the Walon Green–Roy Sickner story, Green's excellent screenplay especially, and Peckinpah's revisions cannot be minimized, in the end it wasn't the writing as such that made for a masterpiece. It was the vision Peckinpah first glimpsed when he imagined Pike riding over the sand dune and saw the Bunch's long walk for Angel stretch out before him, the vision he held to, enlarging, sharpening, clarifying, never letting go until he had raised it to incandescence. His reward – and ours too – was a peerless achievement in the history of film and a great work of art.

NOTES

1 *Sam Peckinpah Collection*. Papers. Gift of the Peckinpah family. Inventory compiled by Valentin Almendarez, supervised by Samuel A. Gill,

archivist, April 1990. Margaret Herrick Library, Academy of Motion Picture Arts and Sciences, Beverly Hills, California.

2 Peckinpah composed his own original screenplays on yellow legal pads, and there is no reason to doubt he used them sometimes in rewriting *The Wild Bunch*. But the pages don't survive in his files, presumably because once the typist had transcribed them, they were thrown away.

3 This passage remained unaltered through the last complete draft, dated 7 February 1968 (with changes as late as 21 March). Unless otherwise noted, all script quotations are either from this draft, which is labeled "Final," or from Green's undated original. Identification and pagination hereafter will follow in parentheses. The passages just quoted are from Final, pp. 39, 120.

4 Unless otherwise noted, all quotations and background information come from interviews and conversations I had with Walon Green (1996–7), L. Q. Jones (1997), Don Levy (1978), Sam Peckinpah (1977–80), Jim Silke (1996), Garner Simmons (1997), and David Weddle (1997). Other principal sources include Stephen Farber, "Peckinpah's Return," interview with Sam Peckinpah (1969), rpt. in *Doing It Right: The Best Criticism on Sam Peckinpah's The Wild Bunch*, ed. Michael Bliss (Carbondale: Southern Illinois University Press, 1994), pp. 37–45 (hereafter "Farber"); Garner Simmons, *Peckinpah: A Portrait in Montage* (Austin: University of Texas Press, 1982), pp. 82–3, 99 (hereafter "Simmons"); David Weddle, *"If They Move . . . Kill 'Em!": The Life and Times of Sam Peckinpah* (New York: Grove Press, 1994), pp. 307–18 (hereafter "Weddle"); and memos and correspondence by Peckinpah, Phil Feldman, and Ken Hyman. All notes, memos, and letters cited in this essay are in the Peckinpah Collection. The epigraph is from Simmons, p. 86.

5 On 15 November 1971 Sickner was the victim of a stunt that went disastrously wrong on the television series *Cade's County*. The "gag," as stuntmen call it, required a Jeep to be jumped over a small ravine, but the Jeep didn't make it. The others, including the driver, jumped clear, but Sickner, inexplicably, held on; when the Jeep struck the far bank, it flipped over and sheared the top of his head off. He was left an invalid, with impaired speech and severely limited brain capacity. As of this writing, he is still alive but unable to provide any information.

In addition to the sources already cited, much of the information on Sickner's involvement in the project comes from interviews I had in April 1997 with Sickner's close friends Buck Holland and Jan Holland and with his son Kane Sickner. I am indebted as well to Lee Ann Fuller (Sickner's stepdaughter).

6 Hayward also went off to other projects – he was John Wayne's regular stunt double – which, as far as Sickner was concerned, ended any claims Hayward might have had, implied or otherwise, to the story.

7 In addition to sources already cited regarding Green's involvement, there is a long interview by Nat Segaloff, "Walon Green: Fate Will Get You," *Backstory 3*, ed. Patrick McGilligan (Berkeley: University of California Press, 1997), pp. 135–6 (hereafter "Segaloff"). Unless otherwise noted, all remarks and attributions to Green are from my conversations with him.

8 For more on this, see Paul Seydor, *Peckinpah: The Western Films – A Reconsideration*, rev. ed. (Urbana: University of Illinois Press, 1980, 1997), pp. 182–3 (hereafter "Seydor"). In the fine cut all references to the Pinkertons and Butch Cassidy were excised, because by then *Butch Cassidy and the Sundance Kid* was a competing picture at 20th Century Fox scheduled to come out within three months of *The Wild Bunch*.

9 With full use of Paramount's research facilities, Peckinpah spent the first part of 1967 poring over all the books, photographs, and newsreels of the Mexican evolution the staff could locate. Both he and his cinematographer, Lucien Ballard, declared on several occasions (see, e.g., Farber, pp. 44–5) that the overall look of *The Wild Bunch* was substantially influenced by the newsreel footage. I'd be amazed if *Memorias de Un Mexicano*, or some of the material used in it, were not among the films Peckinpah watched that winter.

10 "The violence in slow motion is very expressly in the script," Green once said (Segaloff, p. 143), but he later corrected himself. Not only are there no explicit directions for slow motion in his screenplay, there isn't even a suggestion to that effect (which is also true, by the way, of Peckinpah's several drafts). Obviously, however, slow motion was on Green's mind and he did discuss it with Sickner, who must have known that Peckinpah had run high-speed cameras on *Dundee*. Even before then, Peckinpah had used slow motion once on television in *The Losers* (1962) and would use it, again on television, in *That Lady Is My Wife* (1966). Neither was particularly influenced by Kurosawa, nor, for that matter, was the slow motion in *The Wild Bunch*. The synthesis of fast cutting and multiple-speed imagery that Peckinpah forged in 1968–9, while not without its antecedents (see Seydor, pp. 353–4), was as authentic a stylistic innovation as any in films.

11 Green created better than perhaps he knew with the names. "Pike," for example, also means lance or spear, and it is sometimes used as a verb meaning to thrust or pierce; both are appropriate for an embattled old bandit. An archaic meaning is "peak," which is likewise appropriate for a man described as "the best" at what he does and who is eventually given a mythic apotheosis. Thornton, I always assumed, derived from the first syllable, as he is literally the thorn in Pike's side. The similarity of Harrigan to E. H. Harriman, the actual railroad ex-

ecutive whose trains Butch Cassidy robbed, is purely coincidental, Green says; but it was certainly a happy coincidence, as is its similarity to "harry," meaning to harass again and again, exactly Harrigan's relationship to Thornton. As I've observed elsewhere, issues of intention notwithstanding, little in *The Wild Bunch* functions merely by accident or without design.

12 Green has conflicting recollections of when he actually wrote *The Wild Bunch*. He told Segaloff (p. 140) that he did it while on *Morituri*. This is impossible because Carell hired him only after he had proved that he could write by doing the polish on *Winter à Go-Go,* which went into production after *Morituri*. Green first told me that he wrote *The Wild Bunch* in Brazil in November and December 1966. First, I pointed out to him that there seemed to be several inconsistencies about this date too. First, in December 1966 Sickner was already trying to set up a deal for Peckinpah to rewrite and direct the film, for which a dated letter of agreement (that I'll discuss further on) exists. How could Sickner be making a deal for Peckinpah to rewrite a script that hadn't been finished yet? Second, four months later, Peckinpah was starting his rewrite. This doesn't leave a lot of time for Carell to have done the budget break down and passed and for Sickner to have peddled it elsewhere while Green lost interest and returned to documentaries. After thinking about it a little longer and checking on some things, Green got back to me: "You know, it was raining a lot while I was writing that screenplay, and when I first told you November and December of 1966, I was thinking about when *our* rain starts, which is often in December. But *Brazil's* winter rains are during our spring months, and that was when I finished *The Wild Bunch,* in Brazil in the *spring* of 1966."

13 Sam Peckinpah to P.S., letter, 8 April 1977.

14 Speaking of clouded histories, it is not beside the point to note that in these years both Peckinpah and Sickner were part of a loosely connected group of actors and stuntmen (whose number included Lee Marvin, Jason Robards, and many of the supporting casts and crews on Peckinpah's films) who were hard daily drinkers. What with the alcohol, his worries about whether he'd ever make another movie again, and the numerous scripts he was trying to sell as leverage for directing, Peckinpah's memories of this period cannot be absolutely trusted, nor can anyone else's, in particular those of Sickner and Marvin, who drank, if anything, much more than Peckinpah. (In these years the director could at least claim dry periods when he worked.) Interestingly, however, the account from Peckinpah's letter to me, though brief, is, from the standpoint of surviving documents, the

most accurate recollection of anyone's involvement with the project I've come across so far.

According to Buck Holland, not long after arriving in Mexico to begin working on *The Wild Bunch*, Sickner raised so much hell drinking, brawling, and carousing that the Mexican authorities bodily escorted him out of the country and barred him from returning (he tried every entry point he knew and was blocked at each one). The remainder of his involvement with the production was stateside. His "associate producer" credit was part of his deal when Warners purchased the screenplay, but in no serious sense was he a producer on this film (which was the effective beginning and end of any career he might have hoped for in this capacity).

15 Peckinpah himself said on several occasions that the film he really wanted to direct upon returning to features was *The Ballad of Cable Hogue* (1970), which Warren Oates had brought to him. Garner Simmons and I both have doubts about this. While Peckinpah's enthusiasm for the screenplay is evidenced by how quickly he and Feldman managed to get it into production immediately following *The Wild Bunch* (very few directors in his position would have staked such newly gained power on so personal and so uncommercial a project), I've found nothing to indicate that it was even near a front burner at this time in his career. Nor was there studio interest, and the director himself was working on such diverse scripts as *The Hi Lo Country, Castaway, Caravans, Villa Rides, The Diamond Story,* and *The Wild Bunch,* among others, to say nothing of the television projects (see Weddle, pp. 265–306, and Seydor, pp. 170–3).

16 According to correspondence in the Collection, Ryerson might have given Sickner the money as early as February, but it doesn't seem to have found its way to Peckinpah until early spring or later.

17 Just how strapped is evidenced by his selling his share of *The Rifleman,* a television series he helped create, for $10,000, a fraction of its worth at the time (and a tiny fraction of its eventual worth once the syndication and cable markets took off twenty years later).

18 Script credit on screen goes to Green and Peckinpah, in that order. The Guild initially objected to Peckinpah's receiving a credit, but Green felt it was deserved and wrote eloquently on the director's behalf (see Simmons, p. 105).

19 Sam Peckinpah to Ken Hyman, note, 27 October 1967.

20 I have not bothered to do a line count, but my guess is that Peckinpah changed or added almost as much dialogue as he kept.

21 This account glosses over how fully Peckinpah fleshed out Green's opening: All the biblical references are his; so are the mayor's speech about the evils of drink, the hymn "Shall We Gather at the River?,"

many specific bits such as the woman with the package who bumps into Pike, Dutch at full gallop leaning down from his horse to swoop up the saddle bags, and children everywhere, not to mention the whole choreography of the sequence (to which the assistant director, Cliff Coleman, and Roy Sickner himself no doubt made contributions).

22 Peckinpah had Don Jose confess that he ran and hid, "like a coward," during the raid. This confession was included in early cuts but was eventually deleted. The reasons are not known, but an educated guess is that it didn't go anywhere either as plot or as characterization. Another deleted scene has to do with a long bit of comic relief, which Peckinpah wrote, involving Dutch and some villagers trying to shoe an uncooperative mule. Memos between the director and Feldman indicate that this was removed owing to technical problems in the lab timing and because it didn't work very well (the producer was not alone in hating it). If Don José's dialogue had been intercut with this sequence, it may have been impossible to salvage it from the sequence itself – which explains Dutch's curious absence from the scene and perhaps accounts for what has always struck me as the odd editing scheme of the exchange between Pike and Don José, where so much of their dialogue is played off screen.

23 One of the best examples of the bounty hunters' ineptitude comes near the end of the picture, when one of them falls off a galloping horse. However, this was a real, not a planned, fall, which the other stuntmen didn't let the poor man live down for the rest of the production.

24 Peckinpah got the idea for this when Emilio Fernandez, the actor who plays Mapache, told him, "You know, the Wild Bunch, when they go into that town like that, are like when I was a child and we would take a scorpion and drop it on an anthill" (Simmons, p. 86).

25 This exchange is in the theatrical trailer, which is included in the Warner Home Video laserdisc of the 1995 restoration of *The Wild Bunch*.

26 Richard Gentner to P.S., 1996.

27 One big change that Peckinpah made was to reduce drastically the Gorches' bigotry toward Angel and other Mexicans, particularly the racial epithets ("greaser," "bean"); from Pike he removed all traces of it. Memos indicate that Feldman was worried that the Mexican censors would not grant permission to film there unless this material was removed or softened. In the absence of memos by Peckinpah responding to this point, there is no way of knowing if this was a serious concern of his. My guess is that he knew that a little of this attitude goes a long way and revised accordingly.

28 We don't know her name from the film either, as no one speaks it (just as we don't know that Don José is Angel's grandfather). Yet it

was typical of Peckinpah throughout his career to give even bit players and walk-ons a name. According to his friend Don Levy, Peckinpah did this because he never forgot the days when he was struggling to make it. He believed it made an actor feel better about himself if he could say, "I'm playing Joe the deputy in a new movie," as opposed to, "I got a bit as a deputy." Of course, Peckinpah also knew that giving a character a name puts the actor in a more personal relationship to the role, which usually pays off with a better performance.

29 Significantly, the Aurora scene did not assume its final form until *after* Holden was cast. It is easy to imagine Lee Marvin thirsting for vengeance, but who can imagine him pining for a lost woman, as his miscasting in John Frankenheimer's *The Iceman Cometh* (1973) demonstrates? To be sure, Peckinpah directed Marvin in a 1961 episode of *Route 66* in which he played a cuckolded man with a sensitivity and a subtlety rarely seen in his film work. But Holden is so completely Pike Bishop that no one I've talked with who had anything to do with the project when Marvin was still attached to it regrets Marvin's departure. (Peckinpah identified with Holden and put quite a lot of himself into Pike; see Weddle, pp. 334–8, and Seydor, pp. 170–3, 180–1.)

30 Probably thinking of Martin Ransohoff (who fired him from *The Cincinnati Kid*) or Jerry Bresler (his producer on *Major Dundee*) or any number of studio "suits," Peckinpah described Harrigan as "a small, dapper, self-important back-shooting railroad executive" (Final, p. 5).

31 They first appear in the Final script (6) as changes dated 27 February. As with the flashback to Thornton's capture, they were placed differently, and far less effectively, there (on the rooftop before the shooting starts) than in the completed film (where the lashing is dissolved in under Thornton's close-up as the last beat in his bickering with Harrigan before hitting the trail; the rock pile never made the final cut).

32 For more on this point, see Seydor, pp. 168–70.

33 Philip Young, *Ernest Hemingway: A Reconsideration,* rev. ed. (University Park: Pennsylvania State University Press, 1966), pp. 63–74.

34 David Weddle tells me that the editor, Lou Lombardo, said that this was a suggestion of his.

35 "*Playboy* Interview: Sam Peckinpah," *Playboy* 19, no. 8 (August 1972), 72.

36 See "Sam Peckinpah Lets It All Hang Out," interview, *Take One* 2, no. 3 (January–February 1969), 19.

37 Robert Becker to P.S. (1996).

38 Peckinpah *really* loved a parade, and an amazing number of them or their equivalents appear in his work.

2 Peckinpah the Radical: The Politics of *The Wild Bunch*

It is unthinkable that the 1995 rerelease of *The Wild Bunch* (1969) almost didn't happen due to a controversy within the Motion Picture Association of America (MPAA) about the need for the film to carry an NC-17 rating.[1] Considering the amount of violence in the 1990s cinema, particularly in the work of such self-consciously indebted heirs to Sam Peckinpah as John Woo and Quentin Tarantino, suppressing *The Wild Bunch* would have been one of the more dismal ironies of the age. The irony would have been all the more profound considering the relative depthlessness of these newer directors and much of the male-oriented action cinema that trades so heavily in violence. Looking at Peckinpah's work today, one cannot help but perceive the massive social and cultural break that has occurred within the past twenty years; indeed, one could argue that the period and the cultural tendency called "postmodernity" is something post–*Wild Bunch*. Peckinpah, so often referred to as the "master of violence," or similar malarkey, was among the last social critics produced by Hollywood. His use of violence, like all thematics of his work, is deeply involved with profound humanist and antiauthoritarian concerns that sometimes verge on radicalism. Peckinpah's great compassion for the human condition and for the characters he created is

79

something totally alien to the glacial movie-brat worldview of a Tarantino that showcases obsessively various favorite tropes and images of commercial cinema and consumer culture. Even more upsetting, the very hagiography provided Peckinpah by fans such as Tarantino, Woo, Walter Hill (who restaged the opening and closing massacres of *The Wild Bunch* in *The Long Riders* [1980] and *Extreme Prejudice* [1987], respectively), and a host of others tends to entrench Peckinpah in a very specific and limited position in the American cinema, and to perpetuate blinkered or mistaken notions about the politics of his vision.

Sam Peckinpah's death in 1984 produced a few retrospectives, but his eulogists tended to describe a director of some promise who failed to attain the stature of a major hero in the industry pantheon. It is not important that *Cross of Iron* (1977), *Bring Me the Head of Alfredo Garcia* (1974), and *The Killer Elite* (1975) are complex on issues of sexuality, patriarchy, and capitalism; it is sufficient to know that Peckinpah simply ran out of steam, no longer able to attract an audience, a filmmaker whose breakthrough *The Wild Bunch* gave him temporary celebrity in the media spotlight as Hollywood's master of graphic violence.

The inadequate reappraisal of Peckinpah is representative of the misguided strategies of journalistic criticism. Rather than focus on the innovative themes of his work, the inflections of several genres, and the evidence of progressive ideas emerging from the restrictions of industry, critics regard Peckinpah chiefly as a one-shot artist whose contradictions and incoherent body of work diminish him as a subject for serious consideration. But Peckinpah's contradictions, as much as those of any Hollywood director, are at the heart of what makes his films important. That he should be able to produce a work of some ideological coherence in his masterpiece, *The Wild Bunch* (1969), is fairly extraordinary given the resistance of his day. At this point, I do not wish to feign some deconstructionist conceit about "Peckinpah" being a slate, an intertext where a number of narratives and genre conventions meet. Peckinpah's individual contribution can be appreciated precisely as it is viewed within a historical context, and as the progressive impulses of this director are seen simultaneously with their contradictions and their overall relationship to the industry. Many of Peckinpah's films of the 1970s contained progressive, even radical themes (and almost always showed great technical mastery), but for various reasons, such as the tendency of media reviewers to dismiss Peckinpah for his several repetitive themes, the progressiveness of his work was largely unperceived. Yet there is a great deal about Peckinpah's work, including its late phase, that is interesting and will undoubtedly get fuller treatment.

Andrew Britton wrote an important piece about the gay subtext of *Cross of Iron,*[2] a film that could stand closer examination, with attention to Peckinpah's interest in Brecht. The interconnections of government, business, media, and the military-intelligence apparatus, favorite concerns of horror/science fiction in the 1970s and 1980s, keep recurring in Peckinpah. *The Getaway* (1972), an interesting attempt (damaged by the casting of Ali MacGraw) at the type of crime thriller made popular by Raoul Walsh, is a Vietnam/Watergate-era film in its sense of pervasive corruption (the penal system actually controlled by the private sector, both men and women portrayed as prostitutes exchanging favors for personal freedom). *The Killer Elite* says much in its title: the intelligence community is portrayed as a glorified, transnational Murder Inc. employing psychopaths usually associated with the underworld in earlier films. This film and *The Osterman Weekend* (1983) (Peckinpah's last and strongest attack on American society in its ornate conspiratorial vision) are noteworthy in their post-Watergate depiction of betrayal, avarice, internecine rivalry, and the demise of any sense of law and democratic principles. One image in *Bring Me the Head of Alfredo Garcia* poetically sums up these concerns: a gangster/executive gets a pedicure from his secretary while he reads a *Time* article about Nixon's possible impeachment. The apocalyptic gun battles that conclude many of Peckinpah's films (and that immediately put off critics) may be seen as the same expression of rage against the current society represented in the *fantastique* by exploding bodies, reversion to barbarism, or technological Armageddon. *The Wild Bunch* is simply our best model, and one especially useful in that for all its celebrity as a classic Western (and even a landmark film in relation to others by Peckinpah), its radical content has been ignored.

To be sure, prejudices against Peckinpah are not easily overcome, at least in part because of his public profile and intellectual obsessions. A hard-drinking, crusty director in the tradition of Ford and Hawks, Peckinpah championed the "territorial imperative" and similar determinist theories of Robert Ardrey. Embracing such reactionary drivel seemed to supply Peckinpah with a "scientific" rationale not for machismo but for an incipient nihilism. These interests were catered to in the extreme in the pedantic and often repugnant film essay *Straw Dogs* (1971), whose hyperbolic violence was hardly mitigated or rationalized by the flagrant misogyny in its man's-home-is-his-castle thesis centered on an academic weakling transformed into defender of the hearth. Peckinpah's interest in Hemingway and Ford, individualism, and the solidarity of the male group also did not bode well for any sense of Peckinpah as radical artist. The very interesting writing of Jim Kitses[3] and Paul Seydor[4] helped ensure Peckinpah critical respectability, but as late as 1981 a major text on film history contained an entry on *The Wild Bunch* titled simply "Zapping the Cong,"[5] regarding the film chiefly as an allegory of the Vietnam incursion, certainly pertinent but only a component of the film's more general ideological investigation.

While the directorial innovations of *The Wild Bunch* have been noted in full, it was not until around the time of Robin Wood's remark that the film is part of the "apocalyptic phase"[6] of American filmmaking that we see a different disposition toward the politics of this film and a tendency to see it in terms other than a vague parable about American intervention in Vietnam. When one looks at the restored version of *The Wild Bunch,* it is difficult not to appreciate what an extraordinarily adversarial work it is, savaging the Western genre and the American civilizing experience it has mediated. Brecht and Buñuel (much admired by Peckinpah – Buñuel's *Los Olvidados* [1951] was a favorite film) shine through more vividly than Hemingway and Ford, and it was perhaps Peckinpah's downfall that such an amalgamation should present itself unresolved.

Appreciation of the richness of *The Wild Bunch* has been de-layed for some very specific and material reasons. First, the mar-keting of the film by Warner Bros. was callously indifferent, be-ginning with the studio's cutting of the flashbacks concerning Pike's early life (scenes Peckinpah felt were central to the film) and its double-billing of the film with ostensibly similar adventure fare produced by Warners such as *The Green Berets* (1968) and, later, *Dirty Harry* (1971). Second, the film was coopted in several respects by the hyped *Butch Cassidy and the Sundance Kid,* a star vehicle for Paul Newman and Robert Redford, which contained (but treated with a light touch) the theme of men with their backs to the wall, an idea often spoofed and trivialized that would sat-urate the Western as the genre played itself out in the 1960s. Per-haps most important, *The Wild Bunch* could not hold its own against films embraced by the counterculture and recognized as more or less embodying progressive sentiments, such as *Bonnie and Clyde* (1967), *Zabriskie Point* (1970), and *Easy Rider* (1969). It did not seem immediately apparent to audiences of the late 1960s' counterculture that *The Wild Bunch* was a film firmly situated in the crises of that decade, and concerned with making some sweep-ing statements about America and the civilizing process that pro-duced the Vietnam adventure. The unusually graphic (at that date) violence of Peckinpah's film, the presence of such Hollywood mainstays as William Holden, and the very fact that it was a West-ern excluded it at first both from commercial success (its road show presentation never happened, and it was rereleased twice before it achieved an audience) and from appraisal as ideologi-cally provocative. Even a cursory review, informed by the critical practice of recent years, reveals how extraordinarily bold are the gestures of *The Wild Bunch.*

PECKINPAH PERSONAL AND POLITICAL

In his comments on the film in his book *Horizons West,* Jim Kitses remarks, "*The Wild Bunch* is America."[7] The implica-tions of this statement become clear as we understand how in-terwoven the film's critique of the frontier experience is with its insights into the construction of male personality by American culture. The film begins this examination by the critical approach it takes to the general theme of U.S. adventurism in Mexico, a theme popular in the postwar Western as American interventionism escalated internationally. Films such as *Vera Cruz* (1953) or, later, *The Magnificent Seven* (1960) and *The Professionals* (1966) depicted Mexico as an idyllic landscape or arid backdrop to test the mettle of alienated men in disfavor in their own land (an early scene of *The Searchers* [1956] contains this idea, with Ethan Edwards giving his niece a Mexican military decoration). Except for those films that use the Mexican Revolution for a meditation on revolutionary change (*Viva Zapata*, 1952) or for broader statements about warfare and the male group (*They Came to Cordura*, 1959), the attitude of the postwar Western toward Mexico recapitulates notions of the Other from American melodrama. The Mexican, like the Indian, is alternately demonized and romanticized, with death being the "right place to go" (an important reference point for all this is the nineteenth-century play *Metamora).* The landscape of Mexico is an Other as it becomes the inverse of a Conradian jungle: it is a hellish desert where machismo is proven through confrontations with crazed natives (John Wayne's *The Alamo* [1960] is archetypal). In *The Wild Bunch,* the historical specificity of revolutionary Mexico is understood precisely within the context of assumptions about imperialism, seen first in the construction of the male subject, and as a conjunction of Self and Other as the plight of Mexico is related to the self-image of the United States, and the personalities of Peckinpah's Hispanics have correlates in his Anglos.

It has been suggested by various critics that *The Wild Bunch* is finally about Angel/Jaime Sanchez, the young idealist whose utopian dreams and revolutionary fervor are reclaimed when the Bunch make their last stand at Aqua Verde. Pike/William Holden sees in Angel his lost youth and a moral code the Bunch have long since scrapped. But this popular interpretation overlooks the film's sense that if such a code ever existed, it was morally bankrupt at its inception. Angel is a revolutionary, but he is also a belligerent

FIGURE 16
Angel's capture and torture reawaken Pike's lost sense of honor and community.

misogynist; by relating him to the young Pike, we see the doomed nature of Angel's dream. Calling Angel a misogynist does not lend any distinctiveness to Angel's sins since it is clear that Angel's conduct and that of Pike are merely representative of the world of the film. In most respects, Angel, Pike, and in fact most of the characters stand for the norm. Peckinpah's principal concern is to point to some standard assumptions shared by men. Angel's romantic love for Teresa gives him the prerogative to murder her; the youthful Pike causes Aurora's death out of a bravado and arrogance that mask his insecurity. *The Wild Bunch*'s parable of America is concerned with the conflict between the romantic and the real, the ideal and the material, a conflict represented in Pike's agony over the public self (the resourceful outlaw) he sustains versus the insecure, blundering, and vicious man he wants to conceal or rationalize through references to codes of honor.

Angel's relationship to Pike is significant since Angel's capture and persecution reawaken Pike's anguish over lost family and community, a sense of life as it might have been. Yet, although this vision is clearly preferable to the hell represented by Harrigan and Mapache (technocracy, militarism, imperialism), it is not unrelated to the evils of the world. Pike has consistently lived a lie, one that Angel buys into given his unquestioning allegiance to Pike ("I go with you, *jefe"*). His admiration of Pike (the charismatic male who remains undistorted in the eyes of the young) precludes Angel's stated beliefs in democracy and community, in the solidarity he supports to the point of sacrificing his life. It is sensible that Peckinpah should show Mapache standing amid the gunfire during Pancho Villa's assault on the *federales;* Mapache's bravery is reducible here to an absurdly inflated self-image, machismo rampant and ridiculous. Mapache is separated only a little from Pike and Angel by his authoritarianism, but Peckinpah indeed makes the line deliberately thin. Mapache is also chivalrous, romantic, hot-headed, brutal, and blundering, the same amalgam we see in Pike and Angel. (Young children are shown admiring Mapache, much as Angel and the children of his village admire Pike; Mapache's remarks to the children at the battle with Pancho Villa and at Aqua Verde are as banal and deluded as Pike's admonitions to Angel.) The lie of the male code informing Pike/Angel and Mapache is revealed in the relationship between Pike and Thornton/Robert Ryan. We can understand their story only in the unedited version of the film, but this two-character construct, basic to Peckinpah's earlier *Ride the High Country* (1961), is absolutely essential to the narrative.

In the first flashback, showing Pike's escape from a brothel and his consequent betrayal of Thornton, the film suggests that the two men are caretakers of shared memories not easily borne. The flashback occurs just after Pike has bragged to Dutch about his willingness to meet the railroad company and Pershing's army head on ("I wouldn't have it any other way"). Pike is plagued by the memory of the bordello episode ("Being sure is my business"), giving the lie as it does to Pike's entire life. When the Bunch ride out later in the film to rob the train for Mapache, Pike tells Dutch, "This time we do it right." This line is important since it occurs just after Pike recounts the story of Aurora's murder and the origin of his wounded leg (as Kitses pointed out, Pike's bad leg makes us recognize him as a "crippled man burdened by his past"; there is another metaphor here since Pike is an archetypal limping hero who prevails, rather pathetically, over a barren land). Pike has never been "sure" about anything and is not able to "do it right" even when the act is his last chance at personal affirmation. When the bounty hunters find the dead Bunch at Aqua Verde, Coffer breathlessly says: "There he *is,* there's *Pike!,*" to which T.C. responds: "You ain't so damn big now, are you, Mr. Pike?" Thornton is out of earshot, but the point is clear: no one will ever really know the dignity and profound failure of the outlaw, and perpetuating his legend is not a concern of his lost friend. The bordello flashback, shared by Pike and Thornton, is key to understanding the film's conception of the hypocrisy the male lives out. Thornton, sent to prison by his friend's incompetence, continues in his affection for and loyalty to Pike. When Coffer asks Thornton about Pike, wondering "what kind of man we're up against," Thornton responds flatly, "The best. *He* never got caught." Thornton never betrays his old friend, never revealing the real reason Pike wasn't caught. The implication here concerns not just Thornton's affection for Pike, but his need to support Pike's code, on which rests Thornton's own identity and self-worth, even if his reduction to bounty hunter forced to pursue his old comrades works principally to shake Thornton loose from the romanticism to which Pike desperately clings. While Pike practically cringes from the bordello memory (he rebounds from the moment of guilt by telling Dutch, "I made him [Harrigan] change his ways"), Thornton bears it stoically (in Peckinpah's deft cross-cutting), having reconciled for himself the truth about men. The sexual politics are manifest here, since it is clear that the affection men have for each other is consistently translated into violence and bravura acts resulting in destruction, including self-destruction born of denial of a basic reality.

There is no irony in Thornton's most intimate connection with Pike occurring when Pike is dead (Thornton's retrieval of Pike's revolver) as the male code, really the repressed homoerotic code, finally merges eros with thanatos. And Dutch's whittling on a stick outside the bordello as he mourns Angel's fate is indeed concerned with Dutch's affection for Angel about to culminate in a personal apocalypse that connects the libido to the death wish in an essential prescription of the cult of the male group.

Dutch is especially central to the sexual politics of the film and the Bunch's relationship to the world at large; he appears at some significant transitions that underscore the contradictions of *The Wild Bunch*. There is a particularly telling moment in the dissolve that concludes the Bunch's poetic farewell to Angel's village, serenaded by peasants in a moment that seems to pay homage to the pastoral utopianism of the Western. The dissolve fades into a close shot of a woman breast-feeding a baby; across her bosom rests a bandolier of ammunition. The brutal image turns the scene immediately preceding it into myth. We are now in Mapache's stronghold, the real world. Dutch and Angel scout Aqua Verde for bounty hunters; their relationship equals Dutch's camaraderie with Pike. The shot of Dutch and Angel just after the breast/bandolier image underscores the close construction of eros and thanatos, the unbridled id as the consequence of repression so central to the film. Dutch is a support and confidant, challenging Pike on hoary notions such as the sanctity of a man's word ("It's who you give it *to!*"). Yet in many scenes the notion of Dutch as caretaker of the Bunch's moral conscience is thoroughly undercut. Dutch is also another rather blind disciple who mirrors the hero's darker aspects, a kind of negative Sancho Panza. He supports Pike's decision to leave the dead Buck unburied, scoffing at the thick-headed and sadistic Gorch brothers, who sometimes actually display greater humanity ("He was a good man, and I think we oughta bury him!"). Dutch, after being querulous during his campfire talk with Pike, finally supports Pike's machismo ("Pike, I wouldn't have it any other way either"). At the final massacre, Dutch uses a woman as a shield, presaging Pike's murder of a prostitute who wounds him ("Bitch!"). But there is something more ornate to Dutch's character.

Some critics observe half-seriously that Dutch appears to be gay since he doesn't enter the brothel in the scene just before the Bat-

FIGURE 17
Dutch and Pike share a last moment of friendship before their death in the Aqua Verde battle.

tle of Bloody Porch. The obvious response is that Dutch is indeed the most principled and troubled member of the gang. He recalls Angel's rescue of him during the train robbery and his abandoning Angel to Mapache – reality versus the male code is thrown in the face even of the Bunch's soul and arbitrator (Dutch suggested to Pike that Angel be allowed to keep some of the stolen guns). Yet Dutch's sexuality is hardly an outlandish topic for discussion. Considering the intimacy of so many men in the film (Angel–Dutch, Pike–Dutch, Pike–Angel, Pike–Thornton), the film's violence seems manifestly an explosion of the tension and repression under these deeply felt, unspoken, and complicated relationships. Except for a brief dance at Angel's village, Dutch has no heterosexual relationships, not even any horsing around with whores at Mapache's bath house. Even Old Sykes affirms, "I'm a delight with a pretty girl!" Dutch shares intimate moments only with Pike and Angel, the real/romantic axis of the film. He sleeps beside Pike as the two men share doubts with each other. Pike needles Dutch in the good-natured way that suggests a strong emotional bond ("Come on, ya lazy bastard!"). During the final massacre, the two men have some very significant scenes. At a small lull before the final phase of the bloodletting, Dutch and Pike crouch behind an upturned table, sharing a knowing and frightened stare, realizing the end they have created. Dutch cheers at the devastation Pike wreaks with the machine gun ("Give 'em hell, Pike!"), the younger man again applauding the prowess of the older, and is consequently horrified as Pike goes down. Dutch throws himself in the line of fire as he reaches for Pike; the two men collapse looking at each other, Dutch saying Pike's name several times.

Far from being simply a recognition of the Bunch's futility, the film's final moment is an affirmation of men's affection for each other, even as it is displayed in the highly repressed, twisted forms sanctioned by dominant culture (well represented in the Western, the most conservative film genre). *The Wild Bunch* comes very close to suggesting something about the male group that William Burroughs insists on in *The Wild Boys, Cities of the Red Night,* and *The Place of Dead Roads,* that is, male-oriented action-adventure fiction has as its basic subtext the description of a gay utopia where the male libido is unfettered, and takes directions both destructive and liberatory. Peckinpah is more critical than Burroughs in decrying the utopianism of this vision, arguing that male sexuality remains essentially repressed in the most "wild" circumstances and is manifest most often in violence, an idea Burroughs handles rather blithely. Unlike Burroughs, Peckinpah doesn't think sex and violence can exist together felicitously. But Burroughs's concerns are not alien or arcane to Peckinpah – their most overt presentation is the two gay gangsters played by Gig Young and Robert Webber in *Bring Me the Head of Alfredo Garcia,* probably the least condescending portrayal of gay men in the action cinema (admittedly, they are bad guys, but their homosexuality seems incidental to their badness and a straightforward revaluation of the two-character male constructs in the Peckinpah Westerns). The death of the Gig Young character is portrayed tragically, the Webber character crying, "Johnny, Johnny!" as he leans over his dead sidekick. It is not ironic that Peckinpah was a favorite director of Jean Genet. Before producer Dietor Schidor obtained Genet's permission to film *Querelle* (1982), he was required by Genet to provide a letter of introduction from a prominent filmmaker. Schidor went straight to Peckinpah, who promptly obliged.[8]

It may even be argued that the film's paeans to its heroes are in part a classic idolatry of the male, whose beauty, heroism, and virility were conjoined in antiquity, except here again Peckinpah insists on the contradictions of such concepts. Pike's situation, both tragic and pathetic, is rendered best in the sand dune sequence when Pike mounts his horse after a bad fall on his game leg. In the film's most poignant scene, Pike, now clearly an old man, struggles upright amid the laughter of the Gorch brothers. Dutch/ Ernest Borgnine, his face bathed in the preternatural glow of the morning sun, admires the resolute Pike riding off slowly, hunched over his horse in agony but nevertheless determined. The scene is an almost classical homage to the stoic, handsome male form, particularly if we see in it the intertext/back story of William Holden, the archetypal beefcake hero of classical Hollywood (Peckinpah once remarked that *The Wild Bunch* was in a sense "about Bill Holden in his fifties, no longer the glamour boy").

The scene that immediately follows (and effectively undercuts) this brilliant and sensitive sequence is a testimony to Peckinpah's integrity in its insistence on probing the contradictions of the male group and the society encompassing it. Old Sykes rides beside Pike, thanking him for the protection from Tector Gorch, praising Pike for his belief in sticking together, "just like it used to be." At this point Sykes learns that his grandson, Crazy Lee, was killed at San Rafael. Sykes is satisfied to learn that his lunatic grandson "did fine, just fine," but Pike, who only then is aware of Lee's relationship to his old mentor, is momentarily disturbed by the memory of his decision to use the young man as cannon fodder to aid the Bunch's escape. The film does not digress from the idea that Pike is a vicious man for whom "codes" have become abstractions impossible to support. When Thornton claims Pike's gun after the Aqua Verde massacre, he is both affirming his affection and conferring forgiveness; Thornton acknowledges Pike's basic morality, which has managed to coexist with Pike's failure and with the cruelty emerging from an attempt to prop up Pike's idea of himself. What remains most graven in the consciousness of the viewer, however, is the slumped body of Pike, his right hand still clasping the grip of the machine gun, surrounded by shell casings and dead bodies. There has seldom been an image of the male hero, either vanquished or triumphant, so simultaneously spectacular, evocative, and revolting. We are reminded that the sign systems of patriarchy are built on piles of the dead and that mass death reifies these systems.

THE WEST AS WASTELAND

The Wild Bunch is at least as forceful as the Italian Western in debunking the conventions of the genre and in using its thematics to attack fundamental premises of American civilization. The bounty hunter, romanticized in the TV series *Wanted: Dead or Alive,* and at worst depicted as the last-ditch enterprise of the down-and-out gunfighter nevertheless noble (*The Tin Star,* 1957), takes a new turn in the 1960s. Portrayed as amoral pragmatists by Sergio Leone, bounty hunters are in Peckinpah's film simply vermin, lumpenized elements who function as metaphors for the world of the film. The constant bickering of T.C./L.Q. Jones and Coffer/Strother Martin, their avarice, and their stupidity ("Don't fire at the army, you idiots!") is emblematic of the internecine warfare, gangsterism, and betrayal apparent everywhere. T.C. and Coffer are the kind of peripheral comic figures who, as in classical theater, contain in their actions some of the essential points of the narrative. The bounty hunters are associated with predatory birds in several important scenes, particularly the entry into Aqua Verde after the final massacre; we are reminded that Harrigan, Mapache, Pike, and Thornton are all predators, and that the

FIGURE 18
After the Aqua Verde massacre, the bounty hunters descend like
vultures to loot the corpses.

victimization of people is central to this story and the frontier experience.

The railroad has long been regarded in the genre as a symbol
of the harmful effects of technology on the Virgin Land (the "machine in the garden" idea), represented in such disparate films as
The Man Who Shot Liberty Valance (1962) and *Once Upon a Time in
the West* (1967). After a long period in the Western wherein the
railroad represented the essential rightness of the American civilizing process (*The Iron Horse*, 1924), by the time of *Liberty Valance*

FIGURE 19
Harrigan (left) personifies the savagery of unfettered capitalism.

and the Leone films, the railroad had become associated with the falsification of history that has become a preoccupation of the genre. In *For A Few Dollars More* (1965), the railroad is the force that propels Colonel Mortimer, "the finest shot in the Carolinas," into becoming a paid killer. The railroad becomes the embodiment of expansionist industrial capital, and we come to learn who is paying the bills of all the gunmen patrolling the frontier. This is explicit in *Once Upon a Time in the West,* with Frank (Henry Fonda) a murderous emissary of railroad interests. Although Frank is far more malevolent and powerful than Thornton, Frank's relationship to his tycoon boss is roughly equivalent to that of Thornton to Harrigan. A nice Brechtian conflation occurs in the film as Frank momentarily sits at the desk of his tycoon boss, remarking, "It feels almost like holding a gun, only much more powerful." There is a chilling evocation of fascism in the scene (perhaps because of the presence of cowriter Bertolucci), with capital's power finally usurped by its enforcement apparatus. Peckinpah's film shares with Leone's the idea of the railroad as battering ram for industrial cap-

ital. More specifically, *The Wild Bunch* shows the railroad to be the
incarnation of everything hypocritical and morally reprehensible
about capitalism. Harrigan is more than a railroad executive: he
represents the hegemony of capitalism in the affairs of the state.
The simple ideological point is that the police, the military, hired
gunmen, and so on, are the enforcement apparatus *always* owned
by the private sector. (Altman's *McCabe and Mrs. Miller* [1972] and,
much later, Jim Jarmusch's *Dead Man* [1996] expand on the notion of the gunfighter as agent of capital.) When Wainscoat, mayor
of San Rafael, attacks Harrigan for "using our town as a battlefield,"
Harrigan retorts, "We represent the law." Indeed, Harrigan *is* the
law. The sheriff of San Rafael is barely visible, and the voices of
authority among the townsfolk are brushed aside by Harrigan.
Frontier justice and the fair play honored by Ford are reduced here
to the extralegal but absolute power of Harrigan, who relies upon
mercenaries to capture the Bunch, with the U.S. Army an ancillary
weapon of industry; the army's pursuit of the Bunch and Pancho
Villa is really about protecting Harrigan's interests. The massacre
at San Rafael engineered by Harrigan and the bounty hunters
evokes as well capitalism's destruction of the society it supposedly
sustains, the perfect evocation of Vietnam-era, destroy-the-village-
in-order-to-save-it ideology discussed in relation to the film by
Richard Slotkin.[9] Thornton asks Harrigan, "How does it feel to hire
your killings, with the law's arms around you?" Harrigan replies,
"Good." It is noteworthy that Pike's banditry is aimed precisely at
Harrigan and the railroad. Pike's attempt to make Harrigan change
his ways seems to be an assault on the railroad as a particular encroachment on human freedom. While Pike and the rest of the
Bunch are fascinated with technology (the awestruck moment
around Mapache's car) and display typical male professional in-
genuity as they deal with it (Pike saying, "What I don't know
about, I sure as hell am going to learn" as he first hefts the stolen
machine gun), Pike's first instinct at the final massacre after the
killing of Mapache is to kill the German military envoy. Pike's last
stand with the machine gun includes the apocalyptic demolition
of the munitions stolen for the imperialist forces.

Organized religion, also a centerpiece of the classic Western, is shown here as an element of the superstructure brushed aside when it interferes, however marginally, with capitalism's interests. Mayor Wainscoat, leader of the temperance rally, is both the chief civic official and the town preacher. The merger of the two roles recapitulates Captain Reverend Clayton in *The Searchers*, Ford's idealized conjunction of religious and secular authority. In the character of Wainscoat this conjuncture is by no means felicitous since he is incompetent in both roles (Wainscoat had no foreknowledge of the ambush and leads his prayer meeting straight into the battle). More important, religion is an empty force constantly juxtaposed with the world of men, represented by Mapache, Harrigan, and the Bunch.

A discordant version of "Gather at the River" (a favorite Ford theme) is played by the Temperance Union orchestra just before the shooting starts; the song is picked up by Crazy Lee as he murders the railroad depot hostages. Peckinpah is deft in playing with the "Gather at the River" convention, as the song annotates the tension rather than the tranquility of the frontier community. The temperance meeting itself is attended for the most part by the very young and the elderly; the congregation stumbles, uncomprehending, through the temperance pledge Wainscoat recites. We first hear Wainscoat's biblical exhortations ("Do not take wine nor strong drink!") as we watch children playing with a nest of ants and scorpions – this violent image/sound configuration is one of Peckinpah's best evocations of Buñuel, a horrific depiction of society rending itself to pieces while simultaneously trying to support itself with traditional religious bromides. The immediate reference is the donkey devoured by the bees it transports in Buñuel's unnerving documentary *Las Hurdes* (1932). Peckinpah prefers, with Arthur Cravan, "mystery in broad daylight." Like Buñuel, Peckinpah sees the fantastically hideous in the commonplace phenomena most people blithely ignore out of a denial of essential facts of existence. Peckinpah's insistence on the violence of children goes beyond debunking childhood innocence to emphasize the cul-de-sac of civilization as he evokes his *Triumph of*

Death. That many of the children playing with the ants and scorpions are physically impaired underscores Peckinpah's sense of a godless, malevolent universe, and his antiauthoritarian temperament is always circumscribed by this recognition. His hard-nosed insistence on the material aspect of everyday life supports his radicalism and scoffs at the sentimental religiosity of the genre.

The most visceral depiction of the frontier as imperialist adventure appears when the Bunch approach Angel's village. We see a starving dog amid crumbling adobe and hear Dutch's remark, "That damn Huerta scraped it [the countryside] clean." The landscape of Peckinpah, long before Altman, Eastwood, and Jarmusch, is deromanticized. The arid Southwest is thoroughly inhospitable, made more so by the ambitions of men. Peckinpah's wide-angle lens is less about adoring vistas than about showing the scope of the carnage. The idyllic moment in Angel's village is such an abrupt rupture in the narrative that it can be seen only as a landscape of the imagination (perhaps in homage to *The Treasure of the Sierra Madre* [1948], another key source), a glimpse of the utopian possibility that the film knows is unattainable. Throughout the film this scene continues to resonate, its mythic aspect affirmed in the film's final image. Following the scene in the village, we are brought back to the world of men via the reality facing the people of Mexico, their perpetual victimage. It is significant that in the two massacres, particularly the second, there are insert shots not just of the wounded innocents but also of ordinary people forced to observe, the strain of the lives they have already lived on their faces, now registering a final fear or, at points, merely inurement.

THE WILD BUNCH AND REVOLUTION

While Peckinpah insisted laconically that his film was about "bad men in changing times," it is clear that *The Wild Bunch* is a meditation not only on the construction of the male within American culture but also on the nature of evil and the origins of bourgeois notions of the criminal. Here too Peckinpah seems to

depend a good deal on Brecht and Buñuel for a sophisticated notion of criminality since he takes pains to separate the Bunch, finally depicted as noble, from the rest of their world, seen as wholly
corrupt. The most telling scene is the early sequence in Aqua Verde
when the Bunch, seated at an outdoor cafe, first spot Mapache
and his minions. Pike makes a joking comparison between the
Bunch and Mapache's army (and Mapache's German advisors).
Dutch bristles at the equation, angrily telling Pike, "We don't hang
nobody." Through Dutch's insights and Angel's actions, the Bunch
(or, rather, Pike) come to a gradual recognition of a more genuine
sense of honor, but claim it too late and for motives not fully resolved. Like Brecht's gangsters, Peckinpah's bad men are natural if
hyperbolic manifestations of capitalism. Although Dutch is right
to scold him, Pike is not wrong in saying that Mapache (and Harrigan?) is "like some others I could mention." But like *The Three-
penny Opera, The Wild Bunch* asks if it is more evil "to open a bank
than rob a bank." While Peckinpah, like Brecht, emphasizes the
grotesquerie of capitalist civilization, he doesn't interrogate its
attempts to protect its democratic façade. In *The Wild Bunch,* capitalism's veneer of democracy is transparent and irrelevant, and
Peckinpah insists on this rapacity and murderousness as the true
nature of this society. Before other revisionists of the Western,
Peckinpah accomplishes this basic unmasking.

The first scene of the film, with the Bunch approaching in army
gear, is less about playing with audience expectations (we assume
the soldiers are good guys) than about suggesting the true face of
state power and the basic institutions of patriarchal, capitalist society. The Bunch *are* as violent and rapacious as the state apparatus, and the state apparatus is as inept and comical as the Bunch.
Like Pershing's army and Harrigan's paid killers, the Bunch are
representative of the real order of things. As a metonym of the
world that spawned them, they are as proficient at terror – and as
idiotic and incompetent – as their rivals. It is noteworthy that the
comedy of T.C. and Coffer is repeated by the Gorch brothers; for
Peckinpah there is no "outside," no place from which we can watch
from a critical distance. Hence comedy in Peckinpah, unlike, say,

Shakespeare, cannot annotate the action or provide insight concerning the larger world that we watch. Conversely, society's only adversaries to the established order, where they exist at all, are criminal fringe elements (the Bunch) driven by greed, whose transformation in the narrative flows from complex material circumstances rather than lofty idealism and a bent toward redemption. We are not concerned here with mercenaries with a heart of gold, as in *The Magnificent Seven.*

The liberation of Aqua Verde at the end might be said to be largely incidental, and a key issue remains the interchangeability of the various male groups. The Bunch do indeed eventually effectuate revolutionary violence in Mexico, and through much of the film their plight intersects with the plight of the poor. Above all, the Bunch's final "rebellion" has at its base issues of economy and ruptures within a historical moment that become manifest on the micro and macro levels, in terms of individual and group contradictions. The Marxist approach to criminality seems appropriate to understanding *The Wild Bunch* since the film's theme of lost innocence is tied to the search for community and human solidarity, an end to alienation, even if the aims are parochial despite grand-sounding rhetoric (Angel says: "I care about *my* people, *my* village, Mexico"). At Angel's village, Pike says guardedly to Don José, "You know what we are then." Don José responds, "*Si,* the both of you!" Pike, Dutch, and Sykes, now breaking into laughter, retort, "And *you!*" While Pike expects Angel to forget family, village, Mexico itself (these are all the same in Angel's mind) if he wishes to continue in the Bunch's escapades, the village sequence helps to establish the most significant tension of the film: the need for affirmation of self versus the need to transform society. The village sequence tells us that the film is ultimately about Pike, the emblem of American individualism, who realizes the bankruptcy of his position too late.

The contradictions within Pike, the conflict of the real and the ideal, are only partially resolved in the shattering conclusion, with the Bunch's return for Angel, the final massacre, Thornton's reunion with Sykes, and the apotheosis of the Bunch. In the brothel scene before the massacre, Pike's moment of grim self-appraisal/ revulsion seems to affirm Angel's idealism and zeal as Pike recognizes the young prostitute's moral superiority to him. But Angel and Pike are killers of women, and their sexual violence is not unrelated to their romanticism. The point is made as the sensitive moment between Pike and the young whore is violated by the cruelty of the Gorches in the next room. Pike takes up Angel's battle, perhaps without being fully aware of how his self-nullification is also an affirmation of Angel's worst aspects and his own.

Much has been written about the Bunch's attempted rescue of Angel and the basic Anglos-in-Mexico themes of *The Wild Bunch* as a parable of the Vietnam invasion. As Richard Slotkin has noted, it is more useful to see *The Wild Bunch* as an undermining of the myths and conventions of the genre (*The Magnificent Seven, The Professionals*) than merely as a specific comment on the incursion into Southeast Asia, although the film's assault on its genre probably could not happen in a context other than the post-Tet Vietnam era.[10] Above all, *The Wild Bunch* debunks the basic assumption that U.S. interventionism is selfless and benign. As Slotkin has argued, the sacrificial myth of the Last Stand that is essential to "interventionist Westerns" such as *The Alamo* and *The Magnificent Seven* is always an affirmation and sacralization of U.S. imperialist ideology and a demonization of the Other, so closely related is it to myths of antiquity such as the Crucifixion, Thermopylae, and Masada. The Last Stand of the Bunch jettisons this mythology as it recapitulates its basic themes. This Last Stand is an apocalyptic inferno presaged by the early moments of the film showing sick children watching a scorpion being killed by ants as it attempts to kill them, in the process stinging itself to death. As if the gods are no longer amused, the children finally intervene and make a conflagration of the anthill. The devastation of the Battle of Bloody Porch respects the nihilism of the prelude, which is central to the ideology of the film, its view of America. The notion of a "front line," with the good guys stolidly, relentlessly moving against the enemy, is gone, with Peckinpah often violating left–right continuity to upset our sense of space. The feeling of melee also reiterates the confused and conflicted moral code of the Bunch and the world of men they represent. Women are murdered and become murderers; innocent civilians again become incidental targets.

Enough has been said about Peckinpah and childhood innocence; Pike's slaying by a boy gives closure to the anthill scene, the children playing cowboy in the carnage of San Rafael, and the torture of Angel gleefully assisted by children. The self-deception of childhood innocence is the foundation stone, for Peckinpah, of other myths of Hollywood genre cinema, including the goodness of small-town life, the centrality of religion, family, community. Bloody Porch is, after all, the place where Teresa was murdered by Angel (problematicizing our view of Angel as martyr as he is killed by Mapache) and where her funeral was angrily interrupted by an impatient Mapache. (The scene recapitulates the temperance rally, with the elderly Mexican women here reciting the rosary as they walk oblivious in procession past the screaming Zamora and the opulent banquet table laid out for the Bunch; only the Gorch brothers show any courtesy, as they did with the death of Buck, and this out of ignorant superstition that the elder Tector in any event says lacks "class.") The classic march to the showdown that precedes the massacre is a bold, hyperbolic stroke that seems to assert the nobility of the Bunch. Yet it is also apparent that Pike's decision ("Let's go!") has little to do with anything beyond personal interests and failures (about the death of Aurora, Pike says, "There's isn't a day or an hour that goes by that I don't think about it"). That the people of Aqua Verde seem oblivious to the march of the Bunch suggests the questionable nature of this final act of liberation.

There seems little ideological equivocation, however, in the film's final moments, with the Bunch not only liberators (the guns end up with the peasants at least) but with both Thornton and Sykes finally understanding that their only sensible place is with the revolution. The liberation entails, of course, the destruction of Aqua Verde. It is hard to say what Sykes and Thornton think about the ideology of Villa, but the film makes clear what the remainder of the Bunch will be up to. Sykes says, "Me and the boys have some work to do. It ain't like it used to be . . . but it'll do," to which Thornton chuckles, acknowledging Sykes as he rises to join him. A *campanero* carries the machine gun from the gates of Aqua Verde. Sykes rides with Don José, the elder from Angel's village. Just as Don José acknowledged his kinship with the outlaws during their stay at his village, the Bunch (what is left of them) acknowledge kinship with Angel, Don José, and the people of Mexico. Here Peckinpah fully constructs the bandit as outsider and rebel. As Dutch says to Colonel Mohr, "We're not associated with anybody." Of course, the Bunch ultimately find something larger, although rather unconsciously, than their own camaraderie and bankrupt macho code, finally embracing the marginalized people who are either bewildered by them or who idealize them. The laughter at the conclusion (coinciding with the laughter of the dead members of the Bunch, superimposed on the image, suggesting an acknowledgment and blessing of Thornton and Sykes's decision) is not sardonic or cavalier; it suggests quite simply that the path of the Bunch always led to this moment. The final image, the Bunch's entry into Valhalla (with the strains of "La Golondrina" describing a complete utopian space), is Peckinpah's most romantic gesture, but the contradictions are again poignant and compelling.

The scenes in Angel's village, particularly the Bunch's farewell, are among the great evocations of serenity in American cinema. As the Gorch brothers play cat's cradle with a peasant girl, Pike laughingly says, "Now *that* I find hard to believe," to which Don José responds, "Not so hard. We all dream of being a child again, even the worst of us . . . perhaps the worst most of all." Interestingly, on the mention of "worst" the camera cuts to a distraught Angel, the idealist of the group, flying into a rage over the betrayal by Teresa. Is Angel the worst? Don José remarks that for Angel, Teresa was "a goddess, to be worshipped from afar. To Mapache she was a mango, ripe and waiting." Pike says laconically, "Angel dreams of love and Mapache eats the mango." Angel's romantic dream, resulting in the cold-blooded murder of Teresa, shows how his notion of "goddess" is entrenched in the virgin–whore construction of the female so essential to Western civilization. Just before the murder, Pike tries to restrain Angel, who complains, "She was my woman!" Pike consoles Angel: "I know, I know." Pike's consolation refers us to his own culpability in the murder of Aurora and the misogyny at the base of romantic love. The scenes in Angel's village and the subsequent murder of Teresa bring into question the romanticism of the Western itself. Pike and Angel, the older man–young acolyte construct central to the male-oriented genre cinema, are always associated with each other, the terrible failed potentiality of the younger man shown to be a reflection of the history and values of the *jefe* with whom he wants to ride.

Pike (it is really his tale entirely) and the others represent an American idealism long since corrupted, its energies spent, its politics turned into exaggerated individualism. More than any film since *Citizen Kane, The Wild Bunch* is a meditation on America's promise versus its actuality. The seemingly throwaway vignette at the rail depot in the opening shows the importance of an establishing sequence to a skilled artist. The depot supervisor dresses down a clerk: "I don't care what you *meant* to do . . . it's what you *did* I don't like." The promise has no relationship to the realization. In Thornton's words, "What I want and what I need are two different things." Charles Foster Kane in *Citizen Kane* burns his Declaration of Principles (a metaphor for the scrapping of the Constitution by capitalism); Pike flees from Thornton, causes Aurora's death, and sacrifices Crazy Lee and Angel while admonishing his underlings to keep things "just like it used to be."

The film foresees the America that emerged in its wake in the 1970s, 1980s, and 1990s as a cult of nostalgia for a lost America (that never existed) and "traditional values" complemented a savage assault on the public sector and the welfare state and a destruction of the social contract. The remaining remnant of American notions of freedom may have some role in effectuating genuine social change, but the amount of waste and savagery represented in the world of *The Wild Bunch* leaves such a possibility in doubt. While the film suggests that revolution is the only avenue to social transformation, such a conviction cannot mitigate the jaundiced view of the entire American adventure. For this Peckinpah will probably be regarded chiefly as a cynic or nihilist, but the contradictions of his work, particularly as we view them in an era that prefers to ignore contradictions, make his art among the most crucial analyses of the failure of the American experiment. *The Wild Bunch* is involved in more than homage for a dead past; it is a recognition of how that past was probably always a deceit.

NOTES

1 David Weddle, "Dead Man's Clothes: The Making of *The Wild Bunch*," *Film Comment*, May–June 1994, pp. 44–57.
2 Andrew Britton, "Sideshows: Hollywood in Vietnam," *Movie* 27–8, (Winter 1980–Spring 1981), pp. 20–3.
3 Jim Kitses, *Horizons West: Anthony Mann, Budd Boetticher, Sam Peckinpah; Studies of Authorship in the Western* (Bloomington: Indiana University Press, 1969).
4 Paul Seydor, *Peckinpah: The Western Films* (Urbana: University of Illinois Press, 1980).
5 David A. Cook, *A History of Narrative Film* (New York: Norton, 1981), p. 631.
6 Robin Wood et al., *The American Nightmare* (Toronto Festival of Festivals, 1979), p. 17.
7 Kitses, p. 175.
8 See Dietor Schidor's foreword to Rainer Werner Fassbinder, *Querelle: The Film Book*, trans. Arthur S. Wensinger and Richard H. Wood (New York and Munich: Schirmer/Mosel-Grove Press, 1983), p. 6.
9 Richard Slotkin, *Gunfighter Nation: The Myth of the Frontier in Twentieth-Century America* (New York: Atheneum, 1992), pp. 593–613.
10 Ibid.

3   "Back Off to What?" Enclosure, Violence, and Capitalism in Sam Peckinpah's *The Wild Bunch*

Approximately thirty minutes into *The Wild Bunch,* after the disastrous Starbuck job, Pike, obviously weary of his outlaw existence, says to Dutch, "I'd like to make one good score and back off." When Dutch replies, "Back off to what?" we see the core of Peckinpah's intent in the film: to depict the outlaw's violent, materialistic life as a dead end. Indeed, almost from its opening moments, *The Wild Bunch* deals with images of enclosure that suggest a sense of finality. A feeling of enclosure is created when the Bunch ride into Starbuck, where they are surrounded on all sides by bounty hunters, and it is repeated in other actions in the film: during the initial entrance of the Bunch into Agua Verde, the delivery of guns to Mapache's henchman in a canyon, and the final shootout in Agua Verde. What all of these scenes of enclosure naturally involve is the notion of space both as a physical construct and as a metaphor for various kinds of limitation or entrapment. Given Peckinpah's masterful dramatization in the film of significant themes such as loyalty, friendship, and honor, along with *The Wild Bunch*'s continuing influence as a film notable for its breakthrough representational techniques, I think it would be productive to investigate *The Wild Bunch*'s use of space with regard to how it relates to some of the film's major concerns: memory,

105

interpersonal relations, and the influence that money exerts on human behavior.[1]

Let's take a few preliminary examples of the enclosure motif as it emerges early in the film. At *The Wild Bunch*'s beginning, the Bunch ride past a group of children. Two of the men, Pike and Dutch, turn slightly to look down, and what they see is the children torturing some scorpions, which, along with some ants, have been placed within a wooden cage. The despairing Shakespearean citation "As flies to wanton boys are we to the gods – they kill us for their sport" immediately comes to mind at this point, especially given the feeling of arbitrary cruelty that is being dramatized. Equally strong, though, is the notion of entrapment, which is here trebled, since the insects are not only surrounded by the wooden cage and hemmed in by the semicircle of children who stand around gaping as their "sport" proceeds but are also enclosed within the encompassing gaze of the members of the Bunch.

The relation between violence and entrapment should appear obvious given the fascination that the insects' torture holds for the children: violence itself is a trap, a stultifying form of behavior that has negative consequences for both perpetrator and victim, locking individuals into a series of actions and reactions that become self-reinforcing and virtually addictive.[2]

That Pike and Dutch seem, in spite of themselves, fascinated with and appalled by the behavior of the children torturing the ants and scorpions highlights not only the attraction of violence but also its potential for obscuring self-awareness. Were they perceptive enough, what Pike and Dutch would realize on a conscious level while watching the children is what they undoubtedly intuit subconsciously: that the children's game represents these men's lives in miniature – an existence in which brutality and self-gratification are inextricably linked. Indeed, this is perhaps why so much of the laughter in *The Wild Bunch* is caused by the misfortune or ridiculing of characters such as Lyle (when he is denied whiskey after the train heist) or Angel (when he is captured by Mapache).

Given the fact that Peckinpah doubtless wishes the audience

to draw a connection between the children's actions and those of the Bunch, we should recall at this point Don José's comment during the fiesta in Angel's village. "We all wish to be a child again," Don José says, "even the worst of us – maybe the worst most of all." Yet the childlike nature to which Don José alludes, by which he seems to mean a state of innocence, is not present in the film. The children whom we see in *The Wild Bunch* are associated with cruelty and brutality. Aside from the children torturers, there are the youngsters who "replay" the Starbuck massacre, circling a dead man and "shooting" him with their hands; the infant suckled by a Mexican woman whose bandolier strap lies between her breasts (according to Peckinpah, then, violence and dependency are yoked from the time of early childhood; perhaps there is the suggestion here that violence is itself a form of dependency); and the young boy who delivers the coup de grace to Pike at the end of the Agua Verde massacre. The only other child of note is the baby of the woman with whom Pike has sex toward the film's end. Yet this child represents not a peaceful reality but a life involving love and family that for Pike and the Bunch never was and never could have been. We thus feel a strong sense of limited possibilities and obscured self-awareness in the film, which is communicated via its imagery, its ethics, and, as will be seen, its attitude toward capitalism.

In one of the monochrome freeze-frame shots during the film's opening titles, the Bunch, after passing by the children at the ant cage, are seen headed down a row of railroad tracks that seem to represent a narrowing of possibilities, especially given their association with Thornton, who is being blackmailed by the railroad man Harrigan. That the freeze-frame shot emphasizes the tracks' diminishing perspective also suggests a tie-in with Harrigan, whose steely adamancy and lack of humanistic response typify not only the narrowness of his character but also, by extension, the capitalist organization that he represents, which, like all railroads, was doubtless ruthless in its appropriation of land and its manipulation of manpower. Thus, in the film's opening moments, some of its major meanings have already been suggested: enclosure as a metaphor for physical, psychological, and ethical limitation; entrapment; arbitrary violence; fateful inevitability; and capitalism. The relations among these notions will be developed as the film continues.

The opening sequences's freeze-frame monochrome images do more than merely relegate the Bunch to a black-and-white newspaper/historical past; they also have a spatial suggestiveness, since when the image shifts to a stylized black and white, the majority of its depth disappears.[3] The repeated collapsing of physical space in the film suggests a further thematic: that violence involves a type of enclosure that has not only psychological but also ethical ramifications, that it is part of a realm that lacks moral depth, and that it can only be enjoyed if it is abstracted from the context in which it occurs, a realm in which brutality causes real death, real pain, real suffering.

It's quite likely that in making the violence in *The Wild Bunch* so graphic, Peckinpah did indeed intend (as he often claimed) to show people how terrible it really is, and that the only people who could find the film's violence entrancing are those who fail to draw a connection between its reality and its fictive representation. Just as people who are themselves violent may to a degree see their own acts of violence as somewhat unreal (which thereby helps to make its continuation possible), filmgoers who do not treat *The Wild Bunch*'s violence as real may see it as fictively unreal because doing so suits their desire for an aesthetic appreciation of violence that only someone at a safe and pleasant distance from it could achieve. However, in doing so, these individuals fail to react in the complex way that the director wanted them to. As Peckinpah once commented:

> The point of the film is to take this façade of movie violence and open it up, get people involved in it so that they are starting to go in the Hollywood television predictable reaction syndrome, and then twist it so that it's not fun anymore, just a wave of sickness in the gut. . . . It's ugly, brutalizing, and bloody fucking awful . . . and yet there's a certain response that you get from it, an excitement that we're all violent people.[4]

When he made this statement in 1969, Peckinpah was aware of the tremendous effect that *The Wild Bunch*'s violence was having on audiences. Many critics thought that the film's representations of cruelty were self-indulgent and disgusting; others rationalized them. Regardless of one's feelings on this issue, it's questionable if there really is, as Peckinpah claims, a turning point in the violence (the "twist" to which he refers), a juncture at which one can discern a change from representation to overrepresentation. And though the shootouts at the film's beginning and end surpass virtually anything else in cinema, their exaggerations don't guarantee that the audience will stop at Peckinpah's turning points to reflect on their reactions to what they're seeing, which is what Peckinpah implies.

Moreover, although these sequences certainly cause the kind of "excitement" to which Peckinpah draws attention, this doesn't mean that the audience, having been excited, will then become ashamed about their reaction to the violence. Indeed, just the opposite effect was often seen in audience members during the violent scenes in *The Wild Bunch* and in comparable sequences, such as the farmhouse assault sequence in *Straw Dogs,* during the screening of which one audience member yelled out (presumably to Dustin Hoffman's David Sumner, who was defending his house against gang attack), "Kill 'em all!" Perhaps the most that can be said at this point about *The Wild Bunch*'s representation of violence is that, like so much else in Peckinpah's films, it involves a degree of contrariety, precisely what makes the film such a fascinating work of art.

If we turn to a consideration of the Starbuck shootout, we find that these scenes also contain powerfully contradictory forces. The explosiveness of the action – with men, women, and children running and being thrown in all directions – is carefully counterbalanced by the manner in which the scene is shot, for although the rapid-fire editing often seems to "open up" the action (suggesting, at the very least, if not the possibility of freedom then the excitement created by Peckinpah's photographic and editorial technique), the effect of this technique is often undermined by a great deal of what we subsequently witness. We are given images of bodies and animals colliding; of people being hurtled toward the ground; of a man falling into the small enclosure of a store window; of the bounty hunters, virtually shoulder to shoulder, jockeying for better positions from which to shoot. At one point, Thornton fires at Pike. However, instead of hitting Pike, Thornton's shot wounds a tuba player, who passes into a space in front of Pike that hadn't seemed to be there before (thus reminding us that a cinematic image photographed with a telephoto lens poorly represents the amount of space between people). Perhaps this act results from Thornton's slow reaction time, which suggests the onset of an old age characterized by a narrowing down of physical possibilities (as Pike later says of himself, "ain't getting around any better," a statement whose tone of finality is amplified when we later learn of his thigh wound). Possibly the musician is hit because of the speed at which he is moving (which seems less likely given the instrument's bulk and weight). Regardless of which explanation we adopt, the shot's significance is virtually the same: human beings' behavior is governed by forces (the passage of time, external events) over which they have virtually no control. We thus recall the railroad office manager's statement: "I don't care what you meant to do; it's what you did I don't like." Even one's own best intentions collapse under the weight of circumstance. Undoubtedly, Pike and Thornton didn't mean for their lives to turn out as they did, but like virtually everyone else in this film, they are trapped by the weight of present conditions, which are predominantly a function of past actions. Almost all of the characters in *The Wild Bunch* are locked into a loop of determined behaviors, a situation to which they find it extremely difficult to resign themselves, even if they realize that they may, to a degree, have determined these behaviors themselves. In *The Wild Bunch,* then, not only passing time but also progressively limited choices narrow one toward death, an idea reflected in the film's conception of physical and psychological space.

It's only during the ride-out from Angel's village that a dramatic sense of spatial depth – and, thereby, figurative freedom from in-

FIGURE 20
The Bunch leave Angel's village, depicted as a lush world of peace and calm.

evitability – is created. As the Bunch leave, they pass between two rows of villagers. The profusion of background material in the frame (trees, village structures) and the presence of sunlight filtering down through the trees create a great sense of depth. The ride-out is a fitting culmination of the fiesta scenes' sense of celebration and tranquility. For a brief time, the Bunch have entered the apparently limitless and lush green world of repose, freed for the most part from their past-haunted statuses (although Peckinpah reminds us of this aspect when he photographs Pike under a tree, alone, staring wistfully into the distance). Yet one should appreciate that the entire village interlude is suspiciously realized. Supposedly plundered by Huerta's men, the village nonetheless yields up a bounty of food that belies the previous suggestions of its poverty (e.g., the starving dog on its outskirts and Don José's comments about the villagers' cattle and grain being taken from them). The sincerity of the director's romantic intentions is the only genuine part of these scenes; the rest represents Peckinpah's admirable but (given his film's overall tone) inappropriate attempt to invoke feelings of possibility rather than entrapment, freedom rather than determinism, concepts that in the context of the film's emphasis on limitation seem quaint but, ultimately, forced and false. In *The Wild Bunch*'s universe, dimensionality, depth, and possibility are repeatedly set off against, and ultimately yield to, entrapment, inevitability, and death.

One of the notions that the film appropriates is Frederick Jackson Turner's concept of the frontier as a realm of opportunities that is rapidly closing. Turner's thesis concerning the frontier remains as controversial today as when it was first presented at a meeting of the American Historical Society in 1893. Turner advanced the idea that the defining aspect of American territorial settlement was the notion of unexplored territories that, Turner felt, had significance not just as physical land masses but as symbolic realms connoting opportunity and new beginnings. According to Turner, the frontier generated American optimism for the future. Regardless of the validity of the thesis (and it has been widely debated since it was proposed),[5] the essential point is that in *The Wild Bunch,* Peckinpah has chosen to dramatize it. And why not – especially since the kind of tension in the Turner essay between possibility and entrapment is endemic to Peckinpah's vision in this film.

Initially, Turner asserts, the frontier was regarded as promising a new life:

> American development has exhibited not merely advance along a single line, but a return to primitive conditions on a continually advancing frontier line, and a new development for that area. American social development has been continually beginning over again on the frontier. This perennial rebirth, this fluidity of American life, this expansion westward with its new opportunities, its continuous touch with the simplicity of primitive society, furnish the forces dominating American character.[6]

Yet though he generally avoids drawing attention to contradictory forces, Turner nonetheless does so implicitly. From a work he refers to as "Peck's New Guide to the West," Turner quotes the unnamed author's delineation of a tripartite wave of westward migration. This migration begins with pioneers, who have "rude" agricultural tools and who build log cabins; they are followed by people who purchase the pioneers' land and "improve" it with bridges, houses with windows and chimneys, and such things as schools and courthouses. Finally come "the men of capital and enterprise," who buy the land from the previous owners, who in turn push on, themselves eventually to become men of enterprise.[7]

What do we see outlined here but the rise of capitalism, of which Turner implicitly approves? Yet not once in his essay does Turner address the question that his citation from the Peck book implicitly raises: weren't there negative consequences to the so-called progress to which he is here giving his sanction? And how did such "progress" affect the notion of the frontier spirit – that spirit, with its yearning to escape from confinement, that now seems to have mutated into a conventionalism tied to property and acquisition, concepts connotatively opposed to the forces of freedom that the pioneer supposedly embodied?

Turner did recognize that there were some problems with the psychology of Americans. At one point he notes, "as has been indicated, the frontier is productive of individualism. Complex society is precipitated by the wilderness into a kind of primitive organization based on the family. The tendency is anti-social. It produces antipathy to control, and particularly to any direct control."[8] While one might read this resistance to control as a hallmark of admirable individualism, it is also a quality that Turner sees as easily yielding to the capitalist desire for what is really nothing more than fiscal self-aggrandizement. Perhaps not surprisingly, we find that the Bunch embody these characteristics as well. Although the Bunch obviously relish their freedom, they pay a heavy price for it, as we can see from the fact that they are homeless, romantically unattached, and apparently poverty-ridden (e.g., when the Bunch first enter Agua Verde as a group, Dutch draws attention to how little silver he has left). It is thus highly ironic (and, to risk neologizing, Turneresque) that for the sake of money, the Bunch compromise their freedom by entering into an agreement with Mapache that, knowing the "general's" untrustworthy personality, they realize is not only risky but even treasonous (thus Dutch's "that's hitting pretty close to home, ain't it?" – the only indication in the film that the Bunch may have some feeling of loyalty to the United States). Contradiction and irresolution, then, are built into these men's character, and it's quite possible that the conflicted feelings that the Bunch have about the deal with Mapache to a degree reflect Peckinpah's feelings about the deals he felt compelled to make with studio executives so that he could produce his films (projects that, like the train heist, he would repeatedly resolve to "do right"). With the exception of *Bring Me the Head of Alfredo Garcia,* Peckinpah eventually came to feel that all of these deals were not only compromised but compromising.

As Leo Marx points out in *The Machine in the Garden,* although the longing for the type of freedom that Turner's frontier represents seems to be innate, this tendency is also potentially dangerous. Marx refers to "popular and sentimental" pastoralism, which is essentially the desire for freedom and open land on which Turner's thesis rests, as something of an illusion. He characterizes this type of pastoralism as

> an expression less of thought than of feeling. It is widely diffused in our culture, insinuating itself into many kinds of behavior. An obvious example is the "flight from the city." An inchoate longing for a more "natural" environment enters into the contemptuous attitude that many Americans adopt toward urban life . . . wherever people turn away from the hard social and technological realities this obscure sentiment is likely to be at work.[9]

In other words, the frontier doesn't promise freedom so much as a flight from responsibility. At one point in his essay, even Turner recognizes the problem inherent in idealizing the frontier:

The democracy born of free land, strong in selfishness and in-dividualism, intolerant of administrative experience and edu-cation, and pressing individual liberty beyond its proper bounds, has its dangers as well as benefits. Individualism in America has allowed a laxity in regard to governmental affairs which has rendered possible the spoils system and all the manifest evils that follow from the lack of a highly developed civic spirit . . . the colonial and revolutionary frontier was the region whence emanated many of the worst forms of an evil currency.[10]

It doesn't require a major leap from a recognition of the prob-lems implicit in the spirit of freedom proposed by Turner to an acknowledgment of the link between this reckless abandonment of responsibility and the actions of the Wild Bunch. Despite being outlaws who believe that they live by a code, the Bunch continually subvert it. Although the Bunch, like Turner's pio-neers, embody the desire for a new land where they can be free (Pike, wanting to take refuge in Mexico, says, "I'm tired of being hunted"),[11] they nonetheless carry within themselves an impulse toward acquisitiveness that compels them to keep stealing, thereby constantly hazarding the freedom that they so strongly crave. Throughout the film, it is easy to see how Pike's code of "stick[ing] together" is compromised by the Bunch's avarice, self-interest, and (on the part of the Gorches) racism. One might even read the code as a defense of remaining fast with one's possessions, of staying within a group only because it profits one to do so. Peckinpah wants us to realize how conflicted these men's motivations and actions are. He shows us the Bunch wonderfully acting in concert during the train heist, but to what end do they do so? To get gold (which undoubtedly to some extent represents money stolen from the Mexican peasantry) and furnish a pseudogeneral with am-munition in an antirevolutionary campaign, thereby making them pragmatically not very different from the man for whom they are stealing the weapons. They stick together when, before going back into Agua Verde to escape Thornton and his men, they greedily bury their ill-gotten gold "together." Even when Pike offers to buy the captured Angel back from Mapache, he only offers half of his gold for him, an offer spurned for good reason: Mapache is less interested in money than in living up to his own (admittedly some-what corrupt) values. "I need no gold, and I don't sell this one," Mapache says.

Complementing these notions of destructively self-contained self-interest is *The Wild Bunch*'s repeated focus on the past, which is, of course, unchangeable. As they appear in the film, Pike's mem-ories are filled with notions of violence and enclosure. The two extended flashbacks that we see involve sex, violence, and death. In the sequence with the prostitutes, the ambience is claustro-phobic and, given the scene's circumstances (it takes place after a robbery), potentially menacing. If the room in which we see Pike and Thornton has any windows, they are covered with thick drapes. Pike is bracketed by two women; a third is pushed into the already crowded space by Thornton. There is no feeling of cele-bration – or even humor, as there was after the Starbuck robbery. Instead, these men are engaged in what might most accurately be described as enforced (and purchased) pleasure. When the sense of menace becomes concrete with the arrival of two Pinkerton men, one of whom fires, hitting Thornton, Pike escapes through another room's window. Yet as the existence of the flashback makes clear, although Pike avoids capture, he takes with him the memory of selfishly motivated abandonment, a quality with which he con-tinually contends throughout the film.

In the second flashback, which involves Pike's lover Aurora, sex, death, and violence are once again yoked. Like its predecessor, this flashback, which is "replayed" toward the film's end when Pike backs into a room in which there is a soldier and a Mexican woman (thus the trap of painful, repetitive memories), also suggests a poverty of emotional commitment and a concurrent, symbolic spatial restrictiveness. Pike is first seen bearing flowers and gro-ceries, material bribes meant to excuse his tardiness. Later, we see Pike in Aurora's small bedroom. The dim lighting is at once ro-mantic and menacing; once again, a gun-toting, vengeful figure emerges through a doorway and wounds someone. After recount-ing this story, Pike comments, "not a day goes by that I don't think about it." His statement reminds us not only of Thornton's

FIGURE 21
Pike with Aurora in a flashback that reveals his emotional pain and
obsession with the past.

obsessive memory of being whipped in jail but also of another assertion in a comparably revelatory scene with Dutch, during which
Pike talks about his long-standing feud with the railroad. After
Dutch says, "you must have really hurt that railroad bad," Pike
replies, "there was a man there, name of Harrigan. Had a way of
doing things. I made him change his way." The remark reveals
how fixated Pike (and, by extension, Harrigan, who is obsessed
with Pike's capture) is on this particular vendetta. Three characters
in the film, then – Pike, Thornton, and Harrigan – are filled with
memories of betrayal, deceit, and blackmail, memories that produce feelings of either guilt, anger, or shame. Pike feels guilty about
abandoning Thornton; Thornton feels anger at Pike over the abandonment, which placed him in the clutches of Harrigan, who already had an ingrained vendetta against Pike (and, perhaps, Thornton, too, since it seems probable that the robbery that occasioned

Thornton's capture was against the railroad). Other characters in the film are also involved in situations that call forth guilt and resentment: it's likely that Angel's ex-girl friend, Teresa, feels some degree of shame about running off from Angel's village and breaking her engagement with him; Angel is worried that the villagers may find out that he is a member of the Bunch. Because of her daughter's death, Teresa's mother bears a natural antipathy toward Angel, as does Mapache when he finds out that the major betrayer against him is Mexican. All of these people, with the notable exception of the virtually conscience-free Gorches, devote a great deal of psychological energy to thinking about past deeds, done by them or against them, and thereby reveal that narrowing of consciousness that is one of the main qualities in this film about limits.

When we explore some of the apparent textual bases for Peckinpah's ideas about violence in the film, we find in them also repeated citations involving narrowing and circumscription. Although Peckinpah has cited Robert Ardrey's *The Territorial Imperative* and *African Genesis* as sources for his ideas about violence and aggression, this reference seems somewhat curious given the pretentiousness, vapidity, and meandering, argumentative method of these two books, which posit that both the desire for land and an innate tendency toward slaughter are the motivating behavioral principles of human beings. Far more relevant to the attitudes regarding violence in *The Wild Bunch* are Konrad Lorenz's *On Aggression* and Hannah Arendt's *On Violence*.

Lorenz notes that among animals in the jungle, aggression has a rational basis: it is used only in defending territory.[12] Yet even within this designation, Lorenz draws attention to another attribute that implicitly links his ideas about aggression with my assertions about *The Wild Bunch:*

> We can safely assume that the most important function of intra-specific aggression is the even distribution of animals over an inhabitable area, but it is certainly not the only one. Charles Darwin had already observed that sexual selection, the selection of the best and strongest animals for reproduction, was furthered by the fighting of rival animals, particularly males.[13]

If we view territory as relating not only to land but also to people, we can see that much of the basis for the fighting within the Bunch and between the Bunch and others is sexually based. To go back to the flashback sequences, two of the three involve women as (capitalist) property: the whores in the first flashback, the sense on the part of both Pike and Aurora's husband that Aurora is "theirs." This quality surfaces as well in the rivalry between Angel and Mapache concerning Teresa, although Mapache's blithe reaction after Teresa's death seems to echo the usual attitude of the Gorches, who share women all of the time. Yet it is the Gorches who most pointedly draw attention to Teresa as property ("well, she ain't your woman no more") and who taunt Angel regarding the supposedly off-limits status of his sister, mother, and even grandmother when they are about to enter his village.[14]

Hannah Arendt disagrees with Lorenz's implication that violence, which she conceives of in terms of warfare, stems from an "irrepressible instinct of aggression."[15] Rather, she views it as a device that functions as an "arbiter in international affairs for which no adequate substitute has been found."[16] This last observation makes it easy to see that *The Wild Bunch*'s focus on violence necessarily implies the field in which it most obviously manifests itself: politics. Arendt quotes from C. Wright Mills's book *The Power Elite:* "all politics is a struggle for power; the ultimate kind of power is violence."[17] In this context, two of the film's characters immediately come to mind – not Mapache or Huerta or Villa but Harrigan and Mohr, who are conceptually linked. Both men are power-allied individuals who manipulate minor politicians or functionaries. After the Starbuck massacre, when Mayor Wainscoat complains that the railroad "used our town as a battlefield," Harrigan, in a haughty voice, asserts, "we represent the law." The implication is clear: appointed or elected officials are less important than the men who have money, and who use their money to create laws that favor them alone. As for Mohr, the power that he invokes in the film easily dwarfs Harrigan's since it is not regional but international (as a result, our antipathy to Mohr seems greater than our dislike of Harrigan: we're quite glad when Mohr gets shot).

In a tone whose arrogance invites comparison with Harrigan's way of speaking, Mohr identifies himself as "Commander Frederick Mohr of the Imperial German Army." Clearly, Mohr represents the most despicable power of government: the ability to wage war, which is, as Machiavelli points out, the ultimate source of governments' influence over individuals. Both Harrigan and Mohr wage war – Harrigan masterminded the mini-battle of Starbuck; Mohr is in Mexico because his government wishes to enlist Mexico's aid in the impending global upheaval of what would become World War I – and both men wield the influence of money and property, coextensive forces that act in the name of repression. As the presence in *The Wild Bunch* of these two characters so amply demonstrates, economic influence in the film is political influence (and vice versa), and political influence, as we've just seen during the Starbuck shootout, involves the use of violent force.

Although the use of force in *The Wild Bunch* is clearly prevalent, what may not be as clear is that, as Arendt emphasizes, there is an important distinction between force and power, one that brings into relief the impotence of the characters in the film who, like Pike and Dutch, mistake violence for force rather than as an expression of futility. As Arendt points out, "out of the barrel of a gun grows the most effective command, resulting in the most instant and perfect obedience. What can never grow out of it is power."[18] Perhaps more to the point, though, is that in the Bunch's violence we see reflected a state of mind that necessarily involves the limitations of a lifestyle defined by a narrow series of choices. According to Arendt, "It has often been said that impotence breeds violence, and psychologically this is quite true, at least of persons possessing natural strength, moral or physical. Politically speaking, the point is that loss of power becomes a substitution of violence for power . . . violence can destroy power [but] it is utterly incapable of creating it."[19] Keeping these statements in mind, we can see that the Bunch are purveyors not of strength but of weakness. The Bunch's violence is a sign of their futile self-loathing; their bonding is often the result of little more than mutual greed. These aspects are repeatedly dramatized in the film, which pulls us in one direction and then another, first making the Bunch seem admirable, then showing us their brutal side. Ultimately, though, *The Wild Bunch* focuses on the Bunch making mistakes, acting frustrated, carrying out acts of violence in response to whims of frustration. The vendetta against (and by) Harrigan, the drawing of guns during the argument about the Starbuck "silver," the killing of Teresa – all of these situations (and there are many more in the film) demonstrate how much emphasis *The Wild Bunch* places on poor justifications for excessive force.

A further issue raised by the film is whether or not violence is a behavior that is consciously motivated (Arendt's view) or an instinctual act (as Lorenz contends). Again, the film's view is conflicted. There is a great deal of ruminating about violence in *The Wild Bunch* (certainly Pike's and Thornton's constantly reflecting on past events associated with violence tells us this), and situations rife with a potential for violence occur often. However, when violence does finally erupt, the participants in these situations seem to be acting as though they are so caught up in the events that there is simply no time for thought, only action. Violence, then, often seems to be fueled by its own curious energy, which appears to be independent of the energy exhibited by the participants in it. *The Wild Bunch* shows us that there is a line that is crossed in human behavior between reason and a madness allied with ferocity; and when that line is crossed, reason retreats. When a gunfight nearly breaks out between Angel and the Gorches over dividing up the Starbuck booty, Pike comments, "go on, go for it, fall apart," thereby attempting to invoke rationality and self-awareness to prevent bloodshed. It's clear, though, that if a first shot in this scene had been fired, reason would have fled: this is precisely what happens after Mapache is gunned down. The Bunch kill the "general" on impulse as retaliation for Angel's murder. As so often occurs in the film after a violent act (e.g., after Angel shoots Teresa), there's a significant pause as the film's action hangs in the balance. Following Mapache's death, Pike slowly pivots, waits a second, looks at Mohr, takes careful aim, and then fires, shooting Mohr through the head. After that point (with one rare exception to which I'll draw attention later), people aren't acting, they're re-acting.

Yet Peckinpah also makes us aware that even these violent men can become so in awe of violence's destructive potential that they are themselves given to pauses of surprise. I have already drawn attention to the point in the Starbuck massacre when Thornton draws a bead on Pike. Thornton waits for a second, not only re-acting slowly because of his age but also apparently considering what he is about to do. That momentary hesitation allows for the intervention of the tuba player, which makes it possible for Pike to fire and escape. Harrigan is aware of the mistake that Thornton has made by being too thoughtful. "Why didn't you shoot Pike when you had the chance?" he asks Thornton. Thornton, though, doesn't answer, not wanting to admit either to his slowness (he is an old man, asleep when we first see him) or to his contemplative, virtually brooding nature (the pose that he strikes when he leans back against Agua Verde's wall at the film's end is quite similar to that of Pike in Angel's village sitting under a tree and thinking).[20]

Toward the end of the train heist sequence, there's another noteworthy frozen moment. The fuse on the bridge has been lit; Pike and the Bunch are on the Mexican side of the border, look-ing back. Once again, Thornton and Pike regard each other across a physical distance that symbolizes their psychological alienation. As he did in Starbuck, Thornton raises his rifle to shoot Pike; Pike, counting on the inevitability of the dynamite explosion, tips his hat to Thornton in a gesture compounded of both respect and taunting bravado. When the bridge explodes, with horses and rid-ers thrown into the water, Peckinpah shows us Pike's astounded reaction: Pike is shaken by the ferocity of the blast, which he doubt-less feels in both a physical sense (the shock wave) and a psycho-logical one (resulting from the impressiveness of the force that is unleashed). For a moment, though, Pike can only stare at the de-struction he has wrought. Just as he does in the middle of the Agua Verde massacre when he realizes that his men are being shot to pieces (he sees both of the Gorches hit with bullets within a few seconds), this man of violent action is temporarily rendered inert. Given these instances' dramatization of contemplative hesitation, with the nature of and reactions to violence being repeatedly dissected and investigated, it's difficult to avoid concluding that the film in which the Bunch and other violent characters appear is neither a celebration nor a glorification of violence but an inquiry into its limitations and the manner in which it operates.

Mexican cultural attitudes toward violence also not only seem to form the basis for a significant amount of the film's near-the-border action but also throw into relief the attitudes evidenced by the Bunch. As Christina Jacqueline-Johns points out in *The Origins of Violence in Mexican Society,* much of the violence in Mexican society is a result of influences from both the Aztec civilization and the Spanish, the latter of whom conquered Mexico in the sixteenth century. Jacqueline-Johns attributes this violence to the impulse to acquire new land and enslave the population, attitudes that she views as extensions of the movement toward capitalism in sixteenth-century Europe:

> Sometime around the 14th century, [economic] expansion reached its limit and what had expanded began to contract. Population at the time began to reach a saturation point given the state of technology, and food shortages and epidemics were the result . . . the only way out of the stagnation was to expand the economic pie to be shared. What was needed and what capitalism offered was a new and more lucrative form of surplus appropriation, [one that moved beyond the tenets of feudalism with its] "direct appropriation of agricultural surplus in the form of either tribute . . . or of feudal rents."[21]

As a result, to get the valuable minerals out of Mexico's ground, the population was enslaved:

> This process of reorganization [of Mexican society was] especially violent. The history of Conquest Mexico, the first thirty years of Spanish colonial presence . . . was largely the history of a forced change in the labor process . . . in this period of transition, organized violence served to transform the relationship of classes to one another and to the means of production.[22]

FIGURE 22
The bounty hunters quarrel over their spoils after the shootout in San Rafael. Much of the film's violence occurs in contexts geared to capitalist expansion.

When we apply these insights to *The Wild Bunch,* it seems clear that the overwhelming majority of its violence occurs in the context of actions geared to capitalist acquisition. The ambush in Starbuck is set up by a railroad man trying to thwart a robbery against his company and intending to capture men who have stolen from the company before and who have a sizable bounty on their heads; the train heist is carried out on behalf of a man involved in a movement to maintain a repressive military–economic hold on the Mexican government; the first argument that we see among the Bunch concerns money; as previously noted, the Bunch (as well as Mapache) regard women as property; and the final shootout results from the Bunch's disgust with these alienating attitudes and their inability to find a means of countering them.

Predominantly, the film's violence is capitalist violence. For the

Bunch, the past that dominates their present is an economically influenced one. In the violent, regrettable actions of the Bunch, men whose pasts have been a series of one mistake after another, what we witness is nothing less than a dramatization of the history of the United States itself, whose past and present are riddled with treaties ignored, promises broken, agreements unmet. Jim Kitses is thus quite right when he observes, "*The Wild Bunch* is America."[23] Or, as Jacqueline-Johns puts it, "there [is] no way to sensibly extract 'criminal' violence from the more systematic violence that pervade[s] Mexican life, or that violence from the social and historical context in which it occurred, without reducing its meaning beyond sense. Criminal violence was Mexican violence, and Mexican violence was the violence of Mexico's history, its past reproduced in its present."[24] This is just as true for the film's American characters as it is for its Mexican ones. The history of this country is steeped in violence: the carnage of the 1776 revolution; the brutal campaigns against Native Americans; the massive deaths incurred during the war between the states; the Vietnam War; the church burnings, assassinations, and civil unrest that continue up to today. At all times, we are haunted by this country's violence-ridden past and weighed down by its murderous and abusive present. Similarly, the present violence of the Bunch is a function of *their* past, which repeatedly encloses them in an insular, and dangerous, life characterized by murder rather than peace, chaos rather than bonding, abandonment rather than commitment. Limited in sensitivity, intelligence, or foresight, these men can define themselves only through barbarous group behavior or extreme forms of diversion.

Inquiring into the nature of the relation between the Bunch's emotional shortcomings and the economic system to which they so often seem bound brings up one of the basic questions raised by the film: is the essential nature of human beings cooperative or selfish? In his book *The Art of Loving*, Erich Fromm observes, "if love is a capacity of the mature, productive character, it follows that the capacity to love in an individual living in any given culture depends on the influence this culture has on the average person."[25] Fromm makes reference to Sigmund Freud's *Civilization and Its Discontents,* which disparages Marxian economics by asserting that its underlying assumption about the desire of humans to act cooperatively is at variance with observable human nature, which Freud conceives of in terms of aggression and self-interest.[26] Fromm, however, demonstrates that Freud's hypothesis was really nothing more than the unwitting extension of capitalist materialism to the field of human relations:

> The second factor determining Freud's theories lies in the prevailing concept of man, which is based on the structure of capitalism. . . . Freud was largely influenced in his thinking by the type of materialism prevalent in the nineteenth century . . . he did not see that the basic reality lies in the totality of human existence . . . in the practice of life determined by the specific structure of society.[27]

Extrapolating from this quote allows us to see that although *The Wild Bunch* never resolves the issue of human beings' fundamental nature, the film nonetheless functions as a critique of the society that made the Bunch what they are: a group of men unable to penetrate their socialized responses to the ultimate truth – that they are tragically representative of the predominantly anomic society in which they live. Bitter, unloved, wanted only for the money that their "pelts" will bring, they wander without purpose, lost in the capitalist wasteland of a film that at its end tries to romanticize them but that, overwhelmingly, exposes them as pathetic emotional wastrels. In the Bunch's failure to reach self-awareness, we see the failure of contemporary capitalist America, an anhedonic culture that has lost the ability to do anything notable except wage war and experience pain.

One of *The Wild Bunch*'s major ironies is that at its apotheosizing end, its intended emotional effect (to make us miss the Bunch) and its subtext (which reveals them as pitiable men) wildly diverge, almost in the manner of some sort of hysterical confusion.[28] The film tries to move away from a feeling of capitalist ennui, but it cannot. All of the talk about Starbuck "silver," about the ten thousand dollars in gold that Mapache offers, about the payrolls to be delivered to garrisons, about the prices on the heads of the Bunch, even the apparently idealistic gesture of giving Angel guns (Pike requires Angel to give up his share of the gold for them), are linked to and sullied by this fateful corruption. Ultimately, the film collapses back into a wistful reminiscence for men whose badness is not a function of their physical violence so much as the violence that they do to their ideas of their past selves, as men who at one time had hope for a life different from the ones they finally lived. *The Wild Bunch*'s emphasis on claustrophobic despair occurs for the final time out in the open, in the dusty stretch of land outside of Agua Verde's gate, where, despite the reinvoked images of a laughing Bunch, we come to the grim realization that in more ways than one, and long before the film's end, these bad men have really (in Peckinpah's words) reached "the end of the line."[29]

NOTES

1 To the best of my knowledge, the only essay that relates *The Wild Bunch*'s use of filmic space to larger contextual issues is Leonard Engel's "Space and Enclosure in Cooper and Peckinpah: Regeneration in the Open Spaces," *Journal of American Culture* 14:(2) (Summer 1991), pp. 86–93. Unfortunately, Engel tends to refrain from investigating the manner in which Peckinpah uses space allusively in the film.

2 Although I am somewhat hesitant to ascribe biographical significance to this aspect of the film, we are to a degree encouraged in this direction by the similarity between Peckinpah's personal behavior and that of the film's violent characters. It is well known that Peckinpah was prone to violent outbursts, which were often prompted and exacerbated by his drinking (even David Weddle's tasteful biography of Peckinpah is compelled to return to this fact repeatedly). While we can't assert that drinking *causes* violence, it is certainly true that drinking lowers one's tolerance for it. Even when, as with the children at the film's beginning, drinking is not allied with violent action, we can nonetheless posit a further connection between alcohol and violence if we regard violence as an intoxicant, a form of behavior that exerts a powerful, virtually physical pull on those involved with it as a result of its potential for excitation. A whole other essay could be written on the function of alcohol in Peckinpah's films.

3 Perhaps Peckinpah is here suggesting that his own perspective, like that of any artist re-creating past events, is narrow or foreshortened – that he must, by necessity, employ allusion and metonymy, communicating the flavor of life through disparate events; that he is, in essence, somewhat like his protagonists, who often seem at a strange remove from events. (Indeed, the slow-motion violence in the film suggests just this kind of distancing effect, signaling our simultaneous attraction to and repulsion by acts of brutality.)

4 Sam Peckinpah quoted in David Weddle, *"If They Move . . . Kill 'Em!":* *The Life and Times of Sam Peckinpah* (New York: Grove Press, 1994), p. 334.

5 See, e.g., Ray Allen Billington, ed., *The Frontier Thesis: Valid Interpretation of American History?* (New York: Holt, Rinehart and Winston, 1966).

6 Frederick Jackson Turner, "The Significance of the Frontier in American History," in *Frontier and Section: Selected Essays of Frederick Jackson Turner* (Englewood Cliffs, NJ: Prentice-Hall, 1961), p. 38.

7 Ibid., pp. 49–50.

8 Ibid., p. 56.

9 Leo Marx, *The Machine in the Garden: Technology and the Pastoral Ideal in America* (New York: Oxford University Press, 1970), p. 65.

10 Turner, p. 58.

11 One of the major ironies in the film, of course, is that the Bunch are not free in either the United States or Mexico.

12 Konrad Lorenz, *On Aggression* (New York: Harcourt, Brace, and World, 1966), pp. 35–6.

13 Ibid., pp. 38–9.

14 Yet once the Bunch are in the village, a certain amount of this rivalry disappears: the Gorches playfully tag after Angel's sister, with no apparent thought of claiming her; Pike lets his female companion dance with Dutch (although the woman looks to Pike for permission before she does so); and Sykes steals what he refers to as "[Dutch's] gal" away from Dutch, although he does so playfully.

15 Hannah Arendt, *On Violence* (New York: Harcourt, Brace, and World, 1970), p. 5.

16 Ibid.

17 Ibid., p. 35.

18 Ibid., p. 53.

19 Ibid., pp. 54–6.

20 Paul Seydor has pointed out to me an interesting (and, in my view, virtually reciprocal) reaction on Pike's part. After the tuba player is hit, Pike turns and looks back at Thornton. Although he has a clear

shot at his former friend, Pike instead chooses to fire at, and wound, the man to Thornton's right. Neither Thornton nor Pike seems willing to kill the other; introspective men to the end, they are too strongly joined in memories (as in the duplicate flashback ruminations they undergo regarding Thornton's capture by the Pinkerton men) and desires (both want deliverance from their former lifestyles) to really wish the other dead.

21 Christina Jacqueline-Johns, *The Origins of Violence in Mexican Society* (Westport, Conn.: Praeger Publishers, 1995), p. 111. The quote within Jacqueline-Johns's citation is from Immanuel Wallerstein, *The Modern World System* (New York and London: Academic Press, 1974), p. 38.

22 Ibid., p. 131.

23 Jim Kitses, "The Wild Bunch," in Michael Bliss, ed., *Doing It Right: The Best Criticism on Sam Peckinpah's The Wild Bunch* (Carbondale: Southern Illinois University Press, 1994), p. 79.

24 Jacqueline-Johns, pp. xi–xii.

25 Erich Fromm, *The Art of Loving* (New York: Harper Colophon, 1962), p. 83.

26 Sigmund Freud, *Civilization and Its Discontents,* trans. and ed. by James Strachey (New York: W. W. Norton Co., 1961), pp. 60–1.

27 Fromm, pp. 91–2.

28 The term is loosely derived from Geoffrey Nowell-Smith's essay on Vincente Minnelli, "Minnelli and Melodrama," which appears in Christina Gledhill, ed., *Home Is Where the Heart Is: Studies in Melodrama and the Woman's Film* (London: BFI Books, 1987), pp. 70–4.

29 Sam Peckinpah quoted by Stephen Farber in "Peckinpah's Return," *Film Quarterly,* 23 (1) (Fall 1969), p. 9.

DAVID A. COOK

4 Ballistic Balletics: Styles of Violent Representation in *The Wild Bunch* and After

Displays of armed violence in American cinema go back at least to Edwin S. Porter's *The Great Train Robbery* (1903), with its multiple gunfights and its sensational concluding image of a bandit firing his revolver directly into the camera lens. This seeming assault on the audience, which contained the "special effect" of hand-tinted orange-yellow gunsmoke in contemporary prints, marked the beginning of an uneasy relationship between spectators and on-screen gunplay that has been tempered by the cultural/political status of real armed violence in American society at any given point in time and quite obviously persists today. Historically dependent on the current state of motion picture technology and prevailing mechanisms of content censorship, the relationship was aggravated to the point of rupture during the late 1960s when two films broke the bounds of conventional representation to become flashpoints in a heated national debate over gun violence. Produced in the climate of rebellion that followed the assassination of President John Kennedy and President Lyndon Johnson's precipitous escalation of the Vietnam War, Arthur Penn's *Bonnie and Clyde* (1967) and Sam Peckinpah's *The Wild Bunch* (1969) bracketed the assassinations of Martin Luther King and Robert Kennedy and the worst urban riots in the country's history. Both films combined the use of slow motion with blood-filled squibs (explosive devices concealed beneath an actor's clothing and triggered electronically to represent bullet strikes) to depict the impact of bullets on the human body – enhanced, in *The Wild Bunch,* by spurting arterial blood and gaping exit wounds – setting a new standard for ballistic violence on screen that clearly echoed the real-world context of political assassination, ghetto uprisings, and Vietnam.

Yet the history of the representation of gunplay in American films, especially since World War II, had led logically to this conclusion. Most closely associated with the Western and the gangster film (genres proceeding from *The Great Train Robbery* and D. W. Griffith's *The Musketeers of Pig Alley* [1912], respectively), but also endemic to the combat, detective, and espionage film, gun violence in the teens and twenties was often depicted by the real thing. According to John Baxter, a rifleman or sharpshooter was a standard member of any Western film crew during this era, although more cautious directors used slingshots firing marbles or pieces of chalk to simulate gunshots, whisking off their actors' hats with black threads.[1] For gunshot wounds themselves, ink-soaked plugs of sponge rubber were fired from a starting pistol, as at the conclusion of Howard Hughes's *Hell's Angels* (1930) when Ben Lyon is shot at close range in the back. Such methods produced reasonably credible results until the coming of sound added a new dimension of realism to film that demanded a visual counterpart. Machine-gun sprays with live ammunition achieved this effect in such gangster films as *Taxi!* (Roy Del Ruth, 1932) and *G-Men* (William Keighley, 1935), until they were replaced by sophisticated process screen photography in the late 1930s.[2] At about the same time, the invention of a blood-filled gelatin capsule solid enough to be fired from a compressed air rifle but soft enough to explode on impact promised new realism in the depiction of wounds. In the late sixties, these capsules, augmented by the "squib" – a tiny shaped charge detonated by wire to simulate the impact of a bullet without firing any projectile at the actor or stunt man[3] – would produce the spurting wounds of *Bonnie and Clyde* and *The Wild Bunch,*

FIGURE 23
With bullet hits visible on his body, a businessman is shot dead in
Peckinpah's *The Getaway* (1972).

but in the early years of sound, cultural factors arose to ensure
that the level of violence in American cinema would be kept well
within socially decorous limits for decades to come.

In the period 1929–32, the Payne Fund Studies had been undertaken by nationally known researchers to determine the influence
of motion pictures on children, and the conclusions – popularly
summarized by Henry James Forman in his 1933 volume *Our
Movie Made Children* – suggested that the influence was both broad
and pernicious.[4] Almost simultaneously, the advent of sound had
produced a wave of grim, and often brutal, screen realism that was
typified by a trio of gangster films – *Little Caesar* (Mervyn LeRoy,
1930), *The Public Enemy* (William Wellman, 1931), and *Scarface*
(Howard Hawks, 1932) – that provoked censorship battles with
the Motion Picture Producers and Distributors of America (MPPDA)

and many state licensing boards.[5] The public outcry against such violent early sound films, as well as against those thought to be lewd and libidinous, produced the threat of a nationwide boycott by the Catholic Church in April 1934. The ultimate result was the MPPDA's imposition of the Production Code. Best known today for its proscription of sexuality, the Code's most elaborate strictures were reserved for the depiction of crime. It was forbidden to show the details of a crime or to display machine guns, submachine guns, or other illegal weapons; it was further forbidden to discuss these weapons in dialogue scenes or even to represent the sound of their repercussions off-screen. (Gangster films like *Scarface* had made a positive fetish of the sound and image of the recently invented Thompson submachine gun; that film contains a spectacular drive-by Thompson attack on a speakeasy violent and *loud* enough to have been shot forty years later.) The Code also required that law enforcement officers never be shown dying at the hands of criminals and that all criminal activities within a given film be punished.[6] Under no circumstances was crime to be justified; suicide and murder were to be avoided unless absolutely necessary to the plot; and the suggestion of excessive brutality or wholesale slaughter of any kind was absolutely prohibited because, as a 1938 amendment to the Code put it, "frequent presentations of murder tend to lessen regard for the sacredness of life."[7] Members of the MPPDA agreed not to distribute any film denied the Production Code Administration's (PCA) Seal of Approval or, by extension, to book such films into any of the nation's first-run theater chains, nearly all of which they owned.

During America's participation in World War II, the antiviolence strictures of the Code were relaxed (as, to a lesser extent, were the moral ones) for reasons of state. It became important for combat and espionage films to have the hard edge of documentary realism, especially as the war deepened in 1943 and 1944, and for propaganda films to show a formidably brutal enemy. Nazi and Japanese barbarism was on full display in such sensational films as *Hitler's Children* (Edward Dmytryk, 1943), *Hitler's Madman* (Douglas Sirk, 1943), *None Shall Escape* (Andre de Toth, 1944), *Behind the Rising*

Sun (Edward Dmytryk, 1943), and *Blood on the Sun* (Frank Lloyd, 1945), which contained scenes of mass execution, rape, and torture (including blinding, crucifixion, and the bayonetting of children), not shown directly on screen but clearly implied. Newsreels and documentaries from the Army Signal Corps lingered over piles of enemy corpses and exploited a taste for violent revenge (e.g., advertising copy for *With the Marines at Tarawa* [March 1944] encouraged the viewer to see "the real thing at last – no punches pulled, no gory details omitted").[8] By the war's end, the American public had seen an unprecedented array of debased human behavior on screen. Although the PCA never lost its grip on feature film content, there was unquestionably a coarsening of audience taste during the war, a desensitization to death and dying, after which it was difficult to retrench in peacetime.

As a result, the postwar period saw an injection of violence into almost every action genre – especially the Western and the film noir. Starting with *Duel in the Sun* (King Vidor, 1947) and *Ramrod* (Andre de Toth, 1947) and proceeding through *Yellow Sky* (William Wellman, 1948), *Blood on the Moon* (Robert Wise, 1948), *Red River* (Howard Hawks, 1949)and *The Furies* (Anthony Mann, 1950), psychological motivation in the Western became more tangled and the violence more specific.[9] *Film noir,* whose prototype was Billy Wilder's corrosive *Double Indemnity* (1944), became the genre of postwar pessimism par excellence. With their downbeat atmosphere, dark lighting, and antitraditional cinematography, films like *The Blue Dahlia* (George Marshall, 1946), *Out of the Past* (Jacques Tourneur, 1947), *Dark Passage* (Delmer Daves, 1947), *Dead Reckoning* (John Cromwell, 1947), *Raw Deal* (Anthony Mann, 1948), *Criss Cross* (Robert Siodmak, 1949), *They Live By Night* (Nicholas Ray, 1949), *D.O.A.* (Rudloph Mate, 1949), and *White Heat* (Raoul Walsh, 1949) were urban crime melodramas in which violence assumed the status of an existential act. Shootings, beatings, and stabbings become normative behavior in a world where corruption cuts across all moral categories, and the violence in film noir was both more excessive than in earlier crime films and more intense.[10]

Speaking specifically of the postwar Western, Lawrence Alloway characterized the whole postwar aesthetic when he wrote that "violence is calibrated with a new precision" and enlarges the "pattern of behaviour tolerated within the form."[11] Abetting this process was the crippling of the studio system through the "Paramount decrees" of 1948, which forced the major studios to divest themselves of exhibition over the next five years and relinquish their control of the American market. This caused a steady rise in independent production and a weakening of Production Code authority since filmmakers could now book their work into theaters without the PCA seal.[12] Legal challenges were also being mounted to the Code, including one resulting in the *Miracle* decision of 1952, which extended First and Fourteenth Amendment protection to motion pictures for the first time since 1915.[13] Thus, by the mid-fifties, it was possible to see mainstream films noir in which a police officer's wife and son are blown to smithereens in the family car and a gangster's moll is facially disfigured by a cup of boiling coffee (*The Big Heat* [Fritz Lang, 1953]), or a young woman is tied to a bed and tortured to death with pliers off-screen while a private eye is pistol-whipped to a bloody pulp (*Kiss Me Deadly* [Robert Aldrich, 1955]). In the realm of the Western, a group of films appeared in the early fifties treating the the social impact of new weapons technologies on the frontier. Without actually violating the Code's strictures against the display of illegal weapons, films like *Winchester 73* (Anthony Mann, 1950), *Colt .45* (Edwin L. Marin, 1950), *Only the Valiant* (Gordon Douglas, 1951), *Across the Wide Missouri* (William Wellman, 1951), and *The Siege at Red River* (Rudolph Mate, 1954) fetishized such legal automatic weapons as repeating rifles and the Gatling gun. Alloway notes that there was a general increase in technical/operational information in these "weapon Westerns," speculating that this new emphasis may have addressed the large percentage of World War II and Korean War veterans in the domestic audience or may have bled over from pervasive discusssions of Cold War armaments in contemporary news media.[14] Whatever the case, the cycle extended through the decade with such films as *Man Without a Star*

(King Vidor, 1955), *The Young Guns* (Albert Band, 1956), *The Tin Star* (Anthony Mann, 1957), *Gunman's Walk* (Phil Karlson, 1958), and *Saddle the Wind* (Robert Parrish, 1958) – by which time the Production Code, rewritten in l956 to eliminate all remaining taboos but those against nudity, sexual perversion, and venereal disease, had become nearly irrelevant. Standards for the depiction of violence on screen would henceforth depend more on what filmmakers created and the public would tolerate than on what industry self-censorship prescribed.

Concurrently, another trend resulting from divestiture – runaway production – had reached its height. This was the practice of American companies making films abroad to capitalize on cheaper labor and other lower costs. Italy, Spain, and later Yugoslavia were often used as locations for the expensive widescreen epics of the fifties and early sixties, and there was a good deal of industry cross-fertilization between Hollywood and Europe as a result. The Italians began producing "sword and sandal" or "peplum" epics (named for a typical garment worn in ancient times) with the *Hercules* (1958–65), *Maciste* (1959–65), and *Ursus* series (1960–2), and as early as 1961 the Cinecitta Studios started making American-style Westerns with expatriate "B" stars like Richard Basehart, Rod Cameron, and Edmund Purdom. These genre knock-offs, which came to be known as "spaghetti Westerns," were strongly influenced by two American Westerns set in Mexico and directed by Robert Aldrich – *Vera Cruz* (1954) and *The Last Sunset* (1961) – the former through its theme of American mercenaries involved in a foreign revolution and the latter through its elaborate stylization of genre conventions and iconography.[15] During 1961 and 1962, Aldrich himself was in Italy to make the biblical epic *Sodom and Gomorrah* (1962), and hired as his assistant director a young peplum veteran named Sergio Leone (1929–89), who also supervised a more sexually explicit Italian version of the film. The following year, Leone directed the sine qua non of spaghetti Westerns, *A Fistful of Dollars* (1964), which he adapted from Akira Kurosawa's samurai film *Yojimbo* (1961) nearly shot for shot. Casting Clint Eastwood (then costar of the CBS television series *Rawhide*) as a

nameless bounty hunter who cynically manipulates a feud between two warring clans, Leone shaped the features of the classical Italo-Western – baroque framings, a stretching of time through
both long takes and montage, an electronically synthesized score
(here, by Ennio Morricone), a Latinate cast and Mexican setting,
and an emphasis on sudden and shocking violence. (In the explicitness of its swordfights, *Yojimbo* itself had upped the ante on
gore in the samurai film.)[16] *A Fistful of Dollars* was a box-office
smash on both sides of the Atlantic, and Leone followed with the
equally successful sequels *For a Few Dollars More* (1965) and *The
Good, the Bad, and the Ugly* (1966), creating a boom in spaghetti
Westerns on a global scale. Whereas only 25 such films had been
made before 1964, over 300 were produced in Italy between 1965
and 1969, with 66 in the peak year of 1966–7 alone.[17] Artful, nihilistic, and extremely bloody, Leone's *Dollars* series with Eastwood
and Sergio Corbucci's *Django* films,[18] with Franco Nero, were both
widely popular in the United States and upped the ante on what
was acceptable in the realm of violent representation on American screens.

The American response was to match the Italians with Westerns
like *Duel at Diablo* (Ralph Nelson, 1966), *Hang 'Em High* (1967,
nominally directed by Ted Post but largely the creation of its star,
Clint Eastwood), and *A Time for Killing/The Long Ride Home* (Phil
Karlson, 1967), which contained multiple cold-blooded shootings,
as well as scenes of torture and rape. This was possible because the
MPAA had further revised the Production Code in September
1966 to eliminate specifically proscribed behavior and to offer instead a list of ten general guidelines (e.g., "Detailed and protracted
acts of brutality, cruelty, physical violence, torture and abuse,
shall not be presented").[19] These were to be applied contextually,
relative to a film's plot, and a provision was made for borderline
cases to be released with a "Suggested for Mature Audiences" designation, opening the door to the classification and ratings system
that would succeed the Code in 1968. The 1966 revisions left filmmakers considerable creative leeway in the depiction of violence,
where justified by the plot, but stylistically the *representation* of

violence remained tied to the stage conventions from which it had emerged in the early silent period. In fact, for all of their graphic letting of stage blood and piling up of corpses, when it came to showing actual gunshot wounds, the spaghetti Westerns and their American clones were remarkably old-fashioned: however riddled with bullets a character might be, and at whatever range, there was little or no representation of entry and exit wounds. Typically, shots containing the actual moment of impact are quickly cut away from to conceal their lack of verisimilitude, or a stunt fall removes the wound site itself from our field of vision. As late as mid-1967, then, American films that contemporary critics could describe as "brutally realistic"[20] were refusing to represent the physiological effects of violence by suppressing the clinical pathology of gunshots and other wounds.

That the impact of bullets was consistently understated in these films stemmed both from the lingering presence of the Code and from a lack of imagination on the part of filmmakers themselves. Their failure to move beyond nineteenth-century stage conventions of realism in this area is not surprising given the inherent conservatism of the American industry with regard to style. Formally, in fact, most Hollywood films of the 1960s resembled their studio-era predecessors in every way but their widescreen aspect ratio and color. In other parts of the world, however, stylistic variety in the representation of violence was less rare. In Japan, for example, Akira Kurosawa practiced the intercutting of footage shot at different camera speeds to represent violent action in his epic *Seven Samurai* (1954), which was widely seen in the West after winning the Silver Lion at Venice and an Oscar for Best Foreign Film. (Appropriately, *Seven Samurai* was remade by Hollywood as a Western, *The Magnificent Seven* [John Sturges, 1960], but without Kurosawa's use of multiple cameras and dynamic montage; and, as noted earlier, Kurosawa's later samurai film *Yojimbo* [1961] was remade in Italy as *A Fistful of Dollars* [1964], the first spaghetti Western.)

Kurosawa's intercutting of normal and slow-motion footage in the battle sequences of *Seven Samurai* was innovative but not unique. Slow motion, achieved by overcranking the camera and projecting the film at normal speed, had long been the province of the avant-garde (e.g. Dziga Vertov's *Kino-glaz* [1924]) and documentary cinema (Leni Riefenstahl's *Olympiad* [1936]) but was used occasionally in narrative film to achieve some expressive effect (e.g., the pillow fight sequence in *Zero du conduite* [Jean Vigo, 1934] or the dropping of the glass globe that signal's Kane's death in *Citizen Kane* [Orson Welles, 1940]). Kurosawa himself intercut footage shot at different speeds as early as his first film, *Sanshiro Sugata* (1943), and continued the practice selectively in his samurai films of the fifties and sixties. In France, Henri George Clouzot experimented with slow-motion intercuts in both *Le Salaire de la peur* (*The Wages of Fear* [1953]) and *Les Diaboliques* (1955), influencing New Wave directors, who used slow-motion sequences to represent not only violence (e.g., Jean-Luc Godard in *Pierrot le fou* [1965]) but also romance (François Truffaut in *Jules et Jim* [1963]) and existential mystery (Alain Resnais in *L'Année dernière à Marienbad* [1961]). Borrowing from the New Wave, Lindsay Anderson brought slow-motion intercuts to British New Cinema in the rugby match that concludes *This Sporting Life* (1962) and the climactic shootout of *If . . .* (1968), where it was clearly intended to evoke *Zero de conduite;* and, in Spain, Welles shot slow-motion footage to depict the ghastliness of medieval warfare in the Battle of Shrewsbury sequence for *Chimes at Midnight* (1966). Hollywood remained largely resistant to such practices before Arthur Penn's groundbreaking *Bonnie and Clyde* was released by Warner Brothers in August 1967, although Penn himself had used slow motion to represent the fall of a wounded gunfighter in *The Left-Handed Gun* (1957) ten years before, and Peckinpah had shot the river battle that concludes *Major Dundee* (1965) with multiple cameras running at different speeds but stopped short of intercutting his slow-motion footage into the final print.[21] In other American pre–*Bonnie and Clyde* examples, Sidney Lumet used slow motion for the flashback that opens *The Pawnbroker* (1965), John Derek for some brief action sequences in his World War II film *Once Before I Die* (1965), and John Boorman for several flashbacks in *Point Blank*

(1967), but no Hollywood filmmaker before Penn had used it to depict a shooting.

There was, however, a very prominent slow-motion shooting in the recent collective memory that had been seen on American television screens again and again: the murder of alleged presidential assassin Lee Harvey Oswald by Jack Ruby on November 24, 1963. NBC-TV cameras had caught this shooting live as it occurred at 12:21 Eastern Standard Time in the basement of Dallas police headquarters, but it was soon made available to all of the networks by videotape, and it was replayed over and over in slow motion so that viewers could follow the chaotic events of the murder and its aftermath. Throughout that Sunday afternoon and evening, the videotape replay of Oswald's shooting was intercut with live coverage of mourners filing past President Kennedy's flag-draped coffin as it lay in state in the Capitol rotunda. It was from their experience with the Oswald murder that network broadcasters conceived the idea of the "instant replay" for live sporting events. (Broadcast-standard videotape had been introduced by Ampex in 1957; unlike film, it could be replayed – and at variable speeds – as soon as it was shot.) Only five weeks later, on New Year's Eve 1963, it was used in a broadcast of the Army-Navy football game and by the end of 1964 had become a standard feature of televised sports. Indeed, Eric Barnouw credits slow-motion video replay with the rise of football to national prominence on network television by making it both accessible and pleasurable: "[B]rutal collisions became ballets, and end runs and forward passes became miracles of human coordination."[22] Here it seems that the technology of videotape, soon to loom so large in bringing the Vietnam War into America's living rooms, preceded – and quite possibly influenced – film in expressing the poetics of violent action, organized or not.

According to a December 1967 interview with *Cahiers du Cinéma*, Arthur Penn conceived the "ballet of death" that concludes *Bonnie and Clyde* before he began shooting it,[23] and he later acknowledged the influence of Kurosawa.[24] In the process, he used four cameras running at different speeds (twenty-four, forty-eight,

FIGURE 24
The deaths of Bonnie and Clyde established a new level of graphic violence in modern cinema.

seventy-two, and ninety-six frames per second), each equipped with different lenses, and then intercut the footage into a twenty-two-second montage sequence representing the protagonists' agonized death by machine-gun fire. The actors (Faye Dunaway and Warren Beatty), heavily wired with explosive squibs and blood capsules, seem to be blown apart in slow motion, transferring a physical and emotional shock to the viewer that is both wrenching and strangely beautiful. The film, and this sequence in particular, generated a historic controversy over screen violence that was part of a larger ongoing debate about the looming presence of violence in national life. Penn clearly intended this, among others things, by having a piece of Clyde's head fly off, he said, "like that famous photograph of Kennedy"[25] – by which he meant the still frames from the Zapruder film published in the November

29, 1963, and November 25, 1966, issues of *Life* magazine.[26] (The American public did not have a chance to see the Zapruder film itself until it was shown on national television in 1975 [see note 25], by which point – after *Bonnie and Clyde, The Wild Bunch,* and their immediate successors – it must have seemed like a nightmare promise fulfilled.)

But Penn had also hit upon something deeper and more atavistic than an evocation of contemporary political violence, as he indicated in his *Cahiers* interview: "There's a moment in death when the body no longer functions, when it becomes an object and has a certain kind of detached ugly beauty."[27] This is the key to understanding the powerful attraction that the multiple-speed montage style identified here as "ballistic balletics" has for filmmakers and audiences alike. However socially responsible or irresponsible it may be in context, the slow-motion depiction of death by high-powered weapons fire is aesthetically pleasing. As the avant garde had understood for decades (and network television sportscasters had known since 1964), slow-motion photography offers one of the cinema's great aesthetic pleasures. Combined with the thrill of pyrotechnic violence, it functions like an electrode implanted in the collective hippocampus. As proof, *Bonnie and Clyde* went on to become one of the most profitable films of 1967, earning by July 1968 nearly $28 million in rentals worldwide on an investment of $2.5 million.[28] Audiences liked the film for both its entertainment value and its social themes, but they were mesmerized by its conclusion, often sitting in stunned silence while the final credits rolled until the theater lights came up.[29] Many returned to see it again and again, making *Bonnie and Clyde* one of the first films to do significant repeat business. This was not lost on the new leadership team at Warner Bros. that had recently merged with Seven Arts Productions, Ltd., and would subsequently produce *The Wild Bunch.*

According to its special effects director, Danny Lee, *Bonnie and Clyde* was the first film to use synthetic blood capsules together with exploding squibs to simulate bullet strikes on the human body.[30] Squibs had recently been used to replicate the effects of machine-gun fire in gangster films like *Party Girl* (Nicholas Ray, 1958) and *The St. Valentine's Day Massacre* (Roger Corman, 1967),[31] where small explosive charges can be seen to splinter tables, chip walls, and (in the latter) puncture pipes and victims' overcoats during shootings; and artificial blood capsules had been used sparingly to create wounds since the late 1930s. In combining them, *Bonnie and Clyde* broke the last taboo against violent representation in American film. As Charles Champlin wrote in the *Los Angeles Times,* "Under the old [Production] Code, you would see somebody be shot but you never saw the body being torn apart. You didn't make the link."[32] Now, all at once, violent death could be communicated as a nearly physical sensation in full anatomical detail. It was a revolution in perception that paralleled contemporaneous upheavals in American social life and in the film industry, where financial instability and conglomerate buyouts were creating a sense of uncertainty about the future. As Penn himself would later recall of the era: "What was happening at the time in Hollywood was that enormous power had devolved upon the directors because the studio system had kind of collapsed. We were really running it, so we could introduce this new perception of how to make another kind of movie."[33]

Though Peckinpah claimed to have seen *Bonnie and Clyde* only after completing *The Wild Bunch,* several cast and crew members recall remarks to the contrary. (Dub Taylor, who had played C. W. Moss's father in Penn's film and the mayor of Starbuck in *The Wild Bunch,* remembers Peckinpah telling him during production, "It'll be better than *Bonnie and Clyde*";[34] and wardrobe supervisor Gordon Dawson recalls Peckinpah saying, "We're going to bury *Bonnie and Clyde,*" before filming the opening massacre sequence.[35]) Whatever the truth of Penn's influence, that of Kurosawa is indisputable: Peckinpah consistently cited *Rashomon* (1950) as his favorite film, and he told Ernest Callenbach after completing *Ride the High Country* (1962), "I'd like to be able to make a Western like Kurosawa makes Westerns."[36] The Kurosawa "Westerns" he might have seen at this point would have included *Seven Samurai* (1954), *The Hidden Fortress* (1958), *Yojimbo* (1961), and *Sanjuro* (1962), with its famous "explosion of blood" in the climactic swordfight. There Kurosawa depicted his protagonist slashing into an opponent's heart, producing a spectacular geyser of blood – actually carbonated chocolate syrup hidden in a pressurized container beneath the actor's kimono[37] – which was probably the first on-screen arterial spray in the history of mainstream cinema. It seems likely that the slitting of Angel's throat by Mapache in *The Wild Bunch* (which employs similar technology)[38] has its origins here, but whether Peckinpah saw *Sanjuro* or not, he was determined to show the visceral impact of high-powered weaponry in his own film to an extent that exceeded even *Bonnie and Clyde*. To this end, he experimented with larger squibs loaded with a mixture of blood and raw meat, and he ordered his actors squibbed both front and back to simulate a bullet's complete trajectory through the body. (Al-

FIGURE 25

The violence of *The Wild Bunch* went well beyond the level of gore that *Bonnie and Clyde* had established in 1967.

though Penn had shown a piece of Clyde's skull flying off behind his head in the death montage, he had not squibbed either of his protagonists for exit wounds.) Peckinpah even wired concealed charges to his actors' stomachs so that they would receive a real slap of recoil when their bullet squibs exploded and would react physically to being "shot."[39] These techniques combined with Peckinpah's rapidly cut multiple-camera montage to produce the extreme stylization of the Starbuck and Agua Verde massacres, with their countless, seemingly endless slow-motion shots of blood and tissue exploding from flesh.

The "slow-motion leap," as Marshall Fine has called it,[40] represented a convergence of Peckinpah's own long-standing interest in slow motion with that of two collaborators – screenwriter Walon Green and editor Lou Lombardo. Green's original script for the film, adapted from a story by Peckinpah's friend Roy N. Sickner, called for all of its action sequences to be filmed in slow motion,[41] an unthinkable practice for a mainstream Western in 1969 but one that had obvious appeal for the director of *Major Dundee*. Lou Lombardo, for his part, had never cut a feature before *The Wild Bunch* but had worked with Peckinpah as an assistant cameraman on his teleproduction of *Noon Wine* (*ABC Stage 67*, November 1966). He had since become an editor on several filmed television series, and Peckinpah convinced Warner Bros. to hire him after seeing a slow-motion death sequence Lombardo had put together for an episode of *Felony Squad* months before *Bonnie and Clyde*. In it, footage of Joe Don Baker falling after being shot by police had been filmed at twenty-four frames per second but triple-printed optically at seventy-two frames per second.[42] Lombardo then intercut the resulting slow-motion footage of Baker's fall with that of the cops firing on him at normal speed until he finally hit the ground. When Peckinpah and his producer, Phil Feldman, saw this sequence, they were reportedly ecstatic,[43] and it became the catalyst for shooting the film's gunfights at variable camera speeds and integrating the footage into extended montages of violent action. Ultimately, Peckinpah would film both the Starbuck and Agua Verde massacre/shoot-outs with six separate cameras running at 24, 30, 60, 90, and 120 frames per second to achieve a wide range of speeds for subsequent intercutting, speeds that Lombardo could vary even more elaborately through optical printing. Of course, the concept of intercutting slow-motion with normal-speed action sequences was fundamental to the work of both Kurosawa and Penn, but neither had sought the precise temporal elasticity that informs violent death in *The Wild Bunch.* (It's worth noting, though, that other kinds of action are the subject of variable speed montage in the film; these include the long, tumbling fall of horses and men down a sand dune during the Bunch's flight into Mexico, the ramming of the cavalry troop car after the munitions train robbery, and the blowing up of the bridge across the Rio Grande with the bounty hunters in pursuit – none of which, amazingly, involve fatalities [at least, not on screen].)

The extreme violence of *The Wild Bunch* was facilitated during its production by the final dismantling of the Production Code and its replacement by a rating classification system. As chief industry spokesperson, Motion Picture Association of America (MPAA) president Jack Valenti had for several years been promoting a new climate of creative freedom for filmmakers in response to the social revolutions so clearly taking place across the land. He had engineered the Code revisions of 1966 and later become an apologist for the new wave of movie violence represented by films like *The Dirty Dozen* (Robert Aldrich, 1967) and *Bonnie and Clyde,* which in a February 1968 press conference he shrewdly but accurately connected to the escalating war in Vietnam: "For the first time in the history of this country, people are exposed to instant coverage of a war in progress. When so many movie critics complain about violence on film, I don't think they realize the impact of thirty minutes on the Huntley–Brinkley newscast – and that's real violence."[44] Four months later, after Martin Luther King and Robert Kennedy had been murdered on American soil, the national debate over film violence reached crisis proportions, and Valenti led the MPAA in taking self-protective action.[45] Between June and September, he worked with its nine member companies, the National Association of Theater Owners

(NATO), and the International Film Importers and Distributors of America (IFIDA) to craft a rating system on the British model that would respond to public anger over movie violence without reducing filmmakers' creative freedom (or the industry's huge new profits from graphic representations of sex and violence on screen). On October 7, 1968, Valenti announced the creation of the MPAA's new Code and Rating Administration (CARA), with its four classifications by audience category effective November 1 – G (general audience), M (mature audience – changed in 1972 to GP and then PG [parental guidance recommended]), R (restricted – persons under 16 [later 17] not admitted unless accompanied by a parent or guardian), and X (persons under 16 [later 17] not admitted). As Stephen Prince points out, adoption of the CARA system helped to institutionalize the radical shifts in film content that had followed the Code revision of 1966.[46] *Bonnie and Clyde* had pushed the limits of that revision, but *The Wild Bunch* would have broken them altogether and could not have been released with the PCA seal in its final form. The new ratings system, however, enabled its producers to negotiate an R rating downward from an X with most of its violence intact, ensuring that it would reach its target audience: the 17- to 25-year-old age group.

Although the style and level of its violence would influence several generations of directors, *The Wild Bunch* had no immediate imitators. *Butch Cassidy and the Sundance Kid* (George Roy Hill, 1969) might look like a version of Peckinpah's film bowdlerized for Young Republicans, but in fact William Goldman's script predated that of *The Wild Bunch* by at least a year (Phil Feldman had read it in 1967 and unsuccessfully urged Warner Brothers production chief Ken Hyman to buy it),[47] and the two films were released just months apart. (There *is*, however, a suspiciously Peckinpah-like slow-motion sequence of Butch and the Kid shooting some Bolivian bandits near the end of the film that was filmed at four times normal speed.)[48] Penn followed *Bonnie and Clyde* with the nonviolent counterculture ballad *Alice's Restaurant* (1969); and although he used violence selectively in his films of the 1970s (e.g., *Little Big Man* – see note 48), he never again approached the sheer visceral horror of *Bonnie and Clyde*'s "ballet of death." In fact, for all of its screen violence, the next decade featured few practitioners of "ballistic balletics" but Peckinpah himself. The multiple-camera, variable-speed montage effects of *The Wild Bunch* were repeated with suitable differences in the gunfire sequences of *Straw Dogs* (1971), *The Getaway* (1972), *Pat Garrett and Billy the Kid* (1973), *Bring Me the Head of Alfredo Garcia* (1974), *The Killer Elite* (1975), and *Cross of Iron* (1977) before they devolved into the self-parody of *Convoy* (1978) and entered standard industry practice in the 1980s. Outside of Peckinpah's work, there were only a handful of 1970s films that used exploding squib effects to represent gunshot wounds. These include Ralph Nelson's *Soldier Blue* (1970), where there are several close shots of bloody entry and exit wounds during the Sand Creek massacre sequence;[49] Francis Ford Coppola's *The Godfather* (1972), when the character of Sonny Corleone (James Caan) is ambushed by rival gang members with machine guns at a highway tollbooth; and Martin Scorsese's *Taxi Driver* (1976), during Travis Bickle's (Robert De Niro) climactic shooting spree. For *The Godfather,* makeup artist Dick Smith invented the "mole," a squib concealed beneath a mock layer of skin, and rigged Caan with over 100 of them for detonation during the *Bonnie and Clyde*–style attack. *Taxi Driver,* for which Smith also designed makeup effects, used a combination of prosthetics and explosive squibs to show a man's hand blown off by a .44 magnum in a sequence of slaughter so gruesome that Scorsese had to diffuse the color in printing to avoid an X rating.

By the time of Peckinpah's last film, *The Osterman Weekend* (1983), it had become difficult to distinguish his ballistic montages from those of such mainstream action directors as Walter Hill (*The Warriors* [1979]; *The Long Riders* [1980]), Clint Eastwood (*Sudden Impact* [1983]), and George Pan Cosmatos (*Rambo: First Blood Part II* [1985]; *Cobra* [1986]), and slow-motion squib work had passed from innovation to conservative norm. By this time, too, the level of violence that had stirred public outrage in the late 1960s had become normative, if not actually acceptable, so that Charles Champlin could write with dark amusement of the climactic mas-

FIGURE 26
Ballistic montages and slow motion have become routine elements of contemporary action films. Sylvester Stallone in *Cobra*.

sacre in *Rambo:* "I tried a body count the other afternoon, but gave up after two dozen because there was no reliable way even to estimate how many fell to the bombs, rockets, and perpetual load automatic weapons. . . . I can't believe the full toll is less than 100."[50] The escalation of screen mayhem was a direct result of market forces unleashed in the post-CARA, post–*Wild Bunch* era as the enormous box-office power of "ultraviolence" was realized in the success of films like *A Clockwork Orange* (Stanley Kubrick, 1971),[51] *Dirty Harry* (Don Siegel, 1971), *Magnum Force* (Ted Post, 1973), *Dillinger* (John Milius, 1973), *Walking Tall* (Phil Karlson, 1973), *Death Wish* (Michael Winner, 1974), *Taxi Driver* (Martin Scorsese, 1976), and *Marathon Man* (John Schlesinger, 1976), but above all *The Godfather,* whose blockbuster status as the fifth highest-grossing film of the decade ($85.7 million domestically) conferred the mantle of industry respectability on eruptive bloodletting in a way that the paltry earnings of *The Wild Bunch* ($7,503,192 domestic gross for 1969)[52] or even *Bonnie and Clyde* (about $28 million through 1968 – see earlier) could not.

In 1987, self-proclaimed Peckinpah protegé Walter Hill would make *Extreme Prejudice,* a modern-day gloss on *The Wild Bunch,* whose conclusion reprises and updates the Agua Verde massacre with contemporary firepower. (More recent if less specific tributes to *The Wild Bunch* include *Point Break* [Kathryn Bigelow, 1991], *True Romance* [Tony Scott, 1993], and *Heat* [Michael Mann, 1995].) That same year, Stanley Kubrick used extreme slow-motion squib detonations to prolong the agony of the sniper ambush sequence of *Full Metal Jacket* (1987) – the first film named after a bullet casing rather than a weapon, as if to underscore the new obsession with ballistics. In the 1990s, the work of American directors like Quentin Tarentino (*Reservoir Dogs* [1992], *Pulp Fiction* [1994]), Roger Avary (*Killing Zoe* [1994]), Sam Raimi (*The Quick and the Dead* [1995]), and Dutch emigré Paul Verhoven (*Total Recall* [1990], *Basic Instinct* [1992]) makes a positive fetish of ballistic balletics, and Robert Rodriguez (*El Mariachi* [1992], *Desperado* [1995], *From Dusk to Dawn* [1996]) has become famous for choreographing gun battles as if they were dance numbers. In Hong Kong, John Woo (*The Killer* [1989], *Bullet in the Head* [1990], *Hardboiled* [1992]) and others created an entire subgenre of "gunplay" films around the ballistics of high-capacity automatic pistols by conscious analogy with *The Wild Bunch,* and Italian director Carlo Carlei explained of the shooting scenes in his *Flight of the Innocent* (1993), "There is a chain of inspiration like the Bible. . . . Everything comes from Peckinpah. . . ."[53] This is the sense in which footage from *The Wild Bunch* appears in the montage of violent images on Mickey and Malorie's motel TV screen in Oliver Stone's *Natural Born Killers* (1994), not as indictment but as history.

And yet, because it has become virtually impossible to see a killing in film or television that is *not* shot in graphic slow motion, we need to recall what this style meant in the context of its time nearly thirty years ago. Then, as Kathryn Bigelow recalls, it seemed "almost gestalt editing . . . [because] it imploded standard theories . . . and was radical and tremendously vibrant."[54] It was

Hollywood cinema borrowing exultantly from both the avant-garde and from television in ways scarcely imaginable only years before, but doing so, paradoxically, to embody a terrible new knowledge of the pathology of gunshot wounds inflicted by five years of domestic political assassination and the war in Vietnam.

NOTES

1 John Baxter, *Stunt: The Story of the Great Movie Stunt Men* (Garden City, N.Y.: Doubleday & Company, 1974), p. 180.
2 John Culhane, *Special Effects in the Movies: How They Do It* (New York: Ballantine Books, 1981), pp. 116–117.
3 Ibid., p. 181.
4 David A. Cook, *A History of Narrative Film,* 3rd ed. (New York: W. W. Norton & Company, 1996), pp. 281–2.
5 Frank Miller, *Censored Hollywood: Sex, Sin, & Violence on Screen* (Atlanta: Turner Publishing, 1994), pp. 56–61.
6 Cook, p. 283.
7 Quoted in *Jack Vizzard, See No Evil: Life Inside a Hollywood Censor* (New York: Pocket Books, 1971), p. 313.
8 Quoted in Thomas Doherty, *Projections of War: Hollywood, American Culture, and World War II* (New York: Columbia University Press, 1993), p. 58.
9 Lawrence Alloway, *Violent America: The Movies 1946–1964* (New York: Museum of Modern Art, 1971), p. 54.
10 Writing of this trend in 1950, Manny Farber commented: "Hollywood has spawned, since 1946, a series of ugly melodramas featuring a cruel aesthetic, desperate craftsmanship, and a pessimistic outlook ("Films," *The Nation*, October 28, 1950, p. 397).
11 Ibid., p. 54.
12 The test case for this was Otto Preminger's *The Moon Is Blue,* released by United Artists without the PCA seal in 1953.
13 In 1950, *The State of New York* v. *The Miracle* attempted to prevent the exhibition of the Italian film *Il miracolo* (*The Miracle* [Roberto Rossellini, 1948]) on the grounds that it committed "sacrilege." The case finally went to the U.S. Supreme Court, which in May 1952 ruled that "movies were a significant medium for communication of ideas" and therefore were entitled to a constitutional guarantee of free speech.
14 Ibid., 39.
15 *The Last Sunset* became a cult film in Italy and was championed by the prestigious journal *Bianca e nero.*

16 Stephen Prince, *The Warrior's Camera: The Cinema of Akira Kurosawa* (Princeton, N.J.: Princeton University Press, 1991), p. 233.

17 According to Christopher Frayling in *Spaghetti Westerns: Cowboys and Europeans from Karl May to Sergio Leone* (London: Routledge & Kegan Paul, 1981), only about 20 percent of these were distributed internationally.

18 The "Django" character lasted through thirty films, only the first of which was actually directed by Corbucci. More bizarrely violent than Leone's work, *Django* was banned in several countries and produced in its immediate sequel, *Django Kill* (Guilio Questi, 1967), what Phil Hardy calls "the most brutally violent Spaghetti Western made" (*The Western* [New York: William Morrow, 1983], p. 302).

19 Quoted in Richard S. Randall, *Censorship and the Movies: The Social and Political Control of a Mass Medium* (Madison: University of Wisconsin Press, 1968), pp. 201ff.

20 Review of *Duel at Diablo* in *The New York Times,* October 16, 1966, p. E-6.

21 David Weddle, *"If They Move . . . Kill 'Em!": The Life and Time of Sam Peckinpah* (New York: Grove Press, 1994), pp. 243, 250.

22 Eric Barnouw, *Tube of Plenty: The Evolution of American Television,* 2nd rev. ed. (New York: Oxford University Press, 1990), p. 348.

23 Andre Labarthe and Jean-Louis Comolli, "The Arthur Penn Interview," rpt. in Sandra Wake and Micola Hayden, eds., *The Bonnie and Clyde Book* (London: Lorrimer, 1972), pp. 165–73.

24 Gary Crowdus and Richard Porton, "The Importance of a Singular, Guiding Vision: An Interview with Arthur Penn," *Cineaste,* 20,2 (Spring 1993): 9.

25 Labarthe and Comolli, p. 169.

26 The still frames appeared in "The Assassination of President Kennedy," *Life,* November 25, 1963, pp. 24ff., and "A Matter of Reasonable Doubt," *Life,* November 29, 1966, pp. 38–48. Time-Life Corporation paid Zapruder $150,000 for his 8mm film of the assassination on November 25, 1963, and kept it under lock and key for twelve years, except when it was subpoenaed by Jim Garrison for the Clay Shaw trial in New Orleans in 1969, after which bootleg copies began to appear. However, the the first authorized public showing of the Zapruder film did not take place until November 10, 1974, in Boston, and the film was first shown on national television on March 6, 1975 (on ABC's *Goodnight America,* hosted by Geraldo Rivera), at which point *Life* sold the film back to the Zapruder family for $1. It seems virtually impossible, therefore, that either Penn or Peckinpah had seen the Zapruder film as such while *Bonnie and Clyde* and *The Wild Bunch* were

in preparation. However, public awareness of the film as the crucial evidentiary basis of the Warren Commssion's *Report* was very high in 1967 owing to media coverage of the Garrison investigation and the release of Emile de Antonio's film of Mark Lane's *Rush to Judgement* in January.

27 Labrathe and Comolli, pp. 62–63.

28 "Warren Beatty 'Bonnie' Share," *Variety,* August 7, 1968, p. 1.

29 Both this phenomenon and the film's repeat business are recounted in the *Time* magazine cover essay "The Shock of Freedom in Films," December 8, 1967, pp. 66ff. The author can verify both, having seen *Bonnie and Clyde* four times between October and December 1967 at theaters in the suburbs of Washington, D.C., with audiences stunned into immobility by the film's conclusion.

30 Culhane, pp. 120–1.

31 For the record, Corman's film and Penn's were released just weeks apart, in August and September 1967, respectively.

32 Quoted in Laurent Bouzereau, *Ultra Violent Movies: From Sam Peckinpah to Quentin Tarentino* (New York: Carol Publishing Group, 1996), p. 3.

33 Crowdus and Porton, p. 12.

34 Quoted in Marshall Fine, *Bloody Sam: The Life and Films of Sam Peckinpah* (New York: Donald I. Fine, Inc., 1991), p. 124.

35 Quoted in Weddle, p. 331.

36 Ernest Callenbach, "A Conversation with Sam Peckinpah," *Film Quarterly* 17,(2) (Winter 1963–4): 10.

37 Donald Richie, *The Films of Akira Kurosawa,* 2nd ed. (Berkeley: University of California Press), p. 162.

38 According to Jaime Sanchez, who played Angel, a perforated, flesh-colored tube of pressurized stage blood was run across his throat, which burst open on contact with Emilio Fernandez's (Mapache) rubber knife (quoted in Weddie, p. 342). A side view of this action, showing the blood spurt, was eliminated from the final version to avoid an X rating (Fine, p. 144).

39 Weddle, p. 329.

40 Marshall Fine, *Bloody Sam: The Life and Films of Sam Peckinpah* (New York: Donald I. Fine, Inc. 1991), pp. 142–149.

41 Ibid., pp. 144–5.

42 Garner Simmons, *Peckinpah: A Portrait in Montage* (Austin: University of Texas Press, 1982), p. 85.

43 Lombardo, quoted in Weddle, p. 333.

44 "'Brutal Films Pale Before Televised Vietnam' – Valenti," *Variety,* February 21, 1968, p. 2.

45 Two 1969 Supreme Court decisions were also involved in the creation of the ratings system. In *Ginsberg* v. *New York,* the Court ruled that the government could protect minors from sexually explicit materials; in *Interstate Circuit* v. *Dallas,* the Court affirmed the basic constitutionality of local censorship ordinances. Together, the two decisions suggested that communities could establish their own censorship guidelines for minors, so the MPAA set out to beat them to it.

46 Stephen Prince, *Savage Cinema: Sam Peckinpah and the Rise of Ultraviolent Movies* (Austin: University of Texas Press, 1998), pp. 12–27.

47 Weddle, p. 308.

48 According to George Roy Hill in the documentary *The Making of Butch Cassidy and the Sundance Kid,* the sequence was shot with both overcranked and undercranked cameras, with the intention of intercutting the resulting footage. But Hill felt that the fast-motion shots made the sequence too "balletic" and retained only the slow motion shots of the action in the final film. *Butch Cassidy and the Sundance Kid* (released in October 1969) went into production on September 16, 1968, some three months after principal photography was completed for *The Wild Bunch* (released in June 1969), so it seems unlikely that Hill used Peckinpah as the source for his slow-motion violence, whose squib work is in any case nearly bloodless.

49 Arthur Penn's *Little Big Man* (1970) also offered a version of the Sand Creek massacre, less gory than Nelson's, that – surprisingly, perhaps – used only one exploding squib shot, without either spurting blood or slow-motion. Both *Soldier Blue* (released in August) and *Little Big Man* (released in December) intended a parallel between Sand Creek and the My Lai massacre of March 16, 1968, which had recently been revealed in the American press.

50 Quoted in Bouzereau, p. 158.

51 The term "ultraviolence" originated with Anthony Burgess's novel *A Clockwork Orange* (1962) and was popularized by Kubrick's brilliant adaptation of the book.

52 Weddle, p. 373.

53 Quoted in James Greenberg, "Western Canvas, Palette of Blood," *The New York Times,* February 26, 1995, "Arts and Leisure" Section, p. 26.

54 Ibid.

5   Re-Visioning the Western: Code, Myth, and Genre in Peckinpah's *The Wild Bunch*

The Wild Bunch was made just as the Western as a reliably profitable program staple was supposedly dying out after being the most dependably audience-satisfying structural format for more than seven decades. It is worth noting that despite evidence of the current "collapse" of the Western as a marketable commodity, there are still more Westerns in cinema history than any other Hollywood genre. Just as *The Great Train Robbery* (1903), *Stagecoach* (1939), and *High Noon* (1952) reconfigured the landscape of the American Western (and, in the case of *The Great Train Robbery,* helped to create it), Sam Peckinpah's *The Wild Bunch* re-created the genre of the Western for the late 1960s. This film remains fresh and vital today because of the enormity of its revisionist enterprise. In its use of slow-motion photography to accentuate key moments of suspense and/or violence, in its creation of an entirely new set of character values for its protagonists (notably William Holden as Pike Bishop and Ernest Borgnine as Dutch Engstrom), and in its elegiac embrace of the "end of the old West," *The Wild Bunch,* particularly in the extended director's cut (which I saw in a preview screening in 1969 as a writer for *Life* magazine and which is now readily available on home video), it constitutes a complete re-visioning and reconfiguration of classical Western

155

genre values in a way that sweepingly calls all previous examples of the genre into question.

It is also interesting that *The Wild Bunch* should appear at the same time as George Roy Hill's *Butch Cassidy and the Sundance Kid* (1969), a film that offered a far more conventional and sentimental view of the West than *The Wild Bunch,* although it, too, culminated in a fatal shoot-out for the protagonists. There are moments of respite in *The Wild Bunch* (notably the idyllic stopover in Angel's village, discussed later), but for the most part, *The Wild Bunch* is propelled forward through action and violence. Unlike *Butch Cassidy,* which can also be considered a "buddy" Western, the gang in *The Wild Bunch* is held together by greed and a cruel sense of humor that dictate their every move. Romantic interludes in *The Wild Bunch* are "paid affairs" with prostitutes; the film opens with a violent robbery gone wrong and then coalesces into one extended chase sequence for the rest of the film, with time out only for sleeping, fighting, or planning the gang's next illegal escapade. One could hardly imagine the song "Raindrops Keep Fallin' on My Head" being incorporated into Peckinpah's vision of the West, as it was in *Butch Cassidy,* as a prominent set piece in the film.

Unlike the romantic and leisurely world of *Butch Cassidy,* violence in *The Wild Bunch* is insistent and omnipresent, not episodic or sporadic. The cruelty and sadism of the film are everywhere apparent. *The Wild Bunch* presents a new sort of heroic figure to the audience, one that is prefigured only by the lone-wolf protagonists of 1940s American film noir: the hero as antihero, a loner and a violent misfit who seeks only to survive through the disruption and abrogation of the established rules of the existing social contract. Mirroring this interior state of continual destruction and renewal, the editing of *The Wild Bunch* is at once intensive and plastic yet nonintrusive; as David Cook notes, with 3,642 cut points, the film is one of the most intensively edited motion pictures ever produced.[1] The forced sentimentality of John Ford's "coded West" has been replaced by the rampant intensity of mob violence and individual ambition; Howard Hawks's "profession-

FIGURE 27
Violence in *The Wild Bunch* is insistent and omnipresent.

alism" has here been raised to a higher degree of personal accountability than in *El Dorado* (1967) or any other of Hawks's
Westerns. What makes *The Wild Bunch* fresh today is the newness
of its vision, the originality of its stylistic and thematic approach,
and the matter-of-fact fatality of its foredoomed plot line.

Simultaneously, *The Wild Bunch* critiques and/or extends the
thematic domain of the numerous B Westerns that presented a
sometimes schematic yet more often multivalent vision of the
American West for serial generic consumption. In addition to Ford,
Hawks, and Fred Zinnemann, Peckinpah's vision can be traced to
the works of such B-film craftsmen as Joseph Kane, Ray Nazarro,
and Sam Newfield, as well as many others who labored in the
field of the program Western. Working at the same time that Ford,
Hawks, and other A-line directors were making larger-budgeted
Westerns, Kane (working for Republic), Nazarro (for Columbia) and

Newfield (for PRC) were making a bizarre mixture of "singing Westerns" in the Roy Rogers/Gene Autry mold, alternating these modest, nonconfrontational films with such productions as Kane's *Brimstone* (1949), Nazarro's *Last Days of Boot Hill* (1947), and Newfield's *Death Rides the Plains* (1943). Kane also directed numerous TV Westerns, such as *Bonanza, Cheyenne,* and *Laramie.* He even directed a 1941 remake of *The Great Train Robbery* as an homage to the film that began the entire cycle of American Westerns.

Newfield was undoubtedly the most prolific of these three genre craftsmen, directing no fewer than twenty-three Westerns in 1943 (he averaged twenty a year for more than two decades), for a career total of several hundred Western features. Indeed, Newfield was forced by PRC to adopt two directorial aliases to cover his tracks (Sherman Scott and Peter Stewart) simply because he made films so quickly and efficiently. Joseph Kane directed more than 100 Westerns, nearly all of them for Republic, before going over to television in the late 1950s (when Republic collapsed). Nazarro directed many of the B Westerns Columbia produced in the 1940s and also has more than 100 feature Westerns to his credit. Above all other considerations, these directors epitomized the code of professionalism in action that permeates the world of the Western as a genre; Kane's and Nazarro's average schedule was a six-day shoot, with budgets as low as $20,000; Peckinpah would work under many of the same conditions in creating his early series Westerns for weekly television.

Often these program Westerns were unexpectedly subversive. In the post–World War II 1940s, Nazarro directed a curious series of psychological, twist-ending Westerns for Columbia that seemed to suggest that established gender roles in the West were no more solidified than in contemporary psychological thrillers; dutiful daughters are revealed to be pyromaniacal psychopaths, trusted sheriffs are revealed as hopelessly corrupt, and bounty hunters kill their prey in cold blood rather than capture them alive (*Throw a Saddle on a Star, Roaring Rangers, Terror Trail, Two-Fisted Stranger,* and *Heading West* [all 1946]). B Westerns offered creative freedom even as they operated within a zone of physical impoverishment;

as long as you got the film finished on time, you could pretty much do what you wanted. The best of the B Westerns inhabited a phantom zone of imagistic commerce, creating narratives that thrived on continual conflict, strictly observed codes of behavior, and unceasing violence. Lack of financing brought a lack of supervision and the freedom that came with it. We will see the pattern of relative creative freedom of the B American Western repeated in the ultra–low-budget spaghetti Westerns of the early 1960s. Change seldom happens at the top echelons of filmmaking; instead it starts in the trenches and works its way up into our collective spectatorial consciousness.

Thus, these directors (and many others like them during this era, such as Spencer Gordon Bennet, William Witney, and Lesley Selander) began working out, in the 1930s and 1940s, many of the themes that would later surface in the "adult Westerns" of the 1950s and 1960s: the corruption of authority, the uselessness of societal constructs in maintaining order, a questioning of the established code of ethics, the thin line between "civilization" and chaos, the uniform as an unreliable disguise (as in the opening robbery sequence of *The Wild Bunch*), and even (in Nazarro's films) the disguise of expected gender behavior as a mode of criminal operation. Growing up in Fresno, California, during the 1930s and 1940s, Peckinpah no doubt had the chance to see hundreds of program Westerns; indeed, much of his love for the genre may be traced to his recreational filmgoing during this period of his often undisciplined adolescence. Although he was probably not aware at the time of any particular directorial signature in any of the films he viewed, the combined *vision* of the B Western as a world of unremitting violence and down-at-the-heels nihilism could not have failed to influence his later work.

Interviewed more than forty years later, director Joseph Kane revealed that he, in turn, admired Peckinpah's work, commenting in a 1973 interview that "I saw . . . *The Wild Bunch* [and Peckinpah's] *Pat Garrett and Billy the Kid* [1973]. They were pretty bloody. Good Westerns, but a bit too violent. That guy Peckinpah can really shoot Westerns."[2] Clearly, Peckinpah had numerous generic and stylistic models to draw upon in his youth within the cinema, and of all the cinematic myths then being displayed at the local theater, that of the American Western was at once the most pervasive, the most varied (if only through the sheer number of films being produced by a wide variety of filmmakers), and the most adventurous, which certainly would have appealed to the young director-to-be. Indeed, Peckinpah was deeply in love with the Western genre from the beginning of his career, as his early credits within the industry indicated. Between 1955 and 1960, Peckinpah scripted and/or directed numerous episodes of various television Westerns, including *Gunsmoke, Pony Express, Tales of Wells Fargo, Tombstone Territory, Trackdown, Broken Arrow, Klondike, Zane Grey Theatre*, and *The Westerner*, as well as writing and directing one episode (*Mon Petite Chow*) of *Route 66*.

Most important, Peckinpah created the classic television Western series *The Rifleman* with writer/director Arnold Laven, directing and scripting several episodes of the show, before Peckinpah and Laven had a falling out over *The Rifleman*'s target audience. Peckinpah wanted to move away from a muted version of the Western in favor of a more realistic vision, even within the context of the compromised world of series television – a not altogether unreasonable ambition, given the vitality and viciousness of such contemporary television series as *Shotgun Slade, Have Gun, Will Travel*, or *Wanted: Dead or Alive*. This is the quest Peckinpah would pursue during his ascent within the world of feature films, to bring to the screen a vision of the Western that had previously been only hinted at. Westerns weren't juvenile programming for Peckinpah; they were epic tales on the order of the Nibelungen saga, in which death, betrayal, violence, and treachery operated as the primary concerns of the narrative.

Working in series television, Peckinpah developed a lifelong respect for the crew members he worked with on a daily basis; this, too, would carry over into his relationships with key crew members on his theatrical features. Episodic TV is above all a grinding business, in which deadlines simply *must* be met, because the air date for a given program has to be filled with new product. The

FIGURE 28

A beautiful portrait of the friendship between two aging gunfighters (Randolph Scott and Joel McCrea), *Ride the High Country* shows Peckinpah's love for the West and his special regard for the Western.

unspoken credo of a series television director is simply to "get it, then forget it," a strategy directly at odds with Peckinpah's unwavering commitment to his material, no matter how frankly commercial. Veteran Western director Joseph Kane vividly described the relentless pace of directing an episode of a television Western: "[T]ake shows like *Rawhide, Laramie, Bonanza, Cheyenne,* which I did . . . you had to knock off around twenty-eight setups a day. Figure it out – you've got to do a setup every fifteen minutes. . . ."[3] Peckinpah significantly developed his skills as a director on his various series episode assignments, acquiring a respect for professionalism and attention to detail that would be of immeasurable assistance throughout his career as a director of theatrical motion pictures.

Peckinpah's second feature film as director, *Ride the High Country* (1962), was an elegiac Western that combined a number of

Peckinpah's major themes for the first time. Randolph Scott and Joel McCrea star in the film as two aging gunfighters, much like William Holden's and Robert Ryan's characters in *The Wild Bunch;* in addition, the cast members included future members of the Peckinpah Stock Company: R. G. Armstrong, Warren Oates, and L. Q. Jones. *Ride the High Country* is a quiet, almost meditational Western centering on the themes of change, the passing of time, the passages of friendship, honor and responsibility, and changing codes of conduct.

Peckinpah's next film, *Major Dundee* (1964), despite the backing of the star, Charlton Heston, was cut by the studio into an incomprehensible series of violent vignettes, without any of the necessary framing story to keep the film's action in context. The director turned in a first cut of two hours and forty-four minutes and felt confident that he could tighten the film up to a mutually agreeable running time. *Dundee*'s narrative, centering on a sort of *Dirty Dozen* (or *Wild Bunch*) assault on the Apaches led by Heston as a cavalry officer, was bolstered by a gallery of excellent performances by James Coburn, Warren Oates, Slim Pickens, Ben Johnson, R. G. Armstrong, and L. Q. Jones – pretty much the Peckinpah rogues' gallery intact – but Columbia Pictures, the producers of *Major Dundee,* took the film away from Peckinpah after several disastrous previews and cut "forty-four minutes, almost 27 percent of the film's running time," from the final version of the film.[4]

The savage recutting of *Major Dundee* was not well known outside the industry; thus, when *Major Dundee* opened to uniformly negative reviews, Sam Peckinpah was accorded the lion's share of the blame. Nor did Peckinpah help matters by publicly decrying Columbia's actions; between the release of *Dundee* in 1964 and the production of *The Wild Bunch* in 1969, Peckinpah labored as the screenwriter on Arnold Laven's *The Glory Guys* (1964) and Buzz Kulik's *Villa Rides* (1968); Peckinpah was to direct the latter before being fired by the film's star, Yul Brynner. Peckinpah found some measure of critical and commercial salvation during this period in television; his 1966 script and direction of *Noon Wine* for the anthology series *ABC Stage 67* was nominated for Best Television

Adaptation by the Writers Guild of America and for Best Television Direction by the Directors Guild of America.

Then came *The Wild Bunch* (1969), which was seen at the time as Peckinpah's last chance for a major feature breakthrough. For the first time – and, many would argue, for the last time – Peckinpah was afforded a decent budget, a generous shooting schedule, and a minimum of interference both during and after production of the film, resulting in a Western that Peckinpah had been leading up to with all his previous work and one that changed not only the face of the Western but that of American film altogether. As Jean Baudrillard accurately notes, "cinema plagiarizes itself, recopies itself, remakes its classical, retroactivates its original myths . . . [thus] cinema also approaches an absolute correspondence with itself."[5] Peckinpah was about to "retroactivate" the myth of the Western, to "remake" the classics of the Western genre in a totally new fashion, by introducing an entirely new world view into the interior landscape of his characters' motivations.

The Wild Bunch features a nearly perfect ensemble of actors from Peckinpah's stock company in both the major and minor roles: William Holden (Pike Bishop), Ernest Borgnine (Dutch Engstrom), Robert Ryan (Deke Thornton), the amazingly grizzled Edmond O'Brien (Eddie Sykes), Warren Oates and Ben Johnson (as Lyle and Tector Gorch, respectively, two of the less astute members of the group), Jaime Sanchez (the appropriately named Angel, a beatific sacrifice to the gods of violence), and Emilio Fernandez (Mapache). Each of these seasoned veterans plays off against the others as the individual gears in a monstrous mechanism of destruction. The bit parts are also indelibly etched: Strother Martin (Coffer) and L. Q. Jones (T.C.) as the two high-strung bounty hunters; Albert Dekker, porcine and detestable, in one of his last roles as Pat Harrigan, the hatchet man for the railroad; even Bo Hopkins (Crazy Lee) and Dub Taylor (Mayor Wainscoat) add both substance and reality to their relatively brief roles within the film. Add to this Peckinpah's extensive use of location shooting, his insistence on full coverage in both master and close-up shots from numerous angles for all scenes, and the director's determination to shoot as much film as he felt was required (in the case of *The Wild Bunch*, some 333,000 feet of film and 1,288 camera setups) to get the film as close as possible to his original conception, and one can begin to discern to some degree the discipline, teamwork, and sheer drive and determination that finally brought the completed film down from a long and *very* rough cut to the final 145-minute version we have today.[6]

In the domain of *The Wild Bunch*, it is action that rules above all else (recalling, however perversely, F. Scott Fitzgerald's oft-cited axiom that "action *is* character"). As Jane Tompkins notes, "at the beginning of . . . *The Wild Bunch* a temperance leader [actually Dub Taylor's Mayor Wainscoat] harangues his pious audience ['In this here town, it's 5 cents a glass. *Five cents a glass*. Does anyone really think that that is the price of a *drink?*']; in the next scene, a violent bank robbery makes a shambles of their procession through town. The pattern of talk canceled by action [within the Western] always delivers the same message: language is false or at best ineffectual; only actions are real."[7] This insistence upon action as the ultimate test of veracity within an individual or a system can be seen as part of the traditionally dominant structure of the Western, but it can also be turned against itself by being carried to extremes, which is what Peckinpah does in his work. Within the conventional Western, violence exists to question, and then to uphold in opposition, the remnants of the tenuous social fabric of society.

In this embrace of action as the true test of the individual, Peckinpah's film echoes its many generic precedents, all based on *physical action* by their protagonists more than any other motivational/narrational factor. Peckinpah maintained a delicate balance between his scenes of spectacle and violence and the more restrained expository scenes that simultaneously framed and commented on the exploding bridges, flying glass, and falling bodies that punctuate the narrative of *The Wild Bunch*. The film creates an atmosphere of constant tension within the spectator precisely because it is so contained, so controlled, that the violence just beneath the surface seems fully capable of bursting forth at any moment. Indeed, these scenes of excessive spectacle (the opening massacre, the final shoot-out, and the grinning children adorning the edges of the film's framework as their "pet" scorpions and red ants devour each other) *form* a significant section of the film's narrative; they constitute a major portion of the text of the work.

The Wild Bunch is, in fact, a call for a complete revision of what audiences and critics had come to expect from the classical Hollywood Western; in its place, Peckinpah proposed a new model of his own, based on his long apprenticeship within the genre and his personal fascination with those who operate at the margins of conventional society – the losers, the misfits, men who are out of step with the rapidly changing times. Loss and despair permeate Peckinpah's vision of the West, and of the Western, in stark contrast to the sentimentalism of John Ford (*My Darling Clementine,*

FIGURE 29
The alienated, embittered Ethan Edwards (John Wayne) in *The Searchers* is a vivid precedent of the tormented, anguished misfits that Peckinpah would typically portray.

She Wore a Yellow Ribbon) and even the professional codes (the integrity and honor of a group of heroic and admirable men, as distinct from Peckinpah's corrupt outlaws) embraced by Howard Hawks (*Red River, Rio Bravo*). The cynical opportunism of Pike, Dutch, and the other protagonists of *The Wild Bunch* stands in stark contrast to John Wayne's alienated but still sympathetic characters in Ford's *The Searchers* (1956) or in Hawks's *Red River* (1948). In each film, Wayne plays an obsessed individual, bent only on the accomplishment of a single task (reclaiming a young girl kidnapped by Native Americans in *The Searchers,* getting the cattle through to the railroad link-up in *Red River*) at the expense of all other considerations, yet he still retains a good deal of humanity and warmth. Peckinpah's vision is far more bleak. In contrast to Wayne's heroism and victories in the Westerns of Ford and Hawks, there are no easy victories in the world of the Peckinpah Western; in fact, there are no victories at all. There is only the struggle, and the search, for some solidity within the confines of a rapidly changing and often overtly hostile landscape, and the certainty that time, and the human span of years, are quickly being exhausted. Racism and sexism are frankly acknowledged, and they aren't excused, ignored, or condoned. They exist as unfortunate yet unavoidable facts of human existence, and Peckinpah presents these social inequities as part of the tale he has to tell. Exhaustion itself identifies the world of the Peckinpah Western and sets it off from the more conventionally heroic films of Ford and Hawks. Peckinpah's characters are tired, aging, weary from often profitless effort.

Unlike *The Great Train Robbery* (1903), there is no certainty that a hastily rounded-up posse will effect the capture of the film's bandit protagonists; the cavalry will not come to the rescue of the beleaguered passengers, as in *Stagecoach* (1939). Pike Bishop (William Holden) or Deke Thornton (Robert Ryan) are as close to heroic figures as Peckinpah will allow in *The Wild Bunch;* though they may owe a degree of their professionalism to the Hawksian code of ethics, Peckinpah decisively rejects the macho heroics of John Wayne's various on-screen personae in such Ford films as *The*

Searchers, She Wore a Yellow Ribbon (1949), *Rio Grande* (1950), or even *The Man Who Shot Liberty Valence* (1962). Even at his most dissolute, Wayne's character in the films of Ford and Hawks retains a core of almost medieval chivalry; Pike Bishop's most sympathetic moment in *The Wild Bunch* occurs arguably near the conclusion of the film, when Bishop, after having sex with a young woman who has turned to prostitution to feed her infant child, throws a few extra coins in her direction with a momentary twinge of guilt. More emblematic of Pike's true personality is his joking with the other gang members about having sex with two Hondo whores in tandem with his curt instructions to the other members of the gang during *The Wild Bunch*'s initial "set-up" robbery sequence, the oft-quoted "If they move – kill 'em." While Wayne's various characters are quick to dispense advice to, and act as a role model for, a gallery of young acolytes who grace such films as Hawks's *El Dorado* (1967), *Rio Bravo* (1959), and *Rio Lobo* (1970), Pike Bishop makes it clear to his associates that "I don't know a damn thing, except I either lead this bunch or end it right now." Bishop and his gang are not heroic role models, but killers whose residual humanity is simply greater than that of the venal bounty hunters who pursue them.

Yet John Ford and Howard Hawks were not the only influences on Peckinpah's work as a director of Westerns. Andrew V. McLaglen, Budd Boetticher, Michael Curtiz, Edward Dmytryk, Samuel Fuller, Henry Hathaway, Burt Kennedy, Fritz Lang, Anthony Mann, George Marshall, John Sturges, Raoul Walsh, and many others all brought their own series of thematic considerations to the Western genre. In many ways, as the *Cahiers du Cinéma* critics were quick to point out, the films of these genre artists were often more interesting and ambitious (socially and/or artistically) than the works of the more established directors within the genre. While it is true that McLaglen's Westerns are mostly efficient, workmanlike tales designed to offend no one (such as *McClintock* [1963]), they move along with style and assurance; Budd Boetticher created a series of dark, affecting character studies for the aging Randolph Scott in the now-classic Buchanan films (especially *Ride Lonesome* [1959] and *Comanche Station* [1960]). Michael Curtiz and Fritz Lang both brought a sense of doom-laden nostalgia to their visions of the old West (see Curtiz's *Dodge City* [1939] and *Santa Fe Trail* [1940]). Raoul Walsh, whose matter-of-fact cruelty prefigured in some respects Peckinpah's later work (as seen most clearly in his non-Western *White Heat* [1949], the Westerns *The Lawless Breed* [1952] or *Gun Fury* [1952]), treated his subject matter with a more kinetic and, it might be argued, more assured hand. Anthony Mann brought a newly sadistic violence and a gallery of obsessed, neurotically driven characters to the Western in *Bend of the River* (1951), *The Naked Spur* (1952), *The Man from Laramie* (1955), and others. Sam Fuller, particularly in his wildly operatic *Forty Guns* (1957), staged one of the most violent shoot-outs in Western history for the conclusion of the film (a hostage is shot down in cold blood in order that the villain may be apprehended) while indulging along the way in a series of frenzied CinemaScope dollies of seven to ten minutes' duration through the streets of a dusty Western town. Robert Aldrich in *Vera Cruz* (1954) placed a cynical, amoral American adventurer in Mexico in a tale that clearly prefigures Peckinpah's own later work. These and other films helped establish a dark and cynical tradition in the Western, one that was often distinct from the more straightforward heroics of Ford and Hawks, and Peckinpah's work may be seen as a culmination of this line of development.

At the same time that Peckinpah was preparing for *The Wild Bunch,* there was another agency of social rupture at work within the cinema. The American Western was just one of many genres appropriated by the Italian cinema in the 1960s and jump-started by the auteurs of Cinecitta through the use of unprecedented doses of violence. The classical Hollywood Western was reconfigured most effectively by the disruptive figure of Italian director Sergio Leone, who created a compelling vision of monosyllabic nihilism in such films as *A Fistful of Dollars* (1964), *For a Few Dollars More* (1965), and *The Good, the Bad, and the Ugly* (1966), all of which starred ex-television cowboy Clint Eastwood (late of the teleseries *Rawhide,* where he played the character of Rowdy Yates).

FIGURE 30
Sergio Leone's spaghetti Westerns, made in the mid-sixties, were far more violent and cynical than Hollywood films of the period.

Eastwood's trip to Italy was a last-ditch gamble for the actor; he needed to re-create a new image for himself, distinct from the nice-guy image he had used to such effect on television. Shrewdly, Eastwood and Leone cut the dialogue in these films down to almost nothing (which made dubbing the films into English and other "marketable" languages immeasurably easier); more tellingly, they stripped Eastwood's character of both a name and any motivation other than greed, lust, or a desire to kill, dubbing him "the man with no name." In addition, Eastwood urged Leone to directly violate a number of unspoken but still rigidly enforced Hollywood taboos against what was then regarded as excessive violence, such as showing the rapidly firing gun of a hired killer in the extreme foreground of a shot while the corpses of his victims pile up in the background of the frame.

The success of these films marked the public and critical acceptance of a new level of cinematic violence in the depiction of the universe of the Western. Leone's films were followed by numerous imitations, including Enzo Castellari's *Go Kill and Come Back* (1968), Franco Giraldi's *A Minute to Pray, A Second to Die* (1967), Tonino Valeri's *A Taste for Killing* (1966), and many others. But something was missing in these hugely successful, resolutely bloodthirsty films: depth. The spectacle of violent death after violent death, interspersed with rapes, mutilations, hangings, and ritual executions, was accomplished in the spaghetti Westerns without even a modicum of character or motivation. These films raised the bar on the graphic specificity of violence, thus erasing the legacy of the sentimental West, but they were empty at the center. The films were nothing more or less than efficient killing machines, unreeling with mind-numbing, grisly assurance to reveal a core of absolute nonexistence. Peckinpah's films were violent, but they never sacrificed character or thematic development in their pursuit of the director's nihilist vision. Thus, the Italian films were more of a detour than anything else in the development of Peckinpah's career as a director; they simply opened the door to a new level of realism that made it possible for the director to bring his vision to the screen.

In the world of *The Wild Bunch,* Pat Harrigan (Albert Dekker), who works for the railroad and sends Deke Thornton after Pike and the rest of the Wild Bunch at the film's outset, is despicable because he "hires [his] killins' done" (in Deke's words), rather than pulling the trigger himself. As Thornton asks him, "Tell me, Mr. Harrigan, how does it feel getting paid for it? Getting paid to sit back and hire your killings with the law's arms around you? How does it feel to be so goddamned right?" to which Harrigan replies with vehemence, "Good!", indicating that within the social order of *The Wild Bunch,* all constituted authority is necessarily corrupt and appeals for mercy are worthless. When Angel's (Jaime Sanchez) village is pillaged by bandits, and Pike and the Bunch show up in the aftermath of the onslaught, they are disgusted but not all that surprised to discover that the assault has been the work of the *federales* under the malign leadership of the cruel and sadistic Mapache (Emilio Fernandez), a tin god of a feudal warlord, whose authority rests only upon the rifles (and one machine gun) the Bunch agree to provide him with. Deke Thornton's band of hired assassins who search for the Bunch are described by Deke himself as "scum" and "worthless"; as two unctuously rapacious bounty hunters working for Deke, Coffer (Strother Martin) and T.C. (L. Q. Jones) distinguish themselves by the utterly loathsome relish they display as they rob the corpses of their various victims of cash, watches, and even the gold fillings from their teeth.

Although in the cultural landscape of *The Wild Bunch* violence is the only true social force, Bishop realizes that the days of smash and grab are nearly over: "We've got to start thinking beyond our guns" he tells the other gang members after the group's initial failed robbery. "Those days are closing fast." What the characters in *The Wild Bunch* want more than anything else is to do the impossible: turn back the clock to the days of their youth, and relative innocence, as Don José (Chano Urueta) intuitively observes during a conversation with Pike: "We all dream of being a child again, even the worst of us. Perhaps the worst most of all." Beyond innocence, on the twilight side of existence, there is only blind honor to hold to as a value. As Bishop tells his compatriots at one point, "When you side with a man, you stay with him. And if you can't do that, you're like some animal. You're finished! We're finished! All of us!" Above all other considerations, and despite their insistent embrace of violence as the only solution to the travails of existence, the members of the Bunch obey a twisted code of honor, if only to themselves. As Deke Thornton tells his motley crew of assassins, "We're after men, and I wish to *God* I was with them" (as Deke *had* been at one time, when he and Pike rode as outlaws together).

This emphasis upon honor is part of the traditional code of the Western. Honor is what Jane Tompkins refers to when she states that within the world of the Western, "it doesn't matter whether a man is a sheriff or an outlaw, a rustler or a rancher, a cattleman or a sheepherder, a miner or a gambler. What matters is that he be a *man* [original emphasis]. That is the only side to be on." Citing Deke's exclamation in *The Wild Bunch,* Tompkins concludes that Deke's sentiments, "I think, [mirror] the way the audience of a Western feels when things are going right. I wish to God I was with them."[8] *The Wild Bunch* offers us, at least on one level, the spectacle of the corrupt but honor-aspiring being chased by the purely corrupt (with the exception of Deke's reluctant leadership of those whom he so clearly despises). *The Wild Bunch* are *men*, especially men of action, and they will need the skills they possess to survive within the narrative domain Peckinpah forces them to inhabit.

Since all authority is corrupt, the world of *The Wild Bunch* is a brutal one, bereft of emotional solace and comfort. All of Peckinpah's characters are after their own interests at the expense of any and all other considerations; loyalties shift and twist under the pressure of the struggle to survive. No one can be trusted; love is an expensive illusion that is often transmogrified by circumstance into hate. Crime and currency go hand in hand; temperance (in

FIGURE 31
Henry Fonda's Wyatt Earp in *My Darling Clementine* typifies the gentlemanly, virtuous Western hero against which Peckinpah reacted.

all matters) is seen as a joke. The only hope is to keep on running, and death is inevitable. The dead, the dying, and the vultures dot the terrain of *The Wild Bunch,* always observed by the grinning children who will grow up to replicate the deeds of their mothers and fathers.

This bankruptcy of authority differs completely from the typical Fordian strategy of commonplace decency versus unbridled evil in such films as *My Darling Clementine* (1946), in which a sanitized and reformed Wyatt Earp (Henry Fonda) and a sympathetic outlaw loser, Doc Holliday (Victor Mature), join forces to do battle with malevolent Ike Clanton (Walter Brennan) and the other members of his family at the O.K. Corral. When Doc goes down to a martyr's death during the assault, Ford lingers on his consumptive's handkerchief as it flutters over the wooden planks of the corral's fence – Doc's spirit liberated, his atonement complete at last. There is nothing like this in Peckinpah's vision of the West.

In *The Wild Bunch,* the dead die without time for a moment's reflection; no redemption is involved, only the cessation of human existence. When Mapache slits Angel's throat near the conclusion of *The Wild Bunch,* he is cut down in a hail of reflexive gunfire from Pike, Dutch (Ernest Borgnine), and the other members of the gang. No one thinks about it; they all just *act.* Just seconds before, Mapache and his henchmen had been celebrating the acquisition of the rifles and the machine gun with drunken revelry in the town square. In the nervous laughter that haltingly follows their killing of Mapache, Pike, Dutch, and the other members of the Bunch realize that they have embarked upon a road from which there is no retreat. Violence will now be met with violence until all that is human is expunged.

In this regard, Peckinpah's spectacle of the futility of human endeavor builds on previous film work and has in turn been enormously influential. Fred Zinnemann's bleak depiction of the evasion of personal responsibility in *Act of Violence* (1949) and *High Noon* (1952) finds its logical conclusion in such Peckinpah films as *The Wild Bunch, Bring Me the Head of Alfredo Garcia* (1974), and *Straw Dogs* (1971); more recent films such as David Cronenberg's

Crash (1996), Mike Figgis's *Leaving Las Vegas* (1995), and Mathieu Kassovitz's *La Haine* (literally, *Hate,* 1995) have embraced the operational structures and rules of Peckinpah's morally problematic universe and applied it to contemporary society, where, all too sadly, they fit very well. The spaghetti Westerns of Leone and his Italian and Spanish compatriots, the modish violence of John Boorman's *Point Blank* (1967), and the fatalism of Fritz Lang's *Scarlet Street* (1945) all played their part in the formation of Peckinpah's code of perpetual self-examination and solitary defiance, but Peckinpah was the first to coalesce these disparate dystopian universes within the confines of a single narrative. *The Wild Bunch* reconfigured and revitalized the cinema in *all* genres, not just as a medium of moral agency but also as a plastic art. It is for this that Peckinpah's films are remembered, for the melding of violence with social commentary. Far from being a director predominantly of violence, as he is often considered, Peckinpah was more accurately an artist whose subject was the collapse of the Western and the concomitant eclipse of the world in which the Western once operated.

NOTES

1 David Cook, "Essay on *The Wild Bunch,*" in *The International Directory of Films and Filmmakers,* Vol. 1, 2nd ed. (Chicago, 1990): 979–80.
2 Charles Flynn and Todd McCarthy, "Interview with Joseph Kane," in *Kings of the Bs: Working Within the Hollywood System,* ed. Todd McCarthy and Todd Flynn (New York, 1975): 323.
3 Flynn and McCarthy, 322–3.
4 Marshall Fine, *Bloody Sam: The Life and Films of Sam Peckinpah* (New York, 1991): 98.
5 Jean Baudrillard, *Simulacra and Simulation,* trans. Sheila Faria Glaser (Ann Arbor, Mich., 1994): 47.
6 David Weddle, *"If They Move . . . Kill 'Em": The Life and Times of Sam Peckinpah* (New York, 1994): 354.
7 Jane Tompkins, *West of Everything: The Inner Life of Westerns* (New York, 1992): 51.
8 Ibid., 18.

6 *The Wild Bunch:* Innovation and Retreat

To argue that *The Wild Bunch* is something less than the masterpiece it has been taken for (by some since 1969, by most since its time of reclamation more recently) is not to say that the critical fascination with it is misplaced. The film is too rich to deflect hyperbole for long. In generic terms, Sam Peckinpah's first attempt at Western *maudit* has a certain edge over most of the commonly sanctioned "classic" Hollywood Westerns, primarily because it comes closer to what we in this deconstructive and unromantic time imagine to have been *the real truth* of Old Western life: filth and frustration. Additionally, it revels in the bawdy muscularity and brutality that John Ford usually left implied in his hero's sidelong sneer, if at all, and it stripped away many of the tinselly trappings that all those reliable Hollywood hands (Hawks, Mann, their epigones) had draped over the carcass of the genre.

And politically it was the most potent Western since – since when? It came at a time in American history when each drop of movie blood was (probably correctly) felt to be originating from a point somewhere in the vicinity of the Mekong Delta. The film's violence lifted a simple story about what happens when men go to Mexico[1] into the realm of sociocultural comment, enabling the oldest of film schematics, that of the Western, to speak to the most

175

relevant social contingencies. Peckinpah had dismantled a genre and recast it under the heat of modern American history; the artist and his time conspired in creating a work singularly symptomatic of its moment.

Now, this is rhetoric plain and simple, and if there is a part of this writer that wants to believe in what the rhetoric says, there is another part that wonders if the thing itself still holds up. Well, it does and it doesn't. Precisely like *Bonnie and Clyde* – a film that influenced it as much as any Kurosawa samurai epic – *The Wild Bunch* is radical form imposed on pedestrian content, and unsurprisingly, it is only the radical currents that still carry the electricity of something genuinely new and potent, something that was made to change the perception of all who viewed it. (Change it to *what* is another question, one that Peckinpah's inferiors

FIGURE 32

Peckinpah opens the film with an audacious and savage shoot-out in San Rafael that promises to show viewers a West never before seen, felt, or heard on screen.

throw pennies at to this day.) Radical in its violence, the film still communicates death in a way that is both insanely urgent and reflectively distanced, convulsive and appreciative, in the manner of those painters (Picasso, Goya) Peckinpah has so often been allied to.[2] This much is obvious, so obvious as to be as impervious to revision as the hide of a white whale is to the harpoon.

But *The Wild Bunch,* when it is not choking on its violence, is a work as reactionary as the dime novels that in another time had so brazenly mythologized the West, that eagerly constructed false truths and turned to the most bilious of homilies to quantify everything that was wild and inchoate in the youthful country. Taken as a whole, *The Wild Bunch* sags from the weight of the clichés it buys into; it leaks power through holes of complacency. Despite the greatness in it, the film is a failure, and on no terms so much as those Peckinpah set for himself. He opens so audaciously, with a chaotic shoot-out that catches an entire town – old men, corseted matrons, tiny children – in its fire: a surge of bloody and outrageously displacing action to kick things off. What Peckinpah promises us here is a West (not just a Western) we haven't seen, heard, or felt before, shot through the prism of all that was sanitized out of the classic Western – not only filth and frustration, blood and guts, sex and sweat, but the heavy hand of a particularly savage mortality shadowing the Western heroes who used to ward off the buzzards with buffed buckskin and a long-legged stride. It is a promise made with the famous words that, so chilling and clever in the timing, precede Peckinpah's own name in the opening credits: "If they move, kill 'em." It is a promise and a threat, thrown at the audience like a knife – and Peckinpah doesn't make good.

Perhaps he couldn't make good, not at that time. *The Wild Bunch* is a personal film, and so its complacency, its evasions as both art and worldview, are Peckinpah's. It's the work of an auteur all right, but an auteur who, although visually prodigal is emotionally limited in terms of what he can convey with film. This movie, like its maker, does not know whether to go forward or back. It is excited by the thrill of the new but is afraid to relinquish the comfort and moral certainty of the familiar. This is the schism the film inhabits, the internal conflict that defines what it is, the key to its failure.

As an individual, Peckinpah was contradictory in all the classic ways; as a filmmaker he was the same, possessed of a nature that folded inward in a division that determined equally his best choices and his worst. The biographical anecdotes sketch a man capable of surpassing loyalty and abrupt betrayal; a vociferous opponent of America's Vietnamese incursion who nevertheless vaunted his own Marine past; an autodidactic theorist of human aggression apparently powerless to fathom his own bulging veins and hairy chest. He was the scion of a rigid and exclusionary WASP family, yet the wealthy, prominent Peckinpahs were only a generation removed from the decidedly more savage realities of their pioneering forebears, and Peckinpah absorbed this grimier history even as he was living within the protections of an established life. The early-twentieth-century Fresno over which the Peckinpahs and their set held sway was a modem frontier town in which saloons vied for the young man's attention alongside temperance unions, brothels alongside the guardians of sexual rectitude. "This disparity between the romantic myth and the reality of the Wild West," writes David Weddle, "provoked complex reactions in the young Sam Peckinpah. His deeply conflicted feelings toward both would later give his Westerns an incredible emotional charge."[3]

This charge comes from his vacillation between opposite poles, most often those representing a received (social or mythical) response to life and its vicissitudes as opposed to an internalized, personally interpreted response to them. An old story: Peckinpah's was a schizophrenia unique to the male American artist who is caught between what his macho conditioning tells him is true and what his artist's heart feels to be true. It is this schizophrenia that in *The Wild Bunch* allows the director to linger on the destruction wrought by his star killers even while sanctioning them for having their personal loyalties in place. It is this schizophrenia that dictates another film's sympathetic and fleshly portrait of the bawdy, self-motivated woman (Hildy in *The Ballad of Cable Hogue*), only to contradict such a portrait with the next film's misogynistic depiction of sexually driven femininity (Amy in *Straw Dogs*). One reason Peckinpah is not the easiest filmmaker to embrace is that his work is rampant with right angles both ideological and artistic; he offends one's sense of single purpose. But by any realistic measure it would have been wrong to expect of Peckinpah anything other than a divided art, and difficult not to recognize that *The Wild Bunch* is a film fundamentally divided against itself.

But contradictions in and of themselves are no guarantee of aesthetic worth, though in a postmodern age suspicious of formal symmetry they can often be taken as such. Contradictions are productive only insofar as they are both unconscious and to some extent willful. This is to say that the contradictory impulses in an artist's nature must be subliminal enough to have a life and a play of their own, but that the artist must be aware of them and possess the skill and inspiration to make them work in his favor. In Peckinpah's signal work the contradictions are rendered fluid, dynamic; the opposing attitudes speak to, mitigate, reshape one another. When an artist lacks either the skill or the self-awareness, the contradictions register as dumb, immutable facts clashing insensately; witness the Dirty Harry series in which Nixonian law-and-order politics make nonsense of the hymn to rugged (read homicidal) individualism.

What made Peckinpah's contradictions count as aspects of a sensibility was, simply, that he finally was aware of them – even if he was only sometimes able to incorporate them into his works in productive ways. Unlike so many other indulgers in manic-depressive, passive-aggressive, constructive-destructive extremes, he was sufficiently clear of eye to spot the psycho-symbolic portents in his own background; hence his tight connection to those divergent elements that were determining his work. Peckinpah spoke of being raised by a mother who believed "absolutely in two things: teetotalism and Christian Science,"[4] but he was thinking of the loggers and trappers and mountaineers among his ancestors when he said, "My people were all crazy . . . just crazy."[5] Perhaps he was thinking of both when he staged the *Wild Bunch's* opening, with its teetotalers and crazies caught in a conflict so savage and direct that it gives some idea of the acuteness of the contradiction as Peckinpah must have perceived it. This – a schizophrenia realized, in some portion submitted to – was what enabled and even forced Peckinpah to contradict himself more flagrantly than any contemporary moviemaker, to move from the cold, raw condemnations of *Straw Dogs* to the folksy warmth of *Junior Bonner,* in which no character is so harshly judged – with neither the condemnation nor the generosity registering, in its context, as a false posture.

So all right, Peckinpah was large, he contained multitudes; where does this position *The Wild Bunch?* Firmly under the sway of this schizophrenia.

All of Peckinpah's contradictions expressed in their various ways one umbrella contradiction: the impulse toward innovation, the drive forward, weighing against an equally strong draw backward – backward in history, in values, in cinematic style. A man of his moment with the mentality of a frontiersman, Peckinpah saw in the Western a depiction of past times that he could make over in the image of a new world. If his attraction to the Western as a genre indicates his nostalgia, his brutalization of the old materials into a new form evinces a drive far more radical than reactionary.

But all of this is after the fact. Peckinpah had to discover for himself, film by film, everything that appears evident to us now. *The Wild Bunch,* a work constipated and not mobilized by its contradictions, so confident in its violent technique and so needlessly regressive otherwise, is transitional, a lesson Peckinpah was teaching himself. What to hold on to and what to outgrow; how to parlay a radical vision of violence into an inclusively radical vision of the Western genre and of life as it could be portrayed within the confines of a commercial art form. He did not know himself in the sense that we as his analysts pretend to know him, but he learned.

A certain literary orthodoxy has it that the first and last paragraphs of any serious novel are bound to be microcosms front and back of the present project. Let's first consider the opening and penultimate scenes of *The Wild Bunch,* where Peckinpah unleashes in most concentrated form the violence that he became famed for, the violence that gives this film its still-live wire of radical energy. And then let's consider the rest of the film.

As always, Peckinpah's prelude girds several fields of action simultaneously: The bunch ride into town for what they expect will be a routine bank job; Deke Thornton's scurvy ghouls load up for an ambush; the temperance society preaches pieties; giggling children play Lord of the Flies. The flow of imagery is fluid despite being particularly dense with portentous movement, strikingly physical, very much in the present tense. But as each credit appears the on-screen image is fixed in place for several seconds, and all color and definition are excised, leaving only a rough, minimalist version of that fixed image – an approximation, clearly, of frontier photography and lithography, redolent of "Wanted" posters, daguerreotypes, parchments blanched with age.[6]

Surely Peckinpah's motive in imposing this formal tic was to presage the past–present conflict, but in doing so he also gives us the first glimpse of the movie's unproductive schism – that contradiction between Peckinpah's obeisance to outmoded tradition and his fervor for translating it into a new film language. For more than anything, these credits are, in pure film terms, about motion versus stasis, the director's desire for present-tense movement set off against his impulse to crystallize selected moments of time into instant history. Innovation demands a multileveled engagement with the immediate moment, while retreat reaches for the simpler, less detailed evocation of the past.

But if this opening scene defines what will eventually prove to be the film's limits, it is also challenging and dynamic enough in both form and feeling to escape those limits. This is even more true of the sequence that will end the picture, one of the most famously contradictory sequences in any film, the one that horrifies as it thrills, disgusts as it delights, inspires anger as much as approbation. The film's concluding massacre is five or six minutes of pure paroxysm, aurally a concrete block of uninterrupted gunfire and prolonged kamikaze screams, visually a danse macabre composed of clumsy lurchings cut against the most elegant and unlikely balletic movement, with bodies either isolated or in concert wafting sideways, floating skyward, drifting down. Peckinpah maintains both the grace and the pressure until there comes a point where the viewer who is not beaten back into blindness achieves what D. H. Lawrence calls "the pitch of extreme consciousness."[7] Formal beauty issues even from the filth. Bullets raise great plumes of dust in long rows, and each puff is a Busby Berkeley dancer throwing her kick. The sequence is musical in its small symmetries, its syncopations. Ernest Borgnine sinks heavily to earth, his unheard thud a downbeat setting up for the detonating hand grenade and the pinwheeling of a half-dozen Mapache soldiers through the air. The film loses its mind, and with insanity comes an unimagined lucidity.

A passionate, astonishing, genius five minutes – a short film about killing. It's enough to redeem *The Wild Bunch* from its own hackneyed soul and clichéd *longeurs* – if rhetoric carries the day. Otherwise, no. The film that has preceded this climax has been too sane by half: too well adjusted to the very conventions of genre and medium that the massacre makes irrelevant. The aesthetic insanity of it, total enough for the viewer to lose all spectatorial identity in its tide, is not retroactive; it is self-contained, its blood doesn't spill over onto the rest of the picture. Finally, the climax is emotionally overwhelming not because it is itself an emotional act or because it forces a confrontation with loss, but simply because it is so *climactic,* for Peckinpah as much as for any viewer. It releases the largely untapped energies of the previous two hours, energies dammed by schematic characters, melodramatic confrontations, sentimental elisions, and tumescent whorehouse romps. Like many an act of murder in the real world, Peckinpah's kiss-off of the Wild Bunch is a way of breaking the tedium – violating the routine one has set for oneself.

But it's worth asking what the violence and Peckinpah's styling of it have to do with the film's unproductive schism. In a way, the violence itself encapsulates the schism – only here it does, within its limits, function productively. The violent style of *The Wild*

Bunch is Peckinpah's trademark, snippets of real time knotholing the smooth grain of slow motion, the liquid free falls and crash landings versus the jarring, inelegant rip of a moment's brutality. The interruptions of violence in real time represent that same innovative drive, putting across violence with a new force and explicitness, while the rhythmic cuts in and out of slow motion pull back to something less confrontational, more considered. The real-time cuts are in a sense antiaesthetic: blunt, ugly, factual. Slow motion has the other effect, that of reifying the chaotic present-tense action into something only marginally physical and wholly aesthetic, freezing chaos under a cool gaze, the gut-shot body no longer flesh and tissue so much as a sculpted object falling languidly through indeterminate space. The combination of textures, of staccato and legato, militates against the unreflective impact of mere shock, and forestalls the intellectual oblivion that is usually the partner of kinetic excitement. This is where the schism – that tension between backward and forward movement – does not hinder the integrity of the material but achieves it, enlarges rather than cramps one's perception of it. If *The Wild Bunch* is a constipated work, then. the violence has the effect of a laxative in the body of the whole film, allowing the art to flow rather than stopping it up.

But this success points up Peckinpah's inability at this stage of his career to instill his nonviolent scenes with the same kinds of sensual complications. The violent heights of the film – the initial shoot-out, the dynamiting of the bridge, and the climactic massacre – are peaks separated by great lengths of comparatively barren incident and encounter, scenes not freighted with the same weight, not occupying the same matrix of meaning. Because outside of its violence the film is too much a collection of unquestioned surfaces, of obvious exigencies – its life is all exterior, nothing unifies it subliminally. *The Wild Bunch* has *political* subtext to spare, but the Vietnam parallels were an association the film's audience was already prepared to make; these implications are present but thoughtlessly so, a confirmation of the obvious rather than a foray into the ambiguous. The film is notably short on the subtext that derives from visual and emotional styles deployed in the invisible ways that secretly structure a viewer's whole response to a film – just that realm where Peckinpah could have proven himself another kind of master, and later did, though by then few seemed to care.

The film's undercurrent – that hidden auto-critique that all works yield in some form – does not buttress the radical, death-centered implications of the violence. Rather, it reiterates the dewy-eyed macho romance of the screenplay, not to mention that of the Hollywood Western tradition, the limits of which Peckinpah sought to explode. (It makes sense, John Wayne feeling that *The Wild Bunch* "would have been a good picture without the gore."[8]) In this regard it is decidedly inferior to *The Searchers,* an archetypal Hollywood Western, wherein the racist text was qualified by a succession of red-drenched images that suggested something bloody and guilty bubbling up from the unconscious of the Western genre. Granted that Peckinpah seldom worked on the level of purely visual implication: His individual images, unlike those of, say, Antonioni or Kubrick, are not usually fraught with meaning – "meaning" here referring to a symbolic or extratextual level of interpretation, as opposed to the emotional and visceral meanings his best films are rife with. For Peckinpah the meaning most often resides in such subtleties as the juxtaposing of images, the modulating of rhythms and energies from scene to scene, the physical terrain of the actors.

At his best, Peckinpah was able to unify a film in a way that had nothing to do with the standard chinoiserie of auteurist style and everything to do with simple tonalities – visual and emotional moods pervasive enough to communicate ambiguity even when a screenplay mouthed platitudes. The deep blues and blacks of *Pat Garrett and Billy the Kid* – its deemphasizing of the redemptive possibilities of landscape and light – are endemic to its slack-eyed depiction of a new West that is bruised, battered, and sexually spent, and gaunt with age. For *Straw Dogs* Peckinpah used locations and surfaces to instill palpable cold in each frame, to give scenes the taste of metal and the texture of slate, and basted the result in a dirt-colored half-light that mocked any triumphal aspect that might have attended David Sumner's coup de grace.

The Wild Bunch is visually and emotionally generic in comparison, and not simply because there's only so much novelty a director can impart to the same yellow desert, yet another clapboard hamlet, the eternal hacienda. Directors from William Wellman (*The Ox-Bow Incident* [1943] – perhaps the first noir Western) to Monte Hellman (*The Shooting* [1965, released 1967] – horse opera as ghost story) have shown that even this ancient genre can pulse with new blood if squeezed at the right pressure points. Though Peckinpah achieves this level of innovation in his framing and cutting of the violent passages, those long stretches in between – when dialogue and dusty trail must carry the film's whole burden – are put forth in a mode that wavers between nostalgic languor and dyspeptic impatience. Thematically they are loaded with Peckinpah's reactionary temperament (typified by too many scenes of hearty male laughter fatalistically booming in a nonexistent abyss), while texturally they are void of his innovative temperament, which craved new ways to impart to death a beauty and a terror, a meaning and a moral weight.

In these long passages bridging the set pieces – the "character" scenes, the majority of the picture – Peckinpah treats death like weather, talking about it (usually in aphorisms) but not doing anything about it. Such scenes as Dutch and Pike's fireside dialectic on mortality ("Back off to *what?*") may speak to death as a theme, but tonally and as visual realizations they evade the issue by seeming arch, obligatory – felt, perhaps, but in a too-familiar way. So much else in the picture, what should be the emotional guts of it – the guts that all the violence would ideally blow open, spread out in a new context for our reconsideration – is in this way devalued, denied the rude energy, the immediacy of *action lived in the moment.* There is rudeness in the film, to be sure, but of a genre-approved variety; cliché lives at the heart of that rudeness, and freezes it.

There is Peckinpah's dotage on Albert Dekker as Harrigan, the railroad boss who cracks the whip behind Deke Thornton. If this man represents evil, the death force loose in the capitalist mind, no one need lose sleep: As offered to us, the diabolical Harrigan wears a Snidely Whiplash cosmetic scowl, and is so grincing and fulsome in his evil that it is impossible to imagine his like insinuating itself poisonously into the American scene, for who would take him for anything but the backlot villain that he is? In a better film this man would represent himself first of all; then he would represent the railroad, and money, and capitalist rapacity, and the rest. He would have his reasons; he would not subsist merely on the bread and water of undirected sadism.

So many tired pranks in this story. The mangy comedy of Strother Martin and L. Q. Jones has no place in a film of this intended seriousness; meant as comic relief, their byplay only annoys because it is not strikingly comic and because the idea of relief is again the film's trapdoor. Relief from innovation, relief from tension, from the threat of death – Peckinpah is relieving us left and right, letting us off every hook his violence puts up. Then there is the detour to the Mexican village of Angel's birth, quoting a scene from *The Treasure of the Sierra Madre* and posed as an idyll from the Hollywood wax museum: appreciative, gringo-loving Mexicans biding their time until revolution comes, Angel puffing his noble chest with vengeful, noble thoughts. The Bunch move on to Mapache territory, and they are sent off with a song. Pappy Ford himself would weep, and partly out of appreciation: His tradition is not disturbed by these scenes; their dues to the tradition are paid in full.

It is not necessarily mere political correctness to decry the excess of a white American male's macho sentimentality in the picture, from the cultural imperialism of the Bunch being serenaded by worshipful Mexicans to Angel's impulsive murder of his ex-lover Teresa, a wanton act of the phallus swept away in the wake of the men's hysterical laughter. Buffoonery of any kind can be given depth if the perspective is right – if the artist knows it well enough to share in it at the same time he is revealing it. But here it has no depth because Peckinpah, though he is sharing in it only to a degree, is not revealing it at all. If anything, the director shows more complicity with the infantile abandon of the Gorch boys than with Pike's fleeting intimations of disaster. When the Gorches shoot holes in wine barrels and shower in the spray with their whores, or when Mapache's men suck tequila off the compliant legs of village women, there is always an overlay of music to boost the occasion – trumpets and mariachi, music with a hint of parody, but more than a hint of triumph. Visually the camera's eye is anything but critical. The director is prodding along these revels, offering them as the rewards of a man's tiring, dirty work, an entertainment in which we are to share.

Fine – if the buffoonery is going to be complicated by its opposite, the sense that these are grown boys acting out a little boy's fantasies of pillage, that the macho sentiment is an evasion of life because it is an evasion of fear. But Peckinpah does not go far in spelling this out. So the scenes of lusty male bravado lie effectively dormant and unrelievedly asinine. But in the case of *The Wild Bunch,* this is more than the old Hemingway bluster showing itself. It is again the call of nostalgia, and these scenes act as correctives to all the instability thrown up by the violence. A complacent audience takes comfort in the bluster: *This* we understand – this old movie world where men are men and women are receptacles or at best (the treacherous Teresa) the deus ex machina to trip a man's righteous trigger. We're paying homage to the genre, we're situated in a tradition. Relief.

There is one component to the film, aside from its violence, that threatens to defy relief, and it points in a direction Peckinpah would only later follow. This component is Robert Ryan as Deke Thornton – both the actor and the character. It isn't foolish to speak of Deke as the film's symbol of death in life, a man compelled to move forward but arrested in time. Unlike his opposite number, Pike, Deke has no facile escape hatch from the modern predicament. Pike, being an outlaw unreconstructed, can – must – blast his way into the next world, achieve heroism in that final blaze, the heroism obviating his outlaw's weakness, his lack of direction. But Deke, by virtue of the choices he has made, is the one who must go on living in this new America where nothing will

FIGURE 33
Deke Thornton (right) is the film's symbol of death in life, a man whose torments are more complex than those of Pike and the Bunch.

be self-evident, must willingly enter the limbo history has laid in for him. His torments are more complex than those assigned to any of the Bunch, and they are more viscerally present in Ryan's scenes because Ryan plays Deke as a stooped, nearly beaten oak of a man; close to demented by his conflicts but quiet and sure of his movements; dead in the eyes but terse and forceful in action. Physically he is all contradiction, all angles and abrasions that will not resolve, and emotionally he has the sharp edge of real conflict that might conceivably have ennobled and vitalized the contradictions of the work itself.

But Deke is a symbol that nags and never takes hold, for Peckinpah doesn't have him at the center of the story, where he should be. Each time Deke appears, the film deepens and becomes something more haunted, the film haunted by its darkest notion of it-self; but then the scene shifts, the shadow is averted, the film at-tains its relief. Peckinpah gives this pattern away early. Following the opening shoot-out, Ryan walks sad-eyed through the corpse-ridden streets, and Peckinpah looks down with him at the splayed bodies, all that residual hysteria; then, too quickly, the moment is over, foreshortened by Dekker's stagy bark and the imperatives of narrative machinery. More than once in his handling of Deke, Peckinpah leads his audience to the precipice and then whisks it to the next genre banality without allowing time for the impact to sink in. Catharsis is terminated before it begins, the contempla-tion of death not even a memory, more the wisp of a discarded fancy.

This aftertaste, essential if the film is going to constitute a *spir-itually* – if not formally – unified attack on cinematic propriety and the audience's emotional distance, is shortchanged. Other roads are not taken, either, or they are glancingly assayed. The epochal social transformation these characters are meant to embody – cap-italist hegemony in, free-range individualists out – stands mono-lithically at the center of the film. Peckinpah means in some way to excoriate the expediencies of an America newly mechanized, urbanized, and capitalized. But lacking the urgency of something reimagined in terms of a particular kind of social violence, the tragedy of human obsolescence remains a dramatic stratagem rather than a true theme, abstract from the physical violence that fires off around it. The passing of the Old West had been a com-mon movie plaint at least since Ford's *The Iron Horse of* 1924, and Peckinpah makes no radical move to revitalize or subvert the su-perannuated conceit. Perhaps he believed in it too much – or too little – to question it, but whatever the reason, there are scant re-serves in the film of the one emotional element that would have enabled it to put a human face on a hoary cliché. That element is fear – fear of not only one's own physical death, but of the death of the entire world one has known, the consigning to the dustbin of history of one's collective identity and milieu. This is what the drama of social transformation means in human terms, at least

for those not in a position to sit at the throne of a new world order; this is the drama that, if treated comprehensively, might have
set the film tensing with the fear it lacks. Instead Peckinpah bargains low for the predigested inevitabilities of a hundred other
cowboy-movie scenarios. Nostalgia.

And so he defines the drama in terms that are false to the style.
The violence that Peckinpah glories in and devotes his energies
to needs an equally rich insinuation of dread to carry through
emotionally as well as kinetically. The great film that *The Wild
Bunch* is not would make more of the small, everyday deaths that
prefigure the big death, would fortify its geysers of blood with a
strong undercurrent of hot, quiet despair, and would render the
twilight of the gunmen in emotional shades as novel and un-
nervingly subtle as the physical. What all of this means in effect
is that although the violence as artistic form and expression stands
up, it stands too much alone. The bloodshed is not as integral to
the film that surrounds it as it may seem. The world of *The Wild
Bunch* is a world in which violence occurs, but it isn't, as it has
to be, a violent world. The violence of it has been referred to as
"spectacular,"[9] and it is; but were it truly integral, it would not be
so much a spectacle as an intensification of emotional tones and
existential fears already present in the most dispensable mundan-
ities of dialogue and set design, the length of a shot or the cine-
matographic play of light on water.

This yields a clue to the film's ultimate failure of vision, and
points out the singular superiority to it of *Pat Garrett and Billy the
Kid*. For *Pat Garrett* does everything *The Wild Bunch* does not do.
It reimagines its clichés, sometimes word for word, in terms that
are not themselves clichéd; it gives the resonance of tragedy to
the social transformations that render its heroes historically ab-
surd; it uses the filmmaker's particular materials to depict a world
in which violence is not spectacle but only a blunter version of
business as usual. And it is an utterly despairing vision.

This last is especially important. It's not often noted that *The
Wild Bunch* is, despite its violence, finally an attempt at an affirmation – of life, of camaraderie, of manhood. This is inherent in

the material: the clichés of the story themselves affirm the refuge the screenplay takes in generic scenes played out obligingly. But more than this, Peckinpah bolsters that fundamental affirmation in so many ways that it must have been purposeful on his part. The picture is filled with laughter, its sound hollow but not desperate; this isn't the laugh of men drowning out death with the ring of bonhomie, merely men responding obliviously to the onrush of doom. The macho buffoonery, to repeat, is shown not as an evasion of fear but as an embrace of life. And the film's resolution, even coming so soon after the massacre, is ineffably "up." Among the points scored at the last are the rough justice meted out to Thornton's gang of corpse robbers; the assurance that the villagers' resistance will continue; and the reunion of Deke and Sikes, the survivors left to renew a once hearty and potent Bunch. There is the smile on Ryan's face – and here Peckinpah finally gives that one nagging symbol its relief – when Edmond O'Brien delivers the film's last line: "It ain't like it used to be, but . . . it'll do." In the event that we do not take these words to mean precisely what they say, Peckinpah then brings up the music and stretches out O'Brien's enduring cackle – surely the longest continuous laugh in screen history – till it meets a series of curtain calls showing the stars also laughing, carefree, as they were in life. Presumably their spirit lives on in all men. Affirmation. And an affirmation that is nothing if not shamelessly nostalgic, a last sentimental reach for the safety and final moral order of another time, for that dim and ill-defined past.

In the face of all this, it hardly matters whether Peckinpah truly meant for the violence to have the effect of embittering the material and traumatizing the audience, or if he only staged these grand savageries to gratify some personal perversity. (Or, as is most likely, both.) What matters is not intent but effect, what a filmmaker leaves on the screen and what a film leaves on an audience – and by this measure, Peckinpah's postmassacre coda recapitulates everything affirmatively, tidily, and dubiously; picks it up and dusts it off, as it were, and sends it out bravely to face another day. Does the memory of death, which an audience sheds easily enough in any case, stand a chance against the sequential return of our heroes in cross-faded, soft-edged vignettes, enjoying a final belly laugh to the unctuous backing of the Mexican lullaby? Undeniably, the final note is of grace, resurrection from mere temporal death into the nominal afterlife of hagiography. This is what an audience is left with, and it is left with a lie – at the very least, the kind of rhetorical simplicity that, from an artist as bitter as this, will always seem less than the truth, no matter how necessary it may be to the completion of a certain dramatic form.

The sentiment of uplift was not Peckinpah's métier, and he knew it – or came to know it, perhaps in part from having made *The Wild Bunch*. So, when, a few years later, he returned to the development of a long-dormant screenplay about Pat Garrett and Billy the Kid that in its elemental conflict – unregenerate outlaw pursued by self-loathing ex-confederate – is identical to *The Wild Bunch,* it made sense that he should now concentrate on the conflicted pursuer rather than the bandit whose code of honor and moral designations remain relatively undisturbed throughout. *Pat Garrett* is a far deeper, more troubling business than *The Wild Bunch* precisely because its protagonist is not Pike Bishop but Deke Thornton.

Even at his most demoralized, Peckinpah still had a romantic streak, and Pat *Garrett* is sentimentally elegiac to the extent that it finishes off Billy the Kid with a glamorized Christly death in a lachrymose setting. But its elegy is unsettled, hedged, far from absolute, as if Peckinpah now knew what he hadn't known four years earlier – that in the only terms honest to himself, death had to be treated as a true end, not as a mere passageway leading out at the credits to the netherworld of posthumous glory. This is why, as against the laughter and communal singing of *The Wild Bunch's* wistful peroration, *Pat Garrett* closes on its conflicted hero hitting the dust under a mercenary's bullets. Visually it explicitly recalls Joel McCrea sliding out of the frame at the end of *Ride the High Country*. But the meaning of the image has been pulled inside out: Now death is wrapped up in betrayal and defeat, not in the final defense of honor or the anticipation of a secondary life in Hollywood heaven.

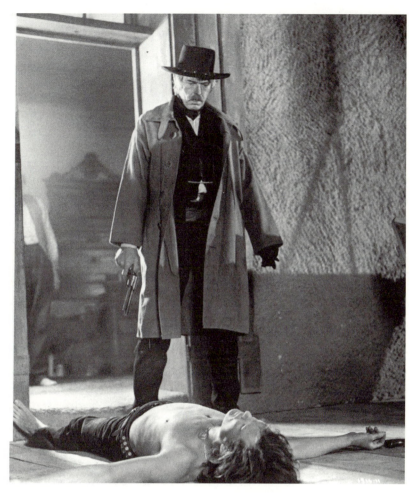

FIGURE 34
Pat Garrett (James Coburn) stands over the body of Billy the Kid.

This would also explain the *Pat Garrett* role Peckinpah reserved for himself. Just before Garrett kills Billy, the filmmaker appears, spitting taunts from a shadowy perch, as the coffin maker.

Peckinpah was a profound pessimist. This is obvious in the craggy, weary, suspicious tone of his films, their cumulative aroma of disgust, their general avoidance of salvation as a viable out. His abiding legacy as a filmmaker precluded any other stance: It was conscious choice as much as family background or anthropological theory that led him to become the Picasso of violence rather than the Renoir of love scenes. And as a profound pessimist, Peckinpah could achieve his greatness only when working toward a vision that realized pessimism, the one value in which he could finally, completely believe.

Everything he produced was pessimistic in the sense that confrontation resulting in death was its natural end point, but Peckinpah at his greatest – his most committed and convincing – exercised the rigor to take the pessimism clear through the climax to the final frames so that one's memory of the film could not escape it. Does *The Wild Bunch* leave us with a memory of *death?* Violence, yes, but not death. Those final guffawing curtain calls – patronizing strokes on the brutalized sensibilities of the audience, the Bunch could be wearing angels' wings – are meant to enfold what came before in a wrap of warmth, to qualify, to soften, even to erase that memory of death; and this they do. The facility of this reversal is in itself impressive – Peckinpah was a pro – but its deliberate retrenchment betrays a director frightened of the implications of the violence he was about to show the world, afraid of going too far into the darkness it threw before him.

But *The Wild Bunch* gave him the notoriety and popular sanction to test himself further; it enabled him to work out his visual strategies of violence on a grand scale; and it gave him a place to deposit several years' worth of frustrated artistic energies and then to consider the components of the result. Peckinpah, to his credit, found the nerve necessary to confront those implications that he had before seemed eager to gloss over: *Pat Garrett,* his final Western, was also his final (disciplined) venture into that darkness and his finest realization of it.

So *The Wild Bunch* was a step in a process – a crucial step, but a step only. This process was one of patricide. Freud called it the "Oedipus complex," and when considering the lives of the poets, Harold Bloom labeled it "the anxiety of influence"; apply it to

Peckinpah's famously mottled, disproportionate career and that career takes on a shape, a sense, a direction it never seemed to have. Peckinpah's patricide was such that he had to kill the Hollywood Western that spawned him before he could create something entirely his own.

If words occur to describe the phenomenon, they are Malraux's: "A heritage is not transmitted; it must be conquered; and moreover it is conquered slowly and unpredictably."[10] Peckinpah conquered his heritage even more slowly and unpredictably than most. Certainly his first important film, *Ride the High Country,* sees him positioned, as a young director, firmly within the very tradition he would ultimately (symbolically) terminate – here following the rules of that tradition with a particular grace but never pushing them past their most comfortable limits, and offering almost no stylistic hint of where his more personal concerns would later lead him. As a Hollywood Western, *Ride the High Country* is exemplary not only for its skillfulness but because it is pure genre. It proves Peckinpah knew the tradition – the first step in violating it.

The aborted epic *Major Dundee* was more genre exercise than subversion, though it did feature early attempts at realistic violence that were hobbled by Peckinpah's evident confusion as to how far be wished to take them. Stilted and impersonal, the film is marginal in Peckinpah's career and represents no significant advance over *Ride the High Country. The Wild Bunch* was his first concerted, self-conscious attempt to radically redefine the Western genre. But again it was only a step in this direction. Its success in subverting the traditional Western is limited entirely to its violence; otherwise, it embraces that tradition, unaware of how moot the violence has rendered the tradition, unwilling to effect a growth in mentality and genre commensurate with the radicalism of the violence. And fatally, it undermines the force of its disturbing and innovative use of violence by trading it for an affirmation that in the film's own terms is conventional, formulaic, and unconvincing.

Peckinpah's step-by-step deconstruction of the traditional Western can be traced through his shifts in attitude with regard to this affirmation and the recurring images he uses to index them. As an interim statement bridging the divergent Western revisions of *The Wild Bunch and Pat Garrett, Straw Dogs* – nothing but a Western in modern dress – is informed by an ambivalence so cutting that it obliterates affirmation even as a fantasy; if anything, affirmation is a structuring absence. Like *The Wild Bunch, Straw Dogs* ends with the hero's smile, the ride of the hero away from the camera and into darkness – but only those watching with one eye shut would claim that David Sumner's smile is unburdened or that his darkness leads to glory rather than merely to a deeper darkness.

Pat Garrett achieves the final synthesis. Its despair, as opposed to the affirmation of *The Wild Bunch,* is seeded throughout the film, from first scene to last, supported meanwhile by a filmic universe of converging details. It is convincing. In its scorn of conventional heroics, its disdain for the moralistic claims of a bought-and-paid-for law, its certainty that commerce as much as murder will out, it kills the Western dead, at least that part of it that had anything to do with Peckinpah.

But the breakthrough would not have happened had *The Wild Bunch* not been made, for if *The Wild Bunch* was an orgasm, *Pat Garrett* is the cigarette afterward. Reflection follows cataclysm in the sequence described by these films. In many ways *Pat Garrett* is a virtual retracing of the steps Peckinpah took in *The Wild Bunch,* a retracing that takes in those depths not countenanced before. This starts with the *Pat Garrett* credit sequence, which also employs real time and stop time, and intercuts the past of Billy the Kid with the present of Pat Garrett – Billy's bullets reaching across the decades to slay his old friend and ultimate killer, two levels of time in a dynamic interaction. This interplay is thematically a very simple idea and cinematically a very profound one. For the dramatization of past and present as *equally* dynamic is precisely what *The Wild Bunch* lacks; and it is Peckinpah's catching up with the full visual and emotional realization of this idea that makes *Pat Garrett* his masterpiece.

The *Wild Bunch* massacre has its echoes in the final scene of *Pat*

Garrett. After Pike's killing of Mapache, the Bunch and the hundreds of soldiers are caught in a long pause, frozen in an uncertain grasp for the nearest gun, the knowledge of what is about to happen dawning on every man's face. The pause goes on, and there is a frisson in these terrible moments unlike anything in cinema. But an even deeper frisson runs through the similar pause that precedes Garrett's symbolic suicide – after shooting Billy he shoots himself in a mirror. The same realization of death that met the Bunch in those moments before the massacre meets Garrett here: The same pause is followed by the same destruction of self. Even the blasted mirror has been seen before. In the midst of the massacre Pike also shoots through one, but there it was plain confusion, it meant nothing; in *Pat Garrett* it is a fully considered, determined act, and it means everything.

The movement Peckinpah has described in the arc between these two climaxes is toward something self-directed and self-eviscerating, a more interior and personalized psychology of violence. The psychology of *Pat Garrett* is just as simple as that of *The Wild Bunch,* but only in the sense that human psychology, as it truly lives and operates under the academic mouthwash, is often simple. But Peckinpah makes the psychologically simple emotionally complex in ways that were not accessible to him at the time of *The Wild Bunch.* He does this, again, by pursuing more than a merely nostalgic, genre-defined connection to the past, by giving its mysteries a weight equal to the contingent realities of the present, and by filling out the abstractions that are genre codes with the specificities of individualized characters.

This is why, when Peckinpah reaches the pinnacle of both his art and his pessimism, the focus is on the individual, not the Bunch. And, accustomed as we are to praising the artful mass deaths of *The Wild Bunch,* it may be quite a while before we realize that each of the killings in *Pat Garrett* – and there are many – occurs singly. There are no wholesale slaughters in which faces and identities disappear and some abstraction of death itself is the only presence. In Peckinpah's masterpiece, each man lives alone; each man dies alone.

It's not only possible but likely that Peckinpah, flush with the freedom of a large scale and large money, added to the violence trail *Bonnie and Clyde* had freshly blazed, approached *The Wild Bunch* with a very particular agenda. Suspecting it might be his last chance to hold the reins of a major commercial film, he rejected moderation and aimed to fill its two and a quarter hours with a career's worth of gory deaths and genre worship. Without a doubt, the film's purchase on greatness resides partly in the sense one gets from the violent scenes of an artist under pressure, straining before time runs down to express all he knows and all he can do, and struggling to do so within the generic bounds of an all but depleted form.

But if *The Wild Bunch* includes virtually everything Peckinpah knew or would ever know about editing, the choreographing of violence, etc. – about technique – it shows us only a very small piece of what he knew about relationships, moods, ambivalences. If his subsequent films demonstrate anything, they demonstrate this. *The Wild Bunch's* limits are not obscured but exposed by its innovations: In doing death so brilliantly the film does life somewhat less well, and serves no real justice at all to those psychological horror regions where life and death shade over and the physical cowers before the existential. This was the resource Peckinpah had to find in himself and that *The Wild Bunch*, in its purgative burst, may have made possible. He had to go past his obvious fascination with violent death as a visual phenomenon in order to see it in its contiguity with everything else – not only life but love and hate, bravado and fear.

Which is to say that if *The Wild Bunch* lacks the contemplative depth of great art, it nonetheless contains the liberating materials that in Peckinpah's case made great art possible. For the most deadly bullet ever fired in a Peckinpah film never pierced any flesh: There is a truer, deeper sense of death in the image of Pat Garrett blowing a hole through his own reflection than there is in any of *The Wild Bunch's* many contorted bodies and flying flashes of red. It seems correct, symbolically and otherwise, that Peckinpah should have had to reject the simplicities of his inheritance in order to breathe into his work not only the innovation he sought but the fierce refusal that it implied – and that only after burning away the underbrush of tradition could he touch the unique truths that had lain hidden inside his art from the beginning.

NOTES

1 Sam Peckinpah, quoted in Georgia Brown, "Once Were Westerns," *The Village Voice* (March 7, 1995): 54.

2 See Peckinpah, *"Playboy* Interview," *Playboy* (August 1972): 65; and Pauline Kael, *5001 Nights at the Movies* (New York, 1991), 837.

3 David Weddle, *"If They Move . . . Kill 'Em!": The Life and Times of Sam Peckinpah* (New York, 1994), 17. See also Marshall Fine, *Bloody Sam: The Life and Films of Sam Peckinpah* (New York, 1991), 11–20.

4 Peckinpah, *Playboy* interview, 72.

5 Peckinpah, quoted in Chris Hodenfield, "Sam Peckinpah Breaks a Bottle," *Rolling Stone* (May 13, 1971): 18.

6 For a more detailed anaylsis of the credit sequence, see Paul Seydor, *Peckinpah – The Western Films: A Reconsideration* (Urbana, IL, 1997), 207.

7 D. H. Lawrence, *Studies in Classic American Literature* (London, 1977), 4.

8 John Wayne, *"Playboy* Interview," *Playboy* (May 1971): 76.

9 William Johnson, *"Straw Dogs," Film Quaterly* (Fall 1972): 61.

10 Andre Malraux, quoted in F. O. Matthiessen, *American Renaissance: Art and Expression in the Age of Whitman* (New York, 1941). xv.

REVIEWS AND COMMENTARY

NEW MOVIES – MAN AND MYTH

(*Time* magazine, June 20, 1969)

"When the legend becomes fact," says the canny newspaper editor in John Ford's *The Man Who Shot Liberty Valance*, "print the legend." Sam Peckinpah is a filmmaker dedicated to telling truths and still preserving the legend of the American West. In feature films (*Ride the High Country, Major Dundee*) and television shows (*The Westerner*), his characters are eminently fallible, their deeds frequently inglorious. They are legends both because and in spite of themselves. *The Wild Bunch* is Peckinpah's most complex inquiry into the metamorphosis of man into myth. Not incidentally, it is also a raucous, violent, powerful feat of American filmmaking.

The script – which Peckinpah wrote with Walon Green – has the sound and rhythm of a rambling campfire yarn. Pike Bishop (William Holden) is the aging leader of a ragtag bunch of bandits who ride through the Southwest trying to scrape together an honorably illegal living. The money from previous jobs has just about run out, and the bunch is being trailed by a group of murderous bounty hunters. After an unsuccessful stick-up in which two of them are killed, the rest light out for Mexico, with the bounty hunters hard on their trail, looking to make what Bishop calls "one good score."

The score turns out to be a crazy scheme to steal a U.S. armaments shipment for a free-booting Mexican general named Mapache, a slow-witted executioner fighting a losing battle against Pancho Villa's army. "We share very few sentiments with our government," Bishop explains lightly as his men prepare to take the required rifles from a U.S. Army supply train. In 1913, this sort of activity is already anachronistic and doomed to failure. Trying to fulfill the terms of the contract, the bunch get doublecrossed. At the same time, they are caught in the vise of their own simplistic code of honor ("When you side with a man, you stay with him," Bishop says). Mapache betrays them from one side while the bounty hunters attack from another, and they are all finally wiped out in the bloodiest battle ever put on film.

"Listen," Peckinpah says, "killing is no fun. I was trying to show what the hell it's like to get shot." Using a combination of fast cutting and slow motion, Peckinpah creates scenes of uncontrolled frenzy in which the feeling of chaotic violence is almost overwhelming. Where the slow motion murders in *Bonnie and Clyde* were balletic, similar scenes in *The Wild Bunch* have the agonizing effect of prolonging the moment of impact, giving each death its own individual horror. Peckinpah repeatedly suggests that the true victims of violence are the young. Children watch the scenes of brutality and carnage wide-eyed, with little fear; a Mexican mother nurses her child by holding her bandolier aside, the baby's tiny fists pressed up against the cartridges. Finally, with mounting excitement, one boy gets to participate in his first fight – and excitedly shoots Pike Bishop in the back.

Peckinpah is sometimes guilty of over-kill himself. Action sequences – like an attack by the Villa forces on Mapache – occasionally destroy the continuity of the elaborate story, and flashbacks are introduced with surprising clumsiness. These, happily, are not typical moments. More characteristic are the sweeping visual panoramas of the whole film (stunningly photographed by Lucien Ballard) and the extraordinarily forceful acting from a troupe of Hollywood professionals. Holden hasn't done such good work since *Stalag 17,* and the bunch – Ernest Borgnine, Warren Oates, Ben Johnson, Edmond O'Brien, Jaime Sanchez – all look and sound as if they had stepped out of a discarded daguerreotype. As the reluctant head of the band of bounty hunters, Robert Ryan gives the screen performance of his career.

For all this, *The Wild Bunch* is Sam Peckinpah's triumph. His hard-edged elegies for the West come from a life spent absorbing its folk-ways. Born into a California pioneer family, Peckinpah is a hard liver who has found some of his script ideas by doing research in barrooms and bordellos. Because he is scrappy and unwilling to compromise, he has spent a good deal of his professional time warring with the money men in the front office who truncated *Major Dundee* and fired him from *The Cincinnati Kid* after three days of shooting. "You have to worry and fight until you get what you want," he once said, and if Peckinpah has battled more than most, his tenacity has finally paid off.

The Wild Bunch contains faults and mistakes, but its accomplishments are more than sufficient to confirm that Peckinpah, along with Stanley Kubrick and Arthur Penn, belongs with the best of the newer generation of American filmmakers.

VIOLENCE AND BEAUTY MESH IN *THE WILD BUNCH*

VINCENT CANBY

(*The New York Times*, June 25, 1969)

Sam Peckinpah's *The Wild Bunch* is about the decline and fall of one outlaw gang at what must be the bleeding end of the frontier era, 1913, when Pancho Villa was tormenting a corrupt Mexican Government while the United States watched cautiously from across the border.

The movie, which opened yesterday at the Trans-Lux East and West Theaters, is very beautiful and the first truly interesting, American-made Western in years. It's also so full of violence – of an intensity that can hardly be supported by the story – that it's going to prompt a lot of people who do not know the real effect of movie violence (as I do not) to write automatic condemnations of it.

"The Wild Bunch" begins on a hot, lazy afternoon as six United States soldiers ride into a small Texas border town with all the aloofness of an army of benign occupation. Under a makeshift awning, the good bourgeoisie of San Rafael is holding a temperance meeting. Gentle spinsters, sweating discreetly, vow to abstain from all spirits.

The "soldiers" pass on to the railroad office, which they quietly proceed to rob of its cash receipts. Down the street, a group of children giggle as they watch a scorpion being eaten alive by a colony of red ants. A moment later, the town literally explodes in the ambush that has been set for the outlaws.

Borrowing a device from "Bonnie and Clyde," Peckinpah suddenly reduces the camera speed to slow motion, which at first heightens the horror of the mindless slaughter, and, then – and this is what really carries horror – makes it beautiful, almost abstract, and finally into terrible parody.

The audience, which earlier was appalled at the cynical detachment with which the camera watched the death fight of the scorpion, is now in the position of the casually cruel children. The face of a temperance parade marcher erupts in a fountain of red. Bodies, struck by bullets, make graceful arcs through the air before falling onto the dusty street, where they seem to bounce, as if on a trampoline.

This sort of choreographed brutality is repeated to excess, but in excess there is point to a film in which realism would be unbearable. "The Wild Bunch" takes the basic element[s] of the Western movie myth, which once defined a simple, morally comprehensible world, and by bending them turns them into symbols of futility and aimless corruption.

The screenplay, by Peckinpah and Walon Green, follows the members of the Wild Bunch from their disastrous, profitless experience at San Rafael to Mexico where they become involved with a smilingly sadistic Mexican general fighting Villa. Although the movie's conventional and poetic action sequences are extraordinarily good and its landscapes beautifully photographed (lots of dark foregrounds and brilliant backgrounds) by Lucien Ballard, who did "Nevada Smith," it is most interesting in its almost jolly account of chaos, corruption and defeat. All personal relationships in the movie seem somehow perverted in odd mixtures of noble sentimentality, greed and lust.

Never satisfactorily resolved is the conflict between William Holden, as the aging leader of the Wild Bunch, and Robert Ryan, as his former friend who, with disdain, leads the bounty hunters in pursuit of the gang. An awkward flashback shows the two men, looking like characters out of a silent movie, caught in an ambush in a bordello from which only Holden escapes.

The ideals of masculine comradeship are exaggerated and transformed into neuroses. The fraternal bonds of two brothers, members of the Wild Bunch, are so excessive [that] they prefer having their whores in tandem. A feeling of genuine compassion prompts the climactic massacre that some members of the film trade are calling, not without reason, "the blood ballet."

Peckinpah also has a way of employing Hollywood life to dramatize his legend. After years of giving bored performances in boring movies, Holden comes back gallantly in "The Wild Bunch." He looks older and tired, but he has style, both as a man and as a movie character who persists in doing what he's always done, not because he really wants the money but because there's simply nothing else to do.

Ryan, Ernest Borgnine and Edmond O'Brien add a similar kind of resonance to the film. O'Brien is a special shock, looking like an evil Gabby Hayes, a foul-mouthed, cackling old man who is the only member of the Wild Bunch to survive.

In two earlier Westerns, "Ride the High Country" (1962) and "Major Dundee" (1965), Peckinpah seemed to be creating comparatively gentle variations on the genre about the man who walks alone – a character about as rare in a Western as a panhandler on the Bowery.

In "The Wild Bunch," which is about men who walk together, but in desperation, he turns the genre inside out. It's a fascinating movie and, I think I should add, when I came out of it, I didn't feel like shooting, knifing or otherwise maiming any of Broadway's often hostile pedestrians.

WHICH VERSION DID YOU SEE?

VINCENT CANBY

(*The New York Times,* July 20, 1969)

Without making any public statement of the fact, Warner Brothers–Seven Arts, the distributor, and Phil Feldman, the producer, have eliminated four sequences from Sam Peckinpah's *The Wild Bunch,* the Western currently at the Trans-Lux East and Trans-Lux West Theaters. The cuts, or, as Feldman likes to call them, the "lifts," which represent a little more than eight minutes in total running time, were made after the movie was reviewed. Thus, technically, "The Wild Bunch" now being shown is not the movie that critics wrote about, some most favorably, as I did. More important, the movie, as a superior work of Hollywood Western art, has been diminished, not fatally (it is still a very good and beautiful film), but certainly to an extent that will be noticeable to everyone who saw the original version and liked it, flaws and all.

I'm not inclined to become indignant about the cuts made in "The Wild Bunch," although I feel that three of the four "lifts" definitely reduce the humanity that runs through the movie in ironic counterpoint to the vividly overstated violence. "The Wild Bunch" has not been butchered the way "Isadora" seems to have been. Rather than being indignant, I'm baffled by the casual way in which moviemakers, even good moviemakers, treat their movies as well as the public. There are a lot of people who like to take movies seriously, but it's difficult when you can never be sure you're seeing a finished movie, or a version hastily assembled to meet a theater opening, or one whose content is dictated by the type of theatrical release it is to receive, or even one whose third reel was lost by the projectionist.

Last week, in checking the report that "The Wild Bunch" has been cut, I called the producer in Hollywood, where he is currently completing post-photography work on another Peckinpah film, "The Ballad of Cable Hogue." "The Wild Bunch" is the second movie that Feldman has produced – the first was "You're a Big Boy Now" – and he seems to be the kind of producer who is genuinely interested in making unusual movies. Feldman was anything but hesitant to talk about the cuts made in the film, all of which, he emphasized several times, had been made with his consent and the consent of the director (who was in Hawaii on vacation last week and could not be reached).

The lifts, said Feldman, had not been made in response to criticism that the film was too savage and brutal. Not touched are the two extraordinary battles, which open and close the movie and, in effect, frame the story of the decline and fall of an outlaw gang on the Texas–Mexican border in 1913. The cuts, he said in more or less one breath, were made to accelerate the pace of the film, to help the "esthetics" and perhaps (he didn't seem too sure) to shorten the running time so as to allow an extra performance in a theater's daily screening schedule. "The fact is," he went on, "we had been considering these lifts for some time, but we didn't have time to make them before the New York opening."

I can understand that problem, which faces all producers, but then Feldman went on to clinch his argument with this statement: "If we had had time to make the cuts before the New York opening, you wouldn't have seen these scenes and you wouldn't have missed them."

At the time I talked to Feldman, I hadn't yet seen the new version, but I still found this a curious avenue of persuasion. It's rather like telling me that if I were an Australian bushman, I'd regard my morning subway ride as an exotic event, so why do I beef about the cattle-car conditions? Well, I had seen the original version of the film, and I'm *not* an Australian bushman.

As if to prove that there is no final, perfect form for any movie, not, at least, for "The Wild Bunch," Feldman reported that the foreign version of the film will run approximately five minutes longer than the version that originally opened in New York. In foreign markets, he said, the movie will be a hard ticket attraction, exhibited in 70 millimeter and stereophonic sound and with an intermission in which candy can be sold. The foreign version he said, also includes a scene that is not in – nor remotely suggested by – the domestic version. This is a flashback that shows how the old leader of the Wild Bunch (William Holden) got his gimpy leg (he was shot by an irate husband).

I can't speak for other "Wild Bunch" aficionados, but now that I know it exists, I'd be interested in looking at it. But, says Feldman, like the scenes eliminated from the domestic version, it is "an interruption of the *flow* of the story."

Now, having seen the re-edited version at the Tran-Lux West, I'd be inclined to agree that one of the four lifts does ease the flow of the story. This is the longest individual cut, about three and one-half minutes, and shows the Mexican Federal forces of the bandit general Mapache (Emilio Fernandez) under attack by the forces of Pancho Villa. Judged simply in terms of the story of the members of the Wild Bunch, the scene is not important, but, like all of the action sequences, it is beautifully staged and enriches the movie's texture – the feeling for time and place.

Each of the three other cuts, I feel, does affect the story itself by eliminating either motivation or dramatization of the outlaw gang's contradictory code of honor. Now gone from the movie is the flashback that shows Holden and Robert Ryan, in their youth, caught in an ambush in a whore house from which only Holden escapes. It was an awkward scene, but it was the only scene in the film that showed the two men together and provided some explanation as to why the two former friends are involved in the death struggle that is the surface story of the film.

Another cut eliminates the strange confession of the oldest member of the Wild Bunch (Edmond O'Brien) that the youngest member, who has just been killed, is actually his grandson, a fact, he says somewhat hesitantly, he didn't mention before because he didn't want any special favors for the boy. The fourth cut is within the dreamy interlude the Wild Bunch spends in a small Mexican village. The gang arrives at the village and in the new version almost immediately departs, as the villagers line the road, waving and singing like Tahitians saying farewell to the crew of the Bounty.

In talking about the cuts, Feldman stressed something that is quite true, that the making of every movie is a joint effort and thus, in effect, not comparable to the creation of a novel.

"Peckinpah and I," he said, "worked from the first to the final frame together. We didn't necessarily always agree, but we agreed between 95 and 96 percent of the time. Some people have accused Sam of wanting to make it more bloody. Actually, he toned down the violence that I wanted, especially in the first fight.

"The first version of the picture that we assembled ran three hours and 10 minutes. I'm sorry that a lot of that footage had to be eliminated, but it was just too long. Every time we made a cut, Lucien Ballard [the cinematographer] chastised me for removing some of his pretty pictures. For Lucien, every cut was a stake driven through Dracula's heart. If 'The Wild Bunch' were to please everyone who worked on it, it would have to be three and one-half hours long."

I'm not sure that there is an absolutely perfect version of "The Wild Bunch" somewhere on a cutting room floor. I do feel, however, that the movie on exhibition here now is just a little less interesting than the one I reviewed. It's still an important work of movie literature, but some chapters have been torn out.

Seeing "The Wild Bunch" at the Trans-Lux West last Saturday reminded me once again that there sometimes is a great difference between the way a movie looks in a private screening room and in a theater. The movie, shot in wide-screen Panavision, looked beautiful in the screening room, where the image completely filled the properly wide screen. At the Trans-Lux West, the image, because it is so wide, can only utilize about three-fourths of the screen height. At the theater you have the feeling that you're peering at the movie through a slightly opened window. I also first saw "True Grit" in a private screening room, a small room where the projector was probably no more than 40 feet from the screen. The colors were rich and deep. When I went back to see the film at the Radio City Music Hall, the color brilliance seemed definitely off, perhaps because of the tremendous distance between the projector and the screen.

PRESS VIOLENT ABOUT FILM'S VIOLENCE, PROD SAM PECKINPAH FOLLOWING "BUNCH"

(*Variety,* July 2, 1969)

– Freeport, Bahamas, June 24. No doubt but that the most disputatious film shown at W7's massive press junket here on Grand Bahama Island, which ended Sunday (22), was Sam Peckinpah's "The Wild Bunch." On the morning after its showing a near-raucous press conference with pic's creators and key actors took place at the King's Inn and Golf Club during which the film's castigators and defenders squared off against each other. Violence was the issue, since the western may be the most violent U.S. film ever made.

The interesting aspect was how the confab changed character as it progressed, beginning as little more than an attack on the film and ending with "The Wild Bunch" defended hotly by its admirers. With Peckinpah absent for the beginning of the session, highlights went something like this:

Virginia Kelly (*Reader's Digest*): "I have only one question to ask: *Why was this film made?*"

Phil Feldman (producer): "The era of escapism is over; the era of reality is here. We in America have to face our problems and resolve them. The American people has been a violent people, from its beginnings; we tend to look away from our violence, as we look away from hunger in America. But these things must be looked at squarely."

Voice: "But do the ends justify the means? Haven't you considered the effect on audiences of such realistic portrayal of violence in films?"

Feldman: "Truth is not beautiful; dying is not beautiful. The entertainment industry has a right and duty to depict reality as it is. If audiences react against the reality that is shown, it may prove therapeutic."

Voice: "I'd like to ask William Holden why he starred in such a film as this. He lives in Kenya and has taken great interest in African game preservation. Films like this encourage violence against every living thing – animals as well as humans."

William Holden (actor): "I just can't get over the reaction here. Are people surprised that violence really exists in the world? Just turn on your tv set any night. The viewer sees the Vietnam War, cities burning, campus riots; he sees plenty of violence. Against this background, the pendulum in motion pictures has swung in one direction. Let us hope that it swings back on matters of sexual morality and violence."

After about a half hour of this, Peckinpah enters.

Stuart Byron (*Variety*): "Perhaps we should just recap what's already been asked of the others. Why did you make this film? What does it say? Why all the violence?"

Sam Peckinpah (writer-director): "I have nothing to say. The film speaks for itself."

Red Reed (*Holiday*): "Then why are we holding this press conference?"

Peckinpah: "That's a good question."

Voice: "I think we deserve an answer to the simple question as to whether Mr. Peckinpah enjoys violence."

Peckinpah: "All right – my idea was that it would have a cathartic effect. No, I don't like violence. In fact when I look at the film myself I find it unbearable. I don't think I'll be able to see it again for five years."

Feldman: "You shouldn't think that this subject is all we're interested in. The next film Sam and I made was a comedy."

Reed: "I can't wait to miss it."

Byron: "What cuts were made in order to get the Motion Picture Association of America to change the film's rating from X to R?"

Feldman: "The original cut ran three hours: we took out 40 minutes. At the request of the MPAA, one line of dialogue was removed, and a few other bits of action. But most of the cutting was our own."

Roger Ebert (*Chicago Sun-Times*): "I suppose all of you up there are getting the impression that this film has no defenders. That's not true. A lot of us think that 'The Wild Bunch' is a great film. It's hard to ask questions about a film you like, easy about one you hate. So I just wanted it said that to a lot of people this movie is a masterpiece."

Voice: "Hear! Hear!"

Peckinpah: "I tried to emphasize the sense of horror and agony that violence provides. Violence is not a game."

Richard Lederer (W7 adpub veep): "I think I should say at this point that we make it very clear in our advertising that this is a violent film. In our teaser ads. You may think that's being a bit tricky, but there's an honesty behind it. We don't want the wrong people seeing the film."

Ernest Borgnine (actor): "I must say that when I received the script I didn't read into it all of these controversial things. We who made the film knew it was violent and even felt repulsed at times, but we felt that we were achieving something. So many significant things are now being read into it that perhaps there is a moral suggestion here."

Ebert: "One thing I'm curious about. There's a scene of a whole bridge collapsing with people still on it, and those look like real people on horses falling into the water to me."

Peckinpah: "Yes, they are. I had a great stunt director on the film."

Sam Lesner (*Chicago Daily News*): "But what about the way the blood spurts practically across a room? Medically, I'm told that only happens when certain arteries are hit by a bullet. Yet in your film it happens all the time. Did you have a doctor advising you?"

Peckinpah: "Yes – the stuntman was a great doctor. No. I'm kidding. Yes, we had a doctor."

Voice: "You juxtapose children with people being killed, and that seems to suggest that the children are dying also. Yet you never show a child being killed. Why?"

Peckinpah: "Because I'm constitutionally unable to show a child in jeopardy."

Voice: "If you want to make a statement against violence and war, why make a western? Why not make a film about Vietnam?"

Peckinpah: "The Western is a universal frame within which it is possible to comment on today."

Mary Knoblauch (*Chicago Today*): "You know, it's all very easy for all of you to sit there and say you're making a film against violence. But the fact is that the people who don't know what violence really is won't go to this picture. They'll be kept away by the ads, and meanwhile they'll aimlessly re-elect the politicians who continue the Vietnam war. It's your intention to reach these people, but they won't come. This film will open the Roosevelt Theatre and get the action crowd – the ones who really like violence."

FILMOGRAPHY

The Deadly Companions (1961)
DIRECTION: Sam Peckinpah
SCREENPLAY: A. S. Fleischman, based on his novel
CINEMATOGRAPHY: William H. Clothier
EDITING: Stanley E. Rabjohn
MUSIC: Marlin Skiles; song "A Dream of Love" by Marlin Skiles and
    Charles FitzSimons, sung by Maureen O'Hara
SOUND: Gordon Sawyer and Robert J. Callen
PRODUCER: Charles FitzSimons
RELEASED BY: Pathe-American
RUNNING TIME: 90 minutes
PRINCIPAL CAST: Maureen O'Hara (Kit Tilden), Brian Keith
    (Yellowleg), Steve Cochran (Billy), Chill Wills (Turkey), Strother
    Martin (Parson)

Ride the High Country (1962)
DIRECTION: Sam Peckinpah
SCREENPLAY: N. B. Stone, Jr.
CINEMATOGRAPHY: Lucien Ballard
EDITING: Frank Santillo
MUSIC: George Bassman
PRODUCER: Richard E. Lyons
RELEASED BY: Metro-Goldwyn-Mayer
RUNNING TIME: 94 minutes

PRINCIPAL CAST: Randolph Scott (Gil Westrum), Joel McCrea (Steve Judd), Mariette Hartley (Elsa Knudsen), Ron Starr (Heck Longtree), Edgar Buchanan (Judge Tolliver), R. G. Armstrong (Joshua Knudsen), James Drury (Billy Hammond), L. Q. Jones (Sylvus Hammond), John Anderson (Elder Hammond), John Davis Chandler (Jimmy Hammond), Warren Oates (Henry Hammond)

Major Dundee (1965)

DIRECTION: Sam Peckinpah
SCREENPLAY: Harry Julian Fink, Oscar Saul, Sam Peckinpah
STORY: Harry Julian Fink
CINEMATOGRAPHY: Sam Leavitt
EDITING: William A. Lyon, Don Starling, Howard Kunin
MUSIC: Daniele Amfitheatrof; title song ("Major Dundee March") by Daniele Amfitheatrof and Ned Washington
SOUND: James Z. Flaster
PRODUCER: Jerry Bresler
RELEASED BY: Columbia Pictures
RUNNING TIME: 134 minutes
PRINCIPAL CAST: Charlton Heston (Major Amos Dundee), Richard Harris (Capt. Benjamin Tyreen), Jim Hutton (Lieutenant Graham), James Coburn (Samuel Potts), Michael Anderson, Jr. (Tim Ryan), Senta Berger (Teresa Santiago), Mario Adorf (Sergeant Gomez), Brock Peters (Aesop), Warren Oates (O. W. Hadley), Ben Johnson (Sergeant Chillum), R. G. Armstrong (Reverend Dahlstrom), L. Q. Jones (Arthur Hadley), Slim Pickens (Wiley), Karl Swenson (Captain Waller), Michael Pate (Sierra Charriba)

The Wild Bunch (1969)

DIRECTION: Sam Peckinpah
SCREENPLAY: Walon Green, Sam Peckinpah
STORY: Walon Green, Roy N. Sickner
CINEMATOGRAPHY: Lucien Ballard
EDITING: Louis Lombardo
ASSOCIATE EDITOR: Robert L. Wolfe
MUSIC: Jerry Fielding
MUSIC SUPERVISION: Sonny Burke
SOUND: Robert J. Miller
ART DIRECTION: Edward Carrere
SPECIAL EFFECTS: Bud Hulburd

WARDROBE: Gordon Dawson
SECOND UNIT DIRECTION: Buzz Henry
ASSISTANT DIRECTORS: Cliff Coleman, Fred Gammon
PRODUCTION MANAGER: William Faralla
ASSOCIATE PRODUCER: Roy N. Sickner
PRODUCER: Phil Feldman
RELEASED BY: Warner Brothers/Seven Arts
RUNNING TIME: 145 minutes (original European release and 1995
   restoration), 143 minutes (initial domestic release), 139 minutes (cut
   domestic release)
PRINCIPAL CAST: William Holden (Pike Bishop), Ernest Borgnine
   (Dutch Engstrom), Robert Ryan (Deke Thornton), Edmond O'Brien
   (Freddie Sykes), Warren Oates (Lyle Gorch), Jaime Sanchez (Angel),
   Ben Johnson (Tector Gorch), Emilio Fernandez (Mapache), Strother
   Martin (Coffer), L. Q. Jones (T.C.), Albert Dekker (Harrigan), Bo
   Hopkins (Crazy Lee), Bud Taylor (Wainscoat), Jorge Russek (Zamorra),
   Alfonso Arau (Herrera), Chano Urueta (Don José), Sonia Amelio
   (Teresa), Aurora Clavel (Aurora), Yolande Ponce (Yolo), Fernando
   Wagner (Mohr),

The Ballad of Cable Hogue (1970)
DIRECTION: Sam Peckinpah
SCREENPLAY: John Crawford, Edmund Penney
CINEMATOGRAPHY: Lucien Ballard
EDITING: Frank Santillo, Lou Lombardo
MUSIC: Jerry Goldsmith
SONGS: "Tomorrow Is the Song I Sing" by Jerry Goldsmith, Richard
   Gillis, sung by Richard Gillis; "Wait for Me, Sunrise" by Richard
   Gillis, sung by Richard Gillis; "Butterfly Mornings" by
Richard Gillis, sung by Stella Stevens and Jason Robards
SOUND: Don Rush
EXECUTIVE PRODUCER: Phil Feldman
PRODUCER: Sam Peckinpah
ASSOCIATE PRODUCER: Gordon Dawson
CO-PRODUCER: William Faralla
RELEASED BY: Warner Brothers
RUNNING TIME: 121 minutes
PRINCIPAL CAST: Jason Robards (Cable Hogue), Stella Stevens (Hildy),
   David Warner (Joshua), Strother Martin (Bowen), Slim Pickens (Ben),
   L. Q. Jones (Taggart), Peter Whitney (Cushing), R. G. Armstrong
   (Quittner), Gene Evans (Clete), Susan O'Connell (Claudia)

Straw Dogs (1971)
DIRECTION: Sam Peckinpah
SCREENPLAY: David Zelag Goodman, Sam Peckinpah, based on the
    novel *The Siege of Trencher's Farm,* by Gordon M. Williams
CINEMATOGRAPHY: John Coquillon
EDITING: Roger Spottiswoode, Paul Davies, Tony Lawson
EDITORIAL CONSULTANT: Robert Wolfe
MUSIC: Jerry Fielding
SOUND: John Bramall
PRODUCER: Daniel Melnick
RELEASED BY: ABC Pictures
RUNNING TIME: 118 minutes (113 minutes U.S. release)
PRINCIPAL CAST: Dustin Hoffman (David Sumner), Susan George
    (Amy Sumner), David Warner (Henry Niles), Peter Vaughan (Tom
    Hedden), T. P. McKenna (Major Scott), Del Henney (Charlie Venner),
    Ken Hutchison (Norman Scutt), Colin Welland (Reverend Hood), Jim
    Norton (Chris Cawsey), Sally Thomsett (Janice), Donald Webster
    (Phil Riddaway), Peter Arne (John Niles), Cherina Mann (Mrs. Hood)

Junior Bonner (1972)
DIRECTION: Sam Peckinpah
SCREENPLAY: Jeb Rosebrook
CINEMATOGRAPHY: Lucien Ballard
EDITING: Robert Wolfe, Frank Santillo
MUSIC: Jerry Fielding
SONGS: "Arizona Morning," "Rodeo Man" written and sung by Rod
    Hart; "Bound to Be Back Again" by Dennis Lambert and Brian Potter,
    sung by Alex Taylor
PRODUCER: Joe Wizan
RELEASED BY: ABC Pictures
RUNNING TIME: 103 minutes
PRINCIPAL CAST: Steve McQueen (Junior Bonner), Robert Preston (Ace
    Bonner), Ida Lupino (Elle Bonner), Joe Don Baker (Curly Bonner),
    Barbara Leigh (Charmagne), Mary Murphy (Ruth Bonner), Ben
    Johnson (Buck Roan), Bill McKinney (Red Terwiliger), Sandra Deel
    (Nurse Arlis)

The Getaway (1972)
DIRECTION: Sam Peckinpah
SCREENPLAY: Walter Hill, based on the novel by Jim Thompson
CINEMATOGRAPHY: Lucien Ballard

EDITING: Robert Wolfe
EDITORIAL CONSULTANT: Roger Spottiswoode
MUSIC: Quincy Jones
SOUND: Charles M. Wilborn
PRODUCERS: David Foster, Mitchell Brower
RELEASED BY: First Artists
RUNNING TIME: 122 minutes
PRINCIPAL CAST: Steve McQueen (Doc McCoy), Ali MacGraw (Carol McCoy), Ben Johnson (Jack Benyon), Sally Struthers (Fran Clinton), Al Lettieri (Rudy Butler), Slim Pickens (Cowboy), Jack Dodson (Harold Clinton), Dub Taylor (Laughlin), Bo Hopkins (Frank Jackson)

Pat Garrett and Billy the Kid (1973)
DIRECTION: Sam Peckinpah
SCREENPLAY: Rudolph Wurlitzer
CINEMATOGRAPHY: John Coquillon
EDITING: Roger Spottiswoode, Garth Craven, Robert L. Wolfe, Richard Halsey, David Berlatsky, Tony De Zarraga
MUSIC: Bob Dylan
SOUND: Charles M. Wilborn, Harry W. Tetrick
PRODUCER: Gordon Carroll
RELEASED BY: Metro-Goldwyn-Mayer
RUNNING TIME: 122 minutes (rough "director's cut"), 106 minutes (original release)
PRINCIPAL CAST: James Coburn (Pat Garrett), Kris Kristofferson (Billy the Kid), Bob Dylan (Alias), Jason Robards (Governor Lew Wallace), Barry Sullivan (Chisum), Richard Jaeckel (Sheriff Kip McKinney), Katy Jurado (Mrs. Baker), Slim Pickens (Sheriff Baker), Chill Wills (Lemuel), John Beck (Poe), R. G. Armstrong (Deputy Ollinger), Luke Askew (Eno), Richard Bright (Holly), Matt Clark (J. W. Bell), Jack Elam (Alamosa Bill), Emilio Fernandez (Paco), Paul Fix (Pete Maxwell), L. Q. Jones (Black Harris), Charlie Martin Smith (Bowdre), Harry Dean Stanton (Luke), Claudia Bryar (Mrs. Horrell), Aurora Clavel (Ida Garrett), Rutanya Alda (Ruthie Lee), Walter Kelley (Rupert), Gene Evans (Mr. Horrell), Sam Peckinpah (Will)

Bring Me the Head of Alfredo Garcia (1974)
DIRECTION: Sam Peckinpah
SCREENPLAY: Gordon Dawson, Sam Peckinpah, from a story by Frank Kowalski and Sam Peckinpah
CINEMATOGRAPHY: Alex Phillips, Jr.

SUPERVISING EDITOR: Garth Craven
EDITORS: Robbe Roberts, Sergio Ortega, Dennis E. Dolan
MUSIC: Jerry Fielding
SOUND: Manuel Topete
EXECUTIVE PRODUCER: Helmut Dantine
PRODUCER: Martin Baum
ASSOCIATE PRODUCER: Gordon Dawson
RELEASED BY: United Artists
RUNNING TIME: 112 minutes
PRINCIPAL CAST: Warren Oates (Bennie), Isela Vega (Elita), Gig Young
    (Quill), Robert Webber (Sappensly), Helmut Dantine (Max), Emilio
    Fernandez (El Jefe),Chano Urueta (bartender), Jorge Russek (Cueto),
    Chalo Gonzalez (Chalo), Janine Maldonado (Theresa), Tamara
    Garina (Grandmother Moreno), Kris Kristofferson, Donny Fritts

The Killer Elite (1975)
DIRECTION: Sam Peckinpah
SCREENPLAY: Marc Norman, Sterling Silliphant, from the novel by
    Robert Rostand
CINEMATOGRAPHY: Phil Lathrop
EDITING: Garth Craven, Tony De Zarraga, Monte Hellman
MUSIC: Jerry Fielding
SOUND: Richard Portman, Charles M. Wilborn
PRODUCERS: Martin Baum, Arthur Lewis
EXECUTIVE PRODUCER: Helmut Dantine
RELEASED BY: United Artists
RUNNING TIME: 122 minutes
PRINCIPAL CAST: James Caan (Mike Locken), Robert Duvall (George
    Hansen), Arthur Hill (Cap Collis), Bo Hopkins (Jerome Miller), Mako
    (Chung), Burt Young (Mac), Gig Young (Weyburn), Helmut Dantine
    (Vorodny)

Cross of Iron (1977)
DIRECTION: Sam Peckinpah
SCREENPLAY: Julius J. Epstein, Herbert Asmodi, from a novel by Willi
    Heinrich
CINEMATOGRAPHY: John Coquillon
EDITING: Tony Lawson, Mike Ellis
MUSIC: Ernest Gold
SOUND: David Hildyard
PRODUCER: Wolf Hartwig

RELEASED BY: E.M.I.
RUNNING TIME: 133 minutes
PRINCIPAL CAST: James Coburn (Sergeant Steiner), Maximilian Schell (Captain Stransky), James Mason (Colonel Brandt), David Warner (Captain Kiesel), Klaus Lowitsch (Kruger), Roger Fritz (Lieutenant Triebig), Fred Stillkraut (Schnurrbart), Michael Nowka (Dietz), Senta Berger (Eva), Veronique Vendell (Marga), Mikael Slavco Stimac (Russian boy soldier)

Convoy (1978)
DIRECTION: Sam Peckinpah
SCREENPLAY: B. W. L. Norton, based on the song by C. W. McCall
CINEMATOGRAPHY: Harry Stradling, Jr.
SUPERVISING EDITOR: Graeme Clifford
EDITORS: John Wright, Garth Craven
MUSIC: Chip Davis
SOUND: Bill Randall
SECOND UNIT DIRECTION: Walter Kelley, James Coburn
EXECUTIVE PRODUCERS: Michael Deeley, Barry Spikings
PRODUCER: Robert E. Sherman
RELEASED BY: United Artists/E.M.I.
RUNNING TIME: 110 minutes
PRINCIPAL CAST: Kris Kristofferson (Martin Penwald, a.k.a. Rubber Duck), Ali MacGraw (Melissa), Ernest Borgnine (Dirty Lyle Wallace), Burt Young (Bobby, a.k.a. Pig Pen), Madge Sinclair (Widow Woman), Franklyn Ajaye (Spider Mike), Brian Davies (Chuck Arnold), Seymour Cassel (Governor Gerry Haskins), Cassie Yates (Violet), Walter Kelley (Federal Agent Hamilton), John Bryson (Texas governor), Sam Peckinpah (news crewman)

The Osterman Weekend (1983)
DIRECTION: Sam Peckinpah
SCREENPLAY: Alan Sharp, based on the novel by Robert Ludlum
SCREENPLAY ADAPTATION: Ian Masters
CINEMATOGRAPHY: John Coquillon
EDITING: Edward Abroms, David Rawlins
MUSIC: Lalo Schifrin
SOUND: Jim Troutman
PRODUCERS: Peter S. David, William N. Panzer
RELEASED BY: Twentieth Century–Fox
RUNNING TIME: 105 minutes

PRINCIPAL CAST: Rutger Hauer (John Tanner), John Hurt (Lawrence Fassett), Meg Foster (Ali Tanner), Dennis Hopper (Richard Tremayne), Craig T. Nelson (Bernard Osterman), Helen Shaver (Virginia Tremayne), Cassie Yates (Betty Cardone), Burt Lancaster (Maxwell Danforth), Chris Sarandon (Joseph Cardone)

Select Bibliography

Arendt, Hannah, *On Violence* (New York: Harcourt, Brace, and World, 1970).

Billington, Ray Allen, ed., *The Frontier Thesis: Valid Interpretation of American History?* (New York: Holt, Rinehart and Winston, 1966).

Bliss, Michael, ed., *Doing It Right: The Best Criticism on Sam Peckinpah's The Wild Bunch,* (Carbondale: Southern Illinois University Press, 1994).

Callenbach, Ernest, "A Conversation with Sam Peckinpah," *Film Quarterly,* Vol. 17, no. 2 (Winter 1963–4), pp. 3–10.

Cook, David A., *A History of Narrative Film,* 3rd ed. (New York: W. W. Norton & Company, 1996), pp. 281–2.

Cook, David A., "Essay on *The Wild Bunch*," *The International Directory of Films and Filmmakers, Volume 1,* (2nd ed.), Nicholas Thomas, ed. (Chicago: St. James Press, 1990), pp. 979–80.

Crowdus, Gary, and Richard Porton, "The Importance of a Singular, Guiding Vision: An Interview with Arthur Penn," *Cineaste,* Vol. 20, no. 2 (Spring 1993), pp. 4–16.

Doherty, Thomas, *Projections of War: Hollywood, American Culture, and World War II* (New York: Columbia University Press, 1993).

Engel, Leonard, "Space and Enclosure in Cooper and Peckinpah: Regeneration in the Open Spaces." *Journal of American Culture,* Vol. 14, no. 2 (Summer 1991), pp. 86–93.

Farber, Stephen, "Peckinpah's Return," *Film Quarterly,* Vol. 23, no. 1 (Fall, 1969), pp. 2–11.

Fine, Marshall, *Bloody Sam: The Life and Films of Sam Peckinpah* (New York: Donald I. Fine, Inc., 1991).

Flynn, Charles, and Todd McCarthy, "Interview with Joseph Kane," *Kings of the Bs: Working Within the Hollywood System,* Todd McCarthy and Charles Flynn, eds. (New York: E. P. Dutton, 1975), pp. 312–24.

Frayling, Christopher, *Spaghetti Westerns: Cowboys and Europeans from Karl May to Sergio Leone* (London: Routledge and Kegan Paul, 1981).

Freud, Sigmund, *Civilization and Its Discontents,* trans. and ed. James Strachey (New York: W. W. Norton, 1961).

Hodenfield, Chris, "Sam Peckinpah Breaks a Bottle," *Rolling Stone* (May 13, 1971) p. 18.

Jacqueline-Johns, Christina, *The Origins of Violence in Mexican Society* (Westport, Conn.: Praeger Publishers, 1995).

Kitses, Jim, *Horizons West: Anthony Mann, Budd Boeticher, Sam Peckinpah; Studies of Authorship in the Western* (Bloomington: Indiana University Press, 1969).

Laurent, Bouzereau, *Ultra Violent Movies: From Sam Peckinpah to Quentin Tarentino* (New York: Carol Publishing Group, 1996).

Lorenz, Konrad, *On Aggression* (New York: Harcourt, Brace, and World, 1966).

Marx, Leo, *The Machine in the Garden: Technology and the Pastoral Ideal in America* (New York: Oxford University Press, 1970).

Miller, Frank, *Censored Hollywood: Sex, Sin, and Violence on Screen* (Atlanta: Turner Publishing, 1994).

"*Playboy* Interview: Sam Peckinpah," *Playboy,* Vol. 19, no. 8 (August 1972), pp. 67–74, 192.

"Press Violent About Film's Violence, Prod Sam Peckinpah Following 'Bunch'," *Variety,* July 2, 1969, p. 15.

Prince, Stephen, *Savage Cinema: Sam Peckinpah and the Rise of Ultraviolent Movies* (Austin: University of Texas Press, 1998).

Sam Peckinpah Collection. Papers. Gift of the Peckinpah family. Material received October 1986. Inventory compiled by Valentin Almendarez, supervised by Samuel A. Gill, archivist, April 1990. Margaret Herrick Library, Academy of Motion Picture Arts and Sciences, Beverly Hills, California.

Seydor, Paul, *Peckinpah: The Western Films: A Reconsideration,* rev. ed. (Urbana: University of Illinois Press, 1980, 1997).

Simmons, Garner, *Peckinpah: A Portrait in Montage* (Austin: University of Texas Press, 1982).

Slotkin, Richard, *Gunfighter Nation: The Myth of the Frontier in Twentieth-Century America* (New York: Atheneum, 1992).

Tompkins, Jane, *West of Everything: The Inner Life of Westerns* (New York: Oxford University Press, 1992).

Turner, Frederick Jackson, "The Significance of the Frontier in American History" in *Frontier and Section: Selected Essays of Frederick Jackson Turner* Englewood Cliffs, NJ: Prentice Hall, 1961), pp. 37–62.

Weddle, David, "Dead Man's Clothes: The Making of *The Wild Bunch,*" *Film Comment,* May–June 1994, pp. 44–57.

Weddle, David, *If They Move . . . Kill 'Em: The Life and Times of Sam Peckinpah* (New York: Grove Press, 1994).

Yergin, Dan, "Peckinpah's Progress: From Blood and Killing in the Old West to Siege and Rape in Rural Cornwall," *New York Times Magazine* (October 31, 1972), pp. 89–92.

Index

WHAT DO UNIONS DO ?

James T. Bennett
Bruce E. Kaufman

editors

WHAT DO UNIONS DO ?

A Twenty-Year Perspective

Transaction Publishers
New Brunswick (U.S.A.) and London (U.K.)

Library of Congress Catalog Number: 2006043757
ISBN: 978-1-4128-0594-0
Printed in the United States of America

Library of Congress Cataloging-in-Publication Data

What do unions do? : a twenty-year perspective / James T. Bennett & Bruce E. Kaufman, editors.
    p. cm.
  "Originally published in a six-part symposium in the Journal of Labor Research"—Acknowledgments.
   ISBN 1-4128-0594-5 (pbk. : alk. paper)
   1. Labor unions—United States. I. Bennett, James T. II. Kaufman, Bruce E. III. Journal of labor research.

HD6508.W44 2007
331.880973—dc22   2006043757

Contents

Acknowledgments

The chapters in this book were originally published in a six-part symposium in the *Journal of Labor Research*, beginning with the Summer 2004 issue and extending through the Fall 2005 issue (vol. XXV, no. 3–vol. XXVI, no. 4). This symposium was sponsored by the John M. Olin Institute for Employment Practice and Policy at George Mason University. Financial support provided by the John M. Olin Foundation is gratefully acknowledged.

1

What Do Unions Do?
A Twenty-Year Perspective

James T. Bennett and Bruce E. Kaufman

I. Introduction

Labor unions are at least as old as industrial economies and have been the subject of debate and controversy for just as long. All sides agree that the objective of unions is to advance the interests of their worker members, and toward this end they exert pressure on employers and governments for improved terms and conditions of employment. Controversy quickly flares, however, once the discussion moves beyond this point. Two issues, in particular, occupy center stage. The first is one of fact, and concerns the effects of unions. Central questions include: how do unions affect wages?, firm performance?, labor market efficiency?, workers' welfare?, and the political process? The second issue involves evaluation and judgment: Are unions good or bad for workers, firms, and the economy? Are the methods unions use to achieve their objectives consistent or inconsistent with widely shared ethical and legal principles? And, would social welfare be advanced by encouraging or discouraging additional unionism?

Twenty years ago this debate was taken to a new level with the publication of *What Do Unions Do?* by Richard Freeman and James Medoff. In the first paragraph of their book, they observe, "For over 200 years, since the days of Adam Smith, economists and other social scientists, labor unionists, and businessmen and women have debated the social effects of unionism. Despite the long debate, however, no agreed-upon answer has emerged to the question: What do unions do?"

In the remainder of the book they attempt to fill in the gaps and holes in our knowledge of "what unions do." Their comprehensive approach brought to the subject new theory, an impressive collection of data sets, and sophisticated statistical tools. Not only did Freeman and Medoff (F&M) cover oft-considered subjects, such as the union effect on wages, but also a variety of new or seldom-treated topics, such as how unions affect employee benefits, turnover, productivity, and firm profitability. Going further, they also gave attention to a variety of noneconomic dimensions not often addressed by economists, such as democracy in unions and the union role in dispute resolution and work force governance.

1

II. Theory

F&M contend that economists and the general public hold two quite different conceptions of unions, one is negative and the other is positive. The negative view they call the "monopoly face" of unions, the positive they call the "collective voice/institutional response" face.

They introduce the monopoly face with the statement (p. 6), "Most, if not all, unions have monopoly power, which they can use to raise wages above competitive levels. Assuming that the competitive system works perfectly, these wage increases have harmful economic effects, reducing the national output and distorting the distribution of income." F&M do not analytically elaborate the monopoly face of unions, but use the concept as a convenient metaphor for the general idea that unions — like monopolistic firms — possess market power and use it to raise the price of labor above the market level. The artificially high price of labor, in conjunction with restrictive work rules and strikes, leads to a number of undesirable outcomes: resource misallocation, inefficiency in production, a bias toward cost-push inflation, and lower capital investment and productivity growth. Unions thus appear in their monopoly guise as a special interest group that uses economic and political "muscle" to gain more income for their members (and leaders) at the expense of the welfare of the larger community.

In constructing the voice/response face of unions, F&M draw on ideas from the public choice area of economics and Hirschman's influential book, *Exit, Voice, and Loyalty* (1970). They contend workers have two ways of dealing with workplace problems: the "exit" option of quitting and the "voice" option of speaking up to management. As F&M note, in a perfectly competitive labor market worker exit and entry among firms produces a situation in which no individual can be made better off without making someone else worse off. Firms are also operating on their efficiency frontiers, so no organizational slack exists. If, however, markets have significant imperfections, such as limited/asymmetric information or mobility costs, the exit option of turnover suffers from two drawbacks: Turnover imposes positive cost on workers and firms and fails to achieve the optimal configuration of working conditions and production methods. Firms may also not minimize costs. Efficiency, therefore, may be promoted by relying on voice as a way to solve workplace problems.

But, argue F&M, voice is also likely to be undersupplied relative to the social optimum if it only takes the form of individual communication between workers and managers due to public good (free-rider) problems and workers' fear of being fired. Effective voice, therefore, has to be *collective* voice, such as a labor union, since only then will workers have the incentive to express their true preferences and the assur-ance that they will not suffer for it. Typically, F&M conceptualize union voice in the relatively narrow sense of a form of communication and information flow and assume it is largely separable from the exercise of union bargaining power. In places (e.g., p. 11), however, the concept is broadened to subsume a political process of rule making, workplace governance, and rights enforcement and couched as a limitation on the employer's power.

According to F&M, the traditional view of unions is largely negative because the assumption of "perfect markets" leaves no room for union voice to play a beneficial role. Illustratively, they state (p. 12), "The greater the imperfection of markets, and the further the real-world management is from a computer programmed by the Invisible Hand, the greater are the possibilities for management's response to unions to improve the operation of the economy." In the presence of market imperfections, however, union voice can promote efficiency in a number of ways, they claim, such as by reducing turnover cost, improving working conditions and production methods, enhancing specific on-the-job training, improving decision making, and by fostering a greater sense of cooperation and trust. Union voice, suggest F&M, can also promote efficiency by inducing/helping management to improve coordination, reduce slack, and implement human resource policies more fairly and professionally.

Another consequence of collective voice, note F&M, is that it leads to a fundamentally different labor contract between the firm and employees. In a regime of individual bargaining, the employer's attention is on keeping/hiring the "marginal" worker — the one just on the margin of going to another firm, while it may ignore or take for granted the preferences of the inframarginal workers who are locked into their jobs by seniority, fringe benefits, or other such factors. Since the marginal worker is more likely to be young, single, and mobile, while the inframarginal workers are more likely to be older, have families, and tied to the community, the preferences of the two groups regarding the mix of wages, benefits, and working conditions may be substantially different. With individual bargaining, the employment package will be structured to appeal to the marginal worker; with collective bargaining the union through a median voter process will articulate the preferences of the "average" employee. Again, the outcome under collective bargaining, by moving the labor contract toward what is desired by a majority of the work force, may promote greater efficiency and employee satisfaction in the labor market.

The bulk of F&M's arguments focus on the efficiency effects of unionism. At points, however, they broaden the analysis to include the effect of unions on other social outcomes, such as income inequality, democracy in the workplace, and representation of workers in the nation's political process. F&M claim that the conventional (monopoly) view of unions also leads to a negative assessment of the contribution of unions in these areas. When unions raise wages, for example, they (allegedly) widen income inequality among workers, while it is claimed that unions themselves are often nondemocratic or corrupt and distort the political process through sizable lobbying and campaign contributions. Acknowledging that all of these criticisms have an element of truth, F&M also claim that a voice/response theory of unions leads to a much more positive picture and one more consistent with the overall performance of unions. The democratic nature of unions, for example, leads to wage-leveling policies that reduce income inequality. Unions also protect employees' rights in the workplace and counterbalance corporate power in the political arena.

The final component of F&M's theory is management's role. The negative monopoly effects of unions, they argue, are real but also potentially more than offset by the positive effects of the voice/response face. The latter, however, are only realized when management takes a constructive approach to collective bargaining, and the parties deal with each other in a spirit of cooperation and mutual gain. The paradox, say F&M, is that while unionism is on net neutral-to-positive for productivity, efficiency, and social outcomes, it nonetheless reduces profits and thus engenders strong employer resistance.

The picture they paint, therefore, is one of missed opportunities — many workers without unions want representation, unions on net are good for the economy and society, and yet management's resistance to unions — coupled with weak labor laws — has been the central force behind a steady erosion in private sector union density from more than one-third in the 1960s to less than one-tenth four decades later. In contrast, union density in the public sector has remained steady at roughly forty percent for several decades, which they hold up as a model for what private sector density might resemble were it not for management resistance.

III. Empirical Evidence

The two contrasting views of unions give markedly different pictures of unionism's economic and social repercussions — the monopoly face predicts social loss, the voice/response face social gain. The critical issue, then, is which model better describes the effects of labor unions.

On a conceptual level, Freeman and Medoff state (p. 19) that both models are relevant: "Since, in fact, unions have both a monopoly and a voice/response face, the key question for understanding the impact of private sector unionism in the United States relates to the relative importance of each." F&M are thus saying that theory alone cannot decide the issue, since both models describe a portion of reality, so the ultimate determination has to come from a weighing and sifting of the empirical evidence. As F&M put it (p. 246), "The central question is not, 'Who in principle is right?' but rather, 'Which face is quantitatively more important in particular economic outcomes?'"

Having proposed the crucial test, F&M devote the remainder of *What Do Unions Do?* to a chapter-by-chapter empirical examination of the effects of unions on a wide variety of economic and social processes and outcomes. Topics included are: wages, fringe benefits, wage inequality, employee turnover and job tenure, employment adjustment to business cycles, the role of seniority, employee job satisfaction, impact on nonorganized workers, productivity, profits, political power, union governance, and union organizing.

What do they find? F&M provide this summary statement (pp. 19–20),

Although additional study will certainly alter some of the specifics, we believe that the results of our analysis provide a reasonably clear and accurate picture of what unions do — a picture that stands in sharp contrast to the negative view that unions do little more than win monopoly wage gains for their members. Our most far-reaching conclusion is that, in addition, to well-advertised effects on wages, unions alter nearly every other measurable aspect of the operation of workplaces and enterprises. . . . On balance, unionization appears to improve rather than harm the social and economic system. In terms of the three outcomes in Table 1.1, our analysis shows that unions are associated with greater efficiency in most settings, reduce overall earnings inequality, and contribute to, rather than detract from, economic and political freedom. This is not to deny the negative monopoly effects of unions. They exist. They are undesirable. But . . . our analysis indicates that, in fact, focusing on them leads to an exceedingly inaccurate representation of what unions do. In the United States in the period we have studied, the voice/response face of unions dominates the monopoly face, though we stress that an accurate portrait must show both faces.

After this statement, F&M list thirteen specific empirical findings from their analysis. Put briefly, they are:

- Unions have a substantial monopoly wage impact, although the exact size of the union-nonunion differential varies considerably over time and across industries and demographic groups. The social cost of union monopoly wage gains is modest — about 0.3 percent of gross domestic product.
- Unions also increase the share of compensation going to employee benefits and shift the composition of the benefits package toward deferred benefits, such as pensions and health insurance.
- Unions reduce the overall level of wage inequality among workers.
- Unionized workers are less likely to quit their jobs and have longer job tenure than similar nonunion workers.
- During recessions unionized firms make more use of temporary lay-offs, rather than wage cuts. On cyclical upswings unionized firms recall relatively more workers, and nonunion firms tend to hire new employees. Unions sometimes agree to wage cuts, but generally only in the face of a substantial threat to employment.
- Unionized workplaces operate under different and more explicit rules than nonunion workplaces. Seniority is more important, dispute resolution more formal, job security protections greater, and management discretion and flexibility restricted.
- The "threat effect" of unions causes nonunion firms, on net, to modestly improve wages and employment conditions of production workers in order to avoid becoming unionized.
- Union workers report greater dissatisfaction with their jobs, particularly with respect to working conditions and relations with supervisors.
- In most cases unionized establishments have higher productivity than nonunion ones.
- Unionized firms earn a lower return on capital and reduced profits. The reduction in profitability is concentrated, however, among firms in concentrated and

otherwise highly profitable sectors of the economy (implying union wage gains largely take the form of a redistribution of monopoly rents from firms to workers).

- The political power of unions has contributed to the enactment of numerous pieces of legislation that promote the general social/employment interests of workers. With respect to labor laws that directly impact union power, unions have been able to preserve existing favorable legislation but not expand on it.
- The popular image of unions as boss-run, corrupt institutions is a caricature. Most unions are highly democratic and corruption problems are concentrated in only a few industries.
- The percent of private sector workers belonging to unions has declined sharply since 1950. The decline is due largely to a dramatic increase in the amount and sophistication of legal and illegal company actions designed to forestall union organizing.

IV. National Labor Policy

With these empirical findings in hand, F&M in the last chapter of *What Do Unions Do?* turn to consideration of the implications for national labor policy, particularly as it bears on union organizing and collective bargaining.

Based on their empirical work, they conclude (p. 247) "in most settings the positive elements of the voice/response face of unions offset or dominate the negative elements of the monopoly face. . . . In an economy where governments, business, and unions work imperfectly — sometimes for, sometimes against the general welfare — there is a place for unions to improve the well-being not only of their members but of the entire society." F&M then ask (p. 248), "Should someone who favors, as we do, a thriving market economy, also favor a strong union movement and be concerned with the ongoing decline in private sector unionism?" The answer they give is: "Accord-ing to our research findings, yes."

This answer leads F&M to the "bottom line" regarding the existing level of unionism. They assert (p. 248), "The paradox of American unionism is that it is at one and the same time a plus on the overall social balance sheet . . . and a minus on the corporate balance sheet." Because unionism hurts profits and employer control of the workplace, companies expend great time and resources in resisting unions — even though seen from a social point of view the nation would benefit from greater unionization. Thus, F&M conclude (p. 250): "While we are not sure what the optimal degree of unionization is in this country, we are convinced that current trends have brought the union density below the optimal level." In a later study, Freeman (1992) suggests that the optimal level of union density in the United States is somewhere between the 25 percent level existing at the time *What Do Unions Do?* was written and the 60 to 80 percent level in Scandinavia, yielding a figure (if conservatively estimated) in the range of 35 to 45 percent. This figure, as earlier noted, approximates the level of public sector union density.

These conclusions lead F&M to suggest, in very broad terms, three directions for change in the American collective bargaining system and national labor policy.

The first is to revise the legal framework to encourage greater unionization, with the purpose of bringing union density closer to the "optimal" level (or range). The principal method they recommend is making the organizing process for workers easier and less costly. Given their conclusion that management resistance is the largest hindrance to greater organizing, F&M advocate that penalties on employers for unfair labor practices be substantially increased and the time taken for representation elections be reduced to no more than 15 days (from an average of 6–8 weeks).

Their second recommended change is to strengthen the voice/response face of unions, thus increasing their positive contribution to firms and society. They do not detail how this should be accomplished, however, other than to suggest that experiments aimed at fostering greater labor-management cooperation in unionized firms should be encouraged and expanded.

Their third recommendation is to weaken the monopoly face of unions, thus reducing the negative effects of unions on firms and society. The principal policy they propose toward this end is promoting greater competition in product markets (thus making it more difficult for unions to raise wages) and avoiding trade barriers that protect high-cost (possibly unionized) firms. They also counsel union leaders to give greater recognition to the negative trade-off between wages and employment and thus (p. 250) "use their economic power more judiciously."

What Do Unions Do? ends with this summation (p. 251):

> All told, if our research findings are correct, the ongoing decline in private sector unionism — a development unique to the United States among developed countries — deserves serious public attention as being socially undesirable. We believe the time has come for the nation to reassess its implicit and explicit policies toward unionism, such as it has done several times in the past. And we hope that such a reassessment would lead to a new public posture toward the key worker institution under capitalism — a posture based on what unions actually do in the society and on what, under the best circumstances, they can do to improve the well-being of the free enterprise system, and of all of us.

V. The Volume: Purpose and Plan

When *What Do Unions Do?* was published two decades ago, it deservedly received great attention and commentary in both academic and public circles. Not only did the book provide the most comprehensive quantitative portrait available of the impact of trade unionism on the economy and society, but it also put forward a new conceptual framework for thinking about these issues. Also noteworthy was the fact F&M went against the current of prevailing thinking — certainly in the economics profession — and concluded that on net unionism serves the social interest and the nation should restructure labor law to promote it.

Twenty years have now passed. The book continues to be frequently cited. And one of its authors, Richard Freeman, continues to produce a steady stream of research on trade unions and worker voice that amplifies and extends the pioneering work in *What Do Unions Do?* In other respects, however, the situation has changed in some striking ways.

A major development is the remarkable outpouring of additional theoretical and empirical research on unionism since *What Do Unions Do?* In part stimulated by F&M's research, and in part made possible by new research methods and data sets, economists and other social scientists have produced over the last two decades hundreds of new books and journal articles that extend our knowledge on unions and their impact on workers, firms, and labor markets. A portion of this new literature extends and develops theoretical models of unions, including the exit/voice model of F&M, while an even larger part pushes forward the empirical exploration of the full range of union effects. The latter covers not only the wage effect of unions, long an object of economic research, but also the numerous other dimensions popularized by F&M.

Given this new literature, an obvious and, we think, critical question waits to be answered: As a positive account of what unions do, how well does F&M's book hold up in light of subsequent research and experience? In particular, did they capture the important economic and social effects of unions? Also, does their conclusion that unionism is a net plus on both the economic and social balance sheets still bear the weight of evidence 20 years later? One purpose of this book is to subject these questions to detailed, in-depth investigation by leading experts in the field.

A second striking development that has taken place over the two decades since the publication of *What Do Unions Do?* is the continued downward trend in union density in the United States. From 1900 to mid-century union density slowly and irregularly moved on an upward trend, starting at 7 percent in 1900 and reaching a peak of 33 percent in 1953. Since then density has retraced much of its path, moving steadily downward decade-to-decade until in 2005 it stood at 12 percent. More remarkable is the path of union density in the private sector. Private sector density peaked in the United States in the early 1950s at 36 percent and then fell steadily and sharply until in 2005 it stood at only 8 percent — very close to the overall level of union density in 1900! Much the opposite trend occurred in the public sector, by way of contrast. Public sector density rose more than threefold between 1960 and 1980, and then remained in the 35-to-40 percent range from the mid–1980s to the present time.

Writing in the early 1980s, F&M concluded that the actual level of union density was below the socially optimal level. They therefore advocated a change in national labor policy to encourage greater unionization. In a more recent book, Freeman and Rodgers (1999) advance the same proposition. Based on a nationwide survey done for the Clinton-appointed Commission for the Future of Worker-Management Relations, they conclude that roughly three times as many workers (about 45 percent) want union representation as currently have it. The shortfall in union representation is, in turn, only one dimension of a larger and more general undersupply of voice and representation at the workplace. According to Freeman and Rogers (F&R), over 50 percent of American workers report they have less influence at work than they desire — a shortfall they call a "representation/participation gap." Paralleling the conclusions of *What Do Unions Do?*, F&R also find that the single most important reason for the gap in voice and influence at work is management resistance, particularly when workers' desire for more voice takes the form of union representation. With regard to the latter point, for example, F&R state (p. 89), "the main reason these [unorganized] workers are not unionized is that the managements of their firms do not want them to be represented by a union." They conclude, therefore, that outmoded American labor law needs to be revised to provide more of all types of employee voice at work, including a substantial increase in union representation. As they state in the book's last sentence (p. 155), "the right choice for private action and public policy would be to help workers gain the voice and representation in workplace decisions that they so clearly want."

Certainly the presumption would have to be that if the level of union density when *What Do Unions Do?* was published in 1984 was significantly below the socially optimal level, then today the shortfall must be that much greater, given the trends outlined above. The flip side of this argument is that the case for reform of the nation's labor law to promote more unionization (and other forms of worker voice) is presumably even more compelling than when F&M advanced it two decades ago. These considerations directly lead to the second major question that motivates this book: Does the weight of the evidence support F&M's contention that the economic and social interests of the nation would be advanced by greater unionization? More particularly, in light of all the research evidence accumulated to date, can it be reasonably concluded that unions on net enhance economic efficiency, as F&M claim? If the scope of analysis is broadened to include social goals beyond efficiency, does the evidence then show unionism to be a net plus? Finally, is it possible or desirable to simultaneously accomplish an overall increase in union density, a reduction in the monopoly power of unions, and expansion of the voice face of unions, as F&M advocate?

This volume contains nineteen additional chapters, written by some of the field's most recognized and respected scholars, that together seek to answer these questions. The book is at once a twentieth anniversary tribute to Freeman and Medoff's pioneering book *What Do Unions Do?*, an in-depth and comprehensive reexamination and reassessment of the theoretical and empirical arguments advanced in *What Do Unions Do?*, and a more wide-ranging state-of-the-art review of the research literature on trade unions. In the latter respect this volume complements two other comprehensive reviews of trade unions edited by Addison and Schnabel (2003) and Fernie and Metcalf (2005).

Several features of this book deserve brief mention. First, the emphasis is on the economic features and impacts of trade unions, as evidenced by the economic orientation of many of the chapter topics and the large representation of economists among the authors. But we also endeavor to round out the volume with topics and authors representing other dimensions of the trade union experience, such as management, industrial relations, law, and politics. Likewise, several of the topics in this symposium were only briefly examined by F&M in *What Do Unions Do?*, but for sake of inclusiveness and comprehensiveness we have given them more emphasis here.

Another way we have tried to broaden the volume is by including a significant international component. *What Do Unions Do?* is written almost exclusively from the vantage point of the American system of collective bargaining and labor law. In later writings, however, Freeman and co-authors have extended the analysis in various respects to other countries. We have attempted to go even further in this direction, believing that the experiences of other countries yield additional valuable "data points" that can help identify the causes and consequences of trade unionism. Also, the union decline that began in America in the mid–1950s has spread in more recent years to many other industrial countries, making the social welfare and public policy issues raised in *What Do Unions Do?* of greater relevance to an international audience. Thus, we have asked the authors to incorporate, where possible, international evidence into their analyses. A separate paper on the international dimension of unions is also included. We note, however, that the symposium does not pretend to cover the entire international experience with regard to unions, and includes evidence drawn largely from countries where trade unions and collective bargaining are well institutionalized and used principally to win workplace-centered concessions from employers.

Also distinctive is our effort to promote balance, fairness, and multiple viewpoints in this symposium. The fact that we publish this symposium in honor of the twentieth anniversary of *What Do Unions Do?* reflects our judgment that the book is a pioneering scholarly achievement. We do not publish this symposium, however, to either promote or criticize the point of view taken by F&M; our only goal is to advance the state of knowledge about labor unions and better inform public policy debates on the benefits and costs of unionism. With this objective in mind, we have chosen authors who have a reputation for high-quality, nonpartisan scholarship. Some have taken positions in past research that support F&M, while others have taken the opposite side. The mandate given to everyone was to be scrupulously fair and balanced. To further promote fairness and balance, we have also deliberately broadened the discussion to include both economic and noneconomic effects of unions, recognizing that while concerns with economic efficiency are of great importance so too are other considerations, such as social justice and democracy in industry. Finally, another element of balance is achieved by including chapters written, respectively, by a representative of management and organized labor.

A few words should also be said about the structure of the symposium. Chapters 2–16 are devoted to individual topics related to trade unionism and its effects, such as wage differentials, fringe benefits, macroeconomic performance, and dispute resolution. (A chapter on workers' rights and workplace democracy was commissioned but not completed.) The next four chapters (17–20) then provide a synthesis and summation. Each author, using the preceding papers as input, builds a composite portrait of "what unions do" and contrasts and compares this portrait with the one developed by F&M. These four papers also reconsider the economic and social case advanced by F&M in favor of greater unionization and the public policy measures they propose to achieve this.

One of these four summary chapters is authored by Richard Freeman. It provides him an opportunity to review and critique all the preceding chapters and to offer his own assessment of how the evidence and arguments presented in *What Do Unions Do?* looks from today's vantage point. Freeman writes this chapter representing both the joint work done with Medoff, as well as the numerous other studies on unions he has published individually or with other co-authors. Although *What Do Unions Do?* is the focal point of the chapters in this volume, Freeman's other union-related research is also woven into various chapters, partly for purposes of inclusiveness and partly because his views and positions have in certain respects evolved over time since *What Do Unions Do?* was published 20 years ago.

References

Addison, John and Claus Schnabel. *International Handbook of Trade Unions*. Cheltenham, U.K.: Edward Elgar, 2003.

Fernie, Sue and David Metcalf. *British Unions: Resurgence or Perdition?* London: Routledge, 2005.

Freeman, Richard. "Is Declining Unionization of the U.S. Good, Bad, or Irrelevant?" In Lawrence Mishel and Paula Voos, eds. *Unions and Economic Competitiveness*. Armonk, N.Y.: M.E. Sharpe, 1992, pp. 143–72.

_____ and James Medoff. *What Do Unions Do?* New York: Basic Books, 1984.

Freeman, Richard and Joel Rogers. *What Workers Want*. Ithaca, N.Y.: Cornell University Press, 1999.

Hirschman, Albert. *Exit, Voice, and Loyalty: Responses to Decline in Firms, Organizations, and States*. Cambridge: Harvard University Press, 1970.

2

What Unions Do:
Insights from Economic Theory

Bruce E. Kaufman

I. Introduction

At the end of *What Do Unions Do?*, Freeman and Medoff (F&M 1984, p. 247) conclude that "unionism on net probably raises social efficiency" and (p. 250) "recent trends have brought the level of union density below the optimal level." For these reasons, they advocate revision in the nation's labor laws in order to foster greater unionization in the American economy.

These conclusions are controversial and, it seems fair to say, go against the mainstream of opinion among economists. In making their case, F&M appeal to both theory and empirical evidence. The empirical evidence is examined in considerable detail in other chapters in this book; my purpose in this chapter is to introduce the theory side of the subject. Other authors will, however, also consider theory, albeit more selectively. To proceed, I first review the theoretical literature on what F&M call the "monopoly face" of unions. The emphasis is on basic models and their implications for the effect of unions on key economic and social outcomes. The same is then done for the voice/response face of unions. I endeavor to present a neutral, straightforward account of the different theoretical perspectives and issues in debate, reserving until my concluding chapter an assessment and commentary.

My focus is on the modern, microeconomics-based theory of unions. Naturally, this perspective emphasizes the economic function and effects of unions over the noneconomic, particularly since the issue of efficiency occupies center stage in modern economics. An alternative, more historical and heterodox perspective is provided in the next chapter.

II. The Monopoly Face of Unions

F&M claim that most economists view unions as akin to a labor market monopoly. The first question that may be asked is whether this characterization is indeed accurate.

Among mainstream economists, and speaking at a broad level of generality, the answer is probably "Yes." In the *Theory of Wages*, Hicks (1932, p. 137) states that "monopolistic combination is common enough in all parts of the economic system; very much the same motives which drive business men to form rings and cartels drive their employees to form unions." A similar point of view is expressed by Friedman (1951, p. 206): "From this strictly economic point of view, labor unions and enterprise monopolies are conceptually similar if not identical phenomena and have similar effects." He then says (p. 239), "It seems to me like all other monopolies labor monopolies are undesirable. This goes back to my belief in a competitive society." More recently, Hirsch and Addison observe (1986, p. 21), "The monopolistic view of unionism, firmly held by most economists, begins with the presumption that unions raise wage rates above competitive levels in the union sector," leading to the prediction that (p. 22), "Society suffers net welfare losses from unionism owing to the resulting inefficient factor mix and the misallocation of resources between the union and nonunion sectors." In a similar vein Booth (1995, p. 51) remarks, "The standard view of trade unions is that they are organizations whose purpose is to improve the material welfare of members, principally by raising wages above the competitive wage level. There is little dispute that unions are frequently able to push wages above the competitive level — what is called the 'monopoly' role of trade unions. . . . In a competitive framework the trade union does introduce into the economy a variety of distortions and inefficiencies."

When economists talk about the monopoly face of unions, they typically have a standard, simplified model in mind as the baseline of comparison (Oswald, 1985; Farber, 1986; Addison and Chilton, 1997), which I show in Figure 2.1, Panel A. Shown there is a competitive labor market, with an equilibrium wage of W_0 and employment of L_0 determined by the market labor demand and supply curves. Now introduce a union into this industry and assume that it successfully organizes all the firms. The union gains market power through its control of the supply of labor to the firms, either through the strike threat or apprenticeship programs and union security provisions (e.g., a closed shop), and uses this power to raise the wage above the competitive level. In this model, it is assumed that the goal of the union is to maximize utility of the membership, and utility is a function of the wage rate and level of employment. This assumption yields union indifference curves, such as I_1. Assuming the union has the bargaining power to obtain its preferred outcome, the optimal wage is W_2 where the indifference curve I_1 is tangent to the labor demand curve. The firm then chooses the employment level L_2.

The market power of the union provides its employed members a wage gain of W_2-W_0. They presumably would report a higher level of satisfaction with their jobs. Employment in the unionized industry in the short run falls to L_2, however, and industry output contracts. In the long run, capital is variable, and the labor demand curve becomes more elastic, leading to a further decline in employment. The costs of production for unionized firms increase and, despite a rise in the market price of the product and a possible long-run increase in productivity (as unionized firms substitute capital for labor), the firms' prof-

Figure 2.1
The Union Effect on Wages and Employment

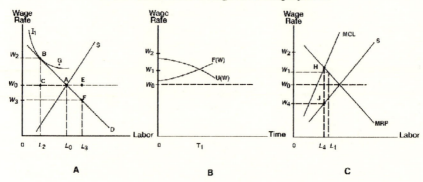

its shrink. If firms were just earning a competitive return on capital before unionization, the higher costs and lower profits drive some out of business. An incentive also opens up for nonunion firms to enter this industry, since they can earn above-normal profit given the higher product price in the market and their lower cost structure.

There are yet other implications. At the wage of W_2, the market supply curve (S) shows L_3 workers want union jobs, creating an excess supply of labor of L_3-L_2. These workers may queue for union jobs, remaining unemployed until a vacancy opens, or migrate to the nonunion sector and search for jobs there. In the case of the latter, the supply of labor in the nonunion sector (assumed for simplicity to have identical labor demand and supply curves) increases, putting downward pressure on the nonunion wage. If the nonunion wage is flexible, it declines to (say) W_3, leading to an expansion in nonunion employment and an expansion of output in that sector. Although nonunion workers suffer reduced wages (W_0-W_3), nonunion firms earn higher profits, temporarily at least. Assuming workers in the two industries are identical except for union status, the introduction of unionism leads to greater income inequality among production workers — before unionization all were paid W_0, after unionization one group gets W_2 while the other gets W_3. Aggregate income inequality may decline, however, if owners of capital originally received much higher incomes than owners of labor and the effect of unionization is to much reduce the former. [Wage inequality also declines if unions standardize wages across firms. In the simple version of the competitive model, however, all firms pay W_0, making this a moot issue.]

Rent-Seeking and the Incidence of the Union Tax

These conclusions lead most economists to take a dim view of unionism and collective bargaining, at least in its economic function. Seen from this perspective, unions are rent-seeking institutions that use monopoly power to transfer economic "surplus" (rents) from other economic agents to union members. This point of view is well captured in Hicks' observation (1932, p. 137), "where it is possible for men to snatch gains, real or apparent, permanent or temporary, from the abandonment of individual action, it would be surprising if they did not sometimes attempt it." In Panel A, one measure of the amount of rent transferred (or "snatched") by the union is the difference in the wage bill before and after unionization — the difference between areas W_0AL_00 and W_2BL_20. It is in principle no different than the income transferred from oil-consuming to oil-producing counties by the OPEC cartel when it uses its market power to restrict oil production and increase the price.

The union wage gain can be thought of as a union-imposed tax on employers, nonunion workers, and consumers. The degree to which unions can transfer rents thus raises issues quite similar to those addressed in the public finance literature on the incidence of a tax (Bronfenbrenner, 1971; Bennett and DiLorenzo, 1984). In general, a tax will raise more revenue the more inelastic (less price sensitive) is the demand for the good being taxed and the less opportunity economic agents have to evade it. Many aspects of union behavior are directly interpretable in this light.

One crucial ingredient for union success is an inelastic demand for labor. The more inelastic is the labor demand curve, the smaller is the loss in employment for any given union wage increase and the greater is the increase in the wage bill for union labor. Indeed, if the labor demand curve were elastic a higher union wage would actually reduce the wage bill — an unattractive result for union members.

Factors contributing to an inelastic labor demand curve are highlighted by the Marshall-Hicks laws of derived demand (Rees, 1989). These laws state that labor demand will be more inelastic: (1) the more inelastic is the product demand curve, (2) the more difficult is substitution in production between union labor and capital or nonunion labor (i.e., the lower is the elasticity of substitution), (3) the smaller the share of union labor cost to total cost (this condition is reversed if the elasticity of substitution is greater than the elasticity of the product demand curve), and (4) the less elastic the supply of other competing factors of production.

It is usually argued that the likelihood of unionization and the potential gains from organization increase as these laws individually and collectively are more fully met (Ulman, 1955; Hirsch and Addison, 1986). These laws also influence who pays the union tax. Consider condition 1, for example. The firm's demand for labor is derived from the consumers' demand for the product and, hence, the less price sensitive is product demand the less wage sensitive is labor demand. Thus, when substitution possibilities for the final product are small, unionized firms are better able to pass to consumers the cost of union wages through higher product prices, given the modest decline in unit sales. One implication is that unions have greater ability to raise wages when they organize all firms in the product market, since the market product demand curve is more inelastic than the product demand curve for any one firm. A second is that union wage gains are also potentially greater among imperfectly competitive firms (e.g., oligopolies and monopolies) since their product demand curves are also more inelastic than those of competitive firms. The same may also apply to public sector organizations.

Condition 2 augments the ability of unions to raise wages and transfer rents by making it more difficult for the firm to replace union workers with nonunion workers in the short run and capital in the long run. The former can be accomplished by various contract restrictions, such as union security provisions mandating a union (or closed) shop, and picketing and threats of violence that deter nonunion workers from taking the jobs of strikers; the latter may be an inherent feature of the production technology or arise from union work rules that restrict the introduction of new technology or mandate a minimum crew size or employment of a particular craft or occupation. Condition 3 facilitates union wage gains because a rise in wages leads to only a small increase in total production cost, thus having only a small negative effect on profits, prices, and product demand. This condition ordinarily favors craft unions over industrial unions, since the former typically represent only one trade or occupation in a plant or company while the latter represent all production workers. Condition 4 also limits the substitution of nonunion labor or capital for union workers, given that an increase in demand for the substitute factor drives up its price and makes it no longer as economically attractive to replace the union labor.

Unions' activities in the political process at the federal, state, and local levels are also interpretable in this economic framework (Johnson, 1989; Delaney and Schwochau, 1993). Union lobbying for import restrictions and defeat of free-trade legislation, for example, are attempts to limit the substitution possibilities of consumers in the product market and firms in the labor market, thus making the demand curve for union labor more inelastic than otherwise. Likewise, restrictive immigration and minimum wage laws reduce the competitive threat of lower cost nonunion labor. In the public sector, unions use their political power to limit substitution possibilities in other ways, such as leading opposition to privatization of public services.

Costs of Unionization

From a monopoly perspective, not only does union rent-seeking appear to lack a compelling public interest rationale, it also imposes a variety of economic costs. These costs were touched on earlier but deserve a more detailed examination. Four major areas of cost are considered.

Allocative Inefficiency. A fundamental insight of microeconomic theory is that competitively determined relative prices lead to an efficient allocation of resources across firms and industries. Efficient resource allocation is a virtue because it is Pareto optimal — e.g., it is impossible to reallocate resources so as to make at least one economic agent better off without simultaneously making another worse off. When unionism is introduced into an otherwise competitive economy, it distorts relative prices, leads to a misallocation of resources, and thus creates inefficiency and a social welfare loss.

For example, economy-wide allocative efficiency requires that units of an identical input be allocated in such a way that the marginal products are equalized across firms and industries. Thus, if the cost of labor is the same in two industries but its marginal product is higher in one, a net gain in output and social welfare could be achieved by redistributing labor from the industry with a low marginal product to the one with a high marginal product. The virtue of wage/employment determination in a competitive market is that market forces bring about exactly this distribution of labor, while a cost of collective bargaining is that it leads to "too little" employment in the unionized sector and "too much" employment in the nonunion sector. The resulting welfare loss is shown in Panel A of Figure 2.1. [Assume the diagram represents the marginal product schedule for two separate but identical industries, one union and one nonunion.] It has two components — a deadweight loss in the unionized industry denoted by the triangle ABC (the value of foregone output above its opportunity cost), and a deadweight loss in the nonunion industry equal to the triangle AEF (the excess of opportunity cost over the value of additional output). Empirical studies provide varying estimates of the size of the union-induced welfare loss, generally in the range of 0.1–0.3 percent of GDP but as high as 0.8 percent (Hirsch and Addison, 1986; Vedder and Galloway, 2002).

A second form of allocative inefficiency arises in the long run. Not only will the higher union wage cause unionized firms to reduce employment and output but it will also induce them to substitute capital for labor. Inefficiency caused by too little labor in the unionized sector is thus exacerbated by too much capital (in relative terms) in the long run. Perhaps, however, the amount of capital employed in the unionized industry may decline in absolute terms if the scale effect (the decline in desired capital as output falls in the unionized industry) dominates the substitution effect (the shift from labor to capital in producing a given level of output). Whatever the case, allocative inefficiency results.

Technical Inefficiency. An economy is technically efficient when the maximum possible output is being produced from a given combination of inputs. Orthodox microeconomics assumes that the forces of competition motivate employers to operate firms with technical efficiency. Technical efficiency implies, in turn, cost minimization and absence of organizational slack.

From a monopoly perspective, unions interfere with the efficient operation of firms, thus contributing to technical inefficiency. Critics of unions cite a long list of restrictive rules and practices that raise cost and retard productivity (Reynolds, 1984; Northrup, 1997). Examples include featherbedding (make-work) requirements, narrow job classifications that split up job tasks among a number of trades or occupations, restrictions on management's ability to promote workers on the basis of merit or to discipline/terminate low-performing workers, and a "work to the contract" attitude toward job performance. The motive of unions in bargaining for these things is partly to restrict employers from shifting higher union wage costs back on to union workers through work intensification ("speed ups") or replacement with lower cost nonunion workers; another part is to gain new benefits for workers, such as improved job security. From an economic perspective, however, these restrictive union practices are again a form of rent-seeking that entail substantial costs in terms of inefficient use of scarce resources. According to one knowledgeable observer (Rees, 1963), the social cost unions create from technical inefficiency may well be two-to-three times as large as those arising from allocative inefficiency.

Reduced Capital Investment and Higher Firm Deaths. It was noted above, in discussing allocative inefficiency, that in response to a higher union wage firms may increase or decrease the amount of capital used in production. The cost in this case comes from an inappropriate mix of labor and capital. But when additional considerations are taken into account, theory suggests that it is quite likely that unionized firms will decrease investment spending on long-lived capital projects and research and development (R&D). The cost of unions in this case is not a static form of inefficiency but a dynamic one and takes the form of reduced productivity growth and innovation. It is also possible that unionism leads to earlier "deaths" (closures) of plants and firms (Freeman and Kleiner, 1999).

The key point is that a higher union wage not only raises the relative price of labor, but it also acts as a tax on capital (Hirsch, 1991). To the extent that firms cannot pass on higher union wage costs to consumers, they must finance them from profits, thus reducing the net return on the firm's invested capital. Faced with a lower return on investment, unionized firms are likely to reduce capital spending, or redirect capital spending from unionized plants (or divisions) to nonunion plants — possibly in another country. The same reasoning applies to investment in R&D.

Since reduced capital spending and R&D means lower output and employment in the future, unions have an incentive to pledge to firms in return for undertaking new capital investment that they will restrain their wage demands and cooperate in improving production efficiency. Firms fear, however, that once they invest in long-lived capital a union will renege and use its bargaining power to extract not only profits but also quasi-rents (revenue above average variable cost), knowing that in the short run as long as the firm can at least cover variable costs it will continue in operation (Grout, 1984; Lawrence and Lawrence, 1985). Thus, rather than have future capital investments held hostage or "milked" by a union, firms forego at least a portion of investment spending, particularly on projects that are highly immobile or have very long payback periods. Union milking of capital is also likely to lead to earlier shutdown of organized firms and plants because they underinvest in maintenance and new equipment or find in cyclical economic downturns that revenue no longer covers operating costs.

Inflationary Bias and Greater Cyclical Instability. The areas of union cost considered so far are microeconomic in nature; the next is macroeconomic. Two aspects are identifiable.

The first is that the monopoly face of unions may impart an inflationary bias or "price creep" to the economy (Mitchell, 1980; Hirsch and Addison, 1986). [The degree of centralization in the bargaining structure is an important intervening variable, however (Naylor, 2003).] Unionization of an industry, such as assumed in Figure 2.1, leads to a one-time rise in the price level, assuming the increase in wages (from W_0 to W_2) is not offset by an increase in productivity. Other things equal, the union wage should then remain stable at W_2 and, for a given level of unionization, the price level is also stable. But other things may not stay equal. One possibility is that the union demands a higher wage in each subsequent bargaining round, thus moving firms gradually up their labor demand curves and causing them to match higher wages with higher prices. This result is not consistent with the simplest monopoly model of unions (per the dictum that "monopoly causes high prices but not rising prices"), but an alternative median voter model of unions (discussed shortly) predicts this form of upward ratchet in prices. A similar result can emerge from models of inter-union rivalry and wage imitation (Ross, 1948; Budd, 1997).

A second possibility is the unions and other special interest groups lobby government officials to use expansionary monetary and fiscal policies to create jobs for the L_3–L_2 people who are (potentially) unemployed at the union wage of W_2. If these policies are implemented, the rightward shift of the aggregate demand curve and increase in national production and employment will likely lead to some increase in the price level (moving along an upward sloping aggregate supply curve). Furthermore, the expansion of employment in the unionized industry shifts out the labor demand curve and, under reasonable assumptions, leads to a new and higher equilibrium union wage (not shown in Panel A, Figure 2.1, but above W_2).

The second form of macroeconomic cost is that unions may exacerbate the cyclical instability of the macroeconomy or lengthen periods of boom and recession (Mitchell, 1980; Neumark, 1993). Union wages are less flexible than market-determined wages because they are typically specified in multi-year contracts. During a cyclical boom, nonunion wages rise under the pressure of increased labor demand, thus helping maintain a balance between supply and demand. Union wage rates, however, are more rigid and thus cannot rise as quickly. Not only does the rigidity of union wages interfere with self-correcting processes in the economy (thus exacerbating instability), policymakers can misread the stability in wages as a sign that there is still more room for fiscal/monetary stimulation. The opposite chain of events happens in recessions, potentially exacerbating downturns. Unions can also make it more difficult for fiscal and monetary policy to end a boom or recession since multi-year contracts impart considerable inertia into union wages and make them more impervious to aggregate demand conditions.

III. Extensions and Qualifications

Although the monopoly model of unions sketched above provides the baseline framework for analyzing the economic effects of unions, it is highly stylized and simplified. To provide a more complete picture, therefore, extensions and qualifications must be introduced. Some of the most important are briefly described below; note, however, that the voice/response function of unions is reserved for separate treatment. In some cases these extensions and qualifications to the monopoly model strengthen the negative picture of unions, while in other cases they lead to a more positive assessment.

Endogenous Union Membership

The simplest version of the monopoly model treats union formation and the level of union membership as exogenous variables. Initially, a labor market has no union; then, without explaining why or how, the workers are assumed to unionize and the economic effects are examined. A more realistic model, however, makes union formation and union membership endogenous.

One approach is to look at union membership (or a union card) as an asset that workers purchase for price P per time period and then hold in order to gain the net benefits that accrue from the services unions provide (Pencavel, 1971). The decision to join a union and the level of union membership can then be modeled as the outcome of a demand/supply process — workers demand union services and unions supply the services (Hirsch and Addison, 1986; Farber and Krueger, 1993). The price of union services is the membership dues and fees workers pay to unions to finance their operations. Other things equal, the larger is workers' demand for unions or the greater the supply of union services, the larger will be observed union membership.

Workers' demand for union services can be modeled as a function of a standard set of variables: own price, price of related goods, net benefit of union services, income, and tastes. Variation in own price (dues) causes movements along a union services demand curve, changes in the other variables cause a shift in the curve. The latter are most important in explaining the level and change over time in union membership.

Perhaps most significant in this regard is the net benefit that workers gain from union membership. One such benefit is a higher union wage, and the usual assumption is that the greater the union-nonunion wage differential the greater workers' demand for union membership (Farber, 1983). This consideration also points out, however, that the relevant variable in the demand function is the *net* benefits of union membership, since higher wages also brings with it potential offsetting costs, such as threat of job loss. Obviously, the more elastic the labor demand curve the greater the threat of job loss and hence the less attractive is unionization.

Job loss, either threatened or real, can also arise from coercive actions undertaken by employers to forestall union formation. In this respect the size of the union-nonunion wage differential has a two-sided effect on the net benefits of union services and workers' demand for unions (Freeman and Kleiner, 1990). On one hand, a larger wage differential increases the benefits of union services and draws workers to unions; on the other it causes employers to resist unions more strongly and undertake actions, such as firing union supporters and closing plants, that reduce the net benefits of unionization. The extent of legal protection and encouragement given to union organizing thus has an important influence on the strength of union demand.

Other factors also influence net benefits. One consideration is demographic characteristics of workers, such as race, gender, age, and education/skills. Workers who suffer discrimination or low pay in labor markets, for example, may well gain more from a union and potentially have a larger demand; while the wage-leveling policies of unions may be unattractive to workers in the top tier of a firm's wage distribution, such as those with advanced degrees or unique talents.

The next important variable in the union demand function is the price (or availability) of related goods. Most important in this regard are substitute goods for unions. Three such unions substitutes are "good markets," "good management," and "good laws" (Bennett and Kaufman, 2002). One reason the monopoly model leads to a relatively negative view of unions is that most often it is built on the assumption that labor markets are competitive. This assumption is double-edged: it suggests, first, that the terms and conditions of employment are already well-adjusted (or "optimal" in an efficiency sense) in light of relative prices and factor supplies/productivities and, second, that workers who have a legitimate dissatisfaction or grievance have a readily available and low (zero) cost means to solve the problem — quit and find a job elsewhere. Competitive markets are thus a good substitute for union services, except in the area of rent-seeking. Where labor markets are less than perfectly competitive, well-adjusted terms and conditions of employment, and corrections to any departures therefrom, can also potentially be obtained from two other union substitutes — professional management and a well-run corporate human resource function and various laws and regulations, such as protective labor legislation, social insurance programs, and income redistribution programs that favor workers. Thus, the more readily available and lower cost are union substitutes the smaller the demand for unions, other things equal.

Two other demand-shift variables are income and tastes. Whether union membership is a normal or inferior good is not well established either theoretically or empirically, so not much can be said. The taste variable reflects individual preferences for union membership, as well as the effect of broader social and cultural factors. Demand for unions, for example, would most likely be stronger in a community with a strong working-class culture but weaker where people have a strong ethos of individualism.

Variations in demand curves for union services thus explains, in part, the extent of trade unionism. The supply side of union services also deserves brief mention, however, for demand by itself will not yield collective bargaining — unions have to be willing and able to provide this service at a reasonable cost. Thus, the supply curve of union services will lie further to the right, other things equal, the larger are bargaining units (providing economies of scale in servicing members), the greater the proportion of dues-paying members in a bargaining unit (e.g., such as union or closed shop, thus eliminating free riders), and the greater the legal protection given to picketing, strikes, and other forms of union pressure (Farber, 1984; Taras and Ponak, 2002).

In most markets economists presume that price adjusts to equilibrate demand and supply. In the market for union services, however, it is likely that disequilibrium prevails. The price of union services — monthly dues— is not flexible and thus cannot clear the market. Equally important, union services are in part a collective good. That is, an individual worker may have a demand for unionism but cannot gain union representation unless a majority of workmates also have a demand for unions. Furthermore, in countries with a Wagner Act model of union recognition, the majority of workers must be willing to express this desire through a formal organizing campaign and election, running the risk of employer retaliation. Many workers, therefore, may have a frustrated demand for unionism (Farber and Krueger, 1993; Freeman and Rodgers, 1999).

The Union's Objective Function

A second aspect of the monopoly model that requires extension and qualification concerns the specification of the union's objective function. This issue is relevant because the objective function specifies the union's goals in collective bargaining — a critical assumption in any effort to predict what unions do.

Analytically, profit maximization is a relatively straightforward objective for a firm. This assumption follows from two facts: first, making a profit is the unambiguous goal of firms in a capitalist economy and, second, everyone who owns part of a firm — whether a sole proprietor, a partner, or individual shareholder — gains when profit increases, thus making each person's goal consistent with the organization's goal.

A union's objective is far more difficult to specify (Pencavel, 1991; Kaufman, 2002). A union does not own the labor it sells but, rather, sets a common price that individual workers and the firm agree to honor. In this respect a union is more like a cartel of independent producers who band together to achieve a monopoly-like outcome. Furthermore, while firms are interested in profit, workers are interested in the full range of terms and conditions of employment, including not only wages but also benefits, job security, working conditions, and style of management. Collapsing all of these disparate items into a meaningful dollars and cents maximand is very difficult, so the only recourse is to either focus on one or two variables at the expense of the others or assume the union's goal is the general (and unobservable) one of maximizing "utility," where utility is a function of all the terms and conditions of employment. Finally, unlike a firm's shareholders, individual union members do not usually share equally in the "profits" (rents) gained from collective bargaining — as the union raises the wage some members gain more income but others lose their jobs and are worse off — and thus it is generally impossible to derive an aggregate union objective function from the diverse and partially conflicting objective functions of the individual members.

No ideal solution has yet been found to these problems. In practice, the theoretical literature goes in two directions (Oswald, 1985; Flanagan, 1993). One is to use the general utility function approach, such as depicted in Panel A and finesse the collective choice (aggregation) problem through simplifying assumptions (e.g., that layoff is by random draw). The second is to develop an explicit collective-choice mechanism that explains how the diverse preferences of the individual union members are aggregated and reconciled to yield a well-defined bargaining goal for the union. Insider-outsider, property rights, and median voter models are among this genre, with the latter most widely used (Martin, 1980; Bennett and Johnson, 1980; Hirsch and Addison, 1986; Kaufman, 2002).

The median voter model assumes that the union's bargaining goals are chosen by the union leader(s). To keep the model tractable, it is often assumed that the only variable on the bargaining table is wages. Once the wage rate is chosen, the firm uses the labor demand curve to determine the level of employment. The union leader's goal is to gain re-election, and to do this he or she must win in negotiations a wage rate favored by a majority of the members. The smallest majority possible is 50 percent plus one of the membership. To make the outcome interesting, it is further assumed that the union members differ in their probability of layoff, say due to seniority provisions (last in, first out). The result gives rise to a well-ordered distribution of union members ranked by their most preferred wage rate — the least senior member prefers the competitive wage since at any higher wage he or she loses the job, the median (middle) member in the seniority queue prefers the wage be raised just up to the point on the demand curve where he or she is threatened with layoff, and the most senior member prefers a yet higher wage on the demand curve until he or she is also threatened with layoff. The most preferred wage demands of the other union members can be determined in similar fashion. Given this, it can be shown that the union leader will adopt the median member's preferred wage as the union's bargaining goal. The reason is that any lower wage will be opposed by the median member and everyone of higher seniority, thus leading to the union leader's electoral defeat, while the same happens (but for opposite reasons) if the leader chooses a higher wage.

The median voter model has several important implications for understanding union behavior. First, it introduces into the monopoly model the important piece of realism that unions are, at least within broad parameters, democratic organizations. Whether "democratic" rent-seeking is any less objectionable on economic efficiency grounds is uncertain, but from a social/ethical perspective the democratic nature of unions undoubtedly frees them from some of the negative stigma imparted by the monopoly/cartel image.

A second implication is that unions not only redistribute income from consumers, firms, and nonunion workers to union members but also redistribute income among the union members themselves (Kaufman and Martinez-Vasquez, 1988; Devinatz, 2002). As the union raises wages and bargains for various benefits and work rules, some union members gain more than others; indeed, some members may be worse off, e.g., if employment declines and they lose their jobs. Union bargaining goals, therefore, always in part reflect internal political dynamics within the organization. "Make work" featherbedding rules, for example, are not likely to be a major bargaining demand of a union with expanding membership, while they may well be a major concern for a union whose members face substantial displacement by new technology. Likewise, a union is likely to reject a company's request for a wage cut unless the threat to jobs is so large that a majority of the members view a "Yes" vote as in their self-interest.

An interesting application of this insight concerns the effect of unions on firms' structure of wages and benefits. Widely noted effects of unionism are wage standardization and wage-leveling (Card, 2001). They can partly be rationalized as unions' attempt to eliminate competition based on labor cost differentials among workers and firms, or as an attempt to promote worker solidarity and internal equity. But Freeman (1980a) has argued that these policies are also likely to arise for median-voter reasons. A majority coalition in a union always has an incentive to use collective bargaining to restructure wages in their favor, in effect taxing the minority. He suggests that most likely the majority coalition will form at the lower end of the wage distribution since a larger amount of income can be redistributed. The result will be a more compressed wage structure (entry-level rates increased and maximum pay rates reduced) and a flatter age-wage profile.

Freeman (1981) also points out another predicted effect of unionism is to increase the share of benefits in total labor compensation and tilt the benefits package toward pensions and health insurance and away from bonuses. Nonunion firms structure their compensation package to attract/retain the "marginal" worker who is more likely to be younger and unmarried or married without children. If these firms are unionized, however, the union will bargain for a compensation package that reflects the preference of the median member — a person likely to be older and with a spouse and children. Freeman reasons that the marginal worker will want most compensation in the form of wages, while the median worker will have a greater demand for benefits. Likewise, the median worker will have a greater demand for certain benefits, such as pensions and health insurance, reflecting his or her greater age.

A third implication of the median voter (not considered by F&M) concerns the dynamic path of the union-nonunion wage differential. Assuming for simplicity that the union can dictate the wage outcome, in the first bargaining around the union raises the wage from the competitive level to the median voter's preferred wage (where he or she is next to be laid-off), forcing the firm up its labor demand curve and cutting employment by one-half. In the next contract period, there is a new median voter and the wage is again forced up, moving the firm further up the demand curve and again eliminating the bottom half of the seniority distribution. This upward ratchet effect (or quest for "more") continues until the union bargains itself out of existence (Burda, 1990; Kaufman, 2002).

This scenario is naïve, partly because the median voter is modeled as a myopic one-period maximizer and partly because the union is assumed to have sufficient bargaining power to attain the median voter's preferred wage in each negotiation. Building in more realistic assumptions, however, does not alter the fundamental conclusion — other things equal, a democratic union with senior-ity-based layoffs will gradually nibble its way up a firm's labor demand curve, leading to declining employment, a widening union-nonunion wage gap, and a bias toward cost-push wage inflation. These predictions led to an early debate (e.g., Shister, 1943) whether it is possible to reconcile union democracy and "responsible" union wage policy (a question still unresolved). Likewise, this model suggests one reason why unions are strong supporters of full-employ-ment macroeconomic policies; such policies shift the labor demand curve to the right and remove the threat of unemployment, thus allowing the upward union wage ratchet to continue.

A final implication of the median voter model concerns the union effect on capital investment and R&D expenditures. Hirsch (1991) argues, for example, that the decision-making horizon of most union members — particularly the senior members who may control the union's wage policy — often may be shorter than the economic life of the firm's long-lived, specialized capital equipment. This fact, combined with the inability of union members to sell or bequeath their property rights in union jobs to others (Martin, 1980), causes unions to act "rationally myopic" and raise wages to the point where firms do not earn a competitive rate of return on capital. The result is a slow process of dis-investment and industrial and union decline.

Union-Firm Bargaining

The next extension to introduce is the bargaining process between the union and firm. To this point it has been assumed that the union has sufficient power to dictate a "take it or leave it" wage outcome to the firm. In reality, wages and the other terms and conditions of employment in unionized firms are determined through a sequential-step bargaining process with the threat and occasional use of a strike.

The bargaining process is depicted in Panel B of Figure 2.1. This model originates with Hicks (1932) and has subsequently been extended and developed in a number of directions (Cross, 1969; Kaufman, 1992; Gallagher and Gramm, 1997). The vertical axis measures the wage rate, the horizontal axis measures bargaining time (e.g., days). Total time available to reach an agreement without a strike is T_1; disagreement past this point necessarily entails a strike of some duration. Without strike costs and other costs of disagreement, the firm and union have no motivation to compromise and reach an agreement. Thus, the firm's desired wage rate is the competitive wage W_0 in Panel A, while the union's preferred wage is W_2. When costs of disagreement are introduced, however, both sides have to calculate the benefits and costs of intransigence. In general, holding out for W_0 and W_2 now carries potentially large costs for the firm and union in the form of a strike and other sanctions, so immediately in the first round of bargaining they are induced to "put some money on the table" in order to move toward agreement. Thus, in Panel B the firm's initial wage offer is modestly higher than W_0 and the union's demand is modestly lower than W_2.

The two lines that originate from the vertical axis are the union's "resistance curve" $U(W)$ and the firm's "concession curve" $F(W)$ which depict the wage rates (presumed to be the only subject of bargaining) that each side offers/demands in each round of the bargaining process. The two lines gradually converge as each bargainer makes compromises — motivated in large part by the looming strike deadline. As shown in Panel B, the two bargainers reach an agreement at the strike deadline T_1. The wage rate is W_1, determined by the intersection point of the resistance and concession curves. In a world of perfect foresight, this bargaining process could be dispensed with and the two sides could immediately move to W_1 (saving themselves the costs of bargaining). Bargaining models based on Nash-type game theory essentially make this theoretical leap (Addison and Chilton, 1997; Manzini, 1998). When the bargainers have bounded rationality and imperfect/asymmetric information, however, they have to grope their way to an equilibrium, as pictured in Panel B. In some cases the parties start out with differences in their positions that are too large for them to compromise in the allotted bargaining time; in other cases one or both sides are inexperienced, maladroit, or opportunistic bargainers, and the compromise process breaks down; and yet in other cases strong emotions or commitment to principle make one party unwilling to consider compromise. Whatever the cause, a strike occurs and lasts until an agreement is reached or one of the parties exits the relationship.

Introducing bargaining into the monopoly model provides several new insights. First, it reveals that union wage policy is shaped by two fundamental constraints — the labor demand curve *and* strike costs (real and expected), rather than just the former as in the simplest monopoly model.

Second, it is evident that the union wage gain with bargaining is smaller than predicted by the simple monopoly model. In Panel A, the wage gain is W_2-W_0; in Panel B it is W_1-W_0. Bargaining thus serves to moderate the size of the union monopoly wage gain, keeping the misallocation of resources and rent transfer smaller than otherwise predicted. Moreover, when the right to strike is limited or banned, as in many public sector situations, the union wage gain is smaller yet. Bargaining's positive contribution to efficiency is counterbalanced, however, by an additional form of resource cost and inefficiency. The restraint bargaining provides on union rent-seeking is not a free good. To "produce" collective bargaining requires scarce time and factor inputs of union, firm, and government negotiators and mediators. More importantly, when coercive weapons are used, such as strikes, boycotts, and slowdowns, production is lost and resources remain idle. Although strikes in recent years have occurred in only a small proportion of union negotiations and, in general, resulted in very modest social cost, in the 1940s–1960s when union density and power was much higher so too were the incidence and cost of strikes (Gunderson and Melino, 1987; Kaufman, 1992). Finally, an intangible but real cost of collective bargaining is that it heightens or gives outlet to an adversarial, sometimes bitter "we against them" relationship between the workers and the firm.

Third, consideration of the bargaining process reveals yet another reason why the efficiency loss from unionism may be overstated by the monopoly model. A large literature on "efficient contracts" has developed showing that a union and firm have an incentive to replace the traditional noncooperative "on the demand curve" bargaining strategy with a cooperative "off the demand curve" approach, given that the latter yields wage/employment outcomes that are potentially more desirable for both sides (Booth, 1995; Addison and Chilton, 1997). Without going into details, the cooperative outcome entails moving from the monopoly (noncooperative) outcome of W_2/L_2 in Panel A to a point off the labor demand curve, such as depicted by Point G, where the wage is lower but the level of employment is higher. Point G is closer to the original competitive outcome of point A and thus less efficiency-distorting. Indeed, under certain conditions, Point G may lie directly above Point A (a vertical contract curve in the efficient bargain model), and the level of employment and output in the union and nonunion sectors remains the same as in the competitive outcome (Abowd, 1989). Since the wage rate at Point G is higher, however, unionism still redistributes rents to the workers.

Note also that the efficient bargain model leads to a more sanguine view of union work rules. An efficient contract moves the firm off its labor demand curve. As this literature demonstrates, once the contract is signed the employer has an incentive to renege on the negotiated employment level and reduce jobs, since by moving leftward from Point G back to the labor demand curve it can increase profits. To prevent (albeit imperfectly) such employer opportunism, a union can negotiate work rules, such as minimum crew sizes (Johnson, 1990). In this interpretation, union work rules are a contract-protection device that helps police a win-win agreement, rather than a productivity-sapping interference in production. Given this optimistic conclusion, a cautionary note is required. Despite superficial appeal, economists have pointed out that the efficient contract model has serious conceptual and practical difficulties that raise significant questions about its validity and relevance. Conceptually, for example, it is not apparent why the senior majority of union members would vote for a wage cut when the increase in jobs goes to unemployed low-seniority workers in the layoff pool (Kaufman, 2002). Empirically, researchers have found little evidence from collective bargaining negotiations and contracts that unions have successfully obtained employment commitments from firms that represent off-the-demand curve settlements (Oswald, 1993).

Labor and Product Market Structure

The final extension is to introduce noncompetitive product and labor market structures into the model. Both are important, the former because it provides a long-lasting source of rents for unions to transfer and the latter because union power gains social and economic legitimacy to protect the underdog and offset employer exploitation of labor (Chaison and Bigelow, 2001).

Consider first imperfect competition in product markets. If product markets are perfectly competitive, the union's ability to raise wages and other labor conditions above market levels is very limited. Ease of entry and exit into the industry means that firms in the long run only earn a competitive return on capital, leaving zero surplus for unions to capture. If unions do push up labor costs in organized firms, in the end the result is self-defeating since these firms go out of business — both because they do not earn a competitive return on capital and because lower cost nonunion rivals underprice them and capture their customers.

This conclusion is modified modestly by further qualifications. First, even in a competitive product market unions can raise wages and other labor standards to the extent they also contribute to greater productivity, since the latter offsets the former and leaves the firm's cost structure the same as nonunion rivals. Second, the "long run" may be ten or 20 years in the future when capital is very bulky and long-lived, so even if unions can only raise labor costs above competitive levels in the short run (by capturing quasi-rents or temporary excess profits) this may be attractive to workers. Third, if some firms have lower cost structures than others, say due to non-reproducible advantages such as superior management or ownership of a strategic natural resource, they are able to earn rents (above-normal profits) even in the long run which are available for union capture. And, finally, if a union can organize the entire product market, including all new entrants, it can then take labor cost out of competition and push up wage rates, moving up an inelastic industry labor demand curve with only modest employment loss. Parenthetically, for this reason employers in very competitive industries have in some cases in the past welcomed industry-wide unionization as a way to stabilize prices during depressions or as a cartelizing device to raise prices and joint surplus (Vittoz, 1987; Maloney et al., 1979).

When product markets are imperfectly competitive, prospects for successful union rent-seeking increase significantly, particularly among regulated firms and large oligopolists with above-normal profits. [A union first has to organize these firms, however, which is frequently a substantial challenge.] In imperfect competition, individual firms have market power and can set the price on their product demand curves to maximize profit. Above-normal profit is not guaranteed for an imperfectly competitive firm, but it is more likely in both the short and long run due to factors such as differentiated products, one or only a few sellers, barriers to entry, collusive price coordination, and government regulatory barriers. Imperfect competition thus helps create additional rents for unions to capture, leading to the prediction (other things equal) that the union wage effect should be greater in this sector (Rees, 1989). This prediction is also supported by the fact (already noted) that the labor demand curve of an imperfectly competitive firm is more inelastic than for a competitive firm, thus diminishing the union's worry of employment loss.

Threat of capital dis-investment and plant shutdown is also reduced to the degree the union transfers the monopoly portion of the firm's rents while leaving untouched the normal rate of profit. To the extent that imperfect competition allows firms to earn large (monopoly) profits, union rent transfer appears less objectionable (or even benign/meritorious) since it redistributes to labor some of the excessive gains or "cream" going to capital. Indeed, redistribution of monopoly rents to labor may increase efficiency in at least two ways. Rent sharing, for example, can increase (or maintain) employee morale and productivity, given that workers feel on equity grounds they deserve a "fair share" of their employer's profits (the "ability to pay" argument) and will reduce work effort and productivity if it is not forthcoming (Blanchflower et al., 1986; Levine, 1993). A second possibility is that rent-sharing, by transferring income from capital owners with a lower propensity to spend to workers with a higher propensity, strengthens aggregate demand in the macro economy and maintenance of full employment (Argyrous et al., 2003).

Next consider labor market structure. As in product markets, imperfect competition in labor markets gives companies a measure of control over price (and other terms and conditions of employment) which they can use to increase profit. Imperfect competition in labor markets arises from a variety of factors, many of which in generic form are similar to product markets: differentiated workers and jobs, one or only a few buyers of labor, barriers to worker mobility, and imperfect/asymmetric information. The key difference is that while companies use market power in product markets to *raise* price above the competitive level, they use market power in labor markets to *lower* price (the wage) below the competitive level. In the former case, consumers are "exploited" whereas in the latter case companies exploit workers, where "exploitation" in labor markets is conventionally defined to mean a wage below labor's contribution to production (marginal revenue product). The classic rationale for labor unions, in turn, is to use collective bargaining to protect the worker underdog and eliminate exploitation of labor by raising wages.

These ideas are illustrated in Figure 2.1. The exemplar of imperfect competition in product markets is monopoly and the analog in labor markets is monopsony (one buyer of labor). Panel C illustrates a monopsonistic labor market. The firm faces an upward sloping supply curve of labor (S), rather than a horizontal labor supply curve as for an individual competitive firm, because the monopsonist is the only labor buyer in the local market and, hence, can lower the wage and not lose all of its labor supply to competitors. Conversely, to acquire more labor it has to offer a higher wage, which by assumption it also has to pay to both new and old hires. These considerations give rise to a marginal cost of labor schedule (MCL) showing the increase in labor cost for every new employee. The equilibrium, profit-maximizing employment level is L_4 (where marginal revenue product, given by the MRP schedule, equals MCL) and the wage is W_4 (given by the supply curve at L_4). Instead of the competitive wage of W_0, workers receive the lower wage W_4. The amount of monopsonistic exploitation is the difference between point H and J.

The monopsony model, strictly defined, applies to a single buyer of labor. The classic form is a "one company town" where the only major employer is (say) a coal mine or textile mill; another close equivalent is a community with only one buyer of a specialized kind of labor, such as firemen. Monopsony-like conditions can arise in any employment situation, however, where the firm faces an upward sloping supply curve of labor. One example is oligopsony where there are only a few buyers of labor, such as the market for nurses in a community with only one hospital and a small number of doctors. Another is inframarginal workers who have some element of immobility or "job lock" due to seniority, firm-specific employee benefits (e.g., health insurance), or employer-specific training. Monopsony-like conditions may also arise when employers face a rising marginal cost of recruiting new employees due to worker heterogeneity and imperfect job market information (Card and Krueger, 1995; Manning, 2003). In each case the firm can pay less than competitive wages (or benefits or other conditions) and not lose most of its work force to competitors.

Several important implications regarding unionism flow from this model. First, it is evident why in a monopsony situation workers have a demand for union representation. The firm has market power and provides below-competitive wages and other conditions of employment. Collective bargaining in this context is thus a form of protection and countervailing power — it gives workers as a group additional bargaining power to confront the employer on a "level playing field" and raise wages closer to what would prevail in a truly free market. This idea is illustrated in Figure 2.1, where the wage rate W_1 determined by the bargaining process in Panel B is closer to the competitive wage W_0 in Panel C than is the monopsony wage of W_4. Thus, while collective bargaining is "monopoly-creating" in Panel A (a competitive labor market), it is "monopsony-reducing" in Panel C (Reynolds and Taft, 1956).

A second implication is that by creating a level playing field in a monopsony labor market collective bargaining can (but not necessarily will) also expand employment and improve economic efficiency — just the opposite results from the case of a competitive labor market. As a nonunion firm, the monopsonist hires L_4 workers at the wage of W_4; as a unionized firm it is forced to pay the higher wage of W_1 and, equating marginal revenue product and marginal cost of labor (no longer the MCL schedule but a horizontal line at W_1 to the supply curve S, after which it jumps to MCL), hires L_1 employees — an increase of L_1–L_4. This expansion of employment, in turn, contributes to a more efficient allocation of resources — output is increased closer to what would prevail in a competitive situation and the marginal value of extra labor (given by the MRP schedule) is brought closer to the opportunity cost of labor (given by the labor supply curve S). [Observe, however, that all of these conclusions depend on the assumption that the union's bargaining power is not so great, or repeatedly applied, that it raises the wage above Point H.]

A third noteworthy implication is that collective bargaining in a monopsony labor market may still drive plants/firms out of business in the short or long run. Just because a monopsonist pays a below-competitive wage does not mean it always makes an above-normal profit, or any profit at all (e.g., an old textile mill in a one-company town that is barely covering operating costs). Collective bargaining, by raising labor costs, may thus hasten the exit of capital. But, broadly viewed, this result is also beneficial for allocative efficiency since the resources can flow to higher valued uses.

Finally, the monopsony case also reveals what appears to be a compelling case for public protection and encouragement of trade unionism and collective bargaining. With collective bargaining three "goods" are attained: exploitation of labor is diminished or eliminated, economic efficiency is improved, and workers are given an independent voice and democratic rights in a workplace and community otherwise dominated by the employer.

Given this positive assessment, why don't the majority of labor economists support unionism and collective bargaining? The answer: most do not think monopsony is prevalent or even a serious problem in labor markets (Reynolds, 1984; Boal and Ransom, 1997; Addison and Hirsch, 1997). Most economists believe labor markets have become more competitive over time with increased geographic mobility, improved job market information, and a larger number of employers in local areas. The "classic" one-company-town form of monopsony is therefore widely seen as an historical curiosum, while other forms of quasi-monopsony (oligopsony, monopsonistic competition) or "dynamic" monopsony (arising from flows of employee quits and new hires) are variously regarded as spotty in occurrence, of modest significance for wage determination, or of a short run, transitory nature (Manning, 2003). Another view is that employers who have a degree of monopsony power nonetheless often refrain from using it for exploitative purposes lest it damage morale and productivity or firm reputation. Yet another is that sources of labor immobility, such as specific on-the-job training, not only lock workers into jobs but also lock employers into workers (because firms invest in training workers and lose the investment if workers quit) and thus create a more balanced situation of *bilateral* monopoly. And, finally, the theoretical case that unions are needed to offset deleterious labor market imperfections has faded badly among economists in the face of new theoretical developments that argue these imperfections are either an economizing response to scarcity (e.g., job search as an adaptation to imperfect information) or do not pose a serious obstruction to competitive forces (e.g., the theory of contestable markets).

Whatever the case, the economics literature seldom emphasizes or even mentions monopsony in labor markets. Perhaps the most telling evidence is that even Freeman and Medoff, who desire to build a positive case for unionism, omit altogether an appeal to monopsony conditions and accept from the start that unionism (on net) distorts a competitive wage structure (also see Naylor, 2003). [As described below, F&M motivate the voice/response face of unions with appeal to various forms of market imperfection, but these (apparently) are not a source of monopsony power for employers.] The contrast in this matter is stark relative to the view of unionists and an earlier generation of economists (see the next chapter this volume). The AFL-CIO's web page (<www.aflcio.org>), for example, declares in the first sentence of the section "How and Why People Join Unions" that "People who work for a living know about the in-equality of power between employers and employees," and shortly thereafter repeats this theme, stating "Workers in unions counterbalance the unchecked power of employers."

In ending this discussion, it is important to note that employers may gain a measure of control over wages and labor conditions for other reasons besides monopsony. As an example, economists have recently developed an "efficiency wage" model of unemployment (Akerlof and Yellen, 1986). The basic idea — to some degree an updated version of Marx's "reserve army of the unemployed" — is that firm's deliberately pay above market-clearing wages so that a positive amount of involuntary unemployment exists in labor markets, giving employers an additional method to motivate employee work effort (lest they be fired). The mainstream literature, however, generally regards this form of employer control from a relatively positive/benign perspective as a legitimate method employers use to curb employee shirking (caused by principal-agent problems) and, certainly, few contemporary labor economists — including Freeman and Medoff and the others just cited — advocate unions as a means to curb it.

IV. The Collective Voice/Institutional Response Face

As Freeman and Medoff suggest, the monopoly model of unions — when combined with a theory of competitive labor markets — leads to a largely negative verdict on the effects of labor unions. In years past, a traditional response to this verdict was to challenge the competitive markets assumption and argue, per the monopsony discussion above, that union power is needed to offset employer power in imperfect labor markets. For reasons related to intellectual and real-world trends, this justification for unions is waning in both generality and influence, certainly in the academic community but arguably also among the public. As this rationale for unions has declined in influence, another has arisen. This new view of unions shifts attention from imperfections in the structure of markets to imperfections in employment contracts and internal firm governance (Williamson et al., 1975; Barker, 1997). Although there are several diverse strands of theory, some of which are direct extensions of traditional microeconomics and others that come from organizational economics and "new institutional economics," all have a common root in transaction costs and incomplete contracts. For expositional simplicity, I refer to this new line of theory as "contract and transaction cost economics" (CTCE), although in reality it comes under different labels. The voice face of unions developed by F&M in *What Do Unions Do?* is interpretable as an early application of CTCE.

Transaction Cost and Incomplete Contracts

One reason neoclassical economics leads to a negative verdict on unions is because the core theory starts with a theory of perfectly rational decision makers and perfectly competitive markets, so even when these parts are amended and qualified it is difficult to avoid the conclusion that a labor union is (largely) an interference in an otherwise well-functioning market system and thus a source of inefficiency and welfare loss.

A CTCE model of unions reaches different and more positive implications because it replaces these two fundamental neoclassical assumptions. Instead of modeling the economic agent as perfectly rational (the "rational actor" model), CTCE theorists use a model of *bounded rationality*. Formally developed by Simon (1982), bounded rationality recognizes that human decision making is impacted by what Commons' (1934) called "stupidity, ignorance and passion" and what in today's literature are called limited cognition, imperfect information, and emotional affect (Kaufman, 1999). In this model, human behavior and decision making are purposeful and largely reasoned ("procedurally rational") but also prone in a substantively important way to suboptimization, inertness or "slack," systematic biases and errors, occasional resort to violence and aggression, and the influence of interpersonal emotional states arising from feelings such as love, hate, anger, and jealousy.

The second amendment is to note that all institutional forms for organizing and carrying out exchanges have imperfections, thus creating a larger potential for organizations such as unions to have positive efficiency effects. The nature and impact of the imperfections in CTCE are different, however, than in standard neoclassical economics (Williamson, 1985; Dow, 1997). CTCE theorists note that in an interdependent economy people must engage in exchange for production and consumption to proceed. What is exchanged, however, are not physical goods and services but property rights to scarce things, including the services of workers. Every exchange, therefore, involves a transfer of property rights and this transfer is governed by an implicit or explicit contract between the two parties. The central research issue in CTCE is to discover how economic agents organize and transact the contracting process and the efficiency implications thereof. With respect to labor, for example, various options potentially exist; firms may use full-time employees, independent contractors, temporary workers or (law permitting) slaves, and will presumably choose the contractual option that minimizes cost. The kind of cost that they seek to minimize, in turn, is transaction *cost* — the real resources used to exchange property rights or, alternatively, to construct, enforce, and administer contracts. [The concept of a transaction comes from Commons (1934); the concept of transaction cost and its use for comparative institutional analysis comes from Coase (1937) and Williamson (1985).]

It is widely agreed (e.g., Reder, 1999) that neoclassical microeconomics omits transaction cost, since its core assumptions allow buyers and sellers to construct complete and fully contingent contracts at zero cost. Since exchange carries no cost, efficiency is always maximized through market exchange — to the point that, as Coase first recognized, there is no rationale for multi-person firms and the economy dissolves into a system of "perfect decentralization" where all production is done by sole proprietorships (Demsetz, 1991; Kaufman, 2003). No employment relationship exists and the labor market disappears! With nonzero transaction costs, however, it may be more efficient to shift from obtaining labor through spot transactions with other firms (operating in the guise of independent contractors) to hiring employees and entering into long-term contracts. That is, positive transaction cost arises from factors such as bounded rationality, imperfect information, asset specificity, incompletely specified or nonpartitionable property rights, and imperfectly enforced contract law. Because of nonzero transaction cost, every new contract thus entails additional expense, providing a motive for the firm to hire longer term employees over short-term independent contractors and to minimize churn through "hiring and firing." Thus, consistent with the argument of F&M, in a positive-transaction-cost world the "exit" option of the free market is not necessarily the most efficient way to re-contract for labor services.

Equally important, nonzero transaction cost means that all employment contracts are *incomplete* — i.e., the employer and employee cannot possibly fully specify in writing all terms and conditions of employment, such as the precise tasks and work effort expected of the employee, the risk of injury or level of noise, and the management style of supervisors. Thus, with incomplete contracts both the employer and employee are exposed to a host of potentially costly contract breaches arising from opportunism, malfeasance, adverse selection, moral hazard, and principal-agent problems (Miller, 1991; Dow, 1997). As examples, an employee may promise to be a diligent worker but then loaf at every opportunity, while the employer may promise a promotion in six months but later renege. Since positive transaction costs make the exit option expensive, the employer and employee need an alternative method to prevent and resolve these problems lest they cause hard feelings and conflict that sap cooperation and efficiency. Following F&M, one solution is to instead construct a "voice" option in the firm, such as a labor union, so employer and employees can communicate, talk out differences, and construct a regime of enterprise rules and regulations that are fair and "win-win" for all parties.

In the presence of bounded rationality and positive transaction cost, a labor union can increase efficiency in a number of ways. The case is far from ironclad, however, and a union may also decrease efficiency or be an inferior solution to transaction cost problems relative to a different type of voice institution.

Public Goods in the Workplace

As earlier described, a central part of F&M's justification for the voice function of unions rests on the idea that many workplace conditions have characteristics of a public good. A public good presents a contracting problem and source of market failure because for technological or cost reasons establishing a well-defined individual property right is impossible or prohibitively expensive. As a result, the good or service is "public": provision to one person means provision to many or all (as with national defense). The problem for market exchange is that individual economic agents have an incentive to understate their true demand for the good, hoping others will pay the full cost and they can free ride and consume it at no (or little) cost. Due to this type of transaction cost problem, the good will be under-provided relative to the socially optimal level. One solution is to have the good provided by a collective organization, such as a government, where each person (voter) is assessed a prorated share of the cost. Unable to free ride, the voters have an incentive to declare their true demand, allowing government to provide a more efficient level of the good than the private market.

Many workplace conditions may have a public goods quality. Increased safety, improved ergonomics, reduced heat and noise, flexible work schedules, and an end to management harassment or insensitivity are nonrivalrous in consumption since enjoyment by one worker does not reduce the amount available for others. Individual workers thus have an incentive to free ride, particularly since confronting the employer may have significant costs. Although many nonunion firms say they have an open-door policy, and many managers express a desire for feedback from subordinates, workers worry that speaking up will brand them as troublemakers or people who are not team players, resulting in a bad image with the boss, lower performance evaluations and pay increases, and perhaps discriminatory treatment or even termination (Lewin, 2004). A union can thus enhance efficiency because it replaces ineffective individual voice with a stronger collective voice, leading to an increase in the supply of workplace public goods closer to the social optimum (Flanagan, 1983).

Higher Productivity

Collective voice provided by a labor union can also promote higher productivity, thus contributing to a second form of efficiency gain. This positive effect can arise through several channels (Kuhn, 1985).

One channel is by reducing turnover costs (Freeman, 1980b). The competitive market model assumes worker mobility and the accompanying hiring and quitting are costless. With bounded rationality and imperfect information, however, firms must invest considerable resources in recruiting and screening prospective employees, while workers invest similar resources in job search and interviewing. Similarly, once an employment relationship commences, in many situations both the employer and employee incur match-specific costs, such as investments in firm-specific job skills and training, that are lost if the worker quits or is terminated. If these forms of transaction cost are sizable, using labor mobility to sort workers into good job matches and provide signals to firms about workers' preferences may be inefficient. A labor union, on the other hand, may promote greater productivity if it reduces employee churn by substituting direct communication with the employer for indirect communication through quitting. An important form of direct communication, for example, is a formal grievance system where management and union representatives meet to resolve work performance, discipline, and discharge disputes (Lewin and Boroff, 1996). Without such a system, the employee separation rate may be higher as workers either quit or are terminated.

Bounded rationality and the existence of organizational slack (sometimes called "X-inefficiency") is a second route through which unions can improve productivity. As long as the firm's profits are above some satisfactory level, managers may "loaf" or pursue other goals at the expense of profits, such as plush offices or "empire building" through numerous mergers and acquisitions. Unionization or a union wage increase, therefore, may reduce the level of organizational slack and force managers to tighten operations, reduce unnecessary expenses, and focus more single-mindedly on profit (sometimes called a "shock effect"). All of these actions will increase productivity and yield a gain in efficiency (Kaufman, 1999; Altman, 2001).

The incomplete nature of employment contracts creates a third channel for unions to stimulate higher productivity. The employment contract commits a worker to provide a certain number of hours of labor, but within some range the employee chooses how much work effort (or "labor power") to provide. If employees provide the minimum required amount of effort, productivity will be low; if they provide their maximum work effort, productivity will be high. One variable that strongly influences work effort is whether employees feel fairly treated by the company. If the company gives employees a "gift" of above-market wages, generous benefits, and employment security, they will reciprocate with a gift of hard work, loyalty, and attention to customer satisfaction; if on the other hand workers feel unfairly treated, they react by punishing the company through greater absenteeism, loafing on the job, and a bad attitude toward customers (Akerlof, 1990). A union may thus contribute to higher productivity by creating conditions that motivate greater employee work effort, either by eliminating practices and conditions that seem unfair or establishing terms and conditions that are superior to other firms.

Another dimension of voice that unions may facilitate is employee involvement in the production process. The traditional management model is "command and control" where managers do the "brain work" and give the orders and employees do the "back work" and follow the orders. Companies using a new "high performance" employment model have found, however, that productivity is higher when workers are empowered and involved, giving them more responsibility, say, and influence in how the work is organized and performed (Levine, 1995). Employee involvement may not develop beyond a superficial level in nonunion firms, however, because managers resist ceding control and fear that empowering workers will lead to a demand for a sharing of the gains (rents). A union, however, can exert greater pressure on companies to expand the breadth and depth of employee involvement, thus promoting greater productivity. Paradoxically, firms will nonetheless often prefer to forego the productivity gains of unionism because their profits are higher when they do not have to share the gains with workers (Freeman and Lazear, 1995).

A final way in which union voice can promote higher productivity is by creating "credible commitments" between companies and workers. Companies try to motivate employees to work harder and smarter with an overt or implicit promise that employees will share in the greater profits in the form of higher wages, better benefits, and other rewards. Employees fear, however, that once they live up to their end of the deal companies will renege and keep all the profits. So, afraid of employers' double-dealing, employees hold back and the potential gain to productivity is lost (Miller, 1991; Kaufman and Levine, 2000). Unionism, however, can solve this type of prisoner's dilemma by getting the employers to agree in a written contract how the gains from cooperation will be shared.

Agency Services

A third way unions can reduce transaction cost and increase efficiency is by providing agency services to workers and firms. The principle involved is well illustrated in sports and entertainment labor markets where professional athletes and rock stars hire agents to represent them. These agents improve the "quality" of the employment contract between the employer and employee; in effect, agents serve as intermediaries and brokers (Barker, 1997). As the employees' agent, a union can provide three kinds of efficiency-enhancing services (Faith and Reid, 1987). The first is to supply relevant labor market information (wages at competing firms, alternative pension plans) and aid in contract negotiation with the employer. A second benefit is monitoring and evaluating the employer's contract performance (governance services). A third benefit is communication (voice services) of the workers' preferences regarding the structure of compensation and personnel practices. While rock stars and professional athletes typically hire individual agents, workers have less money and specialized needs and thus find agent sharing to be more cost effective. A labor union is one such arrangement, a professional employees association is another. Although not directly related to efficiency, it is important to note that a fourth service provided by a collective agent is to represent workers' interests in the political and regulatory process (Delaney and Schwochau, 1993).

Firms can also find it advantageous to hire or create an agent to act as an intermediary with workers (Kaufman and Levine, 2000). Rather than the employer having to meet one-on-one with each employee to negotiate and administer the employment contract, this job can be assigned to the agent, thus reaping economies of scale. The agent may also be granted some independence by the employer, thus increasing the trust of workers that the agent will perform as an "honest broker" in mediating conflicts of interests. A labor union is one such agent; others include a personnel/human resource department and employee representation plan ("company union").

Qualifications

All of the arguments of this section provide theoretical rationales for why union voice may improve economic efficiency. Four significant qualifications to this otherwise positive account have to be noted, however.

First, on a conceptual level F&M's theory has a potential lacuna. They portray the monopoly and voice/response functions as largely separable — the former is the efficiency distorting exercise of "muscle," the latter is the efficiency-enhancing effect of communication or "voice." In reality, however, unions often are only able to induce firms to provide more collective goods or honor workers rights when voice is backed up by muscle. It is not self-evident, therefore, how the muscle function of unions with respect to wages and benefits can be significantly weakened or redirected, per F&M's proposal (p. 248), yet the voice function strengthened.

A second qualification is that on an empirical level the putatively positive effect of union voice may in fact hide a more negative monopoly effect. Unions, for example, may lower the employee quit rate but if this is done by making it difficult for firms to fire "dead wood," the result may be lower productivity. Likewise, unions may achieve economies of scale in negotiating collective contracts with employers, but if the collective bargaining process creates or heightens adversarial relations and feelings of distrust the result may be less effective teamwork and employee involvement.

A third qualification is that many of the gains in efficiency from union voice accrue in the short run, often in the form of a "one-time" improvement. A union is organized and a new governance regime is established, including a written contract, grievance system, and a plant safety committee. For the first several bargaining rounds, a significant proportion of the union's bargaining power may be expended to win these improvements, thus keeping the monopoly wage effect to a modest level. In the long run, however, further gains in the voice area are likely to be subject to substantial diminishing returns, causing the union to shift a growing proportion of its collective bargaining demands to improvements in the economic package. Over time, therefore, one may expect that the negative monopoly face will gradually displace the positive voice face. [A similar conclusion is a reasonable hypothesis with respect to the monopsony-reducing effect of unions.]

Finally, even if unionism contributes to increased efficiency in all the ways enumerated above, the possibility remains that some other kind of workplace institution may perform better. Examples include a works council, employee representation plan, legally binding employee handbook, or labor court. Before one can conclude that national labor policy should encourage more unionism, a comparative institutional analysis should be done to determine that unions are superior to other forms of collective representation and work force governance. Ideally, such analysis should also be performed to determine the optimal form of union and configuration of labor law.

V. Conclusion

I have attempted to distill a quite sizable body of literature written by modern economists on the theory of labor unions, with particular emphasis given to the "two faces" view of unions developed by Freeman and Medoff in *What*

Do Unions Do? Many important ideas and contributions have necessarily been omitted, but hopefully the main contours and implications are captured.

From this review, it seems clear that F&M have correctly called attention to the fact that unions in theory and practice have both a positive and negative face. They are also correct, I think, to suggest that most economists believe, as a generalization, that the negative side of unions outweighs the positive side, at least with respect to resource allocation and efficiency. When other noneconomic outcomes are introduced, such as income and wealth inequality, social justice, and workplace democracy, the verdict of economists may become more favorable (see Rees, 1989, for example). But this conclusion is highly tentative since modern-day economists typically refrain from making pronouncements on what are perceived to be normative issues.

The most controversial aspect of *What Do Unions Do?* is F&M's claim that even on efficiency grounds unionism is most likely a net plus or, at worst, a very small negative. The theoretical models and implications reviewed in this chapter do not provide definitive evidence on this matter, but they do reduce our range of ignorance and inform our priors. In this regard, several points are worth noting.

First, it appears that unions in their economic function have not two faces but three. There is the negative monopoly-creating face and the positive voice face, but F&M and most modern labor economists omit a third face — the positive monopsony-reducing face. The term "monopsony-reducing" endeavors to capture the idea that unions are necessary to offset employer power in the labor market and firm, thus protecting workers from managerial abuse and substandard wages and working conditions. Employer power, however, has broader origins than classic monopsony, for it originates in a variety of restrictions on competition and mobility — including job lock from seniority provisions and health care plans, discrimination and segmented labor markets, and lack of jobs due to involuntary unemployment. A fair generalization is that the most compelling social rationale for unions among citizens and policymakers is the traditional one of "protecting the underdog" and "leveling the playing field," which appears to speak to the monopsony-reducing role. It is thus paradoxical that F&M, who desire to construct a positive rationale for unions, omit this aspect of unionism altogether. Instead, they follow most modern labor economists and assume that labor markets are largely competitive, at least in wage determination. This view may be entirely correct as an empirical matter; my point is that it is too fundamental to "what unions do" to so easily dismiss or assume it away.

When one looks at the theoretical literature on unions, other union "faces" also emerge that seem important but under-emphasized by F&M. One such distinction, for example, is the "short run" and "long run" faces of unions. Much of the theory and analysis in *What Do Unions Do?* is static, cross sectional, and short run. On one hand this emphasis is to a degree unavoidable, given modeling complexities and data availability. But economic theory also suggests that a preponderate focus on the short run is likely to impart a positive bias to the economic scorecard on unionism. One reason is that more of the efficiency benefits from unions are realized in the short run (from the voice and monopsony-reducing effects); a second is that more of the efficiency costs from the monopoly face of unions appear in the long run (due to factor misallocation and lower productivity growth). As a concrete example, F&M use the median-voter model of unions to derive a positive union effect on the short-run provision of collective goods in the workplace but fail to consider the negative long-run implication of this model for employment, capital investment, and cost-push inflation. Another example is the primary (but not exclusive) focus on the determinants of the cross-sectional differences in the level of productivity across firms, rather than on the *dynamic path* of productivity growth between union and nonunion firms. Also largely neglected by F&M are the macroeconomic costs of unions, such as a tendency for cost-creep inflation and higher unemployment in order to restrain union bargaining demands.

Given these shortcomings, it is also evident that F&M in *What Do Unions Do?* have made significant and enduring contributions to the theory and understanding of unions. Certainly their most important contribution is their emphasis on and elaboration of the "voice/response" face of unions. As demonstrated in the next chapter in this volume, some of these ideas were noted by an earlier generation of economists, but F&M gave these ideas a systematic treatment and theoretical foundation grounded in modern economic theory. No subsequent study of unions can discuss union voice without referencing F&M. Two other noteworthy contributions also deserve highlight. Prior to F&M, most of economic theorizing focused on the wage effects of unions. More than any prior study, their book forced economists to broaden their models to include the gamut of union effects, including not only wages but also benefits, productivity, quits, and a variety of other outcomes. And, finally, F&M also made a significant mark on the theoretical literature with their application of the median-voter model to the union effect on the structure of wages, benefits, and personnel practices.

I estimate that twenty years after the publication of *What Do Unions Do?* the large majority of economists remain convinced that economic theory points to a net negative impact of unions on resource allocation and economic efficiency. In this respect F&M have failed to move professional opinion. Without question, however, they have forced economists to carefully reconsider the case for and against unionism and have, possibly, moved the verdict in a modestly more favorable direction. In the grand scheme of things, these are powerful accomplishments for one book.

References

Addison, John and Barry Hirsch. "The Economic Effects of Employment Regulation: What Are the Limits?" In Bruce Kaufman, ed. *Government Regulation of the Em-*

ployment Relationship. Madison, Wisc.: Industrial Relations Research Association, 1997, pp. 125–78.

Addison, John and John Chilton. "Models of Union Behavior." In David Lewin, Daniel Mitchell, and Mahmood Zaidi, eds. *The Human Resource Management Handbook, Part II*. Greenwich, Conn.: JAI Press, 1997, pp. 157–96.

Akerlof, George. "The Fair-Wage-Effort Hypothesis and Unemployment." *Quarterly Journal of Economics* 105 (May 1990): 255–84.

_____ and Janet Yellen. *Efficiency Wage Models of the Labor Market*. New York: Cambridge University Press, 1986.

Altman, Morris. *Worker Satisfaction and Economic Performance*. Armonk, N.Y.: M.E. Sharpe, 2000.

Argyrous, George, Mathew Forstater, and Gary Mongiovi. *Growth, Distribution, and Effective Demand*. Armonk, N.Y.: M.E. Sharpe, 2003.

Barker, George. *An Economic Analysis of Trade Unions and the Common Law*. Brookfield, Vt.: Avebury, 1997.

Bennett, James T. and Bruce E. Kaufman. "Conclusion: the Future of Private Sector Unionismin the U.S. — Assessment and Forecast." In James Bennett and Bruce Kaufman, eds. *The Future of Private Sector Unionism in the United States*. Armonk, N.Y.: M.E. Sharpe, 2002, pp. 359–86.

Bennett, James T. and M. Johnson. "The Impact of Right to Work Laws on the Economic Behavior of Local Unions — A Property Rights Perspective." *Journal of Labor Research* 1 (Spring 1980): 1–28.

Bennett, James and Thomas DiLorenzo. "Unions, Politics, and Protectionism." *Journal of Labor Research* 5 (Summer 1984): 309–14.

Blanchflower, David, Andrew Oswald, and Peter Sanfey. "Wages, Profits, and Rent-Sharing." *Quarterly Journal of Economics* 111 (February 1996): 227–51.

Boal, William and Michael Ransom. "Monopsony in the Labor Market." *Journal of Economic Literature* 35 (March 1997): 86–112.

Booth, Alison. *The Economics of Trade Unions*. New York: Cambridge University Press, 1995.

Bronfenbrenner, Martin. *Income Distribution Theory*. Chicago: Aldine, 1971.

Budd, John. "Institutional and Market Determinants of Wage Spillovers: Evidence from UAW Pattern Bargaining." *Industrial Relations* 36 (January 1997): 97–116.

Burda, Michael. "Membership, Seniority and Wage Setting in Democratic Labour Unions." *Economica* 57 (November 1990): 455–66.

Card, David. "The Effect of Unions on Wage Inequality in the U.S. Labor Market." *Industrial and Labor Relations Review* 54 (January 2001): 296–315.

_____ and Alan Krueger. *Myth and Measurement: The New Economics of the Minimum Wage*. Princeton: Princeton University Press, 1995.

Chaison, Gary and Barbara Bigelow. *Unions and Legitimacy*. Ithaca, N.Y.: Cornell University Press, 2001.

Coase, Ronald. "The Nature of the Firm." *Economica* 4 (November 1937): 386–405.

Commons, John. *Institutional Economics: Its Place in Political Economy*. New York: MacMillan, 1934.

Cross, John. *The Economics of Bargaining*. New York: Basic Books, 1969.

Delaney, John and Susan Schwochau. "Employee Representation Through the Political Process." In Bruce Kaufman and Morris Kleiner, eds. *Employee Representation: Alternatives and Future Directions*. Madison, Wisc.: Industrial Relations Research Association, 1993, pp. 265–304.

Demsetz, Harold. "The Theory of the Firm Revisited." In O. Williamson and S. Winter, eds. *The Nature of the Firm*. New York: Oxford University Press, pp. 159–78.

Devinatz, Victor. "The Fears of Resource Standardization and the Creation of an Adversarial Workplace Climate: The Struggle to Organize a Faculty Union at Illinois State University." In David Lewin and Bruce Kaufman, eds. *Advances in Industrial and Labor Relations,* Vol. 11. New York: Elsevier Science, 2002, pp.145–80.

Dow, Gregory. "The New Institutional Economics and Employment Regulation." In Bruce Kaufman, ed. *Government Regulation of the Employment Relationship.* Madison, Wisc.: Industrial Relations Research Association, 1997, pp. 57–90.

Faith, Roger and Joseph Reid. "An Agency Theory of Unionism." *Journal of Economic Behavior and Organization* on 8 (No. 1, 1987): 39–60.

Farber, Henry. "The Determination of the Union Status of Workers." *Econometrica* 51 (September 1983): 1417–38.

_____. "Right-to-Work Laws and the Extent of Unionization." *Journal of Labor Economics* 2 (July 1984): 319–52.

_____. "The Analysis of Union Behavior." In Orley Ashenfelter and Richard Layard, eds. *Handbook of Labor Economics,* Vol. 1. New York: North-Holland, 1986, pp. 1039–89.

_____ and Alan Krueger. "Union Membership in the United States: The Decline Continues." In Bruce Kaufman and Morris Kleiner, eds. *Employee Representation: Alternatives and Future Directions.* Madison, Wisc.: Industrial Relations Research Association, 1993, pp. 105–34.

Flanagan, Robert. "Workplace Public Goods and Union Organization." *Industrial Relations* 22 (Spring 1983): 224–37.

_____. "Can Political Models Predict Union Behavior?" In R.J. Flanagan, K.O. Moene, and M. Wallerstein, eds. *Trade Union Behavior, Pay-Bargaining, and Economic Performance.* Oxford: Oxford University Press, 1993, pp. 5–62.

Freeman, Richard. "Individual Mobility and Union Voice in the Labor Market." *American Economic Review* 66 (May 1976): 361–8.

_____. "Unionism and the Dispersion of Wages." *Industrial and Labor Relations Review* 34 (October 1980a): 3–23.

_____. "The Effect of Unionism on Worker Attachment to Firms." *Journal of Labor Research* 1 (Spring 1980b): 229–62.

_____. "The Effect of Unionism on Fringe Benefits." *Industrial and Labor Relations Review* 34 (July 1981): 489–509.

Freeman, Richard and James Medoff. *What Do Unions Do?* N.Y.: Basic Books, 1984.

Freeman, Richard and Morris Kleiner. "Employer Behavior in the Face of Union Organizing Drives." *Industrial and Labor Relations Review* 43 (April 1990): 351–65.

_____. "Do Unions Make Enterprises Insolvent?" *Industrial and Labor Relations Review* 52 (July 1999): 510–27.

Freeman, Richard and Edward Lazear. "An Economic Analysis of Works Councils." In Wolfgang Streeck and Joel Rogers, eds. *Works Councils.* Chicago: University of Chicago Press, 1995, pp. 27–52.

Freeman, Richard and Joel Rodgers. *What Do Workers Want?* Ithaca, N.Y.: ILR Press, 1999.

Friedman, Milton. "Some Comments on the Significance of Labor Unions for Economic Policy." In David McCord Wright, ed. *The Impact of the Union.* New York: Harcourt, Brace, 1951, pp. 204–34.

Gallagher, Daniel and Cynthia Gramm. "Collective Bargaining and Strike Activity." In David Lewin, Daniel Mitchell, and Mahmood Zaidi, eds. *The Human Resource Management Handbook*, Part II. Greenwich, Conn.: JAI Press, 1997, pp. 65–94.

Grout, Paul. "Investment and Wages in the Absence of Binding Contracts: A Nash Bargaining Approach." *Econometrica* 52 (March 1984): 449–60.

Gunderson, Morley and A. Melino. "Estimating Strike Effects in a General Model of Prices and Quantities." *Journal of Labor Economics* 5 (January 1987): 1–19.

Hicks, John. *The Theory of Wages.* New York: MacMillan, 1932.

Hirsch, Barry. *Labor Unions and the Performance of Firms.* Kalamazoo, Mich.: W.E. Upjohn Institute for Employment Research, 1991.

_____ and John Addison. *The Economic Analysis of Unions.* Boston: Allen and Unwin, 1986.

Hirschman, Albert. Exit, *Voice, and Loyalty.* Cambridge: Harvard University Press, 1970.

Johnson, George. "Organized Labor's Political Agenda." In Wei-Chiao Huang, ed. *Organized Labor at the Crossroads.* Kalamazoo, Mich.: W.E. Upjohn Institute for Employment Research, 1989, pp. 63–90.

_____. "Work-Rules, Featherbedding, and Pareto-Optimal Union-Management Bargaining." *Journal of Labor Economics* 8 (January 1990): S237–59.

Kaufman, Bruce. "Research on Strike Models and Outcomes in the 1980s: Accomplishments and Shortcomings." In David Lewin, Olivia Mitchell, and Peter Sherer, eds. *Research Frontiers in Industrial Relations and Human Resources.* Madison, Wisc.: Industrial Relations Research Association, 1992, pp. 77–130.

_____. "Emotional Arousal as a Source of Bounded Rationality." *Journal of Economic Behavior and Organization*on 38 (February 1999): 135–44.

_____. "Models of Union Wage Determination: What Have We Learned since Dunlop and Ross?" *Industrial Relations* 41 (January 2002): 110–58.

_____. "The Organization of Economic Activity: Insights from the Institutional Theory of John R. Commons." *Journal of Economic Behavior and Organization* 52 (September 2003): 71-96.

_____ and Jorge Martinez-Vasquez. "Voting for Wage Concessions: The Case of the 1982 GM-UAW Negotiations." *Industrial and Labor Relations Review* 41 (January 1988): 183–94.

_____ and David Levine. "An Economic Analysis of Employee Representation." In Bruce Kaufman and Daphne Taras, eds. *Nonunion Employee Representation: History, Contemporary Practice, and Policy.* Armonk, N.Y.: M.E. Sharpe, 2000, pp. 149–75.

Kuhn, Peter. "Union Productivity Effects and Economic Efficiency." *Journal of Labor Research* 6 (Summer 1985): 229–48.

Lawrence, Colin and Robert Lawrence. "Manufacturing Wage Dispersion: An End-Game Interpretation." *Brookings Papers on Economic Activity* (No. 1, 1985): 47–106.

Levine, David. "Fairness, Markets, and Ability to Pay." *American Economic Review* 83 (December 1993): 1241–59.

_____. *Reinventing the Workplace.* Washington, D.C.: Brookings Institution, 1995.

Lewin, David. "Dispute Resolution in Nonunion Organizations: Key Empirical Findings." In Samuel Estreicher, ed. *Alternative Dispute Resolution in the Employment Arena.* New York: Kluwer, 2004.

_____ and Karen Boroff. "The Role of Loyalty in Exit and Voice: A Conceptual and Empirical Analysis." In David Lewin, Bruce Kaufman, and Donna Sockell, eds. *Advances in Industrial and Labor Relations*, Vol. 7. Greenwich, Conn.: JAI Press, 1996, pp. 69–96.

Maloney, Michael, Robert McCormick, and Robert Tollison. "Achieving Cartel Profits through Unionization." *Southern Economic Journal* 46 (October 1979): 628–34.

Manning, Alan. *Monopsony in Motion: Imperfect Competititon in Labor Markets.* Princeton: Princeton University Press, 2003.

Manzini, Paola. "Game Theoretic Models of Wage Bargaining." *Journal of Economic Surveys* 12 (February 1998): 1–41.

Miller, Gary. *Managerial Dilemmas.* New York: Cambridge University Press, 1991.

Mitchell, Daniel. *Unions, Wages, and Inflation.* Washington, D.C.: Brookings Institution, 1980.

Naylor, Robin. "Economic Models of Union Behavior." In John Addison and Claus Schnabel, eds. *The International Handbook of Trade Unions.* Northampton, Mass.: Edward Elgar, 2003.

Neumark, David. "Declining Union Strength and Labor Cost Inflation in the 1980s." *Industrial Relations* 32 (Spring 1993): 204–22.

Northrup, Herbert. "Construction Union Programs to Regain Jobs: Background and Overview." *Journal of Labor Research* 18 (Winter 1997): 1–16.

Oswald, Andrew. "The Economic Theory of Trade Unions: An Introductory Survey." *Scandinavian Journal of Economics* 87 (No. 2, 1985): 167–93.

_____. "Efficient Contracts Are on the Labour Demand Curve: Theory and Facts." *Labour Economics* 1 (1993): 85–113.

Pencavel, John. "The Demand for Union Services: An Exercise." *Industrial and Labor Relations Review* 24 (January 1971): 180–90.

_____. *Labor Markets and Trade Unionism.* Cambridge: Blackwell, 1991.

Reder, Melvin. *Economics: The Culture of a Controversial Science.* Chicago: University of Chicago Press, 1999.

Rees, Albert. "The Effects of Unions on Resource Allocation." *Journal of Law and Economics* 6 (October 1963): 69–78.

_____. *The Economics of Trade Unions,* 3rd ed. Chicago: University of Chicago Press, 1989.

Reynolds, Lloyd and Cynthia Taft. *The Evolution of Wage Structure.* New Haven, Conn.: Yale University Press, 1956.

Reynolds, Morgan. *Power and Privilege: Labor Unions in America.* New York: Universe Books, 1984.

Ross, Arthur. *Trade Union Wage Policy.* Berkeley: University of California Press, 1948.

Schwartz-Miller, Ann and Wayne Talley. "Technology and Labor Relations: Railroads and Ports." *Journal of Labor Research* 23 (Fall 2002): 513–34.

Shister, Joseph. "The Theory of Union Wage Rigidity." *Quarterly Journal of Economics* 57 (August 1943): 522–42.

Simon, Herbert. *Models of Bounded Rationality,* Vol. 2. Cambridge: MIT Press, 1982.

Taras, Daphne and Allen Ponak. "Mandatory Agency Shop Laws As an Explanation of Canada-US Union Density Divergence." In James Bennett and Bruce Kaufman, eds. *The Future of Private Sector Unionism in the United States.* Armonk, N.Y.: M.E. Sharpe, 2002, pp. 260–91.

Ulman, Lloyd. "Marshall and Friedman on Union Strength." *Review of Economics and Statistics* 37 (November 1955): 384–401.

Vedder, Richard and Lowell Galloway. "The Economic Effects of Labor Unions Revisited." *Journal of Labor Research* 23 (Winter 2002): 41–50.

Vittoz, Victor. *New Deal Labor Policy and the American Industrial Economy.* Chapel Hill: University of North Carolina Press, 1987.

Williamson, Oliver. *The Economic Institutions of Capitalism.* New York: Free Press, 1985.

_____, Michael Wachter, and J. Harris. "Understanding the Employment Relation: The Analysis of Idiosyncratic Exchange." *Bell Journal of Economics* 6 (Spring 1975): 250–78.

3

Historical Insights: The Early Institutionalists on Trade Unionism and Labor Policy

Bruce E. Kaufman

I. Introduction

My prior chapter evaluated trade unionism through the lens of modern economic theory; this chapter pursues the same tact but through the lens of history. The historical dimension examined is the writings of the first group of American labor economists to extensively consider the subject of trade unions and labor policy. This group is the early institutional labor economists, centered on John R. Commons and the Wisconsin School, who founded and dominated labor economics in the United States in the first third of the twentieth century.

My purpose for this review is partly to provide an historical (and heterodox) perspective to the subject of unions and labor policy that is largely omitted by Freeman and Medoff (F&M, 1984) in *What Do Unions Do?* The more important reason, however, is that this early literature provides a substantially different and more positive theoretical perspective on unions than is typically found in more modern writings. The early institutionalists were sympathetic to the mission and accomplishments of the labor movement and attempted to develop a body of theory that gave a public interest rationale for an expanded role for collective bargaining. This project achieved great success in the 1930s with passage of the National Labor Relations Act and the emergence of mass unionism. Although these events and ideas are of interest for their own sake, they seem particularly relevant for this volume given F&M's parallel goals of constructing a more compelling theoretical rationale for unionism and encouraging greater union density through labor law reform.

In developing this study, I proceed in three steps: an overview of the theoretical framework developed by the early institutional economists to analyze labor markets; a more detailed look at their theory of trade unions and collective bargaining; and, finally, a review of the role and function of trade unions in their larger strategy of labor market reform. Implications and conclusions are given at the end.

II. Intellectual Precursors

The economics profession has always been divided on the subject of unions, although it is fair to say that the weight of thinking over the years has tended toward the skeptical-to-negative. But there are also notable exceptions.

Given his stance in favor of relatively unrestricted market competition, one would think, for example, that Adam Smith would have taken a dim view of trade unions. Surprisingly, however, he saw a potentially useful social role for them. In Chapter 8 of the *Wealth of Nations*, Smith (1776: 66) observes, "What are the common wages of labour, depends every where upon the contract usually made between those two parties, whose interests are by no means the same. The workmen desire to get as much, the masters to give as little as possible. . . . It is not, however, difficult to foresee which of the two parties must, upon all ordinary occasions, have the advantage. . . . In all such disputes the masters can hold out much longer. . . . In the long run the workman may be as necessary to his master as his master is to him, but the necessity is not so immediate." In this passage Smith speaks to what has always been the most compelling rationale for unions — to level the playing field and protect the underdog — and it is a thread woven throughout the remainder of this chapter. It is also a justification for unions, as noted in my earlier chapter, that is conspicuously absent from *What Do Unions Do?* and from most of the modern economics literature.

A century later, some economic theorists followed Smith's reasoning and took a similarly open-minded stance on unions. The most prominent example is Alfred Marshall (1961: 335–36) who declares "while the advantage in bargaining is likely to be pretty well distributed between the two sides of a market for commodities, it is more often on the side of the buyers than on that of the sellers in a market for labour." This led him to express cautious support for trade unionism, if practiced in a responsible and moderate manner — a position reinforced by his belief that the primary reason workers combine is due to "the unfairness of bad masters" (Petridis, 1973).

The dominant view in the American economics profession of the late nineteenth century, however, was decidedly more negative with regard to the purpose and effects of trade unions (Bendix, 1956; Perlman and McGann, 2000). Influential at the time were doctrines such as the wage fund, laissez-faire, freedom of contract, and Social Darwinism. Representative of the tenor of the times is this statement by Arthur Latham Perry (1878), who maintains that the solution to the worker's problems is (p. 200) "to look out for his own interest, to know the market value of his own service, and to make the best terms for himself which he can; . . . the remedy . . . is not in arbitrary interference of government in the bargain, but in the intelligence and self-respect of the laborers." He then condemns collective bargaining and strikes as (p. 204) "false in theory and pernicious in practice . . . they embitter relations between employers and employed . . . and rarely or never are permanently advantageous."

Views such as these, and the deductively derived theory of English classical and neoclassical economics that supported them, led a group of socially conscious and reform-minded American economists in the late nineteenth century to seek an alternative in German political economy of the historical-social school (Kaufman, 2004a). German economics stressed that all theories are historically contingent; theory should be "realistic" and thus built from an inductive process of empirical observation and investigation; all economic activity takes place within social and legal institutions; and active state management of the economy is necessary for economic progress and social order (Fine, 1956; Yonay, 2000). Young American economists, such as Richard Ely, came back to the United States from their German studies and endeavored to introduce this new approach here. Toward this end, they created the American Economics Association (1885) and, later, the institutional school of economics. They also became the first scholars to intensively study the labor movement and espouse its broad aims and purposes (Ely, 1886).

III. The Early Institutional Perspective on Labor Markets

The focal point of the institutionalists' research program was the study of labor, given that they saw the conditions of labor as the nation's number one economic and social problem, and their object was to improve the position of labor and balance and harmonize employer-employee relations through wide-ranging institutional reform. To accomplish these reforms, they pursued a three-pronged strategy: documenting the existence of serious labor problems, constructing a body of theory that showed these problems were neither efficient nor unalterable outcomes, and constructing a multi-step program of institutional change to solve the labor problems. One of the steps in their reform program was expanded trade unionism and collective bargaining — an agenda item finally realized in 1935 with the passage of the National Labor Relations Act.

Labor Problems

The concept of "labor problems" is seldom encountered in the modern economics literature but is crucial to understanding why the early institutional economists supported trade unions and expanded collective bargaining. In the first half of the twentieth century the study of labor most often went under the title "Labor Problems," not "Labor Economics" (McNulty, 1980; Kaufman, 1993). The difference in perspective is fundamental, since the existence of numerous "problems" immediately suggests that the status quo may well not be either efficient or welfare maximizing.

Nearly every labor textbook of this early period (e.g., Adams and Sumner, 1905; Estey 1928) began with several chapters devoted to "Evils," "Problems," or "Griev-ances" and included a standard list of topics, such as low wages, excessive work hours, child labor, employment insecurity, industrial accidents, and autocratic shop governance. Individually, each of these outcomes was portrayed in a negative light as socially injurious and often economically wasteful; collectively, they were seen as the source of growing class conflict between Capital and Labor and the cause of mounting strikes, labor violence, and interest in Socialism. The cause of labor problems, in turn, was traced back to defects and maladjustments in the existing institutional structure. Three factors in particular were highlighted: treatment of labor as a commodity in a system of unregulated labor markets; a monarchial system of work force governance in which employers have largely unrestricted rights as to the management and treatment of labor; and a political and economic system in which property rights, wealth, and political power are skewed in favor of the rich and business class. The result, as portrayed in these textbooks, was a lopsided, socially suspect distribution of wealth and power in which an elite enjoyed great luxury and largely unrestricted control of industry while millions of other Americans spent twelve-hour work days earning poverty-level wages in the nation's mills and factories, risking immediate termination for the least offense.

New Economic Theory

Documenting and publicizing the existence of numerous serious labor problems was crucial to the institutional project because it provided empirical evidence that both called the orthodox body of economic theory into question and created a compelling case for social reform (for a critical review, see Fishback, 1998). These economists thus became famous for detailed case studies and field investigations of labor conditions and institutions. But "facts" by themselves are not always persuasive; what is also needed is an intellectual theory or framework that indicates why labor problems occur and how they can be solved. In particular, since the orthodox theory of the day suggested that labor unions (and labor legislation) are either futile or pernicious, legitimating these institutions required a legitimating set of ideas. This was the goal of the early institutional labor economists.

The first and in many respects most influential attempt at institutional theorizing was done by the English historical economists/sociologists Sidney and Beatrice Webb in their book, *Industrial Democracy* (1897). Their ideas were then elaborated and developed by American labor economists, such as John R. Commons, Sumner Slichter, William Leiserson, Henry Seager, Harry Millis, and Paul Douglas. [Although modern economists tend to put Paul Douglas in the neoclassical camp, according to Reder (1982) he was regarded by his colleagues at Chicago as an institutionalist.] In modified form, this body of thought was in turn adopted by a younger generation of "neo-institutional" labor economists, such as Dunlop, Kerr, Lester, and Reynolds, and under their influence dominated research in labor economics through the mid–late 1950s (Kaufman, 1988). This tradition has been largely displaced by modern-day neoclassical economics in the field of labor economics, but remains the intellectual core of the field of industrial relations. Thus, when F&M cite in *What Do Unions Do?* (p. 3) ideas and evidence that supports trade unions by "industrial relations experts," they are referencing this institutional and neo-institutional tradition (Kaufman, 2004b).

The theory of the early institutionalists is not "theory" in the formal, analytic sense in which that term is often used today. They did nonetheless construct a logically connected, coherent body of ideas and relationships that gave a significantly different view of labor markets and the role of unions therein. Three parts of it are important for understanding their perspective on unions.

The first is the effort of the institutionalists to substitute a different set of welfare criteria for evaluating economic performance. Orthodox economics typically takes economic efficiency as the sole criterion, with other social goals ruled out as normative and thus not amenable to scientific analysis. The early institutionalists, however, believed that all economic theory is inherently normative so they felt it permissible to introduce explicit normative criteria. [Commons (1934a) states the goal of institutional economics is to "correlate economics, law, and ethics," based on the idea that the rules of the economic game (a.k.a. "institutions") are determined by human laws, and that all laws rest on ethical beliefs about right and wrong]. In their view, efficiency is important but so too are two other humanistic goals: first, achievement of equity and justice in workplace procedures and outcomes and, second, structuring the work experience so it contributes to human self-development and self-actualization (Kaufman, 1997; 2005).

If efficiency is the only goal, economic activity is judged solely on its contribution to consumption and production of material goods and services, and labor inevitably becomes a means to an end — an expense to be minimized and a source of work to be maximized. In such a situation Slichter (1931: 653) states that the danger is "man is a slave to industry rather than industry a servant to man." He then says (pp. 651–52), "It is vitally important that the methods of production shall be planned not only to turn out goods at low costs but to provide the kind of jobs which develop the desirable capacities of the workers. . . . It is just as important to make work more pleasant as less onerous as it is to make farms and factories produce more commodities." Also illustrative of the point of view is this statement by Commons (1919: 33) in which he contrasts the two schools of thought: "they [workers] are treated [in orthodox theory] as commodities to be bought and sold according to supply and demand," whereas in institutional theory "they are treated as citizens with rights against others on account of their value to the nation as a whole."

The second place these early labor economists modified orthodox theory is in the theory of the human agent. According to Commons (1934a: 870), the neoclassical conception of the human agent is "an infinite being capable of making all of his transactions at a single instant of time." He argues, however, that institutional economic theory should be based on a more realistic model and, in particular, one congruent with empirical research in psychology and sociology. These ideas were later taken up by Herbert Simon and the Carnegie School — most famously in Simon's idea of "bounded rationality" — and today comprise the field of behavioral economics. Thus, Commons (1934: 874) states that human behavior is largely purposive and reasoned but at the same time heavily imbued with elements of "stupidity, ignorance, and passion" — or limited cognition, imperfect information, and emotional affect in modern terms (Kaufman, 1999a).

One element of "passion" is an emotional commitment to fairness, making relative comparisons a ubiquitous influence in wage determination and a major source of discontent in business firms. Another consequence of bounded rationality is that the policies and practices of business firms are often not optimal, even when evaluated against the narrow criteria of profit and efficiency; yet another is that firms often do not minimize cost and thus operate with organizational slack. In this regard, Slichter (1931: 641–42) observes, "Managements, of course, are never as efficient as they might be. . . . When a union succeeds in obtaining a wage increase, managers feel a special need of finding ways to get more work out of the force. In fact, the shock to managerial complacency which is produced many be precisely what is needed to jolt an administration out of a rut." A fourth consequence of passion is that many aspects of workers' behavior connected with unions cannot be completely understood in terms of individualistic, rational calculations, since the decision to organize or strike (as examples) is partly motivated out of emotional states such as frustration, envy, injustice, and hatred (Wheeler, 1985; Kaufman, 1999b).

The third key area of revision is with respect to the structure and operation of labor markets. As described in my earlier theory chapter, the tendency in neoclassical economics is to examine labor markets through the lens of competitive theory and to view competition as a force promoting the social good and the interests of workers. Competition, for example, achieves an optimal allocation of resources, induces firms to pay workers compensating wage differentials for unsafe jobs, and gives workers an opportunity to quit a bad employer for a good one.

The early institutionalists took a more ambivalent stance on competition, seeing it as sometimes a positive force but at other times a negative force. Illustrative is the comment of Adams (1886: 34) that "Competition is neither malevolent nor beneficent but will work malevolence or beneficence according to the conditions under which it is permitted to act," and that of Leiserson (1938: 15), "There is nothing inherent in economic laws that makes them necessarily work out to promote human welfare if allowed free play. They need to be controlled and directed [by institutions] if we want them to accomplish human purposes."

With respect to labor in early twentieth-century America, the early institutionalists concluded that competition, if not regulated and "institutionalized," would often work against human welfare and social progress. For example, Commons states (1919: 29) that competition "tends to bring the advanced employers down to the level of the backward" and (p. 37) "ends in the despotism of powerful individuals." The same perspective is voiced in this statement by Slichter (1931: 195), "This competition [in the labor market], if unrestricted, is likely to result in low wages, a killing speed of work, an excessively long working day, and hazardous and unhealthy shop conditions."

To make competition promote human ends, they concluded, it not only has to be free but also *fair* and *balanced* (Budd, 2004). Competition is fair and balanced when the rules of the game do not unduly favor one side over the other, both sides have reasonably equal opportunities and access to markets, and neither the buyers nor sellers have a lopsided advantage in resources (endowments). The idea of fair and balanced competition leads to what is arguably the single most important positive and normative concept in the early institutional literature — *equality of bargaining power*. Equality of bargaining power was never rigorously defined, but its origin and common-sense meaning go back to Adam Smith (the quotation previously cited) and essentially implies a "level playing field" in wage determination. With an inequality of bargaining power, the wage determination process is tipped against the individual worker, causing wages and working conditions to be lower than otherwise. Thus, Commons and Andrews (1936: 373) state, "The need for collective bargaining arises from the serious discrepancy in 'withholding power' between the individual employer and individual wage earner, a discrepancy which tends to result in terms of employment highly oppressive to the workers and injurious to society in general. It is obvious that the individual laborer is at a great disadvantage in bargaining with an employer. . . . It is a case of the necessities of the laborer pitted against the resources of the employer." On a normative level, the early institutionalists made equality of bargaining power one of the fundamental goals of labor policy, per the comment of Commons and Andrews (p. 532), "equality of bargaining power . . . is a principle so important for the public benefit that it becomes in itself a public purpose."

Equality of bargaining power became a normative purpose because only then will the terms of the labor contract pass the ethical test of "reasonableness" — the standard used in the courts of law and public opinion in determining the need for market regulation (Commons and Andrews, 1936). From this perspective, therefore, the economic case for market regulation thus turns, in significant degree, on the proposition that the worker's disadvantage in bargaining power is so substantial that it results in socially unacceptable, and often economically inefficient, terms and conditions of employment. Such conditions legitimate, in turn, abridgement of freedom of contract in labor markets through government regulation of employment. The institutionalists' legal argument supporting this position is that since the courts had earlier ruled that other forms of commercial contracts could be declared null and void if it could be shown that one side had been coerced into agreement, the state thus had constitutional grounds for abridging freedom of contract in labor markets where conditions of unemployment and dire economic necessity drive workers into agreeing to onerous terms and conditions of employment. Without such regulation, competition and freedom of contract can turn workers into "wage slaves" (Glickman, 1997).

Inequality of bargaining power may arise at two different levels in the market exchange process. One is because of greatly unequal endowments or skewed rules of the game.

To illustrate, one rule of the game that was much disputed in the early twentieth century was immigration law. Business interests, in particular, favored a policy of unlimited immigration, while many social reform groups and the above-cited economists favored legal limits on immigration. In a demand-supply diagram of a competitive labor market, the effect of the legal rule is to determine the location of the labor supply curve — a legal limit on immigration shifts it to the left and wages are high(er) while an unrestricted immigration rule shifts it (far) to the right and wages are low(er). Viewed through the prism of orthodox microeconomics, where the rules of the game are typically taken as a "given" and the welfare criterion is efficiency, the latter outcome, even if very unequal between capital and labor, appears unobjectionable because it passes the test of Pareto optimality.

Based on an alternative welfare test of reasonableness, however, the resulting terms and conditions may well be viewed as unacceptable. With unlimited immigration, the labor market is flooded with workers and the equilibrium price of labor (and associated working conditions) is driven down to a low level. Not only does this legal rule clearly benefit one class over another (the further to the right is the labor supply curve, the smaller is the wage bill paid to labor, given an inelastic demand curve, and the higher are profits earned by employers), it may well lead to wages and working conditions — even if "competitively" determined — that are clearly injurious to the efficiency of the economy and welfare of a large segment of society. Sweatshop conditions in the needle trades and 12-hour/seven-day work weeks in the steel industry are but two examples from this era. From an institutional perspective, therefore, this is a case of competition that is neither fair nor balanced — particularly in light of the fact that manufacturers had successfully lobbied Congress for high tariffs to protect their product markets from "unfair" foreign competition. Going further, to them this looked like a case of "institutional exploitation" — not the low wages that arise from "market exploitation" in orthodox theory (e.g., monopsony) — but from the low wages and dehumanizing work conditions that result from legal rules that result in a contrived oversupply of labor and cutthroat competition among workers (Taylor, 1977).

The second place inequality of bargaining power may arise is because of imperfect competition in labor markets. Abstracting from the size of endowments, a natural reference point for an equality of bargaining power in the labor market is perfect competition (Kaufman, 1989). In perfect competition, the individual employer and worker have equal bargaining power (zero, because both are wage takers) and confront each other on a level playing field. The fact of the matter, however, is that "some of our most imperfect markets are labor markets" (Lester, 1941: 43) and (p. 44) "Generally, it is easier for buyers to dominate the labor market and control the price of labor than it is for them to control the markets and prices of standard commodities." The result is that the individual worker is in an inferior bargaining position, leading to less than competitive outcomes and a measure of (market) exploitation.

The institutionalists advanced a number of reasons why labor markets are imperfect and lead to the worker's disadvantage in wage bargaining. The first is that labor markets are quoted price markets (rather than a bourse, as pictured in competitive theory), so wages are administered prices and workers are placed in a "take it or leave it" situation vis-à-vis the individual employer (Dunlop, 1944). A second is the existence of imperfect and asymmetric information in the labor market. Employers, in their view, are usually more knowledgeable about labor market conditions and can drive the better bargain, while workers are disadvantaged because the quality and quantity of working conditions is known to the employer but not to the worker ex ante to the employment contract (Slichter, 1931). A third imperfection arises from segmented labor markets and discrimination, such as against women, blacks, and foreign-born workers, which artificially limits the demand for their labor (Kaufman, 1991, 1997). A fourth feature of labor markets that tips bargaining power against workers, although not technically a market imperfection per se, is the fact that labor cannot be inventoried and workers typically have only a small financial reserve fund, thus putting extra pressure on them to sell their daily labor at whatever price it can fetch (Webb and Webb, 1897).

An additional source of employer control over wages is due to monopsony and employer collusion. Classic forms of monopsony were more widespread in this historical era. One economist estimated, for example, that two million workers in the 1930s were employed in local communities with only one significant employer (MacDonald, 1938: 77). Also illustrative is the remark of Senator Robert Wagner (quoted in Huthmacher, 1968: 64), after touring company-owned Appalachian coal camps, that "had I not seen it myself, I would not have believed in the United States there were large areas where civil government was supplanted by a system that can only be compared with ancient feudalism." Regarding employer collusion, Millis (National Labor Relations Board, 1985: 1555) states, "Even in a city like Chicago, an industry may dominate a large community, and the firms engaged in it may control the situation within rather wide limits. Going beyond this, I would cite a number of instances where associations of manufacturers or merchants have fixed wage scales or, indeed, maximum wages to be paid and have enforced them more successfully than any American state has enforced its minimum wage standards."

If monopsony is defined broadly to cover any employment situation where an employer faces an upward sloping labor supply curve, then according to the institutionalists, it is widespread to the point of being ubiquitous in medium-to-large companies. In their view (e.g., Slichter, 1931; Reynolds, 1946), firms, for example, often confront a kinked labor supply curve — a horizontal part for new hires but an upward sloping part for the "inframarginal" workers who confront mobility costs from accumulated seniority rights, benefit entitlements, and specific on-the-job training. The firms thus pay competitive market wages to the new hires (the "marginal" workers) but may pay less than competitive wages to the inframarginal employees.

Monopsony and related forms of imperfect competition represent a demand-side problem — not enough employers bidding for labor to maintain competitive conditions. To the early labor economists, there was another demand-side problem that was far more prevalent and a much more serious source of unequal bargaining power and anti-social conditions in labor market — a lack of jobs (Commons, 1921a; Kaufman, 1997).

Due to massive immigration, large-scale migration from farm to city, and long periods of recession and depression, most urban labor markets in the early part of the twentieth century experienced a chronic condition of excess supply, putting continual downward pressure on wages and labor conditions, particularly for the unskilled. This process is vividly described by the Webbs (1897: 660):

> When the unemployed are crowding round the factory gates every morning, it is plain to each man that, unless he can induce the foreman to select him rather than another, his chance of subsistence for weeks to come may be irretrievably lost. Under these circumstances, bargaining, in the case of the isolated individual workmen, becomes absolutely impossible. The foreman has only to pick his man, and tell him the terms. Once inside the gates, the lucky workman knows that if he grumbles at any of the surroundings, however, intolerable; if he demurs to any speeding-up, lengthening of the hours, or deduction; or if he hesitates to obey any order, however unreasonable, he condemns himself once more to the semi-starvation and misery of unemployment. For the alternative to the foreman is merely to pick another man from the eager crowd, whilst the difference to the employer becomes incalculably infinitesimal.

Also illustrative is this statement by Commons and Andrews (1936: 48):

> Another reason for the low wage scale, largely the result of the first [extensive immigration], is the cutthroat competition of the workers for work. Among the unskilled, unorganized workers, the wage that the cheapest laborer — such as the partially supported woman, the immigrant with low standards of living, or the workman oppressed by extreme need — is willing to take, very largely fixes the wage level for the whole group.

The early labor economists recognized that wage adjustments play an important and necessary role in allocating labor and maintaining a balance between demand and supply. They also believed, however, that allowing the general level of wages and labor conditions to sink in response to widespread unemployment is most often ineffective and even counter-productive (Commons, 1921b; Slichter, 1931). One reason, anticipating Keynes, is that they believed wage cuts not only fail to restore equilibrium in labor markets but most often worsen the situation. Wage cuts, for example, reduce purchasing power and aggregate demand and corrode employee morale and productivity. Worse, if allowed to proceed, wage cuts can lead to a deflationary process of "destructive competition" in labor markets in which excess supply conditions, restricted factor mobility (e.g., inability to move to another state or country where jobs are available), and the pressure of fixed costs (e.g., ongoing food, shelter, and medical expenses for families) lead workers to bid down wages to rock-bottom levels (Clark, 1924). Steinbeck's *The Grapes of Wrath* (1939) depicted this process among California fruit pickers during the Depression.

The second reason they opposed this process is because of the human toll it takes on workers and their families. If labor were a commodity like wheat or coal, a downward plunge in the wage and labor conditions might well be an efficient method to restrict supply and stimulate demand. When used in labor markets, however, the result is widespread human misery. [Further aggravating the problem is that the aggregate labor supply curve was viewed as negatively sloped (Lester, 1941), so a general decline in wages actually expands the supply of labor in the market and exacerbates the demand/supply imbalance.]

It is evident from the forgoing that unequal bargaining power is, in the institutional perspective, a fundamental feature of early twentieth-century labor markets. The ill-effects of unequal bargaining power reveal themselves, in turn, in the numerous labor problems previously cited — poverty wages, long hours, frequent accidents, and so on. Particularly damaging to the efficiency of the labor market is that competition no longer gives rise to fully compensating wage differentials (or any differentials at all) and, indeed, crowding of the unemployed and marginalized into a restricted range of jobs causes the least agreeable employments to also pay the worst (Commons and Andrews, 1936; Kaufman, 1997). Because competition does not give rise to fully compensating differentials for factors such as risk of injury and disagreeable job characteristics, the private marginal cost of labor to firms is less than the social marginal cost, and workplace "bads" — such as accidents, heat, and polluted air — are overproduced. Firms are also able to shift part of the social cost of production to workers, their families, and the community (Stabile, 1993) — a form of social subsidization of capital the Webbs (1897) called "industrial parasitism."

This discussion leads to the one class of market imperfections not yet discussed in any detail — externalities and public goods. These imperfections are important, partly because they provide much of the rationale in F&M's theory for the benefits of the voice face of unions.

F&M stress that public goods and external effects are most likely to adversely affect the optimal supply of working conditions, a point also well-recognized by the earlier generation of institutional labor economists. A fundamental source of public good and externality problems is indivisible or poorly specified property rights. The desired working conditions, for example, may be "lumpy" and thus non-partitionable — per Lester's (1941: 39) observation that "the desire [of workers] for a larger measure of security simply cannot be chopped up into small particles — the only form in which the market can handle problems."

Likewise, because slavery is illegal employers cannot purchase property rights to the person but only to an hour of his labor, leading them to seek to maximize short-run work effort and output at the expense of the employee's long-term health and stamina (ibid.: 42). Often, as a result, workers' physical and human capital was rapidly depleted, leaving them "on the scrap heap" by age 40. A third example stems from the indivisible nature of firm's employment practices, per Slichter's (1931: 655) observation that a minority group of employees in a firm will often be unable to trade-off more amenable work conditions for lower wages because the firm cannot provide (as an example) different levels of accident prevention to different groups of workers within the same plant. Finally, due to bounded rationality and imperfect information, it is impossible for the worker to write a fully contingent employment contract that specifies the full range of present and future working conditions (Commons and Andrews, 1936). As a result, many terms and conditions of employment are open-ended and, once employment has commenced, subject to different interpretations and sometimes opportunistic change by the employer.

For these and other reasons, even early critics of trade unionism, such as W.H. Hutt (1980: 74), concluded that competitive determination of working conditions is sub-optimal — declaring that these matters "are not adequately determined by the market process — hours and work conditions . . . are best decided collectively." In a similar vein, Millis (National Labor Relations Board, 1985: 1553) observes, "the great majority of wage-earners are employed under such conditions that they must act in concert with reference to wage scales, hours, and working conditions if they are to have a reasonably effective voice as to the terms on which they shall work."

IV. Theory of Unions and Collective Bargaining

I now examine in more detail theoretical propositions the early institutionalists advanced about trade unions and collective bargaining. It must be kept in mind, however, that their ideas on these matters evolved over time, as is amply illustrated in the next section of this chapter. Indeed, it is a basic plank of the institutional paradigm that there are few economic theories that are "timeless" in their application since all operate in a constantly changing institutional and cultural context (Kaufman, 2004b).

It was observed, first, that unions vary considerably in their aims and how they achieve them. Perhaps the most famous categorization is by Hoxie (1917), who distinguishes five types: revolutionary, business, uplift, predatory, and dependent. The dominant type of unionism in the United States was business unionism, and the institutionalists gave most attention and clearly sought to promote this type. Unions in other countries, such as France and Italy, tended to eschew workplace collective bargaining for methods of class struggle and "direct action" (sabotage, general strikes) — tactics that tend to put them outside the realm of economic analysis (even broadly defined) and at odds with the institutionalists' normative goal of preserving social order through negotiation and compromise.

Second, they conceived of collective bargaining as a method of market and workplace rule making and regulation. In this respect, the justification for trade unions and collective bargaining turns on the same sort of generic considerations that apply to any form of social and economic regulation — does it promote efficient use of resources and valued human/social goals?

Third, as an agency of rule making and regulation, collective bargaining has two broad functions (Slichter, 1939; Kaufman, 2000a). The first is an economic function aimed at improving the terms and conditions of employment. The emphasis is on use of the union's market power to raise wages and improve hours, benefits, job security, and working conditions. This function matches closely F&M's "monopoly face." In this regard, it was clear to the early institutionalists that in their economic function unions were monopoly-like organizations. Slichter (1931: 354) observes, for example, that "trade unions, of course, are monopolies, or at least attempts to create monopolies," while the Webbs (1897: 816) note, "Powerful Trade Unions show no backwardness in exacting the highest money wages that they know how to obtain."

Commons (1950: 59) suggests, however, that the better way to view unions is not as monopolies per se but as cartels. Unions do not own and sell their members' labor but set a uniform market price. Unions are also like cartels in that the cartel leaders must devise a pricing (and entry) policy that promotes the survival of the organization and satisfies the interests of the individual members. This task necessarily involves a political process within the organization, leading the institutionalists to view unions even in their economic function as necessarily a form of political organization (or "industrial government") operating in an economic environment (Commons, 1921b; Ross, 1948). Thus, Slichter (1931: 658) notes that, "unions are democratic organizations and their policies necessarily reflect the desires and the interests of their members," while the Webbs (1897: 836) seem to anticipate the median voter model (described in my earlier theory chapter) with their observation that "whenever the association contains several distinct classes of workers . . . any scheme of equalized finances and centralized administration produces, even with the best of democratic machinery, neither efficiency nor the consciousness of popular control, and hence is always in a condition of unstable equilibrium." With regard to the economic goals of unions, some of the institutionalists were willing to follow Samuel Gompers and take the goal as "more." Commons (1913: 121), however, suggested a three-fold typology of union goals: wealth redistribution, joint aggrandizement, and protection.

Unions also have a second face — a political function in which they use rule making and regulation to introduce joint decision-making, worker participation and representation, and due process into firms' governance structures. This function is a generalization of F&M's "voice face." Commons (1921b), for example, observed that firms are governance structures or a form of industrial government and, as such, have leaders and "citizens," a body of written and unwritten laws and rules that define rights, duties, and procedures, and an executive, legislative, and judicial process for proposing, enforcing, and interpreting workplace rules. The object of the governance face is to transform the firm from one of industrial monarchy and "divine right of capitalists" to what Commons called "constitutional government in industry," the Webbs (1897) called "industrial democracy," and Slichter (1939) called "civil rights in industry."

Fourth, also like F&M, the early institutionalists recognized that unions have both negative and positive effects on economic efficiency and social welfare (to be detailed shortly). They therefore evaluated unions using a benefit/cost analysis similar to that proposed by F&M. Writing in 1926, for example, economist Warren Catlin (p. 316) observes:

> Unionism, as a whole, centering in collective bargaining, is, of course, to be judged according to its effectiveness in meeting the evils of unemployment, overstrain, industrial accidents, occupational disease, inadequate wages, wealth-concentration, and inequality of opportunity, which have been presented as the chief planks in the indictment of labor against modern capitalism. The defenders of unionism need not be expected to demonstrate that it is also positively beneficial and advantageous to employers as a class, desirable as that might be; but they are called upon to show that it does tend to restore balance in the industrial world, and is a substantial help to the workers without doing material injustice to employers or injury to the public. The good that it does one of the three parties must not be counterbalanced by the harm it does to the other two.

Fifth, using this standard, it is noteworthy that American labor economists of this period — even from the University of Chicago — were near unanimous in their belief that the nation would benefit from a higher level of unionism than existed before the NLRA. Representative is this statement made by Millis in his Congressional testimony on the NLRA (National Labor Relations Board, 1985: 1557): "I, therefore, maintain that organization [trade unions] and intelligent and honest collective bargaining has a sound basis in economics." Also providing testimony was Paul Douglas (the period's foremost analytical labor economist and, with Millis, a member of the Chicago faculty), who declared to the same Senate committee (p. 239), "I should like to submit that the organization of labor should be welcomed instead of feared. We might get along with purely individual bargaining in a period of small-scale competitive capitalism. When large-scale enterprises appeared, individual bargaining, even under competition became inadequate."

Finally, the early institutionalists also emphasized the valuable role of unions in giving working people a voice and representation in the larger political process of the nation. In their view, business interests dominated and often corrupted the legislatures and courts of that period, leading Veblen (1904: 286) to state that American democracy "means, chiefly, representative of business interests." In a similar vein, Baker remarks (1904: 378), "They [workers] see the railroad corporations and similar combinations getting class representation in our legislatures, and even higher up, in our Congress, by bribery and purchase; why should not the union men vote for what they want? At least it is honest." Thus, unions provide not only countervailing power and voice in the labor market and internal firm governance but also in the larger political arena.

Having set out the general principles, I turn to a more detailed look at the economic and political faces of unions and the benefits and costs that go with each.

The Economic Function

As previously indicated, the early institutionalists viewed unions as akin to labor market monopolies or cartels. They further recognized that in the "perfect" market of orthodox theory the exercise of this monopoly power by unions would harm efficiency and social welfare. In this spirit, Millis notes in his Congressional testimony on the NLRA (National Labor Relations Board, 1985: 1553–54):

> Of course if there were perfect mobility of labor, keen competition for labor, and no concerted control of wages and hours by employers, the situation would be substantially different from what is has been and the case for collective bargaining would be less conclusive in modern industry. I am aware that many of my academic brethren assume that these conditions just mentioned are generally true, and reason that in the absence of such friction in the market, wages, hours, and all the rest of it rather steadily adjust themselves to what industry, and consumers, should and can bear.

But then he notes (pp. 1553–54),

> The truth, as I see it, is . . . that the competitive demand for labor, while important, does not go far in protecting the workers against long hours, excessive overtime, fines, discharge without sufficient cause, and objectionable working conditions. . . . One is thus driven to the conclusion that . . . hours of work and conditions of work — things which intimately concern workmen, are best decided collectively — through legislation or through collective bargaining, and some of them are not easily subject to legislative control. This is particularly true of a reasonable degree of security of tenure. The case for collective bargaining is only less strong with respect to wages.

Five aspects of this quote deserve comment. First, Millis justifies unionism on grounds that it protects workers from various evils, such as excessive hours and objectionable working conditions. Second, he acknowledges that competitive theory leads to a negative verdict on the economic effects of unionism, but he sets aside this verdict because the theory does not capture the numerous "frictions" that impede the competitive process. Third, he points to problems with the "competitive demand for labor" as the crucial weak spot in the orthodox theory of labor markets. He acknowledges that the competitive demand for labor provides some protection for workers, but claims that it is inadequate. Fourth, he states that the case for collective bargaining is strongest for the determination of working conditions and "less strong" for determination of wages. This conclusion is, in broad outline, parallel to the viewpoint of F&M. Finally, for reasons discussed later in this chapter, it is useful to note that Millis' testimony in favor of collective bargaining was made in 1935 — six years into the Great Depression.

The problems with the competitive demand for labor have already been described — administered wages, imperfect/asymmetric information, segmented markets and discrimination, costs of mobility, monopsony (broadly defined), public goods and externalities, and (most importantly) lack of jobs and unemployment. These labor market imperfections, in turn, lead a system of individual bargaining to yield less than competitive wage rates and other terms and conditions of employment contract. The fundamental rationale for the exercise of unions' monopoly power, therefore, is that it provides a defensive, countervailing form of power — it balances the employers' superiority of power in the market and protects the worker from exploitation and unreasonable conditions. Thus, Slichter (1931: 365) states of monopolies, "The monopoly may succeed in raising the price and even raising it substantially, but this does not necessarily mean that the price is unreasonably high." He goes on to observe, "The best examples of monopolies which merely eliminate cutthroat competition are found among labor unions." A similar perspective is offered by Douglas (1934: 94–95): "the forces which operated against labor's receiving its marginal product were stronger than those which tend to prevent capital from securing its margin. An increased activity by the state in behalf of labor, or further unionization on the part of the wage-earners themselves, would have helped to redress this balance [of bargaining power]."

Unions in their economic function also bring numerous other benefits. Many promote greater efficiency and conservation of the nation's human resources, while others are valued for the humanistic goals earlier described. Among the most important benefits mentioned by the early institutionalists are the following (every item can be found in Millis and Montgomery, 1945; Slichter, 1931; Lester, 1941):

- *Taking Wages Out of Competition.* If unions can organize all competing firms, they can use collective bargaining to establish uniform labor costs across the industry (what the Webbs called "the Device of the Common Rule" and the "Standard Rate") and thus take wages out of competition. Doing so promotes the market stabilization goal because it protects wages and labor standards from downward "nibbling" from lower cost or more desperate competitors in product and labor markets (Commons, 1909). The standard rate can then be gradually raised over time in line with the increase in productivity and industry profits so workers share equitably in the fruits of progress.
- *Promote Efficiency in Other Areas.* Taking wages out of competition also transfers the force of competitive rivalry to other areas, such as managerial efficiency,

product quality, research and development, and human capital investment. Firms are also induced to modernize and update their capital. Another positive effect of a union floor on labor cost is that it drives the least efficient firms out of business and allows a reallocation of capital, labor, and output to their more efficient competitors.

- *Increase Employee Security.* Security is a highly valued "good" for workers, in part for its own intrinsic value and in part to ensure that workers have income to cover ongoing fixed and variable living costs. Competitive markets not only do not provide the "optimal" amount of security for workers, they often represent a daily threat to security — particularly in the real world of scarce jobs and costly, time-consuming search. Unions increase job security in part by making it more expensive/difficult for firms to layoff workers and in part by establishing formal rules (or job property rights) about how layoffs and new job opportunities are distributed.
- *Increase Human Capital Investment.* Unions tend to change labor from a variable to a quasi-fixed cost for the firm. Since workers are thus less likely to turnover and have longer job tenure, firms have greater incentive to invest in on-the-job training and other forms of human capital. For this reason, and also because of higher union wages, organized firms are also able to "skim the cream" of the work force and get the higher quality workers.
- *Standardize the Wage Structure.* Studies of local labor markets and firms' internal wage structures by the early institutional economists revealed that competition did not set one uniform "going wage" like theory predicts but instead permitted a wide range of seemingly haphazard and often discriminatory wage differentials to co-exist even among workers in the same plant doing the same job. A benefit of unions was to standardize and formalize the wage structure.
- *Protect Employees from Overwork.* Employees have to maintain the value of their physical and human capital over a 30–40 year time horizon, and often their financial needs grow over time for family reasons. Employers, however, typically have a shorter time horizon and, particularly for wage workers who are in plentiful supply, want to get from them as much work as possible, even if this means rapid depreciation of the worker's capital (since the workers can be readily replaced). Unions can establish reasonable workloads and work speed, thus preventing this wastage of the nation's human resources.
- *Promote Greater Employee Work Effort.* Paradoxically, unions can also contribute to greater output by creating conditions that promote greater employee work effort. For example, when employees believe they are not being treated fairly, they hold back on work effort and even sabotage production. By establishing fair treatment in the plant, unions help create a positive work environment and promote greater work effort. Likewise, in piecework production workers deliberately hold back, fearing maximum effort will later cause management to cut the piece rate. By protecting piece rates from unilateral change, unions remove this problem.
- *Reduce Turnover.* In nonunion firms, employees who are dissatisfied with conditions and treatment at their place of work are often afraid to speak up or never get their concerns addressed, leading to high turnover rates and numerous forms of additional cost (hiring, training, search, etc.)
- *Threat Effect.* The fear of being organized causes many nonunion firms to pay more attention to their employees' needs and interests than otherwise, leading many to give their workers more competitive wages and implement personnel procedures more efficiently and fairly.

- *Protect High-Road Employers.* By placing a floor under competition, unions protect "high-road" employers (progressive firms with above-market pay and benefit programs) from the competitive threat posed by "low standards" firms that seek competitive advantage through low pay and skimping on work conditions.
- *Promote Aggregate Demand.* Many trade unionists and early institutional economists believed that a capitalist economy is prone to under-consumption. They saw unions as a way to promote purchasing power and full employment by transferring above-normal profits (monopoly rents) from owners of capital to workers, given that the latter have a higher propensity to spend. Failure to correct this imbalance results in aggregate supply growing faster than aggregate demand, eventually bringing about a glut in product markets, a deflationary slump, and risk of destructive competition. In the 1940s, the positive aggregate demand effect of unions evolved into the doctrine of "social Keynesianism" (Kaufman, 1996).

The early institutionalists also saw that the economic function of unions had a number of downsides. While many of the benefits of unions accrue in the short run, a number of the costs only become manifest in the longer run. Some of the most important negative economic consequences of unions are the following.

- *Monopoly Wage Effect.* In the short run, market frictions and unequal bargaining power cause wages for many workers to be depressed below the competitive, full-employment level. Union wage increases are thus defensive or "monopsony reducing" (per the terminology of my earlier theory chapter). When unions have brought wages to a competitive level or perhaps modestly above, they should stop their upward push — per the stricture of the Webbs (1897: 738–89), "When the percentage of the workmen out of employment begins to rise, . . . it [the union] must necessarily check any further advance." [Millis and Montgomery (1945: 374) suggest that union wage policy should aim to place the wage slightly above the marginal value of labor and then let induced productivity growth close the gap.] As the institutionalists recognized, however, unions seek to gain the maximum price for labor and, hence, their drive for joint aggrandizement (or "more") may over the longer run push wages and labor costs significantly above the competitive level. When this occurs, unions shift from a defensive, protective mission to an offensive, aggrandizing one. It becomes "a cold business proposition" aimed at "controlling the market," "crushing competition," and "mulcting the public" (Baker, 1904). The most important factors making possible union monopoly wage effects, according to the institutionalists, are complete organization of the employers, control of the supply of labor, a strategic position in the industry, and supportive government.
- *Restriction of Labor Supply.* The institutionalists noted that unions could raise the wage rate by using bargaining power to either set a standard rate or restrict the supply of labor (Webbs, 1897). The former sets a wage floor above the market equilibrium rate (similar to a minimum wage law) while the latter raises the wage by shifting the labor supply curve to the left. They favored the former, as practiced by industrial unions, because it raises the plane of competition without otherwise interfering with market processes and efficient resource allocation. Most unions of this period, however, were craft unions which sought to limit the supply and utilization of labor through numerous restrictive practices, per

Hansen's observation (1922: 523): "No one is more firmly convinced that a commodity must be scarce in order to be dear than are trade unionists." These restrictive practices were viewed as harmful to efficiency and thus to be condemned — although in muted terms given the view of the institutionalists that they were often necessary to promote the larger good unions accomplish or are no worse than the restriction of output imperfectly competitive firms use to raise product price.

- *Wage Inequality.* The early institutionalists concluded that unions reduce wage dispersion among organized production workers in a plant, but in another respect they worsen income inequality. Most unions of this period were craft unions, and they largely represented skilled workers who tended to be among the higher paid before unionizing (the "aristocracy of labor"), and because of their skills and strategic position in the production process they frequently were able to use collective bargaining to force up wages to relatively high levels. In this respect, unions worsened income inequality between the highly paid skilled workers and the mass of unskilled and semi-skilled workers who remained largely unorganized.

- *Restrict Productivity.* Unions also restrict productivity and efficient plant operations in a number of ways. Commons (1913: 124) observes that "a union's purpose is necessarily and designedly restrictive. It is not designed to increase production — its purpose is to tie the employer's hands." As he elsewhere notes (1913: 122), it is possible that unions nonetheless lead to a net increase in productivity but it is "because they set other forces at work to overbalance their restrictions." Whether the direct negative effect on productivity of union restrictions outweighs the indirect positive effect (such as from increased managerial efficiency) is an empirical (and dynamic) issue, and the early institutionalists found evidence on both sides. But certainly unions, and particularly craft unions, often forced on employers numerous inefficient practices, including "make-work" requirements, restrictions on the introduction of new machinery and technology, and narrow and rigid job classifications. The adversarial climate that often accompanies collective bargaining also works against productivity.

- *Raise Cost and Reduce Profit.* Even if unions raise productivity, in most cases this cost saving is more than offset by other areas of cost increase, such as higher wages. As a generalization, therefore, unionism raises production costs and product prices and reduces profits. In a number of cases, these negative effects are relatively modest, and some lost profit represents merely a redistribution of monopoly rents to labor. However, in some industries, such as coal and apparel, the union effect on cost and profit is quite large.

- *Reduce Employment and Capital Investment.* Slichter (1939) observes that for most unions their bargaining power exceeds their organizing power. Furthermore, they tend to underestimate the long-run elasticity of demand and allow the internal political pressure of the rank and file for "more" to unduly ratchet up wages. The result is that over time unionized firms develop higher cost structures and lower margins of profit, while simultaneously a sector of lower cost nonunion firms (or plants) emerges and grows. The latter partly arises from "capital flight" and "runaway plants" as companies dis-invest in their union facilities and build new, unorganized facilities in other states or countries. Unless the firms are locked into a geographic area (say by mineral deposits or port sites) or the unions can organize the new firms or gain regulatory restrictions on entry, the union sector of firms is likely to shrink over time, as is employment and union membership.

- *Restrict Management.* Although related to productivity and cost, the negative effect of unions on the efficiency and flexibility of management was highlighted for separate attention by the early institutionalists. As already noted, in many cases before unionization the management of an enterprise suffers from inefficiency, slack, and poor leadership. But after unionization a separate set of evils appears. Unions restrict and impede management in numerous respects, such as rigid personnel practices (e.g., promotion is determined solely by seniority, inability to terminate low performers), slower decision making and ability to respond to market developments, and insistence on "working to the contract." Unions also politicize internal firm governance and sometimes management loses effective control of the work force.
- *Strikes and Boycotts.* Collective bargaining cannot work without the right to strike and occasional exercise of that right, along with other pressure tactics. Believing in the overall utility of collective bargaining, the early institutionalists accepted strikes and boycotts as a reasonable price to pay to promote equality of bargaining power and private resolution of industrial disputes. They also recognized, however, that strikes and boycotts impose costs on the public and the economy and sometimes are used irresponsibly by unions. Sympathy strikes, jurisdictional strikes, and secondary boycotts all have large "external" effects, and building trades unions in particular had a propensity to engage in internecine battles over job rights that would frequently disrupt production and inflate costs.

The Governance Function

The early institutionalists also developed a second functional explanation for unions that was political in nature and viewed unions as a part of the governance structure of industry and a vehicle for promoting democracy in the employment relationship.

According to Commons, every formal organization is a "government." In this vein he states (1950: 40), "each kind of collective action is a government, differing in the kind of 'sanctions' employed to bring the individual into conformity with the rules." The highest form of government in society is the political government that claims sovereignty over the land and people and the right to use the sanction of physical violence to enforce the working rules and defend the state against enemies. Below the nation state are a host of other organizations, including corporations, unions, churches, and political parties, forming a diffuse network of jurisdictions and power centers. From an analytical point of view, all such organizations can be viewed as a pluralistic set of governments for each is the product of collective action, is governed by working rules that specify authority relations and the distribution of rights, liberties, duties, and exposures, and employs sanctions to enforce the working rules (Commons, 1950: 75).

In the economic sphere the most important organization is the firm. A firm is a governmental entity since it claims sovereignty over scarce resources, constructs and administers working rules that govern what its members may and may not do, and enforces these rules through various sanctions. Like a political government, a firm also contains an executive, legislative, and judicial process through which the working rules are created, applied, enforced, and interpreted. Employees, in turn, are viewed not just as "hired hands" but citizens (or subjects) of the industrial government.

When the institutionalists looked at the governance structures in the political realm of American life in the early part of the twentieth century, they saw the gradual spread and development of representative democracy. While the political process was often dominated by business interests and public administration suffered from too-frequent incompetence and corruption, the government was nonetheless in broad outline run "by the people, for the people, and of the people" and provided effective law and order in civil affairs. When they looked at the economic sphere of American society, however, a far different and less positive picture emerged.

Commons (1918, Vol. 2: 519) characterized the industrial system in the late 1800s as prone to "despotism and anarchy." Anarchy exists, he states, when the strong rule the weak through the threat of physical harm and people's life and property can be taken without notice or compensation. This situation aptly characterized the laissez-faire labor market of that period, he claims, since the worker had no protected property right in his only source of income — the job — and thus a person's livelihood could be confiscated at a moment's notice through the unilateral action of either the strong (the employer) or the desperate (an unemployed job seeker). Despotism exists, in turn, when the people in control of a government exercise unrestrained power over the citizens and use this power in an exploitative and unjust manner for personal gain at the expense of the common good. Despotism also characterized the labor market of the late nineteenth–early twentieth centuries, the institutionalists thought, since employers were given nearly unrestrained rights to run their enterprises as they saw fit. While the defenders of competition and freedom of contract argued that workers had effective protection through the ability to quit one employer and seek work at another ("voting with their feet"), the institutionalists saw this protection as a weak and often ineffective one.

On the defects of industrial anarchy and autocracy the institutionalists built their case for industrial democracy. As noted in other studies (Derber, 1970; Dickman, 1987; Lichtenstein and Harris, 1993), proponents of industrial democracy at the turn of the century defined it in a number of disparate ways, ranging from profit-sharing to government ownership of the means of production. The institutionalists took a middle-of-the-road position. For them, industrial democracy has four key elements.

The first element is some method for voice, participation, and representation of group (or "stakeholder") interests in the respective unit of industrial government. Thus, Commons states (1919: 40), "Representative democracy in industry is representation of organized interests" and (p. 43) "it is the equilibrium of capital and labor—the class partnership of organized capital and organized labor, in the public interest." Democracy, in this view, requires that workers as "citizens" be given a voice in the determination of the working rules of the enterprise and in the manner the working rules are administered.

The second key element in industrial democracy is to substitute "rule by law" for "rule by men." Rule by law means that the working rules of the industrial government have to be set forth in a written document (a "constitution") and all stakeholder groups must abide by the laws of the workplace. This aspect of industrial democracy is captured in these words by Leiserson (1922: 75), "Whether carved on stone by an ancient monarch or written in a Magna Carta by a King John, or embodied in collective agreement between a union and employer, the intent is the same, to subject the ruler to definite laws to which subjects or citizens may hold him when he attempts to exercise arbitrary power."

The third key feature of industrial democracy is that an impartial judicial procedure be available to all parties when disputes arise over interpretation or application of the working rules. This feature goes under the name *due process of law*. Speaking of industrial constitutions, Commons (1919: 108) states in this regard, "Like the Constitution of the United States, the agreement has become a 'government of law and not of men.' A man is not deprived of his job without 'due process of law.' This is the difference between democracy and autocracy, and the reason why the machinery of democracy is complex and that of autocracy is simple."

The fourth key element of industrial democracy for the institutionalists is a reasonable balance of power between the employer and worker. Power, to the institutionalists, is ability to influence, and if one party to the employment relationship has a preponderance of power, it is likely that it will be used in ways that are both arbitrary and onerous. Since in their view the employer normally has the power advantage over the individual worker, some method must be found to equalize power if mutual discussion and compromise are to take the place of dictation and unilateralism in the workplace. The method the institutionalists advocated was creation of collective forms of organization that represent workers, such as trade unions, political parties, professional associations, and employer-created representation bodies. Thus, Commons (1919: 43) states, "Only through organization can the modern industrial worker . . . have an effective voice either in industry or government. . . . In his individual weakness he gains greater power and liberty through organization."

Given these key elements of industrial democracy, the next issue confronting the institutionalists was how to operationalize it. Not unexpectedly, their first choice was collective bargaining through trade unions. With regard to the representative function in industrial government, the trade union appeared to be ideal since its purpose is to represent workers, and its operation and leadership are controlled by the worker members. Likewise, the institutionalists saw in the process of collective bargaining a direct parallel to the legislative function in political government. Commons described the negotiating meetings of the employers' and workers' representatives as an "industrial parliament," the trade agreement as the "constitution" of the industrial government, and the myriad of rules and regulations hammered out by the parties governing the day-to-day utilization of labor as the "common law" of the shop. Trade unions also brought due process of law to the workplace by requiring that employers abide by written standards of conduct, through establishment of a formal dispute resolution process that protected workers rights to a fair trial, and ensuring that in case of unresolved disputes a decision is rendered not by the employer but by a neutral third party. Sumner Slichter (1941: 1) refers to this adjudicatory function of collective bargaining as "industrial jurisprudence." Finally, trade unions also equalized the bargaining power between the firm and workers.

Clearly, the political dimension of unions provides an entirely separate rationale and justification for collective bargaining. In certain respects it also has greater public appeal. In their economic function, unions necessarily accomplish their purpose through measures that abridge and curtail competition and freedom of contract — principles that are viewed favorably by most of the public as bedrock American values. The early institutionalists sought to shift the terms of the debate over union power from a focus on "competition vs. monopoly" to "democracy vs. autocracy." Since Americans also instinctively favor democratic forms of governance over authoritarian forms, the institutionalists saw the governance (industrial democracy) rationale for unions as an effective way to give union power a positive public purpose (Dickman, 1987).

Although predisposed to favor unionism and collective bargaining on grounds of industrial democracy, the institutionalists also recognized that in reality the balance sheet is more checkered. In particular, they saw that unions themselves were frequently undemocratic and, sometimes, corrupt. Commons (1919: 122) states in this vein, "we know that organized labor is as likely to be as arbitrary as the employer if it has the power. . . . In the name of democracy labor may be as despotic as capital in the name of liberty." Likewise, Hoxie (1917: 177) observes, "unionism in its own organization and conduct is hardly to be called democratic." Many unions of that period also had very restrictive and discriminatory membership policies aimed at rationing high-paying jobs among a select few. Many union constitutions of the period contained a formal bar on admission of black workers, while many craft unions were essentially "closed" organizations with insiders protected by high initiation fees and restrictive apprenticeship requirements. In this regard, no aspect of the "monopoly face" of unions attracted more public disapproval and employer resistance than the practice of the "closed shop." The closed shop — an agreement that the employer will only hire and employ members in good standing of a particular union — was widespread before being banned in the Taft-Hartley amendments to the NLRA in 1947. Unions claimed that the closed shop protected them from "free riders" and the substitution in production of nonunion workers for union workers, while critics claimed it gave unions a virtual monopoly on the supply of labor to the firm and a potent way to control both employers and the union

rank and file. The early institutionalists took a conflicted position on this matter
— admitting the defects of the closed shop in principle and practice but nonetheless condoning it as a necessary device to provide unions bargaining power and
organizational stability (Slichter, 1939). There was, finally, considerable pockets
of corruption in the labor movement, per Cooper's (1932: 654) observation,
"particularly in large cities, where unionism reaches its greatest strength, shady
practices involving the racket and accompanying graft flourish."

V. Labor Reform Strategy

Having described the early institutionalists' rationale for collective bargaining, the final step is to situate unionism and collective bargaining within their
larger strategy of labor reform (Kaufman, 2003). The agenda for reform is the
solution of the numerous labor problems previously described. To accomplish this
task, the institutionalists developed a reform strategy with three major goals.

The first goal is stabilization of product and labor markets to smooth disruptive fluctuations in production and employment, prevent excess supply
conditions from dragging down labor standards, provide workers with secure,
full-time jobs, and eliminate what the institutionalists (Commons, 1921a) saw
as the most important problem of capitalism — unemployment. The second
goal is equality of bargaining power between workers and employers. The aim
is to redistribute property rights, balance endowments, and use countervailing
forms of market power to make competition in labor markets fair and balanced,
creating a "level playing field" in the determination of the terms and conditions of employment. The third goal is industrial democracy or "constitutional
government in industry." The aim is to bring into the industrial sphere basic
democratic practices enjoyed by workers in the political sphere, such as a written agreement, opportunities for participation and representation (or "voice")
in the determination and enforcement of workplace rules, and the protection of
due process in the resolution of disputes and administration of discipline. In the
background was a fourth, superordinate goal — to preserve the basic outlines of
the American system, and its foundation on private property, a market economy,
and representative political government, from overthrow on account of class
struggle between Capital and Labor and the correlative appeal of Socialism,
Fascism, and Communism. As Commons (1934b: 143) put it, his goal was "to
save capitalism by making it good."

The next part of the institutionalists' labor reform strategy was a set of four
methods which collectively and interactively could be used to accomplish the
goals. The four are: trade unionism and collective bargaining, legal enactment
in the form of protective labor law and social insurance programs, progressive
personnel/human resource management, and macroeconomic stabilization and
full employment through monetary, fiscal, and income-redistribution policies.
A fifth instrument, but one outside the scope of this discussion, is a more general program of institutional and political reform to integrate Labor as a class

into American society and make it an equal partner in the economic enterprise — that is, to change it from being an exploited "outsider" to a justly-treated "insider."

Given these general principles, the interesting question is: What is the proper scope and role for trade unionism and collective bargaining as instruments of labor reform? The answer given by the early institutionalists evolved in four phases from 1900 to the mid–1930s, reflecting their effort to adapt and improve their labor strategy in light of new events and ideas (Kaufman, 2003). Space constraints limit me to only indicate the main outline and conclusions.

Phase I of the institutionalists' labor reform strategy starts in the late 1890s and lasted most of the next decade. Their primary instrument they promoted for improved labor outcomes was a form of bilateral monopoly established through industry-wide collective bargaining between an employers' association and a national union. Industry-wide collective bargaining took wages out of competition, thus stabilizing labor markets, established equality of bargaining power, and introduced constitutional government into industry. The other three instruments for reform received little-to-no emphasis, largely because the Supreme Court continually declared protective labor laws unconstitutional and progressive personnel management and counter-cyclical macroeconomic stabilization policies had not yet been developed.

The beginning of Phase II overlapped with the end of Phase I (roughly 1907–1909) and extended to about 1917. In Phase II the institutionalists introduced a second instrument, legal enactment, in the form of protective labor laws and social insurance programs (e.g., minimum wages, unemployment insurance). The former was intended to establish a floor of labor standards across the market; the latter was intended to insure workers and their families against risks to their employment and income (Moss, 1996). Phase II developed in part because the Supreme Court in several rulings approved protective labor laws for women, children, and hazardous trades and in part because the institutionalists realized that industry-wide collective bargaining would remain confined to a small portion of the labor market. Thus, the preferred instrument for stabilizing markets, equalizing bargaining power, and introducing industrial democracy remains unionism and collective bargaining, but legal enactment is used as a complement where unionism is largely absent. The other two instruments still wait to be developed.

In Phase III, covering the years 1918–1931, progressive management ("Welfare Capitalism") and macroeconomic monetary and fiscal stabilization are added to the mix of instruments. Although the place of legal enactment in the institutionalists' labor reform strategy is carried over and even strengthened from Phase II, progressive management and macroeconomic stabilization represent partial substitutes for unionism and collective bargaining and thus the scope and role of the latter in the labor reform strategy are reduced. Counter-cyclical monetary and fiscal policies are now the major device to stabilize product and labor markets and maintain full employment and a reasonable balance in bargaining power. [Although little known today, Commons was a recognized authority on monetary policy, helped found the National Bureau of Economic Research to study business cycles, served as president of the National Monetary Union, and advocated in writings and testimony to Congress that the Federal Reserve practice a price stabilization monetary rule (Whalen, 1993). He and fellow institutionalists also advocated additional public works spending in economic downturns.] Likewise, starting about 1918 a number of progressive companies started to pioneer a new employee relations model subsequently called "Welfare Capitalism" (Jacoby, 1997; Kaufman, 2001). Components of this model were the business function of personnel management, an array of "welfare" (benefit) programs, incorporating principles of "human relations" into management, and a nonunion form of employee representation to provide voice, participation, and equitable dispute resolution. This model of progressive management also helped stabilize labor markets and equalize bargaining power since the employers, in an effort to promote employee goodwill and a "unity of interest," voluntarily provided above-average wages, employment conditions, and job security. Likewise, the institutionalists came to see the employee representation plans as an alternative form of voice and constitutional government in industry and regarded the better run plans as a suitable substitute for union voice — in some respects even superior since they avoid the adversarialism, restrictions, and craft fragmentation of many unions (Kaufman, 2000b).

Given the availability of more policy instruments, the role of trade unionism and collective bargaining in solving labor problems is narrowed and reduced in Phase III. As now envisioned by the institutionalists, the labor market has something like a bell-shaped distribution of employers ranked by the quality of their employment practices, with a group of "high road" Welfare Capitalism employers in the right-hand tail, a group of "low road" employers (a heterogeneous group with disproportionate representation of smaller, undercapitalized firms; companies in "secondary" labor markets; and companies in competitive, labor-intensive industries) in the left-hand tail, and a large group of employers bunched to the left and right of the mean. The entire frequency distribution shifts to the right or left with variations in aggregate demand such that a state of full employment considerably shortens (but never eliminates) the left-hand tail of "bad" employers. The role of collective bargaining (complemented by protective labor legislation) is fivefold: first, to truncate the lower part of the left-hand tail of the distribution of employment practices either by raising standards or forcing these employers out of business (implying some employment loss from union wage gains or a minimum wage law is not necessarily harmful to efficiency and welfare); second, to take wages out of competition in certain "sick" industries (e.g., coal, apparel) through industry-wide collective bargaining so the pressure of excess capacity and destructive competition did not drag down labor standards below the social minimum; third, to use the "threat effect" to pressure unorganized firms (especially those below the mean) to improve their employment practices; fourth, to bring "constitutional government in industry" to firms anywhere in the frequency distribution that use punitive, harsh, or unjust management methods; and, fifth, to gradually shift up the frequency distribution over time through bargaining gains (and legislated increases in minimum labor standards) and the induced improvements in productivity from greater managerial efficiency and other such sources.

On the other (right-hand) side of the of the frequency distribution, the "high-road" employers — typically progressive nonunion firms — define "best practice" in employment relations at a point in time and gradually push forward the leading-edge of employment practices over time. Among these employers collective bargaining typically has no net contribution to make to social welfare, per the comment of Commons (1921a: 15) that "Labor has not come into existence at all to deal with that first class of employers [the high-road employers]. . . . It has come in solely in order to use coercion with . . . those who need it because they will not or cannot meet new conditions."

The Great Depression and New Deal of the Roosevelt administration ushered in Phase IV of the institutionalists' labor reform strategy. As they saw it, monetary stabilization (in conjuction with the gold standard) had dramatically failed, leading to mass unemployment and the reappearance of labor problems on a scale and scope not seen for several decades. With mass unemployment, the frequency distribution of employers shifted dramatically to the left. By 1932 all but the remnants of the "high-road" employers of the 1920s were slashing wages, eliminating job security, and reverting to a harsher regime of labor management. Suddenly, practically every industry was "sick" and wages and labor standards were ratcheting downwards under the pressure of destructive competition. Thus, just as monetary stabilization had appeared to fail, so had progressive management, and neither appeared to offer a way out of the debacle. Since large-scale pump priming through Keynesian-style fiscal policy had not yet been popularized [Keynes' General Theory was not published until 1936], the Roosevelt administration and the institutionalists were left with two remaining instruments — legal enactment and trade unionism. They combined these, with a version of European corporatism and cartel policy, to create the National Industrial Recovery Act (NIRA), the New Deal's central piece of economic recovery legislation (Hawley, 1966).

To stanch destructive competition and stabilize product markets, the NIRA encouraged firms to form industry associations and collectively set price and production quotas through negotiated "codes of fair competition." The same was to be accomplished in labor markets by a combination of much-expanded collective bargaining (encouraged by the NIRA's Section 7a guarantee of the right to organize) and minimum wage and maximum hour provisions. Expansion of collective bargaining considerably beyond its Phase III domain was now seen as desirable for three other reasons. The first was to equalize bargaining power, since the Depression tilted the playing field sharply in favor of employers, and the NIRA paradoxically then compounded the problem by encouraging firms to collude in the setting of wages and hours. The second was to restore full employment through income redistribution. Most of the institutionalists and New Dealers (Commons excepted, who still held a monetary theory of the Depression) thought the cause of the Depression was underconsumption resulting from the 1920s drift toward greater income inequality, so they sought to promote recovery by using collective bargaining to redistribute income from profits to wages and thus expand purchasing power and aggregate demand (Kaufman, 1996). The third was to spread industrial democracy across labor markets, reflecting the widespread perception that employers had treated labor with considerable injustice and harshness.

The NIRA was declared unconstitutional in 1935, but soon thereafter three new pieces of labor legislation were enacted that collectively implemented the institutionalists' Phase IV labor reform strategy. The first was the National Labor Relations Act, which in the Preamble attributed the Depression to labor's unequal bargaining power and therefore declared it in the public interest to "encourage the practice and procedure of collective bargaining." The Act also discouraged alternative forms of employee voice by banning employer-created employee representation plans. The second law was the Social Security Act, which enacted old-age pensions and unemployment insurance. The third law was the Fair Labor Standards Act, which enacted minimum wage, maximum hour, and child labor standards. Together these laws sought to solve the massive labor problems unleashed by the Depression through a comprehensive program of institutional reform. Because monetary stabilization and progressive management appeared impotent, the institutionalists returned to the Phase II version of their labor reform strategy and used trade unionism and legal enactment as the instruments to bring fairness and balance to wage determination, economic security to workers and their families, democracy and voice to the governance of the workplace, and full employment to the macroeconomy. These policies clearly resonated with the American work force and public, because union membership and density more than tripled and the organized labor movement became a central component of a much larger social movement that dominated American intellectual and political thinking for several decades.

VI. Conclusion

The work of the early institutional labor economists provides numerous insights on the economic case for and against unionism and collective bargaining. Contained in their work is clear recognition that unions have two faces — a "monopoly" face and a "voice" face — and that unions both promote and harm economic efficiency and social welfare. In this respect, the ideas advanced by Freeman and Medoff have clear antecedents in the early institutional and industrial relations literature. Where the early institutionalists and F&M differ is that the former do not immediately assume the monopoly face of unions is detrimental, or that the voice face is mostly a matter of communication with management and aggregation of preferences to overcome collective choice problems. As seen by the institutionalists, most labor markets are by nature imperfect so the effect of union monopoly power is frequently to offset employer power in wage determination, resulting (on net) in more efficient and equitable terms and conditions of employment. Similarly, the fundamental contribution of the voice face of unions is to democratize the workplace, replacing unilateral and sometimes arbitrary rule with constitutional government in industry. Unions not only provide workers more "voice" (communication) but also more "muscle" (power) to make this voice heard and effective.

Key to the institutional theory of unions is a heterodox perspective on labor markets that contains a wider set of welfare criteria, a behavioral theory of the human agent, models of imperfect competition, explicit attention to the legal "rules of the game," and recognition of involuntary unemployment and dynamic linkages between microeconomic and macroeconomic aspects of wage/employment determination. With such a model, there is no presumption that market outcomes are necessarily efficient or fair — although they may be — and, thus, there is opportunity for the exercise of union power to do good as well as harm. The positive face of unions in the early institutional perspective comes from the exercise of union power to protect the underdog, level the playing field, promote full employment, bring a measure of justice, dignity, and due process to the workplace, and pressure legislators to pass laws promoting the interests of workers. In this mode, union power is required for both wages and voice and serves the social welfare in both cases (contra F&M). The negative face of unions appears when they pass from this protective and democratic function to an aggrandizing and autocratic function in which they use their power to exploit firms and consumers through excessive wages and restrictive rules, deny their own members genuine voice and representation in internal union governance, and lobby Congress for laws that protect and enhance union monopoly rents at the expense of the welfare of the community. Expressed in this face, union power is detrimental to social welfare in both its bargaining and voice functions.

The other key insight provided by the early institutionalists is that the degree to which unions have a positive versus negative face depends on several important contingencies overlooked by F&M and many other contemporary economists. The first is the level of unemployment in the labor market. The greater the level of unemployment in the labor market, the worse the imbalance in bargaining power between the employer and worker and the greater the need for collective bargaining to protect workers from the emergence of exploitation, sweatshop conditions, and unjust treatment. Explicit in this position is rejection of the orthodox assumption (at least in simple models) that a general decline in wages and labor standards is an effective or socially desirable way to solve an unemployment problem. Conversely, when labor markets operate at full employment, most individual workers confront their employers on a relatively level playing field and the need for union countervailing power is much reduced — but not completely eliminated since there always exists a residual of "low-road" employers and ill-treated workers even in the tightest labor market.

The other important contingency the work of the early institutionalists emphasizes is the availability and effectiveness of good substitutes for union protection. "Good markets" (full employment) are one such substitute, but so are "good employers" and "good laws" (Bennett and Kaufman, 2002). The early institutionalists never wavered in their belief that American labor markets would benefit from higher union density, but over time they significantly scaled-back their "optimal" level of density as these other substitute tools for solving labor problems emerged and developed. As they realized, the more widespread and effective are good markets, good employers, and good laws, the smaller will be the private and social demand for collective bargaining. When both the "good markets" and "good employer" options failed in the 1930s, however, they joined with the Roosevelt administration to aggressively push forward collective bargaining and legal enactment as a way to cope with that decade's enormous labor problems. Over the intervening seven decades the nation has greatly expanded the scope and scale of labor law, succeeded in providing greater stability and full employment in labor markets, and developed far more sophisticated and professional human resource management practices. Although it is conjecture on my part, if the early institutional labor economists were still alive, I believe that they would once again scale back the optimal level of union density in light of these trends, albeit not to current levels in the private sector. These historical developments, and their implications for trade unionism and national labor policy, are largely omitted by F&M from *What Do Unions Do?*, however, with the result their analysis of trade unionism and case for higher union density is less complete and persuasive.

References

Adams, Henry Carter. "Relation of the State to Industrial Action." *Publications of the American Economics Association* 1 (No. 6, 1886): 7–85.

Adams, Thomas, and Helen Sumner. *Labor Problems*. New York: MacMillan, 1905.

Baker, Ray Stanard. "A Corner on Labor." *McClures* 22 (1904): 366–78.

Bendix, Reinhard. *Work and Authority in Industry*. New York: Wiley, 1956.

Bennett, James T. and Bruce E. Kaufman. "Conclusion: The Future of Private Sector Unionism in the U.S. – Assessment and Forecast." In James Bennett and Bruce Kaufman, eds. *The Future of Private Sector Unionism in the United States*. Armonk, N.Y.: M.E. Sharpe, 2002, pp. 359–86.

Budd, John. *Employment with a Human Face: Balancing Efficiency, Equity, and Voice*. Ithaca: Cornell University Press, 2004.

Catlin, Warren. *The Labor Problem in the United States and Great Britain*. New York: Harper, 1926.

Clark, John M. *Studies in the Economics of Overhead Costs*. Chicago: University of Chicago Press, 1924.

Commons, John. "American Shoemakers, 1648–1895." *Quarterly Journal of Economics* 24 (November 1909): 39–83.

————. *Labor and Administration*. New York: MacMillan, 1913.

————. *History of Labor in the United States,* 4 vols. New York: MacMillan, 1918.

————. *Industrial Goodwill*. New York: McGraw-Hill, 1919.

————. "Industrial Relations." In John R. Commons, ed. *Trade Unionism and Labor Problems*, 2nd series. New York: Augustus Kelly, 1921a: 1–16.

————. *Industrial Government*. New York: MacMillan, 1921b.

————. *Institutional Economics: Its Place in Political Economy*. New York: MacMillan, 1934a.

————. *Myself*. Madison, Wisc.: University of Wisconsin Press, 1934b.

————. *The Economics of Collective Action*. Madison, Wisc.: University of Wisconsin Press, 1950.

———— and John Andrews. *Principles of Labor Legislation*, 4th ed. New York: Harper & Row, 1936.

Cooper, Lyle. "The American Labor Movement in Prosperity and Depression." *American Economic Review* 22 (December 1932): 641–59.

Derber, Milton. *The American Idea of Industrial Democracy, 1865–1965*. Champaign: University of Illinois Press, 1970.

Dickman, Howard. *Industrial Democracy in America*. LaSalle, Ill.: Open Court Press, 1987.

Douglas, Paul. *The Theory of Wages*. New York: MacMillan, 1934.

Dunlop, John. *Wage Determination under Trade Unions*. New York: MacMillan, 1944.

Ely, Richard. *The Labor Movement in America*. New York: Thomas Crowell, 1886.

Estey, J.A. *The Labor Problem*. New York: McGraw-Hill, 1928.

Fine, Sidney. *Laissez Faire and the General Welfare State: A Study of Conflict in American Thought, 1865–1901*. Ann Arbor: University of Michigan Press, 1956.

Fishback, Price. "Operations of 'Unfettered' Labor Markets: Exit and Voice in America Labor Markets at the Turn of the Century. "*Journal of Economic Literature* 36 (June 1998): 722-65.

Glickman, Lawrence. *A Living Wage*. Ithaca, N.Y.: Cornell University Press, 1997.

Hansen, Alvin. "The Economics of Unionism." *Journal of Political Economy* 30 (August 1922): 518–30.

Hawley, Ellis. *The New Deal and the Problem of Monopoly*. Princeton: Princeton University Press, 1966.

Hoxie, Robert. *Trade Unionism in the United States*. New York: Appleton, 1917.

Huthmacher, Joseph. *Senator Robert F. Wagner and the Rise of Urban Liberalism*. New York: Atheneum, 1968.

Hutt, W.H. *The Theory of Collective Bargaining,* reprinted. Washington: Cato Institute, 1980.

Jacoby, Sanford. *Modern Manors: Welfare Capitalism since the New Deal*. Princeton: Princeton University Press, 1997.

Kaufman, Bruce. *How Labor Markets Work: Reflections on Theory and Practice by John Dunlop, Clark Kerr, Richard Lester, and Lloyd Reynolds*. Lexington: Lexington Books, 1988.

————. "Labor's Inequality of Bargaining Power: Changes over Time and Implications for Public Policy." *Journal of Labor Research* 10 (Summer 1989): 285–97.

————. "Labor's Inequality of Bargaining Power: Myth or Reality?" *Journal of Labor Research* 12 (Spring 1991): 151–66.

————. *The Origins and Evolution of the Field of Industrial Relations in the United States*. Ithaca, N.Y.: ILR Press, 1993.

_____. "The Evolution of Thought on the Competitive Nature of Labor Markets." In Clark Kerr and Paul Staudohar, eds. *Labor Economics and Industrial Relations: Markets and Institutions*. Cambridge: Harvard University Press, 1994, pp. 145–88.

_____. "Why the Wagner Act?: Reestablishing Contact with Its Original Purpose." In David Lewin, Bruce Kaufman, and Donna Sockell, eds. *Advances in Industrial and Labor Relations,* Vol. 7. Greenwich, Conn.: JAI Press, 1996, pp. 15–68.

_____. "Labor Markets and Employment Regulation: The View of the 'Old' Institutionalists." In Bruce Kaufman, ed. *Government Regulation of the Employment Relationship*. Madison, Wisc.: Industrial Relations Research Association, 1997, pp. 11–55.

_____. "Emotional Arousal As a Source of Bounded Rationality." *Journal of Economic Behavior and Organization* 38 (February 1999a): 135–44.

_____. "Expanding the Behavioral Foundations of Labor Economics." *Industrial and Labor Relations Review* 52 (April 1999b): 361–92.

_____. "The Early Institutionalists on Industrial Democracy and Union Democracy." *Journal of Labor Research* 21 (Spring 2000a): 189–210.

_____. "The Case for the Company Union." *Labor History* 41 (August 2000b): 321–50.

_____. "The Theory and Practice of Strategic HRM and Participative Management: Antecedents in Early Industrial Relations." *Human Resource Management Review* 11 (Winter 2001): 505–34.

_____. "John R. Commons and the Wisconsin School on Industrial Relations Strategy and Policy." *Industrial and Labor Relations Review* 57 (October 2003): 3–30.

_____. *The Global Evolution of Industrial Relations: Events, Ideas, and the IIRA*. Geneva: International Labour Organization, 2004a.

_____. "The Institutional and Neoclassical Schools in Labor Economics." In Dell Champlin and Janet Knoedler, eds. *The Institutionalist Tradition in Labor Economics*. Armonk, N.Y.: M.E. Sharpe, 2004b, pp. 13–38.

"The Social Welfare Objectives and Ethical Principles of Industrial Relations." In John Budd and James Scoville, eds., *Ethics in Human Resources and Industrial Relations*. Champaign, IL.: Labor and Employment Relations Association, 2005, pp. 23-59.

Keynes, John. *The General Theory of Employment, Interest and Money*. New York: Harcourt Brace, 1936.

Leiserson, William. "Constitutional Government in American Industries." *American Economic Review* 12 (March 1922): 56–79.

_____. *Right and Wrong in Labor Relations*. Berkeley: University of California Press, 1938.

Lester, Richard. *Economics of Labor.* New York: MacMillan, 1941.

Lichtenstein, Nelson and Howell Harris. *Industrial Democracy in America: The Ambiguous Promise*. New York: Cambridge University Press, 1993.

Marshall, Alfred. *Principles of Economics*, 9th (Valorium) ed. London: MacMillan, 1961.

MacDonald, Lois. *Labor Problems and the American Scene*. New York: Harper, 1938.

McNulty, Paul. *The Origin and Development of Labor Economics*. Cambridge: MIT Press, 1980.

Millis, Harry and Royal Montgomery. *Organized Labor* (Vol. 3 of *The Economics of Labor*). New York: MacGraw-Hill, 1945.

Moss, David. *Socializing Security: Progressive-Era Economists and the Origins of American Social Policy*. Cambridge: Harvard University Press, 1996.

National Labor Relations Board. *Legislative History of the National Labor Relations Act,* Vols. 1 and 2. Washington, D.C.: U.S. Government Printing Office, 1985.

Perlam, Mark and Charles McGann, Jr. *The Pillars of Economic Understanding: Factors and Markets.* Ann Arbor: University of Michigan Press, 2000.

Perry, Arthur. *Elements of Political Economy.* New York: Scribner's, 1878.

Petridis, Anastasios. "Alfred Marshall's Attitudes to an Economic Analysis of Trade Unions: A Case of Anomalies in a Competitive System." *History of Political Economy* 5 (1 1973): 165–98.

Reder, Melvin. "Chicago Economics: Permanence and Change." *Journal of Economic Literature* 20 (March 1982): 1–38.

Reynolds, Lloyd. "The Supply of Labor to the Firm." *Quarterly Journal of Economics* 60 (May 1946): 390–411.

Ross, Arthur. *Trade Union Wage Policy.* Berkeley: University of California Press, 1948.

Slichter, Sumner. *Modern Economic Society*, 2nd ed. New York: Henry Holt, 1931.

_____. "The Changing Character of American Industrial Relations." *American Economic Review* 29 (March 1939): 121–37.

_____. *Union Policies and Industrial Management.* Washington, D.C.: Brooking Institution, 1941.

Smith, Adam. *An Inquiry into the Nature and Causes of the Wealth of Nations.* New York: Modern Library, 1937 (1776 original).

Stabile, Donald. *Activist Unionism: The Institutional Economics of Solomon Barkin.* Armonk, N.Y.: M.E. Sharpe, 1993.

Steinbeck, John. *The Grapes of Wrath.* New York: Viking, 1939.

Taylor, James. "Exploitation Through Contrived Dependence." *Journal of Economic Issues* 11 (March 1977): 51–59.

Veblen, Thorstein. *The Theory of Business Enterprise.* New York: Scribner's, 1904.

Webb, Sidney and Beatrice Webb. *Industrial Democracy.* London: Longmans Green, 1897.

Whalen, Charles. "Saving Capitalism by Making It Good: The Monetary Economics of John R. Commons." *Journal of Economic Issues* 27 (December 1993): 1155–79.

Wheeler, Hoyt. *Industrial Conflict: An Integrative Theory.* Columbia: University of South Carolina Press, 1985.

Yonay, Yuval. *The Struggle Over the Soul of Economics: Institutionalist and Neoclassical Economists in America between the Wars.* Princeton: Princeton University Press, 1998.

4

What Effect Do Unions Have on Wages Now and Would Freeman and Medoff Be Surprised?*

David G. Blanchflower and Alex Bryson

I. Introduction

> Everyone "knows" that unions raise wages. The questions are how much, under what conditions, and with what effects on the overall performance of the economy" (Freeman and Medoff, 1984, p. 43).

Richard Freeman and James Medoff's (F&M) pathbreaking 1984 book *What Do Unions Do?* has had an enormous impact. According to Orley Ashenfelter, one of the commentators in a review symposium on the book published in January 1985 in the *Industrial and Labor Relations Review*, the response of the popular press to the book "has only been short of breathtaking" (p. 245).[1] It received rave reviews at the time it was written and unlike most books has withstood the test of time. It is certainly the most famous book in labor economics and industrial relations. One of the other reviewers in the symposium, Dan Mitchell called it "a landmark in social science research" and so it has proved (p. 253). We went to the *Social Science Citations Index* and typed in "What do unions do" (hereinafter WDUD) and found that it had been cited by other academics more than one thousand times.[2] Herein we show that the vast majority of their commentary written in the early 1980s is still highly applicable despite the fact that private sector unionization has been in precipitous decline. An old adage is that a classic book is one that everyone talks about but nobody reads. F&M's work is not one of those. It is a true classic because it continues to be a book that anyone — scholar or layman — interested in labor unions needs to read!

Central to the thesis propounded by F&M is that there are two faces to unions — the undesirable monopoly face — which enables unions to raise wages above the competitive level which results in a loss of economic efficiency. This inefficiency arises because employers adjust to the higher union wage by hiring too few workers in the union sector. The second, more desirable face to be examined in detail by others in this book, is the collective voice face which enables unions to channel worker discontent into improved workplace conditions and productivity. Our study concentrates on the monopoly face of unions and its impact on relative wages. We explore the various claims made by F&M about how unions affect wages and update them with new and better data.

We examine in some detail the role of the public sector, which was largely ignored by F&M. This was a perfectly understandable omission at the time but is less appropriate today given the importance of public sector unionism in the United States.[3] In Section I we report F&M's main findings. In Section II we discuss the main labor market changes that have occurred since WDUD was written. Section III reports our estimates of wage gaps disaggregated by various characteristics used by F&M. We also examine wage gaps that F&M did not examine, namely those in the public sector and for immigrants. Section IV examines time series changes in the union wage gap. Section V models the determinants of changes in the union wage premium at the level of the industry, occupation, and state. Section VI outlines our main findings and discusses whether F&M would have been surprised about these findings when they wrote WDUD.

II. Summary of F&M's Findings on Union Wage Effects

F&M reported that early work on union wage effects used aggregate data on different industries, occupations, and areas. Much of this work was summarized in Lewis (1963). The reason that such aggregated data were used was that "data on the wages of union versus nonunion individuals or establishments was neither available nor, given the state of technology, readily amenable to statistical analysis" (1984, p. 44). These studies found a union wage effect on average of 10–15 percent. The more recent studies F&M examined, including a number of their own, used micro data at the establishment level but more usually at the individual level. In Table 4.1 F&M showed that the union differential in the 1970s was 20–30 percent using cross-sectional data (the seven numbers in the table averaged out at 25.3 percent). Such estimates may still suffer from bias because differences due to the skills and abilities of workers are wrongly attributed to unions. F&M also considered "before and after" comparisons and argued that, although they represent a way to eliminate ability bias they also suffer from measurement error problems derived from mismeasurement of the union status measure (Hirsch, 2003). F&M reported 12 estimates using panel data in their Table 2 for the 1970s: these are sizable but smaller than the cross-section estimates they examined, averaging out at 15.7 percent.[4]

F&M used data from the May 1979 Current Population Survey (CPS) to obtain a series of disaggregated estimates using a sample of nonagricultural, private sector, blue-collar workers aged 20–65. They reported that unions raise wages most for the young, the least tenured, whites, men, the least educated, blue-collar workers and in the largely unorganized South and West.[5] Furthermore, F&M found, using data for 62 industries from the 1973–1975 May CPS, that there was considerable variation in the size of the differential.[6]

F&M argued that the amount of union monopoly power is related to the wage sensitivity of the demand for organized labor. The smaller response of employment to wages the greater, they argued, is the ability of unions to raise wages without significant employment loss. Areas where employment is less responsive to wage changes, such as air transport, they argued should be where one would expect to find sizable wage gains.

F&M then argued that the differential likely depends on the extent to which the union is able to organize a big percentage of workers — the higher the percentage the higher the differential (p. 51). F&M found that for blue-collar workers in manufacturing a 10 percent increase in organizing generates a 1.5 percent increase in union wages. In contrast, they argued that the wages of nonunion workers do not appear to be influenced by the percentage of workers organized. In terms of the characteristics of firms and plants F&M obtained the following results: (a) union differentials depend on the extent to which the firm bargains for an entire sector rather than for individual plants within a sector; (b) wage differentials tend to fall with size of firm/ plant/workplace; and (c) there was no clear empirical evidence on the relationship between product market power and differentials primarily as it is so difficult to measure power.

In terms of macro changes in differentials, F&M found that the 1970s were a period of increases in the union wage premium. F&M conjectured that a possible ex-planation was the sluggish labor market conditions then prevailing. Wages of union workers, they argued, tend to be less sensitive to business cycle ups and downs — particularly due to three-year contracts. This implies the union wage premium moves counter-cyclically — high in slumps when the unemployment rate is high and low in booms when the unemployment rate is low. However, F&M found that inflation and unemployment explained less than 50 percent of the rising union differentials in the 1970s. Nor did the rising wage differentials of the 1970s represent an historical increase in union power. The early 1980s, according to F&M, were a period of "givebacks" where unions agreed to wage cuts. Union wage gains were not a major cause of inflation.

F&M ended chapter three by estimating the social cost of monopoly power of unions. Loss of output due to unions they found to be "quite modest," accounting for between 0.2 percent and 0.4 percent of GNP or between $5 billion and $10 billion.

F&M drew six conclusions on the union wage effect: (a) The common sense view that there is a union wage effect is correct; (b) the magnitude of the differential varies across workers, markets, and time periods; (c) variation in the union wage gap across workers is best understood by union standard rate policies arising from voice; (d) variation in the union wage gap across markets is best understood by union monopoly power and employer product market power; and (e) wage premia in the 1970s were substantial but they returned to more "normal" levels in the 1980s; and (f) social loss due to unions is small.

III. Changes in the Labor Market since WDUD

Union density rates in the United States have fallen rapidly from 24 percent in 1977 to 13 percent in 2002 (Hirsch and Macpherson, 2002).[7] The decline was most dramatic in the private sector where in 2002 fewer than one in ten workers were union members. Density remains higher in manufacturing than in services. However, Table 4.1 suggests that union membership has roughly the same disaggregated pattern in 2001 as it did in 1977 — union density is higher among men than women; for older versus younger workers; in regions outside the South; and in transportation, communication, and construction. The exceptions are by race, where in 1977 rates were higher among nonwhites, but there is little difference by 2001, and by schooling. In 1977 membership rates for those with below high school education were nearly double those with above high school education. In 2001 they were approximately the same. So the highly qualified have increased their share of union employment.

The number of private sector union members declined between 1983 and 2002 from 11.9 million to 8.7 million while the number of public sector union members actually increased from 5.7 million to 7.3 million (Hirsch and Macpherson, 2003, Table 1c). Due to the growth in total employment in the public sector, however, the proportion of public sector workers who were union members was exactly the same in 2001 and 1983 (37 percent).[8] By 2002, 46 percent of all union members were in the public sector compared with 32.5 percent in 1983.

IV. Union Wage Gaps since WDUD

What has happened to the union wage differential between 1979 and 2001? Table 4.2 presents union wage gaps obtained from estimating a series of equations for each of the major sub-groups examined by F&M who used the 1979 May CPS file on a sample of nonagricultural about private sector, blue-collar workers aged 20–65. Their sample was very small, 6,000 observations. Rather than use the estimates reported by F&M to ensure large sample sizes we decided to pool together six successive May CPS files from 1974–1979 and compare those to wage gaps estimated for the years 1996–2001 using data from the Matched Outgoing Rotation Group (MORG) files of the CPS. Columns 1 and 2 estimate wage gaps for the private sector for 1996–2001 and 1974–1979, respectively. Columns 3 and 4 present equivalent estimates for the sample used by F&M of nonagricultural, private sector, blue-collar workers aged 20–65.

Hirsch and Schumacher (2002) show a "match bias" in union wage gap estimates due to earnings imputations.[9] This bias arises because workers in the CPS have earnings imputed using a "cell hot deck" method so wage gap estimates are biased *downward* when the attribute being studied (e.g., union status) is not a

Table 4.1
Disaggregated Union Membership Rates, 1977 and 2001, in Percent

	1977	2001
All	24	14
Private Sector	22	9
Public Sector	33	37
Private Sector Employees		
Men	27	12
Women	11	6
Whites	20	9
Nonwhite	27	10
Ages 16-24	12	4
Ages 25-44	23	9
Ages 45-54	27	13
Ages >=55	22	10
< High School	23	7
High School	25	12
> High School	13	8
North East	24	12
Central	25	12
South	13	5
West	22	9
Agriculture, Forestry & Fisheries	3	2
Mining	47	12
Construction	36	19
Manufacturing	34	15
Transportation, Communication,		
and Other Public Utilities	48	24
Wholesale & Retail Trade	10	4
FIRE	4	3
Services	7	6

Source: 1977, *What Do Unions Do?* 2001 authors' calculations from the ORG file of the CPS.

criterion used in the imputation. By construction, the individuals with imputed earnings have a union wage gap of about zero; hence omitting them raises the size of the union wage gap. They show that standard union wage gap estimates such as reported in Blanchflower (1999) are understated by about three to five percentage points as a result of including individuals with imputed earnings.

Unfortunately, consistently excluding those individuals with imputed earnings over time is not a simple matter.[10] Herein we follow the procedure suggested by Hirsch and Schumacher (2002) and that we used in Blanchflower and Bryson (2003).[11] All allocated earners are identified and excluded for the

Table 4.2
Private Sector Union/Nonunion Log Hourly Wage Differentials,
1974–1979 and 1996–2001, in Percent

	Private Sector		Freeman & Medoff's Sample	
	1974-1979	1996-2001	1974-1979	1996-2001
Men	19	17	27	28
Women	22	13	27	24
Ages 16-24	32	19	35	23
Ages 25-44	17	16	26	28
Ages 45-54	13	14	22	27
Ages >=55	19	16	29	28
Northeast	14	11	21	22
Central	20	15	27	27
South	24	19	29	26
West	23	22	31	34
< High school	33	26	31	29
High school	19	21	25	28
College 1-3 years	17	15	28	28
College >=4 years	4	3	17	14
Whites	21	16	28	27
Non-white	22	19	28	30
Tenure 0-3 years	20	20	28	n/a
Tenure 4-10	16	15	19	n/a
Tenure 11-15	10	11	12	n/a
Tenure 16+	17	8	28	n/a
Manual	30	21	n/a	n/a
Non-manual	15	4	n/a	n/a
Manufacturing	16	10	19	19
Construction	49	39	55	45
Services (excl. construction)	34	16	43	29
Private sector	21	17	28	28

Notes: 1996-2001 data files exclude individuals with imputed hourly earnings. Controls for 1996–2001 are 50 state dummies, 46 industry dummies, gender, 15 highest qualification dummies, private nonprofit dummy, age, age squared, log of weekly hours, four race dummies, four marital status, year dummies + union membership dummy (n=546,823). Estimates for 1974–1979 are adjusted upwards by the average bias found during 1979–1981 of .033. Controls for 1974–1979 are nine census division dummies, 46 industry dummies, years of education, age, age squared, log of weekly hours, four race dummies, four marital status dummies, five year dummies + union membership dummy (n=183,881). Tenure estimates for 1974–1979 obtained from the May 1979 CPS and for 1996–2002 files and February 1996 and 1998 Displaced Worker and Employee Tenure Supplements and January 2002 and February 2000: Displaced Workers, Employee Tenure, and Occupational Mobility Supplements. Freeman/Medoff's sample consists of non-agricultural private sector blue-collar workers aged 20-65 (n=64,034 for 1974-1979 and 142,024 for 1996-2001).

years 1996–2001 in the MORG files. Because the May CPS sample files do not report allocated earnings in 1979–1981, the series are adjusted upward by the average bias of .033 found by Hirsch and Schumacher using these May CPS data for 1979–1981. Earnings were not allocated in the years 1973–1978. For the period 1973–1979 total sample size was approximately 184,000 compared with 547,000 for the later period. In each year from 1996–2001 there are approximately 130,000 observations for the private sector in the MORG; in the May files, sample sizes are approximately 31,000.

Comparing F&M's sample and the wider private sector sample for the 1970s (columns 4 and 2, respectively, in Table 4.2), F&M's sample generates a larger wage gap for all, with the exception of the least educated.[12] The difference between the two samples is large, with the F&M sample generating a premium for the entire private sector, which is a third larger (28 percent as opposed to 21 percent) than in the wider sample. However, patterns in the wage gaps across workers are similar. (a) By *sex*, there is little difference in the size of the gap. (b) By *age*, the union effect is U-shaped in age and largest among the youngest who tend to be the lowest paid. (c) By *tenure*, the pattern is also U-shaped. (d) By *education*, unions raise wages most for the least educated, with the most highly educated having the lowest premium. (e) By *race*, unions raise wages by a similar amount for whites and nonwhites. (f) By *occupation*, although not reported in column 4, F&M (1984, pp. 49–50) report larger gains for blue-collar than for white-collar workers. The manual/non-manual gap in column 2 bears this out. (g) By *region*, unions had the largest effects in the relatively unorganized South and West, with more modest effects in the relatively well-organized Northeast. (h) By *industry*, construction and services have the highest premia.

What has happened since the 1970s?

(i) By *sex*, the wage gap has declined for women, but remained roughly stable for men so that, by the late 1990s, the union wage gap was higher for men than for women. The rate of decline in women's union premium is underestimated in F&M's restricted sample, but is still apparent. (j) By *age*, the U-shaped relationship apparent in the 1970s has disappeared because there has been a precipitous decline in the premium for the youngest workers, while the older workers' wage gap has remained roughly constant. In the full private sector sample, young workers still benefit most from unionization, though this is not apparent in F&M's restricted sample. (k) By *tenure*, as in the case of age, the U-shaped relationship between tenure and the union premium apparent in the 1970s has disappeared, because low- and high-tenured workers have seen their wage gap fall substantially while middle-tenure workers have experienced a stable union wage gap. Now, it seems the premium declines with tenure. (l) By *education*, the lowest educated continue to benefit most from union wage bargaining, but not to the same degree as in the 1970s. Although the trend is not so apparent in F&M's sample, the wage gap has fallen most for high school dropouts. (m) By *race*, a three-percentage point gap has opened up between the union premium

Table 4.3
Union Wage Differentials in the Public Sector, in Percent

	1983–1988		1996–2001	
	Wage Gap	Sample Size	Wage Gap	Sample Size
Private	22	(754,056)	17	(567,627)
Public	13	(165,276)	15	(110,833)
Federal	2	(33,633)	8	(20,938)
State	9	(42,942)	10	(34,919)
Local	16	(88,642)	20	(60,981)
Male	8	(77,528)	10	(48,298)
Female	17	(87,748)	16	(62,534)
Age <25	28	(15,603)	23	(7,771)
Age 25-44	13	(93,676)	15	(53,798)
Age 45-54	8	(32,127)	11	(33,830)
Age >=55	13	(23,870)	14	(15,433)
New England	17	(33,540)	17	(20,148)
Central	16	(38,863)	16	(25,930)
South	10	(51,785)	12	(33,522)
West	10	(41,088)	13	(31,232)
<High School	26	(13,217)	18	(29,775)
High School	15	(48,037)	13	(21,536)
College 1-3	13	(35,097)	11	(9,672)
College >= 4 Years	8	(68,925)	11	(50,029)
Whites	13	(131,676)	14	(85,893)
Nonwhites	15	(33,600)	16	(24,939)
Manual	18	(17,874)	18	(9,679)
Non-manual	13	(147,402)	14	(101,150)
Registered nurses (95)	5	(2,945)	6	(1,854)
Teachers (156-8)	15	(25,147)	21	(19,484)
Social workers (174)	12	(2,870)	12	(2,716)
Lawyers (178)	5	(1,014)	17	(1,184)
Firefighters (416-7)	15	(1,866)	19	(1,227)
Police & correction officers (418-424).	16	(6,068)	18	(5,503)

Notes: Sample excludes individuals with allocated earnings. Controls and data as in Table 4.2.

commanded by nonwhites and the lower premium for whites. (n) By *occupation,* the union premium has collapsed for non-manual workers. Despite some decline in the premium for manuals, their wage gap was 17 percentage points larger than that for non-manuals by the late 1990s (compared with only five percentage points in the 1970s). (o) By *region,* the wage gap remains largest in the West and the South though, in F&M's sample, there is no difference in the premium in the South and Central regions. The wage gap remains smallest in the Northeast. (p) By *industry,* the wage gap remains largest in construction and smallest in manufacturing. The decline in the differential was particularly marked in services. We return to industry differentials later.

Two points stand out from these analyses. First, *no group of workers in the broader private sector sample has experienced a substantial increase in its union premium.* Indeed, the only group recording any increase at all is those aged 45–54 whose premium rose from 13 percent to 14 percent. Clearly, unions have found it harder to maintain a wage gap since F&M wrote. Second, with the exception of the manual/non-manual gap, those with the highest premiums in the 1970s saw the biggest falls, so there has been some convergence in the wage gaps. This finding is apparent whether we compare trends using F&M's sample (columns 3 and 4) or the broader private sector sample (columns 1 and 2). This trend may be due to an increasingly competitive U.S. economy, where workers commanding wages well above the market rate are subject to intense competition from nonunion workers. Nevertheless, with the exception of the most highly educated and non-manual workers, the wage premium remains around 10 percent or more.

Public Sector

F&M said little or nothing on the role of unions in the public sector, although, as noted above, Freeman has subsequently written voluminously on the issue. Given that the remaining bastion of U.S. unionism is now the public sector, if F&M were writing today they would likely have devoted a considerable amount of space in a twenty-first century edition of WDUD to the public sector. More evidence on how the role of unions in the public sector has changed since WDUD was written is reported by Gunderson elsewhere in this volume.

The size of the public sector grew (from 15.6 million to 19.1 million or 22.4 percent) between 1983 and 2001, but as a proportion of total employment it fell from 18.0 percent to 16.1 percent. Union membership in the public sector grew even more rapidly (from 5.7 million to 7.1 million or by 24.6 percent). Furthermore, by 2001 public sector unions accounted for 44 percent of all union members compared with 32.5 percent in 1983.

Table 4.3 is comparable to Table 4.2 for the private sector in that it presents disaggregated union wage gap estimates. Because sample sizes in the public sector are small using the May CPS files we again decided to use data from the ORG files of the CPS for the years 1983–1988 for comparison purposes with the 1996–2001 data. Data for the years 1979–1982 could not be used, as no union data are available. A further advantage of the 1983–1988 data is that information is available on individuals whose earnings were allocated who were then excluded from the analysis.

The main findings are as follows: (1) The private sector union wage gap has fallen over the two periods (21.5 percent to 17.0 percent) whereas a slight *increase* was observed in the public sector (13.3 percent to 14.5 percent, respectively); (2) the majority of the worker groups in Table 4.3 experienced *increases* in their union wage premium over the two periods, but wage gaps declined markedly for those under 25 and with less than a high school education; (3) there was little change in public sector union wage gaps for men or women. In marked contrast to the private sector where men had higher differentials than women, wage gaps in both periods in the public sector were *higher* for women than for men; (4) unions benefit workers most in local government and least in the federal government, although the differential for federal workers increased over time;[13] (5) just as for the private sector, the wage benefits of union membership are greatest for manual workers, the young, and the least educated; (6) there are only small differences in union wage gaps for nonwhites compared to whites in both the public and the private sectors; (7) in contrast to the private sector where wage differentials were greatest in the South and West, in the public sector exactly the opposite is found. Differentials are higher in the public sector in New England and the Central region in both time periods whereas the reverse was the case in the private sector; and (8) wage gaps increased over time for teachers, lawyers, firefighters and police.

Immigrants[14]

F&M also said nothing about the extent to which U.S. labor unions are able to sign up immigrants as members and by how much they are able to raise their wages. Using the data available in the CPS files since the mid–1990s we calculate wage gaps for the period 1996–2001. We find little variation in union wage gaps by length of time the immigrant had been in the United States, holding characteristics constant as well as wage gaps for the U.S.-born. However, differentials by source country are large. Differentials for Europeans (11.6 percent for Western Europe and 12.7 percent for Eastern Europe) are well below those of the native born (16.8 percent). Estimates are also in low double digits for Asians, Africans, and South Americans (13.3 percent, 11 percent, and 12.2 percent, respectively). In contrast the wage gap for Mexicans is 28 percent.

V. Time Series Changes in the Union Wage Gap

F&M reported that the 1970s was a period of rising differentials for unions, although they did not separately estimate year-by-year results themselves. Table

4.4, which is taken from Blanchflower and Bryson (2003),[15] reports adjusted estimates of the wage gap using separate log hourly earnings equations for each of the years from 1973 to 1981 using the National Bureau of Economic Research's (NBER) May Earnings Supplements to the CPS (CPS)[16] and for the years since then using data from the NBER's (MORG) files of the CPS.[17] The MORG data for the years 1983–1995 were previously used in Blanchflower (1999).[18] For both the May and the MORG files a broadly similar, but not identical, list of control variables is used, including a union status dummy, age and its square, a gender dummy, education, race, and hours controls plus state and industry dummies.[19]

The first column of Table 4.4 reports time-consistent estimates of union wage gaps for the total sample whereas the second and third columns report them for the private sector. To solve the match bias problem discussed above, as in Tables 2 and 3 we followed the procedure suggested by Hirsch and Schumacher (2002). Results obtained by Hirsch and Schumacher (2002) with a somewhat different set of controls are reported in the final column of the table. For a discussion of the reason for these differences, see Blanchflower and Bryson (2003). The time series properties of all three of the series are essentially the same.

The wage gap averages between 17 and 18 percent over the period, and is similar in size in the private sector as it is in the economy as a whole. The table confirms F&M's comment (1984, p. 53) that "the late 1970s appear to have been a period of substantial increase in the union wage premium." What is notable is the high differential in the early-to-mid 1980s and a slight decline thereafter, which gathers pace after 1995, with the series picking up again as the economy started to turn down in 2000.

Table 4.5 presents estimates of both the unadjusted and adjusted union wage gaps for the private sector. The sample excludes individuals with imputed earnings. In column 1 of Table 4.5 we report the results of estimating a series of wage equations by year that only include a union dummy as a control. These numbers are consequently different from those reported by Hirsch and Macpherson (2002, Table 2a) who report raw unadjusted wage differences between the union and nonunion sectors but do not exclude individuals with imputed earnings.[20] Throughout the unadjusted wage gap is higher than the adjusted wage gap, implying a positive association between union membership and wage-enhancing employee or employer characteristics. However, the unadjusted gap has declined more rapidly than the regression-adjusted gap since 1983. In 1983 the unadjusted estimate was 128 percent higher than the adjusted estimate. In 2002 the difference had fallen to 91.5 percent higher.

To establish what is driving this effect, Hirsch et al. (2002) decompose the unadjusted wage gap into its three components — employment shifts, changes in worker characteristics, and changes in the residual union wage premium. Using CPS data for the private sector only, they find almost half (46 percent) of the decline in the union-nonunion log wage gap over the period 1986–2001 is accounted for by a decline in the regression-adjusted wage gap. Sixteen percent of

Table 4.4
Union Wage Gap Estimates for the United States, 1973–2002, (%)
(excludes workers with imputed earnings)

Year	All Sectors Blanchflower/Bryson	Private Sector Blanchflower/Bryson	Private Sector Hirsh/Schumacher
1973	14.1	12.7	17.5
1974	14.6	13.8	17.5
1975	15.1	14.3	19.2
1976	15.5	14.6	20.4
1977	19.0	18.3	23.9
1978	18.8	18.6	22.8
1979	16.6	16.3	19.7
1980	17.7	17.0	21.3
1981	16.1	16.3	20.4
1983	19.5	21.2	25.5
1984	20.4	22.4	26.2
1985	19.2	21.0	26.0
1986	18.8	20.1	23.9
1987	18.5	20.0	24.0
1988	18.4	19.1	22.6
1989	17.8	19.2	24.5
1990	17.1	17.6	22.5
1991	16.1	16.6	22.0
1992	17.9	19.2	22.5
1993	18.5	19.6	23.5
1994	18.5	18.2	25.2
1995	17.4	18.0	24.5
1996	17.4	18.4	23.5
1997	17.4	17.7	23.2
1998	15.8	16.1	22.4
1999	16.0	16.9	22.0
2000	13.4	14.3	20.4
2001	14.1	15.1	20.0
2002	16.5	18.6	
1973-2001 average	17.1	17.6	22.4

Notes: Wage gap estimates calculated taking anti-logs and deducting 1. Columns 1 and 2 are taken from Table 3 of Blanchflower and Bryson (2003). Column 3 is taken from column 5 of Table 4 of Hirsch and Schumacher (2002). Data for 1973-1981 are from the May CPS Earnings Supplements. a) 1973-1981 May CPS, n=38,000 for all sectors, and n=31,000 for the private sector. Controls comprise age, age^2, male, union, years of education, 2 race dummies, 28 state dummies, usual hours, private sector and 50 industry dummies. For 1980 and 1981 sample sizes fall to approximately 16,000 because from 1980 only respondents in months 4 and 8 in the outgoing rotation groups report a wage. Since the May CPS sample files available to us do not include allocated earnings in

Table 4.4 (cont. notes)

1979–1981, the series in columns 2 and 4 are adjusted upward by the average bias of 0.033 found by Hirsch and Schumacher (2002) using these May CPS data for 1979–1981. The data for 1973–1978 do not include individuals with allocated earnings and hence no adjustment is made in those years. b) Data for 1983–2002 are taken from the MORG files of the CPS. Controls comprise usual hours, age, age squared, four race dummies, 15 highest qualifications dummies, male, union, 46 industry dummies, four organizational status dummies, and 50 state dummies. Sample is employed private sector nonagricultural wage and salary workers aged 16 years and above with positive weekly earnings and non-missing data for control variables (few observations are lost). All allocated earners were identified and excluded for the years 1983–1988 and 1996–2001 from the MORG files. For 1989–1995, allocation flags are either unreliable (in 1989–1993) or not available (1994 through August 1995). For 1989–1993, the gaps are adjusted upward by the average imputation bias during 1983–1988. For 1994–1995, the gap is adjusted upward by the bias during 1996–1998. In each year there are approximately 160,000 observations for the U.S. economy and 130,000 for the private sector in the MORG; in the May files, sample sizes are approximately 38,000 and 31,000 respectively until 1980 and 1981 when sample sizes fall to approximately 16,000 and 13,000, respectively, as from that date on only respondents in months four and eight in the outgoing rotation groups report a wage. The Hirsch and Schumacher (2002) wage gap reported in column 3 is the coefficient on a dummy variable for union membership in a regression where the log of hourly earnings is the dependent variable. The control variables included are years of schooling, experience and its square (allowed to vary by gender), and dummy variables for gender, race and ethnicity (3), marital status (2), part-time status, region (8), large metropolitan area, industry (8), and occupation (12).

the decline is accounted for by changes in worker characteristics and payoffs to those characteristics, chief among these is the increase in the union relative to nonunion percentage of female workers. The remaining 38 percent of the decline in Hirsch et al.'s unadjusted wage gap was due to sectoral shifts and payoffs to the occupational sectors of workers. The sectoral changes that stand out are the substantial decline in union relative to nonunion employment in durable manufacturing, and the decline in relative pay (that is, the industry coefficient) in transportation, communications and utilities, a sector with a large share of total union employment.

The results reported in Table 4.4 are broadly comparable to the estimates obtained by Lewis (1986) in his Table 9.7, which summarized the findings of 165 studies for the period 1967–1979. Lewis concluded that during this period the U.S. mean wage gap was approximately 15 percent. His results are reported in Table 4.6.[21] The left panel contains estimates for the six years prior to our starting point in Table 4.4. It appears that the unweighted average for this first period, 1967–1972, of 14 percent is slightly below the 16 percent for the second interval, 1973–1979. The estimates for the later period are very similar to those shown in Table 4.4 — which also averaged 16 percent — and have the same time-series pattern. In part, Lewis's low number for 1979 is explained by the fact that the 1979 May CPS file included allocated earners and hence the estimates were not adjusted for the *downward* bias caused by the imputation of the earnings data.[22]

Figure 4.1 plots the point estimates of the U.S. union wage premium, taken from the first column of Table 4.5, against unemployment for 1973–2002. The

Table 4.5
The Ratio between Unadjusted and Adjusted Union Wage Gap
Estimates for the United States, 1983–2002 (%)
(excludes workers with imputed earnings)

Year	Unadjusted	Adjusted	Unadjusted/Adjusted
1983	48.3	21.2	2.28
1984	48.3	22.4	2.16
1985	47.0	21.0	2.24
1986	44.8	20.1	2.23
1987	45.2	20.0	2.26
1988	44.6	19.1	2.34
1989	38.0	19.2	1.98
1990	34.3	17.6	1.95
1991	32.8	16.6	1.98
1992	32.5	19.2	1.69
1993	34.0	19.6	1.74
1995	34.6	18.0	1.92
1996	35.8	18.4	1.95
1997	36.1	17.7	2.04
1998	33.2	16.1	2.07
1999	32.5	16.9	1.92
2000	29.4	14.3	2.06
2001	29.8	15.1	1.98
2002	35.6	18.6	1.91

Notes: Column 1 obtained from a series of private sector log hourly wage equations that only contained a union membership dummy and a constant. Reported here is the antilog of the coefficient minus 1. Column 2 is from Table 4.4. Column 3 is column 1/column 2. Sample is employed private sector nonagricultural wage and salary workers aged 16 years and above with positive weekly earnings and non-missing data for control variables (few observations are lost)
Source: ORG files of the CPS, 1983–2001.

premium moves counter-cyclically. There are three main factors likely influencing the degree of counter-cyclical movement in the wage gap. The first, cited by F&M (1984, pp. 52–53) as the reason for the widening wage gap during the Depression of the 1920s and 1930s, is the greater capacity for union workers to "fight employer efforts to reduce wages" when market conditions are unfavorable. Conversely, when demand for labor is strong, employees rely less on unions to bargain for better wages because market rates rise anyway. The second factor is that union contracts are more long term than nonunion ones and, as such, less responsive to the economic cycle, so union wages respond to economic conditions with a lag.

When inflation is higher than expected, a greater contraction in the premium can occur because nonunion wages respond more to higher inflation. However,

Figure 4.1
Movements in the U.S. Private Sector Wage Premium, 1973-2002

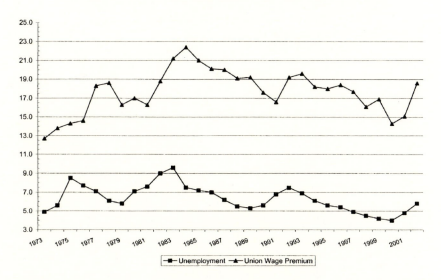

the third factor, which should reduce the cyclical sensitivity of the union wage premium, is the cost-of-living-adjustment (COLA) clauses in union contracts that increase union wages in response to increases in the consumer price level. According to F&M (1984, p. 54) the percentage of union workers covered by these agreements rose dramatically in the 1970s, from 25 percent at the beginning of the decade to 60 percent at the end of the decade. However, F&M's estimates for manufacturing suggest that COLA provisions "contributed only a modest amount to the rising union advantage" in the 1970s. Bratsberg and Ragan (2002) revisit this issue and find the increased sensitivity of the premium to the cycle is due in part to reduced COLA coverage from the late 1980s, but we find no such evidence (see below).

Commenting on the growth of the union wage premium during the 1970s, F&M (1984, p. 54) suggested that "at least in several major sectors the union/ nonunion differential reached levels inconsistent with the survival of many union jobs." They were right. In the 1970s and early 1980s, the wage gap in the private sector rose while union density fell, as predicted in the standard textbook model of how employment responds to wages where the union has monopoly power over labor supply. In the classic monopoly model, demand for labor is given, so a rise in the union premium results in a decline in union membership since the premium hits employment. The fact that unions pushed for, and got, an increasing wage premium over this period, implies that they were willing to sustain membership losses to maintain real wages, or that unions were simply unaware of the consequences of their actions.

Table 4.6
U.S. Mean Wage Gap: 1967–1979

Year	# Studies	Mean Estimate	Year	# Studies	Mean Estimate
1967	20	14%	1973	24	15%
1968	4	15%	1974	7	15%
1969	20	13%	1975	11	17%
1970	8	13%	1976	7	16%
1971	20	14%	1977	10	19%
1972	7	14%	1978	7	17%
			1979	3	13%

From the mid-1990s, the continued decline in union density was accompanied by a *falling* union wage premium because demand for union labor fell as a result of two pressures. The first was increasing competitiveness throughout the U.S. economy: Increasing price competition in markets generally meant employers were less able to pass the costs of the premium onto the consumer, so that pressures for wages to conform to the market rate grew. Second, union companies faced greater nonunion competition. Declining union density, by increasing employers' opportunities to substitute nonunion products for union products, fueled this process. So too did rising import penetration: If imports are nonunion goods, regardless of U.S. union density, they increase the opportunity for nonunion substitution. These same pressures also increased the employment price of any union wage gap (the elasticity of demand for union labor).

VI. Industry, Occupation, and State-Level Wage Premia

So far, we have focused primarily on union wage effects at the level of the individual and the whole economy. However, the literature on the origins of the union wage premium focuses largely on firms and industries because the conventional assumption is that unions can procure a wage premium by capturing quasi-rents from the employer (Blanchflower et al., 1996). If this is so, there must be rents available to the firm arising from its position in the market place, and unions must have the ability to capture some of these rents through their ability to monopolize the firm's labor supply. Individual-level data can tell us little about these processes. Instead, the literature has concentrated on industry-level wage gaps. In this section we model the change in the union wage premium at three different units of observation — industry, state, and occupation.

Industries

As we noted above, F&M reported wage gap estimates by the extent of industry unionism. They (1984, p. 50) comment on substantial variation in the union wage effect by industry, with gaps ranging between 5 percent and 35 percent in the CPS data for 1973–1975. F&M's results are reported in the first column of Table 4.7. We used our data to estimate separate results by two-digit industry for 1983–1988 and 1996–2001. We chose these years as it was possible to define industries identically using the 1980 industry classification. Using these data we also found considerable variation by the size of the wage gap by industry as shown in Table 4.7. There is less variation in the wage gap by industry in the later period than in the earlier period with only three industries, construction (41 percent), transport (36 percent), and repair services (37 percent) having a differential of over 35 percent, compared with six in the earlier period which includes the same three — construction (52 percent); transport (44 percent) and repair services (37 percent) — plus agricultural services (41 percent); other agriculture (56 percent) and entertainment (47 percent).[23]

Where is the union wage premium rising, and where is it falling? We estimated the regression-adjusted wage gaps in 44 industries during the 1980s (1983–1988) and then in the late 1990s (1996–2001). In contrast to the analysis by worker characteristics, which reveal near universal decline in the premium — at least in the private sector — we found that the wage gap rose in 17 industries and declined in 27 — results are presented in an appendix available on request from the authors. The gap rose by more than ten percentage points in autos (+12 percent) and leather (+19 percent). It declined by more than 20 percentage points in other agriculture (–33 percent) retail trade (–20 percent) and private households (–29 percent). Many of the industries experiencing a rise in the union premium between 1983 and 2001 would have been subject to intensifying international trade (machinery, electrical equipment, paper, rubber and plastics, leather) but this is equally true for those experiencing declining premiums (such as textiles, apparel, and furniture). Horn (1998) found that increases in import competition increased union density and decreased in the wage premium within manufacturing industries. This occurred because union density fell slower than overall employment when faced with import competition. Horn also found that imports from OECD countries decreased union density; imports from non-OECD countries tended to raise union density within an industry.

There is a negative correlation between change in union density and change in the premium (correlation coefficient –0.39). Some of the biggest declines in the premium have been concentrated in sectors where the bulk of private sector union members are concentrated, as Table 4.8 indicates. It shows the three industries with more than a 10 percent share in private sector union membership in 2002. In construction and transport, which both make up an increasing proportion of all private sector union members, the premium fell by around 10 percentage points. In retail trade, where the share of private sector union membership has remained roughly constant at 10 percent, the premium fell 20 percentage points. The decline in the wage gap for the whole economy, presented earlier, is due to the fact that the industries experiencing a decline in their wage gap make up a

Table 4.7
Union Wage Effects by Industry Using CPS Data

Estimates by Industry	FM 1973–1975	1983–1988	1996–2001
<5%	13	11	10
5–15%	17	15	19
15–35%	24	12	12
>=35%	8	6	3
# Industries	62	44	44

higher percentage of all employees than those experiencing a widening gap. The results are similar to those presented by Bratsberg and Ragan (2002) who found that, over the period 1971–1999, the regression-adjusted wage gap closed in 16 industries and increased in 16 others. Their analysis is not directly comparable to ours, but where industry-level changes are presented in both studies, they tend to trend in the same direction. Only in one industry (transport equipment) do Bratsberg and Ragan report a significant increase in the wage gap where we find a decline in the wage gap.

These changes in the union wage premium by *industry* over time are worth detailed investigation, even though F&M did not present such analyses. Our first step was to estimate 855 separate first-stage regressions, one for each of our 45 industries in each year from 1983–2001 with the dependent variable the log hourly wage along with controls for union membership, age, age squared, male, four race dummies, the log of hours, and 50 state dummies. The sample was restricted to the private sector and excluded all individuals with allocated earnings. Three sectors with very small sample sizes (toys, tobacco, and forestry and fisheries) were deleted. We extracted the coefficient on the union variable, giving us 19 years * 42 industries or 798 observations in all. The adjustments discussed earlier were made to deal with imputed earnings. The coefficient on the union variable was then turned into a wage gap taking anti-logs, deducting 1 and multiplying by 100 to turn the figure into a percentage. We used the ORG files to estimate the proportion of workers in the industry who were union

Table 4.8
All Private Sector Union Members: Share of Membership

	Share of Membership, 1983	Share of Membership, 2002	Change in Premium, 1983–2001
Construction	9.3	13.5	-10.7
Retail Trade	10.2	10.5	-20.3
Transport	9.7	12.3	-8.0

members both in the private sector and overall and mapped that onto the file. Unemployment rates at the level of the economy are used as industry-specific rates are not meaningful: Workers move a great deal between industries and considerably more than they do between states. (A table providing information on the classification of industries used and the average number of observations each year is included in the data appendix available on request from the authors.) Regression results, reported in Table 4.9, columns 1 and 2, estimate the impact of the lagged premium, lagged unemployment, and a time trend on the level of the industry-level wage premium. The number of observations is 756 as we lose 42 observations in generating the lag on the wage premium and the union density variables.

In the unweighted equation in column (1) the lagged premium is positively and significantly associated with the level of the premium the following year indicating regression to the mean. Unemployment and the time trend are not significant. However, once the regression is weighted by the number of observations in the industry in the first-stage regression, (column (2)) lagged unemployment is positive and significant, indicating counter-cyclical movement in the premium, while the negative time trend indicates secular decline in the premium.

Bratsberg and Ragan (2002) reported that the industry-level premium was influenced by a number of other variables.[24] In particular they found that COLA clauses reduced the cyclicality of the union premium and that increases in import penetration were strongly associated with rising union premiums.[25] They also

Table 4.9
Industry, State, and Occupation-Level Analysis of the Private Sector Union Wage Premium, 1983–2001

	(1)	(2)	(3)	(4)	(5)	(6)
Level of Analysis	Industry	Industry	State	State	Occupation	Occupation
$Premium_{t-1}$	.2584*	.3453*	.2051*	.2366*	.0907*	.1746*
	(.0367)	(.0350)	(.0337)	(.0333)	(.0379)	(.0374)
$Unemployment\ rate_{t-1}$	.6333	.5866*	.4373*	.5366*	.3799	.5823*
	(.4035)	(.2821)	(.1449)	(.1175)	(.5084)	(.2900)
Time	-.0463	-.2344*	-.1547*	-.0651	-.3419*	-.2416*
	(.1056)	(.0762)	(.0468)	(.0379)	(.1343)	(.0788)
State/industry/ occupation dummies	50	50	41	41	41	41
Weighted by # obs at 1st stage	No	Yes	No	Yes	No	Yes
R^2	.6187	.7749	.5071	.5861	.7345	.8453
N	756	756	918	918	756	756

Source: Outgoing Rotation Groups of the CPS, 1984-2001. Samples exclude individuals with imputed earnings.

Table 4.10

Industry Level Analysis of the Union Wage Premium in the Private Sector, 1973–1999

	(1)	(2)	(3)	(4)	(5)	(6)	(7)	(8)	(9)
Premium_{t-1}					.6030*	.2759*	.6001*	.2468*	.3196*
					(.0274)	(.0350)	(.0284)	(.0361)	(.0333)
Time				-.0019*	-.0012*	.0002	-.0011*	-.0001	-.0009*
				(.0004)	(.0003)	(.0004)	(.0003)	(.0004)	(.0003)
Unemployment rate	.0187*	.0131*	.0108*	.0083*	.0064*	.0064*	.0061*	.0070*	.0052*
	(.0017)	(.0017)	(.0011)	(.0014)	(.0010)	(.0021)	(.0011)	(.0022)	(.0010)
COLA	.0763*	.0767*	.0403*	.0155	-.0065	.0139	.0041	.0156	.0141*
	(.0313)	(.0303)	(.0126)	(.0134)	(.0090)	(.0140)	(.0108)	(.0144)	(.0096)
Inflation	-.0182*	-.0077	.0012	.0006	.0024*	.0026	.0020*	.0032	.0002
	(.0065)	(.0069)	(.0008)	(.0008)	(.0007)	(.0015)	(.0008)	(.0016)	(.0008)
Unempt rate*COLA	-.0092*	-.0047							
	(.0038)	(.0036)							
Unempt rate*Inflation	.0026*	.0012							
	(.0009)	(.0009)							
Import penetration Durables	.2048*	.2201*	.2362*	.3090*	.1688*	.1234*	.1738*	.1668*	.1811*
	(.0427)	(.0414)	(.0441)	(.0424)	(.0326)	(.0416)	(.0461)	(.0549)	(.0302)
Import penetration Nondurables	.1655*	.1459*	.1491*	.1698*	.0939*	.0880*	.0914*	.0945*	.1043*
	(.0513)	(.0525)	(.0509)	(.0488)	(.0302)	(.0208)	(.0419)	(.0265)	(.0314)
Dereg. Communications	.0752*	.0609*	.0589*	.0612*	.0451*	.0625*	.0506*	.0734*	.0532*
	(.0316)	(.0244)	(.0246)	(.0248)	(.0200)	(.0307)	(.0234)	(.0261)	(.0193)
Deregulation Rail	.0329	.0400	.0394	.0580	.0200				.0333
	(.0905)	(.0844)	(.0855)	(.0839)	(.0616)				(.0606)
Deregulation Trucking	-.0716	-.0617	-.0630	-.0394	-.0139				-.0332
	(.0560)	(.0570)	(.0565)	(.0518)	(.0429)				(.0398)
Deregulation Air	.0554	.0684	.0661	.0815	.0087				.0214
	(.1262)	(.1217)	(.1190)	(.1161)	(.0852)				(.0804)
Deregulation Finance	-.0614*	-.0599*	-.0587*	-.0329	.0179				-.0174
	(.0191)	(.0188)	(.0195)	(.0203)	(.0160)				(.0150)
Weighted	Yes	Yes	Yes	Yes	Yes	No	Yes	No	Yes
Method	GLS	GLS	GLS	GLS	GLS	GLS	OLS	OLS	GLS
Wald Chi²/ R²	2,325.01	2,781.32	2,686.37	3,190.74	10,961.71	1,220.21	.8973	.6516	6,189.4
N	832	832	832	832	832	832	832	832	806

Notes: All equations also include a full set of 31 industry dummies. Data are taken from Bratsberg and Ragan 2002. GLS regression estimated with industry specific AR(1) process in error term. Where indicated ach observation in the GLS regressions is weighted by the industry observation count of the first step following Berntsberg and Ragan (2002). Column 9 excludes Retail Trade. Standard errors in parentheses.

found some evidence that industry deregulation had mixed effects. Their main equations (their Table 2) did not include a lagged dependent variable. Table 4.10 reports results using their data for the years 1973–1999 using their method and computer programs that they kindly provided to us. Column 1 of Table 4.10 reports the results they reported in column 2 of their Table 2. Column 2 reports our attempt to replicate their findings. We are unable to do so exactly — the problem appears to arise from the use of the xtgls routine in STATA which gives different results on our two machines.[26] There are several similarities — we find import penetration both in durables and nondurables, COLA clauses, deregulations in communications, and the unemployment rate all have positive and significant effects. We also found, as they did, that deregulation in finance lowered the premium. In contrast to Bratsberg and Ragan, however, the inflation rate and the two interaction terms with the unemployment rate were insignificant. The model is rerun in column 3, but without the insignificant interaction term. A linear time trend is added in column 4: this is negative and significant, and eliminates the COLA effect and the negative effect of deregulation in the finance sector. Column 5 adds the lagged union wage premium, which is positive and significant. Its introduction makes inflation positive and significant. In columns (6) to (8) models are run without the four insignificant deregulation dummies. Column (6) indicates that using an unweighted regression, the size of the lagged premium effect drops markedly and the time trend and inflation lose signifi-cance, showing these results are sensitive to the weighting of the regres-sion. The smaller coefficient on the lagged dependent variable is unsurprising given that there is much less likely to be variation in the union wage gap estimates in industries with large sample sizes that have higher weights in the former case. We are able to confirm Bratsberg and Ragan's finding that the unemployment rate, deregulation in communications, and import penetration in both durables and nondurables have positive impacts on the premium but not the findings on COLA, inflation, or any of the other deregulations identified.

That import penetration in durable and nondurable goods sectors increases the premium suggests that union wages are more resilient than nonunion wages to foreign competition. Import penetration is likely correlated with unmeasured industry characteristics that depress the premium inducing a negative bias that is removed once industry characteristics are controlled for. Import penetration has likely reduced demand for union and nonunion labor, with union wages holding up better than nonunion wages, but at the expense of reduced union employment. There are theoretical and empirical reasons as to why this might occur. For instance, since union wages tend to be less responsive to market conditions generally, union wages may be sluggish in responding to increased import competition. Alternatively, industries characterized by "end-game" bargaining may witness perverse union responses to shifts in product demand as the union tries to extract maximum rents in declining industries (Lawrence and Lawrence, 1985). Another possibility is that increased import penetration reduces the share of union employment in labor-intensive firms and increases it in capital-intensive firms. Greater capital intensity reduces elasticity of demand for union labor, allowing rent-maximizing unions to raise the premium (Staiger, 1988).

It isn't obvious that weights should be used if we regard each industry as a separate observation. In cross-country comparisons which, say, contrasted outcomes for Switzerland, the United Kingdom, and the United States, it wouldn't make a lot of sense to weight by population and thereby make the observation from the United States 4.67 times more important than that of the United Kingdom and 39.3 times more important than Switzerland.[27] Columns (1) to (6) are GLS estimates accounting for potential correlation in error terms. Column (7) switches to a weighted OLS and shows that results are not sensitive to the switch. The unweighted OLS in column (8) gives broadly the same results as the unweighted GLS in column (6). Taking off the weights has a much bigger effect than switching from GLS to OLS.

Furthermore, the industries defined by Bratsberg and Ragan are *very* different in size. Some industries are very broadly defined — for example industry 32 Services covers SIC codes 721–900 whereas tobacco, for example, covers one SIC code (130). Retail trade averaged 19,075 observations. Column 9 of Table 4.10 illustrates the sensitivity of the results to industry exclusions. It is exactly equivalent in all respects to column 5 of Table 4.10 except that it drops the 32 observations from retail trade. The lagged dependent variable falls dramatically from .60 to .32. The COLA variable is now significantly *positive* while the inflation variable moves from being significantly positive to insignificant. The unweighted results (not reported) are little changed. Bratsberg and Ragan's results appear to be sensitive to both the use of weights and the sample of industries used.

States

In the United States unions are geographically concentrated by town, county, district, and state. Often towns next to each other differ — one is a union town, the other is nonunion. Waddoups (2000) used this interesting juxtaposition of union and nonunion zones to estimate the impact of unions on wages in Nevada's hotel-casino industry.[28] Although they share many features and are subject to broadly similar business cycles, most of the 50 states in the United States are comparable in size and economic significance to many countries. They also differ markedly in their industrial structures and unionization rates. Assuming union density proxies union bargaining power, this implies different premiums across states. However, as noted earlier, F&M found the union premium at the regional level was inversely correlated with union density, with the premium highest in the relatively unorganized South and West. To explore this issue further, and to assess changes over time, we estimated separate wage gaps for two time periods at the level of the 50 states plus Washington, D.C. Results at the level of the state were also estimated and are summarized in Table 4.11 below — full state-level results are available in the appendix available on request from the authors. The data used are from the Outgoing Rotation Group files of the CPS. It was not possible to identify each state separately in the May CPS, so F&M did not report such results. Hence, we compared results from a merged sample of the 1983–1988 with those obtained from our 1996–2001 files.[29] The correlation between changes in state density and state premia is negative but small (–0.10).

First we notice that *the variation in the union wage premium is much less by state than it is by industry.* Only two states in the earlier period had gaps of at least 35 percent — North Dakota (35 percent) and Nebraska (37 percent) and none in the later period. There has been a downward shift in the premium generally, as indicated by the movement from the 15–35 percent category to the 5–15 percent category. The mean state union wage gap was 23.4 percent between 1983 and 1988, falling by 6.2 percentage points to 17.2 percent in 1996–2001. The premium fell in all but five states, with South Dakota recording the biggest decline (16.8 percentage points). In four of the five states where the premium rose, it only increased by a percentage point or two (Vermont, Massachusetts, Wyoming, and Hawaii). The premium only rose markedly in Maine, where it increased 9 percentage points (from 7 percent to 16.1 percent). Since the early 1980s, union density fell by an average of 5.7 percentage points, with Pennsylvania (–10.6 percent) and West Virginia experiencing the biggest decline (–11 percentage points). The premium appears to have declined more in smaller states than it has in bigger states. The five biggest states of California, Texas, Florida, New York, and Illinois had small changes in their wage gaps (–1.4 percent; –6.7 percent; –10.1 percent; –0.6 percent and –4.5 percent, respectively). The five smallest states measured by employment tended to have big declines in the differentials: New Mexico (–14.10 percent); Alabama (–14.20 percent); Nebraska (–15.00 percent); Arkansas (–15.20 percent); South Dakota (–16.80 percent).[30]

We then ran 969 separate first-stage regressions, one for each state in each year from 1983–2001 with the dependent variable the log hourly wage along

Table 4.11
Union Wage Effects by State Using CPS Data

Estimates by State	1983–1988	1996–2001
<5%	0	0
5–15%	6	21
15–35%	43	30
>=35%	2	0
# States (+D.C.)	51	51

with controls for union membership, age, age squared, male, four race dummies, the log of hours, and 44 industry dummies. The sample was restricted to the private sector, and allo-cated earnings were dealt with as described earlier. We extracted the coefficient on the union variable, giving us 19 years * 51 states (including D.C.), 969 observations in all. We then mapped to that file the unemployment rate in the state-year cell.[31] Once again we ran a series of second-stage regressions where the dependent variable is the one-year level of the premium (obtained by taking anti-logs of the union coefficient and deducting one) on a series of RHS variables including the lagged premium and lagged unemployment and union density rates.[32] Results are reported in columns (3) and (4) of Table 4.9. The number of observations is 918 — we lose 51 observations in generating the lag on the wage premium and the union density variables. Both unweighted and weighted results are presented where the weights are total employment in the state by year. Controlling for state fixed effects with 50 state dummies we find that with an unweighted regression (column (3)), the lagged premium is positive and significant, as it was at industry level. Again, as in the case of industry-level analysis, the effect is apparent when weighting the regression (column (4)). The positive, significant effect of lagged state-level unemployment confirms the counter-cyclical nature of the premium: The effect is apparent whether the regression is weighted or not. There is also evidence of a secular decline in the state-level premium, but only where the regression is unweighted.

State fixed effects account for state-level variance in union density where the effect is fixed over time. However, Farber (2003) argued that there remain potential unobserved variables which simultaneously determine density and wages, but which are time-varying, and thus not picked up in fixed effects, which might bias our results.

Occupations

Finally, we moved on to estimate wage gaps at the level of the occupation pooling six years of data for each of the time periods 1983–1988 and 1996–2001. In each case we used files from the Outgoing Rotation Group files of the CPS. As with our estimates by industry, there is considerable variation by occupation both in the first period and the second. The variation is greater than was found when the analysis was conducted at the level of states — once again results by occupation are reported in an appendix available on request from the authors. The results are summarized in Table 4.12. In the first period 11 occupations had wage gaps over 35 percent — primarily manual occupations. In the second seven of these occupations still had gaps of over 35 percent. Out of the 44 groups, 13 showed increases in the size of the differential over time while the remainder had decreases. We used the same method described above for industries and states, with occupations defined in a comparable way through time. Columns (5) and

Table 4.12
Union Wage Effects by Occupation Using CPS Data

Estimates by Occupation	1983–1988	1996–2001
<5%	10	10
5–15%	9	9
15–35%	14	17
>=35%	11	8
# Occupations	44	44

(6) of Table 6 show that whether the occupation-level analysis is weighted or not, there is clear evidence of regression to the mean, with the lagged premium positive and significant, as well as evidence of a secular decline in the premium. A significant counter-cyclical effect is evident when the regression is weighted, but not in the unweighted regression.

In all three units of observation we have used — industry, state, and occupation — there is evidence that the private sector premium moves counter-cyclically and that it has been declining over time. In all three cases the lagged level of the premium entered significantly positively and was larger when the weights were used than when they were not. The size of the lag was greatest when industries were used as the unit of observation and least when occupations were used. Translating the results from levels into changes — that is by deducting t-1 from both sides — leaves all of the other coefficients unchanged. Using the weighted results in Table 4.6 the results reported below imply mean convergence.

State level	$\Delta \text{Premium}_{t\text{-}t\text{-}1}$	$=$	$-.7949 \text{Premium}_{t\text{-}1}$
Industry level	$\Delta \text{Premium}_{t\text{-}t\text{-}1}$	$=$	$-.6457 \text{Premium}_{t\text{-}1}$
Occupation level	$\Delta \text{Premium}_{t\text{-}t\text{-}1}$	$=$	$-.8254 \text{Premium}_{t\text{-}1}$

The *higher* the level of the premium in the previous period the lower the change in the next period.

VII. What Have We Learned and Would F&M Have Been Surprised about These Results When They Wrote WDUD?

The Private Sector Wage Premium is Lower Today Than It Was in the 1970s

This would not have surprised F&M. Indeed, they predicted that the premiums of the 1970s were unsustainable due to their impact on union density (F&M, 1984, p. 54). Perhaps it is surprising that the premium remains as high as it has. One possibility is that, even though union bargaining power has declined, union density continues to decline, implying that there is some employment spillover into the nonunion sector. If wage setting in the nonunion sector is more flexible than it used to be, this additional supply of labor to the nonunion sector may depress nonunion wages more so than in the past, keeping the premium higher than anticipated.

The Union Wage Premium is Counter-Cyclical

The decline in the premium in good times is what seems to explain much of the decline in the premium since the mid–1990s. Far from being a surprise to F&M, they identified the counter-cyclical nature of the premium. We show the premium is counter-cyclical at the state, occupation, and industry levels. F&M said COLA's could dampen counter-cyclical movements in the premium, but thought their significance had been overplayed. This is confirmed: we find no COLA effect, though this finding is contested by others.

There Is Evidence of a Secular Decline in the Private Sector Union Wage Premium

There is evidence at state, industry, and occupation level of a downward trend in the private sector union wage premium accompanying the marked decline in union presence in the private sector. The effect is sensitive to weighting in the case of the state-level and industry-level premia, but not in the case of the occupational premia. Interestingly, the wage gap appears to have declined most in the smallest states (e.g., New Mexico, Alabama, Nebraska, Arkansas, and South Dakota) and declined least in the bigger states (e.g., California, Texas, New York, and Illinois). It would not have been a surprise to F&M that there had been some reduction in the ability of unions over time to raise wages as the proportion of the work force they bargain for has declined.

There Remains Big Variation in the Premium across Workers

Patterns in the premium across worker types resemble those found by F&M. The F&M sub-sample generally overstated the size of the premium in the population as a whole, but we suspect this would not have surprised F&M. A decline in the premium over time seems to have occurred across all demographic characteristics in the private sector, but there is regression to the mean, the biggest losers being among the most vulnerable and certainly the lowest paid workers (the young, women, and high school dropouts). But perhaps the real surprise is just how large the premium still is for some of these workers (26 percent for high school dropouts, 19 percent for under 25 years old). One puzzle is the remarkable rise in the share of union employment taken by the highly qualified, yet they continue to receive the lowest union premium. Why?

Do they look for something else from their unions, e.g. professional indemnity insurance or voice, or are their unions less effective? In contrast to the private sector, the public sector has experienced a small increase in the premium, an increase apparent for most public sector employees. In the public sector industry-level bargaining remains the norm, maintaining union bargaining power. So, perhaps F&M would not have been surprised by this result. We look at one group of workers that F&M did not consider: immigrants. The premium varies little by year of entry to the United States, but does depend on the country of birth, with Mexicans benefiting from the highest premium. Whether this reflects the human capital, occupational mix, or costs of immigration faced by different groups is a matter for further research, but we suspect the results would not have surprised F&M.

There Is Big Variation in Industry-Level Union Wage Premia

F&M also found wide variation in industry-level premiums and might have expected this to persist because unions' ability to push for a premium, and employers' ability to pay, is determined by industry-specific factors (such as union organization and the availability of nonunion labor, regulatory regimes, bargaining, and product market rents). However, we find convergence in industry-level premiums since F&M wrote, that is, a falling premium where it was once large, and a rising premium where it was once small. (Overall decline at the economy level is due to the fact that the former constitutes a larger share of employment than the latter.) F&M may well have been surprised by this regression to the mean, because in 40 percent of the industries we examined there was a rise in the premium.

State-Level Union Wage Premia Vary Less Than Occupation- and Industry-Level Premia

F&M did not explicitly compare variations in the premia at the state and industry levels. Freeman expressed the view to us that it made sense to him that there would be more variation at the occupation and industry levels as they are more closely approximated to markets. No surprise here.

Union Workers Remain Better Able Than Nonunion Workers to Resist Employer Efforts to Reduce Wages When Market Conditions Are Unfavorable

Import penetration is a good proxy for competition in the traded goods sector. Although the impact of imports on the U.S. wage distribution is often overstated (Blanchflower, 2000a), it may be expected to play a role where imports permit substitution of union products for nonunion products. If imports reduce demand for domestic output and, in turn, demand for labor, this should reduce union and nonunion wages (assuming the supply of nonunion labor is not perfectly elastic). Whether the premium rises or falls with increased import penetration depends on the relative responsiveness of union and nonunion wages to demand shifts resulting from foreign competition. Unions' ability to resist employer efforts to reduce wages when market conditions are unfavorable was cited as one reason for the counter-cyclical premium by F&M (1984, pp. 52–53).

There Has Been a Decline in the Unadjusted Wage Gap Relative to the Regression-Adjusted Wage Gap

Union members do have wage-enhancing advantages over nonmembers, but these have diminished in recent years, implying changes in the selection of employees into membership. It is unlikely that F&M would have predicted this.

Public Sector Wage Effects Are Large and Similar to Those in the Private Sector

F&M did not examine public sector effects and we suspect F&M would not have predicted this.

VIII. Policy Implications

In spite of — or perhaps because of — the inexorable decline in union membership since F&M wrote, and despite some evidence of a recent secular decline in the premium, the union wage premium in the United States remains substantial and is substantial by international standards (Blanchflower and Bryson, 2003). How should U.S. policy analysts treat this piece of information: Should policy support unions or make life more difficult for them?

From a standard economic perspective a substantial union premium has to be bad news: In bargaining on their members' behalf unions distort market wage setting, resulting in a loss of economic efficiency. This may have consequences for jobs and investment for the firms involved and potential impacts for the economy as a whole in terms of inflation and output. However, it is not obvious that markets do operate in the textbook competitive fashion, so there may indeed be rents available that employers are at liberty to share with workers. Furthermore, there is evidence — confirmed herein — that unions are particularly good at protecting the wages of the most vulnerable workers. If the most vulnerable are receiving less than their marginal product — and, perhaps, even if they are receiving it — there may be moral and ethical grounds for supporting unions. Finally, whether analysts like it or not, there is substantial unmet demand for union representation in the United States.[33] People are not getting what they want, raising the question of whether policy should be deployed to assist unions to organize.

F&M found the union premium effect on output was modest, and inflation effects were negligible. There is no reason to alter this judgment. However, the size of the social costs of unionization requires an answer to a fundamental, unanswered question, namely: Where does the premium originate? F&M assume that it necessarily originates in the monopoly rents of employers in privileged market positions, although there are at least three possibilities: (1) unions increase the size of the pie because union workers are more productive than like workers in a nonunion environment; (2) unions operate in firms with excess profits arising from a privileged market position (this may arise either because unions only seek to organize where there are excess profits available, or because these sorts of employers have something particular to gain in contracting with unions); and (3) the premium is simply a tax on normal profits.

It really matters which of these three options it is. If (1) is true, there's no implication for workplace survival or union density, indeed, if this were the case, one might expect a growth in unionization as firms recognize the advantages in unionizing. If it is (2) there is limited damage, but with (3) there are real problems for firms, with potential effects for investment, jobs, and prices. Of course, different employers may be in different positions at any point in time and the weight attached to the three options may differ over time with the business cycle, structural change in the economy, and so on. What evidence is there on the above? Hirsch, in his contribution to this volume, covers these issues in some detail.

Herein we focus on some key points. (i) F&M (1984, p. 54) speculate that at least in some areas, the wage gap has "reached levels inconsistent with the survival of many union jobs." Blanchflower and Freeman (1992) take this issue further and argue that the levels of the union wage differential were so high this gave incentives to employers to remove the union — the benefits of removing the unions appeared to outweigh the costs. Well, what has happened to union jobs? There is a growing body of evidence that employment growth rates are lower in the union sector, suggesting (2) or (3). The evidence is for the United States (Leonard, 1992), Canada (Long, 1993), and Australia (Wooden and Hawke, 2000) and Britain (Blanchflower et al., 1991; Bryson, 2001). However, Freeman and Kleiner (1999) and DiNardo and Lee (2001) find no clear link between unionization and closure. Indeed, F&M record instances in which union workers accepted cuts in normal wages ("givebacks"), sometimes to keep employers in business. (ii) Unionization is more common where employers operate in monopolistic or oligopolistic product markets, suggesting that unions do try to extract surplus rents. (iii) The premium falls when one accounts for workplace heterogeneity. The implication is that some of the premium usually attached to membership is, in fact, due to union workplaces paying higher wages than nonunion workplaces. If this is so, why? Perhaps unions target organization efforts on workplaces that have rents to share; as noted above, they would be foolish not to. Or employers use unions as agents to deliver lower quit rates to recoup investment in human capital (which makes them more productive/profitable). Abowd et al. (1999) stated that higher paying firms are more profitable or more productive than other firms. If this is so for union firms, they are operating at a higher level of performance than other firms. It makes sense that unions are located in higher performing workplaces since, despite higher wages and a negative union effect on performance, they continue to survive, albeit with slower employment growth rates. A central thesis of WDUD was that unions were more productive so this would not surprise F&M. (iv) The evidence that unions have a substantial negative impact on employment growth suggests that the social cost of unions may be larger than F&M calculated. If the premium reduces the competitiveness of union firms, they will lose employees and, as a consequence, union organizing will get tougher for unions. This is exactly what has happened. On the other hand, if unions do not command a premium, they lose their best selling point for prospective customers. It's Catch–22.

From a public policy perspective, it is not obvious from this evidence that unions, taken as a whole, operate to the detriment of the economy or, if they do, that the magnitude of the problem is really that great. Even the evidence on slower employment growth rates is open to the criticism that the link is not causal but arises because unions are often located in declining sectors. What is lacking from the discussion above is a realization that unions and their effects are heterogeneous: Taking wages alone, unions appear to operate very differently across individuals, states, and industries. Before we can make any clear policy prescriptions about what governments should do to, or for, unions we need to know more about the nature of this heterogeneity to establish under what conditions employers and unions can increase the size of the pie.

And then finally we asked Richard Freeman whether he was surprised by any of these findings. He kindly read the paper and gave us three responses. First, he was most surprised by the fact that the public sector wage effects are so large and so similar to those in the private sector. Second, he said he was surprised how little we know about the social costs of unions in the twenty-first century. Consequently he was unsure about the magnitude of the social costs, but would like to see empirical work on the issue although he said would be "stunned" if there were large effects, but as any good empiricist he would let the data speak. Third, he said was not surprised by any of our other findings.

Notes

*   We thank Bernt Bratsberg, Bernard Corry, Henry Farber, Richard Freeman, Barry Hirsch, Andrew Oswald, Jim Ragan, and participants at NBER Labor Studies for their comments. We also thank the UK Economic and Social Research Council (grant R000223958) for funding.

1.   The symposium included an introduction by the editor John Burton along with reviews by Orley Ashenfelter, Barry Hirsch, David Lipsky, Dan Mitchell, and Mel Reder, plus a reply by Richard Freeman and Jim Medoff.
2.   It has been cited an astonishing 1,024 times over its near 20-year life. In 2002 alone it had 34 cites. It is clear that the book continues to be relevant.

3. Richard Freeman has devoted a lot of his subsequent writings to an examination of unionism in the public sector including Freeman (1986, 1988), four chapters written with co-authors in Freeman and Ichniowski (1988), and a co-authored paper on union wage gaps for police (Freeman et al., 1989). Freeman's other post-F&M work on union wage effects includes an international comparative paper with one of the authors (Blanchflower and Freeman, 1992), and the impact of union decline on rising wage inequality in the United States — see for example Freeman, (1993, 1995, 1999); Freeman and Katz (1995); Freeman and Needels (1993); and Freeman and Revenga (1998). For a discussion of the issues involved see Blanchflower (2000a).

4. For further discussions on these issues, see Lewis (1986), Freeman (1984), and Blanchflower and Bryson (2003).

5. In contrast Lewis (1986), who did not restrict his analysis to nonagricultural private sector blue-collar workers aged 20–65 as F&M did, found no differences by either gender or color, although he confirmed F&M's other disaggregated results. Lewis reported a number of additional disaggregated results that were not examined by F&M. Lewis found the wage gap was greater for married workers; U-shaped in age/experience; U-shaped in tenure/seniority minimizing at 22–24 years of seniority and was higher the higher is the unemployment rate. He found mixed results regarding any relationship with the industry concentration ratio.

6. Sample sizes in many cases were likely very small as is made clear from their footnote 11 which says that they limited their sample of industries to ones containing at least five union and nonunion members. The rule resulted in only four industries being dropped.

7. F&M use 1977 union density rates in Table 2.

8. These estimates are obtained from the ORG files. Although numbers for the public and private sectors as a whole are available since 1973, the breakdown by federal, state, and local employee only begins in 1983.

9. We do not deal here with a further problem identified by Card (1996) of misclassification of self-reported union status in the CPS, first identified by Mellow and Sider (1983). Card concludes that about 2.7 percent are false positives and 2.7 percent are false negatives. Given that there are more nonunion workers than union workers, this means the union density rate is biased upwards. See Farber (2001) for a discussion and a procedure to adjust the union density rate for error. In 1998, the observed private sector rate of 9.7 percent translates to an adjusted rate of 7.4 percent (the figures for 1973 were 25.9 percent and 24.5 percent, respectively).

10. The number of wage observations followed by the percentage imputed in parentheses (hourly + non-hourly paid) in the NBER MORG are given below. Note in 1995 allocation information is only available on one-third of the wage observations, hence the small sample.

1979	171,745 (16.5%)	1986	179,147 (10.7%)	1993	174,595 (4.6%)	2000	161,126 (29.8%)
1980	199,469 (15.8%)	1987	180,434 (13.5%)	1994	170,865 (0%)	2001	171,533 (30.9%)
1981	186,923 (15.2%)	1988	173,118 (14.4%)	1995	55,967 (23.3%)	2002	184,137 (30.4%)
1982	175,797 (13.7%)	1989	176,411 (3.7%)	1996	152,190 (22.2%)		
1983	173,932 (13.8%)	1990	185,030 (3.9%)	1997	154,955 (22.2%)		
1984	177,248 (14.7%)	1991	179,560 (4.4%)	1998	156,990 (23.6%)		
1985	180,232 (14.3%)	1992	176,848 (4.2%)	1999	159,362 (27.6%)		

11. A revised version of their paper, due for publication in the *Journal of Labor Economics* in 2004, exploits the unedited earnings data for those years.

12. Although there are some differences in the levels of the wage differences reported in columns 3 and 4 of Table 3, the majority of these results are consistent with the findings reported by F&M in their Figure 3. Major exceptions are F&M's finding that wage gaps were higher for men than women and for nonwhites compared with whites. We suspect such differences arise because of the small sample size in the May 1979 CPS of 6,018 used by F&M.

13. Nearly all federal workers have wages set by civil service pay schedules, but these are not set by collective bargaining in any meaningful sense. Even with workers in the exact same federal job, one will say they are a union member and the other will say they are not. Thus the low union premium for federal workers may not be very meaningful. For state and local workers (and some groups of federal workers like postal workers), the union status variable provides meaningful information. We thank Barry Hirsch for this point.

14. Tables for the analyses presented in this section are available from the authors.

15. We have added data for 2002 as the 2002 ORG has recently become available.

16. The May extracts of the CPS extracts in Stata format from 1969–1987 are available from the NBER at <http://www.nber.org/data/cps_may.html>.

17. Hirsch et al. (2002) have compared union wage gap estimates obtained from the BLS quarterly Employment Cost Index (ECI) constructed from establishment surveys and from the annual Employer Costs for Employee Compensation (ECEC) with those obtained using the CPS. They find that union/nonunion wage trends in the three series "are consistent neither with each other nor with the CPS," and ultimately con-clude that "we find ourselves relying most heavily on results drawn from the CPS" (Hirsch et al., 2002, p. 23).

18. There was no CPS survey with wages and union status in 1982.

19. Following Mincer, it is more usual to include a term in potential experience rather than a direct measure of age. We use education, however, for reasons of comparability as the CPS Outgoing Rotation Group files from 1993 report qualifications rather than years of schooling.

20. Similarly in the 2003 edition of Hirsch and Macpherson's *Union Membership and Earnings Data Book,* recently received.

21. There is a dissonance between the estimates Lewis offers by way of summary in his introductory chapter and those given in his Table 9.7 produced here (Lewis, 1986, p. 9).

22. Lewis (1986) had 35 studies using the CPS, 1970–1979; 16 studies using the 1967 Survey of Economic Opportunity; 25 studies using the Panel Study of Income Dynamics, 1967–1978; 15 studies using Michigan Survey Research Center survey data other than the PSID, including the 1972–1973 Quality of Employment Survey; 22 studies using the National Longitudinal Surveys of 1969–1972; and eight studies exploiting other sources.

23. F&M's smaller sample sizes by industry could account for some of the greater variation in their estimates.

24. Bratsberg and Ragan (2002) also use CPS data. But their analysis differs in several ways. First, they assess trends over the period 1971–1999 whereas we present trends over the period 1983–2001. Second, we adjust for wage imputation as recommended by Hirsch and Schumacher (2002) whereas Bratsberg and Ragan do not. Third, specifications producing the regression-adjusted estimates differ somewhat. Fourth, the samples differ. In particular, Bratsberg and Ragan exclude government workers, and they present results for some different industries. Fifth, their wage premium relates to weekly wages whereas all of our estimates are derived from (log) hourly wages.

25. The import penetration variables are calculated as the ratio of imports to industry shipments. Bratsberg and Ragan (2002) in their footnote 19 report that they tabulated shipments through 1994 from Feenstra (1996) and thereafter from the U.S. Bureau of the Census, U.S. Merchandise Trade, series FT900 (December) and Manufactures' Shipments, Inventories and Orders (<http://www.census.gov>).
26. When the equations are run on the two machines using OLS they are identical. The problem appears to arise from the different tolerances used across computers and not from differences in the STATA programs.
27. According to the 2002 Human Development Report Table 5 (<http://hdr.undp.org/>) the population of the United States in 2000 was 283.2 million compared with 60.6 million in the UK and 7.2 million in Switzerland.
28. He finds wages of highly unionized occupations in Las Vegas's hotel and gaming industry are significantly higher than wages of identical occupations in less unionized Reno.
29. The source of the data is the *Union Membership and Coverage Database* which is an Internet data resource providing private and public sector union membership, coverage, and density estimates compiled from the Current Population Survey (CPS) using BLS methods. Economy-wide estimates are provided beginning in 1973; estimates by state, detailed industry, and detailed occupation begin in 1983; and estimates by metropolitan area begin in 1986. The *Database*, constructed by Barry Hirsch (Trinity University) and David Macpherson (Florida State University), is updated annually and can be accessed at <http://www.unionstats.com>.
30. The main exceptions are Maine, Hawaii, and Vermont which are small and which had increases in the wage gap. Florida is the fourth largest state after California, Texas, and New York but its differential declined by 10 percentage points.
31. Source: <http://data.bls.gov/labjava/outside.jsp?survey=la>.
32. We experimented with both the level of the unemployment rate and the log and the latter always worked best.
33. According to Peter Hart Associates, the percentage of nonmembers saying they would vote for a union hit 50 percent in 2002, the highest percentage since their figures began in 1984 (when the figure was only 30 percent). See <http://www.aflcio.org/mediacenter/resources/upload/LaborDay2002Poll.ppt>.

References

Abowd, John M., Francis Kramarz, and David Margolis. "High Wage Workers and High Wage Firms." *Econometrica* 672 (March 1999): 251–333.

Blanchflower, David G. "The Role and Influence of Trade Unions in the OECD." Report to the Bureau of International Labor Affairs. Washington, D.C.: U.S. Department of Labor, August, 1996. Downloadable at <www.dartmouth.edu/~blnchflr/Projects.html>.

_____. "Changes Over Time in Union Relative Wage Effects in Great Britain and the United States." In Sami Daniel, Philip Arestis, and John Grahl, eds. *The History and Practice of Economics: Essays in Honour of Bernard Corry and Maurice Peston, Volume 2*. Northampton, Mass.: Edward Elgar, 1999, pp. 3–32.

_____. "Globalization and the Labor Market." Report to The Trade Deficit Review Commission, downloadable at <http://www.ustdrc.gov, 2000a>.

_____. "Self-employment in OECD Countries." *Labour Economics* 7 (September 2000b): 471–505.

_____ and Alex Bryson. "Changes Over Time in Union Relative Wage Effects in the UK and the US Revisited." In John T. Addison and C. Schnabel, eds.

International Handbook of Trade Unions. Cheltenham, UK: Edward Elgar, 2003, pp. 197–245.

_____ and Richard B. Freeman. "Unionism in the U.S. and Other Advanced OECD Countries." *Industrial Relations* 31 (Winter 1992): 156–79; reprinted in Michael Bognanno and Morris M. Kleiner eds. *Labor Market Institutions and the Future Role of Unions*. Oxford: Blackwell, 1992, pp. 56–79.

_____, Neil Millward, and Andrew J. Oswald. "Unionism and Employment Behaviour." *Economic Journal* 101 (July 1991): 815–34.

Bratsberg, Bernt and James F. Ragan. "Changes in the Union Wage Premium by Industry – Data and Analysis." *Industrial and Labor Relations Review* 56 (October 2002): 65–83.

Bryson, Alex. "Employee Voice, Workplace Closure and Employment Growth." London: Policy Studies Institute Research Discussion Paper No. 6, 2001.

Card, David. "The Effect of Unions on the Structure of Wages: A Longitudinal Analysis." *Econometrica* 64 (July 1996): 957–79.

Farber, Henry S. "Notes on the Economics of Labor Unions." Working Paper 452, Princeton University Industrial Relations Section, 2001.

_____. "Nonunion Wage Rates and the Threat of Unionization." Working Paper 472, Princeton University Industrial Relations Section, 2003.

Freeman, Richard B. "Longitudinal Analyses of the Effects of Trade Unions." *Journal of Labor Economics* 2 (January 1984): 1–26.

_____. "Unionism Comes to the Public Sector." *Journal of Economic Literature* 24 (March 1986): 41–86.

_____. "Contraction and Expansion: The Divergence of Private Sector and Public Sector Unionism in the United States." *Journal of Economic Perspectives* 2 (Spring 1988): 63–88.

_____. "How Much Has De-unionization Contributed to the Rise in Male Earnings Inequality?" In Sheldon Danziger and Peter Gottschalk, eds. *Uneven Tides: Rising Inequality in America*. New York: Russell Sage Foundation, 1993, pp. 133–63.

_____. "Are Your Wages Set in Beijing?" *Journal of Economic Perspectives* 9 (Summer 1995): 15–32.

_____. "The New Inequality in the United States." In Albert Fishlow and Karen Parker, eds. *Growing Apart: The Causes and Consequences of Global Wage Inequality*. New York: Council on Foreign Relations Press, 1999, pp. 21–66.

Freeman, Richard B. and Casey Ichniowski. *When Public Sector Workers Unionize*. Chicago: NBER and University of Chicago Press, 1988.

_____ and Harrison Lauer. "Collective Bargaining Laws, Threat Effects and the Determination of Police Compensation." *Journal of Labor Economics* 72 (April 1989): 191–209.

Freeman, Richard B. and Larry F. Katz. *Differences and Changes in Wage Structures*. Chicago: University of Chicago Press and NBER, 1995.

Freeman, Richard B. and Morris M. Kleiner. "Do Unions Make Enterprises Insolvent?" *Industrial and Labor Relations Review* 52 (July 1999): 510–27.

Freeman, Richard B. and James L. Medoff. *What Do Unions Do?* New York: Basic Books, 1984.

_____. "Reply." *Industrial and Labor Relations Review* 382 (January 1985): 259–63.

Freeman, Richard B. and Karen Needels. "Skill Differentials in Canada in an Era of Rising Labor Market Inequality." In David Card and Richard B. Freeman, eds. *Small Differences That Matter*. Chicago: University of Chicago Press and NBER, 1993, pp. 45–67.

Freeman, Richard B. and Anna Revenga. "How Much Has LDC Trade Affected Western Job Markets?" In Mathias Dewatripont, Andre Sapir, and Khalid Sekket, eds. *Trade and Jobs in Europe: Much Ado About Nothing?* Oxford: Clarendon Press, 1999, pp. 8–32.

Hirsch, Barry T. "Reconsidering Union Wage Effects: Surveying New Evidence on an Old Topic," mimeo, 2003.

_____ and David A. Macpherson. "Earnings and Employment in Trucking: Deregulating a Naturally Competitive Industry." In James Peoples, ed. *Regulatory Reform and Labor Markets.* New York: Kluwer Academic, 1998, pp. 61–112.

_____. "Earnings, Rents and Competition in the Airline Labor Market." *Journal of Labor Economics* 18 (January 2000): 125–55.

_____. *Union Membership and Earnings Data Book: Compilations from the Current Population Survey 2002 Edition.* Washington, D.C.: Bureau of National Affairs, 2002, 2003a.

_____. "Union Membership and Coverage Database from the Current Population Survey: Note." *Industrial and Labor Relations Review* 56 (January 2002): 349–54.

Hirsch, Barry T., David A. Macpherson, and Edward J. Schumacher. "Measuring Union and Nonunion Wage Growth: Puzzles in Search of Solutions." Paper presented at the 23rd Middlebury Economics Conference on the Changing Role of Unions, Middlebury, Vt., April 2002.

Hirsch, Barry T., David A. Macpherson, and Wayne G. Vroman. "Estimates of Union Density by State." *Monthly Labor Review* 124 (July 2001): 51–55.

Hirsch, Barry T. and Edward J. Schumacher. "Unions, Wages, and Skills." *Journal of Human Resources* 33 (Winter 1998): 201–19.

_____. "Match Bias in Wage Gap Estimates Due To Earnings Imputation," Mimeograph, Trinity University, available at <www.trinity.edu/bhirsch/> or <www.ssrn.com>, 2002.

Horn, John T. "Unions, Firms and Competition: The Effects of Foreign Competition on Unionization and the Impact of Unions on Firm Investment." Ph.D. thesis, Department of Economics, Harvard University, 1998.

Lawrence, Colin and Robert Z. Lawrence. "Manufacturing Wage Dispersion: An End Game Interpretation." *Brookings Papers on Economic Activity* 1 (1985): 47–116.

Leonard, Jonathan S. "Unions and Employment Growth." *Industrial Relations* 31 (Winter 1992): 80–94.

Lewis, H. Gregg. *Unionism and Relative Wages in the United States.* Chicago: University of Chicago Press, 1963.

_____. *Union Relative Wage Effects: A Survey.* Chicago: University of Chicago Press, 1986.

Long, Richard J. "The Impact of Unionization on Employment Growth of Canadian Companies." *Industrial and Labor Relations Review* 48 (July 1993): 691–703.

Mellow, Wesley and Hal Sider. "Accuracy of Response in Labor Market Surveys: Evidence and Implications." *Journal of Labor Economics* 1 (October 1983): 331–44.

Staiger, Robert W. "Organized Labor and the Scope of International Specialization." *Journal of Political Economy* 96 (October 1988): 1022–47.

Waddoups, C. Jeffrey. "Unions and Wages in Nevada's Hotel-Casino Industry." *Journal of Labor Research* 21 (Spring 2000): 345–61.

Wooden, Mark and Hawke, Anne. "Unions and Employment Growth: Panel Data Evidence." *Industrial Relations* 39 (January 2000): 88–107.

5

Unions and Wage Inequality

David Card, Thomas Lemieux, and W. Craig Riddell

I. Introduction

How unions affect the distribution of income is a subject that has long intrigued social scientists. The publication of *What Do Unions Do?* and the related papers by Freeman (1980, 1982, 1984) represented a watershed in the evolution of economists' views on this question. Until the 1970s the dominant view was that unions tended to increase wage inequality (Johnson, 1975). Using micro data on individual workers in the union and nonunion sectors, Freeman (1980) presented results that challenged this view. He showed that the inequality-reducing effects of unions were quantitatively larger than the inequality-increasing effects. The equalizing effect of unions became a key chapter in *What Do Unions Do?* and an important component of the authors' overall assessment of the social and economic consequences of unions.

Recently the relationship between unions and inequality has attracted renewed interest as analysts have struggled to explain increases in wage inequality in many industrialized countries. The fact that two of the countries with the largest declines in unionization — the United States and the United Kingdom — also experienced the biggest increases in wage inequality raises the question of whether these two phenomena are linked. If so, how much of the growth in earnings inequality can be attributed to the fall in union coverage?

We make several contributions to this issue. We begin by presenting a simple framework for measuring the effect of unions on wage inequality, based on the potential outcomes framework that is now widely used in program evaluation. Our framework emphasizes three key aspects of collective bargaining: How does the probability of union coverage vary for workers who would earn more or less in the nonunion sector? How much do unions raise average wages for workers in different skill groups? How do unions affect the dispersion of wages within narrow skill groups? Next, we trace the evolution of economists' views on the impacts of unions on the wage distribution. This section places the contributions of Freeman (1980, 1982, 1984) and Freeman and Medoff (1984) in historical context. Third, we present new evidence on the relationship between unions and wage inequality for three countries — Canada, the United Kingdom, and the United States — during the past three decades. Finally, we assess whether the position put forward in *What Do Unions Do?* regarding unions and wage inequality has held up to the scrutiny of subsequent research, including the new evidence reported herein.

Our analysis of unions and wage inequality in the United States, the United Kingdom, and Canada is motivated by several factors. One is to better understand trends in income inequality. Several previous studies have concluded that falling unionization contributed to the steep increase in wage inequality in the United States and the United Kingdom during the 1980s. Wage inequality did not rise as quickly in these countries in the 1990s. This raises the question of whether the evolution of union coverage and union wage impacts can account for some of the changing trend in wage inequality. More generally, differences across these countries in the timing of changes in unionization and in wage inequality provide an opportunity for further assessing the contribution of institutional change to trends in income inequality.

Our empirical analysis is also motivated by the fact that in these three countries the institutional arrangements governing unionization and collective bargaining provide an environment that is suitable for estimating how unions affect wage inequality. As with other aspects of the economy, collective bargaining institutions in these countries are broadly similar. In particular, negotiations are conducted at the enterprise level, and there is no general mechanism to extend union wage floors beyond the organized sector. The fraction of workers covered by collective agreements in the three countries is also relatively modest — currently under one-third of wage and salary workers. Thus it is possible to compare the structure of wages for workers whose wages are set by union contracts, and those whose wages are not, and potentially infer the effect of unions on overall wage inequality. A similar task is far more difficult in other countries (including the major European countries and Australia) because there is no clear distinction between the union and nonunion sectors. Collective bargaining in these countries is conducted at the industry or sectoral level, and the provisions are formally or informally extended to most of the labor force. Moreover, in many countries, unions exert considerable influence on political decisions (such as minimum wages) that directly affect labor market outcomes.

We also seek to assess whether there are common patterns in the impact of unions on the wage structure in countries with economies and industrial relations systems that are broadly similar. Of particular interest are patterns in union coverage and union wage impacts by gender and skill. To do so, we use micro data samples to compare the incidence and average wage effect of unions by skill level on male and female workers in the three countries, and measure recent trends in union coverage by skill level. Despite some differences in the institutional systems that govern the determination of union status in the three countries, we find remarkable similarity in the overall patterns of union coverage and in the degree to which unions affect wages of different skill groups. Within narrowly defined skill groups, wage inequality is always lower for union workers than nonunion workers. For male workers, union coverage tends to be concentrated at the middle of the skill distribution, and union wages tend to be "flattened" relative to nonunion wages. As a result, unions have an equalizing effect on the dispersion of male wages across skill groups in the three countries, complementing the effect on within-group inequality. For female workers, however, union coverage is concentrated near the top of the skill distribution, and there is no tendency for unions to flatten skill differentials across groups. Thus, unions tend to *raise* inequality between more and less skilled women in the three countries, offsetting their effect on within-group inequality.

As a final step, we use data from the past 25 years to compute the changing effect of unionization on wage inequality. During the 1980s and 1990s, unionization rates fell in all three countries, with the most rapid decline in the United Kingdom and the slowest fall in Canada. These trends contributed to rising male wage inequality, particularly in Britain. Indeed, we estimate that the precipitous fall in U.K. unionization can explain up to two thirds of the difference in the trend in male wage inequality between Britain and the United States.

II. Unions and Wage Inequality

Conceptual Framework. A useful framework for studying the effect of unions on wage inequality is the potential outcomes model now widely used in program evaluation (Angrist and Krueger, 1999). Assume that each worker faces two potential wages: a log wage in the union sector, WiU, and a log wage in the nonunion sector WiN. Ignoring dual job holders, a given individual is either in one sector or the other at any point in time, so one of these outcomes is observed and the other is not. Letting Ui denote an indicator for union status, the observed wage of individual i is

$$W_i = U_i W_i U + (1 - U_i) W_i^N.$$

Let W^U and W^N represent the means of the potential wage outcomes in the two sectors, and let V^U and V^N represent the corresponding variances. Finally, let W and V represent the mean and variance of observed wages in the economy as a whole. In this setting, a natural measure of the effect of unions on wage inequality is $V - V^N$: the difference between the observed variance of wages and the variance that would prevail if everyone was paid his or her nonunion potential wage.

There are two problems with this measure. The first is purely practical: How do we estimate V^N? The second is conceptual. Arguably, any given individual in the union sector has a well-defined potential wage in the nonunion sector. But if the union sector disappeared, the equilibrium set of wage offers in the nonunion sector could change.1 Thus V^N is a function of the size of the union sector, $V^N(u)$, where $0 \leq u \leq 1$ indexes the fraction of workers in the union sector. In the absence of any unionization, the variance of observed wages would be

$V^N(0)$. Thus, the effect of unionization on wage inequality, taking account of the general equilibrium impact of the presence of the union sector, is $V - V^N(0)$.

Despite its theoretical appeal, it is difficult to imagine developing a credible estimate of $V^N(0)$. Under strong assumptions, however, it may be possible to estimate $V^N(U)$, where U is the current fraction of unionized workers. The advantage of this measure is that potential nonunion wage outcomes *under the current level of unionism* are at least partially observed (for all current nonunion workers). Since

$$V - V^N(U) = V - V^N(0) + \{V^N(0) - V^N(U)\},$$

the difference $V-VN(U)$ overstates or understates the "true" effect of unions by a term reflecting how much the variance of nonunion wage outcomes would change if the union sector was eliminated. While acknowledging this potential bias, in the rest of this analysis we focus on comparisons between V, the observed variance of wages, and $V^N(U)$, the variance that would prevail if everyone were paid according to the *current* nonunion wage structure.

Estimating the Variance of Potential Nonunion Wages

In order to estimate V^N we have to make an assumption about how current union workers would be paid if they worked in the nonunion sector. One starting point is the assumption that union status is "as good as randomly assigned," conditional on observed skill characteristics. In this case, the counterfactual variance V^N can be estimated as the variance of wages for a suitably reweighted sample of nonunion workers. In this section we show how the resulting calculations are related to three key factors: the variation in the union coverage rate by wage level in the absence of unions, the size of the union wage effect for different skill groups, and the union-nonunion difference in the variance of wages within skill categories. We then show how the assumption that union status is independent of unobserved productivity factors can be relaxed.

Let $W_i^N(c)$ represent the log wage that individual i in skill group c would earn in the nonunion sector, and let $WiU(c)$ denote the log wage for the same individual if employed in a union job. Assume that

$$W_i^N(c) = W^N(c) + e_i^N \text{ and}$$
$$W_i^U(c) = W^U(c) + e_i^U,$$

where $W^N(c)$ and $W^U(c)$ are the mean nonunion and union log wages for individuals in skill group c, respectively, and the random terms eiN and eiU are *independent* of actual union status (conditional on the observed skill level c). Let $VU(c)$ and $VN(c)$ denote the variances of potential wage outcomes for individuals in skill group c in the union and nonunion sectors, respectively. The union-nonunion gap in average wages for workers in skill group c is

$$\Delta_w(c) = W^U(c) - W^N(c),$$

while the corresponding variance gap is

$$\Delta^v(c) = V^U(c) - V^N(c).$$

Under the independence assumption, $W^N(c)$ and $V^N(c)$ provide unbiased estimates of the mean and variance of nonunion wage outcomes for all workers in skill group c, not just those who are actually working in the nonunion sector. The variance of wages in the nonunion sector will not necessarily equal V^N, however, if the distribution of nonunion workers across skill groups differs from the distribution of the overall work force. A simple way to estimate V^N is to reweight individual observations from the nonunion work force to account for this difference. Letting $U(c)$ denote the fraction of workers in skill group c in union jobs, the appropriate weight for nonunion workers in group c is $1/(1-U(c))$.

While reweighting provides a convenient way to calculate V^N, it is nevertheless instructive to develop an analytical expression for $V-V^N$ under the conditional independence assumption. Analogous expressions were first derived by Freeman (1980) and used extensively in Freeman and Medoff (1984). To begin, note that if a homogeneous group of workers in some skill group c is split into a union and a nonunion sector, and if unions alter the mean and variance of wages by $\Delta^w(c)$ and $\Delta^v(c)$, respectively, then the overall mean and variance of wage outcomes for workers in skill group c will be

$$W(c) = W^N(c) + U(c)\,\Delta_w(c), \tag{1}$$
$$V(c) = V^N(c) + U(c)\Delta_v(c) + U(c)(1-U(c))\Delta_w(c)^2. \tag{2}$$

The first of these equations says that the average wage of workers in skill group c will be raised relative to the counterfactual nonunion average wage by the product of the unionization rate $U(c)$ and the union wage gap $\Delta_w(c)$. The second expression shows that the presence of unions exerts two potentially offsetting effects on the dispersion of wages, relative to the counterfactual $V^N(c)$. First is a "within-sector" effect that arises if wages are more or less disperse under collective bargaining than in its absence. This is just the product of the extent of unionization and the union effect on the variance of wages. Second is a positive "between-sector" effect, reflecting the wedge between the average wage of otherwise identical union and nonunion workers.

If there are many skill groups in the economy, the variance of log wages across all workers is the sum of the variance of mean wages across groups and the average variance within groups:

$$V = \mathrm{Var}[W(c)] + \mathrm{E}[V(c)],$$

where expectations (denoted by E[ ]), and variances (denoted by Var[ ]) are taken across the skill categories. Using equations (1) and (2), this expression be rewritten as:

$$V = \text{Var}[W^N(c) + U(c)\Delta_w(c)] + \text{E}[V^N(c) + U(c)\Delta_v(c) + U(c)(1-U(c))\Delta_w(c)^2]$$
$$= \text{Var}[W^N(c)] + \text{Var}[U(c)\Delta w(c)] + 2\text{Cov}[W^N(c), U(c)\Delta w(c)]$$
$$+ \text{E}[V^N(c)] + \text{E}[U(c)\Delta_v(c)] + \text{E}[U(c)(1-U(c))\Delta_w(c)^2], \tag{3}$$

where Cov[,] denotes the covariance across skill groups. In contrast to equation (3), if all workers were paid according to the wage structure in the nonunion sector, the variance of wage outcomes would be

$$V^N = \text{Var}[W^N(c)] + \text{E}[V^N(c)].$$

The effect of unions on the variance of wage outcomes, relative to what would be observed if all workers were paid according to the current wage structure in the nonunion sector, is therefore

$$V - V^N = \text{Var}[U(c)\Delta_w(c)] + 2\text{Cov}[W^N(c), U(c)\Delta_w(c)]$$
$$+ \text{E}[U(c)\Delta v(c)] + \text{E}[U(c)(1-U(c))\Delta_w(c)^2]. \tag{4}$$

Substituting observed values for $WN(c)$, $U(c)$, $\Delta_w(c)$, and $\Delta_w(c)$ into equation (4) leads to an expression that is numerically equal to the difference between the observed variance of wages V and the "reweighting" estimate of V^N, derived by reweighting each nonunion worker by $1/(1-U(c))$.

To understand the implications of equation (4) it is helpful to begin by considering a case where the union coverage rate, the union wage effect $\Delta_w(c)$, and the union variance gap are all constant across skill groups. In this case the first two terms in equation (4) are 0, and the effect of unions reduces to the simple "two sector" equation introduced by Freeman (1980):

$$V - V^N = U\Delta v + U(1-U)\Delta_w^2, \tag{4'}$$

where U represents the overall unionization rate, Δ_v represents the difference in the variance of log wages between union and nonunion workers, and Δw represents the difference in mean wages between union and nonunion workers.

When union coverage rates or union effects on the level or dispersion of wages vary by skill group, the effect of unions also depends on how the union wage gain $U(c)\Delta_w(c)$ varies with the level of wages in the absence of unions (the covariance term in equation (4)), and on by how much unions raise the variation in mean wages across different groups (the $\text{Var}[U(c)\Delta_w(c)]$ term in equation (4)). In particular, if union coverage is higher for less skilled workers, or if the union wage impact is higher for such workers, then the covariance term will be negative, enhancing the equalizing effect of unions on wage dispersion.

Allowing for Unobserved Heterogeneity

The assumption that union status is "as good as random" conditional on observed skills is convenient but arguably too strong. In this section we show how the presence of unobserved productivity differences between union and nonunion workers biases the calculation that ignores these differences. As before, assume that workers are classified into skill categories on the basis of observed characteristics, and suppose that potential nonunion and union wages are given by:

$$W_i^N(c) = W^N(c) + a_i + e_i^N, \tag{5a}$$
$$W_i^U(c) = W^U(c) + a_i + e_i^U, \tag{5b}$$

where a^i represents an unobserved skill component that is equally rewarded in the union and nonunion sectors. Continue to assume that e_i^N and e_i^U are independent of union status, and let

$$\theta(c) = E[a_i \mid U_i{=}1, c] - E[a_i \mid U_i{=}0, c]$$

represent the difference in the mean of the unobserved skill component between union and nonunion workers in group c. If union workers in group c have higher unobserved skills than their nonunion counterparts, for example, then $\theta(c) > 0$.

The *observed* wage gap between union and nonunion workers in group c includes the true union wage premium and the difference attributable to unobserved skills:

$$D_w(c) = \Delta_w(c) + \theta(c).$$

Similarly, assuming that e_i^N and e_i^U are independent of a^i, the *observed* difference in the variance of wages between union and nonunion workers in group c is:

$$D_v(c) = \Delta_v(c) + \text{Var}[a_i \mid U_i{=}1, c] - \text{Var}[a_i \mid U_i{=}0, c],$$

which is a combination of the true union effect on within-group inequality and any difference in the variance of the unobserved productivity effects between union and nonunion workers. If union workers tend to have a narrower distribution of unobserved skills, for example, the observed variance gap $\Delta_v(c)$ will be biased downward relative to the "true" union effect $\Delta_v(c)$.

Assuming that potential wage outcomes are generated by equations (5a, 5b), it can be shown that the difference in the variance of wages in the presence of unions and in the counterfactual situation in which all workers are paid according to the nonunion wage structure is

$$V - V^N = \mathrm{Var}[U(c)\Delta_w(c)] + 2\mathrm{Cov}[W^N(c),\ U(c)\Delta_w(c)]$$
$$+ \mathrm{E}[U(c)\Delta_v(c)] + \mathrm{E}[U(c)(1\text{-}U(c))\{\ (\theta(c)+\Delta_w(c))^2-\theta(c)^2\ \}]. \qquad (6)$$

Only the last term of this equation differs from equation (4), the expression that applies when $\theta(c)=0$ for all groups.[2] In the presence of unobserved heterogeneity, however, $\Delta_w(c)$ and $\Delta_v(c)$ can no longer be estimated consistently from the observed differences in the means and variances of union and nonunion workers in skill group c. By the same token, it is no longer possible to use a reweighting procedure based on the fraction of union members in different observed skill groups to estimate V^N.

It is instructive to compare the estimated effect of unions under the "as good as random" assumption to the true effect, when potential wages are generated by equations (5a, 5b). The estimated effect is given by equation (4), using the observed within-skill group union differences $D_w(c)$ and $D_v(c)$ as estimates of $\Delta_w(c)$ and $\Delta_v(c)$. The true effect is given by equation (6). The difference is

$$\text{Bias} = \mathrm{Var}[U(c)D_w(c)] - \mathrm{Var}[U(c)\Delta_w(c)] + 2\mathrm{Cov}[W^N(c),\ U(c)(D_w(c)-\Delta_w(c))]$$
$$+ \mathrm{E}[\ U(c)(D_v(c)-\Delta_v(c))] + \mathrm{E}[U(c)(1\text{-}U(c))\ \{D_w(c)^2 - \Delta_w(c)^2 -2\ \theta(c)\ \Delta_w(c)\}].$$

There are various competing factors here. For example, if $D^w(c)$ varies more across skill groups than $\Delta_w(c)$, the sum of the first two terms is likely to be positive. On the other hand, if $D_w(c)$ is more strongly negatively correlated with nonunion wages across skill groups than $\Delta_w(c)$ (as argued in Card, 1996), then the third (covariance) term will be negative, leading to an overstatement of the equalizing effect of unions. We return to this issue below.

III. A Review of the Literature on Unions and Inequality

Until recently, most economists believed that unions tended to raise inequality. For example, Friedman (1956) — appealing to Marshall's laws of derived demand — argued that craft unions will be more successful in raising the wages of their members than industrial unions. Following this logic, Friedman (1962, p. 124) concluded:

> If unions raise wage rates in a particular occupation or industry, they necessarily make the amount of employment available in the occupation or industry less than it otherwise would be — just as any higher price cuts down the amount purchased. The effect is an increased number of persons seeking other jobs, which forces down wages in other occupations. Since unions have generally been strongest among groups that would have been high-paid anyway, their effect has been to make high-paid workers

higher paid at the expense of lower paid workers. Unions have therefore not only harmed the public at large and workers as a whole by distorting the use of labor; they have also made the incomes of the working class more unequal by reducing the opportunities available to the most disadvantaged workers.

As this quote makes clear, Friedman posited two channels for the disequalizing effect of unions. One is the "between-sector" effect — the gap in wages between otherwise similar workers in the union and nonunion sectors. The other is a hypothesized positive correlation between the union wage gain and the level of wages in the absence of unions — that is, an assumption that the covariance term in equation (4) is positive. Even economists more sympathetic to unions than Friedman shared this view. For example, Rees (1962) suggested that "theory and evidence" both predict unions will have a bigger effect on high-skilled workers. Noting that union membership (in 1950) was concentrated among workers in the upper half of the earnings distribution, Rees concluded that the overall effect of unions was probably to increase inequality.

Not all scholars accepted this position. Following their detailed analysis of the evolution of the wage structure in several industries, Reynolds and Taft (1956, p. 194) concluded that: "Summing up these diverse consequences of collective bargaining, one can make a strong case that unionism has at any rate not worsened the wage structure. We are inclined to be even more venturesome than this, and to say that its net effect has been beneficial." Much of the reasoning behind this position was based on evidence of unions negotiating "standard rates" that resulted in greater uniformity of wages within and across establishments.

Evidence on these issues was scanty and inconclusive until the widespread availability of micro data in the 1970s. Stieber (1959) examined the effect of unions in the steel industry and concluded that during the 1947–1960 period collective bargaining did not flatten the wage distribution. In an interesting contribution, Ozanne (1962) tabulated data for McDormick Deering (a farm machine company) over the period 1858 to 1958. During this period many different unions unionized the same plant. He found no tendency for unions per se to reduce or increase intra-firm wage inequality. Skill differentials narrowed during some regimes and they widened during other periods. However, there was a general tendency for industrial unions to lower skill differentials and for craft unions to raise them. In his classic study of union relative wage effects, Lewis (1963) examined the correlation between estimates of the union wage differential and wage levels. He concluded that unionism increased the inequality of average wages across industries by 2 to 3 percentage points.

Some contrary evidence appeared in the late 1960s and early 1970s. Stafford (1968), Rosen (1970), and Johnson and Youmans (1971) found that unions compress the wage structure by raising wages of less skilled workers relative to their more skilled counterparts, while Ashenfelter (1972) found that unions contributed to the narrowing of the black-white wage gap. Nonetheless, in a survey written in the mid–1970s, Johnson (1975, p. 26) concluded that "union members generally possess characteristics which would place them in the middle of the income distribution, . . . so that unionism probably has a slight disequalizing effect on the distribution of income."

The direction of subsequent research was fundamentally altered by the methods and findings in Freeman's (1980) important study, which first laid out the two-sector framework described in Section II.[3] Freeman (1980) also used establishment-level data to measure the effect of unions on the wage gap between blue-collar and white-collar workers. Since few white-collar workers are unionized, this exercise extended the simple two-sector model to incorporate a "between group - within sector" effect analogous to the "between" and "within" effects in the basic two-sector model. The key finding in Freeman's study — and a result that was largely unanticipated by earlier analysts — is that the "within-sector" effect of unions on wage inequality is large and negative, especially in manufacturing. Freeman attributed the compression of wages in the union sector to explicit union policies that seek to standardize wages within and across firms and establishments. Coupled with the tendency for unions to reduce the wage gap between blue-collar and more highly paid white-collar employees, the equalizing effects of unions more than offset the "between-sector" disequalizing effect between union and nonunion workers. In nonmanufacturing industries, Freeman concluded that the net impact of unions was smaller, reflecting both a smaller "within-sector" effect and larger "between-sector" effect. Subsequent research has confirmed that wage differences between different demographic and skill groups are lower, and often much lower, in the union sector than in the nonunion sector.[4] The residual variance of wages within demographic and skill groups is also generally lower in the union sector.

Analysis of longitudinal data by Freeman (1984) confirmed the finding of lower wage inequality in the union sector, even controlling for individual worker effects. In particular, Freeman documented that wage dispersion tends to fall when workers leave nonunion for union jobs and to rise when they move in the opposite direction. The effect of unions on wage dispersion estimated from longitudinal data is, however, smaller than comparable estimates using cross-sectional data. This lower estimate appears to be at least partly due to measurement error in union status.

Freeman (1993), using more recent longitudinal data from the 1987–1988 CPS, confirmed that unionization reduces wage inequality. On the basis of his longitudinal estimates, he concluded that declining unionization accounted for about 20 percent of the increase in the standard deviation of male wages in the United States between 1978 and 1988. Using a more sophisticated econometric approach (see the discussion of Card, 1996, below), Card (1992) also concluded that the drop in unionization explained around 20 percent of the increase in wage inequality during the 1980s. Gosling and Machin (1995) reached a similar conclusion that the fall in unionization accounts for around 15 percent of the increase in male wage inequality among semi-skilled workers in Britain between 1980 and 1990.

Second Generation Studies

Beginning with Freeman (1980), the first generation of micro-based studies significantly altered views regarding the relationship between unionization and wage inequality. But these studies tell an incomplete story. On the one hand, they focus on male, private sector workers. On the other hand, they tended to ignore variation in the union coverage rate and the union wage effect across different types of workers.

A second generation of studies used variants of the framework underlying equation (4) to develop a more complete picture of the effect of unions. DiNardo and Lemieux (1997) implemented a reweighting technique to construct estimates of the sum of the terms in equation (4) for men in the United States and Canada in 1981 and 1988. They estimated that in 1981 the presence of unions reduced the variance of male wages by 6 percent in the United States and 10 percent in Canada. The corresponding estimates in 1988 are 3 percent in the United States and 13 percent in Canada. Thus, they estimated that changing unionization contributed to the rise in United States wage inequality in the 1980s, but worked in the opposite direction in Canada. Their decompositions also showed that in both countries unions lower the variation in wages within and between groups, with a larger net effect within skill groups.

A related study by DiNardo et al. (1996) examined both men and women in the United States in 1979 and 1988. DiNardo et al. (hereinafter, DFL) use the reweighting technique applied by DiNardo and Lemieux. DFL focus on explaining the rise in wage inequality over the 1979–1988 period. For men, their methods suggested that shifts in unionization accounted for 10–15 percent of the overall rise in wage dispersion in the 1980s, with most of the effect concentrated in the middle and upper half of the wage distribution. For women, on the other hand, the estimated contribution of changing unionization was very small. DFL also estimated that falling unionization explains about one-half of the rise in the wage premium between men with a high school diploma and dropouts, and about a quarter of the rise in the college-high school wage gap for men.

The study by Bell and Pitt (1998) used DFL's method to analyze the impact of declining unionization on the growth in wage inequality in Britain. Depending on the data source used, they found that between 10 and 25 percent of the increase in male wage inequality can be explained by the fall in unionization. Machin (1997) reached similar conclusions.

Card (2001) examined the contribution of unions to wage inequality among U.S. men and women in 1973–1974 and in 1993. Card reported estimates based on the simple two-sector formula (equation (4')), and on a variant of equation

(4) obtained by dividing workers into 10 equally sized skill groups, based on predicted wages in the nonunion sector. Two key findings emerged from this analysis. First, the presence of unions was estimated to have reduced the variance of men's wages by about 12 percent in 1973–1974 and 5 percent in 1993. Overall, shifts in unionization can explain about 15–20 percent of the rise in male wage inequality in the 1973–1993 period. Second, although the within-group variance of wages is lower for women in the union sector than the nonunion sector (i.e., $\Delta_v(c)$ is on average negative), this equalizing effect is counteracted by a positive between-group effect, so overall unions had little net effect on wage inequality among U.S. women in 1973–1974 or 1993.

Card (2001) also conducted separate analyses of the effects of unions on men and women in the public and private sectors in 1973–1974 and 1993. The trends in unionization were quite different in the two sectors, with rises in union membership in the public sector for both men and women, and declines in the private sector. Nevertheless, comparisons of the patterns of union wage gaps by skill group suggest that unions affect the wage structure very similarly in the two sectors, with a strong tendency to "flatten" wage differences across skill groups for men, and less tendency for flattening among women. Overall, Card's estimates implied that unions reduced the variance of men's wages in the public sector by 12 percent in 1973–1974 and 16 percent in 1993. In the private sector, where union densities declined, the union effect fell from 9 percent in 1973–1974 to 3 percent in 1993. An interesting implication of these estimates is that differential trends in unionization among men in the public and private sectors can potentially explain a large share (up to 80 percent) of the greater rise in wage inequality in the private sector. The estimated effects of unions on women's wage inequality are all close to zero, except in the public sector in 1993, when the effect is about –5 percent.

Gosling and Lemieux (2001) examined the effects of unions on the rise in wage inequality in the United States and the United Kingdom between 1983 and 1998, using the DFL reweighting method. Their estimates suggested that in both the United States and the United Kingdom, unions have a much smaller equalizing effect on female wage inequality than male inequality. They estimated that shifts in union coverage among men in the United Kingdom can explain up to one-third of the rise in wage inequality there between 1983 and 1998, while in the United States the decline in unions can explain up to 40 percent of the rise in inequality. Consistent with findings in DFL and Card (2001) they concluded that changes in unionization had little net effect on female wage inequality in either country.

Studies That Correct for Unobserved Skill Differences

A potential problem with estimates of the equalizing effect of unions based on equations (4') or (4) is that union workers may be more or less productive than otherwise similar nonunion workers. In this case, comparisons of the mean and variance of wages for union and nonunion workers with the same observed skills confound the true "union effect" and unobserved differences in productivity. Traditionally, economists have argued that union workers are likely to have higher unobserved skills than their nonunion counterparts (Lewis, 1986). This prediction arises from the presumption that in a competitive environment, unionized employers will try to counteract the effect of above-market wage scales by hiring the most productive workers. If total productivity of worker i consists of an observed component p_i and another component a_i that is observed by labor market participants but unobserved by outside data analysts, and if an employer who if forced to pay a union wage W^U hires only those workers with $p_i + a_i > W^U$, then p_i and a_i will be *negatively* correlated among those who are hired. Workers with the lowest observed skills will only be hired if they have relatively high unobserved skills, whereas even those with below-average unobserved skills will be hired if their observed skills are high enough. This line of reasoning suggests that the "flattening" of the wage structure in the union sector arises from selectivity bias, rather than from the wage policy of unions per se.

If unions really flatten the wage structure, however, then there is another side to the story, since highly skilled workers gain less from a union job. A worker with observed productivity skills p_i and unobserved skills ai can expect to earn $p_i + a_i$ in a competitive labor market. Such a worker will only take a union job paying W^U if $p_i + a_i < W^U$. In this case union members are negatively selected: Workers with the highest observed skills will only accept a union job if their unobserved skills are low. This view also implies that the wage structure in the union sector will appear "flatter" than the nonunion wage structure. Combining the two sides of the market, one might expect union workers with low unobserved skills to be positively selected, since for these workers the demand side is the binding constraint, whereas unionized job holders with high unobserved skills are negatively selected, since for these workers the supply side constraint is the more serious constraint.

Some evidence of this "two-sided" view of the determination of union status was developed by Abowd and Farber (1982), who used information on workers who reported that they would prefer a union job, as well as on those who held union jobs, to separate the roles of employer and employee choice. They found that workers with higher experience were less likely to want a union job (consistent with the idea that wages for highly experienced workers were relatively low in the union sector), but were more likely to be hired for a union job, conditional on wanting one (consistent with the idea that employers try to choose the most productive workers).

Several recent studies attempt to assess the effect of unions on the wage structure, while recognizing that union workers may be more or less productive than otherwise similar nonunion workers. Lemieux (1993) and Card (1996) measure the wage outcomes of job changers who move between the union and nonunion sectors, distinguishing between workers in groups defined by observed productivity characteristics. A limitation of these studies is that they implicitly assume that the rewards for unobserved ability are similar in the union and nonunion sectors. Lemieux (1998) adopted a more general approach that allows the union sector to flatten the returns to unobserved ability relative to the nonunion sector.

Lemieux (1993) studied men and women in Canada in the late 1980s, and reported separate estimates of the effect of unions for three skill categories in the public and private sectors separately, and in the overall economy. For men, his results showed that unionized workers from the lowest skill group are positively selected (i.e., they have higher unobserved skills than do nonunion workers in the same group), whereas those in the upper skill groups are negatively selected. This result — which is consistent with a simple two-sided selection model — echoes a similar finding in Card (1996) for U.S. men in the late 1980s. An implication of this pattern is that the between-group "flattening effect" of unions apparent in the raw data is somewhat exaggerated, although there is still evidence that unions raise wages of low-skilled men more than those of high-skilled men. Lemieux also examined the changes in the variance of wages, and concluded that some of the apparent reduction in variance in the union sector may be due to selectivity, rather than to a within-sector flattening effect. Unfortunately, this inference is confounded by the potential selectivity of the group of union status changers, and the fact that the variability of wages may be temporarily high just before and just after a job change. Overall, Lemieux concluded that the presence of unions lowers the variance of male wages in Canada in the late 1980s by about 15 percent. A similar calculation for U.S. men, based on Card (1996), shows a 7 percent effect. These effects are somewhat smaller than corresponding estimates that fail to correct for unobserved heterogeneity.

Lemieux's findings for women in Canada were much different than those for men. In particular, neither the cross-sectional nor longitudinal estimates of the union wage gaps showed a systematic flattening effect of unions. Coupled with the fact that union coverage is lower for less skilled women, these results implied that unions raise the between-group variance of wages for women. This effect is larger than the modest negative effect on the within-group variance, so Lemieux's results imply that on net unions raised wage dispersion among Canadian women.

Lemieux (1998) presented an estimation method that accounts for the potential "flattening" effect of unions on the returns to individual skill characteristics that are constant over time but unobserved in conventional data sets. Using data on men who were forced to change jobs involuntarily, he concluded that unions tend to "flatten" the pay associated with observed and unobserved skills. Moreover, the variance of wages around the expected level of pay is lower in the union sector. As a result of these tendencies, Lemieux's results implied that unionization reduced the variance of wages among Canadian men by about 17 percent — not far off the estimate in his 1993 study.

IV. Estimating the Effect of Unions on Wage Inequality

Data Sources

We use a variety of micro data files to compare the effects of unions on wages in the United States, the United Kingdom, and Canada over the past 30 years. Our U.S. samples are the most straightforward, since the Current Population Survey (CPS) has been collecting data on wages and union status annually since 1973. We use the pooled May 1973 and May 1974 CPS samples as our first U.S. observation. For later years, we use the monthly earnings supplement files (the so-called "outgoing rotation group") for 1984, 1993, and 2001. The earnings and union status information all pertain to an individual's main job as of the survey week.

In 1993 the United Kingdom's Labour Force Survey (UKLFS) began asking questions on union status and earnings that are comparable to the CPS questions. Strictly comparable data are unavailable for earlier years. The 1983 General Household Survey (GHS) is the only large-scale micro data set that contains information on union status and wages in the United Kingdom prior to the 1990s. While this data source has several limitations, we elected to combine the 1983 GHS with the 1993 and 2001 UKLFS samples for our U.K. analysis.

The Canadian Labour Force Survey (CLFS) added questions on earnings and union status in 1997. To supplement these data, we combine two smaller surveys — the 1991 and 1995 Surveys on Work Arrangements — as a source of information for the early 1990s, and the 1984 Survey of Union Membership as a source of information for the early 1980s. All three of these surveys were conducted as supplements to the regular CLFS.

In addition to the usual problems that arise in comparing survey responses over time and across countries, a significant issue for our analysis is the measurement of union status. The 1984 and later CPS files include questions on both union membership and union coverage. The 1973 and 1974 May CPS files, however, only ask about union membership. For comparability reasons, we therefore focus on union membership as our measure of union status in the United States. Our U.K. data sets include data on union membership as well as responses to a question about whether there is a "union presence" at the individual's place of employment. As noted in Bland (1999, Table 6), however, the latter question significantly overstates coverage under collective bargaining agreements. As in our U.S. analysis, we therefore use union membership as our measure of unionization in the United Kingdom. With respect to Canada, consistent information on union membership cannot be recovered from the 1991 and 1995 SWA's, so we use union coverage as our measure of unionization in Canada. We believe that this choice has little effect on the results, since only about two percent of Canadian employees are covered by collective agreements but are not union members.[5]

Figure 5.1
Unionization Rate by Wage Level, United States

1a. U.S. Men

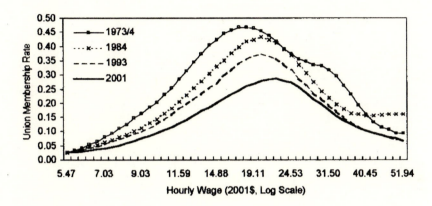

1b. U.S. Women

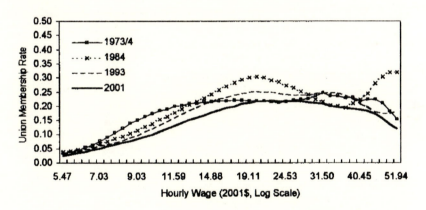

In the data appendix we explain in detail how we process the various data sets to arrive at our final estimation samples. Generally speaking, our samples include only wage and salary workers age 16 to 64 (15 to 64 in Canada) with non-allocated wages and earnings (except in 1984 and 2001 in Canada). We use hourly wages for workers who are paid by the hour and compute average hourly earnings for the other workers by dividing weekly earnings by weekly hours (or earnings for a longer time period divided by the corresponding measure of hours). We also exclude workers with very low or very high hourly wage values. Sample weights are used throughout except in the 1983 GHS for which sample weights are not available.

Figure 5.2
Unionization Rate by Wage Level, Canada

2a. Canadian Men

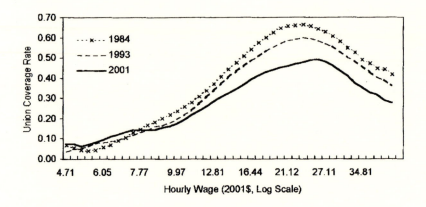

2b. Canadian Women

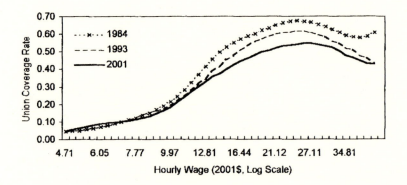

To implement the methods developed in Section II, we divide workers in each sample into skill groups, based on age and educational attainment. The number of skill groups used varies by country, reflecting differences in the sample sizes and the age and education codes reported in the raw data files. In the earlier Canadian data sets, age is only reported in 10-year categories (a total of five categories for workers age 15 to 64), and education can only be consistently coded into five categories. Thus we only use 25 skill groups for Canada. Given the small sample sizes available in the 1983 GHS and the 1993 UKLFS, we use the same number of skill groups for the United Kingdom (five age and five education groups). In our U.S. samples, we are able to use a much larger number of skill categories because of the larger sample sizes and detailed age and education information in the CPS. We have re-analyzed the U.S. data using about the same number of skill groups as in Canada and the United Kingdom, however, and found that this has little impact on our results.

Patterns of Union Coverage and Union Wage Effects

To set the stage for our analysis it is helpful to begin by looking at how union coverage and the size of the union wage gap vary by skill level. Figures 5.1–5.3 show the unionization rates of men and women in the United States, the

Figure 5.3
Unionization Rate by Wage Level, United Kingdom

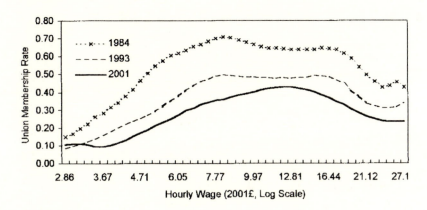

3a. U.K. Men

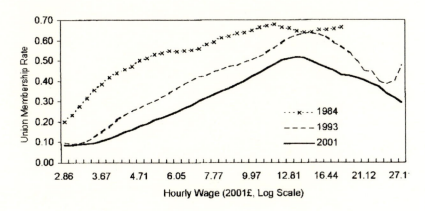

3b. U.K. Women

United Kingdom, and Canada, by the level of real hourly wages. These graphs are constructed by calculating union membership/coverage rates for workers in narrow wage bins, and smoothing across bins.[6] In all three countries, unionization rates of men tend to follow a hump-shaped pattern, peaking for workers near the middle or upper middle of the wage distribution. By comparison, unionization rates of women in the United States and Canada are about the same for highly paid workers as for those in the middle. This pattern is driven in part by relatively high rates of unionization for teachers, nurses, and other public sector workers, who are near the top of the female wage distribution. In the United Kingdom there is more of a fall-off in union membership among the highest paid women, especially in the more recent data. Comparisons of the unionization rates in different years reveal the rapid decline in union membership among U.S. and U.K. men. Declines are also evident for Canadian men and for women in all three countries.

The framework developed in Section II suggests that the effect of unions on wage inequality depends in part on how the union wage gap varies by skill. Figures 5.4–5.6 provide some simple evidence on this variation, using data from the early 1990s for the three countries. These figures plot mean wages for unionized workers in a given age-education group (i.e., $W^U(c)$ in the notation of Section II) against the corresponding mean for nonunion workers with the same skill level (i.e., $W^N(c)$) for 25 age-education groups in Canada and the United Kingdom, and about 150 groups in the United States. In interpreting these figures, note that if union and nonunion workers in a given skill group have the same average wages, the points in these graphs will lie on the 45-degree line. On the other hand, if the union wage gap $\Delta w(c)$ is positive, the points will lie above the 45-degree line. Moreover, if $\Delta_w(c)$ is larger for lower wage workers, the points will tend to be further above the 45 degree line for low-wage skill groups (on the left side of the graph) than for high-wage groups (on the right). This is in fact the case for U.S. men. The best-fitting line relating $W^U(c)$ to $W^N(c)$ is also shown in the figure, and lies above the 45 degree line but with a slope of less than 1.

Interestingly, the same pattern is true for men in Canada and the United Kingdom, as shown in Figures 5.5a and 5.6a. For skill groups with low average wages (e.g., less educated and relatively young men) the mean union wage tends to be substantially higher than the mean nonunion wage, while for groups with high average wages (e.g., middle-age college or university graduates) the mean union wage is not too much above the mean nonunion wage. Thus, in all three countries $\Delta_w(c)$ is larger for low-wage men than high-wage men, implying that unions tend to "flatten" wage differentials across skill groups. As previously discussed, one caveat to this conclusion is that there may be unobserved skill differences between union and nonunion workers in different age-education groups that tend to exaggerate the apparent negative correlation between wages in the nonunion sector and the union wage gap. We address this issue further in the next section.

Figure 5.4
Union Relative Wage Structure in the United States, 1993

4a. U.S. Men, 1993

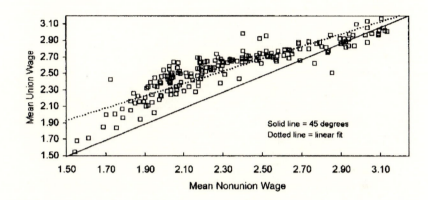

4b. U.S. Women, 1993

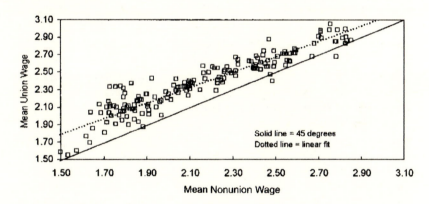

For women, the patterns of union wages relative to nonunion wages are also remarkably similar in the three countries. Unlike the patterns for men, however, the union wage gaps for women are roughly constant. Coupled with the tendency for unionization rates of women to rise across the wage distribution, the absence of a "flattening" effect of unions on female wages implies that covariance between the nonunion wage $W^N(c)$ and the union wage gain $U(c)\Delta_w(c)$ is either zero or positive, limiting the potential equalizing effect of unions on female inequality.

Although the data in Figures 5.4–5.6 pertain to the early 1990s, similar plots from other years show that the basic patterns have been very stable in all three countries over the past 20–30 years. In all our sample years, the union-nonunion wage gap for men tends to be highest for the least skilled workers, and to be relatively small (or even negative) for highly skilled men. The union gap for women, on the other hand, tends to be stable or only slightly declining with skill level. The consistency of these patterns over time and across the three countries is remarkable.

The Effect of Unions on Wage Inequality

With this background, we turn to our analysis of the effect of unions on wage inequality in the three countries. Tables 5.1, 5.2, and 5.3 summarize a variety of facts about unionization and the structure of wages for the United States, Canada, and the United Kingdom, respectively. Reading across the columns of Table 5.1, a comparison of the entries in the first row confirms the steep decline in U.S. unionization rates documented in many studies. As illustrated in Figures 5.1a and 5.1b, however, these aggregate figures hide a sharp difference between men and women. Between 1973 and 2001, the unionization rate of women declined only about 2 percentage points, from 14 to 12 percent, while for men it fell by 50 percent, from 31 to 15 percent. This sharp male-female difference has much to do with the gradual shift of unionization from the private to the public sector. For instance, Card (2001) showed that for both men and women, unionization rates declined by about 50 percent in the private sector between 1973 and 1993. During the same period, however, unionization rates increased sharply in the public sector. Women in general, and unionized women in particular, are much more concentrated in the public sector than their male counterparts. As a result, the rise in public sector unionism has largely offset the decline in private sector unionization among women.

The trends in unionization in Canada between 1984 and 2001 (Table 5.2) are similar to those in the United States. The male unionization rate declined by 14 percentage points, even more than the 9 percentage point decline in the United States over the same period. As in the United States, the decline for women was more modest (4 percentage points). The drop in unionization in our Canadian samples is much steeper than the decline registered in membership tallies obtained from union reports, but is consistent with the trends reported by Riddell and Riddell (2001) based on similar micro-data sources.

Table 5.3 shows that unionization rates have also fallen sharply in the United Kingdom in the past two decades: by 27 percentage points for men and by 14 percentage points for women. As in the United States and Canada, the faster decline in male unionization is linked to the relative shift of unionization from the private to the public sector (Gosling and Lemieux, 2001). In the United Kingdom, this shift was compounded by privatization of many nationalized industries, which transferred sizeable numbers of mainly male workers from the unionized public sector to the much less organized private sector (Gosling and

Figure 5.5
Union Relative Wage Structure in Canada, 1991-1995

5a. Canadian Men, 1991-1995

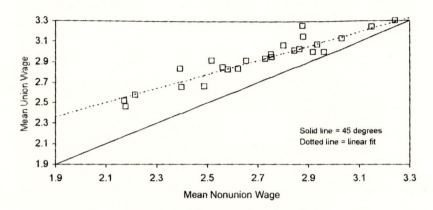

5b. Canadian Women, 1991-1995

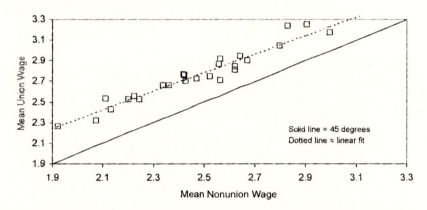

Lemieux, 2001). Interestingly, the relatively faster decline of male unionization in the three countries meant that by 2001, male and female unionization rates were not too different in the United States, Canada, or the United Kingdom. This near equality marks a sharp departure from the historical pattern of greater unionization among men.

The next set of rows in Tables 5.1–5.3 show the evolution of mean wages of nonunion and union workers and the trend in the union wage gap. We also report an adjusted wage gap, calculated from a regression that includes dummies for each skill category. As in the case for the unionization rates, the estimated wage gaps show a remarkably similar pattern across the three countries. The

Figure 5.6
Union Relative Wage Structure in the United Kingdon, 1993

6a. U.K. Men, 1993

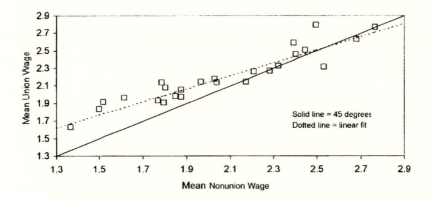

6b. U.K. Women, 1993

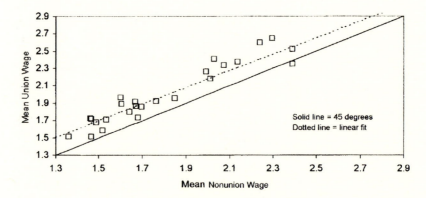

unadjusted wage gaps tend to be larger for women than for men. The adjusted wage gaps are uniformly smaller than the unadjusted gaps, and in all three countries the divergence has increased over time, implying that union membership rates have fallen more for relatively unskilled workers (as is apparent in Figures 5.1–5.3).

Like the unadjusted union wage gap, the adjusted wage gap is typically larger for women than for men. Nevertheless, gender differences in the adjusted gaps are less pronounced than the corresponding differences in the unadjusted gaps, especially in more recent years. For example, the unadjusted wage gaps in the United States in 2001 were 0.233 for men and 0.305 for women, versus adjusted wage gaps of 0.156 and 0.149. This pattern is consistent with Figures 5.1 to 5.3, which show that unionized women are more highly concentrated in the upper end of the skill distribution than unionized men. As a result, controlling for the skill composition of the work force reduces the union wage gap far more for women than for men.

Another trend that is shared by all three countries is a gradual decline in the adjusted union wage gap, by 5 to 10 percentage points (depending on gender and country) between the early 1980s and 2001. Since the rate of unionization also declined sharply during this period, the implied effect of unions on average wages — the union wage gain $E[U(c)\Delta w(c)]$ — has declined dramatically over the last two decades. For example, the adjusted impact of unions on male wages in the United Kingdom went from 9.2 percentage points in 1983 (unionization rate of 0.57 times an adjusted gap of 0.162) to 1.7 percentage points in 2001 (0.307 times 0.045). In the United States, the effect on average wages of men fell from 5.7 percentage points (unionization rate of 0.307 times an adjusted gap of 0.185) to 2.3 percent in 2001 (0.149 times 0.156).

The next rows in Tables 5.1–5.3 report measures of wage dispersion within the union and nonunion sectors. Once again, the results are remarkably consistent across countries. As first documented in Freeman (1980), the standard deviation of wages is always smaller in the union than in the nonunion sector. Moreover, the gap between the standard deviation in the union and nonunion sector is always larger for men than for women. These observations are confirmed by Figures 5.7 to 5.12, which show kernel density estimates of the densities of log hourly wages in the union and nonunion sectors, and for the two sectors pooled together, by gender and time period.[7] For example, Figure 5.7 displays the wage distribution for U.S. males. In all four time periods, wages are more tightly distributed in the union than the nonunion sector. In particular, while the upper tails of the union and nonunion densities look qualitatively similar, the lower tail goes much further to the left in the nonunion sector. By contrast, the inter-sectoral differences in wage dispersion are much less striking for U.S. women (Figure 5.8). In 1984, for example, the union and nonunion distributions show different skewness, and average wages are higher in the union sector. However, whether wages are more narrowly distributed in the union or nonunion sector is unclear.

Inspection of Figures 5.7 and 5.8 (and the corresponding figures for Canada and the United Kingdom) suggests that the minimum wage is an important factor in explaining overall trends in wage inequality, particularly for nonunion female workers.[8] An interesting conjecture is that unions appear to have a more limited effect on the dispersion of female wages in part because minimum wages limit the amount of dispersion in the lower tail of the female wage distribution.

The wage densities for Canadian men (Figure 5.9) and women (Figure 5.10) are qualitatively similar to those in the United States. In particular, it is clear that male wages are more narrowly distributed in the union sector than

Table 5.1
Effect of Unions on Wage Structure of U.S. Workers, 1973–2001

	1973/1974		1984		1993		2001	
	male	female	male	female	male	female	male	female
Fraction Union Members	0.307	0.141	0.236	0.141	0.185	0.132	0.149	0.121
Mean Log Wages (2001$):								
Nonunion Workers	2.646	2.270	2.573	2.276	2.535	2.337	2.667	2.457
Union Workers	2.841	2.499	2.866	2.605	2.838	2.686	2.899	2.761
Union Gap (unadjusted)	0.196	0.230	0.293	0.329	0.304	0.349	0.233	0.305
Union Gap (adjusted)	0.185	0.220	0.208	0.228	0.210	0.210	0.156	0.149
Standard Deviation Log Wages:								
Nonunion Workers	0.553	0.442	0.563	0.467	0.594	0.515	0.601	0.538
Union Workers	0.354	0.383	0.363	0.408	0.399	0.444	0.417	0.460
Union Gap	−0.198	−0.059	−0.199	−0.058	−0.194	−0.071	−0.184	−0.077
Variance Decomposition:								
Overall Variance	0.258	0.195	0.289	0.223	0.331	0.270	0.340	0.289
Two sector model								
Within-sector effect	−0.055	−0.007	−0.044	−0.007	−0.036	−0.009	−0.028	−0.009
Between-sector effect	0.008	0.006	0.015	0.013	0.014	0.014	0.007	0.010
Total effect	−0.047	0.000	−0.028	0.006	−0.022	0.005	−0.021	0.001
Model with skill groups								
Within-sector effect	−0.022	−0.006	−0.020	−0.007	−0.018	−0.009	−0.013	−0.009
Between-sector effect	0.007	0.004	0.010	0.008	0.012	0.011	0.004	0.008
Dispersion across groups	−0.011	0.001	−0.007	0.000	−0.008	−0.003	−0.006	−0.005
Total effect	−0.026	0.000	−0.017	0.001	−0.014	−0.001	−0.015	−0.007
Sample Size	43,189	30,500	77,910	69,635	71,719	69,723	55,813	55,167
Number of Skill Groups	180	180	343	343	244	246	245	246

Note: Samples include wage and salary workers age 16–64 with non-allocated hourly or weekly pay, and hourly wages between $2.00 and $90.00 per hour in 1989 dollars.

Table 5.2
Effects of Unions on Wage Structure of Canadian Workers, 1984–2001

	1984		1991-1995		2001	
	male	female	male	female	male	female
Fraction Union Workers	0.467	0.369	0.408	0.353	0.330	0.317
Mean Log Wages (2001$)						
Nonunion Workers	2.658	2.365	2.661	2.452	2.728	2.495
Union Workers	2.987	2.793	2.972	2.851	2.964	2.853
Union Gap (unadjusted)	0.330	0.428	0.311	0.398	0.236	0.358
Union Gap (adjusted)	0.251	0.321	0.204	0.275	0.153	0.226
Standard Deviation Log Wages:						
Nonunion Workers	0.528	0.446	0.514	0.465	0.501	0.463
Union Workers	0.343	0.368	0.362	0.380	0.386	0.395
Union Gap	-0.185	-0.078	-0.152	-0.084	-0.115	-0.068
Variance Decomposition:						
Overall Variance	0.231	0.218	0.233	0.227	0.229	0.224
Two sector model						
Within-sector effect	-0.075	-0.023	-0.054	-0.025	-0.034	-0.019
Between-sector effect	0.027	0.043	0.023	0.036	0.012	0.028
Total effect	-0.048	0.019	-0.031	0.011	-0.021	0.009
Model with skill groups						
Within-sector effect	-0.041	-0.027	-0.033	-0.028	-0.025	-0.022
Between-sector effect	0.017	0.022	0.010	0.017	0.006	0.012
Dispersion across groups	-0.014	0.014	-0.002	0.014	0.001	0.013
Total effect	-0.037	0.009	-0.025	0.002	-0.017	0.003
Sample size	17,737	15,356	17,981	18,323	24,003	23,703
Number of skill groups	25	25	25	25	25	25

Note: Samples include wage and salary workers age 15–64 with allocated hourly or weekly pay (except in 1991–95), and hourly wages between $2.50 and $44.00 per hour in 2001 dollars.

Table 5.3
Effect of Unions on Wage Structure of U.S. Workers, 1973–2001

	1983		1993		2001	
	male	female	male	female	male	female
Fraction union workers	0.570	0.426	0.392	0.337	0.307	0.285
Mean log wages (2001£):						
Nonunion Workers	1.843	1.416	2.036	1.705	2.170	1.873
Union Workers	2.053	1.685	2.224	2.047	2.306	2.167
Union Gap (unadjusted)	0.210	0.269	0.188	0.342	0.135	0.294
Union Gap (adjusted)	0.162	0.195	0.131	0.184	0.045	0.137
Standard Deviation of Log Wages:						
Nonunion Workers	0.532	0.412	0.586	0.499	0.588	0.510
Union Workers	0.382	0.399	0.438	0.475	0.442	0.468
Union Gap	-0.150	-0.013	-0.148	-0.024	-0.146	-0.043
Variance Decomposition:						
Overall Variance	0.216	0.183	0.293	0.268	0.303	0.266
Two sector model						
Within-sector effect	-0.078	-0.004	-0.059	-0.008	-0.046	-0.012
Between-sector effect	0.011	0.018	0.008	0.026	0.004	0.018
Total effect	-0.067	0.013	-0.051	0.018	-0.042	0.006
Model with skill groups						
Within-sector effect	-0.034	-0.023	-0.031	-0.028	-0.032	-0.025
Between-sector effect	0.009	0.011	0.006	0.008	0.002	0.005
Dispersion across groups	-0.026	0.009	-0.016	0.012	-0.013	0.010
Total effect	-0.050	-0.003	-0.041	-0.008	-0.042	-0.010
Sample size	4,435	3,512	4,009	4,139	7,548	8,113
Number of skill groups	25	25	25	25	25	25

Note: Samples include wage and salary workers age 16–64 with non-allocated hourly or weekly pay, and hourly wages between $2.00 and $90.00 per hour in 1989 dollars.

Figure 5.7
Density of Wages, U.S. Males

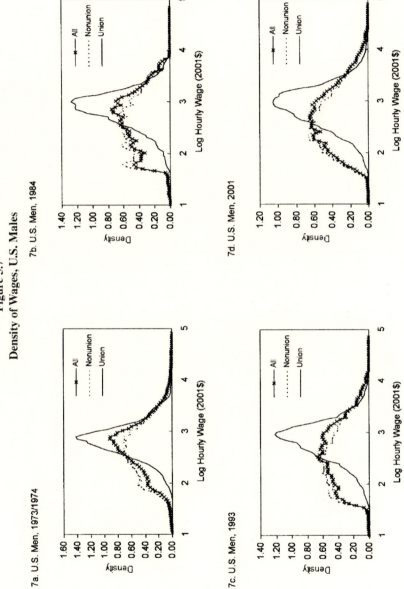

7a. U.S. Men, 1973/1974

7b. U.S. Men, 1984

7c. U.S. Men, 1993

7d. U.S. Men, 2001

Figure 5.8
Density of Wages, U.S. Females

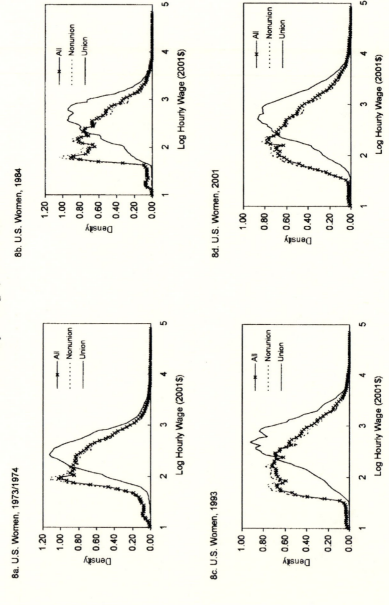

Figure 5.9

Density of Wages, Canadian Males

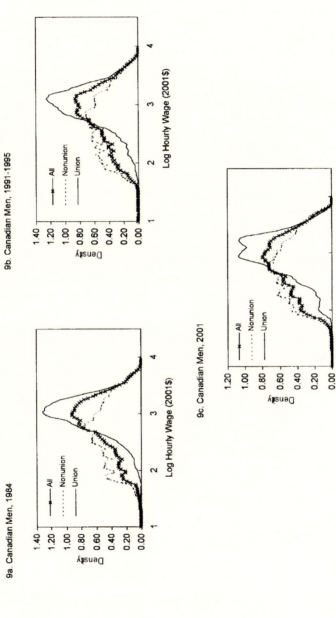

9a. Canadian Men, 1984

9b. Canadian Men, 1991-1995

9c. Canadian Men, 2001

the nonunion sector. Things are not as clear for women, in part because of the minimum wage, which has a surprisingly large visual impact in the nonunion sector, especially in 2001. Relative to the United States or Canada it is more difficult to see union wage compression effects for U.K. males (Figure 5.11) or females (Figure 5.12). Comparing the reported standard deviations of wages in the two sectors in Table 5.3, however, the union-nonunion gaps are nonetheless quite similar to those in Canada or the United States.

The bottom rows of Tables 5.1–5.3 show the various components of our analysis of the effect of unions on wage inequality. For reference purposes, we first present a simplified analysis based on the two-sector model that ignores any differences across skill groups (equation (4')). Comparing the results across countries and over time, the results from this simplified analysis are remarkably consistent. For men, the within-sector effect is substantially larger (in absolute value) than the between-sector effect, implying that unions reduce wage dispersion. Relative to the overall variance, the compression effect ranges from 31 percent in the United Kingdom in 1984, when the unionization rate was 57 percent, to 6 percent in the United States in 2001 (unionization rate of 15 percent). More generally, the compression effect of unions is highly correlated with the overall level of unionization.[9]

In contrast to the situation for men, the simplified analysis of equation (4') implies that unions have either no effect on female wage inequality, or a slightly disequalizing effect. This contrast is attributable to three complementary factors. First, the female unionization rate is lower, reducing the size of the within-sector effect. Second, the gap in overall wage dispersion between union and nonunion workers is much smaller for women than men. Third, the union wage gap is systematically larger for women than men, yielding a larger (more positive) between-sector effect $U(1-U)\Delta_w^2$. Indeed, in the later years of our analysis, the between-sector effect dominates in all three countries. Consistent with findings reported in Card (2001) and Lemieux (1993), unions thus tend to increase the variance of wages among women.

The final rows in Tables 5.1–5.3 show the effect of unions on the variance of wages when we distinguish among skill groups. Recall from equation (4) that this analysis includes three components: an average within-sector effect, $E[U(c)Dv(c)]$, an average between-sector effect, $E[U(c)(1-U(c))\Delta_w(c)^2]$, and the sum of two "between-skill-group" terms, $Var[U(c)\Delta_w(c)] + 2Cov[W^N(c), U(c)\Delta_w(c)]$, that reflect the rise in inequality between groups if the union wage gain varies by skill group and any tendency of unions to raise wages more or less for higher wage workers.

Starting with men, the introduction of controls for observable skill systematically reduces the magnitudes of both the within–and between-sector effects. It is easy to see why this happens in the case of the between-sector effect. As noted earlier, adjusting for characteristics reduces the union wage gap, and thus decreases the size of the between-group effect. In other words, part of the measured between-sector effect in the simple two-sector calculation is a spurious consequence of that fact that union workers are more skilled, on average, than nonunion workers. A similar reasoning can be used to understand why the within-group effect also declines when differences in observed skills are taken into account. Recall from Figures 5.1a–5.3a that unionized men are more concentrated in the middle of the wage distribution than nonunion men. Part of the lower dispersion of wages in the union sector is thus a spurious consequence of the fact that union workers are more homogenous.

Interestingly, adjusting for observed skill characteristics also reduces the magnitude of the between-sector effect for women but increases (or leaves unchanged in the United States) the magnitude of the within-group effect. The latter finding means that union women are no more homogenous (in terms of their observable skills) than their nonunion counterparts, which is consistent with the evidence reported in Figures 5.1b, 5.2b, and 5.3b. Once worker characteristics are taken into account, the within-sector effect tends to dominate the between-sector effect for both men and women. Thus, the results from a simplified analysis which ignores measured skill differences tends to overstate male-female differences in the effect of unions on wage inequality.

The final components of the union effect are the two terms which reflect the effect of unions on the distribution of wages across skill groups. As highlighted in our discussion of Figures 5.4–5.6, the union wage effect $\Delta_w(c)$ is systematically lower for high-wage men, inducing a negative covariance between $W_N(c)$ and $U(c)\Delta_w(c)$. By contrast, the wage gap for women is not much lower for high-wage groups, and the higher unionization rate for those groups induces a positive covariance between $W^N(c)$ and $U(c)\Delta_w(c)$.

The results in Tables 5.1–5.3 are broadly consistent with this prediction. As expected, unions tend to reduce wage dispersion across skill groups for men (except in recent years in Canada where the effect is essentially zero). Also as expected, unions tend to increase wage dispersion across skill groups for women in Canada and the United Kingdom. In the United States, however, unions have little effect on female wage dispersion across skill groups from 1973 and 1993 and actually reduce wage dispersion in 2001. A natural explanation for the difference between the United States on one hand, and Canada and the United Kingdom, on the other, is that the union wage gap for U.S. women tends to decline slightly with higher nonunion wages (see Figure 5.4b). This lowers the covariance between $W^N(c)$ and $U(c)\Delta_w(c)$ for U.S. women relative to the other two countries.

Once all three factors are taken into consideration, our calculations show that unions systematically reduce the variance of wages for men. By contrast, the effects for women tend to be small and slightly positive (i.e., unions raise inequality). This pattern of result is quite similar to what we found with the simpler model, though the magnitude of the effects tend to be smaller when we control for worker's characteristics.

Figure 5.10
Density of Wages, Canadian Females

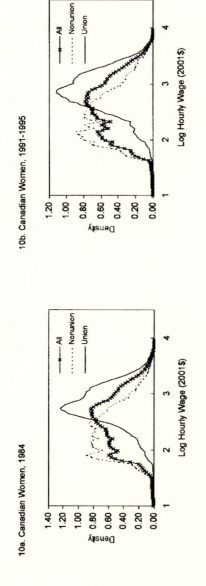

10a. Canadian Women, 1984

10b. Canadian Women, 1991-1995

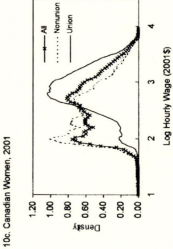

10c. Canadian Women, 2001

Figure 5.11
Density of Wages, U.K. Males

11a. U.K. Men, 1984

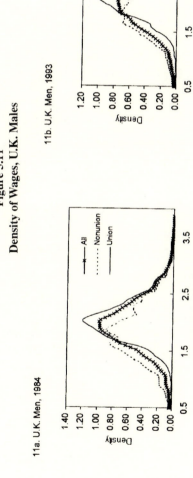

11b. U.K. Men, 1993

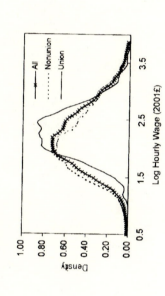

11c. U.K. Men, 2001

Figure 5.12
Density of Wages, U.K. Females

12a. U.K. Women, 1984

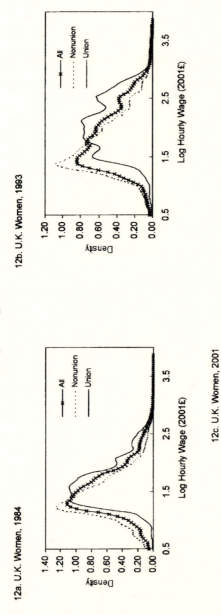

12b. U.K. Women, 1993

12c. U.K. Women, 2001

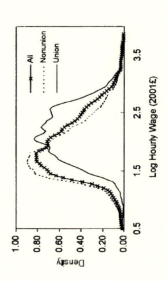

Biases from Unobserved Heterogeneity

As noted earlier, a potential problem with estimates of the equalizing effect of unions based on equation (4) or (4') is that union workers may be more or less productive than otherwise similar nonunion workers. In this case, comparisons of the mean and variance of wages for union and nonunion workers with the same observed skills confound the true union effect and unobserved differences in productivity. Studies by Lemieux (1993), Card (1996), and Lemieux (1998) have attempted to use data on job changers to measure the extent to which union and nonunion workers in different skill groups have different unobserved productivity characteristics.[10] The two Lemieux studies analyzed data for men and women in Canada, while Card examined data for men in the United States. All three studies found that among North American men, unions tend to raise wages more for less skilled workers, but that simple comparisons which ignore unobserved skill components tend to *overstate* the flattening effect. Lemieux's results for Canadian women, on the other hand, show little evidence of flattening, either in simple cross sectional comparisons or in more sophisticated longitudinal estimators. Lemieux (1998) also used longitudinal data to examine the apparent effect of unions on the dispersion of wages controlling for observed and unobserved skill components. This analysis suggested that some of the apparent reduction in variance in the union sector may be due to selectivity, rather than to a within-sector effect. Unfortunately, this inference is confounded by the potential selectivity of the group of union-status changers, and the fact that the variability of wages may be temporarily high just before and just after a job change. Overall, Lemieux (1998) concluded incorporating unobserved heterogeneity effects leads to a small reduction in the apparent effect of unions on male wage inequality. A similar conclusion was reached in Card (1996).

Based on these findings, we conclude that the estimates of the equalizing effect of unions on male workers in the United States, Canada, and the United Kingdom in Tables 5.1–5.3 are likely to slightly *overstate* the true equalizing effects. For women, the estimated effects in Tables 5.1–5.3 are very small anyway, and the existing longitudinal research suggests there is no important bias.

Unions and Differences in the Trends in Wage Inequality

To what extent can changes in the strength of unions explain the evolution of wage inequality over time and the differences in inequality across countries? In light of the results of Tables 5.1–5.3, we look at this question for men only since unions appear to have little effect on wage inequality for women.[11] Starting with the United States, Table 5.1 shows that the variance of male wages increased from 0.258 to 0.340 (a rise of 0.082) between 1973/1974 and 2001. During the same period, the effect of unions on the variance of wages computed using the simplified model declined from –0.047 to –0.021 (a rise of 0.026). If this effect had remained constant over time, overall wage inequality would have grown by 31 percent less (0.026/0.082) than it actually did. The contribution of unions to the growth of inequality remains important though only about one-half as big (14 percent) when we use the more sophisticated estimates of the union effect that control for observable skills.

The results for the United Kingdom are qualitatively similar. Between 9 and 29 percent of the 0.087 growth in the variance of log wages between 1983 and 2001 can be accounted for by the decline in union compression effects. Furthermore, in both the United States and U.K. union wage compression effects remained relatively constant between 1993 and 2001. In particular, the effects from the analysis that controls for workers' characteristics are essentially unchanged in the period from 1993 to 2001. This is consistent with the slowdown in the growth of inequality in both countries in the 1990s, relative to the 1980s.

As in the United States and United Kingdom, the union wage compression effect has been steadily declining for Canadian men since 1984. Unlike the United States and the United Kingdom, however, overall inequality has remained very stable in Canada over time, so overall inequality would have actually declined if union wage impacts had remained at their 1984 levels. Several developments may have offset the pressures toward increased inequality associated with the decline in union strength. The real minimum wage in Canada rose from the mid-1980s to the late-1990s, in contrast to the situation in the United States where the real minimum wage was approximately constant over this period (Kuhn, 2000). In addition, there is some evidence that the much more rapid growth in educational attainment in Canada compared to the United States during the 1980s and 1990s reduced the tendency for widening earnings differentials between less educated and more educated workers (Murphy et al., 1998).

Turning to cross-country differences in wage inequality, first note that in 1983/1984 the variance of wages was lowest in the United Kingdom (0.216) followed by Canada (0.231) and the United States (0.289). By contrast, union wage compression effects (from the model that controls for skill differences) were highest in the United Kingdom (–0.050), followed by Canada (–0.037) and the United States (–0.017). The pattern of cross-country differences in wage inequality is thus consistent with the pattern of union wage compression effects. For instance, differences in union wage compression effects account for 45 percent of the U.K.-U.S. difference in the variance of wages in the early 1980s. By 2001, the U.S.-U.K. difference in the variance of wages had fallen to 0.037, while the U.S.-U.K. difference in the union compression effect had fallen to 0.027. This indicates that over 70 percent of the difference in wage inequality can now be explained by union wage compression effects. In 2001, however, union wage compression effects cannot account for the much lower variance of wages in Canada.

In summary, union wage compression effects help explain a reasonable fraction of the secular growth in male wage inequality and of cross-country differences in male wage inequality. One exception is the surprising lack of growth in male wage inequality in Canada relative to the other two countries. An assessment of the relative importance of the various influences on wage inequality among Canadian men is a worthwhile subject for future research.

V. Summary and Conclusions

The impact of unions on the structure of wages has recently attracted renewed interest as analysts have struggled to explain the rise in earnings inequality in several industrialized countries. Canada, the United Kingdom, and the United States provide a potentially valuable set of countries for examining this question. All three countries now collect comparable data on wages and union status in their regular labor force surveys. Several features of the collective bargaining institutions of these countries make them suitable for studying the relationship between unions and wage inequality. Bargaining is highly decentralized; there are no general mechanisms for extending collective bargaining provisions beyond the "organized" sector; and the fraction of the work force covered by collective bargaining is relatively modest. Thus it is possible to compare the structure of wages for workers covered by union contracts to those who are not covered, and potentially infer the effect of unions on overall wage inequality.

A number of previous studies, including Freeman (1980, 1982, 1984, 1993), Lemieux (1993), Card (1996, 2001), DiNardo et al. (1996), DiNardo and Lemieux (1997), Machin (1997), and Gosling and Lemieux (2001), have examined the relationship between unionization and wage inequality in these countries individually or in country pairs. Most of the previous work has focused on men and on the 1970s and 1980s. One contribution of this study is to provide a comprehensive analysis of the evolution of unionization and wage inequality for both men and women in all three countries over the past two to three decades. Following the approach developed in Lemieux (1993) and Card (1996), we also take into account variation in collective bargaining coverage and union wage impacts across workers with different levels of observable skills.

In his landmark paper, Freeman (1980) concluded that, overall, unions tend to reduce wage inequality among men because the inequality-increasing "between-sector" effect is smaller than the dispersion-reducing "within-sector" effect. Our analysis indicates that this finding is very robust across countries (United States, United Kingdom, and Canada) and time periods (from the early 1970s to 2001). Controlling for worker characteristics alters the magnitudes of the "within-sector" and "between-sector" effects, and introduces additional terms that reflect differences in union coverage and union wage effects across skill groups. For men in all three countries both the "within-" and "between-" sector effects decline when we control for the skill composition of the work force. Because union workers are more skilled, on average, than nonunion workers, adjusting for characteristics reduces the magnitude of the "between-sector" effect. The decline in the within-group effect reflects the fact that unionized men are more homogeneous than their nonunion counterparts.

We find remarkably similar patterns in union representation and union wage impacts across skill groups for men in all three countries. Union coverage tends to be concentrated in the middle of the skill distribution, and union wages tend to be compressed relative to nonunion wages. As a consequence, unions have an equalizing effect on the dispersion of wages across skill groups in the three countries, complementing the effect on "within-group" inequality.

Once all these factors are taken into consideration, our calculations imply that unions systematically reduce the variance of wages for men in all three countries, though the magnitudes of the effects are smaller when we control for the skill composition of the work force.

Interestingly, an equally robust finding that emerges from this paper is that unions do not reduce wage inequality among women. In all three countries, this important male-female difference in the impact of unionism is due to a combination of three factors. First, unionized women are more concentrated in the upper end of the wage distribution than their male counterparts. Second, the union wage gap is larger for women than for men, resulting in a larger "between-sector" effect. Third, the union wage gap is larger for lesser than higher skilled men, while this is not the case for women.

Another important conclusion is that the impacts of unions on the wage structure in the United States, Canada, and the United Kingdom have followed remarkably similar trends over the last two decades. In all three countries, the unionization rate and the union wage differential have declined substantially since the early 1980s. For men, this has resulted in a steady erosion of the equalizing effect of unions that explains a significant fraction of the growth in wage inequality in the United States and United Kingdom. The decline of female unionization has been much smaller than that of men. As a consequence, unionization rates of men and women are nearly equal now in all three countries, marking a sharp departure from the historical pattern. However, the modest decline in union coverage among women had little impact on female wage inequality.

Interestingly, in both the United States and the United Kingdom our estimates of the effects of unions on wage inequality were virtually unchanged between 1993 and 2001. This is consistent with the slowdown in the growth of inequality in both countries during the 1990s, relative to the 1980s. However, in Canada there was little change in wage inequality during the 1980s and 1990s, despite a moderate drop in union coverage among men. The Canadian experience suggests that other factors offset the pressures toward widening inequality associated with the decline in unionization.

Although trends in union coverage and union wage effects are very similar in the three countries, there are substantial differences in the levels of unionization and wage inequality. The pattern of cross-country differences in wage inequality is consistent with the pattern of wage compression effects. Our calculations indicate that differences in union wage compression effects can account for almost one-half of the U.K.-U.S. differential in the variance of wages in the early 1990s, and over two-thirds of the differential in 2001.

In *What Do Unions Do?*, the impact of unions on the distribution of income is a leading example of how the "voice" aspect of unionism (reduced inequality among union workers — the "within-sector" effect) dominates its "monopoly" face (inequality between union and nonunion workers — the "between-sector" effect). Twenty years later, our study confirms that this key finding remains robust to the choice of country and time period. An important qualification, however, is the case of women where we show that these two aspects of the impact of unions on wage inequality more or less offset each other.

What Do Unions Do? recognizes that there is no consensus on the social benefits of the equalizing effects of unions on the distribution of income. It states that "For readers to whom greater inequality is a plus, what unions do here is definitely good. For readers to whom greater equalization of income is undesirable, what unions do is definitely bad" (p. 247). On balance, however, *What Do Unions Do?* clearly sides with those who think that unless the equalizing effects of unions result in large costs due to allocative inefficiencies, what unions do here is socially good. Although we do not assess the impacts of unions on resource allocation and economic performance, we share the view that the consequences of unions for wage inequality are beneficial from a social point of view.

The last paragraph of *What Do Unions Do?* starts with a dire warning: "All told, if our research findings are correct, the ongoing decline in private sector unionism — a development unique to the United States among developed countries — deserves serious public attention as being socially undesirable" (p. 251). By linking the decline in unionism to the dramatic increase in wage inequality in the United States since the 1970s, our research strongly confirms that the ongoing decline in private sector unionism indeed had socially undesirable consequences. In retrospect, this sentence of *What Do Unions Do?* only erred by stating that the decline in private sector unionism was a development *unique* to the United States. In the 20 years following the publication of the book, unionism sharply declined in the United Kingdom and fell moderately in Canada. In the case of the United Kingdom, the decline in unionism has resulted in a steep growth in wage inequality among men. These recent developments show that the social consequences of the decline in unionism deserve even broader attention (north of the border and across the Atlantic) than at the time *What Do Unions Do?* was first published.

Notes

1. This possibility was emphasized by Lewis (1963). The presence of unionized employers may lead to higher wages in the nonunion sector (if nonunion employ-

ers raise wages to deter unionization efforts) or to lower wages (if unionization reduces employment in the union sector, increasing labor supply in the nonunion sector).

2. Equation (6) is only correct if unobserved skills are rewarded equally in the union and nonunion sectors, although it may provide a good first approximation if the rewards for unobserved ability in the union sector are not too much lower than in the nonunion sector. Lemieux (1998) presented a model in which unobserved attributes are rewarded differently in the union and nonunion sectors.

3. A couple of studies in the late 1970s and early 1980s also pointed to the conclusion that unions lowered wage inequality. Hyclak (1979) analyzed the determinants of inequality in wage and salary income in urban labor markets and found that higher union coverage was associated with lower earnings inequality. Hyclak (1980) found a negative relationship between the state mean of union density and the percentage of families with low earnings. Hirsch (1982) performed a cross-sectional study at the industry level using a simultaneous equations model of earnings, earnings dispersion, and union coverage. He concluded that the equalizing effects of unions on earnings inequality are larger when allowance is made for the joint determination of union coverage and wage dispersion. Metcalf (1982) also looked at the dispersion of wages across industries in the United Kingdom (without controlling for the joint determination of earnings and union coverage) but concluded that union coverage widened the pay structure across industries. Metcalf also showed, however, that the variation of weekly earnings was lower in the union sector and that unions narrowed the pay structure by occupation and race.

4. See Lewis (1986) for a review of U.S. studies and Meng (1990) and Lemieux (1993) for Canadian evidence.

5. In the 2001 CLFS, 2.4 percent of male workers and 1.9 of female workers were covered by collective bargaining but not members of a union. The two different measures of unionization lead to nearly identical estimates of the union wage premium in a conventional linear regression of wages on union status, education, and experience.

6. In the United States, for example, we use bins for the log hourly wage of width 0.05. We use smaller bins for our U.K. and Canadian samples.

7. The densities are estimated using a bandwidth of 0.05. See DiNardo et al. (1996) for more detail.

8. This is similar to DiNardo et al. (1996) who showed that the minimum wage has a much larger impact on women than on men.

9. The derivative of the right hand side of equation (4') with respect to the unionization rate is $\Delta_v + (1-2\ U)\Delta_w^{\ 2}$. This is negative as long as Δ_v is large relative to $\Delta_w^{\ 2}$.

10. Taking a more direct approach, Hirsch and Schumacher (1998) examined test-score data and found that union members with high measured skills had relatively low test scores.

11. DiNardo et al. (1996), Card (2001), and Gosling and Lemieux (2001) all concluded that de-unionization explains very little of the increase in wage inequality among women in the United States or United Kingdom.

References

Abowd, John M. and Henry S. Farber. "Job Queues and the Union Status of Workers." *Industrial and Labor Relations Review* 35 (April 1982): 354–67.

Angrist, Joshua D. and Alan B. Krueger. "Empirical Strategies in Labor Economics." In Orley Ashenfelter and David Card, eds. *Handbook of Labor Economics* Volume 3a. Amsterdam: Elsevier, 1999, pp. 1277–366.

Ashenfelter, Orley. "Racial Discrimination and Trade Unionism." *Journal of Political Economy* 80 (June 1972): 435–64.

Bell, Brian D. and Michael K. Pitt. "Trade Union Decline and the Distribution of Wages in the UK: Evidence from Kernel Density Estimation." *Oxford Bulletin of Economics and Statistics* 60 (November 1998): 509–28.

Bland, Paul. "Trade Union Membership and Recognition, 1997–98: An Analysis of Data from the Certification Officer and the Labour Force Survey." *Labour Market Trends* (July 1999): 343–53.

Card, David. "The Effects of Unions on the Distribution of Wages: Redistribution or Relabelling?" NBER Working Paper 4195, Cambridge: Mass.: National Bureau of Economic Research, 1992.

———. "The Effects of Unions on the Structure of Wages: A Longitudinal Analysis." *Econometrica* 64 (July 1996): 957–79.

———. "The Effect of Unions on Wage Inequality in the U.S. Labor Market." *Industrial and Labor Relations Review* 54 (January 2001): 296–315.

Card, David and John DiNardo. "Skill-Biased Technological Change and Rising Wage Inequality: Some Problems and Puzzles." *Journal of Labor Economics* 20 (October 2002): 733–83.

Card, David and Thomas Lemieux. "Wage Dispersion, Returns to Skill, and Black-White Wage Differentials." *Journal of Econometrics* 74 (October 1996): 319–61.

DiNardo, John, Nicole M. Fortin, and Thomas Lemieux. "Labor Market Institutions and the Distribution of Wages, 1973–1992: A Semi-Parametric Approach." *Econometrica* 64 (September 1996): 1001–44.

DiNardo, John and Thomas Lemieux. "Diverging Male Wage Inequality in the United States and Canada, 1981–88: Do Institutions Explain the Difference?" *Industrial and Labor Relations Review* 50 (July 1997): 629–51.

Freeman, Richard B. "Unionism and the Dispersion of Wages." *Industrial and Labor Relations Review* 34 (October 1980): 3–23.

———. "Union Wage Practices and Wage Dispersion within Establishments." *Industrial and Labor Relations Review* 36 (October 1982): 3–21.

———. "Longitudinal Analyses of the Effects of Trade Unions." *Journal of Labor Economics* 2 (January 1984): 1–26.

———. "How Much Has Deunionization Contributed to the Rise of Male Earnings Inequality?" In Sheldon Danziger and Peter Gottschalk, eds. *Uneven Tides: Rising Income Inequality in America.* New York: Russell Sage Foundation, 1993, pp. 133–63.

Freeman, Richard B. and James L. Medoff. *What Do Unions Do?* New York: Basic Books, 1984.

Friedman, Milton. "Some Comments on the Significance for Labor Unions on Economic Policy." In David McCord Wright, ed. *The Impact of the Union.* New York: Kelley and Millman, 1956, pp. 204–34.

———. *Capitalism and Freedom.* Chicago: University of Chicago Press, 1962.

Gosling, Amanda and Thomas Lemieux. "Labor Market Reforms and Changes in Wage Inequality in the United Kingdom and the United States." NBER Working Paper 8413. Cambridge, Mass.: National Bureau of Economic Research, 2001.

Gosling, Amanda and Stephen Machin. "Trade Unions and the Dispersion of Earnings in British Establishments." *Oxford Bulletin of Economics and Statistics* 57 (May 1995): 167–84.

Hirsch, Barry T. "The Interindustry Structure of Unions, Earnings and Earnings Dispersion." *Industrial and Labor Relations Review* 36 (October 1982): 22–39.

Hirsch, Barry T. and Edward J. Schumacher. "Unions, Wages, and Skills." *Journal of Human Resources* 33 (Winter 1998): 201–19.

————. "Match Bias in Wage Gap Estimates Due to Earnings Imputation." *Journal of Labor Economics* 22 (July 2004): 689–722.

Hyclak, Thomas. "The Effect of Unions on Earnings Inequality in Local Labor Markets." *Industrial and Labor Relations Review* 33 (October 1979): 77–84.

————. "Unions and Income Inequality: Some Cross–State Evidence." *Industrial Relations* 19 (Spring 1980): 212–15.

Johnson, George. "Economic Analysis of Trade Unionism." *American Economic Review* 65 (June 1975): 23–28.

———— and Kenwood C. Youmans. "Union Relative Wage Effects by Age and Education." *Industrial and Labor Relations Review* 24 (January 1971): 171–79.

Kuhn, Peter. "Canada and the OECD Hypothesis: Does Labour Market Inflexibility Explain Canada's High Level of Unemployment?" In W. Craig Riddell and France St-Hilaire, eds. *Adapting Public Policy to a Labour Market in Transition*. Montreal: Institute for Research on Public Policy, 2000, pp. 177–209.

Lemieux, Thomas. "Unions and Wage Inequality in Canada and the United States." In David Card and Richard B. Freeman, eds. *Small Differences That Matter: Labor Markets and Income Maintenance in Canada and the United States*. Chicago: University of Chicago Press, 1993, pp. 69–107.

————. "Estimating the Effects of Unions on Wage Inequality in a Panel Data Model with Comparative Advantage and Non–Random Selection." *Journal of Labor Economics* 16 (April 1998): 261–91.

Lewis, H. Gregg. *Unionism and Relative Wages in the United States*. Chicago: University of Chicago Press, 1963.

————. *Union Relative Wage Effects: A Survey*. Chicago: University of Chicago Press, 1986.

Machin, Stephen. "The Decline of Labour Market Institutions and the Rise in Wage Inequality in Britain." *European Economic Review* 41 (April 1997): 647–57.

Meng, Ron. "Union Effects on Wage Dispersion in Canadian Industry." *Economics Letters* 32 (April 1990): 399–403.

Metcalf, David. "Unions and the Dispersion of Earnings." *British Journal of Industrial Relations* 20 (June 1982): 163–69.

Murphy, Kevin M., W. Craig Riddell, and Paul M. Romer. "Wages, Skills and Technology in the United States and Canada." In Elhanan Helpman, ed. *General Purpose Technologies and Economic Growth*. Cambridge, Mass.: MIT Press, 1998, pp. 283–309.

Ozanne, Robert. "A Century of Occupational Wage Differentials in Manufacturing." *Review of Economics and Statistics* 44 (August 1962): 292–99.

Rees, Albert. *The Economics of Trade Unions*. Chicago: University of Chicago Press, 1962.

Reynolds, Lloyd G. and Cynthia H. Taft. *The Evolution of Wage Structure*. New Haven, Conn.: Yale University Press, 1956.

Riddell, Chris and W. Craig Riddell. "Changing Patterns of Unionization: The North American Experience." University of British Columbia, Department of Economics, Discussion Paper 01–23, June 2001.

Rosen, Sherwin. "Unionism and the Occupational Wage Structure in the United States." *International Economic Review* 11 (June 1970): 269–86.

Stafford, Frank P. "Concentration and Labor Earnings: Comment." *American Economic Review* 58 (March 1968): 174–81.

Stieber, Jack. *The Steel Industry Wage Structure*. Cambridge, Mass.: Harvard University Press, 1959.

Data Appendix

U.S. Data

Since 1979, the U.S. Census Bureau has been collecting data on weekly hours, weekly earnings, and hourly earnings (for workers paid by the hour) for all wage and salary workers in the "outgoing rotation group" (ORG) of the Current Population Survey (CPS). Beginning in 1983, the ORG supplement of the CPS also asks about the union status of workers (and union coverage). Similar variables are also available in the May supplement of the CPS between 1973 and 1978, though only union membership (and not coverage) is available for this period.

In both the May and ORG supplements of the CPS, workers paid by the hour are asked their hourly rate of pay. We use this variable, which is collected in a consistent fashion over time, as our measure of the hourly wage rate for these workers. The May and ORG supplements also provide information on usual weekly earnings for all workers. For workers not paid by the hour, we use average hourly earnings (weekly earnings divided by weekly hours) as our measure of the wage rate.

Note, however, that weekly earnings are not measured consistently over time. From 1973 to 1993, this variable was collected by asking individuals directly about their earnings on a weekly basis. From 1994 to 2001, individuals had the option of reporting their usual earnings on the base period of their choice (weekly, bi-weekly, monthly, or annually). Weekly earnings are then obtained by normalized the earnings reported by workers to a weekly basis. The available evidence does not suggest, however, that this change in the way earnings are collected had a significant impact on the distribution of wages (see Card and DiNardo (2002) and Gosling and Lemieux (2001) for more detail).

Another potential problem is that weekly earnings are top-coded at different values for different years throughout the sample period. Before 1988, weekly earnings were top-coded at $999. The top-code was later increased to $1,923 in 1988 and $2,884 in 1998. For an individual working 40 hours a week, the weekly earnings top code corresponds to an hourly wage ranging from of $42.6 in 1984 ($2001) to $99.6 in 1973 ($2001). To keep the wage samples relatively comparable over time, we trim observations with wages above $63 ($2001). We also trim observations with wages below $2.5 ($2001), which typically corresponds to about half of the minimum wage. The wage deflator used is the Consumer Price Index (CPI-U). All the U.S. wage statistics reported herein are also weighted using the CPS earnings weights.

Questions about educational achievement were changed substantially in the early 1990s. Until 1991, the CPS asked about the highest grade (or years of schooling) completed. Starting in 1992, the CPS moved to questions about the highest degree. We have recoded the post–1992 data in term of completed years of schooling to have a measure of schooling that is consistent over time. We then use years of schooling to compute the standard measure of years of potential experience (age – schooling – 6). Only observations with potential experience larger or equal than zero are kept in the analysis samples.

Finally, in the 1979–2001 ORG supplements of the CPS, wages or earnings of workers who refuse to answer the wage/earnings questions were allocated using a "hot deck" procedure. We exclude observations with allocated wages and earnings for two reasons. First, wages and earnings were not allocated in the May 1973–1978 CPS. We thus need to exclude allocated observations from the 1984, 1993, and 2001 ORG supplement data to maintain a consistent sample over time. Second, union status is not one of the characteristics used to match observations with missing earnings to observations with non-missing earnings in the *imputation procedure (hot deck) used by the U.S. Census Bureau. As a result, estimates of union wage effects obtained from a sample with alloca-tion observations included can be severely biased downward (see Hirsch and Schumacher, 2003 for more details).

U.K. Data

As mentioned in the text, for the U.K. we use data from the 1983 GHS and the 1993 and 2001 UKLFS. For the sake of consistency, we exclude observa-tions from Northern Ireland since this region was sampled in the UKLFS but not in the GHS. Real wages are obtained by deflating nominal wages with the Consumer Price Index (Retail Price Index). To limit the effect of outliers, we only keep observations with an hourly wage rate between 1.5 and 50 pounds (in 2001 pounds).

In general, we process the U.K. samples to make them as comparable as possible to the U.S. samples. In both the UKLFS and the GHS, we use observa-tions for wage and salary workers with non-missing wages and earnings. We also use the sample weights whenever available (there are no sample weights in the GHS). Since education is not consistently measured over time, we recode education into five broad categories that are consistent over time: university graduates, higher level vocational training and A-level qualifications, middle-level vocational training or O-level qualifications, lower level vocational training, and no qualifications or diploma.

Canadian Data

As mentioned in the text, for Canada we use the 2001 Labour Force Survey (CLFS), the 1991 and 1995 Surveys on Work Arrangements (SWA), and the 1984 Survey of Union Membership (SUM). These data sets are all relatively comparable since both the SUM and the SWA were conducted as supplements to the Labour Force Survey. Relative to the U.S. and U.K. data, however, there are some important limitations in the Canadian data. First, as mentioned in the text, it is not possible to distinguish union membership from union coverage in the SWA. For the sake of consistency over time, we thus use union coverage as our measure of unionization in Canada.

A second limitation is that in the 1984 SUM and the 2001 CLFS missing wages and earnings were allocated but no allocation flags are provided. We thus have to include observations with allocated wages and earnings in the analysis with generates an inconsistency relative to the SWA (where missing wages and earnings are not allocated) and the U.S. and U.K. data. This likely understates the effect of unions on wages in 1984 and 2001, though it is not possible to quantify the extent of the bias. Another limitation is that age is only provided in broad categories, unlike in the U.S. and U.K data where age is reported in years. In particular, it is not possible to separate workers age 15 from those age 16. This explains why we use all wage and salary workers age 15 to 64 in Canada, compared to workers age 16 to 64 in the two other countries.

A further limitation is that hourly wages are top-coded at a relatively low level in the Canadian data. The top codes are $45 in the 1984 SUM, $50 in the 1991 SWA, $40 in the 1995 SWA, and $100 in the 2001 CLFS. For the sake of consistency, we trim observations with hourly wages above $44 (in $2001). Wages are deflated using the Canadian CPI for all items. We also trim observations with wages below $2.5 in $2001, which represents about half of the minimum wage.

One final limitation is that only five education categories are consistently available over time. These categories are: 0 to eight years of school, high school (some or completed), some post-secondary education, post-education degree or diploma (less than university), and university degree. As in the CPS and the UKLFS, all statistics for Canada are computed using sample weights.

6

The Effect of Unions on Employee Benefits and Non-Wage Compensation: Monopoly Power, Collective Voice, and Facilitation

John W. Budd

I. Introduction

Non-wage forms of compensation are monetary and non-monetary items used to attract, retain, motivate, and reward employees above and beyond traditional wage and salary payments. Monetary, non-wage compensation includes profit-sharing payments, lump-sum bonuses, stock options, and other forms of contingent compensation. Non-monetary, non-wage forms of compensation are employee benefits — these used to be called fringe benefits, but as they now represent a substantial fraction of total compensation, "fringe" benefits has become a misnomer. New York City's pension funding crisis in the 1970s and the billions of dollars of unfunded pension liabilities currently faced by the major U.S. automakers and steel companies further underscore the obsolescence of the "fringe" descriptor. Major employee benefits include employer-provided health insurance and pension plans as well as vacation and sick days, life and disability insurance, supplemental unemployment benefits, paid holidays, dental insurance, educational and legal assistance, and a myriad of other items. With growing concern over work-family balance, recent attention has also focused on family-friendly benefits such as parental and family leave, flexible work hours, on-site childcare, job-sharing, and work-at-home programs.

Issues surrounding non-wage forms of compensation are very important for practitioners, policymakers, and researchers (Butler, 1999). With a U.S. emphasis on private rather than public provision of employee benefits — including health insurance, retirement plans, and family-friendly policies — many employees rely on their employer for benefits, and uneven coverage leaves some individuals vulnerable. But escalating benefits costs are a major concern for employers and perhaps an impediment for improved competitiveness (Broderick and Gerhart, 1997). Conflicts over employee benefits are sharpened by the fact that social as well as economic issues are often central — health care, living standards for retirees, leisure time, childcare, and other complex issues. To further address concerns with labor costs and to provide greater incentives

160

for employees, contingent forms of monetary, non-wage compensation have also increased in importance in recent decades (Fossum and McCall, 1997). But this trend can conflict with employees' preferences for predictability and objectivity. Research on the determinants, effectiveness, and implications of non-wage forms of compensation, therefore, is an important component of analyses of work and the employment relationship.

As with many other aspects of the employment relationship, labor unions can affect non-wage forms of compensation in ways that have both positive and negative economic and social consequences. One of the many outstanding and enduring contributions of Richard Freeman and James Medoff's seminal 1984 book *What Do Unions Do?* is demonstrating both theoretically and empirically these positive and negative aspects of labor unions with regard to employee benefits and other forms of non-wage compensation. In fact, *What Do Unions Do?* has largely shaped the last generation of research on the effects of labor unions on individuals, organizations, and society, and this continues to be especially true for the area of non-wage forms of employee compensation.

Freeman and Medoff's (1979, 1984) two faces of unionism — the monopoly face and the collective voice/institutional response face — both predict that unionized employees will have more generous benefit packages than comparable nonunion workers. But the subject of benefits is an excellent illustration of the differences between the two faces, because the prediction of greater benefits for unionized employees stems from very different routes in each face. And this union-induced increase in benefits has very different implications for aggregate social welfare depending on whether the increase is because of the monopoly or collective-voice face. In contrast, to the extent that monetary forms of non-wage compensation are viewed by employees as attempts to replace predictable wage payments with uncertain, contingent compensation such as profit-sharing payments or bonuses, unions are predicted to be associated with a reduced incidence of these items. Union policies favoring objective, standard-rate wage policies over subjective policies with managerial discretion also suggest that profit-sharing payments and bonuses will be less likely in unionized situations (Slichter et al., 1960; Freeman, 1980, 1982; Freeman and Medoff, 1984). As with employee benefits, however, the differences between union and nonunion patterns of monetary forms of non-wage compensation can stem from both the monopoly and collective-voice face of labor unions.

Union-nonunion differences in non-wage forms of compensation that can be explained by the monopoly face are called "monopoly effects" while differences that result from the collective voice/institutional response face are called "collective voice effects." A review of the research since the publication of *What Do Unions Do?* affirms the importance of this conceptual framework, but also reveals the need to add a third effect which I label the "facilitation effect." To fix ideas, consider a typical survey that asks individual employees whether they are covered by an employer-provided pension plan. Research on the monopoly and collective-voice effects assumes that a positive response to this question indicates that the employee is covered by a pension plan whereas a negative response implies that they are not. In other words, these responses are assumed to indicate true availability of employee benefits.

But there is an alternative possibility: A negative response can result from an employee who is ignorant or unaware that he or she is covered by or eligible for a specific benefit. By increasing awareness of employee benefits programs and providing representation when necessary, labor unions can facilitate receipt of employee benefits — holding actual availability constant. As such, if unionized workers report being covered by various benefit plans more frequently than nonunion workers, this difference may stem from a combination of the monopoly and collective-voice effects in raising availability and of the facilitation effect in raising awareness. Freeman and Medoff's monopoly power and collective-voice effects, along with the facilitation effect, provide the organizing framework for the remainder of this reassessment of the effects of labor unions on non-wage forms of compensation.[1]

II. Monopoly Power, Collective Voice, and Union Facilitation

In the neoclassical economics textbook model of the labor market, competition among individuals for jobs and competition among organizations for workers yields market-clearing compensation packages and employment levels in which individuals are rewarded with the value of their marginal contribution to the organization. Moreover, compensation packages (and working conditions) reflect the preferences of the marginal worker — individuals on the margin of accepting a job or quitting in response to small changes in the compensation package or working conditions. In the neoclassical model with labor market competition, the theoretical basis for differences in employee-benefit packages across firms is compensating differentials (Brown, 1980; Montgomery and Shaw, 1997; Rosen, 1974). Workers with stronger preferences for benefits will take jobs at firms that offer more benefits but to compensate for this richer package of benefits, they must accept a lower wage.

Now consider what happens if the employees at one organization are represented by a labor union. In the textbook model, a union is a monopolizing agent. Monopoly power, derived from the threat of imposing costs on the organization through a strike, can be used to increase the compensation package above the market-clearing, competitive level.[2] In fact, the average wage premium for union relative to nonunion workers in the United States is typically thought to be around 15 percent (Lewis, 1986). The same bargaining power that underlies the union wage premium can be used to win more generous benefits packages. This is the monopoly component of Freeman and Medoff's (1979, 1984) two faces of unionism model. In the monopoly face, labor unions are predicted to increase the receipt of employee benefits, such as health insurance and pension plans, relative to nonunion situations because of monopoly power rooted in the strike threat. Actual increases in unionized benefits levels that stem from this monopoly power represent the "monopoly effect" of labor unions on benefits.

This same monopoly power can be used to win additional monetary forms of non-wage compensation, or to resist the imposition of forms perceived as unfavorable to workers. In particular, to the extent that workers prefer predictable, noncontingent compensation payments, the monopoly effect predicts that unionized workplaces will be less likely to have contingent compensation schemes such as profit-sharing or bonus systems. The monopoly effect of labor unions on non-wage forms of compensation — whether in increasing benefits or decreasing contingent compensation — has negative consequences for economic efficiency and aggregate welfare — if labor markets and the employment relationship work according to the textbook neoclassical model.

By definition, the monopoly effect stems from monopoly power which distorts competitive outcomes. Since competitive outcomes maximize efficiency and aggregate social welfare in standard neoclassical economic theory, any deviations — whether caused by a union's strike threat or the monopoly power of a company or the imposition of regulations by a government — are harmful. Increased levels of employee benefits or resistance to contingent compensation both make unionized labor more expensive than the market-clearing, efficiency-maximizing compensation package. Unionized companies will then employ less-than-optimal amounts of labor which causes unemployment or excess supply in the nonunion sector and also raises prices for unionized products. Unionized workers in the standard neoclassical economics theory, therefore, benefit at the expense of investors, nonunion labor, and consumers. Freeman and Medoff (1979, 1984) refer to this as the monopoly face of unionism.

In contrast, consider what might happen if the assumptions of the neoclassical economic model are not fulfilled. Suppose externalities create workplace public goods — such as safety provisions, heating, lighting, grievance procedures, or pensions (Freeman, 1976; Freeman and Medoff, 1984). With self-interested agents, there is a free-rider problem and too little of these beneficial public goods will be provided. Or suppose that asymmetric information, mobility costs, or other complications make labor markets imperfectly competitive, as emphasized by John R. Commons and other early institutional labor economists (Kaufman, 1993, 1997). Under these conditions, employees might not be willing to express their true preferences for various forms of compensation (Freeman, 1981, 1985). With collective voice in the form of a labor union, the free-rider problem can be overcome, and better information about individual worker preferences can be collected (Freeman, 1976; Freeman and Medoff, 1984). And as unions are political institutions with contract ratification and leadership selection done by majority voting, a median voter model implies that unions will negotiate compensation packages to reflect the preferences of the average worker, not the marginal worker as in the nonunion case.[3]

As the average worker is generally older and less mobile than the worker on the margin of joining or quitting the firm, they are more likely to prefer benefits (Freeman, 1981, 1985; Freeman and Medoff, 1984). As such, Freeman and Medoff's (1979, 1984) collective-voice face of unionism predicts that unionized workplaces will have higher levels of employee benefits than nonunion workplaces.4 Note carefully, however, that this prediction differs significantly from the monopoly effect in that the collective voice effect on benefits is a re-arranging of the total compensation package towards more benefits and lower wages to reflect the preferences of the average worker. In the collective-voice effect, total compensation is held constant. Consequently, the collective-voice effect is not necessarily harmful to efficiency and, by countering market imperfections, can actually increase aggregate economic welfare.

Freeman and Medoff's (1984) seminal research focuses on the possibilities of unions winning additional benefits by using monopoly-based bargaining power or by using collective voice to promote average rather than marginal worker preferences. But there is a third dimension: Labor unions can facilitate workers' knowledge and use of existing benefit packages. For example, unions can provide information to employees about benefit plans through union newsletters and other communication channels. Workshops and training sessions can further help employees learn about various benefits programs. Representation by shop stewards in a union-negotiated grievance procedure can help ensure that employees are able to use the benefits to which they are entitled. In the case of mandated benefits such as workers' compensation and unemployment insurance, unions can also facilitate benefits receipt through assistance with employer challenges to employee claims and through protection against unjust dismissal in retaliation for filing a valid claim. In this "facilitation effect," labor unions do not increase the actual incidence or availability of employee benefits plans, but increase the effective coverage by increasing employee awareness and utilization. Survey results in which unionized individuals are more likely than nonunion workers to respond that they have health insurance or a pension plan are assumed by the monopoly and collective-voice effects to mean increased actual availability while the facilitation effect highlights the possibility that these survey responses reflect differential *awareness* rather than *availability*.

In theory, then, a balanced scorecard of the effects of labor unions on non-wage forms of compensation is mixed. The monopoly effect in which unions increase employee benefits and decrease contingent compensation distorts optimal competitive outcomes and is therefore economically and socially harmful if labor markets are competitive. The collective-voice effect — in which unions also increase benefits and perhaps decrease contingent compensation — occurs in the context of market imperfections and can therefore be economically and socially beneficial. The facilitation effect allowing employees to utilize their legitimate benefits programs is also economically and socially beneficial. But what happens in practice is an empirical question.

III. Results from What Do Unions Do?

It is a testament to the enduring quality of *What Do Unions Do?* that the pioneering empirical analyses in chapter 4 ("Fringe Determination under Trade Unionism") and in the underlying articles by Freeman (1981, 1984, 1985) continue to be among the most thorough and significant empirical contributions on unions and non-wage forms of compensation.[5] A wide range of questions using a variety of individual and establishment-level data sources and standard econometric methods are addressed in these works. The one theme that is repeatedly revealed in these analyses — across various questions and data sets — is that observed patterns of benefits can only be partially explained by the monopoly face of unions; the collective-voice effect of labor unions on employee benefits is significant and must not be overlooked.

The results clearly show that unionized workers and workplaces are significantly more likely than comparable nonunion workers and workplaces to have (or express awareness of) major benefit items. In establishment-level data, workplaces with at least 50 percent union members have total expenditures on nonmandatory benefit items 25 to 35 percent higher than similar nonunion workplaces (Freeman, 1981). Holding total compensation constant, the union effect is still significant, but smaller, ranging between 15 and 20 percent. As such, the union effect on employee benefits appears roughly equally split between a monopoly and a collective voice effect.[6] The union effect is particularly large for lower paid establishments and for small establishments. For specific items, the union effect is also particularly strong for health insurance, pension plans, and vacation and holiday pay, and is negative for bonuses. This pattern is consistent with the collective-voice orientation to the preferences of the marginal worker as they presumably desire health insurance, pensions, and vacations as a function of being older and having greater seniority. These results are also robust to instrumenting for total compensation and for using a paired analysis of blue-collar and white-collar workers in the same establishments to control for an establishment-level fixed effect (Freeman, 1981).

In individual-level data, the standard question is whether the individual respondent has a specific benefit. Freeman and Medoff (1984) show that in the Current Population Survey (CPS), the National Longitudinal Survey of Older Men, the Panel Study of Income Dynamics, and the Quality of Employment Survey (QES), unionized workers are 24 to 32 percentage points more likely than similar nonunion workers to report having a pension plan. The CPS and QES also ask about health insurance and the estimated union effect is 14 to 18 percentage points. Finally, the QES also asks about a wide range of plans, and unionized workers are less likely to report contingent forms of non-wage compensation such as profit sharing and stock options. As a check against unobserved selectivity bias, the analysis of longitudinal data reveals that employees who move into unionized jobs significantly gain employee benefits compared to those who stay in nonunion jobs or move out of union jobs (Freeman, 1984, 1985).

An additional dimension to these pioneering results that further reinforces the importance of the collective-voice aspect is the effect of unions on the nature of employee-benefits programs. The strongest evidence pertains to pension plans (Freeman, 1985). Relative to nonunion plans, pension plans for unionized employees are significantly more likely to be defined-benefit rather than defined-contribution plans. This favors workers who stay at the firm longer — the average rather than marginal worker. Eligibility requirements further favor average employees as predicted by the collective-voice face of unionism. Freeman and Medoff (1984) also note that a much higher fraction of union than nonunion disability-insurance plans include age and years of service eligibility requirements which again reflects greater attention to older, less mobile workers.

In sum, the seminal work of Freeman and Medoff (1984), and the more detailed supporting analyses of Freeman (1981, 1984, 1985), support the two faces of unionism model. In the standard neoclassical economics framework, the monopoly effect on employee benefits is a social cost. But the collective voice aspect — which in this early work was revealed to be roughly half of the overall union effect on non-wage forms of compensation — brings social benefits because a more preferable package of benefits is provided at no extra cost. These results provide the context for much of the subsequent research on unions and non-wage forms of compensation.[7]

IV. Health Insurance and Pension Plans

Since the publication of *What Do Unions Do?*, two benefit items have received the bulk of the attention in the research literature: employer-provided health insurance and pension plans. Given the importance of these two items — for both the social welfare of individuals and retirees as well as the large fraction of employers' benefits costs accounted for by these plans — this importance in the research literature is not inappropriate, even if it has been driven by data availability.[8] And in a variety of data sets, the research continues to find that labor unions are associated with greater levels of health insurance and pension benefits.

Using the National Longitudinal Survey of Youth (NLSY), Wunnava and Ewing (1999) find that union representation increases the probability of medical insurance and retirement plans. As in Freeman (1981) and Freeman and Medoff (1984), the union effects in the NLSY are also largest for smaller firms. Unions are also associated with greater pension benefits in the Survey of Consumer Finances (Montgomery and Shaw, 1997). In a focused study of local government employment, Zax (1988) finds support for the monopoly and collective voice effects: Municipal employees represented by a union have increased benefits (the monopoly effect) and a greater weighting of the entire compensation package towards benefits (the collective-voice effect). Also in the public sector, in a national sample of U.S. cities, police receive higher employee benefits payments when covered by a collective bargaining agreement (Feuille et al., 1985). As in Freeman (1981) and in support of a combination of monopoly and collective-voice effects, there is still a positive union effect after controlling for total compensation.

These results are also reinforced by empirical studies of workers in other countries. Using Canadian data on wages and total compensation, Renaud (1998) estimates a union-nonunion wage gap that is smaller than the total compensation gap, which implies a significant union effect on benefits packages. In a different Canadian data set, unionized workers are around 20 percent more likely to have a pension plan than nonunion workers, even after controlling for unobservable personal characteristics using longitudinal analyses similar to Freeman (1984) (Swidinsky and Kupferschmidt, 1991). In Australian longitudinal data, Kornfeld (1993) also finds that unions positively effect the probability of a pension plan. Lastly, in an analysis that closely parallels that of Freeman (1981) and Freeman and Medoff (1984), Miller and Mulvey (1992) find both monopoly and collective-voice effects of Australian unions on total benefit expenditures.

Freeman's (1981) analyses have not been without criticism, however. Belman and Heywood (1991) assert that researchers should distinguish between direct and indirect effects of unions on employee benefits where the indirect effect is the increase in benefits that comes through an income effect. It's not clear, however, how this differs from the monopoly power and collective voice framework. Increased union member income stems from monopoly power, so this indirect effect is simply capturing the extent to which unions channel their monopoly power into benefits rather than wage and salary payments. Belman and Heywood (1991) estimate the direct effect by holding compensation constant — but this is the collective-voice effect. By instrumenting for the hourly wage and using predicted values to distinguish direct from indirect effects, they find significant magnitudes for both union effects on the incidence of health insurance and pensions. This reinforces, not undermines, the two faces of unionism model of *What Do Unions Do?*

By focusing on the role of fixed costs for benefits (such as administration costs) in generating union-nonunion differences in benefits, Fosu (1993) tries to distinguish a model distinct from the collective voice model of *What Do Unions Do?* However, this distinction seems artificial as union-nonunion differences in Fosu's (1993) framework stem from differences in preferences between average and marginal workers, from public goods aspects of benefits, and from the possibility that unions are more efficient at reducing average fixed costs — all of these elements are consistent with Freeman's (1981) and Freeman and Medoff's (1984) collective voice model.

Methodologically, Belman and Heywood (1991) and Fosu (1993) emphasize the need to use econometric methods appropriate for distinguishing between union effects on the likelihood that a benefits plan exists and on the level of expenditure or type of plan conditional upon its existence. Using probit and tobit models on the same employee expenditure data used by Freeman (1981), Fosu (1993) finds positive union effects on both health insurance plans and pension benefits, but stronger results for pensions compared to health insurance. Fosu (1993) also finds an interesting dichotomy: The union effect for health insurance appears to be related to improving the nature of the plan whereas for pension plans the union effect appears to be focused on increasing the chance that a plan exists. Note, however, that these conclusions come from analyses of employer expenditures, not from information about the nature of specific plans. Lastly, Fosu (1993) claims that this dichotomy undermines the collective-voice model, but this overreaches because the validity of the collective voice model does not require *equal* differences in marginal versus average worker preferences across all types of benefits.

Better analyses of the value of pension plans are Freeman (1985), discussed above, and Allen and Clark (1986) who use U.S. Department of Labor data on employer-provided pension plans to calculate the actual value of pension benefits at retirement. In these data, unionized workers receive significantly higher pension benefits at retirement and also retire a year earlier, on average, than nonunion workers. Moreover, unionized retirees were more likely to receive a post-retirement increase in their pension benefits, especially for individuals who had been retired longer. When these three effects — higher annual benefits, earlier retirement ages, and greater post-retirement increases — are put together, Allen and Clark (1986) estimate that total pension wealth is 50 to 100 percent higher for unionized individuals than for nonunion individuals.

Buchmueller et al. (2002) similarly analyze differences between union and nonunion health insurance plans in greater detail than most studies that either analyze only whether health insurance is offered or the total employer monetary contribution. In Current Population Survey data from five years between 1983 and 1997, union representation is significantly related to increased coverage by employer-provided health insurance benefits, and this increase is larger in smaller firms. Retired workers who were covered by a union contract are also significantly more likely to be covered by an employer-provided health care plan for retirees. Using firm-level survey data, Buchmueller et al. (2002) also find that unionization increases the average amount of the health insurance premiums that are paid by the employer and increases the probability that the employer fully pays the premiums. Among indemnity plans, deductibles for unionized employees are significantly lower than for nonunion employees.

An issue that has not received as much attention as it should, however, is awareness versus availability. Nearly all analyses of individual-level survey data on whether or not a worker has employer-provided health insurance or pension benefits assume that workers have perfect information about their benefit plans (Belman and Heywood, 1991; Buchmueller et al., 2002; Freeman and Medoff,

1984, Table 4–3; Miller and Mulvey, 1992; Swidinsky and Kupferschmidt, 1991; Wunnava and Ewing, 1999). A worker who indicates that he or she is not covered is assumed to be truly uncovered rather than covered but ignorant. But in individual survey data, differing response patterns between union and nonunion individuals regarding employee benefits might reflect differential awareness rather than differential availability. To wit, Leigh (1976) reports that unionized employees were more knowledgeable about their pension plans than nonunion employees whereas Luchak and Gunderson (2000) find that even among union workers, workers' knowledge about their pensions is low on average.

These findings suggest that in addition to a monopoly effect and a collective-voice effect, labor unions might also have a facilitation effect that boosts awareness and use of existing benefit plans. Three sets of findings further suggest the presence of a facilitation effect. One, union members are more likely than covered nonmembers to indicate that they have health insurance and pension plans, even though by law they should be equally covered by existing collective bargaining agreements (Budd, 1998). Two, in linked manager-employee data from Britain, individual employees are significantly less likely than managers to indicate that certain family-friendly policies are available (Budd and Mumford, 2004). Three, research on mandated social insurance benefits, such as workers' compensation and unemployment insurance, finds that unionized workers take up these benefits more readily than comparable nonunion workers (Budd and McCall, 1997; Hirsch et al., 1997). These three issues are discussed in the following sections.

V. CPS Results, 2002

This section presents the union-nonunion coverage rate differentials for the most recently available survey of the Current Population Survey (CPS) with two goals in mind.[9] One, these results document the most up-to-date union and nonunion coverage rates in the United States for health insurance and pension benefits. Two, among those covered by union contracts, the differences between union members and nonmembers will be revealed.

The CPS is a monthly survey of approximately 60,000 households that includes labor market information representative of the U.S. noninstitutional population aged 16 and older and is probably the most widely-used U.S. data set in labor economics. The March 2002 survey includes demographic information as well as questions on union status, employer-provided health insurance, and pension plans. Construction of a sample of private and public sector employed individuals with complete information on the questions of interest yields 15,019 individuals. Of these, 13.6 percent are covered by a union contract. Table 6.1 shows that these union workers are significantly more likely than nonunion workers to report that they are in their employer's health insurance plan (82.9 percent versus 58.5 percent for nonunion) and pension plan (75.7 percent versus 45.9 percent).

As shown in Table 6.2, these union-nonunion differences are statistically significant when controlling for the standard demographic and job-attribute control variables in a probit model. These models do not control for total compensation so these estimates should be considered as the total union effect, not as the monopoly, collective-voice, or facilitation effect singly. The results confirm that the earlier findings of Freeman (1981, 1985) and Freeman and Medoff (1984) are still important in the U.S. labor market of the early twenty-first century. Controlling for demographic and job-attribute differences, workers covered by collective bargaining agreements are predicted to be 16.4 percentage points more likely than nonunion workers to be covered by their employer's health insurance plan, and are 18.8 percentage points more likely to be included in their employer's pension plan. Relative to the sample means, these translate into union effects of 20 percent and 37 percent for health insurance and pension plans, respectively. Tables 6.3 and 6.4 document that the significant union effects are present within a wide range of demographic groups, industries, and occupations. Nontrivial union-nonunion differences are documented for both health insurance and pensions for both men and women, white and nonwhite, all age categories, nearly all educational categories, and many industries and occupations. For health insurance, the union-nonunion differential is slightly greater among smaller firms, but there is no obvious pattern for pensions.

Returning to Table 6.1, note further that of the 2,271 workers covered by union contracts, 2,043 (90 percent) are union members whereas 10 percent are covered nonmembers. By law, unions and employers cannot discriminate against

Table 6.1
Health Insurance and Pension Coverage Rates By Union Status, 2002
[sample sizes in brackets]

	Included in a Health Insurance Plan Offered by Employer (1)	Included in a Pension or Retirement Plan Offered by Employer (2)
Full Sample	0.622	0.504
	[15,019]	[15,019]
Covered by a Union Contract	0.829	0.757
	[2,271]	[2,271]
Union Member	0.838	0.765
	[2,043]	[2,043]
Covered Nonmember	0.746	0.684
	[228]	[228]
Nonunion	0.585	0.459
	[12,748]	[12,748]

Source: Current Population Survey, March 2002.

Table 6.2
Probit Analysis of Employer-Provided Health Insurance and Pension Plans,
March 2002 CPS[a]

	Employer-Provided Health Insurance		Employer-Sponsored Pension Plan	
	(1)	(2)	(3)	(4)
Covered by a Union Contract	0.164*	—	0.188*	
	(0.013)		(0.014)	
Union Member	—	0.175*	—	0.197*
		(0.013)		(0.015)
Covered Nonmember	—	0.068*	—	0.108*
		(0.033)		(0.038)
Additional Controls?[b]	Yes	Yes	Yes	Yes
Sample Size	15,019	15,019	15,019	15,019

Source: Current Population Survey, March 2002.

Notes: [a]Each entry contains the marginal effect and robust standard error (in parentheses) from a probit model. The dependent variables are indicators for whether or not the employee has health insurance or a pension plan provided by their employer. bEach probit model also includes control variables for gender, marital status, ethic background (4 categories), education (6), potential labor market experience, part-time, hourly, employer size (5), public sector (3), industry (19), occupation (11), and region (8). *denotes statistical significance at the 0.05 level, two-tailed test.

covered nonmembers so they are equally entitled to all of the contract's wage, benefit, work rule, and administrative policies and protections (Budd and Na, 2000). But consistent with Budd's (1998) findings using the April 1983 CPS, Table 6.1 shows that covered nonmembers are less likely than union members to report that they have employer-provided health insurance and pension plans. When controlling for demographic and job-attribute characteristics (Table 6.2), there is still a significant difference between the two groups of workers. This might reflect differences in awareness rather than actual availability since nonmembers might not receive union publications or help from a union representative. On the other hand, this difference might reflect (illegal) employer or union discrimination, or unobserved differences between the two groups (Budd, 1998; Budd and Na, 2000). This issue does not affect a large number of workers (less than two percent), but further research might reveal additional insights into what unions do.

That the importance of unions for the provision of employee benefits is not limited to the U.S. merits reinforcing. Table 6.5 therefore presents unadjusted and adjusted differences between unionized and nonunion workplaces for four types of employee benefits in a sample of 1,987 workplaces from the British Workplace Employee Relations Survey 1998 (WERS98) (Department of Trade and Industry, 1999).[10] The WERS98 allows one to identify whether the largest

Table 6.3
The Union Effect on Health Insurance Coverage: Subgroup Differences, 2002

	Sample Size (1)	Uniona (2)	Nonunion (3)	Unadjusted Union – Nonunion Difference (4)	Marginal Effect (5)	Standard Error (6)
		Health Insurance Coverage Rate			Adjusted Difference[b]	
Full Sample	15,019	0.829	0.585	0.245*	0.164*	0.013
Gender						
Male	7,557	0.859	0.639	0.220*	0.154*	0.015
Female	7,462	0.793	0.531	0.262*	0.167*	0.020
Ethnic Background						
White	12,778	0.827	0.586	0.241*	0.155*	0.014
Nonwhite	2,241	0.837	0.577	0.261*	0.211*	0.026
Marital Status						
Not Married	6,244	0.841	0.546	0.295*	0.222*	0.022
Married	8,775	0.823	0.613	0.210*	0.131*	0.015
Age						
16–24	2,007	0.525	0.248	0.277*	0.146*	0.052
25–34	3,283	0.804	0.630	0.174*	0.127*	0.027
35–44	4,091	0.838	0.632	0.206*	0.157*	0.021
45–54	3,502	0.871	0.672	0.198*	0.122*	0.020
55+	2,136	0.861	0.639	0.223*	0.140*	0.028
Highest Grade Completed						
Less Than High School	1,659	0.774	0.293	0.482*	0.392*	0.061
High School Diploma	4,577	0.804	0.559	0.245*	0.160*	0.023
Some College	4,509	0.835	0.580	0.255*	0.166*	0.023
College Degree	2,835	0.853	0.729	0.124*	0.107*	0.023
Graduate Degree	1,439	0.865	0.776	0.089*	0.044	0.029
Private or Public Sector						
Private Sector	12,410	0.814	0.569	0.245*	0.185*	0.016
Public Sector	2,609	0.847	0.696	0.151*	0.101*	0.020
Industry						
Agriculture and Mining	303	0.688	0.439	0.248	0.240	0.132
Construction	843	0.811	0.507	0.303*	0.271*	0.042
Nondurable Manufacturing	1,310	0.876	0.773	0.103*	0.033	0.033
Durable Manufacturing	834	0.888	0.750	0.138*	0.126*	0.030
Transp., Commun., Utilities	1,088	0.891	0.692	0.199*	0.126*	0.030
Wholesale and Retail Trade	3,037	0.675	0.447	0.228*	0.224*	0.046
Finance, Ins., Real Estate	943	0.696	0.686	0.010	–0.060	0.109
Bus. and Personal Services	1,576	0.762	0.479	0.283*	0.305*	0.056
Educ. and Health Services	4,288	0.805	0.594	0.211*	0.131*	0.022
Public Administration	797	0.903	0.815	0.088*	0.055	0.026

Table 6.3

	Health Insurance Coverage Rate			Unadjusted Union – Nonunion Difference	Adjusted Difference[b]	
	Sample Size	Uniona	Nonunion		Marginal Effect	Standard Error
	(1)	(2)	(3)	(4)	(5)	(6)
Occupation						
Executive and Managerial	2,249	0.847	0.769	0.079*	0.040	0.035
Professional	2,486	0.853	0.702	0.151*	0.099*	0.024
Technicians and Sales	2,151	0.734	0.552	0.182*	0.166*	0.049
Administrative Support	2,226	0.822	0.574	0.248*	0.167*	0.035
Services and Farming	2,411	0.766	0.334	0.432*	0.190*	0.041
Craft and Repair	1,513	0.846	0.632	0.214*	0.143*	0.030
Operators	726	0.882	0.630	0.251*	0.124*	0.046
Transportation and Laborers	1,257	0.848	0.498	0.350*	0.265*	0.038
Firm Size (Number of Employees)						
Less Than 10	1,881	0.562	0.297	0.265*	0.212*	0.070
10 – 24	1,541	0.630	0.428	0.202*	0.226*	0.066
25 – 99	2,124	0.791	0.579	0.212*	0.179*	0.038
100 – 499	2,329	0.819	0.655	0.164*	0.145*	0.027
500 – 999	881	0.794	0.719	0.075*	0.034	0.042
1,000 or More	6,263	0.867	0.692	0.176*	0.125*	0.014

Source: Current Population Survey, March 2002.

Notes: [a]Covered by a union contract. [b]Adjusted differences are the marginal effect and standard error from a probit model that includes the control variables listed in Table 6.2. *denotes statistical significance at the 0.05 level, two-tailed test.

occupational group in the workplace has private health insurance benefits, an employer-provided pension plan, sick pay in excess of the legally-mandated minimum, and at least four weeks of paid vacation per year. Workplaces in which pay for the largest occupational group is determined by collective bargaining are less likely to provide private health insurance. This underscores the importance of the institutional environment: Britain has a vast public health care system and less than 20 percent of workplaces report having private health insurance in the WERS98. In contrast, unionized workplaces are 16.2 percentage points more likely to have an employer-provided pension, 9.2 percentage points more likely to have excess sick pay, and 17.6 percentage points more likely to have at least four weeks of paid leave. These are workplace-level responses provided by a manager, so they do not reflect a facilitation effect. Based on the research reviewed above, these affects are likely to reflect a combination of monopoly power and collective voice, though a more detailed analysis is warranted. But more significantly, the important effects of unions on the provision of employee benefits highlighted by Freeman (1981) and Freeman and Medoff (1984) are not limited to the United States.

Table 6.4
The Union Effect on Pension Coverage: Subgroup Differences, 2002

| | Sample Size (1) | Pension Coverage Rate | | Unadjusted Union – Nonunion Difference (4) | Adjusted Difference[b] | |
		Uniona (2)	Nonunion (3)		Marginal Effect (5)	Standard Error (6)
Full Sample	15,019	0.757	0.459	0.298*	0.188*	0.014
Gender						
Male	7,557	0.762	0.482	0.279*	0.208*	0.019
Female	7,462	0.751	0.437	0.314*	0.151*	0.022
Ethnic Background						
White	12,778	0.772	0.468	0.303*	0.190*	0.016
Non-White	2,241	0.691	0.406	0.285*	0.191*	0.033
Marital Status						
Not Married	6,244	0.685	0.351	0.334*	0.209*	0.024
Married	8,775	0.797	0.540	0.257*	0.161*	0.017
Age						
16–24	2,007	0.434	0.132	0.302*	0.156*	0.039
25–34	3,283	0.685	0.456	0.229*	0.170*	0.032
35–44	4,091	0.780	0.532	0.248*	0.180*	0.024
45–54	3,502	0.823	0.568	0.255*	0.159*	0.024
55+	2,136	0.775	0.502	0.273*	0.120*	0.036
Highest Grade Completed						
Less Than High School	1,659	0.571	0.163	0.408*	0.228*	0.050
High School Diploma	4,577	0.711	0.415	0.296*	0.175*	0.024
Some College	4,509	0.765	0.458	0.306*	0.188*	0.026
College Degree	2,835	0.794	0.616	0.177*	0.133*	0.030
Graduate Degree	1,439	0.868	0.681	0.187*	0.099*	0.036
Private or Public Sector						
Private Sector	12,410	0.684	0.432	0.251*	0.197*	0.018
Public Sector	2,609	0.843	0.655	0.188*	0.139*	0.021
Industry						
Agriculture and Mining	303	0.688	0.331	0.356*	0.392*	0.133
Construction	843	0.680	0.332	0.348*	0.310*	0.055
Nondurable Manufacturing	1,310	0.804	0.606	0.198*	0.145*	0.038
Durable Manufacturing	834	0.762	0.590	0.172*	0.193*	0.042
Transp., Commun., Utilities	1,088	0.824	0.535	0.289*	0.230*	0.035
Wholesale and Retail Trade	3,037	0.497	0.315	0.182*	0.133*	0.045
Finance, Ins., Real Estate	943	0.478	0.591	–0.113	–0.076	0.114

Table 6.4 (cont.)

| | | Pension Coverage Rate | | Unadjusted Union – Nonunion | Adjusted Difference[b] | |
| | Sample Size | Uniona | Nonunion | Difference | Marginal Effect | Standard Error |
	(1)	(2)	(3)	(4)	(5)	(6)
Bus. and Personal Services	1,576	0.500	0.327	0.173*	0.144*	0.065
Educ. and Health Services	4,288	0.785	0.503	0.282*	0.157*	0.024
Public Administration	797	0.854	0.754	0.100*	0.092*	0.034
Occupation						
Executive and Managerial	2,249	0.799	0.657	0.142*	0.087	0.043
Professional	2,486	0.849	0.619	0.231*	0.137*	0.027
Technicians and Sales	2,151	0.604	0.434	0.170*	0.103*	0.051
Administrative Support	2,226	0.766	0.469	0.297*	0.140*	0.039
Services and Farming	2,411	0.654	0.213	0.441*	0.149*	0.035
Craft and Repair	1,513	0.773	0.454	0.319*	0.234*	0.037
Operators	726	0.763	0.438	0.325*	0.206*	0.052
Transportation and Laborers	1,257	0.701	0.302	0.399*	0.271*	0.041
Firm Size (Number of Employees)						
Less Than 10	1,881	0.329	0.181	0.147	0.081	0.050
10 – 24	1,541	0.457	0.267	0.190*	0.222*	0.067
25 – 99	2,124	0.645	0.400	0.245*	0.196*	0.043
100 – 499	2,329	0.759	0.516	0.243*	0.187*	0.033
500 – 999	881	0.735	0.592	0.143	0.037	0.053
1,000 or More	6,263	0.816	0.601	0.215*	0.169*	0.016

Source: Current Population Survey, March 2002.

Notes: See Notes to Table 6.3.

Table 6.5
British Workplaces with Employee Benefits by Union Status, 1998

	Employees in Largest Occupational Group Entitled to…			
			Sick Pay in	
	Private Health Insurance	Employer Pension Scheme	Excess of Statutory Requirements	At Least Four Weeks of Paid Annual Leave
	(1)	(2)	(3)	(4)

A. Unadjusted Differences: Sample Means [sample sizes in brackets]

Full Sample	0.179	0.783	0.757	0.897
	[1,987]	[1,987]	[1,987]	[1,987]
Largest Occupational	0.086	0.934	0.877	0.974
Group Has Collective	[665]	[665]	[665]	[665]
Bargaining for Pay				
Nonunion	0.226	0.707	0.697	0.858
	[1,322]	[1,322]	[1,322]	[1,322]

B. Adjusted Differences: Probit Marginal Effect [p-values in brackets]a

Largest Occupational	−0.058*	0.162*	0.092*	0.176*
Group Has Collective	[0.0006]	[0.0007]	[0.0004]	[0.0002]
Bargaining for Pay				

Source: Workplace Employee Relations Survey, 1998.

Notes: [a]Each entry contains the marginal effect and p-value of the union coefficient in a probit model for each of the four employee benefits. The probit model includes sampling weights and the *p*-values account for the stratification in the sampling procedure. Each probit model also includes control variables for employer size, establishment age, multiple worksites, public sector, workplace demographics (proportion female, part-time, youth, older, and non-white), presence of a human resources representative, workplace proportion in teams and quality circles, industry (11), occupation (7), and region (10). The sample size is 1,987. * denotes statistical significance at the 0.05 level, two-tailed test.

VI. Employer Expenditures Results, 2004[11]

To distinguish the monopoly effect from the collective voice effect, Freeman (1981) and Freeman and Medoff (1984) analyze 1970s data from the establishment-level Expenditures for Employee Compensation survey and find three key results. First, total expenditures on nonmandatory benefit items are 25 to 35 percent higher in union workplaces (those with at least 50 percent union members) than in nonunion workplaces. Second, the union effect on benefits is particularly large for lower paid establishments and for small establishments. Third, the union effect on employee benefits is roughly equally split between the monopoly and collective voice effects. These results are robust to instrumenting for total compensation and for using a paired analysis of blue-collar and white-collar workers in the same establishments to control for an establishment-level fixed effect (Freeman, 1981).

To investigate the extent to which their results still hold true 30 years later, I present up-to-date results from the Employer Costs for Employee Compensation (ECEC) data.[12] The ECEC is the successor to the survey analyzed by Freeman (1981) and Freeman and Medoff (1984) and has the advantage over its predecessor of specifically identifying each job as covered by a union contract or not. The analyses reported herein are from the March 2004 survey and are based on 33,776 private sector jobs from 7,863 establishments. For each establishment there is information on industry, total number of employees, and state; for each job there is information on occupational classification, whether the job is covered by a collective bargaining agreement, and employer expenditures on hourly wages and 20 categories of employee benefits.

Table 6.6 presents share of each benefit in the total compensation package for union and nonunion jobs. Perhaps the most striking result is that voluntary benefits account for 26.5 percent of total compensation for private sector jobs covered by a union contract compared to only 16 percent for nonunion jobs.[13] Or in dollar terms, these shares imply that union jobs include $8.51 per hour in voluntary benefits compared to $3.52 per hour for nonunion jobs. While all of the individual differences between union and nonunion jobs are statistically significant at conventional levels, the differences are particularly notable for health insurance, defined-benefit retirement, vacation, and overtime. The only categories for which nonunion jobs have a higher share than union jobs are defined-contribution retirement and nonproduction bonuses — the two benefit items that unions have traditionally resisted. The probability that unionized jobs have each benefit is greater than for nonunion jobs for all of the benefits except for these same two categories.

The pattern of results in Table 6.6 is similar to those for 1974–1977 reported in Freeman and Medoff (1984, Table 4.1).[14] In both sets of results, there are large union-nonunion differences in expenditures on retirement benefits, health, life, and disability insurance, and shift premiums. In fact, in many cases the

Table 6.6
Union-Nonunion Differences in the Private Sector
Total Compensation Package, 2004

	Union		Nonunion	
	Share of Total Compensation (1)	Fraction with the Benefit (2)	Share of Total Compensation (3)	Fraction with the Benefit (4)
Total Compensation	1.000	—	1.000	—
Per Hour	[$32.13]		[$22.01]	
Straight-Time				
Hourly Wage	0.644	—	0.741	—
Benefits, Total	0.356	—	0.259	—
Benefits, Mandated	0.091	1.000	0.099	1.000
Benefits, Voluntary	0.265	0.997	0.160	0.964
Health Insurance	0.102	0.960	0.060	0.685
Defined Benefit				
Retirement	0.044	0.764	0.007	0.162
Defined Contribution				
Retirement	0.012	0.509	0.014	0.563
Life and Disability				
Insurance	0.006	0.913	0.004	0.637
Vacation	0.034	0.911	0.025	0.772
Holidays	0.023	0.904	0.018	0.774
Sick Leave	0.009	0.685	0.006	0.583
Overtime Premiums	0.021	0.870	0.011	0.532
Shift Differentials	0.006	0.496	0.002	0.126
Nonproduction				
Bonuses	0.005	0.362	0.010	0.417
Other[a]	0.006	0.809	0.003	0.536
Sample Size	4,703	[b]	29,073	[b]

Notes: [a]Other benefits include supplemental unemployment benefits, severance pay, and other leave.
[b]Sample sizes vary in columns 2 and 4 because these calculations omit observations with imputed values.
Source: Employer Costs for Employee Compensation data, March 2004.

union-nonunion differences have widened in the 2004 data. For example, the overall relative shares of voluntary benefits were 18 and 12 percent for union and nonunion jobs, respectively, in the earlier data. As noted above and in Table 6.6, these shares are 26.5 and 16 percent in 2004. The union share has therefore increased by almost 50 percent whereas the nonunion share has increased by 33 percent.

The results in Table 6.6 are unadjusted and do not control for other characteristics. Table 6.7 therefore reports the results of regressing the logarithm of voluntary benefits expenditures (columns 1, 3, and 5) and the logarithm of total compensation (columns 2, 4, and 6) on a dummy variable for whether the job was covered by a union contract, two establishment size dummy variables, region effects, and three-digit industry and occupation effects. One drawback

Table 6.7

Estimating Monopoly and Collective Voice Effects from Private Sector Compensation Expenditures, 2004[a]

	All Private Sector Establishments		Small Private Sector Establishments		Low-Paid Private Sector Jobs	
	Log Voluntary Benefits	Log Total Compensation	Log Voluntary Benefits	Log Total Compensation	Log Voluntary Benefits	Log Total Compensation
	(1)	(2)	(3)	(4)	(5)	(6)
1 if Union-Covered Job	0.191*	0.289*	0.397*	0.395*	0.474*	0.116*
	(0.034)	(0.014)	(0.084)	(0.040)	(0.129)	(0.017)
Log Total Compensation	1.795*	—	2.079*	—	3.017*	—
	(0.047)		(0.097)		(0.214)	
3-digit Industry and Occupation Effects?	Yes	Yes	Yes	Yes	Yes	Yes
Implied Voice Effect[b]	26.93 percent		32.62 percent		57.56 percent	
Adjusted R^2	0.643	0.729	0.577	0.681	0.389	0.405
Sample Size	32,804	32,804	6,618	6,618	5,073	5,073

Notes: [a]Each entry reports the OLS coefficient and robust standard error (also adjusted for clustering by establishment). Each regression also includes control variables for establishment size (two categories) (except in columns 3 and 4), and region (eight categories) and is weighted using establishment-occupation weights. Small establishments (columns 3 and 4) are those with fewer than 50 employees. Low-paid jobs (columns 5 and 6) are those with total compensation less than the twenty-fifth percentile. [b]See text. *Denotes statistical significance at the 0.05 level, two-tailed test.

Source: Employer Costs for Employee Compensation data, March 2004.

of these establishment-level data is that there isn't any information on the characteristics of the jobholders so detailed industry and occupation effects are instead relied on to control for differences across jobs. Table 6.7 reports the results for three private sector samples: all establishments, establishments with fewer than 50 employees, and jobs with total compensation less than the twenty-fifth percentile. These last two specifications are important because Freeman (1981) found that the union effect on voluntary benefits expenditures was particularly strong in small and low-paid establishments — comparing the union coefficient in columns 3 and 5 with column 1 shows that the same conclusion is still true 30 years later.

Recall that one of the main advantages of the ECEC data over individual-level data such as the CPS is that the ECEC contains a measure of total compensation. This is important because the collective voice effect implies that unions will increase benefit expenditures holding compensation constant. In columns 1, 3, and 5, the union effect — holding total compensation constant — is positive and statistically significant. In short, the earlier result that the total effect of unions on employee benefits is a mixture of a monopoly effect and a collective voice effect remains true.

To estimate the relative magnitude of these two effects, Freeman (1981, equation 1) decomposes the total union effect into (1) the effect holding compensation constant (the collective voice effect) and (2) the effect of compensation on benefits holding unionism constant multiplied by the effect of unions on compensation. This second effect captures the extent to which union benefits are higher because unions raise total compensation — in other words, the monopoly effect. Applying this decomposition to all private sector establishments, the results in column 1 of Table 6.7 show that the point estimate for the effect of compensation on benefits holding unionism constant is 1.795 while the effect of unionism holding compensation constant is 0.191. To complete the decomposition, we need the effect of unions on total compensation — this point estimate of 0.289 is reported in column 2. The total union effect on benefits is therefore 0.191 + 1.795 * 0.289 = 0.710. This implies that the collective voice effect is 26.93 percent of the total (0.191 ÷ 0.710).[15] The collective voice effect is slightly larger in small establishments and is over 50 percent of the total effect in low-paid jobs.

In alternative specifications, a similar qualitative pattern of results is apparent, but with differing magnitudes for the collective voice effect. For example, using regressions that include both fixed establishment effects and two-digit occupation effects, the estimated union effect on voluntary benefits expenditures is 0.156 with a t-statistic in excess of four and an implied collective voice effect of nearly 70 percent. Using levels instead of logarithms also yields the conclusion that the overall effect of unions on benefits is a combination of monopoly and collective voice effects.[16]

In sum, the broad pattern of results reported by Freeman (1981) and Freeman and Medoff (1984) remains true 30 years later. Jobs that are represented by a union have total expenditures on voluntary benefit items significantly higher than similar nonunion jobs — between 15 and 40 percent higher with total compensation held constant, and perhaps as much as 70 percent higher overall.[17] The union effect on benefits is also more pronounced for lower paid establishments and for small establishments. And the union effect on employee benefits continues to include a mixture of monopoly and collective voice effects. However, depending on the specification, the relative importance of these two effects varies considerably — the collective voice effect might account for as little as 25 percent or as much as 75 percent of the total union effect on employee benefits expenditures.

VII. Family-Friendly Policies

A category of employee benefits that has received substantially greater public attention since the publication of *What Do Unions Do?* is family-friendly policies that aim to help employees strike a balance between work and family responsibilities (Bailyn et al., 2001; Williams, 2000). Examples include paid parental leave, on-site or subsidized childcare, job-sharing arrangements, and flexible work schedules. As these benefits increase in importance, a new question for what unions do to non-wage forms of compensation is whether labor unions increase or decrease the provision of family-friendly benefits. Budd and Mumford (2004) is the most explicit analysis of this question to-date.[18]

Using the British WERS98 data set, Budd and Mumford (2004) find that British workplaces with at least one recognized union are more likely to have parental leave, special paid leave for short-term family issues, job-sharing options, and to a lesser extent, subsidized childcare. Of additional interest for this review, Budd and Mumford further try to distinguish between monopoly and collective voice effects in the provision of family-friendly policies. Lacking good measures of total compensation (the usual method for isolating the collective-voice effect), this study instead analyzes whether family-friendly policies in unionized workplaces are related to measures of monopoly power (such as workplace union density) and collective-voice (such as regular union meetings or workplace demographics). The two benefits that involve paid leave time (parental leave and special-paid leave) appear driven to be by monopoly power. In contrast, childcare, job-sharing arrangements, and work-at-home options — issues with potentially greater integrative rather than distributive aspects — are more strongly associated with measures of collective voice. While this is only one study, these first results support the extension of Freeman and Medoff's (1979, 1984) two faces of unionism beyond the more traditional benefits emphasized in the bulk of the literature to newer family-friendly policies.

In addition to the workplace-level data, the WERS98 data set used by Budd and Mumford (2004) also includes a rich linked component — 25 employees from many of the establishments were also randomly surveyed so the WERS98 data include both establishment and employee-level measures. As such, for several family-friendly policies there is information on both whether a manager indicates the policy is available in the workplace and whether an individual employee thinks it is available to him or her. In addition to the monopoly and collective-voice effects, therefore, the facilitation effect can also be analyzed in these data. Among workplaces with a family-friendly policy (according to the manager), large fractions of employees do not indicate that this policy is personally available to them. In other words, there appears to be a significant discrepancy between availability and awareness. Budd and Mumford (2004) find that this discrepancy decreases in the presence of a labor union for both parental-leave and job-sharing programs. This is consistent with the facilitation effect, such as through union-provided information so that unionized employees have a greater awareness of their benefits programs.[19]

VIII. Mandated Social Insurance Benefits

An aspect of employee benefits that does not receive much attention in *What Do Unions Do?* is required benefits — mandated social insurance programs such as social security, unemployment insurance (UI), and workers' compensation. But an analysis of this area is important because it reveals another aspect of what unions do in terms of benefits, and also provides additional evidence for the facilitation effect. As noted by Freeman (1981) and Freeman and Medoff (1984), expenditures on legally required benefits are not significantly different between union and nonunion employers. But instead of employer expenditures, consider the extent to which *comparable* union and nonunion employees — who are therefore equally entitled to the social insurance benefits — are able to use the social insurance programs in practice. Empirical analyses of a variety of U.S. mandated benefits programs consistently show that labor unions increase the effective implementation of these programs and help workers access their benefits (Weil, 1996).

There are several important reasons why unions might facilitate benefits receipt (Budd and McCall, 1997; Weil, 1996). The complexity of UI, workers' compensation, and the Family and Medical Leave Act (FMLA) can create ignorance and uncertainty among workers — raising such questions as: Am I eligible? What are the benefits? What do I have to do? — and therefore create a barrier to employees exercising their rights. To the extent that these programs are costly to employers, they have a disincentive to provide information and assistance to employees. But a union can internalize the costs and provide information through union newsletters, stewards, and training sessions. Because of the costs involved, employers might also object to requests to take family leaves under the FMLA or to the filing of UI or workers' compensation claims. Or an employer might (unlawfully) retaliate against individuals who try to exercise such rights. Unions can provide contractual protections — such as just-cause discipline and discharge requirements backed by a grievance procedure — as well as technical assistance and representation through administrative dispute resolution procedures — such as occurs for challenged workers' compensation and UI claims.

The empirical research is consistent with this union facilitation effect. Budd and Brey (2003) find that among hourly employees, unionized individuals are significantly more likely than nonunion employees to have heard about the Family and Medical Leave Act. Hirsch et al. (1997) attribute greater levels of workers' compensation receipt among unionized workers, compared to similar nonunion individuals, at least partially to union-provided information on workers' compensation systems and to union-provided help in pursuing workers' compensation claims. Similarly, hourly unionized workers are more likely to receive UI benefits than are comparable nonunion individuals (Budd and McCall, 1997, 2004).

The research on workers' compensation and UI benefits does not directly observe the facilitating behavior — though the anecdotal evidence is quite strong — but the research is careful to control for numerous factors in an attempt to make union and nonunion workers as comparable as possible in the statistical analyses. Moreover, Budd and McCall (1997) explicitly distinguish between incentive effects (which are ultimately rooted in monopoly power) and rights-facilitating effects (which can be socially beneficial like the collective-voice effect) of labor unions in increasing UI benefits receipt. In particular, union-negotiated supplemental unemployment benefit (SUB) plans provide an additional incentive for workers to apply for UI benefits, so in this way unions are not facilitating UI benefits receipt via socially-beneficial information provision and representation. But the union effect on UI benefits receipt is just as strong in industries without SUB plans. Rather, the empirical results are consistent with a union facilitation effect. Facilitation of mandated social insurance benefits receipt should be added to the list of what unions do.

IX. Monetary Forms of Non-Wage Compensation

Most of the research on unions and non-wage forms of compensation pertains to employee benefits, but Freeman and Medoff's (1984) two faces framework can also be (cautiously) applied to monetary forms of non-wage compensation such as lump-sum bonuses, profit-sharing plans, or stock options. As in the provision of benefits, union monopoly power can be used to win additional monetary forms of non-wage compensation as part of an increased total compensation package. In contrast, if there is a choice between a package of straight-time wages and lower employment on the one hand, and contingent compensation and higher employment on the other, the median worker who is likely not in jeopardy of losing his or her job is more likely to favor wages over contingent compensation (Kaufman, 2002).[20] As such, the collective-voice aspect of unionism predicts that unions will decrease the presence of contingent compensation.

There is an important dichotomy between this situation and employee benefits, however. In the benefits case, the collective-voice effect can be welfare-enhancing — total compensation is held constant so the employer is indifferent while workers can be better off with benefits. In the contingent compensation case, an employer is unlikely to be indifferent between contingent and noncontingent compensation. As such, the union might be using its monopoly power to satisfy the preferences of the median worker for wages rather than contingent compensation. In terms of its effect on aggregate welfare, this should be considered as a monopoly effect rather than a collective- voice effect.[21]

Turning to the empirical record, Freeman and Kleiner (1990) compare establishments that undergo a union organizing drive to a nonunion control group that doesn't experience any union activity during the sampling time frame. On average, among the locations that are newly unionized with a first contract successfully negotiated, the incidence of profit-sharing plans falls by 12 percentage points whereas over the same period of time, the control group incidence increased by 8 percentage points. Ng and Maki (1994) also find a negative effect of unions on the incidence of profit-sharing plans. A survey of Michigan manufacturing firms similarly reveals that unionized operations are less likely to have profit-sharing or gainsharing plans than nonunion facilities (Cooke, 1994). Within a sample of worker incentive plans, Ittner and Larcker (2002) find that union representation increases the frequency of worker-related measures of performance, such as productivity or safety, relative to nonworker measures, such as financial performance metrics.

The literature on lump-sum bonuses highlights some of the union resistance to contingent compensation, but estimates of union-nonunion differences in the relative frequencies of these plans are difficult to find. Within the U.S. unionized sector, lump-sum bonuses were rare before the concession bargaining period in the 1980s, but then increased in frequency as business sought to relieve labor cost pressures (Bell and Neumark, 1993; Erickson and Ichino, 1994). Martin and Heetderks (1994) further document negative employee attitudes towards lump-sum payments. These patterns are consistent with monopoly union power being insufficiently strong to resist the substitution of lump-sum payments for wages in a concessionary environment.

X. Conclusions

In the twenty years since the publication of *What Do Unions Do?*, employee benefits and contingent forms of non-wage compensation have increased in importance and scope in human resources and industrial relations practice and policy. Nevertheless, Freeman and Medoff's (1984) seminal work, and the associated research in Freeman (1981, 1985), has stood the test of time. The theoretical and empirical agenda for research on unions and non-wage forms of compensation established in those works continues to be the leading framework for conceptualizing and analyzing this important issue.

Freeman and Medoff's two faces of unionism is clear and extremely insightful. The textbook neoclassical economics model considers labor unions as labor market monopolies. The monopoly effect of labor unions on employee benefits predicts that unions increase benefits because unions can use their monopoly power to extract greater compensation, including benefits, from employers. Breaking out of the textbook neoclassical economics model, unions are institutions of collective employee voice. The collective-voice effect of unions on employee benefits predicts that unions increase benefits because as a democratic, collective institution, unions will promote the preferences of average rather than marginal workers. As average workers have greater seniority and less mobility, they are widely assumed to desire more benefits and less monetary compensation. The key insight is that while the monopoly and collective voice effects both predict that unions increase benefit levels, the aggregate welfare effects are very different. In a textbook model, the monopoly effect distorts the optimal competitive allocation of workers and resources and is therefore economically and socially harmful (to all but the unionized employees). But if the world is more complex than the textbook model, the collective-voice effect — which does not increase total compensation — can be economically and socially beneficial.

The contributions of Freeman (1981, 1984, 1985) and Freeman and Medoff (1984) to the understanding of unions and non-wage forms of compensation are magnified by the fact that these works are still among the most careful empirical analyses of this topic.[22] Using a variety of data sources, these works found that unions do in fact increase benefit levels. Moreover, contrary to the conventional view in the monopoly tradition, Freeman (1981, 1984, 1985) and Freeman and Medoff (1984) document that empirically, the monopoly effect is only half of the story. Roughly half of the estimated union effect on employee benefits in the United States is due to the collective-voice effect.

Subsequent research — in Australia, Canada, and Great Britain as well as the United States — has consistently found that unions increase employee benefit levels, especially for employer-provided health insurance benefits and pension plans. Both the monopoly and collective-voice effects also continue to be supported by the data. And new research implies that this framework also applies to the emerging area of family-friendly benefits. To this catalog of what unions do, however, should also be added the facilitation of awareness and use of existing benefits, including mandated social insurance benefits.

The social importance of the interlinkages between labor unions and employee benefits is underscored by the declining trends in the fraction of workers who have health insurance and pensions — which has coincided with a decline in U.S. union density. In fact, Buchmueller et al. (2002) find that the union density decline can explain approximately 25 percent of the decline in aggregate health insurance between 1983 and 1997. Similarly, Bloom and Freeman (1992) estimate that 20–25 percent of the decline in pension coverage in the 1980s can be linked to the decline in union density. The social importance of the nexus between unions and benefits is also apparent in the problem of unfunded pension liabilities — General Motors' pension plan, for example, was under-funded by $19.3 billion in 2002. The immediate cause of this problem was the extended bear market for stocks, but one underlying issue is the generous defined-benefit pension plans negotiated by unions in autos, steel, airlines, and elsewhere. At the extreme, the quasi-governmental Pension Benefit Guaranty Corporation steps in and covers pension liabilities when companies file for bankruptcy — to a certain extent, then, the costs of labor unions' monopoly face pension gains, and of companies' funding strategies, are shifted to the public at large.

What Do Unions Do? has perhaps had such a great impact on shaping the economic analysis of labor unions because it embraces mainstream economic principles. Freeman and Medoff (1984) concede the core economic belief that labor unions are distortionary monopolizing agents, but go on to show that unions can also have positive welfare effects if there are issues with public goods and externalities. These positive welfare effects are the basis of the collective-voice face, but the underlying market imperfections are never used to question the unquestionable — the validity of the negative monopoly face. In neoclassical economic analysis, the balanced scorecard for labor unions is therefore a mixture of the negative monopoly face and the positive collective-voice face. However, scholars have long questioned whether labor markets are competitive (Kaufman, 1988). With respect to employee benefits, the empirical evidence generally fails to find that benefit levels can be completely explained by compensating differentials that result from competitive market pressures (Montgomery and Shaw, 1997). If labor markets are not perfectly competitive, even the monopoly face of labor unions might be economically and socially beneficial.

In particular, the industrial relations model of the employment relationship is premised on an inherent conflict of interest between employers and employees interacting in imperfect labor markets. The employment relationship is modeled as a bargaining problem between stakeholders with competing interests such that employment outcomes depend on each stakeholder's relative bargaining power (Budd, 2004; Budd et al., 2004). As such, when bargaining power between corporate employers and individual workers is significantly unequal, substantial social and economic ills can result: wages insufficient for a decent life and for sufficient purchasing power to support economic activity; dangerous working conditions that people should not have to tolerate and that impose significant costs on local communities through medical costs, disability payments, and lost productivity; autocratic methods of supervision that violate standards of human dignity and de-motivate workers (Kaufman, 1997).

In the industrial relations model, therefore, the monopoly face of labor unions can be socially beneficial as it offsets corporate monopoly power and other labor market imperfections. In fact, the National Labor Relations Act of 1935 seeks to protect the formation of labor unions at least partly to promote the monopoly face: Labor union power that offsets corporate power and raises wages will boost consumer purchasing and therefore stimulate aggregate demand (Kaufman, 1996). Additionally, if firms have monopoly power in product markets and therefore earn above-normal profits, the monopoly wage gains of labor unions look less like a misallocation of resources (which is unambiguously negative with respect to economic welfare) and more like a redistribution of rents from capital to labor (which has ambiguous effects on economic welfare). Again, the monopoly face of labor unions is not necessarily harmful to aggregate welfare, and might be socially beneficial, if the assumptions of the textbook economic model are not fulfilled.

In conclusion, the effect of labor unions on non-wage forms of compensation is a microcosm of greater debates over the roles of unions in the economy and society. *What Do Unions Do?* demonstrates that unions might benefit some at the expense of others, but also that unions might serve the greater good, both economically and socially. The evidence twenty years later continues to support both faces, as well as the socially-beneficial contribution of facilitating the receipt of existing benefits and mandated social insurance programs. Ultimately, therefore, the evaluation of the balanced scorecard of the effect of unions on non-wage forms of compensation depends more on personal, subjective beliefs about the appropriate balance between efficiency, equity, and employee voice. The continuing power of *What Do Unions Do?* is in providing the framework for approaching this evaluation from an informed perspective.

Notes

*   I thank Bruce Kaufman for helpful comments and acknowledge the Department of Trade and Industry, the Economic and Social Research Council, the Advisory, Conciliation and Arbitration Service, and the Policy Studies Institute as the originators of the 1998 Workplace Employee Relations Survey data, and the Data Archive at the University of Essex as the distributor of the data. I also thank Michael Lettau at the Bureau of Labor Statistics for his help with the Employer Costs for Employee Compensation data and his hospitality while I analyzed these data at the Bureau of Labor Statistics. None of these organizations bears any responsibility for the authors' analysis and interpretation of the data.

1.   For a review of the research on employee benefits or contingent compensation more generally, see Broderick and Gerhart (1997) and Fossum and McCall (1997).
2.   For a more careful discussion of various models of union objectives, including the traditional monopoly model, see Kaufman (2002) and the references therein.
3.   See Kaufman (2002) and the references therein for a discussion of the median voter model and its applications to union objectives. Freeman (1981, 1985) further shows that in addition to the median voter model, if a union acts as an optimizing cartel to maximize total worker surplus, unionized workplaces will be more likely to have employee benefits if average workers have a greater preference for benefits than marginal workers.
4.   If the median worker prefers predictable, noncontingent compensation rather than contingent compensation and higher employment, the logic of the median voter model also suggests that collective voice will lower the incidence of contingent compensation (Kaufman, 2002).

5. Other early examinations of unions and employee benefits include Duncan (1976), Solnick (1978), Leigh (1981), and Feldman and Scheffler (1982).
6. The magnitudes of the various effects reported in Freeman and Medoff (1984) are significantly higher than reported in Freeman (1981), presumably because of differences in the control variables, but the resulting conclusion that the monopoly and collective voice effects are roughly equally important holds true.
7. Freeman and Medoff (1984) and Freeman (1985) also raise the issue of the investment behavior of union pension funds. Dorsey and Turner (1990) subsequently found no differences in investments and rates of return between single-employer union and nonunion funds, but found that collectively-bargained multi-employer funds had less risky investments and lower returns. No evidence of social investing by union pension funds was uncovered.
8. The studies that have data on other employee benefits often also find a positive union effect on their provision, such as for employer-provided life insurance (Wunnava and Ewing, 1999). Sheets and Yuan (1988) find that U.S. firms with a higher fraction of unionized employees are more likely to provide employee termination benefits — employee transition assistance, severance pay, and advance notification of upcoming layoffs. Green and Potepan (1988) find that unions increase paid vacation time among U.S. workers, and Green (1997) finds a similar result for British workplaces. Family-friendly benefits are discussed separately in a subsequent section.
9. The CPS is a monthly survey of approximately 60,000 households that includes labor market information representative of the U.S. noninstitutional population aged 16 and older.
10. WERS98 is the fourth in an on-going series of surveys and follows the 1980, 1984, and 1990 Workplace Industrial Relations Surveys. WERS98 is a nationally representative survey of workplaces with 10 or more employees containing a vast amount of information on diverse aspects of human resources and industrial relations. Face-to-face interviews for WERS98 were conducted with a manager (with day-to-day responsibility for employee relations) at 2,191 workplaces between October 1997 and June 1998. WERS98 is a stratified random sample and larger workplaces and some industries are over-represented; the results in Table 5 therefore use workplace sampling weights. For additional details on WERS98, see Cully et al. (1999) and Forth and Kirby (2000).
11. Technically, the data used herein measure employers' costs of benefits rather than expenditures, but the narrow distinction is not important for the topic at hand. "Expenditure" is used in this chapter for convenience and to be consistent with Freeman (1981) and Freeman and Medoff (1984).
12. The results reported herein are based on the micro data used to calculate the employment cost index estimates that are published quarterly by the U.S. Department of Labor's Bureau of Labor Statistics (BLS). The BLS collects these data as part of the National Compensation Survey.
13. For public sector jobs, the voluntary benefits share for union jobs is 26.4 percent — almost identical to the private sector share — while the nonunion share is 23.5 percent — much higher than in the private sector.
14. The comparisons are not perfect because Freeman and Medoff (1984) report their results for production workers and also because the categories of benefits are not identical between the earlier and later surveys.
15. For the public sector, the overall union effect is smaller, but the amount attributable to the collective voice effect is 42.86 percent of the total effect.
16. Freeman (1981, equation 13) also develops a structural model to account for possible simultaneity bias in the levels specifications. This does not change my conclusions

herein. For example, in a levels regression of voluntary benefits expenditure with three-digit industry and occupation effects, the OLS estimate for unionism, holding compensation constant, is 2.175 and the corrected coefficient is not statistically different (2.215). Instrumenting for total compensation also does not change the results.

17. The overall union effect is lowest for the fixed effects specifications — in the neighborhood of 20–25 percent.

18. Other studies analyze the determinants of employer-provided, family-friendly benefits, and unionization is sometimes included as an explanatory variable in statistical analyses, but unionism is not the focus of attention in these studies (Deitch and Huffman, 2001; Kelly and Dobbin, 1999; Osterman, 1995). Gerstel and Clawson (2001) investigate union leaders' views on work-family issues.

19. Some degree of caution is warranted because in the WERS98 data, discrepancies between the managers' and employees' responses might stem from unequal coverage of family-friendly policies rather than employee ignorance. Budd and Mumford's (2004) analyses try to limit this possibility by focusing on workplaces in which other benefits are equally provided and by excluding part-time and temporary workers. Further research with more precise questions, however, is warranted.

20. Chelius and Smith (1990) investigate profit sharing and employment stability.

21. This effect on the incidence of contingent compensation should not be confused with the operational argument that conditional upon the existence of a contingent-compensation plan, the collective-voice effect of unions can potentially increase aggregate welfare by making the plan more effective relative to a similar plan in a nonunion setting (Cooke, 1994; Eaton and Voos, 1994).

22. Perhaps the most significant methodological advance occurred very recently. Buchmueller et al. (2002) apply a semi-parametric decomposition technique to the analysis of union effects on the employer's share of health insurance premium payments.

References

Allen, Steven G. and Robert L. Clark. "Unions, Pension Wealth, and Age-Compensation Profiles." *Industrial and Labor Relations Review* 39 (July 1986): 502–17.

Bailyn, Lotte, Robert Drago, and Thomas Kochan. *Integrating Work and Family Life: A Holistic Approach.* Alfred P. Sloan Foundation Work-Family Policy Network, 2001. Retrieved November 20, 2002 from http://lsir.la.psu.edu/workfam/WorkFamily.pdf.

Bell, Linda A. and David Neumark. "Lump-Sum Payments and Profit-Sharing Plans in the Union Sector of the United States Economy." *Economic Journal* 103 (May 1993): 602–19.

Belman, Dale and John S. Heywood. "Direct and Indirect Effects of Unionization and Government Employment on Fringe Benefit Provision." *Journal of Labor Research* 12 (Spring 1991): 111–22.

Bloom, David E. and Richard B. Freeman. "The Fall in Private Pension Coverage in the United States." *American Economic Review* 82 (May 1992): 539–45.

Broderick, Renae and Barry Gerhart. "Non-Wage Compensation." In David Lewin, Daniel J.B. Mitchell, and Mahmood A. Zaidi, eds. *The Human Resource Management Handbook, Part III.* Greenwich, Conn.: JAI Press, 1997, pp. 95–135.

Brown, Charles. "Equalizing Differences in the Labor Market." *Quarterly Journal of Economics* 94 (February 1980): 113–34.

Buchmueller, Thomas C., John DiNardo, and Robert G. Valletta. "Union Effects on Health Insurance Provision and Coverage in the United States." *Industrial and Labor Relations Review* 55 (July 2002): 610–27.

Budd, John W. "Fringe Benefits and Union Status: Members Versus Covered Non-members." *Proceedings of the Fiftieth Annual Meeting.* Madison, Wisc.: Industrial Relations Research Association, 1998, pp. 250–58.

———. *Employment with a Human Face: Balancing Efficiency, Equity, and Voice.* Ithaca, N.Y.: ILR Press, 2004.

——— and Angela Brey. "Unions and Family Leave: Early Experience under the Family and Medical Act." *Labor Studies Journal* 28 (Fall 2003): 85–105.

Budd, John W., Rafael Gomez, and Noah M. Meltz. "Nice Guys Can Finish First: Balancing Competing Interests As an Industrial Relations Paradigm." In Bruce Kaufman, ed. *Theoretical Perspectives on Work and the Employment Relationship.* Champaign, Ill.: Industrial Relations Research Association, 2004.

Budd, John W. and Brian P. McCall. "The Effect of Unions on the Receipt of Unemployment Insurance Benefits." *Industrial and Labor Relations Review* 50 (April 1997): 478–92.

———. "Unions and Unemployment Insurance Benefits Receipt: Evidence from the CPS." *Industrial Relations* 43 (April 2004): 331–55.

Budd, John W. and Karen Mumford. "Trade Unions and Family-Friendly Policies in Britain." *Industrial and Labor Relations Review* 53 (January 2004): 204–22.

Budd, John W. and In-Gang Na. "The Union Membership Wage Premium for Employees Covered by Collective Bargaining Agreements." *Journal of Labor Economics* 18 (October 2000): 783–807.

Butler, Richard J. *The Economics of Social Insurance and Employee Benefits.* Boston: Kluwer, 1999.

Chelius, James and Robert S. Smith. "Profit Sharing and Employment Stability." *Industrial and Labor Relations Review* 43 (February 1990): S256–S273.

Cooke, William N. "Employee Participation Programs, Group-Based Incentives, and Company Performance: A Union-Nonunion Comparison." *Industrial and Labor Relations Review* 47 (July 1994): 594–609.

Cully, Mark, Stephen Woodland, Andrew O'Reilly, and Gill Dix. *Britain at Work: As Depicted by the 1998 Workplace Employee Relations Survey.* London: Routledge, 1999.

Deitch, Cynthia H. and Matt L. Huffman. "Family Responsive Benefits and the Two-Tiered Labor Market." In Rosanna Hertz and Nancy L. Marshall, eds. *Working Families: The Transformation of the American Home.* Berkeley: University of California Press, 2001, pp. 103–30.

Department of Trade and Industry. *Workplace Employee Relations Survey: Cross-Section, 1998* (computer file), 4th ed. Colchester: The Data Archive (distributor), 22 December 1999. SN: 3955.

Dorsey, Stuart and John J. Turner. "Union-Nonunion Differences in Pension Fund Investments and Earnings." *Industrial and Labor Relations Review* 43 (July 1990): 542–55.

Duncan, Greg G. "Earnings Functions and Nonpecuniary Benefits." *Journal of Human Resources* 11 (Fall 1976): 462–83.

Eaton, Adrienne E. and Paula B. Voos. "Productivity-Enhancing Innovations in Work Organization, Compensation, and Employee Participation in the Union versus the Nonunion Sectors." In David Lewin and Donna Sockell, eds. *Advances in Industrial and Labor Relations, Volume 6.* Greenwich, Conn.: JAI Press, 1994, pp. 63–109.

Erickson, Christopher L. and Andrea C. Ichino. "Lump-Sum Bonuses in Union Contracts." In David Lewin and Donna Sockell, eds. *Advances in Industrial and Labor Relations, Volume 6.* Greenwich, Conn.: JAI Press, 1994, pp. 183–218.

Feldman, Roger and Richard Scheffler. "The Union Impact on Hospital Wages and Fringe Benefits." *Industrial and Labor Relations Review* 35 (January 1982): 196–206.

Feuille, Peter, John T. Delaney, and Wallace Hendricks. "Police Bargaining, Arbitration, and Fringe Benefits." *Journal of Labor Research* 6 (Winter 1985): 1–20.

Forth, John and Simon Kirby. *Guide to the Analysis of the Workplace Employee Relations Survey 1998*. London: National Institute for Economic and Social Research, 2000. Retrieved November 25, 2002 from http://www.niesr.ac.uk/niesr/wers98/Guide.htm.

Fossum, John A. and Brian P. McCall. "Pay and Reward for Performance." In David Lewin, Daniel J.B. Mitchell, and Mahmood A. Zaidi, eds. *The Human Resource Management Handbook, Part III*. Greenwich, Conn.: JAI Press, 1997, pp. 111–43.

Fosu, Augustin Kwasi. "Nonwage Benefits As a Limited-Dependent Variable: Implications for the Impact of Unions." *Journal of Labor Research* 14 (Winter 1993): 29–43.

Freeman, Richard B. "Individual Mobility and Union Voice in the Labor Market." *American Economic Review* 66 (May 1976): 361–68.

_____. "Unionism and the Dispersion of Wages." *Industrial and Labor Relations Review* 34 (October 1980): 3–23.

_____. "The Effect of Unionism on Fringe Benefits." *Industrial and Labor Relations Review* 34 (July 1981): 489–509.

_____. "Union Wage Practices and Wage Dispersion within Establishments." *Industrial and Labor Relations Review* 36 (October 1982): 3–21.

_____. "Longitudinal Analyses of the Effects of Trade Unions." *Journal of Labor Economics* 2 (January 1984): 1–26.

_____. "Unions, Pensions, and Union Pension Funds." In David A. Wise, ed., *Pensions, Labor, and Individual Choice*. Chicago: University of Chicago Press, 1985, pp. 89–121.

_____. and Morris M. Kleiner. "The Impact of New Unionization on Wages and Working Conditions." *Journal of Labor Economics* 8 (January 1990): S8–S25.

Freeman, Richard B.. and James L. Medoff. "The Two Faces of Unionism." *Public Interest* (Fall 1979): 69–93.

_____. *What Do Unions Do?* New York: Basic Books, 1984.

Gerstel, Naomi and Dan Clawson. "Unions' Responses to Family Concerns." *Social Problems* 48 (May 2001): 277–97.

Green, Francis. "Union Recognition and Paid Holiday Entitlement." *British Journal of Industrial Relations* 35 (June 1997): 243–55.

_____ and Michael J. Potepan. "Vacation Time and Unionism in the U.S. and Europe." *Industrial Relations* 27 (Spring 1988): 180–94.

Hirsch, Barry T., David A. Macpherson, and J. Michael DuMond. "Workers' Compensation Recipiency in Union and Nonunion Workplaces." *Industrial and Labor Relations Review* 50 (January 1997): 213–36.

Ittner, Christopher D. and David F. Larcker. "Determinants of Performance Measure Choices in Worker Incentive Plans." *Journal of Labor Economics* 20 (April 2002): S58–S90.

Kaufman, Bruce E., ed. *How Labor Markets Work: Reflections on Theory and Practice* by John Dunlop, Clark Kerr, Richard Lester, and Lloyd Reynolds. Lexington, Mass.: Lexington Books, 1988.

_____. *The Origins and Evolution of the Field of Industrial Relations in the United States*. Ithaca, N.Y.: ILR Press, 1993.

_____. "Why the Wagner Act? Reestablishing Contact with its Original Purpose." In David Lewin, Bruce E. Kaufman, and Donna Sockell, eds. *Advances in Industrial and Labor Relations, Volume 7*. Greenwich, Conn.: JAI Press, 1996, pp. 15–68.

_____. "Labor Markets and Employment Regulation: The View of the 'Old' Institutionalists." In Bruce E. Kaufman, ed. *Government Regulation of the Employment Relationship*. Madison, Wisc.: Industrial Relations Research Association, 1997, chapter 1.

_____. "Models of Union Wage Determination: What Have We Learned Since Dunlop and Ross?" *Industrial Relations* 41 (January 2002): 110–58.

Kelly, Erin and Frank Dobbin. "Civil Rights Law at Work: Sex Discrimination and the Rise of Maternity Leave Policies." *American Journal of Sociology* 105 (September 1999): 455–92.

Kornfeld, Robert. "The Effects of Union Membership on Wages and Employee Benefits: The Case of Australia." *Industrial and Labor Relations Review* 47 (October 1993): 114–28.

Leigh, Duane E. "The Effect of Unionism on Workers' Valuation of Future Pension Benefits." *Industrial and Labor Relations Review* 34 (July 1981): 510–21.

Lewis, H. Gregg. *Union Relative Wage Effects.* Chicago: University of Chicago Press, 1986.

Luchak, Andrew A. and Morley Gunderson. "What Do Employees Know About Their Pension Plan?" *Industrial Relations* 39 (October 2000): 646–70.

Martin, James E. and Thomas D. Heetderks "An Exploratory Study of Employee Perceptions of Lump-Sum Payments." In David Lewin and Donna Sockell, eds. *Advances in Industrial and Labor Relations, Volume 6.* Greenwich, Conn.: JAI Press, 1994, pp. 163–82.

Miller, Paul and Charles Mulvey. "Trade Unions, Collective Voice, and Fringe Benefits." *Economic Record* 68 (June 1992): 125–41.

Montgomery, Edward and Kathryn Shaw. "Pensions and Wage Premia." *Economic Inquiry* 35 (July 1997): 510–22.

Ng, Ignace and Dennis Maki. "Trade Union Influence on Human Resource Management Practices." *Industrial Relations* 33 (January 1994): 121–35.

Osterman, Paul. "Work/Family Programs and the Employment Relationship." *Administrative Science Quarterly* 40 (December 1995): 681–700.

Renaud, Stéphane. "Unions, Wages, and Total Compensation in Canada: An Empirical Study." *Relations Industrielles* 53 (Fall 1998): 710–29.

Rosen, Sherwin. "Hedonic Prices and Implicit Markets: Product Differentiation in Pure Competition." *Journal of Political Economy* 82 (January 1974): 34–55.

Sheets, Robert G. and Ting Yuan. "Determinants of Employee-Termination Benefits in Organizations." *Administrative Science Quarterly* 33 (December 1988): 607–24.

Slichter, Sumner H., James J. Healy, and E. Robert Livernash. *The Impact of Collective Bargaining on Management.* Washington, D.C.: Brookings Institution, 1960.

Solnick, Loren M. "Unionism and Employer Fringe Benefit Expenditures." *Industrial Relations* 17 (February 1978): 102–17.

Swidinsky, R. and M. Kupferschmidt. "Longitudinal Estimates of the Union Effects on Wages, Wage Dispersion and Pension Fringe Benefits." *Relations Industrielles* 46 (Autumn 1991): 819–38.

Weil, David. "Regulating the Workplace: The Vexing Problem of Implementation." In David Lewin, Bruce E. Kaufman, and Donna Sockell, eds. *Advances in Industrial and Labor Relations, Volume 7.* Greenwich, Conn.: JAI Press, 1996, pp. 247–86.

Williams, Joan. *Unbending Gender: Why Family and Work Conflict and What to Do About It.* New York: Oxford University Press, 2000.

Wunnava, Phanindra V. and Bradley T. Ewing. "Union-Nonunion Differentials and Establishment Size: Evidence from the NLSY." *Journal of Labor Research* 20 (Spring 1999): 177–83.

Zax, Jeffrey S. "Wages, Nonwage Compensation, and Municipal Unions." *Industrial Relations* 27 (Fall 1988): 301–17.

7

What Do Unions Do for Economic Performance?

Barry T. Hirsch

I. Introduction

The publication in 1984 of Richard Freeman and James Medoff's *What Do Unions Do?*, which summarized and synthesized results from their broad-based research program, was a landmark in labor economics and industrial relations. *What Do Unions Do?* quickly changed the subject matter and approach for scholars studying unions. The models (or descriptions) of unions employed by labor economists were extended to include a collective voice face of unions in addition to its microeconomic monopoly face. Empirical analyses of unions, which once focused almost exclusively on union wage effects, began to address the large variety of topics studied in *What Do Unions Do?* Industrial relations scholars, who had never abandoned a broad multi-disciplinary approach to what unions do, increasingly were expected to include data and econometric analysis in their research.

The appearance of *What Do Unions Do?* coincided with the beginnings of the long-term decline in private sector unionism in the United States. Although unionism was declining, the steady stream of research fueled by *What Do Unions Do?* provided us with a far richer understanding of the nature of unions and collective bargaining than we would otherwise have had. Twenty years later, the approach adopted and empirical regularities found by Freeman and Medoff hold up reasonably well. The continuing decline of private sector unionism, however, eventually eroded interest in and research on this topic. Freeman and other scholars increasingly have turned their attention toward issues such as public sector unions, alternative union and nonunion forms of worker representation, and workplace institutions outside the United States.

This essay focuses on perhaps the most contentious topic in *What Do Unions Do?* — union effects on productivity, growth, profits, and investment. Contentious first because the monopoly and voice approaches to unions provide different expectations about union effects on performance, and second, because the empirical evidence on which conclusions were based was extremely limited in 1984 (and remains limited today). Much of their story on unions and economic performance holds up well.[1] Freeman and Medoff rightly emphasize that union effects on productivity vary with respect to the labor relations environment and degree of competition, that unions generally decrease profitability, and that there exists slower growth in the union sector of the economy. Subsequent research suggesting that average union productivity effects are close to zero does not support Freeman and Medoff's conclusion that unions are generally good for productivity. Although they conclude that monopoly profits provide the principal source for union wage increases, subsequent research suggests that unions also tax the normal returns to long-lived tangible and intangible capital investments. And while it is true that much of the negative relationship between unions and growth is not causal, slower growth is partly attributable to the lower profits and investment resulting from union rent seeking.

I first summarize what Freeman and Medoff say about unions and performance in *What Do Unions Do?* A brief section on issues of measurement follows. I then provide an analysis of subsequent evidence on unions and performance, focusing on studies examining the U.S. private sector. This lengthy section is not intended to provide an exhaustive survey of each topic but, rather, to evaluate the themes, evidence, and conclusions presented in *What Do Unions Do?*[2] The next section is rather speculative, looking forward and asking what types of policy changes might better encourage workplace voice and participation in a world of declining unionism. A concluding section follows.

II. What Do Freeman and Medoff Do?

Freeman and Medoff examine the effects of unions on firm performance in two chapters of *What Do Unions Do?* Chapter 11 asks whether unionism is good or bad for productivity. Chapter 12 provides evidence on unions and profitability. They rightly emphasize that: "What unions do to productivity is one of the key factors in assessing the overall economic impact of unions" (p. 180). They conclude that in general unions tend to increase productivity, although the effect varies to no small extent with respect to time and place and the associated labor relations environment. In contrast, unionism almost always lowers profitability. Taken together, these pieces of evidence present a paradox. In Freeman and Medoff's words: "Beneficial to organized workers, almost always; beneficial to the economy, in many ways; but harmful to the bottom line of company balance sheets: this is the paradox of American trade unionism, which underlies some of the ambivalence of our national policies toward the institution" (p. 190).

Freeman and Medoff identify three routes through which unions affect productivity. One is via price-theoretic effects from standard microeconomic theory. Given union monopoly wage gains, firms may shift toward more capital and higher quality labor. As discussed later, a union wage gain need not produce such responses, but this point can be ignored for now. Although capital deepening or skill upgrading increase output per hour, this is not what is being tested (in principle) in the unions-productivity literature. Rather, the thesis is that unions increase "technical efficiency" — output for a given mix of inputs. Empirical literature in this area is clear on the issue, attempting to quantitatively control for capital investment and labor quality. If unions affect output per worker exclusively by moving up a labor demand schedule, such price-theoretic responses should not show up as union productivity gains in the empirical estimates.[3]

As outlined by Freeman and Medoff, what should show up in the empirical literature (which controls for the input mix) is the net effect of restrictive union work rules and voice/response interaction, the former depressing and latter raising productivity (1984, Figure 11–1, p. 163). These categories should be interpreted broadly. "Restrictive work rules" can include not only inefficient staffing requirements ("featherbedding"), but also any decrease in productivity resulting from limited incentives for worker effort or restrictions on management discretion (obviously, union formalization of the workplace governance structure can increase or decrease productivity).[4] As for voice/response, Freeman and Medoff highlight lower quits and improved personnel policies as key to increased productivity, emphasizing that positive outcomes require good labor relations. Productivity enhancing institutional response might also include a "shock effect" to management induced by higher union wages. Whether such a response should be considered a union voice/response effect or a monopoly effect is not clear, raising the more fundamental question as to whether the two faces of unions are truly distinct. I return briefly to this question. Given both positive and negative effects, the net effect of unions on productivity is an empirical question.

Empirical evidence on unions and productivity was rather sketchy in 1984; it remains less than clear-cut today. As Freeman and Medoff state: "This 'answer' to the debate over what unions do to productivity is probably the most controversial and least widely accepted result in this book" (1984, p. 180). Freeman and Medoff summarize evidence on manufacturing studies and sector-specific studies in construction, wooden furniture, cement, and coal (1984, Table 11–1, p. 166). The strongest evidence for a large positive effect of unions on productivity comes from Brown and Medoff's (1978) rightly influential study using manufacturing industry-by-state data. Depending on one's assumption regarding capital usage, one obtains estimates of union effects on total factor productivity of either 20–25 percent or 10–15 percent. Additional unpublished work with Jonathan Leonard using 1972 and 1977 Census of Manufacturers data produces positive estimates of union productivity effects.

In contrast to the Brown and Medoff study, Clark's (1984) analysis of manufacturing lines of business indicated a –2 percent average difference in the productivity of union and nonunion businesses. Freeman and Medoff cite but do not emphasize Clark's results, despite the fact that business-level analysis has numerous advantages over Brown and Medoff's highly aggregated data.

Sector-specific studies using value-added measures of output during the 1970s indicate extremely large union productivity effects in construction and moderate productivity effects in wooden household furniture. Studies using physical output measures confirm large union productivity effects in construction. Clark's studies of cement plants indicate a moderate union productivity advantage (6–8 percent) in his cross-sectional analysis and a roughly similar increase in productivity among the relatively few plants changing from nonunion to union status. Among the more interesting results in Freeman and Medoff's table are productivity results in underground bituminous coal for four years, 1965, 1970, 1975, and 1980, with union productivity effects swinging from highly positive in 1965 to highly negative in 1975 and 1980. Freeman and Medoff link these changes to deterioration in labor relations within the industry, emphasizing that union effects in the workplace vary depending on labor and management policies and their working relationship.

Despite the rather mixed empirical evidence on productivity, even in 1984, Freeman and Medoff interpret these findings as follows: "In sum, most studies of productivity find that unionized establishments are more productive than otherwise comparable nonunion establishments" (1984, p. 169).

Freeman and Medoff recognize the importance of union effects on productivity growth as well as levels. They analyze three alternative data sets, in each case finding industry union density associated with slower productivity growth. The magnitude of the estimates is nontrivial (relative to mean growth rates), but none is statistically significant, reflecting the large variation across industries in growth rates and their relationship to unionism. Freeman and Medoff conclude: "In sum, current empirical evidence offers little support for the assertion that unionization is associated with lower (or higher) productivity advance" (p. 170).

The final sections of Chapter 11 explore *why* or *how* unions affect productivity. There is no single metric to be estimated here; rather the authors assemble various observations or findings across otherwise disparate studies. Each of their explanations fits into their collective voice/institutional response framework, although in different ways. They first give prominence to the Brown and Medoff (1978) estimate that one-fifth of the union productivity effect found in their study can be attributed to lower quit rates. They also emphasize Clark's (1980a) findings that cement plants switching from nonunion to union changed their plant managers, replacing previously authoritarian or paternalistic managerial practices with more professional and structured supervision and governance. Freeman and Medoff next cite studies showing a link between productivity at unionized plants and the industrial relations climate in those plants, as reflected in number of grievances. Returning to the coal industry, where productivity swung from positive to negative, Freeman and Medoff state (italics in original): "The lesson is that *unionism per se is neither a plus nor a minus to productivity. What matters is how unions and management interact at the workplace*" (p. 179). They then note the importance of competition, suggesting that the coal industry's deterioration in labor relations and failure to maintain productivity gains along with wage gains stems in part from limited competition in that sector. In the concluding section of their productivity chapter, the authors declare: "Higher productivity appears to run hand in hand with good industrial relations and to be spurred by competition in the product market, while lower productivity under unionism appears to exist under the opposite circumstances" (p. 180).

Chapter 12, entitled "But Unionism Lowers Profits," summarizes what at the time was very limited evidence on unions and profitability. Freeman and Medoff (1984, Table 12–1, p. 183) rely on their own unpublished work using aggregate industry data from the Census of Manufacturers or from the Internal Revenue Service, as well as line-of-business data subsequently published in Clark's (1984) paper. Clark's study finds that union plants realize a price-cost margin 16 percent lower than nonunion plants, and "quasi-rents divided by capital" 19 percent lower. The aggregate data likewise indicated substantially lower profits associated with unionism, but with a wider range of estimates. The authors also cite Ruback and Zimmerman's (1984) subsequently published study showing that stock values fall as a result of successful union organizing drives. Despite the paucity of data on profitability, they conclude that unions lower profits. Subsequent work fully supports this conclusion.

Evidence is less clear as to *whose profits* are hardest hit. Freeman and Medoff emphasize work using aggregate industry data showing that unions reduce profits substantially in highly concentrated industries, but not in low-concentration industries. They also cite a subsequently published paper by Salinger (1984) arriving at the same conclusion using company data (although concentration is only weakly related to market value in Salinger's study). As discussed below, Salinger's conclusion is based on a restrictive specification that *forces* the union profit effect to interact with concentration and other variables (Hirsch and Connolly, 1987). Freeman and Medoff downplay Clark's (1984) finding that the largest impact of unions on profits is among lines of business with *low* market shares, noting in a footnote Clark's "contrary result . . . limited to a special group of businesses rather than to the entire economy" (1984, p. 278, fn. 7). Freeman and Medoff conclude that "the union profit effect appears to take the form of a reduction of monopoly profits" (1984, p. 186). Freeman and Medoff, however, are quick to point out that lower profits, whatever their source, can be associated with lower investment and growth. They explore the relationship between concentration and growth, find conflicting evidence, and safely conclude that the evidence relating unions, profitability, concentration, and growth is mixed. They rightly recognize "an important point about the impact of unions on profits: there is little normative content in the direction of the effect per se; rather, what matter are the market conditions and routes by which unionism alters profits" (p. 189).

In summary, Freeman and Medoff conclude that "the evidence on profit-ability shows that, on average, unionism is harmful to the financial well-being of organized enterprises or sectors" (p. 190). Beneficial to organized workers but harmful to the bottom line of companies — this paradox of American labor unions is one that Freeman and Medoff fully recognize. I return to this point subsequently.

III. Two Faces Revisited: What Does Theory Do?

By the time that *What Do Unions Do?* was published in 1984, Freeman and Medoff's "two faces of unions" dichotomy (Freeman and Medoff, 1979; Freeman, 1980) had become a standard framework or cataloging device to address the labor market effects of unions and remains so twenty years later. Although not a formal model in the sense that economists typically use the term, the two-faces approach has provided a broad umbrella under which labor economists and industrial relations scholars either have organized their thoughts about what unions do or, less frequently, based their explicit theoretical models of union behavior. The beauty of the framework is that the two faces — monopoly and voice — provide a sufficiently accurate descrip-tion or shorthand for unions' principal activities, while at the same time being sufficiently broad to permit inclusion of a wide range of union effects in the workplace and economy.

The monopoly-voice distinction is not without limitations, however; the most serious is that these categories are neither distinct nor without ambigu-ity. Three examples should suffice. First, worker preferences and demand for wages, benefits, employment security, and working conditions depend in no small part on union bargaining power. Is this union's voice or monopoly face? Second, Freeman and Medoff stress that workplace outcomes depend crucially on management's response to its union. Is tighter management control in re-sponse to a union wage increases (a "shock effect") an example of labor union's voice/response or monopoly face? Or should one speak of a monopoly/response face? Finally, surveys indicate that workers have a desire for greater voice and cooperation in the workplace (Freeman and Rogers, 1999). Should this be considered an unsatisfied demand for union representation and the types of *collective* voice/response associated with unions? Or is it instead a desire for forms of individual voice and workplace interaction more typically found in nonunion than in union establishments (Kaufman, 2001)?

To address such questions, it is necessary to delineate a much clearer theory of what unions do. Fortunately, such an endeavor is not essential for this essay (but see the contribution to this volume by Addison and Belfield on union voice). Herein, it is sufficient to identify those elements associated with unions that are likely to improve or detract from productivity, growth, profits, and invest-ment. The monopoly/voice framework is a useful device to organize parts of the discussion. Once the focus turns to empirical evidence, one typically identifies (at best) the net effect of unions on various outcomes and rarely identifies the specific routes at work.

The monopoly face typically refers to what are mostly negative results emanating from union distortions relative to what might otherwise exist in a competitive labor market.[5] This face emphasizes the role of bargaining power, recognizing that the ability of unions to extract monopoly gains for its members is determined by the degree of competition and constraints on substitution facing both the employer and union. The standard microeconomic model has unions affecting labor (and product) market outcomes via wages above opportunity costs. The wage premium distorts relative factor prices and factor usage, thus producing a (presumably small) deadweight welfare loss. Independent of price distortions, unions may cause losses in output through strikes and decrease productivity in some workplaces through contractual work rules, reduced worker incentives, and limited managerial discretion.

Taken more broadly, the monopoly face can catalog any union effect that decreases efficiency or total value (the "size of the pie") to firm stakeholders (workers and owners) and consumers. Literature since *What Do Unions Do?* emphasizes unions' role in taxing returns on tangible and intangible capital and the resulting effects on profitability, investment, and growth.

The other face of unions is what Freeman and Medoff call "collective voice/institutional response." This face focuses on value-enhancing aspects of unions, emphasizing the potential role that collective bargaining has in improving the functioning of internal labor markets. For example, legally protected unions can effectively allow workers to express their preferences and exercise "collective voice" in the shaping of internal industrial relations policies. Collective bargaining may be more effective than individual bargaining or regulation in overcoming workplace public-goods problems and attendant free-rider problems. As the workers' agent, unions may facilitate the exercise of the workers' right to free speech, acquire information, monitor employer behavior, and formalize the workplace governance structure (Weil, 2003). Unions may better represent average or inframarginal workers, as opposed to workers who are most mobile and hired at the margin. In some settings, the exercise of collective voice should be associated with higher workplace productivity, an outcome that depends not only on effective voice, but also on a constructive "institutional response" and a cooperative labor relations environment. Freeman and Medoff emphasize that supportive management response to union voice is a necessary condition for positive union outcomes. Less clear is whether management actions that produce positive outcomes are responses to union voice (or voice bolstered by bargaining power) or responses to monopoly gains.

The monopoly and voice faces of unionism operate side-by-side, the importance of each being influenced by the economic environment. For a union firm in a reasonably competitive, largely nonunion industry, cost increases cannot be passed forward to consumers through higher prices. Thus, absent a productivity offset, unions should have little bargaining strength. Substantial union wage premiums in a competitive setting absent productivity improvements should lead establishments to contract over time. If a sizable proportion of an industry is unionized, industry-wide wage increases absent productivity offsets increase costs throughout the industry, costs increases are passed through to consumers, and no individual firm is at a severe disadvantage. But such a situation is difficult to sustain in the long run, if entry/expansion of nonunion companies is possible or products are tradable in world markets. On the one hand, the more competitive the market, the more limited is unions' bargaining power and ability to organize. On the other hand, the more competitive the market the greater the pressure on *union* companies to increase productivity. From a measurement standpoint, union companies that prosper or survive in a competitive environment are not a random draw from among all possible (and largely unobserved) union-firm experiences.

Unions have considerably greater ability to organize and to acquire and maintain wage gains in less competitive economic settings. Such settings include regulated industries in which entry and rate competition is legally restricted and oligopolistic industries in which entry is difficult because of economies of scale or limited international competition. Examples of the former include the previously regulated U.S. trucking and airline industries and the currently protected U.S. Postal Service, in each of which unionized workers have captured regulatory rents (Hirsch, 1988; Hirsch and Macpherson, 1998; Hirsch et al., 1999). Examples of the latter include the *deregulated* airline industry and the automobile industry. Following deregulation, unions' considerable strike power in the airline industry was maintained, allowing unions to capture a sizable share of potential profits during periods of strong demand but requiring concessions during downturns (Hirsch and Macpherson, 2000). In the automotive industry, labor relations have adapted in response to more limited market power and union power following the influx of European and Japanese imports, foreign-owned nonunion assembly plants in the United States, and labor-saving technological change and production innovations (Katz and MacDuffie, 1994).

Absent an offsetting productivity effect, a critical question concerns the source from which a union premium derives. Were it entirely a tax on *economic* profits (returns above opportunity costs), union rent seeking might be relatively benign. But for most firms in a competitive economy, above-normal returns are relatively small and short-lived. What appear to be abnormally high profits often represent the reward to firms for developing new and successful products, a reward for implementing cost-reducing production processes, or simply the quasi-rents that represent the normal returns to prior investment in long-lived physical and R&D capital. These profits serve an important economic role, providing incentive for investment and attracting resources into those economic activities most highly valued. To the extent that union gains vary directly with the quasi-rents emanating from long-lived capital, union wage increases can be viewed as a tax on *capital* that lowers the net rate of return on investment. In response, union firms reduce investment in physical and innovative capital, leading to slower growth in sales and employment and shrinkage of the union sector (Baldwin, 1983; Grout, 1984). It no longer follows that capital-labor substitution in union workplaces is optimal, a subject discussed more fully in the section on investment.[6]

Skill upgrading has been a conventional argument in the union literature (Freeman and Medoff, 1984; Lewis, 1986; Hirsch and Addison, 1986). The argument is simple — a union wage premium both allows and provides incentive for employers to upgrade the skill level of their work forces, offsetting part of the higher wage. Yet empirical evidence for skill upgrading is weak. Absence of clear-cut evidence is not surprising, however, once one realizes that such behavior need not follow from theory. Wessels (1994) provides a simple but persuasive challenge to the skill-upgrading hypothesis. If firms upgrade in response to a union wage increase, the union can then bargain in a future contract for an even higher wage in order to restore the premium. Employers, anticipating this, may respond by not upgrading. Firms that upgrade will face higher future wage demands and will have distorted their factor mix, using a higher skill labor mix than is optimal given its technology. Wessels provides an explicit model in which it is assumed that labor quality augments capital productivity and the decision to hire higher (lower) skill workers results if the elasticity of substitution between labor and capital is greater (less) than unity. Wessels concludes that available evidence is not consistent with skill upgrading.

Longitudinal evidence from wage equations also suggests that skill upgrading is not important. Freeman (1986) and Card (1996) conclude that wage-level and change estimates of the union-nonunion wage gap are similar, once one adjusts for bias from measurement error in union status (which is exacerbated in longitudinal estimates). This implies that, on average, *unmeasured* skills do not differ substantially for union and nonunion workers. Were skill upgrading important, we should observe high measured and unmeasured skills among union as compared to nonunion workers. The selection mechanism within union companies might better be characterized as a form of two-sided selection with positive selection among those with low measured skills and negative selection among those with high measured skills (Abowd and Farber, 1982; Card, 1996). Because of a queue of workers for union jobs, employers are able to avoid hiring workers in the lower tail of the skill distribution (skill here is defined broadly to include productivity-related attributes such as motivation and reliability). Yet few workers from the upper-tail of the skill distribution are either in or chosen from the union queue. Wage compression within union firms, both compression in skill differentials and contractually standardized wages, discourages applications by many of the most able workers. And following the logic of Wessels, firms may not have incentive to screen for and select the most able workers in the union queue if such action may lead to an increase in future wage demands. Card (1996) and Hirsch and Schumacher (1998) find clear evidence of two-sided selection.

The lack of strong longitudinal evidence for high unmeasured skills among union workers provides indirect evidence on unions and productivity. Were there a substantial positive union productivity effect (with measured worker skills and other inputs controlled for), then it seems likely that *some* of this higher productivity would be reflected in high unmeasured skills among union workers. We see no such thing. It seems implausible that union productivity effects would be embedded entirely in the workplace environment and not at all in workers, although such an outcome would be compatible with the collective voice view of how unions affect the workplace.

As the above discussion indicates, evidence is required to assess the relative importance of the monopoly and collective voice faces of unionism. Two additional points warrant emphasis. First, the effects of unions on productivity and other aspects of performance should differ substantially across industries, time, and countries. This is hardly surprising given that both the collective voice and monopoly activities of unions depend crucially on the labor relations and economic environment. Second, union effects are typically measured by differences in performance between union and nonunion firms or sectors. Such differences do not measure the effects of unions on aggregate or economy-wide economic performance as long as resources are free to move across sectors. For example, evidence presented below indicates that union companies in the United States have performed poorly relative to nonunion companies. To the extent that output and resources are mobile, poor union performance has led to a shift of production and employment away from unionized industries, firms, and plants and into the nonunion sector. Overall effects on economy-wide performance have been relatively minor.

IV. Measurement: The Binding Limitations of Data and Inference

What unions do is largely an empirical question. The evidence on this topic has greatly enhanced our knowledge and understanding of union effects on performance. But the availability and quality of data leave much to be desired. Even were better data available, identifying causal relationships is difficult. In this section, a few of the inherent problems associated with empirical studies are reviewed. My purpose is not to denigrate the value of this work — we would have far less understanding of what unions do absent such evidence. But given present limitations, caution must be used in drawing inferences. Were it possible to analyze these issues using better data and alternative methods, our assessment of how unions affect economic performance would require modification, certainly quantitatively if not qualitatively.

Most studies utilize cross-sectional data (at single or multiple points in time), measuring differences in outcomes (productivity, profitability, etc.) across establishments, firms, or industries with different levels of union coverage. Regression estimates from production functions, profit equations, and the like provide estimates of union-nonunion differences in performance, controlling for other *measurable* determinants. The key question is whether one can conclude that the estimated difference in performance associated with differences in unionization truly represents the causal effect of unions.[7]

There are several reasons why one must exhibit caution in drawing such a conclusion. First is potential bias from omitted variables. If one fails to control for an important productivity determinant and that factor is correlated with union density, then one obtains a biased estimate of the causal effect of unionism on performance. For example, older plants tend to have lower productivity, and union density is higher in older plants. If a study were to estimate the union impact on productivity among plants, the inability to measure and control for plant age (or its correlates, such as age of capital) would mean that part of the effect of plant age on productivity would be included in the (biased) estimate of the effect of unions upon productivity. Of course, omitted variables always exist in empirical work. One should have concern only where theory and supplemental evidence strongly suggest that there may exist substantial bias owing to some specified omission.

A second concern is bias resulting from union status being endogenous, rather than determined randomly (or independently of other correlates of the outcome measure). For example, unions likely will organize and survive in firms (or industries) with high potential profits; in this case, standard estimates of union effects on profitability (typically negative) would understate the impact of unions on profits. Alternative methods exist to deal with selection, but generally require identification (and measurement) of at least one variable that affects union status (say, state differences in labor law or sentiment toward unions), but not the outcome variable of interest (e.g., profitability).

A third reason for caution in making inferences is concern about "external validity." Even where one has obtained "internal validity" — unbiased estimates of union effects for the population being studied (e.g., a particular industry, time period, or country) — it is not clear whether these results have external validity that permit generalization. The most reliable estimates of union effects on productivity may well be based on specific industries (e.g., cement, sawmills) where output is homogeneous and can be measured in physical units rather than by value added. Yet it is not clear to what extent results in, say, the western sawmill industry (Mitchell and Stone, 1992) can be generalized to the economy as a whole, particularly given that we expect union effects to differ across time, establishment, industry, and country.

Several studies combine cross-sectional and longitudinal (i.e., time-series) analysis, typically examining *changes* in performance over time resulting from changes in union status (or, similarly, controlling for establishment fixed effects). For example, several studies examine changes in firm market value (measured by stock price changes), investment, or employment following the announcement of union representation elections and their outcomes. A limited number of studies examine changes in productivity or other performance measures following changes in unionization within plants. The advantage of longitudinal analysis is that each individual firm (or plant) forms its own control group — that is, a firm's performance once unionized is compared to its performance prior to unionization (as compared to changes among firms not changing union status). In this way, unmeasured, observation-specific, attributes fixed over time are controlled for in estimating the causal effect of unionization. Although such studies have strong advantages, inference can be difficult. Because unions may affect performance gradually over time, it is difficult to correctly correlate changes in unionization and changes in performance.[8] Moreover, firms or establishments changing union status are not randomly determined, making it unclear whether or not the measured effect among those receiving "treatment" (union status change) can be generalized to those not treated.

V. What Have Unions Done? Revisiting the Evidence[9]

As described in the previous section, union effects on performance must be estimated using imperfect data and statistical models and techniques that permit alternative interpretations of the evidence. Because of these limitations, one must carefully assess individual studies and the cumulative evidence before drawing strong inferences regarding unions' *causal* effect on performance. Even where the evidence is reasonably compelling, we often know little about the precise mechanisms through which these results are produced. In most of the studies reviewed below, unionization is treated as exogenous and we have little or no information on differences across unions in behavior or strategy. We can estimate the strength of the relationship between union status and productivity, profits, investment, or other performance outcomes. But we do not learn much else. The industrial relations and human resources literature has shed a bit of light inside the union-performance black box. But the literature provides few answers to the types of questions asked by unions regarding appropriate strategies, by management about personnel policies, or by policy makers about appropriate legislative and regulatory reforms.[10]

Discussion herein is largely restricted to the U.S. private sector, as in *What Do Unions Do?* There is growing international evidence on unions and performance (recent surveys include Aidt and Tzannatos, 2002; Metcalf, 2003; and, tangentially, Nickell and Layard, 1999). It is doubtful that results from other economies can be readily generalized to the United States, or vice-versa. As we have seen, the effects of unions are specific to the economic, legal, and structural environment. The institution of collective bargaining differs substantially across countries, making comparison difficult (the exception may be Canada and the United States). And changes in the economic, legal, and institutional structure surrounding collective bargaining have real effects on outcomes, as seen most notably by the changes in the United Kingdom since 1980 (Addison and Siebert, 2003; Pencavel, 2003). By the same token, variation across countries in the collective bargaining environment and in the legal structure, if clearly correlated with differences in union effects on performance, can offer clues as to the specific routes through which unions affect the workplace, something lacking in much of the U.S. literature. And non-U.S. studies frequently offer superior data. This is hardly surprising, given that in the U.S. data on firm or plant union density are not publicly available in any systematic fashion. Research may well provide more reliable answers to the question *"What Do Unions Do?"* for other countries than for the United States.

Productivity and Productivity Growth

Freeman and Medoff rightly emphasize the importance of what unions do to productivity. If collective bargaining in the workplace were systematically to increase productivity and not to retard growth, a strong argument could be made for policies that facilitate union organizing (this statement assumes that union-induced distortions in factor mix and economy-wide resource allocation are minor). A pathbreaking empirical study by Brown and Medoff (1978), followed by the body of evidence summarized in *What Do Unions Do?*, made for what appeared to many a persuasive case that collective bargaining in the United States is, on average, associated with substantial improvements in productivity.

The thesis that unions substantially increase productivity has not held up well. Subsequent studies are as likely to find negative as positive union effects on productivity. Critics have pointed out that a large union enhancement of productivity is inconsistent with the far less controversial evidence on profitability and employment (Addison and Hirsch, 1989; Wessels, 1985). And attention has focused on the dynamic effect of unions and their apparently negative effects on *growth* in productivity, sales, and employment. Surveys of the unions-productivity literature for the most part have concluded that union effects are highly variable but on average close to zero (see endnote 2). A "meta-analysis" of the unions-productivity literature concludes similarly that the average effect in the United States is very small but positive, while negative in the United Kingdom (Doucouliagos and Laroche, 2003). A survey of labor economists at leading universities asking for an assessment of the union effect on productivity produced a median response of zero and mean of 3.1 percent (Fuchs et al., 1998).[11]

A typical productivity study estimates Cobb-Douglas or (less restrictive) translog production functions in which measured outputs are related to inputs. To fix the discussion, a variant of the Cobb-Douglas production function developed by Brown and Medoff (1978) is:

$$Q = AK\alpha\,(L_n + cL_u)^{1-\alpha}, \tag{1}$$

where Q is output; K is capital; L_u and L_n are union and nonunion labor; A is a constant of proportionality; and α and $(1-\alpha)$ are the output elasticities with respect to capital and labor. The parameter c reflects productivity differences between union and nonunion labor. If $c>1$, union labor is more productive, in line with the collective-voice model; if $c<1$, union labor is less productive, in line with conventional arguments concerning the deleterious impact of such things as union work rules and constraints on merit- based wage dispersion. Manipulation of equation (1) yields the estimating equation

$$\ln(Q/L) \cong \ln A + \alpha\ln(K/L) + (1-\alpha)(c-1)P, \tag{2}$$

where P represents proportion unionized (L_u/L) in a firm or industry or the presence or absence of a union at the plant or firm level (a zero/one categorical variable). Equation (2) assumes constant returns to scale, an assumption relaxed by including a $\ln L$ variable as a measure of establishment size. The coefficient on P measures the logarithmic productivity differential of unionized establishments. If it is assumed that the union effect on productivity solely reflects the differential efficiency of labor inputs, the effect of union labor on productivity is calculated by dividing the coefficient on P by $(1-\alpha)$.

The conclusion that unions in general raise productivity substantially rests almost exclusively on the results of the influential Brown and Medoff (1978) study. Using aggregate two-digit manufacturing industry data cross-classified by state groups for 1972, Brown and Medoff's preferred coefficient estimates on union density are from .22 to .24, implying values (obtained by dividing the union coefficient by $1-\alpha$) for $c-1$ of from .30 to .31. Using alternative assumptions about capital usage (that increase union relative to nonunion capital), estimates of union productivity effects fall roughly in half. Absent this study, it would have been difficult to sustain the conclusion in *What Do Unions Do?* that in general unions raise productivity.

Limitations attach to the production function test and to the results in their paper, many of which were identified by Brown and Medoff. The use of value added as an output measure confounds price and quantity effects, since part of the measured union productivity differential may result from higher prices in the unionized sector. Not surprisingly, estimated effects of unions on productivity tend to be lower when price adjustments are made (Allen, 1986b; Mitchell and Stone, 1992). Union firms can more easily pass through higher costs when they operate in product markets sheltered from nonunion and foreign competition. Use of value added, therefore, is most likely to confound price and output effects in aggregate analyses relating industry value added to industry union density. It is less of a concern in firm- or business-level analyses that measure firms' union status *and* industry union density or other industry controls (Clark, 1984;

Hirsch, 1991a). These studies tend to find small, generally negative, effects of unions on productivity.

It is difficult to reconcile the Brown-Medoff findings with other pieces of evidence. As argued by Addison and Hirsch (1989), parameter estimates from Brown and Medoff would most likely imply an *increase* in profitability associated with unionism, contrary to the rather unambiguous evidence of *lower* firm and industry profitability resulting from unionization. Wessels (1985) casts further doubt on these findings by showing that it is difficult to reconcile the productivity and wage evidence in Brown and Medoff with evidence on employment. Offsetting increases in productivity due to unionization and relative labor costs would imply substantial decreases in union employment (holding output constant) if firms shift toward labor-saving capital. Yet unions appear to have little effect on capital-labor ratios (Clark, 1984).

There are surprisingly few manufacturing-wide or economy-wide productivity studies and, except for Brown and Medoff, none reports consistent evidence of an overall positive effect of unions on productivity.[12] Clark (1984) provides one of the better broad-based studies. He uses data for 902 manufacturing lines-of-business from 1970 to 1980 to estimate, among other things, value-added (and sales) productivity equations. He obtains marginally significant coefficients on the union variable of from −.02 to −.03. The Clark study has the advantage of a large sample size over multiple years, business-specific information on union coverage, and a detailed set of control variables. In Clark's separate two-digit industry regressions, positive effects by unions on productivity are found only for textiles, furniture, and petroleum. A similar study is conducted by Hirsch (1991a), who examines over 600 publicly traded manufacturing firms during 1968–1980 (firm union data, collected by the author, is for 1977). Hirsch finds a strong negative relationship between union coverage and firm productivity when including only firm-level control variables, but the union effect drops sharply after including detailed industry controls. The results prove somewhat fragile when subjected to econometric probing. Hirsch interprets his results as providing no evidence for a positive economy-wide productivity effect and weak evidence for a negative effect. As in the Clark study, Hirsch finds considerable variability across industries.

A particularly rich data set has been developed recently by Black and Lynch (2002). They estimate production functions for a large sample of U.S. manufacturing plants over the period 1987–1993. Their study focuses on the effects of various workplace practices, information technology, and management procedures, but union status is also measured and analyzed. Absent interaction terms, Black and Lynch find slightly lower productivity in unionized plants following inclusion of detailed controls, a result equivalent to that in the Clark and Hirsch studies. The authors, however, find that this result is driven by low productivity among unionized plants using traditional management systems. Unionized plants that adopt human resource practices involving joint decision making (i.e., total quality management or TQM) and incentive-based compensation (i.e., profit sharing for nonmanagerial employees) are found to be more productive than their nonunion counterparts, which in turn had higher productivity than union plants using traditional labor-management relations (Black and Lynch, 2002). These results reinforce the conclusion that union effects are not a given, but depend highly on the specific economic and labor relations environment in which unions operate. Although one is reluctant to put too much emphasis on these specific results, they comport well with our priors. The suggestion is that union plants with high-performance systems, presumably adopted with union agreement, can realize enhanced productivity, whereas traditional top-down managed union plants realize no such enhancement.[13] Such research reinforces the need to get inside the union black box, helping us understand why there is high variation in performance across different unionized settings.[14]

Productivity studies based on firms within a single industry have advantages as compared to the manufacturing-wide studies. Output can sometimes be measured in physical units rather than value added, information on plant or firm-level union status is more readily available, and more flexible functional forms can be reliably estimated. From a methodological perspective, among the best analyses are Clark's studies of the cement industry (Clark 1980a, 1980b), Allen's analyses of the construction industry (Allen 1986a, 1986b), and Mitchell and Stone's (1992) work on western sawmills. Each of the studies provides a rather wide array of evidence. Clark finds positive, albeit small, effects of unions on productivity among cement plants. Allen (1986b) finds positive union effects in large office building construction and negative effects in school construction. Similarly, Allen (1986a) finds positive and negative union effects on productivity, respectively, in privately and publicly owned hospitals and nursing homes. Mitchell and Stone find negative effects of unions on output in sawmills, following appropriate adjustments for product quality and raw material usage. Although methodological advantages of the industry-specific studies are achieved at the price of a loss in generality, they do increase our understanding of how unions affect the workplace.[15]

Despite substantial diversity in the literature about union productivity, several systematic patterns are revealed (Addison and Hirsch, 1989). First, productivity effects tend to be largest in industries where the union wage premium is most pronounced. This pattern is what critics of the production function test predict — that union density coefficients reflects in part a wage rather than a productivity effect. These results also support a "shock effect" interpretation of unionization, i.e., management responds to an increase in labor costs by organizing more efficiently, reducing slack, and increasing measured productivity. Second, positive union productivity effects are typically largest where competitive pressure exists (consistent with the expectations of Freeman and Medoff, 1984, pp. 179–80), and these positive effects are largely restricted to the private, for-profit, sectors. Notably absent are positive productivity effects in public school construction, public libraries, government bureaus, schools, and law enforcement.[16]

This interpretation of the productivity studies has an interesting twist. The suggestion is that a relatively competitive, cost-conscious environment is a necessary condition for a positive effect of unions on productivity, and that managerial response should be stronger the larger the union wage premium. Yet it is precisely in such competitive environments that there should be little managerial slack and the least scope for union organizing and wage gains. This implies that steady-state union density in the U.S. private sector must remain small, absent a general union productivity advantage. By the same token, introduction of unions or the strengthening of other instruments for collective voice into highly competitive sectors of the U.S. economy is unlikely to have large downside risks for economy-wide performance. Although individual firms may fail to be competitive and perform poorly, market pressures should induce other firms and unions to develop labor relations systems providing the voice/response benefits envisaged by Freeman and Medoff. In short, as the U.S. economy has become more competitive over time (White, 2002), we might expect to see more favorable union-productivity outcomes among surviving and newly unionized establishments.

A concern expressed about the production function test is that there might be survivor bias, a form of selection that would bias upward estimates of union performance (Addison and Hirsch, 1989). In workplaces where unions have the most deleterious effects, businesses fail, contract, or grow slowly. Thus, the sample of union establishments sampled at any point in time includes a large proportion of establishments with positive performance outcomes, while those with poor outcomes are underrepresented.[17] Subsequent evidence indicates that survivor bias is not as serious as once believed. As discussed later, differences in failure rates among union and nonunion establishments and firms (following controls) appear small. If there is no union impact on business failure, survivor bias would arise only through use of weighted regressions, the use of current employment weights giving too large a weight to establishments with good performance (and growing employment) and too little to those with slow growth. Much of the literature uses unweighted regression estimates, however, which should avoid this particular form of bias.

Overall, the evidence produced since *What Do Unions Do?* suggests that the authors' characterization of union effects on productivity was overly optimistic. Freeman and Medoff were certainly correct that union productivity effects vary across workplaces, in particular with respect to the labor relations environment. They were correct to emphasize the role of management response, although one might just as readily emphasize the role of union response to management initiatives. And they were correct to note the role that a competitive market environment has on productivity outcomes. What appears incorrect is their conclusion that "productivity is generally higher in unionized establishments than in otherwise comparable establishments that are nonunion. . . "(p. 180). The empirical evidence does not allow one to infer a precise estimate of the average union productivity effect, but my assessment of existing evidence is that the average union effect is very close to zero, and as likely to be somewhat negative as somewhat positive.

Discussion now turns to the effects of unions on the *growth* in productivity. Productivity growth is typically measured by the change in value added after controlling for changes in factor inputs. Studies examining union effects on growth typically control (when possible) for union-nonunion differences in the accumulation of tangible and intangible capital and other measurable factors of production. Thus, what is being measured is a "direct" effect of unions on growth. Unions may also decrease productivity growth indirectly through their effects on investment and capital accumulation, a topic addressed shortly. Union effects on productivity levels and growth need not be the same. For example, unionization could initially be associated with higher levels of productivity, owing to a "shock effect" or "collective voice," but at the same time retard the rate of growth. In the long run, of course, low rates of productivity growth should produce lower productivity levels relative to comparison firms or industries.

As discussed earlier, Freeman and Medoff (1984) find lower (but not significant) union productivity growth using alternative industry-level data sets. They regard their results as inconclusive. A more comprehensive analysis using firm-level data (thus permitting control for industry effects) is provided by Hirsch (1991a), based on a sample of 531 firms and covering the period from 1968 to 1980. Following an accounting for company size and firm-level changes in labor, physical capital, and R&D, union firms have substantially lower productivity growth than nonunion firms. Accounting for *industry* sales growth, energy usage, and trade, however, cuts the estimate of the union effect by more than half. Addition of industry dummies cuts the estimate further, while the remaining effect proves fragile when subjected to econometric probes regarding the error structure. In short, union firms clearly display substantially lower productivity growth than do nonunion firms, but most (if not all) of this difference is associated with effects attributable to industry differences, union firms being located in industries or sectors with slow growth. There exists no strong evidence that unions have a *direct* effect on productivity growth.

Despite the contentiousness surrounding the effects of unions on productivity and growth, the most comprehensive studies find little effect that can be deemed causal. Results are simply too variable and not particularly robust to econometric probing. Five points surrounding this conclusion are worth emphasizing. First, union firms can be found to have lower productivity and productivity growth absent detailed controls. This is important in and of itself, although it tells us little about unions' causal effects. Second, a small or zero impact of unions on productivity is difficult to interpret. Does this mean that the positive and negative effects of unions are each close to zero, or that they simply cancel each other out with each having an important independent effect? Third, economy-wide studies measure the average effects of unions. There is considerable diversity in outcomes across firms and industries, consistent with the considerable emphasis given to the importance of the economic and labor relations environments. Fourth, studies of productivity and productivity growth control for differences in levels or changes in factor-input usage. But unionization is associated with lower rates of investment and accumulation of physical and innovative capital. This indirect route is primarily how we obtain slower growth in sales and employment in the union sectors of the economy. Finally, absence of a large positive union effect on productivity implies that union compensation gains are not offset, implying lower profitability and (typically) lower investment. The most important point to bring away from the productivity evidence may be the *absence* of a large positive effect due to unions.

Profitability

Absent sufficient productivity enhancements in the workplace or higher prices in product markets, union wage gains decrease profitability. The evidence on productivity does not suggest sufficiently higher productivity to offset higher compensation. Nor is it plausible that higher prices can offset wage increases, apart from regulated industries where prices are administered to approximate average costs. In more competitive settings, where union firms compete with nonunion domestic companies and traded goods, there is little possibility for passing forward higher costs. Lower profits will be seen in current earnings, in measured rates of return on capital, and in lower stock market values of a firm's assets. Ex-ante returns on equity (risk-adjusted) should not differ between union and nonunion companies, since stock prices adjust downward to reflect lower expected earnings (Hirsch and Morgan, 1994).

The responses of firms to differences in costs (union-related or otherwise) should in the long run mitigate differences in profitability. These are mitigated through the movement of resources out of union into nonunion sectors — investment in and by union operations decreasing until post-tax (post-union) rates of return are equivalent to nonunion rates of return. Stated alternatively, union coverage will be restricted to economic sectors realizing above-normal, pre-union rates of returns. Because the quasi-rents accruing to long-lived capital may provide a principal source for union gains and complete long-run adjustments occur slowly, however, we are likely to observe differences in profitability as these adjustments take place.

Consistent with Freeman and Medoff's conclusion in *What Do Unions Do?*, subsequent evidence points unambiguously to lower profitability among union companies, although studies differ in their conclusions regarding the source of union gains. Lower profits are found using alternative measures of profitability.

Studies using aggregate industry data typically employ as their dependent variable the industry price-cost margin (PCM) defined by (Total Revenue –Variable Costs) / Total Revenue — and typically measured by (Value Added – Payroll – Advertising) / Shipments. Line-of-business studies and some firm-level studies use accounting profit-rate measures: the rate of return on sales, measured by earnings divided by sales, and the rate of return on capital, measured by earnings divided by the value of the capital stock. Firm-level analyses of publicly traded firms (Salinger, 1984; Hirsch, 1991a, 1991b) use market-value measures of profitability, a common measure being Tobin's q, defined as a firm's market value divided by the replacement cost of assets. Finally, "events" studies in which changes in market value attributable to votes for union representation or to unanticipated changes in collective bargaining agreements have been examined (Ruback and Zimmerman, 1984; Bronars and Deere, 1990; Abowd, 1989; Olson and Becker, 1990; Becker and Olson, 1992).

The finding of lower profitability from unionization is not only invariant to the profit measure used, but also holds regardless of the time period under study and holds for analyses using industries, firms, or lines-of-business as the observation unit. Although results vary, studies typically obtain estimates suggesting that union firms have profits 10 to 20 percent lower than nonunion firms. Firm-level studies that include large numbers of firm and industry controls tend to obtain the lower estimates. Economists are understandably skeptical that large profit differentials could survive in a competitive economy. Because rates of profit are not typically large, small absolute differences can produce large percentage differences. Whether one believes 10–20 percent differences in profitability can be sustained for "long" period of times depends on the definition of "long" and one's beliefs regarding the competitiveness of the U.S. economy.

Two potential sources of bias that can be identified cause the effects of unionization to be *understated.* First, profit functions are estimated only for *surviving* firms, since those for which the effects of unionization are most deleterious may be less likely to remain in the sample. As stated previously, survival rates of firms do not appear to vary substantially with union status, so bias should be minor. Second, one expects unions to be more likely to organize where potential profits are higher; hence, the negative effect of unions on profits should be understated if union density is treated as exogenous. In fact, studies that attempt to account for the simultaneous determination of union status and profitability obtain larger estimates of union effects on profits (Voos and Mishel, 1986; Hirsch, 1991a), although such estimates are not precise. Because unionization in most firms was established long ago, however, the correlation between union status and current potential (i.e., nonunion) profits should be weak.

Although there is a consensus that unions decrease profitability, there is no agreement on the source of union wage gains. Influential early studies cited in *What Do Unions Do?* concluded that monopoly power provides the primary source for union gains, based on evidence that unions reduce profits primarily in highly concentrated industries (Freeman, 1983; Salinger, 1984; Karier, 1985). Subsequent research calls such a result into question. An early paper by Hirsch and Connolly (1987) criticizes this conclusion on several fronts. Market power arises not only from industry concentration, and rents from market power need not be the only source of union gains. Hirsch and Connolly provide firm-level evidence (but with an industry-level union measure) and find that unions gains derive from the returns associated with firm market share (with industry concentration constant), R&D capital, and weak foreign competition. With data similar to that used by Salinger, Hirsch and Connolly replicate the result from which he concluded that unions capture concentration-related profits. They show that the Salinger outcome is entirely the product of a restrictive specification that forces all union gains to vary with concentration. A more general specification rejects a positive interaction between union density and concentration.

Hirsch and Connolly also argue that if concentration were a major source of union gains, one should see union *wage* premiums larger for workers in more concentrated industries. Yet wage studies reject this outcome. In short, there is little evidence from either product or labor markets to support the hypothesis that profits associated with industry concentration provide a source for union rents. In a subsequent analysis using a data set with a firm union coverage measure, Hirsch (1990) more clearly rejects the hypothesis that concentration-related profit is a source of union rents.

The conflict in results with respect to concentration is not simply a result of the use of industry-level versus firm-level data. An industry study by Domowitz et al. (1986) finds no difference in union effects on profitability with respect to concentration. Likewise, using 1977 four-digit manufacturing-industry data, Chapell et al. (1991) find that unions have similar negative effects on price-cost margins among industries with low, medium, and high concentration. They also find that within concentration categories, unions have a larger effect on the profits of large than small firms.

Note that the studies summarized above do not reject the conclusion that union bargaining power and wage gains derive in part from firm market power. They reject the thesis that *concentration*-related profits provide a major source for union gains, in part because of the tenuous link between firm profitability and industry concentration (Ravenscraft, 1983).[18] As discussed above, unions can and do capture rents stemming from sources of limited competition other than concentration, such as limited trade penetration or firm special advantages. Obvious examples of union gains stemming from market power (or specifically, restrictions on entry) include large wage premiums in the unionized U.S. Postal Service and among union workers in the trucking and airline industries under regulation.

Research appearing since *What Do Unions Do?* suggests that in addition to capturing rents stemming from market power, unions appropriate quasi-rents, in particular those that make up the normal returns to long-lived investments.

This has important implications for investment and long-term growth (addressed below). For example, Hirsch (1991a) concludes that unions capture current earnings associated with limited foreign competition, both current and future earnings associated with disequilibrium or growing demand in the firm and industry (sales growth), future earnings emanating from R&D capital, and current and future quasi-rents emanating from long-lived physical capital (for related evidence, see Cavanaugh, 1998).

An interesting question is the extent to which the poor profit performance of unionized companies during the 1970s and early 1980s helps explain the decline in union membership during the 1980s and beyond. Blanchflower and Freeman (1992) note the unusually high union wage premiums in the United States as opposed to other countries (for recent evidence, see Blanchflower, 2003), arguing that this has consequences for employment and membership. Linneman et al. (1990) show that employment declines have been concentrated in the unionized sectors of the economy; nonunion employment has expanded even in highly unionized industries (for an update and extension, see Bratsberg and Ragan, 2003). That is, shifts in industry demand and employment are an insufficient explanation for the decline in private sector unionism. The complement of wage evidence linking large union premiums to declines in membership is the evidence summarized in this section on poor profit performance among union companies. A reasonable inference is that *profitability* differences between union and nonunion firms help explain declining unionization. Hirsch (1991a) finds a negative correlation between firm-level profitability in the late 1970s and subsequent changes in firm union density between 1977 and 1987. But the relationship between the wage premium, profits, and changes in union density is complex, and the verdict is out on how much of the decline in private sector density is related to lower profitability. Although smaller union wage premiums would lessen management response to unionization, they might also weaken the appeal that union representation has to workers.

Investment in Tangible and Intangible Capital

An area of theoretical and empirical research receiving attention since publication of *What Do Unions Do?* has been the union effect on investment, based on rent-seeking models in which unions appropriate (i.e., tax) the returns from investments in tangible and intangible capital. The theoretical origins for this literature reach back to Simons (1944); influential papers include Baldwin (1983) and Grout (1984). The earliest empirical paper in this literature appears to be Connolly et al. (1986). Rent-seeking models focus on the fact that unions capture some share of the quasi-rents that make up the normal return to investment in long-lived capital and R&D. "Rationally myopic" unions (Hirsch, 1991a; 1992b) find it optimal to tax capital when the time horizon of their members is short relative to owners' time horizon for long-lived, nontransferable capital (it need not follow from theory that the union always has the shorter time horizon; Addison and Chilton, 1998). In response, firms rationally reduce their investment in vulnerable tangible and intangible capital until returns on investment are equalized across the union and nonunion (i.e., taxed and nontaxed) sectors. Contraction of the union sector, it is argued, results from the long-run response by firms to such rent seeking.

As discussed earlier, the union tax or rent-seeking framework both complements and contrasts with the standard economic model of unions. In the standard model, a union wage increase causes a firm to move up and along its labor-demand schedule by decreasing employment, hiring higher quality workers, and increasing the ratio of capital to labor. Capital investment can increase or decrease owing to substitution and scale effects working in opposing directions. In the rent-seeking framework, union wage premiums are a tax on the returns to capital. Firms know that if they invest now in long-lived and nontransferable capital, union bargaining power will result in higher future wages. Stated alternatively, *wage* increases to unions are in part a tax on capital and need not lead firms to shift their factor mix away from labor and toward capital (Hirsch and Prasad, 1995; Addison and Chilton, 1996).[19]

Union rent seeking reduces investment not only in physical capital but also in R&D and other forms of innovative activity (Connolly et al., 1986). The stock of knowledge and improvements in processes and products emanating from R&D are likely to be relatively long-lived and firm specific. To the extent that returns from innovative activity are appropriable, firms will respond to union power by reducing these investments. Collective-bargaining coverage within a company is most likely to reduce investment in product innovations and relatively factor-neutral process innovations, while having ambiguous effects on labor-saving processes. Expenditures in R&D also tend to signal — or be statistically prior to — investments in physical capital. Therefore, firms reducing long-range plans for physical capital investment in response to unions' rent-seeking behavior are likely to reduce investment in R&D.

Patents applied for, or granted, are a measure of innovative *output* emanating from a company's R&D stock. Unionized companies may be more likely to patent, given their stock of innovation capital, to reduce union rent appropriation (Connolly et al., 1986). Although the patent application process is often costly and reveals trade secrets, patents offer firms opportunity to license product and process innovations and transform what might otherwise be firm-specific innovative capital into general capital, and lessen a union's ability to appropriate the quasi-rents from that capital.[20]

Hirsch (1991a) provides an empirical analysis of union effects on investment, both tangible and intangible capital. He distinguishes between "direct" and "indirect" investment effects of unions. The direct effect, discussed above, stems from the union tax on the returns to long-lived and relation-specific capital, leading firms to decrease investment to equate the marginal post-tax rate of return with the marginal financing cost. The indirect effect of unions on investment arises from the higher financing costs owing to reduced profits (and, thus, reduces internal funding of investment) for union firms. With data for 1968–1980 for approximately 500 publicly traded manufacturing firms and a model with detailed firm and industry controls, including profitability, Hirsch estimates the effect on investment for a typical unionized company compared to a nonunion company. Other things equal, the typical unionized firm has 6 percent lower capital investment than its observationally equivalent nonunion counterpart. Allowing for the profit effect increases the estimate to about 13 percent; that is, about half of the overall union effect is indirect. Hirsch repeats the exercise for intangible capital (annual investments in R&D), and his findings imply that the average unionized firm has 15 percent lower R&D, holding constant profitability and the other determinants. Allowing for the indirect effects induced by lower profitability only modestly raises the estimate. These deleterious union effects on capital investment have been confirmed in subsequent U.S. studies (e.g., Hirsch, 1992; Becker and Olson, 1992; Bronars and Deere, 1993; Bronars et al., 1994; Cavanaugh, 1998). Fallick and Hassett (1999) examine *changes* in firms' capital investment in response to a union win in a certification election. They find a substantial reduction, likening the effects of a vote for certification to the effects of a 30 percentage point increase in the corporate income tax.

Given reasonable similarities in the Canadian and U.S. collective bargaining systems and economic environment, two studies warrant mention. Consistent with U.S. evidence, Odgers and Betts (1997) conclude that unions significantly reduce investment in physical capital, while Betts et al. (2001) conclude likewise for R&D. Despite use of industry data (for multiple years), the authors make a convincing case that they have measured causal union effects.

A comparative study of the United States and Britain also warrants attention. Menezes-Filho et al. (1998) provide a detailed analysis of the effects of unions on R&D, concluding that although unionized establishments invest less in R&D, in the United Kingdom this is primarily an effect of the industry location and not of unions. They then subject firm-level data from the United States (provided by Hirsch) to the same battery of econometric tests to which they subject the British data. They conclude that, unlike the British evidence, the U.S. evidence of a deleterious effect of unionization on R&D investment is robust. Whereas the union tax model applies well to the United States, the authors speculate that British unions have fewer deleterious effects on R&D than do American unions owing to more explicit bargaining over employment levels and a preference for longer contracts. A recent survey by Menezes-Filho and Van Reenen (2003) reaffirms this conclusion — in the U.S. labor unions appear to substantially decrease R&D investment, but this same effect is not evident in Britain. The R&D evidence is consistent with labor market evidence finding far smaller union wage effects in Britain than in the United States (Blanchflower and Bryson, 2003).

Employment Growth and Survival

The effect of unions on employment growth and survival is not independent of its effects on productivity, profits, and investment. It would be surprising were lower profits and investment not accompanied by slower growth, and this exactly what the evidence indicates. Linneman et al. (1990) show that much of what has been represented as a "de-industrialization" of America was in fact a *de-unionization*. Using Current Population Survey data for the 1980s, they show that within narrowly defined manufacturing industries, most displayed increases in nonunion employment while at the same time witnessing substantial decreases in union employment. The rate of decline in union employment is related to the magnitude of the union wage premium. In one of the few studies to examine firm-level employment growth, Leonard (1992) finds that unionized California companies grew at significantly slower rates than did nonunion companies. Dunne and Macpherson (1994) utilize longitudinal plant-level data (grouped by industry-by-size) to show that there are more employment contractions, fewer expansions, and fewer plant "births" in more highly unionized industries. They find that unions have no effect upon plant "deaths," even after controlling for plant size (larger plants are less likely to fail but more likely to be unionized). Freeman and Kleiner (1999) analyze two sets of data, one including insolvent and solvent firms, each with information on union status, and a second on individuals surveyed in the CPS Displaced Worker Surveys. Using the first data set, Freeman and Kleiner conclude that failed firms or lines of business (most lines of business remain in operation following bankruptcy) have similar union density as do solvent firms and lines of business. Using individual data, they find that being a union worker does not lead to a higher probability of permanent job loss from plant closure or business failure.

Two carefully executed studies examine the results of successful NLRB elections. In a study using longitudinal plant-level data, LaLonde et al. (1996) show that employment (and output) decrease following a vote in favor of union certification. DiNardo and Lee (2002) examine the causal effect of union elections on the subsequent survival of establishments. Previous literature is hobbled by a paucity of firm — and establishment-level unionization data and concerns about exogeneity. The authors address each of these issues. Combining NLRB election data for 1983–1999 with a matched listing of whether establishments named in the NLRB file continue to exist at that address in May 2001, they compare survival rates for establishments that have *just under* and *just over* a 50 percent vote in union elections. The authors make a convincing argument that the only important difference between these two sets of establishments is the union vote, so that subsequent differences in survival probabilities are likely to be causal. DiNardo and Lee conclude that the effects of successful union organizing drives on subsequent survival rates (from one to 18 years after an election) are negligible. The authors make a persuasive case that the results they find are causal and internally valid. It is less clear to what extent their results generalize to the larger population of existing (or previously existing) union establishments.

In short, the empirical literature finds that U.S. unions are associated with slower employment growth, but exhibit little or no difference in rates of business failure or survival.[21] These seemingly inconsistent results require explanation. The argument (Freeman and Kleiner, 1999) is that rent-seeking unions are willing to drive enterprises toward the cliff but not over it.[22] But in an uncertain world, it is implausible that unions will not sometimes miscalculate economic conditions or management actions, resulting in "accidental" business failures in the union sector. An alternative explanation is that because of wage premiums, union firms may have substantial wage flexibility via contract concessions as compared to nonunion firms with close to opportunity cost wages. Thus, nonunion companies are at a disadvantage when they try to cut costs during a prolonged downturn in business. Such wage flexibility may operate only for the minority of union firms at risk for bankruptcy, plant closures, or significant layoffs; the economy-wide evidence indicates that nonunion wages are procyclical but union wages largely acyclic (Grant, 2001).

VI. What Should Unions Do? Assessing the Future of CV/IR and Public Policy

Freeman and Medoff (1984) expressed considerable concern for the future of labor unions and the exercise of voice in the workplace. It is obvious, 20 years later, that such concern was warranted. By 2002, traditional collective bargaining serves few workers in the U.S. private sector; only one in twelve (8.6 percent) are union members and one in eleven (9.3 percent) are covered by a collective bargaining agreement (Hirsch and Macpherson, 2003). Given a competitive world, there is good reason to expect private sector unionism to continue its decline and little reason to predict any "spurt" in organizing success (Freeman, 1998). Such a conclusion is reinforced by the research discussed herein. Given lower profitability in union companies and widespread management resistance to unionization, organizing levels are likely to remain below replacement levels (i.e., normal union job loss) (Farber and Western, 2001).

What does the status quo imply? Continuation of current trends means that workers' desire for effective voice, cooperation with supervisors and management, and participation in decision making will remain unrealized for much of the nonunion (and perhaps union) work force. Absent a formal voice mechanism in the workplace, there is likely to be a continued reliance on governmental regulation and mandates, which by many accounts is insufficiently flexible and overly litigious (for analysis, see Addison and Hirsch, 1997). Labor law reforms could improve fairness, mitigate the contentiousness of the union organizing process, and facilitate organizing, thus slowing the decline in union density.[23] But union representation would remain very much the exception rather than the rule in the private sector. The case for labor law reforms that would *substantially* enhance organizing is weakened by what on balance appears to be a deleterious impact of unions, in their current form, on long-run economic performance. More fundamentally, labor unions as they now operate may not be the ideal organizational form to deliver the individual voice and cooperative work environment that workers want.[24]

Perhaps the fundamental problem with our current collective bargaining framework is the tension between a union's role as an agent of workplace democracy and voice and its role in redistributing income from owners (or consumers) to workers (Freeman and Lazear, 1995). A principal goal of labor law reform should be to encourage collective bargaining that enhances voice and cooperation while discouraging rent seeking. I salute any such efforts, but success is unlikely. Reforms that might work in this direction and that might muster sufficient political support are likely to have at most a modest effect on the steady-state level of union density. It is difficult to envision changes in labor law that will substantially change workplace governance for the more than 90 percent of private sector workers not covered by collective bargaining.

Continuation of the status quo appears likely, perhaps coupled with modest reforms in labor law and a growing role for government regulation in the workplace. Although not a preferred outcome, it is hardly a nightmare scenario. More of the same would permit continued economic growth and improvement in workers' standard of living. The economic pie would get larger and competition among employers would ensure that most (but not all) workers receive shares of the pie roughly commensurate with their economic contribution. Such a labor market, however, may produce less than the optimal level of worker participation and voice, with lower wealth and well-being than is at least theoretically possible (Levine and Tyson, 1990; Freeman and Lazear, 1995; Kaufman and Levine, 2000).

The remainder of this section is speculative, attempting to outline a general direction in which we might head in order to enhance worker voice and participation, an outcome that Freeman and Medoff once envisioned being possible through the positive face of traditional labor unions. As previous discussion has indicated, I am skeptical that labor unions can provide the principal road to enhanced voice in the workplace. If enhanced individual voice and participation are to occur, they must develop using a variety of approaches in multiple types of largely nonunion workplaces. Successful approaches to enhanced voice are unlikely to be mandated from above. Rather, they are likely to evolve through experimentation and cooperation among employers and their workers, with successful forms being imitated throughout the economy. Organized labor either will be reinvigorated and reinvented via competition — or will continue to whither.

I will not describe the specifics of what the future ought to look like. Rather, I first outline a set of criteria that workplace innovations should satisfy in order to evolve and flourish, followed by proposals that appear to satisfy these criteria. Whether beneficial changes (either those proposed here or elsewhere) can be identified and adopted via the political process is a different question, one about which I have little to say.

Criteria for Value-Enhancing Reforms in the Workplace[25]

A prerequisite for discussion of workplace reforms is to identify criteria that labor and employment law changes should satisfy. I offer the following. Reforms should: (1) be value enhancing for the parties and the economy;[26] (2) involve a greater role for individual and group voice within nonunion and union workplaces; (3) should encourage cooperation and participation across and among all levels of workers; (4) allow for variation in workplace governance type across heterogeneous workplaces; (5) allow flexibility within workplaces over time; (6) limit rather than facilitate rent seeking among worker organizations, including but not limited to labor unions; and (7) facilitate the evolution of workplace agents and institutions that best represent workers' interests and rights (Weil, 2003).

Absent major reforms and changes in current labor law, it is difficult to see how the current system can evolve toward adoption of employment governance structures embodying these characteristics. Meaningful change requires several things to occur. First, management must have incentives to initiate and encourage changes in workplace governance, changes that require removal of current legal barriers. Second, competitive pressures in product and labor markets are probably necessary. And third, pro-active changes in employment law and labor market regulations are likely necessary.

I discuss below two general approaches that have the potential to be value enhancing. The first approach is termed *conditional deregulation*. The second approach involves a change in the *labor law default* from no union to some alternative state. For each of these approaches, a move away from either the default regulatory structure or default governance structure within the firm requires approval of both management and workers (discussed below). The requirement for mutual agreement encourages management and workers to develop value-enhancing alternatives to the default structure.

Conditional Deregulation. Here I describe a variant of a proposal suggested by Levine (1995), which he describes as conditional deregulation. Levine recognizes that there are a large number of governmental mandates and regulatory measures regarding workplace safety, hours and overtime requirements, pensions, discrimination, family leave, and the like. Under a system of conditional deregulation, the default for all (or nearly all) firms would be that they are covered by the full extent of these labor market regulations. These requirements would be divided into those that are non-waivable and those waivable. Non-waivable rights would include some minimum set of standards (say, with respect to discrimination or safety) that could not be waived by any employer. Conditional deregulation would permit employers to be exempt from the waivable set of regulatory standards and be subject only to the minimum standards if they voluntarily adopt alternative regulatory systems with employee oversight and approval.

In order to waive the regulations or "deregulate" workplace standards, firms must have in place independent worker committees to perform the approval and oversight functions. For union companies, the union would provide the employee voice with authority to waive government standards (the employer must also approve the waiver). For nonunion employers, worker committees or councils would be created with authority to approve the waiver on behalf of workers. A contentious issue would be the nature of these committees and the permissible employer role. Unlike Levine, I would argue for abolishment or major reform of 8(a)(2) of the NLRA, which restricts the creation of and role for worker associations other than traditional labor unions. (I would support abolishment of 8(a)(2) even absent other reforms.) I would permit a reasonably active role for the firm in setting up such worker councils, as long as the worker groups meet minimum requirements regarding independence, democratic choice of worker spokespersons, secret balloting on key issues, and antidiscrimination provisions protecting workers active in the worker associations.[27]

An important benefit of such an approach would be that it would spur the establishment of worker associations throughout the private sector and provide a vehicle to enhance worker voice and participation, and possibly cooperation between management and its workers. In those establishments where worker associations are formed, its major role will likely be to facilitate the exchange of information and provide workers a collective voice. Such worker groups, however, may also serve as a vehicle to transfer rents or quasi-rents from shareholders to workers, since their approval of waiving workplace regulations is likely to be conditional on the receipt of monetary or non-monetary gains. Because the employer has the option of staying with the default regulatory standard, this makes it likely that any gains to workers through rent transfer will be less than the additional gains to shareholders from deregulation. In short, such a policy encourages value-enhancing choices by the firm and workers, while constraining the extent of rent seeking.

Adoption of conditional deregulation, as outlined above, would likely accelerate Congressional passage of waivable labor market mandates and employment regulations. Moreover, such regulations would likely set more stringent standards and contain fewer exemptions (based on company size and the like) than in the past. More stringent regulations could be costly absent the option to waive coverage. Given the availability of an opt-out, however, those establishments where regulations would prove costly are the ones most likely to agree on a mutually preferred set of alternative standards. The hope is that establishments will create workers' associations that gradually evolve into effective vehicles for voice, encouraging cooperation between management and its employees and facilitating value-enhancing changes in the workplace.

Conditional deregulation and the widespread creation of worker associations would have uncertain effects on unions. To the extent that nonunion worker associations substitute for traditional organizing, workers in some sectors may see even less reason to unionize. Just as likely an outcome is that conditional deregulation would provide the impetus for fundamental changes in and growth of labor unions in the private sector. With independent nonunion worker groups in place, workers in some firms will decide to turn to traditional collective bargaining and a more formalized union voice.

Changing the Labor Law Default. A second proposed approach would shift the labor law default from its current setting of not unionized to some alternative invoking a governance structure providing independent worker voice. The default structure could be waived or replaced following the joint approval of workers and management. A point to emphasize is that the choice of the labor law and employment regulation defaults matter a lot, even where there exist procedures to modify those outcomes (Sunstein, 2001). For example, current labor law has a nonunion default, but allows majority worker choice of union representation. Imagine the opposite, with union representation the default, but workers free to reject representation by majority vote. In a frictionless system in which preferences are unaffected by the initial allocation, one might expect the two systems to produce the same outcomes.[28]

Obviously, eventual representation outcomes would differ enormously depending on a union versus a nonunion default. For one thing, the NLRA union certification and decertification processes are far from frictionless. Even absent such frictions, however, evidence from behavioral economics (Sunstein, 2001; Choi et al., 2003) indicates that workers would be more likely to stick to their initial endowment (collective bargaining) than would have chosen to adopt it through free elections. Were union coverage the workplace default, far more than 10 percent of private sector workers would remain unionized, even with frictionless decertification elections.

Why does the default affect outcomes? First, change is costly. Second, individuals exhibit behavioral inertia, often sticking with an existing rule or environment as long as it does not differ too much from the preferred choice. Third, and very important, is that the default signals a norm that the state (or employer, etc.) has deemed appropriate. That is, the choice of a norm affects individuals' evaluation of alternative arrangements. Whatever the relative importance of these reasons, a default governance structure must be chosen carefully since many workplaces will not change from it.[29] That being said, the default is not a mandate, but a starting point or endowment (or bargaining "threat point") from which the parties can move.

What might be an appropriate labor law default other than the current nonunion default? My preference is for a default that establishes some form of independent worker association, although not one with full collective bargaining rights. As part of any default, workers would retain their current right to form independent unions (without management approval). An important feature of a default mechanism is that it designates a standard procedure by which workers and management might discuss, negotiate, and approve mutually beneficial changes. It would be important that 8(a)(2) of the NLRA be crippled or abolished. This would permit and encourage management to be involved in the development of their firm's labor relations system, but with workers now starting from an enhanced endowment or bargaining position. Although one cannot predict precisely how any given system might evolve and operate, the widespread availability of the Internet makes it likely that both management and employee groups will use electronic communications to provide and exchange information (Diamond and Freeman, 2001; Freeman, 2002).

Note that the proposal for a change in the employment default can be combined with Levine's proposal for conditional deregulation. Assume that the selected default establishes a relatively independent worker association in the workplace. Management and workers could then make a joint decision to opt-out of waivable federal workplace standards.

Whatever default, it will not function well in all workplaces. The same is true for our current labor law default. In these workplaces, the employer and workers (either in the form of unions or worker associations) have incentive to move away from the default and develop proposals for participatory value-enhancing governance structures. Over time, operation of the system and the observed choices of workers and firms will produce legislated and administrative changes in the default. The inability to identify in advance all outcomes of a given reform should not necessarily be regarded as a serious criticism. The same can be said about any change — or the status quo. Laws and regulations do evolve over time.

The important point is that not only can workplaces opt out of the default, but the search for an alternative governance structure involves a productive exchange of information and the exercise of worker and management voice. Adoption of such a proposal should encourage management, workers, and workers' agents (be they traditional unions or worker associations) to communicate, negotiate, and arrive at alternatives that make all parties better off relative to the default. Clearly, the current labor law default provides little incentive for management or traditional unions to develop alternatives. An alternative default that permitted greater flexibility, be it through conditional deregulation or nonunion worker associations, would encourage value-enhancing innovations.

A major change in employment law and the default governance structure obviously requires thorough analysis and careful design.[30] The actual working of such a system, however, will be determined in no small part by the way it evolves in the workplace, courts, and regulatory agencies. Surprises will occur. Unanticipated outcomes may be good or bad. One simply hopes (perhaps naïvely) that policy evolves to minimize undesirable and encourage desirable results. An important concern is that a shift in the default away from the nonunion standard toward one emphasizing collective voice might shift too much power to incumbent workers (insiders), leading to employer cost levels inconsistent with full employment. It may prove difficult to limit the ability of worker associations or works councils to appropriate rents within a framework that promotes voice and the evolution of value-enhancing arrangements (Freeman and Lazear, 1995). But it strikes me that it's worth a try.

I sensibly end this rather speculative section on a sober note. The most likely prospect for the future, or at least the near future, is not adoption of any proposal discussed above, but continuation of the status quo. Changing the status quo in employment law does not appear feasible. Major changes cannot occur politically until there is strong dissatisfaction with our current system and a consensus that change is likely beneficial. While such a consensus may exist among legal and industrial relations scholars, it does not exist among workers or the general public. The emergence of a consensus for major workplace changes could result from some future economic and social upheaval. Whether such an upheaval will occur, its form if it does so, and the nature of a new majority consensus are far beyond the scope of this paper — and my imagination.

An alternative scenario is that major changes in workplace governance will occur, but that they will occur incrementally, absent a major upheaval or a spur via major public policy changes. A premise of my discussion has been that there are potential gains from greater employee voice and worker participation. What is needed is a governance form or workplace arrangements to make these gains possible. If 8(a)(2) were abolished, one can imagine such arrangements gradually evolving, working well in some workplaces, and then being adopted elsewhere in various forms. The Internet will likely play a major role in any such evolution (Diamond and Freeman, 2001; Freeman, 2002). Labor unions, companies, and other workplace organizations already use the Internet heavily to communicate with their members or workers. There are isolated examples (Wal-Mart, IBM) where union-like worker voice groups, with little prospect for collective bargaining coverage, have emerged through the Internet, facilitating exchange of information and sometimes influencing company policies (Freeman, 2002). Employee voice is about communication and information, both of which are facilitated through electronic communication over networks. Whether effective nonunion employee voice and participation, coupled with an evolving and increasingly supportive legal and regulatory structure, will emerge, remains to be seen. Twenty years ago, Freeman and Medoff saw little need to address alternative nonunion forms for worker voice. Were *What Do Unions Do?* being written today, this is no doubt a subject the authors would consider.

VII. Conclusion

A common characterization of *What Do Unions Do?*, one heard largely although not exclusively from outside the research community, is that Freeman and Medoff argue that unions are unambiguously good — good for their members, good for economic performance, and good for society as a whole. Such a simplistic generalization about unions was inaccurate in 1984 and is still inaccurate today. But this is not what Freeman and Medoff say in *What Do Unions Do?* It is true that they tend to emphasize positive aspects of unionism. But this must be seen in context. A major and legitimate goal of *What Do Unions Do?* was to critique neoclassical economists for their then disproportionate focus on the "single face" monopoly aspects of labor unions. (Their challenge to industrial relations scholars has not been to broaden scope but to provide evidence.) They emphasize that there is a second and perhaps primary face of unions — the collective voice/institutional response face. *What Do Unions Do?* establishes that voice or nonmonopolistic aspects of unions should not be ignored and are worthy of serious analysis. Freeman and Medoff then provide a comprehensive empirical analysis of labor unions and interpret their findings in an intellectually honest manner. A broader "multi-face" view of unionism became widely accepted following the book's publication in 1984, and this perspective remains widely accepted today. And the analysis summarized in *What Do Unions Do?* has served as a reference point and stimulant for much of the subsequent literature on unions, much of which is examined in this and other papers in this symposium.

How have the empirical findings summarized in *What Do Unions Do?* held up over time? For the most part, the empirical regularities that they identify as union effects have been sustained in subsequent research. I have focused on the chapters on unions and economic performance — productivity, investment, growth, and profitability. The subsequent literature has proven less favorable for unions than the conclusions reached by Freeman and Medoff. That being said, little literature existed at the time *What Do Unions Do?* was written and, even now, the empirical evidence in this area is (understandably) limited and cannot establish (or reject) causal union effects or their magnitudes nearly so conclusively as one might like. Freeman and Medoff are clearly correct that variation in union productivity effects vary substantially across workplaces. But their conclusion that union effects are generally positive, which I interpret to mean a nontrivial positive average effect, cannot be sustained, subsequent evidence suggesting an average union productivity effect near zero and at most modestly positive (say, 2–5 percent). Their speculation that productivity effects are larger in more competitive environments appears to hold up, but more evidence on this score would be desirable. Subsequent literature has continued to find unions associated with lower profits. Unlike Freeman and Medoff, several of the studies conclude that unions tax not just monopoly profits, but also the quasi-rents or long-run normal returns emanating from long-lived physical capital and R&D. Lower profits and the union tax on tangible and intangible capital has led to slower employment and productivity growth among union companies, reinforcing the downward trend in private sector unionism. Although union firms grow more slowly, Freeman and Medoff appear correct that unions do not lead to higher rates of business failure.

Even adopting a positive view of the evidence on unions and performance, union effects have not been sufficient to offset what are large (by international standards) union wage premiums in the United States. Because the voice face of unions depends so crucially on cooperative labor relations, management resistance to unionism and union organizing in the years since *What Do Unions Do?* has precluded any chance there might have been for this to be a period of expanding, cooperative, value-enhancing unionism. In short, the collective-voice face of unionism has been muted (or swamped) during the 20 years since publication of *What Do Unions Do?* One can argue as to how much of the management opposition is ideological, how much stems from the economic incentives of management to hold down costs in the face of union wage premiums and a highly competitive environment (Freeman and Kleiner, 1990), and how much is the result of labor law enforcement and generally low penalties (Kleiner, 2002). All three explanations clearly matter.

What Do Unions Do? has provided scholars and the public with a comprehensive and innovative documentation of the economic effects of unions. Yet whatever one's assessment of the evidence, old-style private sector unionism will continue to play a smaller and smaller role in the U.S. workplace. The publication date of *What Do Unions Do?* was doubly timely. It could not have appeared much sooner, given that the micro-level data sets on which much of the analysis is based had only recently become available. And although the empirical relationships uncovered by Freeman and Medoff look much the same today as twenty years ago, the focus of the book inevitably would have had to shift toward public sector unionism, alternatives to private sector unionism, or international comparisons (precisely the topics on which Freeman has subsequently focused). Labor economists and industrial relations scholars truly have been fortunate. Freeman and Medoff told us what private sector unions do while there remained unions doing it.

The research program ignited by *What Do Unions Do?* has continued apace as private sector unionism has declined. This program has been a rich one, extending beyond economists' earlier focus on monopoly unionism and union wage gaps and instead pursuing the ambitious agenda set by Freeman and Medoff. A principal concern among scholars has been the same concern made explicit in *What Do Unions Do?* How can we encourage value-enhancing workplace arrangements that facilitate voice among workers, while constraining unions' monopoly face? Freeman and Medoff focus their attention on traditional labor unionism. But with union density unlikely to rebound in the foreseeable future, the focus in recent literature is increasingly on the 90 percent of private sector workers without a formal mechanism for individual or collective voice and on new forms of workplace governance that might facilitate such voice.

I have provided some rather speculative ideas on the future of workplace voice. A likely path is that we will remain with something akin to the status quo, thus foregoing potential benefits from increased voice and participation. I have described new employment law defaults that might encourage the development of value-enhancing workplace governance structures — that is, those that make possible the benefits of voice with minimal rent seeking. "Radical" changes of this sort, however, appear politically impossible absent major social or political upheavals that economists have little ability to foresee (Freeman, 1998). A more likely avenue for change will be the gradual evolution of the workplace environment, employment law, and workplace governance in ways conducive to voice, participation, technological change (affecting what workers do), and the economic environments in which companies and households operate. There is of course no guarantee that the evolutionary changes produced in a competitive world will result in the type of arrangements described in the industrial relations literature. Nor can we envision what precise paths might be taken to effect such changes, although intensive Internet use for exchanging information, coordination of activities, and facilitating collective action appears likely. If future paths lead to workplace governance structures that take advantage of worker voice while restraining collective rent seeking, it will be in no small part a product of the productive discourse fueled by *What Do Unions Do?*

Notes

*   The paper benefited from the detailed comments of Bruce Kaufman and helpful discussion with John Addison.

1.   When I refer to Freeman and Medoff's "story" I refer to what the authors actually state in *What Do Unions Do?* and not to the simplistic (and incorrect) caricature of their work as saying that unions are everywhere good.
2.   There have been numerous surveys or appraisals of unions and performance in the United States and in other countries; see, for example, Becker and Olson (1987), Addison and Hirsch (1989), Booth (1995), Belman (1992), Freeman (1992), Kuhn (1998), Hirsch (1997), Doucouliagos and Laroche (2003), Aidt and Tzannatos (2002), Metcalf (2003), and Van Reenen and Menezes-Filho (2003).
3.   Addison and Hirsch (1989) make this point, largely rejecting the critique of Brown and Medoff (1978) made by Reynolds (1986).
4.   More broadly, what shows up using the production function approach is the effects of any factor (not elsewhere controlled for) affecting productivity and correlated with unionism. For example, the impact of union pay compression, which can positively or negatively affect productivity, would be included in estimated union productivity effects.
5.   Recent literature (Manning, 2003) argues that many firms face upward sloping supply curves (i.e., have a work force with limited mobility) and thus have leeway in their choice of wage policies. Unlike classical monopsony theory, the "new

monopsony" literature downplays the importance of market structure and provides few implications about employment and efficiency (just as price discrimination does not have clear-cut implications for output and efficiency). A principal outcome of new monopsony is wage heterogeneity. It is not clear if this literature has a lot to say about union performance outcomes, apart from the obvious point that the nonunion counterfactual is more complex than a textbook competitive labor market. The empirical importance of the new monopsony literature remains to be seen.

6. Using standard theory, a wage gain can decrease capital if scale effects exceed substitution effects, but the capital-labor ratio unambiguously rises. If unions tax capital (i.e., the returns on capital facilitate wage gains), there is no presumption that the factor mix is either more or less capital intensive in union firms (Hirsch and Prasad, 1995). No distortion in the factor mix also follows from bargaining models with "strong efficiency" outcomes (a vertical contract curve). Empirical tests of contract models are particularly difficult (Farber, 1986; Abowd, 1989; Pencavel, 1991).

7. I provide no discussion of experimental methods, which have so far played little role in the literature on unions and performance. The experimental literature in personnel economics has added much to our knowledge about how workers perceive and respond to alternative compensation schemes and workplace policies. Such results have potential to inform discussion of how unions impact the workplace, getting inside the proverbial black box.

8. This criticism does not apply to events studies measuring changes in equity value, since changes in stock price quickly reflect investors' expectations as to the present value of future changes due to unionism. A separate question is whether investors are good at predicting how unionization will affect firm performance.

9. Portions of this section rely on my earlier survey of unions and performance (Hirsch, 1997).

10. In a paper on "what unions do now" Turnbull (2003) makes this point forcefully, arguing for increased multidisciplinary research on unions and the need for greater relevance.

11. The specific question asked was: "What is your best estimate of the percentage impact of unions on the productivity of unionized companies?" (Fuchs et al., 1998, pp. 1392, 1418).

12. I exclude a study by Cooke (1994), who examines data on 841 Michigan manufacturing firms. Cooke's principal focus is on union-nonunion differences in the effect of employee participation programs and profit sharing on productivity. In his sample of firms, union companies have substantially higher output per worker, but Cooke has no measure of firm capital intensity, instead controlling for two-digit industry capital per employee, which assigns the same capital intensity to union and nonunion firms. Its coefficient is small and barely significant. Prior studies of manufacturing firms or businesses (Clark, 1984; Hirsch, 1991a) find that the capital-labor ratio is the single most important determinant of labor productivity, union firms are somewhat more capital-intensive (unions are more likely to organize successfully in capital-intensive plants), and resulting union-nonunion productivity differences are negative and close to zero. There is little way to know how much of the union-nonunion productivity difference in Cooke's study results from differences in capital intensity; it is unlikely to explain all the difference. The Michigan sample is likely to contain many firms in motor vehicles and transportation supply, an industry where Hirsch (1991) finds union firms to have a large productivity advantage.

13. Nickell and Layard (1999) and Metcalf (2003) reach similar conclusions in their evaluation of international evidence. Human resource management (HRM) practices such as TQM do not automatically increase productivity. It appears that the

circumstances under which they are adopted make a difference (Kleiner et al., 2002). HRM practices that increase productivity typically increase worker compensation; thus, costs need not decline (Cappelli and Neumark, 2001).

14. Ichniowski et al. (1997) also examine the effect of HRM practices on productivity. They collect data on steel finishing lines with a common technology but different HRM practices. They conclude that innovative practices increase productivity when introduced jointly (rather than individually). The authors estimate union effects, but say little about these, no doubt due to the paucity of nonunion lines (8 percent of the 2,190 line months and what may be just 5 of their 60 steel lines). They obtain union coefficients that are generally small and vary across specifications.

15. A general point in the literature is that union productivity effects depend on the state of labor relations. Recent studies provide evidence that productivity or quality suffers as a result of strikes and labor unrest. Kleiner et al. (2002) conclude that the productivity effects of strikes and slowdowns at a commercial airline manufacturer are temporary. Using auction data, Mas (2002) finds that construction equipment produced by Caterpillar at its U.S. plants during periods of labor unrest was more likely to be subsequently resold and sold at a deeper discount. Krueger and Mas (2004) find that tire defect rates were particularly high at a Bridgestone/Firestone plant during periods of labor unrest.

16. See Addison and Hirsch (1989) and Booth (1995) for references (a study not cited is Byrne et al., 1996). There are exceptions to the conclusion regarding productivity effects in noncompetitive settings. An analysis of hospitals by Register (1988) finds higher productivity in union than in nonunion hospitals. A recent paper by Ash and Seago (2004) concludes that there are lower rates of heart attack mortality in California among hospitals with union rather than nonunion registered nurses. This conclusion is based in large part on declines in mortality among a relatively small number of hospitals that became unionized during the sample period.

17. The logic here is identical to the survivor bias argument in measuring returns to mutual funds. If one measures past returns (over, say, ten years) of surviving funds (a balanced panel), average performance is relatively favorable. If one measures the average across all funds in each of the ten years (an unbalanced panel) average performance, which now includes funds that failed, is below the market as a whole (for evidence, see Malkiel, 2003). Even if no funds failed, an upward bias exists if one weights the funds based on current fund assets, since poorly performing funds would have decreased in relative size over time.

18. Using business-level data, Ravenscraft (1983) finds that market share, but not industry concentration, is related to profitability. Following aggregation, he shows that the positive relationship between industry profit measures and concentration derive from the correlation of concentration with mean market share and not concentration per se.

19. An additional challenge to the standard model comes from the literature on efficient contracts. There are settlements off the labor-demand curve, with lower wages and higher employment, preferred by both the union and management. Efficient contracts require simultaneous bargaining (explicit or implicit) over wages and employment rather than sequential determination (agreement on the wage followed by the firm's choice of employment). If settlements are not on the labor-demand curve, the effect of unions on factor mix cannot be predicted in straightforward fashion (for analysis of these models, see Farber, 1986; Pencavel, 1991).

20. Using firm-level Compustat data and union data from Hirsch (1991a), Cavanaugh (1996) shows that the deleterious union effects on market value and investment are directly related to the ease with which quasi-rents can be appropriated.

21. Canadian evidence on unions and employment growth appear consistent with that in the United States. Long (1993) utilizes survey data from a survey of 510 Canadian business establishments in the manufacturing and nonmanufacturing sectors. Union establishments (i.e., establishments with employees covered by collective bargaining agreements) had considerably slower employment growth between 1980 and 1985, although in manufacturing roughly half of the slower growth resulted not from unionism per se but from location in industries showing slower growth (industry effects were not important in the nonmanufacturing sector). After accounting for industry controls, firm size, and firm age, union establishments in the manufacturing (nonmanufacturing) sector had growth rates 3.7 (3.9) percent per year below those of nonunion establishments (union employment growth was negative over the period). For European evidence, see the recent paper by Addison et al. (2003) and the literature survey by Metcalf (2004).

22. In their words: "Unions reduce profits but they do not 'destroy the goose that lays the golden egg'" (Freeman and Kleiner, 1999, p. 526). Using even more colorful language, Kuhn (1998, p. 1039) states: "Like successful viruses, unions are smart enough not to kill their hosts." Kremer and Olken (2001) apply a formal evolutionary biology model to unions, noting that parasites that kill their hosts do not spread, whereas those that do little harm spread and may evolve to become essential to their hosts. They conclude that unions maximizing the present value of members' wages are likely to be displaced by more moderate unions. Exogenous firm turnover lowers equilibrium union density since unions must work harder (organize more) to stay in place.

23. Discussion of labor law reforms is beyond the scope of the paper. Among the recommendations proposed by the Dunlop Commission during the mid-1990s were: narrowing the definition of supervisory and managerial workers who are exempt from the NLRA, shortening the time between the call for union elections and conduct of the elections, increased access of workers to union organizers, procedures such as mediation to facilitate newly certified unions to achieve first contracts, and fast injunctive relief against discriminatory action by employers. Estreicher (1996) discusses various labor law reforms intended to facilitate "value-added unionism" in the workplace. He starts from the premise that labor markets are overregulated and that greater freedom of contract would enhance development of preferred labor-management arrangements.

24. For a description and data on what workers want, see Freeman and Rogers (1999). Kaufman (2001) provides a discussion and critique. Workers appear to desire individual voice and cooperation — not union voice per se.

25. These proposals follow discussion previously presented in Hirsch and Schumacher (2002).

26. For change to be enhancing for the parties, the "value of the enterprise" must increase. Abowd (1989) defines the value of the enterprise as the sum of firm market value and worker rents.

27. The TEAM Act, passed by Congress but vetoed by President Clinton in July 1996, would have limited the scope of 8(a)(2) and allowed employer-organized and employer-funded worker participation groups in nonunion plants and offices. I support such legislation, whereas Levine would continue protections that prevent creation of "company unions." For evidence on how company unions worked prior to passage of the NLRA, see Kaufman (2000).

28. In order to focus on the role of defaults, I assume that majority approval is synonymous with union coverage, ignoring the issue of obtaining a first contract following a union win.

29. Choi et al. (2003) make the interesting point that where preferences are diverse and the firm (or state in our case) cannot readily identify a preferred default rule, it can make sense to assign a highly inefficient default, thus encouraging parties to select a preferred alternative. Where preferences are homogeneous and change is costly, it is important to choose a default close to the parties' preferred outcome. Choi et al. analyze pension contribution rules for workers within a firm. Our situation is more difficult, since a common governance structure is being assigned for workers within the firm who may have heterogeneous preferences.

30. Relevant is the experience that other countries have had or will have with worker councils and alternative forms of organization, particularly in countries with relatively decentralized wage setting. The European Union Charter of Fundamental Rights of December 2000 provides for what appears to be broad-based guarantees for workers to have rights for information, consultation, and collective agreements (European Union, 2000, Articles 27, 28). How the Charter will be interpreted and implemented is unclear, but European experiences deriving from the Charter may well hold lessons for U.S. employment law reforms.

References

Abowd, John M. "The Effect of Wage Bargains on the Stock Market Value of the Firm." *American Economic Review* 79 (September 1989): 774–800.

_____ and Henry S. Farber. "Job Queues and the Union Status of Workers." *Industrial and Labor Relations Review* 35 (April 1982): 354–67.

Addison, John T. and John B. Chilton. "Self-Enforcing Union Contracts: Efficient Investment and Employment." *Journal of Business* 71 (July 1998): 349–69.

Addison, John T., John S. Heywood, and Xiangdong Wei. "New Evidence on Unions and Plant Closings: Britain in the 1990s." *Southern Economic Journal* 69 (April 2003): 822–41.

Addison, John T. and Barry T. Hirsch. "Union Effects on Productivity, Profits, and Growth: Has the Long Run Arrived?" *Journal of Labor Economics* 7 (January 1989): 72–105.

_____. "The Economic Effects of Employment Regulation: What Are the Limits?" In Bruce E. Kaufman, ed. *Government Regulation of the Employment Relationship*. Madison, Wisc.: *Industrial Relations Research Association*, 1997, pp. 125–78.

Addison, John T. and W. Stanley Siebert. "Recent Changes in the Industrial Relations Framework in the UK." In John T. Addison and Claus Schnabel, eds. *International Handbook of Trade Unions*. Northampton, Mass.: Edward Elgar, 2003, pp. 415–60.

Aidt, Toke and Zafiris Tzannatos. *Unions and Collective Bargaining: Economic Effects in a Global Environment*. Washington, D.C.: World Bank, 2002.

Allen, Steven G. "The Effect of Unionism on Productivity in Privately and Publicly Owned Hospitals and Nursing Homes." *Journal of Labor Research* 7 (Winter 1986a): 59–68.

_____. "Unionization and Productivity in Office Building and School Construction." *Industrial and Labor Relations Review* 39 (January 1986b): 187–201.

Ash, Michael and Jean Ann Seago. "The Effect of Registered Nurses on Heart-Attack Mortality." *Industrial and Labor Relations Review* 57 (April 2004): 422–42.

Baldwin, Carliss Y. "Productivity and Labor Unions: An Application of the Theory of Self-Enforcing Contracts." *Journal of Business* 56 (April 1983): 155–85.

Becker, Brian E. and Craig A. Olson. "Labor Relations and Firm Performance." In M. Kleiner, R. Block, M. Roomkin, and S. Salsburg, eds. *Human Resources and the Performance of the Firm*. Madison, Wisc.: Industrial Relations Research Association, 1987, pp. 43–86.

_____. "Unionization and Firm Profits." *Industrial Relations* 31 (Fall 1992): 395–415.

Belman, Dale. "Unions, The Quality of Labor Relations, and Firm Performance." In Lawrence Mishel and Paula B. Voos, eds. *Unions and Economic Competitiveness.* Armonk, N.Y.: M.E. Sharpe, 1992, pp. 41–107.

Betts, Julian R., Cameron W. Odgers, and Michael K. Wilson. "The Effects of Unions on Research and Development: An Empirical Analysis Using Multi-Year Data." *Canadian Journal of Economics* 34 (August 2001): 785–806.

Black, Sandra E. and Lisa M. Lynch. "How to Compete: The Impact of Workplace Practices and Information Technology on Productivity." *Review of Economics and Statistics* 83 (August 2001): 434–45.

Blanchflower, David G. and Alex Bryson. "Changes Over Time in Union Relative Wage Effects in the UK and the US Revisited." National Bureau of Economic Research Working Paper 9395, December 2002.

Blanchflower, David G. and Richard B. Freeman. "Unionism in the United States and Other Advanced OECD Countries." In M. Bognanno and M. Kleiner, eds. *Labor Market Institutions and the Future Role of Unions.* Cambridge, Mass.: Blackwell Publishers, 1992, pp. 56–79.

Booth, Alison L. *The Economics of the Trade Union.* Cambridge: Cambridge University Press, 1995.

Bratsberg, Bernt and James F. Ragan, Jr. "Changes in the Union Wage Premium by Industry." *Industrial and Labor Relations Review* 56 (October 2002): 65–83.

Bronars, Stephen G. and Donald R. Deere. "Union Representation Elections and Firm Profitability." *Industrial Relations* 29 (Winter 1990): 15–37.

_____. "Unionization, Incomplete Contracting, and Capital Investment." *Journal of Business* 66 (January 1993): 117–32.

_____ and Joseph S. Tracy. "The Effects of Unions on Firm Behavior: An Empirical Analysis Using Firm-Level Data." *Industrial Relations* 33 (October 1994): 426–51.

Brown, Charles and James Medoff. "Trade Unions in the Production Process." *Journal of Political Economy* 86 (June 1978): 355–78.

Byrne, Dennis, Hashem Dezhbakhsh, and Randall King. "Unions and Police Productivity: An Econometric Investigation." *Industrial Relations* 35 (October 1996): 566–84.

Cappelli, Peter and David Neumark. "Do 'High Performance' Work Practices Improve Establishment Level Outcomes?" *Industrial and Labor Relations Review* 54 (July 2001): 737–75.

Card, David. "The Effect of Unions on the Structure of Wages: A Longitudinal Analysis." *Econometrica* 64 (July 1996): 957–79.

Cavanaugh, Joseph K. "Asset Specific Investment and Unionized Labor." *Industrial Relations* 37 (January 1998): 35–50.

Chappell, William F., Walter J. Mayer, and William F. Shughart II. "Union Rents and Market Structure Revisited." *Journal of Labor Research* 12 (Winter 1991): 35–46.

Choi, James J., David Laibson, Brigitte C. Madrian, and Andrew Metrick. "Optimal Defaults." *American Economic Review* 93 (May 2003): 180–85.

Clark, Kim B. "The Impact of Unionization on Productivity: A Case Study." *Industrial and Labor Relations Review* 33 (July 1980a): 451–69.

_____. "Unionization and Productivity: Micro-Econometric Evidence." *Quarterly Journal of Economics* 95 (December 1980b): 613–39.

_____. "Unionization and Firm Performance: The Impact on Profits, Growth, and Productivity." *American Economic Review* 74 (December 1984): 893–919.

Connolly, Robert A., Barry T. Hirsch, and Mark Hirschey. "Union Rent Seeking, Intangible Capital, and Market Value of the Firm." *Review of Economics and Statistics* 68 (November 1986): 567–77.

Diamond, Wayne J. and Richard B. Freeman. "Will Unionism Prosper in Cyber-Space? The Promise of the Internet for Employee Organization." National Bureau of Economic Research Working Paper 8483, September 2001.

DiNardo, John and David S. Lee. "The Impact of Unionization on Establishment Closure: A Regression Discontinuity Analysis of Representation Elections." National Bureau of Economic Research Working Paper 8993, June 2002.

Domowitz, Ian R., Glenn Hubbard, and Bruce C. Peterson. "The Intertemporal Stability of the Concentration-Margins Relationship." *Journal of Industrial Economics* 35 (September 1986): 13–34.

Doucouliagos, Chris and Patrice Laroche. "What Do Unions Do to Productivity? A Meta-Analysis." *Industrial Relations* 42 (October 2003): 650–91.

Dunne, Timothy and David A. Macpherson. "Unionism and Gross Employment Flows." *Southern Economic Journal* 60 (January 1994): 727–38.

Estreicher, Samuel. "Freedom of Contract and Labor Law Reform: Opening Up the Possibilities for Value-Added Unionism." *New York University Law Review* 71 (June 1996): 827–49.

European Union. "Charter of Fundamental Rights of the European Union." *Official Journal of the European Communities* C 364 (December 2000): 1–22, at http://www.europarl.eu.int/charter/pdf/text_en.pdf.

Fallick, Bruce C. and Kevin A. Hassett. "Investment and Union Certification." *Journal of Labor Economics* 17 (July 1999): 570–82.

Farber, Henry S. "The Analysis of Union Behavior." In Orley C. Ashenfelter and Richard Layard, eds. *Handbook of Labor Economics, Vol. II.* Amsterdam: Elsevier, 1986, pp. 1039–89.

_____ and Bruce Western. "Accounting for the Decline of Unions in the Private Sector, 1973-1988." In James Bennett and Bruce Kaufman, eds. *The Future of Private Sector Unionism in the United States.* Armonk, N.Y.: M.E. Sharpe, 2002, pp. 28–58.

Freeman, Richard B. "The Exit-Voice Tradeoff in the Labor Market: Unionism, Job Tenure, Quits and Separations." *Quarterly Journal of Economics* 94 (June 1980): 643–74.

_____. "Longitudinal Analyses of the Effects of Trade Unions." *Journal of Labor Economics* 2 (January 1984): 1–26.

_____. "Is Declining Unionization of the U.S. Good, Bad, or Irrelevant?" In Lawrence Mishel and Paula B. Voos, eds. *Unions and Economic Competitiveness.* Armonk, N.Y.: M.E. Sharpe, 1991, pp. 143–69.

_____. "Spurts in Union Growth: Defining Moments and Social Processes." In Michael D.Bordo, Claudia Goldin and Eugene N. White, eds. *The Defining Moment: The Great Depression and the American Economy in the Twentieth Century.* Chicago: University of Chicago Press (NBER), 1998, pp. 265–96.

_____. "The Labor Market in the New Information Economy." National Bureau of Economic Research Working Paper 9254, October 2002.

_____ and Morris M. Kleiner. "Employer Behavior in the Face of Union Organizing Drives." *Industrial and Labor Relations Review* 43 (April 1990): 351–65.

_____. "Do Unions Make Enterprises Insolvent?" *Industrial and Labor Relations Review* 52 (July 1999): 510–27.

Freeman, Richard B. and Edward P. Lazear. "An Economic Analysis of Works Councils." In Joel Rogers and Wolfgang Streeck, eds. *Works Councils: Consultation, Repre-*

sentation, and Cooperation in Industrial Relations. Chicago: University of Chicago Press (NBER), 1995, pp. 27–50.

Freeman, Richard B. and James L. Medoff. "The Two Faces of Unionism." *Public Interest* 57 (Fall 1979): 69–93.

_____. *What Do Unions Do?* New York: Basic Books, 1984.

Freeman, Richard B. and Joel Rogers. *What Workers Want.* Ithaca, N.Y.: Cornell University Press, 1999.

Fuchs, Victor R., Alan B. Krueger and James M. Poterba. "Economists' Views about Parameters, Values, and Policies: Survey Results in Labor and Public Economics." *Journal of Economic Literature* 36 (September 1998): 1387–425.

Grant, Darren. "A Comparison of the Cyclical Behavior of Union and Nonunion Wages in the United States." *Journal of Human Resources* 36 (Winter 2001): 31–57.

Grout, Paul A. "Investment and Wages in the Absence of Binding Contracts: A Nash Bargaining Approach." *Econometrica* 52 (March 1984): 449–60.

Hirsch, Barry T. "Trucking Regulation, Unionization, and Labor Earnings: 1973–1985." *Journal of Human Resources* 23 (Summer 1988): 296–319.

_____. "Market Structure, Union Rent Seeking, and Firm Profitability." *Economics Letters* 32 (January 1990): 75–79.

_____. *Labor Unions and the Economic Performance of U.S. Firms.* Kalamazoo, Mich.: Upjohn Institute for Employment Research, 1991a.

_____. "Union Coverage and Profitability among U.S. Firms." *Review of Economics and Statistics* 73 (February 1991b): 69–77.

_____. "Firm Investment Behavior and Collective Bargaining Strategy." In Mario F. Bognanno and Morris M. Kleiner, eds. *Labor Market Institutions and the Future Role of Unions.* Cambridge, Mass.: Blackwell Publishers, 1992, 95–121.

_____. "Unionization and Economic Performance: Evidence on Productivity, Profits, Investment, and Growth." In Fazil Mihlar, ed. *Unions and Right-to-Work Laws.* Vancouver, B.C.: Fraser Institute, 1997, pp. 35–70.

_____ and John T. Addison. *The Economic Analysis of Unions: New Approaches and Evidence.* Boston: Allen & Unwin, 1986.

Hirsch, Barry T. and Robert A. Connolly. "Do Unions Capture Monopoly Profits?" *Industrial and Labor Relations Review* 41 (October 1987): 118–36.

Hirsch, Barry T. and David A. Macpherson. "Earnings and Employment in Trucking: Deregulating a Naturally Competitive Industry." In James Peoples, ed. *Regulatory Reform and Labor Markets.* Norwell, Mass.: Kluwer Academic Publishing, 1998, pp. 61–112.

_____. "Earnings, Rents, and Competition in the Airline Labor Market." *Journal of Labor Economics* 18 (January 2000): 125–55.

_____. "Union Membership and Coverage Database from the Current Population Survey: Note." *Industrial and Labor Relations Review* 56 (January 2003): 349–54, and accompanying data site http://www.unionstats.com/.

Hirsch, Barry T. and Barbara A. Morgan. "Shareholder Risk and Returns in Union and Nonunion Firms." *Industrial and Labor Relations Review* 47 (January 1994): 302–18.

Hirsch, Barry T. and Kislaya Prasad. "Wage-Employment Determination and a Union Tax on Capital: Can Theory and Evidence Be Reconciled?" *Economics Letters* 48 (April 1995): 61–71.

Hirsch, Barry T. and Edward J. Schumacher. "Unions, Wages, and Skills." *Journal of Human Resources* 33 (Winter 1998): 201–19.

_____. "Private Sector Union Density and the Wage Premium: Past, Present, and Future." In James Bennett and Bruce Kaufman, eds. *The Future of Private Sector Unionism in the United States.* Armonk, N.Y.: M.E. Sharpe, 2002, pp. 92–128.

Hirsch, Barry T., Michael L. Wachter, and James W. Gillula. "Postal Service Compensation and the Comparability Standard." *Research in Labor Economics* 18 (1999): 243–79.

Ichniowski, Casey, Kathryn Shaw, and Giovanna Prennushi. "The Effects of Human Resource Management Practices on Productivity: A Study of Steel Finishing Lines." *American Economic Review* 87 (June 1997): 291–313.

Karier, Thomas. "Unions and Monopoly Profits." *Review of Economics and Statistics* 67 (February 1985): 34–42.

Katz, Harry C. and John Paul MacDuffie. "Collective Bargaining in the U.S. Auto Assembly Sector." In Paula B. Voos, ed. *Contemporary Collective Bargaining in the Private Sector.* Madison, Wisc.: Industrial Relations Research Association, 1994, pp. 181–224.

Kaufman, Bruce E. "Accomplishments and Shortcomings of Nonunion Employee Representation in the Pre-Wagner Act Years: A Reassessment." In Bruce E. Kaufman, and Daphne Taras, eds. *Nonunion Employee Representation: History, Contemporary Practice, and Policy.* Armonk, N.Y.: M.E. Sharpe, 2000, pp. 21–60.

_____. "The Employee Participation/Representation Gap: An Assessment and Proposed Solution." *University of Pennsylvania Journal of Labor and Employment Law* 3 (Spring 2001): 491–550.

_____ and David I. Levine. "An Economic Analysis of Employee Representation." In Bruce E. Kaufman and Daphne Taras, eds. *Nonunion Employee Representation: History, Contemporary Practice, and Policy.* Armonk, N.Y.: M.E. Sharpe, 2000, pp. 149–75.

Kleiner, Morris. "Intensity of Management Resistance: Understanding the Decline of Unionization in the Private Sector." In James Bennett and Bruce Kaufman, eds. *The Future of Private Sector Unionism in the United States.* Armonk, N.Y.: M.E. Sharpe, 2002, pp. 292–316.

_____, Jonathan Leonard, and Adam Pilarski. "How Industrial Relations Affect Plant Performance: The Case of Commercial Aircraft Manufacturing." *Industrial and Labor Relations Review* 55 (January 2002): 195–219.

Kremer, Michael and Benjamin A. Olken. "A Biological Model of Unions." National Bureau of Economic Research Working Paper 8257, April 2001.

Krueger, Alan B. and Alexandre Mas. "Strikes, Scabs and Tread Separations: Labor Strife and the Production of Defective Bridgestone/Firestone Tires."*Journal of Political Economy* 112 (April 2004): 253–89.

Kuhn, Peter. "Unions and the Economy: What We Know; What We Should Know." *Canadian Journal of Economics* 31 (November 1998): 1033–56.

LaLonde, Robert J., Gérard Marschke, and Kenneth Troske. "Using Longitudinal Data on Establishments to Analyze the Effects of Union Organizing Campaigns in the United States." *Annales d' Économie et de Statistique* 41/42 (1996): 155–85.

Leonard, Jonathan S. "Unions and Employment Growth." In Mario F. Bognanno and Morris M. Kleiner, eds. *Labor Market Institutions and the Future Role of Unions.* Cambridge, Mass.: Blackwell Publishers, 1992, pp. 80–94.

Levine, David I. *Reinventing the Workplace: How Business and Employees Can Both Win.* Washington, D.C.: Brookings Institution, 1995.

_____ and Laura D'Andrea Tyson. "Participation, Productivity, and the Firm's Environment." In Alan S. Blinder, ed. *Paying for Productivity: A Look at the Evidence.* Washington, D.C.: Brookings Institution, 1990, pp. 183–237.

Lewis, H. Gregg. *Union Relative Wage Effects: A Survey.* Chicago: University of Chicago Press, 1986.

Linneman, Peter D., Michael L. Wachter, and William H. Carter. "Evaluating the Evidence on Union Employment and Wages." *Industrial and Labor Relations Review* 44 (October 1990): 34–53.

Long, Richard J. "The Effect of Unionization on Employment Growth of Canadian Companies." *Industrial and Labor Relations Review* 46 (July 1993): 691–703.

Malkiel, Burton G. *A Random Walk Down Wall Street,* 8th ed. New York: Norton, 2003.

Manning, Alan. *Monopsony in Motion: Imperfect Competition in Labor Markets.* Princeton, N.J.: Princeton University Press, 2003.

Mas, Alexandre. "Labor Unrest, Fairness and the Quality of Production: Evidence from the Construction Equipment Resale Market." Princeton University, November 2002.

Menezes-Filho, Naercio, David Ulph, and John van Reenen. "R&D and Unionism: Comparative Evidence from British Companies and Establishments." *Industrial and Labor Relations Review* 52 (October 1998): 45–63.

Menezes-Filho, Naercio and John van Reenen. "Unions and Innovation: A Survey of the Theory and Empirical Evidence." Center for Economic Policy Research, Discussion Paper 3792, January 2003.

Metcalf, David. "Unions and Productivity, Financial Performance and Investment: International Evidence." In John Addison and Claus Schnabel, eds. *International Handbook of Trade Unions.* Northampton, Mass.: Edward Elgar, 2003, pp. 118–71.

Mitchell, Merwin W. and Joe A. Stone. "Union Effects on Productivity: Evidence from Western Sawmills." *Industrial and Labor Relations Review* 46 (October 1992): 135–45.

Nickell, Stephen and Richard Layard. "Labor Market Institutions and Economic Performance." In Orley C. Ashenfelter and David Card, eds. *Handbook of Labor Economics,* Vol. 3C. Amsterdam: Elsevier, 1999, pp. 3029–84.

Odgers, Cameron W. and Julian R. Betts. "Do Unions Reduce Investment? Evidence from Canada." *Industrial and Labor Relations Review* 51 (October 1997): 18–36.

Olson, Craig A. and Brian E. Becker. "The Effects of the NLRA on Stockholder Wealth in the 1930s." *Industrial and Labor Relations Review* 44 (October 1990): 116–29.

Pencavel, John H. *Labor Markets Under Trade Unionism: Employment, Wages, and Hours.* Cambridge, Mass.: Basil Blackwell, 1991.

_____. "The Surprising Retreat of Union Britain." National Bureau of Economic Research Working Paper 9564, March 2003.

Ravenscraft, David J. "Structure-Profit Relationships at the Line of Business and Industry Level." *Review of Economics and Statistics* 65 (February 1983): 22–31.

Register, Charles A. "Wages, Productivity, and Costs in Union and Nonunion Hospitals." *Journal of Labor Research* 9 (Fall 1988): 325–45.

Reynolds, Morgan O. "Trade Unions in the Production Process Reconsidered." *Journal of Political Economy* 94 (April 1986): 443–47.

Ruback, Richard S. and Martin B. Zimmerman. "Unionization and Profitability: Evidence from the Capital Market." *Journal of Political Economy* 92 (December 1984): 1134–57.

Salinger, Michael A. "Tobin's *q*, Unionization, and the Concentration-Profits Relationship." *Rand Journal of Economics* 15 (Summer 1984): 159–70.

Simons, Henry C. "Some Reflections on Syndicalism." *Journal of Political Economy* 52 (March 1944): 1–25.

Sunstein, Cass R. "Human Behavior and the Law of Work." *Virginia Law Review* 87 (April 2001): 205–76.

Turnbull, Peter. "What Do Unions Do Now?" *Journal of Labor Research* 24 (Summer 2003): 491–527.

Voos, Paula B. and Lawrence R. Mishel. "The Union Impact on Profits: Evidence from Industry Price-Cost Margin Data." *Journal of Labor Economics* 4 (January 1986): 105–33.

Weil, David. "Individual Rights and Collective Agents: The Role of Old and New Workplace Institutions in the Regulation of Labor Markets." National Bureau of Economic Research Working Paper 9565, March 2003.

Wessels, Walter J. "The Effects of Unions on Employment and Productivity: An Unresolved Contradiction." *Journal of Labor Economics* 3 (January 1985): 101–108.

_____. "Do Unionized Firms Hire Better Workers?" *Economic Inquiry* 32 (October 1994): 616–29.

White, Lawrence J. "Trends in Aggregate Concentration in the United States." *Journal of Economic Perspectives* 16 (Fall 2002): 137–60.

8

Union Voice

John T. Addison and Clive R. Belfield

I. Introduction

The immediate impact of the collective voice model on research into the economic consequences of unions is hard to exaggerate. Up to the publication of *What Do Unions Do?* much of the mainstream economics profession viewed unions as combinations in restraint of trade, as monopolies (almost) pure and simple. Although organization theory had long suggested that positive union impacts on firm performance might result from shock effects (Leibenstein, 1966) — that is, having to pay a union premium shocks management into looking for cost savings elsewhere, in the process eliminating or reducing slack within the organization — neoclassical economists were generally not only leery of shock effects but also prone to emphasize union restrictive practices as the *source* of X-inefficiency.[1] In this accessible, monopoly view of the world (and abstracting from the costs of the union rule book), unions were viewed as having adverse effects on efficiency by distorting factor prices and usage, redirecting higher quality workers and capital from higher to lower marginal product uses. Furthermore, to the welfare triangle loss(es) had to be added some portion of the transfer effect, as unions engaged the polity to protect their monopoly powers. To be sure, the costs of strikes were no longer uncritically laid at the door of unions,[2] but there were already sufficient distortions associated with the union entity to render this advance of marginal interest only.

Into this staid and rather comfortable world intruded the new view of unionism presented by Freeman (1976, 1978, 1980) and Freeman and Medoff (1979, 1983, 1984), building on Hirschman's (1970) exit-voice (and loyalty) paradigm. Largely reflecting the public goods aspects of the workplace, but also containing governance elements consistent with a number of other developments in economics (such as contract theory), these authors argued that the substitution of an average for a marginal calculus could yield improved performance outcomes. Unwilling to jettison the monopoly model, however, the architects of the new view still spoke of the "two faces" of unionism. No less important, the potential gains pointed to by the model could be thwarted by an unfavorable management response to collective bargaining and also by an adverse union response to reorganization of the work process. For this reason, Freeman and

Medoff label the new view of unionism as a *collective voice/institutional response* model. Even with these qualifications the immediate challenge to the monopoly view was no less important.

The decade following publication of *What Do Unions Do?* was marked by a scramble to fit production and cost functions to data from the union and non-union sectors.[3] In addition, union effects on firm profitability and investments in physical and intangible capital were also rigorously scrutinized. (Some of this material is surveyed in Section III below; see also the careful review by Barry Hirsch in this volume). And then it seems there was a petering out of U.S. research, across all outcome indicators, largely due to an emerging empirical consensus. Aspects of this agreement included the findings that union effects on productivity were small on average (i.e., nowhere near as large in absolute magnitude as reported by Brown and Medoff (1978) in their pioneering unions-in-the-production-function test); that union impact on profitability was consistently negative; and that, more damagingly, unions were associated with reduced investment in physical and intangible capital. Also contributing to this hiatus was the continuing black-box nature of the mechanisms through which unions were supposed to improve workplace outcomes. And perhaps the steady hemorrhaging of union membership and decline in collective bargaining coverage also limited the attractiveness of such research.

But this is not the end of the story. First, there was no parallel hiatus in European research. Second, there has been some development of the union voice model since then; in particular, Freeman and Lazear (1995) have addressed the "union" rent-seeking problem in their application of the collective voice model to works councils (see below). Third, the finding that unions have small productivity effects on average has refocused attention on the factors that might produce swings about the average in either direction, and here a new literature has examined environments that appear more propitious to positive union effects. Nevertheless, we shall argue that the union voice model is deficient in under-emphasizing the bargaining problem, in over-emphasizing worker dissatisfaction, in neglecting individual voice, and in uncritically equating collective voice with autonomous unionism. Yet, if critics are thinking of erecting a headstone, it is still premature to complete the legend: "Union Voice, 1976 – ."

Our discussion is as follows. First, we offer a critical statement of the collective voice model while identifying some linking themes from contract theory and property rights (specifically, the divorce of corporate ownership and control). Second, we provide an eclectic review of the empirical evidence which first reviews findings from an older literature focusing on the net effects of unions on firm performance, next charts some more direct evidence on union voice, and concludes with an examination of an emerging literature focusing on the interaction between unionism and employee involvement mechanisms/human resource management systems. In discussing net effects — ceteris paribus associations between unions and performance indicators — we are looking for broad consistencies with either the union voice or the monopoly models, without expecting evidence of a knockout blow. In looking at more direct evidence on union influence, we address the routes through which union voice might find expression. And in looking at various union-workplace practice interactions in the last part of this empirical section, we examine workplace environments that appear more propitious for the exercise of union voice. Our analysis concludes with an extensive interpretative summary.

II. The Collective Voice Model and Related Themes

Viewing Freeman and Medoff's collective voice model as a single unified approach would be a mistake; rather, it has a number of dimensions ranging from narrow (information exchange) to broad (influence/pressure) while also embracing the governance structure of the firm. Moreover, union voice is only one part of this new model of unionism. The other is what is termed "institutional response," namely management's response to collective bargaining (and, in turn, the union's response to management). In effect, voice cannot succeed without an appropriate institutional response. Thus, Freeman and Medoff (1984, p. 165) write: "Some managements will adjust to the union and turn unionism into a positive force at the workplace; others will not. Over the long run, those that respond positively will prosper while those that do not will suffer in the market place." Finally, there is the vexed question of the integrity of collective voice/institutional response model in the sense of its being distinct from the monopoly face.

Before attempting to set down the various strands of the collective voice/institutional response model it is instructive to address the notion of voice more generally. In the model, *voice* is to be contrasted with *exit*. The latter is a market mechanism: faced with a divergence between desired and actual conditions at the workplace, the worker quits the firm to search for better employment. But there is an alternative to exit. The worker may instead engage in voice, discussing with his/her employer the conditions that need changing without quitting the job. By providing the worker with a voice mechanism, the union lowers quits. In the parent model of Hirschman (1970), the context is the product market rather than the labor market: Exit corresponds to switching goods and voice to complaining about the product. In Hirschman's model, the key variable signifying whether or not the individual will engage in voice or exit behavior is *loyalty*. The more loyal the consumer, the less likely exit behavior and the greater the probability that redress will be sought through voice. There is no mention of loyalty in the collective voice/institutional response model, but it is a similar stimulus that drives behavior in both cases, namely, a deterioration in conditions in the Hirschman model (Boroff and Lewin, 1997) and dissatisfaction in the collective voice model. That being said, and as we shall first see in discussing information exchange, voice is more than the expression of dissatisfaction with current conditions. This in turn raises the first of several key questions that arise in seeking to understand the collective voice model. Might not voice be more pro-productive if it comes from more satisfied workers, and might not voice sourced through a union be adversarial — more an expression of dissatisfaction with the status quo than a communication channel facilitating continuing innovation in labor contracts?[4]

Returning to the various dimensions of union voice, we begin with perhaps the best-known element, namely, the union role in providing information. The labor market context is important here, and is one of continuity rather than spot market contracting because of on-the-job skills specific to the firm and the costs attaching to worker mobility and labor turnover.[5] Given the information problem in such complex and multidimensional continuity markets, what mechanisms are available to elicit information on worker preferences or discontent? Quit behavior can provide such information either inferentially or directly (via exit interviews). However, the collective voice model contends that such information is likely to suffer from selection biases, from problems of motivating the worker to disclose information when there is no benefit from doing so (and the certainty of some positive cost), and finally from the sheer cost of the process of trial and error in determining the efficacy of contract innovations.

Collective voice through the agency of a union may outperform individual activity for various reasons. One reason is the public goods problem of preference revelation.[6] Nonrival consumption of shared working conditions (e.g., safety conditions, line speeds, grievance procedures) and common workplace rules create a public goods problem of preference revelation. Without some collective form of organization there will be too little incentive for the individual to reveal his or her preferences since the actions of others may produce the public good at no cost to that individual. Unions collect information about the preferences of all workers and "aggregate" them to determine the social demand for such public goods. Substituting average preferences for marginal preferences and the arbitraging of worker preferences may be efficient in such circumstances.[7] There are two issues here, neither of which is really addressed in the collective voice model. The first is whether or not the union is a pure agent of the member principal since this will affect the quality of the information passed on to management.[8] The second is whether or not autonomous unions are the only form of collective voice, recognizing that labor law may make that case by default. (In the United States, section 8(a)(2) of the Wagner Act, which prohibits employers from dominating or interfering with the formation or administration of any labor organization or contributing financial or other support to it, clearly rules out company unions. Moreover, it may even be construed as requiring one-side conversations and unilateral management.)

A second public goods dimension of the workplace stems from the nature of the input of effort. Without some form of collective organization, so this argument runs, the individual's incentive to take into account the effects of his actions on others may be too small, just as with preference revelation. This problem will only arise where there are significant complementarities in worker effort inputs, so that output may depend on the lowest level of input by any one worker. In short, collective organization may potentially increase output through a joint determination of effort inputs and perhaps more so through increased cooperation between workers in continuity labor markets. Some analysts have even claimed that the union may also be construed as the agent of the employer principal in monitoring worker effort. This argument has recently been used to help sustain the voice argument for "strong" unionism in Britain in an empirical inquiry into plant closings (Bryson, 2004).

For the public goods argument to have force, two further conditions must be met — both of which are recognized in the union voice model (Freeman, 1976, p. 362). First, costs must be incurred in using external markets: If quitting were costless, the individual worker could simply choose the employer whose working conditions most closely approximated his/her own preferences. Second, the workplace must continue to be buffeted by unforeseen shocks that change the nature of the workplace in an informational context; otherwise, there would be no need for the union's demand-revealing function after the formative match between employer and worker.

The expression of collective voice is expected to reduce quits, absenteeism, malingering, and even "quiet sabotage." The reduction in quits is expected to lower hiring and training costs and increase firm-specific investments in human capital. Lower quits may of course also occasion less disruption in the functioning of work groups. Interestingly, apart from the reduction in quits as a result of the union providing direct information about worker preferences as described earlier, the transmission mechanism between voice and performance is opaque in the voice model. And even in this case there is no formalization of optimal quit behavior. The upshot of this imprecision is that any observed reduction in quits/increase in training may be excessive. Moreover, in discussing the reduction in quits the union voice model appears to emphasize dissatisfaction. *Conceptually,* voice is described as directing attention to workplace problems, encouraging expressions of discontent, and keeping dissatisfied workers from quitting (Freeman, 1976, p. 367), even at the same time as good industrial relations are viewed as a key to improved productivity (Freeman and Medoff, 1984, p. 165). *Empirically,* Freeman and Medoff (1984, Chapter 12) find that expressed worker dissatisfaction is higher in union regimes. They interpret the difference in expressed complaints between union and nonunion labor as an expression of democracy rather than as indicating a true shortfall in satisfaction, noting that: "The difference between 'true' and 'voiced' dissatisfaction reflects the nature of the voice institution" (p. 139). Nevertheless, the particular politicization of the work force that is alluded to might also carry implications for the quality of information that is passed on by unions.

This, then, is the information aspect of union voice.[9] The two other aspects are influence and governance. At least as initially presented, the union influence aspect is not only difficult to disentangle from the shock effect but also morphs into governance. Thus, Freeman and Medoff (1984, p. 15) argue that "Unions can also improve efficiency by putting pressure on management to tighten job-production standards and accountability in order to preserve profits in the face of higher wages. Because unionized management can be challenged by the union, moreover, it will tend to discard vague paternalistic, authoritarian personnel policies in favor of practices in which explicit rules govern behavior." For these reasons, it is more tractable to focus on the governance issue.

The context is again the continuity of the employment relation. Governance refers to the policing or monitoring of incomplete employment contracts and thus includes the use of grievance and arbitration procedures and other mechanisms to mitigate what are seen as problems stemming from the authority relation. Such procedures should also help improve the flow of information between the two sides. The problem is that the specialized procedural arrangements typically associated with union regimes are not unique to those settings. Expressed rather differently, there is an extensive (contract theory) literature in economics documenting why employers would introduce procedural safeguards for the settlement of disputes in union-free continuity markets with uncertainty. Thus, in the idiosyncratic exchange variant of contract theory (Williamson et al., 1975), there emerges a distinct governance apparatus geared to maximizing the joint surplus of the firm by suppressing the hazards of unconstrained idiosyncratic trading. The key elements of this apparatus are promotion ladders, formal grievance procedures, and the application of the seniority principle — all components of a structured internal labor market. There is no explicit mention of unions in this particular model, because the bargaining power possessed by idiosyncratically-trained job incumbents produces the governance apparatus. In the absence of unions, therefore, the firm and its workers may agree on procedural arrangements limiting the hazard of unconstrained idiosyncratic trading. That said, subsequent developments of idiosyncratic exchange discuss monitoring and auditing procedures and do reserve a specific role for unions, suggesting that a union may make it easier for the firm to negotiate and administer these practices (Riordan and Wachter, 1983). Acceptance of this argument raises the issue that the extent and form of voice is in part an endogenous variable, partly determined by firms no less than compensation, training, recruitment, and other human resource management practices. (For a transaction cost model of *nonunion* forms of worker representation based on this reasoning, see Kaufman and Levine, 2000.)

Freeman (1976, p. 364) and Freeman and Medoff (1984, p. 11, fn. 11) claim the union governance aspect of the voice model is quite consistent with the modern contracts literature, the argument being that the presence of a union can facilitate long-term efficient contracting of this nature.[10] They argue that a union specializing in information about the contract and in the representation of workers can prevent employers from engaging in opportunistic behavior. Workers may withhold effort and cooperation when the employer cannot credibly commit to take their interests into account. Thus, fearing dismissal, workers may be unwilling to invest in firm-specific skills or disclose information facilitating pro-productive innovations at the workplace. The formation of a union and the introduction of a system of industrial jurisprudence is one way of protecting employees' interests. In this way, unions may generate worker cooperation, including the introduction of efficiency-enhancing work practices. This argument presupposes that the commitment problem cannot be solved by reputation effects, inducing the employer to live up to contractual commitments and to behave honestly rather than opportunistically. However, reputation effects may be strong enough to make contracts self-enforcing after all.

But if we assume that there is a commitment problem in regular markets, an interesting issue is whether the divorce of ownership and control in the modern corporation could make self-enforcing contracts more feasible. More feasible in the sense that management might be less interested in reneging on an implicit contract in the interest of short-term profit maximization than the owner-principal; and conversely where the interests of managers and shareholders are more closely aligned by, say, profit-sharing schemes for managers. In this case much might hinge on whether unions and self-enforcing contracts are substitutes or complements in establishing workplace cooperation. If they are substitutes, any positive effect of unions on performance will be stronger in firms with less severe agency problems. If they are complements, unions will be more effective in firms where agency stimulates self-enforcing contracts. This argument is of course based on a very narrow view of the agency problem in corporations and must be widened to incorporate rent-seeking behavior by managers which may detract from trustful and cooperative industrial relations and may decrease the range of feasible self-enforcing contracts. Jirjahn (2002) has recently examined the relationships between unions (actually works councils) and self-enforcing contracts and also those between agency and trustful, cooperative industrial relations using information on management profit-sharing schemes. (We report some of his findings in Section III.)

We have yet to mention union rent seeking. In contract theory models in which the union can make credible the employers' *ex ante* promises (Malcomson, 1983), there must be some threat of credible punishment by the union which hinges on the union having bargaining power. In other words, the governance argument depends on union monopoly power. The criticism would then be that voice can be kept distinct from power only by making voice so narrow — by which is meant information exchange — that it may lose much of its explanatory punch, while if it is broadened to increase its reach it becomes simply another facet of the exercise of power. For example, if voice includes a grievance system, it may only be through the exertion of its monopoly power that a union wins such a system and keeps it functioning. This is no mean critique because it calls into question the notion that voice is a putative good that it is represented to be in *What Do Unions Do?*

Subsequent development of the union voice model recognizes the problem of bargaining power. We refer to Freeman and Lazear's (1995) purpose-built analysis of the *works council* with "codetermination" (or joint governance) power at the workplace.[11] In this treatment, there is explicit recognition of the bargaining/hold-up problem hitherto skirted in union voice and which dogs the voice solution to the information problem in continuity labor markets. Freeman and Lazear argue that codetermination will be underprovided by the market because institutions that give power to workers will affect the distribution as well as the size of the joint surplus. The content of collective voice is also spelled out in more detail in this treatment in terms of a continuum bounded by information provision at one extreme and participation/codetermination at the other, with consultation occupying the broad middle ground. Thus, the joint surplus of the firm is said to increase with the progression from information exchange through consultation to participation. Among other things, information rights can help verify management claims about the state of nature, rendering them credible to the work force and avoiding costly disputes that can threaten the enterprise's very survival. Consultation for its part allows new solutions to production and other problems by reason of the non-overlapping information sets of the two sides and the creativity of discussion. Finally, participation or codetermination rights increase the joint surplus by providing workers with more job security and encouraging them to take a longer-run view of the firm. (This latter notion is not uncontroversial because the median voter model might produce exactly the opposite result by virtue of the preponderance of older workers in union councils, or it might otherwise pay workers to be rationally myopic.)

However, Freeman and Lazear recognize that unless the rights of the works council are somehow constrained, they will give rise to a bargaining problem. They argue that the workers' share in the joint surplus grows with the surplus while that of capital declines both relatively and absolutely. The workers' share rises because knowledge and involvement are power, so that the same factors that cause the surplus to rise also cause profitability to fall, so workers will demand too much power/involvement because their share will continue to rise after the joint surplus has peaked. Similarly, employers will either oppose works councils or vest them with too little power because profits decline even as the surplus is increasing. Some means of third-party regulation limiting bargaining power has thus to be found if the societal benefits of worker voice are to be realized. In this context, Freeman and Lazear see the *German* institution as attractive. First, German works councils cannot strike (under the so-called "peace obligation"). Second, neither can they formally engage in bargaining over wages and other conditions of employment unless authorized to do so under the relevant industry-level or regional collective bargaining agreement. In this respect, the authors speak of a potential decoupling of the factors that determine the size of the surplus from those that determine its distribution made possible by labor law and the dual system of industrial relations. Left open is whether or not there is a *sufficient* decoupling in practice. A growing literature has focused on this very question, and we will consider its findings in the next section.

This concludes our discussion of the theory of union voice. As seen by its proponents, the basic advantages of union voice are threefold: it offers a direct communication channel between workers and the firm, an alternative mode of expressing discontent other than quitting with attendant benefits in the firm of reduced turnover costs and greater training, and a necessary modification of the social relations of production (Freeman, 1976, p. 364). To these advantages are added those of contract innovation, interpretation, and enforcement. At issue (in terms of the model) is whether these advantages dominate the monopoly effects or would do so if management were prepared to "stand up" to unions (Freeman and Medoff, 1984, p. 12), or indeed whether the market can reasonably be expected to provide its own solutions to the information and contractual problems that to a greater or lesser extent motivate the union voice model.

Opponents of the model can rightly claim that its separation of voice from power is artificial and that if voice is in fact another exercise of power there can be no assurance that working conditions, training investments, and so on will not be pushed up beyond competitive levels any less so than wages. Such opponents can also with some justification then question whether a lack of a "suitable" managerial/institutional response is other than a rational resistance to union-inflated (other) terms and conditions of the employment contract. All of this pertains to the basic model. Subsequent amendments to the model would probably be viewed by its opponents as too little, too late: The scope for improvements in the joint surplus are inherently limited by bargaining (to include the negative, low-trust syndrome in the workplace induced by its innately adversarial nature) and by the different time horizons of capital and labor.

In these circumstances, the architects of *What Do Unions Do?* would argue that recourse to the facts assumes rather more importance than usual. By the same token, the imprecision of the collective voice/institutional response model means that interpretation of those facts is especially difficult even when well-determined union effects are observed.

III. The Evidence

We alluded earlier to there being a number of developments in the empirical analysis of union voice. We next consider that evidence, beginning with the large literature documenting the *net effects* of unions on various indicators of firm performance. Next we note some rather more direct evidence on union voice, before turning to an emerging literature on the link between employee involvement/high performance work practices and firm performance in union and nonunion regimes.

Conventional, Indirect Tests

There is an extensive literature documenting the net effects of unions on productivity, productivity growth, profitability, and investments in tangible and intangible capital.[12] Beginning with productivity and productivity growth, the U.S. evidence has been surveyed by Addison and Hirsch (1989) and by Hirsch in this volume, the British evidence by Addison and Belfield (2004b), and the German evidence (largely pertaining to works councils since they rather than unions are the agencies of workplace representation) by Addison et al. (2004). Although the approaches taken by the various studies differ, there is ultimately some agreement in the cross-country evidence. The U.S. evidence indicates that the optimistic conclusions from Brown and Medoff's (1978) aggregative analysis — a logarithmic (total factor) productivity differential of .22 to .24 in favor of unionized plants — cannot be sustained. In interpreting the evidence, Addison and Hirsch (1989, p. 79) conclude: "the average union productivity effect is probably quite small and, indeed, is just as likely to be negative as positive." Similarly, there is no indication of a *direct* union effect on productivity growth, once one allows for the fact that unions are located in industries or sectors with low growth.

However, the British evidence tended to point to lower productivity in unionized plants in the 1980s and earlier (Metcalf, 1990; Fernie and Metcalf, 1995). That said, unionized plants had increased their productivity most at the end of the 1980s (Gregg et al., 1993). (We note that no such differential movement in productivity growth is observed in the United States.) As a result, some have concluded that there is no longer evidence of a union productivity shortfall in the United Kingdom. This interpretation, as well as the more attenuated conclusion of a marked reduction in the "disadvantages of unionism," is conventionally attributed in large measure to legislation passed by Mrs. Thatcher and her successor that considerably weakened union bargaining power largely by removing union immunities under the law (Addison and Siebert, 2003).

The German evidence on works councils and productivity has run the gamut from strongly negative results in the early literature based on small firm samples to strongly positive estimates (reminiscent of those obtained by Brown and Medoff) in very recent work using nationally representative establishment data (Addison et al., 2004). However, the latter results are something of a chimera because further econometric work reveals that average effects are (a) unstable in individual years, (b) not robust to disaggregation by establishment size, broad sector, and region, and (c) do not survive re-estimation in first differences (Addison et al., 2003). A more accurate reading of the latest German evidence, therefore, indicates an absence of negative works council effects on average rather than clear pro-productive effects.

There is also a real measure of international agreement on the facts — if not the implications — of the association between unions and profitability. The U.S. evidence is again the most developed, using measures not only of accounting profits but also of company market value and abnormal stock returns in events studies of union representation elections. The U.S. evidence is robust across firms, lines of businesses, and industries, and suggests that unions are associated with 10 to 15 percent lower profitability (Addison and Hirsch, 1989). There is no real evidence of a material change in the magnitude of this effect over time (Hirsch, 1991; Hirsch and Morgan, 1994).

The British evidence points in the same direction, with most studies reporting lower profitability in unionized establishments and firms. However, there are two main caveats to this statement. The first is that, in line with the productivity results noted earlier, the negative impact of unions appears to have weakened through time (Addison and Belfield, 2004b; Metcalf, 2003). The mitigation of the negative union effect over time is again commonly attributed to weakened union bargaining power in the wake of the Thatcher reforms (and deregulation as well as heightened international competition). The second caveat is that, unlike in the United States, there has always been some indication that the union profitability effect is strongest where the firm has product market power (Machin and Stewart, 1996). In other words, the implications of profits capture by unions in the British case have been regarded as more ambiguous (for efficiency) and less of a source of concern than in the United States where there is little obvious indication of any association between wages and concentration-related profits (Hirsch, 2004).

The German evidence also points to reduced profitability under works councils (Addison et al., 2001). The only real exception is a study by Hübler and Jirjahn (2003) in which the effect of councils on establishment "quasi rents" (defined as [sales – raw materials – wages]/number of employees) is positive but statistically insignificant throughout.

This brings us to the related issue of investments in physical and intangible capital, where there is something of a divide in the research literatures. Research in the United States has uncovered a strong negative association between unionism and investment in physical and innovation capital (Hirsch, 1991; Bronars and Deere, 1993; Bronars et al., 1994; Cavanaugh, 1998; Fallick and Hassett, 1999). The fullest analysis is by Hirsch (1991) who presents cross-section/time-series results for both types of investment in a sample of more than 500 firms. For capital investment he reports that the average union firm has annual capital investment that is 13 percent lower than its nonunion counterpart. The *union tax* on the returns to long-lived capital — further discussed by Hirsch in this symposium — contributes a little under one-half of this effect, the balance reflecting a reduced profit rate (profits are an important determinant of capital investment). For R&D expenditures, unionized companies invest some 15 percent less than comparable nonunion firms. Well over three-quarters of this effect is direct, that is, resulting from the union tax. Hirsch also finds that union coverage is negatively associated with the ratio of advertising expenditures to sales (and positively related to the propensity to patent which should reduce the liability of the firm to hold up, ceteris paribus).

The early British research also provides evidence of some negative effects of unions on capital investment (Denny and Nickell, 1992).13 The main source of difference therefore resides in the R&D effect. While confirming Hirsch's

(1991) results for the United States, Menezes-Filho et al. (1998) cannot replicate them for the United Kingdom. Indeed, in their recent review, Menezes-Filho and van Reenen (2003) report that the results are not robust for continental Europe either. So, although the association between unionism and R&D is negative in this bloc as well, it is seemingly driven by unions being concentrated in older, low-tech industries. And in interpreting these results, the authors critique the notion that unions will necessarily hold up firms by expropriating sunk R&D investments through demanding higher wages while also observing that the hold-up problem may be mitigated by strategic incentives to compete in R&D races. The latter such considerations imply that the union effect on R&D might exhibit nonlinearities — being positive at lower levels of union density. The latter point is used to justify some German results on R&D, namely, Schnabel and Wagner's (1994) finding that works councils have a positive impact on R&D intensity (R&D expenditures divided by sales) provided that union density is not too high. The only other German study reporting a statistically significant association between works councils and innovation — here the proportion of sales consisting of new products introduced in the preceding five years — simply interacts works council presence with union density *ab initio* and reports that this composite measure of "labor organization" is associated with a statistically significant reduction in innovative activity (FitzRoy and Kraft, 1990).

This, then, is the basic tenor of the evidence on unionism's net effect on firm performance. It scarcely provides a ringing endorsement of collective voice. But, as was noted earlier, the failure to observe positive productivity effects can simply mean that the voice and monopoly effects are a wash or indicate an insufficiently affirmative response from management. That said, the interlocking nature of the productivity, profitability, and investment evidence *for the United States* does not encourage a sanguine view of collective bargaining in that country and thence the model. Even so, the finding of an average productivity effect near zero does redirect our attention to factors that mediate this result in both the United States and other countries where the dynamic effects of unionism seem less unfavorable. Prior to that, however, we have to consider evidence with a more direct bearing on union voice.

More Direct Approaches

According to the union voice model, the expression of voice should reduce quits and increase tenure — effects that will be amplified because of the union wage premium. In an attempt to identify one source of the roughly 20 percent higher productivity they report for unionized establishments, Brown and Medoff (1978, Table 4) introduce a quits variable into their production function. The coefficient estimate for the union measure (fraction unionized) is reduced from 0.204 to 0.160, that is, by around one-fifth. Brown and Medoff (1978, p.

374) conclude that four-fifths of the union effect is presumably the result of factors such as the "better management, morale, motivation, communication, etc." in unionized establishments. In other words, only one-fifth of the union productivity effect can be associated with a specific route or channel — reduced quits — with the rest coming from amorphous combination of influences of uncertain component magnitude, including the institutional response of management. Although nontrivial, the one-fifth contribution has to be seen in the context of the magnitude of the average productivity differential of unionized plants, and the cautionary remarks of Barry Hirsch in this volume concerning the Brown-Medoff estimate are particularly relevant.

Freeman and Medoff (1984, Tables 6–1, 6–2) seek to gauge the relative strength of union voice and wage effects in influencing quits and tenure. They find that the voice effect of unions dominates any effect from wage increases. For example, using data on all workers from the Panel Study of Income Dynamics, 1971–1979, they report that whereas a 20 percent wage increase reduces quits by 8 percent, the union voice effect (controlling for wages) reduces quits by no less than 31 percent. Corresponding results for tenure (in 1979) are 9 percent and 32 percent, respectively. The result appears robust across a range of datasets and time periods for the United States We will examine some evidence for the United Kingdom below, after considering a sharp German critique of the emphasis on *collective* voice.

In an early criticism of the collective voice model, Kraft (1986) argued that it was not the collective representation of workers' rights per se that caused turnover to be lower but rather the individual rights of workers. Kraft's dependent variable is a subjective measure of unskilled worker quits, the employer respondent being asked whether quit rates for this group were high or low. For a sample of 62 manufacturing firms in 1977/1979, he regresses this dichotomous variable ("high quits" = 1, 0 otherwise) on a vector of covariates that include, in addition to wages and training expenditures, etc., two voice arguments: individual voice and collective voice. Individual voice is measured by questions on the decision possibilities of blue-collar workers on investment and rationalization, coordination of work groups and other personnel decisions, and the determination of the (individual) job design. The responses were ordered by "no decision possibilities," "informed in advance," and "active participation." A voice index was fashioned from the weighted responses (the percentage deviations of the individual observations from the mean of the whole sample). For its part, collective voice is simply proxied by the presence (or absence) of a works council.

Kraft reports that individual voice is inversely related to the excessive quits measure. The association is statistically significant at the .01 level. On the other hand, the coefficient estimate for collective voice is positive and poorly determined, while the two human capital variables mentioned earlier have the expected effect in lowering quits. In recognition that voice maybe endogenously determined — with high-tenure workers being granted more decision rights — Kraft also estimates a simultaneous equations (probit) model. Again individual voice has a statistically significant negative effect on quits, and there is no feedback effect from quits to individual voice. Also, as before, the collective voice measure has no discernible impact on quits.

So, one conclusion from this study is that worker representation through a works council has no impact on the quit rates of unskilled workers in this sample of German firms. As a practical matter, subsequent German research has consistently reported a negative association between works council presence and quits, using objective turnover data (Addison et al., 2001). That being said, the qualitative data supplied by management in the Kraft study may address the vexed question of the optimality of quits in a way that objective turnover data cannot. The other conclusion — that individual voice significantly reduces excessive quits — has not further been tested for Germany. We shall return to this topic and the type of information conveyed by individual voice in Section IV, drawing on a Canadian study by Luchak (2003).

We now examine union voice effects and wage effects on tenure and quits for the United Kingdom, estimating both the relative strength of each effect and accounting for other forms of voice. The empirical investigation uses the 1998 Workplace Employment Relations Survey (WERS98), a national sample of interviews with managers from 2,191 British establishments with at least 10 workers (Department of Trade and Industry, 1999). The survey contains detailed information on the organization of the workplace and the deployment of workers. In addition, the WERS98 includes a survey of employees. Up to 25 employees per workplace were randomly selected and information collected on their personal characteristics, occupational status, earnings, and job conditions. In sum, the WERS98 contains both individual- and workplace-level information, including numerous measures of employee voice. Our analysis of the survey data focuses on the private sector — thereby excluding the health, education, and government sectors — and applies survey weights throughout.

Table 8.1 shows the incidence of a range of voice mechanisms in union and nonunion establishments. The results are clear: regardless of the form of voice, union workplaces report significantly more voice and collective participation than do nonunion workplaces. Next, Table 8.2 describes voice as perceived by workers rather than the management respondent, allowing us to see whether workers recognize greater voice in union regimes — and, indeed, whether it is appreciated. Although the questions differ, the results contrast sharply with those in Table 8.1 and are somewhat disappointing for union voice. Thus, the top panel of Table 8.2 shows that workers in nonunion workplaces do not seemingly report weaker voice; that is, discussions with managers occur with the same frequency, and there is little difference regarding workers' needs (e.g., to develop their skills) or managerial requests for workers' views. Seen from a worker's perspective, then, there is equivalent voice in union and nonunion settings. Union voice may take more confrontational forms than are identifiable using WERS98.

Perhaps unsurprisingly, in this light, there is no evidence that union voice is appreciated by workers. Instead, as the middle panel of Table 8.2 shows, workers in nonunion workplaces are more likely to report that their managers are (very) good at "keeping everyone up to date about proposed changes," at "providing everyone with a chance to comment," and in "responding to suggestions." Consistent with some other evidence (Bender and Sloane, 1998), workers' perceptions and attitudes are considerably more positive in nonunion workplaces (so that individual voice may have a stronger effect than collective voice, as will be commented on below). Note also that whereas 19.1 percent of

Table 8.1
Workplace-Level Voice Measures by Workplace Union Status

	Nonunion Workplace	Union Workplace
At least 60% of employees in the largest occupational group at the workplace work in formally designated teams	48.9%	84.3%
Consultative committee of managers and employees that operates at a higher level than this establishment	21.5	53.7
Joint consultative committee	16.1	30.3
Briefing groups (for any section of the work force)	76.0	83.1
Briefing groups (at least fortnightly)	38.9	41.9
Briefing groups (involving >10% of the work force)	18.8	20.1
Quality circles	13.2	20.7
Consultation (management chain)	42.9	71.6
Consultation (regular meetings with entire work force)	37.3	40.1
Consultation (at least three of: regular meetings, management chain, suggestion schemes, newsletters)	5.2	16.6
Information provision (about the finance of the organization)	38.4	64.1
Information provision (on internal investment plans, finance, finance of the organization, staffing plans)	15.1	36.2
Performance-related pay (at least 60% of nonmanagerial employees received performance related pay in last six months)	11.8	16.8
Profit-related pay	27.4	38.3
Share ownership (at least 60% of nonmanagerial employees are eligible for employee share ownership schemes)	5.2	11.0
Formal procedure for dealing with individual grievances raised by any nonmanagerial employee	80.5	96.6
N (workplaces)	768	396

Notes: WERS98; Survey weights applied; private-sector workplaces only.

Table 8.2
Worker-Level Voice Measures by Union Workplace Status

	Nonunion Workplace	Union Workplace
During the last 12 months, have you discussed any of these with your supervisor/line manager?		
How you are getting on with your job	57.9%	55.1%
Your chances of promotion	22.0	20.6
Your training needs	43.3	46.7
Your pay	41.5	26.7
None of these	26.0	29.6
N		8,550
8,599		
Managers here are understanding about employees having to meet family responsibilities: Percent (strongly agree)	55.9	46.3
N	8,096	8,297
Managers here encourage workers to develop their skills: Percent (strongly agree)	50.4	48.2
N	8,298	8,377
Managers sometimes or frequently ask for the views of you and others working here on:		
Future plans for the workplace	46.0	41.6
Staffing issues, including redundancy	25.8	26.7
Changes to work practices	60.0	55.8
Pay issues	29.8	28.9
Health and safety at work	55.7	63.0
N	8,850	8,599
Percent responding managers are (very) good at:		
Keeping everyone up to date about proposed changes?	42.5	37.0
Responding to suggestions from employees?	34.0	25.7
Dealing with work problems that you or others may have?	49.8	40.3
Treating employees fairly?	53.0	43.2
Providing everyone with chance to comment on proposed changes?	29.9	24.2
N	8,550	8,599
In general, how would you describe relations between managers and employees here?		
Very good	19.1	8.3
Good	42.3	36.3
Neither good nor poor	25.6	30.7
Poor	10.3	16.3
Very poor	4.7	8.4

Table 8.2 (cont.)

	Nonunion Workplace	Union Workplace
N	8,411	8,462
How helpful are find meetings of managers and employees?		
(Very) helpful	58.7	55.1
Not very or not at all helpful	15.2	20.9
Not used here	27.0	23.7
N	8,284	8,384
How much contact your do how have with trade union or other worker representatives about workplace matters?		
Frequently in contact	3.8	16.0
Occasionally in contact	10.1	39.9
% Never in contact	20.8%	24.1%
Am a worker representative	1.2	1.8
Do not know any worker representatives	63.1	17.7
N	8,405	8,538
Unions / staff associations take notice of members' problems and complaints		
(Strongly) agree		47.1
(Strongly) disagree		35.3
Unions / staff associations are taken seriously by management		
(Strongly) agree		35.0
(Strongly) disagree		42.5
Unions / staff associations make a difference to what it is like to work here		
(Strongly) agree		30.7
(Strongly) disagree		33.8
N (workers)		8,599

Notes: See Table 8.1.

workers in nonunion workplaces rate relations as (very good) good, the respective figure in union workplaces is 8.3 percent.

The bottom panel of Table 8.2 offers insight into why union voice does not permeate. One reason may be that voice itself — as expressed in meetings between managers and employers — is not always regarded as helpful. But union influence may also be deficient: Only 55 percent of workers are frequently or occasionally in contact with a union representative; less than 50 percent agree that the union takes notice of members' complaints; and only one-third agree that unions are either taken seriously or make a difference. Thus, union presence — and action in promoting voice — might not guarantee union effectiveness in promoting voice, perhaps because more formalized union voice practices may separate workers from direct contact with managers, implying greater distance between the two.

Table 8.3 reports on worker-level satisfaction in union and nonunion workplaces. Workers in union plants report considerably lower satisfaction with their influence over their jobs, their sense of achievement, and the amount of respect they get from managers. Similarly, workers in nonunion workplaces are more likely to share the values of, feel loyal to, and be proud of their organization. The only measure on which there is parity between union and nonunion workplaces is for satisfaction regarding the amount of pay received. Such results are not unfamiliar, with similar findings being reported in *What Do Unions Do?* by Freeman and Medoff. But taken in conjunction with the previous results, they may well imply that the quality of union voice is just as important a consideration as its quantity.

The determinants of workplace quit rates and workplace tenure are investigated in Table 8.4, using OLS estimation. We control for work force composition (e.g., percent female, unskilled, part-time, and professional), workplace characteristics (establishment age and type, and proxies for the capital-labor ratio), and sector. The union effects are strong: unions reduce the quit rate by 34 percent and raise average workplace tenure by 15 percent; higher wages also have a strong effect on quits. On this evidence, whether workers appreciate union voice or not, they are less likely to quit and more likely to have extended tenure. This leaves aside the issue of whether these effects are pro-productive. Incorporating particular voice channels to the estimations on this occasion adds little to the explanatory power of the quits and tenure equations (but see below).

Table 8.3
Worker-Level Satisfaction Measures by Union Workplace Status

	Nonunion Workplace	Union Workplace
Percent satisfied or very satisfied with:		
Amount of influence you have over your job	62.2%	54.5%
Sense of achievement you get from your work	63.8	56.2
Amount of respect from supervisors/managers	56.9	50.1
Amount of pay you receive	32.5	33.2
Percent agree or strongly agree:		
I share the values of my organization	46.2	41.5
People working here are encouraged to develop their skills	48.9	44.2
I feel loyal to my organization	64.8	58.5
I am proud to tell people who I work for	56.4	49.9
N (workers)	5,597	8,659

Notes: See Table 8.1.

Table 8.4
Log Workplace Quit Rate and Tenure Rate
(OLS Estimation)

	Log Workplace Quit Rate		Log Workplace Tenure Rate	
	[1] Union 'Voice'	[2] Union 'Voice' and Voice Channel	[1] Union 'Voice'	[2] Union 'Voice' and Voice Channel
Ln (average wage)	−0.8422**	−0.8417**	0.0591	0.0901
	(0.2017)	(0.2038)	(0.1034)	(0.1096)
Union workplace	−0.4120**	−0.2936**	0.1475**	0.1007
	(0.0785)	(0.1007)	(0.0545)	(0.0585)
Formal grievance procedure		−0.2024		0.0550
		(0.1083)		(0.0614)
Team working		0.0706		−0.0370
		(0.0871)		(0.0515)
JCC		−0.0591		0.0447
		(0.0803)		(0.0508)
Briefing groups		−0.0950		−0.0039
		(0.1137)		(0.0665)
Quality circles		−0.0350		0.0540
		(0.0874)		(0.0450)
Consultation		−0.0975		0.0604
		(0.1061)		(0.0531)
Information provision		−0.2232*		0.0535
		(0.0877)		(0.0486)
Performance pay		0.0328		−0.0532
		(0.1068)		(0.0553)
Profit-related pay		0.1864*		−0.0492
		(0.0854)		(0.0529)
Shareownership		0.0456		0.0122
		(0.0880)		(0.0527)
Good relations		−0.0944		−0.0634
		(0.0853)		(0.0504)
N	1,084	1,084	517	517
R-squared	0.34	0.36	0.54	0.55

Notes: See Table 8.1. * (**) denote significance at the .01 (.05) levels, respectively. Control variables are: dummy variables for sector (manufacturing, utilities, wholesale, catering, transport, and finance); work force composition (percent female, unskilled, part-time, professional, and minority); dummy variables for capital/labor ratio (3 proxies), log establishment age, and single establishment. Constant term also included.

Their introduction does however reduce the impact of unions (while leaving the wage effect unchanged), and there is no longer a statistically significant effect of unions on tenure, controlling for other voice mechanisms. Similar conclusions obtain when using worker-level tenure equations, and when measures of job satisfaction are included in the estimations. Applying 2SLS to account for the simultaneous determination of tenure and wages produces inflated but same signed coefficient estimates for wages and union status.

Summary results of the component contributions of union voice and wage effects on labor turnover/stability are given in Table 8.5. The WERS98 findings for Britain largely mimic those of Freeman and Medoff (1984, Chapter 6) for the United States. As can be seen, the "wage effect" on quits is –15 percent but is dominated by the "union voice effect" which lowers quits by 34 percent. Similar results are found for the tenure equation. Familiarly, unions are associated with reduced labor turnover and increased labor stability. But, to repeat, the relevance of this more direct evidence of union voice is qualified both by the theoretical imprecision of the quits argument and also by the seemingly modest empirical contribution of reduced quits to the union productivity effect, noted at the beginning of this discussion.

We conclude by noting that some other research for the United States has been rather more pessimistic in suggesting that the negative effect of unions on quits may operate through wages alone. In particular, a study by Delery et al. (2000) of U.S. trucking finds that the union effect is not robust to inclusion of the pay and benefit package, most notably annual earnings and the number of times per month the driver is rotated home. (Consistent with the results in Table 8.4, Delery et al. do not find specific voice mechanisms to be statistically significant.) However, the most recent U.S. research suggests that this concern may have been overstated. In an analysis of the quit behavior of

Table 8.5
Estimates of the Effect of Unionism and a Twenty Percent Wage Increase

	Unionism, for Workers Paid Same ('Voice Effect')	20 Percent Wage Wage Increase ('Monopoly Effect')
Approximate percentage amount by which workplace quit rate is reduced:	34	15
Approximate percentage amount by which workplace tenure is increased:	16	1

Notes: Mean (s.d.) quit rate: 0.15 (0.21); mean (s.d.) worker tenure: 6.6 (5.5) years. Percentage amounts are taken from model [1] of Table 8.4: for the voice effect anti-logs of coefficients are used; for the wage effect anti-logs of coefficients*0.2 are used.

unionized public school teachers that controls for compensation, Iverson and Currivan (2003) report that both union participation — termed "voice" — and job satisfaction each have strongly negative effects on turnover. The union participation measure is constructed from four elements: voting in union elections, attending union meetings, serving as a union official, and seeking union assistance. Interestingly, this participation/voice effect remains strongly negative irrespective of whether or not the union member displays high or low satisfaction. On the basis of their findings, Iverson and Currivan reject the suggestion that unions cause dissatisfaction or that they provide a voice outlet for dissatisfied workers. Another study by Batt et al. (2002) of 302 establishments in the telecommunications sector, which controls for compensation and a variety of human resource practices (such as internal labor market structuring), finds that quit rates are some 4.9 to 6.5 percentage points less in union than nonunion establishments. Deploying workers in problem-solving groups or self-directed teams — which the authors also term collective voice — also lowers quit rates by 2.5 to 3.6 percentage points. Finally, for the nonunion sample, the authors report only marginally significant correlations between quit rates and the presence of nonunion arbitration procedures, peer review procedures, and the dispute rate.

Therefore we can, after all, credit unions with lower turnover. But it may be a modest victory. That is to say, we do not know whether the reduction in quits is optimal or, expressed another way, whether it adds materially to productivity. Nor for that matter is the basis for any such effect transparent. This is most obviously the case because of seemingly greater dissatisfaction of union workers.[14] If it can be shown that the reduction in establishment labor turnover is not simply achieved by virtue of discouraging the dissatisfied from quitting that would be an important source of clarification. Finally, although the focus on turnover addresses perhaps the most direct route through which union voice operates in the model, union voice remains indirect. Recently, some analysts have sought to investigate the extent of voice by considering employee involvement in the union, but the use of union channels and representative participation still constitute more formal and less direct expressions of voice than face-to-face mechanisms. The latter may complement or substitute for union voice but they certainly appear to have a stronger impact on employee morale/satisfaction (Hammer, 2000).

The Contribution of Unions, Employee Involvement, and Other Workplace Practices

The most recent literature on unions and economic performance examines the association between unions, employee involvement/high performance work practices, and performance outcomes. This research considers the factors allowing unionized establishments to achieve better than average performance outcomes. This work is (loosely) in the spirit of the voice model, and can be viewed as addressing the institutional response and governance aspects of the model. The empirical results are mixed but they do offer a more positive, albeit circumscribed, view of union impact than either the net effects or labor turnover literatures reviewed above. We shall review results from the United States, the United Kingdom, and Germany.

Perhaps the best starting point is a somewhat neglected study by Cooke (1994), which examines whether unionism positively or negatively influenced the effectiveness of employee-participation programs and group-based incentives on performance among a 1989 cross-section of 841 manufacturing firms in Michigan (but also see Levine and Tyson, 1990). Cooke's measure of performance is value added net of labor cost per employee. To calculate this he estimates three equations: value added per employee, wage rates, and labor cost/total cost. His measure of employee involvement is a dummy indicating the presence or otherwise of team working, and his group incentives variable is another dummy capturing the presence or otherwise of either profit-sharing or gainsharing plans. These dichotomous variables are jointly interacted with the union status of the firm (the omitted category is absence of unionization, teamworking, and group incentive pay). The other covariates include firm size, depreciable assets per employee (albeit measured at the firm's two-digit primary industry), and proxies for work force skill composition, technology, and market power, inter alia. Using the estimated differentials associated with each combination of employee involvement, group incentive pay, and union status, Cooke estimates their performance effects by subtracting the estimated wage differential, adjusted by the labor cost share differential, from the estimated value added per employee differential.

Cooke's results suggest that firm performance is about 13 percent higher in unionized plants without either employee involvement or incentive pay than in comparable nonunion firms. The introduction of team working raises this differential to around 35 percent. By contrast, its introduction in the nonunion sector does not improve the innovating (nonunion) firm's net performance. In the absence of teamwork, group incentive pay has a much larger effect on efficiency in nonunion firms (+18.5 percent) than in union firms (+6.5 percent). In combination, the two measures also have a much bigger performance payoff in nonunion (+21 percent) than union (–0.7 percent) firms. While suggesting that the payoff to employee involvement and incentive pay may sharply differ in union and nonunion regimes, this study clearly paints a much rosier picture of union operation than the generality of the U.S. productivity studies reviewed earlier.

An updated U.S. treatment is provided by Black and Lynch (2001) who have improved and more representative data in the form of the nationally representative EQW National Employers' Survey, matched to the Longitudinal Research Database. The authors first fit an augmented Cobb-Douglas production function to a 1993 cross section of the data. The sample comprises 638 firms. The regression includes in addition to capital, labor, and materials, a vector of technology variables, a detailed set of controls for worker characteristics, no less than six proxies for *high performance work systems* (total quality management {TQM}, benchmarking, number of managerial levels, number of employees per supervisor, the proportion of workers in self-managed teams, and the {log} number of employees in training), two voice measures (unionization and the proportion of employees meeting regularly in groups), and two levels of profit sharing (management and supervisors and production/clerical/technical). In recognition of a potential omitted variables problem stemming from unobserved plant heterogeneity, Black and Lynch also provide estimates using panel estimation methods. Specifically, they employ a two-step method that involves first estimating a fixed, time-invariant firm effect for each establishment using data for the time-variant factors for 1988–1993, and then regressing these fixed effects (firm-level efficiency parameters) on all the time invariant factors (that is, all variables other than labor, capital, and materials).[15]

The cross-sectional estimates indicate that, although most of the high performance work practices are positively associated with labor productivity, only one — namely, benchmarking — is statistically significant at conventional levels. For its part, the proportion of workers meeting regularly in groups is also positively and significantly related to labor productivity, although the unionization coefficient itself is poorly determined. The nonmanagerial profit-sharing variable is positively and significantly associated with labor productivity, albeit not in all specifications. Although the authors do not find evidence of synergistic bundling of workplace practices, the interaction between unionization and nonmanagerial profit sharing is positive and weakly statistically significant, but that between unionization and TQM is not significant. Interactions of the proportion of workers meeting regularly in groups and the same two variables while positive are also statistically insignificant. That said, the authors are able to reject the joint null that all four interaction terms is zero. Finally, the results for the panel data two-step estimation are broadly the same as the cross-sectional results, although selection may of course still be an issue because of the lack of temporal variation in the voice and workplace practices.

Black and Lynch use their estimates to show how unionized establishments that embrace "transformed" industrial relations practices can have higher productivity than a comparable nonunion plant while those that do not will have lower productivity. Specifically, a union plant practicing benchmarking and total quality management, with 50 percent of its workers meeting on a regular basis, and operating profit sharing for its nonmanagerial employees is reported to have 13.5 percent higher labor productivity than a nonunion plant with none of these practices. By contrast, the corresponding differential for a high performance nonunion establishment is just 4.5 percent. If union and nonunion plants possess none of these workplace practices, the nonunion establishments have 10 percent higher labor productivity than their union counterparts. Note there is no attempt in this study to discover whether the workplace practices in question are positively related to *average costs per worker* (for evidence of which, see Cappelli and Neumark, 2001; see also Black and Lynch, 2000).

These U.S. results are of course consistent with the collective voice/institutional response model. But one must be cautious in interpreting the above evidence for a number of reasons. First, there are the issues of the statistical significance of the variables used in benchmarking exercises of this type and the representativeness of the resulting synthetic workplaces. Second, the management literature is not agreed on the contribution of individual human resource management practices to performance outcomes (especially through time), on the synergies between particular practices (Milgrom and Roberts, 1995; Ichniowski et al., 1997), or indeed on the role of workplace representation for that matter. Third, causation remains an issue and we cannot rule out the possibility that unions may have initially agreed to a "transformed" set of human resource practices and flexible work methods *in extremis*, namely, when threatened by mass layoffs or a plant closing.

Although definitions differ, some of these qualifications are explored in an interesting paper by Wood and de Menezes (1998) using British data from the 1990 Workplace Industrial Relations Survey and the Employers' Manpower and Skills Practices Survey. The authors first attempt to test whether the range of employee involvement and participative mechanisms used in the literature form a unity and can be used as indicators of a high commitment orientation on the part of management. Wood and de Menezes use latent variable analysis to search for identifiable patterns in the use of 23 such practices.[16] They are unable to identify high commitment management as a well-defined continuous variable, but they are able to fit a latent class model to the data, i.e., identify a progression of types of high commitment management. There are four such types: high HCM, medium-low HCM, low-medium HCM, and low HCM.

With regard to unionism, Wood and de Menezes first examine the association between union recognition and high commitment management. Neither high HCM nor low HCM workplaces emerge as distinctive with respect to unionism. This suggests among other things that the tendency of some British industrial relations specialists to treat nonunion workplaces as "bleak authoritarian houses" is erroneous.17 Second, the authors include the establishment's HCM class as an argument in conventional performance equations alongside unionism and controls for workplace characteristics and industry affiliation. They examine seven such performance outcomes: labor productivity, change in labor productivity, financial performance, job creation, employee relations climate, quits, and absenteeism. High HCM establishments are not found to be more effective than others. That is, in no case do they perform better than all the others on any performance criteria. For example, although high HCM plants do have better employment growth and better financial performance than the two medium HCM categories, this does not carry over to the low HCM plants. Evidently different types of plants can perform differently according to the outcome measure. The plot only thickens when it comes to the effect of union recognition, since five out of seven coefficient estimates are negative, of which four are statistically significant.

More recent British work has offered a more optimistic but restrictive view in focusing on the effect of cooperative industrial relations. Metcalf (2003) advances two sets of findings from an analysis of the WERS98. First he defines a human resources management (HRM) workplace as one with a formal strategic plan on human resources, and an employee relations manager involved in its development; employing personality or performance tests in recruitment; having most of its employees in the largest occupational group trained in jobs other than their own; and practicing individual or group performance-related pay. He reports that a HRM workplace with no union recognition has superior labor productivity to a union workplace without these defining characteristics but that union recognition when accompanied by HRM is associated with a much improved relative performance — although for only one of the performance outcomes examined is this improvement sufficient to ensure that unionized plants are the best performing establishments. Second, Metcalf looks at the potential effects of "partnership agreements" in the United Kingdom (Trade Union Congress, 1999). He defines a workplace as having a partnership where it negotiates with a union over pay, where management negotiates or consults with unions over recruitment, training, payment systems, handling grievances, staff planning, equal opportunities, and health and safety performance appraisals. Metcalf (2003, p. 158) reports that such partnerships: "significantly raise the probability of above average performance for financial performance and both the level of and change in productivity."

Finally, the German evidence is more mixed. We noted earlier that the early German research pointed to adverse effects of local workplace representation via works councils on firm performance. Yet, in a follow-up of one of the more negative such studies, FitzRoy and Kraft (1995) qualify their earlier harsh interpretation of works council impact on establishment performance (FitzRoy and Kraft, 1987). They now report that works councils in firms practicing profit sharing are positively associated with productivity. Among their counterparts in non-profit-sharing regimes, however, the works council effect on productivity is still negative and statistically significant.

More recent German research has tended to identify the circumstances where positive effects of works councils might be expected. One strand in the literature has looked at the wider industrial relations context, reporting for example that where the works council plant is covered by an external collective agreement — although not otherwise — positive effects on productivity are found (Hübler and Jirjahn, 2003). This result suggests that rent-seeking behavior may indeed be circumscribed by the dual system as Freeman and Lazear (1995) have conjectured (see Section II). The more general approach has followed the modern United States and U.K. literatures in examining — although somewhat more directly on this occasion — the association between works councils and various workplace practices. One early result suggested that works councils and teamwork might be substitutes (Addison et al., 1997). Hübler and Jirjahn (2003) also report a negative association between teamwork and works councils, although this might reflect the greater difficulty for a works council to represent the interests of the overall work force when individual groups directly communicate with management.

More interesting, therefore, is the association between works councils and other workplace practices. We saw earlier that Jirjahn (2002) anticipated on agency and rent seeking (on the part of management) grounds that the association between works councils and productivity would be mediated by profit-sharing schemes for management. In fitting a productivity equation to pooled data for 438 German plants observed in 1994 and 1996, Jirjahn obtains significantly positive coefficient estimates for the dummies capturing works council presence and the existence of management profit-sharing schemes. For its part, the coefficient estimate for the interaction term is negative, which the author interprets as consistent with two hypotheses: *either* profit-sharing management reduces the commitment value of agency in circumstances where the works council cannot foster trust and loyalty absent the cooperation of management, *or* management rent seeking is curbed by profit sharing and the works council is not so important for building cooperation in situations of reduced opportunism on the part of management. Even if ultimately inconclusive, we would argue that the approach taken by Jirjahn is very much in the spirit of the collective voice model.

Altogether less positive results are however reported by Schedlitzki (2002) who examines the effect of works councils, employee involvement, and their interaction on establishment profitability using the same broad dataset as Jirjahn but data for 1996 alone. She finds that establishments where there is employee involvement but no works council have higher profitability than their counterparts with workplace representation. Schedlitzki interprets her findings as consistent with the so-called "management pressure/management competence" hypothesis of FitzRoy and Kraft (1987, 1990) to the effect that efficient managers can institute adequate systems of communication and decision-making without the *impedimenta* of autonomous works councils.

It will be interesting to see whether these more pessimistic findings are reiterated using nationally representative establishment data from the IAB Establishment Panel. Thus far, it does seem from this new data set that works councils increase further training and that *predicted* further training as well as works council presence may be pro-productive (Zwick, 2002). On the other hand, a recent study of high-performance work practices by Wolf and Zwick (2002) that also controls for selection and unobserved plant heterogeneity is less clear cut, and nicely illustrates the difficulties confronting the analyst in this area. In the first place, the association between the works council and such practices is not always positive and well determined. Second, different practices seem to have different (and exactly reversed) effects on productivity once unobserved plant heterogeneity and selection are accounted for. Specifically, "organizational change" bundles made up of practices that foster employee involvement — a shift in responsibility to lower levels of the hierarchy, the introduction of team work and self-responsible teams and work groups with independent budgets — now have a significantly positive impact on productivity, while the effect of "incentive bundles" such as employee share ownership, profit sharing, and incentive training is now statistically insignificant in the preferred specification. And note that the association between works councils and employment practice bundles is much stronger in the case of incentives than organizational change. Also recall that the positive effect of works councils on productivity observed in this new data set is not robust.

The literature on the association between performance outcomes and unions, employee involvement, and various modern work practices is in its infancy. It suggests that the union effect depends on the regime of human resource practices. This contingency is consistent with union governance and more obviously with institutional response. But it is sobering to reflect that the contingency cuts both ways. Firms may upgrade their human resource practices in response to unionism, as suggested by Freeman and Medoff, but this upgrading can also be a response to union (restrictive) practices.

IV. Interpretation

This review of union voice has traced some major shifts over the course of the past quarter century in the perception of what unions do. The start of the period is demarcated by the influential empirical study of Brown and Medoff (1978). This careful empirical study drew on notions of collective voice and did much to prepare the ground for *What Do Unions Do?* Both works brought ideas current in the industrial relations literature before more skeptical economists, largely weaned on notions of union monopoly. It is unclear just how many minds were changed as a result of this challenge. But they were certainly broadened: the proof of which is the slew of unions-in-the-production-function studies and subsequent estimates of union effects on profitability and investment. Yet the number of such studies had slowed to a trickle by the mid–1990s. If we were to stop the action at this point, it might be concluded that the profession had examined the new theory of unionism and had found it wanting given the lack of a convincing evidence of a material increase in the joint surplus under unionism and every indication from profit and investment data that the dynamic implications of unionism were unfavorable.

This interpretation would be too strong. First, there was no conspicuous fall off in British and German research interest in union voice. Second, the common finding of a near zero average "effect" of unions on labor productivity is interesting in and of itself; for example, it addresses the concerns of those much exercised by the cost of the union rule book. Moreover, it really serves to shift our attention to the factors that might mediate this outcome. Third, research findings are less consistently negative for unions in Europe. In the United States, the strongly interlocking nature of the research results — namely, sizable union wage premia, small average productivity effects, consistently negative profit effects, and unfavorable effects on investment in both physical and intangible capital — do not provide a particularly auspicious context for union voice. Fourth, there are enough ambiguities in our mainstream models to call into question the inevitability of the result that unions will have adverse effects. Thus, in terms of dynamic effects, sufficiently firm action by the enterprise (having a discount factor sufficiently close to one) may discourage union opportunism in respect of the quasi-rents to long-lived relation specific capital (Addison and Chilton, 1998), while in other circumstances the hold-up mechanism may be dominated by strategic R&D behavior (Menezes-Filho and van Reenen, 2003). Fifth, the action is still ongoing and we have commented in particular on an emerging literature on union presence, workplace practices, and firm performance. Finally, of course, the new theory does not argue that improvements in productivity are automatic, only that these may be observed given an appropriate concatenation of circumstances: the expression of effective voice, a constructive institutional response, and a cooperative industrial relations environment.

Unfortunately, the voice mechanisms producing increased workplace performance are disturbingly vague outside of reduced turnover/higher training investments, and even here in neglecting the issue of optimal quit behavior the model cannot address whether the induced reduction in quits and increase in training are excessive.[18] The bigger problem is that the collective voice model is sufficiently catholic to accommodate all sorts of finding, even the most negative. Frankly, "institutional response" is something of a *deus ex machina*. More problematic still is the very integrity of collective voice/institutional response mechanism. Bargaining power is necessary if unions are to play a role in the enforcement of contracts, but bargaining power is what defines the monopoly effect. *Vulgo*: if voice is wrapped up with the exercise of power, how can we be sure that it is the putative "good" that the architects of collective voice take it to be? Power also carries consequences for institutional response because management resistance to voice can then be placed on the same footing as resistance to higher wages.

We consider it unlikely that Freeman and Medoff intend that the information function of unions is the sole — even the main — source of the potential benefits of union voice. But assuming for the moment that they do, very little attention is accorded the quality or effectiveness of collective voice. Thus, for example, there is no formal discussion of whether the union will be a faithful agent of the member-principal. More important in this context is the model's reliance on worker dissatisfaction and the neglect of individual voice. We earlier provided some (controversial) German evidence suggesting that it was individual rather than collective voice that delivered the goods as it were and lowered excessive turnover among unskilled workers. However, a recent paper by Luchak (2003) probably makes the point better. Luchak distinguishes between *direct voice* and *representative voice*. By direct voice he means efforts by employees to effect change through two-way communication with another member of the organization, such as a team member. Representative voice is an indirect mechanism working through a third-party intermediary or process, such as a union steward filing a grievance. He argues that the former is a more flexible, integrative process whereas the latter is more structured, issue oriented, and distributive.

Luchak further distinguishes between two types of worker attachment to their firms: *affective commitment* and *continuance commitment*. The former refers to an emotional bond between worker and firm that, among other things, leads that worker to contribute meaningfully to the organization while at the same time seeking dispute resolution that does not threaten the relationship with the firm. The latter is based on a calculation of the costs and benefits associated with staying with or leaving the organization, such as the sacrifice of material firm-specific training investments and non-portable benefits. Such employees may or may not experience feelings of helplessness and frustration but, in this model, they are motivated to do a minimum toward maintaining organizational membership.

While both types of worker are predicted to evince lower quits, Luchak hypothesizes that employees who have an affective bond to the organization will be more likely to use direct voice and less likely to use representative voice, and conversely for continuance committed employees. These hypotheses are tested using data on 429 employees in a Canadian electric utility in 1997. Controlling for perceived effectiveness of union voice, job satisfaction, demographics, salary, and education, it is reported that score on an affective commitment scale is positively associated with use of direct voice (an average over a three-item scaled response) and negatively associated with grievance filing (or being a shop steward). For its part, score on a continuance commitment scale is not associated with any reduction in the use of direct voice, although it is at least positively associated with grievance filing (if not with being a steward). Both forms of commitment emerge as negatively related to an indicator of quit propensity. And not surprisingly the perceived effectiveness of union voice is associated with more direct voice and more grievance filing.

There are two interesting inferences that can be drawn from this treatment. First, to the extent that it is sourced from continuance committed individuals, collective voice may not be worth listening to. For his part, Luchak concludes that there is a need for some fundamental rethinking of the performance-enhancing features of unions in these circumstances. Second, if unionized employees are more dissatisfied than their nonunion counterparts, we might speculate along with Luchak that they have lower levels of affective commitment. Certainly there is a well-determined positive association between job satisfaction and affective commitment in this Canadian data set. Moreover, if dissatisfied workers tend to file grievances rather than engage in direct voice, the relief of disaffection may be but temporary.

The emphasis on dissatisfaction in the collective voice model is probably consistent with the functioning of traditional unionism. If so, the seeming desire among all workers for representation charted in Freeman and Rogers (1999, pp. 68–70) is undercut by a desire for representation that works *cooperatively* with employers, identified by the same authors (p. 5). The decline in United States union density may therefore have more to do with its adversarial nature than the more popular explanations of antiquated labor laws and unfair tactics by employers (Delaney, 2003). Evidence supplied in this chapter on the attitudes of *British* workers to union voice may also speak to the adversarial nature of collective bargaining.

By the same token, cooperation between management and organized labor is a central theme in *What Do Unions Do?* Cooperation, or a favorable set of institutional responses, is seen as the ultimate key to realizing improvements in workplace performance. This theme has been taken up in the most recent empirical literature linking unionism to employee involvement and various high-performance work practices. We have seen that some progress has been made in identifying circumstances in which unionism can be associated with beneficial performance outcomes. But the impetus for much of this new research emanated from the management literature rather than developing organically from the collective voice model. And if the findings of the new studies can be construed as being in the spirit of the union voice model, the fact remains that there is no agreement on the particular practices that "work" in union environments, still less on the contribution of unionism to the development of high-performance work practices (with the possible exception of further training in the German case). In other words, there has been an inadequate integration of the union voice and management approaches. The benchmarking exercises reviewed herein are interesting in suggesting that unionized plants need not suffer from any, say, productivity shortfall and indeed might enjoy higher productivity than nonunion plants. But they do not establish that unions are pro-productive.

The problems in attributing causality identified by Hirsch in this volume are actually elevated in exercises of this kind. Causation continues to cast a long shadow because of the essentially cross-sectional nature of research involving new working practices. Here the German literature, although still in its infancy, contains the suggestion that some practices might appear successful because they are introduced in times/circumstances of prosperity while others might only appear unsuccessful because they were introduced to deal with major structural problems. Much the same discussion on causation attended investigation of union impact in the earlier net effects literature. Suffice it to say that the analytical problem is only compounded when voice and working practices are being considered jointly.

Finally there are two important institutional considerations that have been raised by our discussion. First, there is the apparent sea change in the effect of British unions on economic outcomes (including macro outcomes, not reviewed here, but see Addison and Siebert, 2003). If the U.S. union voice literature was christened in optimism, the opposite is true of the corresponding British research. Over time, however, the disadvantages of British unionism have dissipated — some would say have even disappeared. It is conventional to attribute this favorable development in large part to legislative changes that attacked union immunities or legal privileges. These changes were accompanied by increased competition, both domestic and international. The suggestion is that institutional change/adversity and competition may be the handmaiden of innovations in union effects — their staying power or persistence is another, uncharted issue. Second, there is some evidence from Germany that it may be possible partly to decouple production from distribution issues at the workplace given an appropriate structure of collective bargaining, here the dual system of industrial relations. At issue of course is the portability of institutions if not economic forces.

Union voice is not dead: It has some theoretical conviction, it has witnessed some modest development, and it still manages to summon a modicum of empirical support. But after one-quarter of a century, it is in urgent need of restatement. In the process, it has to tackle the various lacunae identified above. Absent such development its gradual abandonment would seem to be assured.

Notes

1. Industrial relations scholars, such as Dunlop (1944), Reynolds and Taft (1956), Slichter et al. (1960), and Bok and Dunlop (1970), had long pointed pointed out that unions had diverse positive nonwage effects. For an historical accounting, see Kaufman (1993).
2. This is not to dispute the *short-term* costs of strikes or their effects on product quality, but rather to contest the attribution of blame to one side alone; on which, see Siebert et al. (1985).
3. As a practical matter, 1984 does not mark the beginning of the new applied literature. Rather that literature is so delineated by the publication of Brown and Medoff's (1978) influential production function analysis of union impact, which cites (as forthcoming) *What Do Unions Do?*
4. We note that Boroff and Lewin (1997) question the application of the Hirschman model to the workplace because of their finding that more loyal employees are not only less likely to use voice (specifically grieve) but also less likely to quit.
5. In such markets, allocation and remuneration decisions are not directly determined by the price mechanism. The labor contract will be complex and multidimensional because workers care about nonpecuniary terms of employment and workplace rules, and also because such conditions and methods of organization have different

costs. Worker attitudes and morale are therefore potentially important inputs into production.

6. Individual voice is also less likely because of individual fears of retaliation. The traditional master-servant relationship makes it difficult for individuals to express discontent due to the danger of being fired. Collective voice changes the authority relation. As Freeman (1976, p. 364) writes: "it is clearly easier to retaliate against a single worker than the entire work force." The changed authority relation also implies an industrial jurisprudence system and from the perspective of the model the prospect of a better enforcement of workers' rights and contract execution (further commented on below).

7. Average preferences may also yield better outcomes than marginal preferences when desirable conditions or fringe benefits involve substantial fixed costs.

8. As an approximation, faithful behavior by the union agent obtains where the provision of services corresponds to the preferences of the median voter. Within this framework there are a number of factors making for a divergence between union policies and member preferences, such as situations where the leadership can affect the voting agenda and the existence of exclusive representation agreements/union security clauses. Furthermore, the nonproprietary nature of unionism (i.e., union members do not have transferable property rights in the union) may also permit the union leadership significant discretion in framing policy (Martin, 1980). By the same token, a faithful union agent having determined member preferences may not find it easy to satisfy them. Thus, Flanagan (1983) links the difficulty of providing workplace public goods to membership heterogeneity and he proceeds to examine the basic tension between union structures promoting bargaining power and those that reduce internal decision making costs (which are increasing in membership heterogeneity). For a modern treatment of voice within organizations showing how asymmetric information between the leadership and the membership and heterogeneity of the membership come together to shape policy, see Banerjee and Somanathan (2001).

9. Freeman (1976, p. 365) also makes the interesting observation that in larger organizations union voice will also provide central management with information about local conditions and operations of a type that differs markedly from that passed up the organizational chain.

10. We are not referring to "efficient bargains" on the contract curve, which in general will not be efficient in the sense used here. Even in the case of the vertical contract curve, the question of union impact can only be sidestepped temporarily since the assumption here is that capital is held constant.

11. There is also codetermination at the enterprise level, namely, worker representation on the supervisory boards of companies — full parity representation in firms in the coal, iron and steel industries, quasi-parity representation in companies with more than 2,000 employees, and one-third board representation in companies with between 500 and 2,000 employees.

12. We do not discuss the association between unionism and employment, partly because employment growth is a rather more ambiguous outcome indicator; for example, unionized plants shedding restrictive practices might expand employment less than nonunion establishments. But the sobering facts are that, other things being equal, union plants grow around 3 percent less per year than their nonunion counterparts in both the United States (Leonard, 1992) and the United Kingdom (Addison and Belfield, 2004a).

13. Only one German study has investigated works council impact on capital investment. For a 1990 cross section of circa 50 manufacturing firms, Addison et al. (1993)

regress the gross investment-capital stock ratio on works council presence, firm size, product innovation, and proxies for the state of demand (capital utilization and hours of overtime per employee), and modernity (the capital to sales ratio). They find that firms with a works council present have significantly lower gross investment ratios. The caveat is that, despite the strong showing of the worker representation variable, the overall performance of the equation is weak.

14. We should note that there is the suggestion of higher absenteeism rates in unionized plants in the WERS98; see Addison and Belfield (2001).

15. In addition to this estimator, Black and Lynch also deploy a GMM estimator.

16. In addition to the familiar quality circles/problem-solving groups, teambriefing, top management briefing, profit sharing, employee share ownership, and financial disclosure, the measures include human relations skills as a selection criterion, internal recruitment, multiskilling, individual performance appraisal, welfare facilities, and monthly/cashless pay.

17. The Dickensian allusion is that of Sisson (1995).

18. While there are a few U.S. studies pointing to either lower training or no increase in training in union regimes (Duncan and Stafford, 1980; Lynch and Black, 1998), these are the exception.

References

Addison, John T. and John Chilton. "Self-Enforcing Union Contracts: Efficient Investment and Employment." *Journal of Business* 71 (July 1998): 349–69.

Addison, John T. and Clive R. Belfield. "Updating the Determinants of Firm Performance: Estimation Using the 1998 Workplace Employee Relations Survey." *British Journal of Industrial Relations* 39 (September 2001): 341–66.

———."Unions and Employment Growth: The One Constant?" *Industrial Relations* 43 (April 2004a):305–24.

———. "Unions and Establishment Performance: Evidence from the British Workplace Industrial/Employee Relations Surveys." In Phanindra Wunnava, ed. *The Changing Role of Unions.* Armonk, N.Y.: M.E. Sharpe, 2004b, pp. 281–319.

Addison, John T. and Barry T. Hirsch. "Union Effects on Productivity, Profits, and Growth: Has the Long Run Arrived?" *Journal of Labor Economics* 7 (January 1989): 72–105.

Addison, John T., Kornelius Kraft, and Joachim Wagner. "German Works Councils and Firm Performance." In Bruce E. Kaufman and Morris M. Kleiner, eds. *Employee Representation: Alternatives and Future Directions.* Madison, Wisc.: Industrial Relations Research Association. 1993, pp. 305–38.

Addison, John T., Thorsten Schank, Claus Schnabel, and Joachim Wagner. "German Works Councils in the Production Process." Discussion Paper No. 812, Bonn: Institute for the Study of Labor/IZA, 2003.

Addison, John T., Claus Schnabel, and Joachim Wagner. "On the Determinants of Mandatory Works Councils in Germany." *Industrial Relations* 36 (October 1997): 419–45.

———. "Works Councils in Germany: Their Effects on Establishment Performance." *Oxford Economic Papers* 53 (October 2001): 659–94.

———. "The Course of Research into the Economic Consequenses of German Works Councils." *British Journal of Industrial Relations* 42(June 2004): 255–81..

Addison, John T. and W. Stanley Siebert. "Recent Changes in the Industrial Relations Framework in the U.K." In John T. Addison and Claus Schnabel, eds. *International Handbook of Trade Unions.* Cheltenham, England, and Northampton, Mass.: Edward Elgar, 2003, pp. 415–60.

Banerjee Abhijit and Rohini Somanathan. "A Simple Model of Voice." *Quarterly Journal of Economics* 116 (February 2001): 189–227.

Bender, Keith and Peter J. Sloane. "Job Satisfaction, Trade Unions and Exit-Voice Revisited." *Industrial and Labor Relations Review* 51 (January 1998): 222–40.

Batt, Rosemary, Alexander J.S. Colvin, and Jeffrey Keefe. "Employee Voice, Human Resource Practices, and Quit Rates: Evidence from the Telecommunications Industry." *Industrial and Labor Relations Review* 55 (July 2002): 573–94.

Black, Sandra E. and Lisa M. Lynch. "What's Driving the New Economy: The Benefits of Workplace Innovation." Working Paper 7479, Cambridge, Mass.: National Bureau of Economic Research, 2000.

———. "How to Compete: The Impact of Workplace Practices and Information Technology on Productivity." *Review of Economics and Statistics* 83 (August 2001): 434–45.

Bok, Derek C. and John T. Dunlop. *Labor and the American Community.* New York: Simon and Schuster, 1970.

Boroff, Karen E. and David Lewin. "Loyalty, Voice, and Intent to Exit a Firm: A Conceptual and Empirical Analysis." *Industrial and Labor Relations Review* 51 (October 1997): 50–63.

Bronars, Stephen G. and Donald R. Deere. "Unionization, Incomplete Contracting, and Capital Investment." *Journal of Business* 66 (January 1993): 117–32.

———, and Joseph S. Tracy. "The Effect of Unions on Firm Behavior: An Empirical Analysis Using Firm-Level Data." *Industrial Relations* 33 (October 1994): 426–51.

Brown, Charles and James L. Medoff. "Trade Unions in the Production Process." *Journal of Political Economy* 86 (June 1978): 355–78.

Bryson, Alex. "Unionism and Workplace Closure in Britain, 1900–1998." *British Journal of Industrial Relations* 42 (June 2004): 283–302.

Cappelli, Peter and David Neumark. "Do 'High Performance' Work Practices Improve Establishment-Level Outcomes?" *Industrial and Labor Relations Review* 54 (July 2001): 737–75.

Cavanaugh, Joseph K. "Asset-specific Investment and Unionized Labor." *Industrial Relations* 37 (January 1998): 35–50.

Cooke, William N. "Employee Participation Programs, Group-Based Incentives, and Company Performance: A Union-Nonunion Comparison." *Industrial and Labor Relations Review* 47 (July 1994): 594–609.

Delaney, John T. "Contemporary Developments in and Challenges to Collective Bargaining in the United States." In John T. Addison and Claus Schnabel, eds. *International Handbook of Trade Unions.* Cheltenham, England, and Northampton, Mass.: Edward Elgar, 2003, pp. 503–30.

Delery, John E., Nina Gupta, J. Douglas Shaw, J.R. Jenkins, and Margot L. Ganster. "Unionization, Compensation, and Voice Effects on Quits and Retention." *Industrial Relations* 39 (October 2000): 625–45.

Denny, Kevin and Stephen J. Nickell. "Unions and Investment in British Industry." *Economic Journal* 102 (July 1992): 874–87.

Department of Trade and Industry. *Workplace Employee Relations Survey: Cross-Section 1998* [computer file] 4th ed. Colchester, England: The Data Archive [distributor], 22 December 1999. SN: 3955.

Duncan, Gregory M. and Frank P. Stafford. "Do Union Members Receive Compensating Differentials?" *American Economic Review* 70 (June 1980): 355–71.

Dunlop, John. *Wage Determination under Trade Unions.* New York: MacMillan, 1944.

Fallick, Bruce C. and Kevin A. Hassett. "Investment and Union Certification." *Journal of Labor Economics* 17 (July 1999): 570–82.

Fernie, Sue and David Metcalf. "Participation, Contingent Pay, Representation and Workplace Performance: Evidence from Great Britain." *British Journal of Industrial Relations* 33 (September 1995): 379–415.

FitzRoy, Felix and Kornelius Kraft. "Efficiency and Internal Organization: Works Councils in West German Firms." *Economica* 54 (November 1987): 493–504.

———. "Innovation, Rent-Sharing and the Organization of Labor in the Federal Republic of Germany." *Small Business Economics* 2 (1990): 95–103.

———. "On the Choice of Incentives in Firms." *Journal of Economic Behavior and Organization* 26 (January 1995): 145–60.

Flanagan, Robert J. "Workplace Public Goods and Union Organizations." *Industrial Relations* 22 (Spring 1983): 224–37.

Freeman, Richard B. "Individual Mobility and Union Voice in the Labor Market." *American Economic Review, Papers and Proceedings* 66 (May 1976): 361–68.

———. "Job Satisfaction as an Economic Variable." *American Economic Review, Papers and Proceedings* 68 (May 1978): 135–41.

———. "The Exit-Voice Tradeoff in the Labor Market: Unionism, Job Tenure, Quits, and Separations." *Quarterly Journal of Economics* 94 (June 1980): 643–73.

——— and Edward P. Lazear. "An Economic Analysis of Works Councils." In Joel Rogers and Wolfgang Streeck, eds. *Works Councils, Consultation, Representation and Cooperation in Industrial Relations.* Chicago, Ill.: University of Chicago Press, 1995, pp. 27–50.

Freeman, Richard B. and James L. Medoff. "The Two Faces of Unionism." *Public Interest* 57 (Fall 1979): 69–93.

———. "The Impact of Collective Bargaining: Can the New Facts be Explained by Monopoly Unionism?" In Joseph D. Reid, Jr., ed. *New Approaches to Labor Unions.* Greenwich, Conn.: JAI Press, 1983, pp. 293–332.

———. *What Do Unions Do?* New York: Basic Books, 1984.

Freeman, Richard B. and Joel Rogers. *What Workers Want.* Ithaca, N.Y.: ILS Press, 1999.

Gregg, Paul, Stephen Machin, and David Metcalf. "Signals or Cycles? Productivity Growth and Changes in Union Status in British Companies, 1984–9." *Economic Journal* 103 (July 1993): 894–907.

Hammer, Tove Hellend. "Nonunion Representational Forms: An Organizational Behavior Perspective." In Bruce E. Kaufman and Daphne Gottlieb Taras, eds. *Nonunion Employee Representation — History, Contemporary Practice, and Policy.* Armonk, N.Y.: M. E. Sharpe, pp. 176–95.

Hirsch, Barry T. *Labor Unions and the Economic Performance of Firms.* Kalamazoo, Mich.: Upjohn Institute for Employment Research, 1991.

——— and John T. Addison. *The Economic Analysis of Unions — New Approaches and Evidence.* Boston, Mass.: Allen and Unwin, 1986.

Hirsch, Barry T. and Barbara A. Morgan. "Shareholder Risk and Returns in Union and Nonunion Firms." *Industrial and Labor Relations Review* 47 (January 1994): 302–18.

Hirsch, Barry T. and Kislaya Prasad. "Wage-Employment Determination and a Union Tax on Capital: Can Theory and Evidence Be Reconciled?" *Economics Letters* 48 (April 1995): 61–71.

Hirschman, Albert O. *Exit, Voice, and Loyalty.* Cambridge, Mass.: Harvard University Press, 1970.

Hübler, Olaf and Uwe Jirjahn. "Works Councils and Collective Bargaining in Germany: The Impact on Productivity and Wages." *Scottish Journal of Political Economy* 50 (September 2003): 471–91.

Ichniowski, Casey, Kathryn Shaw, and Gabrielle Prennushi. "The Effects of Human Resource Management Practices on Productivity." *American Economic Review* 87 (June 1997): 291–313.

Iverson, Roderick D. and Douglas B. Currivan. "Union Participation, Job Satisfaction, and Employee Turnover: An Event-History Analysis of the Exit-Voice Hypothesis." *Industrial Relations* 42 (January 2003): 101–105.

Jirjahn, Uwe. "Executive Incentives, Works Councils, and Firm Performance." Unpublished paper, University of Hannover, 2002.

Kaufman, Bruce E. *The Origins and Evolution of the Field of Industrial Relations in the United States.* Ithaca, N.Y.: ILR Press, 1993.

———— and David I. Levine. "An Economic Analysis of Employee Representation." In Bruce E. Kaufman and Daphne Gottlieb Taras, eds. *Nonunion Employee Representation — History, Contemporary Practice, and Policy.* Armonk, N.Y.: M. E. Sharpe, pp. 149–75.

Kraft, Kornelius. "Exit and Voice in the Labor Market: An Empirical Study of Quits." *Journal of Institutional and Theoretical Economics* 142 (1986): 697–715.

Leibenstein, Harvey. "Allocative Efficiency vs. X-Efficiency." *American Economic Review* 56 (June 1966): 392–415.

Leonard, Jonathan S. "Unions and Employment Growth." *Industrial Relations* 31 (Winter 1992): 80–94.

Levine, David I. and Laura D'Andrea Tyson. "Participation, Productivity, and the Firm's Environment." In Alan S. Blinder, ed. *Paying for Productivity — A Look at the Evidence.* Washington, D.C.: Brookings Institution, 1990, pp. 183–237.

Luchak, Andrew A. "What Kind of Voice Do Loyal Employees Use?" British Journal of Industrial Relations 41 (March 2003): 115–34.

Lynch, Lisa M. and Sandra E. Black. "Beyond the Incidence of Employer-provided Training." *Industrial and Labor Relations Review* 52 (October 1998): 64–81.

Machin, Stephen and Mark Stewart. "Trade Unions and Financial Performance." *Oxford Economic Papers* 48 (April 1996): 213–41.

Malcomson, James M. "Trade Unions and Economic Efficiency." *Economic Journal* 93 (Supplement 1983): 50–65.

Martin, Donald L. *An Ownership Theory of the Trade Union.* Berkeley, Calif.: University of California Presss, 1980.

Menezes-Filho, Naercio and John van Reenen. "Unions and Innovation: A Survey of the Theory and Empirical Evidence." In John T. Addison and Claus Schnabel, eds. *International Handbook of Trade Unions.* Cheltenham, England and Northampton, Mass.: Edward Elgar, 2003, pp. 293–334.

Menezes-Filho, Naercio, David Ulph, and John van Reenen. "R&D and Union Bargaining Power: Evidence from Union Companies and Establishments." *Industrial and Labor Relations Review* 52 (October 1998): 45–63.

Metcalf, David. "Union Presence and Labour Productivity in British Manufacturing Industry." *British Journal of Industrial Relations* 28 (July 1990): 249–66.

————. "Unions and Productivity, Financial Performance and Investment: International Evidence." In John T. Addison and Claus Schnabel, eds. *International Handbook of Trade Unions.* Cheltenham, England and Northampton, Mass.: Edward Elgar, 2003, pp. 118–71.

Milgrom, Paul and John Roberts. "Complementarities and Fit: Strategy, Structure, and Organizational Change in Manufacturing." *Journal of Accounting and Economics* 19 (March/May 1995): 179–208.

Reynolds, Lloyd and Cynthia H. Taft. *The Evolution of Wage Structure.* New Haven, Conn.: Yale University Press, 1956.

Riordan, Michael H. and Michael L. Wachter. "What Do Implicit Contracts Do?" Unpublished paper, University of Pennsylvania, 1983.

Schedlitzki, Doris. "German Works Councils, Employee Involvement Programs, and Their Impact on Establishment Productivity." Centre for Economic Performance Working Paper No. 1191, London School of Economics, 2002.

Schnabel, Claus and Joachim Wagner. "Industrial Relations and Trade Union Effects on Innovation in Germany." *Labour* 8 (1994): 489–503.

Siebert, W. Stanley, Philip V. Bertrand, and John T. Addison. "The Political Model of Strikes: A New Twist." *Southern Economic Journal* 52 (July 1985): 23–33.

Sisson, Keith. "Human Resource Management and the Personnel Function." In John Storey, ed. *Human Resource Management.* London: Routledge, 1995, pp. 87–109.

Slichter, Sumner H., James J. Healy, and E. Robert Livernash. *The Impact of Collective Bargaining on Management.* Washington, D.C.: Brookings Institution, 1960.

Trade Union Congress. *Partners for Progress: New Unionism at the Workplace.* London, England: TUC, 1999.

Williamson, Oliver E., Michael L. Wachter, and Jeffrey E. Harris. "Understanding the Employment Relation: The Analysis of Idiosyncratic Exchange." *Bell Journal of Economics* 6 (Spring 1975): 250–78.

Wolf, Elke and Thomas Zwick. "Reassessing the Impact of High Performance Workplaces." Discussion Paper No. 02–07, Mannheim: Center for European Economic Research/ZEW, 2002.

Wood, Stephen and Lillian de Menezes. "High Commitment Management in the U.K.: Evidence from the Workplace Industrial Relations Survey and Employers' Manpower and Skills Practices Survey." *Human Relations* 51 (1998): 485–515.

Zwick, Thomas. "Continuous Training and Firm Productivity in Germany." Discussion Paper No. 02–50, Mannheim: Centre for European Economic Research/ ZEW, 2002.

9

What Do Unions Do to the Workplace? Union Effects on Management and HRM Policies

*Anil Verma**

I. Introduction

My objective is to advance our understanding of union effects by examining what unions do to managerial practices in the workplace. Unions can be an instrument of social change, but even when they play a larger role in society, their core activity remains in the workplace. Their principal engagement is with management, though their actions may extend to lobbying, politics, and the community at both local and international levels. Therefore, in considering the question, "What do unions do to the workplace?," it is important to examine how unions affect management, in general, and human resource management (HRM), in particular.

The main focus for Freeman and Medoff (F&M), in their 1984 book, *What Do Unions Do?*, was not on this question but rather on union effects on outcomes such as productivity. Their findings have been influential in advancing our knowledge of union impact on organizational outcomes, and they offer a number of explanations for their finding of a positive union effect on productivity. Apart from lower quit rates, three other possible explanations are suggested: seniority-based rewards, better job production standards (and better management accountability in general), and more employer-employee communications (pp. 14–15). The latter two of these explanations concern managerial practice but were not directly investigated in the study. I fill a research gap by examining empirical support (or lack thereof) accumulated since the early 1980s, for some of these and other explanations for a positive union effect on management practices.

Citing a landmark study by Slichter, Healy, and Livernash (1960) (hereafter SHL), F&M argue that unions can improve efficiency by "putting pressure on management to tighten job production standards and accountability in order to preserve profits in the face of higher wages" (p. 15). The SHL study investigated how unions affect management practices by examining an exhaustive range of management policies such as hours of work, wage incentives, subcontracting, promotions, and discipline, to name only a few. SHL found that unions can have both positive and negative effects on management and hence on efficiency. Among the positive effects of unions, SHL point to better management, a better balance between employer and employee interests, and better communications. Although SHL did not formally define the term themselves, their findings of a positive union effect has been referred to as the "shock effect" of unions on management.[1]

Even though the SHL study reported both positive and negative union effects on managerial practice, it is most often cited only for unions' positive effect on efficiency. Although some efficiencies result from the union exercising its voice role, the SHL study cites numerous other examples to show that union voice does not always contribute positively to productivity. In many instances, union actions and policies restrain productivity or efficiency. Similarly, the monopoly face of unions arguably can also contribute to restraining as well as enhancing efficiency, although it is generally associated with negative outcomes for management. Thus, the relationship of union policies to efficiency, whether it be the voice or monopoly face, is a complex one.

To further develop our understanding of these issues, it is important to examine empirical evidence accumulated since the publication of F&M on union effects on management practice. Studies conducted since the early 1980s allow us to examine union effects on a range of workplace and HRM policies. Accordingly, I re-visit the impact of unions on managerial practice in HRM and related workplace practices. More specifically, I attempt to fill two gaps in the research literature. First, I revisit the theoretical bases for union impact on management. This section attempts to integrate and clarify a variety of explanations offered in the past. Second, I update the SHL study by examining the empirical evidence accumulated by various studies since the early 1980s. The second half of the paper builds on the conceptual framework to survey the empirical evidence accumulated on union effects on managerial practice in HRM and other related workplace policies. In examining union impact, my focus is on managerial practice rather than on employee or firm-level outcomes. For example, I do not include topics such as the effect of unions on productivity or the effects of seniority on employee outcomes.

II. Conceptual Framework

Union impact on management is framed by two dynamic processes: formation of underlying preferences of each party and the interaction between the two parties as each tries to pursue its goals. When unions arrive on the scene by organizing workers, they tend to drive up wages. In the popular mind, union preferences have been understood foremost in terms of obtaining "more" for their members. Empirical evidence confirms that unions use their monopoly power to force employers to pay better wages and benefits (F&M, 1984). However, unions do strive for and achieve other goals that are equally important to them and their members, namely, fair treatment from management. This aspect of unionism is especially important in considering how unions affect management behavior. Demand for fairness leads the union to get into almost every area of day-to-day managerial decision-making at the workplace level. Slichter (1941) called the emergence of labor-management relations in the 1930s a system "industrial jurisprudence" in which the union gains a voice in almost all aspects of management decision-making in the workplace that have consequences for workers.

One possible response of management to a wage increase is to substitute capital for more expensive labor. Even if the firm operates at the same level of overall productivity, i.e., a combination of higher labor productivity and lower capital productivity, the ensuing outcome can be sub-optimal because it would lead to inefficient allocation of resources. This can be called the *price effect* of unions, i.e., the effect of an increase in the price of labor.

The price effect explanation assumes that the workplace was already producing at the efficient frontier before unionization and that no further gains in productivity could be made *ex post*. A second set of explanations has been offered by a number of scholars who have argued that management on its own does not generally operate at maximum efficiency. Notable among economic theorists is Leibenstein who suggested the concept of X-inefficiency as an explanation for why management would operate sub-optimally. This is discussed later in this section. Among industrial relations researchers, the SHL study is widely considered to be the most comprehensive to gather firm-level evidence to document an increase in managerial efficiency in the post-unionization period.

If we assume that management was operating sub-optimally prior to unionization, management can be "shocked" into adopting policies that would extract new efficiencies from the operations. This is the crux of the shock effect argument, and the SHL study offers a substantial body of detailed workplace-level evidence in its support. Although the SHL study is cited frequently to support a positive effect of unions on management, it is important to emphasize, for my purposes, that SHL also documented numerous negative effects of unions on management. For example, they cite a narrowing of the scope of managerial discretion in the post-unionization phase.

For a better understanding of union impact on management, it is important to frame the shock effect within the context of a union's monopoly and voice roles (Freeman and Medoff, 1979). According to SHL, management responds by seeking higher efficiency in response to unionization-induced shock. One way to obtain better efficiency is to make changes in areas over which management has exclusive control. We can call this the "pure" shock effect, i.e., one in which the union is not directly involved in obtaining new efficiencies. For example, SHL cite the development of management by policy in contrast to an *ad hoc* approach and the introduction of changes in management structure (pp. 951–52). These findings point to the standardization and formalization of managerial workplace practice that takes place as result of unionization but without the direct involvement of the union. Such changes are management initiated, e.g., a tightening of quality standards or reduction of waste and may be implemented in many instances without consulting the union. To summarize it in their own words, "The challenge that unions presented to management has, if viewed broadly, created superior and better balanced management, even though some exceptions must be recognized" (SHL, 1960: 951).

However, management's desire to obtain efficiencies is not limited to policies under management's exclusive control. There are other areas where changes could be made for higher efficiency, but because those changes would affect working conditions, management would need to engage the union in this process. Moreover, for unions, giving workers a voice in workplace matters is a primary goal. Therefore, unions are eager to seize every opportunity to question and modify managerial decisions whenever possible. Building on Hirschman's concept of voice (as opposed to "exit"), F&M suggested that union goals include giving their members a voice in workplace decisions. At this juncture, a dialogue between union and management over efforts to increase efficiency can end in a bitter fight settled only by the exercise of their relative power, or it could result in mutual accommodation through constructive give-and-take. Changes brought about by either of these two processes may be called the *voice effect* of unions on management. Descriptions of voice mechanisms that lead to positive union effects can be found in the SHL study. Theoretical explanations for why such voice mechanisms would contribute to higher efficiency in the workplace are in Metcalf (2003) and Hirsch (2004).

The SHL study found that most union-management relationships began with a collective agreement in the form of a brief, simple document. Over time and with successive bargaining rounds, these documents became longer and more complex. SHL interpreted this process as a positive development that yielded "fully developed contracts" (SHL, 1960: 186). These contracts contained "a close meeting of the minds" in key areas such as discipline for wildcat strikes and a general decline in conflict over the interpretation of clauses in the collective agreement. This process of gradual convergence between union and management views of the workplace could have resulted from mutual and gradual accommodation, or it may have involved the use of the union's coercive monopoly power. The SHL study showed that frequent dialogue, both formal and informal, played a major role in bringing about a convergence in union and management views.

Although F&M make a clear conceptual distinction between the union's monopoly and voice roles, it is operationally very difficult to separate the two. Many changes in the SHL study are reported to come out of dialogue and exchange, but it is not clear that the use of coercive monopoly power did not contribute to observed union effects. When union-shocked management goes to workers to obtain additional efficiencies, sometimes management discovers that they can do better by engaging in dialogue, negotiation, and persuasion than by coercion and mistrust. At other times, either or both parties may use their coercive power as well as dialogue to achieve changes in workplace policies. This suggests that monopoly power and voice may not always be independent of each other. For example, a union with greater monopoly power may also enjoy a more effective voice, or alternately, a union with low levels of monopoly power may not be so influential in its voice role. This possible interaction between the two roles makes it hard to empirically separate the pure effect of monopoly power and voice on management (Hirsch, 2004). Thus, the discussion of empirical research that follows in the next section cannot (and does not attempt to) isolate the pure, or sole, application of either monopoly power or voice. Rather, it argues that union effects on management result from the application of both monopoly power and voice.

Theoretical Explanations of a Positive Union Effect

What is less clear from earlier empirical studies, including SHL, is a theoretical explanation for why unions could have a positive effect on workplace practices. If markets were perfectly competitive, firms would be able to arrive at an optimal mix of HRM and workplace policies without any union presence or pressure. Clearly, this theoretical prediction is not consonant with the evidence from SHL, F&M, and some other studies. Unions do appear to force (or persuade) management to adopt efficient practices that management would have ignored otherwise. An explanation can be offered in terms of management failure, or market imperfections, or both. Management failure results, at least partially, from ambiguities in short- versus long-term goals. Depending on how these goals are defined, management may focus on some policies and not on others. A good example would be investment in training which may receive a bigger emphasis in organizations with longer term objectives than in organizations with short-term objectives. Similarly, market imperfections such as limited information, small number of-buyers and sellers, and coordination failures can lead to the firm adopting non-optimal use of certain workplace policies. Kaufman (2001: 505–508) uses a similar approach to show why firms would adopt less than the optimal amount of worker participation and representation in the workplace. Similar arguments can be developed about a range of workplace and human resource management policies.

One of the much discussed explanations for a positive union effect can be found in Leibenstein's (1966) concept of X-inefficiency which hypothesizes that firms are prone to produce above minimum costs or inside the efficient production frontier. In this view, X-inefficiency results from firms not employing least-cost combinations of labor and capital or from not utilizing the factors of production most efficiently (Hirsch and Addison, 1986: 188). Many factors can lead producers to be X-inefficient: incentives for management, organizational structure, and supervision, among others (Leibenstein, 1978). Once the union makes its appearance, it shocks management into finding efficiencies that were hitherto not fully tapped. Of course, this explanation is not without controversy. Some observers have complained that X-inefficiency is an ambiguous concept (Stigler, 1976). It does not clearly lay out a theory of management motivation in which management would willingly exclude the most efficient methods. However, the X-inefficiency explanation has received support from both economic arguments and organizational evidence.

Altman (2001) developed a theoretical argument for the existence of a positive union effect by building on the concept of X-inefficiency. Altman's principal argument rests on the premise that a range of wages may correspond to the same level of unit cost of production. Although unions push up wages, higher wages may not increase costs (pp. 104–106). With union-induced higher wages, the marginal revenue product (i.e., wages 3 marginal product of labor) line shifts outward because both workers and employers adopt practices, sometimes by cooperating together and at other times by forcing the other party to make concessions, to increase the marginal product of labor. As long as wages rise by an amount equal to the *average* (not marginal) product of labor, there should be no negative impact of higher wages on employment. This explanation for observing a positive union effect is consistent with the concept of X-inefficiency.

Econometric evidence consistent with a positive effect of unions on outcomes such as productivity has been well documented by F&M. In addition, some organizational studies provide qualitative evidence supporting the above explanation. Such evidence suggests that it is very hard for management, a hierarchical organization, to develop the most efficient process on its own because of its inherent inability to question hierarchy or the dominant paradigm. The implication is that when unions enter the scene they are able to question management. Such questioning sets up a dialectic, otherwise absent from managerial deliberations, which leads to better, more creative, and, hence, more productive solutions. Rubinstein and Kochan (2001: 36) in their study of the Saturn car plant cite from the notes of a colleague, Bob McKersie, who sat in on many deliberations of labor-management interactions:

> [I]t is clear that the role of the UAW partners is absolutely pivotal for the functioning of Saturn. At the most recent meeting of the SAC [*joint labor-management body*], the only individuals who were willing to take issue and to "tell it like it is" were the UAW representatives. Other participants in the meeting did not speak their minds as freely and tended to back off when the CEO expressed a point of view . . . (emphasis added).

Although this example by itself is not conclusive, it is consonant with a significant theme in industrial relations literature that one of the union's principal contributions is to question management decisions. A related dynamic of labor-management interaction may be called the *learning effect*, i.e., both sides learn of new arrangements that can be used to govern the workplace and to guide efficient production. Such learning would be less likely to occur in the absence of unions and the dialectic they establish. Clearly, the learning effect, as defined herein, forms a part of the voice effect.

From the foregoing discussion it appears appropriate to conclude that unions have both positive and negative effects on workplace efficiency. In the past, the positive effect of unions on organizational productivity or efficiency has commonly been called the "shock effect." However, effects other than management being shocked may contribute to the positive impact of unions, e.g., the union's voice role. It is also simplistic to attach positive and negative labels to monopoly and voice effects, respectively. As shown above, both monopoly and voice roles of the union contribute to positive and negative effects on efficiency. Some monopolistic behavior of the union can have positive outcomes for the organization just as some voice functions can be inefficient for management. Shock effect can be thought of as the sum total of the positive effects resulting from union shock.

Union Effects over Time

Next, it is necessary to examine the underlying theory of a persistent union effect over time. Do union effects persist or is there a more complex dynamic that may influence the union impact we observe at a given point in time? Union effects may dissipate as innovations diffuse across various industries, firms, and workplaces. Assumptions made about this process will help interpret empirical findings of a union impact.

Union effects may persist in time for various reasons. If social, political, and economic institutions do not change over time they would contribute to persistent union effects. In the post-1950 period, union effects such as the union wage premium have persisted for many years. On the other hand, if markets and institutions are more fluid, union effects likely change over time. For example, there is recent evidence of a declining union wage premium (Bratsberg and Ragan, 2002; Fang and Verma, 2002).

One theoretical explanation for ebb and flow in union effects is the theory of diffusion of organizational innovations. In this view, union effects can be viewed as a series of organizational changes that allow better management. These innovations help the union employer pay a wage premium (and other benefits). But as these innovations become better known over time, they are gradually adopted by nonunion employers. For example, initially grievance procedures were found largely in union establishments. However, over time many nonunion employers have adopted similar grievance procedures. As nonunion employers make gains by adopting such innovations, the union wage premium may be less sustainable and may diminish over time. Similarly, innovations introduced by nonunion employers, e.g., work teams or quality circles, were gradually adopted by union establishments over time. Thus, union effects on management practices may vary over time depending on the stage of innovation diffusion within individual firms or industries.

Innovations diffuse because they improve management practices. But there may be other factors aiding this diffusion. For example, the threat of unionization may persuade some nonunion firms to adopt innovations from union workplaces. In such cases, it becomes difficult to discern management motives for adopting these practices. Another factor may be management desire to avoid costly litigation that may arise from not adopting certain practices that are becoming common elsewhere. A good example is the adoption of grievance procedures which may be seen by management as insurance against employees claiming to be disciplined or discharged without "cause." Thus, several factors may contribute to the diffusion of innovative workplace practices across union and nonunion firms. The issue is whether these factors can be linked to unions.

Observing the Union Effect

Lastly, we must consider how best to observe the union effect if, indeed, there is an effect. The SHL (1960) study was close enough to the first large-scale, enduring wave of unionization to be able to study management practice *before* and *after* unionization using recall interviews with key informants. This approach may not be feasible in many places today.

A direct way to observe the union effect may be to examine workplace policies and practices *before* and *after* the event. Such an event-study approach can be useful in many situations but it is not particularly well suited to unionization where the full impact becomes discernible only after a few years. Moreover, we have not witnessed any large waves of unionization in the last 25 years in North America; this approach would cover only a small number of workplaces.

Another way to measure union impact is to directly compare union and nonunion workplaces after applying appropriate controls for effects of size, industry, etc. In the United States, declining unionization has reduced research interest in such comparisons. Many studies, e.g., periodic surveys of organizational practices in human resource management by the Centre for Effective Organizations at the University of Southern California (Lawler et-al., 2001), do not report their results by union status. In European studies, this differentiation is frequently omitted because collective bargaining coverage can be high even when union density is low. Many European workers and organizations are covered by terms of collective agreements either by law (as in France) or by industry-level understandings among employers (as in Germany). A direct union-nonunion comparison in this context would underestimate the true union-nonunion difference.

III. Union Impact on Management

Research evidence on union impact can be divided into three groups. One group of studies points to the lack of flexibility in union systems. For example, union workplaces are associated with wage compression and fixed wages. Nonunion systems, on the other hand, are more likely to adopt various incentive and contingent-pay systems. The second group of studies tends to emphasize the efficiency that comes as a result of union presence, i.e., through formalization and standardization of management policy. For example, union workplaces tend to have more training and other formal systems such as safety policies. A third group finds no significant difference in HR practices, although many of these studies focus primarily on newer, innovative practices such as employee involvement and flexible work arrangements, among other such practices. As suggested earlier, a finding of no differences across the two sectors may indicate diffusion of key innovations from one sector to the other.

The rest of this section reviews empirical evidence from a number of studies that examine the union-nonunion difference descriptively or estimate the union impact analytically on a range of human resource management and related workplace practices. This review is organized by various workplace practices covered by these studies: recruitment and selection, flexible staffing, training, employee voice, teams and job flexibility, job evaluation, promotion and performance appraisal, pay systems, overall human resource strategies, and quit rates as one example of individual and organizational outcomes that is closely watched by all parties.

Recruitment and Selection

Koch and Hundley (1997) examined the impact of unions on recruitment and selection practices using data from a survey originally conducted at Columbia University of executives from 7,765 business units contained in the 1986 Compustat II Industry Segment files. The final sample included useable responses from 495 executives. This study analyzed two subsamples, one covering all industry groups, and another restricted to manufacturing.

The results indicated that in the all-industry sample, union firms were more likely to employ fewer methods of recruitment, such as newspaper, agencies, referrals, and walk-ins, than nonunion entities. The only exception was in the case of government agencies, where both union and nonunion organizations were equally likely to use this channel. In addition, with partly unionized firms, the number of recruitment methods significantly declined with the increase in the degree of unionization of the firm. Partly unionized firms were also found to use fewer recruitment methods for union jobs than for nonunion jobs. However, as explained in a later section, union firms showed a higher tendency to use formal employment tests. Although these two effects are seemingly opposite in nature, i.e., one reducing management flexibility whereas the other encouraging adoption of more rigorous testing, both effects are consistent with union need for greater formalization of management decision-making.

In other areas of HRM, Koch and Hundley (1997) found mixed support for how unions affect selection methods, such as skill, aptitude, drug, and physical tests. For example, they found only mild support for the proposition that union firms were more likely to use a larger number of selection methods. This effect was positive and statistically significant for the all-industries sample, and positive but not statistically significant for the manufacturing sample. Furthermore, these researchers found that within a single firm, there appeared to be a similarity of union and nonunion selection methods indicating the strength of the threat effect with respect to selection methods. Essentially, unions appeared to increase the likelihood of the use of only drug tests and physicals and not skills and aptitude tests, but overall, union firms have an increasing tendency to use formal employment tests.

Ng and Maki (1994) performed a comprehensive study of union-nonunion differences in various human resource management practices using survey data from a sample of 356 organizations across various industries including Food, Furniture, Fabricated Metals, and Electrical/Electronic Equipment. Using multivariate analysis to control for a variety of factors, they examined the impact of unions on a total of 37 HRM practices from hiring policies to training to promotion practices. With respect to hiring and recruitment practices, they found that the presence of a union increased the likelihood that a firm would formally post jobs internally for open competition among current employees. In addition, union firms were more likely to impose formal probationary periods on new hires. However, regarding external recruitment practices, such as employee referrals, external job advertisements, and walk-ins, as well as the amount of previous job experience required of new hires, this study reported no significant difference. In a study of the auto parts industry, Kaufman and Kaufman (1987) found that union plants were nearly twice as likely to post jobs internally as their nonunion counterparts.

The evidence shows that unions appear to insist on promotion-from-within and the related use of internal posting-and-bidding. This, in turn, causes management to limit its channels of external recruiting, and to some extent, use only physical tests in selection. These findings are consistent with the internal labor market view of organizations (Doeringer and Piore, 1985).

Flexible Staffing

Gramm and Schnell (2001) investigated the use of flexible staffing arrangements in core jobs and how these arrangements affect job security of regular core employees. The researchers used their own survey[2] to collect data from a random sample of human resource managers in Alabama establishments that in part employed flexible staff arrangements. Due to cost saving associated with using flexible staffing arrangements (FSAs), Gramm and Schnell argued that organizations pursuing low-cost production strategies would be more attracted to flexible staffing. They hypothesized that companies using FSAs to complete core tasks have a greater ability to adjust to temporary decreases in the demand for labor and therefore are less likely to layoff regular core employees. The union's role is important in this analysis. Gramm and Schnell pointed out that on the one hand, unions act as a barrier to the dismissal of workers without just cause which, in turn, increases the employer's desire employer to use FSAs to control labor costs. Theoretically, the lower costs provide job security for regular core workers by insulating them from changes in the labor market.

However, unions often oppose alternative employment arrangements and, through collective bargaining, i.e., the use of monopoly power, insist on limiting the use of FSAs. Their empirical results indicated that increases in percentage of union representation decreased the likelihood of the use of FSAs. These findings support the view that unions reduce management flexibility, even though the reduced flexibility may jeopardize job security for their members in the longer run.

In addition, Gooderham and Nordhaug (2000) reported that firms that perceived their trade unions as being powerful were less likely to implement HR strategies to increase numerical flexibility. Various indicators of numerical flexibility include the use of temporary employees, part-time employees, and subcontracting. In fact, trade union power was found to have a "consistently more powerful effect" on the indicators of numerical flexibility than the level of competition. The researchers' intent was to examine factors affecting a firm's use of staffing and HR strategies to improve their flexibility in responding to the firm's competitive environment.

In their study of the auto parts industry, Kaufman and Kaufman (1987) found several instances of work rules in union plants that prohibited some workers from doing the job of other workers. Between 25–33 percent of the plants reported prohibiting production workers from doing the job of other production workers either "usually" or "occasionally." All the nonunion plants said that they "never" prohibit workers from doing the job of another. Among the union plants, only 43.8 percent of the sample could make the same claim. Since this study was carried out many union workplaces have negotiated newer work rules. Thus these estimates of union-nonunion differences may be somewhat higher than in 2004 at the time of this writing.

Training

Osterman (1995) examined how American firms train their employees and whether the type and amount of training can be explained by a firm's organizational structure. Their purpose[3] was to determine the utilization and distribution of skill levels in a cross-section of U.S. firms and to quantify the amount of training received by their workers.

Osterman estimated the effects of organizational structure on the percentage of core employees who received formal off-the-job training. He argued that unions could be a positive influence on the amount of training received by employees by pressuring establishments to invest in their workers, or conversely act as an obstacle to increased training with an insistent stance toward the protection of traditional job rights (p. 138). The results of the model showed that the presence of a union significantly increased the likelihood of a core worker receiving off-the-job training. From this study, it is hard to infer whether the positive effect on training is the result of voice or monopoly power.

Using the British Household Panel Survey (BHPS) covering the period of 1991–1995 and with a sample of 2,982 men and 3,117 women, Arulampalam and Booth (1998) examined the intersection of work-related training and labor market flexibility using type of contract, part-time employment, and lack of union coverage as a proxy. Using a probit model, the researchers found that nonunion workers as well as workers covered by short-term contracts and part-time workers were less likely to be involved in work-related skills training. In addition, nonunion males were 7 percent less likely to receive training than union-organized males and nonunion females were 10 percent less likely to receive training than their unionized counterparts.

Similar inferences on training can be drawn from a study using data from AWIRS 1989–1990. Kennedy et-al. (1994) examined the effect of unions on the extent of formal training provided by employers. The random sample of 2,004 workplaces covered firms with a minimum of 20 employees; interview questionnaires were distributed to management and if applicable, union delegates. Kennedy et-al.'s results indicate that the union impact on formally delivered training programs is positive, but only where unions are active. In addition, active unions also appeared to have a positive net effect on the amount of external training received. The researchers attributed this finding to the possibility that active unions "forced" firms to increase the amount of external general training to improve the overall skill development of the employees, or that unions encouraged firms to use general training as a fringe benefit. Further analysis of the results indicated that the connection between tenure and firm-specific training was strengthened in the presence of an active union. Active unions appeared to reduce the association between firm size and in-house training. Kennedy et-al. attributed this finding to the belief that unions negatively affect efficiency.

In another study of training practices, Heyes and Stuart (1998) gathered data drawn from two surveys conducted between February and October 1994 and in early 1995.[4] The survey covered: (1) attitudes towards training, (2) experiences of vocational and non-vocational training, (3) awareness of efforts to promote training both nationally and at the workplace.

According to their findings, unions appeared to have a positive effect on promoting workplace training and development. In fact, Heyes and Stuart found that union employees were more likely to reap the benefits derived from training if the union plays an active role in training decisions. Where members indicated they had experienced unequal access to training opportunities, the researchers attributed this to most likely reflect management favoritism. However, when the union was involved with training issues, members were significantly more likely to indicate equity in the training opportunities. Heyes and Stuart suggest that the union played a strong role in mitigating discriminatory practices and enabled a more equitable distribution of training.

Further evidence of union impact on training comes from a study by Hundley (1989) using data from the May 1979 Current Population Survey. Hundley matched CPS data with the fourth edition of the *Dictionary of Occupational Titles* (DOT) and other industry variables drawn from the 1997 Census of Manufacturing and collected job data on industrial, occupational, and workplace characteristics. The sample covered all private, nonmanagerial employees except for those in construction or extractive industries. Analyses were conducted for manufacturing and nonmanufacturing samples.

His results indicated that for the manufacturing samples, the effect of unions on specific training was positive. This finding supports the argument that unions benefit from increasing the level of specific training of their membership. In jobs where general education was required, the employees were less likely to be unionized. Hundley argued that since the voice effect of unions appears to reduce quit rates, employers may provide union employees with specific training, as they can collect returns on that training over a longer time. Nevertheless, employers may also want to reduce the amount of specific training to decrease "job-based" bargaining power available to the union.

In a Canadian workplace survey of training practices, Betcherman et-al. (1994, 1997), found that union status of a workplace was positively associated with higher levels of job-related training. These findings are not unusual and together with other findings about the workings of unionized workplaces suggest that unions do exert a "shock"-like effect on management.

Job Evaluation

Ng and Maki (1994) examined the adoption of job evaluation techniques across union and nonunion firms and found that both types of firms were equally likely to use a classification or point-system method of job evaluation. However, nonunion firms were more likely to employ more subjective evaluation criteria, whereas union firms employed more objective ranking evaluation such as the benchmark method. Although management may find that using subjective criteria suits its purposes, unions insist on objective criteria in order to reduce favoritism and to maintain their ability to question management decisions.

Promotion and Performance Appraisals

With respect to promotion procedures, the Ng and Maki (1994) study also found that union workplaces were more likely to formalize promotion procedures than nonunion firms. This finding fits the pattern of union preferences for management to formalize all procedures in writing. The formalization of procedures is the basis for the union's ability to question management. The seniority rule is a highly formalized rule that may be inefficient for management, but it gives the union considerable power in challenging managerial decisions.

In their study of the auto parts industry, Kaufman and Kaufman (1987) found that seniority, as the sole basis for promotion, was not common among either union or nonunion plants. However, if a worker could do the job, seniority became the decisive factor in many more union plants than in nonunion plants. Ability as the deciding factor in promotions was much more prevalent in nonunion plants than in union plants. The same pattern of differences was reported in the case of layoff decisions but the union-nonunion difference was statistically not significant.

With regard to performance appraisals, Ng and Maki (1994) found that union firms are less likely to employ a formal appraisal system. This finding can be related to the way performance appraisal data are used. Regarding specific use of performance appraisal data, their empirical results indicated that whereas both union and nonunion firms were equally likely to employ the results of an appraisal in disciplinary and training decisions, union firms were again less likely to use appraisal results in salary, promotion, and layoff decisions. For unions, the efficiency effects of performance appraisal systems are not large enough to overcome the costs of loss of solidarity among its ranks. Since unions generally view management-run performance appraisals as subjective processes that serve management purposes at the expense of union goals, unions logically oppose such systems or, at the margin, limit their applicability to decision-making.

Pay, Variable Pay, and Incentives Systems

There is fairly widespread and robust evidence that the presence of a union greatly reduces the likelihood of a variable pay plan (VPP). Betcherman et-al. (1994) found that VPPs such as profit sharing, employee stock ownership plans, knowledge pay, merit pay, etc., were more often employed in nonunion firms. The overall incidence of VPPs is close to 50 percent higher in nonunion workplaces. They found that the only VPP implemented by more union firms than nonunion ones was productivity gainsharing, and that figure was only marginally higher than in nonunion plants. For other benefits, the study did not find any significant difference in family-care benefits between union and nonunion firms, except for the incidence of employee assistance programs (EAPs) which were higher in union firms. Nearly 45.7 percent of the union firms offered EAPs, whereas only 28.8 percent of nonunion firms provided them.

Further support for this finding comes from the recent Canadian Workplace and Employee Survey (WES) which since 1999 has surveyed over 6,500 workplaces and 25,000 employees each year. Union workplaces are less likely to use individual incentive plans compared to nonunion workplaces (Verma and Fang, 2002). This is not true of group incentive plans, which occurred with similar frequency in both union and nonunion establishments.

This survey showed that union firms have a much lower incidence of individual incentive plans than nonunion firms. Only 13.6 percent of union firms used incentive compensation systems such as merit pay, profit-sharing, and straight-piece-rate plans, whereas 28 percent of nonunion firms had implemented a profit-sharing plan. Kaufman and Kaufman (1987) also reported that nonunion plants were nearly nine times as likely to adopt a profit-sharing plan as union plants. From this evidence, together with union policy opposing pay systems that compensate individual workers differentially on the basis of management-assessed performance criteria, it is logical to infer that the difference in pay policies of union firms reflects the unions' desire to adopt uniform pay rather than pay schemes based on variation in individual performance. Interestingly, as pointed out in a following section, there is no significant difference between union and nonunion firms in their adoption of pay based on *group* performance that can be measured and verified directly. This criterion distinguishes profit-sharing plans from gainsharing plans. Profit sharing is much more likely in nonunion workplaces because unions generally oppose profit sharing. The union's main objection appears to be that accounting profits can be volatile over time and only loosely connected to workplace effort and productivity. Gainsharing, on the other hand, is more likely found in union workplaces, because it is generally based on verifiable group performance.

In another study, using interview and survey data collected over a five-year period from 53 large (greater than 100 employees) greenfield sites in Ireland, Gunnigle et al. (1998) examined the implications of performance-related pay (PRP) systems on the collective aspect of the labor relationship. The researchers found that the use of performance pay based on individual performance appraisals was highly negatively related to the presence of a union. Specifically, nonunion companies were significantly more likely to use PRP systems. In fact, 75 percent of the nonunion firms used performance pay systems based on individual performance appraisals. Gunnigle et-al. suggested that by allowing managerial discretion over the individual performance appraisal, nonunion firms could employ individualist as opposed to collectivist incremental pay decisions, thus challenging the collectivism of a union environment and collective bargaining.

Some studies suggest union effects even when the union status variable was not directly examined. If unions push for policies such as time-based pay systems and if such pay systems reduce organizational flexibility, we may infer that unions can affect organizational flexibility. In one such study, Long (2001) examined the relationship between a firm's pay system and its ability to achieve structural flexibility in a study of 44 large Canadian manufacturers including forest products, hard goods, high technology, petroleum, pharmaceuticals, and mining. The study examined structural flexibility that includes having (a) informed employees, who have (b) training and knowledge, who are (c) empowered to make decisions, operating under a (d) reward system that creates common goals. The types of pay systems examined included: group pay, such as profit sharing and gainsharing, time-based pay, seniority pay, and individual performance pay.

Results showed a significant and positive relationship between group pay and flexibility and a significant negative relationship between time-based pay and flexibility. In addition, multiple regression results indicated that pay-system-related variables explained a "substantial amount" (approximately 20 percent) of the variance in structural flexibility. Long concluded that the empirical results supported the idea that a firm's pay system may affect its structural flexibility. We know that union firms are more likely to adopt time-based pay. The findings of this study suggested that union firms should have less organizational flexibility.

Although unions generally discourage firms from adopting individual pay incentives, they appear to be less averse to group incentives based on directly measurable and verifiable criteria. In the Ng and Maki (1994) study, both union and nonunion firms were equally likely to adopt group-level incentive pay systems and gainsharing plans. This suggests that even though unions have a different preference pattern in many areas of human resource policies, there are some areas where their preferences coincide with management's. This convergence between HR policies of union and nonunion firms conforms to the notion of innovations diffusing from one sector to another.

Although gainsharing is relatively more popular with unions, some studies have found a mixed picture in terms of the impact of unionization (Kim, 1996). Kim explored the relationship between gainsharing programs and employee involvement and found that unions reduce the effectiveness of gainsharing plans even as they marginally improve their survival. The study[5] focused on the overall effectiveness of compensation schemes that included gainsharing and the factors that increased the likelihood of a successful gainsharing program. Included in the analysis were: a measure of unionization, i.e., union presence in the organization, and union support, i.e., whether the union supported or opposed gainsharing.

With regard to the union variables, empirical results indicated that gainsharing programs in union settings were significantly less successful in influencing organization performance in terms of improved quality, improved labor productivity, cost reduction, and improved production process relative to nonunion establishments. There was no significant difference in bonus payouts. However, results from a reduced sample of only unionized companies indicated that when there was support for gainsharing, the program was significantly more likely to yield positive results of quality, cost reduction, improved production process, and bonus payments.

In another study, Kim (1999) examined the survival of gainsharing programs at 211 different organizations in the United States and Canada using data from a 1992 survey (Kim, 1996). As mentioned earlier, unionization slightly increased the likelihood of a gainsharing program's survival, all else being equal. Organizations using outside consultants to develop and maintain their gainsharing programs were more likely to have their programs fail and disappear. Employee approval, new employee training, customization, financial performance, and capital investments signified successful gainsharing programs. While organizations in the manufacturing industry had significantly less success with their gainsharing programs, unionization did not significantly affect the success of these programs.

Organizational Climate and Workplace Culture

Unions affect organizational climate and workplace culture in various ways. Since this topic is vast in scope, only selected aspects are addressed here. One set of studies point to a more formalized and structured communication between management and employees and a related loss of informality in union workplaces. On the other hand, managements in nonunion environments can build a climate of effective communication and strong identification with organizational goals. In one qualitative study, Cohen-Rosenthal and Burton (1993) found that unions were a barrier to effective communications with management. By opposing the HR manager frequently, the union can often cloud management's intended message. As an intervener, a union can impede and increase the costs of direct communications between management and employees. Many nonunion employers can achieve greater clarity in employee communications because they can communicate with them directly.

Citing an earlier study which employed both surveys and interviews to a sample of 248 workers from three large nonunion and four large unionized U.S.-owned plants in Ireland, Flood and Toner (1997) examined whether any advantage can be derived from nonunion firms following best human resources strategies or by practicing union avoidance strategies. They concluded that a union may decrease a firm's ability to design and adopt human resource policies that can assist in increasing employee motivation and cooperation and in building a strong corporate culture. In addition, the researchers found no evidence that nonunion status increases the firm's overall flexibility; however, the nature of the industry needs to be considered as more traditional industries may have a history of inflexibility.

Taras (2000) examined the level of employee representation in the joint industrial council (JIC) that operates as an enterprise-level employee organization at Imperial Oil's upstream division. Through observing meetings, reviewing corporate minutes, and in-depth interviews from 1995 to 1999,[6] Taras found that Imperial Oil and their JIC employed numerous collaborative and competitive HR techniques that demonstrate the "union threat effect." For example, the primary responsibilities and scope of JICs at various levels cover three areas of workplace policies: "competitive" wages, benefits, and working conditions; strengthening corporate culture through employee affiliation; and providing employee voice through committees and sub-committees. One of the reasons that management continued to work with the JIC, even though they were not legally required to do so, is for the positive contribution of the JIC to the culture and climate of the workplace.

Other ways in which Imperial Oil contributed to the relationship was by allowing hourly employees access to typically confidential information such as competitors' compensation structures and other HR-related information. Although the JIC may have little power to influence wages and benefits structures, the various JIC representatives meet collectively and share information, increasing the employees' sense of corporate affiliation. This sets the tone for a positive climate.

Regarding the creation of an integrative corporate culture, the JIC enabled a work site to vote on any workplace issues, except those involving corporate policy. Other recent union-competitive issues in which the JIC has been involved were downsizing and job elimination. In fact, Imperial Oil states that the JIC operates like a union in providing employee voice as it also oversees discipline and grievance procedures; JIC representatives get involved at the initial stages and remain involved until the final grievance steps.

The Australian Workplace and Industrial Relations Survey (AWIRS) conducted by the Department of Industrial Relations in Australia in 1990 and 1995 is also helpful in understanding the union-nonunion difference in organizational climate (Callus, 1991; Morehead, 1997). Among other findings, the AWIRS indicated that more workplaces had adopted a "modern workplace relations style," implying a decrease in the active role of unions coupled with an increase in a more structured approach by management. Thus, unions tend to decrease management's ability to structure workplace practices, and thus, as the role of unions has been diminishing over time, managements may be more active in structuring workplace climate and culture to their perceived operating needs.

Of the managers surveyed in AWIRS, who indicated they wanted to make changes in pay systems (51 percent), 17 percent stated that union resistance acted as a barrier to implementing those changes. Although the degree of unionization declined over the five-year time frame, AWIRS results indicated that union delegates became more actively involved in negotiating key employment issues such as wage increases, perhaps indicating a more communicative relationship between union delegates and management. A rise in the incidence of grievance procedures and joint consultative committees during this same time period supports this statement. The AWIRS study also found that higher than average numbers of union employees believed that the workplace changes over the last 12 months had negatively affected them and, thus, had made them "worse off." In examining employees' attitudes towards trust and satisfaction, unionized employees were also less likely than nonunion employees to indicate satisfaction with and trust of management. Therefore, although different factors may affect both managers' and employees' level of satisfaction and trust, unions appear to negatively affect the type of management relationship and attitudes in the workplace.[7]

In the area of workplace safety and health, another important contributor to organizational climate, Weil (1991, 1992) found that union workplaces were much more likely to have labor inspections than nonunion workplaces even when the safety and health legislation applied equally to both union and nonunion workplaces. The differential inspection rates are rooted in a climate of safety created by union presence. Clearly, unions play a role in the labor inspection process, which in turn impacts management. In a similar vein, Beaumont and Harris' (1996) study using UK 1990 WIRS data suggested that management motivation for the introduction of HRM practices often arises from dissatisfaction with and a desire to improve the existing labor-management relationship.

Taken together, these findings indicate that unions generally reduce the scope of management prerogatives and discretion. A union makes management's efforts to foster a strong identification with corporate goals and vision among employees more difficult. The evidence confirming this inference is the many nonunion workplaces where managers are willing to offer workers greater voice, better wages, and more generous benefits. Without a union, many managers also develop policies to foster a strong corporate culture to persuade workers that their interests are the same as the organization's.

Employee Voice and Communications

There is a considerable body of indirect evidence that suggests that unions provide a significant amount of voice. As noted earlier, some of the best, though indirect, evidence of union impact on management comes from an examination of management policies in the nonunion sector. In this section, I review a number of studies that report on voice mechanisms in the absence of a union. Although the union threat can be a major factor in adopting employee voice and communications by nonunion firms, this is not the only reason for adopting these practices. Other reasons include a desire to improve efficiency, improve employee satisfaction, and a desire to avoid costly lawsuits that may result from inappropriate employee discipline and discharge in the absence of employee voice.

In a sample of 18 cases from the United Kingdom, Gollan (2000) found that only 11 percent of the workplaces have a representative committee. These nonunion employee representation plans (NERs) discuss potentially threat-effect-induced issues, such as pay, basic work conditions, hours, staffing levels, new technology adoption, and the development of new products and services. However, Gollan's evidence indicated that few committees have negotiation and bargaining rights; thus they are not as effective at affecting policy change. In addition, managers, not NERs, are primarily responsible for resolving grievances and conflict resolution. Thus, NERs have a limited ability to influence wages, policies, and strategic issues, and how and when workplace changes are introduced. Aside from these limitations, NERs in the UK and Australia are good communication mechanisms but are less effective at influencing other substantive HR policies.

The evidence from a Japanese survey[8] also provided similar evidence on possible indirect effect of unions on HR practices in the nonunion sector (Morishima and Tsuru, 2000). A wide range of nonunion representation plans exist in Japan, e.g., some nonunion firms work with employee representatives, whereas other nonunion organizations are more similar to trade unions. In addition, employee associations are also called "friendship societies" or staff councils, perhaps in an attempt to facilitate collaboration or affiliation between the employer and employees. These bodies regularly discuss wages, benefits, health and safety, and other issues over which unions bargain. Thus, effectively, many rights of representation are extended to these nonunion workers in response to the threat of unionization.

Morishima and Tsuru (2000) compared the differences between individual and collective voice mechanisms between union and nonunion firms. In this sample of Japanese firms, significant differences exist between the provision of collective and individual voice between union and nonunion workplaces. Not only have nonunion Japanese firms attempted to match direct union workplace benefits such as compensation structures, but they have also provided indirect benefits, such as a wide range of voice mechanisms, beyond those of union firms. On several indicators of collective voice such as communicating the company's strategy, discussions with management at both senior and middle levels, employee associations, and conducting opinion surveys, nonunion firms lead union firms. Of course, when it comes to formal voice mechanisms, such as joint consultation systems and grievance procedures, many more such programs are found in union workplaces. Union workplaces were also marginally more likely to include (53.8 percent vs. 47 percent) forms of written reports at the individual level. This difference is not that great and is likely a product of greater formalization of practices in the unionized sector.

Several studies have found that unions positively affect employee voice mechanisms. In an Australian study, Benson (2000) found that union workplaces were more likely than nonunion firms to implement employee voice mechanisms. Specifically, union firms were more likely to use collective negotiation, employee surveys and meetings, grievance and equal employment procedures, consultative and safety committees, task forces, and health and safety representatives. Other voice mechanisms typically associated with HRM strategies, such as individual employee negotiations, involvement, and consultation, were evenly distributed across the nonunion and inactive and active union workplaces. Yet, nonunion workplaces were still less likely than union workplaces to use many of the HRM-associated voice mechanisms, specifically, quality circles, employee surveys, supervisor-employee meetings, senior management-employee meetings, and semi/fully autonomous work groups. In addition, quality circles, employee surveys, and supervisor-employee meetings occurred at a significantly higher rate in active union workplaces compared to nonunion firms.

Benson concluded that unions significantly increased the number of voice mechanisms available to union employees compared to nonunion employees. In addition, the more active the union, the greater the number of alternative voice mechanisms. More such evidence can be gleaned from a study by Goll (1991) who found that in union settings progressive decision-making positively influenced the number of participative programs and the number of employees in these programs. These relationships did not exist in the nonunion settings.

Using the 1990 Workplace Industrial Relations Survey (WIRS), Fernie and Metcalf (1995) examined the effects of three forms of employee participation: (1)-employee involvement, (2) contingent pay, and (3) forms of representation on workplace outcomes such as productivity levels and employment changes, specifically the labor relations climate, quit rates, and absenteeism rates. Their analysis indicated that compared to a nonunion firm, the union firm experienced lower employment growth and worse labor relations climate. However, a union was also associated with lower quit rates, which Fernie and Metcalf attributed to the union's provision of a collective voice. Their study also found that a union had no significant effect on the absenteeism rate. Furthermore, joint consultative committees had only a weak or no relationship on these workplace outcomes.

There is a wealth of case studies of individual firms that document voice systems being adopted partially in response to the union threat. Delta Airlines, a major U.S. nonunion carrier, has provided employee voice mechanisms since the company's establishment in 1924 (Kaufman, 2003). These actions include providing a competitive work environment; employee stock options; a profit-sharing plan; building strong corporate culture; competitive wages and benefits; and the Delta Personnel Board Council, a management-employee forum used as a communications channel between the board of directors and employees (Cone, 2000; Kaufman, 2003). Some of Delta Air Lines' leading competitors, such as United Air Lines, are highly unionized, and the union threat perhaps keeps Delta from discontinuing employee voice forums. But, given the long-standing policy of providing employee voice, Delta is likely motivated by other factors as well.

At Imperial Oil's Cold Lake facility, employees are given voice through a formal employee forum (Boone, 2000). However, the company maintains direct control over employee-related financial factors, such as pension plan design and compensation philosophy. This Imperial Oil facility combats the threat effect by giving employees the opportunity to participate in decision-making, but does not allow for employee input in more financially strategic aspects of the business operations.

Dofasco, an integrated Canadian steel producer, maintains several voice programs for its employees in a highly unionized industry. Harshaw (2000) reported that Dofasco has adopted employee-involvement policies that match or exceed workplace practices within the union sector. For example, profit-sharing and employee-savings plans were established early in Dofasco's history. Voice is provided on these topics through a formal representation forum where employees can provide feedback and input on activities that affect them. Dofasco employs numerous formal and informal employee representation activities, such as employee focus groups to solicit feedback on employment policies and practices, and the availability of their company policy manual regarding the terms and conditions of employment.

Other forms of employee representation include: the company's open-door policy with access to the company president, if necessary, and an emphasis on teamwork as the company has adopted multi-skilled teams that are compensated based on competency pay. The company also attempts to incorporate employee involvement in most corporate activities, such as recreation, training, equipment selection, job design, customer interaction, and quality improvements.

IV. A Scorecard for Unions

The empirical findings discussed above are mixed in two ways. First, the evidence suggests that union effects on management objectives can be positive, negative, or neutral, depending on the type and scope of management policy (findings are summarized in Table 9.1.). Second, it is hard to disentangle the separate contributions of voice and monopoly power because the two often are mutually reinforcing. The overview of empirical research presented above can be used to develop a scorecard for unions. In the following section, I discuss areas in which unions reduce flexibility for management, areas where unions help improve management practices, areas where unions make little or no significant difference, and finally, areas where unions have indirectly affected managerial practices.

Unions Reduce Management Flexibility

Unions may reduce management flexibility in several ways. For example, union representation decreases the likelihood that management uses flexible staffing arrangements (Gramm and Schnell, 2001). Unions may also contribute to reduced organizational flexibility by opposing policies that could create flexibility for management (Long, 2001).

More specifically, one may cite union effect on personnel practices such as recruitment and promotions as examples of limiting the full range of management prerogatives. Union firms are more likely to employ fewer *methods of recruitment*, such as newspaper, agencies, referrals, and walk-ins, than nonunion firms (Koch and Hundley, 1997) and are more likely to formalize promotion procedures than nonunion firms (Ng and Maki, 1994). In the compensation area, there is fairly robust evidence that a union greatly reduces the likelihood of a variable pay plan. Studies by Betcherman et-al. (1994) and Gunnigle et-al. (1998) supported this finding. Since variable pay is important to many managers, unions can reduce management prerogatives regarding compensation and rewards. Unions can limit management prerogatives in other ways as well, e.g., by preventing management from implementing HR policies that could foster a strong corporate culture to facilitate employee motivation and commitment (Flood and Toner, 1997). Moreover, in many situations, unions may also act as a barrier to communication between management and workers (Cohen-Rosenthal and Burton, 1993). These empirical findings support the view that unions reduce management flexibility, even though the reduced flexibility may jeopardize job security for their members in the longer run.

Unions Help Improve Management Practices

Union workplaces appear to enjoy an advantage in a number of areas of workplace policy. For example, there is fairly robust evidence from several countries and over many years that firms are more likely to offer more training to union workers (Arulampalam and Booth, 1998; Heyes and Stuart, 1998; Betcherman et al., 1997; Osterman, 1995; Kennedy et al., 1994; Hundley, 1989).

Some recent evidence also corroborates the finding of greater formalization in recruitment and selection. Union workplaces are more likely to use a formal procedure to post jobs (Ng and Maki, 1994) and to use more objective, rather than subjective, tests in selection (Koch and Hundley, 1997). Presumably, these practices obtain efficiencies that nonunion organizations forgo given their pursuit of other objectives, including their desire to remain nonunion. Lastly, unions appear to increase the quality and quantity of voice forums. Many studies document the positive association between union status and worker voice (Benson, 2000; Goll, 1991), whereas others show that increases in voice reduce the quit rate (Rees, 1991; Fernie and Metcalf, 1995).

The overall picture that emerges from these studies is that union workplaces are more formal in their adoption of certain HR practices that are known to create efficiencies for management. These practices include, but are not limited to, training, selection and recruitment, employee voice, and group-incentive plans, such as gainsharing. Thus, empirical evidence supports a positive score for unions in these areas of managerial practice.

Table 9.1

Unions and Human Resource Management Practices

HR Category	Author(s)	Union Effect on HRM	Summary of Findings
Compensation, Benefits, & Incentives	Betcherman, McMullen, Leckie, and Caron (1994)	1. Decreases likelihood of variable pay plan. 2. Marginally higher use of gainsharing. 3. Increase in use of EAPs.	Studies indicate a decrease in the likelihood of using individual incentive plans.
	Verma and Fang (2002)	Decrease in the use of individual incentive plans only—(not group plans).	Mixed findings regarding the effect of unions on gainsharing plans.
	Gunnigle, Turner, and D'Art (1998)	Decrease in the use of individual performance pay plans.	
	Ng and Maki (1994)	No significant difference in the use of group incentive plans and gainsharing.	
	Kim (1996)	Reduce the effectiveness of gainsharing plans.	
	Kim (1999)	No significant difference in the success of the gainsharing program.	
	Cohen-Rosenthal and Burton (1993)	Unions appear to reduce the probability of using incentives and use of technology.	
Promotion & Performance Appraisals	Ng and Maki (1994)	1. Decrease the use of a formal appraisal system. 2. Less likely to use appraisal results in salary, promotion, and layoff decisions.	Decrease in the use of formal appraisal systems.
Staffing & Hiring	Gramm and Schnell (2001)	Decreases the use of flexible staffing arrangements.	Decrease in the likelihood of using flexible staffing arrangements.
	Gooderham and Nordhaug (2000)	Union firms less likely to use temporary employees, part-time employees, and subcontracting.	

Table 9.1 (cont.)

HR Category	Author(s)	Union Effect on HRM	Summary of Findings
Recruitment & Selection	Koch and Hundley (1997)	1. Union firms were more likely to employ fewer methods of recruitment. 2. Mixed support for the effect of unions on selection methods, such as skill, aptitude, drug, and physical tests. 3. There appeared to be a similarity of union and nonunion selection methods. 4. Increase the likelihood of the use of only drug tests and physicals and not skills and aptitude tests. 5. Overall, union firms have an increasing tendency to use formal employment tests.	Union firms were more likely to employ fewer but more formal methods of recruitment.
	Ng and Maki (1994)	Increased the likelihood that a firm would formally post jobs internally for open competition among current employees. More likely to impose formal probationary periods on new hires.	
Organizational Climate, Culture, & Related HR Policies	Cohen-Rosenthal and Burton (1993)	Unions were found to be a barrier to effective communications with management.	Unions appear to decrease a firm's ability to: • communicate directly with employees. • create strong identification with the firm and adopt flexible HR policies.
	Flood and Toner (1997)	Decrease a firm's ability to design HR policies that assist in increasing employee motivation, cooperation, and building a strong corporate culture.	

Table 9.1 (cont.)

	Beaumont and Harris (1996)	Management motivation for the introduction of HRM practices often arises from dissatisfaction with and a desire to improve the existing labor-management relationship.
	Taras (2000)	Nonunion Imperial Oil uses numerous collaborative and competitive HR techniques that demonstrate the "union threat effect" such as providing competitive wages, benefits and working conditions, strengthening corporate culture, and providing employee voice.
	Weil (1991, 1992)	More likely to have labor inspections than nonunion workplaces.
	Ichniowski, Delaney, and Lewin (1989)	No significant difference between the progressiveness of HR policies across union and nonunion firms.
Training & Development	Osterman (1995)	Significantly increased the likelihood of a core worker receiving off the job training.
	Arulampalam and Booth (1998)	More likely that union workers involved in work-related skills training.
		Nonunion males were 7 percent less likely to receive training than unionized males and nonunion females were 10 percent less likely to receive training than their union counterparts.
	Kennedy, Drago, Sloan, and Wooden (1994)	Union impact on formally delivered training programs is positive, but only where unions are active in the workplace.
		Unions appear to increase the likelihood of workers receiving workplace training and development.

Table 9.1 (cont.)

HR Category	Author(s)	Union Effect on HRM	Summary of Findings
Training & Development (*Continued*)		Active unions also appeared to have a positive net effect on the amount of external training received.	
	Heyes and Stuart (1998)	The connection between tenure and firm-specific training was strengthened in the presence of an active union.	
		Unions appeared to have a positive effect on promoting workplace training and development.	
		Union employees were more likely to reap the benefits derived from training if the union plays an active role in training decisions.	
	Hundley (1989)	For the manufacturing samples, the effect of unions on specific training was positive.	
	Betcherman, McMullen, Leckie, and Caron (1994)	Positively associated with higher levels of job-related training.	
	Ng and Maki (1994)	Although a union impacts the likelihood of a training program, the impact varied depending on the type of program deployed.	
		Union firms were less likely to use orientation and external, or off-site training programs.	

Table 9.1 (cont.)

Employee Voice	Gollan (2000)	Few Nonunion Employee Representation (NERs) in the United Kingdom have negotiation and bargaining rights; thus they are not as effective at affecting policy change. Aside from some limitations, NERs appear to represent good communication mechanisms but are less effective at influencing other substantive HR policies.	Unions increase the likelihood of offering various methods of employee voice mechanisms. In response to the threat of union-ization, nonunion workplaces also attempt to offer similar programs.
	Morishima and Tsuru (2000)	Nonunion Japanese firms attempted to match direct union workplace benefits such as compensation structures, etc., and have also succeeded in providing indirect benefits such as a wide range of voice mechanisms beyond that of union firms.	
	Benson (2000)	More likely than nonunion firms to implement employee voice mechanisms.	
		Significant increase in the number of voice mechanisms available to unionized employees.	
	Cone (2000) Kaufman (2003)	Delta has used various techniques to oppose the threat effect including a competitive work environment, employee stock options, a profit-sharing plan, building strong corporate culture, and competitive wages and benefits.	
	Goll (1991)	Positive influence the number of participative programs and the number of employees in these programs.	

Table 9.1 (cont.)

HR Category	Author(s)	Union Effect on HRM	Summary of Findings
Employee Voice (*Continued*)	Fernie and Metcalf (1991)	Due to the union's provision of a collective voice, unionized firms experienced lower employment growth and worse labor relations climate but also lower quit rates.	
		No significant effect on the rate of absenteeism.	
	Boone (2000)	This Imperial Oil facility combats the threat effect by giving employees the opportunity to participate in decision-making, but does not allow for employee input in more financially strategic aspects of the business operations.	
	Harshaw (2000)	Dofasco has integrated numerous methods to apparently match workplace practices within the union sector.	
		It also provides numerous employee voice mechanisms such as OH&S committees, employee focus groups, the company's open door policy with access to the company president	

Table 9.1 (cont.)

Organizational Flexibility and Innovation	Long (2001)	Decrease in organizational flexibility.	Unions may decrease flexibility but they generally increase the probability of adopting workplace practices that contribute to productivity.
	Osterman (1995)	Unions do not affect the likelihood of a firm adopting innovative work practices.	
	Cohen-Rosenthal and Burton (1993)	Union workplaces appear more likely to use teams, provide training, use flexible workplace practices, and formal grievance procedures.	Unions do not appear to reduce (or enhance) the ability to adopt innovations in products or processes.
	Verma and Fang (2002)	Union workplaces more likely to adopt teams, training and grievance procedures.	
	Morehead (1997)	Decrease management's ability to structure workplace practices and over time, management has been able to take a more active role in structuring workplace policies and practices.	

No Significant Difference

In an earlier section, it has been argued that union impact on management policy may not endure over time. If an "innovation" in the union sector begins to diffuse through the industry either because it is an efficient practice or due to union threat, empirical observation may show no differences between the union and nonunion sectors, and we may infer that union effects have dissipated over time.

Several studies find little or no impact of unions on some management policies. For example, Osterman (1994) found that unions do not affect the likelihood of a firm adopting innovative work practices; therefore, neither union nor nonunion firms appear more likely to adopt practices such as teams, job rotation, and TQM, etc. Ichniowski et-al. (1989) found no significant difference between the progressiveness of HR policies across union and nonunion firms. However, union firms were less likely to adopt formal performance appraisals and flexible job design programs. Finally, Cohen-Rosenthal and Burton (1993) examined the diffusion of advanced work practices (teams, rotation, TQM, and QC) and found no significant union effect. In all these cases, union effects that may have existed at one time, had dissipated at the time of these studies. These developments are consistent with a finding of decreasing union wage premium over time in the United States (Bratsberg and Ragan, 2002) and in Canada (Fang and Verma, 2002).

When a previously known union-nonunion difference disappears over time, it could be attributed to the diffusion of workplace practices either due to the innovative nature of the practice or due to union threat. However, in the absence of historical information about a union-nonunion difference, a finding of "no difference" may simply reflect the fact there are no differences between the two sectors. Overall, this is a neutral score for unions, as they appear to have neither a positive nor a negative effect on management.

Indirect Effects of Unions on Managerial Practices

A significant impact of unions on managerial practice can be observed in managerial choice of certain workplace policies in nonunion workplaces that provide employees with union-like benefits, due process, and voice. Research evidence shows that some employers respond to the union "threat" by offering employees many services provided by union workplaces. Extensive voice forums in nonunion firms such as Imperial Oil (Taras, 2000; Boone, 2000; Chiesa and Rhyason, 2000), Dofasco (Harshaw, 2000), and Delta Airlines (Cone, 2000; Kaufman, 2003), to name just three such firms, point to this indirect effect of unions. Thus, these indirect union effects are not as strong as the direct effects discussed earlier, but our observation of the union impact on management would be incomplete if we were to ignore these milder, yet significant, effects.

This indirect effect of unions on managerial behavior can be observed only in the longer run. Cross-sectional snapshots of union-nonunion differences do not adequately capture management's strategic choices (Kochan et-al., 1986). If there are union-nonunion differences in managerial practice in the near term, management will likely incorporate such impacts into their long-term decision-making about where to invest in the future. Some studies have documented the tendency of management to invest away from union operations and into green-field sites that can be run as nonunion shops (Verma, 1985). Since some these workplace practices are adopted in direct response to the unionization threat, it is logical to view such adoption as a managerial response to unionism.

V. Conclusions: Unions and Managerial Practice

A scorecard for union impact on management policy can be drawn up in various ways. I first examined union effects by substantive areas of workplace and HRM policy. Next, the same results were summarized according to their impact on management: positive, negative, neutral, or indirect. Almost 45 years after Slichter et-al. (1960) published their findings of a positive union effect (including the shock effect) on management, many recent studies continue to find empirical support for contemporary versions of a positive union effect. Confronted by union's independent voice, management tends to develop formal systems and procedures that contribute to efficiency and organizational effectiveness. Some of these responses are unilateral management initiatives (shock effect) while others involve dialogue with unions (voice effect). Subject to more refinements in research methodology used by these studies, these findings interpreted collectively suggest a positive score for unions.

There is evidence that some aspects of union effects erode over time. The principal evidence comes from studies that find no difference between management in union and nonunion operations. The erosion is possibly from both ends: Union firms find it increasingly difficult to provide a union premium in a more competitive market, while nonunion firms continue to catch up to (and in many cases lead) practices in the union firm. From a management perspective, this is a neutral score for unions because unions are inconsequential to workplace outcomes in these areas. From a worker perspective, this is a negative for unions as it reduces a union's appeal to workers. Unions find it increasingly more difficult to recruit members based on the instrumental belief that joining a union will lead to gains in terms and conditions of employment. Some writers have argued that such instrumental beliefs are no longer sufficient to attract new members and hence unions need to turn to other types of appeals (Kochan et al., 2004; Verma et al., 2002).

The evidence also suggests that unions do limit flexibility, at least from the management perspective. Part of this effect can be attributed to unions' need to curb management prerogatives. But, in many other instances the inflexibility originates in union unwillingness (or foot-dragging) to accommodate changes to established practice. Rapidly changing markets or technologies require faster adaptation. Although ideology frequently prevents unions from agreeing to introduce flexible work practices, it is the difficult task of selling such concessions politically within the union that accounts for many instances of observed workplace inflexibility. This is a negative score for unions independent of the underlying reasons. When firms are in financial difficulty, this inability to adapt to the external environment hurts the image of unions in the eyes of not only employers but also employees, the government, and the public opinion.

To the credit of unions, many unions have agreed to introduce changes. Several studies of change and adaptation in the union sector document mutual gains and adoption (Kochan and Osterman, 1994; Applebaum and Batt, 1994; Cohen-Rosenthal and Burton, 1993). This would give unions a positive score except that the small victories are frequently considered by many to be swamped by the large negative score on the pace and magnitude of adaptation to the market and new technologies.

Unions are strongly associated with giving workers a voice in the workplace. This is true in the union sector where practices such as formal grievance procedures are almost ubiquitous. Unions are associated with various voice forms including joint committees and representation at the board of directors or other senior-level forums for policy consideration and deliberation. This counts as a positive score for unions.

Unions can also claim partial credit for improving voice in the nonunion sector. While other factors such as the high cost of litigation (e.g., in the case of unjust dismissals) and proactive adoption of "best practice" may be forcing some nonunion firms to adopt voice systems such as grievance procedures, there is ample case-study evidence that the threat of unionization has also played a role in the diffusion of employee voice systems in nonunion firms (Kaufman and Taras, 2000). This can be interpreted as a mildly positive score for unions.

It appears reasonable to conclude that based on the evidence since the publication of F&M, unions continue to make a significant impact on management and on the workplace. Of the three factors cited by F&M and mentioned in my introduction to this study, I did not address the effect of seniority but found considerable evidence to support the shock- and voice-effect explanations. This conclusion must be tempered with several caveats. First, few of these studies consider whether unions create inefficiencies by distorting prices that result in a misallocation of resources. For example, although unions appear to increase training, the issue to be addressed is whether too many resources are being devoted to training. Second, there is evidence that some union effects are eroding over time. Standard economic theory predicts that in the long run unions would have no real impact in a perfectly competitive market. If globalization of the marketplace keeps making markets more competitive in the coming decades, we would need to revisit many of these studies to see if union impact endures or dissipates over time. Third, the direct effect of unions is often confounded with other effects such as the threat effect or the effect of other environmental factors. To answer the question of union effects on management more precisely, more carefully designed studies are needed that control for the effect of other factors. Until better data and results are available, static differences in workplace practices between union and nonunion sectors will remain indicative if not always definitive of the impact of unions.

Notes

*   Comments on an earlier manuscript by Bruce Kaufman are appreciated. Excellent research assistance by Katherine Lee is gratefully acknowledged.

1.   The term "shock effect" is not formally defined in the SHL (1960) book, but positive effects of unionization on management practice are reported throughout the study. Neither is the term formally defined in Slichter's (1941) original study of union impact on management. As Kaufman points out in his historical chapter in this volume, Slichter (1931: 641–42) mentions union "shock to managerial complacency" suggesting that management of its own is never as efficient as possible. Chamberlain (1958: 287) writes that the term "shock effect" was popular among economists at the time of his writing in the late 1950s. By the early 1980s, most researchers were using the term to describe key findings of the SHL study. Among others, Kochan (1980: 332) is a good example of such association of the term with the SHL study.

2.   These firms were identified using the *Alabama Industrial Directory 1993–1994*. The survey was completed between 1994 and 1996; of the initial 394 managers contacted 112 returned completed surveys.

3.   Osterman analyzed data collected from an original telephone survey completed in 1992, containing 875 records of American establishments. The criteria for inclusion required that the establishment be from a nonagricultural industry and have 50 or more employees. The questions pertained to the type and amount of skill required by the work be done, the type and amount of training provided to workers, hiring practices, and the establishment's organization structure including the presence of unions.

4.   The surveys were distributed to a random sample of the Manufacturing Science and Finance union members covering 27 organizations across seven sectors; they received 1,120 responses (or a response rate of 40 percent) and 792 responses (or 55 percent response rate), respectively.

5.   Data were collected in a survey of U.S. and Canadian firms. Kim contacted gainsharing consultants and researchers, labor unions, and labor education institutions and examined U.S. Department of labor publications to determine what establishments used gainsharing. This search yielded a sample of 622 establishments (269 were usable). Questionnaires were mailed out to the human resource or industrial relations manager at each establishment. The managers where asked to rate the effectiveness of their gainsharing program in terms of improved quality, improved labor productivity, cost reduction, improved production process, and bonus payouts.

6.   Information was collected from seven operating areas—six in Alberta and one in the Northwest Territories in 1995 with ongoing follow-ups until 1999. Over 85 managers and workers across all seven areas and involved in the JIC were interviewed. Taras divided the findings into three categories: (1) the nature of the relationship between employees and managers, (2) advantages and disadvantages associated with JICs, and (3) the adaptability of nonunion plans regarding threats to JIC longevity.

7. For example, only 39 percent of union employees indicated they were "satisfied" with the way management treated them and other employees, while 52 percent of nonunion employees indicated satisfaction. AWIRS findings with respect to job satisfaction reflect those of general satisfaction and trust in management, as nonunion employees (68 percent) were more likely to indicate higher levels of job satisfaction than unionized employees (58 percent). These findings corroborate the robust finding in the literature that unionized workers are generally less satisfied with their jobs and employment compared to similar nonunion workers.
8. Data were gathered from responses to written questionnaires by head managers of personnel departments in 1,250 private firms in the Tokyo area with at least 50 employees. The response rate was 41.3 percent.

References

Altman, Morris. *Worker Satisfaction and Economic Performance: Microfoundations of Success and Failure.* Armonk, NY: M.E. Sharpe, 2001.

Appelbaum, Eileen and Rosemary Batt. *The New American Workplace: Transforming Work Systems in the United States.* Ithaca, NY: ILR Press, 1994.

Arulampalam, Wiji and Alison L. Booth. "Training and Labor Market Flexibility: Is There a Trade-Off?" *British Journal of Industrial Relations* 36 (December 1998): 521–36.

Batt, Rosemary, Alexander J. S. Colvin, and Jeffrey Keefe. "Employee Voice, Human Resource Practices, and Quit Rates: Evidence from the Telecommunications Industry." *Industrial and Labor Relations Review* 55 (July 2002): 573–94.

Beaumont, Phillip B. and Richard I.D. Harris. "Good Industrial Relations, Joint Problem Solving, and HRM." *Relations Industrielles/Industrial Relations* 51 (Spring 1996): 391–402.

Benson, John. "Employee Voice in Union and Nonunion Australian Workplaces." *British Journal of Industrial Relations* 38 (September 2000): 453–59.

Betcherman, Gordon, Kathryn McMullen, Norm Leckie, and Christina Caron. *The Canadian Workplace in Transition.* Kingston, Ont.: IRC Press, 1994.

Betcherman, Gordon, Norm Leckie, and Kathryn McMullen. *Developing Skills in the Canadian Workplace: The Results of the Ekos Workplace Training Survey.* Ottawa, Ont.: Canadian Policy Research Networks, 1997.

Boone, David J. "Operation of the Production District Joint Industrial Council, Imperial Oil." In Bruce Kaufman and Daphne Taras, eds. *Nonunion Employee Representation: History, Contemporary Practice, and Policy.* Armonk, NY: M.E. Sharpe, 2000, pp. 457–62.

Bratsberg, Bernt and James F. Ragan, Jr. "Changes in the Union Wage Premium by Industry." *Industrial and Labor Relations Review* 56 (October 2002): 65–83.

Callus, Ron. *Industrial Relations at Work: The Australian Workplace Industrial Relations Survey.* Canberra, Australia: Australian Government Publishing Service, 1991.

Chiesa, Rod and Ken Rhyason. "Production District Joint Industrial Council at Imperial Oil Ltd.: The Perspective from the Employee's Side." In Bruce Kaufman and Daphne Taras, eds. *Nonunion Employee Representation: History, Contemporary Practice, and Policy.* Armonk, NY: M.E. Sharpe, 2000, pp.-474–76.

Cohen-Rosenthal, Edward and Cynthia Burton. *Mutual Gains: A Guide to Union-Management Cooperation,* 2nd ed., rev. Ithaca, NY: ILR Press, 1993.

Cone, Cathy. "Delta Personnel Board Council." In Bruce Kaufman and Daphne Taras, eds. *Nonunion Employee Representation: History, Contemporary Practice, and Policy.* Armonk, NY: M.E. Sharpe, 2000, pp. 469–73.

Doeringer, Peter B. and Michael J. Piore. *Internal Labor Markets and Manpower Analysis, With a New Introduction.* Armonk, NY: M.E. Sharpe, 1985.

Fang, Tony and Anil Verma. "Union Wage Premium." *Perspectives on Labor and Income* 14 (Winter 2002): 17–23.

Fernie, Sue and David Metcalf. "Participation, Contingent Pay, Representation and Workplace Performance: Evidence from Great Britain." *British Journal of Industrial Relations* 33 (September 1995): 379– 415.

Flood, Patrick C. and Bill Toner. "Large Nonunion Companies: How Do They Avoid a Catch-22?" *British Journal of Industrial Relations* 33 (January 1997): 257–77.

Freeman, Richard B. and James L. Medoff. "The Two Faces of Unionism." *Public Interest* 57 (Fall 1979): 69–93.

———. *What Do Unions Do?* New York: Basic Books, 1984.

Goll, Irene. "Environment, Corporate Ideology, and Employee Involvement Programs." *Industrial Relations* 30 (Winter 1991): 138–49.

Gollan, Paul J. "Nonunion Forms of Employee Representation in the United Kingdom and Australia." In Bruce Kaufman and Daphne Taras, eds. *Nonunion Employee Representation: History, Contemporary Practice, and Policy.* Armonk, NY: M.E. Sharpe, 2000, pp. 410–52.

Gooderham, Paul N. and Odd Nordhaug. *Flexibility in Norwegian and British Firms: New Challenges for European Human Resource Management.* New York: St. Martin's Press, 2000.

Gramm, Cynthia L. and John F. Schnell. "The Use of Flexible Staffing Arrangements in Core Production Jobs." *Industrial and Labor Relations Review* 54 (January 2001): 245–59.

Gunnigle, Patrick, Thomas Turner, and Daryl D'Art. "Counterpoising Collectivism: Performance-Related Pay and Industrial Relations in Greenfield Sites." *British Journal of Industrial Relations* 36 (December 1998): 565–79.

Harshaw, Mark. "Nonunion Employee Representation at Dofasco." In Bruce Kaufman and Daphne Taras, eds. *Nonunion Employee Representation: History, Contemporary Practice, and Policy.* Armonk, NY: M.E. Sharpe, 2000, pp. 463–68.

Heyes, Jason and Mark Stuart. "Bargaining for Skills: Trade Unions and Training at the Workplace." *British Journal of Industrial Relations* 36 (September 1998): 459–67.

Hirsch, Barry T. "What Do Unions Do for Economic Performanc?" *Journal of Labor Research* 25 (Summer 2004): 415–55.

——— and John T. Addison. *The Ecnomic Analysis of Unions: New Approaches and Evidence.* Boston, MA: Allen and Unwin, 1986.

Hundley, Greg. "Things Unions Do, Job Attributes, and Union Membership." *Industrial Relations* 28 (Fall 1989): 335–55.

Ichniowski, Casey, John T. Delaney, and David Lewin. "The New Resource Management in US Workplaces: Is It Really New and Is It Only Nonunion?" *Relations Industrielles* 44 (Winter 1989): 97–119.

Kaufman, Robert S. and Roger T. Kaufman. "Union Effects on Productivity, Personnel Practices, and Survival in the Automotive Parts Industry." *Journal of Labor Research* 8 (Fall 1987): 332–50.

Kaufman, Bruce E. "The Employee Participation/Representation Gap: An Assessment and Proposed Solution." *University of Pennsylvania Journal of Labor and Employment Law* 3 (Spring 2001): 491–550.

———. "High-Level Employee Involvement at Delta Air Lines." *Human Resource Management* 42 (Spring 2003): 175–90.

Kennedy, Sean, Robert Drago, Judith Sloan, and Mark Wooden. "The Effect of Trade Unions on the Provision of Training: Australian Evidence." *British Journal of Industrial Relations* 32 (December 1994): 565–80.

Kim, Dong-One. "Factors Influencing Organizational Performance in Gainsharing Programs." *Industrial Relations* 35 (April 1996): 227–44.

———. "Determinants of the Survival of Gainsharing Programs." *Industrial and Labor Relations Review* 53 (October 1999): 21–42.

Koch, Marianne J. and Greg Hundley. "The Effects of Unionism on Recruitment and Selection Methods." *Industrial Relations* 36 (July 1997): 349–70.

Kochan, Thomas A., Harry C. Katz, and Robert B. McKersie. *The Transformation of American Industrial Relations.* New York: Basic Books, 1986.

——— and Paul Osterman. *Mutual Gains Enterprise.* Boston, MA: Harvard Business School Press, 1994.

Kochan, Thomas A., Richard Locke, Paul Osterman, and Michael Piore. "Extended Networks: A Vision for the Next Generation Unions." In Anil Verma and Thomas A. Kochan, eds. *Unions in the 21st Century: An International Perspective.* London: Palgrave Macmillan, 2004, pp. 30–43.

Lawler III, Edward E., Susan Albers Mohrman, and George Benson. *Organizing for High Performance: Employee Involvement, TQM, Reengineering, and Knowledge Management in the Fortune 1000 (The CEO Report).* San Francisco, CA: Wiley, 2001.

Leibenstein Harvey. "Allocative Efficiency vs. 'X-Efficiency'." *American Economic Review* 56 (June 1966): 392–415.

———. *General X-Efficiency and Economic Development.* New York: Oxford University Press, 1978.

Long, Richard J. "Pay Systems and Organizational Flexibility." *Revue Canadienne des Sciences de l'Administration/Canadian Journal of Administrative Sciences* 18 (March 2001): 25–32.

Metcalf, David. "Unions and Productivity, Financial Performance and Investment: International Evidence." In John T. Addison and Claus Schnabel, eds. *International Handbook of Trade Unions.* Cheltenham, UK: Edward Elgar, 2003, pp. 118–71.

Morehead, Alison. *Changes at Work: The 1995 Australian Workplace Industrial Relations Survey: A Summary of Major Findings.* Canberra, Australia: Australia. Department of Workplace Relations and Small Business, 1997.

Morishima, Motohiro and Tsuyoshi Tsuru. "Nonunion Employee Representation in Japan." In Bruce Kaufman and Daphne Taras, eds. *Nonunion Employee Representation: History, Contemporary Practice, and Policy.* Armonk, NY: M.E. Sharpe, 2000, pp. 386–409.

Ng, Ignace and Dennis Maki. "Trade Union Influence on Human Resource Management Practices." *Industrial Relations* 33 (January 1994): 121–35.

Osterman, Paul. "Skill, Training, and Work Organization in American Establishments." *Industrial Relations* 34 (April 1995): 125–46.

———. "How Common Is Workplace Transformation and Who Adopts It?" *Industrial and Labor Relations Review* 47 (January 1994): 173–88.

Rees, Daniel I. "Grievance Procedure Strength and Teacher Quits." *Industrial and Labor Relations Review* 45 (October 1991): 31–42.

Rubenstein, Saul A. and Thomas A. Kochan. *Learning From Saturn: Possibilities for Corporate Governance and Employee Relations.* Ithaca, NY: ILR Press, 2001.

Slichter, Sumner H., James J. Healy, and E. Robert Livernash. *The Impact of Collective Bargaining on Management.* Washington, DC: Brookings Institution, 1960.

———. *Union Policies and Industrial Management.* Washington, DC: Brookings Institution, 1941.

Stigler, George J. "The X-istence of X-efficiency." *American Economic Review* 66 (March 1976): 213–16.

Taras, Daphne Gottlieb. "Contemporary Experience with the Rockefeller Plan: Imperial Oil's Joint Industrial Council." In Bruce Kaufman and Daphne Taras, eds. *Nonunion Employee Representation: History, Contemporary Practice, and Policy.* Armonk, NY: M.E. Sharpe, 2000, pp. 231–58.

Verma, Anil, Thomas A. Kochan and Stephen Wood. "Union Decline and Prospects for Revival." *British Journal of Industrial Relations* 40 (September 2002): 373–84.

———— and Tony Fang. "Do Workplace Practices Contribute to Union-Nonunion Wage Differentials?" *Paper presented to Conference on Workplace and Employee Survey, Statistics Canada, Ottawa,* November 21– 22, 2002.

————. "Relative Flow of Capital to Union and Nonunion Plants within a Firm." *Industrial Relations* 24 (Fall 1985): 395–406.

Weil, David. "Enforcing OSHA: The Role of Labor Unions." *Industrial Relations* 30 (Winter 1991): 20–36.

————. "Building Safety: The Role of Construction Unions in the Enforcement of OSHA." *Journal of Labor Research* 13 (Winter 1992): 121–32.

10

Unionism and Employment Conflict Resolution: Rethinking Collective Voice and Its Consequences

*David Lewin**

I. Introduction

Twenty years ago, in *What Do Unions Do?*, Freeman and Medoff (1984; hereafter F&M) argued that unionism has two faces, namely, a monopoly face and a collective voice/institutional response face. This imaginative argument was grounded in Hirschman's (1970) well-known exit-voice framework, which attempted to explain why customers don't necessarily switch to other firms and, more broadly, why dissatisfied citizens sometimes rise up to challenge established authority. Yet even though they drew from Hirschman's exit-voice framework to concentrate their attention on unionism's two (ostensible) faces, F&M tended to treat employment relationship conflict in subordinate or secondary fashion. F&M's twin focus was on the efficiency (i.e., monopoly) effects of unionism, which they concluded are largely negative, and on the governance (i.e., voice) effects of unions, which they concluded are largely positive *and* more than counterbalance unionism's negative efficiency effects. To the extent that F&M addressed employment relationship conflict and the effectiveness of unions in dealing with such conflict, they embedded it in their "two faces" argument.

In the two decades following the publication of F&M's book, a substantial amount of research has appeared that directly addresses employment relationship conflict. Therefore, in this study, I use this research to (1) retrospectively evaluate F&M's theoretical perspective on conflict resolution and grievance systems; (2) identify and empirically assess six specific implications of F&M's analysis of employment relationship conflict resolution; and (3) provide an alternative view of F&M's broader, exit-voice-based recommendations for reversing the decline of unionism.

II. F&M's Theoretical Perspective on Conflict

Employment relationship conflict can take many forms, including strikes, sabotage, working to rule, withholding effort, shirking, and more. Whether conflict is seen as central or ancillary to the employment relationship, however, depends on one's conceptualization or larger view of the origins, function, and structure of this relationship. From one perspective, historically and contemporaneously reflected in the work of industrial relations scholars, the employment relationship is a pluralist, mixed-motive relationship featuring two parties, labor and management, with opposing interests; hence, conflict is inevitable. From this perspective, it follows that the role of unions is to help improve efficiency by institutionalizing/mediating employment relationship conflict such that wildcat strikes, sabotage, and other manifestations of primitive employment relationships are replaced by relatively more peaceful and professional collective bargaining and grievance processes. In addition, through collective bargaining and grievance procedures, unionism enhances equity in the employment relationship because, without these institutional mechanisms, workers will be at a power disadvantage and employment relationship conflicts will be resolved in the employer's favor (Kaufman and Lewin, 1998). In short, the pluralist perspective on employment relationship conflict implies that unions reduce the incidence of such conflict and help to efficiently and equitably resolve such conflicts.

An alternate view is that, for various institutional and political reasons, unions exacerbate employment relationship conflict with consequent negative efficiency and equity effects. For example, unions have an incentive to manufacture conflict in order to justify their existence to their members. More fundamentally, the very essence of collective bargaining is to have an adversarial approach to the employment relationship so that conflict resolution inherently takes the form of bargaining in an we-versus-them struggle — a struggle that endures and for which there is no resolution. But this is where the unitarist or cooperative perspective on the employment relationship, a perspective historically reflected in the work of management scholars and contemporaneously reflected in the work of human resource management (HRM) scholars, enters the picture. From this perspective, it is possible to restructure the employment relationship from one in which there is an inherent conflict of interests to one in which there is (more or less) a unity of interests. Because employment relationship conflict is considered dysfunctional to the interests of both sides, it should and can be substantially reduced and restructured so that such conflict is resolved not through an adversarial struggle but, instead, through cooperative problem-solving and other "innovative" HRM policies and practices (including alternative grievance-like procedures). From this unitarist perspective, unions have little or nothing to contribute to the employment relationship except, perhaps, heightened conflict (Lewin, 2001).

Instructively, the positive case for unions made by F&M seems not to depend at all on whether the employment relationship is conceived from a pluralist (IR) or, alternatively, from a cooperative (HR) perspective, even though F&M drew from economics and labor relations to blend disciplinary with institutional analysis.[1] By itself, this was hardly novel given the many precedents for a combined economics-institutional approach to the study of labor relations (Kerr, 1964; Chamberlain, 1948; Ross, 1948; Dunlop, 1958, 1944; Slichter, 1941, 1929; Commons, 1934, 1928). What was novel about F&M's work, as suggested by Bennett and Kaufman in this volume's introductory chapter, was their formulation of the "collective voice/institutional response" face of unionism and subsequent empirical operationalization of this concept.

The theoretical inspiration for F&M's development of unionism's voice face was provided by Hirschman (1970), who sought to explain why dissatisfied citizens don't necessarily leave their communities (governments) and move elsewhere, and why dissatisfied customers don't necessarily switch to other firms. Such movements and switches are key behaviors that classical and neo-classical microeconomic theory postulate will occur and thereby serve to equilibrate markets for public as well as private goods. Adopting a more institutional perspective, Hirschman focused on stayers rather than movers or switchers. That is, some dissatisfied citizens and some dissatisfied customers choose to stay rather than leave and, as part of staying, attempt to get their dissatisfactions redressed. This is what Hirschman refers to as the exercise of voice, or the voice option, which he then sharply contrasts with moving or switching behavior, which he refers to as exit, or the exit option.

F&M adopted this theoretical perspective and extended its application to union-management relations. They apparently did so because of their view that if worker voice is effective it must be collective voice. This is because individual worker voice will be under-supplied due to potential free-rider problems and worker fear of reprisal for exercising voice individually (Bennett and Kaufman, this volume). The collective worker voice mechanism that captured F&M's attention was the labor union rather than, say, a labor party. The union would serve to represent workers' interests and would communicate with employers and managers on behalf of the worker collective. F&M then strongly contrasted this collective voice/institutional response face of unionism with the monopoly face of unionism, presenting the argument that both faces must be taken into account in reaching overall judgments about unions' roles, effectiveness, and outcomes.

Framed this way, however, F&M's main line of reasoning can be seen as relatively narrow. It is one thing for a union to communicate its member-employees' concerns to management, but quite another thing to expect those concerns to be addressed or redressed. In the latter circumstance, negotiations and bargaining power become relevant as they influence both a union's willingness to press its members' concerns to management and management's willingness to redress those concerns. By relying so heavily on exit-voice theory to analyze union-management relations, F&M seem to downplay that employment relationship conflict and the resolution of such conflict are strongly shaped by the parties' relative bargaining power. Stated differently, union-management relations involve more than a union "communicating" or "voicing" its members concerns to management.

Further in this vein, if the efficiency payoff to voice is merely the collective aggregation of worker preferences, a 1920s-type employee representation plan seems better suited than a union to providing collective voice since it avoids unionism's monopoly effects. As Kaufman and Taras (2000) have observed, modern alternative dispute resolution (ADR) and employee involvement (EI) programs have their antecedents in 1920s Welfare Capitalist practices of firms, which were adopted in part for voice-type reasons. Anomalously, such employee representation plans were eliminated (that is, made illegal) by the 1935 Labor-Management Relations Act. Although F&M criticize 1920s-type employee representation for "lacking power" (p. 108), their own invocation of exit-voice theory to analyze union-management relations can be criticized on the very same ground. While voice may be a useful construct in any theoretical framework of employment conflict resolution, power is a necessary construct in such a framework; F&M strongly emphasize the former, while de-emphasizing and perhaps ignoring the latter.

Similarly, the construct of exit, as advanced by F&M, apparently presumes that the exit option is actually available to workers — a presumption embedded in F&M's assumption that product and especially labor markets are, in general, competitive. Here however, F&M seem to ignore that high unemployment has often undercut employees' exit option and, correspondingly, that employers have often exercised significant power in external labor markets, leaving workers largely in a take-it-or-leave-it position. From an historical perspective and to counter this power imbalance and "level the playing field" in wage determination, workers sought protection though unionism and grievance procedures. And, while the relatively low levels of unemployment that have prevailed in recent years have contributed to the decline of unionism (Kaufman and Lewin, 1998), the genesis of the particular voice mechanism central to F&M's analysis, namely, the employee union, developed largely to correct the power imbalance in the labor market rather than merely to communicate employee voice to management. Hence, in applying the constructs of exit and voice to union-management relations, F&M tend to overemphasize unionism's communication role and underemphasize unionism's power imbalance correction role.

There is little question that unionization and collective bargaining did in fact enhance employee power relative to employer power, contributed markedly to the peaceful settlement of industrial disputes, and provided a hitherto unknown measure of industrial democracy to millions of workers, most especially during the immediate post-World War II period and into the 1950s when unionism, covering roughly one-third of the U.S. nonagricultural private sector work force, was at its peak. During those times, moreover, there was a clear dichotomy in the labor market and in employment relationships between union workers covered and to some extent protected by collective bargaining agreements containing formal grievance procedures, and nonunion workers uncovered and unprotected by alternative voice/dispute resolution mechanisms in the firm or by legislation codifying, protecting, or conferring one or another employee right or benefit.

Ironically, by the time F&M's work appeared, this dichotomy had already changed considerably. Not only had unionization declined to about one-fifth of the private sector work force, nonunion employers had increasingly adopted workplace dispute resolution procedures; national legislation covering such matters as anti-discrimination in employment, occupational safety and health, and pension protection had been enacted; and judicial decisions established the doctrines of implicit employment contracts and wrongful termination in cases involving nonunion employees. Hence, while the practice of employment-at-will had by the mid-twentieth century been partially mitigated with regard to union workers, by a quarter century or so later this practice had become increasingly mitigated with regard to nonunion workers. Nevertheless, F&M chose to empha-size the stronger rights and protections offered workers by unionism and collec-tive bargaining than by employer voluntarism, legislation, or judicial decisions, and they constructed an imaginative analysis (grounded in Hirschman) that led to their main conclusion that the benefits of the collective voice/response face of unionism exceeded the costs of the monopoly face of unionism.

In my judgment this conclusion does not stand the test of time well, in part because F&M's conceptual framework is grounded in a narrow application of Hirschman's exit-voice-loyalty framework, and in part because of F&M's overly narrow empirical analysis of workplace dispute resolution in union and nonunion contexts. Regarding conceptualization, the role, indeed, the existence, of unions fundamentally depends on whether the employment rela-tionship is conceived of in pluralist or in unitarist terms. The pluralist perspec-tive posits employment relationship conflict as a given, with management and unions as well as collective bargaining and grievance procedures constituting an adversarially-oriented system of dispute resolution. The unitarist perspec-tive, by contrast, posits employment relationship cooperation as a given, with management and labor sharing the same rather than having opposing interests, unions having little or no role, and grievance procedures being a little used component of "progressive" HRM practices. Ironically, by ignoring so critical a matter as the pluralist versus unitarist conceptualization of the employment relationship, F&M seem to overstate their positive case for unions, such as when they claim that union voice is most effective when management is cooperative while also criticizing management for not being cooperative. Stated differently, F&M's exit-voice-loyalty-based analysis of union-management relations does not address the fundamental structure of the employment relationship or the origins and function of conflict in pluralist- versus unitarist-type employment relationships.

Regarding F&M's empirical analysis, my research and that of other scholars has shown that while it sometimes serves to "correct" the power advantage of employers over workers, workplace dispute resolution under unionism sometimes exacerbates rather than redresses employment relationship conflict. This is in part because the grievance procedure is not only a mechanism for providing voice to union members; it also serves as an additional or "extra" bargaining mechanism through which a union attempts to win "more," such as more protective work rules, more slack from supervisors, more money to settle grievances, and more influence for union representatives. Furthermore, and following the pluralist conception of the employment relationship in which conflict is endemic to all such relationships, union workers' exercise of voice through the grievance procedure can have a variety of outcomes ranging, probabilistically, from highly positive to highly negative. Ideally, and empirically, such outcomes should be compared with those that occur in nonunion firms in which, following the unitarist perspective, "aberrant" employment relationship conflict is more likely to be suppressed and HRM-bundled grievance procedures are relatively little used.

Moreover, and following the exit-voice model in which F&M's analysis of union-management relations is grounded, the grievance procedure will be invoked when an employee's relationship with an employer has deteriorated. From this perspective, ex-post efforts to correct employment relationship deterioration through formal grievance procedures, whether in union or nonunion settings, may result in negative consequences for — that is, additional deterioration among — the parties to the employment relationship. Perhaps this is why, in both research and practice, attention has increasingly turned away from reactive, adversarial approaches and toward relatively more proactive, positivist approaches to workplace conflict resolution.

Pursuing these "alternative" conclusions about F&M's two faces argument more deeply, consider what F&M's theoretical perspective specifically implies about conflict and dispute resolution in the employment relationship. First, it implies that union workers will be less likely than nonunion workers to leave their jobs, that is, to quit in response to workplace conflict. Second, it implies that union firms and workers will be more likely than nonunion firms and workers to have workplace governance and dispute resolution arrangements, such as a grievance procedure, in place. Third, it implies that union workers will be more likely than nonunion workers to exercise voice in the employment relationship. Fourth, and closely related, it implies that union workers will be more loyal to their employers than nonunion workers. Fifth, it implies that union workers' exercise of voice will be more effective in redressing employment-related grievances than nonunion workers' exercise of voice. Sixth, it implies that the existence of dispute resolution procedures and worker exercise of voice through such procedures will have positive effects on efficiency and firm performance. To what extent are these implications of F&M's theoretical perspective on workplace dispute resolution supported by empirical research?

III. Empirical Analysis – Unions and Quits

The first implication of F&M's theoretical perspective on conflict and dispute resolution is that union workers will quit their jobs less than nonunion workers. Of all the aforementioned implications, this one appears to have the strongest empirical support, in particular, from earlier studies by Stoikov and Raimon (1968), Burton and Parker (1969), Pencavel (1970), Brown (1978), Leigh (1979), Freeman (1980), Blau and Kahn (1981), Mitchell (1982), and Long and Link (1983), and more recent studies by Addison and Belfield (2004), Batt (2003), and Delerey et al. (2000). As summarized by F&M (pp. 94–101) and controlling for wages and other factors, union workers are much less likely than nonunion workers to quit their jobs, with the reduction in quits under unionism estimated at between 31 and 65 percent. Furthermore, these estimates are much larger than the estimated effects of a 20 percent "monopoly wage" increase on worker quits (F&M: 95–96). Not surprisingly, therefore, the increase in worker job tenure associated with unionism is also significant, with estimates ranging between 23 and 32 percent relative to nonunion workers. In these respects, conclude F&M, "the voice effect dominates the monopoly wage effect" (p. 95).[2]

What explains these quit-reducing, tenure-increasing effects of unions on workers? Put differently and consistent with the title of their (1984) book, F&M ask specifically, "What do unions do to a workplace that causes this change in worker behavior?" (p. 103). They answer this question by citing two union-induced "innovations," namely, development of grievance and arbitration systems and seniority-based personnel policies. Grievance and arbitration systems are especially notable, claim F&M, because they "provide workers with a judicial-type mechanism to protest and possibly to redress unfair or incorrect decisions of their supervisors" (p. 104). In other words, the grievance procedure is the key avenue through which (union) workers can exercise voice and thereby potentially reverse the deteriorated state of their relationships with their employers.

Attributing so large a reduction in worker quit behavior to the presence of grievance and arbitration procedures — that is, voice mechanisms — is questionable, however, because unionism influences other aspects of the employment relationship as well. These include fringe benefits, work assignments and jurisdictions, working conditions, and more, which are not captured by F&M's controls for wages in their quit rate equations (or in similar analyses conducted by Freeman and Rogers, 1999). Indeed, and as observed by Kaufman (2001), the totality of gains obtained by unions may be viewed as a form of "golden handcuffs" that tie union workers much more strongly to their firms than nonunion workers. Voice may well play a role in union workers' relatively low quits and relatively high tenure, but it is unlikely to be so dominant a role as that assigned to it by F&M.

In addition, F&M address the question of "why nonunion firms don't mimic union firms and offer workers the benefit of voice as part of a profit-maximizing strategy" (p. 107). F&M answer this question by proposing that nonunion firms respond primarily to the desires of young, mobile workers (the "marginal" worker), who prefer exit over voice, rather than to the desires of older, more permanent ("inframarginal") workers, who prefer voice over exit. Therefore, "as long as nonunion firms are attuned to the desires of potentially mobile workers, they are unlikely to see the need for grievance and arbitration" (pp. 107–108).

IV. Empirical Analysis – Grievance Procedures

Taken together, these arguments underlie the second implication of F&M's theoretical perspective on conflict and dispute resolution, namely, that union firms will be more likely than nonunion firms to have dispute resolution arrangements, such as a grievance procedure, in place. But this implication is called into question by the rising incidence, scope, and complexity of dispute resolution procedures — often referred to as alternative dispute resolution (ADR) — in nonunion firms. Estimates of the incidence of dispute resolution procedures in nonunion firms range between one-third and two-thirds, with a proximate mean of a little over one-half (Colvin, 2003; Bingham and Chachere, 1999; Lipsky and Seeber, 1998; USGAO, 1997; Feuille and Chachere, 1995; Feuille and Delaney, 1992; Edelman, 1990; Delaney et al., 1989; Ichniowski et al., 1989; Ewing, 1989; McCabe, 1988; Westin and Felieu, 1988). Such estimates should be treated with caution because nonunion ADR practices vary markedly with respect to procedural alternatives, procedural steps, protections of employee rights, and ultimate decision-making authority. They should also be treated cautiously because of potential selection bias problems in that union and nonunion firms with grievance procedures may not be drawn from the same population. That is, workers generally form and join unions when employment relationships are already conflictual and use grievance procedures to resolve such conflict, whereas nonunion firms that adopt ADR practices, especially as part of high-involvement work systems, generally do so to prevent employment relationship conflict.

Nevertheless, longitudinal studies consistently find a growing incidence of ADR procedures in nonunion firms, a widening scope of employment-related issues covered by these procedures, and an expansion of the steps included in these procedures (Colvin, 2003; Feuille and Chachere, 1995; Delaney et al., 1989; Ichniowski et al., 1989). With such widespread diffusion of this "innovation," it is difficult to sustain F&M's proposition that nonunion firms favor and respond to the preferences of young, mobile workers over those of older, more permanent workers.

This proposition is supported by the differential incidence of arbitration in the dispute resolution procedures of union and nonunion firms, respectively. While arbitration is the final step in all but a handful of union firms' grievance procedures, it is estimated to be the final step only in roughly one-sixth to one-third of nonunion firms' dispute resolution procedures. (Colvin, 2003; Delaney et al., 1989; Freeman and Medoff, 1984). Other nonunion dispute resolution procedures, however, provide peer review or mediation or an ombuds or combinations thereof (Colvin, 2004; Bingham and Chachere, 1999; Feuille, 1999; Kaminski, 1999), so that there is both more experimentation with various dispute resolution practices — alternatives — in nonunion than in union firms, and a smaller gap between nonunion and union firms' procedural approaches to conflict resolution than when arbitration alone is considered. Moreover, while grievance procedures in union firms cover only employee-members of bargaining units, grievance procedures in nonunion firms typically cover all nonmanagement personnel and often cover some levels of management personnel (Lewin, 2004, 1997). In sum, when the rising incidence of dispute resolution procedures in nonunion firms is taken together with the continued downward trend in union density, it appears that far more nonunion than union workers are covered by dispute resolution procedures — and perhaps as well by arbitration.

Why has the incidence of dispute resolution procedures grown so substantially in nonunion firms? Following F&M, who argued that "union work rules and procedures for labor relations also spill over to effect nonunion firms" (pp. 153–54), the threat of unionization may primarily explain the rising incidence of dispute resolution procedures in nonunion firms; this may be dubbed a union substitution explanation. Following this line of reasoning, however, the continued long-term decline of unions should reduce pressure on nonunion firms to adopt dispute resolution procedures. Alternatively, recent decisions of the U.S. Supreme Court, such as in *Gilmer v. Interstate/Johnson Lane* (1991) and *Circuit City v. Adams* (2001), have ruled that the full range of employment laws, including Title VII of the Civil Rights Act, the Age Discrimination in Employment Act, and the Americans With Disabilities Act, are subject to arbitration clauses contained in the employment contracts of nonunion employees. This mandatory arbitration doctrine requires "diversion of all employment litigation … into an employer-designed arbitration procedure from which there is no right of appeal or only very limited possibility of court review" (Colvin, 2003). In other words, nonunion employers who adopt an arbitration-type dispute resolution procedure can require employees to submit to this procedure and can also exercise strong control over the procedure itself, including by selecting and paying for the arbitrator (Stone, 1999). Such employer domination of ADR systems and practices can be analogized to employer domination of company unions in an earlier era (Kaufman and Taras, 2000). In any case, nonunion employers who perceive substantial employee litigation threats have an incentive to adopt dispute resolution procedures, in particular, procedures featuring and requiring arbitration. This may be dubbed a litigation threat explanation, one which also suggests that nonunion employers' adoption of ADR procedures does not stem primarily from a desire to prevent employment relationship conflict.[3]

Yet another factor potentially influencing the growth of nonunion dispute resolution procedures is the extent to which such procedures are components of high-involvement or high-performance work systems that have been widely adopted by nonunion (and some union) firms. Such systems, often described as strategic human resource management initiatives, are claimed to promote high levels of employee commitment and thereby enhance productivity, product and service quality, customer satisfaction, and, ultimately, firms' financial performance (Batt, 1999; Ichniowski et al., 1996; Osterman, 1996; MacDuffie, 1995; Huselid, 1995). Although most research and practice regarding high-performance work systems focuses on the use of self-managed teams, employment security, employee training and development, and variable pay, formal dispute resolution procedures are sometimes also included as components of these systems (Huselid, 1995; Arthur, 1992; Cutcher-Gershenfeld, 1991); this may be dubbed a high-performance work system explanation.

To what extent are these contrasting explanations for nonunion firms' adoption of dispute resolution procedures supported empirically? Several studies (Colvin, 2003; Feuille and Delaney, 1993; McCabe, 1988) find that nonunion firms adopt a dispute resolution procedure primarily as part of broader strategic initiatives, such as introducing and developing high-performance work systems, work process re-engineering, and human resource information systems — in this instance for the identification, diagnosis, and resolution of organizational/workplace issues and problems. Similar rationales have been offered for adoption of the ombuds-type dispute resolution procedure (Fernie and Metcalf, 2004). In these studies, union substitution is either not significantly associated or only modestly significantly associated with nonunion firms' adoption of dispute resolution procedures — findings that are also consistent with the notion that declining unionization reduces the pressure on nonunion firms to adopt dispute resolution procedures. Related research, however, finds that union substitution is significantly associated with nonunion firms' adoption of a peer-review-type dispute resolution procedure but not an arbitration-type dispute resolution procedure (Colvin, 2003; Edelman, 1990). By contrast, the threat of employment litigation is significantly associated with nonunion firms' adoption of an arbitration-type dispute resolution procedure but not a peer-review-type dispute resolution procedure. Furthermore, this research finds a stronger association between high-performance work practices and nonunion firms' adoption of a peer-review-type dispute resolution procedure than between high-performance work practices and nonunion firms' adoption of an arbitration-type dispute resolution system.

Despite the recent growth of ADR systems in nonunion firms, there is no one dominant system akin to the grievance system that characterizes union firms. Stated differently, there are widely varying alternative dispute resolution practices in nonunion firms as well as substantial variation in the rights and protections provided to nonunion workers under ADR systems. Moreover, empirical research suggests that ADR systems are most likely to be found in large, publicly traded, "progressive" firms that also tend to adopt high-performance work practices (Colvin, 2003). Rather similar to unionism and bargaining, therefore, ADR systems are least likely to be found in small firms and to cover workers in secondary labor markets in which transient, zero-sum-type employment practices predominate.

Nevertheless, a substantial body of research and practice, much of which emerged since the publication of F&M's (1984) book, leads to the conclusion that nonunion firms have increasingly adopted some type of dispute resolution procedure. In this regard, the gap between union and nonunion firms on which F&M concentrated much of their attention and which informed their analysis of the institutional response/collective voice face of unionism appears to have narrowed considerably. Moreover, and based on strategic human resource management and litigation threat considerations, the proportion of nonunion firms adopting formal dispute resolution systems is likely to rise even further.[4]

V. Empirical Analysis – Exercise of Voice

The third implication of F&M's theoretical perspective on conflict and dispute resolution is that union workers are more likely than nonunion workers actually to exercise voice in the employment relationship. This implication is only partially borne out, however, based on empirical evidence from studies of grievance filing in union and nonunion settings. To illustrate, a multi-sector study of union firms conducted by Lewin and Peterson (1988) found annual grievance filing rates (i.e., the number of written grievances annually per 100 workers) ranging from about eight percent for public school teachers and retail department store clerks to about ten percent for hospital workers and to about 16 percent for steel workers. The overall mean grievance filing rate across all sectors, organizations, and (union) workers covered in this study was about ten percent, which is quite similar to the findings of other researchers in their studies of union workers' grievance filing rates in the United States and Canada (Bemmels, 1994; Stewart and Davy, 1992; Cappelli and Chauvin, 1991; Bemmels et al., 1991).

Evidence of grievance filing by nonunion workers typically comes from research on single (nonunion) firms or several such firms rather than from industry- or sector-level studies. In this research, nonunion workers covered by grievance or equivalent complaint-handling procedures had "grievance" filing rates ranging from about three percent to about six percent, with an overall mean of about five percent (Lewin, 2004, 1992, 1987; Colvin, 2004). Thus, the grievance filing rate of nonunion workers covered by dispute resolution procedures appears to be about half that of union workers.[5]

Consider, however, that not all grievances filed by union workers stem from incidents of unfair workplace treatment or, in exit-voice terminology, a deteriorated state. For example, Kuhn (1961) and Lewin and Peterson (1988) found that grievance activity was highest when the collective bargaining agreement was about to be re-negotiated and lowest at the mid-point of the bargaining cycle, indicating that unions use the grievance procedure in part to extract more economic benefits from employers. Other studies have found that grievance activity sometimes rises because a newly elected local union official wants to show his mettle or a union leader is up for re-election (Chamberlain and Kuhn, 1961; Sayles, 1956). By contrast, these types of economic and political factors are not present in nonunion contexts and thus do not influence the grievance activity of nonunion workers. This, in turn, suggests that grievance filing rates in union settings should be adjusted downward to take account of the effects of union-management bargaining and union political considerations — especially when comparing union and nonunion workers' grievance (voice) activity. If such adjustments were made on a broad scale, they would likely reduce the aforementioned two-to-one ratio of union worker-nonunion worker grievance filing rates, perhaps considerably.

In both union and nonunion firms, grievance procedures typically feature multiple, escalating steps. Comparisons of initial step grievance filing rates between union and nonunion workers therefore provide only a partial picture of differences in grievance activity among these two worker groups. F&M's theoretical perspective on conflict and dispute resolution (further) implies that union workers are more likely than nonunion workers to pursue redress of their grievances to and through higher steps of the grievance procedure. Is this proposition borne out empirically? For the most part, no, it isn't. Studies of grievance activity in union firms find that the large majority of grievances are settled at the first (written) step of the grievance procedure, that about one-third of grievances are taken beyond the first step, and that between three and four percent proceed to the last grievance step, which is almost always arbitration (Feuille, 1999; Kleiner et al., 1995; Bemmels, 1994; Lewin and Peterson, 1988). Studies of grievance activity in nonunion firms report similar findings. Specifically, about 70 percent of nonunion workers' grievances are settled at the first step of the grievance procedure, most of the rest are settled at the second step (or second and third steps) of the procedure, and about two percent proceed to the final step of the procedure (Lewin, 2004, 1992, 1987).

In nonunion firms, this final grievance step is more varied than in union firms and typically features a senior member of management — e.g., the Chief Executive Officer (CEO), senior human resource officer, chief administrative officer or general manager — as the final decision maker (Kaminski, 1999; Feuille and Delaney, 1992; Lewin, 1992, 1987). Where arbitration is the final step in nonunion firms' grievance procedures, the percentage of grievances that reach the final step — a little over three percent, on average — is somewhat higher than when a management official constitutes the final step — a little under two percent, on average. On balance, then, nonunion workers who are covered by dispute resolution procedures are only marginally less likely than union workers to pursue their grievances beyond the first step of the grievance procedure, including to the final grievance step.

Grievance filing is only one part of conflict and dispute resolution dynamics in firms. Industrial relations scholars have often pointed out that most employment-related grievances are never put in writing. Instead, they are "resolved" informally in discussions between workers and supervisors, including but not limited to direct supervisors (Feuille, 1999; Bemmels, 1994; Lewin and Peterson, 1988; Chamberlain and Kuhn, 1965; Kuhn, 1961; Sayles, 1956). The extent of such informal grievance resolution is of course unknown, but it is estimated that in union firms there are about ten unwritten grievances for every one written, or formally filed. Is there reason to believe that this type of informal grievance resolution occurs more or less frequently in nonunion firms than in union firms?

If, as F&M imply, union workers are more likely than nonunion workers to exercise (collective) voice in the employment relationship, this should hold for both formal grievance filing and informal grievance discussion and resolution. Hence, informal grievance activity would be greater in union than in nonunion firms. Alternatively, if nonunion firms are more likely than union firms to adopt high-performance work system practices or what some scholars describe as "proactive" voice mechanisms — e.g., workplace teams, worker consultation, information-sharing, business issues forums, peer performance assessments — nonunion workers may be more likely than union workers to exercise (partly individual, partly collective) voice in the employment relationship. In this instance, the incidence of informal grievance activity would be greater in nonunion than in union firms.

Given their emphasis on expanded worker participation in decision-making, high- performance work system practices and proactive voice mechanisms may be said to legitimize individual differences regarding particular decisions and stimulate internal communication about such differences. In this context, informal grievance activity may occur not because workers experience deterioration of their relationships with their employers but, rather, because of the expanded opportunities for workers to contribute to the functioning and performance of their firms. This reasoning is consistent with the finding of organizational behavior researchers that conflicts over work coordination and task integration can be beneficial to firms (Bendersky, 2003; Jehn, 2001).

Alternatively, high-performance work system practices and proactive voice mechanisms may pose more challenges than workers are able or willing to accept. Workers may not have the skills and knowledge required to participate in or be consulted about a broadened set of decisions; they may find that their jobs have been enlarged to the point where they cannot perform the full range of tasks required or requested of them; and they may become members of work teams that function ineffectively due to free riding, excessive heterogeneity, and lack of cohesion. In these circumstances, informal grievance activity may occur because workers have experienced conflict in — deterioration of — their employment relationships. This reasoning is also consistent with the finding of organizational behavior researchers that personality conflicts are harmful to work groups and firms more broadly (Jehn, 1997; Amason, 1996).

Theorizing about the extent to which informal grievance activity occurs in union and nonunion firms as well as the underlying causes of such activity can take us only so far. Such activity may be more or less prevalent among nonunion than among union workers, but even if it were more prevalent it would not necessarily reflect relatively more conflictual or deteriorated employment relationships among nonunion than among union workers. In the absence of empirical evidence, it is prudent to conclude that informal grievance activity is likely to be far more common than formal grievance activity in nonunion and union firms alike. And, because differences between union and nonunion firms in the incidence of formal grievance filing and the progression of unsettled grievances to the higher steps of grievance procedures are quite small, the implication drawn from F&M that union workers are significantly more likely than nonunion workers to exercise voice in the employment relationship should be regarded as unproven until more definitive empirical studies are conducted.

VI. Empirical Analysis – Unions and Worker Loyalty

The fourth implication of F&M's theoretical perspective on conflict and dispute resolution is that union workers will be more loyal to their employers than nonunion workers. It may be argued that this implication is erroneous because worker loyalty received no explicit attention from F&M. Yet, loyalty is a key variable in the Hirschman framework on which F&M otherwise rely so heavily. Hirschman (1970) postulated that the extent to which organizational members are willing to trade off the certainty of exit against the uncertainties of exercising voice "is clearly related to that special attachment to an organization known as loyalty" (p. 77). While this formulation is at best imprecise and at worst tautological, some scholars have operationalized loyalty as "giving private and public support to the organization" (Rusbelt et al., 1988), others as "organizational citizenship" (Cappelli and Rogovsky, 1998), and still others as "organizational commitment" or "the degree to which a person identifies with an organization" (Boroff and Lewin, 1997). Its particular empirical specification aside, loyalty is posited by Hirschman as being positively correlated with the exercise of voice and negatively correlated with exit behavior. Yet, F&M drew on Hirschman's concepts of exit and voice but apparently not on the concept of loyalty in developing their collective voice/institutional response face model of unionism and labor-management relations.

A different reading of F&M, however, suggests that rather than disregarding loyalty, they took Hirschman literally and regarded loyalty as moderating worker

To illustrate, in a study of grievance behavior in a large, union telecommunications company, Boroff and Lewin (1997) found that, consistent with F&M, union membership was significantly positively associated with grievance filing (i.e., the exercise of voice). Inconsistent with F&M (and Hirschman), however, grievance filing was not significantly associated with worker exit intent. Furthermore, worker job tenure, satisfaction, and perceived effectiveness of the grievance procedure were all insignificantly associated with grievance filing, while both worker loyalty and fear of reprisal were significantly negatively associated with grievance filing. These findings run counter to F&M's (and Hirschman's) propositions about the determinants of worker exercise of voice. By contrast, Boroff and Lewin's (1997) findings that worker loyalty, satisfaction, and perceived effectiveness of the grievance procedure were all significantly negatively associated with worker intent to leave the firm are consistent with F&M's (and Hirschman's) propositions about exit behavior.

Another way of assessing the effectiveness of grievance procedures as a voice mechanism, whether among union or nonunion workers, is to examine post-grievance settlement behavior. For this purpose, Lewin and Peterson (1999) analyzed individual worker data drawn from four union organizations over two three-year periods. Employing a modified pre-test, post-test, control-group design, these researchers found that worker performance ratings, promotion rates, and work attendance rates declined, and worker turnover rates increased significantly for grievance filers compared with non-filers following grievance settlement. These findings contrasted markedly with the absence of significant differences in performance ratings, promotions rates, and work attendance rates between grievance filers and non-filers before or during grievance filing and settlement. In related research, Olson-Buchanan's (1997, 1996) laboratory studies found that grievance filers had significantly poorer job performance than non-filers after grievance filing and settlement, and Klass and DeNisi (1989) found that workers who filed grievances against their supervisors subsequently received lower performance ratings than workers who filed grievances over management policies. Hence, contrary to F&M, it appears that union workers who exercise voice through grievance filing subsequently experience further deterioration rather than improvement of their employment relationships, including increased rather than decreased exit behavior.

Such additional deterioration may, on the one hand, stem from management reprisal against workers for filing grievances. If so, empirical evidence provides stronger support for an organizational punishment-industrial discipline theory of the employment relationship (Sheppard et al., 1992; Arvey and Jones, 1985; O'Reilly and Weitz, 1980) than for an industrial relations-due process theory (Lewin and Peterson, 1988; Peach and Livernash, 1974) or an exit-voice theory of the employment relationship. On the other hand, the negative post-grievance filing and settlement outcomes for union workers summarized above may reveal "true performance." Following this reasoning, grievance filing and settlement

choice between voice and exit behavior. This interpretation is cons
F&M's emphasis on the quit-reducing effect of unionism, which in
say) results from the greater opportunities available to union than
workers for exercising voice in the employment relationship. Inferen
F&M explicitly analyzed job satisfaction as a moderating variable
ing worker choice as between voice and exit behavior. In this rega
reasoned that more dissatisfied workers are more likely to file grieval
less dissatisfied workers, so that the (negative) union impact on quits s
greater on workers with the greatest dissatisfaction. And, citing prior
Freeman (1980) and by Kochan and Helfman (1977), F&M concluded
rates "rise much more modestly among union than among nonunion
as dissatisfaction rises" (p. 105).

But if this is so, an equally plausible proposition is that quit rates ris
more modestly among union than among nonunion workers as loy.
the employer) declines. In one of the only empirical studies that direc
dresses this proposition, however, Lewin and Boroff (1996) found tha
worker loyalty was significantly negatively associated with worker exit
(that is, the intent to leave the job), the (standardized) regression coe
was larger for nonunion than for union workers. In this same study, mor
worker loyalty was also more strongly negatively associated with the ex
of voice (that is, grievance filing) among nonunion than among union wo
Consequently, and despite the paucity of studies directly comparing unio
nonunion worker loyalty, the available (inferential) empirical evidence
not support the proposition drawn from F&M that union workers will be
loyal to their employers than nonunion workers.[6]

VII. Empirical Analysis – The Effectiveness of Voice

The fifth implication of F&M's theoretical perspective on conflict and
pute resolution is that union workers' exercise of voice will be more effec
in redressing employment-related grievances than nonunion workers' exerc
of voice. In this regard and given their theoretical perspective, one wo
have expected F&M to analyze grievance filing, handling, and resolution
samples of union firms, or to compare grievance behavior in samples of uni
and nonunion firms having grievance and grievance-like systems, respective
in place. But F&M did not do this; rather, and as noted earlier, they focuse
more narrowly on how unionism affects quits of workers with varying degre
of job satisfaction. That analysis is too limited and perhaps even off the marl
however, if one is interested in knowing whether and to what extent grievanc
and arbitration systems provide workers an effective voice mechanism. T
answer this question, grievance behavior itself must be studied. Fortunately
several researchers have done just that, both in union and nonunion contexts.
The results of this research appear to confirm some and disconfirm other of
F&M's findings and conclusions.

spur management to pay closer attention to assessing worker job performance. When doing so, "management discovers (ex-post) that grievants ... are indeed poorer performers than non-grievants" (Lewin, 1999: 160). Notably, additional support for this "true performance" explanation of post-grievance filing and settlement employment relationship deterioration inheres in the well-known "shock" theory of the union impact on management developed by industrial relations scholars (Rees, 1962; Chamberlain, 1948; Slichter, 1941, 1929; Commons, 1934, 1928). According to this theory, unionization of a firm's work force shocks that firm's management into improving organizational performance, thereby resulting in higher productivity which offsets higher labor costs and thus leaves unit labor costs unchanged. The shock theory of unionism, it should be noted, is in many respects quite similar to F&M's "two faces of unionism" theory except, of course, that it is not grounded in concepts of exit and voice (or loyalty).

The reprisal explanation for further deterioration of union workers' employment relationships following grievance filing and settlement is strengthened by Lewin and Peterson's additional findings that supervisors of grievance filers in the organizations they studied had significantly lower job performance ratings, promotion rates, and work attendance rates and significantly higher turnover rates than the supervisors of non-filers following grievance filing and settlement. Moreover, no significant differences in job performance ratings, promotion rates, or work attendance rates existed between these two groups of supervisors prior to or during the grievance filing and settlement periods. Alternatively, the fact that grievances were filed against them implies that the supervisors of grievance filers are systematically poorer performers than the supervisors of non-filers, which would also be consistent with firms' closer monitoring of supervisors following rather than prior to or during grievance filing and settlement. Thus, whether and to what extent a reprisal explanation fits the empirical evidence better than a true performance explanation of grievance filers' supervisors' post-grievance filing and settlement employment relationship deterioration is problematic.[7] In any case, empirical evidence indicates that the grievance procedure does not, as F&M would have it, necessarily provide union workers an effective voice mechanism that serves to redress their particular grievance issues or restore the deteriorated state of their relationships with their employers. Therefore, it is also difficult to accept F&M's proposition that the positive effects of the collective voice face of unionism fully or more than fully offset the negative effects of the monopoly face of unionism.

Turning to grievance procedures for nonunion workers, the effectiveness of such procedures may also be gauged by analyzing post-grievance settlement behavior. Relevant evidence in this regard comes from a series of studies (Lewin, 2004, 1997, 1992, 1987) that used the same type of pre-test, post-test, control-group design as was employed by Lewin and Peterson (1999, 1988) in their studies of post-grievance settlement behavior in union settings. Drawing on individual worker data from several large nonunion firms with dispute resolution procedures in place, this research found no significant differences between samples of grievance filers and non-filers in job performance ratings, promotion rates, and work attendance rates prior to and during the grievance filing and settlement periods. By contrast, grievance filers had significantly poorer job performance ratings and lower promotion rates and work attendance rates as well as higher turnover rates than non-filers during the one- and two-year periods following grievance settlement.

Some of these studies were also able to replicate the analysis of post-settlement grievance behavior using samples of supervisors of nonunion grievance filers and non-filers. Once again, the research found a pattern of no significant between-group differences during the pre-grievance filing and grievance settlement periods, but significant between-group differences thereafter. That is, the supervisors of nonunion grievants had significantly poorer post-grievance settlement job performance ratings, lower promotion rates and work attendance rates, and significantly higher turnover rates than the supervisors of nonunion workers who did not file grievances. Hence, and closely similar to the experience in union settings, nonunion workers who exercise voice through grievance filing as well as their supervisors subsequently experience further deterioration of their employment relationships, including increased exit behavior.[8] Taken as a whole, this body of empirical evidence largely fails to support the implication derived from F&M that union workers exercise more effective voice in the employment relationship than nonunion workers.

Also supporting the notion that union workers who exercise voice by filing grievances experience further deterioration rather than redress of their employment relationships are findings from studies of employee reinstatement. The bulk of these studies use samples of arbitration awards in dismissal cases and analyze the incidence of reinstatement, factors affecting reinstatement, and the viability of employment relationships following reinstatement (Bemmels and Foley, 1996; Barnacle, 1991; Rocella, 1989; Lewin and Peterson, 1988; Ponak, 1987; Labig et al., 1985; Shantz and Rogow, 1984; Dickens et al., 1984; Williams and Lewis, 1982; Malinowski, 1981; Adams, 1979). All in all, this research finds that reinstatement occurs in about half of the grievance cases, and for this half less severe discipline is substituted for dismissal. The proportion of dismissed workers who actually return to work following decisions to reinstate varies widely, however, from 88 percent reported in a U.S.-based study (Barnacle, 1991) to 46 percent reported in a Canadian-based study (Malinowski, 1981). Thus, there is some reluctance to return to work among workers who are reinstated with lesser penalties than dismissal (Bemmels and Foley, 1996).

Especially notable, dismissed workers who are partially exonerated by arbitrators apparently have less difficulty following reinstatement than fully exonerated workers. In a study of unionized Canadian workers (Adams, 1979), for example, quit rates for partially and fully exonerated workers were 13 percent and 31 percent, respectively, following arbitrator reinstatement decisions. A related study of unionized U.S. workers (Lewin and Peterson, 1988) found that workers who won their grievance cases (at any step of the grievance procedure) were more likely to quit during the post-grievance settlement period than workers who lost their grievance cases. More broadly, research by Rocella (1989) on reinstated Italian workers and by Shantz and Rogow (1984) on reinstated U.S. workers found combined voluntary and involuntary turnover rates of 28 percent and 58 percent, respectively, in the two-year period immediately following reinstatement.

Some studies (Chaney, 1981; Stephens and Chaney, 1974) conclude that reinstated workers who decide not to return to work are motivated by fear of employer reprisal. These same studies also conclude that unfair workplace treatment is the main reason why reinstated workers who do return to work decide to quit their jobs following reinstatement. Regarding employers, survey-based research finds that whereas the bulk of employers believe that workers reinstated to their jobs with lesser penalties than discharge perform satisfactorily, and also that the incidence of post-reinstatement disciplinary infractions by reinstated workers does not differ significantly from the incidence of disciplinary infractions among other workers, these same employers believe that the reinstatement of dismissed workers negatively affects work force morale as well as working relationships between reinstated workers and other workers (Ponak, 1987; Barnacle, 1981). Taken as a whole, this research suggests that substantial proportions of union workers who exercise voice after their employment relationships have deteriorated to the point of dismissal and who successfully achieve redress of their grievances by being reinstated to their jobs nevertheless subsequently experience additional employment relationship deterioration, culminating in quitting or termination (that is, exit).

VIII. Empirical Analysis – Voice and Organizational Performance

The sixth and final implication of F&M's theoretical perspective on conflict and dispute resolution is that the existence of dispute resolution procedures and workers' exercise of voice through such procedures will positively affect efficiency and firm performance. In this regard, however, empirical research distinguishes the existence or availability of voice from the actual use or exercise of voice in terms of effects on organizational performance. To illustrate, studies of grievance procedure usage by union workers in automobile manufacturing plants (Northsworthy and Zabala, 1985; Katz et al., 1985, 1983) and paper manufacturing plants (Ichniowski, 1992, 1986) found that grievance rates were significantly negatively associated with labor productivity, total factor productivity, and product quality and significantly positively associated with labor costs and unit production costs. In one of these studies (Ichniowski, 1992), moreover, a reduced grievance rate, attributed to the introduction of a labor-management cooperation program, was significantly associated with improved productivity and product quality. On the basis of these and related studies, therefore, grievance procedure usage, that is, the exercise of voice by union workers, is inimical to organizational performance.[9]

A different conclusion emerges from studies of human resource management (HRM) practices and business performance that include the presence of a formal grievance procedure or the percentage of employees covered by a grievance procedure as one among several component or bundled HRM practices. For example, Mitchell et al. (1991) found significant positive relationships between an index of the formality of HRM practices, including a grievance procedure, and return on assets, return on investment, and revenue per employee in a sample of 495 business units of U.S. companies. Huselid (1995) included the percentage of employees covered by a grievance procedure in one of two main indexes of high-performance work practices and found significant positive relationships between these indexes and worker productivity and significant negative relationships between these indexes and worker turnover in a sample of 855 U.S. companies. That study also found that worker productivity was significantly positively related and worker turnover significantly negatively related to both market and accounting-based measures of company financial performance — findings similar to those reported by Arthur (1992) in his studies of steel manufacturing firms. In another study, also set in steel manufacturing, Ichniowski et al. (1997) included the presence of a formal grievance procedure in their measures of innovative bundles of HRM practices and found broader bundles to be significantly positively associated with plant productivity and product quality. Similarly, MacDuffie (1995) found significant positive relationships between expansive HRM bundles and plant performance in a multi-country study of the automobile industry. These various empirical findings are consistent with theoretical frameworks offered by other scholars (Levine, 1995; Eaton and Voos, 1994, 1992), who contend that for innovative HRM practices, especially employee participation in decision making, to have positive effects on organizational performance, these practices must be part of a larger HRM system that includes guarantees of worker due process — in particular, a grievance procedure.

In sum, the main conclusion to be drawn from extant studies of HRM and business performance is that the presence or availability of a grievance procedure is positively associated with organizational performance, especially when bundled with certain other high-involvement-type HRM practices. By contrast, actual grievance procedure usage, that is, grievance filing, is negatively associated with organizational performance. Consequently, when union workers actually exercise voice in the employment relationship, not only is the conflict resolution effectiveness of such voice problematic, efficiency and overall organizational performance appear to be negatively affected. This is a far cry from the positive collective voice/institutional response face of unionism celebrated by F&M that forms the core of their theoretical perspective on workplace conflict and dispute resolution.

IX. Conclusions and Overall Assessment

The central proposition advanced by F&M is that the collective voice/response face of unionism more than counterbalances the monopoly face of unionism. Following this reasoning, it may be concluded that union workers would remain unionized and nonunion workers would become unionized. But what if the collective voice/response face of unionism does *not* more than counterbalance (let alone "dominate") the monopoly face of unionism? Suppose that, consistent with the evidence presented herein, the exercise of voice in the employment relationship leads to further deterioration of the employment relationship rather than to the effective redress of worker grievances? In this circumstance, existing unions would lose members, and unorganized workers would choose not to become union members.

Supposition aside, there is no question that unionization continues to decline sharply. When F&M's book first appeared, about one in five private sector workers belonged to a union; today, less than one in ten private sector workers belongs to a union. But while F&M and, later, Freeman and Rogers (1999), attributed the decline in unionization to employer/management opposition and weak labor law, some of this decline can be attributed to *worker* resistance. Such resistance may stem, in turn and following F&M, from recognition of the net negative consequences of unionism's monopoly face, but also, and contrary to F&M, from recognition of the net negative consequences of unionism's collective voice/response face. If workers judged unions' voice response face, in particular, grievance procedures, to be effective in redressing worker grievances, more union workers would likely remain union members and more unorganized workers would join unions — even in the "face" of employer opposition. While there is little question that there are widely varying types of real-world employment relationships or that unions are best suited to protecting worker interests in certain of these (usually highly adversarial) relationships, the fact that workers as a whole decreasingly choose to become union members suggests that they do not perceive union voice to be effective in redressing deteriorated employment relationships or to be more effective in this respect than nonunion voice options. Such reasoning is consistent with the picture sketched in this paper — a different picture from that forwarded by F&M — of unionism and grievance procedures as largely reactive, adversarial-oriented mechanisms for dealing with workplace conflict resolution, especially in a pluralist, mixed-motive type of employment relationship.

Furthermore, this reasoning is helpful for understanding how F&M so strongly concluded that the positive effects of unionism's collective voice/response face counterbalance the negative effects of unionism's monopoly face. In particular, F&M appear to have adopted an extreme interpretation of a key assumption made by Hirschman, namely, that deterioration in the organization-member relationship is the starting point — the necessary condition — for an individual to choose between the voice and exit options. Hirschman's (1970) book is subtitled *Responses to Decline in Firms, Organizations and States*, meaning that "exit and voice are options to be weighed once one has experienced deterioration, perceived or actual, in one's relationship to an organization" (p. 31). In the context of the employment relationship, therefore, workers who experience deterioration of their relationships with employers will respond either by exiting (that is, quitting) or by exercising voice so as to redress their deteriorated employment relationships. Following F&M's reasoning, workers in a deteriorated state choose unionism as their voice mechanism and exercise voice by negotiating collective agreements that include grievance procedures culminating in arbitration. This, in essence, is what F&M mean by the collective voice/institutional response face of unionism. But, if so, how can the claim that F&M are overly extreme in following the deteriorated state condition of Hirschman's framework be substantiated?

Consider that by comparing union with nonunion workers, as in F&M's analysis of unionism's effects on worker quits, all union workers are in effect presumed to be in a deteriorated state with respect to their employment relationships and all nonunion workers are presumed not to be in a deteriorated state with respect to their employment relationships. Yet, if formal grievance activity is regarded as an indicator of employment relationship deterioration, most union workers don't experience employment relationship deterioration (that is, don't file grievances), and some nonunion workers (covered by grievance procedures) do experience such deterioration (that is, file grievances). In other words, when it comes to employment relationship deterioration, recent grievance procedure research suggests that the record is more mixed than is reflected in the singular union worker-nonunion worker dichotomy that characterizes F&M's theoretical perspective on and empirical treatment of conflict and dispute resolution.[10]

Furthermore, for both union and nonunion workers who do experience deteriorated employment relationships, exit and voice are not the only available response options. An additional response option is "silence," as has been reported in several empirical studies (Rusbelt et al., 1988; Boroff and Lewin, 1997; Lewin and Boroff, 1996), including those that limit the analysis to workers who believe that they experienced unfair workplace treatment (a specific measure of employment relationship deterioration). Silence in the face of unfair workplace treatment may result from workers' fear of reprisal for filing grievances (Lewin and Peterson, 1999; Boroff and Lewin, 1997; Bemmels, 1997), but may also result from workers' judgments that the cost of exercising voice, such as through filing a grievance, will exceed the value to be gained from exercising voice, or that a particular episode of unfair workplace treatment is not substantial or severe enough to warrant filing a grievance. This reasoning also applies to certain non-workplace examples discussed by F&M (pp. 7–8), such as when a diner whose soup is too salty decides neither to complain nor to stop patronizing the restaurant, or when an unhappy couple choose neither to argue nor seek divorce. Silence as a response option in the face of unfair workplace treatment is further supported by the finding that older, more experienced workers are less likely to file grievances than younger, less experienced workers. The inference from this finding is that age and experience bring with them a certain maturity such that not every instance of unfair treatment is regarded as serious enough to merit exit (quitting) or voice (filing a grievance) or incurring the risks of either choice.

F&M's particular interpretation of the deteriorated state condition of Hirschman's framework may also in part be responsible for their portrayal of unions as typically battling overzealous, combative employers as well as for their call for labor law reform to, in effect, increase unionization. If the deteriorated state of worker's relationships with their employers is indeed the primary motivation — the antecedent condition — for such workers to unionize and negotiate with employers to reach collective agreements that contain formal grievance procedures, unionization and grievance procedures are in effect reactive institutional mechanisms in so far as conflict and dispute resolution are concerned. Positioned this way, union-management bargaining and labor relations are more likely to be adversarial than cooperative, and grievance filing reflects a relatively negative exercise of voice, especially if such voice is exercised in a pluralist, mixed-motive type of employment relationship.[11] By contrast, and as noted earlier, much of the research on and practice of high-involvement human resource management as well as ADR that has evolved over the last two decades or so, and that focuses primarily on nonunion firms and workers, can be said to reflect a unitarist conception of the employment relationships featuring relatively more proactive, positive approaches to workplace conflict and dispute resolution — approaches that may also presuppose a relatively high degree of worker loyalty to the employer/firm and a relatively high degree of worker interest in intrinsic rewards (Benabou and Tirole, 2003).

This contrast not only provides a basis for assessing F&M's larger conclusion that "the voice/response face of unions dominates the monopoly face" (p. 20), but also for assessing F&M's normative judgment that "the ongoing decline in private sector unionism...deserves serious public attention as being socially undesirable" (p. 251). It is quite clear — and F&M helped to make it clear — that the monopoly face of unionism has contributed to the sharp decline in worker unionization. This monopoly face plays out such that while unions achieve higher, above market, collectively bargained pay and benefit rates for their members, unionism is also significantly negatively associated with firms' research and development expenditures, capital investment, profitability, and market value. Union firms thus have incentives to reduce the employment of union workers, shift work to nonunion workers and to lower (labor) cost regions and nations, substitute capital and technology for union labor, and even exit a business or industry segment altogether.[12] And, if these incentives were present when F&M's book appeared, they have surely grown stronger in light of the rapid increases in global competition, deregulation, and technological change that occurred since then. It is hardly surprising, therefore, that nonunion firms strongly resist the unionization of unorganized workers.

F&M went further, however, and claimed, "managerial opposition to unionism has increased by leaps and bounds" (p. 230). Writing 15 years later, Freeman and Rogers (1999) went still further and concluded, "the main reason . . . workers are not union is that the management of their firms does not want them to be represented by a union" (p. 89). In this regard, Freeman and Rogers' (1989) survey data indicated that 40 percent or more of nonunion workers want union representation. On the one hand, there is little question that F&M as well as Freeman and Rogers are correct in emphasizing employer opposition to unions as an important contributing factor to the decline in unionization — an argument also made by numerous other industrial relations scholars. On the other hand, because industrial relations research has long emphasized employer opposition as an important barrier to union growth, it is questionable whether such opposition is quantitatively or qualitatively different today (or when F&M wrote their book) from earlier periods. Indeed, it may validly be argued that employer opposition to worker unionization is a constant or enduring feature of U.S. industrial relations.

Let us suppose, however, that there is another dynamic at work in all of this, namely, the worker as a "customer" or potential customer of a union. As with a firm that is unable to attract customers or whose customers switch (exit) to other firms or choose to stop purchasing a particular product entirely, a union that is unable to attract worker-members or whose members choose to sever their membership or work elsewhere must consider the underlying reasons for such behavior. From this perspective, and consistent with F&M's reasoning, workers, like employers/managers, learn about the monopoly face of unionism and decide that union membership is, on balance, too costly. In addition, however, and consistent with the reasoning advanced in this paper, workers learn about the collective voice/institutional response face of unionism and decide that union membership is, on balance, similarly too costly. From this perspective, the decline of private sector unionism continues in part because of worker preferences rather than, or in addition to, rising employer opposition to unionism. Following this reasoning, F&M's recommendations for revising labor law, strengthening unions' voice/response face, and weakening unions' monopoly face are also unlikely to reverse unionism's decline.[13]

In retrospect, there is no question that F&M (1984) produced one of those rare, admirable books that importantly influences a field of scholarly inquiry, shapes the types of questions posed by scholars in that field, explicitly (and readably) argues a particular point of view about the key issue under study, draws clear conclusions from the evidence assembled for the study, and offers specific recommendations for public and private action regarding the key issue. In all these respects and more, F&M's book is a hallmark of industrial relations scholarship.

A related hallmark of scholarship, however, is critique, new analysis, and re-assessment of received knowledge. In these respects, I have argued that F&M's theoretical perspective on conflict and dispute resolution, conclusions about the collective voice/institutional response face of unionism, and recommendations for public and private action to reverse the decline of unionism, are for the most part not supported by the scholarly research that has appeared since the publication of *What Do Unions Do?*.

Notes

* The helpful comments of Corinne Bendersky, Sanford Jacoby, and Bruce E. Kaufman on earlier versions of this manuscript are gratefully acknowledged, as is the research assistance of Wei Hua.

1. Space limitations preclude discussion of other discipline or problem-based approaches to the study of conflict and dispute resolution, including organizational psychology (Nye, 1973; Leavitt, 1964) and sociology (Pondy, 1967; March and Simon, 1958), game theory (Shubik, 1964; Luce and Raiffa, 1957), labor relations (Kochan and Verma, 1983; Barbash, 1964), bargaining and negotiation (Ertel, 2000; Lax and Sebenius, 1986; Chamberlain and Kuhn, 1965; Dunlop and Healy, 1953), international relations (Ikle, 1964; Schelling, 1960) and third-party dispute resolution (Stevens, 1963; Kagel, 1961). For a review, see Lewicki et al. (1992).

2. Following F&M, union-induced reductions in quits and increases in job tenure should provide incentives to employers to invest more heavily in human capital (through training, for example), with consequent productivity increases. But as Addison and Belfield (2004) observe, "we can . . . credit unions with lower turnover. But it may be a modest victory . . . we do not know whether the reduction in quits is optimal or, expressed another way, whether it adds materially to productivity. Nor for that matter is the basis for any such effect transparent. This is most obviously the case because of seemingly greater dissatisfaction of union workers" (p. 21).

3. This litigation threat also strongly implies that, among nonunion firms with dispute resolution procedures, the proportion of those procedures that include arbitration as a settlement step will rise considerably beyond the one-sixth to one-third of such procedures presently estimated to contain an arbitration step.

4. Though ancillary to the focus of this paper, F&M's characterization (pp. 103–104) of seniority-based personnel policies as a union-induced innovation seems misplaced. While initially observing that "one of the major differences between union and nonunion work settings is the greater importance of seniority under unionism" (p. 135), F&M later say, "some nonunion firms place as much weight on seniority in layoffs as do union firms" (p. 154). This suggests that seniority-based personnel policies are not a union-induced innovation. Support for this view is provided by Selznick (1969), who found that seniority was the- principle criterion used by nonunion firms (and by partially union firms for their nonunion workers) to make promotion, layoff, transfer, work assignment, and other personnel decisions.

5. Notable as well is the finding from several studies of grievance dynamics in union and nonunion firms that younger workers are significantly more likely than older workers to file grievances (Lewin, 1999; Lewin and Peterson, 1988; Labig and Greer,

1988). This finding runs counter to F&M's argument that the grievance procedure is a conflict resolution mechanism especially favored by older, more permanent, inframarginal workers.

6. Hirschman's concept of loyalty appears one-dimensional, that is, focused on a customer's loyalty to the firm or a citizen's loyalty to the community. In the employment context this translates into a worker's loyalty to the employer, and empirical studies of grievance behavior that rely in part or in whole on Hirschman's framework are also one-dimensional in that they measure only worker loyalty to the employer (Boroff and Lewin, 1997; Lewin and Boroff, 1996). In union settings, however, it would be possible to measure dual loyalty, that is, worker loyalty to the employer and to the union. This would enable comparisons of union-nonunion worker loyalty to the employer to determine if such loyalty is moderated by loyalty to the union and how, if at all, dual loyalty is related to worker choice of voice or exit behavior. On the modeling and measurement of dual loyalty to the employer and union, see Magenau and Martin (1999) and Fullager (1991).

7. That this reprisal explanation applies even more strongly to supervisors of union grievance filers than to the grievance filers themselves is reflected in the post-grievance settlement turnover analysis conducted by Lewin and Peterson (1999). That analysis found significantly higher involuntary turnover, that is, termination, among supervisors of grievance filers than among supervisors of non-filers, and a significant negative regression coefficient on a supervisor grievance procedure involvement variable in an involuntary turnover equation but not in a voluntary turnover equation. By comparison, grievance filers had significantly higher voluntary but not involuntary turnover rates than non-filers in the post-grievance settlement period, and significant positive regression coefficients on a worker grievance filing variable were found in separate total turnover and voluntary turnover equations.

8. Unlike in the union firms, however, supervisors of grievance filers in the non-union firms had significantly higher voluntary *and* involuntary post-grievance settlement turnover rates than supervisors of non-filers. When combined with findings from the union firms, this evidence suggests that supervisors of union grievance filers are more likely to experience reprisal, specifically in the form of termination, than supervisors of nonunion grievance filers. Because supervisors are not covered by the grievance procedures in union firms but are often covered by such procedures in nonunion firms, these findings further suggest that, by sharpening the distinction between workers and supervisors, unionism increases the probability that supervisors will be terminated for their "involvement" in grievance activity.

9. A similar conclusion is reached by Belman (1992), whose review of the literature on grievance procedure usage and manufacturing plant performance emphasizes the grievance rate as a measure of labor-management relationship conflict. One study (Kleiner et al., 1995) found that the lowest levels of labor costs in aerospace manufacturing plants were associated with moderate (rather than low) levels of grievance activity.

10. This observation is also relevant for assessing empirical studies of grievance initiation and settlement, most of which fail to distinguish among workers who have and have not experienced employment relationship deterioration (for an exception, see Boroff and Lewin, 1997).

11. It may also be useful in this regard to think of strikes as a "macro" form of employee voice, as compared with grievance filing as "micro" form of employee voice. Both forms manifest conflict that requires resolution, with strikes more clearly reflecting

the mix of voice and power and the tendency of union-management relations to be adversarial. That, as noted earlier, grievance filing by union workers increases as the time to re-negotiate a collective bargaining agreement draws nearer further supports the notion that grievance procedures largely operate in and contribute to an adversarial labor-management climate. Thanks to a referee for suggesting this macro-micro distinction.

12. F&M (1984) contend that unionism increases worker productivity, which, ceteris paribus, should reduce employer opposition to unionism and perhaps even stimulate employer support for unionization. But of course union-induced increases in productivity must be offset against union-induced increases in labor costs. If the net effect is to reduce unit labor costs, employers should support worker unionization; if the net effect is to increase unit labor costs, employers should oppose unionization. The sharp decline in the unionization of U.S. workers implies that unit labor costs, on balance, increase under unionism.

13. While labor law has not been revised since publication of F&M's (1984) book, employment laws such as the (1964) Civil Rights Act and the (1970) Employee Retirement Income Security Act have been revised, and new laws, such as the (1993) Family and Medical Leave Act, have been enacted. The extent to which such legislation is effective in protecting employee rights and resolving employment-related conflicts is, to this point, an open question, as is the relative effectiveness of legislation, unionism and ADR in these respects.

References

Adams, Roy. *Grievance Arbitration of Discharge Cases: A Study of the Concepts of Industrial Discipline and Their Results.* Kingston, Ont., Canada: Industrial Relations Center, 1979.

Addison, John T. and Clive R. Belfield. "Union Voice." *Journal of Labor Research* 25 (Fall 2004): 563–96.

Amason, Allenan C. "Distinguishing the Effects of Functional and Dysfunctional Conflict on Strategic Decision Making: Resolving a Paradox for Top Management Teams." *Academy of Management Journal* 39 (February 1996): 123–48.

Arthur, Jeffrey B. "Effects of Human Resource Systems on Manufacturing Performance and Turnover." *Academy of Management Journal* 37 (September 1994): 670–87.

Arthur, Jeffrey B. "The Link Between Business Strategy and Industrial Relations Systems in American Steel Minimills." *Industrial and Labor Relations Review* 45 (April 1992): 488–506.

Arvey, Richard D. and Anthony P. Jones. "The Uses of Discipline in Organizational Settings." In Barry M. Staw and Larry L. Cummings, eds. *Research in Organizational Behavior.* Vol. 7. Greenwich, CT: JAI Press, 1985, pp. 367–408.

Barbash, Jack. "The Elements of Industrial Relations." *British Journal of Industrial Relations* 2 (March 1964): 66–78.

Barnacle, Peter J. *Arbitration of Discharge Grievances in Ontario: Outcomes and Reinstatement Experiences.* Kingston, Ont., Canada: Industrial Relations Center, Queens University, 1991.

Batt, Rosemary. "Work Organization, Technology, and Performance in Customer Service and Sales." *Industrial and Labor Relations Review* 52 (July 1999): 539–64.

_____, Alexander J.S. Colvin, and Jeffrey Keefe. "Employee Voice, Human Resource Practices, and Quit Rates: Evidence from the Telecommunications Industry." *Industrial and Labor Relations Review* 55 (July 2002): 573–94.

Bazerman, Max H. and Margaret A. Neale. *Negotiating Rationally.* New York: Free Press, 1992.

Belman, Dale. "Unions, the Quality of Labor Relations, and Firm Performance." In Lawrence Mishel and Paula B. Voos, eds. *Unions and Economic Competitiveness.* Armonk, NY: M.E. Sharpe, 1992, pp. 41–107.

Bendersky, Corinne. "Conflict and Control: Control System Constraints on Conflict Behaviors in Organizations." *Academy of Management Review* 28 (October 2003): 643–56.

Bemmels, Brian. "The Determinants of Grievance Initiation." *Industrial and Labor Relations Review* 47 (January 1994): 285–301.

———— and James Foley. "Grievance Procedure Research: A Review and Theoretical Recommendations." *Journal of Management* 22 (September 1996): 359–84.

Bemmels, Brian, Yusef Sheref, and Kaye Stratton-Devine. "The Roles of Supervisors, Employees, and Stewards in Grievance Initiation." *Industrial and Labor Relations Review* 45 (October 1991): 15–30.

Benabou, Roland and Jean Tirole. "Intrinsic and Extrinsic Motivation." *Review of Economic Studies* 70 (July 2003): 489–520.

Bendix, Reinhard. *Work and Authority in Industry.* New York: Wiley, 1956.

Bingham, Lisa B. and Denise R. Chachere. "Dispute Resolution in Employment: The Need for Research." In Adrienne E. Eaton and Jeffrey H. Keefe eds. *Employment Dispute Resolution and Worker Rights in the Changing Workplace.* Champaign, IL.: Industrial Relations Research Association, 1999, pp. 95–135.

Boroff, Karen E. and David Lewin. "Loyalty, Voice, and Intent to Exit a Union Firm: A Conceptual and Empirical Analysis." *Industrial and Labor Relations Review* 51 (October 1997): 50–63.

Cappelli, Peter and Keith Chauvin. "A Test of an Efficiency Model of Grievance Activity." *Industrial and Labor Relations Review* 45 (January 1991): 3–14.

Cappelli, Peter and N. Rogovsky. "Employee Involvement and Organizational Citizenship: Implications for Labor Law Reform." *Industrial and Labor Relations Review* 51 (July 1998): 633–53.

Chamberlain, Neil W. *The Union Challenge to Management Control.* New York: Harper, 1948.

———— and James W. Kuhn. *Collective Bargaining*, 2nd ed. New York: McGraw-Hill, 1965.

Chaney, William. "The Reinstatement Remedy Revisited." *Labor Law Journal* 32 (August 1981): 357–75.

Commons, John R. *The Economics of Collective Action.* New York: Free Press, 1928.

————. *Institutional Economics: Its Place in the Political Economy.* New York: Macmillan, 1934.

Colvin, Alexander J.S. "Adoption and Use of Dispute Resolution Procedures in the Nonunion Workplace." In David Lewin and Bruce E. Kaufman, eds. *Advances in Industrial and Labor Relations.* Vol. 13. London, UK: Elsevier, 2004, pp. 71–97.

————. "Institutional Pressures, Human Resource Strategies, and the Rise of Nonunion Dispute Resolution Procedures." *Industrial and Labor Relations Review* 56 (April 2003): 375–92.

Cutcher-Gernshenfeld, Joel. "The Impact on Economic Performance of a Transformation in Workplace Relations." *Industrial and Labor Relations Review* 44 (January 1991): 241–60.

Delery, John E., Nina Gupta, J. Douglas Shaw, J.R. Jenkins, and Margot L. Ganster. "Unionization, Compensation, and Voice Effects on Quits and Retention." *Industrial Relations* 39 (October 2000): 625–45.

Dickens, Linda, Moira Hart, Malcom Jones, and Brian Weekes. "The British Experience under a Statute Prohibiting Unfair Dismissal." *Industrial and Labor Relations Review* 37 (July 1984): 497–514.

Druckman, D., ed. *Negotiations, Social-Psychological Perspectives*. Beverly Hills, Calif.: Sage, 1977.

Dunlop, John T. *Industrial Relations Systems*. New York: Holt, 1958.

_____. *Wage Determination Under Trade Unions*. New York: Macmillan, 1944.

_____ and James J. Healy. *Collective Bargaining: Principles and Cases*, rev. ed. Homewood, IL.: Irwin, 1953.

Eaton, Adrienne A. and Paula B. Voos. "Productivity-Enhancing Innovations in Work Organization, Compensation, and Employee Participation in the Union Versus the Nonunion Sectors." In David Lewin and Donna Sockell, eds. *Advances in Industrial and Labor Relations*. Vol. 6. Greenwich, CT: JAI Press, 1994, pp. 63–109.

_____. "Unions and Contemporary Innovations in Work Organization, Compensation, and Employee Participation." In Lawrence Mishel and Paula B. Voos, eds. *Unions and Economic Competitiveness*. New York: M.E. Sharpe, 1992, pp. 173–215.

Edelman, Lauren B. "Legal Environments and Organizational Governance: The Expansion of Due Process in the American Workplace." *American Journal of Sociology* 95 (May 1990): 1401–40.

Ewing, David W. *Justice on the Job: Resolving Grievances in the Nonunion Workplace*. Boston, MA: Harvard Business School Press, 1989.

Ertel, Danny. "Turning Negotiations into a Corporate Capability." *Harvard Business Review* 77 (May-June 1999): 55–64.

Fernie, Sue and David Metcalf. "The Organisational Ombuds: Implications for Voice, Conflict Resolution and Fairness at Work." In David Lewin and Bruce E. Kaurman, eds. *Advances in Industrial and Labor Relations*, Vol. 13. London: Elsevier, 2004, pp. 99–137.

Feuille, Peter. "Grievance Mediation." In Adrienne E. Eaton and Jeffrey H. Keefe, eds. *Employment Dispute Resolution and Worker Rights in the Changing Workplace*. Champaign, IL.: Industrial Relations Research Association, 1999, pp. 187–217.

_____ and Denise R. Chachere. "Looking Fair or Being Fair: Remedial Voice Procedures in Nonunion Workplaces." *Journal of Management* 21 (March 1995): 27–42.

Feuille, Peter and John T. Delaney. "The Individual Pursuit of Organizational Justice: Grievance Procedures in Nonunion Workplaces." In *Research in Personnel and Human Resource Management*. Vol. 10. Greenwich, CT.: JAI, 1992, pp. 187–232.

Freeman, Richard B. "The Exit-Voice Trade-off in the Labor Market: Unionism, Job Tenure, Quits, and Separations." *Quarterly Journal of Economics* 94 (September 1980): 643–73.

_____ and James L. Medoff. *What Do Unions Do?* New York: Basic Books, 1984.

Freeman, Richard B. and Joel Rodgers. *What Workers Want*. Ithaca, NY: Cornell University Press, 1999.

Fullager, Clive. "Predictors and Outcomes of Different Patterns of Organizational and Union Loyalty." *Journal of Occupational Psychology* 64 (June 1991): 129–43.

Hirschman, Albert O. *Exit, Voice and Loyalty: Responses to Decline in Firms, Organizations and States*. Cambridge, MA: Harvard University Press, 1970.

Huselid, Mark A. "The Impact of Human Resource Management Practices on Turnover, Productivity, and Corporate Financial Performance." *Academy of Management Journal* 38 (June 1995): 635–72.

Ichniowski, Casey. "Human Resource Practices and Productive Labor-Management Relations." In David Lewin, Olivia S. Mitchell and Peter D. Sherer, eds. *Research Frontiers in Industrial Relations and Human Resources*. Madison, WI: Industrial Relations Research Association, 1992, pp. 239–71.

_____. "The Effects of Grievance Activity on Productivity." *Industrial and Labor Relations Review* 40 (October 1986): 75–89.

_____, John T. Delaney, and David Lewin. "The New Human Resource Management in U.S. Workplaces: Is It Really New and Is It Only Nonunion?" *Relations Industrielles/Industrial Relations* 44 (Winter 1989): 97–119.

Ichniowski, Casey, Thomas A. Kochan, David Levine, Craig Olson, and George Strauss. "What Works at Work: Overview and Assessment." *Industrial Relations* 35 (Fall 1996): 356–74.

Ichniowski, Casey, Katherine Shaw, and Giovanni Prennushi. "The Effects of Human Resource Management Practices on Productivity: A Study of Steel Finishing Lines." *American Economic Review* 87 (June 1997): 291–313.

Ikle, Fred C. *How Nations Negotiate*. New York: Harper and Row, 1964.

Jehn, Karen. "A Multimethod Examination of the Benefits and Detriments of Intragroup Conflict." *Administrative Science Quarterly* 40 (June 1995): 256–82.

_____. "A Quantitative Analysis of Conflict Types and Dimensions in Organizational Groups." *Administrative Science Quarterly* 42 (September 1997): 530–57.

_____ and Elizabeth A. Mannix. "The Dynamic Nature of Conflict: A Longitudinal Study of Intragroup Conflict and Group Performance." *Academy of Management Journal* 44 (April 2001): 238–51.

Kagel, Samuel. *Anatomy of a Labor Arbitration*. New York: BNA Books, 1961.

Kahneman, Daniel and Amos Taversky. "Prospect Theory: An Analysis of Decision under Risk." *Econometrica* 47 (June 1979): 263–91.

Kakalik James, Terence Dunworth, Laurel Hill, Daniel McCaffrey, Marian Oshiro, Nicholas M. Pace, and Mary Vaiana. *An Evaluation of Mediation and Early Neutral Evaluation under the Civil Justice Reform Act*. Santa Monica, CA: Rand Institute for Civil Justice, 1996.

Kaminski, Michelle. "New Forms of Work Organization and Their Impact on the Grievance Procedure." In Adrienne E. Eaton and Jeffrey H. Keefe, eds. *Employment Dispute Resolution and Worker Rights in the Changing Workplace*. Champaign, IL: Industrial Relations Research Association, 1999, pp. 219–46.

Katz, Harry C., Thomas A. Kochan, and Mark R. Weber. "Assessing the Effects of Industrial Relations and Quality of Work Life Efforts on Organizational Effectiveness." *Academy of Management Journal* 28 (July 1985): 509–27.

Katz, Harry C., Thomas A. Kochan, and Kenneth R. Gobeille. "Industrial Relations Performance, Economic Performance, and QWL Programs: An Interplant Analysis." *Industrial and Labor Relations Review* 37 (January 1983): 3–17.

Kaufman, Bruce E. "The Employee Participation/Representation Gap: An Assessment and Proposed Solution." *University of Pennsylvania Journal of Labor and Employment Law* 3 (2001): 491–92.

_____ and David Lewin. "Is the NLRA Still Relevant to Today's Economy and Workplace?" *Labor Law Journal* 49 (September 1998): 1113–26.

Kaufman, Bruce E. and Daphne G. Taras. "Nonunion Employee Representation: Findings and Conclusions." In Bruce Kaufman and Daphne Taras, eds. *Nonunion Employee Representation: History, Contemporary Practice, and Policy*. Armonk, NY: M.E. Sharpe, 2000, pp. 527–57.

Kerr, Clark, ed. *Labor and Management in Industrial Society*. New York: Doubleday-Anchor, 1964.

Kleiner, Morris M., Gary Nickelsburg, and Adam Pilarski. "Monitoring, Grievances, and Plant Performance." *Industrial Relations* 34 (April 1995): 169–89.

Kochan, Thomas A. and Anil M. Verma. "Negotiations in Organizations: Blending Industrial Relations and Organizational Behavior Approaches." In Max A. Bazerman and Roy J. Lewicki, eds. *Negotiations in Organizations*. Beverly Hills, CA: Sage, 1983, pp. 13–32.

Kochan, Thomas A., Brian Lautsch, and Corinne Bendersky. "An Evaluation of the Massachusetts Commission Against Discrimination's Alternative Dispute Resolution Program." *Harvard Negotiation Law Review* 5 (2000): 233–78.

Kolb, Debra M. and Jean M. Bartunek. *Hidden Conflict in Organizations: Uncovering Behind-the-Scenes Disputes.* Newbury Park, CA: Sage, 1992.

Kornhauser, Arthur, Robert Dubin, and Arthur M. Ross. *Industrial Conflict.* New York: McGraw-Hill, 1954.

Kuhn, James W. *Bargaining in Grievance Settlement: The Power of Industrial Work Groups.* New York: Columbia University Press, 1961.

Labig, Chalmer E. Jr., I.B. Helburn, and Robert C. Rogers. "Discipline History, Seniority, and Reason for Discharge as Predictors of Postreinstatement of Job Performance." *Arbitration Journal* 40 (September 1985): 44–52.

Lax, David and Sebenius, James K. *The Manager As Negotiator: Bargaining for Cooperation and Competitive Gain.* New York: Free Press, 1986.

Leavitt, Harold J. *Managerial Psychology*, rev. ed. Chicago: University of Chicago Press, 1964.

Levine, David I. *Reinventing the Workplace.* Washington, DC: Brookings Institution, 1995.

Lewicki, Roy J., Stephen E. Weiss, and David Lewin. "Models of Conflict, Negotiation and Third Party Intervention: A Review and Synthesis." *Journal of Organizational Behavior* 13 (Fall 1992): 209–52.

Lewicki, Roy J., Bruce Barry, David M. Saunders, and John W. Minton. *Negotiation*, 4th ed. Boston: McGraw Hill Irwin, 2003.

Lewin, David. "Dispute Resolution in Nonunion Organizations: Key Empirical Findings." In Samuel Estreicher, ed., *Alternative Dispute Resolution in the Employment Arena.* New York: Kluwer, 2004, pp. 379–403.

_____. "IR and HR Perspectives on Workplace Conflict: What Can Each Learn from the Other?" *Human Resource Management Review* 11 (Fall 2001): 453–85.

_____. "Theoretical and Empirical Research on the Grievance Procedure and Arbitration: A Critical Review." In Adrienne E. Eaton and Jeffrey H. Keefe, eds. *Employment Dispute Resolution and Worker Rights in the Changing Workplace.* Champaign, IL.: Industrial Relations Research Association, 1999, pp. 137–86.

_____ and Richard B. Peterson. "Behavioral Outcomes of Grievance Activity." *Industrial Relations* 38 (October 1999): 554–76.

Lewin, David and Karen E. Boroff. "The Role of Exit in Loyalty and Voice." *Advances in Industrial and Labor Relations*, Vol. 7. Greenwich, CT: JAI Press, 1996, pp. 69–96.

Lewin, David. "Conflict Resolution and Management in Contemporary Work Organizations: Theoretical Perspectives and Empirical Evidence." *Research in the Sociology of Organizations.* Greenwich, CT: JAI Press, 1993, pp. 167–209.

_____. "Conflict Resolution in Nonunion Workplaces: An Empirical Analysis of Usage, Dynamics, and Outcomes." *Chicago-Kent Law Review* 66 (September 1992): 823–44.

_____ and Richard B. Peterson. *The Modern Grievance Procedure in the United States.* Westport, CT.: Quorum, 1988.

_____. "Conflict Resolution in the Nonunion Firm: A Theoretical and Empirical Analysis." *Journal of Conflict Resolution* 31 (September 1987): 465–502.

Lipsky, David and Ronald Seeber. *The Appropriate Resolution of Corporate Disputes: A Report on the Growing Use of ADR by US Corporations.* Ithaca, NY: Cornell/PERC Institute on Conflict Resolution, 1998.

Luce, Robert D. and Howard Raiffa. *Games and Decisions.* New York: Wiley, 1957.

MacDuffie, John-Paul. "Human Resource Bundles and Manufacturing Performance: Organizational Logic and Flexible Production Systems in the World Auto Industry." *Industrial and Labor Relations Review* 48 (January 1995): 197–221.

Magenau, John M. and James E. Martin. "Dual and Unilateral Loyalty: Methodological, Conceptual, and Practical Issues." In David Lewin and Bruce E. Kaufman, eds. *Advances in Industrial and Labor Relations*, Vol. 9. Greenwich, CT: JAI Press, 1999, pp. 183–210.

Malinowski, Arthur A. "An Empirical Analysis of Discharge Cases and the Work History of Employees Reinstated by Labor Arbitration." *Dispute Resolution* 36 (March 1981): 31–46.

March, James G. and Herbert R. Simon. *Organizations*. New York: Wiley, 1958.

Mareschal, Patrice M. "Resolving Conflict: Tactics of Federal Mediators." In David Lewin and Bruce E. Kaufman, eds. *Advances in Industrial and Labor Relations,* Vol. 11. Oxford, UK: Elsevier, 2002, pp. 41–68.

McCabe, Douglas M. *Corporate Nonunion Complaint Procedures and Systems.* New York: Praeger, 1988.

McDermott, E. Patrick, Anita Jose, Ruth Obar, Mollie Bowers, and Brian Polkinghorn. "Has the EEOC Hit a Home Run? An Evaluation of the Equal Employment Opportunity Commission Mediation Program From the Participants' Perspective." In David Lewin and Bruce E. Kaufman, eds. *Advances in Industrial and Labor Relations*, Vol. 11. Oxford, UK: Elsevier, 2002, pp. 1–40.

Mitchell, Daniel J.B., David Lewin, and Edward E. Lawler, III. "Alternative Pay Systems, Firm Performance, and Productivity." In Alan S. Blinder, ed. *Paying for Productivity: A Look at the Evidence.* Washington, DC: Brookings Institution, 1990, pp. 15–94.

Nash, John. "The Bargaining Problem." *Econometrica* 18 (1950): 155–62.

Norsworthy, James R. and Craig A. Zabala. "Worker Attitudes, Worker Behavior, and Productivity in the U.S. Automobile Industry, 1959–1976." *Industrial and Labor Relations Review* 38 (July 1985): 544–57.

O'Reilly, Charles A. and Barton A. Weitz. "Managing Marginal Employees: The Use of Warnings and Dismissals." *Administrative Science Quarterly* 25 (June 1980): 467–84.

Ponak, Allen. "Discharge Arbitration and Reinstatement in the Province of Alberta." *Arbitration Journal* 42 (August 1987): 39–46.

Pondy, Louis R. "Organizational Conflict." *Administrative Science Quarterly* 12 (June 1967): 296–320.

Pruitt, Dean. *Negotiation Behavior.* New York: Academic Press, 1981.

Rocella, Martin. "The Reinstatement of Dismissed Employees in Italy: An Empirical Analysis." *Comparative Labor Law Journal* 10 (June 1989): 166–95.

Ross, Arthur. *Trade Union Wage Policy.* Berkeley, CA: University of California Press, 1948.

Rees, Albert J. *The Economics of Trade Unions.* Chicago: University of Chicago Press, 1962.

Rusbelt, Caryl E., Dan Farrell, Glen Rogers, and Arch G. Mainous, III. "Impact of Variables on Exit, Voice, Loyalty and Neglect: An Integrative Model of Responses to Declining Job Satisfaction." *Academy of Management Journal* 31 (September 1988): 599–627.

Sayles, Leonard R. *Behavior of Industrial Work Groups.* New York: McGraw-Hill, 1956.

Schein, Edgar. *Process Consultation.* Reading, Mass.: Addison Wesley, 1969.

Schelling, Thomas. *The Strategy of Conflict.* New York: Academic Press, 1960.

Selznick, Phillip O., with the collaboration of Philippe Nonet and Howard M. Vollmer. *Law, Society, and Industrial Justice.* New York: Sage, 1969.

Shantz, Edward and Richard Rogow. "Post-Reinstatement Experience: A British Columbia Study." Paper presented at the annual meeting of the Canadian Industrial
Relations Association, Guelph, 1984.

Sheppard, Blair H. "Third Party Conflict Intervention: A Procedural Framework." In
Max A. Bazerman and Roy J. Lewicki, eds. *Research in Organizational Behavior*,
Vol. 6. Greenwich, CT: JAI Press, 1984, pp. 141–89.

_____, Roy J. Lewicki, and John W. Minton. *Organizational Justice: The Search for
Fairness in the Workplace*. New York: Lexington, 1992.

Shubik, Martin. *Game Theory and Related Approaches to Social Behavior*. New York:
Wiley, 1964.

Siegel, S. and Lawrence Fouraker. *Bargaining Behavior*. New York: McGraw-Hill,
1960.

Slichter, Sumner. "The Current Labor Policies of American Industries." *Quarterly Journal
of Economics* 43 (May 1929): 393–435.

_____. *Union Policies and Industrial Management*. Washington, DC: Brookings
Institution, 1941.

Stephens, Edward and William Chaney. "A Study of the Reinstatement Remedy under the
National Labor Relations Act." *Labor Law Journal* 25 (November 1974): 31–41.

Stevens, Carl M. *Strategy and Collective Bargaining Negotiation*. New York: McGraw-
Hill, 1963.

Stewart, Gary L. and James A. Davy. "An Empirical Examination of Resolution and
Filing Rates in the Public and Private Sector." *Journal of Collective Negotiations*
21 (August 1992): 323–35.

Stone, Katherine V.W. "Employment Arbitration under the Federal Arbitration Act." In
Adrienne E. Eaton and Jeffery H. Keefe, eds. *Employment Dispute Resolution and
Worker Rights in the Changing Workplace*. Champaign, IL.: Industrial Relations
Research Association, 1999, pp. 27–65.

U.S. General Accounting Office. *Alternative Dispute Resolution: Employers' Experiences
with ADR in the Workplace*. GAO/GGD–97–157. Washington, DC: GAO, 1997.

Walton, Richard E. *Interpersonal Peacemaking*. Reading, Mass.: Addison-Wesley,
1969.

_____ and Robert B. McKersie. *A Behavioral Theory of Labor Negotiations*. New
York: McGraw-Hill, 1965.

Westin, Alan F. and Alfred G. Felieu. *Resolving Employment Disputes without Litigation*. Washington, DC: Bureau of National Affairs, 1988.

Williams, Keith and Donald Lewis. "Legislating for Job Security: The British Experience of Reinstatement and Reengagement." *Employee Relations Law Journal* 8
(March 1982): 482–504.

Zeuthen, F. *Problems of Monopoly and Economic Warfare*. London, UK: Routledge &
Kegan, 1930.

11

The Impact of Unions on Job Satisfaction, Organizational Commitment, and Turnover

*Tove Helland Hammer and Ariel Avgar**

I. Introduction

The purpose of unions is to further the economic interests of their members by negotiating on their behalf over terms and conditions of employment. People join unions both to rectify dissatisfying circumstances and to increase the gains from employment. A pro-union vote is determined primarily by job dissatisfaction and a belief that the union will be able to improve one's work life by ensuring higher wages and benefits, job security, and protection against arbitrary and unjust treatment (Getman et al., 1976; Hammer and Berman, 1981; Zalesny, 1985). According to the neoclassical economic model of union joining, workers choose union jobs over nonunion jobs because the former will have higher utility, which has certainly been born out with respect to wages, benefits, and pensions (Farber and Kruger, 1993; Hirsch and Macpherson, 1998; Hirsch and Schumacher, 2002). In addition, union jobs entail social benefits in the form of a system of due process and participation in decisions about employment and working conditions.

Union membership is not a free good, however. It carries both economic and social costs. The most obvious economic costs to the individual worker are union dues and potential loss of income due to strikes. In addition, job security, supposedly a benefit of union status, is not a certainty for all members. The monopolistic model of unions shows that they lower the demand for union labor by raising wage rates above competitive levels, which results in a shift of jobs to the nonunion labor force (Farber, 1986; Hirsch and Addison, 1986; Addison and Chilton, 1997). This increases the probability that low-seniority union workers may lose their jobs the more unions are achieving success in increasing the wage premium (Kleiner, 2002; Thieblot, 2002).[1] The social costs of union status can include a more adversarial relationship with the employer, a more rigid or bureaucratic organization of work, and more narrowly defined job tasks with less individual discretion.

One can look at union joining as an asset purchase (Pencavel, 1971). As long as the benefits outweigh the costs, and there are no alternative ways of obtaining the benefits at lower costs, there should be a queue of workers wanting union jobs (Abowd and Farber, 1982). Although the gap between union and nonunion wages has narrowed over time, and there are substitutes available for at least some of the services unions provide (Bennett and Taylor, 2002; Fiorito, 2002), there is still an economic advantage to union status (Farber and Western, 2002). Thus, the utility of union jobs should exceed the utility of nonunion jobs, at least for those workers who retain their jobs in the face of a shrinking demand for union labor, and one would therefore expect union workers to be more satisfied with their jobs relative to nonunion workers (the Kaufman theory chapter in this volume). Attitude surveys among U.S. workers have shown repeatedly that it is the other way around: union workers report less overall job satisfaction than nonunion workers. Despite lower job satisfaction, however, union workers are less likely to quit (Freeman, 1978; Borjas, 1979; Kochan and Helfman, 1981; Leigh, 1986; Addison and Castro, 1987; Schwochau, 1987).[2] Recent studies in other countries have reported similar findings (Lincoln and Boothe, 1995; Renaud, 2002; Bryson et al., 2003).

The data show that union workers are at least as satisfied with wages, benefits, and job security as are nonunion workers, but are less satisfied with supervision, job content (the nature of the tasks they are given to do, the skills required, and the freedom to make decisions about their job), the resources available to do their job, and opportunities for promotion (Freeman, 1978; Kochan and Helfman, 1981; Meng, 1990; Miller, 1990; Pfeffer and Davis-Blake, 1991; Lincoln and Boothe, 1995; Renaud, 2002; Bryson et al., 2003). When workers are asked about their overall, or general, job satisfaction, the negative job facets seem to outweigh the positive, resulting in the lower job satisfaction scores for union workers.

Two questions arise from these studies: Why are workers less satisfied with union jobs that, on the face of it, have higher utility than nonunion jobs, and why, if dissatisfied, do they stay? If we assume that union workers are rational economic actors and we assume a competitive labor market where jobs and workers are more or less identical, we would expect, if behavior follows attitudes, that dissatisfied union workers would leave the employer for more pleasant jobs.

II. The Exit-Voice Hypothesis

Freeman and Medoff (1984) suggested that one reason why union workers report less job satisfaction than nonunion workers is that union jobs are less attractive than comparable nonunion jobs on certain job dimensions, such as the quality of supervision, the nature of job tasks, or working conditions. Unpleasant jobs are more likely to lead to unionization to begin with, or the jobs may have become less attractive after unionization if management responded to higher labor costs by increasing demands for production and decreasing allocations to the physical work environment.

Their explanation for the attitude-behavior inconsistency is that union workers become primed to detect dissatisfying conditions in the workplace through the opportunity to bargain with the employer for improvements and the ability to grieve breaches in the union contract, essentially becoming politicized. But because the union also acts as a voice mechanism vis-à-vis management for its members' discontent, workers stay. The effect increases with exposure to, and experience in, the job, so tenure is negatively related to job satisfaction (Borjas, 1979).

The fact that workers do not quit when dissatisfied led Freeman and Medoff to argue that their expressed dissatisfaction does not indicate their true attitudes, but rather their politicization. In other words, if union workers were truly dissatisfied with their jobs, they would look for new ones. Nonunion workers, not being equally politicized and lacking both a voice mechanism and union protection, act on their discontent and quit, in full accordance with economic theory.

In the remainder of this article, we examine the different alternative explanations that have been offered to the exit-voice hypothesis and the research conducted to examine them. We then discuss the research findings in light of theoretical and empirical models of job satisfaction, turnover (quits), and absenteeism. We also briefly examine the relationship between unions and organizational commitment.

III. Alternative Explanations of the Union Effect on Job Satisfaction

A number of possible explanations have been offered for why union members would be less satisfied with their jobs than nonunion workers and also remain in their jobs.

An obvious hypothesis, suggested by Freeman and Medoff (1984), is selection — unions tend to organize among workers who have unpleasant, unsafe, and economically unrewarding jobs and who are therefore likely to vote the union in. Union status is thus a rational response to the objective characteristics of the job (reverse causality).

According to the exit-voice hypothesis, the dissatisfaction of union members does not come from the evaluation by workers of the tangible benefits of the job. Instead, it is the result of a psychological process whereby workers' own *experiences* of seeking redress, or *observing* others doing the same, become translated into attitudes — an inevitable and unanticipated consequence of working within structures and processes that demonstrate the conflicting interests of labor and management.

A third explanation for the negative union effect on job satisfaction is that union leaders "manufacture" discontent by raising members' expectations about job outcomes beyond what is realistic. Dissatisfaction comes from the knowledge that there is always something lacking in the job that the union will strive to attain in bargaining. This argument, which has its origin in Ross' (1948) political model of wage bargaining, is not part of Freeman and Medoff's (1984) thesis. The exit-voice model does not imply that union leaders, on purpose, encourage members to adopt a negative view of the workplace, even if they do provide workers an opportunity to remedy dissatisfying conditions. Union members' dissatisfaction comes from the fact that collective bargaining is adversarial. As others have argued, it would not make sense for union leaders to fuel discontent among their members after a certification election because they would only be reminding the workers that the union was not delivering on its promise to fix the problems it identified during the organizing campaign (Kochan and Helfman, 1981; Pfeffer and Davis-Blake, 1990; Barling et al., 1992; Gordon and DeNisi, 1995).

Other alternative explanations are based on theoretical and methodological objections to the studies used to support the exit-voice model, in particular, the argument that researchers did not control for the effects on job satisfaction of all the differences between union and nonunion jobs and other work environment factors.

A fourth hypothesis is that the negative union effect on job satisfaction arises from differences in the content, or nature, of union and nonunion jobs. If unions, through narrow job classifications and restrictive work rules, limit union workers' full use of their skills and abilities, and offer few opportunities for challenge, achievement, autonomy, and promotions, job satisfaction will suffer (Hackman and Oldham, 1980; Cranny et al., 1992).

A fifth hypothesis is that union and nonunion workers have different preferences for job outcomes or different frames of reference for evaluating job outcomes. The relevant argument is that unions "teach," or socialize, their members to value those facets of the job the unions aim to improve, viz., wages, hours, and working conditions (Berger et al., 1983; Barling et al., 1992), and, by implication, to downgrade those aspects of the work environment the unions have tended to ignore, such as job content. Unions also create more homogeneity among workers in terms of what they consider desirable or find satisfactory, which means that individual differences — an important determinant of job attitudes (Motowidlo, 1996) — will be less important in a union setting than in a nonunion workplace.

A sixth hypothesis is that differences in job satisfaction between union and nonunion workers occur because the industrial relations climate is poorer in union workplaces. Although part of the industrial relations climate is embedded in the exit-voice model through the conflictive nature of bargaining, labor-management relations are also a function of the levels of management's resistance to unionization and union leaders' willingness to work towards a collaborative relationship with the employer. Freeman and Rogers' (1999) national survey of what workers want in the way of workplace representation demonstrated the importance of positive labor-management relations for both union and nonunion workers. The hypothesis assumes that there is a main effect on job satisfaction of the industrial relations climate (Kochan and Helfman, 1981; Gordon and DeNisi, 1995; Kleiner, 2002).

A seventh explanation, which we can call the expanded utility hypothesis, is a merger of previous hypotheses with the utility concept.

Freeman and Medoff (1984) suggested that the dissatisfaction reported by union members is not "real," because it is not based on an assessment of the utility of the union jobs. In the debates about the union effect on job satisfaction, there is an implicit assumption that the utility of a job translates to satisfaction with it. In economic theory the concept of utility is indeed a measure, or indicator, of the satisfaction a person gains from the consumption of a bundle of goods and services. Yet, union workers are clearly dissatisfied with jobs that, seemingly, have high utility. The counterintuitive union effect may come about because utility has been defined, conceptually and operationally, in a rather narrow way. In the wage and employment effects model, utility is function of the wage rate and employment. In a model of union goals or objectives, maximizing the utility for members may include *all* the terms and conditions of employment (Pencavel, 1991). But the bundle considered by union workers in their personal definition of utility may well include items that the union has not been willing or able to obtain for them, such as intrinsically motivating and interesting jobs, harmonious and cooperative relations with supervisors and managers, or investment in new facilities and technologies to ensure future job security.

So far the alternative hypotheses for the negative union effect on job satisfaction have focused on the unit level — either on the workplace and its management, or on the union. A more recent suggestion — an eighth hypothesis — puts the focus on the individual employee by proposing that people who are drawn to unions, and therefore prone to choose union jobs or vote for union representation, have personal characteristics different from those who prefer nonunion status (Bryson et al., 2003). The nature of these differences is not specified, but go beyond demographic characteristics, moving more towards basic values and personalities. The worker heterogeneity hypothesis may have some support in the research showing that American workers prefer nonunion status, everything else being equal, because of societal cultural values that encourage people to define themselves as independent, where personal goals have priority over communal or group goals, and social behavior is guided by attitudes, personal needs, and rights of the individual members (Triandis, 1995; Hammer and Hartley, 1997). According to the standard economic model of union joining, Americans must therefore be "pushed and pulled" into unions by dissatisfaction and expectations of improvements, respectively (Bennett and Kaufman, 2002). The individual difference, or worker heterogeneity, hypothesis suggests that some may be attracted to union status beyond the promise of prospective gains.

IV. The Nature and Consequences of Job Satisfaction

In a well-known treatise on job satisfaction, Locke (1976) defined the construct as a pleasurable or emotional state "resulting from the appraisal of one's job as attaining or allowing the attainment of one's important job values, providing these values are congruent with or help to fulfill one's basic needs. These needs are of two separable but independent types: bodily or physical needs and psychological needs, especially the need for growth. Growth is made possible mainly by the nature of work itself" (p. 1319). Exit-voice researchers have based their studies on a shorter variant of this definition — the view that job satisfaction is determined by job outcomes. Some (e.g, Berger et al., 1983) have recognized that satisfaction depends on how well job outcomes match values, and some have, implicitly, recognized the importance of psychological growth needs (Kochan and Helfman, 1981; Pfeffer and David-Blake, 1990).

Locke's (1976) definition is not a complete model of job satisfaction, however. To understand and predict job satisfaction, more complex models are needed. The most complete, and probably the most relevant, job satisfaction model was developed by Hulin et al. (1985) based on prior theoretical work and empirical research. They describe job satisfaction as a function of four factors or psychological processes: work role (or job) outcomes, work role contributions, the frame of reference used to evaluate job outcomes, and the subjective utility of contributions and outcomes.

Employees evaluate the outcomes they receive in relation to what they expect to receive given their work role contributions, that is, their skills, effort, time, training, and foregone opportunities. The evaluation is influenced by their *frame of reference*, an internal standard of what is acceptable or good, that is shaped by past work experiences and local economic conditions. Employees with a history of high-wage jobs with good benefits, supportive managers, and interesting job tasks will have a different frame of reference than employees who have experienced less munificence — their criteria for assessing the value of jobs are stricter. The frame of reference is also influenced by local economic conditions. Living and working in an area with high unemployment and general decrepitude will lower the internal standard, which means that the same job outcomes will be evaluated more positively than if one lived and worked in a prosperous area with a tight labor market. Having a job when others around do not will increase job satisfaction.

Subjective utility is the value a person places on what he or she brings to the labor exchange and the costs of foregone options that are conditioned on local and occupational unemployment and available alternatives. Being in a tight labor market with high employer demands for one's job qualifications will increase subjective utility because what one can contribute is in short supply. High unemployment and low demand for one's skills and experience will lower subjective utility because many other workers in the local labor market can make equal or better contributions.

The frame of reference construct is directly applicable to the exit-voice hypothesis because union membership should affect the internal standard workers use when they assess the relationship between their contributions and their outcomes. The relative munificence of their job outcomes and their experience of being protected against lay-offs and employer idiosyncrasies give union members a frame of reference that should lower the assessment of present job outcome values. One can say that union members have higher expectations of the present than nonunion members, everything else being equal, because the past has been more benevolent.

Most studies of job satisfaction are based on the assumption that affective responses to the job come entirely from the match between individuals' needs, values, and experiences and characteristics of the work environment, including the job, the employer, and the local economic situation. If this is true, we should be able to design jobs and employment conditions to maximize positive affect. In other words, if workers are dissatisfied, somebody is to blame. Most often than not, the employer gets the blame; in the exit-voice model, the union shares it. But how we feel about our jobs may also lie within us.

Research linking personality traits to affective responses has shown that people are predisposed to respond negatively or positively to events and circumstances in their lives. Two personality traits, in particular, underlie affect: *positive affectivity,* or Extraversion, and *negative affectivity,* or Neuroticism (Emotional Stability).[3] Positive affectivity (PA) is the predisposition to experience positive emotions and moods. High PA individuals have an overall sense of well-being, feel good about themselves and what they do, and perceive stimuli, think, and behave in ways that will maintain their positive feelings (Tellegen, 1985). Negative affectivity (NA) is the predisposition to experience negative emotions and moods. High NA individuals tend to have negative feelings and an overall negative orientation towards themselves and their environment. They think and behave in ways that result in negative feelings.

Positive and negative affectivity are independent personality traits, not endpoints of one continuum. They have a genetic base, which means that they are enduring parts of personality, unlikely to change over time (Tellegen et al., 1988). In other words, there are happy and unhappy people (Costa and McCrae, 1980). Not surprisingly, positive affectivity is positively related to job satisfaction and negative affectivity is negatively related to job satisfaction (Cropanzano et al., 1993; George, 1991). There is no information in either theory or research to suggest that the people who join unions have higher levels of negative affectivity than those who prefer nonunion status, however, but it would be an interesting hypothesis to test if studies were to show that there is meaningful variance in union members' job satisfactions scores that can only be attributed to worker heterogeneity.

V. The Relationship between Job Satisfaction and Turnover

The exit-voice paradox — that dissatisfied workers stay with their employers instead of leaving for better jobs elsewhere — runs counter to the assumption that that workers are rational actors who seek to maximize their utility wherever possible. The relationship between job satisfaction and turnover is not straightforward, however.

All psychological models of turnover (voluntary quits) list job satisfaction as one among several determinants of organizational withdrawal, and not necessarily the most important one (see Hulin, 1991; Rosse and Noel, 1996; Griffith and Hom, 2001 for reviews). Meta-analyses have found that job satisfaction correlates –.26 with actual turnover and –.38 with intention to quit (Cartsen and Spector, 1987). These relationships are weaker when the number of available job alternatives decreases, as when local unemployment is high.

Turnover models focus more on the processes that lead to the decision to quit than on identifying long lists of predictors, which has led to research on the various ways employees can adapt to dissatisfying jobs. Different forms of withdrawing from work, such as tardiness, absenteeism, retirement, and quitting are forms of adaptation. The list of possible adaptive responses is long (Hulin, 1991), and leaving the job is but one among many. It is far from obvious, based on conceptual analyses, that quitting would be the most frequently used response to a dissatisfying job. As long as quitting is costly, and there are other less costly ways to adapt, the dissatisfied are likely to remain in their jobs. For people covered by a collective bargaining contract, the costs of quitting are high when union members believe that they will not be able to find new jobs with the same outcomes (Kochan and Helfman, 1981).

VI. Methodological Problems with Studies Testing the Exit-Voice Model of Job Satisfaction

Most of the studies testing the exit-voice hypothesis and its alternatives have used data sets from national probability samples, like the National Longitudinal Surveys (NLS), the Quality of Employment Survey (QES), or the Panel Survey of Income Dynamics (PSID) (Freeman, 1978; Borjas, 1979; Kochan and Helfman, 1981; Leigh, 1986; Schwochau, 1987) with model specifications that include a number of controls for different alternative explanations. Some studies control for narrow characteristics of the work environment, such as the intrinsic quality of the job, or a mixture of job content and physical workplace factors; others focus on broader constructs like the industrial relations climate or labor-management conflict.

The most obvious methodological problem with the use of large probability samples is the trade-off between generalizability and control. The benefit is that they increase the generalizability of the results across organizations and employers. The drawback is that they confound union membership with working conditions that influence both job satisfaction and unionization. Even when data sets contain variables that allow researchers to control for respondents' perceptions of aspects of the work environment, such as job content or physical characteristics, they do not contain enough measures of sufficient fidelity to hold constant all the important variables that can influence the correlation between being a union member and job satisfaction.

A second problem is that the measures of job satisfaction available in national probability sample data sets are often general (measuring overall job satisfaction) and few in number, which is a threat to reliability. The measurement of perceptions, beliefs, and attitudes is subject to a number of systematic and random biases or sources of error (Ghiselli et al., 1981; Motowidlo, 1996). To guard against random error, in particular, an attitude towards any object, event, or situation should be measured with a series of items representing the domain that defines the object, where each item elicits one or another part of the domain (see Nunnally, 1978, for an explanation of domain sampling theory). Measures with large random error components lower the validity coefficient. A reliable and valid measure of job satisfaction should include sets of items that tap different parts of the respondent's attitude towards the job (such as pay, promotional opportunities, co-workers, supervision, job complexity, skill requirements, etc.) as well as different aspects, or psychological properties, of each job facet (see, for example, the Cornell Job Description Index [Smith et al., 1969] or the Minnesota Satisfaction Questionnaire [Weiss et al., 1967]).

In most of the large-scale probability sample studies, overall job satisfaction and job facet satisfaction have been measured with one question per facet. One-item attitude measures are unreliable. Even when researchers have recognized the statistical problems caused by one-item scales and have tried to create a more reliable indicator of job satisfaction, they have met with modest success because the survey questions available for scale construction have not come from the same domain. For example, Pfeffer and Davis-Blake (1990) combined an overall job satisfaction item from the 1977 Quality of Employment Survey with four other items believed to be related to job satisfaction (intention to quit, likelihood of recommending the job to someone else, extent to which the job measured up to expectations, and whether the respondent would take the job he or she had now if given the choice). Their scale had a modest inter-item reliability coefficient (.75), which reflected the lack of domain sampling precision.

One way around the confounding and measurement problems is to control for work situation heterogeneity by judiciously choosing research samples and attitude measures with known psychometric properties. For example, Gordon and DeNisi (1995) tested the exit-voice hypothesis among union and nonunion workers employed by the same organization where union membership was independent of working conditions, industrial relations climate, and other possible employer-related differences. The costs of controlling for confounding factors through sample selection are lack of generalizability and modest sample sizes. Samples sizes in the Gordon and DeNisi's (1995) study comprised 151 and 1,513 employees. One benefit, however, is that the measures of job satisfaction, and, where relevant, job and firm-level controls, are more reliable and valid indicators. For example, the job satisfaction measure in the Gordon and DeNisi (1995) study was a 13-item scale built from questions covering different job facets, with an inter-item reliability coefficient of .92.

VI. A Review of the Research on the Union Effect on Job Satisfaction and Turnover

Most of the studies done to develop, and challenge, the exit-voice hypothesis have used data from large probability samples. The research covers workers in the United States, the United Kingdom, Canada, and Australia, which allows for comparisons of union effects on job satisfaction and turnover across societal cultural values and industrial relations systems. We review the evidence from these studies first before turning to the studies that have focused on union-non-union comparisons with the controls for work environment differences built into the research design.

The exit-voice hypothesis has received at least partial support from the national probability sample data (Borjas, 1979; Blau and Kahn, 1983; Schwochau, 1987; Miller and Mulvey, 1991). Other studies using the same data sets, but different model specifications, have reached different conclusions about the negative effect of unionization on job satisfaction, the argument that union members' dissatisfaction is not "real," or "true," and the voice explanation for the negative correlation between tenure and job satisfaction (Kochan and Helfman, 1981; Berger et al., 1983; Hersch and Stone, 1990; Pfeffer and Davis-Blake, 1991).

Early studies by Freeman (1978), Borjas (1979), Kochan and Helfman (1981), and Schwochau (1987) attempted to control for reverse causality, the first and most obvious explanation for low job satisfaction among union workers, but found that there was still a significant amount of variance left in job satisfaction scores that could not be explained by the dissatisfied having voted for union representation.

Kochan and Helfman (1981), using data from the 1977 QES survey, found that a positive effect of union membership on satisfaction with pay, benefits, and job security was mediated by union wages. Once wage level was held constant, the relationship between unionization and satisfaction with "bread and butter issues" became insignificant. A significant negative union effect on satisfaction with supervisors, promotion opportunities, job content, the adequacy of resources and information available to do the job did not disappear when wages were held constant, however.

Data on turnover intentions were more in line with the exit-voice hypothesis. Union membership, not controlling for wages, was negatively related to propensity to quit, and job dissatisfaction had much less of an effect on the probability of leaving the job for union members than nonunion workers. But there was no significant relationship between being a union member and intention to quit once wages and job satisfaction were held constant. Union workers were significantly less likely than nonunion workers to believe that they could find new jobs with the same wages and benefits should they quit, which led Kochan and Helfman (1981) to argue that the beneficial union effect on turnover (that is, staying) is caused by wages and benefits.

Two studies using the same data set reached similar conclusions about the absence of a union voice effect on job satisfaction, but arrived at slightly different explanations for their findings. The conceptual frameworks in which these early studies were anchored make them important for the application of job satisfaction theories and data to the exit-voice model.

Berger et al. (1983) argued that unions influence workers' preferences for different job outcomes. In particular, union members should be more satisfied with pay and fringe benefits than nonunion workers because union members have been socialized to consider these as more important. Similarly, union members should be less satisfied with nonpecuniary job outcomes, such as supervision, co-workers, the nature of work, and opportunities for promotion, because these job facets would be perceived as less important. Not surprisingly, the results supported the hypotheses, in the sense that there were no significant union effects on satisfaction with the various job facets when importance ratings and perceptions were held constant. This study is more important for the theoretical proposition that unions influence worker attitudes through their effects on values and perceptions than for some of the results. This is because the measures of job facet importance and satisfaction are not independent, and the mediation effect may therefore be spurious.[4]

Schwochau (1987), building on the Berger et al. study (1983), proposed that union members and nonmembers have different weighing schemes for job outcomes based on differences in job values and expectations. By comparing the actual job satisfaction of union members with derived satisfaction scores based on weights calculated from the nonunion sample, and vice versa (a procedure not entirely transparent), Schwochau showed that the pay satisfaction of union members, which was higher to begin with, declined, while the pay satisfaction of nonunion members increased. Applying the weights derived from the nonunion sample to the union members' satisfaction with supervision, co-workers, and the adequacy of resources increased these scores. The results are not completely in line with the politicization interpretation of the exit-voice model because the negative union effect on job satisfaction came from the adoption of a specific frame of reference for evaluating job outcomes, not from the socialization of union members to a political interest-group model of the workplace.

Pfeffer and Davis-Blake (1990) argued that union membership should, if anything, *increase* job satisfaction because unionized workers should suffer less from wage inequality and employer arbitrariness in the allocation of work, and benefit more from fair work rules and procedures. In addition, the actual efforts union members exert to improve their employment and working conditions should generate more positive perceptions of the workplace through cognitive dissonance.[5] Previous studies (Borjas, 1979; Kochan and Helfman, 1981) had failed to find positive relationships between being unionized and job satisfaction because they had not controlled with sufficient statistical precision for the poor employment and working conditions that motivated decisions to unionize to begin with. Using data from the 1977 Quality of Employment Survey and controlling for worker perceptions of autonomy (freedom and responsibility to make decisions about how one's job gets done), quality of supervision, the amount of role conflict experienced, and work pace — all job attributes related to the propensity to unionize — Pfeffer and Davis-Blake (1990) found a positive correlation between union membership and job satisfaction. This relationship was stronger where union members felt that they had more control over their work situation and were more involved in union activity, as was the case in craft and white-collar unions.

Renaud (2002) replicated Pfeffer and Davis-Blake's (1990) findings with data from a sample of 3,352 respondents to the 1989 Canadian General Social Survey of Education and Work, showing that the significant negative relationship between union membership and job satisfaction disappeared when controls for promotional opportunities, the pleasantness of the physical work environment, freedom to decide how to do one's work, and the routine nature of the job were added to the equation.

Miller (1990) used a sample of approximately 2,800 of young male workers (15- to 25-year-olds) from the 1985 Australian Longitudinal Survey to examine differences between union and nonunion workers' satisfaction with wide variety of physical, psychosocial, and job task characteristics, as well as promotional opportunities, job security, wages, and company policies. Because individual job facet satisfaction scores are usually correlated, one cannot treat comparisons of group means as independent events, but the general pattern in the data showed that the Australian union members were less satisfied than nonunion workers with most aspects of their job and employment situations. The union effect remained significant when controls for firm location, education, occupation, skill level, experience, and public vs. private sector employment were added to the equations. Although the union members in the sample had a 13 percent wage premium, their satisfaction with pay was not higher than that of non-unionists, nor did they report having more of a say in their jobs. Miller (1990) concluded, as had others before him, that the negative relationship between union status and job satisfaction comes from the incentive to unionize in an unpleasant work environment.

In a separate analysis of the union effect on tenure, Miller and Mulvey (1991), using the same data set, found that being unionized had a stronger positive effect on tenure among young Australians than what Freeman (1980) had discovered among young Americans, in support of the exit-voice hypothesis. The stronger effect of Australian unions, however, was due more to the unions' ability to limit employer-initiated lay-offs than it was to voluntary turnover. Still, there was a significant negative union effect on voluntary quits, which the authors attributed to the exercise of collective voice at the workplace level.

Tentative support for a favorable exit-voice effect on tenure comes from a study of 49,000 unionized public school teachers in New York State which showed that teachers with stronger grievance procedures in 1975–1978 had a lower probability of quitting than teachers whose contracts had weaker grievance procedures (Rees, 1991). The study did not include job satisfaction as a variable, however, nor did it have controls for other features of union strength that could have influenced turnover decisions.

Quitting is the permanent escape from a dissatisfying job. Being absent from work on occasion is a form of temporary escape (or, in the language of absenteeism research, "withdrawal"). If the exercise of union voice succeeds in eliminating unsatisfactory working conditions, unionized workers should have less reason to be absent. On the other hand, if job satisfaction is lower among union workers, they should have more reasons to be absent. Testing these competing hypotheses with data from the May 1973–1978 Current Population Survey, the 1973 Quality of Employment Survey, and the first five waves of the Panel Survey of Income Dynamics, Allen (1984) found that the probability of being absent was higher among union members than nonunion workers, controlling for industry, occupation, geographic location, education, gender, race, and marital status. When wages were held constant, absence rates were much higher among union members, suggesting that the wage penalties for being absent are lower for them. Allen (1984) concluded that the results did not support the voice hypothesis, perhaps because unions had not been effective in improving the intrinsically motivating and satisfying aspects of work.

Bender and Sloan (1998) tested the exit-voice hypotheses and alternative explanations on a sample of 1,509 full-time employees between the ages of 20 and 60 using data from the 1986–1987 Social Change and Economic Life Initiative Survey of employment conditions in six local UK labor markets. When controlling for firm-level industrial relations climate, they found that the negative relationships between overall job satisfaction, as well as satisfaction with pay, job security, and promotional opportunities were insignificant across gender and occupation (manual vs. non-manual workers). Contrary to early findings by Borjas (1979), but consistent with Kochan and Helfman (1981) and Schwochau (1987), there were no significant union-tenure interactions. They could not completely rule out the reverse-causation hypothesis, however, and concluded that the relative dissatisfaction of unionized workers is due either to a poor industrial relations climate or the propensity to unionize among the already dissatisfied.

Although the conceptual models of the union-job satisfaction relationship have become more sophisticated across studies and time, as one would expect, the obstacles to empirical testing imposed by limitations in data sets that have been constructed for other purposes remain. One can only control for confounding variables when the data are available, which means that we often find gaps between conceptual models and empirical testing. To compound the difficulty of drawing firm conclusions about union effects on attitudes, the measures that are available to test hypotheses are not the most reliable and valid indicators of the relevant constructs. In other words, most of the large-scale probability studies suffer from under-defined equations and questionable operational definitions.

Gordon and DeNisi (1995) circumvented these problems by examining the effects of union membership on job satisfaction in two samples of public sector employees where the union members and nonmembers within each sample worked for the same employer and were covered by the same collective bargaining contract. They found no significant effects of union membership on job satisfaction when controlling for demographic characteristics (age, education, race, and gender). A second study of job satisfaction and turnover intensions among union and nonunion faculty members organized by the American Association of University Professors (AAUP) also showed that union membership had no significant effects on job satisfaction, nor was it related to turnover intensions, when controlling for rank, length of service, perceptions of faculty influence in decision making, and political liberal values. Union members had more liberal political values and were more concerned about lack of faculty influence in university governance than nonunion faculty, however.

In a comparative study of manufacturing employees in the United States and Japan, Lincoln and Boothe (1993) examined the role of job characteristics — skill requirements and job complexity, discretion or control over work, Quality Circle membership, expectations about promotion, and earnings — as intervening variables between union membership and job satisfaction and organizational commitment. Given the history of union reluctance to support, much less champion, job redesign and employee participation programs (Kochan et al., 1994), and earlier studies which showed that union members were less satisfied than nonunion workers with job content and supervision (Kochan and Helfman, 1981; Berger et al., 1983; Schwochau, 1987), they hypothesized that a negative union effect on employee attitudes in U.S. firms would be caused by poor job quality. In contrast, Japanese enterprise unions with their emphasis on union-management cooperation and an absence of restrictive work rules and narrow job classifications should have a positive effect on job satisfaction and commitment.

Data came from a 1982–1983 survey, developed especially for the study, of 2,788 rank-and-file employees from 51 manufacturing plants in Indiana and 1,894 workers from 43 plants within one geographic region in Japan. Results showed that quit rates in the United States and Japanese firms were similar, with unionized employees less likely than nonunion employees to leave their jobs. Job satisfaction was significantly lower among the Japanese workers, while organizational commitment levels were similar. As expected, there were significant negative union effects on both job satisfaction and organizational commitment in the U.S. sample. These dropped sharply, but remained significant, when controls for job quality, promotion expectations, and earnings were added to the equations. Wages were higher in unionized firms, although the union differential shrank when individual and plant characteristics were added as controls (which makes sense in a within-state manufacturing labor market), but the differences in job complexity, work autonomy, promotion expectations, and Quality Circle membership remained substantial.

In the Japanese sample, there was no significant union effect on job satisfaction, but contrary to expectations, there was a small negative union effect on commitment. Japanese unions, however, were associated with employees having greater job complexity, autonomy, and opportunities for promotion while U.S. unions were associated with lower job quality. Lincoln and Boothe (1993) concluded that the difference in the intrinsic job quality between union and nonunion jobs in the U.S. plants, everything else being equal, not a politicization of the work force, drives the negative union effect on job satisfaction. They suggested further that had their measures of job attributes been better — that is, more reliable — and more comprehensive, the union effect on job attitudes would have been insignificant.

The conclusion we can draw from the research reviewed so far is that the union effect on job satisfaction is determined primarily by the differences between union and nonunion workers' experiences with job content, wages, and workplace industrial relations climate. Thus, when all these factors are held constant, evidence of a job satisfaction differential should disappear. But the story does not end here. The most recent study of why union members are unhappy has a surprising conclusion.

With data on 18,012 employees in 2,192 organizations drawn from the 1998 British Workplace Employee Relations Survey (WERS), Bryson et al. (2003) were able to examine, in a ten-step processes, every alternative explanation that has been offered for the negative union effect on job satisfaction. The WERS data set is unusually rich for a national probability survey, coming from matched samples of senior workplace managers and a random samples of their respective subordinates. It contains four job satisfaction items: satisfaction with pay, the amount of influence experienced over the job, the sense of achievement from work, and the respect received from supervisors and line management. For this study, the items were combined into an overall satisfaction score. In addition, Bryson et al. (2003) examined satisfaction with pay.[6]

As expected, union members reported significantly lower job satisfaction than nonmembers, and continued to do so when demographic characteristics were held constant, although the pay satisfaction gap narrowed. When occupational and job characteristics were added to the equations, however, the coefficient on union status dropped substantially, showing that union members were most frequent in occupations and jobs where job satisfaction is low. There were no significant effects of workplace heterogeneity — industry, size, region, work force composition, establishment characteristics, and union density. Perceptions of the industrial relations climate and respondents' opinions of trade unions, on the other hand, reduced the union membership coefficient. Controlling for pay and hours of work increased overall job dissatisfaction — evidence of the compensating effect of a union wage premium.

By using propensity score matching to control for the problem that union membership is not independent of job situations and occupational and job characteristics, Bryson et al. (2003) found that union members were less satisfied with their jobs than they would have been had they not become members. Union members were less satisfied than a perfectly matched sub-sample of nonmembers with all aspect of the their jobs, although the wage premium served to alleviate some of the dissatisfaction. But higher wages were not sufficient to compensate for other aspects of the job. Additional controls for union strength and union voice (accomplished by removing union activists from the analyses) did not narrow the satisfaction gap between union members and nonmembers. Finally, instrumenting for membership using the employer's perception of the workplace industrial relations climate, the association between membership and dissatisfaction apparent when controlling for observable individual, job, and workplace characteristics disappeared, leading the authors to conclude that the association was accounted for by unobservable factors by which individuals become union members.

In summary, most of the difference in job satisfaction was accounted for by occupational, job, and workplace characteristics, which matches the findings from previous studies. At the end of the day, however, there remained a small but significant negative union effect on job satisfaction that could not be ascribed to anything but "unobserved heterogeneity." What kinds of individual differences are left?

The authors suggest that there are certain innate personal characteristics that predispose union members to be less satisfied with their jobs than other people, and also to join unions. For example, people with higher expectations of, and aspirations towards, their work might be more likely to unionize and also have their aspirations thwarted.

Models of, and research on, union voting include a number of attitudinal variables, such as job satisfaction, perception of equity, trust in management, feelings of powerlessness, or attitudes towards unions (for a summary of the psychological research, see Barling et al., 1990). The research is silent on the role of personality characteristics as predictors of the pro-union vote,[7] but as we discussed earlier, there is ample empirical evidence that dispositions influence job attitudes (Arvey et al., 1989; Staw and Ross, 1985; George, 1996). We return to this research when we examine the findings from the tests of the exit-voice model in light of theories and research on jobs satisfaction and turnover. First, however, we examine the union effect on another attitudinal factor of relevance to the exit-voice model: organizational commitment.

VII. Some Observations on Unions and Organizational Commitment

Organizational commitment is defined as the extent to which an employee identifies with the employer, wants to remain with the organization, and is willing to exert extra effort on its behalf (Mowday et al., 1979). Affective commitment, or the emotional attachment of the employee to the organization, has a number of behavioral consequences, such as retention, work attendance, citizenship behavior, and, under certain circumstances, job performance (Hulin, 1991; Meyer and Allen, 1997).

In Freeman and Medoff's (1984) adoption of the exit-voice model, organizational commitment is a latent variable. Its presence is implied, embedded in organizational tenure. Hirschman (1970), in his description of the exit-voice-and-loyalty model, defined loyalty as an attachment to the organization that helped determine people's decisions to exit or stay and use voice. Loyal employees remain with the employer and strive to correct dissatisfying conditions if they have a voice mechanism available, while the emotionally unattached leave. Most studies based on Hirschman's model have ignored the loyalty component, making an implicit assumption that if employees decide to stay, they must be loyal. An exception is Boroff and Lewin's (1997) study of the relationship between grievance filing and turnover intentions, in which loyalty was conceptually defined and measured as organizational commitment.

Organizational commitment is not the same as tenure. It is one of many determinants of voluntary turnover and is therefore negatively correlated with intentions to quit (Meyer and Allen, 1997; Griffith and Hom, 2001). It is positively correlated with job satisfaction, but it is a different construct with different psychological properties.[8] Because union members are more likely to remain with their employer despite poorer attitudes towards their job, we might expect a positive relationship between union membership and organizational commitment, irrespective of job satisfaction levels. The results of the Lincoln and Boothe (1993) study, however, showed that the union effect on organizational commitment was negative, especially among U.S. employees, even when job quality, wages, and promotional opportunities were held constant. In essence, the results for commitment mirrored the results for job satisfaction. Unfortunately, there were no controls for job satisfaction in the commitment regressions, and no information about the commitment-job satisfaction correlations, so it is not possible to uncover the pure effect of union status on commitment.

Hammer et al. (1981) examined the effect of voice and loyalty on absenteeism among workers in a unionized manufacturing plant that had been bought out by managers, rank-and-file employees, and local citizens to avoid closure. Drawing on Hirschman's model, they expected that job satisfaction, amount of stock ownership (financial commitment), and organizational commitment would be negatively related to voluntary (unexcused) absenteeism if workers perceived the union as an effective voice mechanism. With controls for occupational level, age, and job involvement, job attendance was determined primarily by financial and organizational commitment and union voice, which provides some support for the EVL model. Job satisfaction was unrelated to absenteeism and only weakly correlated with perceptions of union voice. There was also no significant relationship between perceptions of union voice and commitment.

By and large, studies of organizational commitment have paid scant attention to the role of union status. The exception is a small subset of studies of union commitment that have examined the causes of dual loyalty or dual allegiance — that is, union members' commitment to both the employer and the union. Unfortunately, this line of research is by definition confined to union members and can therefore not be used to test hypotheses about union-non-union differences. The one consistent finding from the dual loyalty studies of some relevance to the exit-voice model is that positive correlations between organizational and union commitment are conditional on the industrial relations climate. Where relations between management and labor are positive, there is dual loyalty. Where labor relations are poor, the commitment correlations are either insignificant or negative (see Gordon and Ladd, 1990, for a summary of this research). Again we see the importance of the industrial relations climate as a contributor to employee job attitudes.

VIII. Conclusion

The research on the exit-voice hypothesis, both in the United States and abroad, shows convincingly that most of the variance in the negative union effect on job satisfaction can be accounted for by job quality, industrial relation climate, and wages. Union members see their jobs as less attractive than do nonunion workers in terms of skill requirements, task complexity, the amount of autonomy or discretion available, and opportunities for promotion. Union members also perceive the supervision they receive and the labor-management relations they experience as less satisfactory. They are, however, clearly better off with respect to wages, benefits, and pensions. But when it comes to job satisfaction, the economic advantages of union jobs are not sufficient to compensate for job content and work environment factors.

It comes as no surprise to the job satisfaction researcher that job content — the nature of the tasks people are given to do — weighs heavily in overall job satisfaction scores. While there are individual differences in the degree to which people prefer intrinsically interesting jobs, there is ample empirical evidence showing that autonomy, skill variety, complexity, challenge, and advancement are important determinants of people's affective reactions to their jobs (Deci, 1975; Hackman and Oldham, 1980; Kanfer, 1990). The relative importance of job content factors to overall job satisfaction is also mirrored in the most commonly used measures of job satisfaction (Weiss et al., 1967).

It may be more surprising from a theoretical perspective that the industrial relations climate should have a significant effect on job satisfaction since it is part of the context in which jobs are embedded and therefore not experienced as directly as are work tasks. On the other hand, an adversarial labor-management climate may translate to unfriendly supervisors and tense interpersonal relations, which certainly can be experienced directly. The data from the dual commitment studies (Gordon and Ladd, 1990) and the Freeman and Roger (1999) survey provide additional empirical evidence for the value workers ascribe to non-adversarial, cooperative industrial relations.

One could argue, based on the research evidence, that there is not much support for the exit-voice hypothesis. By the time we control for demographic characteristics, job characteristics, industrial relation climate, and labor market factors, the union effect on job satisfaction is small. It is not insignificant, however, which means that we still need to explain what it is that can make union members different from nonunion workers. Freeman and Medoff (1984) argued that the job satisfaction of union members declines because the workers become politicizied through personal experiences with grieving dissatisfying events and conditions and bargaining to get them improved.[9] A politicizied labor force may contribute to more adversarial labor relations, which could mean that at least a part of the union effect on job satisfaction, which Freeman and Medoff identified as an inevitable result of having a union job, is accounted for by the industrial relation climate. Studies have not examined if union members are more primed to detect dissatisfying events than are nonunion workers, or whether they become more primed to do so with tenure in union jobs as one would expect if the explanation is correct.

We believe a more likely answer can be found in job satisfaction theory: Union members have different expectations, values, or frames of reference for evaluating their job outcomes than nonunion workers. It is worth noting that early tests of the exit-voice hypothesis recognized, somewhat obliquely, that union members evaluated their jobs through a different lens than nonunion members. An example is Schwochau's (1987) hypothesis that union workers weigh outcomes differently than nonunion workers, with a subsequent effect on job satisfaction. Schwochau also made an implicit frame-of-reference argument by suggesting that union members will evaluate wages and benefits higher than other job outcomes because they have learnt that what the union works to obtain in collective bargaining is valuable. Berger et al.'s (1983) findings about the importance union members place on pecuniary job outcomes fit this argument as well. Interestingly, the recognition that union members may have different internal standards for evaluating their jobs was lost in later studies as the focus shifted to more elaborate controls for job and work environment characteristics. Bryson et al. (2004) interpreted their significant effect of worker heterogeneity on job satisfaction to mean that union members seek out union jobs (or vote for union representation) because they have higher job aspirations and expectations to begin with, an argument that also recognizes a frame-of-reference effect. It is not possible based on research to date to determine whether union members arrive at their expectations and frames of reference because of their experiences in union jobs, or search out union jobs because they have higher internal standards for what a good job should contain than workers who opt for nonunion status.

Explaining the exit-voice paradox with respect to turnover is relatively easy. Turnover theory and research have shown that quitting is not an obvious response to lack of job satisfaction. As long as there are less costly ways to adapt to the dissatisfying facets of one's job, one is not likely to leave. The costs of quitting extend beyond pure economic calculations, because leaving the job often involves a separation from a community with a network of friends and relations, and the uprooting of family members from their jobs and schools. Economic utility models do not take into account the psychological costs of leaving behind the investments workers have made over time in jobs and communities. Certainly some union workers quit, presumably in response to the dissatisfaction. But many stay, because, as the research on turnover has shown, the path of least resistance in coping with job dissatisfaction is to adapt.

We disagree with Freeman and Medoff's (1984) hypothesis that the dissatisfaction union workers report in attitude surveys is not "real," in the sense that it does not indicate true attitudes. Implicit in their argument is that workers' true attitudes towards the job are based on objective circumstances only, that is, job outcomes that can be quantified in terms of dollars and cents. As we have tried to show in our discussion of job satisfaction theory and research, however, people's affective, or emotional, reactions to their jobs are based on a number of outcomes, of which wages, benefits and job security are but a subset. The job (dis)satisfaction of union workers, when measured with reliable and valid instruments that cover all important facets of the job, is real.

What are the practical or policy implications of this reality? What, if anything, should be done to correct it, and would it be worth the effort? There are two points to consider before one recommends action. One is the positive union effect on retention. To the extent that unionized workplaces have relatively low rates of dysfunctional turnover, that is, voluntary exit of workers who are trained or highly skilled and therefore not easily replaced, unionized employers are ahead. Turnover rates are high in the United States, and they are costly (Cascio, 2000; Griffith and Hom, 2001). Second, we need to keep the magnitude of the difference in job satisfaction scores between union and nonunion workers in perspective. Union workers are only less satisfied — they are not desperately dissatisfied.

However, there are still good reasons for being concerned about the lower levels of job satisfaction in union workplaces. One is the positive relationship between job satisfaction and job performance. For decades it was thought to be of little practical significance (Petty et al., 1984; Iaffaldano and Muchinsky, 1985), but a recent meta-analysis has estimated the mean true correlation between the two to be .30 (Judge et al., 2001), which is sufficiently large to be important. The relationship is bidirectional, in the sense that job satisfaction can lead to better job performance, especially in complex jobs requiring worker discretion and initiative, and job performance can cause job satisfaction when desirable job outcomes are contingent on performance (Vroom, 1964; Hulin, 1991; Judge et al., 2001).

There is also the argument that job satisfaction is a good in itself irrespective of economic utility. Both employers and unions ought to be interested in ensuring that the workers they employ and represent, respectively, are satisfied with their jobs. Our review of the research suggests strongly that union workers would be more satisfied with their jobs if the quality of job content was higher and labor-management relations were more positive. Both of these conditions can be met with the adoption of a union-management partnership model that allows for participation of workers in decisions about the execution of their jobs and a redesign of work at the point of production. Over the past two decades the employment relationship in many U.S. organizations has been restructured (Batt and Appelbaum, 1994; Kochan et al., 1994). Adoption of participatory work patterns, such as online work teams, increased in American workplaces throughout the 1980s and 1990s (Osterman, 2000), and direct worker participation has been recommended as a new arena for industrial relations (Kochan and Osterman, 1994).

There is disagreement about both the economic and labor-management relations benefits of participatory employment patterns (Godard and Delaney, 2000; Kochan, 2000). Their impact on job performance seems to be modest (Wagner, 1994), but there is consistent evidence that intrinsically interesting jobs and direct worker participation increase job satisfaction (Miller and Monge, 1986; Cohen and Bailey, 1997; Applebaum et al., 2000; Hunter et al., 2002). Unions have been slow in placing work redesign and other direct forms of worker participation on their agendas, but where they have made an effort to work with the employer to improve job content, labor-management relations have also improved (Kochan and Osterman, 1994; Rubinstein and Kochan, 2001). Based on the research to date, there is room for the claim that it would be worth the effort of both unions and employers to collaborate on designing participatory work structures.

Our final point is aimed at researchers. Job satisfaction is not a simple construct. A complete model of its causes and consequences goes beyond an external, objective assessment of job outcomes to include the job holder's personality, past work experiences, and present economic and social environment. Modeling job satisfaction requires a relaxation of the assumptions behind the standard economic model of unions. First and foremost, we must acknowledge that the utility of a job includes both extrinsic and intrinsic outcomes as well as work environment characteristics. Secondly, workers are not always able to move freely in an open, munificent labor market. Only a finite number of jobs is available that provide the kinds of economic benefits union workers enjoy, and it may not be possible for union members to meet their economic obligations by moving to jobs with lower financial returns. It must also be recognized that workers are not purely rational economic decision makers. Noneconomic, non-job-related concerns can influence job choice and turnover decisions. This does not have to mean that people do not make rational choices based on the best information they have available, only that there are nonpecuniary variables in their personal equations. Third, it should not be assumed that worker heterogeneity is random error. There are true individual differences, beyond demographic characteristics, that cause attitudes and behaviors. If research on the union effect on job satisfaction, or on organizational commitment, is to progress, researchers must pay more attention to the complex nature of these variables. Pure economic theories are too simple as models of the causes and consequences of job attitudes.

Notes

* We acknowledge helpful comments from Rose Batt and Ronald Seeber on an earlier draft of this study.

1. The union wage premium is not a threat to job security as long as the demand for union labor is inelastic, or labor costs can be transferred to consumers, but these conditions have become rare, at least in the private sector (Bennett and Kaufman, 2002).
2. Data on job separations from the Panel Study of Income Dynamics show that quit rates of nonunion workers were more than twice the quit rates of union members between 1976–1981, and the gap increased between 1986–1991 (Polsky, 1999).
3. Extraversion and Neuroticism, or Emotional Stability, are part of the "Big Five" personality traits. The Five Factor model of personality has both conceptual and empirical credibility (Costa and McCrae, 1988; George, 1996).
4. Job satisfaction scores already contain an importance component, which means that controlling for importance when regressing job satisfaction on union status will remove part of the true job satisfaction variance from the relationship (Ewen, 1967).
5. According the theory of cognitive dissonance, perceptions, or attitudes, must be consonant with (follow from) behavior, or vice versa. If employees expend efforts to improve the workplace, it follows that they will perceive the workplace as improved.
6. The correlation between overall job satisfaction and satisfaction with pay will be artificially high because pay satisfaction appears on both sides of the equation. The pattern of results should therefore be very similar for the two indicators.
7. The tiny number of studies that have a examined personality characteristics are dated and inconclusive.
8. Meta-analyses of studies examining the job satisfaction-commitment relationship show an average correlation of .44 (Kinicki, McKee-Ryan, Schriesheim, and Carson, 2002).
9. The explanation Freeman and Medoff gave of union members "becoming politizied" is very close to the definition of instrumental conditioning (learning), whereby the job itself becomes associated with a series of unpleasant experiences (grieving and bargaining) and ends up producing negative feelings. It is doubtful that this is what they had in mind, however.

References

Abowd, John M. and Henry S. Farber. "Job Queues and the Union Status of Workers." *Industrial and Labor Relations Review* 35 (April 1982): 354–67.

Addison, John T. and Alberto C. Castro. "The Importance of Lifetime Jobs: Differences Between Union and Nonunion Workers." *Industrial and Labor Relations Review* 40 (April 1987): 393–405.

Addison, John T. and John Chilton. "Models of Union Behavior." In David Lewin, Daniel Mitchell, and Mahmood Zaido, eds. *The Human Resource Management Handbook*, Part II. Greenwich, CT.: JAI Press, 1997, pp. 157–96.

Allen, Steven G. "Trade Unions, Absenteeism, and Exit-Voice." *Industrial and Labor Relations Review* 37 (April 1984): 331–45.

Appelbaum, Eileen, Thomas Bailey, Peter Berg, and Arne L. Kalleberg. *Manufacturing Advantage: Why High Performance Work Systems Pay Off.* Ithaca, NY: ILR Press, 2000.

Arvey, Richard D., Lauren M. Abraham, Thomas, J. Bouchard, and Nancy L. Segal. "Job Satisfaction: Environmental and Genetic Components." *Journal of Applied Psychology* 74 (April 1989): 187–92.

Barling, Julian, Clive Fullagar, and E. Kevin Kelloway. *The Union and Its Members: A Psychological Approach*. New York: Oxford University Press, 1992.

Batt, Rosemary and Eileen Appelbaum. "Worker Participation in Diverse Settings: Does the Form Affect the Outcome and If So, Who Benefits?" *British Journal of Industrial Relations* 33 (September 1995): 353–78.

Bender, Keith A. and Peter J. Sloane. "Job Satisfaction, Trade Unions, and Exit-Voice Revisited." *Industrial and Labor Relations Review* 51 (January 1998): 222–40.

Bennett, James T. and Bruce E. Kaufman. "Conclusion: The Future of Private Sector Unionism in the U.S. — Assessment and Forecast." In James T. Bennett and Bruce E. Kaufman, eds. *The Future of Private Sector Unionism in the United States.* Armonk, NY: M.E. Sharpe, 2002, pp. 395–85.

Bennett, James T. and Jason E. Taylor. "Labor Unions: Victims of Their Own Political Success?" In James T. Bennett and Bruce E. Kaufman, eds. *The Future of Private Sector Unionism in the United States.* Armonk, NY: M.E. Sharpe, 2002, pp. 245–59.

Berger, Chris J., Craig A. Olson, and John W. Boudreau. "Effects of Unions on Job Satisfaction: The Role of Work-Related Values and Perceived Rewards." *Organizational Behavior and Human Performance* 32 (June 1983): 289–324.

Blau, Francine D. and Lawrence M. Kahn. "Unionism, Seniority, and Turnover." *Industrial and Labor Relations Review* 22 (Fall 1983): 362–73.

Borjas, George J. "Job Satisfaction, Wages, and Unions." *Journal of Human Resources* 14 (Spring 1979): 21–40.

Boroff, Karen E. and David Lewin. "Loyalty, Voice, and Intent to Exit a Union Firm: A Conceptual and Empirical Analysis." *Industrial and Labor Relations Review* 51 (October 1997): 50–63.

Brett, Jeanne B. "Behavioral Research on Unions and Union-Management Systems." In Barry Staw and Larry L. Cummings, eds. *Research in Organizational Behavior*, Vol. 2. Greenwich, CT: JAI Press, 1980, pp. 177–214.

Brett, Jeanne M. and Tove H. Hammer. "Organizational Behavior and Industrial Relations." In Thomas A. Kochan, Daniel J. B. Mitchell, and Lee Dyer, eds. *Industrial Relations Research in the 1970s: Review and Appraisal.* Madison, WI: Industrial Relations Research Association, 1982, pp. 221–81.

Brief, Arthur P. *Attitudes in and around Organizations.* Thousand Oaks, CA: Sage, 1998.

Bryson, Alex, Lorenzo Cappellari, and Laidio Lucifora. "Does Union Membership Really Reduce Job Satisfaction?" London: Centre for Economic Performance Discussion Paper No. 569, London School of Economics, 2003.

Carsten, Jeanne M. and Paul E. Spector. "Unemployment, Job Satisfaction and Employee Turnover: A Meta-Analytic Test of the Muchinsky Model." *Journal of Applied Psychology* 72 (August 1987): 374–81.

Cascio, Wayne F. *Costing Human Resources.* Cincinnati, OH: South-Western, 2000.

Cohen, Susan G. and Diane E. Bailey. "What Makes Teams Work: Group Effectiveness Research from the Shop Floor to the Executive Suite." *Journal of Management* 23 (3 1997): 219–90.

Costa, Paul T. and Robert R. McCrae. "Influence of Extraversion and Neuroticism on Subjective Well-Being: Happy and Unhappy People." *Journal of Personality and Social Psychology* 38 (April 1980): 668–78.

_____. "Personality in Adulthood: A Six-Year Longitudinal Study of Self-Reports and Spouse Ratings on the NEO Personality Inventory." *Journal of Personality and Social Psychology* 54 (May 1988): 853–63.

Cranny, C.J., Patricia C. Smith, and Eugene F. Stone. *Job Satisfaction. How People Feel about Their Jobs and How It Affects Their Performance.* New York: Lexington Books, 1992.

Cropanzano, Russell, Keith James, and Mary A. Konovsky. "Dispositional Affectivity as a Predictor of Work Attitudes and Job Performance." *Journal of Organizational Behavior* 14 (November 1993): 595–606.

Deci, Edward L. *Intrinsic Motivation.* New York: Plenum Press, 1975.

Ewen, Robert B. "Weighing Components of Job Satisfaction." *Journal of Applied Psychology* 51 (January 1967): 68–73.

Farber, Henry S. "The Determination of the Union Status of Workers." *Econometrica* 51 (September 1983): 21–23.

_____ and Alan Kruger. "Union Membership in the United States: The Decline Continues." In Bruce Kaufman and Morris Kleiner, eds. *Employee Representation: Alternatives and Future Directions.* Madison, WI: Industrial Relations Research Association, 1993, pp. 105–34.

Farber, Henry S. and Bruce Western. "Accounting for the Decline of Unions in the Private Sector." In James T. Bennett and Bruce E. Kaufman, eds. *The Future of Private Sector-Unionism in the United States.* Armonk, NY: M.E. Sharpe, 2002, pp. 28–58.

Fiorito, Jack. "Human Resource Management Practices and Worker Desires for union Representation." In James T. Bennett and Bruce E. Kaufman, eds. *The Future of Private Sector Unionism in the United States.* Armonk, NY: M. E. Sharpe, 2002, pp. 205–26.

Freeman, Richard B. "Job Satisfaction as an Economic Variable." *American Economic Review* 68 (May 1978): 135–41.

_____ and Joel Rogers. *What Workers Want.* New York: Russell Sage Foundation, 1999.

Freeman, Richard B. and James L. Medoff. *What Do Unions Do?* New York: Basic Books, 1984.

Fullagar, Clive and Julian Barling. "A Longitudinal Test of a Model of the Antecedents and Consequences of Union Loyalty." *Journal of Applied Psychology* 74 (April 1989): 213–27.

George, Jennifer M. "Time Structure and Purpose As a Mediator of Work-Life Linkages." *Journal of Applied Social Psychology* 21 (February 1991): 296–314.

_____. "Trait and State Affect." In Kevin R. Murphy, ed. *Individual Differences and Behavior in Organizations.* San Francisco, Calif.: Jossey-Bass, 1996, pp.145–74.

Getman, Julius G., Stephen B. Goldberg, and Jeanne B. Herman. *Union Representations Elections: Law and Reality.* New York: Russell Sage Foundation, 1976.

Ghiselli, Edwin E., John P. Campbell, and Sheldon Zedeck. *Measurement Theory for the Behavioral Sciences.* San Francisco: W.H. Freeman, 1981.

Godard, John and John T. Delaney. "Reflections on the 'High Performance' Paradigm's Implications for Industrial Relations as a Field." *Industrial and Labor Relations Review* 53 (April 2000): 482–502.

Gordon, Michael E. and Angelo DeNisi. "A Reexamination of the Relationship Between Union Membership and Job Satisfaction." *Industrial and Labor Relations Review* 48 (January 1995): 222–36.

Gordon, Michael E. and Robert T. Ladd. "Dual Allegiance: Renewal, Reconsideration, and Recantation." *Personnel Psychology* 43 (Spring 1990): 37–69.

Gordon, Michael E., John W. Philpot, Robert E. Burt, Cynthia A. Thompson, and William E. Spiller. "Commitment to the Union: Development of a Measure and an Examination of Its Correlates." *Journal of Applied Psychology* 65 (August 1980): 479–99.

Griffith, Roger W. and Peter W. Hom. *Retaining Valued Employees.* Thousand Oaks, CA: Sage Publications, 2001.

Hackman, Richard J. and Greg R. Oldham. *Work Redesign.* Reading, MA.: Addison-Wesley, 1980.

Hammer, Tove H. "Relationships Between Local Union Characteristics and Worker Behavior and Attitudes." *Academy of Management Journal* 21 (December 1978): 560–77.

———— and Michael Berman. "The Role of Noneconomic Factors in Faculty Union Voting." *Journal of Applied Psychology* 66 (August 1981): 415–21.

Hammer, Tove H. and Jean F. Hartley. "Individual-Union-Organizational Relationships in a Cultural Context." In P. Christopher Early and Miriam Erez, eds. *New Perspectives on International Industrial/Organizational Psychology.* San Francisco: New Lexington Press, 1997, pp. 446–92.

Hammer, Tove H., Jacqueline C. Landau, and Robert N. Stern. "Absenteeism When Workers Have a Voice." *Journal of Applied Psychology* 66 (October 1981): 561–73.

Hersch, Joni and Joe A. Stone. "Is Union Job Dissatisfaction Real?" *Journal of Human Resources* 25 (Autumn 1990): 736–51.

Hirsch, Barry T. and David A. Macpherson. *Union Membership and Earnings Data Book: Compilations from the Current Population Survey* (2000 ed.). Washington, DC: Bureau of National Affairs, 2000.

Hirsch, Barry T. and Edward J. Schumacher. "Private Sector Union Density and the Wage Premium." In James T. Bennett and Bruce E. Kaufman, eds. *The Future of Private Sector Unionism in the United States.* Armonk, NY: M. E. Sharpe, 2002, pp. 92–128.

Hirschman, Alberto O. *Exit, Voice, and Loyalty: Responses to Decline in Firms, Organizations, and States.* Cambridge, MA: Harvard University Press, 1970.

Hulin, Charles. "Adaptation, Persistence, and Commitment in Organizations." In Marvin D. Dunnette and Laetta M. Hough, eds. *Handbook of Industrial and Organizational Psychology*, 2nd ed., Vol. 2. Palo Alto, CA: Consulting Psychologists Press, 1991, pp. 445–506.

————, Mary Roznowski and Donna Hachiya. "Alternative Opportunities and Withdrawal Decisions: Empirical and Theoretical Discrepancies and an Integration." *Psychological Bulletin* 97 (March 1985): 233–50.

Hunter, Larry W., John Paul MacDuffie, and Lorna Doucet. "What Makes Teams Take? Employee Reactions to Work Reforms." *Industrial and Labor Relations Review* 55 (April 2002): 448–72.

Iaffaldano, Michelle T. and Paul M. Muchinsky. "Job Satisfaction and Job Performance: A Meta-Analysis." *Psychological Bulletin* 97 (March 1985): 251–73.

Judge, Timothy A., Joyce E. Bono, Carl J. Thoresen, and Gregory K. Patton. "The Job Satisfaction-Job Performance Relationship: A Qualitative and Quantitative Review." *Journal of Applied Psychology* 127 (May 2001): 376–407.

Kanfer, Ruth. "Motivation Theory and Industrial and Organizational Psychology." In Marvin D. Dunnette and Laetta M. Hough, eds. *Handbook of Industrial and Organizational Psychology*, 2nd ed., Vol. 1. Palo Alto, CA: Consulting Psychologists Press, 1990, pp. 75–170.

Kinicki, Angelo J., Frances M. McKee-Ryan, Chester A. Schriesheim, and Kenneth P. Carson. "Assessing the Construct Validity of the Job Description Index: A Review and Meta-Analysis." *Journal of Applied Psychology* 87 (April 2002): 14–32.

Kleiner, Morris M. "Intensity of Management Resistance: Understanding the Decline of Unionization in the Private Sector." In James T. Bennett and Bruce E. Kaufman, eds. *The Future of Private Sector Unionism in the United States.* Armonk, NY: M.E. Sharpe, 2002, pp. 292–316.

Kochan, Thomas A. "On the Paradigm Guiding Industrial Relations Theory and Research." *Industrial and Labor Relations Review* 53 (July 2000): 704–11.

_____ and David E. Helfman. "The Effects of Collective Bargaining on Economic and Behavioral Job Outcomes." In Ronald G. Ehrenberg, ed. *Research in Labor Economics*, Vol. 4. Greenwich, CT: JAI Press, 1981, pp. 321–65.

Kochan, Thomas, A. and Paul Osterman. *The Mutual Gains Enterprise.* Boston, MA: Harvard Business School Press, 1994.

Kochan, Thomas A., Harry C. Katz, and Robert B. McKersie. *The Transformation of American Industrial Relations.* Ithaca, NY: ILR Press, 1994.

Leigh, Duane E. "Union Performance, Job Satisfaction, and the Union-Voice Hypothesis." *Industrial Relations* 25 (Winter 1986): 65–71.

Lincoln, James L. and Joan N. Boothe. "Unions and Work Attitudes in the United States and Japan." *Industrial Relations* 32 (Spring 1993): 159–87.

Locke, Edwin A. "The Nature and Causes of Job Satisfaction." In Marvin D. Dunnette, ed. *Handbook of Industrial and Organizational Psychology.* Chicago: Rand McNally, 1976, pp. 1297–349.

Meng, Ronald. "The Relationship Between Unions and Job Satisfaction." *Applied Economics* 22 (December 1990): 1635–48.

Meyer, John P. and Natalie J. Allen. *Commitment in the Workplace: Theory, Research, and Application.* Thousand Oaks, CA: Sage Publications, 1997.

Miller, Katherine I. and Peter R. Monge. "Participation, Satisfaction, and Productivity: A Meta-Analytic Review." *Academy of Management Journal* 29 (December 1986): 727–53.

Miller, Paul W. "Trade Unions and Job Satisfaction." *Australian Economic Papers* 29 (December 1990): 226–48.

_____ and Charles Mulvey. "Australian Evidence on the Exit-Voice Model of the Labor Market." *Industrial and Labor Relations Review* 45 (October 1991): 44–57.

Motowidlo, Stephan J. "Orientation Toward the Job and Organization." In Kevin R. Murphy, ed. *Individual Differences and Behavior in Organizations.* San Francisco, CA.: Jossey-Bass, 1996, pp. 175–208.

Mowday, Richard T., Richard M. Steers, and Lyman W. Porter. "The Measurement of Organizational Commitment." *Journal of Vocational Behavior* 14 (October 1979): 224–47.

Nunnally, Jum C. *Psychometric Theory.* New York: McGraw-Hill, 1978.

Osterman, Paul. "Work Reorganization in an Era of Restructuring: Trends in Diffusion and Effects on Employee Welfare." *Industrial and Labor Relations Review* 53 (January 2000): 179–96.

Pencavel, John H. "The Demand of Union Services: An Exercise." *Industrial and Labor Relations Review* 24 (January 1971): 180–90.

_____. *Labor Markets and Trade Unionism*. Cambridge: Blackwell, 1991.

Petty, M. M., Gail W. McGee, and Jerry W. Cavender. "A Meta-Analysis of the Relationship between Individual Job Satisfaction and Individual Performance." *Academy of Management Review* 9 (October 1984): 712–21.

Pfeffer, Jeffrey and Alison David-Blake. "Unions and Job Satisfaction: An Alternative View." *Work and Occupations* 17 (August 1990): 259–83.

Polsky, Daniel. "Changing Consequences of Job Separation in the United States." *Industrial and Labor Relations Review* 52 (July 1999): 565–80.

Rees, Daniel I. "Grievance Procedure Strength and Teacher Quits." *Industrial and Labor Relations Review* 45 (October 1991): 31–43.

Renaud, Stephane. "Rethinking the Union Membership/Job Satisfaction Relationship: Some Empirical Evidence in Canada." *International Journal of Manpower* 23 (2 2002): 137–50.

Ross, Arthur M. *Trade Union Wage Policy*. Berkeley, CA: University of California Press, 1953.

Rosse, Josph, G. and Terry W. Noel. "Leaving the Organization." In Kevin R. Murphy, ed. *Individual Differences and Behavior in Organizations*. San Francisco: Jossey-Bass, 1996, pp. 451–506.

Rubinstein, Saul A. and Thomas A. Kochan. *Learning from Saturn*. Ithaca, NY: ILR Press, 2001.

Schwochau, Susan. "Union Effects on Job Attitudes." *Industrial and Labor Relations Review* 40 (January 1987): 209–24.

Smith, Patricia Cain, Lorne M. Kendall, and Charles L. Hulin. *The Measurement of Satisfaction in Work and Retirement: A Strategy for the Study of Attitudes*. Chicago. IL.: Rand-McNally, 1969.

Staw, Barry M. and Jerry Ross. "Stability in the Midst of Change: A Dispositional Approach to Job Attitudes." *Journal of Applied Psychology* 70 (August 1985): 469–80.

Tellegen, Auke. "Structures of Mood and Personality and Their Relevance to Assessing Anxiety, with an Emphasis on Self-Report." In A.H. Tumas and J.D. Masters, eds. *Anxiety and the Anxiety Disorders*. Hillsdale, NJ: Erlbaum, 1985, pp. 681–709.

_____, David T. Lykken, Thomas J. Bouchard, Kimberly J. Wilcox, Nancy L. Segal, and Stephen Rich. "Personality Similarity in Twins Reared Apart and Together." *Journal of Personality and Social Psychology* 54 (June 1988): 1031–39.

Thieblot, Armand J. "The Fall and Future of Unionism in Construction." In James T. Bennett and Bruce E. Kaufman, eds. *The Future of Private Sector Unionism in the United States*. Armonk, NY: M.E. Sharpe, 2002, pp. 149–71.

Triandis, Harry C. *Individualism and Collectivism*. San Francisco: Westview Press, 1995.

Vroom, Victor H. *Work and Motivation*. New York: John Wiley, 1964.

Wagner III, John A. "Participation's Effects on Performance and Satisfaction: A Reconsideration of Research Evidence." *Academy of Management Review* 19 (April 1994): 312–30.

Weiss, D. J., R. W. Dawis, G. W. England, and L. H. Lofquist. *Manual for the Minnesota Satisfaction Questionnaire*. Minneapolis: Industrial Relations Center, University of Minnesota, 1967.

Zalesny, Mary D. "Comparison of Economic and Noneconomic Factors in Predicting Faculty Union Vote Preferences in a Union Representation Election." *Journal of Applied Psychology* 70 (May 1985): 243–56.

12

De-Unionization and Macro Performance: What Freeman and Medoff Didn't Do

Daniel J. B. Mitchell and Christopher L. Erickson

Most, if not all, unions have monopoly power,
which they can use to raise wages above competi-
tive levels.
                                    – Freeman and Medoff (1984: 6)

The inequality of bargaining power between
employees who do not possess full freedom of
association or actual liberty of contract and
employers who are organized in the corporate or
other forms of ownership association substantially
burdens and affects the flow of commerce, and
tends to aggravate recurrent business depressions,
by depressing wage rates and the purchasing power
of wage earners in industry and by preventing the
stabilization of competitive wage rates and working
conditions within and between industries.
                         – Preamble to the Wagner Act of 1935

I. Introduction

Freeman and Medoff's seminal book, *What Do Unions Do?*, covered the gamut of research on collective bargaining and its economic impact with one major exception. It had little to say about the macroeconomic impacts of unions. Of course, no book can cover everything, and judgments must be made about what issues are most critical. Moreover, the decision to downplay the macro side in a book that was published in the mid–1980s is understandable, although unfortunate in hindsight for reasons described below.

By the early 1980s, union representation in the private sector had been slipping relative to the size of the U.S. work force for almost three decades. Gradual relative erosion had turned into dramatic absolute declines in union representation during the years immediately preceding the book's appearance. And concession bargaining was in full swing in the union sector — with freezes and cuts in nominal wages and benefits in many industries. Looking to the future, observers could see little sign of a union turnaround.

The political climate was unfriendly to unions in the 1980s. And product markets in sectors with relatively high union concentrations were reeling from such diverse forces as deregulation, an appreciating dollar, low-wage competition from abroad, etc. At the same time, union organizing, as measured, for example, by the number of NLRB representation elections, had fallen sharply. It was hard to conceive of unions having an influence much beyond their immediate declining sector.

Prior to the 1980s, the macro literature on unions, outlined more fully below, largely revolved around some version of "wage-push." In this view, powerful unions used their bargaining power to push up wages. Their influence extended to the nonunion sector through spillover mechanisms. The push on wages contributed to a wage-price spiral that could be checked (perhaps) by governmental direct intervention or — if that approach didn't work — by sufficiently high unemployment. Thus, unions were seen as potentially raising the unemployment rate over the long term.

Whatever might be said about that view, going forward from 1984 — the year in which the Freeman and Medoff book appeared — it could not have seemed likely to them that unions would in the future be able to trigger wage-price spirals. Freeman and Medoff wrote about more micro-level concerns, e.g., the voice effect of unions, the contrast between union and nonunion benefit packages, issues surrounding internal union affairs and corruption, etc. In a two-page segment, they dismissed the idea that unions could be a cause of inflation mainly on the grounds that the union share of total labor costs had become too small (Freeman and Medoff, 1984: 58–59). Reasonable as their decision to limit discussion of such issues may seem to many readers, it nonetheless left the macro side open. To the extent that macro appears in the book beyond the two-page segment, it involves how unions react to the business cycle (pp. 111–21). Since macro performance with union influence was not much discussed, macro performance without that influence was inherently omitted as well.

As the introductory quote from Freeman and Medoff suggests, they did think that unions had "monopoly" power. Perhaps readers were simply to infer that if there were wage-price spirals related to union monopoly power in the past, there wouldn't be in the future. Wages would no longer be subject to an "artificial" push from unions except within a shrinking union sector; presumably wages would be determined in the dominant nonunion sector by competitive supply and demand forces. Left unanalyzed by Freeman and Medoff was how a nonunion labor market would actually function.

The micro side was more clear, although — we argue later — incomplete for the same reasons. Unions provided extra employee voice. Nonunion employers would provide less voice. Unions tilted the benefit package toward health insurance and defined-benefit pensions, programs that favored more senior workers. Nonunion employers would be less generous with their benefit offerings.

In short, a reasonable hypothesis is that Freeman and Medoff looked to the future and saw union macro effects as yesterday's issue, with "yesterday" being the post-World War II period ending around 1980. But as the quote above from the 1935 Wagner Act suggests, if "yesterday" had been extended back to the Great Depression and before, the authors might not have been so quick to drop macro as an important topic. There was a significant body of opinion in the 1930s and before that saw the alternative to the union monopoly face featured in Freeman and Medoff not as textbook competition but as monopsony. In turn, some who held that opinion saw monopsony as affecting macro performance adversely and therefore looked to unions as a corrective force.

We take a somewhat different view of the union-macro interaction below than those pre-war observers. However, we do agree with the older view that monopsony is a good way to look at nonunion labor markets, even if we see some of its macro implications differently. And we note that once monopsony is seen as the default alternative to union representation, there are also *micro* implications that would have rounded out that side of Freeman and Medoff's analysis. That is, omission of the earlier pre-Wagner Act view left gaps in the book on both the macro and the micro side. Although we focus here primarily on the former, we provide brief reference to the latter as well.

Finally, we point out below that although it may have seemed to Freeman and Medoff that no one going forward from the mid–1980s would be much worried about unions from a macro perspective, with hindsight we know that wasn't entirely so. There developed a European literature, which we touch on below, that linked macro performance to the nature of the industrial relations system, distinguishing between corporatism, atomistic wage determination, and systems in between. And in the United States, records now available show that macro policymakers — particularly at the Federal Reserve — persisted with viewing unions through the lens of wage-push — despite union erosion. Indeed, even when unions are not explicitly discussed, contemporary macro policy makers and academics often seem stuck on an implicit bargaining model of wages. In effect, they seem to maintain a model of union-style wage setting without unions. In sum, if there ever is a second edition of *What Do Unions Do?*, it would benefit greatly from an added chapter on what nonunion employers do, both in macro and micro terms.

II. Unions and Macro Thought Before World War II

The early idea that union upward pressure on wages would benefit the macro economy was largely based on notions of income distribution and consumer behavior. In essence, the idea was simple enough: Workers were consumers who spent the bulk of their incomes. If their wages were higher, they would have more to spend on consumer goods. But businesses, left to their own devices, would push down wages, a rational strategy for each firm but one leading to a Marxist-type contradiction in capitalism collectively. By pushing down wages, firms would in aggregate cut demand for their own products, thus fomenting business depressions. Unions could prevent this Marxian contradiction, in modern terminology a "coordination failure" on the part of employers, by counteracting the downward pressure on wages.

However, it was not just those on the left of the political spectrum who perceived a danger in competitive wage setting. Herbert Hoover, in the early 1930s, famously urged employers not to cut wages as the economy declined on the same logic followed by those with leftist leanings. Wage cuts would mean reduced worker incomes and therefore reduced demand for consumer goods (Hoover, 1953: 43–46). Note that the Hoover view that wages were set by employers in discretionary fashion (and so could be kept up by businesses in the face of a business downturn at presidential urging) is implicitly a monopsonistic view. Buyers in truly competitive markets (T-bills, wheat futures) do not have discretion in the prices they pay. They are price takers. In contrast, monopsonistic employers do not take wages as given; they are wage makers, not takers.

In the period before the Great Depression, the federal government was small. Federal expenditures were less than 3 percent of GDP (in contrast to about 15 percent in the early post-World War II period and about one-fifth today). The Keynesian notion of using fiscal policy as an anti-Depression instrument would not have seemed an option to most observers. Moreover, fiscal orthodoxy emphasized the virtue of balanced federal budgets. Thus, in depressions — with revenue declining — cutting expenditures to match revenue seemed prudent (and was attempted). Monetary policy to resist business downturns was also not seen as appropriate. Yes, the monetary authorities might provide liquidity in the short term if a financial "panic" occurred. But policy should otherwise focus on maintaining the gold standard and allow the economy to function on its own. In any event, business downturns were not necessarily seen as exclusively bad outcomes. Rather, they were inherent adjustments of the economy that would clean out prior excesses.

If monetary and fiscal policy were not to be used to cushion the downturns, that left doing something on the wage side as the option. Herbert Hoover on the right was not anti-union. He signed the Norris-LaGuardia Act of 1932 that limited injunctions in labor disputes. Earlier in his presidency, Hoover toyed with the idea of making John L. Lewis, president of the United Mine Workers, Secretary of Labor (Hoover, 1952: 221–22). But although Hoover reported that he supported "collective bargaining by representatives of labor's own choosing" (Hoover, 1952: 101), he was not about to promote unions actively. So he contented himself with the exhortations noted earlier. Those further to the left, however, were more likely to see encouragement of unions and collective bargaining as a desirable form of anti-depression public policy (Kaufman, 2003: 20–21; 1996).

When the Roosevelt administration came into power, it abandoned many of the orthodoxies of the past. But it continued the Hoover notion that wage cutting was a process that could only aggravate the Depression. The administration first pursued a strategy — embodied in the 1933 National Industrial Recovery Act (NIRA) — of fostering industry codes with minimum labor standards and encouragement of collective bargaining. There was admittedly fuzziness in the administration's approach to macro policy since raising prices ("reflation") seemed also to be part of the agenda. A policy of raising both wages and prices might end up not raising real wages.

In fact, there was a complex of agendas at work in the early New Deal. These involved such matters as the abandonment of the gold standard, pleasing the remnants of the free-silver movement still represented in Congress, supporting farm prices and preventing farm foreclosures, avoiding bank failures, etc. (Mitchell, 2000). While it would be inappropriate to try and elaborate on these varied objectives here, suffice it to say that the Wagner Act's wage-boosting objective was one of the main survivors. By 1935, the NIRA had been declared unconstitutional and the National Labor Relations Act (NLRA), or Wagner Act, thereafter continued its approach in fostering collective bargaining. In 1937, the Wagner Act survived a Supreme Court challenge to its constitutionality. And in 1938, minimum wage standards reappeared at the federal level in the form of the Fair Labor Standards Act.

It is sometimes said that the New Deal's support of wages through unions was an application of "Keynesian" policy in the United States. This interpretation is not entirely correct. It is true that Keynes thought that wage cuts wouldn't cure the Depression. Nonetheless, raising wages was also not the primary Keynesian cure for underconsumptionism. Keynes emphasized fiscal policy and socialization of investment to increase aggregate demand in the face of business downturns. Thus, it is also worth stressing the influence of the other main logic behind the NLRA, which is not strictly Keynesian: to take wages out of competition in order to stop what was widely labeled as "destructive competition." But Keynes' doctrines spread only gradually across the Atlantic. In the postwar period, American Keynesians advanced his agenda, later acknowledging a major role for monetary policy as well by the 1970s.

The fact that unions were not seen as central to avoiding depression after World War II may have been one factor in Freeman and Medoff's lack of discussion of the macro side of collective bargaining. But that can't have been the whole story. While unions were not seen as a key to boosting the economy, they were — as outlined below — seen as potentially inflationary. And while inflation (reflation) in the 1930s was an objective of official policy, rising prices were seen as a major problem to be avoided from the 1940s onward. In short, the Wagner Act view was that unions would stabilize the economy by averting wage deflation. But the post-World War II perspective was that unions might destabilize the economy by causing inflation. Both approaches regarded unions as playing a macro role, but the normative nature of that role was quite different: In the 1930s, inflation (and thus the main implication of the monopoly face of unions) was viewed as a desirable outcome, while in the post-World War II era inflation was viewed as undesirable. One might thus say that there are in effect "two faces of the union macro effect," depending on whether or not the economy is at full employment and in danger of the deleterious effects of inflation.

III. Macro Policy and Union Wages in the Post-World War II Period

Before the 1980s, the importance of union wage determination was reflected in official economic policy. Indeed, much of what might be termed empirical Keynesianism was based on an implicit notion that a bargaining process explained such phenomena as downward wage rigidity. Explanations of wage rigidity from Keynes onward were generally phrased in terms of what workers would "demand," what they expect and believe is fair, and what they would accept. Downward pressure on the nominal wage would not be acceptable, either because it would likely cut the real wage or because — in the presence of decentralized wage determination — it would lower one group's wage relative to others (Mitchell, 1993).

As we indicate later, this bargaining approach to wage setting persists in contemporary rhetoric, despite substantial de-unionization of the American work force. But in the era following World War II, the bargaining model was more plausible. Many workers could effectively make their demands and notions of acceptability felt through collective bargaining. The idea that nonunion employers were potentially monopsonistic continued in the literature (e.g., Bronfenbrenner, 1956). But the focus on the union sector and its spillovers tended to eclipse this approach; if there were sufficient spillovers, nonunion employers would be unable to activate their monopsony potential.

During World War II, and again during the Korean War, formal wage-price controls were imposed in the United States to hold down inflation. That is, the official view was that too much wage push would cause inflation — a "Bad Thing" that direct controls were designed to avert. The assumption underlying controls was that wages and labor costs were a key element in pricing. Thus, these programs sought to constrain wages and then allow businesses a markup form of pricing above their costs.

In the Eisenhower years following the Korean War, however, use of formal controls in peacetime was viewed as distortionary and an overreaching of government. Nonetheless, there was much fretting in that period about an upward inflationary creep in wages relative to productivity (Gordon, 1975). And when empirical Keynesianism came to power in the Kennedy-Johnson era, "voluntary" wage-price guideposts were put into place in an explicit attempt to link (and limit) wage setting to national productivity gains (Sheahan, 1967).

As might be expected, the Kennedy-Johnson guideposts program — even with its voluntary character — was controversial and sparked much debate among economists of that period (Shultz and Aliber, 1966). But econometric work supported the notion that union-sector wage "rounds" played an important part in overall wage setting, a belief that was already widely held among labor relations specialists. "Key" settlements in a few major union situations were viewed as setting the pattern for others. Survey research also seemed to provide empirical support for key settlements and wage imitation (Eckstein and Wilson, 1962; Rees and Schultz, 1970: 44–46).

The key settlement idea had a macro implication. If government could affect these key settlements through an "incomes policy," it could achieve a faster rate of economic growth with lower unemployment and less inflation. The idea was usually phrased in terms of shifting the "Phillips curve" to the left, thus improving the trade-off between inflation and unemployment. Views of this type were not found solely in the United States. Such notions were widely held in other developed countries — especially in Western Europe and Australia, where various forms of incomes policy could be found (Edelman and Fleming, 1965; Ulman and Flanagan, 1971; Hancock, 1981). In turn, the foreign experience with incomes policy was seen in the United States as informing American macro policy (Galenson, 1973).

Clearly, the simplistic view that a few union settlements not only determined most other union wages but also mechanically fixed nonunion wages — through some sort of threat effect — was an overstatement. Union wages could move up or down relative to other wages over time. Thus, there tended to be a widening of the union wage differential in the period after the Korean War. But given the substantially higher unionization rate than exists at present, it was nonetheless plausible to think that union pay practices influenced nonunion practices, even if they did not completely determine them. Moreover, because union workers received more pay per hour in both wages and benefits and because union workers were more likely to be full-timers than nonunion workers, the private compensation bill in the 1950s disproportionately reflected union wages, even apart from any spillover effects (Jacoby and Mitchell, 1988).

A combination of the rise of union wages relative to nonunion and a recession in the early 1960s, provoked an employer backlash. There followed a concession movement that proved to be a milder version of the concessions that developed in the early 1980s. However, the early 1960s episode occurred without the dramatic membership losses seen in the 1980s. Still in both cases — the early 1960s and the early 1980s — union weakness corresponded to a period of decreased strike incidence. But strike incidence rose again after the early 1960s, although it diminished after the early 1980s. In sum, union militancy, measured by strike activity, did not return in the 1980s as it had two decades before. The early 1960s proved to be a lull; the 1980s, in contrast, proved to be a more durable era of declining union representation with a continued undertow of concession bargaining.

Job insecurity worries related to concerns about displacement due to "automation" seemed to play a role in repressing union wage demands in the early 1960s, along with sluggish economic performance. Thus, wage moderation in exchange for job security was a feature of union wage bargains in such diverse industries as longshoring, meatpacking, and metals. The Kennedy-Johnson guideposts may also have had an initial influence in retarding wages and strikes (Perry, 1967). Notably, a number of unions gave up escalator clauses that linked wages to consumer prices by the mid–1960s. Thus, when the economy recovered and inflation accelerated during the Vietnam build-up, union wage gains under long-term contracts tended to fall behind those in the more frequently adjusted nonunion sector. The result was a drop in the union wage premium during the late 1960s.

Significantly, during this period of temporary reduction of union bargaining power, there were growing complaints of worker scarcity and yet only a gradual uptick of wage inflation. Without upward wage pressure from unions, the result was not demand = supply in the labor market but labor shortages. These transitional phenomena foreshadowed more permanent tendencies seen again in the late 1980s and 1990s (Mitchell, 1989). As we note later, labor shortages in the face of union weakness do not fit well with a model of nonunion wage setting as simple textbook competition. But they do dovetail with monopsony as the default alternative to union influence. The proponents of the Wagner Act would not have been surprised.

IV. Direct Controls and Guidelines in the 1970s

A move by unions to catch up in wages (restore the union wage premium) began at the end of the 1960s, just as the Nixon administration and the Federal Reserve hoped to engineer a modest anti-inflation slowdown of the economy. The upward push on union wages — even if it could be rationalized as catch-up for an earlier inflation surprise — was seen as a threat to the official anti-inflation strategy. When the attempt at a soft landing turned into outright recession, a new economic policy was announced in 1971.

The history of incomes policy in the United States up through the 1960s might have suggested that such direct interventions were the province only of Democrats. Democrats had imposed controls during World War II and the Korean War and had promulgated voluntary guideposts in the Kennedy-Johnson era. But in 1971 — much to the consternation of some of his key advisors — Republican Richard Nixon imposed formal wage-price controls as an anti-inflation device (Stein, 1994: 159–63). Although it was never officially stated that the program was focused on union wage settlements, officials of organized labor certainly perceived the program that way (Robinson, 1981: 304–20, esp. 312). In much the same manner as their Kennedy-Johnson predecessors, those in the Nixon administration who designed the program had in mind a mechanism to deal with (union) wage push. They even adopted the Kennedy-Johnson notion that the national productivity trend should be factored into the program guideline for wage settlements.

The Nixon controls program went through various phases before being abandoned in the face of inflationary shocks from dollar devaluation and an OPEC oil price hike (Weber, 1973; Weber and Mitchell, 1978; U.S. Office of Economic Stabilization, 1974). Controls did temporarily retard the wage catch-up movement in the union sector during 1972. Strike incidence also fell briefly. However, demand pressures — combined with the abovementioned dollar depreciation and the OPEC oil shock — led to an abrupt resumption of inflation. Termination of controls in 1974 coincided with a period of anti-inflation Federal Reserve restraint and deep recession.

Although inflation declined after the recession of the mid–1970s, there continued to be an upward push on union wages and on the union wage differential. In place of Nixon's formal controls, the Ford administration substituted a vague "Whip Inflation Now" (WIN) voluntary program. Ford created a new Council on Wage and Price Stability to monitor inflationary developments and make reports on troubling trends.

By this time, the notion of a "natural rate of unemployment" — later termed the "Non-Accelerating Inflation Rate of Unemployment" or NAIRU — was replacing the Phillips curve as a macro construct in the economic literature (Friedman, 1968). Pessimism increased about the degree to which unemployment could be reduced without causing inflationary pressure, i.e., about a high NAIRU. However, even on the assumption that there was no long-run Phillips curve, direct intervention might still be rationalized as lowering the NAIRU. Following this logic, the Carter administration created a new program of "voluntary" wage-price guidelines. It also recommended that Congress enact a program of "real wage insurance," essentially tax incentives for workers whose wage settlements met the federal standards.

Congress never enacted Carter's complex tax proposal. But the guidelines program was maintained through the end of Carter's term and the Council on Wage and Price Stability that Carter had inherited from Ford was continued. The focus on union settlements under Carter was clear; the director of the Council adhered to the longstanding notion of key settlements that set the wage pattern.[1] However, the appointment of Paul Volcker as the new chair of the Federal Reserve in the later years of the Carter administration led to a shift in policy at the nation's central bank.

Volcker officially moved the Fed to a monetarist policy focused on control of the money supply rather than control of interest rates. Whether Volcker and his Fed colleagues were ever confirmed monetarists — or whether monetarism was simply a pragmatic choice of an instrument thought necessary to wring inflation out of the system — has been disputed (Neikirk, 1987: 5, 35, 68). Strict monetarism as guide to policy was more plausible in 1979 than it later became, as financial deregulation in the 1980s changed the relationship between measures of the money supply and inflation (Hafer, 2001: 19). Nonetheless, the Volcker appointment by Carter seemed to foreshadow a move toward monetary policy as the key anti-inflation instrument and away from direct intervention in wages and prices.

Organized labor criticized this Fed shift as a violation of its anti-inflation "accord" with the Carter administration. But Carter's policy makers had no hand in the design of the new Fed policy apparently and learned of it after the fact (Greider, 1987: 113; Neikirk, 1987: 65–66). And the new monetary approach continued into the Reagan years where it was to have its major impact on the macro economy and on unions. Moreover, the Reagan administration brought an immediate end to wage-price controls and guidelines. Upon taking office, the Reagan administration dismantled what remained of the Carter guidelines. In the era of deregulation, direct government involvement in wage and price setting was quickly viewed as an anachronism.

V. Weitzman's Solution for Stagflation in the 1980s

Reducing inflation through recession alone in the early 1980s proved to be a painful process, as many had predicted. By that time, the phrase "stagflation" was commonly applied to a situation in which unemployment and inflation were both high, as they were in the early 1980s. Although Freeman and Medoff did not dwell on union wages from a macro perspective, others in academia did view wage setting as a contributor to stagflation. In particular, Martin L. Weitzman proposed that tax incentives should be provided to move pay practices away from the traditional wage system and towards a "share economy." Weitzman's popular book on the subject with its subtitle — "Conquering Stagflation" — was put out by the same publisher and in the same year (1984) as Freeman and Medoff's volume (See also Weitzman, 1983, 1985, 1987).

Practices such as profit sharing, revenue sharing, and gain sharing were to be encouraged under the Weitzman "share economy" plan through a tax subsidy. Weitzman's view was that the wage system was rigid in the sense that nominal wages did not move (down) to clear the labor market. He argued for an alternative system in which the share parameter, rather than the wage parameter, would be the rigid element. Thus, workers would have, say, a rigid percentage share of profits or revenue rather than a rigid wage. Weitzman assumed that micro incentives were insufficient to produce widespread share economy pay systems. Firms would not internalize macro-level gains in selecting share economy pay practices and, therefore, a tax incentive was needed to change their pay systems.

The Weitzman plan attracted considerable media attention — far more than the Freeman and Medoff book. Weitzman's proposal was labeled by the *New York Times* as the "best idea since Keynes."[2] The idea also had resonance because some highly visible union concession settlements had already incorporated profit sharing, notably in the auto industry. Unions, which had traditionally been hostile to profit sharing prior to the 1980s, were being induced to accept such plans as an offset to concessions. The promise was that if their concessions paid off and made their employers more competitive, workers would eventually share in the resulting future profitability.

In Weitzman's model, share economy pay systems expand labor demand by reducing the marginal cost of labor. If all or most employers were induced to shift to a share system, a chronic labor shortage would be created, thus lowering the NAIRU and lessening the impact of recession. In effect, modest negative demand shocks would result in "layoffs" of vacancies rather than of real workers. Only if the shocks were sufficiently severe would employers resort to actual layoffs. Thus, the macro economy would tend to be more stable since it would have a built-in anti-layoff cushion. The NAIRU would be lowered and, despite chronic labor shortages, inflation would not be triggered by the resulting persistence of low unemployment.

Given the interest in alternative pay systems, and Martin Weitzman's close physical proximity (in the Harvard economics department) to Freeman and Medoff at the time he was writing, we can again only speculate on the lack of a macro focus in their volume. One factor may simply have been timing. There were discussions of the macro effects of alternative pay systems prior to Weitzman's proposal. Weitzman's work began to circulate before Freeman and Medoff's book appeared. However, it may nonetheless have come into prominence too late for inclusion. Another factor may have been that Weitzman was not particularly interested in union wage setting, as opposed to wage setting in general. In fact, he tended to think that unions might get in the way of a share economy by limiting employer hiring (so that the share would not be diluted).

With the benefit of hindsight, however, we can see that had some discussion of Weitzman found its way into Freeman and Medoff, the authors might have been led to a deeper analysis of macro wage setting processes under alternative institutional arrangements. Weitzman's share economy plan in essence produced its macro benefits by creating a chronic labor shortage. There was certainly dispute in the economic literature as to whether a Weitzman share economy would work as advertised (Nordhaus, 1988; Weitzman, 1988). However, the main idea in Weitzman had a certain similarity to monopsony that we explore below more fully. Wages would be lowered (because the tax-favored share would be a substitute) to produce the shortage. In monopsony, of course, wages are also repressed. So under monopsony and under Weitzman the macro economy gets the shortage. But workers don't get the share under monopsony, unlike under the Weitzman approach.

If nonunion employers operate normally as monopsonists, not perfect competitors, we might expect Weitzman effects to occur as a result of de-unionization, even without the tax-based inducements for share plans.[3] And, of course, we did begin to see Weitzman effects without the Weitzman plan by the late 1980s: low unemployment without surging inflation, labor shortages, and only a mild recession when one occurred. Such effects were even more pronounced in the following decade.

VI. Union Decline and Monopsony

[T]he want ads are not a reliable measure of the actual jobs available at any particular time. They are ... the employers' insurance policy against the relentless turnover of the low-wage workforce. Most of the big hotels run ads almost continuously, if only to build a supply of applicants to replace the current workers as they drift away or are fired, so finding a job is just a matter of being in the right place at the right time and flexible enough to take whatever is being offered that day.

–Ehrenreich (2001: 15)

It might be assumed that union decline should have made the U.S. labor market more "competitive." But a key question is what being "competitive" implies for macro analysis in the context of a nonunion labor market. Truly competitive markets are highly sensitive to shortages and surpluses and quickly eradicate both through price adjustments. Thus, one might have expected that if U.S. labor markets were highly competitive by the late 1980s, the labor shortages that developed then should have produced dramatic wage increases. And the same result should certainly have been expected during the labor shortages of the late 1990s, since even more union erosion had occurred.

The fact that there was no wage explosion suggests that if indeed labor markets are now more competitive, the expected characteristics of such "competitive" (i.e., nonunion) markets need further elaboration. Those markets clearly do not work the way competitive markets for Treasury bonds or wheat futures do. Where were the wage increases in the late 1980s and late 1990s that should have been clearing nonunion labor markets? Since such market-clearing wages were not seen, we argue below that a reasonable model of what nonunion employers do is monopsony, not perfect competition. While the union monopoly face is prominent in Freeman and Medoff, the nonunion monopsony face is missing.

It could be argued that for purely empirical micro purposes, Freeman and Medoff did not need to provide much analysis of the nonunion sector. What unions provided "more" of, nonunion employers would provide less of, e.g., more voice in the former, less in the latter. However, as a justification for unions, Freeman and Medoff did provide a rationale for why the union "more" was better than the nonunion less. In the voice case at least, they could argue that voice is valuable to employers, but that voice requires an outside party to induce workers to provide it. However, if standard classical supply = demand is taken as the default case for nonunion employers, other aspects of unionism at the micro level are suspect as "distortions."

After all, in the textbook view, "competitive" labor markets match up worker and employer preferences, producing just the right amount of safety, pensions, or whatever. Any deficiency in an area such as safety is made up by a compensating wage differential. On the other hand, if the default model for the nonunion sector is monopsony, there will be underprovision of benefits and of other positive conditions just as there is underprovision of wages.

Thus, it is not enough to argue — as some do — that under competition nonunion employers will be led to "follow principles of human resource management" (Wachter, 2003: 348). Monopsony doesn't foreclose such practices but it does suggest an insufficiency of them. To make the matter concrete, consider the difference between the ornate hotel lobby — where the hotel operator competes for guests — and the hotel employees' entrance, where the hotel competes for workers. The lobby and the employees' entrance both reflect "competition," but the consequences are not similar. Competition does not lead hotel operators to cater to employee preferences to the same extent that they cater to those of hotel customers.

If it is important to look at the operation of the nonunion sector explicitly to evaluate the union impact at the micro level, the same can reasonably be expected to be true at the macro level. Below we provide some reasons for analyzing the nonunion sector in monopsonistic terms. We then focus on the implications, implications that were not described in the Freeman and Medoff volume.

Monopsony in the Labor Market

Traditionally, labor-market monopsony models were confined to special cases such as company towns or employer collusion in certain occupations. These cases were put forward as an exception to the notion that unions inevitably faced a wage-employment trade-off in bargaining, i.e., a negatively-sloped labor demand curve. In the monopsony case, a counteracting union monopoly effect could raise wages without necessarily decreasing employment. The union monopoly vs. employer monopsony idea, however, typically has been depicted as a curiosity. It was seen as pedagogically useful in helping students learn the microeconomics of the labor market and, perhaps, helpful in explaining unionization of certain odd groups such as nurses and professional athletes (Kaufman, 2003).

Figure 12.1 depicts three alternative positions for wage setting. The labor demand curve of the firm is the marginal revenue product of labor (MRP_L). For reasons we discuss later, the firm faces an upward-sloping supply curve of labor (S). Such a firm, for profit-maximizing purposes, should set the wage at W_M because the marginal wage (MW) intersects the marginal revenue product of labor curve at that point.

If a powerful union entered the scene, it could raise the wage as high as W_U without a loss in employment ($L_U = L_M$). An in-between position — which is analogous to textbook competition — is at a wage = W_C where labor supply = labor demand.[4] Note that at any wage below W_C, the firm faces a labor shortage since the act of adding an additional worker *willing to accept the going wage* provides marginal revenue in excess of that wage. It is, however, rational for the employer to allow the shortage to persist, rather than raise wages to eliminate it. Monopsony, therefore, creates a chronic labor shortage similar to the shortage envisioned by Weitzman for his share economy. We should expect, therefore, that the macro dynamics of a monopsonistic labor market would be similar to those of the Weitzman model.

Although originally seen as a curiosity, the monopsony model was applied more generally to low-wage labor markets by Card and Krueger (1997: 355–86) who used it to explain the seeming lack of disemployment effects when minimum wages were boosted. Their empirical findings with regard to the minimum wage led to considerable professional and policy debate. But labor-market monopsony more generally began receiving wider attention in microanalysis (Bhaskar et al., 2002; Boal and Ransom, 1997; Manning, 2003).

Figure 12.1
Wage Setting Alternatives

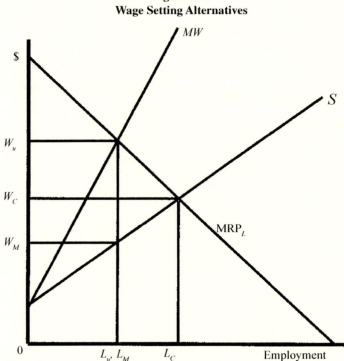

The rationale for depicting the labor supply curve facing a nonunion employer as upward sloping is based on reasonable assumptions about labor market flows. We note later some other rationales for assuming nonunion monopsony, apart from the flow model. However, the flow model is useful to sketch out, à la Card and Krueger.

The Flow Model of Monopsony

A firm which sets a relatively high wage compared to the general average in the relevant labor market will experience low turnover (a low quit rate) and a high absolute inflow of quality workers from the outside labor market. Similarly, a firm that sets a relatively low wage will experience a low absolute inflow of quality workers and a high turnover (quit) rate. These standard personnel assumptions are hardly controversial.

Imagine a firm that is in equilibrium at a low wage so that its high turnover rate is just balanced by new hires. By equilibrium we mean that it is achieving some target level of employment. At such a level, labor inflows and outflows must match, or employment will be changing. Thus, if ten workers arrive in a period, their number must be just balanced by ten quits to keep employment constant.

Now imagine that for some reason the firm raises its wage offer. More workers, say 20, initially are hired per period and a smaller percentage of its work force quits (the higher wage essentially acts as a minimum wage for the monopsonist firm, moving it to expand employment). The firm's work force therefore grows. Eventually, however, a new equilibrium is reached in which the 20 arrivals are just balanced by 20 quits. Although the quit *rate* is lower, the internal work force grows until the quit rate x employment = 20 departures. In short, a high wage produces a big work force for the firm and a low wage rate produces a small one. That is the essence of an upward-sloping supply curve of labor, a necessary and sufficient condition for monopsony power unless a union with Freeman and Medoff's monopoly face is present to offset that power.

Coordination and Monopsony

We have shown that a nonunion employer will typically have monopsony power, once the dynamics of labor flows are considered. Monopsony does *not* depend on there being a single employer in the labor market, e.g., the old company town example. However, the inherent monopsony in nonunion wage setting could be reinforced by employer coordination of wage policies, a *de facto* buyers' cartel. The longstanding stories of monopsony in the nursing labor market have involved explicit coordination by health provider/employers in urban areas, for example.

Notions of wage imitation in the union sector (pattern bargaining) are a traditional fixture of the industrial relations literature (Ross, 1948; see also Erickson, 1996 for a discussion of change and continuity in patterns in the "post-concession" era). The idea that pay should be set in comparison with relevant groups has long been held by arbitrators called in to settle "interest" disputes (Bernstein, 1954: 51–71). But it has also been found that in the nonunion sector, setting wages through comparisons is widespread.

In fact, formally or informally, an almost universal element of wage setting involves finding out what someone else is paying for similar workers. The information might be gathered through trade associations, government surveys, or simply a phone call to the firm down the street (Bewley, 1999: 92–95). "Benchmarking" is a common management practice for evaluation of, and decision making concerning, all internal policies. How-to-do-it books for personnel managers emphasize such comparisons in setting pay (Parus, 2002).

The line between innocent information gathering and cartel-like collusion is a fine one. There are so-called "safe harbor" guidelines in U.S. antitrust law that attempt to prevent pay surveys from being used for collusive purposes. However, many employers are not aware of these guidelines, and the guidelines themselves seem arbitrary and unlikely to prevent collusive behavior[5] (Davis,

2003). In any event, the existence of tacit agreements not to compete for labor has long been noted in the research literature (Myers and Maclaurin, 1943: 40–43). It need not be the case that all firms pay the same wage — they clearly do not — or that all provide the same percentage wage increase. As long as pay at one firm "influences" pay at others, a certain level of *de facto* coordination is occurring.

In a labor market where unions represent a significant fraction of the work force and in which the threat of organization is real to nonunion employers, union wage setting will have a more general influence than just in the bargaining units where it occurs. Nonunion firms in the 1970s reportedly watched union settlements "very carefully" — and made pay decisions based on their observations — to avoid being unionized (Foulkes, 1980: 166). Under such conditions, firms — union or not — were likely to operate in the wage range at or above W_C on Figure 12.1, either because they were forced to do so through bargaining or because they thought it prudent to do so as a defensive measure.

However, such labor markets can be "tipped" into the below W_C monopsony range, if the union sector declines sufficiently and the threat of new organizing recedes. Such decline and threat reduction characterized the 1980s and 1990s.[6] Thus, it is credible that the U.S. labor market moved away from monopoly towards monopsony wage determination in that period. Wage imitation hasn't disappeared. Rather, the nonunion firms that once were influenced by the union sector now focus on other nonunion employers as reference points and do not pattern their pay policies on union settlements (Erickson and Mitchell, 1995).

Risk and Monopsony

In the European context in particular, it has been argued that legal mandates providing job security for incumbent workers actually reduce employment and hiring. The explanation for this outcome is said to be one of risk avoidance. Employers know that if they hire workers and later need to reduce their work forces, terminations may be difficult. As a result, they are said to avoid risk by hiring fewer workers than might be the case under *laissez-faire* conditions (OECD, 1999: 47–132). Employers can be said to "insure" themselves against the risk of expensive layoffs by paying the costs of having too few workers (or using routes around the mandates such as temps or off-the-books hiring).

The United States does not have European-style mandates related to job security. However, there is a downward inflexibility with regard to nominal wage cuts that we explore below in the context of monopsony dynamics. As a legal matter, wage cuts can occur — no law prevents them so long as the minimum wage is paid. But empirically worker morale is hurt by such cuts, and employers seek to avoid them. Thus, American employers face a risk in offering a nominal wage increase that may be difficult to reverse in the event of subsequent falling demand.

Under such circumstances, nonunion employers might "insure" themselves against the downward wage rigidity risk by offering a lower wage than otherwise. They would, of course, pay a cost in the form of increased worker turnover and vacancies. But just as employers in the European model rationally hire too few, it is rational for U.S. employers to pay too little. A lower-wage "insurance" policy, particularly when adopted by many employers, would be sustainable and monopsonistic in its effect.

VII. Macro Dynamics of Monopsony in the Post-Freeman-and-Medoff Era

Thus, many plausible reasons indicate that monopsony prevails in nonunion labor markets, particularly in the context of a declining union threat effect. In our view, the monopsony model can be usefully extended to the macro arena to explain the puzzles that became evident as unions declined. These puzzles were not foreseen in Freeman and Medoff as a consequence of de-unionization, since they did not explore monopsony or macro. Later authors did sometimes cite the union decline as a possible factor in the drop of the NAIRU (Stiglitz, 1997: 7). But a formal explanation of why and how the union decline would have such an effect on the NAIRU was not fully explored.[7] Even where a connection was made to de-unionization and "a decline in labor rents" or to a fear of reduced job security, the monopsony implication was not explored[8] (Cohen et al., 2002; Stiglitz, 2003: 183).

Under monopsony, however, there is a chronic labor shortage. So, for example, if there is an increase in the labor supply, employers will tend to absorb it. During the 1990s, many observers were surprised by the apparent absorption of welfare recipients pushed into the labor market by welfare reform legislation. Note the parallel with the Weitzman model; the marginal additional worker is sucked into employment in both the Weitzman model and the monopsony model. As Weitzman (1984: 98–99) put it, "A share system looks very much like a labor-shortage economy. Share firms (are) ever hungry for labor — cruising around like vacuum cleaners on wheels, searching . . . for extra workers to pull in at existing compensation. . . ."

Weitzman's model also tended to provide a cushion in the event of a demand decline. So does monopsony with one addition: downward nominal wage rigidity. During the 1990s and beyond, economists continued to document the phenomenon of such rigidity (Bewley, 1999; Lebow et al., 2003). In fact, this characteristic of the labor market has been well known for decades, although the precise rationale for it has varied. When combined with monopsony as the nonunion default, such rigidity produces Weitzman-type effects.

Figure 12.2 provides an example. Under monopsony, the wage is set at W_M. A moderate drop in labor demand from MRP_L to MRP_L' produces *no* drop in employment. Even a sharp drop in demand to MRP_L'' produces only a moderate decline in employment to L''. The pre-existing labor shortage cushions employment against negative demand shocks. The contrast with the higher union wage W_U is instructive here. Any drop in demand with initial wage = W_U shows up as reduced employment. Thus, the fall to MRP_L' cuts employment to L^*. The fall to MRP_L'' would cut employment to zero. In short, monopsony produces chronic labor shortages. Unemployment is low but wages are not raised to eliminate the shortages. When negative demand shocks occur, monopsony tilts the results toward mild recession instead of major downturns.[9]

Given these macro dynamics, it should come as no surprise that early job creation after a recession often comes in the form of temp hiring. The flow monopsony model, with its easy entrance and exit, should be particularly linked to temp arrangements. Employers "owe" least to temps and add or subtract them at the margin. In the 1990s, researchers noted the connection between low unemployment without wage pressures and the growth of temporary employment (Houseman et al., 2001). The chronic labor shortage associated with monopsony should especially show up in the temp sector. Rapid growth of temp agency employment was just beginning when Freeman and Medoff wrote, and such employment was not analyzed in their book.

Figure 12.2
Monopsony with Demand Decline

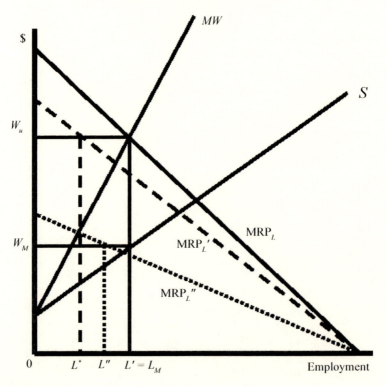

VIII. Monopsony, Macro Performance, and the Pros and Cons of Unions

As noted, Freeman and Medoff did not devote much attention to the macro side of unions, perhaps because they believed that union erosion made the old concerns about wage-push irrelevant. Of course, wage-push does indeed seem unlikely under current circumstances with unions representing less than one in ten private sector workers. There were, we suggest, macro effects in terms of a lower NAIRU and milder recessions (along with micro losses) that Freeman and Medoff did not discuss.

But if Freeman and Medoff had discussed the macro side, and if they had come to the conclusions we do, what would have been their verdict on the pros and cons of unions? In the early 1990s, Freeman reported that he continued to think that on net the balance was positive. On the macro side, he noted that unions no longer had much spillover influence and so could not be charged with causing inflation or unemployment. But since he had no monopsony model of nonunion employers, his analysis did not factor in the macro implications of monopsony (Freeman, 1992: 153–55).

Clearly, a full cost/benefit analysis would have to include macro effects of monopsony as well as micro losses. Monopsony, as indicated earlier, undermines the notion of a competitive matching of employer and employee preferences and gives rise to a host of undesirable economic and social consequences. It suggests that employers, other things equal, will tend to underprovide voice, benefits, and good working conditions absent a union to offset their monopsony power.[10] It suggests downward pressure on wages and a shift of income distribution from labor to capital. The macro effects are thus achieved at the cost of workers' bargaining power and wage outcomes. In a way, it harks back to the concerns about inequality of bargaining power cited by institutionalists in the late nineteenth and early twentieth centuries (the Kaufman history chapter). By the 1990s, analogous concerns about income inequality, decline in health insurance coverage, and unmet voice needs were again commonplace (Mishel et al., 2003: 113–216; Freeman and Rogers, 1999).

Moreover, while unions might produce macro consequences were they to regain the representation rates seen before the 1980s, there are remedies for such effects. One comes from European literature of the 1980s and beyond and has little direct relevance to the United States. But the other does represent an alternative role for unions in the American context.

During the 1980s, there developed a body of literature — especially in Europe — focusing on different industrial relations systems and their macro consequence. Calmfors and Driffil (1988) argued that the NAIRU would have a humped shaped relationship to the degree of wage setting centralization in the labor market. And Freeman (1988), in the same symposium, came to similar conclusions. In a highly corporatist or centralized situation, unions, government, and business could coordinate wage policy to account for adverse macro effects.

At the other extreme, atomized competition would keep wage pressures down. So it was in the middle — presumably as in the U.S. case before the 1980s — that the NAIRU would be higher than at either extreme. However, from the U.S. perspective, the notion that unions could somehow ever become significant enough to make strict corporatism a realistic alternative seems far-fetched.[11] Is there a possibility that if unions could make it back to their pre–1980s level of influence, adverse macro consequences could be avoided?

Most researchers are doubtful that even that more modest comeback is likely (Bennett and Kaufman, 2002). However, suppose that such a comeback did occur. As we have stressed, monopsony produces Weitzman effects but without the Weitzman share. Unions could redirect their bargaining objectives toward share systems rather than the traditional wage system. Indeed, unions could play a vital part in a Weitzman-style economy. Adoption of programs such as profit sharing could be aided by an entity that could verify that profits were being appropriately accounted, and perhaps by a limited European-style corporatism, or at least greater union and worker voice in company strategy and profit formation. That being said, unions in the private sector are a long way from regaining their pre–1980s position. So concerns about the possible macro consequences were that to occur would now have very low weight in a weighing of unions' pros and cons.

IX. The Persistence of Wage-Push Thinking

Up to this point, we have conjectured that Freeman and Medoff did not focus on the macro side because they assumed that the topic had become irrelevant due to union decline. But while that might have seemed a reasonable judgment in the mid–1980s, with hindsight we know now that wage-push thinking by macro policy makers proved resilient. This persistence is remarkable since in academia the kind of "institutional" analysis associated with unions and with the field of industrial relations was in marked decline (Kaufman, 1993).

In the executive branch, monetarist thinking in the Reagan-Bush administrations may have led to a disinterest in union developments.[12] But even within those administrations, some policy makers — after the fact — put great stress on the breaking of the air controllers' strike as an event leading to a low-inflation economy.[13] At the Federal Reserve, however, wage-push thinking seemed to continue into the 1980s and 1990s. Thanks to the posting of transcripts of the Federal Open Market Committee (FOMC) meetings and related staff documents, we now have inside information on monetary policy.[14]

Consider, for example, discussion of the 1997 United Parcel Service-Teamsters strike. When a settlement was reached, Dallas Fed Bank President Robert McTeer said at the FOMC that the new contract had done "a good deal of damage in the past couple of weeks. The settlement may go a long way toward undermining the wage flexibility that we started to get in labor markets with the air traffic controllers' strike back in the early 1980s." Fed Chairman Alan

Greenspan voiced a similar opinion: "The air traffic controllers' confrontation with President Reagan set in motion a fundamental change in policy for this country more than 15 years ago. It is conceivable that we will look back at the UPS strike and say that it, too, signaled a significant change." In effect, both statements suggest that a union wage deal involving 185,000 workers at a single package delivery firm could somehow undermine Fed policy. That idea is the old key-settlement/wage-push approach.

Apart from the focus on particular settlements, more general discussion of the NAIRU in policy circles and academia is still permeated with notions of bargained wages. Workers are said to "demand" certain conditions or to be unwilling to accept others. These rhetorical descriptions do not sit comfortably with a perfect competition model of the labor market and certainly not with a monopsony approach.

The *Annual Reports* of the Council of Economic Advisors (CEA) in the 1990s provide ongoing examples of this tendency. In its February 1994 *Report*, the CEA gave some credibility to the notion that corporate restructuring of the early 1990s might be raising the NAIRU (pp. 109–13). But the CEA was sure the actual unemployment rate was above the NAIRU so that "wage-push inflation is unlikely to be a factor constraining economic growth in the near future." The implication, however, was that "wage-push" was latent, but poised to arise again, as the labor market tightened.

In its February 1997 *Report*, the Clinton CEA provided an extended discussion of the NAIRU concept. It continued the union-like language: the NAIRU would depend on "workers' real wage expectations," "workers' demands," etc. (pp. 45–50). Presumably, if wages didn't meet those expectations, workers would not accept them. De-unionization was cited as a possible factor in the NAIRU's decline, although it was not clear exactly what the CEA saw as the connection. The CEA also cited job insecurity as a factor, so that "workers may be relatively unwilling to press for the wage gains they could normally command...." (pp. 57–63). Again, the implication was that wage-push (wage-press?) was latent but could reassert itself once the insecurity worries subsided. (And one might expect that low unemployment would lead to reduced anxiety about job loss.)

The final Clinton CEA *Report*, issued in January 2001, had the NAIRU down to 5.1 percent. The lack of inflation in the 1990s at unemployment rates below that level was attributed to a "productivity surprise" that would eventually wear off (pp. 71–74). That is, workers would eventually press (somehow) to capture the gains in productivity once they realized those gains existed.

While insider-outsider/implicit contract models, efficiency wage, and reservation wage models might be used to rationalize such demand/accept terminology, those models are not really compatible with wage-push thinking (Kaufman and Hotchkiss, 1999: 665–68). Rather, they serve to explain downward nominal wage rigidity. Workers experience (possibly costly) morale problems when there are take-aways. Employers may wish to avoid such adverse reactions among their insider employees. Similarly, displaced workers seeking new jobs may initially base their pay expectations on their prior wage level and be reluctant to accept offers for less at new jobs. But such reasoning is a far cry from saying that nonunion workers will take the initiative to push up pay because the labor market tightens.

Perhaps if Freeman and Medoff had had access to Federal Reserve transcripts (not available when they wrote) or if they had foreseen the persistence of bargaining/wage-push thinking among macro policy makers, they would have devoted more attention to the macro side of unions. All we can say, however, is that the macro consequences of de-unionization were not explicitly considered in their book.

X. Conclusions

In evaluating unions circa 1984, Freeman and Medoff already knew that union-representation as a proportion of the work force had been declining for some time and had taken a sharp drop recently. They appear to have concluded that the pre–1980 concerns about unions and macroeconomic performance no longer merited much analysis. Certainly, the post–1984 evidence reveals further union erosion and ongoing pessimism among researchers about a union comeback. However, the Freeman and Medoff analysis of the macro impact of unions — with the benefit of hindsight — could usefully have been extended to a more focused appraisal of how a largely nonunion economy would function for three main reasons.

First, the older wage-push approach seems to have persisted in macro policy circles long after Freeman and Medoff might have reasonably supposed it would disappear. Discussion of the determination of the NAIRU — even absent explicit consideration of unions — still often seems to be posed in bargaining terms. Workers "demand" certain wages and conditions. They eventually accept particular terms but won't accept others that don't meet their expectations.

Second, the removal of Freeman and Medoff's union monopoly face from employers does not lead to textbook competition in the labor market as the default. Monopsony seems a more useful construct of the nonunion workplace. And monopsony has consequences that help explain the stylized facts of the U.S. macro economy since Freeman and Medoff wrote. Monopsony also has normative implications for employer provision of working conditions ranging from safety to health insurance and other benefits. Those implications do not follow from modeling the nonunion labor market as perfect competition.

Third, explanations after-the-fact of the macro performance of the U.S. economy — especially low unemployment with low inflation in the 1990s — tend to focus on a variety of *ad hoc* explanations ranging from "good luck" to globalism to various "new economy"/surge of productivity stories. Workers nervous about job security are also invoked, although the low unemployment was accompanied by declining probabilities of job loss (Mankiw, 2002; Krueger and

Solow, 2001). As one review article noted, "there is no shortage of hypotheses to explain... why (the NAIRU) fell during the 1990s" (Ball and Mankiw, 2002: 134). Put less kindly, there is a surplus of hypotheses, most of which are not closely linked to the most dramatic institutional change in the U.S. labor market: de-unionization. This dramatic institutional change has resulted in a de facto monopsonistic labor market, with low unemployment rates (but perhaps more discouraged workers) and low wages, opposite conditions from what might be expected if the economy were to experience a substantial increase in union density. Perhaps a more systematic, monopsony-based approach to what nonunion employers do would have made subsequent macro developments less surprising.

Notes

1. The director of the Council of Wage and Price Stability stated that if the administration "could get the Teamsters to agree to 20 percent for three years, the United Auto Workers would sign a contract for the same thing. So would steel. Each of these unions wants what the other one has got." Cited in Mitchell (1980: 191).
2. "Best Idea since Keynes," *New York Times*, editorial, March 28, 1985.
3. It is important to note that not every alternative to simple time-based wages constitutes a Weitzman share system. In particular, grants of stock — as through an Employee Stock Ownership Plan (ESOP) or through stock options — do not necessarily lower the marginal cost of labor. Much depends on the plan's detailed provisions through which such assets are allocated. Moreover, many "pay for performance" arrangements, such as piece rates or merit bonuses, do not have Weitzman-type properties (and have been part of standard pay practices for many decades). Generally, journalistic reports have tended to exaggerate the incidence of "new" pay practices. Contrary to the media hype concerning stock options, for example, a 1999 U.S. Bureau of Labor Statistics survey (Crimmel and Schildkraut, 2001) found that very few workers were covered by such plans. Those employees who were covered tended to be highly paid managers and professionals. Similarly, BLS surveys suggest that ESOP coverage was very limited as well. Union negotiators began reluctantly accepting lump-sum bonuses in lieu of base pay increases in the 1980s and there was some potential for these bonuses to evolve into *de facto* profit-sharing plans. The evidence on whether such evolution actually occurred is mixed (Bell and Neumark, 1993; Erickson and Ichino, 1994). Thus, while the American pay system will undoubtedly change over time, it is hard to tell a share economy story sufficient to explain the macro performance surprises of the 1990s and beyond.
4. In the textbook model, the demand curve faces a plethora of employers, each one perceiving the supply curve as a horizontal line at *WC*.
5. Monopsonistic behavior by employers is subject to antitrust laws but there has been comparatively little litigation in this area. Some cases have been settled out of court. The main exemption is for multiemployer bargaining in union situations (Blair and Harrison, 1993: 110–11).
6. Farber (2003) finds little empirical evidence of a union threat effect during 1977–2002, a period largely corresponding to substantial de-unionization.
7. By the mid–1980s, the suggestion was being made that de-unionization could produce a lower NAIRU than was incorporated into the forecasting models of that period (Mitchell, 1986). In more formal terms, a model was proposed in which the labor market produced a real wage, conditional on the unemployment rate allowed by the monetary authority, and product markets produced a cost markup, also condi-

tional on the unemployment rate as a proxy for general economic conditions. Since at the macro level the real wage W/P is essentially the inverse of the cost markup P/W, the NAIRU is the unemployment rate that harmonizes the product and labor markets (Mitchell and Zaidi, 1992). This approach appears to have been picked up by the Federal Reserve staff (Brayton et al., 1997). Weakened unions under this approach would lead to a lower real wage and hence a lower NAIRU. However, the approach does not pick up the monopsony effects with its macro dynamics as demand declines. That is, it does not predict mild recessions.

8. The "nervous worker" explanation was often made as an explanation of low upward wage pressure. Note, however, that low unemployment in the 1990s brought with it low probabilities of falling from employment into unemployment, (Stewart, 2002). Unemployment insurance new claims — a proxy for layoffs — were also low.

9. Although we focus in this paper on the United States, the Asian financial crisis illustrates this tendency. Unions in a number of the countries adversely affected by the Asian financial crisis — which bottomed out in 1998 — are either almost non-existent, weak, or government controlled (Kuruvilla and Erickson, 2002). Thus, we might expect that there would be chronic labor shortages and a relatively quick rebound from the negative shock the crisis represented. In fact, that seems to be what occurred. A Nexis/Lexis article count for "labor shortage" and each of the "four-tiger" countries (Singapore, Hong Kong, South Korea, Taiwan) produced the following results for 1995–2000: 1995–538; 1996–563; 1997–608; 1998–376; 1999–526; 2000–730.

10. For evidence that monopsony extends to conditions of work, see Currie et al. (2002).

11. In a cross-country study for the World Bank, Aidt and Tzannatos (2002: 79–120) review the empirical literature and find on weak evidence that the Calmfors-Driffil (1988) finding persisted into the 1990s. However, they do find evidence of poorer macro performance in countries with high rates of "bargaining coverage." In the U.S. there is no substantial difference between membership coverage and bargaining coverage so that we would expect macro performance to improve as coverage fell.

12. A working paper is available from the authors concerning union settlement interpretations at the FOMC and within the Reagan administration (Mitchell and Erickson, 2003).

13. There is no evidence that the breaking of the strike was viewed as a macro policy before the decision was made to fire the striking air controllers.

14. The Federal Open Market Committee consists of the Federal Reserve Board of Governors plus a rotating group of presidents of the regional Federal Reserve Banks. For details and transcripts, see http://www.federalreserve.gov/fomc/.

References

Aidt, Toke and Zafiris Tzannatos. *Unions and Collective Bargaining: Economic Effects in a Global Environment.* Washington, DC: World Bank, 2002.

Ball, Laurence and N. Gregory Mankiw. "The NAIRU in Theory and Practice." *Journal of Economic Perspectives* 16 (Fall 2002): 115–36.

Bhaskar, V., Alan Manning, and Ted To. "Oligopsony and Monopsonistic Competition in Labor Markets." *Journal of Economic Perspectives* 16 (Spring 2002): 155–74.

Bennett, James T. and Bruce E. Kaufman, eds. *The Future of Private Sector Unionism in the United States.* Armonk, N.Y.: M.E. Sharpe, 2002.

Bernstein, Irving. *The Arbitration of Wages.* Berkeley, CA: University of California Press, 1954.

Bewley, Truman F. *Why Wages Don't Fall During a Recession.* Cambridge, MA: Harvard University Press, 1999.

Blair, Roger D. and Jeffrey L. Harrison. *Monopsony: Antitrust Law and Economics*. Princeton, NJ: Princeton University Press, 1993.

Boal, William M. and Michael R. Ransom. "Monopsony in the Labor Market." *Journal of Economic Literature* 35 (March 1997): 86–112.

Brayton, Flint, Eileen Mauskopf, David Reifschneider, Peter Tinsley, and John Williams. "The Role of Expectations in the FRB/US Macroeconomic Model." *Federal Reserve Bulletin* 83 (April 1997): 227–45.

Bronfenbrenner, Martin. "Potential Monopsony in Labor Markets." *Industrial and Labor Relations Review* 9 (July 1956): 577–88.

Calmfors, Lars and John Driffil. "Bargaining Structure, Corporatism, and Macroeconomic Performance." *Economic Policy* 6 (April 1988): 13–61.

Card, David and Alan B. Krueger. *Myth and Measurement: The New Economics of the Minimum Wage*. Princeton, NJ: Princeton University Press, 1997.

Cohen, Jessica, William T. Dickens, and Adam Posen. "Have New Human-Resource Management Practices Lowered the Sustainable Unemployment Rate?" In Alan B. Krueger and Robert M. Solow, eds. *The Roaring Nineties: Can Full Employment Be Sustained?* New York: Russell Sage, 2002, pp. 219–590.

Currie, Janet, Mehdi Farsi, and W. Bentley MacLeod. "Cut to the Bone: Hospital Take-overs and Nurse Employment Contracts." Working Paper 9428. National Bureau of Economic Research, 2002.

Davis, John. *Salary Surveys and Antitrust: An Overview for the HR Professional*. Scottsdale, AZ.: WorldatWork, 2003.

Eckstein, Otto and Thomas Wilson. "The Determinants of Money Wages in the American Economy." *Quarterly Journal of Economics* 76 (August 1962): 379–414.

Edelman, Murray and Robben W. Fleming. *The Politics of Wage-Price Decisions: A Four-Country Analysis*. Urbana, IL.: University of Illinois Press, 1965.

Ehrenreich, Barbara. *Nickel and Dimed: On (Not) Getting By in America*. New York: Henry Holt, 2001.

Erickson, Christopher L. "A Re-Interpretation of Pattern Bargaining." *Industrial and Labor Relations Review* 49 (July 1996): 615–34.

_____ and Andrea C. Ichino. "Lump-Sum Bonuses in Union Contracts." *Advances in Industrial and Labor Relations* 6 (1994): 183–218.

_____ and Daniel J.B. Mitchell. "Pattern Indifference: The Response of Pay Setters to the 1993 GM-UAW Settlement." *Journal of Labor Research* 16 (Spring 1995): 230–34.

Farber, Henry S. "Nonunion Wage Rates and the Threat of Unionization." Working Paper 9705. National Bureau of Economic Research, 2003.

Foulkes, Fred K. *Personnel Policies in Large Nonunion Companies*. Englewood Cliffs, NJ: 1980.

Freeman, Richard B. "Is Declining Unionization of the U.S. Good, Bad, or Irrelevant?" In Lawrence Mishel and Paula B. Voos, eds. *Unions and Economic Competitiveness*. Armonk, NY: M.E. Sharpe, 1992, pp. 143–690

_____. "Labour Markets." *Economic Policy* 6 (April 1988): 63–80.

_____ and James L. Medoff. *What Do Unions Do?* New York: Basic Books, 1984.

_____ and Joel Rogers. *What Workers Want*. Ithaca, NY: ILR Press, 1999.

Friedman, Milton. "The Role of Monetary Policy." *American Economic Review* 58 (March 1968): 1–17.

Galenson, Walter, ed. *Incomes Policy: What Can We Learn from Europe?* Ithaca, NY: New York State School of Industrial and Labor Relations, 1973.

Gordon, H. Scott. "The Eisenhower Administration: The Doctrine of Shared Responsibility." In Crauford D. Goodwin, ed. *Exhortation and Controls: The Search for a Wage Price Policy, 1945–1971.* Washington, DC: Brookings Institution, 1975, pp. 95–134.

Greider, William. *Secrets of the Temple: How the Federal Reserve Runs the Country.* New York: Simon and Schuster, 1987.

Hancock, Keith, ed. *Incomes Policy in Australia.* Sydney: Harcourt Brace Jovanovich, 1981.

Hoover, Herbert. *The Memoirs of Herbert Hoover: The Cabinet and the Presidency, 1920–1933.* New York: MacMillan, 1952.

_____. *The Hoover Memoirs: The Great Depression, 1929–1941.* London: Hollis and Carter, 1953.

Houseman, Susan N., Arne L. Kalleberg, and George A. Erickcek. "The Role of Temporary Help Employment in Tight Labor Markets." Working paper 01–73. Upjohn Institute, 2001.

Jacoby, Sanford M. and Daniel J.B. Mitchell. "Measurement of Compensation: Union and Nonunion." *Industrial Relations* 27 (Spring 1988): 215–31.

Kaufman, Bruce E. 1993. *The Origins and Evolution of the Field of Industrial Relations in the United States.* Ithaca, NY: ILR Press, 1993.

_____. 1996. "Why the Wagner Act?: Reestablishing Contact with Its Original Purpose." *Advances in Industrial and Labor Relations* 7 (1996): 15–68.

_____. "John R. Commons and the Wisconsin School on Industrial Relations Strategy and Policy." *Industrial and Labor Relations Review* 57 (October 2003): 3–30.

_____ and Julie Hotchkiss. *Economics of the Labor Market*, 5th ed. Fort Worth, TX: Dryden Press, 1999.

Krueger, Alan B. and Robert Solow, eds. *The Roaring Nineties: Can Full Employment Be Sustained?* New York: Russell Sage, 2001.

Kuruvilla, Sarosh and Christopher L. Erickson. "Change and Transformation in Asian Industrial Relations." *Industrial Relations* 41 (April 2002): 171–227.

Lebow, David E., Raven E. Saks, and Beth Anne Wilson. "Downward Nominal Wage Rigidity: Evidence from the Employment Cost Index." *Advances in Macroeconomics.* Vol. 3 (Issue 1) 2003, electronic journal at http://www.bepress.com/bejm.

Mankiw, N. Gregory. "U.S. Monetary Policy During the 1990s." In Jeffrey A. Frankel and Peter R. Orszag, eds. *American Economic Policy in the 1990s.* Cambridge, MA: MIT Press, 2002, pp. 19–43.

Manning, Alan. *Monopsony in Motion: Imperfect Competition in Labor Markets.* Princeton, NJ: Princeton University Press, 2003.

Mishel, Lawrence, Jared Bernstein, and Heather Boushey. *The State of Working America: 2002/2003.* Ithaca, NY: ILR Press, 2003.

Mitchell, Daniel J.B. "Dismantling the Cross of Gold: Economic Crises and U.S. Monetary Policy." *North American Journal of Economics and Finance* 11 (August 2000): 77–104.

_____. "Expansion Without Inflation: We Can Have It in the Late 1980s?" In UCLA Business Forecasting Project, *The UCLA National Business Forecast* (June 1986): 35–42.

_____. "Keynesian, Old Keynesian, and New Keynesian Wage Nominalism." *Industrial Relations* 32 (Winter 1993): 1–29.

_____. "Wage Pressures and Labor Shortages." *Brookings Papers on Economic Activity.* (1989): 191–231.

_____ and Christopher L. Erickson. "Not Yet Dead at the Fed: Unions, Bargaining, and Economy-Wide Wage Determination." Working Paper, UCLA Anderson School, 2003.

_____ and Mahmood A. Zaidi. "International Pressures on Industrial Relations: Macroeconomics and Social Concertation." In Tiziano Treu, ed. *Participation in Public Policy-Making*. New York: Walter de Gruyter, 1992, pp. 59–72.

Myers, Charles A. and W. Rupert Maclaurin. *The Movement of Factory Workers: A Study of a New England Industrial Community, 1937–1939 and 1942*. New York: John Wiley, 1943.

Neikirk, William R. *Volcker: Portrait of the Money Man*. New York: Congdon and Reed, 1987.

Nordhaus, William. "Can the Share Economy Conquer Stagflation?" *Quarterly Journal of Economics* 103 (February 1988): 201–17.

Organisation for Economic Co-Operation and Development. *Employment Outlook, July 1999*. Paris: OECD, 1999.

Parus, Barbara. *Market Pricing: Methods to the Madness*. Scottsdale, AZ: WorldatWork, 2002.

Perry, George L. "Wages and the Guideposts." *American Economic Review* 57 (September 1967): 897–904.

Rees, Albert and George P. Schultz. *Workers and Wages in an Urban Labor Market*. Chicago: University of Chicago Press, 1970.

Robinson, Archie. *George Meany and His Times*. New York: Simon and Schuster, 1981.

Ross, Arthur M. *Trade Union Wage Policy*. Berkeley, CA: University of California Press, 1948.

Sheahan, John. *The Wage-Price Guideposts*. Washington, DC: Brookings Institution, 1967.

Shultz, George P. and Robert Z. Aliber, eds. *Guidelines: Informal Controls and the Market Place*. Chicago, IL: University of Chicago Press, 1966.

Stewart, Jay. "Recent Trends in Job Stability and Job Security: Evidence from the March CPS." Working paper 356. U.S. Bureau of Labor Statistics, 2002.

Stiglitz, Joseph E. "Reflections on the Natural Rate Hypothesis." *Journal of Economic Perspectives* 11 (Winter 1997): 3–10.

_____. *The Roaring Nineties: A New History of the World's Most Prosperous Decade*. New York: W.W. Norton, 2003.

Ulman, Lloyd and Robert J. Flanagan. *Wage Restraint: A Study of Incomes Policies in Western Europe*. Berkeley, CA: University of California Press, 1971.

U.S. Office of Economic Stabilization, Department of the Treasury. *Historical Working Papers on the Economic Stabilization Program, August 15, 1971 to April 30, 1974*. 2 volumes and data appendix. Washington, DC: GPO, 1974.

U.S. President. *Economic Report of the President*. Washington, DC: GPO, Various years.

Wachter, Michael L. "Judging Unions' Future Using a Historical Perspective: The Public Policy Choice Between Competition and Unionization." *Journal of Labor Research* 24 (Spring 2003): 339–57.

Weber, Arnold R. *In Pursuit of Price Stability: The Wage-Price Freeze of 1971*. Washington, DC: Brookings Institution, 1973.

_____. and Daniel J.B. Mitchell. *The Pay Board's Progress: Wage Controls in Phase II*. Washington, DC: Brookings Institution, 1978.

Weitzman, Martin L. "Comment on 'Can the Share Economy Conquer Stagflation?'" *Quarterly Journal of Economics* 103 (February 1988): 219–23.

_____. *The Share Economy: Conquering Stagflation*. Cambridge, MA: Harvard University Press, 1984.

_____. "The Simple Macroeconomics of Profit Sharing." *American Economic Review* 75 (December 1985): 937–53.

_____. "Some Macroeconomic Implications of Alternative Compensation Systems." *Economic Journal* 93 (December 1983): 763–83.

_____. "Steady State Unemployment Under Profit Sharing." *Economic Journal* 97 (March 1987): 86–105.

13

Two Faces of Union Voice in the Public Sector

*Morley Gunderson**

I. Introduction

In their classic article on the "Two Faces of Unionism," and their subsequent book, *What Do Unions Do?*, Freeman and Medoff (1979, 1984, respectively) emphasized the positive-voice face of unions in contrast to the conventional monopoly face that emphasized rent extraction. Under its monopoly face, unions can have negative effects on resource allocation, productivity, and social welfare by fostering strikes and restrictive work practices as well as by raising wages above the competitive norm. In contrast, by serving as the institutional embodiment of voice at the workplace, unions could have positive effects on productivity, cost, and social welfare. This could occur through various voice mechanisms: articulating the preferences and internal trade-offs of workers; improving communications between workers and management; fostering due process and restricting the capricious actions of managers; reducing quits; and "shocking" management into more efficient work practices. Even in the case of strikes, positive cathartic effects may ensue and pent-up frustrations may be released, highlighting how the same mechanism can have positive as well as negative effects. Unions can foster such voice mechanisms by providing protection for the use of voice and by providing workers collectively with the incentive to use voice given its public goods nature whereby all workers can benefit, and it is not possible to exclude free riders or non-payers from the potential benefits (Freeman and Medoff, 1984: 8; Kaufman, theory chaoter this volume, p. 35).

The voice function is potentially beneficial to *employers* as well as employees, or at least it may reduce some of the costs associated with the monopoly face. Voice can do so, for example, by improving morale, enhancing loyalty and commitment, reducing costly turnover, ensuring the receipt of deferred compensation, and providing information to employers. Of course, the voice function also has the potential to be costly to employers through various means: shifting loyalty from the employer to the union; fostering adversarialism rather than co-operation; fostering costly grievances and work-to-rule; inhibiting

401

turnover that may be beneficial to employers; and extracting information that employers may not want to divulge. There are two faces to voice, just as there are two faces to unions.[1]

Somewhat surprisingly, the discussion in Freeman and Medoff (1984) and the subsequent reassessments in Freeman (1992) focused on the voice function of unions in the *private* sector but not in the public sector. The subsequent application of the concept in the myriad of studies on union voice also focused on the private sector, as is the case with the articles providing evidence on the union effect on productivity, firm performance, and profitability.[2] This likely reflects the fact that concepts like productivity, organizational performance, and profitability are easier to measure in the private, compared to the public, sector.

Nevertheless, there are reasons to believe (outlined subsequently) that the voice function of unions may be more prominent in the public sector than in the private sector. There are also reasons to believe that union voice in the public sector is likely to take on a more muscle-type bargaining face than the positive communication face. That is, the union voice function in the public sector takes on a cloak that is closer to the monopoly face of unions in the private sector.

My purpose herein is to examine the two faces of union voice in the public sector. Both Canada and the United States are discussed, because in Canada unionization is "alive and well" or at least "alive and kicking," and the public sector is predominantly unionized. The next section provides a theoretical perspective on why voice should be more important in the public sector than the private sector, and why that form of voice is increasingly likely to take on a muscle-flexing, bargaining face. I then outline different forms or manifestations of voice and the implications of voice in the public sector in four areas: unionization as the institutional embodiment of voice; strikes as the loudest form of voice; political activity as an external channel of voice; and employee involvement in the management of the organization as an internal channel of voice. For each area a "scorecard" is provided. That scorecard suggests that the more muscle-flexing bargaining face of voice has increasingly dominated the more positive communication form of voice in the public sector. This likely reflects the fact that these negative forms of voice are not being disciplined by the same competitive global market pressures that are affecting private sector unions and dissipating their monopoly face. I conclude with a summary and some concluding observations.

II.   Why Voice and Muscle Forms of Voice Are Expected To Be More Prominent in-the Public than in the Private Sector

Various reasons can explain why voice should play a more prominent role in the public sector compared to the private sector and why the negative muscle-flexing and influence-peddling face of public sector unions is becoming more prominent in the public sector, compared to the declining monopoly face of unions in the private sector.

First and foremost, exit from the public sector may be reduced because of a public sector wage premium or rent[3] over and above what comparable private sector workers receive and over and above any union wage premium (the latter discussed subsequently). The pure public sector wage premium implies that public sector employees will tend not to leave or exit the public sector. That is, high wages reduce exit, which in turn fosters voice, with unions being the institutional embodiment of voice at the workplace. While this direction of causality is not emphasized by Freeman and Medoff, it is consistent with their perspective that reduced exit increases voice. In such circumstances, unions will try to institutionalize muscle forms of voice to protect and sustain those rents. Since the public sector premium is generally higher for lower level occupational groups,[4] the incentives for staying are generally strongest at the lower wage levels. As such, the desire to have unions provide such voice is enhanced since unions also tend to emphasize wage compression and hence are likely to increase and protect the rents at the lower wage levels. As well, since public sector workers are likely to remain in their jobs, they will also use the communication form of union voice to improve their working situation.

In addition to a pure public sector wage premium, unionized public sector workers also receive a union wage premium as do unionized private sector workers. While the monopoly power of unions has garnered union wage premiums in the neighborhood of 15 percent in the private sector, the *earlier* evidence suggested that the union wage premium in the public sector is smaller, more in the neighborhood of 5 percent.[5] Much of this smaller union impact may reflect the fact that public sector workers are already getting a public sector rent (as discussed previously) making it more difficult to add a further union wage premium. Freeman (1986: 42–43) conjectured, however, that this smaller union impact in the public sector may understate the actual longer run impact for a number of reasons: It is based on the early years of public sector organizing when unions were focusing on establishing themselves rather than garnering wage gains; it did not include fringe benefits which tend to be disproportionately larger in the public sector;[6] the public sector is largely white-collar where union impacts are generally smaller; and spillover wage gains to nonunion public sector workers may lead to the union-nonunion differential understating the wage gains for union workers. His conjecture appears to be correct. More recent evidence suggests that the union wage premiums tend to be similar in the public and private sectors, in part because they have fallen in the private sector but have increased in the public sector. Belman et al. (1997), for example, find union wage premiums to be slightly higher in the public compared to the private sector. Blanchflower and Bryson (this volume) find that the union wage premium in the United States had risen since the 1980s in the public sector but had fallen substantially in the private sector so that by the late 1990s, the union wage premiums were similar in both sectors. Specifically, the union wage premium was 15 percent in the public sector and 17 percent in the private sector in the recent 1996–2001 period, compared to 13 percent and 22 percent, respectively, in the earlier 1983 to 1988 period. They indicate in the Conclusion (p. 108) that Freeman was "most surprised by the fact that the public sector wage effects are so large and so similar to those in the private sector." Even though he had conjectured that the earlier evidence of a 5 percent union wage premium in the public sector may understate the actual longer run impact, even he was surprised at the magnitude of the change.

Blanchflower and Bryson also provide detailed information on how the union wage differential in the public sector varies by different characteristics in the 1996–2001 period: highest at the local level (20 percent) than the state level (10 percent) and lowest at the federal level (8 percent); higher for females (16 percent) than for males (10 percent); highest for younger workers under age 25 (23 percent); higher in New England (17 percent) and Central states (16 percent) compared to the South (12 percent) and the West (13 percent); higher for nonwhites (16 percent) than for whites (14 percent); higher for manual workers (18 percent) than for nonmanual workers (14 percent); highest for teachers (21 percent) and lowest for registered nurses (6 percent) and social workers (12 percent), with police, firefighters, and lawyers around 17–19 percent. Importantly, the union wage premium in the public sector increased since the 1983–1988 period for almost all groups, falling by a substantial amount only for the two outlier groups that had the highest premium in the earlier period—youths under age 25 and persons with less than high school education.

The rising union wage premium in the public sector (both absolutely and especially relative to the private sector) is consistent with the increased aggressiveness and militancy of public sector unions and highlights an increased willingness and ability of public sector unions to use muscle to win wage gains. While private sector unions also have such a willingness, their ability to win wage gains is more circumscribed by global competitive market forces—forces that are not as binding in the public sector.

The addition of a union wage premium (when unions are present) over and above the pure public sector wage premium discussed previously, further enhances the lower exit from the public sector compared to the private sector. Exit from the public sector is reduced even further because many public sector jobs do not have alternatives in the private sector—at least the range of alternatives is reduced. Since reduced exit increases the desire for voice, employee demand for voice should be greater in the public compared to the private sector. This is true for both the communication form of voice to deal with their working conditions and issues, as well as the muscle-flexing and influence-peddling form of voice to protect the rents.

Voice can also be encouraged by loyalty—the third part of the exit-voice-loyalty trilogy. Loyal employees may use voice to improve the workplace and the institution to which they are committed out of loyalty.[7] Public sector employees may have entered "public service" in part out of loyalty to their clientele (as in the teaching, health care, and "caring" professions in general). They may also have a stronger sense of public duty and civic responsibility[8] and have entered public service in part since it provides the opportunity to "do good" (Reder, 1975: 28). All of these loyalty-related attributes may increase the use of voice either directly (because loyalty fosters voice to improve the work environment) or indirectly (because loyalty reduces exit and hence increases the demand for voice).

Public sector workers are also disproportionately more educated and from the professional ranks and thereby likely to be more engaged in their work and informed about it. Their loyalty to their profession means they will want more of a say in their work, and they are less likely to be content with "punching the clock" and "checking their brains at the door." As such, they are more likely to demand voice and to be able to provide effective voice.

As well, their professional status gives them a degree of credibility in the minds of the public when they bargain over issues that may appear to be in the "public interest" but that can also be a manifestation of using muscle to bargain for featherbedding or other rules that enhance their own employment well-being. This can be the case in many areas: when teachers bargain over class size, professional development days, the use of paraprofessionals, or control over the curriculum; when professors bargain over teaching loads and the use of instructors; when police bargain to have two officers in every cruiser; and when health professionals bargain to restrict the use of paraprofessionals.

The union as an institutional form of voice can also be particularly important in the public sector, given the realities of bargaining in that sector. In their muscle-flexing bargaining role, public sector unions can do "end runs" around management, often appealing directly to politicians or the general public through the media when their effectiveness at the bargaining table is stifled. Employers in the public sector may be reluctant to use their full bargaining power against their employees because of public pressure to be a model employer, especially when dealing with disadvantaged employees. That is, there may be considerable public support for what Kaufman (theory chapter, this volume) termed the "third face of unions" of "protecting the underdog" and "leveling the playing field" against otherwise powerful employers.

Restrictions on the range of issues that can be bargained for in the public sector may also redirect voice into other areas. Civil servants may not be allowed by statute, for example, to bargain over wages or to strike (e.g., U.S. federal government). In such circumstances, unions may redirect their attention to other areas, such as having a greater say in workplace issues. Freeman (1986: 51) takes the high degree of unionization in the federal government in spite of their inability to bargain over wages as evidence of the importance of the role of voice: "The high unionization in the federal sector thus provides evidence for workers' desire for representation in a large bureaucratic organization, exclusive of the 'monopoly' power of unions to raise wages through collective bargaining." Of course, union voice in such circumstances can also be interpreted as protecting the overall rents of which wages may be only one component.

The previous discussion highlighted the *potential* importance of voice in the public sector, especially when compared to the private sector. The next section illustrates that the *potential* importance has been translated into greater *actual* importance in the public sector. The form of that voice in the public sector, however, is more in the nature of muscle flexing and influence peddling to garner favorable outcomes for public sector workers, especially when otherwise constrained by more restrictive bargaining laws regarding such areas as dispute resolution and wage determination. This is illustrated in four areas of voice: unionization as the institutional embodiment of voice; strikes as the loudest form of voice; political activity as an external channel of voice; and employee involvement in the management of the organization as an internal channel of-voice.

III. Unionization as a Manifestation of Voice in the Public Sector

Unionization itself as the institutional embodiment of voice is much higher in the public sector compared to the private sector in all advanced industrialized countries (Bordogna, 2003; Freeman, 1996: 61). In the United States[9] where the overall union density rate is slightly under 14 percent, it is almost 40 percent in the public sector compared to 9 percent in the private sector, with almost half of all union members now being in the public sector. In Canada where the overall union density rate is slightly over 30 percent, it is slightly over 70 percent in the public sector compared to around 18 percent in the private sector. In both countries, collective agreement coverage is slightly higher than union density, because some employees who are covered by the collective agreement are not union members. Given the large numbers of managerial and other employees who cannot be unionized, the unionization and coverage rates would be even higher if expressed as a percent of the potentially eligible workforce. In Canada, almost all public sector employees who could be covered by a collective agreement are covered. Over half of all union members, and the two largest unions, are in the public sector in Canada (Gunderson, 2002a; Gunderson and Hyatt, 1996: 247).

Public sector unions had their origins in informal employee associations that effectively provided employee voice and consultation to management, but consultation only whetted appetites for more influence and provided a building block for stronger forms of voice involving more muscle-flexing power and less consultation.[10] These associations were transformed into formal unions in the 1960s and 1970s largely through legislative changes that extended private sector collective bargaining rights to many public sector workers.[11] The legislative changes were fostered by the strong voice of the social protest movement and the willingness to challenge authority that was occurring in the 1960s and 1970s.[12] As well, survey evidence indicates that public sector workers have slightly greater preferences for influence or voice than do private sector workers.[13] In essence, consultative forms of voice provided the foundation for public sector unions as well as the catalyst for their transformation into more conventional muscle-flexing unions and for their dominance in the union movement today. Given that there is little "birth and death" of firms in the public sector, public sector unions also do not have to contend with the issue that new firms are "born" nonunion and, therefore, have to be certified to sustain union membership, as in the private sector. Importantly, management is also more willing to share author- ity and not to resist a union in the public sector compared to the private sector. Freeman (1996) attributes the higher union density in the public compared to the private sector mainly to the slightly greater demand for unionization on the part of public sector workers interacting with the considerably lower resistance to unions on the part of public sector managers.

The lower resistance to unionization on the part of public sector managers reflects the fact that the survival of public sector organizations is not jeopardized by unions flexing their muscle. This is in contrast to private sector firms—and increasingly so under global competition. In the public sector there is no "residual claimant" who profits by resisting unions; there is no great cost to following the "path of least resistance." As such, voice in the form of consultation was easily transformed into voice in the stronger form of bargaining with unions that were fully prepared to flex their muscle.

What grade would the high degree of unionization in the public sector receive in a scorecard that assessed the social optimality of that degree of unionization when compared to the private sector? Certainly, if the degree of unionization in the private sector is taken as a benchmark of the degree that is optimal in the sense that the demand for unionization on the part of workers is required to confront the cost of unionization to employers and hence their resistance to unionization, the degree of unionization in the public sector would be re- garded as "too high." The degree of unionization in the public sector is simply not disciplined the same as in the private sector by such forces as the threat of bankruptcy or plant closing or moving offshore, or by competitive pressures to contain costs to be profitable, or by the need for managerial flexibility. In essence, muscle on the part of unions in the public sector is not met by the same muscle or resistance on the part of employers in the public sector as is the case in the private sector.

IV. Strikes and Other Dispute Mechanisms as Manifestations of Voice

Strikes are the clearest form of union voice at the workplace—voice at its loudest and in its most muscle-flexing form. Those who view strikes as part of the monopoly face regard strikes as a result of unions flexing their monopoly power as the exclusive bargaining agent, immune from anti-trust regulation, and imposing costs on upstream suppliers and downstream customers as well as the struck employer. Strikes can jeopardize the competitiveness of a country and deter inward foreign investment, as well as leaving a legacy of "scarred" relationships between the parties after they return to work.

In the public sector, such strikes are regarded as particularly invidious because services are often regarded as "essential" (which is why they are provided by the public sector), and consumers usually have few alternatives given the monopoly provision by the public sector. As well, consumers generally keep paying for the services (through taxes) even though the services are not provided during the strike. This is in contrast to the private sector where consumers have options to purchase goods produced by non-struck employers, and they do not pay for goods and services that are not consumed because of the strike.

Those who view strikes as part of the more positive voice face of unions, emphasize their positive effect in pressuring the parties to articulate their internal trade-offs and to have those trade-offs confront the legitimate concerns and claims of the other side. Moreover, they emphasize the positive cathartic effect of strikes in releasing pent-up pressures. The "safety-valve" perspective of strikes emphasizes that if strikes as a form of voice are restricted, as is common in the public sector, this will simply redirect conflict into other forms such as increased grievances, unfair labor practices, job actions, political activities, or health and safety complaints.[14] This can be important in the public sector where restrictions on the right-to-strike can take many forms.

The fact that governments in recent years have increasingly restricted the right-to-strike in the public sector suggests that the negative muscle-flexing aspects of strikes are regarded as dominating any positive cathartic or safety-valve aspects. In Canada,[15] for example, in response to fiscal crisis, the federal and most provincial governments over-rode collective agreements in the public sector and imposed wage freezes in the early 1980s. From 1991 to 1997, the federal government suspended collective bargaining for federal employees. Seven other provinces followed with wage freezes and mid-contract pay rollbacks for public sector employees. Numerous provincial governments imposed "social contracts" that mandated employees take a number of days off without pay.[16] Larger proportions of public sector bargaining units were designated as "essential employees" who were denied the right to strike. Ad hoc back-to-work legislation has been increasingly imposed on public sector strikes. Arbitrators are increasingly required by statute to pay attention to the ability-to-pay of governments. While governments effectively decreed collective bargaining in the public sectors in the 1960s and 1970s through legislative initiatives, they restricted—some would say emaciated—collective bargaining in the 1980s and 1990s. What the state giveth, the state can taketh away . . . especially when loud voice meets a hard budget constraint. Similar responses occurred in the United States (Hebdon, 1996; Lund and Maranto, 1996).

Strikes as a form of voice clearly can be circumscribed in the public sector, and strike activity is lower in the public than private sector largely because of the prohibitions and restrictions. Overall, strikes are declining in both the private and public sectors. Nevertheless, the decline is much slower in the public sector so that public sector strikes are accounting for a larger share of total strike activity.[17] Although strikes in the private sector may be described as a declining to a whimper, they are increasing to more of a bang in the public sector. Furthermore, their impact is obviously more widely felt given the essential and monopoly nature of many public services.

What grade would strikes receive on a scorecard that evaluated their social utility as a form of voice in the public sector? There is certainly no consensus on this issue. However, global competitive market forces disciplined the use of strikes in the private sector, suggesting that they had little survival value as a mechanism for solving differences when their costs are internalized by the private parties—and increasingly so under global competition. The public sector is much more immune to such pressures, so the muscle flexing that is manifest in this loudest form of voice is not so constrained by its cost consequences. As indicated, the fact that governments since the 1980s increasingly imposed restrictions on public sector unions with respect to bargaining and strikes, indicates that governments must regard the negative muscle-flexing aspects of public sector unions in this area as dominating any positive cathartic or safety-valve effects. That is, their experience with the bargaining and strikes from the public sector unions they effectively created suggested that more resistance was merited. This would only be the case if the costs of allowing such bargaining and strikes were perceived as outweighing any benefits. Governments may not be able to put the genie back in the bottle once they let it out, but they may contain it.

V. Political Activity as Manifestation of Voice in the Public Sector

Even though individual civil servants, and especially senior ones, are often inhibited from engaging in direct political activity, public sector unions have used their muscle to exert considerable influence-peddling forms of voice in the political arena[18]—especially important given their high turnout in elections (Bennett and Orzechowski, 1983). This can be an effective mechanism for "shifting out the demand curve" for public sector employees and hence enhancing both their wages and employment (Freeman, 1986: 61).[19] Public sector unions have provided political support for opposition to government budget cuts, privatization, and deregulation, all of which can adversely affect public sector workers.[20] They often engage in "social unionism" with community groups to support "living wage" campaigns for municipal employees. Teachers' unions have opposed initiatives that would enhance school choice (vouchers, magnet schools, charter schools, tax credits for private school tuition, and allowing students in public schools to go to schools out of their district). Such choices could otherwise lead to school closings and pressure for schools to compete by means that may put more pressure on teachers.[21] Teachers' unions have also engaged in political actions to improve their compensation (Murphy, 1990) and to inhibit school restructuring (Biond, 1997; Smith, 1989).

Partly in response to the negative image from exhibiting their muscle form of voice in resisting such reforms, a number of teachers' unions have embraced a more positive form of voice, supporting initiatives in such areas as teacher discipline and improvement, national standards and testing, peer review of teachers, school safety and discipline, and school infrastructure.[22]

Public sector unions are also a main force behind the passage of comparable worth legislation in both the United States (Evans and Nelson, 1989; Wesman, 1988) and Canada (Gunderson, 1995; Hart, 2002). Such initiatives have been applied mainly in the public sector and invariably through union complaints or initiatives which are viewed by unions as ways of injecting additional funds into the "pot" over and above those achieved through collective bargaining. For that reason, public sector unions have tried to keep comparable worth settlements separate from bargaining settlements, so that comparable worth settlements are not subject to the give-and-take of the bargaining process where, for example, higher settlements in female-dominated jobs would have to come from lower settlements in male-dominated jobs. Public sector unions have also tried to have comparable worth settlements not advertised as such so that employees may think they are settlements won by the union.[23] In Iowa in the 1980s, public sector unions effectively lobbied for alterations in comparable worth awards that were initially announced but that would have led to pay cuts to male union members. The lobbying led to an infusion of additional public funds as well as a reallocation of the awards towards male union members (Orazem and Mattila, 1990). Unions have also been able to obtain exemptions for seniority in comparable worth legislation (Weiner and Gunderson, 1990: 112), effectively allowing male-female wage differences if they are the result of seniority. In Ontario, they have even obtained an exemption for "bargaining strength." That is, after comparable worth has been achieved, pay differences between male and female jobs are allowed if they result from differences in bargaining strength (Gunderson, 2002).

A scorecard on the social value of political activity as a manifestation of union voice in the public sector would not give a high grade for unions in this area. Their activities, while often in the guise of the public interest, appear more consistent with using their muscle flexing and influence peddling in this area to protect their own interest. Whether political pressure or threats of privatization and market reforms in the public sector will induce a shift to more positive forms of voice is an open question.

VI. Employee Involvement in Management of the Organization in the Public Sector and Associated Productivity Effects

Though unionization and strike activity are the clearest and loudest manifestations of voice in the public sector, a more subtle form of voice occurs in the form of employees wanting their say in how the organization is run on a daily basis. In the private sector, this is jealously guarded by management under the rubric of management rights. Certainly, "progressive" human resource management schemes and employee involvement programs have led to a sharing of some of those rights in the private sector, but generally as ways to tap into the knowledge of workers and to foster commitment to the organization. True power sharing is rare or non-existent and even employee buyouts generally revert back to the situation where "workers work and managers manage."

In contrast, in the public sector, employees appear to have been fairly successful in using their influence form of voice to have a prominent impact on managing the organization.[24] Freeman and Medoff (1984) argued that the positive effect of voice depends on management co-operation. They and others have also documented that management resistance to unions is much less in the public sector compared to the private sector, suggesting that management willingness to work with unions on other aspects of organizational governance and performance should also be greater in the public sector. This in turn suggests that, in theory, any potential positive voice effects on performance and productivity should also be greater in the public sector.[25]

Empirically, the impact of union activity on productivity in the public sector is difficult to measure given the well-known problems of measuring output and productivity in the public sector. After outlining these difficulties, Freeman (1986: 62) reviews 11 earlier studies prior to 1986 on how unions affect productivity in the public sector. He ascertains that seven find no effect, two a positive effect, and two a negative effect, and concludes that they "reject the presumption that public sector unionism necessarily has adverse effects on productivity." Addison and Hirsch (1989: 81) also review a number of earlier studies and conclude that "The apparent absence of a sizable productivity effect in public libraries . . . government bureaus . . . schools . . . and hospitals . . . despite significant union premiums in all but the library sample, supports the thesis that product market competition is a spur to greater efficiency in unionized markets." Subsequent studies also find mixed results. Byrne et-al. (1996) find police unions to have an insignificant effect on productivity with respect to serious crimes and a negative effect for minor crimes. Unionized hospitals are found to have higher productivity (Register, 1988) and lower mortality rates (Ash and Seago, 2004). That latter study also discuss other health care studies that find positive union effects on reducing turnover.

More recently, union effects on productivity in the public sector have been analyzed more extensively in education, where teachers' unions bargain over curriculum, class sizes, student/teacher ratios, student discipline, and student transfers.[26] Such bargaining is often regarded as restricting the flexibility of school districts to adjust to the changing environment (Goldschmidt and Stuart, 1986), although the outcomes obviously could positively affect student performance. The evidence on the effect of teacher's unions on teacher productivity (as generally measured by test scores) is also mixed. Positive but generally small effects were found in Eberts and Stone (1987), Kleiner and Petree (1988), Nelson and Rosen (1996), and Register and Grimes (1991).[27] Recent evidence from Iverson and Currivan (2003) also found that voice (as measured by participating in union activities) was associated with significantly lower quits. A substantial number of studies also find an inverted U-shaped effect, whereby teachers' unions have a positive effect for students of average ability, but a negative effect for students of low and of high ability.[28] Negative effects of teachers unions, however, have been found in Eberts and Stone (1986), Meador and Walters (1994), and Kurth (1987). That last study concluded that the growth of teachers' unions from 1972 to 1983 was a significant determinant of the decline of SAT scores over that same period.

Strong negative effects of teachers' unions were also found in the comprehensive analysis in Hoxby (1996), a study that controlled for the fact that powerful teacher unions could use their muscle and influence to augment school budgets and that true productivity effects require controlling for the level of the inputs or budget. She finds that teachers' unions did increase school budgets which in turn led to higher teacher salaries and teacher-student ratios. These enhanced inputs, however, did not improve student performance suggesting a decreased productivity of school inputs in unionized schools. This leads to her strong conclusion: "It is striking that unionization is associated with more generous school inputs and worse student achievement. This is strong evidence that teachers' unions serve, at least in part, a rent-seeking purpose. Teachers' unions are, indeed, a potential answer to the puzzle of increasing school spending and stagnant student performance in the post-1960 period" (Hoxby, 1996: 708–709). She also finds that this negative effect is stronger in school districts where schools have local monopoly power and do not have to compete for students. This theme emerges from her subsequent work emphasizing that enhanced school choice (vouchers, charters schools, magnet schools, tax credits for private school tuition, and student choice in public schools) increases the demand on the part of schools for more skilled teachers who also put forth more effort. This comes about in part because such schools pay a lower base wage but a higher premium to such skills[29] (Hoxby, 2000).

By way of a "scorecard" assessment of the effect of public sector unions on productivity, the evidence is too mixed to assign a clear grade. As Freeman indicated, the earlier evidence rejects the presumption that public sector unionism necessarily adversely affects productivity. But it certainly does not support the notion that unions have positive effects and certainly not large enough to offset any wage cost effects (which increasingly appear to be positive and more in the range of normal union wage premiums). Nor does the evidence support the conjecture, outlined previously, that any potential positive voice effects on performance and productivity will be greater in the public sector than in the private sector—that conjecture being based on the notion that management resistance is less in the public sector and management co-operation is necessary for the positive form of voice to operate. As well, more recent systematic evidence, especially in the education sector, suggests more substantial negative effects on productivity.

Clearly more empirical work is merited to determine the productivity of public sector inputs and how that productivity is affected by different forms of employee voice including unionization. It is particularly important to link that determination to alternative forms of market structure for the delivery of public sector services, given the growing tendency towards privatization, deregulation, outsourcing, competition in public service delivery, and the provision of public services through private sector delivery agencies. The increased emphasis on output performance measures in the public sector (in part because budgets are often based on such measures) means that "output" measures are increasingly available in the public sector so that such productivity studies are increasingly feasible.

VII. Summary and Concluding Observations

Employee voice through unions is manifest in various ways in the public sector including unionization itself, strikes, political activity, and challenging managerial prerogatives. In each of these areas there are two faces to voice just as there are two faces to unions. Voice can be used in a more influence-peddling and muscle-flexing bargaining fashion to enhance rent seeking and noncooperative behavior with negative effects on productivity, competitiveness, and resource allocation. Voice can also be used more positively by articulating preferences and trade-offs, improving communications, and involving employees and enhancing their commitment to the organization.

In all likelihood both faces of voice apply to unions in the public sector just as they do in the private sector. In the private sector, however, the negative monopoly face of unions has been increasingly constrained by competitive market forces such as globalization and trade liberalization as well as by the industrial restructuring to services and the information economy. Rents are obviously harder to obtain when there are fewer rents on the bargaining table. There is little survival value to pricing yourself out of the market now that market forces are more prominent. In such a private sector environment, unions have generally declined, strikes have dissipated, and managerial prerogatives have been enhanced.

Public services, in contrast, are less subject to the pressures of globalization and trade liberalization, but they are not immune. Countries, and political jurisdictions within countries, are increasingly competing for business investment and the jobs associated with that investment,[30] creating stronger incentives to provide public services and infrastructures more cost effectively. Physical capital, financial capital, and human capital are increasingly mobile and footloose—able to escape jurisdictions that have excessive taxes and costs for the public services and infrastructures. They can increasingly vote with their feet, moving to jurisdictions that provide the Tiebout-type tax and public expenditure package that suits their needs and preferences compelling governments to face a harder rather than soft budget constraint. Governments may not go out of business, but the may not survive the next election.

Such pressures are likely to increase managerial and public opposition if the muscle-flexing bargaining voice dominates the positive communication aspect of voice. As discussed previously, this increased employer resistance has occurred, suggesting that the negative aspects of voice have dominated and are perceived as increasingly costly.

The economic case for and against unions to a large degree depends on the extent to which markets (in the private sector) and organizations (in the public sector) operate efficiently or cost effectively. In the private sector, the increased number of "sellers" arising from trade liberalization, global competition, and deregulation as well as greater consumer choice arising from improvements in information and reductions in transactions costs have helped meet the assumptions required for private sector markets to be efficient, invariably moving them in the direction of greater efficiency. The accompanying decline in private sector unions suggest that any positive voice function was insufficient to offset the monopoly face of unionization in the private sector.

In the public sector, there is no clear benchmark or "competitive norm" from which to develop a scorecard for evaluating the pros and cons of public sector unions. There is certainly more potential for organizational slack and hence a positive shock effect from voice—but this also means more potential for muscle forms of voice for purposes of rent seeking. There is also less rationale for unions to "protect the underdog" in the public sector given the already existing public sector rents and the pressure for public sector employers to be model employers, but this also means that unions may use muscle to protect those rents.

Efficiency is not the only social welfare criteria for evaluating unions. In the industrial relations literature, for example, concepts like "industrial democracy," "social justice," and "freedom of association" are important, and processes are often regarded as ends in themselves as evidenced by the importance attached to concepts like "due process." This is the case in the private as well as the public sector as evidenced by the emphasis on "social unionism" and ties to community and other social activist groups as part of attempts to revive private sector unionism. These coalitions and emphasis on process factors, however, can be part of attempts to restore a monopoly face in the private sector (e.g., resisting the market imperatives of globalization and deregulation) and to establish the potential for more muscle forms of voice in the public sector (e.g., resisting privatization and budget cuts). Clearly, these broader issues have to be kept in mind in framing a scorecard for evaluating public sector unions.

The overall scorecard assessment that I provide herein suggests that the more negative muscle-flexing and influence-peddling form of union voice in the public sector has dominated the more positive form of voice. This was the case in the four manifestations of voice I examined: unionization as the institutional embodiment of voice; strikes as the loudest form of voice; political activity as an external channel of voice; and employee involvement in the management of the organization as an internal channel of voice. This dominance of the more negative face of voice likely reflects the fact that these negative forms of voice are not being disciplined by the same competitive global market pressures that affect private sector unions and dissipate their monopoly face.

Gazing into the crystal ball of the future suggests the following scenarios. Public sector unions will neither grow nor decline substantially reflecting the offsetting forces of increased demand for employee voice to deal with the changes having to confront the realities of lower unionization in many of the out-sourced and privatized public services. Public sector unions will be less confrontational and seek alternative and less adversarial forms of dispute resolution given that their survival can be jeopardized by costly forms of voice. As well, their power will continue to be circumscribed by government restrictions on their right to strike either directly (by requiring binding arbitration) or indirectly through such means as back-to-work legislation, designating essential workers who cannot strike, or freezing agreements. Public sector unions, however, will continue their voice in the political realm and through community groups. With respect to managerial prerogatives, public sector unions will try to have a more constructive voice rather than resisting changes that can otherwise enhance productivity in public services. They will do so by walking the fine line between their self-interest and the public interest, given that their motivations are under the increased scrutiny that comes with governments facing a harder budget constraint.

These predictions all flow from the notion that governments are facing increasing competitive pressures and harder budget constraints and that public sector unions will have to respond to these pressures. The forecasting errors around these predictions, however, are quite substantial suggesting a cloudy and not clear crystal ball.

Notes

* Financial assistance from the SSHRC is gratefully acknowledged, as is the excellent research assistance and insights of Pauline James, and the extensive comments and suggestions of Bruce Kaufman.

1. Various mechanisms or channels through which these positive and negative aspects of union voice operate are outlined in the Kaufman theory chapter and Kaufman and Levine (2000).
2. Addison and Belfield in this volume review that evidence and cite other reviews.
3. Reasons for the existence of a pure public sector wage premium and summaries of Canadian evidence of such a premium are given in Benjamin et al. (2002: 309–11) and Gunderson (2002b) and for U.S. and international evidence in Borland and Gregory (1999).

4. There is some variability in the public sector wage premium across different groups, with some, like teachers, receiving higher premiums at higher levels, possibly reflecting median voter preferences within unions (Zwerling and Thomason, 1995).

5. Reviews of evidence on union wage premiums (including references to other reviews) in the public and private sectors for the United States are given in Freeman (1986), and for the United States and Canada in Benjamin et-al. (2002: 484), Gunderson (2002b), and Gunderson and Hyatt (2004).

6. Freeman (1986: 59) summarizes 11 studies, ten of which find that "public sector unions raise fringe benefits considerably more than they raise wages" suggesting the importance of median voters in shaping preferences for that form of compensation in the public sector.

7. Based on data from private sector firms, Lewin and Boroff (1996) confirm only part of the exit-voice-loyalty notion in that loyal employees tend not to exit but they also tend *not* to use voice (grievances), suggesting that they "suffer in silence."

8. This is evidenced by the much greater extent of volunteer activity by persons who work in the public sector compared to the private sector (Gomez and Gunderson, 2003).

9. Figures on unionization and collective agreement coverage are given in Bennett and Masters (2003: 537) and Thomason and Burton (2003) for the United States, and Gunderson (2002a), Murray (2004), and Swimmer and Bartkiw (2003: 581) for Canada.

10. Kaufman argues in his theory chapter that in general the negative monopoly face will gradually displace the positive voice face over time. Obviously, these early forms of consultation could have continued, given the current array of nonunion form of employee representation that exist (Kaufman and Taras, 2000). Their transformation into more formal unions likely reflected the desire for power to further their interests—some would say to transform "collective begging" into "collective bargaining."

11. The importance of legislative initiatives in establishing public sector unions is documented in Freeman (1986, 1996), Lewin et al. (1988), Saltzman (1985, 1988), Troy (1994), Zigarelli (1996), and various chapters in Freeman and Ichniowski (1988) for the United States, and Gunderson (2002a) and Gunderson and Hyatt (1996: 247) and references cited therein for Canada. For the United States, Walters et al. (1994) provide evidence of the simultaneous relationship whereby public sector unions have a positive effect on the passage of pro-union legislation which in turn fosters additional public sector unionization. Fine and Baktari (2001) find that state bargaining laws do not provide public sector workers with union-democracy protections (e.g., membership voting rights, rights to sue the union or its officers, financial disclosure, protection from coercion) as provided by the Landrum-Griffin Act for private sector workers. While this could reduce the demand for unions, it can also make it easier to establish and sustain unions in the public sector. Ichniowski and Zax (1991) provide evidence that right-to-work laws that ensure workers the right to decline membership in the union that represents them has significantly reduced unionization in the local public sector in the United States.

12. The importance of the general social environment at the time is discussed in Kearney (2003: 508) and Turner and Hurd (2001: 17) for the United States, and Gunderson (2002a) and Gunderson and Hyatt (1996: 248) for Canada.

13. Survey evidence on preferences for unionization is provided in Freeman (1996) and Fiorito et al. (1996).

14. The "safety valve" perspective, and supporting evidence, is provided by various articles by Hebdon: Hebdon (1996, 1998), Hebdon and Stern (1998, 2003), and

Hebdon et al. (1999). Hebdon (1998) also indicates how banning strikes in the public sector reduces positive voice effects of the normal bargaining process such as eliciting information, adjusting expectations, and providing catharsis.

15. See Gunderson (2002a), Gunderson and Hyatt (1996), and Swimmer and Bartkiw (2003: 581) and various references cited therein for Canada.

16. Hebdon and Warrian (1999: 211) find that "despite the coercive environment of the [Ontario] Social Contract Act, superior restructuring outcomes were achieved where workers were able to voice their concerns collectively."

17. For Canadian evidence on public sector strikes, see Gunderson (2002a), Gunderson and Hyatt (1996), and Gunderson et al. (2004); for U.S. evidence see Hebdon (1996).

18. The voice function of public sector workers in political activities is documented and discussed in Bennett and Orzechowski (1983), Chandler and Gely (1995), Courant et-al. (1979), Ehrenberg and Schwarz (1986), Freeman (1986), O'Brien (1994), Masters (1985), Scheurman (1989), Swimmer and Bartkiw (2003), Zax (1989), and Zax and Ichniowski (1989).

19. Freeman (1986: 62) reviews five studies that provide evidence of public sector unions increasing public budgets in areas such as education, police, and general municipal services. Consistent with his perspective on the positive face of unions, he emphasizes that this need not be regarded as negative since productivity effects and the optimal size of public budgets are not considered. Trejo (1991) reviews empirical studies that find a positive correlation between public sector union power and employment growth. He finds evidence, however, of reverse causality whereby large public sector workforces foster unionization because of economies of scale in organizing. Valetta (1993) also finds that the ability of public sector unions to increase demand did not occur based on estimates from longitudinal data that control for unobserved factors.

20. The oppositional activities of public sector unions in a number of areas are discussed in Craft (2003) and Johnson (1994).

21. Teacher union opposition to such reforms is discussed in Boyd et al. (2000), Engval (1995), Kearney (2003), Lieberman (1997), Thomason and Burton (2003), and Troy (1999).

22. For a discussion of this more positive face of teacher unions, see Cibulka (2000), Johnson and Kardos (2000), Kearney (2003), and Kerchner (2002).

23. Evans and Nelson (1989) discuss how the comparable worth awards to state employees in Minnesota in the 1980s were not announced and were added incrementally to pay checks. If they were announced as comparable worth awards, "credit" may go to management for making such awards, whereas if they simply appeared in paychecks, credit may go to the unions.

24. Freeman (1996) provides U.S. survey evidence indicating a greater incidence of employee involvement in the public sector (60 percent) compared to the private sector (55 percent). LeRoy (1990) and Riccucci and Knowles (1993) provide evidence of public sector union resistance to drug testing on the part of employers.

25. I am indebted to Bruce Kaufman for making this point to me.

26. Teacher bargaining over these issues is discussed in Eberts (1986), Eberts et-al. (2002), Hall and Carroll (1973), Goldschmidt and Stuart (1986), Hanushek (1986), and Woodbury (1985).

27. Register and Grimes (1991) specifically provide a voice interpretation to their positive results: "Following the work of Freeman (1976) it may simply be that education is an environment that is extremely sensitive to employee satisfaction; the provision of a collective voice through unionization yields significant benefits

in the form of increased productivity." They also suggest that shock effects may be at work as well as higher quality hiring from the larger queue.

28. This inverted-U pattern is found in Argys and Rees (1995), Eberts and Stone (1984, 1987), and Eberts et al. (2002).

29. For state and local employees, Lewin (2003) found that unions did not inhibit the use of incentive compensation.

30. For a discussion of both the theory and evidence in this area, see Gunderson (1998).

References

Addison, John and Barry Hirsch. "Union Effects on Productivity and Growth: Has the Long Run Arrived?" *Journal of Labor Economics* 7 (January 1989): 72–105.

Argys, Laura and Daniel Rees. "Unionization and School Productivity: A Reexamination." *Research in Labor Economics* 14 (1995): 49–68.

Ash, Michael and Jean Ann Seago. "The Effect of Registered Nurses on Heart-Attack Mortality." *Industrial and Labor Relations Review* 57 (April 2004): 422–44.

Belman, Dale, John S. Haywood, and John Lund. "Public Sector Earnings and the Extent of Unionization." *Industrial and Labor Relations Review* 50 (July 1997): 610–28.

Benjamin, Dwayne, Morley Gunderson, and Craig Riddell. *Labour Market Economics: Theory, Evidence and Policy in Canada.* Toronto: McGraw-Hill, 2002.

Bennett, James and Marick Masters. "The Future of the Public Sector Labor-Management Relations." *Journal of Labor Research* 24 (Fall 2003): 533–44

Bennett, James T. and William P. Orzechowski. "The Voting Behavior of Bureaucrats: Some Empirical Evidence." *Public Choice* 41 (1983): 271–83.

Biond, Azalia. "Implications that Downsizing Could Have for Public Sector Unions." *Journal of Collective Negotiations in the Public Sector* 26 (No. 4, 1997): 295–301.

Bordogna, Lorenzo. "The Reform of Public Sector Employment Relations in Industrialized Democracies." In Jonathan Brock and David Lipsky, eds. *Going Public: The Role of Labor-Management Relations.* Champaign, IL: Industrial Relations Research Association, 2003, pp. 69–106.

Boyd, William Lowe, David N. Plank, and Gary Skyes. "Teachers Unions in Hard Times." In Tom Loveless, ed. *Conflicting Missions? Teachers, Unions and Educational Reform.* Washington, DC: Brookings Institution, 2000, pp. 210–74.

Byrne, Dennis, Hashem Dezhbakhsh, and Randal King. "Unions and Police Productivity: An Econometric Investigation." *Industrial Relations* 35 (October 1996): 566–84.

Chandler, Timothy D. and Rafael Gely. "The Determinants of Public Employee Unions' Political Activities." *Proceedings of the Forty-Seventh Annual Meeting.* Washington, DC: Industrial Relations Research Association, 1995, pp. 295–304.

Cibulka, James G. "The NEA and School Choice." In Tom Loveless, ed. *Conflicting Missions? Teachers, Unions and Educational Reform.* Washington, DC: Brookings Institution, 2000, pp. 150–73.

Courant, Paul N., Edward Gramlich, and Daniel Rubinfeld. "Public Employee Market Power and the Level of Government Spending." *American Economic Review* 69(December 1979): 806–17.

Craft, James. "Future Directions in the Sector Labor Relations: A 2020 Perspective." *Journal of Labor Research* 24 (Fall 2003): 545–60.

Eberts, Randall. "Union Effects on Teacher Productivity." *Industrial and Labor Relations Review* 37 (April 1984): 346–48.

——— and Joe Stone. *Unions and Public Schools: The Effect of Collective Bargaining an American Education.* Lexington, MA: Lexington Books, 1984.

————. "The Effect of Teachers Unions and Student Achievement." *Industrial and Labor Relations Review* 40 (April 1987): 354–63.

Eberts, Randall, Kevin Hollenbeck, and Joe Stone. "Teacher Performance Incentives, Collective Bargaining, and Student Outcomes." *Proceedings of the Fifty-fourth Annual Meeting.* Atlanta: Industrial Relations Research Association, 2002, pp. 180–92.

Ehrenberg, Ronald and Joshua Schwarz. "Public Sector Labor Markets." In Orley Ashenfelter and Richard Layard, eds. *Handbook of Labor Economics*, Vol. 2. New York: Elsevier, 1987, pp. 1219–68.

Engval, Robert P. "Public-Sector Unionization in 1995: Or It Appears the Lion King Has Eaten Robin Hood." *Journal of Collective Negotiations in the Public Sector* 24 (September 1995): 255–69.

Evans, Sara and Barbara Nelson. *Wage Justice: Comparable Worth and the Paradox of Technocratic Reform.* Chicago: University of Chicago Press, 1989.

Fine, Cory and Paul Baktari. "Public Sector Union Democracy: A Comparative Anaylsis." *Journal of Labor Research* 22 (Spring 2001): 391–404.

Fiorito, Jack, Lee P. Stephina, and Dennis P. Bozeman. "Explaining the Unionism Gap: Public-Private Sector Differences in Preferences for Unionization." *Journal of Labor Research* 17 (Summer 1996): 463–79.

Freeman, Richard. "Unionism Comes to the Public Sector." *Journal of Economic Literature* 24 (March 1986): 41–69.

————. "Is Declining Unionization of the U.S. Good, Bad, or Irrelevant?" In Lawrence Mishel and Paula Voos, eds. *Unions and Economic Competitiveness.* Armonk, NY: M.E. Sharpe, 1991: pp. 143–67.

————. "Through Public Sector Eyes: Employee Attitudes toward Public Sector Labor Relations in the U.S." In Dale Belman, Morley Gunderson, and Douglas Hyatt, eds. *Public Sector Employment in a Time of Transition.* Madison, WI: Industrial Relations Research Association, 1996, pp. 59–83.

———— and Casey Ichniowski, eds. *When Public Sector Workers Unionize.* Chicago: University of Chicago Press, 1988.

Freeman, Richard and James Medoff. "The Two Faces of Unionism." *Public Interest* 7 (April 1979): 69–93.

————. *What Do Unions Do?* New York: Basic Books. 1984.

Goldschmidt, Steven M. and Leland E. Stuart. "The Extent and Impact of Educational Policy Bargaining." *Industrial and Labor Relations Review* 39 (April 1986): 350–60.

Gomez, Rafael and Morley Gunderson. "Volunteer Activity and the Demands of Work and Family." *Relations Industrielles/Industrial Relations* 58 (Fall 2003): 573–89.

Gregory, Robert and Jeffrey Borland. "Recent Developments in Public Sector Labor Markets." In Orley Ashenfelter and David Card, eds. *Handbook of Labor Economics.* New York: Elsevier Science, North Holland, 1999, pp. 3573–690.

Gunderson, Morley. "Gender Discrimination and Pay Equity Legislation." In Lou Christofides, Ken Grant, and Robert Swidinsky, eds. *Aspects of Labour Market Behaviour.* Toronto: University of Toronto Press, 1995, pp. 225–47.

————. "Harmonization of Labour Policies Under Trade Liberalization." *Relations Industrielles/Industrial Relations* 53 (No. 1, 1998): 11–41.

————. "Collective Bargaining and Dispute Resolution in the Public Sector." In Christopher Dunn, ed. *Handbook of Canadian Public Administration.* Don Mills: Oxford University Press, 2002a, pp. 517–32.

————. "Compensation in the Public Sector." In Christopher Dunn, ed. *Handbook of Canadian Public Administration.* Don Mills: Oxford University Press, 2002b, pp. 533–45.

———— Robert Hebdon, Douglas Hyatt, and Allen Ponak. "Strikes and Dispute Resolution." In Morley Gunderson, Allen Ponak, and Daphne Taras, eds. *Union-Management Relations in Canada,* 5th ed. Toronto: Addison-Wesley, 2004, pp. 332–70.

Gunderson, Morley and Douglas Hyatt. "Canadian Public Sector Employment Relations in Transition." In-Dale Belman, Morley Gunderson, and Douglas Hyatt, eds. *Public Sector Employment in a Time of Transition.* Madison, WI: Industrial Relations Research Association, 1996, pp. 243–82.

————. "Union Impact on Compensation, Productivity and Management of the Organization." In Morley Gunderson, Allen Ponak and Daphne Taras, eds. *Union-Management Relations in Canada,* 5th ed. Toronto: Addison-Wesley, 2004, pp. 394–413.

Hall, W. Clayton and Norman Carroll. "The Effects of Teachers' Organizations on Salaries and Class Size." *Industrial and Labor Relations Review* 26 (January 1973): 834–41.

Hanushek, Eric. "The Economics of Schooling: Production and Efficiency in Public Schools." *Journal of Economic Literature* 24 (September 1986): 1141–77.

Hart, Susan. "Unions and Pay Equity Bargaining." *Relations Industrielles/Industrial Relations* 57 (Fall 2002): 609–27.

Hebdon, Robert. "Public Sector Dispute Resolution in Transition." In Dale Belman, Morley Gunderson, and Douglas Hyatt, eds. *Public Sector Employment in a Time of Transition.* Madison, WI: Industrial Relations Research Association, 1996, pp. 85–126.

————. "Behavioural Determinants of the Public Sector Illegal Strikes." *Relations Industrielle/Industrial Relations* 53 (Fall 1998): 667–90.

———— and Robert Stern. "Trade-offs among Expressions of Industrial Conflict: Public Sector Strike Bans and Grievance Arbitrations." *Industrial and Labor Relations Review* 51 (January 1998): 204–21.

————. "Do Public Sector Strike Bans Really Prevent Conflict?" *Industrial Relations* 42 (July 2003): 493–512.

Hebdon, Robert, Douglas Hyatt, and Maurice Mazerolle. "Implications of Small Bargaining Units and Enterprise Unions on Bargaining Disputes." *Relations Industrielles/Industrial Relations* 54 (May 1999): 503–24.

Hebdon, Robert and Peter Warrian. "Coercive Bargaining: Public Sector Restructuring Under the Ontario Social Contract, 1993–1996." *Industrial and Labor Relations Review* 52 (January 1999): 196–212.

Hoxby, Caroline. "How Teachers' Unions Affect Production." *Quarterly Journal of Economics* 111 (August 1996): 671–718.

————. "Would School Choice Change the Teaching Profession?" NBER Working Papers 7866, National Bureau of Economic Research, 2000.

Ichniowski, Casey and Jeffery Zax. "Right to Work Laws, Free Riders, and Unionization in the Public Sector." *Journal of Labor Economics* 9 (July 1991): 255–76.

Iverson, Roderick D. and Douglas B. Currivan. "Union Participation, Job Satisfaction, and Employee Turnover: An Event-History Analysis of the Exit-Voice Hypothesis." *Industrial Relations* 42 (January 2003): 101–105.

Johnson, Susan Moore and Susan M. Kardos. "Reform Bargaining and Its Promise for School Improvement." In Tom Loveless, ed. *Conflicting Missions? Teachers, Unions and Educational Reform.* Washington, DC: Brookings Institution, 2000, pp. 7–46.

Johnston, Paul. *Success Where Others Fail: Social Movement Unionism and the Public Workplace.* Ithaca, NY: ILR Press, 1994.

Kaufman, Bruce and David Levine. "An Economic Analysis of Employee Representation." In Bruce Kaufman and Daphne Taras, eds. *Nonunion Employee Representation: History, Contemporary Practice, and Policy.* Armonk, NY: M.E. Sharpe, 2000, pp. 149–75.

Kaufman, Bruce and Daphne Taras, eds. *Nonunion Employee Representation: History, Contemporary Practice, and Policy.* Armonk, NY: M.E. Sharpe, 2000.

Kerchner, Charles. "The Modern Guild: Prospects for Organizing around Quality in Public Education." In Jonathan Brock and David Lipsky, eds. *Going Public: The Role of Labor-Management Relations.* Champaign, IL: Industrial Relations Research Association, 2003, pp. 235–67.

Kearney, Richard. "Patterns of Union Decline and Growth: An Organizational Ecology Perspective." *Journal of Labor Research* 24 (Fall 2003): 561–78.

Kleiner, Morris and Daniel Petree. "Unionism and Licensing of Public School Teachers: Impact on Wages and Educational Output." In Richard Freeman and Casey Ichniowski, eds. *When Public Sector Workers Unionize.* Chicago: University of Chicago Press, 1988, pp. 305–19.

Kurth, Michael. "Teachers' Unions and Excellence in Education: An Analysis of the Decline in SAT Scores." *Journal of Labor Research* 8 (Fall 1987): 351–67.

Le Roy, Michael H. "Drug Testing in the Public Sector: Union Member Attitudes." *Journal of Collective Negotiations in the Public Sector* 19 (No. 3, 1990): 165–74.

Lewin, David. "Incentive Compensation in the Public Sector." *Journal of Labor Research* 24 (Fall 2003): 597–619.

———— and Karen Boroff. "The Role of Loyalty in Exit and Voice," In David Lewin, Bruce Kaufman, and Donna Sockell, eds. *Advances in Industrial and Labor Relations.* Greenwich, CT: JAI Press, 1996, pp. 69–96.

Lewin, David, Peter Feuille, Thomas Kochan, and John Delaney. *Public Sector Labor Relations.* Lexington, MA: Lexington, 1988.

Lieberman, Myron. *The Teachers' Unions.* New York: Free Press, 1997.

Lund, John and Cheryl Maranto. "Public Sector Law: An Update." In Dale Belman, Morley Gunderson, and Douglas Hyatt, eds. *Public Sector Employment in a Time of Transition.* Madison, WI: Industrial Relations Research Association, 1996, pp. 21–58.

Masters, Marick. "Federal-Employee Unions and Political Action." *Industrial and Labor Relations Review* 38 (July 1985): 612–29.

Meador, Mark and Stephen Walters. "Unions and Productivity: Evidence from Academe." *Journal of Labor Research* 15 (Fall 1994): 373–86.

Mehay, Stephen and Rodolfo Gonzalez. "District Elections and the Power of Municipal Employee Unions." *Journal of Labor Research* 15 (Fall 1994): 387–402.

Murray, Gregor. "Unions: Membership, Structures, Actions and Challenges." In Morley Gunderson, Allen Ponak, and Daphne Taras, eds. *Union-Management Relations in Canada.* 5th ed. Toronto: Addison-Wesley, 2004, pp. 79–112.

Murphy, Marjorie. *Blackboard Unions: The AFT and the NEA.* Ithaca NY: Cornell University Press, 1990.

O'Brien, Kevin M. "The Impact of Union Political Activities on the Public-Sector Pay, Employment, and Budgets." *Journal of Economy and Society* 33 (July 1994): 322–46.

Orazem, Peter and Peter Mattila. "The Implementation Process of Comparable Worth: Winners and Losers." *Journal of Political Economy* 98 (February 1990): 134–53.

Reder, Melvin. "The Theory of Employment and Wages in the Public Sector." In Daniel Hamermesh, ed. *Labor in the Public and Non-profit Sectors.* Princeton, NJ: Princeton University Press, 1975, pp. 1–48.

Register, Charles. "Wages, Productivity and Costs in Union and Nonunion Hospitals." *Journal of Labor Research* 9 (Fall 1988): 325–45.

———— and Paul Grimes. "Collective Bargaining, Teachers, and Student Achievement." *Journal of Labor Research* 12 (Spring 1991): 99–109.

Riccucci, Norma M. and Eddie Knowles. "Drug Testing in the Public Sector: The Role of Unions." *International Journal of Public Administration* 16 (July 1993): 891–920.

Saltzman, Gregory. "Bargaining Laws as a Cause and Consequence of Teacher Unionism." *Industrial and Labor Relations Review* 38 (April 1985): 335–51.

———. "Public Sector Bargaining Laws Really Matter: Evidence from Ohio and Illinois." In Richard Freeman and Casey Ichniowski, eds. *When Public Sector Workers Unionize.* Chicago: University of Chicago Press, 1988, pp. 41–78.

Scheureman, William. "Politics and the Public Sector: Strategies for Public Sector Unions." *Policy Studies Journal* 18 (Winter 1989): 433–42.

Smith, Susan Kay. "The Teacher Union Contract: A Constraint on 'Downsizing' the Public Sector." *Journal of Collective Negotiations in the Public Sector* 18 (No. 3, 1989): 229–40.

Swimmer, Gene and Tim Barkiw. "The Future of Public Sector Collective Bargaining in Canada." *Journal of Labor Research* 24 (Fall 2003): 579–96

Thomason, Terry and John F. Burton, Jr. "Unionization Trends and Labor-Management Cooperation in the Public Sector." In Jonathan Brock and David Lipsky, eds. *Going Public: The Role of Labor-Management Relations.* Champaign, IL: Industrial Relations Research Association, 2003, pp. 69–106

Trejo, Stephen J. "Public Sector Unions and Municipal Employment." *Industrial and Labor Relations Review* 45 (October 1991): 166–79.

Troy, Leo. *The New Unionism in the New Society: Public Sector Unions in the Redistributive State.* Fairfax, VA: George Mason University Press, 1994.

Turner, Lowell and Rick Hurd. "Building Social Movement Unionism: The Transformation of the American Labor Movement." In Lowell Turner, Harry Katz, and Richard Hurd, eds. *Rekindling the Movement: Labor's Quest for Relevance in the 21st Century.* Ithaca, NY: Cornell University Press, 2001, pp. 9–26.

Valetta, Robert. "Union Effect on Municipal Employment and Wages: A Longitudinal Approach." *Journal of Labor Economics* 11 (July 1993): 545–74.

Waters, Melissa, R. Carter Hill, William Moore, and Robert Newman. "A Simultaneous-Equations Model of the Relationship between Public Sector Bargaining Legislation and Unionization." *Journal of Labor Research* 15 (Fall 1994): 354–72.

Weiner, Nan and Morley Gunderson. *Pay Equity: Issues, Options and Experiences.* Toronto: Butterworths, 1990.

Wesman, Elizabeth C. "Unions and Comparable Worth: Progress in the Public Sector." *Journal of Collective Negotiations in the Public Sector* 17 (No. 1, 1988): 13–27.

Woodbury, Stephan A. "The Scope of Bargaining and Bargaining Outcomes in the Public Schools." *Industrial and Labor Relations Review* 38 (January 1985): 195–209.

Zax, Jeffery. "Employment and Local Public Sector Unions." *Industrial Relations* 28 (Winter 1989): 21–31.

——— and Casey Ichniowski. "The Effects of Public Sector Unionism on Pay, Employment, Deparment Budgets, and Municipal Expenditures." In Richard Freeman and Casey Ichniowski, eds. *When Public Sector Workers Unionize.* Chicago: University of Chicago Press, 1989, pp. 323–64.

Zigarelli, Michael. "Dispute Resolution Mechanisms and Teacher Bargaining Outcomes." *Journal of Labor Research* 17 (Winter 1996): 135–48.

Zwerling, Harris and Terry Thomason. "Collective Bargaining and the Determinants of Teachers' Salaries." *Journal of Labor Research* 16 (Fall 1995): 467–84.

14

Unionism Viewed Internationally

John Pencavel

I. Introduction

The principal research mission of *What Do Unions Do?* (hereinafter *WDUD*) was to persuade economists to adopt a broader perspective on the activities of labor unions. Freeman and Medoff (1984) maintained that economists riveted on the wage effects of unions and neglected other important features of collective bargaining. The authors certainly recognized the wage-unionism nexus and acknowledged "the negative monopoly effects of unions" (p. 19), but also they drew attention to other dimensions of U.S. unionism, some of which might encourage a more favorable view of unions.

Above all, drawing on Albert Hirschman's (1970) insightful distinction between "exit" and "voice" in expressing dissatisfaction, Freeman and Medoff emphasized how unions provide employees with a mechanism to shape their working environment. This participatory role, together with the higher wages that unions negotiate, discourage employees from quitting their jobs and, typically, so Freeman and Medoff argued, this lower turnover causes union establishments to be more productive than nonunion establishments. There are exceptions to this generalization and, indeed, productivity will be harmed by antagonistic union-management relations, but in general unions enhance productivity.

What was new about this argument? The role of unions as participatory institutions had been long recognized by industrial relations scholars who had noted that productivity benefits might emanate from this form of "economic democracy."[1] No doubt, some economists were ignorant of this work or took an unnecessarily skeptical view of it so Freeman and Medoff's attention to it was welcome. In addition, economists knew that, holding wages constant, unionism reduces quits.[2] The novel element in *WDUD* was in documenting these facts with a wealth of statistical information, piecing them together in a coherent and distinctive portrait of U.S. unionism, and drawing out their implications. The whole was very much more than the sum of its parts. The result was a highly influential, though controversial, characterization of U.S. unionism.

The research in *WDUD* was influential not only in stimulating research on U.S. unionism, but also in provoking research on unionism in other countries.

To what extent does Freeman and Medoff's portrait of U.S. unionism apply to unions in other countries and what can be learned from international unionism that informs our understanding of U.S. unionism? I address these questions. It is impossible to do justice in a relatively short article to the wealth of information that has been collected on unionism and collective bargaining in all other countries and what I present herein must necessarily be highly selective. However, I argue that the international dimension provides a useful perspective on unionism and that there is much to learn about unionism from the experience of other countries. American unionism is distinctive, and it is hazardous to draw inferences about unionism in other countries informed solely from knowledge of unionism in the United States. Indeed, I contend that an international perspective confirms some themes in *WDUD* especially the constructive role that unions may play in providing individuals with an opportunity to participate in fashioning their work environment, but as a pressure group on government the international evidence suggests a less favorable portrait of unionism than Freeman and Medoff's.

In what follows, I distinguish three classes of union activities: the wage-making activities of unions and their implications; the political activities of unions; and the role of unions in regulating the employment relationship. Unions in many countries regard their political ventures as no less important than the pursuit of their wage bargaining goals so that an international perspective on unionism requires a discussion of their political activities. First, I offer a brief sketch of how unionism has changed over the past few decades in some key economies and place these changes in the context of the labor markets of these countries.

II. Recent Developments in Unionism Common to Developed Economies

In *WDUD* Freeman and Medoff described the decline in U.S. private sector unionism as "a development unique to the United States in the developed world" (p. 251). However, looking back from the year 2003, we can now see that the U.S. experience provided something of a portent and the decline in private sector unionism in the United States has been replicated in a number of high-income economies. Figure 14.1 shows that union membership density in four English-speaking countries and Japan declined over the last ten years or more in all except perhaps Canada.[3] There may be indications of this also in three of the four Continental European countries graphed in Figure 14.2, but it certainly does not describe Sweden's experience.

In some countries, such as Britain and New Zealand, this decline in union density has been mirrored by a decline in the role of unions in labor market activities in general. In other countries, the coverage of collective bargaining contracts has remained high and virtually unchanging. For example, union membership rates in France have declined by over one-half since the 1970s whereas the coverage of collective bargaining agreements seems to have changed

Figure 14.1
Union Membership Density, 1950–2001: U.S.A., U.K., Australia, Canada, Japan

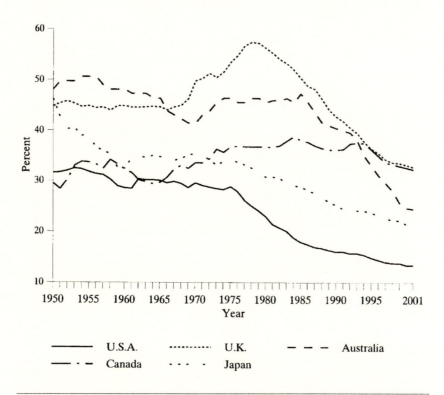

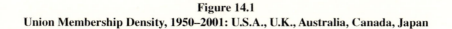

Sources: The data for the United States are from: for 1950–78 Leo Troy and Neil Sheflin, *Union Sourcebook: Membership, Finances, Structure Directory,* first edition, 1985 (Industrial Relations Data and Information Services, P.O. Box 226WOB, West Orange, NJ); for 1979–2001 Barry Hirsch and Daniel MacPherson, *Union Membership and Earnings Data Book,* 2002 edition, The Bureau of National Affairs, Washington, D.C., 2002. The figure for 1982 is linearly interpolated. The data for the United Kingdom are from: for 1950–1995, Bernhard Ebbinghaus and Jelle Visser, *Trade Unions in Western Europe since 1945,* Grove's Dictionaries, Inc., 2000; for 1996–2001, these are spliced with data from *Labour Market Trends,* Vol. 110, No. 7, July 2002, pp. 343–354. The data for Australia are from annual issues of the *Official Year Book of the Commonwealth of Australia;* a change in coverage and definitions cause a break in the series in 1986. The series in the graph above tries to overcome the break by splicing the pre–1986 data using the overlap in 1986 of the two series. For Canada, the data from 1950–75 are from *Historical Statistics of Canada;* from 1976–1994, they are from Morley Gunderson and Allen Ponak, *Union-Management Relations in Canada,* third edition. Data after 1994 are interpolated from the 1997 and 2001 Canadian Labour Force Surveys on union coverage. Data for Japan were kindly provided by Professor Toshiaki Tachibanaki of the Kyoto Institute of Economic Research, Kyoto University.

Figure 14.2
Union Membership Density, 1950–1997: Germany, France, Italy, Sweden

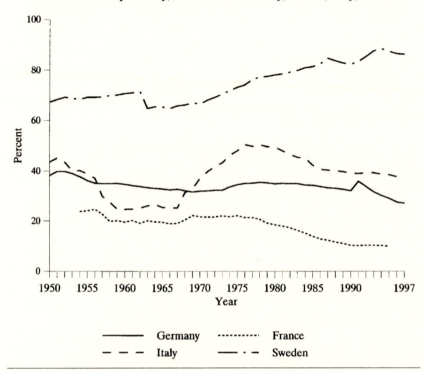

Source: These data are taken from Bernhard Ebbinghaus and Jelle Visser, *Trade Unions in Western Europe since 1945*, Grove's Dictionaries, Inc., 2000. For Germany, France, and Italy, these correspond to what the authors call "net density employed" meaning that pensioners and students are omitted from membership and the denominator consists of employed wage and salary earners (excluding the unemployed). For Sweden, the denominator consists of the labor force (that is, the unemployed are included). For Italy, the data from 1968 onwards are not strictly comparable with those earlier.

little and still embraces a very large fraction of employment. Thus, the mapping from changes in union density to changes in collective bargaining coverage varies markedly across countries. Nevertheless, the decline in union density puts pressure on the financial resources of unions and on unions' social and political influence. In this way, the last 25 years or so have seen unions very much on the defensive in many economies. What accounts for this pressure on unionism in many developed countries?

Elementary price theory suggests that competitive product market environments offer a less hospitable environment for the wage-making activities of unions than oligopolistic or state-protected markets. The cost disadvantage is less if all firms in a competitive industry can be unionized, but this happens rarely without government support for union organization. There is no cushion of supernormal, monopoly profits or public financing for private firms in competitive industries to help absorb unions' wage-push activities so, for a competitive firm, labor demand functions tend to be wage-elastic. Hence, competitive firms paying higher union-negotiated wages must find cost savings elsewhere to avoid declines in their market share. These pressures operate less vigorously when firms are product market monopolies or oligopolies or when entire industries pay union-negotiated wages or when the state protects the organization. Labor demand functions for private or public monopolists or for an entire industry tend to be less wage-elastic than is the case for a single competitive firm. Therefore, unions and product market monopolies (both private monopolies and public monopolies) may co-exist for much longer.

Essentially, in the last few decades, product markets in the developed world have become much more competitive and, therefore, less accommodating to the wage-making activities of labor unions. There are three reasons why product markets have become more competitive.

The first reason is increased international trade between the developed and the emerging economies and among developed economies themselves.[4] Foreign trade converts national product markets into international product markets and the number of product market competitors and potential competitors increases. Because the demand for labor derives from the demand for the product, greater product market competition implies more wage-elastic labor demand functions.

The second reason is the great increase in the international mobility of labor and capital. This has been driven both by falling transport costs and by greater information available about alternative possibilities. Increased factor mobility has also made labor demand and labor supply functions in each economy more elastic because high labor and capital mobility implies that a given wage change induces larger quantity reactions.

The third reason is technological change including the changes associated with the development and advancement of computers. Many business practices have been transformed and manufacturing processes made cheaper. Technological change has reduced the advantages associated with incumbency and allowed new firms to enter industries and compete successfully with older, more experienced firms. The importance of scale economies in many activities has diminished and this has promoted decentralization. Hence, barriers to competition have been trimmed.

In these ways, product market competition in developed economies has increased since the 1970s, the effects of which have been seen in the growth of contingent contracts,[5] the drive toward deregulation and privatization, and the growth of union-free workplaces (Katz and Darbishire, 2000). Some workers in developed economies have been affected more than others by this shift toward a more competitive product market environment. In particular, low-skill workers have suffered relative to those with high skills.

The impact on low-skill workers has been greater because the three reasons listed above to explain why labor markets have become more competitive have especially affected low-skill workers. Thus, with respect to foreign trade, developed economies have tended to import commodities that unskilled workers in developed economies make and cheaper imports reduces the demand for low-skill workers. In addition, a large fraction of immigrants to developed countries have been unskilled workers with lower reservation wages than native unskilled workers which has put downward pressure on the real wages of native unskilled workers. Some firms in developed economies — especially those employing less skilled workers — have shown a readiness to move their operations to low-wage economies. This capital mobility has increased the vulnerability of low-skill labor in developed economies.

Independently of these pressures from trade and factor mobility, technological change has not been neutral with respect to different types of labor. On the contrary, many have argued that modern technological methods require well-educated labor to manage and operate them while machines are apt to replace the work of unskilled workers. In short, some have suggested that technological changes embodied in capital have tended to be complementary with skilled labor and they have tended to substitute for unskilled labor.

The relative importance of these explanations — technological change, trade, immigration, the movement and threat of movement of capital — is subject to controversy. Regardless, together, these factors have put pressure on unskilled workers relative to skilled workers in developed economies. How this pressure has been manifested has depended on an economy's institutions and the pressure itself has affected these institutions including unionism.

In economies with extensive wage-setting by labor unions or governments, these pressures caused falling labor utilization rates of low-skill workers. These falling labor utilization rates may take various forms: a rise in unemployment rates; a slow growth or a fall in employment-population ratios; a drop in work hours; or an increase in the incidence of early retirement. Many other factors influence these labor utilization rates so it is not straightforward to isolate the pressures arising from the drop in demand for low-skill workers.[6]

A rough indicator of these effects on labor utilization rates is provided by changes in male unemployment rates. By examining "changes," constant differences across countries in how unemployed workers are matched with employers can be accommodated and, by focusing on men, cross-country differences are avoided in attitudes to and opportunities for women to work in the market and to count themselves as unemployed. Proportionate changes in male unemployment rates from 1979 to 2000 for ten developed economies are shown in column (1) of Table 14.1.[7] The largest increase in male unemployment is recorded in Sweden and Germany while the United States has experienced a small decrease.

In economies where labor union and government wage-setting institutions are less important or where they have been undermined by competition, these labor market pressures are felt less in changes in labor utilization and more in changes in earnings inequality. Column (2) of Table 14.1 provides a measure of the change in earnings inequality of male workers in recent decades. Using the ratio of earnings at the 90th percentile to earnings at the 10th percentile to indicate inequality, it shows inequality has increased most in Britain and the United States while it has actually fallen in Germany. Other indicators of inequality are correlated with the ratio of earnings at the 90th percentile to earnings at the 10th percentile.

Increases in earnings inequality have tended to substitute for growth in unemployment across these ten countries as shown in Figure 14.3 which graphs the data in columns (1) and (2) from Table 14.1. This negative association is not strong, but a strong link would be surprising given the different possible manifestations of changes in labor utilization and given problems of measurement.[8]

The position that developed countries have occupied on this trade-off between changes in unemployment and changes in earnings inequality is intimately related to unionism. Column (3) of Table 14.1 lists the percentage changes in the fraction of workers covered by collective bargaining contracts. It indicates the substantial reduction in the scope of unionism in Britain, the United States, and Japan over the past twenty years or so. By contrast, the coverage of collective bargaining contracts appears to have expanded between 1980 and the 1990s in France, Sweden, and Germany. Consequently, Figure 14.4 shows a positive association (again not a close one) between changes in unemployment and the change in the coverage of collective bargaining contracts in these ten countries. Where the extent of collective bargaining contracts has grown (in France, Sweden, and Germany), unemployment rates have tended to increase most; where unionism has contracted most (Britain and the United States), unemployment rates have increased little or not at all.[9]

Note that the links here are loose and there is no suggestion that the connection among changes in unemployment, wage inequality, and unionism is precise. There are many reasons for the cross-national variation in unemployment and pay experiences, and some of these reasons are quite independent of one another and of unionism. Nevertheless, some general and approximate patterns are associated with the scope of collective bargaining contracts.

Not merely has the extent of unionism changed in different degrees across developed countries, but also the character of collective bargaining has altered. Multi-employer and multi-sector agreements have become less common within the union sector and more issues are settled at the single-employer level or perhaps the single workplace. This holds not only in economies where the reach of collective bargaining contracts has declined, but also in countries where the scope of collective bargaining remains broad (e.g., Australia and Sweden). Other factors are also at work as evidenced by flatter hierarchies of management structures and greater use of work teams especially in unionized places.

Table 14.1
Changes in Male Unemployment Rates, Male Earnings Inequality, and the Coverage of Collective Bargaining Contracts from the late 1970s to 1990s: Selected Countries

	(1) Proportional Changes in Male Unemployment Rates	(2) Percent Changes in Male Earnings Inequality	(3) Percent Changes in Coverage of Union Contracts
Australia	0.32	7.30	−9.09
Canada	0.06	8.96	−2.70
France	1.13	1.18	11.76
Germany	2.08	−5.46	1.10
Italy	0.75	15.28	−3.53
Sweden	2.32	4.27	3.49
Finland	0.44	3.69	0
Japan	1.32	6.95	−25.00
United Kingdom	0.11	35.10	−32.86
U.S.A.	−0.22	36.79	−30.77

Definitions and Sources: Column (1). Let $U(i, t)$ be the male unemployment percentage of country i in year t. Column (1) lists $[U(i,2000) - U(i,1979)]/U(i,1979)$. The data are drawn from the September 1984 (Table B) and June 2001 (Table B) issues of OECD's *Employment Outlook*. Column (2). Let $D(i,t)$ be the ratio in year t and in country i of the earnings of male workers at the 90th percentile to the earnings of male workers at the 10th percentile. Column (2) lists $100*[D(i,1995) - D(i,1979)]/D(i,1979)$. The data are drawn from the July 1996 (Table 3.1) issue of OECD's *Employment Outlook*. Column (3). Let $C(i,t)$ be the percentage of workers in country i and year t covered by collective bargaining contracts. Column (3) lists $100*[C(i,1994) - C(i,1980)]/C(i,1980)$. The data are drawn from the July 1997 (Table 3.3) of OECD's *Employment Outlook*.

Performance-related pay has grown in all countries and workplace procedures have become less formal.

There is little evidence that developed countries are "converging" on a similar set of institutions, processes, and outcomes. This is not surprising. Notwithstanding greater factor mobility and increased international trade, relative factor prices are quite different across countries so that, even if all economies had access to the same technology, they would select different factor combinations. Moreover, land and climate are inherently immobile and this generates differences in factor proportions across countries even when other input prices are similar. Hence, even if they produced the same combination of goods, countries will use different technologies to do so and these technologies will tend to bring about different institutions and outcomes.

Figure 14.3
Changes in Male Earnings Inequality and in Male Unemployment Rates:
Selected Countries

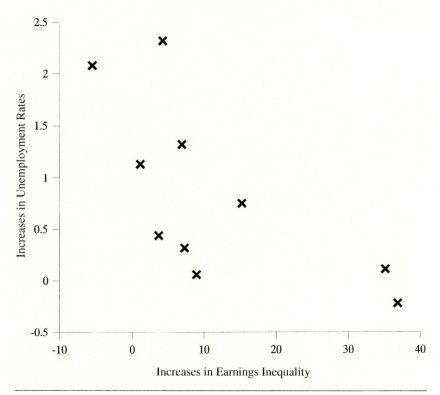

Source: See Table 14.1.

In addition, the preferences and values of people seem to be quite different across countries (at least beyond the most fundamental of needs), and it is not evident that these have become more similar: Continental Europeans appear more concerned with wide disparities of consumption and income, much less enamored of long work hours, and much more troubled if workers lack mechanisms for representation at their workplaces compared with, say, Americans. Such country-specific values mean that different economies adhere to specific institutions and processes so that labor markets in developed countries are not converging on the same organizations and procedures.

These generalizations overlook the rich complexity of specific-country experiences.[10] However, in a broad-brush way, they illustrate the pressures facing contemporary unions. As we shall see, unions probably raise the wages of low-skill workers more than the wages of high-skill workers, but given the

Figure 14.4
Changes in Unemployment Rates and in the Coverage of Collective Bargaining
Contracts: Selected Countries

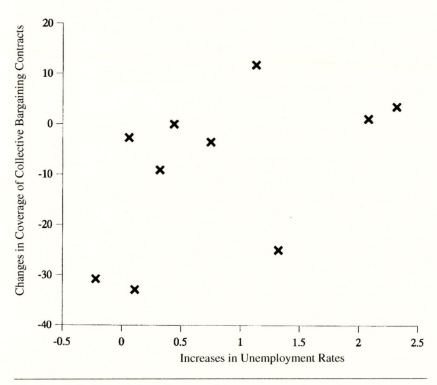

Source: See Table 14.1.

pressures on low-skill labor markets this activity risks higher unemployment
of the low-skill. In Continental Europe, unions may have helped to prevent
increased earnings inequality, but this achievement is largely at the cost of
greater unemployment. Moreover, the unions have been unable to resist the
growth of other factors that undermine union influence — the decentralization
of collective bargaining, the growth of privatization, and the use of contingent
contracts. It is difficult to avoid the conclusion that, to be durable without
enjoying special protection from the state, unions must emphasize their part
in making workplaces more productive and in serving their members' needs
in representing them in a constructive fashion at their place of work. With
these experiences as a backdrop, I consider now three classes of labor union
activities.

III. The Wage-Making Activities of Unions

Union Wage-Push

To economists, the most familiar and well-researched activity of unions is their role in negotiating contracts with employers. These collective bargaining agreements normally cover wages and, in richer economies, they embrace other issues including work hours and days, fringe benefits, layoff procedures, work organization, and grievance procedures. In bargaining over wages, unions typically push wages (and other components of total compensation) above the level that would obtain in their absence. By how much have unions pushed wages above these levels? The difference between union wages and the wages paid to the same workers in the absence of the union is called the "wage gain" of unionism. This gain is difficult to determine because the wages of union workers in the absence of unionism are intrinsically unobserved.

One approach to calculating the wage gain is to compare the wages paid to union workers with the wages paid to nonunion workers, a difference called the "wage gap." The defect in using the wage gap to measure the wage gain of unionism is that the wages of nonunion workers are probably affected by the union's presence. There are several reasons for this. First, in some countries, it is common practice for wages negotiated by unions to be extended to all workers in the same industry or sector. This is the case in a number of Continental European countries where wage-extension rules render the coverage of collective bargaining agreements much greater than the extent of union membership. Also, in the arbitration systems of Australia and New Zealand, the wage "awards" issued by the courts were usually extended to many workers in firms similar to those expressly represented in the cases.[11]

Wage-extension rules encourage employer confederations. An employer has the choice of remaining outside the confederation and have his wage scales set for him or joining the organization in the hope of influencing the level of wages. In this way, the oligopolization of markets is furthered.[12] Wage-extension rules give both unionized employers and unions the comfort of knowing that their labor costs will not be undercut by competitors. Such competition curbs union wage push. When wage-extension rules were lifted by New Zealand's Employment Contracts Act in 1991, the result was a drastic reduction in the extent of multi-employer bargains and of unionism.

Even in the absence of extension rules, the wages of nonunion workers are likely to be affected by the presence of unions. If nonunion employers believe there is a serious threat of their workers becoming unionized and if these employers prefer not to deal with unions, they may pay their workers higher wages simply to reduce the incentive for unionization. In this way, nonunion firms may pay wages comparable to those in union establishments. This phenomenon is known as the threat effect of unionism. The employers who act in this way tend to be those operating in places or industries where unions have recently demonstrated their ability to organize workers. The threat effect of unionism reduces the wage gap between union and nonunion workers below what would obtain in its absence.[13]

In the absence of the threat effect, if workers are disemployed from union firms because of wage-push by unions, some of these workers may seek employment in the nonunion sector. The rightward shift of labor supply curves in the nonunion sector reduces wages for nonunion workers. Again, the wages of nonunion workers are affected by unions elsewhere in the economy. In this instance, the wages of nonunion workers are below those that would obtain in the absence of unionism.

For these reasons, the union wage gain differs from the union wage gap. These explanations are compatible with the research on estimating union wage gaps in different economies. Union wage gaps tend to be largest in the United States and Canada where wage-extension rules are unusual and where, at least in recent years, union threat effects have been modest.[14] On average, in the last decade or so, union-nonunion wage gaps in the United States and Canada have been around 15 percent. In Britain and Australia, where wage-extension rules are more common than in North America but less common than in Continental Europe, union-nonunion wage gaps have been around 10 percent. On the European Continent, union-nonunion wage gaps have usually been estimated to be much less. But this hardly allows the inference that unionism and collective bargaining has not affected wages in Continental Europe; it means that collective bargaining has affected nonunion wages about the same as union wages.[15]

The estimates of the union-nonunion wage gap in the previous paragraph are the average across all workers in an economy. There are systematic differences in the wage gaps for different classes of workers. Thus they tend to be larger for low-skill workers than for high-skill workers. For instance, Card (2001) estimates union-nonunion wage gaps for the United States in 1993 of about 30 percent for low-skill working men and women but about zero for men and twelve percent for women at the top of the skill distribution. Similarly, using microdata across countries, Kahn (2000) finds greater coverage of union contracts is associated with higher pay for low-skill workers relative to medium-skill workers. Schultz and Mwabu (1998) compute a union-nonunion wage gap in South Africa of about zero for highly paid African men but of 41 percent at the tenth wage percentile.[16] Union wage gaps are higher for women than for men (Card et al., this volume). Not only are union-nonunion wage gaps larger among unskilled than skilled workers, but also unions appear to attenuate the sensitivity of wages to other characteristics. For example, the wage-age profile tends to be flatter and the wage premium attached to more schooling is lower among union workers than among nonunion workers.[17]

More generally, earnings inequality tends to be less in developed economies where unions are strong. It is not merely the extent of unionism that is correlated with earnings inequality, but the degree to which collective bargaining is decentralized: In economies where the locus of bargaining is the firm or workplace (as in the United States, Canada, Japan, or Britain), wage inequality within the union sector is apt to be greater than in economies where bargaining takes place at the industry, regional, or economy-wide level (as in Germany, Austria, or Norway) (e.g., Blau and Kahn, 1996). What causation (if any) lies behind these correlations? The collective bargaining structure is not some datum, but is the outcome of a country's economic and social fabric. Thus, when differences in wages among workers are relatively wide and firms are paying quite dissimilar wages, negotiating broad contracts covering a wide variety of people and firms is more difficult. In such circumstances, centralized bargaining procedures are less likely to emerge. Centralization of collective bargaining tends to materialize in economies where wage disparities are already relatively small. Viewed this way, wage dispersion is as much a cause as a consequence of the bargaining structure.

Perhaps this correlation between the extent of unionism and earnings inequality does embody a real causal influence of unionism: By collective bargaining and political pressure, unions push up the wages of low-skilled workers more than those of high-skilled workers and, thereby, they reduce wage dispersion. However, another explanation is that a society's underlying preferences, attitudes, and conventions are reflected both in the extent of unionism and in the degree of wage dispersion. Obviously, it is difficult to be sure of the causal mechanism: If attitudes toward inequality were given and public policy in a country encouraged unionism, would wage inequality decline as a result? From the strength of the time-series and cross-section correlation between unionism and wage inequality in developed economies, it is difficult to resist the inference that a policy change of this sort is likely to reduce wage inequality even though a thoroughly convincing episode of this sort is lacking.[18]

Employment

The cross-country patterns in changes in male unemployment rates in Figures 14.3 and 14.4 are approximately replicated in changes in male employment-population ratios and it has been conjectured that differences in the industrial relations systems across countries have played a role in these employment variations. (See, for instance, the *OCED Job Study 1994.*) Unions and collective bargaining are important features of these industrial relations systems. Conventional economic analysis suggests that, if the union imposes a higher wage on a single firm in a competitive industry and there is no offsetting cost reduction, employment in this firm will shrink.[19] In this way, economists usually expect union wage-making activity to reduce employment or slow employment growth.

Kahn's (2000) micro-data on wages and employment across countries suggest elements of this relationship: He reports an association between, on the one hand, the extent of collective bargaining coverage and, on the other hand, higher relative wages and lower relative employment for low-skilled men.[20]

This process in which unionized firms in incompletely unionized competitive industries shrink and ultimately close may take years. To survive in the long run, unions must find ways to offset this cost disadvantage placed on unionized employers (perhaps by burdening nonunion employers with the same cost) and they must continually organize new workers to prevent a decline in union density. This is why unions care deeply about the rules regulating the organization of new firms: When new organization is costly, it is difficult for unionism to remain a viable presence.

The difficulties unions face in organizing single firms in competitive industries explains why unions attempt to organize either entire industries or firms with some market power. Single firms must have some rents in order that unions can succeed in their wage-making activities. In this event, the union seeks to gain some of these rents. But when the union captures some of the rents and reduces the return to capital for the current producers, new nonunion firms may see an opportunity to enter the industry and make a larger return. Hence unions prefer markets where the entry and exit of firms are costly or regulated by the state. A well-organized union may be able to "capture" the regulatory authority of the state to benefit the union's wage-making activities.[21]

There are other ways in which unions try to frustrate the tendency for nonunion establishments to expand at the expense of union workplaces. One is to attenuate the cost disadvantage of union establishments by using the power of the state to raise the wages of nonunion competitors. One device is the "wage-extension" rules already mentioned. Also, unions have consistently supported state-mandated minimum wage laws. Union workers' wages are usually above these minimum levels so they apply to nonunion workers and they raise the costs of competing firms. For example, until the 1990s, in Britain a number of industry-specific Wage Councils operated where union representation was low to set minimum wages throughout the industry. Union officials often sat on the Wage Councils and the minimum wages tended to be adjusted upwards after union wages went up. This had the effect of preventing the appearance of a large gap between union wages and the wages of nonunion workers in Wage Council industries. These Wage Councils had the strong support of the union movement.[22]

In these instances, how are unions able to secure the power of the state to extend their wage-making influence? The answer is in much the same way as other pressure groups lobby for influence with government. Not only is a well-financed union movement able to provide largesse to a political party, but it may also be able to deliver the votes of union members and the organizational structure to help legitimize the political party's positions. As noted below in the section "Gainers and Losers," unions tend to be effective politically when they succeed in portraying themselves not as a narrow interest group but as advocates for all workers.

Product market competition or the threat of competition is usually least when the employer is the state and it is a regularity of developed economies that, where unionism is not outlawed, it tends to be stronger in the public than in the private sector. This pattern is observed in developing countries, too. It is not merely the case that product markets tend to be less competitive when production takes place in the public sector, but also the state sometimes feels it should provide an example to private industry of a "good" employer and this may mean supporting union organization.

The notion that unions find competitive product markets a less hospitable environment for their wage-push activities is supported by empirical research on union-nonunion wage gaps in both the United States and Britain. For instance, in Britain, Stewart (1990) finds union-nonunion wage differentials for most workers in competitive industries to be zero whereas they are between 8 and 19 percent in firms with some product market power. Union-nonunion wage gaps are absent in firms that operate in international markets. Qualitatively similar results have been derived for U.S. manufacturing industries (Mishel, 1986).

Gainers and Losers

Suppose unions engineer higher wages in some firms. Who gains and who loses? Clearly workers employed at the higher wages gain at least for their duration of employment at this wage. However, in the absence of offsetting cost-reducing activities, employment will not expand in these firms and, more likely it will fall.[23]

I have already noted that when unions raise wages for unionized workers, nonunion workers' wages rise or fall: There are wage-extension rules and threat effects that suggest that the wages of these other workers will rise and there are labor supply effects that suggest that the wages of nonunion workers will fall. However, not all workers can gain: If the size of the pie is fixed, one group of workers can increase its income only if the incomes of another group of workers falls.[24] Some workers gain from the wage-making activities of unions and some workers lose: The gainers are those employed at collectively bargained wages and those who are employed in jobs where the threat of successful union organizing is real; the losers are nonunion workers.[25]

In contrast, some observers characterize union wage-making activity as a struggle over the division of total income between wages and salaries on the one hand and profits on the other hand rather than a struggle among groups of workers. There may well be cases in which a union raises its members' pay by channeling income that would otherwise be distributed as profits or dividends. However, this sort of income redistribution can only be temporary and cannot be typical. There are two reasons for this. One reason is because the profits of incorporated firms in most economies represent a small fraction of total income and, if these profits are distributed over all the workers, they constitute a relatively small fillip to wages.

Consider this example for the United States where data on corporate profits are excellent. If all pre-tax corporate profits in 1999 were confiscated and distributed equally among all employees, the average annual compensation per employee would rise by 14.6 percent.[26] This once-and-for-all boost would need to be repeated the following year to preserve the wage increase. This number varies from country to country, but it is usually not much larger than this value for the United States in 1999.[27] This wage increase from confiscating all corporate profits is considerably smaller than the popular impression of what such a transfer would produce. The potential to transfer corporate profits to workers in this manner is constrained by two considerations: First, most incomes take the form of payments to labor, not payments to "passive" agents as profits, interest, and rent;[28] and, second, any confiscated profits would have to be spread among a very large number of workers. As a result, for the whole economy, union-firm bargaining is less of a contest between labor and capital over the partition of national income and more of a struggle among various groups of workers plus those who receive transfer income from the state.

The second reason why wage increases secured by collective bargaining are not enjoyed principally at the expense of profits is that firms do not passively respond to attempts to appropriate their surpluses. On the contrary, firms will attempt to recover any loss of profits through union activity by passing increased costs on to consumers in the form of higher prices.[29] The prices of commodities produced by unionized firms will tend to rise and consumers of those products will experience a reduction in their real income. The distributional consequences of these relative price changes have not been examined although they may be important. If unions tend to organize firms producing commodities that figure heavily in the expenditures of rich households, the price effects will be borne more by well-off households; if unions organize firms producing goods that figure more in the budgets of poor households, the distributional impacts of relative price changes are regressive. These consumer price effects have not been the subject of scholarly research, and it is not easy to assess their distributional importance.[30]

Firms will respond to a union wage push also by changing the type of workers it employs. If the firm finds itself obliged to pay higher wages, it will alter its hiring policies to employ people whose productivity comes closer to the higher wages. If management upgrades the quality of the work force, the union is affecting not merely workers' wages, but also the type of workers hired. Indeed, if a firm can upgrade its work force completely to match the union-imposed higher wage, wages are higher than in a comparable nonunion firm but the skills of the unionized firm are also higher so that, *holding worker quality constant,* there is no union-nonunion wage gap. The fact that union-nonunion wage gaps tend to be higher when worker quality is not held constant than wage gaps that hold constant (observed) worker quality is evidence of this process.[31]

In conclusion, how unions affect wages and employment in an incompletely unionized economy has a number of different dimensions. When union wage push is unaccompanied by changes in productivity, the size of the economy's resources is necessarily constant and hence increased incomes enjoyed by union workers must come out of the incomes of others. Although commentators some-times assume that union wage gains are secured at the expense of profits, this is largely wishful thinking. Firms protect their profits by cutting employment and passing on higher wage costs to consumers in the form of higher prices. Moreover, the share of national income received as profits and dividends is small relative to the number of workers so the potential for redistribution of this sort is considerably less than is widely thought. Union wage gains will then come out of the incomes of unorganized workers and out of transfer incomes.

IV. Unions As a Pressure Group on Government

The welfare of union members is often materially affected by the legislative, executive, and judicial activities of government. Consequently, labor unions serve their members' interests by influencing government policy by forming alliances with political parties, by calling on their members and supporters to deliver votes for particular people or particular legislation, and by using union incomes to campaign for various people or statutes and regulations.

Microeconomic Issues

As a rule, unions have been skeptical of markets and have supported mea-sures that obstruct untrammeled market forces. As examples, unions routinely support minimum wage legislation, tariffs and quotas on foreign imports, and government regulation — if not ownership — of large industries. In each case, unions are furthering their members' immediate interests. With respect to mini-mum wages, union workers usually earn wages higher than the state-mandated minimum wage so a higher minimum wage reduces competition from nonunion firms. With respect to foreign trade, unions seek to raise the incomes of their members by curtailing foreign competition. With respect to the state regulation or ownership of industry, unions aim to "capture" the administrators and use the administration to raise their members' incomes.

Of course, unions are not the only group to pressure government. Indeed, some observers espouse lobbying activity by unions to offset lobbying activity by employers. However, this argument misses the fact that, on a number of is-sues, the interests of unions and employers coincide. Government regulation of industry often results in the unions and the employers in the regulated industry collaborating to raise their joint incomes at the expense of the poorly represented consumer. Both employers and unions in industries subject to foreign competition petition government for protection from foreign competition to raise their joint incomes. Employers of union labor have testified in favor of minimum wage laws alongside unions and for the same reason: To increase the costs and decrease competition from nonunion employers and nonunion labor. In each instance, the interests of employers and unions are in harmony: Employers and unions seek to enhance their shared incomes at the expense of consumers before proceeding to split this income between themselves.

Unions advocate policies that provide for a vital role for the state in various social welfare activities including health, pension, and unemployment benefits. Indeed, in some countries such as Belgium and Sweden, the unions help in the administration of various social insurance schemes.[32] The unions' strong preference for state intervention in markets suggests that these schemes involve a heavy element of redistribution toward union members. These social welfare issues are likely to matter deeply to their members as suggested by the fact that, in many instances, the first union activities focused on such practices. That is, in the early days of the Industrial Revolution, many unions were established to serve as "friendly societies" for their members providing from union funds an array of insurance benefits covering sickness, unemployment, old age, and death. These mutual insurance activities remain in some unions and, indeed, are growing in Britain where unions offer subsidized legal services.

Macroeconomic Issues

The pressure group activities of unions are not restricted to microeconomic issues. On macroeconomic issues, unions usually advocate expansionary policies whose immediate impact is to increase employment even if this is accompanied by greater inflation. The bargaining power of unions is greater when labor is relatively scarce so expansionary monetary policies that decrease unemployment give unions more leverage over management. Successful assaults on entrenched union prerogatives have often been proceeded by deflationary macroeconomic policies that undermine union bargaining power.[33] The experience of several countries in Latin America in the last thirty years is by no means singular, but it provides a telling set of examples of what has been called the macroeconomics of populism in which labor unions have played an important part.

The macroeconomics of populism starts with radical policies designed to effect a substantial shift in the distribution of incomes (Dornbusch and Edwards, 1991; Sachs, 1990). These policies include expansionary budgetary measures and shifts in taxation, and they are often joined with populist rhetoric that raises workers' expectations. The immediate impact is a rise in real wages and in employment. In due course, the induced balance of payments deficit causes a reduction in the exchange rate and a fall in real wages. Not merely are the initial gains in real wages erased, but real wages fall below their initial level as the country tries to restore its foreign exchange reserves. The failure of the original attempt to raise real wages induces more aggressive redistribution programs and even higher rates of inflation that are often addressed with price controls and accompanying black markets and shortages.

Instances of this populist cycle are provided by Juan Perón's policies in Argentina in 1946–1949, Salvador Allende's in Chile in 1971–1973, José Sarney's in Brazil in 1986–1988, and Alan Garcia's in Peru in 1985–1988. In each case, the policies were supported by most of the labor unions even though, at the end of these cycles, workers were worse off than at the beginning. Thus in Chile in 1971 real wages rose by 17 percent before falling by 10 percent in 1972 with a further fall of 32 percent in 1973. Labor union support is by no means necessary for the implementation of these disastrous policies, and the policies have been pursued by governments of different persuasions including both military regimes and those of the far left. As voices for groups of urban workers, unions have typically advocated these policies in misguided attempts to effect a redistribution of incomes in societies where income inequalities are very large.[34]

These policies may have been manifested most vividly in Latin America, but they are evident in other countries also. For instance, in Britain in the 1970s, a left-wing Labour Government tried to effect a substantial change in the distribution of incomes, a policy urged by the militant union movement at the time. An eruption of inflation, critical balance of payments deficits, and a wave of strikes in public sector monopolies caused the policies to be abandoned and then a totally different stance was taken by the new Conservative Government in 1979. Nevertheless, for a few years, aspects of the macroeconomics of Populism were evident in Britain.

Consider also the industrial relations systems in Australia and New Zealand at the heart of which, for most of the twentieth century, were labor courts that had the authority to impose wages ("awards") and other features of the labor contract on a broad range of firms including those that were not a party to the arbitration. Though the courts were established with the express purpose of eliminating strikes, the incidence of strikes in Australia and New Zealand was no lower than in comparable countries. The system encouraged a zero-sum game approach to labor relations and stimulated not merely the growth of unionism, but also the development of confederations of employers. Even though many agreements were reached directly between unions and employers, these agreements were reached in the knowledge that, in the last resort, either party could take the dispute to arbitration.

The determination of wages at above-equilibrium levels became the fixed point in the system and this had two important consequences: The tendency for higher priced imports to substitute for more expensive domestically produced goods required a system of extensive protection from foreign trade; and the tendency for labor to price itself out of employment required both expansionary monetary and fiscal policies to keep unemployment low and foreign exchange controls, budgetary deficits, and economy-wide controls on prices, rents, and interest rates. The relative living standards of the two countries fell throughout the twentieth century. Again, with highly politicized industrial relations systems, distributional goals propelled macroeconomic policies of accommodation that harmed economic growth and caused the economies continually to flirt with inflation.[35]

Centralization and Coordination of Bargaining and Macroeconomic Performance

The previous paragraphs have argued that unions tend to advocate expansionary macroeconomic policies. In questioning that argument, some maintain that, when virtually all workers' wages are touched by collective bargaining agreements and when the level of coordination of agreements among unions and employers is high,[36] unions tend to be more restrained in advocating expansionary policies and less aggressive in their wage demands. A principal reason is that, when a small group of workers bargain over their wages, they may disregard as of negligible importance the consequences of their wage bargaining on the prices of consumer goods they purchase. However, so the argument goes, this negative externality is internalized when virtually all workers are simultaneously negotiating their wage increases and this inclines the centralized union to adopt a more moderate stance in wage bargaining.

Using reasoning such as this, some economists speculate that highly centralized and coordinated bargaining structures may deliver more favorable macroeconomic outcomes. An empirical literature has developed that examines the relationship between countries' bargaining structures — essentially the degree to which wage bargains are centralized and the extent to which wage increases are coordinated — and various indicators of these countries' macroeconomic performance.[37] Unfortunately, this econometric research has generated few robust results. Estimates are often sensitive to small changes in sample composition, in the measurement of variables, and in the inclusion and exclusion of other variables (Flanagan, 1999). There are several explanations for this.

First, this research treats the collective bargaining structure as given and investigates the association between indicators of this structure and certain macroeconomic outcomes. In fact, countries choose their collective bargaining structure no less than their macroeconomic performance and the omitted variables affecting macroeconomic performance include factors that also affect the collective bargaining system. Thus countries whose political sympathies incline toward an especially low tolerance for unemployment have sometimes thought to be those countries sympathetic to union representation and to the centralization of collective bargaining. If so, the collective bargaining variables and the macroeconomic outcomes are jointly determined variables. Indeed, reforms to the collective bargaining system (such as those in New Zealand and Britain) have often come from dissatisfaction with macroeconomic performance in which case the line of causation is from recent macroeconomic performance to the character of collective bargaining.[38]

Second, this research concentrates on a few aspects of the collective bargaining system — especially the degree to which wage bargaining is centralized and coordinated — and neglects others that would appear to be important. For instance, I suspect the extent of product market competition, the degree to which nonunion labor markets are competitive and serve as a check to monopolistic wage setting in the union sector, and the frequency with which the state is a party in adjudicating labor market disputes are no less important for macroeconomic performance than the degree of centralization and coordination.

Third, there are serious concerns about the measurement of key variables such as the degree of centralization and extent of coordination. It is not merely that scholars disagree over how to categorize various countries, but that the indicators of collective bargaining centralization and coordination are usually not cardinally measured, but are ordinal measures. When a variable is measured in the form of a ranking, it is difficult to interpret the meaning of the estimated regression coefficient attached to it unless bargaining systems are equally spaced on the ordinal scale. Thus consider Calmfors and Driffill's (1988) ranking of countries by degree of centralization. Using low numbers to represent decentralized systems and high numbers centralized systems, their variable places Canada and the United States as first and second, respectively, on the ordinal scale and Australia and France as seventh and eighth, respectively. The use of this variable in a regression context implies that the increase in centralization in moving from Canada to the United States is the same as the change in moving from France to Australia. But the Canadian and United States systems are so similar and those of France and Australia are so very different that it is difficult to comprehend what meaning can be attached to the claim that the difference between Canada and the United States is equal to the difference between France and Australia.[39]

Fourth, in this research, usually, macroeconomic outcomes such as unemployment or price inflation or economic growth are related to indicators of collective bargaining structure but, in computing this relationship, information about the conduct of fiscal or monetary policy or government policy toward monopolies in various countries is neglected. The values of these policy variables may be uncorrelated with the indicators of collective bargaining structure, although anecdotal evidence suggests the converse. For example, in a number of countries, governments adopted accommodating monetary and fiscal policies to neutralize the unemployment-increasing effects of union wage-push policies so that, where unions have the power to raise wages, so governments are presented with a policy dilemma about how accommodating their monetary and fiscal policies should be. Because the ability of unions to raise wages is related to the attributes of the collective bargaining system, the government's macroeconomic policies will tend to bear some association with the extent and character of collective bargaining systems.

Finally, in these studies, there are precious few degrees of freedom from which to draw inferences. Usually twenty or fewer countries constitute the sample space and, because the measures of collective bargaining change slowly in most instances, there is little information contained by adding different periods of time. After holding constant the effects of other variables, there are few degrees of freedom remaining to draw inferences about collective bargaining systems. As an example, in Bleaney's (1996) research on the effect of Central Bank independence and wage bargaining structures on price inflation and unemployment, two or three slope parameters are estimated with a sample of 17 country observations.

All this does not mean that collective bargaining structures are irrelevant to economic performance — far from it. The correct inference is that the econometric methods applied to this issue have yielded fickle results that do not compare well to the sort of robust relationships that are the hallmark of modern empirical Labor Economics.[40] There are surely instances in which centralized and coordinated collective bargaining systems have permitted countries to make adjustments that would be much more costly to effect in decentralized systems. Whether these instances constitute a general and definitive finding that might serve to endorse policy recommendations for, say, emerging economies is another matter. On the basis of the research on this topic, should economists be recommending to countries such as Indonesia or Thailand that their labor markets would operate much better if, for the setting wages by collective bargaining, they organized all employers in a central federation and all workers in a centralized labor union? I do not think so.

V. The Employment Relationship: The Union As the Employee's Agent

Labor contracts are regulated in every country. In many cases, the state's regulation of labor contracts is profound and extensive. For instance, the Labor Codes in many Latin American countries are far-reaching. The legal system in all countries forbids some contracts (such as those involving slavery and child labor) while other contracts are carefully delineated (such as stipulating days that a worker is not obliged to work or activities that an employee may refuse to undertake or wages that an employer must exceed). Why has the legal system so regulated exchanges in labor markets?

The principal reason is that, at least tacitly, it has been recognized that the exchange of labor services has features that are distinctive and that make the buying and selling of labor services different from the buying and selling of other things. Labor contracts are manifestly incomplete: Typically a worker is delivering to firms not merely his time, skills, and effort to management, but also a subset of his liberties. As noted by Coase (1937), whereas resources are allocated outside firms by means of the price mechanism, within firms, orders replace prices as the means by which resources are allocated to one rather than another activity. Usually workplaces are hierarchical — one group of employees follows the instructions given by another group. In these circumstances, what each worker is expected to do and what he may legitimately refuse to do are not always well-defined. In effect, the employee concedes to management the right to assign him to a set of jobs, the range of which is usually poorly delineated. The vagueness of most labor contracts results in disputes over whether the terms of the contract have been breached. These disputes arise because the exchange of labor services provides opportunities for one side to pursue its interests at the expense of the other party's. Hence transactions require some sort of oversight or regulation.

Usually, the state's regulations are general and, necessarily, they are not tied to a firm's particular circumstances. Moreover, the state's regulations are sometimes evaded or they are cosmetic. They are supplemented with other mechanisms to manage the exchange of labor services. The most common of these mechanisms is custom and convention. Such customs are inherited from previous exchanges and give rise to repeated relationships. The labor union is another mechanism to regulate the exchange of labor services.

In poor economies, a union may do no more than attempt to alter wages and leave the rest of the employment contract unchanged. However, as economies become richer, unions respond to their members' concerns over other aspects of the employment relationship. Indeed, some surveys suggest that union members do not identify higher wages as the most valuable aspect of their union's activities. Members are more often inclined to value most the protection that their union provides against arbitrary treatment by the firm's supervisors. In many developed countries, union contracts are characterized by the setting down of rules by which a worker's grievance against his supervisor may be addressed. In effect, these rules constitute a system of jurisprudence internal to the firm where the union acts as an employee's agent.

Evidence that unions may serve as the worker's agent is provided by the role played by unionism in enforcing various statutory requirements of the workplace. As an example, consider safety issues. Most developed countries have regulations governing workplace safety and, if these regulations are more than cosmetic, resources must be devoted to their enforcement. Research from Britain, Canada, and the United States suggests that the level of enforcement in unionized workplaces is considerably higher than in nonunion workplaces.[41] This is the case even when, as in some provinces in Canada and some states in the United States, employee-management safety committees are mandatory. Unions tend to increase the level of awareness of safety issues in the workplace and to protect from management retaliation employees who bring safety complaints to the notice of officials. More generally, there is evidence that unions raise the effectiveness of other statutory workplace regulations such as the receipt of workers' disability insurance, the filing of benefits for unemployment insurance, and the advanced notice procedures of plant closings and layoffs (Hirsch et al., 1997; Weil, 1996).

Using different language, the union provides a "voice" for workers to express their values and preferences. In the absence of such an organization, workers' preferences will be manifested through other mechanisms such as by "exit," that is, by quitting employment and seeking work elsewhere.[42] When there are workplace public goods such as safety and complementarities among workers, a "voice" mechanism may deliver efficiencies compared with a firm lacking such a formal organization for workers. Indeed, in some circumstances, these efficiencies have caused firms to welcome unionism. Thus, in late Victorian Britain, the enlightened opinion was that unions contributed to the smooth functioning of labor markets.[43] When the nonunion market place is disruptive and chaotic (including strike prone), the union may help replace turmoil and unrest with order. Strikes may be conducted not only by unionized but by unorganized workers and a strike managed by a union may be less damaging than one stemming from unruly worker protest.[44]

An alternative mechanism to address employment grievances is through the legal system and the growth in employment litigation in a number of countries may well be the result of the absence of a meaningful union voice at work. In effect, in taking up employment grievances, the plaintiff attorney has replaced the union shop steward and one wonders whether this has been a welcome change. The rise of nonunion arbitration schemes in the United States may portend their development in other countries too.

Once a union is involved in helping to adjudicate workers' grievances, it is really sharing with the employer the task of managing an aspect of the workplace. Although some nonunion companies have established grievance committees and arbitration mechanisms to deal with employees' complaints of mistreatment, these nonunion instruments are sometimes viewed by workers as lacking the definitive clout that a union can provide.[45] Hence, once a union serves as an agent for a firm's employees, it participates in the regulation of the employment relationship. It is not merely in its role in processing employees' grievances that the union participates in managing human resources in a company. In negotiating and helping to administer rules for hiring, training, promoting, disciplining, firing, and laying off workers, a union is participating with supervisors in managing the company.

Industrial relations scholars have conjectured that participation begets greater efficiency, that firms with unions involved in regulating labor contracts may be more efficient than firms that lack a union serving as the agent of workers.[46] Indeed, a number of empirical studies now suggest that, in some circumstances, greater worker participation enhances productivity. See, for instance, Freeman and Dube (2000). In effect, these studies imply that the production technology embraces the conventions and rules associated with the use of labor and that the unionized firm's production function differs from that of the nonunion firm. This has given rise to an extensive research on estimating production functions for the two types of firms. This research sometimes finds that union firms are more efficient than nonunion firms, but there are also instances of the reverse, of union firms being less efficient than their nonunion counterparts. A general finding seems not to be justified.[47] When a union protects or enforces inefficient work practices such as demarcation rules that impede substitution among different types of labor and capital, it reduces productivity.

Whether unionized establishments are more or less productive than their nonunion counterparts depends on the degree to which the parties — the workers and management representing the owners — see themselves engaged in a zero-sum game. If a zero-sum game posture prevails, a mentality develops of "us versus them": It is believed that a fixed income is allocated between rank-and-file workers on one hand and managers and owners on the other hand. This attitude is associated with antagonistic relations between labor and management. When the union and management see themselves involved in a non-zero-sum game in which cooperation augments the pie to be divided, union-management relations are productive. Modern human relations practices are designed to foster — though do not always secure — cooperation.

A labor union is not the only possible vehicle to serve as an agent of employees. Indeed, in many continental European countries, a separate and distinctive role is assigned to works councils operating side-by-side with — or sometimes in place of — the union. Many countries welcome employer-designed employee representation associations though, in the United States, they have to be crafted carefully so as not to conflict with the National Labor Relations Act. Worker-owned and worker-managed firms provide other another way in which individuals may express their "voice" at the workplace.

Public policy has to determine whether and how to encourage these alternative expressions for providing workers with "voice." A portfolio of these various "voice" mechanisms exists in many countries. In Italy, for instance, there is a strong union movement, but also many firms have works councils whereas worker-owned firms have enjoyed considerable tax benefits, and public contracts have been directed to them. Freeman and Medoff's *WDUD* is silent about these alternative expressions of worker "voice," but if the principal defect with unions is the monopoly wage effect (as *WDUD* maintains) why should public policy not support works councils, employee involvement committees, and worker co-ops instead? The record from other countries suggests that there may be a place for these other "voice" mechanisms alongside that of conventional unionism.

VI. Conclusions

How does this international evidence inform an evaluation of *WDUD*? My assessment herein has tended to look unfavorably on the wage-making activities of unionism and to view more favorably unions as a vehicle for workers to participate in shaping their work environments. This is entirely consistent with the perspective in *WDUD*. This participatory role is extremely important and fulfills a key function. Witness the fact that, in the United States, increasingly the plaintiff attorney has substituted for the union shop steward in adjudicating employment grievances. If this pattern is replicated in other countries, that is, if the decline in unionism in the rich economies implies a growth in formal litigation in the courts, the quality of dispute resolution mechanisms in these societies is likely to deteriorate.

In *WDUD*, Freeman and Medoff studied U.S. unionism and, in most workplaces in the United States, employees have little say over their environment. They do what their supervisors tell them to do. In some circumstances, there are efficiency reasons for this, but in many other cases efficiency might be enhanced by the supervisors consulting with rank-and-file workers. The qualities of liberty and uncoerced expression of preferences that are so lauded in the political domain are not enjoyed by most individuals in their capacity as workers except in a narrow sense. If local governments denied citizens an opportunity to voice their preferences and responded to citizens that "if you don't like living here, move," most would declare this both inefficient and unjust. However, this is exactly the situation presented to most workers who find profound decisions affecting their lives being taken by a relatively small group of managers. The local labor union can help offset the disenfranchisement of employees at their work. At its most basic, *WDUD* made the case for the union as an agent of workplace democracy and, with this, I am entirely sympathetic. My difference with *WDUD* is that it did not entertain other workplace mechanisms for worker voice. Yet the evidence from other countries suggests there is a role for these other expressions of worker preferences and information, and such a role might be envisaged for the United States.

Other workplace voice mechanisms do not necessarily bring the baggage of higher wage costs that unionism typically entails and so the case for these other expressions of worker representation is perhaps reinforced in a world in which "globalization" will make the old rationale for unionism of "taking wages out of competition" more difficult for many workers. Employees producing goods and services protected from such competition can continue to enjoy the wage advantages of unionism, but for others the notion of unions in relatively rich countries imposing costs on employers with the aim of establishing a floor under labor conditions is going to be increasingly undermined. To survive, unions in these countries must tailor their activities to avoid imposing costs on employers and to provide more services to their members in the form of monitoring the balance sheets of their companies and providing advice on their pensions, taxes, insurance, and legal issues.

In addition to their wage-making practices and their participatory role, unionism has a third dimension, their activities as a pressure group on government. On this, Freeman and Medoff (1984) offered the following judgment: "unions, for the most part, provide political voice to all labor and . . . they are more effective in pushing general social legislation than in bringing about special interest legislation in the Congress" (p. 247). This constitutes a very selective reading of the political activities of unionism, and it does not comport well with the international evidence reviewed herein. This evidence maintains that, in many countries, unions use the language of representing the interests of all workers, but this language does not correspond to the typical situation. Usually, some workers benefit from unions' political activities, and some workers lose. As examples, unions tend to oppose free trade, to support the direction and ownership of industry by government, to champion statutory minimum wage regulation, and to side with expansionary macroeconomic policies. In each of these cases, the public policies pit one group of workers against another, one group of workers stands to gain and another group stands to lose, and the notion that there is a well-defined interest representing "all labor" is difficult to maintain.

If it is the participatory role of unionism that forms its most valuable feature, it is worth emphasizing that it serves this role at the *workplace*. The focus of industrial relations should be at the workplace. In extending Freeman and Medoff's perspective on unionism to other countries, one must remember that WDUD was describing unions in the United States, a country with a highly decentralized system of collective bargaining, a feature which tends to bring out the better aspects of unions and to mitigate the undesirable features. Not only is U.S. unionism highly decentralized, the state is also largely disengaged from collective bargaining and markets tend to be highly competitive. All these features make U.S. unionism and collective bargaining different creatures from unionism and collective bargaining in many other countries. It would do a disservice to the careful discriminating arguments in *WDUD* to characterize it as a general argument for unionism in all its various guises. As a piece of research emphasizing the contribution that unions can make to economic democracy in a highly decentralized economy, Freeman and Medoff are to be acclaimed for their outstanding and durable scholarship.

Notes

*   This paper is prepared for a symposium on the twentieth anniversary of the publication of Richard Freeman and James Medoff's *What Do Unions Do?* I am grateful to Bruce Kaufman for comments on an earlier draft. For their help with union membership data in Canada and Japan, I thank David Card, Morley Gunderson, and Toshiaki Tachibanaki.

1.   Thus, for instance, in discussing the involvement of unions in influencing the work environment, Sumner Slichter (1941: 575, 579) argued, "The very fact that the workers have had an opportunity to participate in determining their working conditions is in itself favorable to efficiency. . . . [E]fficiency depends upon consent. Even though the specific rules and policies adopted in particular instances may not be ideal, the process of joint determination of working conditions at least offers the possibility of achieving greater efficiency than could be obtained

under rules and conditions dictated by one side. . . . [O]ur survey indicates that in important respects trade union shop rules and policies may contribute to more efficient management."

2. See Pencavel (1970) or Stoikov and Raimon (1968). Pencavel (1970: 13) wrote, "workers typically derive from membership in trade unions numerous nonpecuniary benefits like seniority and grievance procedures. To the extent that job dissatisfaction encourages voluntary mobility — and the removal of the sources of job dissatisfaction is obviously one of the prime functions, if not *the* prime function of American unionism — the effect of trade unionism is to discourage quits." In the empirical results, a fully unionized industry was estimated to have a 0.70 lower quit rate (the mean of the monthly quit rate being 1.36 per one hundred employees) than a totally nonunion industry.

3. The Canadian data in Figure 14.1 depict union membership density until 1994. The density figure for this year is close to that on union coverage reported in micro data sets in the early 1990s. These micro data sets (the Canadian Labour Force Survey) suggest union coverage in Canada fell to 33.7 percent in 1997 and to 31.7 percent in 2001. I have used these coverage figures from 1995 onwards. I thank David Card for providing these data. A discussion of Canadian union membership data appears in Riddell and Riddell (2001).

4. As an indicator of this, for the world as a whole, merchandise exports represented 10.5 percent of GDP in 1990 prices in 1973 and 17.2 percent 25 years later (Maddison, 2001: Table F–5).

5. "Contingent contracts" are compensation methods relating the worker's earnings to indicators of the firm's or the worker's performance. These schemes often result in greater pay differences among workers.

6. So, for instance, where incomes are rising, one might expect income effects in labor-supply behavior to reduce time spent by individuals in the labor market. This would give rise to similar reductions in labor utilization rates even in the absence of the changes in the demand for low-skill workers.

7. Data from the OECD's *Employment Outlook* on changes in male unemployment, male earnings inequality, and collective bargaining coverage to complete Table 14.1 are available for these ten countries only.

8. Year-to-year movements in unemployment rates are usually greater than annual movements in earnings inequality. This implies that the association between changes in unemployment and changes in wage inequality will be more sensitive to choice of years to compute unemployment rate changes than earnings inequality changes. Note that not merely the level of unemployment, but also the movement of workers into and out of unemployment is different in North American labor markets from those in Europe. That is, the probability of an individual entering unemployment in North America is much greater than it is in continental Europe; however, once unemployed, the European worker remains in that state very much longer than the North American.

9. Some economies do not fit this account. For instance, though the absence of OECD data prevent us from including New Zealand in the countries graphed, it does seem as if New Zealand has seen increases in unemployment, increases in earnings inequality, and a reduction in unionism. Another interesting, small country, case is provided by Norway in the late 1980s. Wage differentials at the bottom of the pay distribution appear to have narrowed, not risen, in these years. Kahn (1998a) attributes this to the fact that, unlike most other economies, bargaining became more centralized in Norway and raising the relative pay of low-wage workers received a priority in the collective agreements. At the same time, the employment-population

ratio of low-skilled workers fell with the public sector acting increasingly like the employer of last resort.

10. For instance, increases in earnings inequality in the United States have taken place around declining real wages at around the median whereas increases in earnings inequality in some other countries have occurred around constant or rising real wage levels. Therefore, in some countries, not merely are low-skill workers experiencing lower relative real earnings; they also suffer from lower absolute real earnings.

11. This system of arbitration was dismantled in New Zealand by the Employment Contracts Act of 1991. Australia's system has also been modified in recent decades although not as radically.

12. At the same time, extension rules discourage individual workers from becoming union members. If a worker's compensation is the same regardless of union membership, he might as well save on union dues and remain outside the organization. Hence, in France, less than ten percent of workers are members of unions and yet collectively bargained wages are estimated to cover well over 90 percent of wage and salary workers.

13. Union threat effects in the United States were probably greatest during and immediately after the Second World War when union membership was growing rapidly, and unions demonstrated their capacity to organ-ize large groups of workers. Sure enough, union-nonunion wage gaps were least after the Second World War (Pencavel and Hartsog, 1984), and the threat effect is one of the likely explanations for this. Even today with unionism in decline in the United States, the wages of nonunion workers are higher (other things equal) in industries with an important union presence, something that has been attributed to the threat effect of union activity.

14. Farber (2003) estimates small threat effects in the U.S. economy in recent decades.

15. These estimates of union-nonunion wage gaps are derived from a number of sources including Blanchflower (1996, 1999), Blanchflower and Bryson (this volume), Card et al. (this volume), Grant et al. (1987), Hirsch and Schumacher (2000), Kahn (1998b), Kornfeld (1993), and Wooden (2001).

16. Card's (2001) estimates are "raw," that is, hold constant no other variables. Kahn's (2000) estimates hold constant gender, schooling, age, marital status, and part-time work. Schultz and Mwabu's (1998) estimates hold constant schooling, age, rural-urban residence, and major industry.

17. See Bloch and Kuskin (1978), Booth et al. (2001: 63–65), Lewis (1986), and Schultz and Mwabu (1998).

18. So, for example, the decline in unionism, the greater decentralization of collective bargaining agreements, and the growth in wage inequality in Britain from the late 1970s onwards provides a striking example of this correlation. However, by 1979, the electorate was clearly disillusioned with unionism and ready to embrace a less corporatist vision of society and these changed attitudes contributed to the retreat of collective bargaining. This experience is discussed in Pencavel (2004).

19. Slichter (1941: 345–70) provides examples of how "the differential in costs between union and nonunion plants limits the employment of union members" (ibid.: 370). By contrast, the more formal statistical exercises do not usually deliver as clear results. See the useful review of research in Booth (1995: 216–21). Inputs that are complements to union labor will also suffer from a reduction in employment. Thus, the employment of supervisory management also seems to be lower when unionism is more extensive and where the union-nonunion wage gap is greater. See DiNardo et al. (2000). In a case study of U.S. coal mining, Boal and Pencavel (1994) measured small employment effects of unionism, but much larger effects

on the days the mines were operating. This serves to make the point that there are other types of quantity responses in addition to employment.

20. Feeman and Medoff in *WDUD* (pp. 117–20) also expected union wage push to result in lower employment. However, when they compared employment-population ratios in "low" union states with that in "high" union states in the United States, they detected no difference, a result they did not really explain.

21. The U.S. trucking and railroad industries provide a few good examples. See Hirsch (1988), MacDonald and Cavalluzzo (1996), and Rose (1987).

22. Another example is provided by the "prevailing wage" laws in U.S. states in the construction industry. These laws require private contractors on government projects to pay higher wages than they would otherwise pay. The elimination of these laws in some states between 1979 and 1988 increased the union-nonunion wage gap by about ten percentage points (Kessler and Katz, 2001).

23. I assume that union-management bargaining results in contracts where wages and employment are on the employer's labor demand function. There is a rich literature in labor economics that examines other bargaining outcomes including so-called "efficient contracts" that lie on the parties' contract curve (which may lie to the right of the employer's labor demand function). Surely there are contracts off the employer's labor demand function, but these are not typical. This is because most collective bargaining contracts grant management considerable latitude in determining employment. Even if the employer is forced off the labor demand function, the reduction in profits will ultimately cause a reduction in employment below what would exist in the absence of unionism. These issues are discussed more fully in Pencavel (1991).

24. Will the size of the pie remain unchanged? I discuss below some productivity effects of unionism, but it suffices to note here that these productivity effects are sometimes positive and sometimes negative. On balance, I believe it is appropriate to assume the size of the pie is given.

25. There may be workers who leave the labor market altogether because they are rationed out of the union sector and yet their reservation wages are higher than the wages paid in the nonunion sector.

26. In calculating this transfer, I omit the self-employed and their incomes so they are left unaffected. This is a transfer from the profits of corporations to all employees leaving the self-employed neither better off nor worse off. This estimate of the value of this transfer is very approximate as the accounting issues in defining profits and employee compensation are complex. For instance, with the growth of pension funds and employee stock ownership plans and with the use of salaries to compensate top company executives, capital and labor do not separate cleanly into well-defined groups. Nevertheless, the general sense of the per employee value of corporate profits is indicated by this exercise. This is an accounting exercise. In practice, a confiscatory policy of this sort will set in train offsetting behavior by the owners of corporations to protect their incomes.

27. Thus, in an earlier paper (Pencavel, 1997), I calculated the earnings increase from this exercise for Peru as 11 percent in 1980 and for Colombia as 15 percent in 1985. Because of the cyclical sensitivity of corporate profits, the amount of the earnings increase from this experimental transfer tends to be larger in a boom (as was the year 1999 in the United States) and smaller in a recession.

28. Thus employee compensation consists usually of between two-thirds and three-quarters of national income. The small movements in labor's share of national income over time in the presence of drastic changes in technology and institutional structure have been a frequent topic for research.

29. Indeed, the drop in product demand resulting from increased prices is a principal source for the decline in employment induced by a union's wage push. Because the employer of union workers tries to pass along union wage increases to consumers in the form of higher prices and to nonunion workers in the form of lower wages, one might envisage this situation as one in which union workers and the employer of union workers together are imposing costs on consumers and nonunion workers.

30. Part of the problem for researchers is that many commodities are not sold to households, but they are sold to other firms as intermediate goods. Thus a union-organized steel plant will pass on its higher labor costs as higher prices to firms purchasing steel. How this will ultimately affect households is difficult to assess. This does not mean the distributional effects are small, only that they are difficult to compute.

31. Thus, in the United States, the average "raw" union-nonunion wage gap (that is, wage differences that do not control for skill or other attributes) is about 20 percent whereas the union-nonunion wage gap falls to about 15 percent when skill characteristics are held constant. In South Africa, "raw" union-nonunion wage gaps among African workers in 1995 were of the order of 85 percent. After accounting for differences in the characteristics of these workers, the union-nonunion wage gap falls to about 20 percent (Butcher and Rouse, 2001). Among male production workers in South Korea, Kim (1993) reports union-nonunion monthly earnings differentials in 1988 on the order of 30 percent. Once skill is held constant, the union-nonunion differentials fall to merely 2 percent. In Mexico in 1989, "raw" union-nonunion differentials of over 30 percent fall to 14 percent once skill and other variables are held constant (Panagides and Patrinos, 1994). This argument suggests that unionized employers tend to select workers with high skills, some of which are unobserved by researchers. On the other hand, if union-nonunion wage gaps are lower for highly skilled workers, among highly skilled workers, union jobs will be most attractive to those workers with low skills that are unobserved to researchers (Abowd and Farber, 1982).

32. The Ghent system is the custom whereby the unions play a role in managing the unemployment insurance scheme even though it is financed by compulsory taxation by the state. Some have argued that union involvement in these matters encourages the unions to be concerned with the welfare of the unemployed (sometimes labeled the "outsiders") as well as the employed (the "insiders"). See the review of these issues in Brugiavini et al. (2001).

33. Thus, consider the attack on what were called labor union privileges by Margaret Thatcher in Britain in the 1980s. One reason for their success was that, before making major changes in the law on unionism and collective bargaining, a shift in macroeconomic policy resulted in the largest rise in unemployment in Britain since the 1930s (Pencavel, 2004).

34. East Asian economies have been less prone to these populist tendencies. This may be because the income disparities in East Asia are not so large and intractable as those in Latin America. Also, in East Asia, the fear that unions constituted a Trojan horse for Communism resulted in a greater suppression of collective bargaining so the political clout of unions was considerably attenuated. Correspondingly, the diminished threat of Communism in the last ten years has resulted in greater toleration of unionism in several East Asian countries.

35. As noted earlier, these arbitration systems in New Zealand and Australia have been altered in recent decades especially in New Zealand. An analysis of Australia's and New Zealand's labor markets along these lines is contained in Pencavel (1999).

36. "Coordination refers to the extent to which decisions taken by trade unions and employers' associations at the different bargaining levels (national, sectoral or company) are concerted so as to foster a mutually beneficial strategy" (Scarpetta, 1996: 54). Coordination is more likely when bargaining is centralized, but there are instances of decentralized structures being coordinated as in Japan's system (where employer associations and national trade union centers provide guidelines for their constituent members) or whenever one collective bargaining agreement emulates a previous one (pattern bargaining).

37. There is a long history of this research, but its recent reincarnation was stimulated by Bruno and Sachs' analysis (1985). They entered an index of "corporatism" in a regression equation intended to account for variations across 17 countries in changes in inflation in the 1970s. Corporatism was conceived in terms of "the extent to which wage negotiations proceed at the national level rather than at the plant level; the power of national labor organizations vis-à-vis their constituent members; the degree of organization on the employer side; and the power of plant-level union stewards (the more powerful they are, the less corporatism there is)" (ibid.: 222–23). Bruno and Sachs reported that the acceleration in inflation between 1973 and 1979 was significantly lower in corporatist countries. In subsequent research by others, these various components of corporatism were investigated separately with emphasis on the coverage of collective bargaining and the degree to which bargaining agreements are decentralized and coordinated.

38. As another example of the dependence of collective bargaining structure on macroeconomic outcomes, consider Germany. Recently, there have been clear indications of a move toward greater decentralization of bargaining induced (in part) by persistently high unemployment especially in East Germany.

39. So suppose reform of industrial relations in New Zealand causes collective bargaining there to become less centralized. This reform alters the ranking not only of New Zealand, but necessarily of some other countries even though these other countries' systems have not changed. The relationships that have been estimated with these ordinally measured variables imply that New Zealand's reforms will affect the macroeconomic performance of countries whose collective bargaining systems have not changed because the ranking of at least some of these other countries has shifted!

40. There is an important exception to this general result and this concerns the relationship between collective bargaining and pay inequality: As noted earlier, countries with a large union sector and where bargaining is centralized tend to have a more compressed wage distribution. It is noteworthy, however, that our confidence in this finding derives principally from the use of data on individual workers and not from aggregate data. For instance, see the research of Blau and Kahn (1996) and Kahn (2000). There remains the caveat expressed in Section III: How much of this correlation between wage inequality and unionism is causal?

41. See Reilly et al. (1995), Bernard (1995), and Weil (1999). The British study found no difference in workplace injuries between union and nonunion establishments provided employees participated in the safety committees, but workplace safety was less in establishments where safety was monitored exclusively by the representatives of management. Of course, in addition to the issue of the enforcement of safety legislation, unionism may require management to spend more resources on preventing accidents. A convincing case study is provided by Boal (2002) for the coal mining industry.

42. The distinction between "exit" and "voice" originates with Hirschman (1970), and Freeman (1976) applied it to unionism.

43. Thus, "In the experience of Victorian employers it was the most skilled, responsible, and steady workmen who took the lead in the unions and unionism had a uplifting influence on the weaker brethren. Industrial relations were found to be at their best when strongly organized unions entered into voluntary negotiations with stable associations of employers" (Phelps Brown, 1983: 19). More recently, describing the Kenyan labor markets after the Second World War, Collier and Lal (1986: 164) write, "It is potentially easier to enforce a collective agreement on unskilled labour than several hundred individual ones, partly because of reduced information costs and partly because the union has a contractual continuity which the individual worker lacks and hence has more need to maintain a reputation for sticking to contracts. This is not fanciful. Recall that in Kenya labour unrest, including strikes, preceded by many years the formation of unions. The KFE [Federation of Kenya Employers] welcomed unions as a means of replacing anarchy by order."
44. Thus, Edwards (1996: 22) observes of Indonesia in the 1990s, "in a number of these [strike] cases, public protest is the first step in the negotiation process between 'unorganized' workers and managers. A significant proportion of these strikes takes place outside of any process of negotiation, and among unorganized workers, that is, workers who are not affiliated to the official union or to workers' councils."
45. Some of these nonunion grievance systems have been set up by managements as part of a union-avoidance strategy. Here the "threat effect" operates on governance instead of on wages.
46. For instance, in his classic study, Sumner Slichter (1941: 575) explicitly put forward this conjecture.
47. See Metcalf (2002) for a recent and authoritative review and assessment of this research for six countries (United States, Canada, Britain, Germany, Japan, and Australia). He concludes, "there is no one generalised or average productivity effect of unions — it all depends on the quality of management and unions" (p. 66).

References

Abowd, John M. and Henry S. Farber. "Job Queues and the Union Status of Workers." *Industrial and Labor Relations Review* 35 (April 1982): 354–67.

Bernard, Elaine. "Canada: Joint Committees on Occupational Safety and Health." In Joel Rogers and Wolfgang Streeck, eds. *Works Councils: Consultation, Representation, and Cooperation in Industrial Relations.* Chicago: University of Chicago Press, 1995, pp. 351–74.

Blanchflower, David G. "The Role and Influence of Trade Unions in the OECD." Dartmouth College, unpublished paper (August 1996).

_____. "Changes over Time in Union Relative Wage Effects in Great Britain and the United States." In Sami Daniel, Philip Arestis, and John Grahl, eds. *The History and Practice of Economics: Essays in Honour of Bernard Corry and Marurice Peston.* Cheltenham, UK: Edward Elgar, 1999, pp. 3–32.

Blau, Francine D. and Lawrence M. Kahn. "International Differences in Male Wage Inequality: Institutions and Market Forces." *Journal of Political Economy* 104 (August 1996): 791–837.

Bleaney, Michael. "Central Bank Independence, Wage Bargaining Structure, and Macroeconomic Performance in OECD Countries." *Oxford Economic Papers* 48 (January 1996): 20–38.

Bloch, Farrell E. and Mark S. Kuskin. "Wage Determination in the Union and Nonunion Sectors." *Industrial and Labor Relations Review* 31 (January 1978): 183–92.

Boal, Wlliam M. "The Effect of Unionism on Accidents in Coal Mining, 1897–1929." unpublished paper (December 2002).

_____ and John Pencavel. "The Effects of Labor Unions on Employment, Wages, and Days of Operation: Coal Mining in West Virginia." *Quarterly Journal of Economics* 109 (February 1994): 267–98.

Booth, Alison L. *The Economics of the Trade Union.* Cambridge: Cambridge University Press, 1995.

_____, Lars Calmfors, Michael Burda, Daniele Checchi, Robin Naylor, and Jelle Visser. "The Future of Collective Bargaining in Europe." In Tito Boeri, Agar Brugiavini, and Lars Calmfors, eds. *The Role of Unions in the Twenty-First Century.* Oxford: Oxford University Press, 2001, pp. 1–155.

Brugiavini, Agar, Bernhard Ebbinghaaus, Richard Freeman, Pietro Garibaldi, Bertil Holmlund, Martin Schludi, and Thierry Verdier. "What Do Unions Do to the Welfare States?" In Tito Boeri, Agar Brugiavini, and Lars Calmfors, eds. *The Role of Unions in the Twenty-First Century.* Oxford: Oxford University Press, 2001, pp. 157–277.

Bruno, Michael and Jeffrey D. Sachs. *Economics of Worldwide Stagflation.* Cambridge: Harvard University Press, 1985.

Butcher, Kristin F. and Cecilia Elena Rouse. "Wage Effects of Unions and Industrial Councils in South Africa." *Industrial and Labor Relations Review* 54 (January 2001): 349–74.

Calmfors, Lars and John Driffill. "Bargaining Structure, Corporatism, and Macroeconomic Performnce." *Economic Policy* 6 (April 1988): 13–61.

Card, David. "The Effect of Unions on Wage Inequality in the U.S. Labor Market." *Industrial and Labor Relations Review* 54 (January 2001): 296–315.

Coase, Ronald, H. "The Nature of the Firm." *Economica* 4 (November 1937): 386–405.

Collier, Paul and Deepak Lal. *Labour and Poverty in Kenya: 1900–1980.* Oxford: Clarendon Press, 1986.

DiNardo, John, Kevin F. Hallock, and Jorn-Steffen Pischke. "Unions and the Labour Market for Managers." Center for Economic Policy Research, Discussion Paper No. 2418 (April 2000).

Dornbusch, Rudiger and Sebastian Edwards, eds. *The Macroeconomics of Populism in Latin America.* Chicago: University of Chicago Press, 1991.

Edwards, Alejandra Cox. "Labor Regulations and Industrial Relations in Indonesia." The World Bank, Poverty and Social Policy Department, Policy Research Working Paper 1640 (August 1996).

Farber, Henry S. "The Nonunion Wage and the Threat of Unionization." Working Paper No. 472, Princeton Industrial Relations Section (February 2003).

Flanagan, Robert J. "Macroeconomic Performance and Collective Bargaining: An International Perspective." *Journal of Economic Literature* 37 (September 1999): 1150–75.

Freeman, Richard B. "Individual Mobility and Union Voice in the Labor Market." *American Economic Review, Papers and Proceedings* 66 (May 1976): 361–68.

_____ and Arindrajit Dube. "Shared Compensation Systems and Decision-Making in the U.S. Job Market." Harvard University Department of Economics and the Centre for Economic Performance, London School of Economics, unpublished paper (2000).

_____ and James L. Medoff. *What Do Unions Do?* New York: Basic Books, 1984.

Grant, E. Kenneth, Robert Swidinsky, and John Vanderkamp. "Canadian Union-Nonuniuon Wage Differentials." *Industrial and Labor Relations Review* 41 (October 1987): 93–107.

Hirsch, Barry T. "Trucking Regulation, Unionization, and Labor Earnings: 1973–85." *Journal of Human Resources* 23 (Summer 1988): 296–319.

_____, David A. Macpherson, and J. Michael DuMond. "Workers' Compensation Recipiency in Union and Nonunion Workplaces." *Industrial and Labor Relations Review* 50 (January 1997): 213–36.

_____ and Edward J. Schumacher. "Private Sector Union Density and the Wage Premium: Past, Present, and Future." Unpublished paper (November 2000).

Hirschman, Albert O. *Exit, Voice, and Loyalty.* Cambridge: Harvard University Press, 1970.

Kahn, Lawrence M. "Against the Wind: Bargaining Centralisation and Wage Inequality in Norway 1987–91." *Economic Journal* 108 (May 1998a): 603–45.

_____. "Collective Bargaining and the Interindustry Wage Structure: International Evidence." *Economica* 65 (November 1998b): 507–34.

_____. "Wage Inequality, Collective Bargaining, and Relative Employment from 1985 to 1994: Evidence from Fifteen OECD Countries." *Review of Economics and Statistics* 82 (November 2000): 564–79.

Katz, Harry C. and Owen Darbishire. *Converging Divergences: Worldwide Changes in Employment Systems.* Ithaca, N.Y.: Cornell University Press, 2000.

Kessler, Daniel P. and Lawrence F. Katz. "Prevailing Wage Laws and Construction Labor Markets." *Industrial and Labor Relations Review* 54 (January 2001): 259–74.

Kim, Hwang-Joe. "The Korean Union Movement in Transition." In Stephen Frankel, ed. *Organized Labor in the Asia-Pacific Region: A Comparative Study of Trade Unionism in Nine Countries.* Ithaca, N.Y.: ILR Press, 1993, pp. 133–61.

Kornfeld, Robert. "The Effects of Union Membership on Wages and Employee Benefits: The Case of Australia." *Industrial and Labor Relations Review* 47 (October 1993): 114–28.

Lewis, H. Gregg. *Union Relative Wage Effects: A Survey.* Chicago: University of Chicago Press, 1986.

MacDonald, James M. and Linda C. Cavalluzzo. "Railroad Deregulation: Pricing Reforms, Shipper Responses, and the Effects on Labor." *Industrial and Labor Relations Review* 50 (October 1996): 80–91.

Maddison, Angus. *The World Economy: A Millennial Perspective.* Paris: Development Centre Studies, OECD, 2001.

Metcalf, David. "Unions and Productivity, Financial Performance, and Investment: International Evidence." In John Addison and Claus Schnabel, eds. *International Handbook of Trade Unions.* Cheltenham, UK: Edward Elgar, 2003, pp. 118–71.

Mishel, Lawrence. "The Structural Determinants of Bargaining Power." *Industrial and Labor Relations Review* 40 (October 1986): 90–104.

Organization for Economic Cooperation and Development. *The OECD Jobs Study: Evidence and Explanations.* Paris: OECD, 1994.

Panagides, Alexis and Harry Anthony Patrinos. "Union-Nonunion Wage Differentials in the Developing World: A Case Study of Mexico." World Bank Policy Research Working Paper 1269, March 1994.

Pencavel, John. *An Analysis of the Quit Rate in American Manufacturing Industry.* Princeton: Industrial Relations Section, Princeton University, 1970.

_____. *Labor Markets under Trade Unionism: Employment, Wages, and Hours.* Oxford: Blackwell, 1991.

_____. "The Legal Framework for Collective Bargaining in Developing Countries." In Sebastian Edwards and Nora Lustig, eds. *Labor Markets in Latin America: Combining Social Protection with Market Flexibility.* Washington, D.C.: Brookings Institution Press, 1997, pp. 27–61.

_____. "The Appropriate Design of Collective Bargaining Systems: Learning from the Experience of Britain, Australia, and New Zealand." *Comparative Labor Law and Policy Journal* 20 (Spring 1999): 447–81.

_____. "The Surprising Retreat of Union Britain." In David Card, Richard Blundell, and Richard Freeman, eds. *Seeking a Premier Economy.* Chicago: University of Chicago Press, 2004, pp. 181–232.

_____. and Catherine E. Hartsog. "A Reconsideration of the Effects of Unionism on Relative Wages and Employment in the United States." *Journal of Labor Economics* 2 (April 1984): 193–232.

Phelps Brown, Henry. *The Origins of Trade Union Power.* Oxford: Clarendon Press, 1983.

Reilly, Barry, Pierella Paci, and Peter Holl. "Unions, Safety Committees, and Workplace Injuries." *British Journal of Industrial Relations* 33 (June 1995): 275–88.

Riddell, Chris and W. Craig Riddell. "Changing Patterns of Unionization: The North American Experience, 1984–1998." Department of Economics, University of British Columbia Discussion Paper No. 01–23 (June 2001).

Rose, Nancy L. "Labor Rent Sharing and Regulation: Evidence from the Trucking Industry." *Journal of Political Economy* 95 (December 1987): 1146–78.

Sachs, Jeffrey D. "Social Conflict and Populist Policies in Latin America." In Renato Brunetta and Carlo Dell'Aringa, eds. *Labour Relations and Economic Performance.* New York: New York University Press, 1990, pp. 137–69.

Scarpetta, Stefano. "Assessing the Role of Labour Market Policies and Institutional Settings on Unemployment: A Cross-Country Study." *OECD Economic Studies* 26 (1996): 43–98.

Schultz, T. Paul and Germano Mwabu. "Labor Unions and the Distribution of Wages and Employment in South Africa." *Industrial and Labor Relations Review* 51 (July 1998): 680–703.

Slichter, Sumner H. *Union Policies and Industrial Management.* Washington, D.C.: Brookings Institution, 1941.

Stewart, Mark B. "Union Wage Differentials, Product Market Influences, and the Division of Rents." *Economic Journal* 100 (December 1990): 1122–37.

Stoikov, Vladimir and Robert L. Raimon. "Determinants of Differences in the Quit Rate among Industries." *American Economic Review* 58 (December 1968): 1283–98.

Weil, David. "Regulating the Workplace: The Vexing Problem of Implementation." In David Lewin, Bruce Kaufman, and Donna Sockell, eds. *Advances in Industrial and Labor Relations,* Vol. 7. Greenwich, Conn.: JAI Press, 1996, pp. 247–86.

Weil, David. "Are Mandated Health and Safety Committees Substitutes or Supplements to Labor Unions." *Industrial and Labor Relations Review* 52 (April 1999): 339–60.

Wooden, Mark. "Union Wage Effects in the Presence of Enterprise Bargaining." *Economic Record* 77 (March 2001): 1–18.

15

Has Management Strangled U.S. Unions?

*Robert J. Flanagan**

I. Introduction

Why has the collective representation of private employees declined in the United States? "The Slow Strangulation of Private Sector Unions," the title of the penultimate chapter of Freeman and Medoff's *What Do Unions Do? (WDUD)*, signals the authors' conclusion that declining union representation largely results from factors external to the labor movement itself. Writing in the early 1980s, they document the decline in unionization in the opening pages of the chapter and state the chapter's agenda: "What has caused this dramatic fall in unionization in the U.S. — a fall that contrasts sharply with increases in unionism in most other Western countries, including Canada?" (Freeman and Medoff, 1984: 222).

Freeman and Medoff explore four hypotheses: Union decline reflects (1) changes in economic structure that favor nonunion over union employment, (2) a declining intensity of union organizing, (3) a diminution in workers' interest in union representation, and (4) increasing management opposition. After examining a variety of evidence, they conclude that the decline is attributable to a combination of management opposition (25–50 percent), lower union organizing effort (25–33 percent), and structural change (up to 72 percent). Data assessed by the authors did not permit an empirical estimate of the importance of changing worker interest in unionization. Their lengthy discussion of management opposition follows a common theme of U.S. unions in emphasizing employers' strategic use of the National Labor Relations Act (NLRA), the main regulatory legislation governing U.S. private sector collective bargaining.

With the benefit of 20 more years of data and research, we now know that declining union membership is hardly unique to the United States. In fact, the U.S. experience was not unique in the late 1970s and early 1980s. Among advanced nations the pattern of union decline is now simply too broad to insist that the U.S. record must be explained by distinctive U.S. institutions (Ebbinhaus and Visser, 2000; OECD, 1991, 1994; Calmfors et al., 2001). At the close of the twentieth century, moreover, union representation was also falling in many less developed countries (Section II).

After reviewing union representation trends, I appraise the hypotheses considered by Freeman and Medoff in the light of 20 more years of observation and research. The evidence now supports several conclusions. Structural change favoring nonunion employment is a ubiquitous but minor factor in all countries (Section III). Now, as in 1984, the challenge is to explain declining union membership within most private sector industries and among most demographic groups. A key fact is that the growing attrition of existing union members "accounts" for much of the erosion of U.S. union membership. Yet, the discussion in *WDUD*, in subsequent research, and in policy debates instead focuses on what forces may have "strangled" replacement inflows of new members.

One suspect is organized labor itself. Union organizing effort has received the least research attention, although it has become an important area of policy discussion within the labor movement itself (Section IV). Renewed organizing efforts have not reached sufficient scale or effectiveness to compensate for membership attrition, however. Diminishing worker demand for union representation also reduces new membership inflows. The adoption of advanced human resource management policies in many companies and increasing similarities between union and nonunion employment arrangements contribute to diminished demand for unionization (Section V). The final suspect, management opposition to unions, takes many forms. *WDUD* and much of the subsequent literature emphasize management's well-documented strategic use of the NLRA and produce many proposals for labor law reform. In contrast, I find that strategic use of the National Labor Relations Act and other forms of management opposition are symptoms of a more fundamental determinant of management's aggressive stance toward unions. Since frequently proposed reforms of the NLRA do not address the source of management opposition, they are unlikely to change inflows sufficiently to reverse the decline in private sector union density, a conclusion supported by evidence from other countries (Sections VI–VIII).

II. How Distinctive Is the Union Decline?

"The Slow Strangulation. . . . " portrays declining union representation in the private sector as virtually unique to the United States, a construction of the facts that encouraged the search for an explanation based on distinctive features of the U.S. labor market. The fact that the decline of unionization in the private sector (where the federal regulation of labor relations applies) contrasted with the growth of unionization in the public sector (where it generally does not) increased the appeal of focusing on the effects of the National Labor Relations Act (NLRA).

It is now clear that declining union density characterizes most industrialized countries and many developing countries. Comparative data on the level and changes in union density in industrialized countries appear in Table 15.1,[1] which provides information for both the decade before Freeman and Medoff were writing (left-hand columns) and the period since the 1984 publication of *WDUD* (right-hand columns). The 1970–1980 data measure density as employed union members as a percent of wage and salary workers (OECD, 1994);

the 1985–late 1990s data measure density as union membership as a percent of "formal sector employment for wages and salaries, including agriculture" (Visser, 2003). By shifting sources it is possible to update data for industrialized countries into the late 1990s and to compare recent unionization trends in industrialized countries with those in developing countries (Table 15.2). But one cannot use Table 15.1 to infer changes in union density between 1980 and 1985. Whenever there is a choice, the Tables report data from labor force surveys rather than administrative data.

Even in the 1970s, declining unionization was not unique to the United States. Between 1970 and 1980, the union density rate fell more rapidly in Australia, Austria, France, Japan, the Netherlands, and Spain than in the United States. The density rate for all of Europe began to decline in 1978 (Visser, 2002: 404). Union membership losses visible in a number of industrialized countries during the 1970s broadened and deepened in years following the publication of *WDUD*.[2] Most countries with declining union density during the

Table 15.1
Union Density Rates, Major Industrial Countries
(percent)

	1970	1980	Change	1985	Late 1990s**	Change
Australia	50.2	48.0	-2.2	45.6	24.7	-20.9
Austria	62.2	56.2	-6.0	51.6	38.0	-13.6
Belgium	45.5	55.9	10.4	50.7	53.4	2.7
Canada	31.0	36.1	5.1	34.6	29.9	-4.7
Denmark	60.0	76.0	16.0	78.2	75.4	-2.8
Finland	51.4	69.8	18.4	69.1	76.1	7.0
France	22.3	17.5	-4.8	13.9	10.0	-3.9
Germany, W.	33.0	35.6	2.6	34.3	32.1	-2.2
Ireland	53.1	57.0	3.9	48.3	43.5	-4.8
Italy	36.3	49.3	13.0	42.5	38.0	-4.5
Japan	35.1	31.1	-4.0	28.8	21.5	-7.3
Netherlands	38.0	35.3	-2.4	25.2	24.5	-0.7
Norway	51.4	56.9	5.5	57.5	55.6	-1.9
New Zealand	n.a.	56.0	n.a.	53.1	21.4	-31.7
Portugal	60.8	60.7	-0.1	51.4	25.1	-26.3
Spain	27.4	25.0	-2.4	9.3	16.4	7.1
Sweden	67.7	79.7	12.0	83.7	81.3	-2.4
Switzerland	30.1	30.7	0.6	28.6	21.7	-6.9
United Kingdom	44.8	50.4	5.6	39.0	30.7	-8.3
United States	23.2*	22.3	-0.9	17.4	13.0	-4.4

*1977 data. **2000: Japan, United States. 1999: Austria, Denmark, Netherlands, New Zealand, Switzerland. 1998: Canada, Finland, France, Italy, Sweden, United Kingdom. 1997: Ireland, Norway, Spain. 1996: Australia. 1995: Belgium, Portugal. 1990: West Germany. n.a. not available.

Source: 1970–80: OECD, 1994, Table 5.7, p. 184. 1985– Visser, 2003, Tables 1A, 1C, 1D

1970s experienced much larger declines after 1985, and with the exception of Belgium, countries with increasing unionization during the 1970s experienced losses after 1985. For countries with plant- or company-level representation through works councils, the union membership data underlying Table 15.1 may understate the diminished collective representation of workers. Between 1981 and 1994, for example, the share of employees in plants with works councils in total employment fell from 50.6 to 39.5 percent in Germany, leading one scholar to conclude that "the decline in works council coverage has been more profound than the erosion of collective bargaining" (Hassel, 1999: 487). Decentralization of collective bargaining arrangements accompanied falling collective representation in many European countries. This broader pattern of decline cautions against over-reliance on uniquely U.S. influences in explaining union membership trends.

Although more sparsely documented and less frequently analyzed, union density rates have also declined in much of the less industrialized world since the mid–1980s (Table 15.2). Visser (2003) discusses the variety of economic, social, and political factors influencing changes in unionization in many of these countries. These countries receive no further attention here, however, because *WDUD* focused on the situation of unions in industrialized countries.

Freeman and Medoff argue that comparisons with Canadian experience reveal the importance of distinctively U.S. factors in explaining declining union density in the U.S. private sector. ("Perhaps most telling is the fact that in the country most like the United States, Canada, where many of the same unions and firms operate, the percentage unionized went from below the U.S. percentage unionized to above it" (1984: 227).) Along with Weiler (1983), they argue that this development reflected an important institutional difference between the two North American countries: Despite similar bargaining structures and similar approaches to regulating collective bargaining in the two countries, the fact that Canadian provinces certified unions on the basis of authorization cards rather than contentious representation elections accounted for the stronger position of Canadian unions. With the passage of time, the force of this comparison has also weakened. To some extent, discussions of trends in private sector union density can be muddied by the use of unionization figures that include public employees. Private sector unionization in Canada may have peaked as early as 1958 (Troy, 1990, 1992). Even the overall figures show that Canadian union density declined steadily from the early to mid–1980s, and between 1984 and 1998 the declines were quite similar in the two countries (seven percentage points in Canada and eight percentage points in the United States (Riddell and Riddell, 2001)). Whether the similarity of the post–1984 unionization trends in the two countries undermines the emphasis on management opposition as an explanation of U.S. unionization trends is addressed in Section VII.

In short, the hypothesis that declining U.S. unionization results from distinctive U.S. policies and institutions cannot be established by claiming that the

U.S. membership decline is unique. With union representation falling or failing to keep up with labor force growth in so many countries, general explanations merit priority, and the remaining sections consider several alternatives.

III. Structural Change and Union Representation

Since unionization rates vary by industry, geographical location, and personal characteristics, changing employment and demographic patterns may alter aggregate union density. Countries that share similar changes in employment structure should share similar trends in union representation. Through an accounting exercise based on 1973–1975 regression estimates of the effect of personal characteristics and the industrial, occupational, and geographic structure of employment on union membership Freeman and Medoff (1984: 225) observe that 72 percent of the decline in U.S. unionization could result from changes in these factors. They objected to explanations based primarily on structural shifts in employment, however, on the belief that similar changes in the structure of employment did not produce declining unionization in other advanced countries. "Instead, outside the U.S. unionization has increased, often in large numbers" (p. 227). Evidence in the previous section showed the limitations of this view.

In fact, changing employment patterns account for some of declining union representation in most countries. An OECD analysis found that shifts in employment between one-digit industries accounted for about 17 percent of the 1980–1988 decline in union density in the United States. For other OECD countries the contribution of structural change ranged from 18 to 36 percent (OECD, 1991: 115). Presumably the role of structural shifts would be larger in analyses that also incorporated the occu-pational, geographic, and demographic dimensions found in Freeman and Medoff's analysis.

In a reexamination of the U.S. data, Farber and Krueger (1993) find that changes in employment structure accounted for about 35 percent of the decline in unionization between 1977–1984 but only seven percent of the subsequent decline between 1984–1991. An analysis of the very similar U.S. and Canadian union membership changes between 1984 and 1998 likewise found that structural change explained only a small fraction of the U.S. decline and none of the almost identical Canadian decline (Riddell and Riddell, 2001). Thus, while the exact contribution of changing employment patterns to falling union density varies somewhat from country to country, it is never the dominant factor. To fully understand the decline in collective representation, one must determine what factors explain declining unionization rates within most industries, occupations, areas, and demographic groupings. Table 15.3 describes the industrial and occupational dimensions of the continuing decline in union membership since the publication of WDUD. Although the membership losses in traditional bastions of union strength, such as manufacturing, communications, and transportation, are particularly notable, one must find a sector that is

Table 15.2
Union Density Rates, Other Countries
(percent)

	1980s	1990s	Change	First year	Last year
Latin America					
Argentina	67.5	50.5	-17.0	1986	1995
Chile	23.1	26.7	3.6	1985	1998
Columbia	24.9	17.1	-7.8	1985	1995
Costa Rica	29.1	16.6	-12.5	1985	1995
Mexico	42.8	18.9	-23.9	1991	1997
Uruguay	31.2	20.3	-10.9	1988	1993
Venezuela	29.8	17.1	-12.7	1988	1993
Asia					
Hong Kong	16.8	22.3	5.5	1985	1996
"Korea, South"	12.4	11.8	-0.6	1985	1999
Malaysia	13.5	11.7	-1.8	1986	1995
Philippines	24.1	29.9	5.8	1985	1996
Singapore	20.6	16.9	-3.7	1985	1998
Thailand	3.3	1.4	-1.9	1985	1999
Africa					
Egypt	42.7	38.8	-3.9	1985	1995
Kenya	41.9	33.3	-8.6	1985	1995
South Africa	17.7	40.5	22.8	1985	1998
Uganda	10.2	6.8	-3.4	1989	1995
Zambia	40.0	58.2	18.2	1985	1995

Source: Visser (2003), Tables 1D, 1E, 1F, and 1G

substantially in the public sector (educational services, public administration) to identify even a modest increase in union density. Unreported data for the more narrowly defined industries that underlie the aggregates reported in Table 15.3 reveal the same pattern.

Broad macroeconomic developments may also influence a nation's employment structure in ways that affect unionization rates. A recent analysis of union representation trends in several European countries found that both the unemployment rate, which generally has risen in Europe since the 1970s, and the employment-population ratios are negatively related to union density (Calmfors et al., 2001). Unions seem strongest in cyclically sensitive industries. Increases in the employment-population ratio often signal greater participation by groups, such as youth, who are less likely to join unions or who go into nonstandard employment. Other factors equal, comparatively low unemployment and high

Table 15.3
Union Density Rates, United States, 1984–2001

Industry	1984	2001	1984 - 2001	
			Pct. Point	Percent
Agriculture	1.9	1.7	-0.2	-10.5
Mining	17.6	12.4	-5.2	-29.5
Construction	24.3	19.4	-4.9	-20.2
Nondurable man.	23.8	13.9	-9.9	-41.6
Durable man.	27.5	15.2	-12.3	-44.7
Transportation	45.4	33.2	-12.2	-26.9
Communications	41.4	20.5	-20.9	-50.5
"Utilities, etc."	38.6	30.7	-7.9	-20.5
Wholesale Trade	8.6	5.4	-3.2	-37.2
Retail Trade	7.8	4.6	-3.2	-41.0
FIRE	3.3	2.5	-0.8	-24.2
Bus.& Repr. Ser.	6.4	3.3	-3.1	-48.4
Personal Serv.	6.1	5.2	-0.9	-14.8
Entertainment	13.1	9.5	-3.6	-27.5
Hospitals	17	13.6	-3.4	-20.0
Oth. Medical Ser	9.9	6.7	-3.2	-32.3
Education Serv.	34.3	34.6	0.3	0.9
Social Services	10.8	6.6	-4.2	-38.9
Oth. Prof. Serv.	3.9	3.2	-0.7	-17.9
Public Admin.	28.5	32.2	3.7	13.0
Wage & Salary	18.8	13.5	-5.3	-28.2
Private Sector	15.3	9	-6.3	-41.2

Source: http://unionstats.com/. See Hirsch and MacPherson (2003) for a discussion of the data.

labor force participation rates in the United States should have narrowed union density differentials between the United States and Europe in the 1990s.

To summarize, diverging employment trends in union and nonunion firms have produced a "natural attrition" of union membership. Freeman and Medoff estimated an annual attrition in the union share of the work force of three percent per year and noted that if the annual new organization rate of .3 percent of the nonagricultural work force in the late 1970s and early 1980s persisted, union density in the United States would eventually level off at about 10 percent. They also expressed the view that a steady state union density rate as low as ten percent was unlikely to materialize, because they expected an increase in new organization (1984: 241–42).

In fact, the natural attrition of union membership subsequently increased, while the new organization rate fell further. In virtually every year since 1980, the employment growth rate in the union sector has been negative, while the employment growth rate in the nonunion sector has been positive (Farber and Western, 2002: 43). Remarkably little interpretation of this extraordinary development appears in discussions of declining membership. Research into the role of increasing competition on the divergent employment trends in the union and nonunion sectors would deepen our understanding of declining union density. Import penetration grew throughout the period. While the average union wage premium diminished, at almost 18 percent (net of work force characteristics) it remained about the highest among industrialized countries in the late 1990s (Blanchflower and Bryson, 2002) and provided a significant incentive for consumers to shift to nonunion or foreign products and for companies to established new plants in nonunion parts of the country.

While union membership attrition increased, the new organization rate fell from .3 to .1 percent of the nonagricultural labor force. Most of the decline occurred in the early 1980s when both representation elections and the number of nonunion workers voting in those elections dropped sharply. The union success rate in representation elections actually increased somewhat (to over 50 percent), consistent with the hypothesis that unions chose organizing targets more selectively. Notwithstanding greater selectivity, higher success rates were not sufficient to completely counter the declining election activity. Throughout the period since 1984, actual new organization rates have been well below the rates that would have stabilized the density rate. Farber and Western (2002: 53) estimate that the steady-state union density rate implied by current attrition and new organization rates is 2.1 percent.

Understanding why it has become so difficult to offset natural attrition with new organization requires an evaluation of three interrelated hypotheses: (1) Union organizing efforts have diminished; (2) workers no longer believe that unions can effectively represent their workplace interests; and (3) management opposition undermines union organizing efforts.

IV. Union Organizing Efforts

Do the weak trends in new organization reflect a diminution of union organizing efforts? The decline in representation elections, which are almost always initiated by a petition from a union, is suggestive, as is evidence from the United Kingdom on the importance of establishing union representation at new firms to sustaining union membership (Pencavel, 2001: 19). Unfortunately, there has been no direct evidence produced on the scale of resources allocated by labor unions to organizing new members since the study by Voos (1984, cited in Freeman and Medoff, 1984).

Institutional developments indicate that the U.S. labor movement has been slow to respond to the challenge of new private sector organizing. Historically, new organizing has been the responsibility of individual national unions, which were expected to confine organizing efforts to their traditional jurisdictions. In contrast, the American Federation of Labor and Congress of Industrial Organizations (AFL-CIO), the federation of national unions, led in pursuing organized labor's general political agenda. Shortly after the private sector union density rates peaked in the 1950s, a few national union leaders, worried that many national unions were more concerned with representing current members than organizing new members, urged greater federation involvement in organizing projects. The AFL-CIO leadership rejected such proposals until the 1990s when it gradually responded with a number of initiatives, including the development of an Organizing Institute to train new organizers and a Committee on the Future of Work, which considered novel union services and membership categories. Nevertheless, John Sweeney, a critic of the prior regime became president in 1995 after a difficult internal battle for leadership of the federation. Sweeney pledged $20 million/year to hire and train new organizers, developed a center for Strategic Campaigns, and initiated a program to hire 1,000 college students a year as summer organizers (Dark, 1999). A few large national unions have also significantly shifted resources toward new organizing.

Most recently, the AFL-CIO announced the formation of an organization for *nonunion* workers who wish to support organized labor's actions on political issues. In a departure from traditional union organizing, Working America is not based at the workplace, will not deal with employers, and relies on volunteer contributions rather than obligatory membership dues. The AFL-CIO hopes that Working America will enlist a million workers to lobby and demonstrate for labor's political objectives, although the initial efforts were limited to pilot projects in Cleveland and Seattle (Greenhouse, 2003). Whether this initiative enhances organized labor's presence at the workplace depends in part on whether the development of Working America diverts resources from traditional organizing activities.

To what extent have the new organizing initiatives altered organizing resources and outcomes? There is indirect evidence that U.S. unions have maintained the share of their resources devoted to organizing new members. Total union resources should be roughly proportional to the number of members. When Farber and Western compare new organization to union membership, they find that "New organization per union member has been roughly constant since the early 1970s" (2002: 51), which is consistent with a relatively constant share of resources devoted to new organization. To actually counter the effects of natural attrition of membership, however, unions need to allocate an increasing proportion of union resources to organizing or use existing resources more effectively.

How efficiently are union organizing resources allocated? At the macro level, the earlier cited evidence that unions have improved their success rate while seeking fewer representation elections is consistent with more efficient resource allocation. Micro studies of links between organizing strategies and organizing outcomes are scarce, however. One study of 261 certification elections held in the late 1980s finds that the particular union organizing strategy adopted had an important impact on election outcomes. After relating the union vote to union and management tactics during organizing campaign (as reported by union organizers), the author concludes that the use of a "rank-and-file organizing strategy" substantially raised a union's odds of success. This time-intensive strategy involves the target company's employees' participation in a bargaining committee, the formulation of novel campaign issues, house calls to prospective voters, etc. Yet only one-third of the elections studied followed such a strategy. Consistent with union claims, the study also finds that many management resistance tactics have a negative impact on voting outcomes (Bronfenbrenner, 1997).

How has new organization changed since the 1995 regime change at the AFL-CIO? Both the number of representation elections and the numbers of workers voting in the elections rose slightly after 1996. But at roughly 3,000 elections per year and 200,000 workers voting in the elections at the end of the century, organizing activity remained below half its level in the early 1980s. The modest increase in the union win rate noted earlier preceded the accession of the new leadership. Not all new organizing occurs through NLRB elections, but even if these data understate new organizing, the bottom line is unchanged. In 2002 there were 788,000 fewer union members in private nonagricultural employment than in 1995, when the change in AFL-CIO leadership occurred (Hirsch and Macpherson, 2002). The rate of membership loss did diminish during the economic boom of the late 1990s, but then increased with the recession that began in 2000.

As yet, there is no convincing evidence that the renewed institutional emphasis on organizing has produced sufficient change in the scale of organizing resources or the effectiveness of their use to significantly raise the new organization rate, let alone offset natural attrition of union membership. Moreover, even the effects of an increase in organizing resources could be countered by declining demand for union representation or increasing management opposition, factors addressed in the following sections.

V. Worker Demand for Union Representation

The demand for union representation consists of unionized workers plus nonunion workers who say they would vote in favor of union representation if given the chance. (Supply consists of the actual number of jobs filled by union workers.) By these definitions, the fraction of nonunion workers desiring union representation dropped about six percentage points between 1977 and 1984 (Farber and Krueger, 1993). Since the mid–1980s the fraction has remained stable at about one-third of nonunion employment. In contrast, about 90 percent of workers in union jobs say that they would still vote for union representation (Freeman and Rogers, 1999).3 According to Farber and Krueger's computations, declining demand for union representation fully accounts for falling union density and, in contrast to Freeman and Medoff, they conclude that "There is no evidence that any significant part of the decline in unionization is due to increased management resistance other than the sort of resistance that would be reflected in lower demand for unionization by workers" (1993: 118). Freeman and Rogers (1999) report similar data (from the Worker Representation and Participation Survey (WRPS)) for late 1994.

Why is a majority of workers in the increasingly large nonunion sector uninterested in unionization? What explains the decline in the interest of nonunion workers in union representation in 1977–1984? Job satisfaction is a natural point of departure. Nonunion workers are almost twice as likely to say they would vote for a union if they are dissatisfied with their job. The job satisfaction of nonunion workers increased significantly between 1977–1984 (when the demand for union representation de-creased) but grew more slowly in later years (Farber and Krueger, 1993, pp. 119–20). The job satisfaction measures emphasize dissatisfaction over the wage and job security concerns of workers.

The 1994 data in the WRPS confirm that job satisfaction erodes the willingness of nonunion workers to vote for union representation. An analysis of these data links job satisfaction to specific employer human resource management (HRM) policies. Fiorito (2002: 219) finds that high performance HRM policies "exert a modest negative impact on nonunion worker intentions to vote for a union." Freeman and Rogers (1999) also note that nonunion workers at workplaces with employee involvement programs are more likely to vote against union representation.

Collective representation notwithstanding, union workers feel they have *less* influence at the workplace than do nonunion workers. Nonunion workers who are dissatisfied with their influence in the workplace are more likely to vote for a union, but a key finding from the WRPS data is that dissatisfaction over influence in the workplace does not necessarily translate into union representation. In fact, employees are about evenly divided on whether they prefer a collective or individual approach to addressing workplace problems. An under-appreciated effect of modern employee involvement practices may have been to convince nonunion employees that union representation is not the only method of influencing workplace decisions. Moreover, employees prefer cooperative relations with management to representation by strong, but adversarial, employee organizations. They also prefer that workplace representation have some degree of independence from management, a feature that most employers seem reluctant to grant.

There are other reasons why so many nonunion workers conclude that unions no longer can effectively address their job dissatisfaction. Over the past 25 years, workers have increasingly confronted evidence of the limitations of organized labor's ability to protect wages and working conditions in the face of increasingly competitive markets. Concession bargaining in the early 1980s and the inability to halt layoffs in traditional union jurisdictions in the face of

increased international competition and deregulation may have eroded workers' confidence that unions could deliver on their promises regarding income
and job security.

Workers may increasingly see other institutions as the source of improvements in working conditions. Unions find it more difficult to differentiate their
product from nonunion employers in a world in which management adopts
employment practices originally introduced by unions, and legislation increasingly provides many of the benefits that formerly were only available in union
contracts. Ironically, much of the legislation providing these benefits passed
with strong union support. But are labor unions complements or substitutes
for statutory provision of workplace rights and benefits? Early in the history
of U.S. labor, the American Federation of Labor held the substitute view and
opposed the legislative provision of many items that it felt should be reserved
for collective bargaining.4 The labor federation abandoned this stance by
the 1930s, but the question of whether the growing legislative provision of
workplace benefits makes it increasingly difficult for unions to differentiate
their contracts from nonunion employment arrangements remains. Support
for the hypothesis that union representation and legislation are substitutes
also comes from findings of (a) a significant inverse relationship between
unionization and social welfare expenditures as a percent of GDP and (b)
lower union density rates in states that recognize an "implicit contract" exception to the legal doctrine of employment at will (Neuman and Rissman, 1984).
States that recognize this exception effectively provide greater job security to
nonunion employees.

The complementarity argument holds that unions may supplement legislation
by ensuring the effective implementation of statutory rights. Evidence on this
issue also remains sparse. A study of workplaces in Oregon finds that OSHA
inspections increased more at union workplaces than at nonunion workplaces
(Weil, 1999). This union "supplement" may be important for explaining the
continued allegiance of union members to union representation, but may mean
little to prospective union members, who are more likely to know of general
statutory protection than details of implementation.

Some European scholars advance a "social custom" hypothesis to explain
declining worker demand for unionization. To the attraction of unions for
improving working conditions and job satisfaction, this hypothesis adds the
need for workers to acquiesce in the social norms of family members and co-
workers regarding collective action (Naylor, 1990; Visser, 2002). Visser cites
some European survey evidence that many workers join a union to achieve a
"psychological safety" in their relations with work or family groups holding
pro-union attitudes (2002: 406–408). Like tipping models of segregation, this
motivation for union membership can unravel at sufficiently low unionization
rates as the group norm deteriorates. While the importance of this motivation
in the representation decisions of U.S. workers is not known, it explains why

the large attrition of U.S. union membership noted earlier could itself reduce subsequent worker demand for representation.

Diminished worker demand for union representation, the most under-explored explanation of declining private sector union density in *WDUD*, has become an important explanation for the continued decline of unions over the past 20 years. Consistent with the U.S. facts, the hypothesis can also address the broad pattern of union decline observed in industrialized countries, since it does not rest on the effects of distinctive national institutions. This section stressed the effects of job satisfaction and views of the institutional effectiveness of unions on the worker demand for representation, but the views and actions of management may also play a role.

VI. Management Opposition in the United States

Over half of "The Slow Strangulation of Private Sector Unions" discusses the opposition of U.S. management to unions, concluding "[management] opposition, broadly defined, is a major cause of the slow strangulation of private sector unionism" (Freeman and Medoff, 1984: 239). Freeman and Medoff claim that their research shows that a quarter to a half of declining union success in NLRA representation elections reflects *increased* management opposition as reflected in the increasing number of unfair labor practice charges filed against employers (p. 237). (They do not mention that during the same period allegations of unfair labor practices *by unions* also rose substantially.) Their discussion includes a review of research on management's strategic use of NLRA procedures to oppose the formation of unions or negotiation of first contracts. Since the NLRA procedures are unusual in comparative perspective,[5] this focus fits nicely with their view that declining union density was a uniquely U.S. phenomenon. Missing from their discussion is any historical perspective on the relationship between management opposition and union representation. The fact that the dramatic surge in union membership during the mid–1930s occurred in the face of arguably the most intense management opposition of the twentieth century receives no mention or interpretation, for example.

With the benefit of 20 more years of research and experience, the perspective taken on the role of management opposition in *WDUD* now seems too narrowly conceived and nonetheless too overstated. Too narrowly conceived because the scope of management resistance is much greater than the book's focus on activities regulated under the NLRA. Overstated because the focus on opposition to the formation of new unions ignores the powerful influence of attrition of union jobs on union density, the declining number of jobs in the union sector, and the expanding number of jobs in the nonunion sector.

Broadly speaking, management opposition policies take the form of union substitution or union suppression activities. Efforts to thwart union organizing by preemptively adopting union wages and working conditions appear to be the oldest example of union substitution by nonunion firms. Under U.S. labor law, this tactic is illegal only if undertaken after an organizing campaign begins. (Statutory regulation of occupational health and safety, pensions, employment discrimination and other aspects of the employment relationship also narrows differences between union and nonunion employment conditions.) The adoption of the employee involvement policies discussed in the previous section represents a more recent union substitution approach that appears to have expanded substantially since the publication of *WDUD*. Whether this development falls under the rubric of willful management opposition is debatable, since employee involvement policies may be adopted because they have or are believed to have positive effects on organization performance, quite apart from their impact on unionization. Whatever the motivation, they do seem to dissuade new unionization.

Turning to union suppression activities, management's use of the legal system to oppose the formation of new unions is now much broader than the conflict that registers in the administration of the NLRA. Since the 1970s, employers have increasingly refused to accept the finality of the NLRB's representation decisions. By exercising their legal right to appeal Board decisions, they have moved their cases into the federal courts, where they expect to get a more favorable hearing. Simply lengthening the adjudication period also tends to produce employer-favored outcomes. Moreover, the federal judiciary has increasingly permitted employers to bring tort actions under state law against alleged defamatory claims made during union organizing campaigns and alleged violence during economic strikes. Gradually, the regulation of labor relations policy has drifted back to the courts, an outcome that the passage of the Norris-LaGuardia Act and the NLRA were intended to circumvent (Getman, 2003).

WDUD focuses on the most widely publicized approach to union suppression — working within the NLRA framework to oppose efforts to establish new unions or, when unions win representation rights, to negotiate a first contract. Most research available to Freeman and Medoff indicated that various forms of management opposition, including the use of anti-union consultants to manage the employer's campaign, legal maneuvers designed to delay either elections or the resolution of associated unfair labor practices, or outright illegal behavior, such as discharging employees who support unionization, all inhibit the formation of effective unions and reduce the odds that unions will win representation elections (1984: 233–37). Subsequent studies and a national commission have further chronicled the tactics used by labor-management consultants and attorneys who specialize in opposing union efforts to establish a collective bargaining relationship (Logan, 2002; Commission on Future of Worker-Management Relations, 1994).

In principle, such management opposition tactics need not result in union suppression. While tough tactics may convince employees that union representation will be futile or ineffective, they may also backfire and convince employees of the need for a collective force to counter a determined employer. In practice, most empirical evaluations continue to conclude that opposition tactics inhibit the formation of new unions, but the evidence is not unanimous. While the earlier-cited study of 261 election campaigns by Bronfenbrenner (1997) finds that management opposition tactics reduce union election success, the study by Fiorito (2002) on a much larger sample of the work force finds that nonunion workers say they are more likely to vote for union representation where there is *greater* management opposition to a unionization campaign. Given wide variations in the balance of power between labor and management in specific labor relations settings, it should not surprise us that the outcome of opposition as well as the effectiveness of labor law may be context-specific. Commenting on the contents of anti-union speech by employers, a shrewd observer of the practice and regulation of labor relations noted (Cox, 1960: 44): "Words which may only antagonize a hard-bitten truck driver in Detroit may seriously intimidate a rural textile hand in a company village where the mill owners dominate every aspect of life."

To summarize, management opposition to union representation may take various forms which differ in their likely benefits and costs to management and in their observability to outsiders. Rational employers will choose the approach that best fits their situation, given the benefits and costs. One implication is that the full scope of management opposition is difficult to observe. So are trends in management opposition, as discussed more fully below. A second implication is that efforts to raise the costs of one type of management opposition, such as the labor law reforms discussed in Section VII, may induce many employers to shift to other methods of opposition. Missing from most discussions of management opposition is an analysis of why it exists in the first place, the topic of Section VIII. The remainder of this section maintains Freeman and Medoff's focus on the NLRA.

Trends in Management Opposition

Given the role accorded increasing management opposition prior to 1984 by Freeman and Medoff, one must ask whether management opposition continued to increase as unionization continued to decline over the subsequent 20 years. The absence of a clear measure of management opposition hampers a clear answer to this question in any period. When we look for measures of management opposition or union militancy, we find instead measures of labor-management conflict, such as strikes and unfair labor practice charges that reflect choices or actions by both parties. Strike activity provides an instructive example. The number of work stoppages involving 1,000 or more employees fell from an annual average of 114 (.06 percent of estimated work time) in 1980–1984 to 30 (.02) during 1997–2001. Does the decline reflect less management opposition or less union militancy? Information on strikes over union recognition, which could be more informative about management opposition to union organizing, remains rare.

Figure 15.1
Unfair Labor Practice Charges, 1970–1999

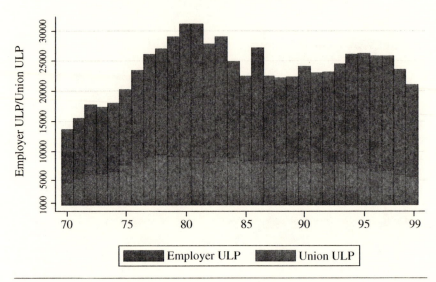

Source: National Labor Relations Board

Figure 15.2
Unfair Labor Practice Charges per Election

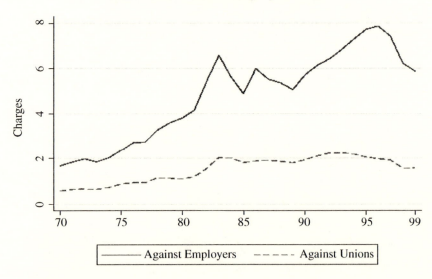

Source: National Labor Relations Board

Figure 15.3
Employees Awarded Reinstatement or Back Pay

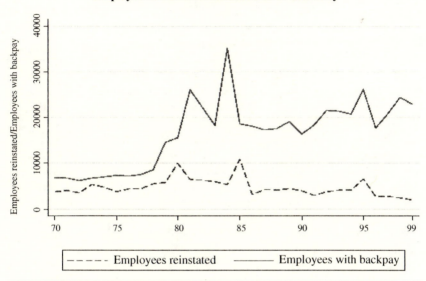

Source: National Labor Relations Board

Figure 15.4
Backpay per Employee

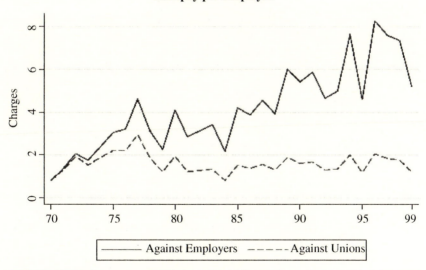

Backpay in thousands of dollars; real backpay in 1970 dollars

Source: National Labor Relations Board

Regulatory regimes that register management resistance as violations of a list of approved labor relations practices provide an alternative measure, but are also subject to similar interpretive ambiguities. The NLRA regulatory system rests on "victim" enforcement, so the volume of charges against employers reflects the joint outcome of employers' choice of labor relations behavior and union decisions to challenge the behavior by filing an unfair labor practice charge with the NLRB. In principle, an increase (decrease) in unfair labor practice charges against employers can reflect an increase (decrease) in employer opposition, an increase (decrease) in the likelihood that a union will challenge suspect behavior, or both. Both the management and union actions are influenced by an incentive structure discussed in Flanagan (1989). Some of the incentives governing the benefit-cost calculation are governed by details of labor law and its administration (e.g., the probability that an unfair labor practice charge will be successful and penalties for violations), but others reflect factors that motivate employer opposition in the first place (e.g., competitive pressure, the compensation premium associated with union representation).

With these caveats in mind, Figures 15.1–15.4 trace the evolution of several potential indicators of U.S. management opposition to unions. Figure 15.1 shows the path of unfair labor practice charges filed against employers and against unions over a 30-year period. Roughly three times as many charges are filed against employers as against unions in an average year. The two series are closely correlated from 1970 until about 1993 ($r > .9$), when a rapid drop in charges filed against unions preceded a later and slower decline in charges filed against employers. These data are not conditioned on changes in the level of regulated activity, however. The data reported in Figure 15.2 "deflate" those in Figure 15.1 by reporting the number unfair labor practice charges per representation election. (The numerator and denominator are not an exact match, since union election campaigns are not the only source of unfair labor practices.) While annual unfair labor practice charges declined in the 1980s, the number of representation elections fell much faster, so that the number of charges per "regulatory incident" has been increasing. Whether this represents increasing management resistance or increased union aggressiveness remains ambiguous.

When the National Labor Relations Board finds that employees have been illegally discharged for exercising their rights to concerted activity, it awards reinstatement or back pay, an approach it views as consistent with the "compensatory" approach to remedies of violations of the NLRA required by the U.S. Supreme Court. The annual number of employees awarded these remedies by the NLRB therefore provides a measure of management opposition that is not polluted by variations in non-meritorious unfair labor practice charges. (The measures only address one type of prohibited labor practice, however.) Back pay is the more important remedy as many discharged employees refuse re-employment with an obviously hostile employer. Beginning in the late 1970s, the number of employees receiving back-pay awards rose steeply, peaking in

1984 (Figure 15.3). The subsequent plateau was about three times the level of the early 1970s, but a gradually diminishing share of the growing nonunion work time. By this measure, management opposition rose to a new plateau between 1978 and 1985, but then drifted up only slightly during a period of continued decline in union density.

Figure 15.4 describes the annual average back-pay award per worker receiving NLRB-ordered back pay. In nominal terms, average back-pay awards increased about tenfold, from roughly $400 in 1970 to $4,000 in the mid 1990s. The amounts reflect the wage level of illegally discharged employees and the length of their period of discharge. Through the dependence on wages, nominal back-pay awards follow the price level in broad terms. Real back-pay awards per discharged worker rise with nominal awards during the 1970s, but are trendless thereafter. Since real wage trends follow productivity trends, the absence of a trend in the real back-pay series is puzzling particularly in the 1990s. While diminishing periods of illegal discharge could offset the effect of wage growth on back pay awards, the lengthening periods of adjudication under the NLRA render this interpretation unlikely.

Writing in the early 1980s, Freeman and Medoff attributed a significant part of declining union density in the private sector to increasing management opposition, and all measures are consistent with a marked increase in opposition in the late 1970s. By the measures reviewed in Figures 15.1–15.4, the surge in management opposition observable in NLRA conflict probably halted by the mid–1980s. Other forms of management opposition probably have increased, although by an unknown amount.

VII. Labor Law Reform

Freeman and Medoff argue that labor law reforms will counter management opposition and facilitate union organizing. After referring to experience with Canadian labor legislation, public sector collective bargaining legislation, and state right-to-work laws, they conclude "that labor law does indeed influence the success of unions in representing workers. Under a different legal environment, U.S. employers would behave differently and unions might fare better in organizing the work force" (p. 243). Judging by the intensity of political battles over proposed reforms of the NLRA, both management and union practitioners of collective bargaining share this view. Freeman and Medoff do not, however, supplement their general claims with an estimate of the extent to which labor law reforms would raise U.S. union density. Given the large attrition of union members, success in representation elections, the main focus of the management opposition evidence, is not the only or necessarily the main source of changes in union density. Other scholars and one national commission have also suggested a number of legal reforms, including immediate certification on the basis of bargaining authorization cards signed by employees (as in some Canadian jurisdictions), special dispute resolution procedures for first-contract negotiations, and punitive damages for serious labor law violations (Getman, 2003; Gould, 1993; Commission on Future of Worker-Management Relations, 1994). The rest of this section examines evidence on the proposition that labor law reforms can counter management opposition sufficiently to reverse the decline of private sector union density.

Canadian Labor Law Reform

The Canadian experience provides a probative comparison with the United States because of national similarities of industry structure, demographics, and approach to regulation of labor relations. Freeman and Medoff emphasized the difference in unionization trends in the two countries, and fewer unfair labor practice charges accompany attempts to gain union recognition in Canada (Thomason, 1994). In 1998, overall union density in Canada (32.5 percent) remained higher than in the United States,[6] but the *decline* in Canadian union density has paralleled that of the United States. (See discussion in Section I.) Does this development undermine the argument that different implementations of a similar labor law account for differences in unionization between the two North American countries?

In fact, the legal environment for union organizing in Canada has changed over the past quarter century. In contrast to the United States, the exact features of Canadian labor law are established at the provincial level. Since 1976, several Canadian provinces revised their labor laws in the direction of U.S. practice, notably by substituting mandatory union representation elections (favored by employers) for authorization card checks (favored by unions).[7] The mandatory election approach increases the scope for employer opposition by lengthening the period between the request for certification as the official bargaining agent and the determination of whether a union has the support of a majority of employees in the bargaining unit. (It might also provide a check on whether employees understood that they were authorizing union representation when they signed the cards.) The shift to mandatory elections therefore increases the cost of bargaining certifications and hence should reduce the number of certification attempts as unions abandon the most difficult organizing opportunities. Evidence for British Columbia indicates that certification attempts declined with the institution of mandatory elections and then increased when the province returned to certifications based on a card check (Riddell, 2001).

A panel study of certification attempts in nine Canadian provinces between 1978–1996 provides the most convincing evidence of the effects of changing bargaining certification procedures (Johnson, 2002). This analysis controls for industrial and demographic characteristics, provincial fixed effects, and provincial time trends before estimating the impact of the institutional changes. The study finds that the shift from card checks to mandatory elections reduces the certification rate by nine percentage points (13 percent). How this result relates to the overall union density rate depends on the scope of union organizing activity and union membership attrition. The study also estimates the effect of changing certification procedures on the percentage of *all firms* granting new bargaining certifications. Unions won certification at about one quarter of one percent of all firms in an average year during the sample period. Assuming that nonunion firms constitute 65 percent of the total (extrapolating the overall unionization rate of the labor force), .004 percent of the nonunion work force is organized in an average year. With a mandatory election procedure, this figure falls to .002 to .003 percentage of the nonunion work force, depending on the estimation procedure. Changes in the legal procedure appear secondary to the scale of organizing activity.

The Johnson study also assesses the impact of two other changes in labor law that occurred in some Canadian provinces over the same time period: compulsory dues check off and first agreement arbitration (which requires that impasses between the parties to a new bargaining relationship be taken to arbitration). Each change tends to raise the benefits of union membership, although first agreement arbitration should have the more powerful effect. Yet, these potential benefits to unions should also stimulate greater employer opposition, raising both the benefits and costs of union certification. Consistent with the ambiguous prediction, these changes in labor law are not significantly related to either the certification rate or the win rate in the empirical analysis (Johnson, 2002: Table 3).

The Canadian evidence therefore supports the view that a shift from mandatory elections to certification based on authorization cards would produce some increase union election success in the United States, but it also indicates that the size of the increased success would not be sufficient to reverse the decline in union density. Moreover, applying the Canadian estimates to the United States may overstate the effects of changes in labor law. In general, the response to the change should depend on the degree of employer opposition in a country. The effects observed in one country can in principle be larger or smaller in another setting. For example, the wage incentives for employer opposition are larger in the United States than in Canada; union wage premia are 17.6 and 8.3 percent in the United States and Canada, respectively. In short, adopting the card-check procedure may mitigate but is unlikely to reverse union density trends.

U.S. Public Sector

Writing in 1984, Freeman and Medoff could contrast the growth of union representation in the U.S. public sector with its decline in the private sector to support their assertion that differences in labor law influence union success. This comparison now seems far less probative than the Canadian evidence reviewed above. Any effort to characterize and contrast labor law in the U.S. public and private sectors must be seen as heroic. While the NLRA covers most of the private sector, a crazy quilt of laws and regulations, some modeled on the NLRA, govern labor relations in the thousands of federal, state, and local governments around the country. The surge in public sector unionism in the 1960s and 1970s more likely reflects the removal of longstanding prohibitions to public sector collective bargaining.

Consistent with this interpretation, the surge in public sector union density halted in the early 1980s. Public sector union density stood at 36.7 percent in 1983 and 37.5 percent in 2000, reflecting slight increases in union representation among state and local employees, largely offset by small decreases among federal employees (Hirsch and Macpherson, 2002). Since 1983 union density in the public sector has approximated the peak density achieved in the U.S. private sector some 30 years earlier. Whether public sector unionization ultimately follows the history of private sector unionization remains to be seen. But one should be cautious about making too much of legal influences. Persistent differences in unionization between the public and private sectors are more likely to reflect different incentives for management opposition. Notwithstanding the ability of taxpayers to vote with their feet, public sector employers face less product market competition than private sector managers. Use of the voice option may encourage vote-conscious politicians to monitor adherence to labor practices favored by public employees.

Regulation vs. Market Incentives for Management Opposition

The remainder of this section explores the roles of incentives and regulation in explaining variations in management opposition over time. The number of unfair labor practice charges filed by unions against employers per representation election (*CHARGES*) and the number of employees awarded back pay by the NLRB (*EMPBP*) are the measures of management opposition. Unfair labor practice charges are observed when an employer chooses arguably illegal behavior, and a union decides to challenge the behavior by filing a charge. Each party's behavior depends on an evaluation of the gains and losses from taking the action. Employers consider the additional profits from successfully resisting a union balanced against the costs incurred if they are found to have violated the NLRA. The fact that the NLRB applies compensatory rather than punitive damages informs this decision, as do the probabilities that the union will challenge the decision and the NLRB will find the charge meritorious. Unions also balance the benefits (e.g., higher wages if the challenge is successful) of challenging an employer's action against the costs. The odds that the NLRB will rule in the union's favor are again an important consideration. In contrast, back-pay awards to (illegally discharged) employees only occur when the NLRB seeks to remedy an actual violation.

These considerations underlie the analysis of two U.S. databases covering the period from the early 1970s to the late 1990s. A time series of annual data covering the private sector for 1970–1999 provides superior measurement of some variables but fewer observations. The following model is estimated on these data.

$$(MGT\ OPP)_t = a_0 + a_1\ WAGEDIFF_t + a_2\ TRADE_t + a_3\ RBPAY_t + a_4\ DELAY_t + e_t. \quad (1)$$

$WAGEDIFF_t$ measures the union-nonunion wage difference in the private sector in year t, adjusted for imputation or match bias.[8] As a measure of the added costs of a unionized work force to employers and the benefit of unions to workers, WAGEDIFF is a key incentive governing both employer and union choices governing strategic use of the NLRA. In order to remove the effects of other influences on the wages of union and nonunion employees, the variable is measured as the coefficient on a dummy variable for union status in a regression of the log of hourly earnings on variables for schooling, experience, gender, race, marital status, part-time status, region, industry, and occupation (Hirsch and Schumacher, 2004).

International competition provides further pressure on employer profits and may raise the consequences of granting union wage increases. Both import penetration of domestic markets and efforts to export to foreign markets provide incentives to keep labor costs low. The ratio of exports plus imports to gross domestic product in year t, $TRADE_t$, therefore represents the importance of international trade (U.S. President, 2002: Table B-1).[9] Both the trade share and the union wage premium rose in the late 1970s. After stabilizing in the early 1980s, the trade share resumed a steady but less rapid increase in the mid 1980s, while the wage premium declined beginning in the 1980s and then more sharply following 1994 (Figure 15.5).

No single variable will capture all aspects of regulatory activity under the NLRA. Two persistent issues concern the effectiveness of NLRB remedies in reducing unfair labor practices and the effect of the length of regulatory procedures on management opposition. Supreme Court rulings that corrective actions under the NLRA must be remedial rather than punitive constrain the Board's choice of remedies. Virtually all meritorious unfair labor practice charges therefore produce a cease and desist order from the NLRB. In discriminatory discharge cases, the Board may go further, awarding reinstatement and back pay (Figures 15.3 and 15.4). In the regression analysis of unfair labor practice charges, $RBAY_t$, real back pay per illegally discharged worker in year t, provides both an assessment of the effects of the NLRB's past efforts to redress employer unfair labor practices and a method to simulate the probable effects of a regime of punitive damages one of the most commonly advocated reforms of the NLRA. There is considerable evidence that the NLRB can influence the outcome of union representation elections and regulatory disputes by the expediency of its procedures. Several studies reviewed in Freeman and Medoff (1984: 234–35) and Flanagan (1987: 59–60) find that lengthy procedures favor management, encouraging strategic congestion of the regulatory system. The overall importance of the length of regulatory procedures is captured by DELAY_t, the number of days between the filing of an unfair labor practice charge and the issuance of an NLRB decision. In the late 1980s and late 1990s, this lag has been as long as two years. The annual reports of the NLRB provide data on $RBAY_t$ and $DELAY_t$.

The industry panel database provides more variation and permits controls for industry fixed effects. On the other hand, the EMPBP measure of management opposition is not available at the industry level, so the panel data are used to estimate:

$$CHARGES_{it} = a_0 + a_1\,WAGEDIFF_{it} + a_2\,TRADE_{it} + a_3\,RBPAY_t + a_4\,DELAY_t + \delta_i + e_{it} \quad (2)$$

in which i indexes industry and t indexes year. The industry-specific fixed effect, δ_i, may capture the effects of unobserved industry-specific differences in profitability or ideology that influence management opposition to unionization, unobserved industry-specific factors influencing union incentives to file charges, or measurement error in the observed incentive variables. Bratsberg and Ragan (2002) provide data on the net union-nonunion wage differential by industry (unadjusted for match bias) estimated from the Current Population Survey.[10] $TRADE_{it}$ is the ratio of imports plus exports to total shipments in an industry. These data were developed by Professor Robert Feenstra and are available at the National Bureau for Economic Research website for four-digit manufacturing industries for 1958–1994. The data were aggregated to 20 two-digit manufacturing industries for 1971–1994. Neither of the regulatory variables is available on an industry-specific basis. $DELAY_t$ continues to measure congestion in the regulatory system. Each additional charge filed delays the resolution of all unfair labor charges by the NLRB, irrespective of the industry in which it originates.

All variables are specified in natural logarithms. The results of the analysis of the aggregate time series appear in rows 1 through 5 of Table 15.4. All variables have the expected signs. Both the number of employer unfair labor practice charges filed by unions per representation election and the number of employees awarded back pay rise with the size of the union wage premium and the trade sector. Increased real back-pay awards limit management opposition, while longer periods of adjudication increase it. When included in the same regression, the effects of the two regulatory influences are more difficult to disentangle (regression 3), although the effects of back pay clearly are the dominant influence on $EMPBP$ (regression 5).

How have incentives and regulatory influences contributed to the evolution of the number of unfair labor practice charges per election since 1984? The growth of the trade sector from 18 to 24 percent of GDP constituted the main upward pressure on employer opposition in this period. In contrast to the late 1970s and early 1980s, the union wage premium declined from 1984 to 1999, offsetting about half the upward pressures from increased trade on unfair labor

Figure 15.5
Union Wage Premium, Trade/GDP Ratio

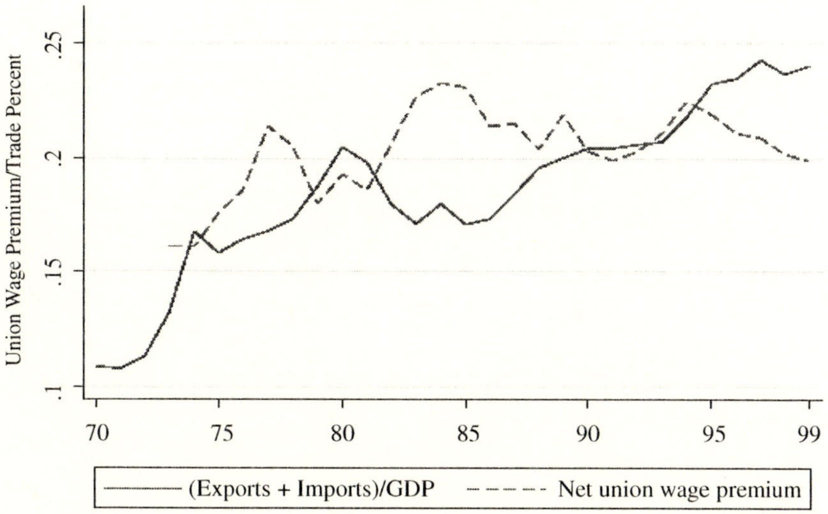

Source: Hirsch and Schumacher; U.S. President

practice charges (Figure 15.5). NLRB actions pulled in two directions; growing real back-pay awards per illegally discharged worker tended to reduce charges, while lengthening adjudication periods raised the number of charges.

More importantly, the impact of the NLRB is small in comparison to the role of incentives that are beyond its sphere of influence. Between 1984 and 1999, for example, the back pay awards countered only about 25–30 percent of the increased unfair labor practice charges associated with the growth of the trade sector. Put differently, if the NLRB were permitted to assess punitive damages (a frequent element of labor law reform proposals), it would have needed the authority to assess nearly quadruple damages to offset the effects of the growing international competition. If the union wage premium had been growing during the period, the multiple would have been even higher. The results on *DELAY* tell a similar story. In 1984, *DELAY* was 660 days. The period of adjudication would have had to decline to 104 days by 1999 to offset the effects of the growing trade sector. The lowest value of *DELAY* in the sample period is 327 days (1974). From a different perspective, the union wage premium declined by only half the amount necessary to offset the effects of trade. In short, the most powerful determinants of management opposition lie outside the sphere of influence of actual or contemplated regulatory actions.

The analyses of the same model on the panel of two-digit manufacturing industries for 1971–1994 appear in regressions 6–8 of Table 15.4. Preliminary

Table 15.4
Explaining Management Opposition
(robust standard errors)

Annual Time Series, 1973–99

Dept. Variables	Constant	lnWAGEDIFF	lnTRADE	Independent Variables lnRBPAY	lnDELAY	R^2	MSE	D-W
1. lnCHARGES	7.514 (.446)*	2.131 (.360)*	1.595 (.245)*	−.322 (.152)**		0.89	0.151	1.44
2. lnCHARGES	3.769 (1.981)**	1.584 (.520)*	1.429 (.233)*		0.424 (.197)**	0.88	0.156	1.14
3. lnCHARGES	5.18 (1.860)*	1.76 (.493)*	1.486 (.237)*	−0.235 (0.152)	0.251 (0.189)	0.90	0.149	1.28
4. lnEMPBP	14.636 (.403)*	1.616 (.301)*	1.569 (.203)*	−0.902 (.105)*		0.91	0.151	1.78
5. lnEMPBP	13.104 (1.799)*	1.373 (.448)*	1.497 (.193)*	−0.845 (.128)*	0.165 (0.192)	0.91	0.152	1.71
Industry Panel, 1971–94								
6. lnCHARGES	−1.12 (.202)*	−0.015 (0.038)	0.886 (.064)*	−0.421 (.081)*		0.40		
7. lnCHARGES	5.463 (.457)*	−0.034 (0.034)	0.523 (.071)*		0.863 (.085)*	0.49		
8. lnCHARGES	−5.166 (.508)*	−0.029 (0.034)	0.536 (.071)*	−0.11 (0.083)	0.807 (.094)*	0.50		

Note: */** p-value < .01 (.05). All variables defined in the text.

Sources: See text.

tests confirmed the presence of significant industry-specific fixed effects that were correlated with independent variables, so the regressions report fixed effects estimates. Exploratory regressions also indicated that *TRADE* is marginally superior to import penetration (the ratio of imports to total shipments) as a measure of the effects of international competition on management opposition. *TRADE, RBPAY,* and *DELAY* all have the expected signs, although the size of the trade effect is smaller than in the aggregate time series estimates. The effects of *RBPAY* and *DELAY* are again difficult to disentangle when both variables appear in the same regression (regression 8).

WAGEDIFF is not statistically significant in the panel data regressions, a finding that is difficult to reconcile with the aggregate time series results. The aggregate time series data confirm the tendency for union wage gains to stimulate management opposition identified in studies of earlier periods (Flanagan, 1987, 1989; Freeman, 1986). The fact that the *WAGEDIFF* series in the industry panel is not adjusted for match bias (see footnote 7) is unlikely to be the main source of the discrepancy. When the aggregate time series regressions are estimated with a *WAGEDIFF* variable that has not been corrected for match bias, the *WAGEDIFF* coefficient diminishes but remains statistically significant. There is a second difference between the samples: The aggregate time series and industry panel *WAGE-DIFF* variables are derived from hourly and weekly wage data, respectively. Differences in hours worked in the union and nonunion sectors may muddy the relationship between hourly rates and management opposition.

VIII. Management Resistance Abroad

Extrapolating the argument of *WDUD* to the rest of the world would imply that the widespread international decline of private sector union representation reflects a worldwide rise in management opposition to unions. Yet, a striking feature of international labor relations is that management opposition to unions is rarely observed in the rest of the industrialized world to the degree found in the U.S. Prominent, well-informed analyses of union decline in Europe consider the role of structural change in employment, the extent to which national legislation addresses threats to employment and income security, the role of unions in administering unemployment insurance systems, the political attitude of national governments towards unions, and macroeconomic conditions, but never mention management opposition as a factor in union membership losses (e.g., Calmfors et al., 2001). Legal restraint of management does not provide an explanation; foreign national labor law systems generally place fewer restraints on management resistance than the NRLA.

Instead, differences in management resistance around the world appear to reflect differences in bargaining structure that influence the extent to which union activity threatens the competitive position of employers. Countries with industry-wide bargaining structures, contract extension, and the like tend to take labor costs out of domestic competition by establishing a common floor for domestic producers. The labor cost floor often is set to permit less efficient firms to remain in business — a policy that thwarts departures from employer associations while permitting comparatively efficient firms to pay more than the negotiated minimum rate. In contrast, unions really can make a difference to an employer's competitive position in the decentralized bargaining structures found in North America, and employers resist such pressure. Labor laws can influence a country's collective bargaining structure, but in ways that are rarely addressed in proposals for labor law reform in the United States. Over the years, for example, the NLRA has facilitated the spread of decentralized bargaining by encouraging representation elections in bargaining units with relatively narrow employee communities of interest.

Union impact on competitive position varies widely among collective bargaining systems. Table 15.5 shows how widely the union wage impacts vary across countries. In five European countries with high union coverage or broad bargaining structures — France, Germany, Italy, the Netherlands, and Sweden — unions have no statistically perceptible effect on wages. Broad bargaining structures effectively weaken management incentives to oppose union representation by taking domestic labor costs out of competition, although they do not insulate management from international competition. During the same period, the wage premium in the United States averaged 17.6 percent, presenting a much stronger incentive for management opposition. But the bottom panel of Table 15.5 also shows that the United States is not the only country with a statistically and economically significant impact of unions on wages. Like the United States, most of the countries with significant union wage impacts have decentralized bargaining structures (Flanagan, 1999: Table 1). Why such union wage differentials do not provoke noticeable management opposition in these countries remains unresolved by research on comparative labor markets, although there is case study evidence that European labor laws do not thwart determined opposition by American multinational companies (Royle, 2002).

In short, there is little or no convincing evidence that the widespread decline in union representation outside of North America can be attributed to increasing management opposition. Nor do labor laws in most of these countries appear to be structured to limit management opposition. Rather the absence of management opposition appears to be related to bargaining arrangements that historically have removed most of the incentives to oppose union representation found in countries with decentralized bargaining arrangements. While U.S. labor law has contributed to the decentralization of bargaining, proposals for revising the NLRA typically address implementation details rather than the bargaining decentralization that provides the main incentive for employer opposition. As such they focus on symptoms — the strategic use of the NLRA by employers trying to avoid perceived threats to their competitive position — rather than the root causes of employer opposition.

Table 15.5
Union Wage Gaps, by Country

	Coefficient	Years
France	.029	1996-1998
Germany	.037	1994-1999
Italy	-.003	1994, 1998
Netherlands	-.006	1994-1995
Sweden	-.002	1994-1999
United States	0.176*	1994-1999
Australia	.118*	1994, 1998-1999
Austria	.150*	1994-95, 1998-1999
Canada	.083*	1997-1999
Denmark	.159*	1997-1998
Japan	.258*	1994-1996, 1998-1999
New Zealand	.099*	1994-1999
United Kingdom	.120 -.134*	1994-1999

Note: * p-value ≤ .05; Estimated from ordinary least squares regressions of log of earnings on age, age-squared, years of schooling, private sector dummy, hours and union status.

Source: Blanchflower and Bryson (2002), Tables 1, 4, 1F, and 1G.

VI. Conclusions

The view that declining unionization is a distinctive U.S. development different from the experience of our structurally similar neighbor, Canada, and different from the experience of the most advanced industrial countries in Europe and the Pacific clearly has not survived the 20 years since the publication of *WDUD*. If the alleged distinctiveness of U.S. experience supported the search for a cause in U.S. institutions 20 years ago, what now appears as a broad social trend almost as ubiquitous as unions themselves argues for explanations that cross international borders. Structural change is an appealing candidate, for the comparatively high income elasticity of demand for products and services produced in sectors where unions are sparse render declining union density a more or less inevitable consequence of economic growth. Yet, employment shifts from heavily unionized to lightly unionized sectors are only a minor source of the fall in aggregate unionization rates in most countries.

There is much stronger evidence of declining demand for union representation among nonunion workers. With many of the benefits formerly associated with union contracts now provided by public policy or modern human resource management policies and with global competition often constraining the gains achievable through domestic collective bargaining, many workers appear to doubt the ability of unions to provide what they want from their jobs and prefer less conflictual approaches to collective activities in the workplace. Management attitudes and actions can also influence worker demand for union representation, but most nonunion workers who prefer nonunion status have not experienced employer opposition in the heat of an organizing campaign.

To date, sustained management opposition to unions and collective bargaining has been largely a North American phenomenon and appears to play little, if any, role in other industrialized countries with declining unionization. Management opposition surely has something to do with lower union density in the United States, but there is no convincing research that demonstrates the scope of the influence. The opposition is multifaceted, and no one measure captures the various methods of resistance available to employers. Nevertheless, by several measures there appears to have been a significant increase in management opposition in the late–1970s that was largely complete by the mid–1980s. Since the mid–1980s the measures provide no consistent message that support a claim that a substantial part of private sector union decline over the past 20 years can be assigned to *increasing* management opposition.

The root cause of greater management opposition is relatively decentralized collective bargaining arrangements under which union compensation gains expose unionized employers to significant competitive pressure. In contrast, public policy discussion (along with *WDUD*) focuses on reforming collective bargaining law (the NLRA). But evidence reviewed and developed herein shows that while some of the proposed reforms are likely to have small effects on union election success, North American labor laws are not the root cause of the problem, except to the extent that the legal system produces more decentralized bargaining. Changes in the details of labor law can influence union win rates in representation elections, but not by enough to counter the attrition in union membership. In short, frequently advocated reforms in U.S. labor law are unlikely to reverse the decline in union density.

Efforts to forecast the major changes in union density in the United States have a notoriously poor record. Nonetheless, the evidence reviewed herein provides no basis for predicting a reversal of union fortunes within the foreseeable future, even if the political climate changed to permit some of the more frequently urged alterations in labor law. Given the growing decentralization of collective bargaining arrangements outside of North America and the continuing expansion of international trade, it seems more likely that discernible management resistance to unions may appear in other countries for the same reason that it emerges in the United States. There already is evidence of a growth of more hostile management attitudes, if not outright opposition, in the United Kingdom, which has experienced considerable decentralization of bargaining structure.

Notes

*   This project benefited from financial support from the Stanford Graduate School of Business, research assistance from Vidya Reddy and Alexei Tchistyi, and comments from William Gould, Bruce Kaufman, Melvin Reder, Leo Troy, and Jelle Visser.

1. Data available for extensive international comparisons, both here and in *WDUD*, report aggregate union density (combining private and public sectors). Where disaggregated data are available, private sector changes appear to dominate the trends.
2. Table 15.1 omits data on transition economies (available in Visser, 2003). While including data from these countries would provide an even stronger picture of declining unionization in Europe, the declines in these countries partially reflect shifts from union roles under central planning that were not typical of other countries in the comparison.
3. Questions on voting intentions are meaningless in countries without representation elections. Consistent with the views of U.S. trade unionists, however, 86 percent of Dutch union members agree that "unions are needed for collective interests, like the negotiation of collective pay agreements." Contrary to U.S. findings, the Dutch survey also found that most (71 percent) nonmembers shared this feeling. Yet, "[o]nly 29 percent [of all employees] thought membership personally useful, while 20 percent said that membership was not of any use to them (Visser, 2002: 413).
4. In the early twentieth century, for example, the AFL opposed minimum wage and maximum hours legislation (for men), compulsory health insurance, and unemployment insurance (Pelling, 1960: 123, 139; Ulman, 1961: 388).
5. The procedures are not unique, however. Canada and Japan have regulatory systems that resemble the NLRA, although in each case there are important differences in implementation (Weiler, 1983; Gould, 1984).
6. Given the greater importance of the public sector in Canadian unionization, comparisons of the overall union density rates can provide a misleading guide to union density in the private sectors of the United States and Canada (Troy, 1992).
7. Mandatory voting laws were adopted in Nova Scotia (1977), Alberta (1998), Newfoundland (1994), Ontario (1996), and Manitoba (1997). One province, British Columbia, reverted to card checks in 1993 after introducing mandatory elections in 1984.
8. The U.S. Bureau of Labor Statistics imputes wages to workers above a wage-reporting ceiling on the basis of several observable characteristics of such workers. Since union status is not one of the imputation characteristics, (a) unionized workers above the wage reporting ceiling are highly likely to be assigned the wage of a nonunion "twin," while (b) nonunion workers are somewhat likely to be assigned the wage of a union "twin." Both effects bias reported union-nonunion wage differences downward by about 5–6 percentage points in an average year. Hirsch and Schumacher (2003) provide a full discussion. As the unionized fraction of the labor force declines, effect (a) increases, and effect (b) decreases.
9. The *TRADE* variable was superior to a measure of import penetration, imports divided by GDP.
10. The estimates of $WAGEDIFF_{it}$ are obtained by regressing the natural logarithm of weekly earnings on union status and control variables for education, experience and its square, part-time status, region, occupation, and detailed industry for separate samples of employees in each industry i in each year t. See Bratsberg and Ragan (2002), who kindly provided the data, for details.

References

Blanchflower, David G. and Alex Bryson. "Changes Over Time in Union Relative Wage Effects in the UK and the US Revisited." NBER Working paper # 9395, December 2002.

Bratsberg, Bernt and James F. Ragan, Jr. "Changes in the Union Wage Premium by Industry Data and Analysis." *Industrial and Labor Relations Review* 56 (October 2002): 65–83.

Bronfenbrenner, Kate. "The Role of Union Strategies in NLRB Certification Elections." *Industrial and Labor Relations Review* 50 (January 1997): 195–212.

Calmfors, Lars, Alison Booth, Michael Burda, Daniele Checchi, Robin Naylor, and Jelle Visser. "The Future of Collective Bargaining in Europe." In Tito Boeri, Agar Brugiavini, and Lars Calmfors, eds. *The Role of Unions in the Twenty-First Century.* Oxford: Oxford University Press, 2001, pp. 1–134.

Committee on Future of Worker-Management Relations. *Final Report.* Washington, D.C.: U.S. Government Printing Office, 1994.

Cox, Archibald. *Law and the National Labor Policy.* Los Angeles: UCLA Institute of Industrial Relations, 1960.

Dark, Taylor E. "Debating Decline: The 1995 Race for the AFL-CIO Presidency." *Labor History* 40 (August 1999): 323–44.

Ebbinghaus, Bernhard and Jelle Visser. *Trade Unions in Western Europe since 1945.* New York: Grove's Dictionaries, 2000.

Farber, Henry S. "The Decline of Unionization in the U.S.: What Can Be Learned from Recent Experience?" *Journal of Labor Economics* 8 (January 1990): S75–S105.

_____ and Alan B. Krueger. "Union Membership in the U.S.: The Decline Continues." In Bruce Kaufman and Morris Kleiner, eds. *Employee Representation: Alternatives and Future Directions.* Madison, Wisc.: Industrial Relations Research Association, 1993, pp. 105–34.

_____ and Bruce Western. "Accounting for the Decline of Unions in the Private Sector, 1973–1998." In James T. Bennett and Bruce E. Kaufman, eds. *The Future of Private Sector Unionism in the United States.* Armonk, N.Y.: M. E. Sharpe, 2002, pp. 28–58.

Fiorito, Jack. "Human Resource Management Practices and Worker Desires for Union Representation." In James T. Bennett and Bruce E. Kaufman, eds. *The Future of Private Sector Unionism in the United States.* Armonk, N.Y.: M. E. Sharpe, 2002, pp. 205–26.

Flanagan, Robert J. "Compliance and Enforcement Decisions Under the National Labor Relations Act." *Journal of Labor Economics* 7 (July 1989): 257–80.

_____. *Labor Relations and the Litigation Explosion.* Washington, D.C.: Brookings Institution, 1987.

_____. "Macroeconomic Performance and Collective Bargaining: An International Perspective." *Journal of Economic Literature* 37 (September 1999): 1150–75.

Freeman, Richard B. "The Effect of the Union Wage Differential on Management Opposition and Union Organizing Success." *American Economic Review* 78 (May 1986): 92–96.

_____ and James Medoff. *What Do Unions Do?* New York: Basic Books, 1984.

_____ and Joel Rodgers. *What Workers Want.* Ithaca, N.Y.: Cornell University Press, 1999.

Getman, Jack. "Another Look at Labor and the Law." *Conference on Future of Labor Unions,* Washington, D.C., April 2003.

Gould, William B. *Japan's Reshaping of American Labor Law.* Cambridge: MIT Press, 1984.

_____. *An Agenda for Labor Law Reform.* Cambridge: MIT Press, 1993.

Hassel, Anke. "The Erosion of the German System of Industrial Relations." *British Journal of Industrial Relations* 37 (September 1999): 483–505.

Hirsch, Barry T. and David A. Macpherson. *Union Membership and Earnings Data Book: Compilations from the Current Population Survey* (2002 Edition). Washington, D.C.: Bureau of National Affairs, 2002.

Hirsch, Barry T. and Edward J. Schumacher. "Private Sector Union Density and the Wage Premium: Past, Present, and Future." In James T. Bennett and Bruce E. Kaufman, eds. *The Future of Private Sector Unionism in the U.S.* Armonk, N.Y.: M. E. Sharpe, 2002, pp. 92–128.

_____. "Match Bias in Wage Gap Estimates Due to Earnings Imputation." *Journal of Labor Economics* 22 (July 2004): 689–722.

Johnson, Susan. "Card Check or Mandatory Representation Vote? How the Type of Union Recognition Procedure Affects Union Certification Success." *Economic Journal* 112 (April 2002): 344–61.

Logan, John. "Consultants, Lawyers and the 'Union Free' Movement in the USA Since the 1970s." *Industrial Relations Journal* 33 (April 2002): 197–214.

National Labor Relations Board, *Annual Report,* various issues.

Naylor, Robin. "A Social Custom Model of Collective Action." *European Journal of Political Economy* 6 (October 1990): 201–16.

Neuman, George R. and Ellen Rissman. "Where Have All the Union Members Gone?" *Journal of Labor Economics* 2 (April 1984): 175–92.

OECD. *Employment Outlook.* Paris: OECD, July 1991, 1994.

Pelling, Henry. *American Labor.* Chicago: University of Chicago Press, 1960.

Pencavel, John. "The Surprising Retreat of Union Britain." *Stanford Institute for Economic Policy Research Paper* No. 00–31, March 2001.

Riddell, Chris. "Union Suppression and Certification Success." *Canadian Journal of Economics* 34 (May 2001): 396–410.

_____ and W. Craig Riddell. "Changing Patterns of Unionization: The North American Experience." Discussion Paper 1–23, Department of Economics, University of British Columbia, June 2001.

Royle, Tony. "Worker Representation Under Threat? The McDonald's Corporation and the Effectiveness of Statutory Works Councils in Seven European Union Countries." *Comparative Labor Law and Policy Journal* 22 (Winter/Spring 2001): 395–431.

Thomason, Terry. "The Effect of Accelerated Certification Procedures on Union Organizing Success in Ontario." *Industrial and Labor Relations Review* 47 (January 1994): 207–26.

Troy, Leo. "Is the U.S. Unique in the Decline of Private Sector Unionism?" *Journal of Labor Research* 11 (Spring 1990): 111–43.

_____. "Convergence in International Unionism, etc.: The Case of Canada and the USA." *British Journal of Industrial Relations* 30 (March 1992): 1–43.

Ulman, Lloyd. "The Development of Trades and Labor Unions." In Seymour Harris, ed. *American Economic History.* New York: McGraw-Hill, 1961, pp. 366–419.

U.S. President. *Economic Report of the President.* Washington, D.C.: U.S. Government Printing Office, 2002.

Visser, Jelle. "Why Fewer Workers Join Unions in Europe: A Social Custom Explanation of Membership Trends." *British Journal of Industrial Relations* 40 (September 2002): 403–30.

_____. "Unions and Unionism Around the World." In John Addison and Claus Schnabel, eds. *International Handbook of Trade Unions.* Brookfield, Vt.: Edward Elgar, 2003, pp. 366–414.

Voos, Paula B. "Trends in Union Organizing Expenditures, 1953–1977." *Industrial and Labor Relations Review* 38 (July 1984): 52–63.

Weil, David. "Are Mandated Health and Safety Committees Substitutes for or Supplements to Labor Unions?" *Industrial and Labor Relations Review* 52 (April 1999): 339–60.

Weiler, Paul. "Promises to Keep: Securing Workers' Rights to Self-Organization under the NLRA." *Harvard Law Review* 96 (June 1983): 1769–827.

16

Organized Labor's Political Scorecard

Marick F. Masters and John T. Delaney

I. Introduction

In Chapter 13 of their book, Richard Freeman and James Medoff (F&M) observed that "[l]ike other interest groups, labor organizations operate in the political sphere as well as in the economic marketplace, seeking as best they can to obtain outcomes beneficial to their members and, in their view, to society as a whole" (1984: 191). This observation set the stage for an analysis of organized labor's political activities and power that led F&M to conclude (p. 206):

> Union political power—myth or reality? Measured by resources used in the political arena, influence on congressional voting, and contributions to the passage of general social legislation, unions are . . . [a] political powerhouse. . . . Measured by ability to obtain special interest legislation favorable to unions over the opposition of business groups, however, unions are far less of a powerhouse. The reality is that unions have considerable political power in some areas. The myth is that they can use this power for the purpose of strengthening unionism and union economic power without general public consent.

Over the two decades since F&M made their assessment, political action has arguably become more salient to organized labor as union membership and bargaining power have declined significantly. Since the election of President George W. Bush in 2000, the U.S. economy has lost nearly three million manufacturing jobs (many held by union workers); American firms have capitalized on productivity improvements to meet market demand with fewer workers; and the government has adopted a host of public-policy initiatives hostile to union workers, such as the narrowing of eligibility for overtime pay, imposition of onerous union financial disclosure requirements, and waiver of union rights in large parts of the federal service. The situation has stimulated a massive political response. At the AFL-CIO's annual Executive Council meeting in March 2004, John Sweeney pledged labor's biggest political effort ever in 2004 to influence the national elections: "America's unions are united for the biggest and earliest mobilization effort for the 2004 elections in the union movement's history" (Sweeney, March 10, 2004).

Accordingly, on the twentieth anniversary of F&M's classic book, it seems appropriate to take stock of what labor has done politically, what we have learned about union political action and influence, and how such involvement may have changed in the larger institutional and social context of American society. In this study, our purpose is to update and expand on F&M's assessments of union political action. First, we put U.S. union political action into institutional and social perspective in order to highlight its limited political objectives. Second, we present a strategic-choice framework to show the array of union strategies, including political action. Third, we review research on union political action that has emerged since F&M examined the topic. Fourth, we present new evidence to update labor's political scorecard on the electoral and lobbying fronts. Finally, we speculate about the wisdom of political action as a strategy for union revival.

II. U.S. Trade Unionism in Perspective: Political Implications

Political action is one of the strategies unions use to achieve their goals. The nature and scope of organized labor's political action depends on how unions see their role in society and how society views the labor movement (Bok and Dunlop, 1970). As a result, for more than a century, conceptualizations of unions have sought to explain political and nonpolitical objectives. For example, theorists such as Sidney and Bea-trice Webb (1894), Robert Hoxie (1920), and Richard Hyman (2001) offered distinctive explanations of union political activities (Figure 16.1).

As the Webbs' (1894: 1) saw it, political action (or legal enactment) was one of three methods used by unions to improve the lot of workers. Whereas "mutual insurance" allowed unions to aid needy members directly and "collective bargaining" focused on negotiating agreements with employers covering represented workers, "legal enactment" focused on securing laws mandating general and specific work regulations at all levels of government. Hoxie (1920) identified four different union agendas to characterize the operating approach of organized labor. According to Hoxie (1920: 45), business unionism, which was characteristic "of local and national craft and compound craft organizations," stressed trade rather than class consciousness and relied principally on collective bargaining to improve working conditions. What were referred to as "friendly" or "uplift" unions, behaved more idealistically, emphasizing mutual insurance. Revolutionary unionism represented a radical strand that stressed class-based political action rather than collective bargaining and mutual insurance. Lastly, Hoxie depicted a "predatory" type of union, which was incurably selfish and self-gratifying.

Writing many years later, Hyman (2001: 1) identified "three ideal types of . . . trade unionism." First, he noted that some unions acted primarily as economic agents and resembled Hoxie's business unionism. A second union type displayed an anti-capitalist purpose. These unions emphasized "militancy and socio-political mobilization" (Hyman, 2001: 2). Hyman's third ideal union type

Figure 16.1
Alternative Types of Unionism and Political Implications

Source	Perspective	Conceptualization	Methodology
Webbs	British Unions	Trade Unionism "Common Rule"	Mutual Insurance / Collective Bargaining / Legal Enactment
Hoxie	U.S. Unions	Business Unionism / Friendly or Uplift / Revolutionary / Predatory	Collective Bargaining / Mutual Insurance / Class/Political Mobilization / Selfish Gain
Hyman	European Unions	Business Unionism / Social Integration / Anti-Capitalist	Collective Bargaining / Legal Enactment / Class-Political Mobilization

Social Integration

Business Unionism

Anti-Capitalist

focused on "social integration," stressing evolutionary rather than revolutionary change. Hyman posited that unions move within this "triangle" of union types as need and circumstance required.

These conceptualizations reveal that the institutional character of unions has direct political implications. Pure business unionism eschews political involvement, à la Gompers' doctrine of voluntarism (Zeigler, 1964). At the other extreme, revolutionary unions act politically to disrupt and overthrow the capitalistic economic order. Between these polar ends, union political activism may take many shapes and forms. In Hyman's (2001: 3) framework, socially integrative unions emerge as integral parts of political parties with "a priority for gradual improvement in social welfare and social cohesion, and hence a self-image as representatives of social interests."

A Continuum of Political Involvement

From these perspectives, the boundaries of union political action may be identified. Where unions operate on this continuum is partly a function of the interplay of the surrounding economic and political systems (Greenstone, 1977), as well as the legal regulation of union political activities, which reflects the broader distribution of economic and political power. At the same time, we should not assume that union political activism is strictly a result of environmental forces. Unions exercise some degree of choice over how much to engage politically and the manner in which such engagement is manifested. As Hyman (2001: 4–5) observed:

> Hence in practice, union identities and ideologies are normally located *within* the triangle. All three models typically have some purchase; but in most cases, actually existing unions have tended to incline towards an often contradictory admixture of two of three ideal types. In other words, they have oriented to one side of the triangle: between class and market; between market and society; and between society and class. These orientations reflect both material circumstances and ideological traditions. In times of change and challenge for union movements, a reorientation can occur.

At one boundary is noninvolvement in politics. This option may reflect a matter of tactical convenience more than ideology as when the AFL-CIO refused to endorse a presidential candidate in the 1972 election. Its eschewal of George McGovern's candidacy signaled the federation's disapproval of the Democratic Party's leftist bent that year. At the opposite boundary, labor may participate through an independent political party. An examination of the biographies of the key activists in today's American Labor Party indicates the involvement of many trade unionists. In between the extremes, unions may select alternative routes, which vary in terms of extensiveness and partisanship. They may opt to participate minimally on a nonpartisan basis. In contrast, they may participate extensively with partisan fervor. It is within these modes, between noninvolvement and independent party that unions behave as *interest groups*.

An Interest-Group View of U.S. Unions

The economic harshness of the Great Depression forced organized labor to abandon the twin philosophies of business unionism and voluntarism, which had "developed in a period characterized by hostile public sentiment and antagonistic employer attitudes" (Zeigler, 1964: 140). Since the New Deal, organized labor has engaged in various forms of electoral and lobbying activities to influence public policy. As a matter of both choice and realism, unions have operated as interest groups within the political system, falling between the market and social-integration points on Hyman's triangle.

As interest groups, however, unions have tilted heavily towards extensive partisan involvement. In fact, organized labor has become an integral part of the Demo-cratic Party, taking on many traditional party functions, such as financing campaigns and mobilizing voters. This union-party nexus has amounted to what Greenstone (1977: 361) labeled "a *partial* equivalence to the Social Democratic . . . party-trade union alliance in much of Western Europe."

The contemporary alliance between organized labor and the Democratic Party emerged as a result of two factors. First, government became increasingly involved in economic and other concerns that affect unions and their members. As Barbash (1956: 246) commented: "Unions are concerned with government at all levels because there is scarcely a phase of wages, hours, working conditions, labor-management relations, union functioning, and the general social and economic welfare which government does not affect in one way or another." Governmental intervention did not make political action "the *central* concern of most unions" (Barbash, 1956: 246) but rather made it largely unavoidable. Second, labor found an ideologically compatible partner in the Democratic Party, as a whole (Barbash, 1947). Simply put, organized labor has never had a sufficient independent base to win elections on any significant scale. As Barbash (1956: 1) noted: "No political democracy has offered a more hostile environment to unionism than has the United States." Labor brought needed organizational resources and skills to a party that advocated expanding political rights and economic and social justice through progressive, yet limited, government involvement. Like any marriage, unions and the Democrats have had their share of disagreements. More important, however, they have developed inseparable political fates.

III. Strategic Choices and Industrial Relations System Outcomes

Unions make various strategic choices to influence outcomes of the industrial relations (IR) system (Kochan et al., 1984). Borrowing from organizational theory, IR scholars have argued that the actors in the system (government, employers, and unions) influence important outcomes through their strategic actions. Kochan et al. (1986: 13) stated that: "*choice* and discretion on the part of labor, management and government affect the course and structure of industrial relations systems." Increasingly, these choices have become interrelated. Labor has had to become more adept at leveraging one strategy to maximize the effect of other options as the political, economic, and industrial relations systems have grown more interconnected (Katz et al., 2003).

In recent years, IR scholars have tried to explain why unions make certain strategic choices. Campling and Michelson (1998) presented an integrated strategic choice and resource dependency framework to explain why unions merged. Katz et al. (2003) developed a contingency and resource dependency model to assess how the Communications Workers of America (CWA) responded strategically to a changing environment. They (2003: 587) found "that the CWA turned to increased political action, growth, and interorganizational linkages to deal with heightened environmental complexity and uncertainty," thereby recognizing strategic interdependencies.

We employ a strategic-choice framework to highlight how political action fits into organized labor's broader strategic picture. To achieve a variety of common objectives, unions may choose from several options. The choices they make, though constrained, are influenced by environmental and organizational contingencies and resource dependencies. Unions respond to change by adapting strategies to maintain the flow of resources on which they depend for success. Obviously, the critical resource for unions is dues-paying membership. With the IR system and wider political economy so integrated, unions will need to be strategically adroit and flexible. The nature, scope, and effect of one strategic choice hinges on the viability of the alternative choices.

Unions' strategic choices are motivated by various factors. Union density, as mentioned, is an essential precondition. Organized labor's ability to raise working and living standards, promote social and economic justice, and expand political democracy depends on its relative presence and strength in the workforce. We do not argue a perfectly linear relationship between membership and power but rather that a shrinking base generally diminishes economic and political influence, unless offset by other factors, such as the emergence of strong public and social sympathy. At a certain point, declining union membership, as has occurred in the U.S. private sector over the past several decades, inevitably raises questions about the relevance of organized labor in society.

To achieve these goals, unions may pursue several options, which vary in terms of their internal or external and immediate or longer-term focus. Relevant strategies include: organizing, collective bargaining, restructuring (e.g., merging with another union), community action, legal or regulatory initiatives, and political action. Union choices depend on resource dependencies and environmental and organizational contingencies. In this regard, unions rely on numerous constituencies or stakeholders to maintain and expand their essential membership and thereby affect other relevant outcomes. They depend, for example, on government to create a legal environment friendly to organizing and collective bargaining. They depend on employers to negotiate in good faith in order to improve working conditions. In addition, unions need alliances with social and financial institutions to promote the good-faith conduct of employers. Furthermore, they need alliances with other interest groups, such as civil rights activists and environmentalists, to influence lawmakers on important economic and social issues. In a similar vein, unions require support from their current members and the willingness of nonunion workers to organize.

These resource dependencies, in turn, are affected by the nature of the environment and the organizational conditions of unions. A union such as the CWA, which faced an environment of rapid technological change amid the extensive legal breakup of the telecommunications industry, had to change strategy as its membership base was being seriously eroded. Political and legal action with other interest groups became essential to influencing employer conduct and creating organizing opportunities.

In sum, unions select from a menu of options to influence a more or less common set of objectives. From this perspective, political action emerges as one among several strategies in the union arsenal. It is a means of securing public policies that impose union goals on society. These policies, in turn, affect broader outcomes. We can therefore draw a scorecard in which union political action is assessed in terms of its (1) mobilization of resources and support (2) aimed at achieving public policies (3) instrumental to the goals of union strength, higher working and living standards, social and economic justice, and political democracy.

IV. The Legal Regulation of Union Political Action

The participation of union and business interests in the political process has long provoked controversy (Corrado, 2003; Mann and Corrado, 2003; Sabato, 1984). As a result, Congress has enacted various laws since 1943 to restrict union political involvement, particularly with respect to the financing of congressional and presidential campaigns. During the past 20 years in particular, several major developments occurred in the area of campaign financing that forced Congress to enact major reform in 2002. These changes have significant implications for how organized labor participates in elections.

Electoral Regulation

In general, Congress has focused on regulating participation in electoral activities rather than on involvement in lobbying activities. Since the early 1970s, two federal election laws have prevailed: the 1971 Federal Election Campaign Act (FECA) and the Bipartisan Campaign Reform Act (BCRA) of 2002, popularly known as McCain-Feingold. The FECA, as amended in 1974, allowed unions (and corporations) to establish political action committees (PACs) to raise money on a voluntary basis and contribute PAC funds to federal candidates under a $5,000 cap for primary and general elections (i.e., $10,000 maximum for both). The amended FECA also allowed unions to spend their treasury money on various electioneering activities aimed at union members and the general public. Basically, the FECA allowed unions to engage in partisan election activities when targeted to their membership. To use treasury funds to influence the wider public, the law required that the money be spent on at least nominally nonpartisan activities.

In the late 1980s and through the 1990s, two related political developments occurred which emasculated the FECA. To escape the limits on treasury contributions, corporations and unions took advantage of a loophole that allowed unlimited contributions to the nonfederal accounts of national party organizations, such as the Democratic National Committee (Rosenberg, 1996). These donations had two intended effects: freeing up money for federal accounts and financing partisan state-party activities that benefited federal candidates. This "soft money," so called because it escaped federal regulation, rapidly surpassed "hard money" (PAC contributions) as the preferred method of interest-group campaign financing.

"Issue advocacy" emerged as another legal escapist device used to channel treasury money to influence the wider public through media advertisements (principally radio and television). Businesses and unions could pay for advertisements that portrayed federal candidates in positive or negative light, as long

Table 16.1
Federal Restrictions on Union Political Action

Type of Activity	FECA		BCRA	
	Hard Money[a]	Soft Money[b]	Hard Money[a]	Soft Money[b]
Financial Contributions				
Candidate	Permitted $5,000 per Candidate per Election	Prohibited	Permitted $5,000 per Candidate per Election	Prohibited
National Party	Permitted $15,000 Cap	Permitted	Permitted $15,000 Cap	Prohibited
Electioneering Communications[c]	NA	NA	Permitted	Prohibited 60/30 Days before election
Express Advocacy[c]	Permitted	Prohibited	Permitted	NA
Issue Advocacy[c]	Permitted	Permitted	Permitted	NA
Internal Communications[d]				
Partisan	Permitted	Permitted	Permitted	Permitted
Nonpartisan	Permitted	Permitted	Permitted	Permitted

Notes: [a]"Hard money" is more specifically regulated by federal election law that can be contributed, within specified limits, to political candidates and parties. Because it may be contributed, it must be raised on voluntary basis. Unions and corporations are generally limited to raising hard money from their so-called "restricted class," which, in the case of unions, includes union members and their families. [b]Soft money is unregulated by federal election law. It emerged from a loophole in the Federal Election Campaign Act of 1971. The loophole allowed individuals, unions, and corporations to give unrestricted amounts to national political parties "nonfederal" accounts. Such money could be used to finance issue advocacy and party-building activities. Because this money was technically unregulated, unions and corporations could make unrestricted contributions from their regular treasury accounts, funded in the case of unions by dues. [c]"Electioneering communications" is a term defined in the Bipartisan Campaign Reform Act of 2002. It is "any broadcast, cable or satellite communication which fulfills each of the following conditions: The communication refers to a clearly identified candidate. . . . The communication is publicly distributed. . . . The communication is distributed during a certain time period before an election. . . . In the case of Congressional candidates only, the communication is targeted to the relevant electorate" (U.S. FEC 2003:8–9). This term is internationally more encompassing than the terminology that emerged under the FECA. "Express advocacy" is a communication that refers unambiguously to a federal candidate, leaving the listening audience with the clear impression that they should oppose or support that candidate on Election Day. "Issue advocacy" is a communication that advocates a particular political position or cause, often associated with a party or candidate, but not specifically urging the election or defeat of a candidate. In practice, it is often difficult to distinguish between express and issue advocacy. Under the BCRA, unions and corporations cannot make electioneering communications in the restricted time period: 60 days before a general election and 30 days before a primary election. Electioneering communications are made to unrestricted classes, that is, the general public. [d]"Internal communications" is a term referring to partisan or non-partisan communications to a restricted class. As mentioned above, in the case of unions, the restricted class is composed of union members and their families.

Source: U.S. Federal Election Commission (2003).

as the ads did not specifically endorse one candidate or urge people to vote for one. A blurry distinction emerged between "issue" and "partisan," or "express" advocacy. The viewing public clearly understood the partisan intent, but the ad sponsors avoided legal culpability.

Eventually, soft money and issue advocacy precipitated a vicious spiral of unrestrained political spending, which provoked a public outcry for reform. Congress responded in 2002 by passing McCain-Feingold (see Table 16.1, which compares the major provisions of the BCRA to the FECA regulating union political action). In brief, the BCRA banned so-called soft-money contributions and prohibited union-sponsored electioneering communications, either issue or partisan, 60 days before a general election and 30 days before a primary contest.

Lobbying Regulation

Federal law allows unions to finance lobbying Congress and the White House as long as such lobbying does not involve bribery and is properly reported. Unions and companies may lobby for or against any legislation before Congress or under review at the White House. In an attempt to promote fuller public disclosure of lobbying activities by interest groups, Congress passed the Lobbying Disclosure Act of 1995, requiring unions and companies to list their lobbyists, identify the issues on which they lobby, and estimate the amount spent for such purposes. Accordingly, we now have broad disclosure requirements covering labor and corporate electoral and lobbying expenditures.

V. Insights from Freeman and Medoff

What did we learn from F&M about union political action? F&M examined the electoral record of union-endorsed candidates over the 1970–1980 period; labor's record of legislative support on key bills voted on in Congress between 1947–1982; and the extent to which union density influenced electoral and legislative support. Six lessons emerged from their research:

1. *Political Mode.* Unions engaged in politics principally as interest groups to influence both the "special" and wider "social" interests of their memberships.
2. *Tactical Variety.* As interest groups, unions pursued various electoral and lobbying activities, within a two-party political structure, to elect supportive candidates and influence lawmakers.
3. *Resource Advantage.* Labor's relative advantage in politics rested on its ability to mobilize voters, not in contributing money, where business readily outspent it.
4. *Density and Influence.* Labor's political influence depended on its density and hence its direct and indirect base within the electorate at large. A decline in density implied a drop in influence over election outcomes and lawmakers' legislative preferences.

5. *Labor's Legislative Record.* Labor garnered more legislative support on broad social issues than special interests where it is possible to form wider coalitions to combat political opposition.
6. *Political Power.* F&M concluded that unions have considerable political power in some areas, but that organized labor was unable to use that power to strengthen unions without public consent.

F&M underscored their bottom-line conclusion in a brief case study on the defeat of Labor Law Reform legislation in the 1977–1978 Congress. To strengthen themselves institutionally, unions had sought to reform labor law to expedite certification procedures; stiffen penalties on employers who violated the law; and grant labor greater access to employees in organizing campaigns. When Jimmy Carter captured the White House in 1976, labor moved quickly to advance this proposal. The time seemed propitious, as Democrats controlled both houses of Congress by large majorities and labor had vigorously supported Carter to end eight years of Republican occupation of the presidency.

Despite high hopes and vigorous lobbying, however, organized labor failed. The reform bill died in the Senate. The principal reason, according to F&M, was fierce business opposition. This *pro-union* legislation invited trench warfare in Congress. Business united in its opposition and galvanized support among the ideological kindred, while isolating labor as a selfishly motivated special interest: "When it comes to special interest legislation, unions do not face an amorphous majority but, rather, powerful business special interest groups" (Freeman and Medoff, 1984: 201). More broadly, labor lacked sufficient density and broad-based interest-group support to prevail on an issue so clearly tied to its "special" concerns. One lesson of this experience was that even in the best of times, unions are limited in their ability to use political power to achieve narrow objectives.

VI. A Literature Update

Over the 20 years since F&M's book was published, researchers from many disciplines have examined union political action. As has been the case historically, however, over that time, the volume of research on union political action is small relative to the amount of research on other union activities (e.g., strikes, collective bargaining). In Table 16.2, we classify empirical research on union political action into five categories: (1) general examinations of union political action; (2) union member voter turnout and preferences; (3) union PAC allocations to congressional candidates; (4) labor's legislative records in Congress, including the effects of PAC money and union density on legislators' votes; and (5) case studies on issues that have provoked intense controversy, such as congressional voting on passage of the North American Free Trade Agreement (NAFTA) in 1993, labor law reform efforts, and striker replacement initiatives.

Table 16.2
Selected Research on Union Political Action, 1984–2004

General	Voting Behavior	PAC Allocations	Legislative Record and Voting	Empirical Case Studies
Masters and Delaney (1984, 1985, 1987b)	Patton and Marrone (1984)	Gopian (1984)	Peltzman (1984)	1) *NAFTA*
Goldfield (1986)	Juravich and Shergold (1988)	Masters and Delaney (1984)	Wright (1985)	Kahane (1996)
Fields, Masters and Thacker (1987)	Delaney, Masters and Schwochau (1988; 1990)	Masters and Zardkoohi (1984, 1987)	Masters and Delaney (1987a)	Steagall and Jennings (1996)
Fiorito (1987)	Uhlaner (1989)	Grier and Munger (1986)	Masters and Zardkoohi (1987)	Box-Steffensmeier, Arnold and Zorn (1997)
Coleman (1988)	Sousa (1993)	Wilhite and Theilmann (1986)	Saltzman (1987)	Engel and Jackson (1998)
Delaney, Fiorito, and Masters (1988)	Clark (1998)	Endersby and Munger (1992)	Wilhite (1988)	Francia (2001)
Masters, Atkin, and Delaney (1989)	Jacobson (1999)	Hurd and Sohl (1992)	Wright (1990)	2) *Striker Replacement*
Delaney (1991)	Clark and Masters (2001)	Masters (1999)	Moore, Chachere, Curtis, and Gordon (1995)	Logan (2003a)
Delaney and Masters (1991)	Radcliff and Davis (2000)	Masters and Jones (1999)	Burns, Francia, and Herrnson (2000)	3) *Labor Law Reform*
Form (1995)	Radcliff (2001)		Dark (1996; 2000)	Kochan (1995)
Masters and Atkin (1996a; 1996b)	Leighley and Nagler (2003)			Logan (2003b)
Masters (1998)				4) *Paycheck Protection*
Dark (1999)				Hogler (1998)
Delaney, Fiorito, and Jarley (1999)				Clark (1999)
Dark (2000)				
Asher, Heberlig, Ripley, and Snyder (2001)				
Bennett and Taylor (2001)				
Wilson (2002)				
Zullo (2002, 2003)				
Masters (2004)				

Our review of the research yields several conclusions, some of which can be made with more confidence than others. Generally speaking, the research corroborates and extends F&M's findings. First, unions have continued to engage in various electoral and lobbying activities to affect public policies (Masters, 2004; Delaney and Masters, 1991). Union political activities have become more sophisticated and extensive, however, to offset a declining membership base (Asher et al., 2001; Dark, 1999). While unions, for the most part, have remained strongly allied with the Democratic Party, labor leaders have become increasingly disappointed with the positions of Democrats on key labor matters (e.g., free trade). Were it not for the openly hostile attitude toward unions displayed by many conservative Republicans, organized labor would probably support Democrats less.

Second, unions have encouraged voter turnout and voting for labor-endorsed candidates, who are primarily Democratic (Clark and Masters, 2001; Sousa, 1993; Juravich and Shergold, 1988; Patton and Marrone, 1984). Research has demonstrated that this strategy is effective as union members and their families are more likely to vote for candidates endorsed by labor than are nonmembers (Zullo, 2003; Delaney et al., 1990, 1988). At the same time, the persistent decline in union density over the past two decades has contributed to a more general decline in voter turnout (Leighley and Nagler, 2003). To a certain extent, organized labor has offset its declining density by raising turnout among its members and union households (Masters, 2004), though labor's effect on election outcomes has suffered from predictable defections to socially conservative candidates (Clark and Masters, 2001; Clark, 1998).

Third, research generally supports an association between PAC contributions and legislative voting (Moore et al., 1995; Saltzman, 1987). Similarly, it shows a correlation between union density and pro-union legislative voting (Box-Steffensmeier et al., 1997; Kahane, 1996). Since F&M wrote, however, the growth of political spending by corporations has dwarfed union political donations. In such an environment, it is impossible for organized labor to "buy" legislative support from Congress. Moreover, union density remains too limited and geographically concentrated to sway sizable numbers of Democratic officeholders today. This has meant that unions get marginally smaller returns from their ever-increasing campaign donations.

Fourth, organized labor's legislative success has varied systematically across the type of issue under consideration. Significantly, unions have enjoyed no success in gaining new *pro-union* legislation over the past 20 years (Logan, 2003a, 2003b), though they have succeeded in blocking many efforts to roll back protective labor laws, such as the Davis-Bacon Act (Dark, 1999), and to advance anti-union laws, such as paycheck protection efforts (Masters, 2004; Hogler, 1998). Unions have had limited success, at certain times, in advancing legislation promoting the general welfare and social justice, such as raising the minimum wage. In general, organized labor's legislative record has correlated strongly with party control in Congress (Masters and Delaney, 1987a). In recent years, Republican control of both Houses of Congress has put unions on the defensive.

Fifth, empirical examinations of specific legislative case studies are almost uniform in reporting on labor's losing causes. Although unions were able to defeat the Team Act in Congress and forestall efforts to enact paycheck protection (Hogler, 1998), such victories seemed inconsequential as unions lost their critical political battles. For various reasons, vehement union opposition to NAFTA did little more than slow down approval of the free trade law (Francia, 2001; Engel and Jackson, 1998; Box-Steffensmeier et al., 1997; Steagall and Jennings, 1996; Kahane, 1996). Logan's (2003a) thoughtful analysis of the union campaign for striker replacement legislation similarly revealed the lack of union political power in the face of united business opposition, increasingly conservative electoral politics, and growing perceptions of the weakness of potential union sanctions on defecting politicians. Even a concerted effort for labor law reform, initiated under a pro-labor president at a time when Democrats controlled both houses of Congress, went down to defeat. Recommendations from the blue-ribbon Dunlop Commission (Kochan, 1995) were essentially dead on arrival (Logan, 2003b). In the end, each of the cases illustrates that unions were facing an uphill battle, as their positions were not seen as reflecting the national interest. At the start of the twenty-first century, business was the darling of the American people, and union efforts were viewed as attempts to constrain capitalism.

Sixth, because the union movement has been unsuccessful at increasing the number of organized workers during favorable economic conditions, it has intensified its political operations. Political action at times appears to be the primary emphasis of organized labor today (Troy, 2001: 245). For example, the 2004 presidential election promises to showcase the most sophisticated and expensive union political effort that has ever occurred. The payoffs from this political strategy are difficult to measure. Whereas union-friendly politicians have done poorly in many recent elections, it is unclear what the political landscape would look like if organized labor had not undertaken monumental political action.

VII. The Political Scorecard: Recent Evidence

To understand organized labor's record, we calculate a current political scorecard by examining several dimensions of union political efforts. First, we examine aggregate patterns in union electoral and lobbying spending. Second, we compare labor's political involvement to other groups' participation. Third, we examine recent evidence on the voting behavior of union members. Fourth, we present labor's legislative record based on congressional votes used by the AFL-CIO to rate lawmakers.

Trends in Union Political Spending, 1990–2002

We examine available data on contributions made by unions to congressional and presidential candidates in the six election cycles over the years 1990–2002. In addition, we report more recently disclosed data on union lobbying expenditures. Campaign spending includes PAC donations, soft money, and contributions made by individuals who are officers or employees of a union.

Table 16.3 shows that union contributions more than doubled in current dollars over the years 1990–2002, rising from $41.4 million to $96.5 million. On a per-member basis, those contributions rose from about $2.50 to nearly $6.00 over the same period. Contributions showed a sizable jump between 1998 and 2000 as a result of the growth of soft money and the intensely competitive

Bush-Gore presidential race. A somewhat different picture emerges, however, when these figures are adjusted for inflation. In real dollars, union contributions peaked in 1992 and fell to their lowest level in the past decade in 2002.

Table 16.3 breaks down union contributions into categories and shows the explosion in soft money contributions, which were not reported separately before 1992. Table 16.3 also shows that over the years 1990–2002, the great majority of union contributions to federal candidates came from PACs: 79 percent of the total of $458.3 million. As suggested, the PAC share of contributions fell dramatically over time. In 1990, PACs made over 99 percent of the total union contributions. By 1998, 82.5 percent of contributions came from PACs. Because of the spike in union soft money in the late 1990s, PACs provided only 62.5 percent of labor's total contributions in 2002. As individuals, officers and employees of unions have made minuscule contributions to candidates.

To provide a more complete picture of labor's political involvement, Table 16.4 reports organized labor's total lobbying expenditures and electoral contributions for the 1998 and 2000 election cycle. The Table 16.4 data show that labor spent about $44.5 million lobbying in Washington during the 1998 election cycle and about $51.1 million in the 2000 cycle. Overall, organized labor spent $105.2 million on political action in the 1998 cycle and $141.2 million in the 2000 cycle. In nominal terms, these totals translate to about $6.50 per member in 1998 and $8.70 per member in 2000, sums that reflect a spending level of about $2.40 per member in real dollars in each of the years.

Union Money in Interest-Group Perspective

Standing alone, in the aggregate, labor's political spending seems impressive. Unions, however, represent just a sliver of the overall interest-group pie of thousands of corporations, trade associations, and nonaffiliated ideological groups. Table 16.5 reports data placing labor's electoral contributions into the broader context of interest-group activity in this area. Specifically, the data show total contributions (PAC, soft money, and individual) made by interest groups in several categories: business, labor, ideological, lawyers/lobbyists, and a miscellaneous "other."

Focusing on the 1992 and 2002 election cycles, several points are noteworthy. First, labor provides less than 10 percent of campaign revenue from interest groups. In 2002, labor provided less than eight cents of every dollar contributed, the smallest percentage among all major categories of donors. Second, labor's share remains small across each of the three modes of contributions. On an individual basis, labor provides a pittance. Note that this has important implications under the new campaign-finance law, which raised the amount individuals can give to a candidate's campaign from $1,000 to $2,000 per primary or general election. Third, labor stands out from the other groups in the overwhelmingly partisan slant in the allocation of contributions: Labor gives over 90 percent

Table 16.3
Union Political Contributions and Funding Sources, 1990–2002

Election Cycle	Non-Treasury Contributions from Individuals	Non-Treasury Contributions from PACs	Treasury Soft Money Contributions	Total Contributions	Per-Member Contributions	Total Contributions Adjusted for Inflation (1982–1984 5 100)	Per-Member Contributions Adjusted for Inflation (1982–1984 5 100)
1990	$123,022	$41,289,235	N/A	$41,412,257	$2.47	$28,698,694	$1.71
1992	$297,666	$48,730,354	$4,313,188	$53,341,208	$3.25	$31,844,701	$1.94
1994	$197,968	$46,431,345	$4,415,075	$51,044,388	$3.05	$26,440,992	$1.58
1996	$399,129	$55,003,484	$9,546,686	$64,949,299	$3.99	$27,993,147	$1.72
1998	$306,986	$50,230,845	$10,322,136	$60,859,967	$3.76	$22,518,187	$1.39
2000	$744,472	$58,988,914	$30,418,895	$90,152,281	$5.54	$25,062,334	$1.54
2002	$438,305	$60,277,966	$35,868,006	$96,584,277	$5.89	$19,402,350	$1.21
GRAND TOTAL	$2,507,548	$360,952,143	$94,883,986	$458,343,677	N/A	N/A	N/A

Source: Center for Responsive Politics, Washington, D.C.

Table 16.4
Total Union Electoral and Lobbying Spending

Year/Cycle	Electoral Contributions	Lobbying	Total Spending	Per-Member Spending
1997–1998	$60,859,967	$44,481,999	$105,241,966	$6.49
1999–2000	$90,152,281	$51,090,923	$141,243,204	$8.67

Source: Center for Responsive Politics, Washington, D.C.

of its dollars to Democrats. Businesses are much more balanced, but their Republican bent grew noticeably during the 1992–2002 decade, reflecting the GOP's takeover of Congress in 1994.

Last, and most important, businesses as a whole dominate all aspects of campaign financing. In 2002, business gave more than $800 million, or close to two-thirds of the total. While the "business" category includes a multitude of disparate and sometimes competing interests, its aggregate financial capacity remains impressive. Indeed, given this capacity, business is capable of exerting considerable influence when it unites on class or ideological grounds, as was the case in Labor Law Reform in the late 1970s and the passage of NAFTA in the early 1990s. As Dreiling (2000: 21) observed: "When unified, the resources of corporations (and business more generally) nullify or crowd out the resources of all other societal interests. Thus, the type and extent of corporate unity is a pivotal problem for observers interested in the characteristics of, prospects for, and limits to democracy in the USA."

Voting Behavior and Election Success

Organized labor, as Greenstone (1977) demonstrated, provides an important party-related function in mobilizing voters. It encourages its members, their families, and similarly situated (in socioeconomic terms) others to register to vote. It operates phone banks and organizes transportation to get out the vote. And it saturates its membership with campaign literature that provides "talking points" to inform and influence other voters. In the 2000 election, for example, the AFL-CIO claims to have organized 100,000 volunteers to get out the vote; registered 2.3 million new voters; made eight million telephone calls; and mailed 12 million pieces of political literature (Masters, 2004). Without question, it is in this voter-mobilization realm that labor is most respected or feared by political operatives.

Obviously, labor's capacity to mobilize voters depends on several factors. One is the sheer size of its base. Another is its effectiveness in mobilizing its base. A third is the extent to which it links to the voter-mobilization of other interests with a similar purpose or preferred electoral outcome. In this regard, Table 16.6 reveals the obvious but nonetheless disturbing trend facing organized

Table 16.5
Spending [in thousands] on Federal Elections by Interest Group, 1992 and 2002
(Percentage of Overall Total in Parentheses)

1992 Election Cycle	Group Total	Individuals	PACs	Soft Money	Democrat	Republican
Business	$399,495 (66.0%)	$201,179 (63.7%)	$132,099 (62.4%)	$66,216 (84.8%)	47%	53%
Labor	$53,341 (8.8%)	$298 (0.1%)	$48,730 (23.0%)	$4,313 (5.5%)	94%	5%
Ideological	$41,563 (6.9%)	$16,221 (5.1%)	$23,381 (11.0%)	$1,961 (2.5%)	68%	31%
Lawyers/Lobbyists	$62,494 (10.3%)	$52,320 (16.6%)	$7,078 (3.3%)	$3,097 (4.0%)	72%	28%
Others	$48,518 (8.0%)	$45,690 (14.5%)	$370 (0.2%)	$2,458 (3.1%)	43%	55%
OVERALL TOTAL	$605,411	$315,707	$211,659	$78,045	54%	45%

2002 Election Cycle	Group Total	Individuals	PACs	Soft Money	Democrat	Republican
Business	$800,064 (63.9%)	$292,487 (59.8%)	$192,896 (54.7%)	$314,680 (76.6%)	39%	61%
Labor	$96,584 (7.7%)	$438 (0.1%)	$60,278 (17.1%)	$35,868 (8.7%)	93%	7%
Ideological	$135,707 (10.8%)	$24,352 (5.0%)	$87,510 (24.8%)	$23,846 (5.8%)	53%	47%
Lawyers/Lobbyists	$112,118 (9.0%)	$77,694 (15.9%)	$10,759 (3.1%)	$23,665 (5.8%)	71%	29%
Others	$108,110 (8.6%)	$94,374 (19.3%)	$926 (0.3%)	$12,810 (3.1%)	45%	55%
OVERALL TOTAL	$1,252,583	$489,345	$352,369	$410,869	48%	52%

Source: Center for Responsive Politics. Washington, D.C.

Table 16.6
Union Share of Electorate, 1980–2000

Presidential Election Year	Voting Age Population (VAP) (thousands)	Voter Turnout (VT) (thousands)	Union Membership (thousands)	Union % VAP	Union % VT
1980	164,597	86,515	20,968	12.7%	24.2%
1984	174,466	92,653	17,340	9.9%	18.7%
1988	182,778	91,595	17,002	9.3%	18.6%
1992	189,529	104,405	16,390	8.6%	15.7%
1996	196,511	96,456	16,269	8.3%	16.9%
2000	205,815	105,586	16,258	7.9%	15.4%

Source: (1) Voting groups: U.S. Federal Election Commission; (2) Union membership: U.S. Bureau of Labor Statistics.

labor. Its electoral base shrinks commensurately with its workforce density. In 1980, union membership equaled 12.7 percent of the entire voting age population and 24.2 percent of the voters who cast ballots. By 2000, these figures had fallen to 7.9 percent and 15.4 percent, respectively. Bluntly, labor per se has a small base from which to work. And we know, based on decades of research, that union members do not march lock step to the political instructions of their leaders (Masters and Delaney, 1987b).

The good news for organized labor is that it has evidently had some success in offsetting the membership decline by increasing turnout. In a study on voting between 1964 and 2000, Leighley and Nagler (2003: 1) found that "unions increase turnout by increasing turnout of union members as well as turnout of nonmembers." They estimated preliminarily that "overall turnout would have been approximately 10.4% higher in 2000 had union strength remained at its 1964 level" (Leighley and Nagler, 2003: 14). This increase would have predominated at the bottom two-thirds of the economic ladder, which tends to vote Democratic. In this vein, the AFL-CIO has reported from its polling that union households comprised 26 percent of the turnout in the 2000 presidential election, compared to 15 percent of the registered voters (Masters, 2004).

In addition, union members have consistently shown a propensity to vote Democratic, even when they run against the broader electorate. For example, Table 16.7 suggests that union members have shown an increasing likelihood of voting Democratic in each of the congressional elections between 1980 and 2000. The union/nonunion differential, in fact, peaked at 16 percent in 2000, when 67 percent of the union voters voted Democratic compared to 51 percent of the electorate at large. While not a solid voting bloc by any means, union voters display a clear preference for Democratic candidates, which can be pivotal

Table 16.7
National Election Studies (NES)
Union Voting Behavior, 1980–2000

Year	Percentage Union Household	Democratic Congressional Vote Percentage		Union-Nonunion Difference
		Total	Union	
1980	26	54	65	11
1982	21	57	70	13
1984	21	55	62	7
1986	20	60	64	4
1988	19	59	68	7
1990	17	64	72	8
1992	16	59	66	7
1994	18	47	61	15
1996	18	49	59	10
1998	17	49	57	8
2000	15	51	67	16

Source: University of Michigan National Election Studies, Ann Arbor, Mich.

in close races. A slight increase in union turnout in battleground states in 2000 would undoubtedly have elected Al Gore to the presidency.

Despite promoting turnout and favoring Democrats, unions have had mixed success at best at the national level in actually electing candidates to office. Labor-endorsed presidential candidates have lost in four of the last six elections. And the Republicans have controlled both houses of Congress since 1994, with a brief hiatus in the Senate due to the defection of Vermont Senator James Jeffords.

The Legislative Record

We report summary statistics on labor's legislative record based on data reported by the AFL-CIO. Historically, the federation has selected a set of "key votes" in the House and Senate in each congressional session and reported whether a legislator voted "right" or "wrong." Table 16.8 reports the win-loss record of the AFL-CIO in these "key votes" over the years 1996–2003. As votes occurred on many different bills, we summarize the roll calls in four legislative categories: (1) legislation pertaining to unions; (2) general labor legislation (e.g., minimum wage); (3) trade legislation (e.g., fast-track authority on free-trade agreements and Most Favored Nation (MFN) status for China); and (4) all other legislation (e.g., fiscal policy, education, and the budget).

The data reveal a generally disappointing record for labor. Overall, labor "won" only 35 percent of the key roll calls. Labor lost a majority of the votes in three of the four categories (Trade, General Labor Legislation, and All Other Legislation). Moreover, within these three categories, some of the union victories occurred because it was not possible to attain the 60 votes needed to break a filibuster in the U.S. Senate. Note that unions lost nearly three-fourths of the votes in the "All Other Legislation" category, which is a hodgepodge of social, budget, fiscal, and welfare issues. This stands in marked contrast to research of decades earlier, which revealed labor tended to do better on the broader issues. But the result is not surprising. It reflects Republican control of Congress and the more conservative, partisan brand of politics practiced in Washington today. In general, fiscal, tax, and budget policies are predictably more pro-business when the GOP runs Congress. Similarly, social policy tilts in a conservative direction during Republican rule. What differs today, however, is the aggressive partisanship displayed by the Republican leadership. This, in turn, has placed organized labor on the defensive in the political arena. For example, on budget matters (which establish funding for regulatory agencies supported by unions and programs advocated by labor), labor has lost virtually every vote in recent years.

One might expect organized labor to suffer more losses than wins on legislation pertaining to unions in an era of Republican congressional control and declining union density. While labor enjoyed nominal victories in two-thirds of these roll calls, its success rings hollow. Invariably, the winning votes occurred on proposals to weaken labor's power. While unions defeated paycheck

Table 16.8
Organized Labor's Legislative Record, 1996–2002

Type of Bill	House Win	House Loss	Senate Win	Senate Loss	Total Win	Total Loss	Percent Wins
Legislation Pertaining to Unions:	6	2	8	5	14	7	66.7%
a) Union/Bargaining Rights	2	2	2	4			
b) Paycheck Protection	1	0	2	0			
c) Labor Agency Budgets	2	0	1	0			
d) Union Reporting			1	0			
e) Prevailing Wage Law	1	0	2	0			
f) Team Act			0	1			
General Labor Legislation:	9	12	6	9	15	21	41.7%
Trade Legislation:	3	8	1	9	4	17	19.0%
All Other Legislation:	12	33	13	30	25	63	28.4%
Overall Union Record:	30	55	28	53	58	108	34.9%

Source: AFL-CIO, Washington, D.C.

protection and efforts to roll back prevailing wage law, they did not advance union interests in a single case. Accordingly, organized labor has needed to spend increasing resources on political action to preserve its past legislative gains. It is not clear how long a declining labor movement can maintain such resource commitments.

In another sense, the key votes selected by the AFL-CIO reflect the fact that unions have had little to celebrate over the past decade. Since the early 1990s, when unions lost close votes on labor law reform and striker replacement legislation (Logan, 2003a, 2003b), most big legislative fights have involved bills opposed by organized labor. Even during the Clinton presidency, unions were not able to count on Demo-cratic support for many critical votes—such as those covering free-trade agreements.

The NAFTA Vote

On December 8, 1993, President Clinton signed the North American Free Trade Agreement (NAFTA) into law. His signature culminated an intensive lobbying effort against great odds. He expended political capital to overcome strong opposition within his own party and uniform opposition by organized labor. A poll taken a few weeks before the November 1993 votes in the House and Senate showed that a majority of Americans opposed NAFTA. Labor unions had threatened to punish Democrats who voted for an agreement they argued could cost thousands if not millions of good-paying jobs on American soil.

With labor so opposed and Democrats in control of both Houses of Congress, how did Clinton prevail? Without question, he used the power and prestige of the presidency to twist arms. According to a controversial report by the Public Citizen's Global Trade Watch (2000: 2), to win on NAFTA "the Clinton White House offered an array of special deals to the few Members [of Congress] still publicly undecided on NAFTA."

More important, the Clinton administration, with the enormous assistance of business, framed the issue in a way that made organized labor look anti-growth, obstructionist, and dangerously out of step with global realities. In fact, labor's intense opposition provoked an unprecedented business response. It has been estimated that business spent $30–50 million lobbying for NAFTA (Dreiling, 2000: 24). It created a "panbusiness effort" under the USA*NAFTA banner. USA*NAFTA mobilized at the grassroots through local chambers of commerce and small employers. Business lobbying was well financed, well timed, ideologically inspiring (free trade, opportunity, growth), and carefully orchestrated.

While the vote, particularly in the U.S. House of Representatives (where then Majority Leader Gephardt was fiercely opposed) was expected to be close, NAFTA passed comfortably. As Table 16.9 reports, 102 Democrats voted for it, making the end result look significantly bipartisan. In the Senate, almost half of the Democrats voted to pass NAFTA, pushing the final vote in favor to 61.

Table 16.9
Legislative Voting on NAFTA, 1993

| Party | House Vote | | Senate Vote | | |
	Yes	No	Yes	No	Not Voting
Democratic	102	156	27	28	1
Republican	132	43	34	10	
Independent		1			
TOTALS	234	200	61	38	1

In the end, organized labor had nothing but egg on its face. A centrist Democratic president had openly gone against it and did so with relentless lobbying. Sizable numbers of Democratic House members voted against labor, as did nearly half the Senate Democrats. And the threat of punishing defiant Democratic legislators, to the extent exercised (Engel and Jackson, 1998), backfired, as Republicans won Congress in 1994. What lesson did this NAFTA vote provide? The same one the defeat of Labor Law Reform taught: Labor loses when it is seen as selfishly motivated and opposed to wider social-economic interests, especially when those interests employ the majority of the workforce.

VIII. Union Political Action: A Critical Assessment

Has organized labor benefited from its political involvement? Is the labor movement's continued political involvement likely to help its desired revival? These are important questions, which require an honest look at the past and a realistic look into the future.

Our analysis identifies a potential paradox for organized labor: Union political success may erode workers' demand for unions. Many of the laws governing the workplace—taken for granted by employees today—were advanced, advocated, and obtained with union support. For example, over the past century, unions have supported federal, state, and local government legislation regulating minimum wages, working hours, overtime, unemployment insurance, pension and old age support, disability and injury protection (e.g., workers' compensation laws), safety and health, and equal employment opportunity (for a review, see Bennett and Taylor, 2001). Such laws have extended to most workers benefits that were formerly secured in bargaining by individuals represented by unions. Historically, union leaders have been concerned about protective labor legislation precisely for this reason (Freeman, 1987). Because researchers have generally ignored this paradox, a systematic accounting is not available. Moreover, available studies of the paradox have suggested mixed results. For example, while some scholars have reported evidence of a trade-off between protective labor legislation and union density (Bennett and Taylor, 2001; Neumann and Rissman, 1984; Reder, 1951), others have observed no relationship (Chaison and Rose, 1991; Freeman, 1987; Stepina and Fiorito, 1986). Accordingly, it is difficult to determine whether the association between union density levels and the availability of protective labor legislation is causal or coincidental. The current environment may portend a test of this relationship. Specifically, efforts by conservatives to reduce some of the protections enjoyed by workers (e.g., recent changes in overtime regulations and proposals to limit the bargaining rights of certain federal government workers) will boost workers' demand for unionism if there is a causal relationship between protective labor laws and union density. It would be worthwhile for researchers to study this relationship.

Despite the paradox, some conclusions seem clear. In terms of promoting union membership and enacting laws favorable to union growth, labor's political record is at best disappointing. Organized labor seems to be incapable of electing Democratic majorities and even of ensuring Democratic fealty on watershed issues. For the most part, *labor*'s agenda cannot find the light of day when Republicans control both the Congress and the White House, unless an otherwise compelling reason emerges. The declining presence of unions in the workforce translates inevitably into diminished political power. Without the capacity to inflict harm through strikes and to move large blocs of voters, labor simply cannot exert the power it once did on either the economic or political scene.

Does this mean that there is no payoff to political action? The answer is clearly "no." Consider what would happen if labor were to disengage politically. One certainly can paint a dark scenario. Congress might repeal laws supporting basic union and collective bargaining rights. The recent evidence suggests that unions have been successful to some extent in resisting conservative-led attacks on labor rights and labor standards, especially when these proposals are successfully framed as anti-union. A union political presence undoubtedly provides the means of building such resistance. Disengagement, therefore, is a high-risk strategy. At least now labor can cover itself somewhat on the downside and take advantage of unexpected opportunities on the upside. There is a lot to be said for simply being a player; you at least have a seat at the table, though you may be dining with few friends.

By maintaining their political involvement, unions have an opportunity to discuss many issues with policy makers and to advance views to the public. Today, in light of emerging information on the nation's war on terror and problems in Iraq, a nonzero potential exists for the emergence of a new coalition of groups and officials that would support different policies across the board. At a time when the nation is sharply (and evenly) divided about a general course of action, unions must participate in the political debate, or cede their positions to others. Hence, even in bad times, unions must be politically active.

In general, our observations are consistent with F&M's conclusions. Union political activity has continued and perhaps increased over the past two decades. The record of union political success has been mixed. And case studies of critical political efforts by the labor movement have ended in defeat. By providing much more detail on union political efforts, our analysis extends F&M's work and identifies specific issues in need of further research. Two decades and many studies have not diminished F&M's assertion that unions need public consent to secure political victories on issues narrowly related to unions' self-interest. Today's conservative political environment promises, however, to challenge organized labor significantly. In particular, the dominance of business in the political spending arena and the increasing power of conservatives in government could create conditions in which unions lose some of the legislative gains achieved in years past.

Is political action likely to contribute to union revival? This is the key question facing the labor movement today. On its present course, the answer is "no." Labor is good at much in politics: It can arrange meetings with legislators, register voters, produce slick mailings and advertisements, and target get-out-the-vote drives. It is, in other words, good at the mechanics. It is more sophisticated in terms of using technology to transmit information than many of its interest-group counterparts. However, labor fails at the critical test: It simply does not inspire. Public policies that generate favorable outcomes are the desired effects of union political action. Policy enactment, unfortunately, can take time, a lot of time, as the campaign for national health care still shows through its lack of success. Political action will only be an effective tool for revival if it inspires the movement of large segments of the workforce and broader public into labor's corner.

For this to happen, labor needs the passion of ideas, not the tools of technology. It needs a cause that transcends divisions and projects a positive future. In opposing free trade, labor can be portrayed, as it has, as being opposed to the future. Unions must seek progress, not regress, if they are to inspire people to action. Therefore, the task becomes one of identifying those unifying, progressive themes that inspire enough to mobilize workers in far greater numbers and with much higher energy than has occurred since the 1930s.

If labor does strike such a resonant chord, it still faces a paradox. Political action is a risky revival strategy. Its benefits accrue to union members and nonmembers alike, especially the more general the social and economic legislation involved. Thus, as F&M noted, if unions are more successful on these legislative matters, they unavoidably encourage free riding. This result works against the very objective of expanding and revitalizing the union movement. For political action to revive organized labor, it must not only inspire but also facilitate union growth, which suggests a focus on those policies that benefit unions institutionally. In such an environment, the right to join a union would be seen as a basic human and political right. More importantly, if unions are to thrive, workers must see joining the union movement as an obligation to promote their own welfare as well as the welfare of the wider society.

References

Asher, Herbert B., Eric S. Heberlig, Randall B. Ripley, and Karen Snyder. *American Labor Unions in the Electoral Arena.* New York: Rowan & Littlefield, 2001.

Barbash, Jack. "Unions, Government, and Politics." *Industrial and Labor Relations Review* 1 (October 1947): 66–79.

———. *The Practice of Unionism.* New York: Harper & Brothers, 1956.

Bennett, James T. and Jason E. Taylor. "Labor Unions: Victims of Their Political Success." *Journal of Labor Research* 22 (Spring 2001): 261–74.

Bok, Derek C. and John T. Dunlop. *Labor and the American Community.* New York: Simon and Schuster, 1970.

Box-Steffensmeier, Laura, W. Arnold, and Christopher J.W. Zorn. "The Strategic Timing of Position Taking in Congress: A Study of North American Free Trade Agreement." *American Political Science Review* 91 (June 1997): 324–39.

Burns, Peter F., Peter L. Francia, and Paul S. Herrnson. "Labor at Work: Union Campaign Activities and Legislative Payoffs in the U.S. House of Representatives." *Social Science Quarterly* 81 (June 2000): 507–22.

Campling, John T. and Grant Michelson. "A Strategic Choice-Resource Dependence Analysis of Union Mergers in the British and Australian Broadcasting and Film Industries." *Journal of Management Studies* 35 (September 1998): 579–600.

Chaison, Gary N. and Joseph B. Rose. "The Macrodeterminants of Union Growth and Decline." In George Strauss, Daniel G. Gallagher, and Jack Fiorito, eds. *The State of the Unions.* Madison, WI: IRRA, 1991, pp. 3–45.

Clark, Paul F. "Conservative Interest Group Impact on Union Voters: The Link between Social and Economic Issues." *Labor Studies Journal* 22 (Winter 1998): 47–52.

———. "Using Members' Dues for Political Purposes: The Paycheck Protection Movement." *Journal of Labor Research* 20 (Summer 1999): 329–42.

——— and Marick F. Masters. "Competing Interest Groups and Union Members' Voting." *Social Science Quarterly* 82 (March 2001): 105–16.

Coleman, Vernon. "Labor Power and Social Equality." *Political Science Quarterly* 103 (Winter 1988): 687–705.

Corrado, Anthony. "A History of Federal Campaign Finance." In Anthony Corrado, ed. *The New Campaign Finance Sourcebook.* Washington, DC: Brookings Institution, 2003, Chapter 1.

Dark, Taylor E. "Organized Labor and the Congressional Democrats: Reconsidering the 1980s." *Political Science Quarterly* 111 (Spring 1996): 83–104.

———. *The Unions and the Democrats: An Enduring Alliance.* Ithaca, NY: Cornell University Press, 1999.

———. "Labor and the Democratic Party: A Report on the 1998 Elections." *Journal of Labor Research* 21 (Fall 2000): 627–40.

Delaney, John T. "The Future of Unions as Political Organizations." *Journal of Labor Research* 12 (Fall 1991): 373–87.

———, Jack Fiorito, and Paul Jarley. "Evolutionary Politics? Union Differences and Political Activities in the 1990s." *Journal of Labor Research* 20 (Summer 1999): 277–96.

Delaney, John T., Jack Fiorito, and Marick Masters. "The Effects of Union Organizational and Environmental Characteristics on Union Political Action." *American Journal of Political Science* 31 (August 1988): 616–42.

Delaney, John T. and Marick F. Masters. "Unions and Political Action." In George Strauss, Daniel G. Gallagher, and Jack Fiorito, eds. *The State of the Unions.* Madison, WI: IRRA, 1991, pp. 313–45.

————, and Susan Schwochau. "Unionism and Voter Turnout." *Journal of Labor Research* 9 (Summer 1988): 221–34.

————. "Union Membership and Voting for COPE-Endorsed Candidates." *Industrial and Labor Relations Review* 43 (July 1990): 621–35.

Dreiling, Michael C. "The Class Embeddedness of Corporate Political Action: Leadership in Defense of NAFTA." *Social Problems* 47 (February 2000): 21–48.

Endersby, James W. and Michael C. Munger. "The Impact of Legislator Attributes on Union PAC Campaign Contributions." *Journal of Labor Research* 13 (Winter 1992): 79–90.

Engel, Steven T. and David J. Jackson. "Wielding the Stick Instead of the Carrot: Labor PAC Punishment of Pro-NAFTA Democrats." *Political Research Quarterly* 51 (September 1998): 813–28.

Fields, Mitchell W., Marick F. Masters, and James W. Thacker. "Union Commitment and Membership Support for Political Action: An Exploratory Analysis." *Journal of Labor Research* 8 (Spring 1987): 143–57.

Fiorito, Jack. "Political Instrumentality Perceptions and Desires for Union Representation." *Journal of Labor Research* 8 (Summer 1987): 271–90.

Form, William H. *Segmented Labor, Fractured Politics.* New York: Plenum Press, 1995.

Francia, Peter L. "The Effects of the North American Free Trade Agreement on Corporate and Labor PAC Contributions." *American Politics Research* 29 (January 2001): 98–109.

Freeman, Richard B. "Unionism and Protective Labor Legislation." In Industrial Relations Research Association, *Proceedings of the Thirty-Ninth Annual Meeting.* Madison, WI: IRRA, 1987, pp. 260–67.

———— and James L. Medoff. *What Do Unions Do?* New York: Basic Books, 1984.

Goldfield, Michael. "Labor in American Politics—Its Current Weakness." *Journal of Politics* 48 (February 1986): 2–29.

Gopoian, J. David. "What Makes PACs Tick? An Analysis of the Allocative Patterns of Economic Interest Groups." *American Journal of Political Science* 27 (May 1984): 259–81.

Greenstone, J. David. *Labor in American Politics.* Chicago: University of Chicago Press, 1977.

Grier, Kevin B. and Michael Munger. "The Impact of Legislator Attributes on Interest Group Campaign Contributions." *Journal of Labor Research* 7 (Fall 1986): 349–62.

Hogler, Raymond L. "Unions, Politics, and Power: The Ideology of Paycheck Protection Proposals." *Labor Law Journal* (October 1998): 1195–204.

Hoxie, Robert F. *Trade Unionism in the United States.* New York: D. Appleton, 1920.

Hurd, Richard and Jeffrey Sohl. "Strategic Diversity in Labor PAC Contribution Patterns." *Social Science Journal* 29 (January 1992): 65–86.

Hyman, Richard. *Understanding European Trade Unionism: Between Market, Class and Society.* London: SAGE Publications, 2001.

Jacobson, Gary C. "The Effect of the AFL-CIO's 'Voter Education' Campaigns on the 1996 House Elections." *Journal of Politics* 61 (February 1999): 185–94.

Juravich, Tom and Peter R. Shergold. "The Impact of Unions on the Voting Behavior of Their Members." *Industrial and Labor Relations Review* 41 (April 1988): 374–85.

Kahane, Leo. "Congressional Voting Patterns on NAFTA: An Empirical Analysis." *American Journal of Economics and Sociology* 55 (October 1996): 395–410.

Katz, Harry C., Rosemary Batt, and Jeffrey H. Keefe. "The Revitalization of the CWA: Integrating Collective Bargaining, Political Action, and Organizing." *Industrial and Labor Relations Review* 56 (July 2003): 573–89.

Kochan, Thomas A. "Using the Dunlop Report to Achieve Mutual Gains." *Industrial Relations* 34 (July 1995): 350–66.

———, Harry C. Katz, and Robert B. McKersie. *The Transformation of American Industrial Relations.* New York: Basic Books, 1986.

———, Robert B. McKersie, and Peter Cappelli. "Strategic Choice and Industrial Relations Theory." *Industrial Relations* 23 (Winter 1984): 16–39.

Leighley, Jan E. and Jonathan Nagler. "Unions as Mobilizing Institutions in the U.S., 1964–2000." Unpublished manuscript, October 17, 2003.

Logan, John. "Labor's 'Last Stand' in National Politics? The Campaign for Striker Replacement Legislation, 1988–1996." London School of Economics, unpublished working paper, 2003a.

———. "The Dunlop Commission and the Elusive Search for Consensus on Labor Law Reform." London School of Economics, unpublished working paper, 2003b.

Mann, Thomas and Anthony Corrado. "The How of Money in Federal Elections." In Anthony Corrado, ed. *The New Campaign Finance Sourcebook.* Washington, DC: Brookings Institution, 2003, Chapter 3.

Masters, Marick F. "AFSCME As a Political Union." *Journal of Labor Research* 19 (Spring 1998): 313–49.

———. "Union Money, Political Action, and Government Regulation: Introduction." *Journal of Labor Research* 20 (Summer 1999): 271–76.

———. "Unions in the 2000 Election: A Strategic Choice Perspective." *Journal of Labor Research* 25 (Winter 2004): 139–82.

——— and Robert S. Atkin. "Financial and Political Resources of Nine Major Public Sector Unions in the 1980s." *Journal of Labor Research* 17 (Winter 1996): 183–98.

———. "Local Union Officers' Donations to a Political Action Committee." *Relations Industrielles* 51 (Winter 1996): 40–61.

——— and John T. Delaney. "Unions, Political Action, and Public Policy: A Review of the Past Decade." *Policy Studies Journal* 18 (Winter 1989–90): 471–80.

Masters, Marick F. and John Thomas Delaney. "Interunion Variation in Congressional Campaign Support." *Industrial Relations* 23 (Fall 1984): 410–16.

———. "The Causes of Union Political Involvement: A Longitudinal Analysis." *Journal of Labor Research* 6 (Fall 1985): 341–62.

———. "Union Legislative Records During President Reagan's First Term." *Journal of Labor Research* 8 (Winter 1987a): 1–18.

———. "Union Political Activities: A Review of the Empirical Literature." *Industrial and Labor Relations Review* 40 (April 1987b): 336–53.

Masters, Marick F. and Ray Jones. "The Hard and Soft Sides of Union Political Money." *Journal of Labor Research* 20 (Summer 1999): 297–328.

Masters, Marick F. and Asghar Zardkoohi. "Congressional Support for Unions' Positions Across Diverse Legislation." *Journal of Labor Research* 9 (Spring 1988): 149–66.

———. "Labor Unions and the U.S. Congress: PAC Allocations and Legislative Voting." *Advances in Industrial and Labor Relations,* Vol. 5. Greenwich, CT: JAI Press, 1987, pp. 79–118.

———. "The Determinants of Labor PAC Allocations to Legislators." *Industrial Relations* 25 (Fall 1984): 410–16.

Moore, William J., Denise R. Chachere, Thomas D. Curtis, and David Gordon. "The Political Influence of Unions and Corporations on COPE Votes in the U.S. Senate, 1979–1988." *Journal of Labor Research* 16 (Spring 1995): 203–22.

Neumann, George R. and Ellen R. Rissman. "Where Have All the Union Members Gone?" *Journal of Labor Economics* 2 (April 1984): 175–92.

Patton, David B. and John J. Marrone. "The Impact of Labor Endorsements on the 1980 Presidential Vote." *Labor Studies Journal* 9 (Spring 1984): 3–18.

Peltzman, Sam. "Constituent Interest and Congressional Voting." *Journal of Law and Economics* 27 (April 1984): 181–210.

Public Citizen's Global Trade Watch. *The Clinton Record on Trade-Vote Deal Making: High Infidelity.* Washington, DC: Public Citizen's Global Trade Watch, May 15, 2000.

Radcliff, Benjamin. "Organized Labor and Electoral Participation in American National Elections." *Journal of Labor Research* 24 (Spring 2001): 405–14.

––––––– and Patricia A. Davis. "Labor Organization and Electoral Participation in Industrial Democracies." *American Journal of Political Science* 44 (January 2000): 132–41.

Reder, Melvin W. *Labor in a Growing Economy.* New York: John Wiley, 1951.

Rosenberg, Lisa. *A Bag of Tricks: Loopholes in the Campaign Finance Systems.* Washington, DC: Center for Responsive Politics, 1996.

Sabato, Larry J. *PAC Power: Inside the World of Political Action Committees.* New York: W.W. Norton, 1984.

Saltzman, Gregory M. "Congressional Voting on Labor Issues: The Role of PACs." *Industrial and Labor Relations Review* 40 (January 1987): 666–86.

Sousa, David J. "Organized Labor in the Electorate." *Political Research Quarterly* 46 (December 1993): 741–58.

Steagall, Jeffrey W. and Ken Jennings. "Unions, PAC Contributions and the NAFTA Vote." *Journal of Labor Research* 17 (Summer 1996): 515–21.

Stepina, Lee P. and Jack Fiorito. "Toward a Comprehensive Theory of Union Growth and Decline." *Industrial Relations* 25 (Fall 1986): 248-64.

Sweeney, John J. "Remarks by AFL-CIO President John J. Sweeney to AFL-CIO Executive Council Meeting Political Program Press Briefing." Bal Harbour, FL, March 10, 2004. <http://222.aflcio.org>.

Troy, Leo. "Twilight for Organized Labor." *Journal of Labor Research* 22 (Spring 2001): 245–59.

Uhlaner, Carole. "Rational Turnout: The Neglected Role of Groups." *American Journal of Political Science* 33 (May 1989): 390–422.

U.S. Federal Election Commission. "BCRA Supplement to All FEC Campaign Guides." *Record* (January 2003).

Webb, Sidney and Beatrice Webb. *The History of Trade Unionism.* London: Longman, 1894.

Wilhite, Al. "Union PAC Contributions and Legislative Voting." *Journal of Labor Research* 9 (Winter 1988): 79–90.

––––––– and John Theilmann. "Unions, Corporations, and Political Campaign Contributions: The 1982 House Elections." *Journal of Labor Research* 7 (Spring 1986): 175–85.

Wilson, Graham K. "In the Shadows of Social Democracy? U.S. Unions in a Time of Adversity." Paper presented at the ECPR Workshops, Turin, March 2002.

Wright, John R. "PACs, Contributions, and Roll Calls: An Organizational Perspective." *American Political Science Review* 79 (June 1985): 400–14.

Zeigler, Harmon. *Interest Groups in American Society.* Englewood Cliffs, NJ: Prentice Hall, 1964.

Zullo, Roland. "Revitalizing AFL-CIO Political Outreach: Can a Direct Informational Campaign Do the Trick?" *Advances in Industrial and Labor Relations*, Vol. 11. Greenwich, CT: JAI Press, 2002, pp. 123–44.

–––––––. "Shaping Political Preferences through Workplace Mobilization: Unions and the 2000 Election." *Advances in Industrial and Labor Relations,* Vol. 12. Greenwich, CT: JAI Press, 2003, pp. 173–96.

17

What Do Unions Do?
Evaluation and Commentary

Bruce E. Kaufman[*]

I. Introduction

To conclude this volume, we (the editors) thought it useful to have several people from diverse backgrounds take the preceding chapters as input, add to them their own perspectives, and provide a broad-ranging review and evaluation of Freeman and Medoff's *What Do Unions Do?* (*WDUD*, 1984). Toward this end, the chapters in this part of the symposium provide, respectively, an academic, a management, and a labor perspective. The positions taken by each author, of course, are their own and do not necessarily represent the views of others. Ending the symposium is a chapter by Richard B. Freeman in which he assesses how the theory, findings, and policy recommendations of *WDUD* look after 20 years and also a response to points made by the various contributors to this symposium.

This chapter assesses *WDUD* from an academic perspective. As noted in the Introduction to this volume, *WDUD* is a widely acclaimed work on trade unions and, in our view, the most influential book on the subject written in several decades. Having re-stated this important accolade, the remainder of this chapter reviews and evaluates *WDUD*. I start with issues of theory, then I review empirical evidence on what unions do, and finally, I consider national labor policy regarding unions.

The most important conclusions I reach are fourfold: Freeman and Medoff (F&M) are correct that unions have both pluses and minuses on the social balance sheet, but in *WDUD* they tend to overstate the former and understate the latter; the economic environment since *WDUD* was written has changed in ways that on net increase the minuses and reduce the positives for unions; the theory and evidence in *WDUD* (and later research by Freeman) provides a relatively weak case for a substantial expansion of union density through policy reform but, paradoxically, provides a much stronger case for a substantial expansion of alternative forms of employee representation and voice; and in theorizing about unions the more narrowly economic and orthodox (neoclassical) the framework the more inevitable is a negative verdict on unions.

II. Theory

The most novel and path breaking aspect of *WDUD* is the detailed empirical estimation of the non-wage effects of unionism (Freeman, 1992: 45). But also noteworthy is the new theoretical model of unionism presented by F&M who call this model the "two faces of unionism." One face is the negative *monopoly* side of unionism; the second face is the positive *voice/institutional response* side. Neither are analytically developed but are used more as a conceptual framework for generating implications and structuring the empirical work. Nonetheless, the two faces theory is widely cited and utilized (Turnbull, 2003; Blanchflower and Bryson, 2004). The thesis of *WDUD* is that the positive voice/institutional response face outweighs the negative monopoly face, implying unions on net contribute positively to economic and social welfare. Nissen (2003) describes this as a theory of "value-added" unionism and distinguishes it from "social movement" unionism.

Intellectual Context and Constraints

A fair and informed evaluation of the theory in *WDUD* is facilitated by brief consideration of the intellectual context and constraints within which it was written. This review also provides an entrée to establishing my fourth point listed in the introduction.

First, it must be recognized that *WDUD* was developed largely in a North American context and from the disciplinary perspective of economics. Although at a broad level both the theory and empirical analysis in *WDUD* are relevant to other types of industrial relations systems, in main outline the book is about American-style business unions in an institutional framework of Wagner Act legislation and decentralized bargaining. Likewise, both authors are economists, and thus the intellectual orientation of the book, while broadly conceived, is toward economic questions, models, and methodology. As Freeman (1992) has noted, the book is also largely a-historical.

Second, one must appreciate that F&M took on a very difficult intellectual mission in *WDUD*. Their task was twofold: first, to present theoretical arguments showing that labor unions can on net promote economic efficiency and, second, do so in a way that is respectable and credible among mainstream economists. This is not an easy needle to thread.

In building a positive theoretical (and empirical) case, F&M were not starting out *de novo*. The institutional economists of the Wisconsin School and neo-institutional economists of the 1940s–1950s (e.g., Dunlop, Kerr, Lester, Reynolds, and Ross)—a group Johnson (1975) in a well-known review article on unions refers to as comprising the "old labor economics"—had written extensively on unions for over eight decades (Kaufman, 1988, this volume's history chapter). This literature, while largely non-formalized, put forward three propositions that support the major thesis advanced by F&M.

The first proposition advanced by the old labor economists is exactly what F&M claim in *WDUD*: that unions have not one face but two—an economic bargaining face and a political voice face. Sumner Slichter (1939: 122), a predecessor of F&M at Harvard, observed for example, "Collective bargaining has two principle aspects. First, it is a method of introducing *civil rights into industry*; that is, of requiring that management be conducted by rule rather than by arbitrary decision. Second, it is a *method of price-fixing*—fixing the price of labor." Earlier, John Commons (1913: 121) described the economic goal of unions as *wealth redistribution*, *aggrandizement*, and *protection* and the political function as *constitutional government in industry*.

The second proposition advanced by the old labor economists that seems to promote F&M's cause is that labor markets are not appropriately modeled as competitive (in the neoclassical sense). John Dunlop, a colleague of F&M at Harvard, declared for example (quoted in Kaufman, 2002: 338), "I reject out of hand any argument that the economy would be better off without unions. Unions do not come into the picture and distort some 'perfect' wage structure, because there is no such thing. In the real world there are all kinds of distortions and inequities built into the wage structure, as any person who has set wages knows. To assume in a model that wages are 'competitive' is to assume away a large part of the problem."

The third proposition the old labor economists advanced was that because nonunion labor markets are imperfectly competitive one cannot assume *a priori* that unions have a negative effect on resource allocation and firm performance. Conclusions, therefore, have to be based on detailed empirical analysis. Thus, in *The Structure of Labor Markets* (1951: 223) Reynolds concludes from his empirical research that competitive forces are "weaker and less effective [in labor markets] than they are in most commodity markets," leading him to observe (p. 256) "the effects of collective bargaining (and other labor market institutions) can be discovered only by patient investigation of concrete situations" and (p. 260) "Whether the results of collective bargaining are better or worse than those of unilateral wage administration by employers . . . is basically a problem for empirical study."

One must conclude from these quotations that there is a long line of work in labor economics not only consistent with the position taken by F&M in *WDUD* but in fundamental respects antecedent to it. F&M chose to downplay these connections, however. They make occasional reference to supporting arguments by "industrial relations experts" and in several places in the text and endnotes cite individual authors or works from the old labor economics. In general, however, *WDUD* is positioned independent from this older tradition and, indeed, independent of nearly any historical context regarding unions. Perhaps of equal or greater substantive importance for their argument, F&M also in large part abandon one of the three central propositions of the old labor economics. That is, F&M start from page one with the assumption that labor markets are competitive, at least regarding the wage (monopoly) face of unions. To the uninitiated it might seem strange for proponents of greater unionism to immediately cede half the argument to the critics. This is particularly so since around the time *WDUD* was written Freeman also wrote two lengthy reviews of the old labor economics literature (Freeman, 1984, 1988) and concluded in the first (with specific reference to Reynolds' book) that it was "on target in its picture of the labor market" (p. 219).

But this puzzle introduces one of the major constraints facing F&M: presenting a positive case for unions that is credible to and respected by mainstream economists. As Johnson (1975) observed, the labor economics field at that time was in the midst of transitioning from the old labor economics to what he called the "new labor economics." The new labor economics had its intellectual home at the University of Chicago and found its theoretical inspiration in neoclassical microeconomics and the work of economists such as Friedman, Stigler, Lewis, and Becker. The hallmark of the Chicago approach is a thorough and uncompromising application of the tools of microeconomic theory to any and all issues. At its core, in turn, is the presumption that markets are highly competitive, prices are parametric to individual economic agents, and resources are efficiently allocated (Reder, 1982; Lazear, 2000; Kaufman, 2004a). Also part of the Chicago approach is a strong strain of disciplinary imperialism that permits inclusion of nonmarket concepts and behaviors only as long as they are nested within the maximizing benefit/cost framework.

Freeman taught at Chicago, and when he and Medoff were writing *WDUD*, the new labor economics had largely displaced the old version. The latter's decline is traceable to a number of factors but, according to Johnson (1975), the most important is methodological. He states (p. 23), for example, "the resultant theory of wages and income distribution was not very satisfactory, and perhaps more importantly, it [the old labor economics] could not be readily integrated into the mainstream of the discipline." The mainstream of the discipline, in turn, is microeconomic price theory with competitive markets at its core. The upshot is that if F&M wanted *WDUD* to get a serious hearing in the seminar rooms at Chicago and Harvard and among the readers of the *Journal of Labor Economics*, they had to largely disassociate the book from the old labor economics, which by now carried a significant intellectual discount, and present a theoretical model that had solid microeconomic foundations. At this point, however, the intellectual needle becomes very difficult to thread for F&M want on one hand to develop a positive efficiency rationale for unions but on the other are heavily constrained to do so by a theory that starts with the null hypothesis that resources are already efficiently allocated. How can this be done?

Here is where F&M creatively, perhaps even brilliantly, get out of the intellectual handcuffs and rescue unions from an otherwise certain "guilty" verdict. Probably estimating (correctly) that a direct assault on the Chicago position is futile, F&M cede to the opposition the claim that unions are labor market monopolies that distort an otherwise competitive wage structure. This becomes the negative monopoly face of unions in their two faces theory. But they then do an end-run on the Chicago position and bring in Hirschman's (1971) *exit/voice model* to provide the theoretical core for the positive voice/response face of unions. Hirschman's exit/voice model is a marriage of modern economics and political science in the mold of public choice theory. Using basic microeconomic principles, Hirschman explores the conditions under which organizational mal-performance is most efficiently corrected by market adjustment through exit (e.g., quitting one restaurant and patronizing another) versus an organizational adjustment through voice (e.g., staying at the restaurant and complaining to the chef). Under certain conditions (e.g., positive mobility costs, when quality is important relative to quantity), the voice option is superior to the exit option. With the Hirschman model, F&M can thus allow that unions have negative monopolistic wage effects and yet still win (or neutralize) the efficiency argu-ment by demonstrating in a way that passes the "respect and rigor" test among economists that they also have a compensating positive voice effect.

So, given these constraints and intellectual crosscurrents, the question is: How does F&M's two faces theory perform as a tool of understanding and prediction with regard to the role and impact of labor unions? My conclusion is that F&M's theory is on balance both innovative and insightful and, more importantly, captures well many facets of union function and performance. Yet, at the same time, it also suffers from some shortcomings and omissions. Here is my evaluation.

The Monopoly Face

F&M do not formally develop the monopoly face of unions. One can reason-ably surmise, however, that the baseline model they have in mind is the standard "on the demand curve" model depicted in Figure 1 of my theory chapter. The basic idea is that in the absence of a union firms pay workers a competitive wage determined by demand and supply in the labor market; when the workers form a union, the union has bargaining power that induces the company to pay workers a higher wage and to also improve other terms and conditions of employment. The main predicted results are higher wages for union workers, a decline in employment and profits in unionized firms, higher prices for consumers, lower wages and employment prospects for nonunion workers, and a misallocation of resources and loss in economic efficiency. In effect, the union wage increase is like a tax that both distorts relative prices and redistributes income with a consequent gain in welfare for organized workers but a more than compensating loss in welfare for other groups and the nation as a whole.

F&M accept this picture of the monopoly face of unions without significant amendment. My judgment is that it captures a large and important core of truth. In their economic function unions operate akin to a cartel in the labor market and raise the price of labor through the exercise of market power gained from the strike threat and various other pressure tactics and restrictions. The fact that California janitors recently unionized and increased their pay from (roughly) $8.00 to $11.00 an hour testifies to this fact, as does the fact that unionized senior commercial airline pilots earn an annual salary in excess of $200,000 a year for a flying time of 40 hours a month.

The crucial question is whether this rise in the price of labor and the methods used to bring it about benefit or harm the economy and social welfare. Based on the standard "union as a monopoly" model, F&M reach a negative verdict. I believe as a first approximation they are probably correct. But I also believe in the short run they overstate the harmful monopoly effect and, conversely, understate it for the long run. These are important qualifications to any account of what unions do.

F&M want to present a more balanced and favorable portrayal of unions, but they largely neglect several considerations regarding the monopoly face that could have significantly aided their cause. F&M cannot, of course, include everything in one book but even modest attention to these considerations could have helped shift the scorecard for unions in a more positive direction. The most important of these factors are the following.

Countervailing Power. F&M assume labor markets are competitive and thus employers have no market power over individual employees. Firms are wage-takers; workers can easily quit one job and find another; and the labor market is at a demand/supply equilibrium ("full employment"). But these assumptions may not be true in many circumstances even as a central tendency. Most firms set wages on a take-it-or-leave-it basis and many have significant discretion in pay rates; employees face substantial constraints on mobility due to prospective loss of health care benefits, pensions, and seniority (tenure); and in most years there are more job seekers than job vacancies. Under these conditions, market forces do not fully protect workers, and the terms and conditions of employment may be substandard relative to the competitive ideal of economic theory (Manning, 2003; Turnbull, 2003). In an earlier era this situation was labeled "labor's inequality of bargaining power" and provided the classic public policy rationale for encouragement of trade unions (Commons and Andrews, 1936; Kaufman, 1989, this volume's history chapter). That is, collective bargaining is a form of countervailing power that balances the wage determination process ("levels the playing field") and thereby promotes improved economic efficiency and social welfare. In this role union wage increases, at least initially, are not "monopoly-creating" but "monopsony reducing," where monopsony is defined very broadly to include any factor that limits competition for labor. When F&M portray in *WDUD* that labor markets are competitive they assume away this classic rationale for unions.

Social Cost of Labor. Union monopoly power can also promote efficiency by ensuring that employers pay the full social cost of labor (Stabile, 1993).

Due to market imperfections and tilted legal rules employers may be able to shift some of the cost of labor to workers, their families, and the community. Examples include inadequate compensation for workplace injuries and illnesses, laying-off workers during recession so families and society bear the upkeep and maintenance expense of labor (while employers keep and maintain their capital input), and an intense work pace or long hours that leads to the rapid depreciation of labor but with no obligation on the employer for ongoing financial support after the worker is used up and discharged.

Macroeconomic Stability/Growth. A third way unions can promote efficiency is by stabilizing and expanding aggregate demand in the economy, thereby promoting macroeconomic stability and growth. Unions stabilize aggregate demand by taking wages out of competition and preventing a deflationary downward spiral of wages and conditions during recessions and depressions; they expand aggregate demand in recessions and depressions by redistributing income from employers and shareholders with a lower propensity to consume to workers with a higher propensity to consume (Mitchell and Erickson, this volume).

Threat Effect. Unions may also promote greater efficiency by using the threat of organization to induce nonunion firms to bring labor standards up to a competitive level. Unions in this function are a form of positive externality. F&M mention the threat effect of unions but could have given it more emphasis as a positive contribution of the monopoly face.

Labor Is Not a Commodity. On purely social welfare grounds union monopoly power may also yield benefits in a way that F&M do not address. Competitive market theory treats labor as a commodity input such as steel or coal, albeit with a utility function. Although society has no vested interest in whether coal or steel receives a low price, is utilized 24 hours a day in a hot temperature, or is harshly treated by the firm, labor is embodied in people and thus carries a much higher moral significance (Budd, 2004; Kaufman, 2005). Thus, although competitive trading in labor may promote efficiency and be consistent with a demand/supply equilibrium, from a social viewpoint it is unacceptable and injurious to the public interest to permit child labor or less than living wages or, alternatively, to require that workers "buy" basic human rights (e.g., a measure of job security, respect from the boss) by agreeing to work for a lower wage (Gross, 2003). Because free markets and the quest for efficiency are likely to lead to an under-supply of these social goods and a concomitant over-emphasis on consumers' interests at the expense of workers' interests, a certain degree of labor market regulation and protectionism by unions and other institutions gains social legitimacy.

All of these positive rationales for unions involve their wage-raising function and suggest that the monopoly face of unions may promote rather than harm efficiency and social welfare. Indeed, it was precisely these kinds of arguments that Senator Wagner and a number of well-regarded labor economists (including two from the University of Chicago) used to support increasing union density through passage of the National Labor Relations Act (NLRA, or Wagner Act) in 1935 (Kaufman, 1996, this volume's history chapter). Also, union monopoly power seems essential in today's economy if they are to achieve one of F&M's social goals: reducing income inequality.

Counterbalancing these positive rationales for the union monopoly face are several negative blemishes that F&M also omit or downgrade. While several of the positive factors operate primarily in the short run, these negative blemishes operate more in the long run. They include the following.

Upward Creep in Wages/Benefits. The standard monopoly model of unions that underlies *WDUD* predicts that unions lead to a one-time mark-up in the level of wages and benefits (other things equal). But incorporating the median voter model into the monopoly face suggests the combination of majority voting and layoff by seniority in unions may lead to a gradual upward movement in the union/nonunion labor cost differential as unions nibble their way up the firm's labor demand curve in response to the senior majority's pressure for "more" in each contract negotiation. This upward ratchet may be particularly true for benefit costs because the senior majority of members have a greater preference for benefits and firms may have less resistance to giving them since the costs are often back lóaded. Amplifying the upward creep in union labor cost is the fact unions also only give concessions, according to the median voter model, when potential job loss is so large it threatens a majority of the membership.

More Elastic Labor Demand. F&M give considerable attention to the wage impact of unions but relatively little to the employment impact. Had F&M considered employment in more depth they would have had to consider something largely omitted: the tendency of labor demand curves to become more elastic over time. The issue of labor demand elasticity receives surprisingly modest attention in *WDUD*, particularly in light of economic events that have undoubtedly made labor demand curves considerably more wage sensitive. Examples include industry deregulation, the globalization of product markets, greater capital mobility, the information/computer revolution, and greater financial market pressure. Some of these developments were already well in sight at the time F&M wrote *WDUD* but their negative implication for the employment impact of the union monopoly face were not much considered.

Capital Investment and Productivity Growth. F&M also give relatively little theoretical attention to two other important determinants of long-run economic performance: capital investment and productivity growth. Microeconomic theory suggests that a union wage increase may lead a firm to either increase or decrease capital investment, depending on the size of the scale and substitution effects. However, two other considerations suggest the union impact on capital investment is more likely to be negative (Hirsch, this volume). The first is that the union wage premium acts as a tax on the returns from capital investment; the second is that organized firms are deterred from making long-term capital commitments fearing that the union will appropriate the rents and quasi-rents. Even if unions do not lower the total amount of capital expenditure, they are likely to cause firms to re-direct it toward lower-cost nonunion production facilities in other parts of the country or overseas. For these reasons theory would suggest that unions may well have a negative effect on productivity growth as well, particularly in the union sector.

The Voice/Response Face

The second dimension of unionism is what F&M call the voice/institutional response face. The monopoly face is where the undesirable features of unionism reside, the voice/response face is the countervailing positive side of unions. Union voice is exercised at two places: internal firm governance and the national polity. The former is examined here.

F&M generate the voice/response face of unions by grafting onto the monopoly model a second channel through which unions affect firm and worker behavior. They call this the exit/voice model, adapted from Hirschman's book *Exit, Voice and Loyalty* (1971). The central idea is that when workers feel dissatisfied with some aspect of employment they have two modes of adjustment: quit the firm and find a new job that provides superior conditions (the exit option) or stay with the firm and try to solve the problem by talking it over with the employer (the voice option).

Two questions may be asked about F&M's voice/response model: first, does it provide new and interesting predictions/implications?; and, second, does it provide an accurate and balanced account of what unions do?

My assessment is that the scorecard is mixed but on net significantly positive. As with union monopoly power, however, F&M both understate and overstate the benefits and costs of union voice.

An earlier reviewer of *WDUD* observed that part of the explanatory power of F&M's exit/voice theory comes from the median voter model (Mitchell, 1985). He pointed out that if the median voter objective function is incorporated into the standard monopoly model, many of F&M's voice/response predictions are just as easily interpretable as union monopoly effects. An example is the hypothesis that collective bargaining will shift labor compensation from wages to benefits. The force of this observation is that the independent contribution of the exit/voice model may be modest.

This point is well-taken but I nonetheless think the exit/voice model does make a substantive net addition to the theory of union behavior. The important insight from the exit/voice model is that there is not one mode of coordination and allocation but two—exit into markets and voice through organizations.

With two modes of adjustment it becomes both a theoretical and empirical question to assess which mode is the most efficient. As F&M note (p. 8) in the first chapter of *WDUD*, for example, "The basic theorem of neoclassical economics is that, under well-specified conditions, the exit and entry of persons (the hallmark of the free-market system) produces a situation in which no individual can be made better off." Viewed from the perspective of institutional economics, these well-specified conditions boil down to a condition of zero transaction cost. With zero transaction cost, using markets is the most efficient way to coordinate and allocate resources since all other governance mechanisms are by implication a higher cost alternative. With positive transaction cost, on the other hand, it pays firms to develop an employment relationship and internal labor market (Williamson et al., 1975). But now labor becomes to some degree immobile, and the exit option thus loses a portion of its effectiveness as a coordinating and allocating device. Furthermore, positive transaction cost also leads to other contracting problems that the market exit option cannot effectively resolve, such as principal-agent problems, contractual opportunism, moral hazard, and adverse selection. And yet another problem, caused by poorly defined and nonseparable property rights, is public goods and externalities in the workplace—the former being particularly emphasized by F&M. Thus, as the exit option loses effectiveness and efficiency another coordinating and allocating device is needed, with the voice option providing such a substitute.

Viewed through the lens of transaction cost theory, F&M's two faces theory seems to provide a valuable and illuminating insight. That is, when unions are examined only in standard neoclassical terms of a competitive labor market and the "firm as a production function" it is a near-inescapable conclusion that they harm efficiency. When these assumptions are relaxed in a direction that surely better matches the real world, markets work imperfectly and voice may yield superior results to exit, giving rise to the possibility that unions improve rather than diminish economic (and social) performance. Correlatively, if exit from employment relationships is to some degree a blunt instrument, F&M may well be on solid ground to argue that by reducing quits unions promote efficiency.

F&M (p. 164) also cite two other ways unions and collective voice may increase firm efficiency through the voice/response face: "more rational personnel policies" and "reducing organizational slack." These union effects are often omitted in standard microeconomic studies of unions on grounds they are either theoretically *ad hoc* or empirically insignificant. Transaction cost theory again suggests that F&M may well be on the right side of this issue, although they do not analytically develop it in *WDUD*.

The key insight is that with positive transaction cost the labor contract is incomplete and thus subject to the principal-agent problem. Also, labor is not taken to be a commodity, as in the core version of neoclassical theory; rather, labor is distinctly human because it is embodied in people and thus inseparable from the seller. This fact means that the workers' labor power (effort) that goes into the production function is variable, rising and falling with factors such as morale, wage level, job satisfaction, fairness of treatment, and quality of working conditions. Another implication is that the motivation of managers to exert effort and attention to maximizing profit and minimizing cost is also variable.

The incomplete nature of the labor contract implies, therefore, that the amount of labor power contributed to production by workers and to maximizing profits by managers can never be treated as a contractual datum determined *ex ante* to production by supply and demand but, rather, is the variable outcome of a continuous bargaining game within the firm (Malcomson, 1999).

Seen in this light, the existence of organizational slack within firms is fully consistent with economic theory and is to be expected in most cases since the interests of managers are seldom fully and completely aligned with or served by the goal of maximum profit. As long as the firm's profits are above the survival level for the firm or managers, they will satisfice with respect to profit by pursuing other valued goals, such as empire building through mergers and acquisitions, rewarding themselves with exorbitant salaries and stock options, and tolerating various inefficiencies and organizational slack. When the workers form a union and collectively bargain, the resulting increase in labor cost may reduce profits to the point where the firm's survival (or managers' career survival) are imperiled, causing management to tighten up and in various ways reduce other areas of cost and improve efficiency (Altman, 2001; Kaufman, 1999a). Earlier called the *shock effect* in the old labor economics, the net effect may well be that productivity rises enough to offset the increase in union labor cost, resulting in higher wages for workers and more efficient firm performance at the expense of managers who now must forgo discretionary perquisites and concentrate more fully on the difficult job of maximizing shareholders' returns.

Similar theoretical support can be adduced for F&M's claim about the positive productivity effect of union-induced improvements in firms' human resource management (HRM) practices. The presumption of the standard price theory model of the firm is that the drive to maximize profit causes managers to adopt the most efficient array of HRM practices, leaving no route for unions to improve economic performance. But at least two theoretical reasons suggest this viewpoint is challengeable.

The first again stems from the principal-agent problem. A competitive labor market will not have principal-agent problems because of the perfect information and perfect contract enforcement assumptions. But the existence of an employment relationship and set of HRM practices implies the existence of positive transaction cost and, hence, the likelihood of principal-agent problems in the firm. With principal-agent problems, in turn, managers presumably will in various ways design and enforce the "web of rules" governing the system of workforce governance (of which HRM practices are a subset) so that their self-interest is advanced at the expense of-both shareholders and workers. A union, therefore, may well promote efficiency if it uses collective bargaining to change the workplace rules toward a more efficient configuration.

The second reason has to do with fairness and workplace morale. The monopoly view of unions F&M criticize provides no analytical room for fairness and morale, at least in the price theory version most economists use to evaluate unions (Rees, 1993). Efficiency is independent of distributional fairness by the fundamental welfare theorem, while the link between fairness, morale, and work effort is typically obviated by the assumption that labor supply is a commodity-like service of a certain determinate quality/quantity. It has long been recognized among practitioners and the old labor economists, and more recently captured in modern behavioral and efficiency wage models by Akerlof (1990) and others, that fairness, morale, and efficiency in the workplace are tightly linked both theoretically and empirically. When employees feel distributive justice has been violated, they deliberately cut back on work effort and shirk on the job in order to re-establish an equilibrium in the wage/effort bargain. Similarly, when norms of procedural justice are violated, morale falls and dispirited employees exert less work effort. Unions can thus improve workplace productivity, as F&M's voice/response model predicts, by reducing the morale and effort-sapping effects of unfairness and injustice, achieved in part by better HRM policies and practices—including more formal and balanced dispute resolution procedures.

So far the thrust of the argument suggests that the positive union voice/response effect on productivity does have a sound theoretical basis. But closer analysis also reveals that the union effect on management and productivity is for other reasons far less likely to be positive. These dimensions of the voice/response face are largely omitted by F&M. The most important concerns the adversarial nature of collective bargaining and its corrosive effect on trust, cooperation, and commitment in the workplace.

A central tenet of management thought is that organizations achieve higher performance when, first, the goals of the employer and employees are aligned (a "unity of interest") so all organizational energy is directed toward a common end and, second, when each side has a high degree of trust in the other, thus overcoming prisoner-dilemma problems and fears of opportunistic behavior (Miller, 1991; Kaufman, 2003a). Collective bargaining, however, emphasizes divergent interests, creates a conflictive "we versus them" environment, and is prone to communicate to the workers the message that management is frequently not competent or trustworthy. A large question exists, therefore: Is collective bargaining compatible in the general case with a mutual gains, high-performance work model? Framed in terms of Hirschman's model, the question is: Does collective bargaining tend to create or perpetuate what he calls a "deteriorated relationship"? One reason for concern is a key construct in Hirschman's theory that F&M largely neglect: employee loyalty. Hirschman posits that workers who feel greater loyalty to the employer will use voice more often and to more constructive effect, yet greater job dissatisfaction and adversarialism in union firms arguably works to corrode employee loyalty (Lincoln and Kalleberg, 1996; Boroff and Lewin, 1997; Luchak, 2003).

Heightening these concerns is the political process in unions where competition for office may lead candidates to accentuate criticism of the employer and take a militant position toward future bargaining demands, while cooperation with management can quickly become tagged as a sell out (Kleiner and Pilarsksi, 2001). Going further, unions introduce a third party into the employment relationship that may pursue organizational goals counterproductive to firm performance. For example, union locals may have a self-interest in promoting or perpetuating animus and distrust of management in order to maintain membership loyalty and militancy, while at the industry level a national union may insist on a uniform pattern of wages and benefits even if this means certain plants or companies go out of business. F&M omit all of these negative features of union voice.

Not only do F&M omit most of these negative aspects of union voice, but they also appear to put management in a contradictory, no-win situation. On one hand, F&M (p. 12) say that it is management's responsibility to say "no" when the union monopoly quest for "more" threatens the economic viability of the firm, yet they also say (pp. 11, 176) that it is management's responsibility to make union voice a "plus" for the firm's economic performance by creating a labor-management climate that is cooperative and relatively conflict free. But are these mandates consistent and mutually attainable, or will cooperation purchase short-term peace at the cost of long-term economic decline?

The attention to this point has been on the interaction between worker voice and firm performance. But voice also has other rationales. A central one is to protect and promote workers' interests and, more generally, provide a more democratic form of workforce governance. Although F&M gave this factor more weight than many economists, they arguably could have gone further given their desire to construct a positive case for unions.

Viewing firms as production functions and markets as competitive, neoclassical economists typically do not accept the argument that workers need protection from managerial abuse of power or greater democratic rights and channels for voice. Illustratively, Alchian and Demsetz (1972: 777) remark,

> It is common to see the firm characterized by the power to settle issues by fiat, by authority, or by disciplinary action superior to that available in the competitive market. This is delusion. It has no power of fiat, no authority. . . . Telling an employee to type this letter rather than file this document is like telling a grocer to sell me this brand of tuna rather than that brand of bread. I have no contract to continue to purchase from the grocer and neither the employer nor the employee is bound by any contractual obligations to continue the relationship.

This is one view (also see Reynolds, 1984). Viewed from the perspective of institutional economics, however, a different conclusion emerges. This theory models the firm not as a production function but as a form of industrial government (or workforce governance). Both the law and operation of markets, in turn, give firms and their owners/managers a power advantage over individual workers. Although the firm and worker are legal equals when bargaining the employment contract (both free to accept or reject), once the contract is consummated the employee is legally mandated to follow the orders and accept the policies of the employer. The law of the employment relationship thus sets up an asymmetrical authority relation in the firm where the employer is the order-giver and the worker is the order-taker. But, as Alchian and Demsetz argue, employers are restrained in their use of this power by competitive market forces and reputational concerns, implying the authority advantage given to the employer by the law may be empty of substantive content. But for an employment relationship to exist there must be positive transaction cost, implying labor markets are imperfectly competitive. Market forces and the threat of quitting are thus imperfect protectors of workers' rights and interests—especially so when in many years involuntary unemployment exists and firms have an excess supply of job seekers.

In such a situation, and without government or union regulation, the workplace can become a form of industrial autocracy with only weak checks and balances, no forum for voice by the worker "subjects," and modest or no protection of due process for employees in disputes over termination, discipline, and other such matters. Of course, for business and philosophical reasons some (perhaps many) employers exercise their power with enlightened paternalism and professionalism, but others—more pressed by economic survival pressures or less constrained by humanitarian ethics—manage employees in an oppressive, unjust, and inhumane manner. To correct this power imbalance, institutionally oriented labor economists have favored unions as one method to bring greater democracy to the workplace (Turnbull, 2003; Budd, 2004; Kaufman, this volume's history chapter). Doing so, they believe, leads (within bounds) to more of both efficiency and fairness, given the complementary link between the two as previously described. A relevant example is the decision of Harvard clerical workers to unionize because they lacked voice and influence and their use of collective voice to generate win-win outcomes for workers and the employer (Hoerr, 1997).

F&M fall somewhere in the middle of these two viewpoints, but their model of and justification for voice are in certain respects heavily neoclassical. In places F&M cite the positive role of unions in democratizing the workplace and protecting workers from arbitrary management authority. These aspects involve a shift of *power* and *rights* from capital to labor. But these considerations are secondary to their argument. Instead, as pointed out earlier, F&M justify union voice on other grounds: correcting a public goods problem in the supply of workplace conditions, employment terms that better match majority preferences in the workforce, and a reduction in wasteful employee quits. What all three have in common is that the positive function of voice originates from improved *communication* and *information* in the workplace.

I personally find all three explanations insightful and to some degree persuasive. But there are also several problems with this scenario. The first is that F&M largely treat union voice and union power as separable constructs and, further, portray the former as good and the latter as bad. With respect to separability, one may ask: Can union voice be effective without some collective power to force the employer to not only listen but also act? For example, is it not through the exercise of power that unions gain the accoutrements of voice cited by F&M, such as seniority and grievance systems, and is it not union power that prevents the employer from unfairly firing or disciplining workers? More generally, can industrial democracy be more than an empty slogan if unions do not have the power to force the firm to give workers new rights, representation, and due process? And, if it is granted that unions need power to effectuate voice, then how is it possible conceptually or practically to separate the exercise of power to improve wages from the exercise of power to improve treatment?

Finally, the thrust of my remarks in the previous section was to argue that F&M paint an unduly negative portrait of unions' short-run monopoly face by assuming *a priori* that it always harms economic efficiency. My contention here is that they sin in the opposite direction with the union voice face. F&M portray union voice as an almost unambiguous plus for economic/social welfare. But just as union wage raising can be good for welfare (rather than uniformly bad), so too can union voice be bad (rather than uniformly good).

For example, F&M assert that union voice benefits efficiency by lowering quit rates. But this argument is far from ironclad. A problem is that F&M do not address what is the optimal level of quits in the labor market, but without knowing this datum it is impossible to determine the plus or minus effect of unions. Furthermore, they assume that the level of quits in a nonunion labor market is excessive, but this is by no means self-evident. After all, if labor markets are competitive, is not the quit level already at its efficient level? Equally serious, F&M do not consider that unions could reduce the quit rate *below* the optimal level—an omission exacerbated by their tendency to emphasize the benefits of reducing quits but neglect the costs. In this regard, unions may lower quits but they may do so by making it very difficult for firms to induce the "deadwood" to voluntarily leave. Firing the deadwood also becomes more difficult.

Similar considerations apply to other dimensions of the union voice face. If union seniority systems are good for efficiency, one must ask: Why do most nonunion firms not adopt them voluntarily and, once unionized, why do they resist putting them in place? Or, contra F&M, are these systems another form of monopoly tax levied on the firm's profits in which unions through a form of price discrimination extract additional rents for senior workers (Kuhn, 1988)? It is also far from self-evident that union arbitration and grievance systems are on balance a plus for efficiency or, more broadly, bring more social benefits than costs, particularly relative to alternative systems of dispute resolution (Lewin, this volume). Unions, for example, can use the grievance system, not for voice, but as another source of bargaining power to pressure the employer and extract monopoly rents (e.g., by flooding the system with grievances, which the employer settles by "buying them off" through a better contract settlement). Even if used purely for voice, these systems can be relatively expensive and time consuming, requiring months to reach a settlement and often thousands of dollars in fees for lawyers and arbitrators.

One also finds the same ambiguity about another dimension of union voice—giving workers democratic voice in the workplace. On one hand, nonunion workplaces can be quite oppressive when workers are exposed to the unilateral, arbitrary, and unfair decisions of managers and supervisors. Instructive evidence, for example, comes from a recent case study of work in a poultry processing plant (Striffler, 2002). Setting the tone, a sign hangs prominently on the wall of the small classroom where new hires go for orientation and says in English and Spanish "Democracies depend on the political participation of its citizens, but not in the workplace." The author then details how the old supervisors were laid-off, new supervisors brought in with instructions to reduce headcount and increase production, and workers either submitted to "intolerable and economically unsound" decisions or quit (p. 310). Unions help protect workers from this kind of abuse and give them a voice in the rules and operation of the workplace, quite possibly improving both equity *and* efficiency. But not all unions are themselves democratic and some are significantly corrupt and dictatorial (Strauss, 2001). F&M downgrade union blemishes in this area, but the nation's oldest and most knowledgeable observer of union democracy recently stated, "The reality is that in wide sections of the American labor movement, crudely or subtly, democratic rights are suppressed, or in peril, or viewed with contempt. No discussion of union democracy can be taken seriously unless it faces up to these facts" (Benson, 2002: 73).

Monopoly and Voice: The Political Sphere

The interplay of the monopoly and voice faces in *WDUD* largely takes place in the labor market (wage determination) and the performance and governance of the firm. In Chapter 13, however, F&M examine the role of unions in the political arena.

The monopoly and voice faces of unions are modestly reconfigured in this chapter. F&M accept that unions have political power and pose the issue as: first, how much political power do unions have?; and, second, do they use this power to promote their narrow organizational interests in greater membership and collective bargaining power or, alternatively, do they use this power to promote a broader social and economic agenda benefiting a wide cross section of workers, consumers, environmentalists, and other groups? If the former, F&M treat this as a manifestation of the negative monopoly face; if the latter they treat it as part of unions' positive voice face. Thus, in this formulation the distinction is not between alternative *forms* of union influence (power versus voice) but alternative *uses* of this influence.

On my theory scorecard are three substantial pluses from this part of *WDUD* and also several significant minuses or missed opportunities. The first plus is that F&M bring into the analysis the political dimension of union activity, a dimension typically neglected by economists; the second is that they again highlight the co-existence of a positive and negative side of unions; and the third is that the monopoly characterization usefully captures the aggrandizing economic side of union political action and the voice face usefully captures unions' role as a representative and spokesman for the broad social/class interests of workers.

But there are also drawbacks and shortcomings. Space allows me to discuss only what I consider is the most important (for more detail, see my history chapter). A basic insight of institutional economics is that the labor market and the employment relationship are embedded in a legal and social system and their operations and outcomes thus reflect the endowments and "rules of the game" established by national political leaders. While neoclassical labor economics typically takes these endowments and rules as a given, institutional economics notes the following: first, the rules and endowments determine the labor market outcomes (wages, hours, conditions) by influencing the structure of the market and the position and slope of the labor demand and supply curves; second, the rich and powerful (e.g., employers, property owners, the social elite) have preponderant influence in establishing these rules and endowments; and, third, self-interest will lead the political rulers to structure these rules and endowments to maximize the monopoly rents of the dominant groups (e.g., capitalists, white native-born men) at the expense of the excluded and marginalized groups (e.g., workers, women, blacks).

What this perspective usefully highlights that F&M miss is that part of the historical function of trade unions is to act as a *labor (working class) movement* and exert political power in order to change the rules and endowments so that labor as a class shifts from being an oppressed/marginalized outsider to a justly treated, listened-to insider living in a progressive welfare state where workers have economic security and opportunities for personal self-actualization and self-development (Boeri et al., 2001; Hyman, 2001; Turnbull, 2003; Kaufman, 2004b). In this respect, the labor movement is no different from other social "liberation movements," such as the civil rights, feminist, and gay/lesbian movements. Thus, a well-known refrain of nineteenth century English trade unionists was (Thompson, 1964: 822) "From the laws of the few have the existing inequalities sprung; by the laws of the many shall they be destroyed," while Sidney and Beatrice Webb (quoted in Dickman, 1987: 104) observe, "What the workers are objecting to . . . is a . . . feudal system of industry . . . of the domination of the mass of ordinary workers by a hierarchy of property owners." This kind of social domination and oppressive economic conditions represents "institutional exploitation."

Examined this way, a labor market can be highly competitive in the neoclassical sense yet institutionally structured so that employers as a group earn very high profits and workers get very low wages, long hours, and sweatshop conditions (e.g., if the labor supply curve is shifted far to the right along an inelastic labor demand curve by, say, an open immigration law). Furthermore, the entire judgment about the "monopoly face" of unions changes. Given a competitive labor market, neoclassical economists and F&M are prone to view unions as a negative force that undesirably raises wages and causes a welfare loss to society. From an institutional perspective, however, the erstwhile competitive wages and conditions are artificially depressed by monopolistic political and social rules, and unions thus simultaneously perform two useful functions: First, they use collective bargaining to directly raise wages and conditions to what would be the competitive level with balanced rules and endowments (an institutional form of monopsony-reducing wage increase) and, second, they use political power to level the playing field and win expanded social welfare protection by changing the rules and endowments in workers' favor through legislation and electoral politics.

The gist of the foregoing is that union monopoly power in the political realm, just as in the economic realm, cannot on an *a priori* basis be put on the minus side of the social balance sheet, at least if one gives any weight in the social welfare function to providing workers with humane, balanced, and just wages and conditions (Budd, 2004; Kaufman, 2005). But it is also true that unions in their quest for "more" can also cross the line in the political sphere and use their power for purposes that unduly tilt the playing field in favor of their narrow organizational interests, as F&M claim. At some point, for example, one can surmise that the labor movement accomplishes its historic purpose of integrating labor into the polity and leveling the political playing field. To some degree unions remain necessary as a political counterweight to employers' political power. But one can also imagine that a strong labor movement will use political power to increasingly tip the rules and endowments in labor's favor, increasing the share of economic rents going to union labor at the expense of profits, consumers, and economic growth. Indeed, unions can use political power to gradually strangle capitalism in their quest for greater control and economic rents. In Europe, for example, many unions in the twentieth century promoted plans of "economic democracy," the central idea being to "euthanize capitalism" by using labor control of the government to pass legislation transferring corporate control from shareholders to unions (Kaufman, 2004b). U.S. unions have not gone this far in their political agenda but they do, nonetheless, seek to protect their monopoly gains through various political stratagems and regulatory measures that may well harm the public interest. Opposition to free-trade agreements, promotion of "industrial policy," a wide variety of restrictive labor laws, and getting taxpayer bail-outs of bankrupt union pension and health care programs are examples (Bierhanzl and Gwartney, 1998; Masters and Delaney, this volume).

Summary

My conclusion is that at a fairly high level of abstraction, or when used as a heuristic device, the two faces theory in *WDUD* performs relatively well in framing important issues about unions and informing our priors about expected empirical effects. This is largely what F&M intended it to do, so on these grounds they well succeeded. Examined more closely, however, the theory needs further conceptual development: In some cases it omits important dimensions of what unions do, and in some respects the model overstates and understates the benefits and costs of unions. The most important places for improvement in the theory are twofold. First, the issue of *power* is key to any theoretical analysis of the pros and cons of unions and a convincing case for greater collective bargaining has to demonstrate that efficiency or social welfare is advanced by giving workers greater collective power. F&M do not do this. Second, the monopoly and voice faces are not uni-dimensional constructs but both have beneficial and harmful sides that capture two alternative union functions: a "protection/improvement" face (beneficial) and an "aggrandizement/restriction" face (harmful). Thus, a useful extension of the two faces theory would be to re-frame it in terms of a 2 x 2 matrix with the monopoly and voice faces along one dimension and the protection/improvement and aggrandizement/restriction faces along the other. The four cells (the four faces of unions) would better capture the diverse roles and effects of unions. When these different faces of unions are considered, the combination of theory and real world developments (e.g., globalization of markets, greater geographic labor mobility, a transition from demand-side to supply-side economic growth) leads me to think that some of the pluses on the union scorecard have diminished since *WDUD* was written and some of the minuses have become larger. But this leads to the next section.

III. Empirical Evidence

The empirical part of F&M's book remains quite impressive for the breadth and depth of topics covered and the sophisticated statistical analysis of numerous data sets. When *WDUD* was published, union wage effects had been studied in some detail, most particularly by Lewis (1983). The non-wage effects of unionism were also starting to receive attention (see Table 1 in Freeman and Medoff, 1981), but the empirical literature was relatively spotty and not well integrated. F&M stepped into this situation and, in a major *tour de force*, raised the entire plane of empirical knowledge about unions, including challenging and unexpected results and an integrated portrait of what it all means.

In the introduction to *WDUD* F&M frame the empirical analysis with this observation (p. 19): "Since, in fact, unions have both a monopoly and a voice/response face, the key questions for understanding the impact of private-sector unionism in the United States relate to the relative importance of each. Are unions primarily monopolistic institutions, or are they primarily voice institutions that induce socially beneficial responses?" Striking a similar theme in the conclusion, they state (p. 246), "The central question is not, 'Who in principle is right?' but rather, 'Which face is quantitatively more important in particular economic outcomes?' "

And what is the grand picture of unionism that all of these empirical findings paint? F&M provided this summary statement (p. 19): "On balance, unionization appears to improve rather than harm the social and economic system. In terms of the three outcomes in Table 1.1, our analysis shows that unions are associated with greater efficiency in most settings, reduce overall earnings inequality, and contribute to, rather than detract from, economic and political freedom."

In this chapter I cannot cover all the separate empirical findings presented in *WDUD*. But provided below is modest commentary and assessment on those findings I consider most important.

Wages

The statistical portrait of private sector union wage effects presented by F&M is largely an accurate one (Blanchflower and Bryson, this volume). The aggregate union wage premium, according to their results, seems to fall in the 15–20 percent range. Calling for remark, however, is the slow downward drift of the aggregate union wage premium since the mid-1980s, despite a substantial decline in density, and a concomitant increase over time in the public sector union premium in the face of largely stable density. One could interpret this as evidence of a median voter mechanism at work, leading to an asymmetric pattern of wage changes (widespread wage rigidity with selective concessions in response to leftward labor demand curve shifts, an upward wage creep with stable or right- ward demand curve shifts) and an upward tendency in the wage premium over time. But interpretation is tricky since density and the union premium are jointly determined and, furthermore, observed trends in aggregate wage differentials can reflect underlying changes in the population of unionized firms. Nonetheless, if this hypothesis is accurate, it suggests that F&M modestly understate the long-run harm of the negative monopoly face. More seriously (discussed below), F&M also probably understate the degree to which union wage gains come at the expense of long-run employment, capital investment, and growth.

Benefits

The statistical portrait of the union effect on benefits presented by F&M is also largely confirmed by subsequent analysis of more recent data (Budd, this volume). Unions raise employer compensation on benefits by as much as 70 percent in the United States, with a portion of this increase representing a redistribution of labor cost from wages to benefits (the voice effect) and the other portion representing a net add-on to wages (the monopoly effect). Both theory (the median voter model) and recent evidence (the increasingly onerous pension and health care obligations of a number of union companies) suggests, however, that F&M again understate the long-run negative impact of the union monopoly effect.

Earnings Inequality

Also accurate is F&M's conclusion that unionism reduces inequality in the distribution of labor market earnings and that the decline in unionism is a significant contributing factor to the rise in overall earnings inequality in the United States and other countries in the last several decades (Card et al., this volume). A partial exception, however, is that the inequality reducing effect of unions appears to largely apply to men but not women (ibid.). Whether this equalizing effect is good or harmful to the economy and social welfare is a largely unanswered question, although Pencavel (this volume) suggests a definite cost in reduced employment growth.

Quits and Tenure

Addison and Belfield's analysis for this symposium suggests that F&M also accurately captured the overall union effect on employee quits (negative) and job tenure (positive). They also find, as F&M report, that the voice effect on quits and tenure is larger than the monopoly wage effect. F&M conclude the reduction in quits and lengthening of job tenure is a significant plus for firm performance and efficiency. I suspect, however, that they overstate the case.

Some empirical research finds that union voice contributes very little to lower quits (Delery et al., 2000). Also, F&M do not, as previously pointed out, provide evidence that the nonunion level of quits and tenure is suboptimal, or by how much. Furthermore, union wage leveling, promotion-by-seniority, and restrictions on termination may well reduce quits the greatest amount for the least productive workers but increase quits for the most productive (Bishop, 1990). In addition, a recent study shows that it is not unionism *per se* that reduces quits but, most importantly, the provision of health insurance benefits and the presence of job ladders, seniority provisions, and other features of internal labor markets (Fairris, 2004). Union firms have more of these variables, as F&M note, but, nonetheless, omitting them from the quit regressions is likely to overstate the union effect and the voice component thereof. And, finally, is it correct to infer, as F&M do, that lower quits from seniority clauses and grievance systems are, on net, a positive voice effect or, alternatively, do these factors have a predominantly negative monopoly effect on quits to the extent they represent, like higher wages, a source of additional rents for union workers?

Macroeconomic Effects

WDUD does not provide much coverage of the macroeconomic effects and consequences of unions. The cyclical adjustment of labor cost is considered in Chapter 7, and Chapter 3 briefly discusses how unions affect inflation. F&M conclude that union wages are a negligible contributor to inflation for three reasons: the union wage premium has little long-run trend; the share of union labor cost in total cost is modest; and union wage changes do not have significant spillover effects on nonunion wage changes. I believe, however, this interpretation is too optimistic.

Simply eyeballing the data from 1950 to the present, in countries with a decentralized bargaining system, one sees a link between union density and macroeconomic performance that is hard to slough-off as all correlation and no causation. Is it coincidence, for example, that in the United States the inflation rate gradually ratcheted upward during the period of strong unionism (1950–1980) or that government policy makers felt compelled to resort to various forms of wage controls to restrain union settlements, while in the period of declining union power (1980–present) the nation has enjoyed a remarkable period of strong job growth and price stability? Furthermore, inflation behavior in Britain, Canada, and Australia shows much the same time-series pattern. Thus, is it coincidence that in the era of strong unionism in the United Kingdom the economy was the inflation-prone "sick man of Europe," while in the post-Thatcher years of much-weakened unionism Britain has enjoyed the best record in Europe of robust employment growth and price stability? Obviously, many other factors play a role in explaining this pattern, but to argue that unionism had a zero effect seems a stretch.

In a Phillips curve framework, unionism may either affect the slope or intercept of the inflation/unemployment trade-off. For median voter reasons, unions may exert some upward cost-push pressure on wages and prices at any given unemployment rate (steeping the slope). As F&M argue, however, the direct quantitative effect is likely to be modest and, furthermore, structural change since 1980 appears to have weakened the linkage between union wages and inflation (Budd and Nho, 1997). F&M ignore, on the other hand, the potential indirect union effect which operates through pressure on the central bank to accommodate union wage push through monetary expansion (Pencavel, this volume). Mitchell and Erickson (this volume) suggest that this channel was well recognized by the U.S. Federal Reserve Bank, and Flanagan (2003) notes that a major argument for European-style centralized bargaining is that it better contains union wage settlements and thus relieves pressure on the central bank to choose between low unemployment/rising inflation and high unemployment/low inflation. In an American context, a good case can be made that high union density, when combined with decentralized bargaining and business unionism, is likely to shift rightward the intercept of the Phillips curve, leading to a higher NAIRU (non-accelerating inflation rate of unemployment). Several time-series studies find that the NAIRU increased in the 1960s and 1970s and then fell in the 1980s and 1990s, mirroring the trend in union membership and power (Gordon, 1997; Ball and Mankiw, 2002), whereas cross-sectional studies find a positive relationship between union density and the unemployment rate across cities, states, and regions (Pantuosco et al., 2001). In their calculations of the economic balance sheet of unionism, F&M ignore this macroeconomic source of welfare loss. A back-of-the-envelope calculation suggests, however, that it could easily swamp the positive voice effect. For example, a one-half percentage point increase in the NAIRU implies, via Okun's law, an approximate $100 billion loss of GDP in order to maintain price stability.

Job Satisfaction

F&M find that union workers report, on average, a lower level of job satisfaction than nonunion workers and that the bulk of this dissatisfaction comes from unhappiness with supervisors and working conditions. They also note an (alleged) paradox: If union workers are more dissatisfied with their jobs, they should quit more often, but in fact quit rates are considerably lower. So, F&M argue that the dissatisfaction union workers feel is not a genuine, objectively accurate unhappiness but a perceived, subjective unhappiness that arises from greater use of voice ("complaining loudly") and the feeling of politicization that accompanies it.

Subsequent empirical research, surveyed by Hammer and Agvar (this volume), supports F&M's finding on the negative union effect on job satisfaction. As they note, however, the cause and interpretation of this finding is complex and not in all respects in agreement with F&M.

There is, first, a sample-selection problem since union workplaces tend to come from the bottom-end of the job satisfaction distribution. One reason is that the characteristics of union jobs tend to be undesirable, such as assembly line work and jobs involving higher safety risks. But also pertinent is F&M's observation (pp. 146–48) that the most important reason unorganized workers seek a union is significant dissatisfaction with the employer, and Hammer and Agvar's conclusion that a negative industrial relations climate is a major cause of low job satisfaction. In terms of Hirschman's model, the employment relationship is already often deteriorated when the union enters the picture. One must then question, given this deteriorated situation, what effect the introduction of collective bargaining will have on workers' job satisfaction. Even if it rises, satisfaction may not rise to the level of well-managed nonunion companies with a positive (non-deteriorated) industrial relations climate. And, paradoxically, the quit rate among the dissatisfied union employees can still be lower if mobility costs, such as a union-negotiated health plan, lock them into jobs with the firm—suggesting that the behavioral response to dissatisfaction may then appear in other less functional and possibly negative-sum ways, such as surly relations with supervisors and a "work to rule" mentality (Luchak, 2003; Lewin, this volume).

One also must ask the question whether it is in the self-interest of unions as institutions to have satisfied workers? The answer would seem to go both ways. Unions presumably attract new members and retain existing members by "delivering the goods" and presumably doing so leads to more satisfied workers. But, on the other hand, if unions eliminate the sources of employee dissatisfaction, will the workers continue to see a reason to pay monthly dues? Or, is part of the adversarial dynamic of collective bargaining a certain penchant on the part of unions to "manufacture" discontent in order to maintain worker militancy and solidarity against the employer?

The conclusion I reach is that the issue of job satisfaction is a complicated one with multiple interpretations, but that on net the reduced job satisfaction reported by union members is more real than F&M suggest and arises in significant part from an adversarial, low-trust employee relations climate that is more likely to exist in organized firms both *ex-ante* and *ex-post* to the union.

Productivity, Employment, and Capital Investment

F&M conclude that (p. 180), "productivity is generally higher in unionized establishments than in otherwise comparable establishments that are nonunion [and] higher productivity appears to run hand in hand with good industrial relations and to be spurred by competition in the product market." Because the positive productivity advantage of union firms remains after controlling for differences in capital intensity, educational skills of the workforce, and other such factors (monopoly face responses as firms substitute physical and human capital for higher cost union labor), F&M conclude that the positive union productivity effect comes from the voice/response face.

F&M note in *WDUD* that their findings on productivity are (p. 180), "probably the most controversial and least widely accepted result in the book." Twenty years later this remains an accurate statement. The chapters by Hirsch, Addison and Belfield, and Gunderson in this symposium survey the evidence for, respectively, the United States, Great Britain, and the North American public sector. Hirsch concludes (p. 209), "Overall, the evidence produced since *What Do Unions Do?* suggests that the authors' characterization of union effects on productivity was overly optimistic. . . . [M]y assessment of existing evidence is that the average union effect is very close to zero, and as likely to be somewhat negative as somewhat positive." Likewise, Addison and Belfield report that the evidence for Great Britain shows a negative union effect on productivity up to the 1980s but since then a diminution of this effect, due, they suggest, to the fact the conservative Thatcher government enacted legislation that considerably weakened union bargaining power. For Germany they find that works councils have a neutral (zero) effect on productivity, leading them to conclude (p. 249) that collective worker organizations have "an average productivity effect near zero." Gunderson reaches similar conclusions for the public sector, observing

(p. 412) that the empirical evidence "does not support the notion that unions have positive effects and certainly not large enough to offset any wage cost effects." He further notes that since management opposition, and perhaps union bargaining power (due to restrictions on the right to strike), are less in the public sector one could reasonably hypothesize that positive union voice effects would be more noticeable, yet such evidence is lacking.

A fair conclusion based on these studies, as well as others (Metcalf, 2003), is that F&M likely overstated the positive union effect on productivity, with the actual effect being approximately zero. They appear on solid ground, however, in arguing that productivity varies with the industrial relations climate. After a review of the evidence, Hirsch concludes that union plants with cooperative labor relations and high-performance HRM practices have above-average productivity, whereas union plants with adversarial relations and traditional "job control" HRM practices have below-average productivity. The problems, however, are threefold: first, only a distinct minority of union establishments are in the cooperative, high-performance category; second, this configuration may be a difficult equilibrium to attain and maintain since it appears to depend on a high degree of union organizational security; and, third, other forms of workforce governance may yield even better results (Pencavel, 2001).

Productivity is a static indicator of firm performance; also important is the time path of firm performance. Three key indicators are productivity growth, employment growth, and capital investment. F&M examined productivity growth and concluded the union effect is zero, but they largely did not cover employment and capital investment.

In his survey article, Hirsch examines the subsequent evidence from the empirical literature on productivity growth. He concludes (p. 210, emphasis in original), "There exists no strong evidence that unions have a *direct* effect on productivity growth." This result is in agreement with F&M. But Hirsch inserts and emphasizes the important caveat "*direct* effect."

Most empirical studies of the union effect on productivity growth control for differences in levels or changes in factor-input usage. But most studies find that unionism has a statistically significant negative effect on capital investment (Hirsch, this volume; Metcalf, 2003). Hirsch concludes this negative effect arises from two sources: higher union-induced labor cost reduces the return to capital and the incentive to invest; and higher union labor cost also reduces firm profits and thus raises the cost of investment funds. Thus, in this respect unionism does have an *indirect* negative effect on productivity growth through the channel of reduced capital investment. A modest body of empirical research also suggests that a second indirect negative effect comes from union resistance to organizational and technological change (Lieberman, 1997; Schwarz-Miller and Talley, 2002) and, at least for North America, lower corporate spending for research and development (Menezes-Filho and Van Reenen, 2003).

F&M did not empirically examine the union effect on employment growth. Subsequent research finds that unionism is associated with slower employment growth in both the United States and other countries (the Hirsch and Pencavel chapters). A study of UK firms between 1990 and 1998, for example, finds that employment grew 29 percent slower in private sector union firms and 18 percent slower in unionized public sector organizations, while an Australian study reported union employment grew at a 2.5 percent slower annual rate (Addison and Belfield, 2004; Wooden and Hawke, 2000). These results suggest that the union sector gradually loses competitive advantage over time due to a combination of higher costs and lower capital investment and innovation, reflected in a shrinking employment base in relative terms and, often, absolute terms. The most notable exception to this rather bleak picture is provided by Freeman and Kleiner (1999). Their empirical analysis finds that firms with a union actually have a lower "death rate" relative to comparable nonunion firms, although this relationship is contingent on the percent of the firm's workforce organized, and past a moderately high density level unionized enterprise death rates are greater. They interpret these conclusions to mean that unions reduce profitability but, in general, not to the point firms are driven from the industry. As Hirsch observes, however, this result is significantly at odds with the substantial body of negative evidence on capital investment and employment growth.

Profitability

F&M examine the effect of unionism on profits and find (p. 190) "the evidence on profitability shows that, on average, unionism is harmful to the financial well-being of organized enterprises or sectors." As they note, however, the economic and social consequences depend greatly on the source of the profits that unions capture. That is, are unions capturing large-sized monopoly rents that otherwise accrue to shareholders as above-normal returns or, alternatively, are they capturing profits that represent part of the competitive rate of return on capital needed to keep the enterprise a going concern? They conclude it is much more the former than the latter, stating (p. 186): "These data suggest that unionism has no impact on the profitability of competitive firms. . . . What unions do is to reduce the exceedingly high levels of profitability in highly concentrated industries toward normal competitive levels."

Research conducted in the 20 years since *WDUD* also finds consistent evidence that unionism reduces profitability. Hirsch (this volume), for example, concludes, "The finding of lower profitability from unionization is not only invariant to the profit measure used, but also holds regardless of the time period under study and holds for analyses using industries, firms, or lines-of-business as the observation unit." He estimates that union firms earn on the average 10–20 percent less profits than comparable nonunion firms. Addison and Belfield (this volume) examine the research literature for Britain and Germany and also find fairly clear evidence of a negative profit effect, in the case of Germany for works councils.

The more controversial and less determined part of the issue concerns the source of the unions' encroachment on profit: competitive returns or monopoly rents? Hirsch concludes in his survey paper that unions most likely capture both; that is, part of their bite on corporate profits comes out of monopoly rents but another part comes out of competitive returns on long-lived capital investments. He argues, therefore, that part of the decline of the union sector stems from the negative effect unions have on profits (the combined effect of higher union wages and a zero productivity differential), but that the verdict is still out on the size and importance of this effect.

HRM Practices

The union effect on specific aspects of enterprise operations and human resource management (HRM) practices receive very modest empirical investigation in *WDUD*. Theoretically, F&M argue that one of the channels through which unions promote higher productivity is by causing management to professionalize, formalize, and standardize employment practices. They note, for example, that after successful union organizing campaigns the plant management is frequently replaced, while econometric analysis indicated that any reductions in management flexibility from unionism has a negligible effect on productivity.

Verma's review of the research literature on this subject provides evidence on both the plus and minus columns of the union scorecard. On one hand, unions are associated with more employee training, longer lasting employee participation systems, and more formalized rules and procedures for discipline and discharge. Whether these are voice effects or monopoly effects is unclear, however. On the other hand, unions also impose numerous restrictions on management that arguably hurt productivity, such as inflexible work rules, limits on transfer and termination, strict promotion by seniority, and inability to base pay on individual performance. The net outcome is theoretically ambiguous, and no empirical study has provided conclusive, broad-based evidence. However, since F&M's argument rests heavily on unions' hypothesized positive effect on productivity, it is worrisome that the empirical evidence does not reveal a significant and quantitatively important transmission mechanism between unionism, HRM practices, and productivity.

The Political Arena

F&M came to three broad conclusions about the union political effect. The first is that unions are quite successful in mobilizing resources and exerting power in the political process. The second is that this exercise of union power leads to a mixed, but generally significant, amount of success in securing legislation that promotes a progressive or liberal social agenda. The third is that the union movement is mostly unsuccessful in using its political power to gain new legislation that promotes its own interests, such as expanded legal immunities, stronger protections of the right to organize, and enhanced bargaining power, but seems able to rally enough support to defeat efforts to weaken this type of legislation. Masters and Delaney (this volume) re-examine these findings and conclude that they continue to describe the American situation, but with important caveats. They observe that since *WDUD* was published the union movement has shifted more of its efforts and resources to political action, reflecting a constellation of developments: a decline in its bargaining reach and effectiveness, a severe erosion of membership and threat to organizational survival, and a stronger and more assertive political attack by conservative social/business groups on unions in particular and the New Deal social welfare state in general. Masters and Delaney find that despite investing greater resources in the political arena the yield for unions is disappointing. That is, the ability of unions to enhance and protect both the broad corpus of social/employment legislation and the more narrow body of union-related legislation has discernibly declined over time. The reason, they cite, is "labor fails at the critical test: it simply does not inspire. . . . Unions must seek progress, not regress, if they are to inspire people to action." I conclude this evidence supports F&M in broad outline but also indicates that over time unions have lost political influence and persuasiveness along a broad front. If unions are on net good for the social balance sheet, as F&M claim, one has to wonder why the public and its political leaders seem increasingly out-of-step with this fact?

Management Resistance and Union Decline

Chapter 15 of *WDUD* is devoted to "The Slow Strangulation of Private Sector Unionism." F&M note that while union membership from 1950 to 1980 had grown in absolute terms when looked at relative to the size of the nonagricultural workforce it had declined by one-third. They call this drop in density "unprecedented," claim that it "contrasts sharply with increases in unionism in most other Western countries," and note that if this pattern continues "the American labor movement will experience a precipitous decline in the next decade."

F&M then examine the causes of this decline. They note that changes in membership and density are a function of the net difference between inflows and outflows of workers from union membership. They estimate the annual outflow to be about 3 percent (implying if density is one-third it will fall by a percentage point in three to four years). They then look at the inflow and see that it dropped in half from the 1950s to the late-1970s-early 1980s—from 0.6 to 0.3 percent. The conclusion they reach is that the much larger size of the outflows from membership relative to the inflows portends a further substantial decline ("slow strangulation") in density until a point of stability is reached at about 10 percent.

F&M do not explicitly examine the outflow side of the equation and give very modest attention to possible causes of the attrition of union membership. Rather, they focus on the inflow side, with one partial exception. The first candidate for union decline they consider is structural economic change, a factor that likely affects both inflows and outflows. They conclude that structural change probably accounts for a modest portion of the decline in density. Focusing on the inflow side, they note that declining union organizing success could reflect diminished worker interest in unions. This factor is not empirically examined, however. Rather, much of the chapter is devoted to reasons the inflow of workers into unions through the NLRB (National Labor Relations Board) election process has shrunk so much. They conclude that part of the explanation is a decline in resources devoted to organizing by unions but that the most important factor is the interactive effect of much-heightened management opposition to unions and increasingly ineffective labor laws protecting workers rights to organize and collectively bargain. They buttress this conclusion by observing, first, that Canadian labor law provides stronger protection of the right to organize and Canadian union density was twice as high and rising and, second, that management opposition was much weaker in the American public sector and public sector density was also much higher and stable.

I believe F&M correctly capture part of the explanation for union decline but omit or misinterpret other parts. As they claim, the breadth and depth of management opposition to unions has increased since the 1960s and 1970s. This trend was remarked upon by management specialists in the 1980s (e.g., Mills, 1981) and has continued as "union-free" status has become both more acceptable and attainable. The statistical picture is admittedly mixed but data on workers fired during NLRB campaigns and unfair labor practices per NLRB election support this long-run trend (Commission on the Future of Worker, Management Relations, 1994; Flanagan, this volume). My own research on this matter (Kaufman and Stephan, 1995) also leads me to believe that these statistical series significantly understate the upward trend in the breadth, depth, and effectiveness of management opposition. The labor law has over the years been interpreted in ways that on balance tip the advantage to employers; a growing share of organizing now takes place outside the NLRA election framework; a number of unions have given up filing NLRA charges in the belief that doing so is futile; employers' tactics have grown far more sophisticated; and over time employers and their consultants learn how to cloth illegal anti-union actions in ways that avoid legal sanctions.

Anyone familiar with the world of work recognizes that the forces of weak labor law, determined employer opposition, and sometimes weak administrative enforcement makes successful organizing and winning first contracts a very difficult task (Hurd and Uehlein, 1994; Bronfenbrenner, 2001; Kleiner, 2002). This fact is reflected, in turn, in the significant long-term decline in new workers organized and represented by unions. On the inflow side, therefore, I believe F&M are correct to attribute a significant (but far from complete) portion of union decline to the interactive effect of employer opposition and weak labor laws.

But there are also important caveats to this conclusion and other factors to consider. For example, evidence indicates that sometimes management opposition actually increases worker commitment to seek union representation (Koeller, 1992; Fiorito, 2002). Also, one has to ask: Why has management opposition increased so much? F&M (p. 239) recognize this issue and tie it (in part) to the increase in the union wage premium in the 1970s and early 1980s. But the union wage premium has fallen since the mid-1980s so the logic of their argument suggests management resistance should follow. But most union supporters (Levin, 2001) claim that it is greater than ever. To reconcile this discrepancy I put forward this hypothesis: The cost penalty of being unionized has actually worsened in the last two decades, since the degree of competition in product markets has increased faster than the union wage premium has fallen, so management resistance continues to increase. Unions and their supporters may decry this heightened opposition, but one can argue that their monopoly gains are partly responsible and, furthermore, that firms are serving not only the interests of shareholders but also the larger public by signaling unions that these monopoly gains are increasingly noncompetitive.

As Troy (1999) and Flanagan (this volume) note, another likely factor behind the smaller inflow of new union members is a long-term decline in worker demand for union representation. F&M almost completely bypass this consideration, and it remains seriously under-researched. On one hand, strong reasons exist to think that part of the lackluster success unions have in gaining new members is because fewer workers find unions an attractive option. American workers join unions, for example, largely because they are dissatisfied with job conditions and treatment and believe that unions can improve these. But over the years unions have lost part of their appeal because of the incorporation of significant parts of the working class into the middle class, improvements in the quality of jobs and remuneration, and the growth of substitute solutions to labor problems. Three examples of the latter (Bennett and Kaufman, 2002) are more competitive, full-employment labor markets ("good markets"), more professional and effective human resource management practices ("good bosses"), and far more extensive legal regulation of the economic and social dimensions of the employment relationship ("good laws"). Union decline, therefore, may be more tied to "union substitution" than "union suppression." A prime example is the negative relationship between worker desire for union representation and the existence in nonunion firms of some form of employee involvement plan or formal dispute resolution program (Belfield and Heywood, 2004). Then, compounding the problem is that unions have also lost a good deal of bargaining power and effectiveness in raising wages and improving conditions for newly organized workers due to more competitive markets, the greater threat of striker replacement, and other such factors.

This story, while having considerable common-sense appeal and some empirical support (Farber and Krueger, 1993), nonetheless also faces problems. The major problem is that surveys find that between 31 and 48 percent of nonunion workers in America say they would like union representation, particularly if their companies did not oppose it (Freeman and Rogers, 1999; Lipset and Meltz, 2004). In addition, some evidence suggests worker interest in unions is *increasing* (Freeman and Rogers, 2001). These pieces of evidence strongly suggest that the demand for unions remains quite robust, but a large part of it is a "frustrated demand" in the sense workers are not able to actually to obtain representation. This shortfall may arise from employer opposition, weak labor laws, lack of resources and commitment to organizing by unions, or some combination of these factors.

F&M emphasize a low inflow into unions as the principle source of the "strangulation." A recent study by Farber and Western (2002) suggests, however, that it is actually the outflow side that is the far more important explanation. They state (p. 53), "The striking finding of this analysis is that the decline of the union organization rate in the U.S. over the last three decades is due almost entirely to declining employment in union workplaces and rapid employment growth in nonunion firms." Likewise, Pencavel (this volume) points out that union decline is not unique to the United States (which, if true, would point the finger of blame at American employers and laws) but has been proceeding for two decades or more in a number of the major economies of the world.

Thus, the implication is that the long-term decline in union density arises far more from the shrinkage of the existing base of union jobs due to plant closings, downsizings, and layoffs than from blocked organizing. This conclusion implies, in turn, that F&M significantly misidentify the source of the union strangulation. Employer opposition remains a significant factor, but it primarily arises as a profit reaction and takes the form of capital investment decisions that favor nonunion facilities in the United States and other countries. Unions also play a role in their demise by raising labor costs to noncompetitive levels, leading to lower capital investment and shrinking employment in union firms. And, finally, part of the strangulation of unions comes from more competitive, globally inter-connected product markets; increased capital mobility; and heightened financial pressures on companies for rising earnings and stock prices. In a case study of the Southern paper industry (Kaufman, 1997), I find clear evidence that it is these factors, coupled with union resistance to high performance work practices, that were primarily responsible for greater management opposition and the marked decline of the union sector.

Summary

Many of the empirical findings reported in *WDUD* have held up quite well over the subsequent two decades. This is an impressive accomplishment, particularly since the world has changed in some significant ways that F&M could not fully anticipate. Several empirical conclusions in *WDUD*, however, appear with the benefit of hindsight and better data to be off-target. The three most important areas of adjustment, in my opinion, are: a downward revision of the union productivity effect to zero; a downward revision of the macroeconomic effect of unions from neutral to harmful; and a shift from attributing the principal cause of union decline to a combination of "suppression" forms of management opposition and weak labor laws to the poor growth performance of union firms and, possibly, a decline in worker demand for unions. I conclude that the bottom line for unions on the economic balance sheet has to be given a minus sign, not a neutral or positive mark as F&M suggest, and that the direction of change is on balance toward the negative side. They are certainly correct, however, that the record on unions is mixed with significant pluses and minuses. Whether inclusion of the noneconomic effects of unions, e.g., industrial democracy, shifts the bottom line to a neutral or positive sign is difficult to answer given the more overtly normative character of the issues at stake and the lack of quantifiable evidence. Certainly some respected economists besides F&M believe so (Rees, 1989), and I shall offer reasons below in support of this argument.

IV. National Labor Policy

In *WDUD*'s concluding chapter F&M summarize the implications of their work for national labor policy. They state (p. 251), "the ongoing decline in private sector unionism . . . deserves serious public attention as being socially undesirable. . . ." and (p. 250) "While we are not sure what the optimal degree of unionization is in this country, we are convinced that current trends have brought the union density below the optimal level." F&M then provide three suggestions for changes in labor policy: strengthen the voice/response face of unions by encouraging more innovative and cooperative forms of labor-management relations; weaken the negative monopoly face by fostering greater product market competition and encouraging unions to be more cognizant of the long-run harm of always seeking "more;" and strengthen and better protect the ability of workers to join unions and collective bargain by expediting the NLRB election process and increasing the penalties for anti-union discrimination and refusals to bargain.

When F&M wrote *WDUD*, union density was 22 percent. They claimed that the optimal level of density was higher than this figure. In a later article Freeman (1992: 167) suggests the optimal density number is somewhere between the American and Scandinavian levels. As a rough and conservative approximation, this translates into a union density figure of 35–40 percent, or roughly equivalent to density in the U.S. public sector. Twenty years after *WDUD* density stands at 13 percent in the American economy, nearly one-half the level existing in 1984, and has fallen all the way to 8 percent in the private sector. If density was sub-optimal in 1984, as F&M claim, then is it several times more sub-optimal today? And, if so, would the nation really be better off by changing national labor policy to substantially raise union density?

These are difficult questions to answer. My judgment, however, is that neither theory nor empirical evidence support such a conclusion.

The kernel of the argument in *WDUD* is that worker voice in nonunion firms is under-supplied due to market failure. This argument was given much publicized and widely cited empirical evidence in a later study by Freeman and Rogers (F&R, 1999). They document from a large-scale survey the existence of a large "participation/representation gap" in the American workplace, indicating that workers want significantly more voice and influence in the workplace than they currently have. Although F&R probably over-state the size of the gap, theory suggests there are indeed good reasons to think competitive labor markets fail to provide the socially optimal amount of employee voice (Kaufman, 2001).

Nonunion firms provide voice only to the extent that it adds to profit. Freeman and Lazear (1995) and Kaufman and Levine (2000) show that for several reasons nonunion firms will undersupply voice relative to the efficient social optimum. Freeman and Lazear emphasize the divergence between private and social marginal benefit of additional collective voice. That is, employers stop short of the optimal level of collective employee voice because more voice also gives workers more leverage to capture some of the additional profits. Kaufman and Levine also point out other reasons voice is likely to be under-supplied, such as prisoner-dilemma problems, principal-agent problems, and adverse selection.

If voice is undersupplied in nonunion labor markets, is more collective bargaining the best solution to the problem? F&M say yes. Their suggested approach (or my interpretation of it) is to expand voice through greater union-ism but then neutralize the negative monopoly face of unions by promoting greater competition in product markets (e.g., through reduction of trade barriers) on the belief that unions will be effectively constrained from rais-ing labor cost lest they force organized firms out of business. This idea, I note, has a long heritage. It was espoused, for example, in the 1940s by Chicago libertarian economist Henry Simons (1948: 60) who, in a spirit similar to F&M, argued "If trade-unions could somehow be prevented from indulging in restrictive monopolistic practices, they might become invaluable institutions." I question, however, whether this approach is either workable or the best solution.

For example, why would millions of additional workers want to join unions if unions have no effective bargaining power to win gains at the negotiating table but, rather, largely function to make firms more efficient by solving free-rider and preference revelation/aggregation problems inside the enterprise? Likewise, it is unlikely that unions will forgo raising labor cost even in very competitive product markets. One reason is because their members may have shorter time horizons than capital owners (or national union leaders may follow a wage policy that promotes their organizational interests at the expense of members' employment) and are therefore willing to milk the quasi-rents even at the cost of eventual demise of the enterprise (a possibility recognized by Simons, 1948: 131); a second reason is because with sufficiently high density in local/regional markets unions are able to take labor cost out of competition and raise wages with only modest short-run employment loss. And, finally, one must ask if adversarial collective bargaining is really the most effective form of employee voice for fostering higher productivity and competitive advantage for American firms in global competition?

This last thought raises the more general question of whether there is some alternative way to remedy the voice shortfall but avoid the negative side of collective bargaining. The answer appears to be a potential yes. If the goal is greater collective voice for workers but without the negative monopoly effect of trade unions, the most obvious and direct solution would be more "company unionism" (broadly defined), such as nonunion employee involvement/representation programs, joint plant councils, alternative dispute resolution programs, or perhaps some variant of European works councils. These devices give employees a negligible-to-relatively-modest increase in power, thus leaving undisturbed the (presumed) competitive wage structure and overall workforce governance regime, but at the same time solve the voice shortfall by giving workers a formal mechanism for collective voice. Furthermore, because they lack the power and adversarialism of a trade union, and arguably contribute more to firm performance and profit (or subtract less), these forms of collective voice engender a smaller amount of employer opposition and may be more effective for workers.

But critics of these nonunion voice schemes, at least of the type that are voluntary and employer-created, reject them because they do not give workers power and influence and, as with some nonunion dispute resolution systems, can have procedurally unfair rules that favor the employer. F&M are in this camp. In *WDUD*, F&M (p.-108) say these schemes "lack power to affect decisions," are frequently "mere window-dressing," and fail to provide adequate voice because of workers' "fear of retaliation." Other critics condemn these nonunion devices because they give workers little power to affect wages, hours, and terms of employment; have no market reach and thus cannot raise and standardize wages in labor markets (take wages out of competition and equalize the earnings distribution); do not challenge the core of unilateral management authority in the firm; and give workers no voice in the political process.

Although all of these criticisms have varying degrees of truth, the empirical evidence suggests a blanket condemnation of employer-created nonunion forms of representation is far too negative. Indeed, modern research suggests these nonunion bodies can yield (with considerable variance) a variety of gains for both workers and firms (Kaufman, 2000, 2003b; Pencavel, 2003; Bryson, 2004). Possibly even better results could be obtained from some hybrid form of enterprise-level employee representation that combines the best of North American-style company unionism and European-style works councils. Both theory and evidence suggest, however, that relatively independent and legally mandated works councils along European lines are an inefficient "one size fits all" approach to voice that likely entails many of the negative costs of unions (Kaufman and Levine, 2000; Addison et al., 2004).

I conclude that F&M appear inconsistent on the subject of employee voice and seem to draw the wrong conclusion. If the exit/voice model and negative monopoly face of unions are taken at face value, the implication seems to be that the voice shortfall would be better served *not* by more trade unionism but by an expansion of nonunion forms of voice (Kaufman, 2001). This conclusion is buttressed by the survey findings of F&R that the majority of Americans want a form of employee representation that de-emphasizes power bargaining, adversarialism, and independence from the employer in favor of closer cooperation and win-win problem-solving and communication. This shift would require, however, a major change in American labor law since provisions of the NLRA (the "company union ban" in Sections 2.5 and 8.a.2) currently severely limit the ability of nonunion companies to operate worker representational committees (Kaufman, 1999b). F&M are silent on this matter but the inference is they did not then support it, nor did the Dunlop Commission of which Freeman was a member, nor did Freeman and Rogers in *What Workers Want*. Rather, F&M (and the Dunlop Commission and, less clearly, F&R) instead recommend changes in labor law to promote more trade unionism. I note, in this regard, that the most vociferous opponents of removing the company union ban in the NLRA are American trade unions, in part I speculate because the law preserves their near-monopoly in the supply of formal employee voice. American unions thus have *two* monopoly faces, one in wage determination and another in the supply of voice. Paradoxically, therefore, unions both expand and restrict voice and, contrary to the hypothesis of F&M, the net effect could be negative.

The bottom line is that if F&M are to give a convincing argument in favor of substantial labor law reform and greater unionism they must address the *power* issue and, in particular, show that society would be better off by augmenting workers' collective power in wage determination in *external labor markets*, workforce governance in *internal labor markets*, and political participation in the *national polity*. They reject nonunion forms of representation because they lack power but do not adequately make the case that independent unions are a superior option for voice in internal labor markets. Then, with respect to external labor markets, F&M contend that unions already have too much power, while they take a somewhat ambiguous position about the optimal degree of union power in the national polity. In my view this position does not add up to a clear and compelling case for greater unionism.

My personal belief is that a compelling, but limited, case can be made for public protection and encouragement of unionism in each of the three arenas just cited. In the short run, labor markets are often imperfect and a combination of limited jobs, costly mobility, imperfect information, and externalities can lead to various labor problems for workers that individual action and competitive market forces cannot fully resolve. In other cases, labor markets are highly competitive and lead to other serious labor problems for workers, such as long hours, greater work intensity, and job insecurity. Some form of protective institutional mechanism, such as unionism or labor law, thus gains social legitimacy. This conclusion is buttressed by four other observations. The first is that societies work best when economic outcomes are regarded as fair and balanced (Kitson et al., 2000; Budd et al., 2004); the second is that on ethical grounds workers should not be treated as commodities (Kaufman, 2005); the third is-that promoting consumers' interests over workers' interests is not distributionally neutral since the largest consumers also happen to be the wealthy who own considerable capital and property (according to Krugman, 2002, the wealthiest 13,000 families in America have almost as much income and thus consuming power as the poorest 20 million families); the fourth is that the union threat effect usefully policies labor conditions in nonunion firms, and, as a form of positive externality, deserves a degree of public encouragement (Bennett and Kaufman, 2002). Likewise, theory and evidence readily show that employers often have a power advantage over the individual employee and sometimes exercise it in ways that range from petty and arbitrary to oppressive and unjust. Again, a social rationale exists for some form of protective device such as a trade union. And, finally, a stable, democratic society requires that all major stakeholder groups have effective interest representation and voice in the creation and enforcement of the rules of the game. Without unions it is difficult to see how labor will be adequately represented or what political counterweight will exist to balance the substantial influence of the wealthy and business class. These are all classic arguments in favor of unions and continue to have merit, albeit on a smaller and more circumscribed scale (Kaufman and Lewin, 1998).

It is hard to convincingly demonstrate but I surmise for the reasons just given that the "optimal" level of unionism in the private sector is probably modestly higher than the current level (8 percent). Much easier to demonstrate is the proposition that the nation's labor law does not adequately protect workers' right to organize and collectively bargain. On these grounds a *prima facie* case exists for selective reforms to strengthen the NLRA, such as a somewhat shorter election period, higher and speedier penalties for anti-union discrimination, and some method to end first-contract impasses.

Having laid out the positive case for unions and labor law reform, I must also note that there is a substantial negative case that strongly suggests substantially higher union density is not in the nation's best interest—at least in the current social and economic milieu. First, a growing portion of employment problems are not well addressed by traditional collective bargaining because of the increasingly diverse nature of the workforce, the changing nature of jobs and employment, and the limited reach of collective bargaining to many sectors of the economy. In addition, many workers simply do not want collective bargaining. Second, the bulk of the evidence suggests that over the long run unions unduly raise labor cost and harm firm performance, leading to capital flight, poor productivity growth, and declining employment. The idea that the U.S. economy would perform better and gain competitive advantage with significantly higher union density in a decentralized bargaining system and a supply-side driven global market place cannot be given serious credence. Third, there remain serious and even growing labor problems for workers, particularly for the tens of millions in the lower end of the job market, due to the globalization and commodification of labor markets and erosion of the social safety and privatization of economic risk. It is not evident, however, that more collective bargaining is in many cases the best solution to these problems, at least absent a worldwide union movement that can once again take labor cost out of competition. Better would be measures such as immigration reform, improved school systems, more responsible corporate governance, and expanded labor law protection. Above all of these measures stands one other: full employment. If the labor market can remain close to full employment the case for expanded unionism is significantly reduced; to the degree labor markets are dragged down by unemployment workers will want and need greater protection. And fourth and finally, there also appear to be more efficient and effective ways to solve some of these labor problems at the workplace than collective bargaining. Examples include nonunion alternative dispute resolution systems, legally binding employee handbooks, and expanded employee involvement plans

This last thought leads me to my final conclusion. The most significant implication coming from the two books *What Do Unions Do?* and *What Workers Want?* is that the American labor market suffers from a significant shortfall of employee voice. Although I question the magnitude reported by F&R, the existence of a participation/representation gap seems eminently plausible. What is the best solution? I counsel a two-pronged approach. It has the advantage of substantially increasing the supply of employee voice in a way that is balanced toward unions and employers, is cost effective and easily implemented, and moves in the direction that American workers say they want. One prong is modest strengthening of the right to organize and collectively bargain, as outlined above. The second is to significantly encourage more nonunion and hybrid forms of employee participation, representation, and dispute resolution by dropping the company union ban in the NLRA and providing incentives for the parties to use in-house methods of joint consultation, mediation, and arbitration. The net effect is an increase in employee voice of *all* types and greater *competition* among the suppliers of voice. This proposal, I note, is exactly in the spirit of the one that F&M's Harvard predecessor Sumner Slichter recommended in Congressional testimony seven decades ago (Slichter, 1935; Kaufman, 2000).

V. Conclusion

Most books in the social sciences quietly slip into oblivion soon after publication. Very few remain frequently cited 20 years later and only a handful merit a retrospective symposium. One of these books is Freeman and Medoff's *What Do Unions Do?* When it was published, a reviewer (Mitchell, 1985: 253) labeled the book "a landmark in social science research." Two decades later this verdict still rings true. The authors of *WDUD* should be justifiably proud.

The thesis of *WDUD* is that unions have both beneficial and harmful effects on the social balance sheet but that the former outweighs the latter. F&M first developed a new "two faces" theory of unions to provide intellectual support for this proposition; they then subjected each facet of union behavior to empirical scrutiny through detailed statistical analysis of numerous data sets. The theory and empirical evidence spoke with one voice: unions are neither entirely saints nor sinners but on balance make a positive contribution to our economy and society.

No book gets everything right and certainly no set of authors can escape criticism from their peers. F&M and *WDUD* are no exception. Each paper in this symposium has in various ways pinpointed weaknesses in the theory, gaps in the evidence, and conclusions that in hindsight appear off-target. In this paper I have taken my turn and have suggested a number of places where F&M could have strengthened their argument, brought in different perspectives, or reached different conclusions. In particular, F&M might have presented a more convincing argument for unions if they had more broadly challenged and gone beyond the standard neoclassical model. Also, I believe in certain respects F&M understate the positive contribution of unions; in others they understate the harm of unions; and that their overall scorecard is modestly too optimistic. Also, in the two decades since publication of *WDUD* the economic and political environment has shifted in ways that are adverse to both unions and F&M's empirical work and policy conclusions. My judgment, however, is that while all of these criticisms and unforeseen events have dented the body of *WDUD* the book's central message, evidence, and scholarly contribution still stand tall.

Note

*   I acknowledge with appreciation the helpful comments of Richard Freeman, Barry Hirsch, Morris Kleiner, and John Pencavel.

References

Addison, John, Claus Schnabel, and Joachim Wagner. "The Course of Research into the Economic Conseuences of German Works Councils." *British Journal of Industrial Relations* 42 (June 2004): 255–81.

————. "Unions and Employment Growth: The One Constant?" *Industrial Relations* 43 (April 2004b): 305–23.

Akerlof, George. "The Fair-Wage-Effort Hypothesis and Unemployment." *Quarterly Journal of Economics* 105 (May 1990): 255–84.

Alchian, Armen and Harold Demsetz. "Production, Information Costs, and Economic Organization." *American Economic Review* 72 (December 1972): 777–95.

Altman, Morris. *Worker Satisfaction and Economic Performance: Microfoundations of Success and Failure*. Armonk, NY: M.E. Sharpe, 2001.

Ball, Laurence and Gregory Mankiw. "The NAIRU in Theory and Practice." *Journal of Economic Perspectives* 16 (Fall 2002): 115–36.

Belfield, Clive and John Heywood. "The Desire for Unionization, HRM Practices, and Coworkers." In Phanindra Wunnava, ed. *The Changing Role of Unions: New Forms of Representation*. Armonk, NY: M.E. Sharpe, 2004, pp. 251–80.

Bennett, James T. and Bruce Kaufman. "Conclusion: The Future of Private Sector Unionism in the U.S.—Assessment and Forecast." In James T. Bennett and Bruce E. Kaufman, eds. *The Future of Private Sector Unionism in the United States*. Armonk, NY: M.E. Sharpe, 2002, pp. 349–85.

Benson, Herman. "Strengthening Union Democracy." *Working USA* 5 (Spring 2002): 71–83.

Bierhanzl, Eward and James Gwartney. "Regulation, Unions, and Labor Markets." *Regulation* 21 (3 1998): 40–53.

Bishop, John. "Job Performance, Turnover, and Wage Growth." *Journal of Labor Economics* 8 (July 1990): 363–86.

Boeri, Tito, Agar Brugiavini, and Lars Calmfors. *The Role of Unions in the Twenty-First Century*. Oxford: Oxford University Press, 2001.

Boroff, Karen and David Lewin. "Loyalty, Voice, and Intent to Exit a Union Firm: A Conceptual and Empirical Analysis." *Industrial and Labor Relations Review* 51 (October 1997): 50–63.

Bronfenbrenner, Kate. "What Do Workers Want: Reflections on the Implications of the Freeman and Rogers Study." *University of Pennsylvania Journal of Labor and Employment Law* 3 (Spring 2001): 385–90.

Bryson, Alex. "Managerial Responsiveness to Union and Nonunion Worker Voice in Britain." *Industrial Relations* 43 (January 2004): 213–41.

Budd, John. *Employment with a Human Face: Balancing Efficiency, Equity, and Voice*. Ithaca, NY: Cornell University Press, 2004.

———— and Yongjin Nho. "Testing for Structural Change in U.S. Wage Determination." *Industrial Relations* 36 (April 1997): 160–77.

————, Rafael Gomez, and Noah Meltz. "Why a Balance Is Best: The Pluralist Industrial Relations of-Balancing Competing Interests." In Bruce Kaufman, ed. *Theoretical Perspectives on Work and the Employment Relationship*. Champaign, IL: Industrial Relations Research Association, 2004, pp.-195–228.

Commission on the Future of Worker-Management Relations. *Fact-Finding Report*. Washington, DC: U.S. Department of Labor and U.S Department of Commerce, 1994.

Commons, John R. *Labor and Administration*. New York: MacMillan, 1913.

———— and John Andrews. *Principles of Labor Legislation*, 4th ed. New York: Harper & Row, 1936.

Delery, John, Nina Gupta, Jason Shaw, G. Douglas Jenkins, Jr., and Margot Ganster. "Unionization, Compensation, and Voice Effects on Quits and Retention." *Industrial Relations* 39 (October 2000): 625–45.

Dickman, Howard. *Industrial Democracy in America*. LaSalle, IL: Open Court Press, 1987.

Fairris, David. "Internal Labor Markets and Worker Quits." *Industrial Relations* 43 (July 2004): 573–95.

Farber, Henry and Bruce Western. "Accounting for the Decline of Unions in the Private Sector, 1973–1988." In James Bennett and Bruce Kaufman, eds. *The Future of Private Sector Unionism in the United States.* Armonk, NY: M.E. Sharpe, 2002, pp. 28–58.

Farber, Henry and Alan Krueger. "Union Membership in the United States: The Decline Continues." In-Bruce Kaufman and Morris Kleiner, eds. *Employee Representation: Alternatives and Future Directions.* Madison, WI: Industrial Relations Research Association, 1993, pp. 105–34.

Fiorito, Jack. "Human Resource Management Practices and Worker Desires for Union Representation." In-James Bennett and Bruce Kaufman, eds. *The Future of Private Sector Unionism in the United States.* Armonk, NY: M.E. Sharpe, 2002, pp. 205–26.

Flanagan, Robert. "Collective Bargaining and Macroeconomic Performance." In John Addison and Schnabel, eds. *International Handbook of Trade Unions.* Northampton, MA: Edward Elgar, 2003, pp.-172–96.

Freeman, Richard. "The Structure of Labor Markets: A Book Review Three Decades Later." In Gustav Ranis, Robert West, Mark Leiserson, and Cynthia Taft Morris, eds. *Comparative Development Perspectives.* Boulder, CO: Westview, 1984, pp. 201–26.

———. "Does the New Generation of Labor Economists Know More than the Old Generation?" In Bruce Kaufman, ed. *How Labor Markets Work: Reflections on Theory and Practice by John Dunlop, Clark Kerr, Richard Lester, and Lloyd Reynolds.* Lexington, MA: Lexington Books, 1988, pp. 205–32.

———. "Is Declining Unionization Good, Bad, or Irrelevant?" In Lawrence Mishel and Paula Voos, eds. *Unions and Economic Competitiveness.* Washington, DC: Economic Policy Institute, 1992, pp. 143–72.

——— and James Medoff. *What Do Unions Do?* New York: Basic Books, 1984.

———. "The Impact of Collective Bargaining: Illusion or Reality?" In Jack Steiber, Robert McKersie, and Daniel Mills, eds. *U.S. Industrial Relations 1950–1980: A Critical Assessment.* Madison, WI: Industrial Relations Research Association, 1981, pp. 47–97.

Freeman, Richard and Edward Lazear. "An Economic Analysis of Works Councils." In Joel Rogers and Wolfgang Streeck, eds. *Works Councils: Consultation, Representation, and Cooperation in Industrial Relations.* Chicago, IL: University of Chicago Press, pp. 27–52.

Freeman, Richard and Morris Kleiner. "Do Unions Make Enterprises Insolvent?" *Industrial and Labor Relations Review* 52 (July 1999): 510–27.

Freeman, Richard and Joel Rogers. *What Workers Want.* Ithaca, NY: Cornell University Press, 1999.

———. "Introduction: Worker Representation . . . Again!" *University of Pennsylvania Journal of Labor and Employment Law* 3 (Spring 2001): 375–84.

Gross, James. *Workers' Rights as Human Rights.* Ithaca, NY: Cornell University Press, 2003.

Hirschman, Albert. *Exit, Voice, and Loyalty.* Cambridge, MA: Harvard University Press, 1971.

Hoerr, John. *We Can't Eat Prestige: The Women Who Organized Harvard.* Philadelphia, PA: Temple University Press, 1997.

Hurd, Richard and Joseph Uehlein. "Patterned Responses to Organizing: Case Studies of the Union-Busting Convention." In Sheldon Friedman, Richard Hurd, Rudy Oswald, and Ronald Seeber, eds. *Restoring the Promise of America Labor Law*. Ithaca, NY: ILR Press, 1994, pp. 61–74.

Hyman, Richard. *Understanding European Trade Unionism: Between Market, Class, and Society*. London: Sage, 2001.

Johnson, George. "Economic Analysis of Trade Unionism." *American Economic Review* 65 (May 1975): 23–38.

Kaufman, Bruce. *How Labor Markets Work: Reflections on Theory and Practice by John Dunlop, Clark Kerr, Richard Lester, and Lloyd Reynolds*. Lexington, MA: Lexington Books, 1988.

———. "Labor's Inequality of Bargaining Power: Changes over Time and Implications for Public Policy." *Journal of Labor Research* 10 (Summer 1989): 285–97.

———. "Why the Wagner Act?: Reestablishing Contact with Its Original Purpose." In David Lewin, Donna Sockell, and Bruce Kaufman, eds. *Advances in Industrial and Labor Relations*, Vol. 7. Greenwich, CT: JAI Press, 1996, pp. 15–68.

———. "The Growth and Development of a Nonunion Sector in the Southern Paper Industry." In Robert Zieger, ed. *Southern Labor in Transition*. Knoxville, TN: University of Tennessee Press, 1997, pp.-295–329.

———. "Emotional Arousal as a Source of Bounded Rationality." *Journal of Economic Behavior and Organization* 38 (February 1999a): 135–44.

———. "Does the NLRA Constrain Employee Involvement and Participation Programs in Nonunion Companies? A Reassessment." *Yale Law and Policy Review* 17 (2 1999b): 729–81.

———. "The Case for the Company Union." *Labor History* 41 (August 2000): 321–50.

———. "The Employee Participation and Representation Gap: An Assessment and Proposed Solution." *University of Pennsylvania Journal of Labor and Employment Law* 3 (Spring 2001): 491–550.

———. "Reflections on Six Decades in Industrial Relations: An Interview with John Dunlop." *Industrial and Labor Relations Review* 55 (January 2002): 324–48.

———. "The Quest for Cooperation and Unity of Interest in Industry." In Bruce Kaufman, Richard Beaumont, and Roy Helfgott, eds. *Industrial Relations to Human Resources and Beyond*. Armonk, NY: M.E. Sharpe, 2003a, pp. 115–46.

———. "High-Level Employee Involvement at Delta Air Lines." *Human Resource Management* 42 (Summer 2003b): 175–90.

———. "The Institutional and Neoclassical Schools in Labor Economics." In Dell Champlin and Janet Knoedler, eds. *The Institutionalist Tradition in Labor Economics*. Armonk, NY: M.E. Sharpe, 2004a, pp. 3–38.

———. *The Global Evolution of Industrial Relations: Events, Ideas, and the IIRA*. Geneva: International Labor Organization, 2004b.

———. "The Social Welfare Objectives and Ethical Principles of Industrial Relations." In John Budd and James Scoville, eds. *Ethics in Human Resources and Industrial Relations*. Champaign, IL: Labor and Employment Relations Association, 2005, pp. 23–59.

——— and Paula Stephan. "The Role of Management Attorneys in Union Organizing Campaigns." *Journal of Labor Research* 16 (Fall 1995): 439–54.

——— and David Lewin. "Is the NLRA Still Relevant to Today's Economy and Workplace?" *Labor Law Journal* 49 (September 1998): 1113–26.

——— and David Levine. "An Economic Analysis of Employee Representation." In Bruce Kaufman and Daphne Taras, eds. *Nonunion Employee Representation: History, Contemporary Practice and Policy*. Armonk, NY: M.E. Sharpe, 2000, pp. 149–75.

Kitson, Michael, Ron Martin, and Frank Wilkinson. "Labour Markets, Social Justice, and Economic Efficiency." *Cambridge Journal of Economics* 24 (November 2000): 631–41.

Kleiner, Morris. "Intensity of Management Resistance: Understanding the Decline of Unionization in the Private Sector." In James Bennett and Bruce Kaufman, eds. *The Future of Private Sector Unionism in the United States*. Armonk, NY: M.E. Sharpe, 2002, pp. 292–316.

———— and Adam Pilarski. "Does Internal Union Political Competition Enhance Its Effectiveness?" In Samuel Estreicher, Harry Katz, and Bruce Kaufman, eds. *The Internal Governance and Organizational Effectiveness of Labor Unions*. New York: Kluwer Law International, 2001, pp.-103–19.

Koeller, C. Timothy. "Employer Unfair Labor Practices and Union Organizing: A Simultaneous Equation Model." *Journal of Labor Research* 13 (Spring 1992): 173–85.

Krugman, Paul. "For Richer or Poorer." *New York Times Magazine* (October 20, 2002): 62–7.

Kuhn, Peter. "A Nonuniform Pricing Model of Union Wages and Employment." *Journal of Political Economy* 96 (3 1988): 473–508.

Lazear, Edward, "Economic Imperialism." *Quarterly Journal of Economics* 115 (February 2000): 99–145.

Levin Andrew. "What Thirty Million Workers Want—But Can't Have." *University of Pennsylvania Journal of Labor and Employment Law* 3 (Spring 2001): 551–61.

Lewis, H. Gregg. "Union Relative Wage Effects: A Survey of Macro Estimates." *Journal of Labor Economics* 1 (January 1983): 1–27.

Lieberman, Myron. *The Teacher Unions*. New York: Free Press, 1997.

Lincoln, James and Arne Kalleberg. "Commitment, Quits, and Work Organization in Japanese and U.S. Plants." *Industrial and Labor Relations Review* 50 (October 1996): 39–59.

Lipset, Seymour Martin and Noah Meltz. *The Paradox of American Unionism: Why Americans Like Unions More Than Canadians Do but Join Much Less*. Ithaca, NY: Cornell University Press, 2004.

Luchak, Andrew. "What Kind of Voice Do Loyal Employees Use?" *British Journal of Industrial Relations* 41 (March 2003): 115–34.

Malcomson, James. "Individual Employment Contracts." In Orley Ashenfelter and David Card, eds. *Handbook of Labor Economics*, Vol. 3B. New York: North Holland, 1999, pp. 2291–372.

Manning, Alan. *Monopsony in Motion: Imperfect Competition in Labor Markets*. Princeton: Princeton University Press, 2003.

Menezes-Filho, Naercio and John Van Reenen. "Unions and Innovation: A Survey of the Theory and Empirical Evidence." In John Addison and Claus Schnabel, eds. *International Handbook of Trade Unions*. Northampton, MA: Edward Elgar, 2003, pp. 293–334.

Metcalf, David. "Unions and Productivity, Financial Performance and Investment: International Evidence." In John Addison and Claus Schnabel, eds. *International Handbook of Trade Unions*. Northampton, MA: Edward Elgar, 2003, pp. 118–71.

Miller, Gary. *Managerial Dilemmas*. New York: Cambridge University Press, 1991.

Mills, D. Quinn. "Management Performance." In Jack Stieber, Robert McKersie, and D. Quinn Mills, eds. *U.S. Industrial Relations 1950–1980: A Critical Assessment*. Madison, WI: Industrial Relations Research Association, 1981, pp. 99–128.

Mitchell, Daniel J.B. "Comment." *Industrial and Labor Relations Review* 38 (January 1985): 253–56.

Nissen, Bruce. "The Recent Past and Near Future of Private Sector Unionism in the U.S.: An Appraisal." *Journal of Labor Research* 24 (Spring 2003): 323–38.

Pantuosco, Lou, Darrell Parker, and Gary Stone. "The Effects of Unions on Labor Markets and Economic Growth: An Analysis of State Data." *Journal of Labor Research* 22 (Winter 2001): 195–205.

Pencavel, John. *Worker Participation: Lessons from the Worker Co-ops of the Pacific Northwest*. New York: Russell Sage Foundation, 2001.

———. "Company Unions, Wages, and Work Hours." In David Lewin and Bruce Kaufman, eds. *Advances in Industrial and Labor Relations*, Vol. 12. New York: Elsevier, 2003, pp. 7–38.

Reder, Melvin. "Chicago Economics: Permanence and Change." *Journal of Economic Literature* 20 (March 1982): 1–38.

Rees, Albert. *The Economics of Trade Unions*, 3rd ed. Chicago: University of Chicago Press, 1989.

———. "The Role of Fairness in Wage Determination." *Journal of Labor Economics* 11 (January, pt. 1 1993): 243–52.

Reynolds, Lloyd. *The Structure of Labor Markets*. New York: Harper & Bros., 1951.

Reynolds, Morgan. *Power and Privilege: Labor Unions in America*. New York: Universe Books, 1984.

Schwarz-Miller, Ann and Wayne Talley. "Technology and Labor: Railroads and Ports." *Journal of Labor Research* 23 (Fall 2002): 513–34.

Simons, Henry. *Economic Policy for a Free Society*. Chicago: University of Chicago Press, 1948.

Slichter, Sumner. "Testimony." In National Labor Relations Board, *Legislative Hearings on the National Labor Relations Act, 1935*. Washington, DC: Government Printing Office, 1985, pp. 88–95.

———. "The Changing Character of American Industrial Relations." *American Economic Review* 29 (March 1939): 121–37.

Stabile, Donald. *Activist Unionism: The Institutional Economics of Solomon Barkin*. Armonk, NY: M.E. Sharpe, 1993.

Strauss, George. "What's Happening Inside U.S. Unions: Democracy and Union Politics." *Journal of Labor Research* 21 (Spring 2000): 211–26.

Striffler, Steve. "Inside a Poultry Processing Plant: An Ethnographic Portrait." *Labor History* 43 (3 2002): 305–13.

Thompson, Edward. *The Making of the English Working Class*. New York: Pantheon, 1964.

Troy, Leo. *Beyond Unions and Collective Bargaining*. Armonk, NY: M.E. Sharpe, 1999.

Turnbull, Peter. "What Do Unions Do Now." *Journal of Labor Research* 24 (Summer 2003): 491–527.

Williamson, Oliver, Michael Wachter, and Jeffrey Harris. "Understanding the Employment Relation: The Analysis of Idiosyncratic Exchange." *Bell Journal of Economics* 6 (Spring 1975): 250–78.

Wooden, Mark and Anne Hawke. "Unions and Employment Growth: Panel Data Evidence." *Industrial Relations* 39 (January 2000): 88–107.

18

What Do Unions Do?
A Management Perspective

Kenneth McLennan

I. Introduction

I assess and critique Freeman and Medoff's (F&M, 1984) seminal research on *What Do Unions Do?* from a management perspective which holds that business' perspectives on unions are influenced importantly by management's major goals. These goals include enhancing long-run profitability by maximizing market opportunities and revenues through innovation and at the same time controlling unit production costs.

Any management assessment of unions is likely to evolve over time and vary from industry to industry depending on changing competition in product markets. On many economic policy issues, such as trade, tax, and government regulation of industry, there is rarely a business consensus, and indeed, managements in different industries often have divergent interests. Labor and management in the same industry may be united in their opposition to policies to expand trade or deregulate the industry. On broad labor policy issues, however, labor and management usually have conflicting interests, and while senior executives in different industries may have similar views on labor relations policies, a management consensus on specific policy proposals is often difficult to achieve. Consequently, I offer a typical or modal business assessment of F&M's research conclusions and subsequent academic research on what unions do.

I present an economic context for management's likely reaction to F&M's conclusions and to the findings of subsequent research on the impact of unions and briefly overview how management responded to the changing economic conditions before and after the publication of *What Do Unions Do?* and how the economic environment influenced management views on the role of unions in 1984 and today. I question whether the union's institutional role of providing workers with voice is more effective and efficient than the range of worker participation practices now offered by management human resource policies.

What Do Unions Do? was intended to show unions in a favorable light and that a much higher rate of private sector unionization was socially beneficial.

Subsequent research published in *What Workers Want* (Freeman and Rogers, 1999) developed this theme and concluded that 32 percent of nonunion workers would join a union if given an opportunity. I challenge this assertion and dispute the claim that management anti-union tactics are primarily responsible for the continued decline of private sector union membership.

I conclude with a discussion of the major labor law reforms favored strongly by F&M in 1984 and by Freeman and Rogers in 1999 and comment briefly on several reform proposals. I also suggest labor law changes that will increase economic performance in both union and nonunion businesses, a goal clearly in the public interest.

II. Management's Evolving Assessment of What Unions Do

There is no monolithic or even consensus management view of what unions do. Management's position on industrial relations issues varies with the firm's economic conditions. In the 1960s and early 1970s, for example, many industries with high union density were oligopolies. In such industries as steel, autos, trucking, and airlines, a significant degree of monopoly power enabled management to raise prices and accommodate union demands for wage increases and more generous fringe benefits. The unions' ability to capture part of the economic rent in these industries was, however, diminished greatly by import penetration of the U.S. steel and auto markets and by deregulation in the trucking and airline industries (Block and McLennan, 1985). By the end of the 1970s increased competition had changed management's collective bargaining strategy and management's view of what unions were likely to do in much more competitive product markets.

To maintain profitability in the early 1980s management in many industries had to aggressively cut the unit cost of production. The tendency for unionization to raise labor costs simply reinforced management's preference for a union-free workplace. In industries with high union density, management began to question some of the traditional features of collective bargaining, such as industry-wide bargaining, master agreements, and in some industries management and labor engaged in concession bargaining.

Although the unusually extensive structural changes in the U.S. economy in the 1970s was beyond the scope of F&M's research, many politicians, labor leaders, and businessmen were asking the same question as Lawrence (1984): *Can America Compete?* In the early 1980s it was not clear how to restore the competitive position of U.S. industry. Many advocated greater government intervention in the economy through industrial policy (Magaziner and Reich, 1982; Bluestone and Harrison, 1882). This proposed policy recommended "tripartisan" decision making with government, along with labor and management, selecting the future "winners" and "losers" among industries. The government would provide selective protection of U.S. industries from foreign competition and provide special subsidies and tax preferences to industries of the future.

Unions representing workers in industries which experienced much more competition in product markets favored an industrial policy as a way to legitimize the union's role in public policies affecting industry and to stem the decline in union density.

In contrast to industrial policy's proponents most economists and most businessmen favored reversing the main sources of loss of competitiveness—poor productivity performance, poor product quality, and poor management practices. In the 1970s the U.S. average annual productivity growth rate was about 1 percent, and the rate came to a virtual halt by the end of the decade. This long-run trend reduced the ability of the economy to raise real wages and made it difficult for management and labor to negotiate wage increases without adversely affecting employment.

The productivity performance of U.S. manufacturing was weak compared to that of major competitor economies. In the 1960s, the United States had a higher *level* of productivity than other major industrial countries—United Kingdom, Canada, West Germany, France, and Japan. In the period 1960–1973, however, productivity growth rates were higher, and in some cases much higher, in those industrial economies compared to the performance of U.S. manufacturing. As a result, this long-run trend of at least 15 years produced a convergence of manufacturing productivity *levels* between the United States and its major industrial competitors (Baumol and McLennan, 1985). This adverse comparative productivity performance accelerated import penetration in many U.S. markets. Unions (and management) were no longer able to capture the economic rent from lack of product market competition which had existed in markets in a number of heavily unionized industries.

Management's response to F&M's 1984 conclusions was deeply influenced by the need to meet the competitive challenges facing U.S. industry at the beginning of the 1980s. Unless unions were willing to negotiate collective agreements that contributed to profitability and provided flexibility to encourage productivity growth, management likely opposed unionization.

III. A Management View of F&M's Conclusions

F&M summarize their research findings and conclusions in Chapter 1 of their book. Table 1 summarizes management's overall assessment of F&M's findings and whether the conclusions are of little or great significance to management goals.

A number of F&M's conclusions are of great concern to management, because most of them are closely linked to management's ability to meet the growing competitive challenge in product markets. The following conclusions conflict with management's goal of long-run profitability.

The conclusion that union plants have higher productivity than nonunion plants is rejected by management. F&M argue that a union's ability to raise wage rates force employers to improve management practices, i.e., unionization

Table 18.1
Summary of Management Assessment of F&M's Findings

Type of Union Impact	F&M's Findings	Significance for Management
Profitability	Unionization lowers profitability	Highly
Productivity	Unionized plants have higher productivity	Highly
Union monopoly power and wage increases	Unions mark up wages, lower employment, output, and reduce efficiency	Highly
Internal labor market rigidity	Seniority and formal job security reduce managerial flexibility	Highly
Wage distribution	Unions widen union/non-union wage external differential but narrow internal wage dispersion	Highly
Unionization threat and wage increases	Threat increases non-union wages	Moderately
Workforce turnover	Job security, seniority, reduce turnover, and cost of hiring	Moderately
Union bargaining and deferred compensation	Unions increase proportion of compensation for deferred compensation	Moderately
Adjustment to economic downturn	Unions favor temporary layoffs vs. slower wage growth	Moderately
Decline in unionization	Employer antiunion actions is the major reason	Moderately
Employee morale	Union workers have lower job satisfaction	Insignificant
Unions and social legislation	Union political action promotes socially beneficial legislation	Insignificant
Union corruption	Unions are democratic institutions and corruption in leadership is minimal	Insignificant

gives management an incentive to increase the capital/labor ratio which results in higher productivity. Also, union security reduces quit rates thereby avoiding hiring and reducing training costs. These advantages, it is claimed, overcome the negative productivity effect of rigid work rules and featherbedding.

Business executives believe that some union bargaining strategies, such as pattern bargaining, can be a major detriment to greater productivity. In addition, F&M's reliance on the study by Brown and Medoff (F&M: 167–68) to support the claim of higher productivity in states with high union density is unconvincing. Aggregate productivity statistics depend on the accumulation of productivity gains at the disaggregate plant level and in the operational divisions.

Management's major concerns are productivity at each plant and in the dispersion of productivity-enhancing practices throughout the organization. Brown and Medoff's claim that productivity is greater in highly unionized states than in states with low rates of unionization is much too aggregate a measure of productivity and of no practical significance to management's goal of raising productivity to compete in increasingly global markets.

Managements' assessment of the union impact on productivity leads to management's strong reaction to several other F&M conclusions outlined in Table 18.1. The finding that unionization narrows the internal wage distribution is a significant concern to most businesses. Human resource policies designed to improve productivity require that compensation be closely related to performance. Union bargaining strategies to negotiate uniform and narrow wage structures reduce management's ability to relate wages to performance and provide incentives to raise output.

Flexibility to adjust the internal labor market has become an increasingly important element in management's human resource policies to improve operational efficiency. As a result, management is generally very concerned about F&M's finding that union collective bargaining for seniority provisions affects hiring, firing, and the firm's wage structure. Also, job security provisions in union contracts reduce managerial flexibility. When unionization increases internal labor market rigidity, management will prefer a nonunion environment.

Since management has an incentive to minimize production costs, the ability of unions to exercise monopsony power to "mark up" wages and lower efficiency is of great concern to business operating in competitive markets, so management will typically oppose unionization.

Perhaps the F&M conclusion of greatest concern to management is the effect on profitability. F&M (1984: 183) state that "The calculations (based on several studies) show clear negative union impacts on both price-cost margins and the return-to-capital measures of profitability. On the basis of these results, managements of unorganized firms have good reason, in general, to oppose unionization: organization will penalize them on the bottom line."

F&M also argue that higher labor costs associated with unionization will encourage the substitution of capital for labor, which in turn will raise productivity. There is no question that high rates of capital investment are necessary for businesses to innovate and reap the advantages of the latest technologies, but there are more effective ways of improving productivity than trusting to some theoretical indirect effect of higher wages.

The firm's ability to finance R&D and innovation and apply the successful results of innovation depends on profitability. The riskier the R&D investment and the more complex the innovation process the higher the rate of return required to attract capital. Long-run profitability increases retained earnings and is critical to financing the firm's future success. Management agrees strongly with F&M's conclusion that business has good reason, in general, to avoid unionization.

Business disagrees with a number of F&M's research conclusions, even though they likely have little direct impact on business' economic performance. F&M devote an entire chapter to employer anti-union activities and conclude that the increase in unfair labor practices during union organizing campaigns is the major reason for the decline in unionism. Business disagrees strongly with this assessment. Even though private sector union density is less than 10 percent, the charge that employers are increasingly anti-union is moderately significant since this is the justification offered for labor law reform—reforms that business opposes.

F&M's claim that unions promote socially beneficial legislation is factually questionable and unlikely to be accepted by management. In the early part of the twentieth century, unions did play an important role in protecting workers against unfair and abusive personnel policies of some employers. By the 1960s, however, few unions were "protecting the little guy." Increasingly most unions were protecting the vested interests of middle-class workers in industries with aging workforces.

In the 1960s and 1970s unions were not always in the vanguard of significant social legislation. For example, equal employment legislation was implemented by the Nixon Administration and unions, with some employer complicity, were often the source of labor market discrimination. Similarly, unions were late to endorse the goals of the Occupational Health and Safety Act, an act authored by two Republicans, Congressman Steiger and Senator Javits.

Management in most businesses probably agrees with several of F&M's 1984 research findings, but they are not of great significance in shaping industries' approach to industrial relations, including the following: the claim that union corruption among union leaders is minimal and that unions are essentially democratic institutions; the conclusion that union workers have lower morale and job satisfaction than nonunion workers; and the assertion that unions favor layoffs rather than wage adjustments in response to recessions.

Management also agrees that unions tend to place greater emphasis on deferred compensation, in the form of pension and health benefits, than do employers. For example, unions favor defined-benefit pension plans, because these plans provide employees with an incentive to remain employed with the same employer and continue to be long-term dues-paying union members. Younger workers tend to favor defined-contribution plans which vest within a year and are more beneficial for workers with relatively high job mobility. Employers who are more interested in workforce flexibility tend to also favor defined-contribution pension plans.

On the issue of employee turnover, business likely agrees that the union goal of job security reduces worker turnover, but in dynamic labor markets, this does not appear to be a significant benefit to employers.

F&M find that the threat of unionization raises nonunion wages. Many companies have adopted a "union substitution" strategy which has given business more flexibility in its human resource strategy even if it has resulted in somewhat higher wage costs. This is simply a compromise management is willing to make in order to avoid unionization and greater rigidity in the internal labor market.

While management's view on F&M's conclusions is likely to differ among industries the advent of more competitive markets changed management's approach to industrial relations and personnel policies. By 1984 management evaluated these policies on the basis of their contribution to efficiency and organizational innovation.

IV. Business Innovations in Response to "Globalization" of the 1990s

The 1990s was the era of globalization—the growing economic interde-
pendence among more and more economies around the world arising from the
expansion of trade in goods and services and the increased flow of international
investment. For the U.S., exports and imports which represented only about 10
percent of the U.S. gross domestic product (GDP) in the 1960s rose to about
24 percent by the end of the 1990s. Between 1970 and 2000 U.S. direct investment abroad and foreign direct investment in the United States had escalated
fivefold (McLennan, 2002).

The 1990s also witnessed another round of deregulation of domestic markets
in banking and telecommunications which exposed a much larger portion of the
U.S. economy to intense competition in the markets for goods and services. To
compete in domestic and global markets, U.S. industry had to match competitors'
unit production costs. Industry achieved this goal in the following ways.

Increased Investment in R&D and Capital Equipment

Successful R&D and the availability of new equipment incorporating the
latest technological advances are the two most important sources of improved
productivity. Since the early 1980s, investment in R&D in the U.S. has continued
to increase until it reached $160 billion in 1997—even though federal expen-
ditures on industrial R&D have declined since 1987, tracking the slowdown in
defense expenditures. A trend, important for the economy's overall productivity
performance, has been the increase in R&D in the nonmanufacturing sector. In
1985 nonmanufacturing R&D accounted for 5 percent of all R&D expenditures;
by 1997 it had risen to 20 percent and contributed to the rapid overall R&D
investment acceleration since 1993 (McLennan, 1998: 2).

Capital accumulation, particularly in machinery and equipment, is critical
to future productivity growth. In the 1990s private capital investment growth
doubled to some 24 percent of GDP growth compared to 13 percent of the
growth in the 1980s (McLennan, 1998: 3). In addition, an increasing portion
of private investment was devoted to producers' durable equipment rather than
to structures.

Investment in equipment varied by industry. For example, in 1980 almost
10 percent of the net capital stock of nonresidential equipment was in informa-
tion-processing equipment—computers, peripherals, and telecommunications
equipment—and by 2000 had grown to about 17 percent (Leonard, 1998). This
higher rate of capital investment along with management innovations in business organization and work processes produced a productivity upsurge which
reduced unit production costs. Table 18.2 shows the extraordinary manufacturing productivity gains since 1990 with an outstanding average annual increase
of 5.1 percent for 1995–1999. During the April 2000–June 2001 recession,

productivity growth fell significantly as output declined but has recovered to a high rate since 2001.

Accelerating productivity in the nonmanufacturing sector of the U.S. economy has raised the performance of the entire nonfarm business sector. For example, productivity growth rates in the major sectors of retail trade, finance, insurance, and real estate and services more than doubled in the 1990s compared to the 1980s (Meckstroth, 2003). The breadth of the improvement in productivity is especially significant since the nonmanufacturing sector represents some 80 percent of the output of the economy.

Management Innovations in Work Organization and Human Resource Strategies

Although the increase in capital investment and innovation in high-tech industries was critical to the acceleration of manufacturing productivity, management's response to the new competitive environment of global markets stimulated many innovations in work organization and human resource practices. These management initiatives involved significant structural changes at the operations level of management which required much more workforce flexibility.

The management innovations included a dramatic new approach to manufacturing processes. The new concept of "lean manufacturing" involved a shift away from batch manufacturing in which a supply of products was produced to meet an anticipated future demand. In lean manufacturing production begins only when the customer places an order. This new approach required reengineering of assembly lines so that workstations were flexible modules capable of modifying the product during the manufacturing process.

The advantages of lean manufacturing are maximized when linked to a just-in-time (JIT) inventory system. Frequently, the supplier's plant is located close to, or even adjacent to, the customer's facility so that supplies can be delivered shortly, even within hours, after an order is placed. One survey indicated that 59 percent of manufacturing respondent companies indicated that selected inputs were supplied on a JIT basis, whereas 26 percent replied that most of their inputs were on a JIT basis. Some 5 percent said they planned to adopt a JIT system (McLennan and Meckstroth, 2001: 6).

Lean manufacturing greatly reduced production costs. Capital, inventory, and warehousing costs were cut substantially. Figure 18.1 shows the trend in the manufacturing inventory-to-sales ratio for the period 1968–2004.[1] Over the past 25 years the manufacturing industry-to-sales ratio has declined 25 to 30 percent. This new approach to supply chain management has reduced capital costs significantly and permitted industry to adapt quickly to customer demand.

Increasing global competition made it very difficult, if not impossible, for businesses to raise prices. With input costs including energy, wages, and fringe benefits, rising, management had to constantly increase efficiency to maintain

Table 18.2

U.S. Productivity: Average Annual Rate of Growth in Output per Hour

Years	Manufacturing (Percent)	Nonfarm Business (Percent)
1973–1980	1.9	1.3
1981–1990	3.0	1.5
1991–1999	4.3	2.0
1990–1995	3.5	1.5
1996–1999	5.1	2.6
2000	4.1	2.9
2001	0.9	1.1
2002	4.5	4.8

Source: U.S. Department of Labor, Bureau of Labor Statistics, data available on web site, www.bls.org.

profitability. Industry's human resource strategies, including management's assessment of what unions do were deeply affected by the continuous cost reduction pressures.

Since the mid-1970s, all businesses have recognized that quality improvement and the pursuit of zero defects in goods and services was an important source of lower unit costs. Not until the late 1980s, however, did U.S. businesses develop quality systems throughout their organizations. Senior management in companies like Motorola and General Electric developed quality-training programs for all their employees, including their corporate staffs.

By the late 1980s most businesses had started to reduce corporate overhead by moving decision making down to the operational level. Middle-level management employment was reduced significantly as part of a cost-reduction strategy, a trend that has continued through the recent recession and the current recovery. Indeed, prior to the onset of the 2000–2001 recession, manufacturing white-collar employment was cut earlier than production-worker employment and more rapidly than in previous recessions. This strategy, in part, accounts for the delayed decline in manufacturing output and continued productivity growth during this recession compared to typical recessions (McLennan and Meckstroth, 2001: 2–4).

In most manufacturing companies a close link now exists between lean manufacturing and quality control, and a new approach is taken to work organization. Various forms of worker participation have existed since the mid-1970s when companies formed quality circles in which workers discussed how to improve the manufacturing process and output. Over the past two decades, as decision making moved to the operational level, division general managers in many companies have established worker participation teams, many of which

Figure 18.1
Manufacturing Inventory-to-Sales Ratio, 1968–2004

Source: Economic Report of the President, February 2004 and Economic Indicators, November 2004.

are self-directed with considerable authority to modify manufacturing processes. Worker participation groups have now become a potentially importance source of productivity improvement.[2] How unions reacted to this new form of work organization obviously affected management's view of unions.

Implications of Globalization for What Unions Do

Macroeconomic benefits of globalization are substantial for both the U.S. economy and many developing countries whose economies are entering the global trading system. For the United States the advantages of globalization are low inflation, lower costs, and higher business profits that stimulate greater investment which in turn produces more rapid economic growth and a higher standard of living for Americans. Developing countries also benefit from higher wages for a portion of their workforce and more rapid economic growth.

When globalization involves offshore outsourcing of jobs, some U.S. workers are laid off and may have to find reemployment, perhaps at a lower wage (Fay, 2005). Outsourcing domestically has been occurring for many decades as businesses increasingly concentrated on their core competency and sought lower cost suppliers. In the 1970s and 1980s offshore outsourcing increased as businesses contracted for low-skill labor in developing countries.

In the 1990s U.S. businesses increasingly outsourced jobs to semi-skilled and skilled workers in other countries by using electronic communications. There is no accurate estimate of the number of jobs outsourced annually, although one estimate is that offshoring could result in an average of some 250,000 layoffs per year through 2015 (Brainard and Litan, 2005). In a workforce of 140 million this is an extremely small number of laid-off workers. The job loss from outsourcing is a little more than 20,000 a month in an economy which typically generates *net* job gains of about 150,000 each month. The U.S. Bureau of Labor Statistics estimates that in the first quarter of 2004 only 4,633 workers were laid off due to outsourcing (Drezner, 2004). It is also important to recognize that U.S. businesses are significant exporters of high-tech services and that many jobs are the result of "insourcing" through direct foreign investment in the United States.

The sustained competitive environment associated with globalization simply reinforced management's concern that unions were likely to resist economic change and in most cases do little to assist businesses to become more efficient. The issue for management is whether the performance of unions over the past 20 years, as analyzed by-an impressive body of academic research, is sufficient to justify a new and different management assessment of what unions do.

V. Post-1984 Research on What Unions Do: Impact on Management Views of Unions

Management has an interest in the post-1984 research findings in the following areas which affect business performance. First, management is concerned about how unions affect the macroeconomic environment. Management favors an environment which produces strong, noninflationary economic growth since the ultimate market test for business is long-run profitability which depends importantly on *real* economic growth.

Second, in an era of global competition management must control production costs. Research on how unions affect the ability of management to improve supply-chain management and control wage escalation and increasingly the cost of fringe benefits is critical to industry's ability to compete in both domestic and overseas markets.

Third, as productivity levels of other countries converge with that of the U.S., businesses must continually innovate. How unions affect management's innovation and productivity goals is of major concern to business.

Fourth, management has an interest in the labor movements' dramatic shift from business unionism to political action. Management believes that union success in the political arena would likely lead to labor legislation unfavorable to business interests.

Finally, the significant decline in private sector unionism since the 1950s is in itself not a problem for management. Managements, however, are very wary of the views of some academics and labor leaders who claim that the workforce, and society, would benefit economically and socially from a much higher rate of unionism. The underlying fear of business is that the public policy changes required to encourage much higher rates of unionization would be detrimental to business interests. Each of these of concerns is discussed briefly.

Macroeconomic Environment

In their historical review of unions and the macroeconomic environment, Mitchell and Erickson (this volume) correctly point out that F&M focus almost entirely on the microeconomic impact of unions. For the most part, Mitchell and Erickson accept the traditional view that the role of unions in nonunion labor markets is to correct the monopsony power of employers. The macro implication of this view is similar to John Kenneth Galbraith's (1956) view of American capitalism, where unions act as a "countervailing power" in both product and labor markets.

Mitchell and Erickson (this volume) point out that over the last century most views on the macro effect of unions involved the potential for unions to produce cost-push inflation. In 1984 F&M claimed that unions cannot cause cost-push inflation or unemployment, and Mitchell and Erickson confirm that Freeman continued to support this position into the 1990s. There is, however, evidence that in other countries a significant decline in unionism can contribute to improved macro performance.

In the United Kingdom union density declined from about 45 percent in the mid-1980s to about 30 percent in 2000; in the private sector union density dropped below 20 percent. According to Nickell and Quintini (2002: 208), this decline "contributed to the decline in inflationary pressure at given levels of labor-market slack and, hence to the fall in equilibrium unemployment." These authors estimate that the equilibrium unemployment rate fell by 2.7 percentage points. Over the period 1985–2000 the unemployment rate in the United Kingdom fell from about 11 percent to less than 6-percent and the rate of inflation dropped from about 7 percent to less than 3 percent.

Hirsch (this volume) also confirms the adverse affect of unionism on the macroeconomic environment: "Literature since *What Do Unions Do?* emphasizes unions' role in taxing returns in tangible and intangible capital and the resulting effects on profitability, investment, and growth." Hirsch also points out that in increasingly competitive product markets the typical union premium in wages and benefits is not derived from "abnormal" profits, which even if they exist are short-lived, but from a reduction in the rate of return on past investments. This, in turn, reduces future economic growth. Although low union density restricts this adverse economic impact to a limited number of industries, it does affect management's reaction to unionization threats. In addition, any reduction in growth in output in any part of the economy has a small adverse indirect macro effect on labor, management, and the public generally.

Controlling Increases in Labor Costs

The attitude of business executives toward what unions do is influenced how unions affect labor costs, benefit costs, and management's flexibility to change operations and lower unit costs. The wage-cost implications of unionization are discussed by Blanchflower and Bryson (this volume) who compare the wage premium of union employees over nonunion workers for two time periods—the second half of the 1970s and the second half of the 1990s.

In the 1970s the private sector union wage premium was 21 percent and declined to 17 percent in the second half of the 1990s. The union wage premium was greatest for workers aged 16–24, had less than a high school education, were over 55 years old, and for workers in jobs requiring manual skills. These findings may reflect a more rigid union wage schedule and the tendency for union-negotiated wages to have less dispersion around the median wage in the bargaining unit. While the union wage premium is declining over time, union facilities will require a significant productivity advantage over nonunion facilities to avoid a unit wage cost of production disadvantage compared to the average nonunion facility.

Budd (this volume) acknowledges that non-wage forms of compensation have put upward pressure on unit labor costs. Since the late 1930s, management and labor negotiations in the union sector and management human resource policies in nonunion firms have increased the importance of non-wage compensation for attracting, motivating, and rewarding employees over and above wages and salaries. Budd also identifies the various forms of non-wage compensation and points out that, as in F&M, the monopoly face of unions is an important source of higher benefits for union workers than the benefits received by comparable nonunion workers. F&M conclude that this monopoly power, while beneficial to union workers, has an adverse effect on aggregate economic welfare.

Budd claims that unions' ability to improve non-wage benefits may not adversely affect economic welfare. First, the institutional voice of unions simply results in a rearranging of total compensation toward more benefits, is not harmful to efficiency, and may increase aggregate economic welfare. Second, in his view, if the monopoly face of unions offsets corporate monopoly power and other labor market imperfections, the union's role can be socially beneficial.

The growth of a wide range of benefits now available to both union and nonunion employees cannot be attributed entirely to unionization. The original impetus to the increasing importance of benefits came from a U.S. Treasury Department tax ruling toward the end of World War II which held that employer-paid premiums for health insurance should be excluded from employees' taxable income. The growth of employer-provided health insurance accelerated greatly until the 1980s when some 80 percent of employees had health insurance.

The growth of benefits in total compensation was also stimulated by employer human resource policies. Indeed, up to the 1980s the mark of a successful human relations executive in union and nonunion firms alike was innovation in introducing new benefits. As suggested by Lewin (this volume), over the past 40 years, private sector management has been responsive to employee interests and provided employees with voice in the absence of a union.

The post-1984 research on non-wage compensation reviewed by Budd clearly shows that union workers have a higher rate of employer health insurance and pension plans. In an era of global competition, if the cost of financing benefits is not offset by a trade-off with wage and salary compensation, management will be concerned about the effect on unit labor costs.

Budd appears to recognize this management concern and the social significance of the problem of overly generous benefits in many union contracts. "[T]he nexus between unions and benefits is also apparent in the problem of pension liabilities—General Motors' pension plan, for example, was under-funded by $19.3 billion in 2002." Budd blames the pre-2000 bear stock market for the problem but admits that "one underlying issue was the generous defined-benefit pension plans negotiated by unions in autos, steel, airlines, and elsewhere."

The problem of overly generous benefits is also apparent in many union-negotiated employer health plans. It has been widely reported that, on average, every new General Motors car includes some $1,400 in health care costs. General Motors now has fewer than 200,000 employees supporting 1.1 million beneficiaries participating in the company health care plan—with 450,000 of them retirees who get close to first-dollar coverage for health care costs with retirees paying only $3 per prescription. This ratio of beneficiaries to workers for GM's health care plan is much higher than the ratios for the Social Security and Medicare programs, both of which have serious long-run financing problems.

Budd suggests that some of the generous defined-benefit pension plans may fail and require a government bailout. There may be pressure from unions and management for similar assistance to save overly generous union-negotiated health care benefits from bankrupting some businesses.

As Budd pointed out, there may be a relationship between a decline in the proportion of workers covered by employer-provided health insurance and pensions (presumably defined-benefit plans) but the industrial relations performance of labor and management with regard to non-wage compensation in some of the industries cited by Budd is likely to discourage management in general from welcoming unionization of their facilities.

Business generally prefers compensation systems that give management the freedom to adjust to changing economic conditions. For example, defined-benefit pension plans are less desirable for both employers and employees as product markets become more competitive, and the proportion of workers covered by defined-benefit plans has declined significantly. By 1995, only 23 percent of workers were covered by defined-benefit plans compared to 39 percent in 1975

(Watson Wyatt, 2000). Employers tend to favor defined-contribution and hybrid pension plans, such as cash-balance and pension-equity plans which have a high degree of portability. As the labor force became more mobile with the average number of years of job tenure for workers declining, pension portability has become more advantageous for most workers, especially younger workers. Employers also favor defined-contribution plans since the problem of a huge unfunded liability is avoided.

In a period of rapid change, employers also favor the flexibility of monetary forms of non-wage compensation including lump-sum bonuses, profit-sharing plans, and stock options. If business faces more intense competition and profit declines, adjustments can be made through one or more forms of this type of contingent compensation without adversely affecting the employees' wage base. Budd presents research results which confirm that union operations are less likely to have profit-sharing or gain-sharing plans than nonunion operations and, indeed, that unionization results in a decline in such contingency forms of monetary compensation.

Unions and Productivity Growth

Unless union firms can demonstrate higher productivity growth rates than comparable nonunion firms, union claims that they can reduce unit labor costs sufficiently to offset the union wage gap and the relatively high cost of non-wage benefits negotiated by unions are not supportable. If the rates of investment in R&D and capital equipment are lower in union than in nonunion firms, productivity performance in union facilities will almost certainly trail nonunion productivity growth. Hirsch (this volume) reviews the post-1984 research on this issue. Although in 1984 F&M conclude that productivity is probably somewhat higher in union operations than in nonunion firms, Hirsch's review does not support this conclusion.

Hirsch points out that "union firms clearly display substantially lower productivity growth than nonunion firms, but most (if not all) of this difference is associated with effects associated to industry differences, union firms being located in industries or sectors with slow growth." Hirsch also points out that the effect of unions on productivity tends to be indirect, through "lower rates of investment in accumulation of physical and innovative capital." Hirsch concludes that absence of a large positive effect on productivity means that the union wage gap cannot be offset, resulting in lower profitability.

Addison and Belfield (this volume) confirm Hirsch's conclusions and note that the average union firm has 15 percent lower annual R&D expenditures, 13 percent lower annual capital expenditures, and 10 to 15 percent lower profitability than its nonunion counterpart.

It is very difficult for businesses to increase prices in competitive markets. If unions are successful in negotiating wage and benefit increases management may reduce capital investment, leading to slower growth in sales and employment and shrinkage of the union sector. Hirsch concludes that despite the fact that "unionization could initially be associated with higher levels of productivity, owing to a 'shock effect' or 'collective voice,' but at the same time retard the rate of growth. In the long run, of course, low *rates* of productivity growth should produce lower productivity *levels* relative to comparison firms or industries" [italics added]. Facing the prospect of the adverse effect of unions on productivity, management will try to avoid unionization.

Labor Unions and Political Activism

Political activism is not new to the U.S. labor movement. Early U.S. labor history is replete with examples of unions, and in some cases groups of unions, as leading proponents of various ideologies such as syndicalism, socialism, and communism. Following World War II labor unions increasingly advocated the need for economic gains within the capitalist system. Although unions generally favored the Democratic Party and supported Democratic candidates for office, most unions worked with Republicans on some legislative issues, and some unions supported Republicans in federal, state, and local elections.

Unions' pragmatic approach to political action changed in the 1990s as the rate of private sector unionism continued to decline. At the 1997 AFL-CIO convention, then Vice President Al Gore committed the Clinton Administration to adopting a new federal contracting regulation that would have essentially "blacklisted" companies that are *alleged* to have violated laws concerning overtime, union organizing, and other labor relations regulations.[3] By 2000 the AFL-CIO and most national unions, in part in response to the Gore commitment, dedicated more resources both to finance Democratic candidates and get out the vote for the election campaign of Vice President Al Gore (McLennan, 2001a).

John Sweeney, president of the AFL-CIO, and the presidents of all private sector unions and most government unions made political activism a central role of U.S. unions. Though labor unions delivered the vote for Vice President Gore in a number of states (McLennan, 2001a), unprecedented union support was not sufficient to win the presidential election for the Democrats. As a result unions had failed in their effort to have a Democratic Administration and Democratic majorities in Congress to enact union-friendly legislation, such as labor law reform, which would make it easier for unions to be represented as bargaining agents and stem the continuing decline in private sector unionism.

Masters and Delaney (this volume) assess the labor movement's strengths and weaknesses in political action and note that union members vote at a higher rate than their proportion of the voting age population. In 1980 union members were 24.2 percent of the votes cast, but as union density declined, they were only 15.4 percent by 2000. Masters and Delaney's evaluation of labor's political activism in terms of electing candidates and winning legislative battles is that labor's record is "at best disappointing" (p. 386).

Masters and Delaney attribute labor's lack of success to conservative Republican leadership in the White House and Congress and to the large financial resources that business devotes to political campaigns. In contrast to labor unions, business typically donates a significant portion of its political action funding to Democrats as well as Republicans. Business financing of campaigns had little to do with labor's lack of success in the 2004 Presidential election since Democrats outspent Republicans. In businesses' view the poor outcome of unions' political activism is more likely related to the unions' ideological public policy positions. Indeed, Masters and Delaney admit that on some issues, such as trade, organized labor is made to look anti-growth.

Masters and Delaney propose (p. 515) that the labor movement should continue its political activism strategy, and "identify progressive themes that inspire enough to mobilize workers in far greater numbers and with much higher energy than has occurred since the 1930s." If these progressive themes include labor law reforms which allow unions to be certified as a bargaining agent by a majority of signed card authorizations rather than a majority vote in a secret ballot, business will continue to oppose unionization.

Perhaps part of the problem facing union leaders is that they continue to take public policy positions that may have been important in the mid-twentieth century, but are less relevant for the economy and the workforce of the twenty-first century. Labor political strategists have failed to recognize that while union members cast some 15 percent of the ballots in elections, a sizeable proportion vote Republican. The majority of middle- and lower-middle-income workers can no longer be counted on to vote for Democrats, and a substantial portion of the workforce is unlikely to support unions if part of their payment in union dues is used to support political candidates they oppose.

F&M claim that unions provide political voice for all labor and are more successful in pushing general social legislation than in bringing about special-interest legislation in Congress. As Pencavel (this volume) points out, this is a very selective reading of the political activities of unionism. As discussed earlier, many labor unions opposed equal employment opportunity legislation and were slow to endorse occupational health and safety legislation. In addition, in supporting public policies affecting pensions and health care, for example, and in their bargaining strategies, many unions have favored older members with seniority over younger low-tenure workers. In policy debates unions automatically lobby to preserve the status quo of major social programs, such as Social Security and Medicare, even though these programs will become financially insolvent in their present forms.

To succeed in the legislative process, unions may have to reassess their policy goals and return to a business unionism model with more discriminating political action. Unions may have to work with moderate Republicans and Democrats to promote legislation that benefits *all* workers.

Sources of the Decline in Unionism

The reasons for the precipitous decline in unionism over the past 25 years are important to business mainly because labor leaders and some academics attribute employer anti-union actions during union organizing campaigns as the major reason for the decline. F&M addressed this issue, and in a later book Freeman and Rogers emphasized the role of employer opposition as the source of declining union density:

> Most firms welcome the steady decline of private-sector unions and oppose any reform that might reverse that decline, however justifiable the reform. Once only Neanderthal ideologies dreamed of a "union free" economy, now however, as that reality approaches many businesses support this goal and are prepared to expend substantial resources to achieve it—lobbying to prevent union-friendly changes in existing law and resisting attempts at new organizing (Freeman and Rogers, 1999: 67).

This line of argument is the justification for labor law reform proposals offered by labor leaders and some academics. Business rejects this view and opposes the type of reforms frequently proposed, including those contained in the recommendations of the Commission on the Future of Worker-Management Relations appointed by the first Clinton Administration to consider changes in labor law.

Management believes that unionism has declined for the following reasons: Globalization and structural changes in the economy which reduced the number of employees in many manufacturing industries where unions had substantial membership; a huge growth in the service sector which had a very low rate of unionization; union failure to provide the services demanded by the workforce; a major shift in human resource strategies which gave workers voice without the collective voice of the union; and extensive growth in government labor market policies which protected workers in the workplace supported by legal options available to workers with a potential grievance.

Management dismisses the claim that anti-union activities directed by high-paid consultants hired by business is a major reason for the precipitous fall in unionization. Management believes this view is simply not credible (McLennan, 2001b). Freeman and Rogers (2001) disagree strongly with this management view.

F&M have a separate chapter on the reasons for the decline in unionism. They reject the structural change reason for the decline in unionism by pointing out that other countries have experienced similar structural changes without experiencing a decline in unionism, and from their interpretation of other studies, F&M claim that company opposition accounts for a quarter to a half of the decline in union electoral success in NLRB representation elections.

Flanigan (this volume) analyzes F&M's views on the role of employer anti-union behavior. First, he rejects the F&M view that the United States is the only country experiencing a decline in private sector unionism. Even before 1984 unionism was declining in a number of countries, and since 1984 the decline has been pervasive among industrialized nations and even in some developing countries.

Pencavel (this volume) also provides a detailed review of declining union density in a number of other industrialized countries, and he points out that in other countries there is a tendency for wages to be "taken out of competition" which results in higher unemployment compared to that in the United States. For F&M's employer anti-union theory to prove correct, employers in all countries must be engaging in similar anti-union behavior. There is little evidence that this is occurring.

As Flanagan observes, although most studies continue to conclude that employer opposition reduces the growth of new unionism, according to one study, employer anti-union tactics can cut the other way. The greater the management opposition the more likely nonunion workers will feel they need a union.

Flanagan presents evidence suggesting that workers' preferences for unions are not accurately measured by signed authorization cards. He points out that five Canadian provinces have dropped the authorization card checks and required a mandatory election as in the United States. One study found that this change reduced the certification rate by 13 percent, a result that confirms management's view that although surveys of employees' attitude or intentions are interesting, management feels there is no substitute for the secret ballot as an accurate measure of workers' preferences.

Flanagan demonstrates that union-friendly labor law reforms will have little effect on union density. He also concludes that since the mid-1980s there is no consistent message that supports a claim that a substantial part of the private sector union decline over the past 20 years can be assigned to *increasing* management opposition.

Freeman and Rogers (2001) claim that many businesses support the goal of a union-free economy which implies that there is a broad-based business movement working to banish unions. No such anti-union conspiracy exists. Management's view of unions depends on how unionism is likely to affect each individual business' economic performance. Most senior business executives prefer a union-free environment, but managements in many businesses have developed constructive union-management relations even though both parties have conflicting interests on many employment-related issues.

Management does not share F&M's position that the decline in union density is harmful to workers' interests and to the general welfare. Nor does management believe that the nation would benefit from a much higher rate of private sector unionization. Business executives do not speculate about the optimal rate of union density in the private sector, and they do not advocate a zero rate with a union-free economy. Executives in almost all private sector industries recognize that intense competition has forced business to be much more efficient in order to achieve the goal of long-run profitability. If any part of the workforce is unionized, management expects the union to respond to the new economic reality. While competition forces management to be more efficient and reduce unit costs of production through product and process innovations, it also encourages businesses to improve and utilize the skills and knowledge of the workforce. To maintain a productive workforce, management must provide attractive employment conditions whether or not the threat of unionization exists.

Those favoring a higher rate of unionization cite Freeman and Rogers's (2001) telephone survey in which 32 percent of the nonunion respondents said they would vote for a union if given the opportunity. In addition, some 82 percent of those respondents said their colleagues would also vote for a union. This method of determining what workers want is highly questionable.

There is considerable difference between a telephone answer to a hypothetical question about an individual's view about joining a union and the individual's binding decision to support a union financially and give the union authority to affect decisions concerning employment conditions. To assume that what anyone says in a telephone interview guarantees future behavior stretches reality. As pointed out previously, the certification rate of unions dropped 13 percent when a number of Canadian provinces dropped authorization card checks and required mandatory secret ballots for determining union representation. A secret ballot is a clear indication of intent; a response to a question from a telephone interviewer is an extremely uncertain indication of intent.

Workplace Democracy

Pencavel (this volume, p. 448) claims that "[t]he qualities of liberty and uncoerced expression of preferences that are so lauded in the political domain are not enjoyed by most individuals in their capacity as workers except in a narrow sense." He continues by advocating the need for greater workplace democracy since most U.S. employees have little say over their work environment. "They do what their supervisors tell them to do . . . in many cases efficiency might be enhanced by supervisors consulting with rank-and-file workers." The advocates of the justice and benefits of greater union density have seized upon industrial democracy—the opportunity for workers to influence every aspect of the work environment—as the ultimate justification for union-provided institutional voice. Pencavel supports the need for voice in the workplace but rejects the view that it can only be provided by unions.

The issue of the power that supervisors exert over those who report to them has been recognized for over 200 years. Kaufman (this volume) cites Adam Smith's concern that the bargaining power of the master is always greater than the power of workmen. Smith believed that economic progress was based on individuals' desire to improve their economic status, but at times this desire should be restrained by justice, a concept developed in his first book, *Theory of Moral Sentiments*, written in 1759. For example, he felt that governmental enforcement of justice was necessary in the relationship between master and servant [slave] to avoid the "love to domineer." The issue of the relationship between order givers and order takers was also recognized by Alexis de Tocqueville who described how an order taker can be a lackey (lacquais in French), the lowest ranked domestic servant of the aristocracy. "[T]he servant occupies a subordinate position from which he cannot escape; close to him stands another man with a higher rank which he cannot lose" (Tocqueville, 1969: 574–75, first published in 1835).

The early institutionalists emphasized the importance of unions and collective bargaining for providing workers with industrial democracy by giving workers status and protecting their security in the workplace (Kaufman, this volume). In his two books, *The Labor Movement* (1921) and *A Philosophy of Labor* (1951), Frank Tannenbaum described how workers join unions to achieve workplace and social status and experience psychological satisfaction. Writing in 1921 he predicted that union power would produce a radical solution in the form of syndicalism within the U.S. industrial structure.

By 1951 Tannenbaum recognized a changing union-management labor relations environment. He continued to emphasize noneconomic as well as economic reasons for unionization and the existence of a conflict of interest between management and union goals but he predicted much more harmony and cooperation in industrial relations. He felt that the union would gradually share in management decisions and accept responsibility for them. "[T]he union is the conservative force of our time. It is conservative because through bickering over details and by continuous compromise it-seeks to preserve the older values by integrating a nonmoral essentially corrosive power (the corporation) into a society possessed of the ethical basis for survival." He assumes that the union will become part of the modern corporation by buying into it through the investment of union funds and through the extension of fringe benefits (Tannenbaum, 1951: 169).

Most in the workforce are order takers whether working in a private sector for-profit or nonprofit organization, a government agency, or an academic institution. No order taker wants to be treated as a lackey, and over a period of some 70 years management in most organizations has recognized that there are economic and social benefits from giving order takers respect and some degree of freedom in how work is performed.

Budd (this volume, p. 186) supports the need for workers to have institutional voice in the workplace. He points out that there is an inherent conflict of interest between employers and employees and when bargaining power heavily favors employers, adverse outcomes are likely:

Wages insufficient for a decent life and for sufficient purchasing power to support economic activity; dangerous working conditions that people should not have to tolerate and that impose significant costs on local communities through medical costs, disability payments, and lost productivity; autocratic methods of supervision that violate standards of human dignity and de-motivate workers.

Some features of this description of the workplace environment may still exist in some industries and in some companies, but it is an extremely unusual exception rather than common. Progressive human resource policies have, in management's view, made this rationale for union institutional voice unnecessary. Management is well aware that workers join unions for psychological as well as economic reasons. The benefit of group participation and influence on decision making in operations give workers psychological satisfaction.

Kaufman (this volume) points out the role of the institutionalist's industrial democracy proposals. Management was well aware of the proposals for industrial democracy, and although many in industry initially resisted these new ideas, business eventually did respond to them. There is no evidence that unions or the threat of unionization were the major stimuli for improvements in employment conditions through out industry. The long gradual decline in union density has not led to adverse working conditions in the United States.

The 1940s witnessed the beginning of an extensive body of human relations writings, based on industrial psychology research, which demonstrated the value of worker job satisfaction to job performance. Over the last 60 years business has improved working conditions dramatically, and most workers now have some degree of participation in business decision-making. Is a progressive human resource strategy by management motivated by union avoidance? Perhaps in some cases it is. In most cases, however, management has recognized that worker participation can improve organizational performance. According to Freeman and Rogers (2001), 55 percent of unionized workers participated in an employee involvement program, and 49 percent of the much larger population of nonunion workers had an employee involvement program at their workplace.

F&M focus on the monopoly face of unions and promote the advantages of institutional voice. Since 1984 research on labor unions has followed a similar pattern. Indeed, the value of exit has been largely ignored and to some extent regarded as an undesirable labor market adjustment (Pencavel, this volume). Management can learn a great deal from employees who leave voluntarily because they are unhappy with wages and conditions of employment. Employers like to avoid turnover costs but it only requires job exiting at the margin of the workforce before management has to reassess its human resource policies. Most employees also benefit from a voluntary exit. While unions have a vested interest in reducing the rate of exit, many who voluntarily move to another employer do so to gain better compensation and improved working conditions.

The emergence of Wal-Mart as a major force in the retail business has dramatically changed the degree of competition in the industry. Opposition to

Wal-Mart has become a *cause célèbre* for unions, existing retail businesses, liberal environmental groups, and some local politicians who charge that Wal-Mart fails to provide its workforce with any degree of industrial democracy and is frequently in violation of labor standards.

Wal-Mart's entry into the retail market has clearly benefited consumers and generated significant employment, albeit in mostly relatively low-wage jobs. The underlying issue in the criticism of Wal-Mart is not the few highly publicized wage-and-hour and immigration violations which the company has admitted. It is the reaction of other retailers to greater competition which makes it difficult for them to raise prices. Union opposition is based on Wal-Mart's success in avoiding unionization. Unions recognize that if they are unable to organize Wal-Mart it will be difficult for them to negotiate wage and benefit improvements in other retail businesses with union representation.

VI. Conclusions

Over the past 30 years, progressive human resource policies and government regulation of the workplace have improved working conditions. Today unions are no longer exercising union power to "protect the underdog" or "level the playing field" (Kaufman, this volume). Unions are using their power to pass legislation to benefit their narrow special interests. There are two groups in the workforce that may provide unions with organizing opportunities. One segment of the workforce is the growing number of nonpermanent employees or contingent workers. Another is the growing low-wage part of the service sector. The Service Employees International Union has been one of the few unions to expand membership among these employees. The aging of the baby boomers will raise the demand for service workers in health care facilities and in hotel and office maintenance which will increase organizing opportunities for unions in this industry (Kosters, 2004).

The authors of some of the symposium chapters support labor law reforms to give workers collective voice to influence their working environment which business will certainly oppose. Business feels that card certification campaigns can result in extensive personal pressure on individual employees to go along with the views of other employees. In the final analysis, there is no substitute for secret ballots to determine the will of individuals.

Business may be willing to accept mediation and perhaps even *voluntary* binding arbitration of first-contract negotiations. Mandatory binding arbitration proposals will always be opposed by business because it inevitably leads to unrealistic bargaining positions on the part of labor since the arbitrator's award is typically in between the final positions of the parties. In most cases management evaluates a collective bargaining settlement in terms of its long-run effects on the firm. On the other hand, unions typically try to maximize short-term gains, and the arbitrator's award will usually be based on current labor market conditions.

Finally, business strongly feels that punitive damage awards by the National Labor Relations Board would not be in the public interest, let alone business interests. There is too much adverse experience with the outcome of punitive damage and pain and suffering awards in product liability and medical malpractice awards to seriously consider this type of legislative change, especially in an era when there is considerable public support for liability reform.

Over the next several decades there are two major industrial relations issues facing management and labor. First, management and labor need to recognize the long-run implications of negotiated non-wage compensation arrangements on employment and on future profitability. This primarily involves decisions on pension and health care plans and applies equally in union and nonunion environments.

In the past the unions and management often settled on overly generous pension and health benefits since, unlike wage improvements, the full cost of defined pension benefits and defined health plans did not occur for many years. The tragedy of the failure to recognize the inevitable future costs of non-wage benefits is clearly demonstrated in the current insolvency plight of the pension plans of several major airlines. Overly generous defined-benefit health benefits may also result in similar insolvency problems for some union-negotiated health benefits.

The health care industry now represents over one-seventh of the U.S. GDP and is an industry which has virtually no price competition among health care providers. Prices throughout most of the industry are determined by a huge, complex government-administered price control system which over the past decade has resulted in annual cost increases in the range of 7 percent to 10 percent in both the public and private sectors. In contrast, businesses in most other private sector industries face severe competition and have had great difficulty raising prices; indeed, in some industries real prices have declined. As a result, many private sector employers are now, or soon will be, unable to provide overly generous health care benefits. Labor and management must continue to move to defined-contribution pension plans and start adopting defined-contribution health care plans, such as Health Saving Accounts, as part of employer-provided health care insurance.

The second industrial relations challenge facing management and labor is how to utilize the skills of the workforce to maximize productivity. Fewer levels of management, decentralization of decision making, and greater worker participation in some types of business decisions are essential to economic performance. Public policy should encourage these trends. Management believes that advocates of the need for greater workplace democracy should support efforts to reform the NLRA to encourage nonunion facilities to establish self-directed work groups. Congress tried to amend §-8(a) (2) of the NLRA by enacting the Teamwork for Employees and Management Act (TEAM)[4] which would have modified § 8(a)(2) by permitting employers to establish work groups, which would improve quality and productivity, provided that such groups would not negotiate collective agreements or attempt to amend any existing labor contracts. This legislation passed the House of Representatives and the Senate, but was vetoed by President Clinton in 1996 (McLennan, 2001).

Since workers and employers, as well as the public, appear to benefit from participative management, labor laws must be modified in order to disperse these benefits throughout the economy. Management believes that the public policy toward increasing workers' participation in business decisions should support a pluralistic approach by encouraging participation in both union and nonunion environments. This is management's perspective on how to provide the workforce with voice.

Notes

1. Monthly averages are the ratio of inventories at end of month to sales for the month. In 1992 the standard industrial classification (SIC) system was modified slightly. The publishing industry was removed from manufacturing and petroleum refining added to form the new North American Industrial Classification System (NAICS). Since these industries are relatively small in output, the change had no effect on the trend in the ratio.
2. For a review of the development of worker participation teams described as high performance work systems and how they pay off, see Applebaum et-al. (2000).
3. As part of the record-breaking "midnight" regulations on December 20, 2000, President Clinton issued such a regulation which a year later was revoked by the Federal Acquisition Regulation Council during the Bush Administration. The December 20, 2000 Clinton regulation allowed government contracting officers to make unilateral determinations of "nonresponsibility" about prospective contractors on the basis of "relevant creditable information" that a contractor has, within the past three years, violated various labor, employment, environmental, antitrust, or consumer protection laws, whether relevant or not to the work or services to be procured by the government. Any deficiency in these areas would deem the company disqualified—or blacklisted—from future contract competitions. For further information, see Guth (2002).
4. The Team Act was introduced in the 105th Session of Congress as H.R. 1529 and S. 669. For a discussion of the TEAM Act, see Manufacturers Alliance/MAPI Report EL-162 at pp. 9–11 (August 1994) which contains testimony of Kenneth McLennan before the U.S. Department of Labor's Commission on the Future of Worker-Management Relations.

References

Applebaum, Eileen, Thomas Bailey, Peter Berg, and Arne L. Kolleberg. *Manufacturing Advantage*. Ithaca, NY: Cornell University Press, 2000.

Baumol, William J. and Kenneth McLennan, eds. and contributors. *Productivity Growth & U.S. Competitiveness*. New York: Oxford University Press, 1985, pp. 3–16.

Block, Richard N. and Kenneth McLennan. "Structural Economic Change and Industrial Relations in the United States' Manufacturing and Transportation Sectors Since 1973." In Hervey Juris, Mark Thompson, and Wilbur Daniels, eds. *Industrial Relations in a Decade of Economic Change*. Madison, WI: Industrial Relations Research Association, 1985, pp. 337–82.

Bluestone, Barry and Bennett Harrison. *The Deindustrialization of America.* New York: Basic Books, 1982.

Brainard, Lael and Robert E. Litan. "Services Offshoring, American Jobs, and the Global Economy." *Perspectives on Work* 8 (Winter 2005): 9.

Drezner, Daniel W. "Where Did All the Jobs Go? Nowhere." *New York Times*, September 29, 2004.

Fay, Timothy A. "The Carrier Move from Syracuse." *Perspectives on Work* 8 (Winter 2005): 4–6.

Freeman, Richard B. and James L. Medoff. *What Do Unions Do?* New York: Basic Books (1984).

Freeman, Richard B. and Joel Rogers. *What Workers Want.* Ithaca, NY: Cornell University Press, 1999.

———. "Introduction: Worker Representation . . . Again!" *Journal of Labor and Employment Law* 3 (Spring 2001): 381.

Galbraith, John Kenneth. *American Capitalism.* Boston: Houghton Mifflin, 1956.

Guth, Elaine J. *Controversial Government-Wide Regulation Contractor Responsibility to Labor Relations and Other Noncontractual Standards Is Revoked—At Last!* Arlington, VA: Manufacturers Alliance/MAPI, E-159, January 2, 2002.

Kosters, Marvin. "Unions and the Economy." *The World and I.* Washington, DC: News World Communications (April 2004): 54–59.

Lawrence, Robert Z. *Can America Compete?* Washington, DC: Brookings Institution, 1984.

Leonard, Jeremy A. *Stimulating Manufacturing Productivity Growth through Investment in Computers.* Arlington, VA: Manufacturers Alliance/MAPI, ER-449, June 1998.

Magaziner, Ira and Robert Reich. *Minding America's Business.* New York: Harcourt Brace Janovich, 1982.

McLennan, Kenneth. *Globalization: Implications for U.S. Industry and the Work Force of the Future.* Arlington, VA: Manufacturers Alliance/MAPI, ER-493 (1998): 2–3.

———. "Globalization: Some Implications for 21st Century Labor Markets." In David Lewin and Bruce E. Kaufman eds. *Advances in Industrial Relations*, Vol. 11. Oxford: JAI Elsevier Science, 2002, pp. 201–13.

———. *Union Membership Continues 25-Year Decline.* Arlington, VA: Manufacturers Alliance/MAPI, PR-149, February 2001a.

———. "Worker Representation and Participation in Business Decisions Through Employee Involvement Programs." *Journal of Labor and Employment Law* 3 (Spring 2001b): 568–81.

——— and Daniel J. Meckstroth. *Adjusting to Economic Change: Industry's Response to Economic Slowdowns.* Arlington, VA: Manufacturers Alliance/MAPI, ER-521 (August 20, 2001): 2–4, 6.

Meckstroth, Daniel J. "The Changing Structure of U.S. Manufacturing and Its Labor Force." In Thomas J. Duesterberg and Ernest H. Preeg, eds. *U.S. Manufacturing: The Engine for Growth in a Global Economy.* Westport, CT: Praeger, 2003, pp. 35–66.

Nickell, Stephen and Glenda Quintini. "The Recent Performance of the U.K. Labour Market." *Oxford Review of Economic Policy* 18 (2002): 202–20.

Tannenbaum, Frank. *The Labor Movement.* New York: G.P. Putnam, 1921.

———. *A Philosophy of Labor.* New York: Alfred A. Knopf, 1951.

de Tocqueville, Alexis. *Democracy in America* II. Garden City, NY: Anchor Books Edition, 1969: First published in 1835.

Watson Wyatt Worldwide. *The Unfolding of a Predictable Surprise: A Comprehensive Analysis of the Shift from Traditional Pensions to Hybrid Plans iii.* Washington, DC: Watson Wyatt Worldwide, 2000.

19

What Do Unions Do?
A Unionist's Perspective

Stephen R. Sleigh[*]

I. Introduction

In 1984, Richard B. Freeman and James L. Medoff (F&M), published *What Do Unions Do?* (*WDUD*). The title alone was provocative, suggesting at once the possibility that unions do little and at the same time, maybe there were some unanswered questions that might lead one to think that unions perform something useful. The rigorous neoclassical economic training of both Freeman and Medoff provided a launching point to reassess what unions do. The framework that F&M applied to answering the questions about what unions do set the book apart from previous research and has spawned a small academic industry that continues to look critically at the economic role of unions in American society. These Symposium chapters attest to the depth and continuing importance of F&M's contribution to the research on labor and employment relations.

For practitioners of labor relations in the United States and elsewhere, F&M also had an impact. As a union research person, I will describe my personal story with *WDUD*, the realities that I face every day in representing American workers through research and strategy, and conclude with some thoughts on what unions should do in the future. This is not intended as an academic contribution to the ongoing labor economic research or the history of labor economics but rather a reflection on the impact this book has had on one person in a senior staff position in the American labor movement and how that translates into actions. The authors, especially Freeman, continue to play a vital role in thinking about the future of labor and employment relations and the role unions play in society.

I begin with an overview of *WDUD*'s major findings and comment, briefly, on my union view of those findings then and now. Section III is a snapshot of unionism circa 1984; Section IV provides an example of how unions are addressing one of the most difficult issues in employment relations today: providing affordable, quality health care; Section V details the IAM's (International Association of Machinists) efforts at understanding how to prioritize our members concerns through the use of surveys; and Section VI provides an example of how unions address the competitiveness of firms through productivity and efficiency. These three sections provide a snapshot of how unions actually put the "voice" mechanism into practice. The last section summarizes my critique of *WDUD* and my perspective on what unions should do, and why that is important for society.

II. Overview of WDUD

WDUD was the most important economic assessment of the role of American labor unions in over 20 years, and has remained a touchstone for academic work for the past 20 years. F&M concluded that, on balance, unions were a good thing for the American economy and society as a whole. The innovation F&M used in their analysis of unions' impact on the economy was the application of a theory from political science to economic theory contained in Hirschman's *Exit, Voice, and Loyalty* (Hirschman, 1970). He argued that "voice" is an important mechanism that requires analysis and integration into standard economic theory. F&M called this "the two faces of unionism." On the one hand, unions raise labor costs (wages and benefits), and in some circumstances where such increases reflect monopoly power in the labor market, they may be economically harmful. That is the traditional view of unions espoused by most neoclassical economists. On the other hand, unions provide workers a voice, and that translates into improved productivity, lower quit rates, and other economically beneficial attributes.

Given the context of the U.S. economy in the early 1980s F&M found that the monopoly wage effect was modest, less than 1 percent of gross national product (p. 57). The past 20 years has seen significant erosion of union power and density, due in large part by several large, interrelated trends that greatly impacted heavily unionized sectors: globalization, which introduced very low-wage labor costs in manufacturing and was hastened by substantial expansion of regulatory protection of the interests of mobile capital such as NAFTA and the WTO; deregulation, especially in transportation—trucking and airlines most notably; loosening of labor market regulations in the search for flexibility; and, more recently, privatization of public services. Taken together, these trends were supported, to greater or lesser extents, by both U.S. political parties. The combination of these trends caused substantial loss of union jobs in manufacturing and transportation and with it the power of unions to negotiate wage and benefit increases for the same proportion of the workforce as in the early 1980s. The monopoly wage effect, from a union perspective in 2005, is but a dream of times past. From a management perspective the problem with unions, in 1980 and 2005, is that they tend to reduce profitability by redistributing income to labor away from capital and that restrictive work rules keep organizations from adopting best practices resulting in the loss of competitiveness in relation to nonunion organizations which have flexibility to implement best practices.

On the positive side, *WDUD* found that unions provide a number of socially beneficial functions. Among these were: (1) allocating a larger share of labor costs to the provision of benefits, especially retirement income and health care; (2) unions reduce income inequality, even while achieving a significant premium for their members; (3) by providing a system of workplace justice, through a grievance and arbitration mechanism, unions help reduce the arbitrary rule of supervisors, which in turn increases employee morale; (4) through explicit provisions of a collective bargaining agreement, unions provide a framework for the professional management of an organization, rather than a haphazard set of individual deals; and (5) these positive attributes can lead to increased productivity and efficiency (pp. 20–23).

F&M collected significant datasets on each of these issues, and others, and came to the conclusion that the voice mechanism, on balance, outweighs the monopoly wage face of unionism. Over time, F&M's conclusions appear correct, but increasingly irrelevant. As American unions have continued to decline, what F&M termed "the slow strangulation of private sector unionism," the ability of American unions to express workers voice has greatly diminished to dangerous levels, in my view. The economic analysis of the voice mechanism in *WDUD* was, in my view, the most important and lasting contribution of the book. But voice alone is not enough to deliver what workers want. At 8 percent of the private sector workforce in the United States, organized workers' voices have become barely audible whispers. What workers want, and in my view what is best for society, is to have a voice with power in the workplace. Given the context of the early 1980s, unions had some power. The issue was how to expand it in ways that benefited the entire society. Today, the issue for the American labor movement is how unions survive the slow strangulation that is on the verge of asphyxiating the labor relations system of the past seventy years. To make it clear, I clearly have a vested interest in such survival. The case I try to make below is that the social benefits of a revived labor movement far outweigh the negative consequences of continued erosion of union power.

III. The End of the Gravy Train

In 1984 I was working as a machinist, a very specialized machinist, who installed and maintained newspaper printing presses. The company I worked for, Goss Graphic Systems, was a division of Rockwell International. In addition to printing presses, Rockwell produced the space shuttle and related aerospace manufacturing and services, industrial automation, and other industrial products. As a successful conglomerate, Rockwell compared to General Electric in terms of revenues and profits in the early 1980s. Goss was known throughout the world as the leading producer of newspaper printing presses. With nearly 60 percent market share in the noncommunist bloc countries, Goss was globally dominant in the manufacture and servicing of newspaper printing presses. As a result of market position, complexity of work performed, and the requirement of a four-year apprenticeship, we printing press erectors were a well-compensated group of workers. As a member of the International Association of Machinists and Aerospace Workers (IAM), the union that represented machinists at Goss, I reaped the rewards of significant pay increases every year of my machinist career. I was, in some respect, a recipient of the "monopoly wage" face of unionism described by F&M. In reality, my high wages were the result of being highly skilled within a company that had market share in a profitable industry. Nothing wrong with that!

I became a printing press erector in 1979 after serving a four-year apprenticeship to learn the machinist trade. My work as a printing press erector took me to seven different countries and 50 different newspapers from 1979 to 1984. In 1984, I received a scholarship from the IAM to cover college expenses. I quickly completed my bachelor's degree in labor relations at the University of Massachusetts and then went on in 1986 to attend Harvard University's Kennedy School of Government. It was there, in the spring of 1987, that I took a labor economics class with James Medoff and turned to Richard Freeman for advice on how to deal with my advisor, the notoriously cantankerous John Dunlop. Not only was Richard a noted economist but, moreover, from my point of view, he knew how to get things done! *WDUD* had only come out a few years before so the atmosphere of the class, and discussions on unions overall, were filled with energy. Having been on the shop floor, as a beneficiary of union-negotiated wages, and now in the classroom as a beneficiary of a union scholarship, I was inspired then, and now, by the work of Freeman and Medoff (and Dunlop!).

Having spent the better part of the years since 1987 working in and around the labor movement, and the last 11 years as director of strategic resources at the IAM, a position that encompasses research and strategy, I have experienced and participated in some of the biggest challenges facing unions. A lot has changed since 1984 when *WDUD* first appeared. The story of my former employer, Goss, is emblematic of those changes, at least for skilled blue-collar workers. After dominating the newspaper printing press business for nearly a century, foreign competition began to encroach on Goss's market share in the late 1980s. By the mid-1990s, after a series of sales and reorganizations, Goss was facing serious financial difficulties. In the fall of 1999 Goss filed for Chapter 11 bankruptcy protection, and months later emerged from bankruptcy and shed all of its U.S. manufacturing by the fall of 2001.

The president of Goss, Richard Sutis, cited unfair competition from Japan and Germany for Goss' demise: "The illegal dumping [by Japanese and German manufacturers] caused Goss to lose sales and profits and forced our company to file for Chapter 11. . . . We relied on a valid U.S. anti-dumping law that allows damages for such predatory practices."[1] In short, Goss had fallen victim to competitive practices that allowed foreign producers an untenable advantage through massive government subsidies. Despite the efforts of the IAM and Goss, the predatory practices of Japanese and German printing press manufacturers continue. For months we worked with private equity investors and legislators to see if Goss' manufacturing could be saved, but in the end the company closed all of its manufacturing in the United States in the fall of 2001. Although the name lives on, the Goss product is now made primarily in Asia, resulting in the loss of nearly 600 well-paying jobs in the United States. When Goss' main production facility closed in Cedar Rapids, Iowa, the pain of plant closure was felt directly by IAM-represented members, their families, and the community at large. The loss was far more than economic, and this is a critical point that is lost in econometric studies. These people had invested their lives in this facility, had used their skills to build the best product in the world, and forged friendships that had lasted decades. The labor market is different from any other market, and when a plant closes we're not talking about a market-clearing event but rather a human loss. *WDUD* fails to capture, or even address, the third part of Hirschman's analysis, that of loyalty. Workers, somewhat more than supervisors and managers who have more professional opportunities, and far more than shareholders who have little or no personal attachment to an investment, have the highest personal stake in the success of an organization. Their loyalty to the organization, and the work they perform, differentiates workers' outlooks from all other stakeholders. As Hirschman notes, "the likelihood of voice increases with the degree of loyalty" (Hirschman, 1970: 77).

The Goss story has been repeated a thousand times over the past ten years, and especially over the last five years in the manufacturing sector. The once strong manufacturing sector of the U.S. economy, and with it a strong labor movement, is a mere shadow of what it was when I joined the workforce in 1974. Today, for workers in manufacturing, the gravy train is over.

The manufacturing core of the labor movement at the time *WDUD* was published has been decimated and with it the ability to set standards that lifted all workers. In the past four years over three million U.S. manufacturing jobs were lost, and those jobs that remain are increasingly nonunion. The dramatic exodus of manufacturing jobs from the United States is due to a variety of causes as noted above. F&M could not have foreseen such a dramatic change in the landscape of unionism, but the outcome of the decline in manufacturing jobs is a completely unbalanced distribution of power between workers who fear the loss of their jobs and owners who can effectively "put any factory on a barge" in Jack Welch's phrase. The social result is increased income inequality and declining opportunities for middle-income pay and benefits for those without college educations. Other capitalist economies, especially the Scandinavian countries, have navigated these same forces with similar outcomes, increasing inequality, but to far lesser extent then experienced in the United States (Kenworthy, 2004). Neither increasing inequality or declining opportunities for upward mobility is good for the United States.

IV. Responding to Change: The Health Care Crisis in the United States

One issue that cuts across all sectors of the economy that has confounded unions and management alike is the rising cost of health care. In 2004 75 percent of the labor disputes that ended up in strike payments being made in the IAM identified health care cost shifting as the key issue in dispute. Health care cost shifting was the key issue in the largest work stoppage in 2003 and 2004 involving the United Food and Commercial Workers (UFCW) and west coast supermarkets, the most visible strike in the past few years.

Back in the day when *WDUD* came out, health care was not even listed in their index, instead appearing lumped together in the category of "fringe benefits." Even the phrase "fringe benefits" has a quaint ring to it: "a decorative border" according to the dictionary. In fact, when the War Labor Board was negotiating with business and labor to contain wage increases during World War II, the idea was floated to add health insurance and retirement benefits into the mix since these benefits cost so little. Apparently a creative person at that table came up with the term based on the popular play *Oklahoma!* that included a popular tune, "Surrey with a Fringe on Top." Thus was born the term "fringe benefits."[2]

The historical significance should not be lost. It was unions negotiating with the government and big business that brought about the introduction of health care insurance and pension benefits in the 1940s and 1950s, and it was unions that set the standard for such benefits throughout the next 40 years. When F&M published *WDUD* unions still represented nearly one in four workers in the private sector and that representation density spilled over to a significant portion of the nonrepresented workforce.

Today, of course, union density in the private sector has fallen below 8 percent and with it the "union wage (and benefit) effect" has likewise shrunk. Health insurance, along with life and accident insurance, accounted for 4 percent of total compensation according to *WDUD* in 1977. Virtually every union worker, 99 percent, was covered for health insurance, versus 79 percent of nonunion workers.

The current share of health care expenditure is 9.1 percent of total labor cost, and in some cases that the IAM is involved with can range as high as 15 percent of total labor cost. The rapid escalation of health care cost, to $5,267 per person per year in 2002, with annual increases in the first five years of this decade averaging 14 percent, is nearly double the cost from 1999.[3] Coming at a time of economic slowdown after the stock market and "new economy" exuberance burst, combined with the paralyzing effects of September 11, 2001, especially on the air transportation and tourism sectors of the economy, health care costs created a crisis for labor relations in the United States.

Employers responded to the crisis by shifting costs to workers and dropping coverage for many. Indeed, Wal-Mart, the nation's largest employer, set the corporate example by containing its health care expenditures by hiring older workers eligible for Medicare coverage, spouses who were covered by another organization's health care, and encouraging low-wage "associates" to get subsidized health care through state Medicaid programs. In the labor market, the union wage and benefit effect has now become the Wal-Mart wage and benefit effect in a spiral downward for workers and their families. Union workers by and large have medical care (81 percent) versus barely half for nonunion workers.

At the IAM we developed a strategic approach to dealing with the crisis in health care costs that has been used in a number of negotiations over the past six years. In analyzing the health care issue we realized an important fact: Our efforts at the bargaining table were limited to negotiating over the cost of health care and the benefit plan design of health care coverage. The key item missing is the quality of care our members and their covered dependents get for those benefits. What we found was troubling: While the United States spends more on health care as percent of gross domestic product (nearly 15 percent in 2004) we rank thirty-seventh in the world in health outcomes according to the World Health Organization. In what other area would we accept spending the most and getting such poor returns? The WHO rankings put the United States between Costa Rica and Slovenia in health outcomes. Would we as a country accept spending the most on defense in the world (we do) and yet rank between Costa Rica and Slovenia's military? Clearly not.

The shortcomings of the health care system in the United States, what we get for our health care expenditures, were documented in a seminal study published in 2000 by the National Academy of Science's Institute of Medicine (IOM). The study, *To Err Is Human*, raised national awareness as to the shortcomings of our health care delivery system. Among the findings:

- As many as 98,000 Americans die per year due to preventable medical errors;
- More people die in a given year as a result of medical errors than from motor vehicle accidents, breast cancer, or AIDS; and
- Medication errors alone cause as many deaths as all workplace related accidents (Corrigan et-al., 2000).

The report identified two key obstacles to improving the health care delivery system: the decentralized and fragmented nature of the care delivery system and the fact that group purchasers have made few demands for improvements in safety.

The IAM had already launched a series of quality initiatives with some of its large companies, notably the Boeing Company, in the mid-1990s. Armed with the information from *To Err Is Human*, the IAM made patient safety a national bargaining objective. Why should we continue to fight over marginal increases in cost sharing when the product being purchased was of inferior value? While bargaining still focuses on costs, and the overall impact those costs have on total labor costs and thus on organizational performance, our strategy was to focus a mutual-gains approach with employers, especially large employers with concentrations of employees in a given health care market, on this value added proposition.

In 1999, just prior to the release of *To Err Is Human*, the IAM and Boeing agreed on a framework for working together on patient safety. Specifically, we put into our collective bargaining agreement three standards for measuring improvements in patient safety that health policy experts identified as providing the most immediate benefit. These three improvements were: requiring doctors to enter prescription drug orders via computer; require hospitals to have only doctors trained and certified as being able to handle work in the intensive care unit provide such staffing; and, to refer employees and covered dependents to hospitals that perform more than a minimum number of specified procedures per year, or evidenced-based referrals. Later in 2000, these three improvements in patient safety became the basis for a national effort launched by the Business Round Table known as the Leapfrog Group. The IAM was the first labor organization to join Leapfrog and has been among its most active participants in regional roll-outs of patient safety.

Since putting the quality agenda forward in 1995, with the patient safety focus in 1999, the IAM has taken the lead among unions in developing a value agenda for health care purchasing that focuses on what we get for our money. Holding providers accountable, including health plans, hospitals, and doctors, is an added responsibility the union has taken on. The outcome of that work is that today hospitals respond to our requests for action on implementing patient safety. In Puget Sound, where the IAM and Boeing are significant players in health care purchasing, every hospital has responded to the Leapfrog Group's request for information on the status of patient safety initiatives. No other area of the United States has consistently achieved that level of hospital responsiveness. Because of the joint efforts of the IAM and Boeing, consumers in Puget Sound have more information available to them, and their hospitals are reducing preventable medical errors. As an added benefit, and one that requires further research, high-quality health care and reducing preventable medical errors also results in overall lower costs. If ever there was a mutual-gains opportunity, this example would seem to provide a good model to follow.

Still, much work remains but the example is an important one from the perspective of F&M's *WDUD*. The central idea of *WDUD* is that unions provide a voice for workers. Indeed, in annual surveys we conduct of our members' priorities for the coming year, preserving health care benefits has ranked as the number one issue in each of the last three years. Preserving benefits, especially health care, is a clear enough task for a union to work on. Taking on the delivery system of health care involves something altogether more complex. In more detailed surveys on health care alone, most IAM members view the quality of services as quite good. In other words, the voice mechanism alone is inadequate to address the structural failure of the health care system. Since medical errors are not usually seen, and the health care delivery system is cloaked in the veil of professionalism and licensure, everyday people's understanding of the extent of the problem needs to be raised.

The downside for union leaders is getting too far ahead of the membership. Since union leaders' jobs depend on the assent of the membership, through direct election in the case of the IAM, they need to stay closely in tune with the members' needs and desires. The next section details an effort we have undertaken to better understand the members' needs and desires, but we'll come back to the notion that F&M developed that "voice" is the key to what unions do.

V. Pulse of the Union: What Workers Want (and Get) from Their Union

Starting in 1999 the IAM's Strategic Resources Department began conducting annual surveys of IAM members in a project called The Pulse of the Union. The annual survey, which randomly selected 1,000 members weighted by region and gender, is a self-administered mail instrument. Typical response rates over the years have hovered around 35 percent. After conducting these surveys internally for several years, the IAM partnered with researchers from the University of North Carolina and Rutgers to do a more formal phone survey. While the annual Pulse of the Union survey continues as a snapshot of members' desires and needs, the phone survey project broke new ground in assessing member attitudes toward the union, their job, the company they work for, and society in general.

During the summer of 2002 we conducted in-depth interviews with 840 IAM members for this project. We were particularly interested in looking at generational differences in union member attitudes toward the union, work, and society. The coming wave of Generation-X into the workforce is seen as a challenge not only for business but also for unions. The standard lament in union halls and among leadership is that the new generation doesn't know what was done for them years ago. As with any survey, timing is an issue. Coming at a point of extreme economic contraction following the September 11, 2001 attacks, the results need to be viewed through the lens of economic insecurity that gripped our members in the summer of 2002. Notwithstanding the timing issue, the Taking the Measure survey was the most extensive ever conducted to my knowledge by a union of its members.

The key question that motivated this research is how much our members trust the union and management where they work, and what explains that trust, or lack thereof. Getting the voice of the members right is largely a matter of trust. How that plays itself out is complicated—trust can be directed towards individuals and organizations, and can change over time. From an economic point of view, how does trust translate into organizational effectiveness? Does trust in the union indicate less trust in the company, translating into lower productivity? The results of the Taking the Measure survey didn't definitively answer those questions, of course, but they do point in the same direction that F&M were heading 20 years ago.

A few of the key findings on workers attitudes toward management:

- Workers in companies that have downsized trust their managers less than do workers in companies that have not experienced downsizing;
- Workers who have more autonomy in their work report that they trust their managers more than those who are closely supervised;
- Workers who regard work as central life interest and believe in a just world are more likely to trust the company's managers and union leadership; and
- Workers with longer seniority trust managers less than workers with fewer years on the job.

Trust in union leaders follows a similar path with a few notable differences:

- Workers with more autonomy trust union leaders less than those closely supervised; and
- Seniority appeared to have no effect on trust in union leaders (Kalleberg et-al., 2004a).

The conclusion of the study is that trust appears to strongly enhance organizational citizenship behaviors: "trust in the company is strongly and positively related to citizenship behaviors that are performed on behalf of the company; similarly, workers who place greater trust in their union leaders are more likely to perform union citizenship behaviors" (Kalleberg et-al., 2004b). In general, the view of younger members (30 and under) was consistent with that of more senior union members. Somewhat to our surprise, we did not find a significant generation gap except on some obvious issues like retirement income (older workers want more pension benefits more than younger workers).

Understanding the desires and needs of union members is received in many forms, most directly by union leaders at the ballot box. By conducting a systematic, detailed survey of our members' attitudes toward the union, their work, the company they work for, and society in general, the IAM now has a better understanding of how to satisfy the voice mechanism that F&M identified as the key function of unions.

VI. Towards a High-Performance Work Place

One management criticism of American unions is that collective bargaining agreements tie the hands of managers from achieving productivity and efficiency gains. Examples abound of restrictive work rules found in collective bargaining agreements, such as the printing trades where manning standards set before the introduction of computer-assisted offset presses added twice as many pressmen to a newspaper line as were necessary to complete the task. A related complaint is that unions keep management from installing state-of-the-art systems of production, thus reducing competitiveness.

The IAM was often cited as an American union opposed to workplace innovation in the 1980s. Indeed, the view of IAM leadership in the 1980s and early 1990s was to oppose workplace cooperation on the grounds that management should manage and workers should work, and that capital was always interested first and foremost in extracting profits from the combination of the former and latter. The union's job, in this view, was to always and everywhere fight for the direct and immediate improvement of the wages and working conditions of our members.

The early 1990s saw a significant change in our perspective on workplace cooperation. The effects of globalization, deregulation, and privatization were being felt throughout the IAM manifested in a precipitous drop in membership from just over one million members in 1969 to fewer than 600,000 in the early 1990s. If employers truly wanted to engage the union in a partnership to improve productivity, become more competitive and preserve or expand jobs, we should be prepared to engage them in such a conversation. The underpinning of the IAM's strategy on high performance workplace organization (HPWO) was detailed in Ray Marshall's (1987) *Unheard Voices: Labor and Economic Policy in a Competitive World*. The core argument Marshall made, that the participation of workers in production-level decisions, whether on the shop floor or the corporate boardroom, is critical to the competitive ability of the organization.

After a thorough and intense discussion among the leaders of the IAM, a new program was launched in 1994 that dedicated union resources to developing internal capacity to engage management in the discussion about transforming workplace processes. A new department, the High Performance Work Organization Partnership department, was charged with the responsibility of developing a consistent union-wide policy for IAM districts and locals to follow in terms of engaging in productivity and quality improvement programs.

At the same time, the IAM became an active participant in the Lean Aircraft Initiative (later to become the Lean Aerospace Initiative or LAI). The premise of LAI was to adapt the best practices of lean production from the Toyota system of automobile production and apply them to the production of military fighter jet aircraft. Over the next ten years, from 1994 to 2004, the IAM actively collaborated with the top-tier aerospace companies and second-tier suppliers, the Air Force, and researchers at the Massachusetts Institute of Technology (MIT), in seeking ways to reduce the cost of fighter jet aircraft through the application of lean practices. In a parallel research effort known as the Labor Aerospace Research Agenda, the IAM and UAW worked with MIT researchers to detail best practices in aerospace collective bargaining, ways to reduce job instability through changes in procurement processes, and how to make "lean work for the workforce." The premise was simple: By reducing the cost of future fighter jets Congress could afford to modernize and stay globally dominant in air superiority, and provide for more secure jobs for our members.

The HPWO approach adopted was based on several key principles:

- A full partnership between the IAM and management including union participation in developing a business plan that commits the organization to a growth strategy;
- Shared decision making around the vital functions that are critical to the organization, its costs, and the processes used to the work;
- Development of continuous learning and skill building for the entire organization;
- Continuous integration of leading-edge technology that builds on the skills, knowledge and insights of union-represented front line workers; and
- Acceptance by the company of the union as an independent source of power for the workers.

After ten years and a substantial investment of time and effort, the IAM has a number of well-documented success stories for both the LAI/LARA work and the HPWO program. On the LAI/LARA front, the IAM and Boeing were able to apply lean principles to collapsing the number of job categories from 42 to eight in one collective bargaining agreement in 2000. The flexibility this accorded the Company was groundbreaking in the industry. At the same time, it gave IAM members increased opportunities to acquire additional skills, compensation, and job security. With HPWO, the IAM's longest standing effort dates back to the start of the program in 1994 with the Harley-Davidson Company. Over the years, the IAM partnership with Harley has often been cited as a critical source of their competitive advantage and rescue from near bankruptcy in the late 1980s.

Despite these initiatives very few employers have responded to the promise that increase cooperation with the union could bring. After ten years of participating in LAI, and seeing aerospace companies maintain profits and extravagant executive compensation while IAM jobs steadily disappeared, to the point where employment in the aerospace sector hit a fifty-year low in early 2004, the IAM withdrew from LAI in 2005. With HPWO, fewer than 1 percent of all IAM agreements have achieved a full partnership as described by the principles above. While the IAM is still committed to the idea of workplace partnership, the fact is that few employers are ready to cede the kind of control that a partnership implies. The key issue that keeps emerging is whether management is serious about competitiveness and growing the workforce or are they more interested in control and keeping their jobs secure despite the deleterious effect that has on organizational performance. In our experience management has shown far more desire to remain in control than in truly trying to find ways to increase productivity and expand job opportunities for production employees.

VII. *What Do Unions Do?* in Perspective

"[T]here is a place for unions to improve the well-being not only of their members but of the entire society. . . ." (*WDUD*). F&M thought in 1984 that U.S. unions would most likely stabilize membership, and even laid out some interesting ideas for the rejuvenation of labor. After seeing a slow decline from the peak density years of the mid-1950s, F&M saw unionization leveling off around 20 percent of the workforce if historical rates of organizing were maintained; otherwise they foresaw a slow decline to 10 percent of the workforce over the next 20 years. Unfortunately, from a union perspective, the latter scenario has come to pass. A few years of stability, and a few areas of growth, particularly in the fast-growing service sector, could not stem the overall loss of union density. Just as with the loss of bone density, at some point the loss of union density will result in the collapse of the house of labor as we now know it. That time is not here yet, but just as it was unthinkable in 1984 that unionization in the private sector would fall below 10 percent, as it now has, the emergence of a new form of worker voice is sure to follow if present trends continue.

Some hope does seem to be emerging. A recent survey of collective bargaining indicated that more than a third of the parties to contract negotiations were engaged in strategic workplace-level innovations. In our experience at the IAM, strategic bargaining, where the parties identify common interests rather than competing claims, is slowly taking hold. Despite the fact that the union has dedicated significant resources to developing high-performance work organization partnerships, which grow out of a strategic bargaining approach, less than 1 percent of IAM agreements have such a partnership.

Turning back to F&M, one critical point they made was succinctly put: "When unions are more costly to employers, employers are more hostile to unions." The "union advantage" now stands at roughly 20 percent for wages and 28 percent for total compensation. While such a markup from nonunion workers is certainly worth the cost of union membership, the cost in employer opposition is not sustainable. In an ever more competitive economy, and where competition is not constrained by national borders, unions need to find new ways to organize and express workers voice beyond raising pay and benefit costs.

F&M correctly identified voice as the issue for unions. What they may have missed through their prism of neo-classical economics is that unions, in order to express voice effectively, need to act more as an agent for group, or class, needs rather than as maximizers for individual economic welfare. The model of U.S. labor relations is rooted in individual-, firm-, or even plant-level negotiations. The structure of collective bargaining creates barriers to seeking industry-wide or society-wide solutions. While our efforts to deal with surging health care costs and uneven quality at individual bargaining tables is a creative approach, it lacks a social movement necessary to truly carry out reform. The true innovation in the health care example will come when labor joins together to form purchasing pools for large groups of people in a given region. By aligning our purchasing power with that of a broader social good, in this case reduced cost, greater transparency in health care outcomes, and improved patient safety, the labor movement may recapture the social high ground and start to build a mechanism for delivering a social good to our members and society at large.

Finding the right set of institutional mechanisms to carry out a social agenda that is consistent with labor's role of giving workers a voice is, in my view, the central challenge for American unions. In comparing labor market and unionization trends in other countries one can see a wide range of such institutional mechanisms. Bruce Western (1993: 7), a political scientist, gets it right: "Where class has no institutional reality, unions and employers appear to each other as market agents. In this setting, collective action is insecure, fluctuating with market power."

Collective action is indeed insecure in today's U.S. labor market. The challenge to the labor movement is to find a way to express workers' voice, as so well described by F&M, in a society that has erected a virtual obstacle course to keep unions from delivering the economic benefits once enjoyed by a majority of American workers, and now by fewer and fewer. Perhaps 20 years from now we can look back in retrospect to see what innovations workers and their organizations developed and the conclusion will be, as F&M concluded *WDUD*, that what unions actually do is "to improve the well-being of the free enterprise system, and of us all" (p. 251).

F&M did a monumental job aggregating data in a systematic way to answer the question of what unions do. Their conclusions were that unions' monopoly wage effect was generally harmful to the economy, but that the "voice" effect of unions was positive both economically and socially. On balance, the data in *WDUD* support the idea that unions provide a useful mechanism for workers and the economy.

The past 20 years have seen significant structural change in the U.S. economy, particularly in the decline of manufacturing described anecdotally above, and a number of long-term trends that were evident in the early 1980s continue today. The impact on unions of these long-term trends is worth considering in light of the U.S. labor movement's struggle to remain relevant. The debate within the labor movement is important not just to unions, but more broadly to the entire society. If unions don't exist to provide workers a voice, what mechanisms will?

Five broad trends will shape what unions do in the future in the United States: (1) continuing employer hostility to relinquishing control of corporate and workplace governance; (2) slower growth in the workforce and with it an aging workforce; (3)-increasing application of information technology to production; (4) continued increase of globalization of production; and (5) increasing skills for many occupations at the same time there is downward pressure on wages for unskilled work.

Perhaps these challenges can be met through innovative tactics within the existing framework of collective bargaining. Taking a page from F&M, and focusing on how voice is actually translated into action, suggests to me that the existing framework of collective bargaining will continue in those situations where relationships are mature, but that a new form of representation will emerge for the 90 percent of workers who currently have no voice in setting the terms and conditions of employment. We know from various surveys that a far larger proportion of the workforce want to have the benefit of union representation than the 14 percent who currently have an organized voice through which to speak to management. Developing institutional mechanisms to express voice will depend on our ability in organized labor to aggregate our power. Finding ways to lessen management opposition to ceding some control of organizational governance is the key. This may take the form of regulatory changes such as real penalties for violating workers' rights to organize and mandatory arbitration of first contract negotiations. I for one am not going to hold my breath until that happens! Another approach is to start building on our existing source of strength: the collective power inherent in a block of 15 million union members, who also happen to represent nearly 50 million consumers if you count dependents and unrepresented employees at unionized organizations, and the pension assets of millions of workers totaling over $3 trillion.

F&M underestimated the difficulty in changing the organizational culture of American unions. Unlike corporations, which can impose change with little resistance from shareholders and unrepresented employees, unions need to have the assent of their members to make significant changes. The very problem with unions that F&M identify, monopoly wages, is exactly what our members want! Many sectors that F&M studied still had globally dominant positions in the early 1980s, like Goss did in printing presses. Within the IAM the average age of a member is 48 with 18 years of seniority. That means they came into the union, on average, in 1987, just as the era of U.S. manufacturing dominance was coming to an end. Now we find ourselves in highly competitive markets, going up against workers who are paid a fraction of well-established union wages and benefits cost.

Economists still tend to focus on "exit" rather than "voice." In many respects exit is certainly easier to measure and quantify. Voice, on the other hand, is messy. In my view, voice is another way of thinking about commitment, trust, and loyalty. Those are not values you hear often from corporate America. The relentless focus on creating shareholder value has tended to push commitment, trust, and loyalty aside. For unions operating in post-monopoly sectors the key to survival is finding ways to enhance commitment, trust, and loyalty of the workforce while improving organizational performance. F&M touch on this lightly in their discussion of the efficiency effects of unions, but again the appreciation of the difficulty in sustaining workplace transformation is lacking. Experience has taught union leaders that high-performance workplace relationships require a lot of time, resources, and energy. In a time of contraction and embattlement, those are all hard to come by.

Looking forward, we could re-pose the question F&M asked over 20 years ago as "What Will Unions Do in the Future?" Responding to the five challenges listed above is a place to start, and F&M's analysis informs each of the strategic approaches I think will work best.

Employer hostility to unions is a fact of life in the United States, even within well-established bargaining relationships within firms. One example is General Electric which has steadily and methodically moved work out of unionized facilities and regions into nonunion facilities in the United States and abroad. Of the roughly 132,000 production employees at General Electric in 1963, approximately 90 percent belonged to one of ten different unions. Today, GE's unionized workforce in the United States barely consists of 20,000 employees (Schatz, 1983).

Organizing new employers is notoriously difficult in the United States. As mentioned above, the "union advantage" in wages and benefits, acts as a strong incentive for nonunion employers to keep wages and benefit levels down. F&M correctly identified these twenty years ago, and the problem has only gotten worse as the few pockets or islands of unionism recede to the rising tide of lower wage nonunion facilities. One way to bridge the gap between union and nonunion wage and benefit levels is to create two-tier systems wherein new hires get substantially less than current employees. That often appears as the path of least resistance, especially when you are trying to get a contract ratified. Sacrificing the unborn may seem relatively painless, but in the long run, and in industries with high employee turnover the long run is not very long, such an approach is bound to create more problems than it solves.

The answer to employer hostility to unionism needs to come through a combination of lessening the economic sting of higher wages and benefits through productivity and quality improvement and bringing additional goods to the table that an employer, especially a small one, could not bring. Health care is one such example. Pooling together pension assets in multi-employer plans is another.

A second trend that will shape what unions do in the future is the slowing growth in the size of the workforce. In the 1970s the U.S. workforce grew by an average of 2.6-percent per year; by the 1990s growth had slowed to 1.1 percent per year, and is projected to decline to .3 percent per year by the 2020s. Slow growth of the workforce will likely mean that the workforce in place will steadily get older. In the IAM we have seen this trend in the aerospace sector. In 1984 the average age of an IAM member in aerospace was 42; today it is approaching 50. As employment opportunities contracted, and as less senior employees were laid off, the workforce inexorably gets older. With generous retirement income benefits including defined-benefit pensions and employer contributions to savings plans, a large segment, perhaps as much as a third, of aerospace workers will leave the industry in the next five years. The resulting loss of skill and experience will resonate throughout the industry.

Reinventing apprenticeship and training programs is a role unions should lead in response to the coming slowdown in employment growth. Another area where unions can lead is in finding ways to make work more appealing for older workers. Being flexible and responding quickly to changing conditions is difficult for unions due, in large part, to our democratic structure: It's not easy to get a majority of people to agree on any change that benefits only a few. Changing working hours to shorten the workday for more senior employees might be one response; job sharing and phased retirement are two others that we are working on.

A third challenge runs in an opposite direction from that of an aging workforce and slow employment growth: increasing application of information technology to production and service jobs. Over the past 20 years the cost of one megahertz of information processing power fell from $7,500 to $.17! Younger workers have, in general, had greater exposure to information technology and feel more comfortable using interactive software than generations of workers who have come to expect to work by a rigid set of rules and procedures. Again, there is an opportunity for unions to mediate the process by which workplace transformation takes place, to give all workers a voice in how best to apply the advances available through information technology.

Globalization was an emerging trend when *WDUD* was published and today represents one of the greatest challenges to unions. Over the last 40 years trade-related economic activity (both imports and exports) have increased from 10 percent of the U.S. gross domestic product to 25 percent, and that percentage is growing. In manufacturing, as was described earlier in the story of Goss, foreign competition hangs over every workshop. Often the threat is not from a foreign competitor per se, but more so from the threat of a U.S. manufacturer relocating work outside the United States. The search for lower production costs, especially lower labor and environmental costs, has led to an exodus of manufacturing jobs to Mexico and China. The threat of globalization is now moving into areas once thought immune: Research and development work is joining call centers as the outsourcing activity of choice. F&M, putting on their economist's hats, sided with increased trade liberalization and removing of barriers and deregulating the economy while calling for adjustment assistance for workers impacted by structural change. Overall, U.S. consumers have clearly benefited from deregulation in airlines and reducing trade barriers to such things as apparel. Workers and their unions, however, bore the brunt of these changes with the level of adjustment assistance in reality woefully inadequate. Coming to grips with continued global economic integration poses a great challenge to unions. Merely forming cross-border alliances between unions has proven ineffective. Transcending national borders will require a fundamental change in how unions operate and how they view themselves. Again, F&M identified the problem, but failed to understand that the organizational logic of American unions makes such a response extremely difficult.

Finally, and somewhat optimistically, the aging of the workforce combined with increasing information technology, and the globalization of a consumer market along with production and service processes, may create opportunities for high-value-added work. Customization and tailored solutions may become widespread consumer demands in the future, requiring a highly skilled workforce adept at moving quickly to meet consumer demand. In a return to the days of craftsmanship more than a century ago, unions may find themselves as organizers of skilled workers prepared to work a variety of complex tasks. Unions in this new world of production may look more like the guilds of yesteryear.

In this review of the impact of F&M's *WDUD*, I sought to connect my personal story to my professional work as a union researcher and strategist. *WDUD* sits on my shelf at work and at home, and I often find myself referring to ideas they developed over 20 years ago. I have not tried to critique their economics or the excellent analyses in this Symposium. Rather, I hope the reader takes away one thought from this paper: Unions are embattled institutions in the United States, and F&M's work two decades ago remains a source of inspiration and hope that society in general will come to agree with the statement that "[t]here is a place for unions to improve the well-being not only of their member but of the entire society."

Notes

*   I thank Bruce Kaufman for helpful suggestions and encouragement throughout the writing of this piece; Ron Blackwell for reviewing the next-to-last draft of this paper; Ann Greiner for her observations on the health care section; and Teresa Canning for multiple assists in pulling this paper together. The views expressed herein are mine alone and not necessarily those of the International Association of Machinists and Aerospace Workers.

1.   "Goss Graphic Systems Plans to Shift All Manufacturing Overseas," *Graphic Arts Monthly*, October 1, 2001, and "Goss Urges Congress to Preserve Right to Pursue Anti-Dumping Claim," *Business Wire*, July 27, 2001.

2.   This anecdote was supplied by Joel Cutcher-Gershenfeld whose father, Walter Gershenfeld, was at the meeting with Cyrus Ching, then director of the War Labor Board, and George Taylor of the University of Pennsylvania who was chairing the meeting.

3.   U.S. Department of Labor, "Employer Cost Employee Compensation–September 2004," released January 27, 2005.

References

Corrigan, Janet, et al. *To Err Is Human*. Washington, DC: National Academy Press, 2003.

Freeman, Richard and James L. Medoff. *What Do Unions Do?* New York: Basic Books, 1984.

Freeman, Richard and Joel Rogers. *What Workers Want*. Ithaca, NY: Cornell University Press, 1999.

Hirschman, Albert. *Exit, Voice, and Loyalty*. Cambridge, MA: Harvard University Press, 1970.

Kalleberg, Arne, Eileen Appelbaum, Stephen Sleigh, and John Schmitt. "For Better or Worse: Union and Company Trust and Citizenship Behaviors." Champaign, IL: IRRA *Proceedings*, 2004.

———. "Taking the Measure of Workers and Jobs: Surveying What Workers Want (and Get) from the Union and Company." Report to the Alfred P. Sloan Foundation, 2004.

Kenworthy, Lane. *Egalitarian Capitalism*. New York: Russell Sage Foundation, 2004.

Marshall, Ray. *Unheard Voices*. New York: Basic Books, 1987.

Mishel, Larry and Matthew Walters. "How Unions Help All Workers." Washington, DC: Economic Policy Institute, 2003.

Schatz, Ronald. *The Electrical Workers*. Champaign, IL: University of Illinois Press, 1983.

Western, Bruce. *Between Class and Market: Postwar Unionization in the Capitalist Democracies*. Princeton, NJ: Princeton University Press, 1997.

20

What Do Unions Do?
The 2004 M-Brane Stringtwister Edition

Richard B. Freeman[*]

I. Introduction

When Bruce Kaufman first told me that he was organizing a twentieth anniversary review of *What Do Unions Do?* in which researchers would assess
the book's findings and arguments in light of ensuing research and events,
I was both honored and worried. Honored that he and so many other labor
experts felt that the book was sufficiently durable to merit re-assessment
and criticism and worried that some of the criticisms might be harsh. Our
knowledge of unions has advanced over 20 years. The economy and unions
have changed over the period. I know more than I had known in 1984, and
so too would the reviewers. If before the reviews began, I could rewrite a few
chapters . . . add another chapter . . . modify some sentences . . . improve,
update, correct . . . I would be more comfortable. With the benefit of hindsight
revision, I could guarantee that the reviews would be encomiums . . . huzzahs
. . . bravissimos.

Then a friendly member of the Union of String Theorists offered me the
opportunity of a lifetime—a chance to travel in his 11-dimensional M-brane
stringtwister back in time through the nearest Gott loop to improve and revise
the book. "Think of how you can outmaneuver and stymie and unnerve your
critics!" my union friend said. "It would be like re-recording the Nixon tapes!"
"But what if string theorists, even the unionized band, have it wrong, and there
are just four dimensions to space-time?" I replied, a bit nervous at trusting the
latest M-brane string theory. Like other economists, I have more faith in the
Invisible Hand than in hands-on economic engineering, and like other labor
specialists, I prefer evidence to theory. "Don't worry," came the reply, "The
Union of String Theorists reduces turnover, increases pay, raises productivity,
lowers inequality, and improves fringe benefits. And, if by chance, there are
only four dimensions, the M-brane stringtwister will do nothing worse than
scramble your brains into chaotic perturbation. That would be a disaster for a
physicist, but who knows what it will do to a labor economist? Scrambled brains
and chaotic perturbation might turn your neurons on and give you a new start

in life. If you wrote about economies in Calabi-Yau space, you'd be eligible to join our union. Our health plan covers scrambled brains."

So I have considered the corrections, revisions, and changes I would make in the book if the 11-dimensional M-brane stringtwister works . . . and new ideas for the next phase of research on trade unionism if the world has fewer than 11 dimensions. To guide my deliberations, I read the papers in the *What Do Unions Do?—A Twenty-Year Perspective* and reviewed the large literature on unionism in the United States and other countries that followed *What Do Unions Do?*

As the Symposium papers make clear, some findings and interpretations in *What Do Unions Do?* have held up well over time and across settings. But the book also missed some things and . . . (*sotto voce*) may even have got some others wrong. In the period since the book, research by many scholars, including participants in the symposium and myself—older and presumably wiser than when the book appeared—has enriched and altered thinking about unionism. In areas where I believe the book got the story right but where controversy remains, I will argue that the evidence favors *WDUD*. In areas where the reviewers have correctly identified weaknesses, I will make the appropriate changes or, if the 11-dimensional M-braner doesn't work, shout uncle. I conclude by unscrambling ideas for future work.

II. Basic Themes

There are three main themes in *WDUD*.

As many commentators have stressed, the first theme is that studying the effects of unions on wages as if unions were a textbook monopoly misses critical aspects of what unions do and, indeed, of what any democraticizing institution does at the workplace. Following Albert Hirschman's (1970) exit-voice terminology, I labeled the missing component "collective voice" (Freeman, 1976). This placed unions as a social institution front and center. Going beyond the standard exit-voice model, *WDUD* sought to capture the two-sided nature of collective bargaining by stressing that management's response to unionism or worker voice was critical in determining outcomes. For employee voice to be effective at the workplace, management must listen. For employee voice to be effective more broadly, the state and society must listen. The stress on voice as a mode of communication and information in *WDUD* fit well with the emerging economics of information of the 1980s. The notion that unions could improve compensation packages by obtaining workers' preferences for non-wage benefits was influenced by Michael Spence's work in industrial organization and the development of new goods. The combination of information via voice and union bargaining power should enable unions to improve firm-level economic outcomes in compensation and other areas. Union facilitation of information flows from workers to the firm allows the firm to provide the best benefit package for a given expenditure. Union bargaining guarantees that the firm listens to worker concerns and that the firm does not take the lion's share of the gains from the better flow of information.

I recognize now but was oblivious then to other ways in which collective voice can and does operate in variegated institutional settings. Throughout the European Union, mandated works councils provide collective voice without extracting monopoly wages at the workplace. As union density has fallen in the United States and the United Kingdom, firms have created mechanisms for worker participation through employee involvement committees, joint consultative councils, and so on. My analysis with Joel Rogers in *What Workers Want* (1999) highlights that many workers want unions or other labor institutions to help them give input into workplace decisions—the voice face of unionism. I take the criticisms of *WDUD* for ignoring nonunion voice as valid. But note that voice without power is too often ignored by higher-ups in organizations as the early institutional economists stressed (Kaufman, this volume).

The second theme of the book is that any evaluation of the benefits and costs of unionism has to balance the costs due to monopoly wage or compensation setting against the economic benefits that unions bring through lower turnover, improved productivity, more desirable distributions of compensation between wages and benefits, reduced dispersion in pay for workers, and the political success of unionism in advancing the well-being of workers broadly. *WDUD* took the view that union wage or compensation gains imposed efficiency losses on the economy that showed up in "Harberger triangles." This rejected the theoretical possibility that management and labor would reach efficient bargains over wages and other workplace conditions and transfer income from firms to workers without loss of employment or output (Leontief, 1946). Even without Coase-style efficient bargaining, the empirical calculations showed that the allocative losses due to unionism were relatively modest, of a magnitude that the benefits of unionism could largely offset or even dwarf. The fall in the union wage gap in recent years (Hirsch et-al., 2004; Blanchflower and Bryson, 2004) implies that the monopoly-face losses have become even less debilitating for the aggregate economy. But the book had a serious weakness in analyzing the economic cost of unionism: Its social calculus was based almost exclusively on a comparative statics allocative analysis. *WDUD* gave little attention to the effects of unions on growth—be it employment growth, output growth due to investment, or research and development—that should enter any social evaluation of unionism.

The third theme was that unionism does most social good when union workplaces compete with nonunion workplaces. That competition is good for firms is a cardinal principle of economics. That competition between unions and other institutional forms or among unions is good for the labor market is contestable. At one extreme, some opponents of unionism find it hard to believe that any rate of unionization above zero could benefit the economy. At the other extreme some analyses imply that centralized bargaining is optimal. Examining Nordic labor relations, Mancur Olson (1990) argued that all-encompassing unions are optimal since they internalize the negative externalities (usually, loss of jobs) that result from union wage gains. In a similar vein, Calmfors and Driffil (1988) claimed that unions that cover only a moderate share of the workforce have the greatest allocative losses. By contrast, my work with Lazear (1995) argues that the curve relating worker power within a firm to output has an inverse U-shape, so that the ideal level of worker power is intermediate between what workers/unions want and what management wants. Kaufman and some others in this volume are on the right track to critique the simplistic way *WDUD* dealt with the complex issue of the optimal level of unionization.

As Pencavel notes in his chapter, empirical evidence on the optimal level of unionization and associated mode of collective bargaining is mixed. At times Scandinavian countries and Austria which operate with high levels of unionism and "neocorporatist" arrangements have had superior economic performances, but these are small open economies that may not need domestic competition to keep noses to the grindstone. At other times, countries with middling levels of unionism, such as Ireland or the Netherlands, have done well, using social pacts that cover the entire workforce to resolve macroeconomic problems. And countries with low levels of unionization, such as the United States, have outperformed other capitalist economies in some periods—for example, from the mid-1990s through the mid-2000s.

As a devotee of competition, I wish the evidence spoke clearly that unions bring more positive things to an economy in a competitive setting. But the cross-country, time series regressions that analysts use to make inferences about the effects of different levels and forms of unionism on aggregate economic outcomes give what Pencavel generously calls "fickle results" from which it is not possible to make valid generalizations.[1] If the M-brane stringtwister works, I will modify the discussion of the optimal level of unions considerably, stress how little robust evidence we have, and make the theoretical point that institutional details may matter a lot. I would also stress that the problem is a Coasian one of whether or not the institutions help or impede labor and management to reach efficent bargaining outcomes and that current theory provides little help in sorting out this issue.

Kaufman makes two other critical comments about the assessment of the optimal level of unionization that also deserve attention. First, accepting that unions reduce turnover, which most firms find desirable, he notes that we lack evidence that turnover was excessive absent unionism in the economy as a whole. Given the high rate of mobility in the United States, I would be shocked if turnover is sub-optimal, but even so the point is valid: What is good for the firm may not be good for the economy. Moreover, views about the optimal level of turnover for the economy have changed over time. In the 1950s some American labor economists worried that declines in mobility were creating "industrial feudalism" (Ross, 1958; Kerr, 1997). In the 1970s and 1980s, many heralded Japanese lifetime employment as economically beneficial, since guaranteed tenure would induce workers and firms to invest more in specific human capital. In the 2000s many view the high mobility in the United States as superior to longer-term job tenures. The changes in views are not rooted in research on the economy-wide benefits and costs of higher turnover, presumably because no one has devised a convincing research strategy to identify the optimal level of turnover in the United States or elsewhere.

Second, Kaufman notes that the optimal level of unionism depends on two factors that *WDUD* did not treat: the presence (and presumably effectiveness) of other institutional mechanisms for worker voice; and the ability of unions to redress imbalances in bargaining power in external labor markets and in the national polity. Alternative institutions of effective worker voice would reduce the optimal level of unionism, as mandated works councils have arguably done in the European Union. But greater union bargaining power could also lead non-union employers to provide greater channels of voice to their workers, as they seek to avoid unionization, as arguably occurred in the U.S. when firms developed non-union channels of voice to fend off unionism. From this perspective, a stronger union movement strengthens non-union voice as well, making the two complements. Finally, the ability of unions to redress imbalances in bargaining power in the national arena can produce greater investments in schooling, more occupational health and safety protections, and the like, which benefit all workers and the nation. Recall Sam Gompers' famous statement in 1893: "What does Labor want? Labor wants more schoolhouses and less jails; more books and less arsenals; more learning and less vice; more leisure and less greed; more justice and less revenge; in fact, more of the opportunities to cultivate our better natures" (quoted at http://www.the-tidings.com/2004/0910/laborhomily.htm).

In the M-brane stringtwister revision, I have added a long chapter on the optimal level of unionization, but must admit that, for all the mathematical twisting and turning, not even the symmetries in Calabi-Yau manifolds identify a single answer.

III. Errors of Omission

There were (at least) three serious errors of omission in *WDUD*.

1. The Rest of the World

The first is that the book dealt almost exclusively with the U.S., as if the rest of the capitalist world had no unions or as if there was nothing to learn from what unions did outside the United States. Looking back, it is easy to shake one's head at the American hubris of entitling the book *What Do Unions Do?* with so little attention to the rest of the world. Having spent considerable time in the United Kingdom and elsewhere learning about how unions and labor institutions operate outside the United States, I am acutely aware of differences in the rules governing labor practices among advanced countries and in the difference between confrontational U.S. labor-management relations and the more—dare I say?—civilized relations in most EU countries. Retitling the volume *What Do U.S. Unions Do?* would surely be the first change I will make in the 2004 stringtwister edition (with a promise of further volumes on other advanced economies).

As a *mea culpa* for ignoring the rest of the advanced world, I note that prior to the National Bureau of Economic Research's Comparative Labor Markets project, labor economics in the United States was itself highly U.S.-centric. We left the experiences of other countries to area specialists, sociologists, comparative industrial relations, and the few residual Marxists. Assessing the extent to which *WDUD* offers a general analysis of unionism requires evidence on what unions do outside the United States as well as within the U.S.[2] There was also, however, a powerful practical factor that limited *WDUD* to the United States: the difficulty of obtaining for other countries micro data of the type that formed the heart of our research. Hard as it may be to believe, the Workplace Industrial Relations Survey was not yet readily available and the OECD had yet to publish the *Employment Outlook*, which helped spur analysis and micro-data gathering on labor issues in advanced countries. Nowadays, with international students in our classes, labor economist colleagues and micro-data sets in virtually every country, entire censuses on laptops, and the potential of web-based surveys covering many countries, there is no such excuse.

In any case, Pencavel's Symposium chapter on unionism from an international perspective is on target. We have as much to learn about unionism from the experiences of other countries, particularly countries with more centralized and state-influenced economic systems, as we do from the decentralized U.S. economic system. The fall in union density in many OECD countries shows some convergence in the position of unions among advanced countries, but Pencavel correctly rejects the notion of convergence in labor institutions broadly. Collective bargaining coverage has diverged across countries, as countries with mandatory extension of contracts continue to rely on union-management negotiations to set pay. France, with a smaller percentage of workers unionized than the United States has nearly all of its workforce covered by collective bargaining.

Going beyond the OECD, there is also much to be learned from the experiences of unionism in developing countries which *WDUD* and the Symposium have ignored. At one stage the World Bank, the IMF, and other international financial institutions viewed unions and collective bargaining as adverse to desirable economic policy. The ILO necessarily took the opposite view. But as research has proceeded, the World Bank (though not the IMF) has moved toward a perspective closer to that in *WDUD*. In 1995 the Bank's *World Development Report* stated (p. 79) that "Free trade unions are a cornerstone of any effective system of industrial relations that seeks to balance the need for enterprises to remain competitive with the aspirations of workers for higher wages . . . unions can help raise workplace productivity and reduce workplace discrimination." In 2003, the Bank published Toke and Tzannatos' review of studies of unions, *Unions and Collective Bargaining: Economic Effects in a Global Environment*, that concluded that unions were more likely to improve than harm developing economies. Part of the Bank's message has been that repression of unions in developing countries can be associated with excessive intervention and regulation by the state.

Going beyond the microeconomic analyses of *WDUD* and related research, there is a missing element in *WDUD* and the Symposium commentary that the experience of developing countries brings to the fore. This is the role that unions have historically played as a democratic voice institution fighting for democracy and free markets. *Solidarnosc* helped overturn the Soviet Empire. COSATU helped undo the Apartheid regime in South Africa. The trade unions in Zimbabwe have stood against President Mugabe's seizure of private property and destruction of the economy. The Peronist unions helped stabilize Argentina in the aftermath of its 2001 economic crisis and have been a responsible force in Argentina's ensuing recovery. At some unknown future date, free trade unions will help China move toward democracy.

The big lesson from bringing the rest of the world into the *WDUD* analysis is that unions are mutable social institutions that operate differently in different institutional settings. Unions have a monopoly face and a voice face. The mix between them and the impact of unions on economic and political outcomes depends on the environment in which unions operate. The United States is one environment. There are many others.

2. The Public Sector

The second important error of omission is that the book deals solely with private sector unions. Police workers, firemen, teachers, and government employees of diverse sorts make no appearance. This was not because we believed, as George Meany once claimed, that public sector workers were non-organizable, but because the public sector environment differs so much from the private sector environment as to require a different analytic model. In both sectors, unions and management have a mutual interest in increasing the demand for the products or services and a conflict over the division of revenues. In the private sector, unions can do little to raise demand for goods or services made by union labor, so most managements oppose unions as an institution that reduces profits. In the public sector, unions are often an effective advocate of increased public services, producing a different attitude among managers. Police unions and police departments gain from greater budgets for security, teachers' unions and school boards gain from greater resources for education, and so on. A realistic analysis of public sector unions has to factor in their role in shifting demand for public services through lobbying legislatures or city government and through campaigns to convince citizens that they need more public services, as well as their role in shifting the allocation of budgets toward workers.

Given that the public sector has maintained its density in the United States and in other countries while private sector density has fallen, omission of the public sector is a serious weakness of *WDUD*.[3] If one were to analyze the impact of unionism by sector proportionate to collective bargaining coverage or membership today, nearly half of one's research effort would be devoted to the public sector.[4] Thus, *WDUD* is about a declining proportion of the U.S. unionized workforce. Blanchflower and Bryson include estimates of union wage effects on public sector workers in their analysis, and Gunderson reviews other evidence on public sector unionism, but the Symposium in general has followed the *WDUD* concentration on the private sector. In succeeding work, I have tried to remedy the *WDUD* exclusion of the public sector by examining the growth of public sector unionism (Freeman, 1986), the effect of public sector unions on wages and benefits using a before/after design (Freeman et al., 1989), and, working with NBER colleagues, have tried to illuminate how public sector unions affect outcomes differently than private sector unions and why they have developed so differently (Freeman and Ichniowski, 1988).

3. Dynamics, Growth, and the Macroeconomy

The most egregious error of omission in *WDUD* is the cursory treatment that the book gave to the effect of unions on growth and dynamics. As the book was nearing publication, I became concerned about this and undertook some last second regressions of productivity growth on union density across industries, which gave insignificant negative coefficients on the rate of unionization. Reviewing the current state of work in this area, of which his own is the most important (Hirsch, 1991), Hirsch (this volume, p. 210) concludes that "there exists no strong evidence that unions have a *direct* effect on productivity growth," consistent with the *WDUD* analysis.

But productivity growth is not the same as economic growth at the firm or industry level. The standard growth accounting equation relates output growth to total factor productivity growth *and* to the growth of capital and labor. Hirsch's analysis of investment in physical capital and R&D spending in the United States shows that union firms and sectors invest less than otherwise comparable nonunion firms and sectors, which implies lower rates of growth for organized parts of the economy. The logic for the lower investments is the union impact on profits and quasi-rents. If union firms earn lower profits from given investments because unions shift some of those profits to workers, they will invest less than otherwise comparable nonunion firms. These results have been replicated in different data sets, models, and time periods in the United States. In addition, a wide body of research has found that employment growth in union sectors falls short of that in nonunion sectors, which further adds to the picture that unions reduce the growth of firm or sectoral output primarily by affecting usage of factors. By contrast, work on unionism in the United Kingdom has not found adverse union effects on investment or R&D, possibly because United Kingdom unions have a modest impact on wages and presumably profits. Still, even in the United Kingdom, unions are associated with lower employment growth. Given a choice between current members and possible new members in the future, unions will favor the former, sacrificing growth and future members for the benefit of current members, as Peter Kuhn (1982) pointed out in his PhD dissertation (written as *WDUD* was nearing publication). This view is consistent with the findings, including Freeman and Kleiner (1999) and that of DiNardo and Lee (2004), that unionism does not increase the risk of plant or firm closure, even while it reduces employment growth.

But the fact that U.S. unions cut into quasi-rents and reduce R&D spending and investment in physical capital and lower growth of employment at the level of firms or sectors does not mean that unionism reduces economic growth nationally. If union firm A does not make a given investment because unions lower the prospective profit on that investment, nonunion firm B may make the investment, so that the rate of national investment and growth is unchanged. But in the United States, unions have arguably contributed to aggregate economic growth through a very different mechanism: by increasing the savings of American workers through union-negotiated, defined-benefit retirement plans. My analysis of 1979 Current Population Survey showed that 83 percent of union workers had pension coverage compared to 39 percent of nonunion workers (Freeman, 1985). Budd's Symposium paper finds a similar, though modestly smaller, difference in the 2002 Current Population Survey: 76 percent of workers covered by a union contract having a pension plan compared to 46 percent of nonunion workers. Since pension fund moneys are deferred compensation and thus savings, these figures show that unions increase the savings of American workers and thus the supply of capital for economic growth. Given that saving and investment rates are highly correlated by country (Feldstein-Horioka, 1980), this should increase investment and growth. Whether this effect of unions on growth is more or less important than the reduction growth at the industry or firm level due to union capture of profits is an unexplored issue that deserves scholarly attention.

Turning to macroeconomic fluctuations, Mitchell and Erickson in their chapter note that *WDUD* failed to address the impact of union wage setting and other policies on macroeconomic adjustments, and in particular on the prevalence of profit-sharing modes of compensation that could help maintain full employment and low inflation. While some unions have negotiated substantial profit sharing, for instance the UAW in its bargaining with the Ford Motor Company, workers and unions generally prefer greater certainty in wage payments. Given the less than stellar 1990s–2000s economic performances of France, which has the highest rate of profit sharing in the European Union, and of Japan, which relies substantially on profit sharing through its spring and winter bonus system (Freeman and Weitzman, 1987), I find it difficult to believe that this is a major factor in macroeconomic performance. But, then, like most microeconomists, I find macroeconomics to be highly problematic since it seeks to reach generalizations and to judge theories on so few data points.

From the international perspective, unions play a bigger role in macroeconomic policy making and political developments outside the United States than in the United States. In some settings, as Pencavel notes, unions have supported disastrous populist macroeconomic policies. But in Scandinavia, unions have been in the forefront of linking labor market policies and macro policies in ways designed to strengthen markets and in pushing the frontier of economics in thinking about these issues. When one talks with a Latin American economist, there is often a deep suspicion of what unions do to the macroeconomy. When one talks with a Scandinavian economist, there is no such suspicion—in part because the unions regularly consult with the best macroeconomists and make decisions in a macroeconomic context. Even within advanced Europe, moreover, there are strikingly different experiences. McLennan (this volume) associates the successful macroeconomic performance of the United Kingdom with the decline in private sector unionism that followed the Thatcher industrial relations reforms. But over the same period, Ireland adopted an EU social pact for wage-setting, maintained union density and influence, and outperformed the United Kingdom. OECD analyses of the impact of collective bargaining and unionization on macro outcomes published in various *Employment Outlooks* tell no clear story. Again, the message I draw is that unions are mutable social institutions that operate differently in different institutional settings.

IV. The Test of Time: Do the Empirics Stand Up?

*"Give me your evidence or shut the #**,! up."*—
Punk Labor Economist, circa 1984

WDUD was written when structural modeling, usually of labor supply behavior, was the vogue among labor economists. To those lucky enough to have missed this phase of research, structural modeling meant developing sophisticated models of optimizing behavior and then estimating those models with as much econometric sophistication as possible on data that was rarely rich enough to yield clear conclusions nor to illuminate real behavior. Little time was given to finding the pseudo experiments or valid instruments that might truly identify responses to economic incentives. Since none of the modelers knew the right structure and most dismissed behavioral economics as outside the space of economic investigation, this research taught us more about modeling than about the world. My view then and now is that this approach does not add greatly to our knowledge of economies. Taking a very different approach, the institutional economists and industrial relations experts whose work Kaufman summarizes built their knowledge of the world largely on case studies.

As the punk economist quote at the outset of this section indicates, the methodological approach of *WDUD* differs from these modes of analyses. Research on *WDUD* was motivated by a (sometimes aggressive punk) belief that progress in understanding unions would come more from analyses of large bodies of statistics covering multiple outcomes than from blackboard theorizing or case studies. It is on large bodies of statistical evidence, generated in the ensuing 20 years, that nearly all of the Symposium reviewers have judged the durability of the book's message.

My reading of the state of research on what unions do, which the Symposium chapters summarize admirably, is that the *WDUD* claims that have undergone the most substantial and rigorous empirical analysis remain valid today. The empirical assertions about what unions do to wages, dispersion, and inequality of pay; fringe benefits; quits and turnover; profitability; job satisfaction; human resource management policy; and political activity and outcomes appear robust over the past two decades. Research on union effects on productivity gives a wide range of estimates that are consistent with the *WDUD* claim that "Unionism *per se* is neither a plus nor a minus to productivity. What matters is how unions and management interact at the workplace" (Freeman and Medoff, 1984: 179), though not with some of the more positive gloss put on that generalization in the book, which Hirsch softly critiques as being "overly optimistic" about where the average effect would ultimately lie. I will reduce the gloss if the M-brane stringtwister gives me the chance.

Overall, however, since the Symposium participants agree, sometimes enthusiastically and sometimes grudgingly, that *What Do Unions Do?* got most things right, I don't see great need for M-brane stringtwister improvements, much less for Richard Nixon erasures of the record. To be sure, I would have chosen adjectives from a more benign thesaurus on some contested points than did some of the Symposium participants, but I have no problem with their substantive assessments. What unifies empirical labor economists as a group is that our conclusions are data driven rather than prior driven. Our priors can be found in the adjectives or gloss/spin we give to particular findings, but not in the findings themselves. Stripped of verbiage, we let the evidence do the talking. But, adjectives aside, there is one *WDUD* claim with which some Symposium participants disagreed strongly enough that I feel the need to put on my "punk labor economist" outfit and go to battle. This is the claim that management opposition to unionism has been a major cause of the precipitous drop in private survey sector unionism. After commenting on the research results about which there is general agreement, I will defend this claim against the criticisms.

1. Union Wage Effects (Blanchflower and Bryson)

When I think union wage effects, I do not think *WDUD*. I think H. Gregg Lewis. The *WDUD* research on union wage effects dovetails closely with Lewis's later work, in part because Gregg visited NBER and Harvard to analyze CPS files, where research assistants working on *WDUD* did some work for him as well. Our analyses of the micro data showed substantial differences in union wage effects among groups of workers and industry, occupation, and region. Thanks to Hirsch et al. (2004) and Blanchflower and Bryson (this volume), we know now that the CPS estimates were biased downward because the Census hot-deck procedure of imputing earnings to missing observations did not include unionism as a hot-deck variable. Still, Blanchflower and Bryson show that this does not affect the patterns of differentials among workers or sectors. They confirm the finding that there is no single union wage effect, but a set of effects that depend on worker and sectoral characteristics. In addition, *WDUD* argued that declines in union density should make the demand curve for union labor more elastic and thus lead to a decline in the union differential; and that the differential should vary countercyclically, as nonunion wages respond more rapidly to immediate market pressures than union wages. Blanchflower and Bryson show that both of these expectations are supported empirically. The falling union premium in the private sector in turn means that the estimated monopoly effect of unionism through static reallocation of labor is smaller than stated in the book.

2. Inequality (Card, Lemieux, and Riddell)

When I first analyzed the effect of unionism on dispersion of pay, most economists (at least around Chicago) believed that unions raised inequality by increasing the pay of labor's elite and reducing the pay of nonunion workers by displacing labor from union sectors. The analysis summarized in *WDUD* showed that union-induced reductions in the dispersion of pay among union workers and union-induced reductions in the white-collar/blue-collar pay differential dominated these factors, so that on net unions reduced pay inequality. Because this finding ran counter to the then prevailing wisdom, I compared inequality within firms and across the entire economy with cross-sectional data and examined longitudinal data that followed workers from union to nonunion employment or conversely. Much of this work focused on men in the private sector. Ensuing research on wage inequality, reviewed and extended by Card et al., has covered more groups—women, public sector workers—with more powerful models that deal with variation in coverage and with differing union wage effects among groups of workers—and found that the union impact on dispersion of earnings is robust across time, models, and data.

As Card et al. note, it is harder to examine the union impact on dispersion of pay outside the United States and in countries with decentralized labor relations systems. If nearly everyone in Sweden is covered by collective bargaining, if the Netherlands extends collective bargaining agreements to non-covered workplaces, and if Italy changes pay nationally through the Scala Mobile, as it did for many years, one cannot use comparisons of union wages and nonunion wages to infer the effects of unionism. There are two ways to deal with this problem. First, one can compare dispersion of pay across countries with differing levels of collective bargaining coverage. Such comparisons invariably show lower dispersion of earnings in economies where collective bargaining is more prevalent. The other and potentially stronger test is to exploit changes in wage-setting institutions over time to test if changes in collective bargaining coverage or modes of determining pay are accompanied by changes in dispersion. The evidence for Italy, where the dispersion of pay narrowed when Italy set pay through the Scala Mobile, and widened when Italy abandoned that form of pay-setting for more decentralized market-driven wage determinination, shows the same pattern. For better or worse, unions and other wage-setting institutions reduce dispersion of pay.

3. Quits, Turnover, and Dispute Resolution (Addison and Belfield; Lewin; Verma; Hammer and Avgar)

"We can after all credit unions with lower turnover" (Addison and Belfield, this volume, p. 258). The essence of the exit-voice analysis of unionism is that there are two substitute ways for workers to deal with workplace problems: quitting or voicing their problems to management. High exit should accompany low voice and conversely. The innovation of *WDUD* was to test this analysis with individual-level data and then to use these data to break the inverse relation between unionism and turnover into a part due to the monopoly face of unionism—higher wages and better benefits—and a part purportedly due to union voice. The individual-level data showed overwhelmingly that union workers have lower quit rates and greater years of job tenure, which reflects the cumulation of turnover—a result that has stood up in ensuing work. Standard econometric analysis shows, moreover, that the wage and benefit effects on turnover fell far short of explaining the full union impact on turnover. This leaves the question: Does voice or something else explain the remaining effect?

When I gave seminars on the union-quit relation in the early 1980s, some economists proposed a simple alternative—that union workers quit less because they were less able than nonunion workers and would get bad jobs outside of the union setting. This is an interesting hypothesis, but one inconsistent with the argument that some of the same economists raised against estimates of union wage differentials—that those estimates were biased upward because union firms hired more able workers drawn to the firm by higher wages. In any case, the "union workers quit because they are less able" story died a quick death.

Longitudinal data on quit behavior showed that the same worker had a lower propensity to quit in a union job than in a nonunion job.

The work reviewed by Addison and Belfield, Lewin, and by Hammer and Avgar confirms that, yes, unions reduce quits and turnover in ways that go beyond the effects of unions on wages and benefits. Addison and Belfield's analyses of the British WERS data file offers a particularly powerful test of the generality of claims about union effects on turnover and satisfaction. The analysis relates to the United Kingdom and uses data gathered with a different sampling design than I used to analyze the union effect on quits and tenure in the United States. That the magnitudes of the union "voice" effects in their Table 8.5 for the United Kingdom "largely mimic those of Freeman and Medoff" (p. 257) for the United States made my day when I read it.

But what we call the voice part of the union effect is essentially a residual—the reduction in quits/increase in tenure that the monopoly face of unionism fails to explain. In the first issue of the *Journal of Labor Research* (Freeman, 1980), I gave some modest evidence that the union effect was correlated with measures of voice, but my analysis was at best suggestive. There remains, as Addison and Belfield stress, more to do to identify the route by which unionism lowers turnover beyond improving wages and benefits. We need measures of the effectiveness of nonunion voice as well as union voice at workplaces. We need to exploit matched employee-employer data sets to test the voice interpretation of the union impact and to suggest alternative interpretations, as well. We could also benefit from some experiments, in laboratories or in the field, to illuminate the exit-voice trade-off.

Lewin argues convincingly that individual workers' use of grievance systems cannot account for the large quit-reducing and tenure-increasing effects of unions. He points out that workers who file grievances are often less productive and may experience worse employment relations or even higher quit or turnover behavior than other workers. Clearly, a high grievance rate is no measure of collective voice working to improve labor conditions or productivity, but of its opposite. A good worker-management relation resolves problems early, without going to formal dispute channels. If management listens to collective voice, and if the union is responsible, problems are solved before they produce formal grievances. Unlike Lewin, I view the finding "from extant studies of HRM and business performance . . . that the presence or availability of a grievance procedure is positively associated with organizational performance, especially when bundled with certain other high-involvement-type HRM practices" (p. 332, this volume) as precisely the positive collective voice/institutional response face of unionism. The word collective means group-level activity, and the words institutional response means organization-level activity. When union voice works successfully and management responds positively, there should be few grievances and lots of collaboration to solve problems.

Looking at workplace-level data, Verma highlights the fact that union work-places are more likely than nonunion workplaces to have formal mechanisms for collective voice. In Japan joint consultation committees and grievance procedures are more commonly found in union than in nonunion workplaces. In Australia, employee surveys and meetings, grievance and equal employ-ment procedures, consultative and safety committees, task forces, and health and safety representatives are more likely in union than in nonunion workplaces. He concludes that "unions are strongly associated with giving workers a voice in the workplace" (p. 445, this volume), the *sine qua non* for the exit-voice model to offer insight into union-nonunion differences in turnover and other outcomes.

The problem in reaching closure on the analysis of collective voice is that we lack measures of the amount and quality of collective voice at particular workplaces. If workplace or organizational-level measures explained some of the substantial union residual in quit or tenure equations above and beyond union effects on compensation, the voice hypothesis would gain support. If they explained none of the residual union effect, we would have to look for explana-tions in other ways. If well-operating voice mechanisms, nonunion as well as union, were associated with lower turnover, analyses would be pushed back a stage to try to determine why collective voice works well in some settings and not in others. The phenomenon to explain is not simply the large union impact on quits and tenure, with compensation fixed that *WDUD* identified, but also the variation in impacts across settings.

4. *Unions and Benefits* (Budd)

WDUD claimed that unions raised fringe benefit spending and that roughly one-half of the increase in fringe spending was the result of the voice face of unions amalgamating worker preferences toward public goods at the workplace and getting workers to reveal those preferences to management. The public goods argument was right out of a standard public economics course. The assertion that union voice would lead workers to reveal their true preferences toward benefits was also rooted in basic theory. The argument was that absent some control over how the employer would use information about workers' preferences, workers would not tell employers their true valuation of benefits for fear that the employer would extract all of the surplus, as a discriminating monopolist would do. A union or some organization was needed to guarantee that some of the benefit from the information went to workers and, thus, to give workers an incentive to reveal their true preferences.

Budd's review of the post *WDUD* literature on benefits supports both propo-sitions for the United States and extends the results to the United Kingdom, where he finds that employer pensions, sick pay, and annual leave are positively impacted by unionism. The U.S. evidence from March Current Population Surveys on the prevalence of health insurance and pension plans shows massive difference between union and nonunion workers, with "in many cases the union-nonunion differences have widened" in the regression analyses compared to the *WDUD* results (p. 178, this volume). Similarly, his evidence from the Employer Costs for Employee Compensation strongly supports the impact of unionism on spending on fringe benefits. Budd's estimated voice effect of unionism accounts for about one-quarter of the total impact of union coverage on fringe benefits overall and over 50 percent of the union impact in low-wage jobs—part and parcel of the union impact in reducing dispersion by raising the economic position of the lower paid more than of the higher paid.

Budd advances the analysis of the impact of unions on employee benefits by identifying two effects that *WDUD* did not examine. These are the impact of unionism on employee awareness of benefits and the impact of unions on employee use of those benefits, which together he labels the *union facilitation effect*. The evidence shows that union members have greater knowledge of benefits than covered nonmembers and, what is perhaps more important, are more likely to take-up benefits than nonunion workers. The finding that union members know more about legally mandated benefits and are more likely to receive them than are nonmembers supports the basic thrust of the voice model: that unions can improve the functioning of the job market through provision of information and assistance to workers in obtaining their rights at workplaces. As the union share of employment falls, not only is the provision of important privately negotiated benefits, such as pensions and health coverage at risk, so too is the delivery of socially mandated benefits.

5. Unions Reduce Profits (Hirsch)

That unions reduce profits is central to the theme of *WDUD*. It is central to the redistribution of earnings from employers to workers. It is central to the argument that management has economic motivation to-oppose unions. Surprising as it may seem, when I sought to determine what unions do to profits in NBER Working Paper 1164, which was the back-up for the chapter in *WDUD*, there were virtually no econometric investigations of unionism and profitability. Industrial organization economists focused on the relation between product market concentration and profits whereas labor economists were concerned with wages, not with profits. Talk about low-hanging fruit. As Hirsch summarizes, ensuing work in this area "points unambiguously to lower profitability among union companies" (p. 211, this volume) irrespective of the particular measure of profits, mode of analysis, level of data, or time period covered. What has not been clarified is the extent to which the union reduction in profits comes from economic rent or monopoly profit (which would make it pure redistribution) and the extent to which the reduction comes from normal returns—quasi-rents—with undesirable efficiency consequences. Hirsch's and other's findings on lower R&D and investment in union firms or sectors implies that at least some of the reduction comes from unions reducing normal profits or quasi-rents and thus affecting growth.

6. *Job Satisfaction* (Hammer and Avgar)

That union workers express less satisfaction with their workplace situation than nonunion workers even though unions bring better material rewards and opportunity to exercise collective voice is one of the puzzles that *What Do Unions Do?* uncovered by examining the relation of unionism to outcomes other than wages. The finding that union workers report less satisfaction has been replicated in many studies in different countries, so the key research question is what explains this pattern. The exit-voice interpretation was that reported dissatisfaction differed from the "true" dissatisfaction that leads to quits because union workers developed more critical attitudes about what they should get from their workplace. Hammer and Avgar list eight possible explanations, including some interesting variants of the exit-voice analysis such as unions socializing members to be attuned to particular job outcomes, and the natural alternative hypothesis, that the content of union and nonunion jobs differs greatly, with union jobs intrinsically less satisfying.

Ensuing work has found that while much of the union/nonunion difference in job satisfaction can be accounted for by detailed characteristics of the job and workplace, there often remain significant negative effects of unionism on satisfaction. Accounting for the negative satisfaction result with detailed measures of job content does not by itself, however, resolve the satisfaction puzzle. This is because the puzzle is not simply that union workers report less satisfaction but that they also quit less. The correlation between unionism and job satisfaction is seemingly inconsistent with the correlation between unionism and turnover, since one would expect that any variable that lowers turnover would raise satisfaction, as wages do. Thus, a job content/workplace characteristics explanation of the satisfaction result must show not only that content/workplace variables eliminates the negative correlation with satisfaction but that it also eliminates the negative correlation with quits. This has not been done, to my knowledge.

Hammer and Avgar correctly criticize the terminology in *WDUD* regarding the way union voice affects attitudes. We called the dissatisfaction not "real," which does not capture properly what the analysis says. I much prefer the Hammer and Avgar statement (p. 349) that "union members have different expectations, values, or frames of reference for evaluating their job outcomes." The methodological implication that follows from this is that any model of how unions affect job satisfaction must analyze its effect on both the expectations/values/frames and on objective outcomes. Since I left Chicago many years ago, I can also agree that "pure economic theories are too simple as models of the causes and consequences of job attitudes," (p. 367) without fear of being instantly slapped down by the Invisible Hand.

7. *Political Activity* (Masters and Delaney)

"Clear it with Sidney"—purported statement by Franklin Delano Roosevelt, referring to Sidney Hillman, president of the Amalgamated Clothing Workers Union. Unions devote considerable resources to politics. They seek two goals: legislation or administrative policies that allow them to function successfully as organizations; and laws that benefits workers broadly. The *WDUD* analysis found that despite the heavy involvement of unions in the Democratic party, unions were unable to get Democratic administrations to enact laws favorable to them as institutions but that by working with other groups, unions helped enact pro-worker legislation more broadly.

Masters and Delaney's review of union political activity in the past 20 years corroborates this picture. As union density has fallen, unions increased their political efforts, offsetting at least part of their reduced share of the workforce. In 2002 AFL-CIO political operatives claimed that they had increased the union share of the electorate in the face of falling density, but this was the result of erroneous analysis of exit poll data (Freeman, 2004). The National Election Studies data given in Masters and Delaney's Table 16.7 show a continuous drop in the percentage of the electorate from union households from 26 percent in 1980 to 15 percent in 2000. They also show that the union-nonunion difference in voting Democratic in Congressional elections increased over this period, but the increase was insufficient to compensate for the decline in the union share of voters. In addition, although union financial contributions to political campaigns are large, they are dwarfed by business contributions.[5]

The efforts of unions to gain advantage for their organizations and workers broadly through politics were largely unsuccessful in the 1990s. During the Clinton Administration unions failed to get striker replacement or labor law reform and failed to stop the NAFTA treaty that they believed, rightly or wrongly, would harm American workers. The most they could do, Masters and Delaney report, was to prevent Congress enacting laws that could weaken unions. But, as density has fallen, so too has union ability to deter anti-union policies. At the state level in the early 2000s, Oklahoma enacted a right-to-work initiative, and the Republican governors of Indiana, Missouri, and Kentucky rescinded state-level collective-bargaining regulations.

Why has the huge union effort in politics borne so little fruit? One hypothesis is that the union movement has become so linked to the Democratic Party that the Democrats take them for granted and see little value in battling for union goals, while the Republicans see them as their main political opponent,[6] and thus seek to weaken them. Another possible hypothesis consistent with the Masters and Delaney analysis is that union political campaigning provokes massive responses by business, which can draw on much larger resources, which influence Democratic as well as Republican politicians. Masters and Delaney offer a third hypothesis, that while labor is good at the mechanics of politics, it lacks "the passion of ideas," that while difficult to test, has the flavor of a correct assessment of the state of trade unions. In any case, the message from *WDUD* that political action is unlikely to revive union fortunes seems as or more valid today than it did twenty years ago.

8. *The Illusive Productivity Effect* (Hirsch)

Prior to the Brown and Medoff (1978) production function analysis of the effect of unions on productivity, discussion of unions and productivity often revolved around horror stories of featherbedding, for instance by the musicians' union or printing unions. The cross-state, two-digit industry production function analysis, by contrast, suggested that unions had a huge positive productivity effect. As additional and more refined evidence accrued, however, estimates of union productivity effect shrunk—for instance, Kim Clark's 6–8 percent estimated productivity effect for cement (Clark, 1981) or his -2 percent effect in business line data (Clark, 1984). The cross-state production function analysis was too aggregate to hold up under scrutiny. Yes, value added in a two-digit industry was higher in unionized Minnesota than in nonunion Mississippi, controlling for capital and labor inputs, but the difference was more likely due to manufacturers producing goods of different quality for different markets than that unions massively raised productivity.

Ensuing work has supported the modest magnitudes found in the more refined estimates. Belman (1992, Appendix I) reported that approximately two-thirds of the studies of unionism on productivity found positive effects, though estimates varied across sectors and sometimes in the same sector. Doucouliagos and Laroche (2003) performed a meta analysis of 73 union productivity studies in the United States, Japan, and United Kingdom and found a near zero effect among all studies, but a positive one for U.S. manufacturing. Hirsch correctly stresses the "substantial diversity in the literature about union productivity" and views the existing evidence as showing that the average union effect is very close to zero. Based on the three reviews, I regard the evidence as more favorable to a positive union effect than he does but agree that the strongest conclusion from this research is that there is a lot of variation in estimated union effects.[7]

Why is the estimated impact of unions on productivity so varied? There are two plausible explanations. The first is that the production function methodology is too crude to uncover anything more than the basic link between capital and labor, and perhaps quality of labor, and output. Measures of output almost never capture the same physical units: There are subtle variations even in tons of cement that would escape any econometrician. The second explanation, which is consistent with the *WDUD* story, is that what matters is not unionism *per se* but the interaction of unions with management, which can differ across industries, firms, and even establishments within a firm. If this is the case, the only way to progress in understanding union productivity effects is to replace the 0/1 union variable with new measures of "collective voice/institutional response" in union (and nonunion) settings—the true quality of labor and management relations, which no major U.S. survey even seeks to uncover, but where the UK WERS surveys and their clones provide a valuable model.

9. Management Flexibility and HRM Workplace Practices (Verma; Lewin; Hirsch; Addison and Beldfield)

The claim that unions reduce management flexibility and alter human resource management is not a *WDUD* original. The encyclopedic *The Impact of Collective Bargaining on Management* by Slichter, Livernash, and Healey, published in 1960, told in excruciating detail the multiple ways in which management operated differently under collective bargaining than in its absence. The book exhausted me and probably all other students assigned to read its 9001 pages. The innovation of *WDUD* and ensuing research was to go beyond case studies to measure quantitatively the presence or absence of procedures that limited management flexibility in decision-making and that institutionalized personnel or HRM policies.

Verma's analysis shows that the generalization that unions formalize decision-making and reduce discretion and increase the time spent in making decisions holds today. Some of the formalizations, such as formal job posting, probationary periods for new workers, and formal off-the-job training, are likely to increase productivity. Others, such as less use of temporary help, use of more formalized promotion procedures but less reliance on appraisals in salary, promotion, or layoff decisions, have no clear impact on productivity. Less use of performance-related pay and individual incentives in union settings is likely to reduce individual effort, but may increase workers' willingness to help other workers and thus add to team productivity. Whatever the effects of formalization on productivity, there is no gainsaying that unions limit the range of managerial decision-making.[8]

Lewin's evidence on grievance procedures tells a similar story: greater prevalence of formal procedures at union workplaces than at nonunion workplaces, though it is the growth of nonunion dispute resolution systems that is the most striking development in the past two decades or so. The diminution of the union-nonunion gap raises the question of why nonunion firms have mimicked grievance procedures (and possibly other aspects of union workplaces that limit managerial discretion). If Verma's hypothesis (p. 307) that unions can "claim partial credit for improving voice in the nonunion sector" through threat effects is valid, we would expect to see some of the formal systems weakening in nonunion firms, as union density continues to fall.

10. The Decline of Union Density (Flanagan; McLennan; Lewin)

The final chapter of *What Do Unions Do?* attributed much of the decline in private sector union density to the anti-union activities of management and predicted that density would keep dropping below ten percent in the forseeable future on the basis of a stock-flow model of membership. While the chapter is cautious to call this a projection rather than a prediction, Lane Kirkland, then head of the AFL-CIO, dismissed the analysis as academic tomfoolery (though he probably used somewhat different words) and discouraged me from organizing an NBER conference to explore the decline in depth. After all, F&M were young whippersnappers with no practitioner experience. I remember thinking, maybe he knows things that we don't and maybe we will get caught extrapolating trend declines just before density suddenly turns up. Twenty years later, with private sector density at 8.5 percent and falling, the numbers clearly told the story.

Seeking to understand the fall in density, Medoff and I examined and rejected the then common belief that the fall primarily reflected changes in the structural composition of industries. Instead, we argued that economically motivated management opposition to unionism was the major driving force for the fall in density and estimated that by itself management opposition accounted for about one-quarter to one-half of the drop.

Flanagan, McLennan, and Lewin disagree with this finding. In their world, the decline in union density results largely from a loss of worker interest in organizing, with management opposition presumably contributing much less than our estimated 25–50 percent. I have no sympathy with their arguments. The neoclassical economics part of me finds it incomprehensible that firms, seeking to preserve profits against union wage and benefit increases, would spend large sums of money and management time to defeat unions in NLRB representation elections if this was not effective. The industrial relations part of me finds it incomprehensible that field observation of organizing campaigns, descriptions by union organizers, claims by anti-union consultants, and statements by workers, could be so wrong about the role of management. The common sense part of me wonders why management would oppose card checks, fast elections, and neutrality clauses in collective agreements if management had little impact on the outcomes of union organizing campaigns.

To be sure, management opposition is not the sole cause of the decline of unionism in the United States: The *WDUD*-estimated share fell far short of 100 percent. As Flanagan points out, density has fallen in many EU countries where management opposition is nil. But EU countries often mandate extension of collective bargaining, so that union contracts cover workers regardless of their membership. Free-riding behavior, which is minimal in the United States, not management opposition, leads some workers to stay out of unions under those circumstances. As long as collective contract coverage remains high, union density is not a battlefront between labor and management, as it is in the U.S. Foreign experiences aside, Flanagan agrees that management makes economically rational decisions in opposing unionism, and argues (p. 488) that "the root cause of greater management opposition is relatively decentralized collective bargaining arrangements under which union compensation gains expose unionized employers to significant competitive pressure." This is consistent with the book and with ensuing work I have done with Blanchflower (Blanchflower and Freeman, 1992). Where Flanagan and I disagree (aside from rhetoric) is on whether management opposition, proxied by charges of illegal management practices per NLRB election, must rise continuously, as it did in the 1960s and 1970s, for opposition to deter unionization. He believes that the measured stability of this proxy from the mid-1980s to the 1990s invalidates the *WDUD* analysis that opposition is important. I do not see the logic of this claim. Once firms have found the level of opposition that succeeds in deterring unionization, why should they give more resources to opposing unions? The economic principle is to spend until the marginal benefit equals the marginal cost, and then to maintain that level. By the 1980s, management had achieved the level of opposition necessary to deter union organizing drives.

Building on Flanagan's analysis, McLennan (p. 580) rejects "the claim that anti-union activities directed by high-paid consultants hired by business is a major reason for the precipitous fall in unionism" as not credible. Again, I have great faith in the rationality of management. If consultants are not helping defeat unions, why would management hire them? If spending company resources to defeat union drives does not succeed, why do it? Given that McLennan stresses that the finding that unionization lowers profitability was of greatest concern to management, standard economic anlaysis suggests that management will seek to protect those profits by opposing unions. Management does not fight unions in the interests of workers. The WRPS asked managers in organized firms whether they thought unions benefited workers, and the majority said yes.[9] This suggests that they share rather than disagree with "F&M's position that the decline in union density is harmful to workers' interests," as McLennan says(p. 581).[10]

The principal alternative hypothesis for the fall in union decline is that nonunion workers no longer seek to unionize as much as in the past. Flanagan says (p. 487) "there is much stronger evidence of declining demand for union representation among nonunion workers." To the contrary, the "declining worker interest" hypothesis runs counter to the survey evidence that shows that a large and increasing proportion of-workers want unions in the United States. The WRPS showed that 32 percent of nonunion workers would vote for a trade union, with approximately 8–12 percent of workers reporting that management's attitude would shift their vote in an NLRB election. Lipset-Meltz (2004) found that 48 percent said they would vote union in an NLRB election[11]—a proportion higher than in Canada. Comparable questions for other English-speaking countries show that the United States has the highest proportion of nonunion workers who support unionism (Boxall et al., 2006). The Peter Hart (Peter Hart Polls, "today," 2003) survey evidence (in his Figure 1) shows the percentage of nonunion workers who have said they would vote union has risen over time.

Apparently accepting that the survey evidence shows a huge number of workers wanting but unable to gain union representation, McLennan questions how much faith we should put in workers' responses. He notes (p. 582), "there is considerable difference between a telephone answer to a hypothetical question . . . and the individual's binding decision to support a union." I agree. It is harder to support a union at a workplace, particularly if your management and supervisor are telling you to oppose the union than it is to say, yes, I favor a union on a telephone survey. But there is no reason to believe that "the telephone response bias" has grown over time (which is needed to account for the trend in the Hart results); differs among countries (which is needed to account for the greater expressed desire for unions in the United States than elsewhere); or is so large as to invalidate the survey evidence (if only 10 percent or nonunion workers were in workplaces where a majority favored unions but where opposition deterred them, density would more than double).

In any case, in summer 2005 the AFL-CIO undertook an experiment that effectively tested whether what people were saying on surveys truly meant they would join a union organization, albeit in a different institutional setting than voting in an NLRB election against the wishes of management. The AFL-CIO sent organizers into ten cities to ask people to join WorkingAmerica (,www. workingamerica.org.), a non-collective bargaining affiliate. The organizers signed up 800,000 members in six months and signed up thousands more on the Internet. This, despite the fact that WorkingAmerica offered uncertain benefits beyond information about labor issues and solidaristic support. The ease with which organizers signed up workers shows a deep hunger for an employee organization to help them with workplace and labor market problems, consistent with the survey results. Whether American trade unions can tap this hunger and deliver services to the millions who favor unions but cannot gain collective bargaining at the workplace will go a long way to determining whether unions can reinvent themselves in the United States (Freeman, 2005a).

In sum, I give both management and workers credit for knowing their economic interests and give management credit for competence in defending their economic interest, and workers credit for telling the truth about what they want.

V. New Braners: What Next for Unions and Research?

"F&M told us what private sector unions do while there remained unions doing it" (Hirsch, this volume, p. 226). The Symposium chapters show that *What Do Unions Do?* identified empirical regularities about trade unions that have stood the test of ensuing analyses and changing economic developments and which appear to apply broadly to unions across the world. The reason that ensuing research has corroborated most *WDUD* results is not that the book's analyses were flawless—the diverse criticisms invalidate that interpretation—but rather that the book relied on micro data sets with thousands of observations that allow us to differentiate fact from fancy and uncover general patterns, rather than on structural modeling or limited case studies.

Some Symposium participants disagree with how Medoff and I packaged the factual regularities—the interpretation or spin that we put on them. Our analysis reflected our priors, based on the Hirschman exit-voice model, and also a benign view of unions as an institution that tries to improve the well-being of normal employees. By examining a diverse set of outcome variables, rather than concentrating on union wage effect as in previous literature, we gave ourselves a difficult conceptual task. Research on the multiplicity of effects of unions does not easily lend itself to a single theme which a book demands, as our editor, Martin Kessler, continually reminded us. We struggled to weave all the findings together to give a unified picture of this complex social institution.

Symposium critics point out that the exit-voice/institutional response model that we used was incomplete in various ways.[12] We did not examine potentially complicated interactions between the voice and monopoly faces of unionism nor their relation to loyalty. We did not investigate the operation of nonunion voice institutions. Kaufman correctly infers that our analysis sought to balance economists' concern with monopoly issues with institutional concerns—to walk the narrow path between devotees of the Invisible Hand and observers of visible hands. Today, with globalization having augmented the imbalance of power between labor and capital that he stresses, I would use the stringtwister to add a chapter on that issue. Even with stringtwister amendments, however, I accept that the facts established in the book would be open to alternative interpretations. This is because the extant data, generated by the world rather than by controlled experiments, does not provide definitive tests as to whether variables are causally linked as *WDUD* claimed or are linked for other reasons.

Some participants in the Symposium disagree with the *What Do Unions Do?* bottom line that the positive voice face of unionism dominates the negative monopoly face, so that society as well as workers lose from the decline of unionism. However, many of those dubious that traditional unionism is the appropriate institutional vehicle for voice accept the notion that workers need some institutional support in navigating the workplace and labor market. They direct attention at firms developing nonunion channels of voice. Given the continual decline in private sector union density,[13] their perspective and that of *What Do Unions Do?* converges in one important way: recognition that the nation needs to reform private sector labor institutions that have changed little since the New Deal. By reform I do not mean labor law reform AFL-CIO style nor management style per McLennan's chapter but reforms that give labor and management greater leeway, protection, and incentive to experiment with institutions of worker representation and participation that fit a 21st century economy.

From this perspective, post-*WDUD* research should be guided not by the F&M issue of "what private sector unions do while there remain unions to do it" but by the question "what new labor institutions can give workers sufficient voice at workplaces to improve their well-being and the national economy?"

To answer this question, we need new knowledge in three broad areas. The first is in determining what workers and management want from labor institutions and labor laws. Joel Rogers and I (1999) took a first cut at finding out what workers want from our book with that title, but we barely touched on what management wanted. Someone should undertake a detailed analysis of the attitudes of managers toward labor relations and unions, covering the gamut from CEOs to direct supervisors. Moving beyond surveys, we need experimentation with institutions beyond what current law allows. My preferred way to open the door for experiments with new labor codes would be to turn legal regulation of private sector labor over to the states, as Canada does to provinces, and then to assess what works or does not on the basis of state practice.

The second area where we need additional knowledge is in the potential for new forms of unionism to deliver collective voice and other services to workers outside of collective bargaining. Rogers and I have suggested a particular form—open-source unionism—in which the organization combines inexpensive provision of information and advice over the Internet with geographically based meetings and minority unions at particular work places (Freeman and Rogers, 2002a, 2002b). The key to this form is that it enrolls members irrespective of employer agreement to collective bargaining and thus takes management opposition out of the equation. Some unions are experimenting with open-source forms, with the AFL-CIO's WorkingAmerica being arguably the most extensive variant (Freeman, 2005a). Historically, the Knights of Labor fit our open-source model, but without modern information technology to reach members. Prior to the enactment of state collective bargaining legislation, state and local employees had associations that did not bargain. Some government unions, including federal government unions, operate without collective bargaining contracts today. Whether this or some other restructuring of unionism [See Lerner (2002) for a very different proposal.] would enable unions to improve the lot of workers despite low union density and global economic competition should be on every labor researcher's agenda.

The third area where we need additional knowledge to illuminate the road toward institutional reform is the link between the economic and social environment and union performance, which arguably underlies the variability in union wage and productivity effects. This would require better measures of labor-management relations than 0/1 collective bargaining dummy variables and analysis of the factors that lead to varying union policies and management "institutional response." Most important, since 92 percent of private sector workers in the United States are nonunion, we need to explore the variation in the effects of nonunion institutions on outcomes and the factors that lead firms to choose one set of institutions over another. Finally, since 94 percent or so of the world's workforce resides outside the United States more research resources should go to studying how unions operate under the far wider range of economic and social structures outside the United States, in particular to the potential development of real unions in China, and union activity in India and other large developing countries, that compete with us in world markets through low wages.

At the end of his Symposium chapter, Hirsch offers some "rather speculative ideas on the future of workplace voice" with which I have considerable sympathy. Like him, I am favorably inclined to some variant of Levine's (1998) proposal for "conditional deregulation"—exempting firms from some labor regulations when they have formed independent worker committees that take responsibility for compliance in national regulations. This would require the abolition or major reform of section 8(a)(2) of the NLRA. The Dunlop Commission discussed the idea of conditional deregulation, but did not endorse it as "practical" since neither unions nor employers wanted it. I am also favorable to widening the choice of labor representation that U.S. managers and workers currently face: from a collective bargaining majority union or nothing to a choice that would include intermediate organizations, joint committees, or works council type arrangements, which also would require changes in section 8(a)(2). However, as noted, I think that the best path toward a new labor code in the United States is to weaken federal preemption of private sector labor. If the United States turned large parts of labor law to the states, there would be a ferment of innovation. States would experiment with conditional deregulation or with alternative labor organization defaults or with different ways of ascertaining worker desires for unionism and of moving parties to first contracts. They could experiment with different ways to penalize firms or unions that act unfairly. There is no reason why "right to work" provisions should be the only place where states can choose alternative ways of regulating union and management-labor relations activity within their jurisdiction. Weakening federal preemption and giving the states more leeway to experiment with alternative forms seems to be the best way to open the door to these and other possible innovations.

In conclusion, we should direct post-*WDUD* research on labor relations toward providing ideas and evidence to help labor, management, and the country move beyond Depression Era labor institutions. Thankfully, we can contribute to this policy relevant research agenda without risking having our brains scrambled in the 11 dimensional M-brane stringtwister or writing our papers about labor relations in Calabi-Yau space.

Notes

*   I thank Bruce Kaufman and James Bennett for organizing the 20-year perspective and the *Journal of Labor Research* for supporting the Symposium. I owe much to John T. Dunlop and H. Gregg Lewis, who were my mentors in studying trade unionism, and to Martin Kessler, who was editor-extraordinaire in developing the book. This paper is dedicated to Martin, who was an incredible editor, a first-rate intellectual, and a wonderful person.

1.   My interpretation is harsher. These data and the measures used to reflect collective bargaining systems across countries are sufficiently weak to allow analysts with different priors to reach contrary conclusions from comparable data (Freeman, 2005b).

2.   Even today, while U.S. economists are more aware that there are interesting things to learn from economies beyond our own, colleagues from other advanced countries have trouble publishing papers in leading U.S. journals on labor issues. And articles on labor markets in developing countries are found largely in development journals.

3.   While private sector union density has trended downward since the mid-1950s to reach 8.5 percent in 2004, public sector density rose in the 1970s and 1980s and then stabilized at about 35 percent of the public sector workforce.

4.   In 2004 48 percent of workers covered by collective bargaining agreements were in the public sector, and 47 percent of members were in the public sector http://www.bls.gov/news.release/union2.nr0.htm.

5.   McLennan suggests that business is reasonably even-handed in its political donations between the parties and that Democrats outspend Republicans in the 2004 election. Delaney and Masters' chapter shows reasonably even division of business spending between parties in 1992 but a huge difference in 2002. Data on party spending in the Presidential Election show higher expenditures by Republicans www.opensecrets.org/presidential/index.asp.

6.   Republicans had a more positive agenda toward unions and workers in years past. McLennan reminds us that the Nixon Administration enacted considerable pro-worker legislation. George Schultz, John Dunlop, and Bill Usery were among the most professional distinguished Secretaries of Labor in U.S. history—all three appointed by Republican presidents.

7.   Analysis of union impacts on productivity outside the US also give a mixed picture. Addison and Beldfield (this volume) note that UK studies found negative union productivity effects in the 1980s but not in the 1990s, as the economy became more competitive and that some German studies of the effects of works councils on productivity find high productivity effects while others find essentially no effects.

8.   Limiting management decisions arguably should improve productivity in badly managed firms but may lower it in well-managed firms. This suggests that the second moment of the distribution of productivity among union firms would be smaller than the second moment of the distribution of productivity among nonunion firms. This, however, would seem to run counter to the evidence that union firms with the most advanced HRM practices have particularly high productivity.

9.   Sixty-four percent of managers in firms with unions reported that unions improved the lives of workers in their firm (Freeman and Rogers, 1999: 88).

10.   I am also puzzled by McLennan's criticism of the claim by Freeman and Rogers that business spends money to keep unions out of workplaces when they can, since he observes that "most senior business executives prefer a union-free environment."

11. The WRPS used a 3-point scale: yes, no, don't know. The Lipset-Meltz survey used a 5-point scale, differentiating the yes into definitely yes (16 percent) and probably yes (32 percent).
12. Verma (this volume) states that "Although F-M make a clear conceptual distinction between the union's monopoly and voice roles, it is operationally very difficult to separate the two." Addison-Belfield (this volume) assert: "Union voice . . . is in urgent need of restatement . . . to tackle various lacunae."
13. Given that unionism has grown in sudden unexpected spurts, I have a more open view than most researchers that union fortunes could change rapidly, at least if unions managed to develop new forms and innovate their mode of operation (Freeman, 2004a, 2004b, 2005a).

References

Aidt, Toke and Zafiris Tzannatos. *Unions and Collective Bargaining: Economic Effects in a Global Environment.* Washington, DC: World Bank, 2002.

Becker, Brian E. and Craig A. Olson. "Labor Relations and Firm Performance." In M. Kleiner, R. Block, M. Roomkin, and S. Salsburg, eds. *Human Resources and the Performance of the Firm.* Madison, WI: Industrial Relations Research Association, 1987, pp. 43–86.

Belman, Dale. "Unions, the Quality of Labor Relations, and Firm Performance." In Lawrence Mishel and Paula B. Voos, eds. *Unions and Economic Competitiveness.* Armonk, NY: M.E. Sharpe, 1992, pp.-41–107.

Blanchflower, David G. and Richard B. Freeman. "Unionism in the United States and Other Advanced OECD Countries." In M. Bognanno and M. Kleiner, eds. *Labor Institutions and the Future Role of Unions.* Cambridge: Blackwell Publishers, 1992, pp. 56–79.

Boxall, Peter, Richard Freeman, and Peter Haynes, eds. *What Workers Say: Employee Voice in the Anglo-American World.* Ithaca, NY: Cornell University Press, 2006.

Brown, Charles and James Medoff. "Trade Unions in the Production Process." *Journal of Political Economy* 86 (June 1978): 355–78.

Calmfors, Lars and John Driffil. "Bargaining Structure, Corporatism and Macroeconomic Performance (Centralization of Wage Bargaining)." *Economic Policy* 6 (April 1988): 13–61.

Card, David. "The Effect of Unions on Wage Inequality in the U.S. Labor Market." *Industrial and Labor Relations Review* 54 (January 2001): 296–315.

Clark, Kim B. "The Impact of Unionization on Productivity: A Case Study." *Industrial and Labor Relations Review* 33 (July 1981): 451–69.

———. "Unionization and Productivity: Micro-Econometric Evidence." *Quarterly Journal of Economics* 95 (December 1980b): 613–39.

———. "Unionization and Firm Performance: The Impact on Profits, Growth, and Productivity." *American Economic Review* 74 (December 1984): 893–919.

Coase, Ronald. "The Federal Communications Commission." *Journal of Law and Economics* 2 (October 1959): 1–40.

DiNardo, John and David S. Lee. "Economic Impacts of New Unionization on Private Sector Employers: 1984–2001." *Quarterly Journal of Economics* 119 (November 2004): 1383–441.

Doucouliagos, Chris and Patrice Laroche. "What Do Unions Do to Productivity? A Meta-Analysis." *Industrial Relations* 42 (October 2003): 650–91.

Feldstein, Martin and Horioka, Charles. "Domestic Saving and International Capital Flows." *Economic Journal* 90 (June 1980): 314–29.

Freeman, Richard B. "Individual Mobility and Union Voice in the Labor Market." *American Economic Review, Papers and Proceedings* 66 (May 1976): 361–68.

———. "The Effect of Unionism on Worker Attachment to Firms." *Journal of Labor Research* 1 (Spring 1980): 28–61.

———. "Unionism, Price-Cost Margins, and the Return to Capital." Cambridge, MA: NBER Working Paper No. 1164 (July 1983).

———. "Unions, Pensions, and Union Pension Funds." In David A. Wise, ed. *Pensions, Labor and Individual Choice.* Chicago: University of Chicago Press for NBER, 1985, pp. 89–121.

———. "The Effect of the Union Wage Differential on Management Opposition and Union Organizing Success." *American Economic Review* 78 (May 1986): 92–96.

———. "Unionism Comes to the Public Sector." *Journal of Economic Literature* 24 (March 1986): 41–86.

———. "Contraction and Expansion: The Divergence of Private Sector and Public Sector Unionism in the United States." *Journal of Economic Perspectives* 2 (Spring 1988): 63–88.

———. "Is Declining Unionization of the U.S. Good, Bad, or Irrelevant?" In Lawrence Mishel and Paula B. Voos, eds. *Unions and Economic Competitiveness.* Armonk, NY: M.E. Sharpe, 1991, pp.-143–90.

———. "How Much Has De-unionization Contributed to the Rise in Male Earnings Inequality?" In Sheldon Danziger and Peter Gottschalk, eds. *Uneven Tides: Rising Inequality in America.* New York: Russell Sage Foundation, 1993, pp. 133–63.

———. "What Do Unions Do . . . to Voting?" Cambridge, MA: NBER Working Paper # 9992 (September, 2003).

———. "The Road to Union Renascence in the U.S." In Phanindra V. Wunnava, ed. *The Changing Role of Unions: New Forms of Representation.* Armonk, NY: M.E. Sharpe, 2004a, pp. 3–21.

———. "Searching Outside the Box." In Julius Getman and Ray Marshall, eds. *The Future of Labor Unions: Organized Labor in the 21st Century.* Austin: University of Texas, LBJ School of Public Affairs, 2004b, pp. 75–110.

———. "From the Webbs to the Web: The Contribution of the Internet to Reviving Union Fortunes." Cambridge, MA: NBER Working Paper 11298 (May 2005a).

———. "Labour Market Institutions Without Blinders: The Debate Over Flexibility and Labour Market Performance." *International Economic Journal RIEJ* 19 (June 2005b): 129–45.

——— and Casey Ichniowski. *When Public Sector Workers Unionize.* Chicago: NBER and University of Chicago Press, 1988.

——— and Harrison Lauer. "Collective Bargaining Laws and Threat Effects of Unionism in Determination of Police Compensation." *Journal of Labor Economics* 72 (April 1989): 191–209.

——— and Morris M. Kleiner. "Do Unions Make Enterprises Insolvent?" *Industrial and Labor Relations Review* 52 (July 1999): 510–27.

——— and Edward P. Lazear. "An Economic Analysis of Works Councils." In Joel Rogers and Wolfgang Streech, eds. *Works Councils: Consulation, Representation, and Cooperation in Industrial Relations.* Chicago: University of Chicago Press, 1995, pp. 27–50.

——— and James Medoff. *What Do Unions Do?* New York: Basic Books, 1984.

——— and Joel Rogers. *What Workers Want.* Ithaca, NY: Cornell University Press, 1999.

———. "Open-Source Unionism: Beyond Exclusive Collective Bargaining." Working Paper (Fall 2002).

———. "A Proposal to American Labor." *The Nation*, June 24, 2002.

——— and Robert J. Valletta. "The Effects of Public Sector Labor Laws on Labor Market Institutions and Outcomes." In Richard B. Freeman and Casey Ichniowski, eds. *When Public Sector Workers Unionize*. Chicago: NBER and University of Chicago Press, 1988, pp. 81–106.

——— and Martin L. Weitzman. "Bonuses and Employment in Japan." *Journal of the Japanese and International Economies* 1 (1987): 168–94.

Hirschman, Albert. *Exit, Voice, and Loyalty: Responses to Decline in Firms, Organizations, and States*. Cambridge: Harvard University Press, 1970.

Hirsch, Barry T. *Labor Unions and the Economic Performance of U.S. Firms*. Kalamazoo, MI: Upjohn Institute for Employment Research, 1991.

———, David A. Macpherson, and Edward J. Schmumacher. "Measuring Union and Nonunion Wage Growth: Puzzles in Search of Solutions." In Phanindra V. Wunnava, ed. *The Changing Role of Unions: New Forms of Representation*. Armonk, NY: M.E. Sharpe, 2004, pp. 115–47.

Kerr, Clark. *Labor Markets and Wage Determination: The Balkanization of Labor Markets and Other Essays*. Berkeley: University of California Press, 1977.

Kuhn, Peter J. "A New, Integrated Theory of Unions and Life Cycle Employment Contracts Microform: Voice, Malfeasance, and Welfare." Harvard University PhD Dissertation, 1982.

Leontief, Wassily. "The Pure Theory of the Guaranteed Annual Wage Contract." *Journal of Political Economy* 54 (February 1946): 76–79.

Lerner, Stephen. "Three Steps To Reorganizing and Rebuilding the Labor Movement," December 2002, ,http://www.labornotes.org/archives/2002/12/e.html..

Levine, David. *Working in the Twenty-First Century: Policies for Economic Growth Through Training, Opportunity, and Education*. Armonk: M.E. Sharpe, 1998.

Lewis, H. Gregg. *Union Relative Wage Effects: A Survey*. Chicago: University of Chicago Press, 1986.

Lipset, Seymour Martin and Noah Meltz. *The Paradox of American Unionism: Why Americans Like Unions More Than Canadians Do but Join Much Less*. Ithaca, NY: Cornell University Press, 2004.

Olson, Mancur. *How Bright are the Northern Lights? Some Questions About Sweden*. Lund: Lund University Press, 1990.

Ross, Arthur M. "Do We Have a New Industrial Feudalism?" *American Economic Review* 48 (December 1958): 903–20.

Slichter, Sumner H. *Union Policies and Industrial Management*. Washington, DC: Brookings Institution, 1941.

———, James J. Healey, and E. Robert Livernash. *The Impact of Collective Bargaining on Management*. Washington, DC: Brookings Institution, 1960.

About the Editors and Contributors

John T. Addison is Hugh C. Lane Professor of Economic Theory at the University of South Carolina.

Ariel Avgar is a doctoral student at the New York State School of Industrial and Labor Relations, Cornell University.

Clive R. Belfield is associate professor of economics at Queens College of the City University of New York.

James T. Bennett is William P. Snavely Professor of Political Economy and Public Policy and director of the John M. Olin Institute for Employment Practice and Policy at George Mason University.

David G. Blanchflower is Bruce V. Rauner Professor of Economics at Dartmouth College.

Alex Bryson is principal research fellow at the Policy Studies Institute, London.

John W. Budd is professor of industrial relations and human resources at the University of Minnesota.

David Card is Class of 1950 Professor of Economics at the University of California, Berkeley.

John T. Delaney is professor of management and dean at the Katz School of Business, University of Pittsburgh.

Christopher L. Erickson is professor and associate dean in the Anderson Graduate School of Management, University of California, Los Angeles.

Robert J. Flanagan is Konosuke Matsushita Professor of International Labor Economics and Policy Analysis at the Stanford Graduate School of Business.

Richard B. Freeman is Herbert S. Ascherman Professor of Economics at Harvard University and director of the Labor Studies Program at the National Bureau of Economic Research.

Morley Gunderson is CIBC Chair in Youth Employment at the Industrial Relations Centre, University of Toronto.

Tove Helland Hammer is professor of organizational behavior at the New York State School of Industrial and Labor Relations, Cornell University.

Barry T. Hirsch is E.M. Stevens Distinguished Professor of Economics at Trinity University.

Bruce E. Kaufman is professor of economics and senior associate of the W.T. Beebe Institute of Personnel and Employment Relations, Georgia State University.

Thomas Lemieux is professor of economics at the University of British of Columbia.

David Lewin is Neil H. Jacoby Professor of Management and senior associate dean at the Anderson Graduate School of Management, University of California, Los Angeles.

Marick F. Masters is professor of business administration at the University of Pittsburgh.

Kenneth McLennan is retired president of the Manufacturers Alliance and adjunct professor in the Thomas Jefferson Program in Public Policy, The College of William and Mary.

Daniel J. B. Mitchell is Ho-Su Wu Professor of Management at the Anderson Graduate School of Management, University of California, Los Angeles.

John Pencavel is Pauline K. Levin-Robert L. Levin, and Pauline C. Levin-Abraham Levin Professor in the School of Humanities and Sciences, Stanford University.

W. Craig Riddell is professor of economics at the University of British Columbia.

Stephen R. Sleigh is director of strategic resources for the International Association of Machinists and Aerospace Workers.

Anil Verma is professor of industrial relations and human resources at the University of Toronto.

Index